PIERS PLOWMAN

The Malvern Hills and River Teme from Bransford. Photograph by Bill Meadows.

Medieval Institute Publications is a program of
The Medieval Institute, College of Arts and Sciences

 WESTERN MICHIGAN UNIVERSITY

WILLIAM LANGLAND

Piers Plowman

A Parallel-Text Edition
of the A, B, C and Z Versions

VOLUME II, Part 1.
INTRODUCTION AND TEXTUAL NOTES

By

A. V. C. SCHMIDT

Revised Edition

MEDIEVAL INSTITUTE PUBLICATIONS
Western Michigan University
Kalamazoo

Library of Congress Control Number: 95126458

ISBN 978-1-58044-159-9

P 5 4 3 2 1

ALTERVM·HOC·VOLVMEN·IAM·AD·LVCEM

IN·IMPERFECTIS·VLTIME·PERFECTVM

DECEM·POST·ANNOS·AMICE·PRAETENDO

In memory of Colin Macleod (1943–1981)

Where shal man fynde swich a frend with so fre an herte?

CONTENTS

EDITORIAL PREFACE

The present work completes a two-volume edition of *Piers Plowman* begun some twenty years ago, of which Volume I (the Text) was published by Longman in 1995 and is now out of print. It is the plan of the publisher, Medieval Institute Publications of Western Michigan University at Kalamazoo, first to issue Volume II (the Introduction, etc) in a similar format, and at a later date to reprint it as a set, together with a corrected edition of Volume I, in paper covers at a reasonably affordable price. This was always my hope with the original Longman project, and I am therefore grateful to Medieval Institute Publications and especially to its Director of Publications for exploring the feasibility of the book and saving from interment in permafrost what one reviewer called a 'mammoth' enterprise. It gives me great satisfaction that my edition should appear under its imprint, and I am much obliged to Andrew Galloway for suggesting this to me at a time when commercial pressures had made the work too costly for its original British publisher. Nonetheless, I wish to express my thanks to Andrew MacLennan, Longman's Director of Publishing in 1985, for sharing my sincere (if ingenuous) belief that, with the appropriate single-mindedness and energy on my part, the two volumes might appear together within a decade. In fact they have taken as long to complete as Skeat spent on his EETS and Oxford editions together, and nearly as long as Langland did on writing *Piers Plowman*. As the manuscript was delivered in 2005, I have not been able to take account of scholarship since that date, except for citing a handful of important recent publications, which are recorded in the Bibliography. Langland's poem continues to find enthusiastic students in countries its author had never even heard of; the present edition is intended to help those who have got beyond a first acquaintance to probe more deeply into this endlessly fascinating masterpiece. I hope that the reader will find most of what he needs between these covers and conclude that 'A bouhte such a bargayn he was the bet evere'. For myself, I am content to make the poet's words my own: 'And yf Y be laboure sholde lyven, and lyflode deserven, / That laboure that Y lerned beste, therwith lyven Y sholde'.

AVCS

Oxford
2008

ACKNOWLEDGEMENTS

I am much indebted to Balliol College and Oxford University for four terms of leave from teaching that enabled me to work on this project, and for help with the cost of books, computing equipment and travel to libraries. I am grateful to Patricia Hollahan of Medieval Institute Publications at Kalamazoo for her faith in this project, and to the Institute for undertaking to publish it in the present form.

I wish to thank Helen Barr for her comments on part V of the *Introduction*; she of course bears no responsibility for the opinions expressed or the errors that remain. I am also grateful for help on particular points from John Burrow, Miriam Griffin, Jeremy Griffiths, Stuart Lee, Seamus Perry and Lawrence Warner. The friendly support and interest of Andrew McNeillie, Charlotte Brewer, Chacotta Bunting, Andrew Galloway, Anne Hudson, Tomonori Matsushita, Sarah Ogilvie-Thomson and Tim Wilson has been a heartening experience. I am immensely grateful to Gwen Appleby for putting me in touch with Bill Meadows and Glenys Burrows, who provided the photographs that form the frontispieces of this volume. My indebtedness to the previous editors of *Piers Plowman*, especially Walter Skeat, George Kane and E. T. Donaldson is writ large on every page of this edition. Indispensable for preparing the *Commentary* and *Glossary* have been the edition of the C Version by Derek Pearsall, of which a new edition has now been published by Exeter University Press (2008), the Glossaries of John Alford, *The Yearbook of Langland Studies* (*vade-mecum* of every wanderer in the wilderness of books and articles on *Piers Plowman*) and that *merveille* of twentieth-century collaborative learning, the *Middle English Dictionary*. A more general debt I wish to record is to the inspiration and example of two great Langland scholars whom it was my misfortune to know too little and too late, Jack Bennett and Elizabeth Salter: *Of hir wordes thei wissen us for wisest in hir tyme.*

To Judith Schmidt, finally, my obligations in respect of this entire work are beyond reckoning. Her lesser contributions included typing and pasting up the Apparatus of Vol I, producing the Concordance for the *Glossary*, printing the copy of Volume II and reading *forceres* of proofs of the first volume; her greatest has been patient submersion in *Piers Plowman* at sometimes unsociable hours, without (too often) *slomberyng into a slepyng*. Had I lacked the serene certainty of her support, the enterprise would never have been begun, let alone (after some twenty years) completed.

The second volume of this edition is dedicated to the memory of the brilliant scholar and poet, *Animae dimidium meae*, who first proved to me that *Treuthe is tresor trieste on erthe*.

ABBREVIATIONS

AC	*Analecta Cartusiana*
AM	*Annuale Medievale*
Archiv	*Archiv für das Studium der neueren Sprachen und Literaturen*
BJRL	*Bulletin of the John Rylands Library*
CHMEL	*The Cambridge History of Medieval English Literature,* ed. Wallace
CCSL	*Corpus Christianorum, series Latina* (Turnhout, 1954ff)
CCCM	*Corpus Christianorum, Continuatio Medievalis* (Turnhout, 1967ff)
ChR	*Chaucer Review*
EETS	*Early English Text Society*
EHR	*English Historical Review*
ELH	*English Literary History*
E&S	*Essays and Studies*
ELN	*English Language Notes*
e.s	*extra series* (EETS)
ESt.	*English Studies*
HLQ	*Huntington Library Quarterly*
IMEV	*Index of Middle English Verse*
JEGP	*Journal of English and Germanic Philology*
JLH	*Jahrtausend Lateinischer Hymnendichtung,* ed. Dreves-Blume
JWCI	*Journal of the Warburg and Courtauld Institutes*
LSE	*Leeds Studies in English*
MÆ	*Medium Ævum*
MED	*Middle English Dictionary*
MLN	*Modern Language Notes*
MLQ	*Modern Language Quarterly*
MLR	*Modern Language Review*
MP	*Modern Philology*
MS	*Medieval Studies*
NM	*Neuphilologische Mitteilungen*
NML	*New Medieval Literatures*
NQ	*Notes and Queries*
OCL	*Oxford Companion to Law*
OED	*Oxford English Dictionary*
o.s.	*ordinary series* (EETS)
PBA	*Publications of the British Academy*
PBSA	*Papers of the Bibliographical Society of America*
PG	*Patrologia Graeca*
PL	*Patrologia Latina*
PMLA	*Publications of the Modern Language Association of America*
PQ	*Philological Quarterly*
RES	*Review of English Studies*

SAC	*Studies in the Age of Chaucer*
SB	*Studies in Bibliography*
SP	*Studies in Philology*
Spec	*Speculum*
s.s.	special series (EETS)
YES	*Yearbook of English Studies*
YLS	*The Yearbook of Langland Studies*
AF	Anglo-French
Alf*C*	Alford, ed. *Companion to PP*
Alf*G*	Alford, *PP: Glossary of Legal Diction*
Alf*Q*	Alford, *PP: A Guide to the Quotations.*
AN	Anglo-Norman
AMA	*Alliterative Morte Arthure*
AP	Alan of Lille, *De Arte Praedicatoria*
AW	*Ancrene Wisse*
B&T-P	Burrow and Turville-Petre
Bn	Bennett, *PP: Pr & Passus I–VII*
CA	Gower's *Confessio Amantis*
CH	Alan of Lille, *Contra Haereticos*
CT	Chaucer's *Canterbury Tales*
DC	*Distichs of Cato*
DPN	Alan of Lille, *De Planctu Naturae*
E	Eastern
FM	*Fasciculus Morum*
GO	*Glossa Ordinaria*
HME	Mossé, *Handbook of Middle English*
IG	Indexical Glossary
IPN	Index of Proper Names
Ka	Kane, *PP: A Version*
K–D	Kane & Donaldson, *PP: B Version*
K–F	Knott & Fowler, *PP: A-Text*
L	Langland
M	Midland
MES	Mustanoja, *Middle English Syntax*
MS	*Mum and the Sothsegger*
N	Northern
NT	New Testament
OE	Old English
OF	Old French
OT	Old Testament
Pe	Pearsall, *C-text*
PP	*Piers Plowman*
PPCr	*Pierce the Ploughman's Crede*
PTA	*Parlement of the Thre Ages*

R–H	Robertson and Huppé, *PP & Scriptural Tradition*
R–K	Russell & Kane, *PP: C Version*
RRe	*Richard the Redeless*
RR; Rom	*Roman de la Rose*; Chaucerian translation (*Romaunt*)
S	South(ern)
SC	Bernard, *Sermones in Cantica Canticorum*
Sch¹	Schmidt, *B Text, 1st edn*
Sch²	Schmidt, *B Text, 2nd edn*
SEL	*South English Legendary*
SGGK	*Sir Gawain and the Green Knight*
Sk	Skeat
SS	*Summer Sunday*
SW	South-Western
SW	*Sawles Warde*
TC	Chaucer's *Troilus and Criseyde*
TL	Usk's *Testament of Love*
TN	Textual Notes
Vg	Vulgate Bible
VA	*Verbum abbreviatum*
VL	*Vetus Latina*
W	Western
WPal	*William of Palerne*
Wr	*Wright*
WSEW	*Select English Works of Wyclif*
WW	*Wynnere and Wastoure*

FOREWORD

The second volume of this PARALLEL-TEXT edition of *Piers Plowman* is divided into six parts: A, an *Introduction*; B, *Textual Notes*; C, a *Commentary*; D, a *Bibliography*; E, an *Indexical Glossary* to the four versions; and F, Four *Appendices* dealing with the Language and Metre of the poem, the Rubrics, the poet's 'Repertory', and corrections to errors in Volume I. Although a preferred status is not implied for the C-Text, all references in parts B, C and E follow the practice of Skeat's parallel-text edition in referring for convenience to this, the final version of the poem.

The *Introduction* consists of *five* sections: an analytical list of the manuscript sources; a critical survey of the editorial tradition, placing the present work in relation to its predecessors; an examination of the textual evidence for the four versions printed in volume I; an explanation of editorial principles and methods; and a concise account of the poem's authorship, audience and date, the order of the versions and *Piers Plowman*'s reception and influence. The *second* section of the Introduction requires no specialised textual knowledge and may be consulted in conjunction with the *fifth* by readers wanting a general perspective on the texts in volume I but not a detailed study of the manuscript sources and the problems of transmission. Familiarity with the first two sections is, however, presupposed by the more technical account in the *third* and *fourth*. The Notes to the *Introduction* will be found separately at the end of each of its five sections.

The *Textual Notes* contain a detailed sequential account of all major problems, justifying the readings adopted and, where space allows, discussing rejected emendations of other editors. The *Commentary* aims principally to elucidate the verbal and historical meaning of the text; but while it includes some critical discussion, there is no attempt to offer a conspectus of past or current debate on the wider interpretative issues touched on in parts of section V of the *Introduction*. The *Bibliography* lists the works cited and a selection of those consulted but not specifically mentioned. The *Glossary* offers a comprehensive and indexed explanation of all words appearing in the edited texts of the four versions. Finally, the *Appendices* cover in detail particular topics referred to only briefly in the *Introduction*, *Notes* and *Commentary*. Together, these six sections aim to provide the necessary material for advanced study of the poem's text and context.

A. INTRODUCTION

I. THE MANUSCRIPTS OF *PIERS PLOWMAN*

§§ 1–3 The Manuscripts. § 4 Single-Version
Manuscripts (nos. 1–41). § 5 Conjoint Manuscripts
(nos. 42–52). § 6 Conflated **ABC** Text (no. 53).
§ 7 Fragments (nos. i–iv).

§ 1. In his edition of *Piers Plowman* for the Early English Text Society (1867–88), W. W. Skeat (*Sk* hereafter) recognised five 'shapes' of the text. Three of these are authorial, the 'single' versions **A**, **B** and **C** (manuscripts nos. 1–41 listed below). The present edition also accepts as authentic a fourth version known as **Z**, a text of Prologue–VIII 92 surviving only in a 'conjoint' form with a text of **C** added later (no. 52 in the list below). Skeat also recognised two scribally-produced 'conjoint' forms combining portions of **A** and **C**, or of **B** and **C** (*Sk* II i, III ix, IV 832).[1] Of the conjoint texts (nos. 42–52) six are of **A** and **C** (46–51), of which one (no. 49) conflates parts of its **A** portion from **C**, and three are of **B** and **C** linked by a passage of **A** (nos. 43–5). Additionally there is one of **B** and **A** (no. 42) and one (no. 53) that conflates its text of **B** through-out with material from **A** and **C**. The fact that of the fifty-three manuscripts eleven (including the early copies nos. 43–5 and 52) are of the conjoint type suggests that non-authentic shapes of the poem were known, perhaps widely, in the generation after Langland's death. The following list acknowledges as much in the way it divides the witnesses (into 'single-version' and 'conjoint'). The manuscripts are through-numbered from 1–53; but for convenience in relating this section to the Textual Apparatus, the order *within* each division is that of the sigils after classification of the manuscripts, as printed in Vol. I, x–xii. Crowley's *editio princeps* of the poem (no. 13) has been accorded manuscript status, since it apparently derives from a source that is not among the manuscripts now extant (*Sk* II xxxvi–vii; see III, *B Version*, §§ 13–16).

§ 2. Detailed accounts of the *Piers Plowman* codices have appeared in Skeat's EETS editions, in the three volumes of the Athlone edition (1960–97) edited by Kane (*Ka*), Kane and Donaldson (*K–D*) and Russell and Kane (*R–K*), in that of the Z-Text (1983) by Rigg and Brewer (*R–B*), and in a number of special studies. The early manuscript copies in which the texts are preserved continue to attract much scholarly interest for the light they throw on the work's 'reception' and cultural context and hence potentially on its contemporary meaning. The manuscripts of **A** are described in *Sk* I, xii–xxvii and *Ka* 1–18; those of **B** in *Sk* II, vi–xxxix and *K–D* 1–15, adding no. 14 (unknown to Skeat), but most fully now in Benson and Blanchfield (*B–B* hereafter), who also reproduce marginal and other scribal additions; those of **C** in *Sk* III, xix–l and *R–K* 1–18, adding seven important copies not in *Sk*; that of **Z** in *R–B* and also in Brewer and Rigg's facsimile of Bodley 851 (1994). There are lists of the manuscripts of all versions in Brewer, *Editing 'PP'* (1996) 448–51 and (with notes) in Hanna, *Langland* (1993) 37–42, and valuable discussion by Doyle of many individual copies in Kratzmann & Simpson (1986) 33–48. Published facsimiles include a plain reproduction of Crowley's print (**B**) and full facsimile editions with detailed introductions of Bodley 851 (**Z**), of the Vernon ms and Trinity Cambridge R. 3. 14 (both **A**), of Trinity Cambridge B. 15. 17 (**B**), and of Hm 143 and the illustrated Douce 104 (both **C**), while full-page half-tone plates illustrating all the **B** copies appear in *B-B*. Full-colour facsimiles of the highest quality are becoming available through the *Piers Plowman Electronic Archive* (ed. Duggan *et al*.), in which hypertext editions of nos. 11, 17, 20, 21 and 23 of the B-Text have already appeared on CD-Rom.

§ 3. The following account, which is much indebted to the works mentioned above, provides for the *Piers Plowman* content of each copy concise information on the material, script, date, language, number of lines per page, and corrections; it also notes points relating to ownership and companion texts (if any). Since textually important material on the rubrics appears in the critical apparatus to the text in Vol. I, deviant varieties of the presumed sub-archetypal forms are noticed here only in cases of exceptional interest (for further details and discussion see Appendix Two). Occasional comments are included on the textual value of the copy, an asterisk before a sigil signifying that the manuscript has proved indispensable for establishing the text of the version in question. The list is complete except for the sixteenth- and seventeenth-century transcriptions and excerpts in Bodleian mss James 2, Wood donat. 7, the BL ms Sloane 2578 and the Caius College Cambridge ms 201 (a transcript of Owen Rogers' 1561 print), which have no textual value.

§ 4. Single-Version Manuscripts

A-TEXT

1 **D** *Oxford, Bodleian Library ms Douce 323*
Paper; a semi-cursive hand of late C15. 28–34 ll. per p. Mixed EW dialect. Contains Pr–XI. A member of group d of the sub-family r^1.

2 ***R** *Oxford, Bodleian Library ms Rawlinson Poetry 137*
Vellum; bastard anglicana of mid-C15; scribe signs *Tilot* at end. 30–4 ll. per p. SW Sussex dialect. The sole copy to have *prologus* as first heading. Contains entire text, the only one with Passus XII complete (see Matsushita, *Facsimile* 2010:71–4, with diplomatic transcription 139–42); VII 70–213a misplaced after I 179. A member of the sub-family r^1; substantively the most important **A** ms, but less suitable than T as copy-text (cf. L of **B**, no. 20 below). See further S. Horobin, 'The Scribe of Rawlinson Poetry 137 and the Copying and Circulation of *Piers Plowman*' in *YLS* 19 (2005) 3–26.

3 **U** *Oxford, University College ms 45*
Vellum, anglicana formata of C15^1; paper, bastard anglicana of C15^2. 30–8 ll. per p. (vellum); about 28 (paper). S. Cambs. dialect. Lacks I 33–99, X 211–XI 47, XII 20–117 through loss of leaves and (like R) misplaces VII 70–213a after II 23.

4 **V** *Oxford, Bodleian Library ms English Poetry a.1* (*the Vernon ms*)
Vellum; anglicana of *c*.1400. 160 ll. per p. in two cols. N.Worcs. dialect. Lacks XI 184–313 and perhaps an original XII through loss of final leaf. No title or rubrics except at IX. *PP* followed by *Joseph of Arimathea*. Used by *Sk* as base-text but (though early) only moderately good member of sub-family r^2. Facsimile ed. Doyle 1987.

5 H *London, British Library ms Harley 875*
Vellum; two anglicana hands of C15$^{2-3}$. 36–41 ll. per p. N-W. Warws. dialect. Lacks VI 48–VII 2 through loss of leaf. Rubrics for only II–VI, VIII. The genetic twin of V.

6 *J *New York, Pierpont Morgan Library ms 18 (the Ingilby ms)*
Paper; anglicana hand of *c.* 1450. 29–38 ll. per p. Lincs. dialect. *PP* text preceded by *Pistill of Susan* and Rolle's *Form of Perfect Living.* The major representative of the *r²* sub-family (see III, *A Version,* § 19) and the only one with any of XII (this last printed entire *Sk* IV ii 857–59).

7 L *London, Lincoln's Inn Library ms 150*
Vellum; anglicana hand of C15^1. Tall narrow 'holster' book; 50–55 ll. per p. Two leaves probably lost which could have contained VIII 157–end. *PP* preceded by two metrical romances and *Seege of Troye.* For a study see Horobin & Wiggins 2008.

8 E *Dublin, Trinity College ms 213 (D.4.12)*
Paper; scrivener's hand; from watermarks C15$^{3-4}$. 27–34 ll. per p. Durham or Northumberland with a more southerly element. Contains Pr–VII 44, with VII 70–213a misplaced after I 182 (cf. R and U). *PP* text followed by alliterative *Wars of Alexander.*

9 A *Oxford, Bodleian Library ms Ashmole 1468*
Paper; bastard anglicana hand of C15$^{3-4}$. 22–30 ll. per p. W Suffolk dialect. Pr–I 141 lacking through loss of leaves.

10 *M *London, Library of the Society of Antiquaries no. 687*
Paper; free hand tending to cursive, of *c.* 1425. 28–35 ll. per p. NW Suffolk dialect. Unusual division at IX treating it as *prologus* to Dowel etc. Important as the only complete representative of the **m** family (see III, *A Version,* §§ 24–47 below). Facsimile by Matsushita (2007).

B-TEXT

11 *W *Cambridge, Trinity College ms B. 15. 17*
Vellum, 147 leaves (*PP* on ff.1r–130v); anglicana formata hand of *c.* 1400 resembling that of the scribe of Ellesmere ms of *Canterbury Tales* and a Staffordshire scribe of the same period [Doyle 1986:39]; display script bastard anglicana with Latin boxed in red. Carefully paragraphed with blue and red parasigns and blank line between paragraphs (cf. L, M, Y and R below). 33–5 ll. per p. Punctuated with raised points at caesuras and raised hooks or points at many line-ends. Possibly the product of a London or Westminster workshop. Dialect of Middlesex or London type. See further *Sk* II xiii–xiv; *K–D* 13–14; *B–B* 56–9, with facsimile pl. of f. 19v. *PP* text followed by Rolle's *Form of Living* and a devotional lyric *Crist made to man a fair present* (see *IMEV* 611). Substantively less good than **L** but has unusually consistent spelling and systematic grammar, close to that of the Hengwrt and Ellesmere mss of *The Canterbury Tales* (see Horobin and Mooney 2004). Printed by Wright (1842) and used as copy-text by Kane-Donaldson (1975), Schmidt (1978) and in the present edition. Now Vol 2 in the *PP Electronic Archive*, ed. Turville-Petre & Duggan (2000), reviewed by J. Sebastian in *YLS* 15 (2001). Facsimile with diplomatic transcription by Matsushita (2010).

12 Hm; Hm^2 *San Marino, Huntington Library ms Hm 128*
Vellum; six anglicana hands with occasional secretary features, those of the *PP* texts anglicana formata of early C15. About 40 ll. per p. The product more probably of a clerical group than of a commercial workshop. S. Warws. dialect. Hm^2 preceded by *The Prick of Conscience*, Hm by *Siege of Jerusalem* and *How the Good Wife Taught her Daughter.* Pastedown has inscription 'Robert or William Langland made pers plow[man]', possibly by William Sparke, and John Bale's inscription 'Robertus langlande natus in comitatu salopie in villa Mortymers Clybery in the claylande, within viij myles of Malborne hylles, scripsit peers ploughman, li 1', followed by first line of *PP*. See Turville-Petre 2002:43–51. Electronic edition by Calabrese, Duggan and Turville-Petre (2008).

13 **Cr** *Robert Crowley's* Three Printed Texts *of* 1550

a Cr[1] *British Library C. 71. c. 29*
Title *The Vision of Pierce Plowman, now fyrste imprynted by Roberte Crowley, dwellyng in Ely rentes in Holburne. Anno Domini, 1505* [error for 1550; Colophon has *M.D.L*]. The *editio princeps*, based on a lost ms of β type. Facsimile ed. by Bennett 1976.

b Cr[2] *British Library C. 71. c. 28*
Title-page *The vision...nowe the seconde time imprinted...Whereunto are added certayne notes and cotations in the mergyne, geuynge light to the Reader. And in the begynning is set a briefe summe of all the principall maters spoken of in the boke.* A reset reprint of *a* based on another lost ms compared throughout with it.

c Cr[3] *British Library C. 122. d. 9*
A reprint of Cr[2] with readings from yet another one or more mss. Cr is not included in *B–B* but Crowley's address to the reader is given in full in *Sk* II xxxii–iv. On *Cr* see Crawford 1957, King 1973, Thorne and Uhart 1986, Brewer 1996:7–19, Hailey 2007.

14 **S** *Tokyo, collection of Toshiyuki Takamiya ms 23* (formerly *London, Sion College Ms Arc. L. 40 2/E. 76*)[2]

Paper; secretary hand of mid-16C (?George Hewlet). About 42 ll. per p. The ms was discovered in 1966; described in *K–D* and fully in *B–B* 112–15, with pl. A β-family text of w-type, very inaccurate and heavily modernised. Rejected for editing by K–D and likewise here.

15 **G** *Cambridge, University Library ms Gg. 4. 31*

Paper; secretary hand of C16[1]. 33–45 ll. per p. Spelling somewhat modernised; passus-headings only as explicits, one out throughout, with Pr treated as Passus I. Table of contents by original scribe (*B–B* 133–36; and see Jefferson in Burrow & Duggan 2010: 140–52).

16 **Y** *Cambridge, Newnham College ms 4* (*Yates-Thompson ms*)

Vellum; anglicana formata of *c*.1430. About 40 ll. per p. Paragraphs separated by blank line; caesurae marked with various pointings. Dialect London with diluted W forms (possibly N Oxon). *PP* text followed by *Lay Folk's Mass Book,* in another hand.

17 **O** *Oxford, Oriel College ms 79, pt. 1*

Vellum; anglicana formata, of C15[1]. About 39 ll. per p. Dialect N. Herts. Lacks XVII 97–342, XIX 283–362 through loss of leaves. Title *Pers plowman*. Marginal glosses and corrections by main scribe; further corrections by another C15 hand. Electronic edition ed. Heinrichs (2005).

18 **C**[2] *Cambridge, University Library ms Ll. 4. 14*

Paper; small anglicana, of C15[2]. About 35 ll. per p. Dialect Cambs. (?Ely). *PP* followed by *Richard the Redeless,* English educational texts and a glossary of *PP* in secretary hand of mid-C16, possibly Robert Crowley (printed *Sk* II 421–6, with comments; *B–B* 148–9). Interlinear and marginal corrections by both scribe and glossator.

19 **C** *Cambridge, University Library ms Dd. l. 17*

Vellum; anglicana formata, with headings and quotations in bastard anglicana, of *c*.1400. 61 ll. per p. (two cols.). Dialect mixed with N and SWM forms. A large folio of historical and religious works with *PP* in pt. 3 followed by English texts *On Visiting the Sick,* Mandeville's *Travels, Seven Sages of Rome,* and a Latin Gospel Concordance.

20 ***L** *Oxford, Bodleian Library ms Laud Misc. 581*

Vellum; anglicana formata, of *c.* 1400. Paragraphed and punctuated with mid-point caesurae. Possibly the product of a commercial London workshop (cf. Y, M, R). Dialect S Worcs. overlaid with some N and E forms from intermediate London copying. Corrections and notes by main scribe, including some interlinear glosses; many cross-shaped marginal marks, apparently for intended corrections, some actually made. Annotations in later hands, one of mid-C16 on f.1: 'Robart Langelande borne by malborne hilles.' Printed by Sk and Bn; substantively the best member of the β family, but less suitable as copy-text than W (no. 11 above). Electronic edition ed. Duggan and Hanna (2005).

21 **M** *London, British Library ms Additional 35287*
Vellum; varying anglicana, of early C15[1], resembling hand of Hengwrt-Ellesmere scribe (cf. 11). Paragraphed with blank lines but no parasigns. Heavily altered through erasure and overwriting by at least two correctors, one identified as Adam Pinkhurst by Horobin 2009. About 40–1 ll. per p. Dialect mixed with relict Herefordshire forms. See Turville-Petre 2002:51–64. Electronic edition ed. Eliason, Turville-Petre and Duggan (2005).

22 ***R** *London, British Library ms Lansdowne 398*
Oxford, Bodleian Library ms Rawlinson Poetry 38
Vellum, the Lansdowne portion (ff. 77–80) being leaves 3–6 of the first quire, with 1–2, 7–8 lost, as also are leaves between ff. 95–6 of Rawl. (orig. quire 14); anglicana formata, with incipits and Latin in bastard anglicana, of *c.* 1400. Paragraphs separated with blank lines; frequent parasigns (cf. L, M, Y). 36–8 ll. per p. No title, and in place of final explicit *Passus ii^{us} de dobest*; passus-numbering one out from XI to XVIII (= X–XVII). Dialect basically S Worcs. with overlay of N and Suffolk from London copying. Ownership names include 'William Butte(s)' of early C16 (f. 101r). Imperfect representative of the α family, but the only sound one; unique portions first printed by Sk, subsequently by K–D, Sch; regarded as preserving a later recension of B-Text by Hanna (1996:215–29) and Taylor (1997), and see also Taylor, Dissertation 1995; but cf. III, *B Version*, §§ 52–5 below.

23 ***F** *Oxford, Corpus Christi College ms 201*
Vellum; current anglicana with Latin in 'fere-textura' (Doyle 1986:40), of *c.* 1400. Historiated opening initial of dreamer [Schmidt 1991, cover]. About 42 ll. per p. Dialect Essex. Title *Incipit pers þe plowman*; idiosyncratic passus-divisions (counting Pr as I and XX as XVI); see Adams 1985:228–9, Weldon 1993, *B–B* 207, and *Sk* II xxvii–xxx (entire). Corrupt and sophisticated but still important as the only α witness for the portions missing from R (Taylor 1996:530–48 maintains dependence of F on R). A facsimile hypertext edition is Vol. I of the *Piers Plowman Electronic Archive*, ed. R. Adams *et al.* (1999); reviewed by S. Shepherd in *YLS* 14 (2000).

C-TEXT

24 ***X** *San Marino, Huntington Library ms Hm 143*
Vellum, occupying the whole (ff. 1–106v), preceded by three leaves of Chaucer's *Troilus*. Current anglicana formata, of *c.* 1400. Corrected a.h., the name 'Piers (Plouhman)' almost everywhere erased. Paragraphed with red and blue parasigns; foreign words and some keywords underlined, mostly in red. 36 ll. per p. Dialect SW Worcs. with signs of London copying. No incipit or final explicit; standard **x**-family passus divisions and '.W.' after 'Willielmi' in explicit to IX. Photostatic facsimile by Chambers *et al.* (1936) and in colour by Matsushita, *Facsimile* (with diplomatic transcription) 2008; opening as frontispiece in Alford 1988. Discussion in Chambers 1935:1–27, Russell 1984:275–300, Bowers 1992:24–6, 2005:137–68, Calabrese 2005:169–99, Horobin 2005:248–69. Unknown to Sk but selected by Chambers as base for **C** on grounds of completeness, language and early date; printed first by Pe, then used as copy-text by Sch and R–K.

25 ***Y** *Oxford, Bodleian Library ms Digby 102*
Vellum; one anglicana hand, of C15[1]; on ff. 97v, 139v a *Dispute between the Body and the Soul*. Belonged to Kenelm Digby in C17 (cf. nos. 40, 49). But for want of Pr–II 156 (probably through loss of leaves) would be the best substantive witness of this version. See Schaap 2001 on marginalia and Horobin 2010 (forthcoming).

26 **I (J)** *London, University of London Library ms S.L.V. 88 (the Ilchester ms)*
Vellum; anglicana formata with secretary features, of *c.* 1400–10, ascribed to London 'Scribe D' [Doyle & Parkes 1973]. About 31 ll. per p. Severely damaged with text missing through loss of leaves at XI 276–XII 19, XV 296–XVII 59*a*, XVIII 102–161, XXI 79–XXII 81; XXII 82–end only partly legible. Dialect S Worcs. (See Horobin & Mosser 2006). Not a conjoint text but Prologue the product of a compiler, setting passages from C IX in a frame-text of A Pr with C Pr 91–157

inset in second of three A-Text passages (printed entire *R–K* 186–94; 105–24 in Vol. I, App.; see Pearsall 1981). Highly valued as a **C** witness by earlier editors but of limited textual worth.

27 **P²** *London, British Library ms Additional 34779*

Vellum; anglicana formata of *c.* 1400–10 (that of scribe of Rylands ms Eng. 90). Corrections by several later hands. About 39 ll. per p. Much damaged, esp. ff. 1, 5, 92. Dialect SE Shropshire.

28 **U** *London, British Library MS Additional 35157*

Vellum; anglicana formata, of *c.* 1400. About 32 ll. per p. Mostly unparagraphed with red underlining of foreign and some keywords. Corrections by main scribe (signed 'Preston' f. 124v). Dialect NW Worcs. from a SW Worcs. exemplar. Important as **x** witness where Y is defective. See Grindley 1996.

29 **D** *Oxford, Bodleian Library ms Douce 104*

Vellum; anglicana formata of C15¹; much erased and altered, partly by another anglicana hand. About 34–5 ll. per p. Stained with loss of text at ff. 49v, 50v and esp. 1r, 60v, 61r–3. After final *Explicit liber de Petro ploughman* the date of completion in m. h. [1427]. Dialect Hiberno-English. The only copy with illustrations; facsimile with colour pls. of these by Pearsall & Scott 1992, and study by Kerby-Fulton & Depres 1999.

30 *****P** *San Marino, Huntington Library ms Hm 137*

Vellum; anglicana formata, of *c.* 1400; scribe signed Thomas Lancastre (or Dancastre) at end. Rubrics, foreign words, names and some keywords in red textura. 43 ll. per p. Dialect of Gloucester-Monmouthshire border. Important as complete early representative of *p¹* branch of **p** family. The former Phillipps 8231, and the first **C** copy to be printed, by Whitaker 1813 (on which see *Sk* III li–lxvi, Brewer 1996:37–45) and then by Sk; see *Intro.* II, § 30.

31 **E** *Oxford, Bodleian Library ms Laud Misc. 656*

Vellum; anglicana, of *c.* 1400 (frontispiece to *Sk* III). About 40 ll. per p. *PP* text preceded by *Siege of Jerusalem* and followed by three religious works. Dialect N Oxon. Final *Explicit passus secundus de dobest. incipit passus tercius.*

32 **A** *London, University of London Library ms S.L.V. 17*

Vellum; anglicana formata, of *c.* 1400–10. About 37 ll. per p. Dialect W Worcs. *PP* lacks VII 236–83, XXII 88–end (cf. next). Originally the last portion of larger volume containing *Handlyng Synne* and Mandeville's *Travels* Text D. See Perry 2007.

33 **V** *Dublin, Trinity College ms 212 (D.4.1)*

Vellum; anglicana formata, of *c.* 1390–1400 (ff. 88v, 89r as pl. II in Kane 1965). Some corrections m.h. and l.h. About 41 ll. per p. Lacks VII 236–83, XXII 88–end (cf. *A.*). Dialect NW Gloucs. On f. 90v the important memorandum about Langland's paternity (pl. I in Kane 1965; *Intro.* V, § 4). See further Brooks 1951:141–53; Kane 1965¹:26–33.

34 **R** *London, British Library ms Royal 18 B xvii*

Vellum; bastard secretary hand, of C16¹; corrections and alterations on early ff. in three hands. 31–45 ll. per p. *PP* text preceded by *Piers the Plowman's Creed*. Sole witness to the *p¹* sub-group <RM> where M is defective (see next).

35 **M** *London, British Library MS Cotton Vespasian B xvi*

Vellum; bastard anglicana, of *c.* 1400; some correction by erasure. About 41 ll. per p. Dialect W Warws. *PP* text preceded by four short pieces, including on ff. 2v–3v a poem against the Lollards [Robbins 1959:187], and followed by a Latin account of the Holy Blood of Hailes.

36 **Q** *Cambridge, University Library ms Additional 4325*

Vellum; anglicana formata, *c.* 1410; alterations m. h. and some corrections in another early hand. About 47 ll. per p. Dialect NW Gloucs. Damaged with some loss of text between V 131 and VII 96.

37 F *Cambridge, University Library ms Ff. 5. 35*
Vellum; textura quadrata of C15$^{1-2}$. 37 ll. per p. Dialect mid-Oxon. Imperfect through loss of leaves at VII 264–IX 181, XIII 93–XV 179. *PP* preceded by Mandeville's *Travels,* A-Text.

38 S *Cambridge, Corpus Christi College ms 293*
Vellum; anglicana formata with some secretary features, of C15$^{2-3}$. To p. 78. about 35 ll. per p., thereafter about 42. Dialect S Herefs. Imperfect (probably from defective exemplar) at VIII 267–X 95, XV 82–157, XXI 8–323.

39 G *Cambridge, University Library ms Dd. 3. 13*
Vellum; anglicana, of *c.* 1390–1400; heavily corrected m. h. 30–40 ll. per p. Dialect SE Herefs. and NW Gloucs. borders. Imperfect through loss of leaves at Pr 1–153, XIII 225a–XIV 40, XV 288–XVI 40, XXII 40–end; also lacks numerous other lines singly or in groups.

40 K *Oxford, Bodleian Library ms Digby 171*
Vellum; anglicana formata of *c.* 1400. About 33 ll. per p. Dialect SE Herefs. Imperfect from loss of leaves at beginnning and through defective exemplar at end, lacking Pr–II 216, XV 66–end. Belonged to Kenelm Digby in C17 (cf. nos. 25, 49).

41 *N *London, British Library ms Harley 2376*
Vellum; anglicana formata, of C15^{1}. Dialect SE Herefs. The only complete representative of the group *p^{2}* (III, *C Version,* §§ 54–6). For a study see Black in *MAE* 67: 257–90.

§ 5. Conjoint Manuscripts

B *and* **A**

42 H^{3} *of* A-Text; ***H** *of* B-Text *London, British Library ms Harley 3954.*
Vellum, anglicana formata, of 1400–25, written by Heron (cf. no. 25). About 40 ll. per p. Dialect S Norfolk. Title *Perys Plowman;* final *Explicit tractatus de perys plowman.* Rubrics from I to VII and at end of X. Contains B Pr–V 125 foll. by A V 105–XI. H is much contaminated but important as perhaps representing an independent line of descent within the β tradition of the B-Text. For a study see Horobin 2008.

C, A *and* **B**

43–5 B *of* B-Text; **b** *of* C-Text

43 Bm *of* B-Text; **L** *of* C-Text *London, British Library ms Additional 10574*
Vellum; anglicana formata, of *c.* 1400–10. Missing XX 356–87 added by C19 owner Dr Adam Clarke.

44 Bo *of* B-Text; **B** *of* C-Text *Oxford, Bodleian Library ms Bodley 814*
Vellum; anglicana formata, two alternating hands, both of *c.* 1400–10.

45 Cot *of* B-Text; **O** *of* C-Text *London, British Library ms Cotton Caligula A xi*
Vellum; anglicana with secretary features, of C15^{1}. Corrections m. h. and others.

All three members contain C Pr–II 128, then an expanded version of A II 86–198 followed by B III–XX, the transitions being carefully patched; have about 40 ll. per p. (Cot has 32); and are in a dialect with N Gloucs forms residual from the common exemplar. (On the relations of the three mss see *Sk* II xxv–xxvii, 391–2; *K–D* 40–2; Davis 1997)

A *and* C

46–8 **t** *of* A-Text *and* C-Text

46 *T *Cambridge, Trinity College ms R. 3. 14*

Vellum; anglicana formata of *c.* 1400. 74 leaves; illustration on f. iii verso, with arms of Thomas Nevile, Master of Trinity 1593–1614 (frontispiece to Vol. I). 41–46 ll. per p. Dialect mixed, mainly EM with some relict W forms. Idiosyncratic passus-divisions: continuous from I throughout **A** and **C** portions. At end of XI *Passus tercius de dowel. Breuis oracio penetrat celum*, then C XI 301ff; [XII] *Passus secundus de dobet*; [XVI] *P. sextus de dowel*; [XVII] *P. septimus de dowel & explicit*; [XVIII, XIX, XX] *P. pr., sec., ter. de dobet*; [XXI] *Expl. de dobet Et inc. de dobest*; [XXII] *secundus passus de dobest*. Final Explicit. The A-Text has no major omissions, lacking only 13 ll. of its *r¹* ancestor. Collated *Sk* I and adopted for its completeness and good spelling as copy-text in *K–F, Ka* and the present edition. Facsimile with transcription by Matsushita (2010).

47 **H²** *London, British Library ms Harley 6041*

Paper; anglicana formata, of *c.* 1425. 31 ll. per p. One leaf missing and five as fragments. The **A** portion lacks some 200 whole and 70 part ll; **C** portion some 350 ll.

48 **Ch** *Liverpool, University Library ms F. 4. 8 (Chaderton ms)*

Vellum; anglicana formata, of *c.* 1420. 30–6 ll. per p.

All three members of **t** contain A Pr–XI completed by C XI 301–end, with C XI 300*a* forming the conjuncture, and are in EM dialect with some W relict forms, esp. *heo, hy* in T.

49 **K** *of* A-Text; **D²** *of* C-Text *Oxford, Bodleian Library ms Digby 145*

Paper; free cursive hand, written 1531 by Sir Adrian Fortescue (see Turville-Petre 2000). 24–8 ll. per p. Contains A Pr–XI 313 [K], with rubric *Finis de dowell*, followed by C XI 301–end [D²], but omitting 300*a* (cf. **t** above). Standard **A** rubrics as in **t**; for **C**, standard **x**-type rubrics except that XII–XVII are *quartus-nonus de dowell*.

50 **W** *of* A-Text and C-Text *formerly Duke of Westminster's ms, Eaton Hall; now York, University Library, Borthwick Add. ms 196³*

Vellum; court hand of C15¹. Contains A Pr–XI followed by C XII–end. Rubrics [I–VIII] *Passus primus-octauus de visione*; [IX] *prologus de dowel dobett & dobest*, [X, XI]; *primus, secundus de dowel*, [after XI 166] *Tercius passus de dowel*, [after XI 313] rubricator's guide *passus iiij de dowel*; [XIII–XVI] are *vᵘˢ~viiijᵘˢ de dowel*, [XVII–XXII] as in standard **p**-type rubrics.

51 **N** *of* A-Text; **N²** *of* C-Text *Aberystwyth, National Library of Wales ms 733B*

Vellum; anglicana hand of C15¹. 29–35 ll. per p. Contains A I 76 (legible only from 104)–VIII 185 [N], followed by C X–XXI 428 [N²]. **A** portion strongly contaminated from **C** in VI; **C** portion of mixed **x** and **p** character with sporadic contamination from a **B** source of β-type.

Z *and* C

52 *Z *(the Z Version)*; **Z** *of* A- and C-Texts *Oxford, Bodleian Library ms Bodley 851*

Vellum; 209 leaves, bound and foliated after 1439. Contains (ff. 124r–39v) *1:* the **Z** Version of *PP* [= ms Z of **A** for *Sk, Ka*]; small anglicana formata hand of late C14 ('Hand X' [Rigg-Brewer]), perhaps that of John Wells, monk of Ramsey, owner of the book. 50 ll. per p. *2:* A VIII 89–185, followed by a rhyming conclusion and *Explicit Vita et Visio Petri Plowman* (here treated as sigil Z of **A** Version), in anglicana hand with secretary features of C15¹⁻² ('Hand Q' [Rigg-Brewer]). *3:* C X–XXII in same hand (sigil Z of **C**). Dialect of SW Worcs. The *PP* text preceded by well-known Latin pieces incl. Map, *De nugis curialium*, Bridlington's *Prophecies* and *Apocalypsis Goliae*. See the edition by Rigg-Brewer

1983 and their *Facsimile* of the Z-Text 1994, also Matsushita, *Facsimile* (with diplomatic transcription) 2008; Schmidt 1984; Kane 1985; Duggan 1987[1]; Green 1987; Hanna 1993. The sole representative of what is here taken as the 'Z' Version of *Piers Plowman*.

§ 6. Conflated **ABC** Text

53 **Ht** *San Marino, Huntington Library ms Hm 114*

Paper; anglicana formata, of C15[2]. 26–36 ll. per p. Dialect SE Essex. A-Text of **B** type heavily conflated from **C** and to a less extent from **A**, with re-arrangements, substitutions and introduction of spurious matter. Title *Piers plogman* before Prologue, final *Explicit pers ploughman*. See *Sk* III xix–xx; Russell & Nathan 1963; *K–D* 114–15; Scase 1987; Hanna 1989.

§ 7. Fragments

i **P** *Cambridge, Pembroke College ms 312 C/6*

Vellum bifolium, C15. Dialect E Anglian. Contains most of A IV 106–V 29, VII 84–93, 212*a*–41, 242–82. See *Ka* 13.

ii **Hm**[2]

See no. 12 above.

iii **H** *Yale University, Beinecke Rare Book and Manuscript Library, Osborn ms fa45 (the 'Holloway' fragment; previously Oslo, Martin Schøyen Collection, ms 1953).*

Vellum bifolium; anglicana formata, of c. 1400. Dialect SW Worcs. Contains C I 199–II 44, III 123–174, with 149–58 mostly lost through damage. Substantively and linguistically identical with X (no. 24 above);[4] described in Hanna 1993[2]:1–14.

iv **Ca** *Cambridge, Gonville and Caius College ms 669* / 646*

Vellum; bastard anglicana (scribe John Cok) of C15[1]; p. 210 in a ms of religious works by Rolle and others. Contains C XVI 180–199*a*.

THE MANUSCRIPTS: NOTES

1 Skeat further specifies in IV xvii–xviii an early **A** form ending at Passus VIII (as in Harley 875), an **A** form without XII (Douce 323), an uncompleted revision to **B** (ms Harley 3954), a version intermediate between **B** and **C** (Rawlinson Poetry 38), and an early version of **C** (Ilchester). But none of these 'shapes' identified as authorial affected his treatment of the three edited versions, which represent the complete non-conjoint forms of the poem now known as **A**, **B** and **C**.

2 Discovered 1966.

3 Sold to an anonymous purchaser at Sotheby's, July 1966; now on loan to University Library, York. A microfilm of the ms kindly provided by the Liverpool University Library was used for this edition.

4 After collation of a photocopy of H in the Cambridge University Library, the original was made available for examination through the kindness of the late Jeremy Griffiths, who was holding it for purchase by the Schøyen Collection.

II. THE EDITORIAL TRADITION OF *PIERS PLOWMAN*

The Present Edition and Previous Editions

i. *Towards a Parallel-Text Edition of* Piers Plowman

§ 1. *Piers Plowman* has received a great deal of attention from interpretative critics in the second half of the last century. The time now seems to be ripe for a fully-annotated and glossed critical edition of the poem in all its versions, to provide for our age what the Oxford Edition of W. W. Skeat did so well for his.[1] A partial example of a major single-version commentary is the excellent Clarendon Press edition by J. A. W. Bennett of the B-Text *Visio*.[2] But despite a five-page table of variants including some select readings from the **A** and **C** versions, the edited text of **B** to which Bennett's notes are geared, based on Bodleian Library manuscript Laud Misc. 581, differs little from that of Skeat's 1869 Student Edition of B Prologue–Passus VII. Bennett's work appeared only three years before the pioneering Athlone Press Edition of **B** by George Kane and E. Talbot Donaldson.[3] But any modern *Commentary* answering to Skeat's in fullness will have to take proper account of the important twentieth-century developments in our understanding of the poem's textual history most challengingly represented in the successive Athlone editions of **A**, **B** and **C**.[4] And these developments have such far-reaching implications for understanding of the poem as to require that a new interpretative Commentary should also be based on a freshly-edited text of *Piers Plowman* in all its versions. The multi-volume Athlone enterprise by many hands[5] will correspond when finished to the five-volume Early English Text Society edition produced single-handedly by Skeat between 1867 and 1885.[6] What it will not provide is an equivalent to his two-volume Oxford Parallel-Text of 1886. This provided the basis of most critical studies until the last quarter of the twentieth century. The edition now completed by this second volume is intended in part as a modern successor to it.

§ 2. The present edition, however, differs from Skeat's in five main features. The first is its inclusion, as a *fourth version*, of the unique **Z-Text** in manuscript Bodley 851. The second is its provision in Vol. I of a substantial *Critical Apparatus* to all the texts printed (Skeat's Oxford edition cited only a few of the variants given in his EETS volumes). In Vol. II a third feature is the long *Introduction*, including an extended account of the editorial issues, followed by a briefer treatment of non-textual matters such as authorship and background. The fourth is the body of *Textual Notes*, which are of the kind provided briefly in the EETS edition but in technical detail corresponding to parts of the Athlone Introductions. Finally, the *Indexical Glossary* resembles that in the EETS Vol. IV ii rather than the condensed form of it in Skeat's Oxford edition. The four Texts have been printed in parallel in one volume and the *Textual Notes, Commentary* and *Glossary* in a second so as to make it possible to study the texts and the relevant editorial material together. The choice of a *parallel* rather than a sequential format has been made only after consulting potential users of the edition. For though the reasons for adopting it may be evident, this way of printing *Piers Plowman* is not wholly free of drawbacks. Skeat's ingenious layout, which also recorded the poet's structural transpositions by a double presentation in smaller type of deferred or anticipated 'parallel' material, can distract if not confuse a reader wishing to read one version through. It is visually unappealing; it is quite unlike any text of the poem a medieval reader might have encountered; and its advantages for comparative study of the revision-process are probably now outweighed by the need to give each version its proper due. Though the last consideration most obviously affects the uncouth newcomer on the scene, **Z**, which can only suffer by being juxtaposed with its comelier successors, it applies as much to the mature but neglected **C** Version, the mere existence of which signifies Langland's reluctance to rest content with **B**. In the end, however, choice of a parallel format has been dictated by the nature of the texts themselves.

§ 3. Skeat, in producing his EETS volumes, did not systematically compare the readings of the **A**, **B** and **C** Versions, each of which he edited and published successively, though he did consult the **B** manuscripts when editing **A**.[7] And since the Oxford Edition reprinted his EETS texts with virtually no alteration, it is evident that he did not re-edit the poem in a 'parallel' or comparative way. This was understandable, given the pioneering nature of Skeat's enterprise, his initial lack of access to all the known copies of any one (let alone every) version, and his wish to complete the Oxford project rapidly after nearly twenty years spent on the EETS volumes. But as an editor, Skeat very seldom identified textual problems in **A**, **B** or **C** that could be solved, or best solved, only by recourse to one or both of the other versions. It seems that he made limited use of the numerous manuscript copies of each version he published. And, in fact, his main shortcoming as an editor was excessive trust in the readings of his chosen base-manuscripts, the *Vernon*, *Laud* and *Phillipps* copies of **A**, **B** and **C** respectively.

§ 4. For Skeat's successors, the solution to particular textual difficulties has not lain simply in choosing a better base-manuscript or making wider use of the diverse witnesses to the three versions. To take the case of **B**, what Elsie Blackman acutely perceived in 1918 and George Kane and E. Talbot Donaldson demonstrated at length some sixty years later, was that the archetype of the extant manuscript copies was itself very corrupt.[8] Many of its errors, they argued, could be corrected only by turning to the superior text of **C** and, in the half of the poem where it was present, that of **A**. Although open to dispute, this part of the Athlone editors' procedure proved indispensable to the present editor in preparing an annotated student's text of **B** twenty-five years ago.[9] When, a few years after this appeared in 1978, the opportunity arose to replace Skeat's Oxford Edition, it became quickly clear that **A**, **B** and **C** would have to be systematically edited in parallel. That is, every reading in each version would have to be established in the light of all variants not only in that version but also, where they existed, in the corresponding parts of the other versions. To some extent, Kane and Donaldson ('K–D' hereafter) had already done this for **B**; but the degree to which they had embraced the 'parallelist principle' only became explicit in 1988 when, in a 'Retrospect' to the second edition of his A-Text, Kane revealed that he now would have taken 'full account' of both **B** and **C** when emending corruptions in the archetypal text of **A**.[10]

George Russell and Kane, the editors of the third Athlone volume (1997), showed no hesitation in taking such 'account' of the implications of **A** and **B** for their edition of **C**. The present editor had reached the same position shortly before, when beginning work on the text of **C**, but unlike Russell and Kane ('R–K' hereafter) has made much less use of **B**, and none of **A**, for emending apparent archetypal errors in **C**.

§ 5. Less obvious than the need for 'parallel editing' was the requirement to print Langland's texts in parallel. Its advantage lay in complementing rather than duplicating the Athlone multi-volume format, and also in highlighting the manner in which the texts had been edited. Further, the familiar Skeatian layout would serve to focus attention on the readings of the **Z** Version even more effectively than would placing it as the first of four successive texts, let alone in the ambiguous isolation of an Appendix. But while choice of this format was more pragmatic than polemical, some reply is owed to the objection made by a reviewer of Vol. I[11] that a 'standard edition' was an inappropriate place for special pleading on behalf of **Z**. Firstly, then: a parallel-text edition provides an immediate stimulus to debate about the authenticity of **Z**. Secondly, printing **Z** alongside **A** is arguably not much more alarming than the Athlone editors' extensive use of **A** and **C** to emend the text of **B** or, more particularly, of **A** and **B** to emend that of **C**. Finally, given the peculiar difficulties posed by a multi-version work preserved in some fifty divergent copies, it may not even in principle be possible to produce a 'standard' edition that at once obeys the imperatives of parallel-editing and acknowledges current disagreements over the nature of the Z-Text. Thus, despite outwardly recalling the Oxford Edition accepted as 'standard' for nearly a century, this edition cannot take for granted what Skeat did when he digested his EETS volumes into parallel format. In relation to the Athlone texts, a growing divergence in approach on the part of the present editor has combined with differences of formal presentation to make of the present edition less of the supplement it was originally envisaged as and more of an alternative.

§ 6. Since the former aspect is explored fully below (§§ 55–134), it is enough here to illustrate the latter from a single major difference. Thus, while the Athlone Critical Apparatus provides a complete corpus of variants, the present edition prints variant readings only where the given version's archetypal text is in doubt. This economy is imposed by the parallel-text format, which rules out lavish citation of variants. But there is no need in any case to duplicate materials assembled with skill and thoroughness by the Athlone editors (and used with gratitude by the present editor in preparing the apparatus for **A** and **B**). This edition concentrates instead on foregrounding the parallelistic editorial process by the use of group sigils to bring out with maximum clarity the dual textual traditions attested in the **A**, **B** and **C** Versions. Its Apparatus therefore separates in an Appendix such information as the rejected unique readings of each version's base-manuscript. The purpose of this is to avoid distracting attention from the variants given, which are those relevant to establishing the key pairs of contrasted family readings. The rationale of the Apparatus is thus selection rather than comprehensive inclusion; it interprets, instead of simply recording, the mass of substantive manuscript data. Accordingly, textual information with no bearing on the establishment of the adopted text is usually not included.

A Version by T. A. Knott and D. C. Fowler (1952),[23] a worthwhile undertaking that suffered an (undeserved) eclipse thanks to Kane's critique of it in his edition of **A**.[24]

§ 12. The procedure adopted by Knott-Fowler ('K–F' hereafter) is not that of simply printing their base-manuscript, *Trinity College Cambridge R. 3. 14*, 'with occasional readings from other mss' (a close enough description of Skeat's eclectic positivism). Instead K–F follow, at least in theory, the alternative method of editing known as 'recension'. This aims to establish, by critical or comparative analysis of the variants, the text of the source or archetype from which they derive. But K–F make a point of allowing that their 'critical readings' are established 'by the weight of evidence, genealogical *and other*' (p.28; italics mine), an important rider that tacitly recognises a twofold problem. Just as the 'direct' method (described at § 8 above) is effective mainly with major readings, recension works only when the dependence of one extant witness (or convincingly inferrable lost source) upon another can be shown from the cumulative weight of their agreements in error. But since K–F's stemma acknowledges that none of the **A** manuscripts is a direct copy of any other,[25] no manuscript can be eliminated as a potential bearer of an original reading by direct descent. On the other hand, as both branches of their stemma derive independently from their postulated common original, neither branch can be proved secondary, and so neither can be eliminated. A third line of transmission, that of the **A** readings preserved in the **B** Version, though also perhaps independent, is judged by K–F to be merely ancillary. Their genealogy, therefore, since it cannot determine the choice of readings, is in effect otiose, and is in practice not relied on by K–F to any noticeable degree.

§ 13. Now, if the manuscripts in a textual tradition *can* be shown to descend vertically from a single archetype, even where lost group-ancestors or sub-archetypes must be posited, editing by recension reveals itself on examination to be a variety of positivism. But it is a more *logical* variety than the ordinary kind, and so nearer to rationalism, since its ultimate interest is less the facts *per se* than the causes that explain them. In other words, the main quarry that the 'logical positivist' editor has in view is the *archetype*, and nothing that may lie beyond it. However, in the *Piers Plowman* traditions, application of the recensional method is impeded by extensive convergent variation that confuses the relations between the witnesses forming the postulated genetic groups. K–F consequently end in the same eclecticism as Skeat, because their 'other' evidence (§ 12) acquires as much weight as the 'genealogical.' But the fact that this evidence is little else except the intrinsic value of the readings effectually opens the door to the 'direct method', the method associated with Kane and his colleagues. And it is replacement of the (at least in theory) near-mechanical operation of the stemma by critical *reasoning,* at all stages up to and beyond the archetype, that constitutes 'textual rationalism'.

§ 14. The Athlone *Piers Plowman*, when completed with its five-volume Commentary by Stephen Barney and others (the 'Penn Commentary') will form an even more massive work than the EETS edition produced single-handedly by Skeat. As the **A** Version was edited by Kane, **B** by Kane and Donaldson, and **C** by Russell and Kane, the three volumes perhaps inevitably show certain differences of handling. The first was based on the **A** manuscripts only, while the collaborative editions take the witness of the other two versions into account (see § 4 above). In other words, Kane's original approach to **A** has been abandoned, and **B** and **C** edited more or less 'parallelistically'. But while the three volumes embody a common attitude to the problems of

Langland's text,[26] it is nevertheless Athlone **A** that has exerted a far-reaching, even a constraining influence upon that of **B** and, to a less extent, **C**.[27] This is because the basic editorial principles of the later volumes remain those established by Kane in his edition of **A**.

§ 15. The Athlone project's continuity is reflected in its uniform layout. Each critical apparatus provides a complete corpus of variants, while the discussion of the text, from the classification of the manuscripts to the emendation of corruptions, forms a systematic introductory treatise. With the abandonment of end-notes in **B** and **C** has gone any residual resemblance to Skeat's EETS editions.[28] The Athlone Introductions' vast body of carefully organised and analysed primary material offers an enormously valuable resource for any subsequent editor. But it is perhaps less in their meticulous examination of the variational groups than in their wider view of the history of the texts, the character of the archetypes and the editorial obligation to restore (where possible) the originals, that the Athlone editions have proved so innovative and controversial. The attempt to recover the authorial text has been prosecuted most energetically in the edition of **B**. The edition of **A** was much more cautious about emending the archetype and that of **C** stops short of 'restoring' what its editors profess to believe was a work in progress and opts instead for the 'pre-archetypal' form as 'edited' by the poet's 'literary executor'. But allowing for these differences, which will be examined more fully below, the whole project can be fairly described as in essence 'rationalist'.

§ 16. The Athlone editors believe that the text of *Piers Plowman* was corrupted by the copyists from the earliest stages of its transmission. Not only was the archetype of the **A** manuscripts corrupt, so was the **A** copy used by the poet for revision to **B**. The text of **B** underwent massive deformation when the archetype of the extant witnesses was generated. As before, the scribal **B** manuscript used by the poet in composing **C** contained many errors, some of which provoked him to particular acts of revision. This latest (unfinished) version was in certain respects further damaged by the medieval 'editor' of the material from which the archetype of the **C** manuscripts was copied, as finally was that archetype itself. Editors who aim to recover what Langland wrote thus cannot avoid fashioning for themselves, as an instrument of guidance, something like an 'ideal' conception of the poet's *usus scribendi*. The latter term denotes the specific features of metre, style and expression that are criterial for authenticating the variants examined in the quest for each archetypal text and for assaying the 'originality' of that text where its readings are not in doubt. It is fundamental to this conception that scribal and authorial characteristics can be distinguished in most contested cases. In consequence, where the surviving evidence suffices, even one version's identifiably inauthentic archetypal readings may be drawn upon for reconstructing the hypothetical original in the light of one or both of the other versions. Moreover, in editing the 'middle' version, the most corrupt of the three, agreed **AC** readings can reliably guide correction of archetypal errors. In particular cases, even individual **A**, **B** or **C** copies may be judged to preserve their originals by 'good correction' from superior lost manuscripts of these versions. Finally, in the absence of direct textual evidence, an experienced understanding of the poet's *usus* and of the scribes' customary tendencies to vary from it may authorise conjectural emendation even of unanimously attested readings. For in the end, all the witnesses to a version, being descended from a bad archetype, may prove to be as untrustworthy as the chosen copy-text itself.

§ 17. It should be clear from this summary account how far editorial 'rationalism' differs from Skeat's 'eclectic' and Knott-Fowler's 'logical' kinds of positivism. In principle, it allows greater freedom in the choice of readings; most important, though, it does not stop at the archetypes, but aims to recover their lost originals through inferential reasoning from the known character of scribal variation. Texts produced by such editing are bound to differ substantially from those available to Langland's contemporaries, in proportion to the rigour with which the direct method is followed through. Any 'ideal' conception of the poet's mind and art in general, and of his syntax, lexis and versification in particular, must of course be based on the witness of the extant copies. But this consideration does not inhibit the Athlone editors, where they believe the scribes have consciously or unconsciously substituted their own words for the poet's, from exerting to the full the force of their editorial 'reason' (which excludes neither imagination nor intuition) in order to recover or restore the 'original' poem. Rationalist editing may begin with the manuscripts, but it does not end with them.

§ 18. A judiciously mild form of 'rational' editing was Derek Pearsall's aim in his 1978 edition of **C** for the York Medieval Texts. This was the second of the three complete single-version editions to appear between the Athlone B-Text and Volume I of the present edition, published by Longman in 1995. It was dedicated to Skeat's memory and it follows his eclectic positivism, eschewing Knott-Fowler's claim to be 'critical'. But Pearsall's edition ('*Pe*' hereafter), admirably as it brings up to date its predecessor's notes in the light of a century's work on the sources and background, does more besides. Skeat had printed manuscript *Phillipps 8231* (now *Huntington 137*), as had Thomas Whitaker, who published the first edition of **C** in 1813 (see § 30 below). But Pearsall based his text on ms *Huntington 143*, the one also selected for the Athlone and the present edition. This copy, which represents a much better **C** tradition, was unknown to Skeat, as was the one (*BL Additional 35157*) that Pearsall used to correct errors in Hm 143. He further consulted two other manuscripts of the same family, the *Ilchester* and the *Trinity College Cambridge* copies, which Skeat had collated throughout and drawn on sporadically; but he also turned to Hm 137 to supply lines missing from all members of the family of Hm 143. Very occasionally, too, Pearsall resorted to **B** (in its edited Athlone form) to emend presumed archetypal errors in **C**, notably in the last two passūs, where both versions are almost identical. Use of Hm 143 as copy-text, as has already been noted, had been recommended by Chambers, who published a facsimile of it in 1936; and in 1967 Pearsall and Elizabeth Salter had co-edited for the York Medieval Texts *Selections* from **C** based on Hm 143 corrected from Add. 35157.[29] The York complete edition demonstrated what the *Selections* had adumbrated: that **C**'s poetic excellence, too often concealed by the 'prosiness, pedantry and fussiness' (*Pe*, p. 21) of Skeat's 'standard' text of the inferior Phillipps copy, deserved recognition in its own right. The high esteem **C** now enjoys (attested by a recent verse translation),[30] is due mainly to its first modern editor's advocacy. And it was in fact a detailed examination of Pearsall's text that convinced the present editor that the **C** version would offer an immensely interesting editorial challenge.

§ 19. A major stimulus to produce the annotated edition of **B** that appeared in the same year as Pearsall's **C** came from a similar scrutiny of the Athlone text of **B** a few years earlier. The remainder of Bennett's Clarendon B-Text (see § 1 above) then lay some distance ahead; and, even if completed, it seemed as though this would possess a 'pre-Athlonean' or at best a 'post-Skeatian' character. Although a new edition of **B** could obviously not be *based* on Kane-Donaldson, it seemed inevitable that its text would have to draw deeply on their material and take significant account of their methods. Thus, by contrast with the York C-Text, the present editor's 'Everyman' text (though designed for students) carried a *Critical Apparatus* and *Textual Notes* of equal length to its interpretive *Commentary*. The first of these features it shared with Knott-Fowler's **A** version, which had been re-printed in 1964. The Everyman edition did not, however, dispense with the use of square brackets around emended readings (as did *K–F* and *Pe*), and it printed the apparatus on the text-page (where *K–F* placed it at the end). But because it was setting out, like the Parson in the *General Prologue*, 'to winne folk...by fairnesse' to the poetry of Chaucer's great contemporary, it provided marginal glosses of difficult words and treated the work's textual problems only summarily (as had *K–F*). In modernising obsolete Middle English letter-forms, it was following Knott-Fowler and, before them, Wright (*Wr*; see § 31 below). But in its focus on structure, meaning and literary qualities, the Everyman Introduction's model was the Salter-Pearsall *C-Text Selections*. It was this inspired little work that prepared a way in the editorial wilderness for seeing Langland as a great religious poet rather than as the colourful chronicler of medieval society familiar since the days of Skeat.

§ 20. The provision of a Glossary in the 1982 reprint of the Everyman edition brought it into line with those of Knott-Fowler, Bennett and Pearsall. But in its handling of the text, its indebtedness to Kane and Donaldson was obvious (even if, while adopting their methods, it sometimes reached very different conclusions). Thus, despite greater caution in rejecting archetypal readings, the Everyman showed its 'rationalist' leanings in two ways. One was its citation of 'K–D' after a number of readings and emendations; the other was its use of the 'versional' sigils **A**, **C** or **AC** to support a variant or indicate the source of a reading not found in any **B** witness. Here, moreover, the referent of '**A**' was the Athlone A-Text of Kane, that of '**C**' the Hm 143 text that would form the basis of the forthcoming Russell-Kane C-Text and had been cited by K–D in the Introduction to their recently published B-Text. These 'Athlonean' sigils contained the germ of a fully 'visible' parallel-edited text. Though no longer required in volume I of the present edition, which prints all the texts on facing pages, in the Everyman Second Edition (1995) they still serve their original purpose. However, since the latter has been extensively altered to accord with the Longman B-Text, what they now denote is the **A** and **C** Versions as printed in that text. But in the *Visio* section of the revised Everyman they are sometimes joined by a new versional sigil, **Z**.

§ 21. The addition of the sigil **Z** is explained by the publication of a third single-version edition some five years after the Everyman first appeared. Consisting of the first part of the *Piers Plowman* text in manuscript Bodley 851, it was designated by Skeat's sigil 'Z', though Skeat (like Knott-Fowler and Kane after him) made no use of it when preparing his A-Text. However, George Rigg and Charlotte Brewer, the editors of this neglected text, saw it not as an eccentric abbreviation of **A** with spurious interpolations and lengthy omissions but as a substantive version anterior to **A**. And **Z**, they maintained, was not only unfinished, like **A**, but in a draft state, although they identified Bodley 851 as an early scribal copy, not a holograph.[31] Their argument is based on the 'Z'-Text's formal coherence, linguistic integrity, stylistic consistency and unique textual relationship to **A**. But Rigg and Brewer ('R–B' hereafter) judge it independent in possessing some authentic readings that show the archetypal A-Text to be in error.

18

§ 22. The case for **Z** made by R–B was antecedently unlikely to receive a disinterested appraisal from the Athlone editor of **A**, who had dismissed it without consideration, and its wider reception was also somewhat muted. However, though the present project was still only a gleam in its editor's eye, what Bodley 851 suggested *prima facie* to that eye (still as sceptical about **Z** as any) was something more remarkable than an **A** copy re-written by an inventive scribe (like the singular B-Text in manuscript Corpus 201).[32] Its unique passages, in particular, appeared not simply expansions of an oddly truncated source but (at their best) novel and arresting. Its 'author' was evidently no mere follower of Langland, like the poets of *Pierce the Ploughmans Crede* and *Mum and the Sothsegger*. Strikingly, too, **Z**'s equivalent of **A**'s *Visio* differed not just in degree but in kind from other scribal 'versions,' despite revealing (like certain of them) what looked like contamination from **B** and **C**. Despite all these features, however, **Z** seemed initially interpretable as a remarkably 'creative' response by one reader-author-scribe who had encountered *Piers Plowman* in its earliest and probably in its later forms as well. If this was the case, then it properly belonged to the history of the poem's reception, not to that of its text. But for a prospective editor of a parallel-text there appeared no Gowerian *middel weie* between rejecting **Z** as spurious and accepting it as authentic. Manuscript Bodley 851 should either prove classifiable or have to be rejected as an irretrievably aberrant witness to the **A** tradition. To place **Z** apart in an Appendix as simply too interesting for total oblivion while unusable in editing would only defer judgement instead of making it. And if 'the business of textual criticism' was 'to produce a text as close as possible to the original,'[33] then an editor prepared to identify 'original' readings in any individual manuscript of an accepted version should not quail from doing as much in a text proposed but not yet accepted as a 'version.' To hypothesise **Z**'s authenticity during the process of systematic parallel-editing would, it seemed, facilitate discovery of its true nature through a minute comparison with the divergent manuscript texts of **A**, **B** and **C**, which could each, for the purpose of this exercise, be regarded as a scribal 'version'.

§ 23. The result (somewhat surprising in the event) was a conviction that, despite certain residual problems, R–B's case appeared sound. There was thus no alternative, after editing **Z** in parallel, but to print it as **A, B** and **C** were to be printed, in parallel. A cautionary example, however, lay ominously at hand: Skeat's bold attribution of *Richard the Redeless* to Langland, which is now universally rejected. Nonetheless, it was plain to see that the two cases differed in essence. For Skeat, the question of printing *Richard* in parallel with *Piers Plowman* obviously never arose; but one positive effect of his mistaken attribution was to bring *Richard the Redeless* an attention it would not otherwise have received. The editors of Bodley 851 had shown it to have at the least major textual implications for the **A** Version. These would be more vividly (though more provocatively) highlighted if **Z** did not figure as a mere sigil following its (at times perforce extended) variant readings in the critical apparatus to **A**.[34] Arguments in support of this decision have been offered below that it is hoped may prove convincing (see III, *Z Version*). But whatever doubts may persist in the minds of readers, **Z**'s inclusion here is not intended to assume its claims established once for all so much as to arouse rigorous debate on the proper criteria for recognising authenticity in the *Piers Plowman* tradition (there has been very little such as yet). The same may be said for citing **Z** in the revised Everyman Apparatus, which encourages its users to assess **Z**'s evidence and not (like Skeat and Kane) to ignore it.

§ 24. The preceding paragraphs have described what may be called, despite ruptures and changes in theory, a true editorial 'tradition', extending from the mid-nineteenth century to the present time. It is also one to which many notable contributions have been made by scholars who did not themselves succeed in producing editions. Amongst these, Chambers stands out as the second father of *Piers Plowman* editing, without whose pioneering studies the Athlone project might never have come into being.[35] Skeat's edition, which this section began with, was not the first, and the present one will doubtless not be the last. But while acknowledging its place in the tradition, this edition is intended as more than a continuation of earlier undertakings, if less than a total substitute for them. Drawing extensively on the efforts of the nine editors discussed, its aim is to offer an equivalent to what the earliest of them accomplished (like the present editor) with no collaborators, and also (unlike him) no true predecessors: a *Piers Plowman* for our time.

iii. *Earlier Editions: from* Crowley *to* Wright

§ 25. Both the distinctiveness of the present edition and its place in the tradition should emerge from the following examination of the strengths and limitations of those predecessors. Its purpose is to bring out through an extended historical critique the dimensions of and the most effective way of handling the textual problem. But it starts by considering the earlier editorial undertakings (now largely of historical interest) that kept knowledge of *Piers Plowman* alive between the manuscript period and the age of Skeat, with whom the scholarly tradition began. The *editio princeps* of the poem was the **B** Version published at Holborn in 1550 by Robert Crowley, who reprinted it twice in the same year.[36] Crowley the Protestant controversialist has the credit of rescuing Langland from the neglect into which most medieval writers except Chaucer fell under the combined impact of the Renaissance and the Reformation. His lost manuscript source, which was distinct from any of the extant manuscripts and which he seems to have reproduced rather inaccurately, contained few unique variants of real value (see *Introduction* III, B Version, §§ 13–16, esp. § 16, below). But a couple of major readings in Crowley's first print (Cr[1]) will illustrate two positive features of his editorial work. The first shows him apparently consulting other versions to correct an unsatisfactory reading, initiating a procedure used by his successors from Wright onwards. In the famous description of divine love at B I 152 *And also þe plante of pees, moost precious of vertues*, Crowley's *plant* (as in parallel **A** and **C**) is both intrinsically 'harder' than the archetypal **B** reading *plente* and (*pace* Skeat) one that is unlikely to be a spelling-variant of the latter. Unless *plante*, a reading accepted as authentic by all modern editors, had entered his source from a lost **B** manuscript superior to the archetypal text, it must derive from one of the other 'auncient copies' (of other versions) mentioned in his prefatory Address to the Reader.[37] By contrast, *provided* at B V 165 is not too hard to be his own conjecture, though more probably a modernisation of an original **purveiede* introduced in his manuscript source to correct the unmetrical archetypal reading *ordeinede*. Crowley's second impression (Cr[2]), re-set from another lost manuscript and collated throughout with Cr[1], lacks unique right readings. But Cr[3], mainly a reprint of Cr[2], provides in *wishen vs* a basis for reconstructing the original at B XII 270 from the corrupt archetypal reading *wissen*. Further, as Crowley's reading here could have been a correction prompted by the verb *wenen* at corresponding C XIV 195, his text may even reveal the rudimentary beginnings of a 'parallel' approach to editing the poem.

§ 26. These corrections, however, mark the limits of Crowley's achievement; for in other respects his own practice does not bear out his exhortation 'to walke in the waye of truthe'.[37] In the summary added in Cr² his confusion of Piers with the dreamer in Passus VIII helped mislead generations of readers, and it no doubt underlies the further error in William Webbe's 'commendation' (1586) of the 'auncient poet...*Pierce Ploughman*' as 'the first that...obserued the quantity of our verse without the curiosity of Ryme.'[38] More culpably still, to further his polemical aims Crowley (in Skeat's words) 'falsifies his text of set purpose'.[39] Thus for *And Marie his moder be oure meene bitwene* at B VII 197 he substitutes *And make Christe our meane, that hath made emends,* which preserves Langland's metre while reforming his theology. At B XII 85, instead of *For Goddes body myȝte noȝt ben of breed wiþouten clergie,* he has *For bread of gods body myght not be without cleargy,* another change designed 'to make this line...more suitable for his Protestant readers,'[40] though at the cost of barely making sense. In XIII 259 for *Ne mannes masse make pees* Crowley prints *There may no man make peace.* Here Langland's later replacement of *masse* by *prayere* at C XV 230 doubtless implies his own dissatisfaction with the original. But the poet's revision, so far from being 'Wycliffite,' may show rather an awareness that **B**'s phrase '*man's* mass' expresses a less than fully orthodox sense of the priestly minister as performing his ritual act *in persona Christi*. Finally, at XV 181 *He kan portreye the Paternoster and peynte it with Aues,* for *Aues* Crowley (as Skeat notes) 'ingeniously substitutes *Pitie*, thus adding a fourth initial *p*, contrary to Langland's usual custom.'[41] Here (as in VII 197) Crowley's 'ingeniousness' resides only in his *following* the poet's use of a fourth alliterating stave (by no means unusual, as Prologue 1 should have reminded Skeat). More serious is his deletion of Langland's emphasis on saying the Rosary as a penitential exercise similar to the Psalms and the Lord's Prayer (XV 179–81).

§ 27. Of a piece with Crowley's corruptions of the poet's Marian and Eucharistic emphases are the 'notes and cotations in the mergyne,' with what Brewer calls their 'clear polemical orientation',[42] offered for the reader's assistance on the title-page of Cr². One concerns confession, the importance of which in the **B** Version is shown by its threefold treatment in Passūs V, XIII and XX. Crowley's note against III 51ff ('The fruites of Popishe penaunce'), as J. N. King showed, elicited from a seventeenth-century Catholic reader Andrew Bostock a rejoinder ('Not the fruits but abuse of Penaunce') indicating a much better comprehension of the poet's purpose. The same reader (on f. xxxix^r of Douce L 205) answers Crowley's comment on B VII 172–73 ('Note howe he scorneth the auctority of Popes Math.vi') by succinctly stating the orthodox doctrine of indulgences, which Langland understood and (at 174–81) apparently endorsed.[43] These (fairly typical) examples suggest that Charlotte Brewer understates in finding 'perhaps a little strong' King's assertion that Crowley 'kidnapped' the poem in an attempt to 'interpret it as reformist propaganda.'[44] Kidnapping is a serious crime, even if the victim is one's spiritual rather than bodily offspring; but it fits the bill. Crowley's 'notes and cotations', far from 'geuynge light to the Reader,' belong with 'the worckes of darcknes' that he believed the poet, like Wycliffe, 'crye[d] oute agaynste.'

§ 28. Crowley is not, however, directly responsible for the 'faultiness and imperfection' that Thomas Tyrwhitt attributed to his lost manuscript source.[45] Being of the 'β' type, this source (necessarily) lacked the many lines and passages unique to the 'α' tradition (see *B Version*, §§ 7, 58 below); and his other 'auncient copies' presumably did not include any that, like the Rawlinson and Corpus manuscripts, preserve this tradition. Again, Crowley is not to blame that as late as Wright's edition (1842) his was the only form of **B** to have been published (as noted at § 31, Wright was much influenced by his print). Nor, finally, is it Crowley's fault that Owen Rogers, by including the Lollard-related *Pierce the Ploughman's Crede* in his 1561 re-issue of Cr[3], initiated the unhappy coupling of these texts that was repeated three centuries later by Wright. But Rogers's suggestion that the *Crede* was by the author of *Piers Plowman* could only lend colour to his predecessor's strong implication that the poet was a sympathiser with, if not a supporter of, John Wycliffe. All this adds up to a major failure of Crowley's in his editorial duty to print what the author wrote and explain what he meant, not what he thought Langland should have written or meant. His edition's contribution to the understanding of *Piers Plowman* is thus almost entirely negative, and its place is in the history of the poem's reception rather than of its editing. All the same, insofar as the text derives from a lost manuscript copy, 'Crowley' should have found a place in Benson and Blanchfield's volume describing the manuscripts of the B-Text.[46]

§ 29. Although it was never re-published entire until our time (see *Intro.* I, no. 13 above), parts of Crowley's text were reprinted in the eighteenth century. First Thomas Warton the younger included some 500 lines of extracts from Cr[2] in Vol. I of his *History of English Poetry* (3 vols., 1774–81), with glossarial and historical annotations foreshadowing Skeat's and, unlike Crowley's, genuinely 'geuing light to the reader.' Next, the antiquary Joseph Ritson in Vol. I of his *English Anthology* (3 vols., 1793–94) gave Passus V 1–441 from Cr[1] with some variants from Cr[2] and emendations of his own, but without annotation. It was, however, not until 1824 that Richard Price, a librarian at the British Museum, in a new edition of Warton's *History*, replaced his extracts with a text based on the early fifteenth-century manuscript *Cotton Caligula A xi*,[47] recording Crowley's readings in a critical apparatus. He also gave in an Appendix to Vol. II parallel passages from the antiquary Richard Heber's **C** manuscript (subsequently Phillips 8231 and now Huntington 137), corrected from two other British Museum C-Text copies, *Cotton Vespasian B xvi* and *Harley 2376*.[48] Price probably contributed more to the understanding of the textual situation than anyone before Skeat. He printed a selection of critical texts based on the manuscripts and recognised the value of comparing parallel passages in the different versions. More important still, he identified in manuscripts *Harley 875* and *6041*[49] a third version of *Piers Plowman*, known since Skeat as **A**, which he surmised was perhaps 'the first draught of the poem' (Vol. II, 482–83). Skeat, without naming Price, acknowledged his acuity, which has at last received due recognition from Brewer.[50]

§ 30. Price, however, was not the first to make available for comparison a version other than the one that Skeat, as late as 1869, still called 'the "Crowley" type, or Type B' (*Sk* II, p. i). That was the achievement of the Lancashire topographer Dr Thomas Whitaker, who in 1813 published an elaborate black-letter folio edition entitled the *Visio Willi de Petro Plouhman*. Based on his friend Richard Heber's manuscript (later Phillipps 8231, now Hm 137), this first complete Langland edition since Crowley was the *editio princeps* of the version Skeat named **C**. As well as an Introductory Discourse, Whitaker provided a glossary, a 'perpetual commentary' or continuous paraphrase on the page, brief notes and a detailed summary of the poem's content. He anticipated Price in illustrating the description of Wrath with parallel extracts from Crowley, the B-Text *Oriel College* manuscript[51] and another manuscript of Heber's now recognised as a conflated copy of **A**, **B** and **C**.[52] His edition, which has been recently examined by Brewer, was extensively cited by Skeat.[53] The latter recognised Whitaker's ignorance of Middle English as a disabling deficiency in his text and glossary, but offered what are comfortable words for any editor of the poem: 'if there are numerous inaccuracies, the desire to be accurate is none the less clear'.[54] Concerning Langland's supposed heterodoxy, Whitaker correctly observes that the poet's belief in 'almost all the fundamental doctrines of Christianity has no tendency to prove him a Wickliffite or Lollard' (p. xviii), proving that the 'historical' nineteenth century had early achieved a more balanced perspective on the turbulent fourteenth century than was possible for the sanguinary sixteenth. Whitaker's notion of Crowley's text as representing a later revision of the Phillipps version, which he calls 'the first but vigorous effort of a young poet' (p. xxxi), now seems hard to credit. But given Whitaker's ignorance of **A**, it seems only a degree more eccentric than Jill Mann's proposal that **A** may have been written after both **B** and **C**.[55] The worst to be said of his view is that it overlooks what internal evidence exists for dating the longer versions, e.g. **C**'s removal of **B**'s allusion to the coronation of the young heir and its bold new reference to popular disaffection with the king for encouraging 'custumes of coueytise.'[56]

§ 31. The title of *The Vision and the Creed of Piers Plowman*, which Thomas Wright published in 1842 and reprinted with a few extra notes in 1856, echoes Crowley's, while his inclusion of the *Crede* follows Owen Rogers's reprint. Familiar with medieval historical works, Latin satirical writings and over half the extant manuscript copies of the poem, Wright was much better equipped for his task than was his immediate predecessor. Yet he arguably advanced understanding of the poem less than Whitaker (whom he treated more unkindly than did Skeat after him) and certainly less than Price. As Wright admits, his edition 'differs very little' from Crowley's (*Vision*, p. xliv), perhaps unsurprisingly since its base-text *Trinity Cambridge B. 15. 17* belongs to the same sub-group of 'β' copies as did the Tudor printer's lost manuscript source.[57] Wright helpfully modernises its obsolete Middle English letter-forms; but his printing of the poem in half-lines misrepresents its metrical structure, wastes space and produces a line-numbering incompatible with any other edition. His transcription is generally accurate and his glossary greatly improves on Whitaker's. But a fault in the former can lead to error in the latter, as when for *bonched* he reads *bouched* in Pr 74 and glosses it 'to stop people's mouths.' The non-existent word *bouched* perhaps seemed real to Wright, as Crowley has it too, and his conjectured sense is historically plausible. This particular mistake, moreover, may be *lightly forȝyuen*; for in this manuscript *n* is often indistinguishable from *u*, as at XVI 20 where, again following Crowley, he has for a probably original *loue dreem* the reverse error of *lone dreem* (the manuscript could read either). Wright's attractive emendation *giltles* for *synneles* in Pr 34 (rejected by Skeat but adopted by K–D and the first Everyman edition) illustrates his adventurous acceptance of an other-version reading (here from **A**) solely for what he understands to be its superior metre.[58] His textual comments are few, his frequent citations of Whitaker highlighting the differences between the latter's version and his own, and his explanatory annotation, if sporadic and unsystematic, is not without interest. But Wright's edition made little difference to later understanding of the text or its meaning. Skeat's observations on it (*Sk* II xxxvi–xxxix) may seem neutral compared with his warm appreciation of Whitaker's more defective work; but it is hard to see how he could have learnt much from Wright.

iv. Skeat's *Editions*

§ 32. Walter Skeat brought to his editing of Langland far more philological and historical learning than any of his predecessors. But any comparison of his B-Text with Wright's had to wait until two years after the appearance of his A-Text, which initiated a twenty-year project for the Early English Text Society.[59] Begun in 1866 and published in 1867, this first volume pre-empted misapprehension with its lengthy admonitory title *The Vision of William concerning Piers Plowman, together with Vita de Dowel, Dobet, et Dobest, Secundum Wit et Resoun* and its subtitle 'The "Vernon" Text; or Text A.' Its limitations, such as excessive confidence in the base-manuscript[60] and inadequate use of the other collated manuscripts to correct its errors, persisted throughout the later editions. These defects might be largely discounted had Skeat used his 1886 Parallel-Text as an occasion for revision and improvement (he did not). But given that he had to make his own way, some of his A-Text's weaknesses may be due to his having no predecessor, as Wright had in Crowley. When compared with Whitaker's edition of **C**, which offered a negative model, its superiority is quickly evident. However, Skeat's naming of the **B** and **C** Versions the 'Crowley' and 'Whitaker' types respectively reveals his early awareness of working in an editorial 'tradition.'

§ 33. Skeat published before his edition a pamphlet that made available for comparison an eleven-line passage (= B III 76–86 //) drawn from manuscripts of all three versions.[61] Seven are from **A**, eleven from **B** (including Rogers's valueless reprint of Crowley) and eleven from **C**. Its main purpose was to elicit information about as yet unidentified copies of the poem. Among those that came to light was *Ashmole 1468*, which Skeat used in Passus XI together with *Harley 3954* to correct errors in *Trinity R. 3. 14* (his base here after the cessation of his main copy-text).[62] These two manuscripts, with one from Dublin (*TCD 213*) that he heard of too late to use and another not known till 1922 (*Society of Antiquaries 687*),[63] belong to a distinct family of the **A** tradition.[64] But it is very doubtful whether Skeat would have identified them as such, even had all four been ready to hand. For his declared method at this stage was to print the single manuscript he judged 'the oldest and best written' as having 'readings...on the whole better than those of any other' and to correct it from the copies collated only 'where it seemed to need it.'[65] Vernon (V) is indeed the earliest **A** copy and coaeval with most of the oldest **B** and **C** manuscripts (*c.* 1400),[66] though not as early as Skeat's 1370–80 (p. xv), which would have brought it to within a few years of **A**'s probable date of composition.[67] Unfortunately, however, Vernon lacks Passus XI's last 130 lines through loss of a final leaf; but Skeat's attraction to this imposing manuscript and mistaken belief that the 'conjoint' **AC** Trinity ms (T) was much later in date led him to discountenance T as his base-text, and this despite resorting to it in XI 184–313 and also for earlier corrections, including the supply of whole lines.[68] It is harder to understand why he included from *Harley 875* (H) some 27 lines absent from V and all other copies 'for completing the sense, in passages that seem incomplete', while acknowledging that a few were spurious (later editors unanimously reject all of them).[69] The last point indicates Skeat's initial inability to detect scribal interpolations by applying rigorous metrical and stylistic criteria.

§ 34. In the matter of A Passus XII, however, Skeat gave an admirably judicious treatment of the one text he had, the opening eighteen lines found in *University College ms 45*, which he printed with comments.[70] The full form with John But's ending, uniquely preserved in ms *Rawlinson Poetry 137* (R), came to light only after publication. This material he issued with his B-Text in 1869, numbering the pages *137–44 for binding-up with his A-Text. Skeat's identification of Passus XII as substantially authentic is supported in the present edition but for his acceptance of lines 99–105 (which is nonetheless defensible).[71] The third copy containing Passus XII, the *Ingilby ms* (J),[72] became known to Skeat only after the publication of **C**. This he duly printed in 1885 with emendations and notes in the second part of Vol. IV.[73] In his parallel-text edition five years later Skeat placed Passus XII in the main text and not in an Appendix as did Knott-Fowler and Kane later, and he was right to do so. This portion of his final edition, with its use of all extant authorities, its apparatus and its shrewd emendations, is as 'critical' a piece of editing as could be asked for. The inadequacies of Skeat's *A-Text* elsewhere are partly due to his incomplete access to the manuscripts, but more to his editorial inexperience at this stage. However, Skeat's early awareness of the relevance of **B** to the editing of **A** is implicit in his brief comparison of the two versions on pp. 156–58; and it is well illustrated by his inclusion (after V 201) of manuscript U's lines about Clement the Cobbler on the grounds that 'they appear in all later versions...and are certainly genuine.'[74] This greatly improves on his editorial treatment of the Harley 875 lines mentioned above. Skeat may overlook possible cross-version contamination in U; but the example is a delicate one, because the lines' appearance in the **A** family called **m** below (III, *A Version*, §§ 24ff) allows that they might also have been present in the original text of **A**.[75]

§ 35. More open to criticism is Skeat's neglect of another conjoint text, the **C** portion of which he was to designate 'Z'. As he observed in his *C-Text* Preface, Bodley 851 was completely overlooked because it lacks the lines B III 76–86 // chosen as the 'test-passage' for identifying *Piers Plowman* manuscripts, and so Skeat received no notice of it. His later judgement of its first part as 'an extremely corrupt text, mere rubbish...written out from imperfect recollection'[76] suggests that his notion of the poem's organisation and development had by then become fixed. As already noted, Skeat could have corrected his earlier oversight in the Parallel-Text edition; and, given the peculiar textual problems of a multi-version poem surviving in multiple copies, the necessity to do so was matched by a singular opportunity. But he was never to re-consider **A** in the light of Bodley 851's unique text. Skeat's EETS volume, the *editio princeps* of the **A** Version, with its original spelling, paragraphing, side-notes and introduction, nonetheless represents a great advance on its predecessors. Over thirty of his emendations to the base-text (whether Vernon, Trinity or Rawlinson) have stood the test of time and witness to his taste and understanding.[77] But the edition is now of mainly historical interest, and a measure of its inadequacy is that the first two twentieth-century Langland texts undertaken for editing should both have been of **A**.

§ 36. Skeat's B-Text of two years later is much superior, and it may still be regarded as a usable 'conservative' edition of the poem's only completed version. His base-manuscript Laud Misc 581 (L) has not been favoured by most recent twentieth-century editors.[78] But by contrast with the drawbacks he laboured under with both **A** and **C**, Skeat had access from the start to nearly all extant **B** witnesses. The exception is the *Sion College* manuscript, which was found as recently as 1966, but is a corrupt modernised copy of no use for editing.[79] However, Skeat managed to omit from his list of manuscripts, which is numbered consecutively through the versions, the **B** portion of the conjoint Harley 3954, which he had described and dismissed in his *A-Text*[80] and completely ignored in editing **B**. This copy, though contaminated from **A**, is now acknowledged to contain some readings with a good claim to be original, and has at least the value of a collateral authority.[81] But more than compensating for this omission is Skeat's effective recognition of the existence of two **B** traditions, one represented by Laud and the remaining copies except Corpus 201, and one by Rawlinson Poetry 38, of which copy he happily discovered some missing leaves in *BL Lansdowne 398* (joint sigil R).[82] Skeat did not attempt a genealogical classification of the **B** manuscripts, any more than he had done for **A**. But he recognised the affinity between both Wright's manuscript (W) and Crowley and that between the eight copies with the current sigils G, Y, O, C^2, C, Bm, Bo (= *Sk* B) and Cot (= *Sk* B.M.).[83] And of the relations between the last three, which K–D assign the joint sigil B, he gave a basically correct preliminary account.[84]

§ 37. Though Skeat had ignored ms Bodley 851 (Z) as relevant to establishing the text of **A**, he observed the 'peculiarities' of ms *Corpus 201* (F), a **B** copy in some ways comparable to Z, and he recorded in detail its eccentric passus-divisions (pp. xxviii–xxx). But though Skeat did not perceive that F is descended from the same common original as R, he did note (*pace* Brewer)[85] how F agrees with R at XIV 189 in the important right reading *pouke* against *pope* in L and the rest. It is nonetheless unfortunately true that, while he found F 'worth consulting in a case of difficulty' (p. xxx), Skeat gave no thought to the source of its good readings. But as these are many more than he realised, the oversight had adverse consequences, given that R remains incomplete even after the addition of the separated Lansdowne leaves. The main losses in L occur at XIX 56–9, 237a–38b and 337, where Skeat's omission of some evidently original lines preserved only in F leaves his B-Text defective. However, his bold step of incorporating Rawlinson's distinctive material in its entirety was wholly justifiable, even though his judgement of R as a **B** Version '*with later improvements and after-thoughts*' (p. xii), recently revived by Taylor and others, is rejected in the present edition.[86] Skeat's view of R can become tortuous, as in relation to X 291–303, lines present in both R and **A** but missing from all other **B** manuscripts except F. These, he maintains (pp. 406–07), were 'first cut out' but 'on second thoughts' retained, whence they reappeared in the C-Text in a different part of the poem [i. e. at V 146–55]. Skeat's is a much more complicated explanation than that of K–D, who argue that the lines were lost from the RF ('α') tradition by mechanical error.[87] His notion of Langland's compositional methods is nonetheless one that for Brewer (if not for the present editor) has 'a good deal to recommend it.'[88] Whatever the case, it seems clear that Skeat's interpretation of Rawlinson inhibited him from comparing it closely with Laud (L) and thus from acquiring manuscript authority to correct many errors that L shares with the other members of its family 'β' (see *Introduction* III, *B Version* §§ 41–3). It is evident, too, that while he recorded R's variants and compared the readings of his chosen **B** witnesses with those of the other versions, he did not see the significance of the frequent agreement of **A** and **C** with R against L and the remaining β copies. Thus at IV 94 *Thanne gan Mede to* meken *hire, and mercy she bisouȝte*, L's *mengen* is challenged on intrinsic grounds by R's *meken* supported by all other versions, including **Z** (which of course Skeat ignored). His notion of R as a 'transition stage' between **B** and **C** (p. xii) would here require Langland's supposed 'afterthought' to have been either a restoration of **A** or an anticipation of **C**, a possible explanation but not the most economical available (cf. *Introduction* IV, *Editing the Text*, § 2). Though at times he corrected the text from other versions where his base-manuscript was hopelessly corrupt, Skeat did not systematically weigh L's readings against R's in the light of **A** and **C**. So when he draws on R to emend a reading attested by the other **B** copies, as at X 429a (*Sunt* for *Siue*), his emendation is on grounds of common sense and does not appeal to **C**'s authority for additional support.

§ 38. Skeat included as an appendix a sixteenth-century glossary found in manuscript *CUL Ll. 4. 14* and written in a hand that he suggests may be Crowley's.[89] As in his *A-Text*, he gives side-notes with helpful page-references to parallel passages and also the sources of Langland's abundant Latin quotations. His Critical Notes contain interesting comparisons with **C**, as at XIII 152–56 (on Patience's riddle) and 293–99, in relation to R as 'a copy of the B-Text with all the latest additions' (p. 411). But most notable is his very full record of the variants of Cr^l and many of its annotations, while his detailed account of it on pp. xxxi–xxxvi of the Preface usefully reprints Crowley's Address to the Reader entire. Skeat's textual notes often display shrewd insight, as at X 366 (*Sk* 368) where he supports his judgement of *non mecaberis* (*slee noȝt*) as 'the author's own mistake' by apt reference to A XI 254 = *Sk* 247. At XIX 434 = *Sk* 428 likewise, his restoration of L's deleted *pur* in *pursueth*, though made primarily on the basis of the five **B** witnesses collated, takes proper account of parallel **C**.

§ 39. Judged as a whole, Skeat's edition of **B** has lasting value as an accurate print of Laud Misc 581 supplemented by the distinctive portions of the almost equally important Rawlinson copy. Its success is due partly to his having had access to all the manuscripts, but much more to his skill in producing a text that is intelligently 'conservative' without being rigidly positivistic. Its impact was considerable, particularly through the annotated *editio minor* of Prologue–Passus VII (the '*Visio*') based on it, which provided the first taste of Skeat's remarkable abilities as a commentator.[90] Continuously in print until replaced by Bennett's Clarendon edition of 1972, the latter made *Piers Plowman* accessible to a far wider audience than the subscribers who read the parent work. The complete *B-Text* was incorporated without change into the Oxford edition and became the basis of nearly all interpretative studies for a century.[91] In his Preface, Skeat maintained that 'of the three forms of the poem in its integrity, the B-Text is the best' (p. xl). This view became universal and was to be repeated over a century later by the present editor,[92] though it can no longer be maintained without qualification in many respects. Whatever the case, as the next four paragraphs will bear out, the best of Skeat's three EETS editions is undoubtedly his text of **B**.

§ 40. The EETS edition of the C-Text appeared in 1873, accompanied by *Richard the Redeless,* which Skeat ascribed to Langland, and *The Crowned King*, which he regarded as an imitation[93] (only the latter judgement finds support today).[94] The unique text of *Richard* survives along with the glossed **B** copy (C^2) in manuscript CUL Ll. 4. 14 (see § 38 above).[95] Skeat's arguments for this poem's Langlandian authorship are weak, his point about the *f / v* alliteration it shares with *Piers* probably confusing metrical idiolect with dialect.[96] But as noted at § 23, the attention attracted to *Richard* by its inclusion with *Piers* perhaps offsets Skeat's unfortunate following of Crowley in treating as Langland's a piece of accomplished imitation. Both works have been omitted since the 1959 re-issue of the *C-Text*, which contains corrections by J. A. W. Bennett of its mistranscriptions and the original Critical Notes, but not Skeat's one-hundred pages of prefatory material. As Bennett rightly states,[97] much of the latter remains in concise form in the Parallel-Text Introduction; but omitting its valuable 30-page description of the manuscripts (*C-Text* xix–li) rendered the reprint much less useful than that of the (unchanged) EETS *B-Text*. Also removed in 1959 was Skeat's pioneering comparative account of the versions (pp. lxxvi–xciv) and his critique of Whitaker's edition (li–lxiii), as lengthy as the treatment of Crowley in his edition of **B**. All references to his *C-Text* here are accordingly to the first edition of 1873.

§ 41. By this time, Skeat understood the poem's text far better than when he embarked on **A**; but he regrettably did not have access to all the important **C** manuscripts as when working on **B**. The **C** Version is now recognised as surviving in two main recoverable lines of transmission, described below as 'x' and 'p', of which the **x** tradition is much the better (see *Introduction* III, *C Version* §§ 62–4). Skeat knew several examples of both, and as many as ten of the twenty-two copies he described were of the **x** type. They are *Ilchester* (I), *Digby 102* (Y), *Additional 34779*, formerly Phillipps 9056 (P^2), *Douce 104* (D), *Bodley 814* (B), *Cotton Caligula A xi* (O), *Additional 10574* (L), *Trinity Cambridge R. 3. 14* (T), *Harley 6041* (H^2) and *Digby 145* (D^2).[98] But of these the last six are conjoint copies and the first four variously imperfect or damaged. Moreover, of the three extant **x**-type copies complete enough for consideration as a base-text, Skeat knew only Douce 104, which he judged (p. xlvi) an inferior member of 'the same sub-class as I and T' [i. e. the **x** family]. Of the other two that might have impressed him more favourably, *Additional 35157* (U) was acquired by the British Museum more than twenty years after Skeat's text appeared, and *Huntington 143* (X) came to light only as late as 1924.[99] Not surprisingly, therefore, Skeat based his text on a **p** manuscript, of which he knew thirteen of the sixteen surviving copies, over half of them complete. The eleven Skeat described were *Phillipps 8231*, now *Hm 137* (P), *Laud 656* (E), *Trinity Dublin D. 4. 1* (V), *Royal 18 B xvii* (R), *Cotton Vespasian B xvi* (M), *CUL Ff. 5. 35* (F), *Corpus Cambridge 293* (S), *CUL Dd. 3. 13* (G), *Digby 171* (K), *Harley 2376* (N) and the conjoint *Bodley 851* (Z). A second conjoint text, the *Westminster* manuscript (W, now York, University Library, Borthwick Add. MS 196) was to be described only in an Index of Additions in Part IV of the completed work (1885).[100] Having chosen P as his base-text, Skeat collated four other **p** manuscripts E, M, F and G, resorting also to S where G was defective. But while appreciating the **p** copy Z's **C** portion 'as furnishing collateral evidence' (p. xxxiii) for emendations to P made 'after collation with other MSS' (p. xxxii), he declined to cite Z in his apparatus (see further § 44). Of the **x** manuscripts, Skeat collated I and T throughout; but again, though noting that Digby 102 (Y) belonged to the 'IT sub-class' (p. xlvii), he passed it over. This was unfortunate, since this manuscript descends from a superior branch of the family now best represented by the complete copies X and U (*Intro.* III, *C Version* § 17).

§ 42. Skeat's *C-Text*, with an apparatus, summarising side-notes, and versional cross-references, now to both earlier texts, gives some sense of being 'parallelistic' in spirit if not in form. But his comparisons with **A** and **B** had no consistent critical impact on his editorial practice. Thus at Prologue [= *Sk* Passus I] line 41 Skeat replaces *tho gomes* PS by *god wot* from MF with no indication that this is also the **AB** reading, a fact which might be thought to have prompted scribal contamination. But *tho gomus* is certainly the archetypal reading, of which *wrecches* E and *gromes* N are scribal replacements of a neutral by a more hostile term. Skeat might have avoided emendation had he checked an accessible **p** copy such as R or an **x** copy like D. This he should have done, since both I and T are useless here, one being a jumbled **AC** composite in the opening, the other an A-Text, while Y does not begin until II 157. Skeat also ignored manuscript B at this point, citing few readings from it on the grounds that it 'cannot be much depended on' (p. xxxix). Quite possibly, it was instinctive distrust of B as a conjoint text that deterred him from ascertaining the quality of its **C** portion through comparison with other copies. But in this case he would have found B to agree not only with the 'IT type' manuscript D but also with the **p**-type manuscript R. Skeat thus adopts *god wot* simply because he prefers it, neither recording the weight of support for his base-text's reading nor suspecting that M and F could be contaminated from **B**, as they very probably are.

§ 43. Skeat's 'eclectic positivism' is illustrated at Pr 72, where for PE *bulles* (again the probable archetypal reading) he substitutes *breuet* from I and M,[101] a reading shared also by B (in this case arguably through contamination from the **B** Version). But he gives no reason for preferring *breuet*, whether for its superior sense, or because supported by **B**, or for both reasons. Earlier in the same line, by contrast, Skeat accepts **p**'s *blessed* where **x** has *bounchede* (known to him through I), a reading which seems more likely to be original than to be a sub-archetypal contamination from **B**.[102] But he would probably not have adopted *bounchede* even had he been aware that X and U here agree with I, since that reading is in fact attested by the other **x** copies P², D and B, which he knew. For Skeat generally seems to have relied not on 'critical' comparison but on personal taste and the privileged witness of his base-manuscript, as is illustrated by his unwise retention of **p**'s *vnwyse* at l. 49. At this point, manuscript I is unavailable to endorse M's superior alternative *wyse*; but had Skeat observed how M is supported by R, a **p** copy not suspect of contamination, comparison with the **x** witnesses B, P² and D might have made him recognise in *vnwyse* a scribal flattening of an original identical with **A** and **B**.[103] The number of such 'flattened' readings in P and its frequent padding-out of the text[104] have helped to form the still current opinion of **C** as poetically inferior to **B**. So it is ironic that Skeat should have been the first to reach that conclusion and his 'standard' edition be responsible for others' coming to share it.

§ 44. Skeat's edition of **C** is thus of limited value by comparison with his **B** (though, unlike his **A**, it does not contain any plainly spurious lines). This is mainly because he took insufficient account of the **x** family witnesses available to him and rarely corrected errors in P from G, K and N, which he was unaware belong to a better branch of **p** than EVRMFSZ (to name just those he used).[105] Skeat's suggestion that P and Z were both made 'from an early copy of the poet's own autograph copy' (p. xxiv; cf. pp. xxx) has no real basis. All the same, Brewer has no cause to wonder why Skeat, given his belief that Z was 'even more correct in its readings than P' (p. li), 'did not take [Z] as his copy-text in preference to P;'[106] for since its **C** portion begins only at Passus X, this manuscript is intrinsically unsuitable. But as with his view of the **B** copy R's 'intermediate' status, which still has supporters (see § 37 above), there is little to be said for Skeat's opinion of Ilchester as 'clearly an earlier draught of the C-Text' (p. xxxvii).[107] Nor is there for Brewer's recent commendation of Skeat's view that ms I represents a separate branch of the **C** tradition as 'confirmed by later scholarship'; it is not.[108]

§ 45. The final part of Skeat's edition appeared in two sections.[109] Of these the first (1877) contained Notes to the three versions, Indexes to the notes and a Bibliography. The second (1884) had a Glossary, General Preface, Proper-Name Index and chronologically-arranged List of Historical References to the poem, together with a revised form of the initial Parallel Extracts, which now brought the project full circle. Though these nearly thousand pages have dated in many respects, their positive qualities far outweigh the shortcomings of the earlier volumes. Skeat's explanations show a profound grasp of the poem's historical meaning and an even more impressive understanding of its copious and idiosyncratic language. The Glossary alone, produced without the aid of modern historical dictionaries or concordances, but clearly organised, comprehensive, etymological and indexed, makes the fourth part an invaluable resource. It shows Skeat as by natural leaning more of a lexicographer than a textual critic. This fourth part has been mined by later editors without the leisure or capacity to replicate his painstaking researches. Only Bennett has surpassed Skeat in the range and depth of his first-hand enquiries into the poem's sources and background; but his commentary unfortunately covers only B Prologue–Passus VII. Skeat's notes and glossary, though geared to the C-Text, refer to parallel passages in the other versions and annotate matter unique to them. This arrangement helped greatly to shorten the time he was to spend on the final work that rounded off his twenty-year stint as an editor of *Piers Plowman*.

§ 46. The two-volume Oxford Parallel-Text of 1886 made the poem available in the format of a classic 'standard edition' rather than one for Middle English specialists.[110] Skilfully condensing the material in the earlier six volumes, it contained little that was new. The Notes kept the essence of the EETS fourth part, while dispensing with illustrative material that was occasionally superfluous even in the original setting. The Glossary omitted all but a few select etymologies and the abundant orthographic variants, but still occupies nearly thirty per cent of the second volume. By contrast, textual discussion was drastically limited to a brief description of the manuscripts and the editions of Crowley and Wright. The ten pages Skeat gave to *Richard the Redeless* could have been better spent bringing to bear on the text of *Piers Plowman* the comprehensive knowledge of all three versions he had lacked at the start of the project. His failure to do so may have been due to a wish to complete the work with a minimum of delay; but it is perhaps not surprising that he felt no need to re-think the C-Text, as he might have done if manuscripts X and U had already come to his attention.

§ 47. With the **B** and **C** Versions on facing pages and **A** running across the upper portions of both, the layout of the Clarendon Press text-volume is a triumph of simplicity and clarity. Skeat also had the inspired idea of printing again, in smaller type, material in **B** and **A** that was transposed in **C**, as well as **C** passages moved a significant distance from their previous positions, particularly in Passūs XI and XIII of **B**. His treatment of the accidentals is ambivalent, using a raised medial point for the manuscripts' variously-shaped metrical markers, and only half-heartedly modernising letter-forms, replacing *þ* with *th* but retaining *ȝ*. Skeat's textual apparatus records the rejected reading of the base-manuscript and the source of the variant adopted; but the absence of even an abbreviated equivalent to the EETS Critical Notes is a lack. The result (doubtless unintended) is to make the text appear more certain than, by this stage, he knew it both was and would have seemed with fuller apparatus and textual annotation. These reservations aside, the edition fully deserved its warm reception. What it did above all was to make clear to a wider audience that Langland's work was not marginal, but belonged with Chaucer's at the centre of medieval English literature. No later editor of *Piers Plowman* has achieved as much.

v. *Towards a Critical Edition*

§ 48. Skeat's edition was nonetheless found wanting within a generation of its completion, as a result of major advances in the understanding of the textual traditions. In 1909 R. W. Chambers accordingly embarked on a new EETS edition of **A**, the obvious starting-point, as this was the least satisfactory of Skeat's three texts. It was never achieved, but the editorial principles put forward in an important article of that year with J. G. Grattan, a sort of equivalent to Skeat's 1867 pamphlet on the manuscripts, had far-reaching effects.[111] Chambers and Grattan initially conceived their text along expanded Skeatian lines, aiming to use as its base either *Rawlinson Poetry 137* (R) or *Trinity Cambridge R. 3. 14* (T), 'with collations of all the other MSS.'[112] But their article recognised, as Skeat had not, the observed fact of scribal 'improvement' and the consequential obligation for an editor to prefer the better of two available variants instead of adhering to the base-manuscript's reading except where it was plainly mistaken or nonsensical. What they really desiderated was a 'critical' edition, arrived at through comparing the readings of all witnesses so as to establish a family tree of their textual relationships.[113] Such was also the aim of T. A. Knott, the American scholar whose important article of 1915 criticised both the 'older' (Skeatian) eclecticism guided by personal taste and the new approach of Chambers and Grattan, who applied their analysis of the internal and external evidence of readings only to some manuscripts and not to others.[114] Knott also wished to use the Trinity manuscript, but as what is more accurately called a copy-text, being 'little more than the basis for spelling and dialect.'[115] The main difference between Chambers and Knott seems to lie in their views of how the genealogical method would operate in relation to the *Piers Plowman* manuscripts. Knott believed that persistent agreement in significant errors indicated their clear presence in the copy from which the manuscripts agreeing derived. Chambers wished to accord due importance to contamination, coincidence and change of exemplar as causes of the convergent variation in the witnesses that obscures vertical transmission and thereby hinders the construction of a stemma.

§ 49. Neither side brought out an A-Text, and their disputes can seem after nearly a century exaggerated in their espousal of supposedly antithetical standpoints. But the differences in theory have had a real bearing on subsequent editorial practice, even though, if Chambers' observation is limited mainly to minor variants, it will be seen to complement rather than contradict Knott's, which holds of major readings. The Chambers-Grattan approach was taken up and developed by George Kane as editor of the Athlone Press A-Text; and an edition of Knott's A Pr–VIII was published by D. C. Fowler, who completed the work by editing Passūs IX–XII himself. The competing views of editing now seem after a century in some ways matters of emphasis more than of irreconcilable principles. Chambers-Grattan and Knott-Fowler were each partially right about the text of Langland. Thus it now seems uncontroversial first, that selecting even the variants on which to classify manuscripts necessitates a measure of editorial 'judgement' and second, that extension of this judgement towards the making of 'critical' decisions cannot be dismissed as the mere exercise of 'personal taste', when its grounds are explicitly stated and rationally defended. For it is obvious that textual arguments to support the preferred readings in a poetic text cannot attain the impersonality possible in the case of legal or theological writings; nor should they be expected to. At the same time, the gradual emergence of variational groupings will affect assessment of the stemmatic weight of variants judged 'significant' on intrinsic grounds. But however hard a 'critical' editor may aim at theoretical consistency, the value of the text achieved will depend to a great degree on the strength of the argument for each specific choice of reading; and with major readings it is usually possible to make a genuine case. This case cannot exclude 'personal taste', but can recognise it openly in order to control it by reference to more objective criteria (on what these criteria might be, see further IV, *Editing the Text* §§ 14–22 below). Editorial decisions should ideally be neither mechanical nor arbitrary; but the reasoning behind them, however convincing, will often fall short of demonstration. This said, the true test of an editorial method's worth is not the absolute consistency of the theory it exemplifies but the credibility of the text it produces. It is not the text that is validated by the theory but the theory that is vindicated by the text. There may be a real, if limited, analogy here between critical editing and experimental science; but the crucial question with both is, does it work? The theory underpinning an editorial method should be as rigorous and lucidly expounded as the nature of its object allows, and that has at least been the present editor's aim. But if what has just been said is true, the determining 'test' of the arguments in part IV of this *Introduction* and in the *Textual Notes* must be the edited text presented in Volume I. In the end, a good edition will meet the needs of a specific readership; a better will serve several classes of reader; the best will be one that most nearly satisfies the largest number of different kinds of reader.

vi. *The* Knott-Fowler *Edition of the* A-Text

§ 50. To meet the needs particularly of the student rather than the specialist was the clear aim of the first modern Langland edition, although its critical apparatus (called 'Textual Notes') will interest primarily the latter. The Knott-Fowler A-Text (*K–F*) has the advantage of being based on all the extant **A** manuscripts, of which it gives a concise account. The three copies that remained unknown to Knott as to Skeat became available for Fowler to use in completing Knott's work: *National Library of Wales 733B* (N), *Society of Antiquaries 687* (M) and *Liverpool University F. 4. 8*, the 'Chaderton' manuscript (Ch).[116] Additionally at hand from the outset was the Ingilby ms (J), which ranks with M and Rawlinson Poetry 137 (R) as one of the three most important **A** copies. The *K–F* Textual Notes are printed at the end, an arrangement that has drawbacks but allows a full and clear presentation. So, for example, at I 127, II 83, IV 24, 61 (the last a major crux) the variants may be inspected even more conveniently than if the manuscripts were directly before the reader; produced half a century before electronic technology, K–F's textual data remain useable and useful. They include a valuable list of lines absent from each copy, and all variant rubrics (a feature omitted by Athlone **B** and **C**). Their main presentational defect, which they share with Athlone, is to provide sigils only for the variants and not for the manuscripts supporting the lemma. Requiring the reader to work out the strength of manuscript support for the reading preferred, this was a needless economy, given the generous layout adopted. But while the variants recorded are 'only a selection', the criteria for inclusion are (sensibly enough) 'wherever the critical reading is not readily apparent' or 'deviates from the reading of T' (p. 171). However, the want of 'critical notes' like Skeat's (and Kane's) is felt, since K–F's Introduction gives under ten pages to textual questions (their editorial principles, having been sketched at §§ 12–13 above, will not be described again). Textual information is therefore largely located in the genealogical trees on pp. 26 and 27, two being provided because three copies (H, E, L) fail, while one (N) ceases as an **A** witness before Passus IX, and because K–F see the *Visio* and *Vita* as distinct parts of the poem, though not as different works that circulated separately.[117]

§ 51. Knott-Fowler's section on Historical Background, seven times the length of that on the poem, belongs in spirit to the age of Skeat, in effect ignoring the important recent studies of its thematic content and literary character[118] (it was to be a generation before the fruits of twentieth-century literary criticism enriched the introduction and annotation of editions aimed at the non-specialist).[119] Their text is more attractive than Skeat's with its border of side-notes or Kane's later with its austere lack of paragraphing. The replacement of obsolete letter-forms and avoidance of square brackets around readings that depart from the copy-text combine to render the work as accessible as Chaucer's in a modern standard edition. Of these two economies (one followed by the Everyman, the other by the York edition), the second is linked to the editors' refusal of conjectural emendation. But while this decision lessens the need for 'critical notes,' the absence of any sign of intervention by the editors unintentionally conceals their avoidance rather than solution of textual difficulties. As will emerge,[120] K–F's classification of the manuscripts is also unsatisfactory. They find three lines of descent from the 'original' (either archetype or holograph): *x*, from which descend V (Skeat's base-text) and its genetic twin H; *y*, ancestor of all the other **A** manuscripts; and *z*, source of the **A** material preserved in the **B** Version (whether or not revised). However, as will be shown (III, *A Version* § 14ff), K–F's 'x' has the same common ancestor (to be designated r^2) as five of their 'y' copies, I [J], L, Di [K], W and N; the manuscripts T, H^2, Ch, D, R and U possess an exclusive common ancestor (r^1); and both r^1 and r^2 derive independently from one sub-archetypal source (to be designated **r**). Secondly, **r**'s line of descent is wholly distinct from that of K–F's 'minor' group EAMH^3 (called **m** at §§ 24ff below, and there argued to be far from minor). Thirdly, both **r** and **m** stand in immediate independent descent from a single archetype (Ax). Finally, Ax's errors show that it cannot be the author's original. This last point implies that some conjectural emendation may be inescapable in a genuinely 'critical' edition once the archetype has been arrived at. But in K–F's text the dagger of corruption is no more in sight than the bracket of correction. Their basic grouping of the manuscripts needs no significant modifications; but to judge from the edited text, it matters little that their identification of the sub-archetypes is faulty or that, given the lack of direct dependence of any extant copy upon another, neither diagram looks like a true stemma. For K–F evidently do not pay much heed to the constraints of the genealogy; and so if their text reveals a 'y' rather than an 'x' character, it is not because they have shown x to be secondary (derived from y), but because they have preferred the y readings on intrinsic grounds. The stemma has little to do with K–F's frequent rejection of r^1 readings, either where r^2 or where r^2**m** retain presumed archetypal readings from which r^1 diverges. But as they do not recognise **m**'s independent descent, they not surprisingly dismiss readings found *only* in **m**, whether or not x and y here agree, although comparison with the other versions shows these readings as very likely to be archetypal (see III, *A Version* § 48).

§ 52. To illustrate this last point more fully: in about 160 instances (nearly seventy of them major) where the present edition follows *K–F*,[121] 33 are r^2 readings, and in 20 of these r^2 is accompanied by **m**.[122] In some cases, however, the stemma has only partly influenced the choice of variant, and does not explain the variant rejected. Thus at II 83 *of mendis engendrit*, r^2 is supported by **B** but has been wholly corrupted in x, which has *a Mayden of goode* (the reading accepted by Skeat). This example would appear to confirm K–F's view of M as belonging to y, since its variant *for monnys engendryng* looks like a further smoothing of N's nonsensical *of mennis engendrid*, a misreading of *mendes*. However, the postulate of a y-family reading distinguishable from x is contradicted by *fendis* r^1, of which E's *frendis* is a corresponding smoothing. This, of course, is one case where dependence of both r^1 and M upon r^2 could plausibly be maintained, and the beginnings of a true stemma discerned. But since both r^1 and **m** are later found to be right against r^2, e. g. at (*a*) X 214 *same] schrewe*, with support from **B** (= K–F's source z), neither can be inferred to derive from r^2. Secondly, since r^1 is uniquely right at (*b*) XI 19 *construe* against both r^2 *conterfeteth* and **m** (*om*), r^1 cannot derive from either. Lastly, since **m** (supported by **B**) is uniquely right at (*c*) I 106 *mene] om* **r**, group **m** cannot be descended from r^1 or r^2. The r^2 variant (*a*) *schrewe*, which K–F properly reject, tells against their x / y division, since it is attested by both V and two of their y copies J and K. So they must be presumed to prefer *same* on 'other' (non-genealogical) grounds such as intrinsic character, majority support and the witness of **B**. In example (*b*), where K–F read *conterfeten*, their sole criterion must be intrinsic quality, since the majority have *construe* (the r^1 reading) and *contreuen* appears in only one **A** witness, K [Di], which they no doubt diagnose as contaminated from **B** or **C**. Here K–F's procedure is not easily distinguishable from either Kane's 'direct method' or Skeat's 'eclecticism'; and this is unfortunately a case where none of the editors explain their choice in a note.

§ 53. The last instance discussed illustrates K–F's inadequate notion of the poet's metre, which adversely affects their text in several places. For in following the majority reading here and ignoring the evidence of **m**, they are led to include among their acceptable 'variations' on Langland's 'basic pattern' [of *aa / ax*] the demonstrably inauthentic *aa / bb* (p. 16), despite the fact that the reading of **m** [= their T²M] is here supported by **B** [= their source z]. It is partly owing to this defective understanding that K–F have no incentive to emend archetypal readings on metrical grounds. A notable such example is at V 200 *þrumblide*, where the reading of V *prompelde* would actually support their view of x as a family directly derived from the archetype. But in choosing *stumblide* they seem unhappily misled by the presence of this unmetrical substitution-error in most **B** copies and in Skeat's C-Text, though the probable **C** and the possible archetypal **B** reading supports Vernon (and may be its source). K–F's unawareness of **m**'s critical significance[123] allows them not only to print an unmetrical form of VII 270 (and to accept another spurious pattern *aa / xa* at p. 16) but even to omit the AMH³ variant from their textual notes (p. 231). If they thus overlook **m**, it comes as no surprise that, following Skeat and anticipating Kane, they make neither use nor mention of **Z**, a text which, as Rigg-Brewer were to show, cannot be ignored by an editor of the **A** Version. Neglect at I 110 of both **Z** and M (here the sole **m** witness) accordingly leaves their line with a metrical pattern of the form *ax / xa* found nowhere on their list.

§ 54. Many of these incoherences arise out of K–F's failure (like that of Kane after them) to edit the A-Text in the light of the other versions. This prevents them from formulating an empirically based theory of Langland's metre powerful enough to enable them to discriminate and correct scribal errors decisively. In part, the refusal to edit parallelistically may be due to K–F's belief that **B** was not written by the same author as **A**, although the Introduction remains uncommitted on this question. Where their text convinces, this is often due simply to the same good sense and feeling for style on which Skeat relied, but which Knott himself had called in question. Thus in so straightforward a case as Pr 44 *þo Robertis knaues* K–F presumably adopt the minority variant *þo* of H²LM against that of their copy-text and the majority not because it appears archetypal (VH *þese* arising from *þo* and not from *as*) but simply because it gives sharper sense in the context. A similar instance is *Fayteden* Pr 42 as against *Flite þan* of the copy-text T and the whole *r¹* subfamily supported by E and the *r²* manuscript K. Here such factors as the **BC** reading might have played a part in their decision; but without significant support from the variants, the genealogy itself cannot have been criterial. For since V's *feyneden hem* is likely to derive homœographically from *fayteden*, K–F can have adopted the latter only on grounds of 'intrinsic' superiority.[124] In conclusion, when they are right or wrong, it is owing to a successful or unsuccessful act of 'personal judgement.' Their reasons are not given, but on evidence like that examined, the genealogical imperative cannot have been the strongest. If K–F's text is better than Skeat's, it is in part because they have tested many readings 'critically'; but if it is often preferable to that of Kane, whose method is more rigorous and consistent, this is in spite of their theory, not because of it. In that paradox lies a lesson any editor of Langland would do well to ponder.

vii. *The Athlone Editions:* Kane's *Edition of the* A-Text

§ 55. The Athlone edition of the A-Text edited by George Kane (1960), based once again on the Trinity Cambridge copy, is aimed at scholars. Its focus is so exclusively textual that it dispenses with the literary and historical discussion and the supplementary material on date and authorship found in Knott-Fowler and Skeat. Five years later, Kane showed in a magisterial mono-graph that all three versions were written by William Langland,[125] a conclusion accepted from the outset as fundamental to the idea of the present edition (see further Part V, §§ 1–6). But the 'parallel' principle played no direct part in Kane's editing, and had he offered a stemma it would presumably not have contained the source *z* postulated (and to some extent used) by K–F (see § 51). Thus, in defining **A**'s distinctive character, while Kane takes account of text absent from, echoed in or revised by **B** and **C** (p. 21), he ignores text present in **B** and / or **C** with no or with minimal alteration. By strict definition, material in this last category is not 'distinctive'; but that K–F were right to think it relevant to editing **A** is a conclusion that Kane, after working on **B**, was tacitly to acknowledge in his 1988 'Retrospect'.[126] Like K–F, Kane uses all the witnesses except Bodley 851; but his implied view of the latter as a corrupt scribal **A** copy does not save him in his initial sentence from misdescribing the 'first version' as preserved in seventeen manuscripts and one fragment; for counting Z, the number is eighteen. This is a rare error in a work that sets the standard of accuracy for subsequent editors (a point to remember when reading the criticism of it below).

§ 56. Kane's *A Version* is printed with an *apparatus criticus* at the foot of the page, critical end-notes and a long *Introduction* on the problems of editing the text. Even without this last, the Apparatus alone, which is lucidly explained and justified on pp. 170–72, is invaluable to any subsequent editor. It improves in intelligibility on K–F's in always placing after a lemma the source of a reading selected in preference to that of the Trinity manuscript. Unlike theirs, it is also a comprehensive corpus of variants (a luxury that a parallel-text format precludes). And while its dense columns crowd the page-space in a ratio of 2:1 with the text, the arrangement has such obvious advantages that it has been followed in the present edition. The overflowing fullness of the Athlone Apparatus is partly due to its including non-substantive variants that could have been omitted without loss: e.g. at I 26, after the lemma *shuldist* come the immediate source-reading *schuldest* and five variants, all non-significant and two purely orthographic (*scholdist*; *scholdest*). Despite its historical-linguistic interest, which shows the residual influence of Skeat, such mate-rial is unnecessary for understanding the basis of the edited text, except in a few ambiguous cases. Kane's omission of the **A** rubrics from his apparatus is not a problem here, since they are recorded for each copy in the section on the manuscripts. Moreover, they could arguably be regarded not as authorial but as part of the scribal layout (though no argument to this effect is offered). None-theless, since the rubrics can be examined to reveal how the poem's divisions were understood as far back as the archetypal stage, their absence from later volumes becomes a fault, and the present editor has judged it necessary to include and analyse them (Appendix II). The want of any cross-references to discussions of particular readings in the *Introduction* is made good in the *Critical Notes*, which comment on conjectural emendations and problematic cases of discrimina-tion among variants. But the omission of such notes in subsequent Athlone editions becomes a source of frustration. Like the latter, **A** makes no reference in the apparatus to the scholars who first printed the readings adopted, a courtesy surely obligatory for a 'critical' editor using earlier solutions to a difficult text's many problems. Thus (except for Skeat's emendations in Passus XII) some fifteen readings adopted after the **A** Version's first editor receive no acknowledgement, while some fifty of Knott-Fowler's major readings (about two-thirds of those accepted in the present edition) have no sigil to compensate for the strictures to which K–F's edition is subjected in the Introduction (esp. pp. 90–114). The unhappily Olympian suggestion of owing nothing to any predecessor is one that an editor should be strenuously at pains to avoid.

§ 57. Kane's text outwardly resembles Skeat's rather than K–F's in keeping the original spelling while introducing modern punctuation (with some reluctance, as Kane notes on p. 170). But inconsistently it eschews paragraphing, an unhelpful practice repeated in later Athlone volumes even where the copy-text is paragraphed (T itself has none). This makes Kane's edition (*Ka* hereafter) harder to use than K–F's, which employs modern paragraphing, or Skeat's, which preserves that of the Vernon manuscript. Following traditional practice, square brackets enclose any reading that diverges from Trinity's. Although not a difficulty in **A**, this procedure becomes one in **B** and **C**, which have many more conjectural readings not derived from an extant source, but no cross-references or critical notes to provide any help. Since the Athlone editors treat each base manuscript as a copy-text chosen for completeness, linguistic consistency and orthographic regularity rather than for substantive superiority, there is little gain even for the specialist in signalling every departure from it indifferently. Brackets that constantly remind of the 'edited' character of the text may be salutary in discouraging undue confidence in the uniformity of the witnesses. But as used here, they obscure a textually important distinction between readings rejected as non-archetypal and archetypal readings judged unoriginal. The present edition has accordingly followed a *middel weie* between the 'cleared' Knott-Fowler and the 'cluttered' Athlone layout, using brackets only around readings unattested in *any* manuscript of the version in question (see IV § 51). There are aesthetic arguments for reducing visible signs of editorial intervention, but they rank after the need for an open (if discriminating) recognition of the copy-text's 'instrumental' character.

§ 58. Kane's *Critical Notes* throughout display more penetrating textual insight than can be found in Skeat's *A-Text*. Where dealing with recurrent minor features like *ful* for *wel*, they helpfully cross-refer (as on Pr 26) to discussion in his *Introduction* of a whole category of scribal substitutions. The notes on lexical variants sometimes do the same, as at X 136 where *mynchons* Ch is preferred to *martires* r^2**mBC** and the r^1 reading *nonnes* is judged a scribal substitution for the former (on these sigla see *Introduction* III, *A Version*, §§ 1–5). Kane is certainly right (pp. 161–62) to say that this and the other Chaderton variants he favours 'stand or fall as a group', and thus to consider them together (for the argument that his assessment here is mistaken see here *Intro.* IV §§ 32–3 below and the relevant *Textual Notes*). But his treatment of major lexical variants can be unsatisfactory, as at Pr 34 where he adopts the Trinity / Chaderton reading *giltles* as 'the only possible original of all the variants' and as 'also metrically superior.' The first statement is demonstrably untrue and is formally rebutted in the present edition's note to this line. For the second, Kane gives no reason; and this proves a revealing weakness of the enterprise, since a later discussion in the Kane-Donaldson *B-Text*[127] will accept as authentic the metrical pattern *aaa / xx*, which is that of the majority (and probably archetypal) reading here in **A**. Finally, in adopting the variant *giltles*, Kane omits to mention that Wright used it to emend B Pr 36 on the assumption that three staves confined to the a-half are impermissible. Although K–D convincingly refute this notion, they nonetheless retain Kane's emendation in their text of **B**, again without acknowledging its first proponent. Such is the confusion besetting the editor who does not consistently tread the 'parallel' way which, though winding *by many a wente*, alone offers egress from the *wilde wildernesse* of scribal variants. For this example graphically displays the later Athlone theory as at once in conflict with the earlier Athlone practice and, paradoxically, as determined by it. Similar inconsistencies persist into Athlone **C** and are neither few nor negligible.

§ 59. The smooth functioning of Kane's introductory discussions, apparatus and critical endnotes indicates that this procedure should have been retained in Athlone **B** and **C**. The present edition therefore retains separate critical notes in this second volume so as to facilitate consultation alongside the parallel text, discussing problems of a particular version and others shared by more than one version together as they arise rather than subsuming them under general categories of scribal error. For a wider danger of the Athlone approach adumbrated in **A** becomes clear from considering a particular case mentioned above. It is partly his judging Chaderton's *mynchons* original that leads Kane to interpret the majority variant *martires* as evidence that Langland used a corrupt scribal copy of **A** in revising to **B**, which has the latter reading. Despite this troubling (and significant) implication, *martires* is nonetheless printed in the a-half of parallel B IX 112 [= *K–D* 114], possibly under influence from *martres* in the b-half of parallel C X 206 [= *R–K* 205]. Here, K–D's acceptance in **B** of an **A** variant that Kane diagnosed as scribal fails to cohere with their earlier retention of *giltles* in B Pr 34 against *synnelees* in the **B** archetype (Bx). It must therefore raise a doubt whether the poet's supposed use of a 'scribal' **A** manuscript (an *a priori* possibility) can satisfy the critical canon of economy of explanation (IV, §§ 19–21 below), as it ought. For if *synnelees* supported by **B** and *martires* supported by **BC** are both retained, the need to postulate a 'scribal revision copy' disappears. Now, in itself, a particular inconsistency may not invalidate use of this latter postulate in relation to the revision of **B** to **C**.[128] But it suggests a need for caution in invoking it; for consistency here would entail adopting the 'harder' *mynchons* not only in **A** but also in **B** and **C**, a step too radical even for the Athlone editors. What becomes evident is that, while each decision purports to depend on what they judge original for any one version by intrinsic criteria, such judgement verges on the arbitrary when exercised without disinterested examination of the parallel evidence *throughout*. The inadequacy of such an examination in the second and third Athlone volumes indicates the constraining, even constricting effect of the first of them.

§ 60. For any later editor, Kane's specific failures when editing **A** without regard to **B** and **C** obviously carry a warning, with an implied imperative. But other deficiencies were remediable from the outset on the basis of the **A** tradition alone. Most notably, the Athlone A-Text retains inferior **r** readings in the face of better ones in the family **m**, readings later adopted in the second edition of 1988 (Ka^2). Thus at V 256 [254] *seke*] **r**; *go to* **m** and VIII 100 *to helle shalt þu wende*] **r**; *þe deuel shal haue þi soule* **m** Kane prints lines with the metrical pattern *ax / ax* that he and his collaborators (unlike K–F and the present editor) consider inauthentic; but at VII 233 *Actif lif oper contemplatif*] **r**; *transposed* **m** (where **B** is at hand supporting **m**), Ka^2 abandons **r** for **m** to adopt a line with this same 'inauthentic' scansion. At VII 270 *cole plantis*] **r**; *trs* **m**, Ka^2 will reject **r**'s unmetrical *aa / xa* line for *plaunte coles* in accordance with K–D's emendation of the (possibly) archetypal text at B VI 285 [286]; yet support for the ultimately accepted reading was already available in an 'A' source independent of **m**, manuscript **Z** (at VII 290). However, since Kane had earlier overlooked this copy as a possible **A** witness (see § 54), it should hardly cause surprise that his 'Retrospect' ignores **Z**'s attestation of the reading he now considers correct (Ka^2 p. 461).

§ 61. These four cases do more than betray only the inconsistency that any editor would be wise to admit may be at times unavoidable. They reflect a deep incoherence in the Athlone approach to Langland's text that persists from Kane's **A** through the collaborative editions of **B** and **C**. Thus *Ka²*'s statement that corrections of such *Ka¹* readings as VII 270 are based not only on other-version evidence but on better understanding of the poet's 'metrical practice and of the quality of archetypal manuscripts' is only partly true. For the witness of **m** at VII 290 implies that the *archetype* of **A** (Ax) was correct, and was accurately preserved in this one family. The presence of the presumed scribal reading *cole plantis* in both the **A** family **r** and in the **B** family β may, initially, suggest that Langland revised from a scribal copy of **A** and overlooked the unmetrical line. But this particular error, as argued in the *Textual Notes* on C VIII 309, is of a type that could easily have recurred independently in the archetype of **B** (Bx), which is in any case strictly indeterminable here in the absence of the α family witness. What is clear is that there lay to hand from the outset a reading superior in metre and 'harder' in sense that Kane could not recognise as such. This might have been because, like Knott-Fowler, he failed to discern in **m** a line of descent from Ax independent of **r**. But even *Ka¹* not only prefers three major **m** readings supported by **B** (I 37, V 87, 243 [241]), it adopts two important ones (XI 195, 245) with no parallel in **B**. Kane's explicit response to the challenge of these lines in the original Critical Notes stops short, however, at opining that the **m** copies 'were at some stage corrected' or that their right readings are 'due to restoration' and that it was 'the archetype of the surviving manuscripts' that was corrupt (*A-Text*, pp. 434, 441). This problematic notion of 'good correction' from a lost source superior to the archetype is one that the Athlone editors will invoke again in relation to both the **B** ms Corpus 201 (F) and the **C** ms NLW 233B (N²). But as will be seen later, logically simpler explanations of these copies' right readings, such as contamination from the **A** and **B** traditions, are available without multiplying hypothetical entities beyond necessity. So here likewise in **A**, the postulate (III, *A Version* §§ 52–4) of **r** and **m**'s independent descent from a single archetype both explains the data economically and provides a firm basis for editing **A**. And it does this even before taking into account the witness of the other versions (including **Z**), which is confirmatory even where not indispensable.

§ 62. Three weaknesses are thus responsible for the edition's main lapses in congruity with the subsequent Athlone volumes. The first is Kane's failure to acknowledge **m** as a primary sub-archetypal branch of the **A** tradition, which contrasts markedly with the Athlone editors' later recognition of two independent lines of transmission in the longer versions.[129] There is of course no reason why the textual situation in **B** and **C** should have been reproduced in **A**, nor why 'good correction' of **m** should be ruled out in principle; for such correction is perceptible in the **A** tradition below the sub-archetypal level, e.g. in the group <TH²Ch>. But since **m** consistently displays the same positive and negative characteristics of excluded, included, correct and incorrect material as later enable the Athlone editors to identify the sub-archetypal traditions of **BC**, there is little to favour a hypothesis that is intrinsically weaker by the canon of explanatory economy (see IV, §§ 19–21). More important, even *Ka²* apparently fails to grasp the significance of **m**. This is revealed by the *ad hoc* quality of Kane's comparison of the **m** readings that he adopts with those of **r** (pp. 461–62), as consultation of the present text will disclose.[130]

§ 63. The second weakness of Kane's editing lies in his unsatisfactory understanding of Langland's metre. This results in unmetrical archetypal lines printed without comment in 1960 being judged in 1988 to indicate that the poet 'once or even twice missed or did nothing about them' (*Ka²*, p. 463), with the consequence that the editor need do nothing about them either. But if the ten lines Kane lists[131] are examined in the present edition together with the textual notes discussing them, their value as evidence that Langland used a scribal **A** manuscript for his **B** revision virtually disappears. Only three contain assured archetypal errors, and that two of these might have recurred coincidentally in archetypal **B** will hardly strain belief.[132] Nor are these the only incongruities; for lines left metrically defective in *Ka* persist unnoticed in *Ka²*, though all may be corrected on the evidence of **m** and / or (an)other version(s), and still others may be emended by unadventurous conjecture.[133]

§ 64. The third defect in Kane's edition relates to the witness of manuscript Bodley 851, where *Ka²*'s support of *Ka*'s silent dismissal of Z as 'useless for editing, if not actually misleading' (p. 459) proves a serious misjudgement. For at I 110, when *Ka²* diagnoses archetypal 'misreading of *l* as long *s*' and corrects *siȝt* to *liȝt* in the phrase *louelokest of liȝt,* Kane (whether in ignorance or defiance) overlooks that this is what Z reads. Now, even if Z were judged only an eccentric **A** copy, that would hardly make it more 'useless for editing' **A** than is, say, Corpus 201 for editing **B** or NLW 733B for editing **C**. For notwithstanding their gross corruptions, both those manuscripts win respect from the Athlone editors for their occasional 'superior' readings. So, if it registers a 'good correction' here, Z should merit similar recognition. But it could be, on the other hand, that Z is right because it preserves an authorial form of the poem *independent* of Ax, and of **A** itself, as Rigg-Brewer argue (and as will be maintained in *Intro*. III, *Z Version* §§ 1–12). Further significant information in **Z**'s version of line I 110 is also neglected by Kane; for the agreement of its b-half with the probable **m** form *Oure Lord seluen* obviates the need for his 'hard' scansion with two staves in *lóuelókest* by yielding a perfect line of standard metre. Loss of the last lift *seluen* in **r** is, moreover, mechanically ascribable to homoteleuton, since line 111 ends *hym*seluen. This example serves both to challenge Kane's understanding of **m** and his negative valuation of **Z**; but it has further implications for the Athlone text of **B**. For though K–D regard this line as archetypally lost from **B** (p. 205n154), they fail to observe that the form they conjecture is that of an extant manuscript. The distinction between ignorance and defiance now begins to look as fine as that between John Donne's 'air and angels'.

§ 65. Kane's *Introduction* is, nevertheless, outstandingly important for providing the most thorough account of the editorial process given to any Middle English text since *The Canterbury Tales* in the edition of Manly and Rickert.[135] Its description of the manuscripts, though more concise than Kane would have wished, is deficient only in omitting Bodley 851.[136] Equally exemplary in clarity and comprehensiveness is its discrimination of the poem's seven scribally-produced manuscript 'shapes' with **C** endings and interpolated **B** or **C** material from an authentic one characterised by 'some 400 lines not found in the other two versions' (p. 42). The scribal shapes are attested in seven copies, the authentic one in ten copies consisting of a prologue and eleven passūs (preserved in whole or part), and three containing some or all of a twelfth (Kane's conclusion, following K–F, that the latter passus was probably not in the archetype is accepted here). The 'literary examination' of XII deferred to another occasion remains unprovided in *Ka²*. This lack is made good in the present edition, which finds XII authentic but for its last nineteen lines, and so differs from *Ka* and *K–F* in not treating it as an 'appendix' (III, *A Version*, §§ 65–71).

§ 66. In his classification of the **A** manuscripts, Kane rejects simple recourse to either the 'striking' or the 'commonplace' category of variants, respectively those designated 'major' and 'minor' readings in the present work (see IV §§ 25–36). This is because the first could be the product of 'correction' or conflation and the second of coincident variation. Abandoning classification with reference to selected variants, Kane also renounces editing on the basis of the resulting genealogy as proposed by Knott-Fowler. Instead, he treats major and minor variants alike at the classification stage and establishes his text after scrutinising all the variants so as to uncover 'the scribal tendencies of substitution' and thus determine the direction of variation from the authorial text. This way of identifying inauthentic readings depends on W. W. Greg's two-pronged criterion for recognising originality, according to which the preferred reading 'is itself satisfactory, and...explains the origin of the erroneous alternative' (p. 62).[137] A preliminary text obtained by applying this 'direct' method forms the required point of reference for Kane's subsequent analysis of the variational groups. Some groups are found very persistent, several less persistent and mutually conflicting, and over a thousand random, indicating conflation and / or coincident variation. Concluding that in these circumstances a stemma cannot be established, Kane proceeds to a summary and critique of K–F. He accepts some of their smaller variational groups as probably genetic but finds many more to conflict with the presumed genetic groups, and expresses scepticism about both the anomalous and the smaller, less stable groups they recognise. He ends by showing that, since K–F's division of their groups into two families x and y (see § 51) cannot be sustained, and the genetic relations between their constituents are qualified by 'an enormous amount of convergent variation...the use of recension for determining this text is unauthorised' (p. 68).

§ 67. Most of this section convincingly applies Greg's foundational editorial principle; but while Kane's judgement of many, perhaps most minor readings as coincidentally generated is plausible, few of the major ones can be convincingly shown to arise from conflation or 'correction' (sound or mistaken). Accordingly, there are no real grounds for rejecting a classification on the basis of some degree of selection, nor for assuming that, if K–F's stemma is unsustainable, no better one may be found on that basis (see *Intro*. III, *A Version*, § 5). For since the two categories of variants are qualitatively different, there are grounds for asking whether the major type generally may indicate genetic relationship, while the minor type may be in various instances (not always determinable) *either* genetic in origin *or* produced by random scribal substitution according to recognisable processes. But while in principle a classification by major readings alone might be expected to produce different groupings from one based on *all* readings taken together, in practice the differences turn out to be slight. This is because it is in minor readings, many or most of which are (as allowed) ascribable to coincidental variation, that numerically telling 'challenges' to postulated genetic groupings tend to occur. But where such challenges are major and conflation or 'correction' may or must be invoked, neither the number nor the proportion is ever significant enough to undermine the antecedent likelihood of a genetic relationship.[138] Kane's reasonable insistence (p. 68) that 'all conclusions about genetic relations' must be necessarily qualified, together with the fact (already recognised in K–F's stemma) that no **A** group or family ancestor derives from any other, effectively rule out recension as a sufficient means of 'fixing' the text. And these considerations also compel recognition of genetic evidence as 'only one of a number of available indications of originality' (p. 63). But such a conclusion does not entail that a recensional hypothesis is without indicative value, especially if based upon the evidence of *all major readings* taken as a distinct and comprehensive category. Nor, it need hardly be said, is it wholly at odds with K–F's opinion that the 'critical readings' are those 'attested in every case by the weight of evidence, genealogical and other.'[139] Kane's chief difference from his predecessors lies rather in his decision that those 'critical readings' are attainable 'without using recension' (p. 63), and in his attaching much less weight to the genealogical than to the 'other' evidence accumulated through discerning the 'direction' of scribal variation. Nonetheless, however skilfully this is applied, it remains doubtful to the present editor that such a 'direction' can be anywhere near as reliably ascertained for minor as for major readings as Kane appears to think (see *Intro.* IV, §§ 27 ff).

§ 68. Of enduring value in Kane's *Introduction* is his painstaking examination of variational groups made up of two to five witnesses. Since Kane's lemma is adopted after evaluating in the light of the genealogical evidence the readings initially produced by the 'direct method', it is obvious that different lemmata would generate a different number of readings within any group classed as 'variational.' This consideration, however, does not in itself render use of the method misleading, since the absolute number of agreements between any two or more manuscripts obviously cannot change. And while a lemma in itself contains no genetic information, and does not rigidly determine the composition of the groups, it is a valuable heuristic device for identifying, and a point of reference for classifying and displaying, readings relativistically designated 'variants'. It should moreover be observed that when, as it often does, the adopted text has (near)-unanimous manuscript support, it is antecedently likely to represent the archetypal reading.[140] Although Kane's agreements are sometimes miscounted to a not insignificant degree,[141] this section's accuracy and clarity make it indispensable. (The same holds good of the later Athlone editions, which follow the pattern laid down in **A**).

§ 69. Kane's most original contribution to the theory of editing is found in the account of his methods and resources. He begins uncontroversially enough by discussing the mechanical errors to which all scribes were prone through inattention, distraction and visual confusion from difficult copy. Under this category come larger errors of omission caused by similarity or identity of line-endings and beginnings (hom(œ)oteleuton; hom(œ)oarchy). But some are traceable to grammatical or semantic features of the authorial text that provoked copyists to shorten or simplify; and others are the scribes' deliberate substitution of their own words and phrases for those of the copy, through desire for what they considered greater correctness, intelligibility, emphasis or elegance (p. 128). Although an element of 'subjectivity' now starts to show through, Kane in practice vindicates his procedure by opening it to critical assessment at every stage. This is well shown in his analysis of the 'homœograph', the substitution of a word of similar shape for one the scribes found difficult for some reason. Two examples (p. 133) reveal Kane's general conviction that their main motive for altering the text was a wish to make it 'easier.' The likelier original will therefore be the *lectio difficilior*, the 'harder' reading that both gives satisfactory sense and explains the easier variant(s). This notion is central to the direct method of editing.

§ 70. In one example, for *kete* at XI 56, found only in manuscripts VKW, Kane recognises three variants as homœographic, *ked* DRU, *kid* TH²Ch and *cowrte* JA. A fourth he does not record here, though arguably *grete* MH³ is no less a homœograph than *cowrte* (as acknowledged in his critical note, which conflicts with the list on p. 133) or else, like *cowrte*, a semantically-motivated replacement of *kete*, which looks unlikely to be a substitution for any of the others. This is a case where r^1 and the common original of MH^3 err disjunctively while Skeat's base-text Vernon (presumably following its immediate source) seems to preserve the original by direct descent: < v < r^2 < **r** < Ax < **A**. But the convergence of the genetically distinct **m** copy A with the r^2 copy J would seem to bear out Kane's belief that stemmatic relations based on major readings are distorted through scribal interventions in response to difficult sense. Here the context (*Clerkes and kete men*) indeed seems to have prompted copyists in two separate traditions to interpose a social group (nobles) conventionally associated with clerks, while another plausible category (the famous) has been introduced coincidentally by the scribes of D, <RU> and <TH^{2}Ch> or, more probably (given these copies' persistent affiliation), that of their exclusive common ancestor r^1. Such a complex situation invites more than one 'genetic' interpretation. Thus MH^3 may preserve **m**, and A may have replaced its reading with a term alliterating more exactly. Alternatively, **m** read *kete* and the MH^3 ancestor introduced one easier term, A another one that coincided with J's substitution for r^2's presumed correct reading *kete*. Where genealogical evidence is so ambiguous, it may indeed appear that only the direct method can suffice both to discriminate one reading as archetypal and to assess its originality.

§ 71. As it happens, in the above case of *kete clerkes* all four editors of **A** happily agree; but another of Kane's homœographs proves that significantly divergent conclusions may be reached even when applying the same method. It occurs at X 47, where for the majority reading *help* the group TH^{2}Ch have *halle*. Unlike the variants at XI 56, this must be considered only doubtfully a homœograph, since Kane's postulated original *allie* is not an extant variant but a conjecture (as is discoverable from a critical note cross-referring to the *Introduction*). Here, however, despite his acute analysis, Kane's emendation does not undermine Skeat's and K–F's belief that *help* is what the author wrote. The *Textual Notes* in the present edition should be consulted with a view to seeing if the variant *halle* can indeed be, as Kane insists, 'fairly accounted for'. But his judgement of *help* as a 'guess-gloss...very probably directed by [*help* in] line 49 below' (pp. 164–65) suffers from two weaknesses. Firstly, for *help* not to have been the archetypal reading (as Kane's explanation entails) assumes its fourfold coincidental substitution in the ancestors of D, RU and the unrelated r^2 and **m** (something theoretically possible). Secondly, however, if *halle* TH^{2}Ch is a homœograph, it must uniquely reflect the postulated archetypal reading *allie*. And that (unless 'superior correction' is invoked) could only have occurred via **r**, the exclusive ancestor this group shares with RU, D and r^2. The last three must therefore have coincidentally substituted a variant both distinct from the postulated archetype and further in form from it than that of TH^{2}Ch. This explanation, though historically possible, is much less economical than to see **r** as at once faithfully transmitted by RUDr^2 and as identical with **m**, and both traditions as here preserving Ax. That *help* should be both archetypal and original, far from being excluded, is arguably confirmed by its repetition at 49. What cannot be doubted is that, instead of its presence distracting from the effective operation of the direct method, as Kane holds, the lack of parallel evidence here measurably *lessens* the method's cogency. For while *allie* may in an absolute sense be 'harder' than *help,* it remains only a possibility, given that the majority reading is unexceptionable on grounds of sense and metre. This example illustrates what difficulties attend textual rationalism in the absence of other-version evidence, without which it is more or less hazardous to resort to reconstruction. (The wider aspects of the conflict between 'historical' and 'logical' approaches to textual problems will be touched on in IV § 36 below).

§ 72. No less problematic are those substitutions that Kane traces to active scribal involvement in the content of *Piers Plowman* as 'a living text' (p. 136). He argues very convincingly that, since copyists who censored or toned down readings often needed to 'smooth' syntactical or metrical damage caused by their own interference, studying recurrent instances of this enables the editor 'to deduce the existence of several general tendencies of scribal substitution' (p. 143). That some manuscript readings may actually be 'author's variants,' however, Kane judges an undemonstrable hypothesis. Agreeing with this, the present editor would find it also an *unnecessary* one to account for what is more economically explained in terms of securely identifiable scribal variation alone. Pursuing the important question of the authority of the archetypal text, Kane argues (again very plausibly) that, while majority or even unanimous agreement does not in itself prove, it is a presumption of originality '*in the absence of all other considerations.*' Here he concedes that even the 'limited' results of genetic analysis 'may help to estimate the strength of the majority support' (p. 148). But Kane remains convinced that identifying scribal tendencies of substitution is the editor's 'final means of determining originality,' though he rightly sees his decisions as 'provisional only, subject to modification or rejection if further manuscript evidence should come to light' (p. 149). The laudably 'scientific' character of this conclusion should be acknowledged as a real advance in the theory of editing (see further IV, §§ 16–17 below).

§ 73. The foregoing account of the 'direct method' immediately raises an issue of principle that it is convenient to consider here, although Kane does not address it explicitly. Reliable identification of scribal 'tendencies' may be a major tool for discriminating the archetypal reading among conflicting variants; and archetypal readings may be capable of authentication by the same criteria. But the approach retains an *a priori* element in its presumption that 'authorial' characteristics *can* be securely recognised in being essentially different from those of 'scribal' variants. Thus several features of the poet's *usus scribendi* (his style, lexis and metre) are appealed to as criterial for authenticating the archetypal text of **A**, although the basis for identifying these features remains the versional archetype itself. The sole solution to this dilemma, one which Kane ignores, would seem to be reference to the other versions of *Piers Plowman*; for only when two or more versions agree in a line or reading can a valid claim be made for judging the text securely 'authorial.' This is because, on the basis of such 'common' readings, an analytical use of the term 'authorial text' becomes available which is also empirically sound; for what it denotes is the agreed text of the poem in its several versions. Now, that text appears, with varying degrees of ratification, only in these 'core-lines' of the poem (see IV, §§ 1–12). Consequently, what should emerge as properly criterial for Langland's practice is 'all and only those features found in these (doubly or trebly attested) lines and readings'. Other features found in lines archetypally attested in only one version, in order to avoid being classed as authentic only *a priori*, must satisfy stylistic and other 'norms' derived from the 'core-text'. Such 'universional' lines may (and in principle must be allowed to) contain some features absent from the core-text; but not being empirically validated, they obviously cannot furnish a sufficient standard for authenticity. Kane's claim that 'identification of the scribal tendencies of substitution equips the editor with his final means of determining originality' therefore strikes the present editor as mistaken. It is, at the least, very misleading; for the only 'final' means of establishing Langland's text is to use criteria derived from an analysis of the poem's core-lines. Kane's failure to reach this conclusion in his edition of **A** has adverse consequences, notwithstanding the penetration that enables him to achieve convincing results where his predecessors failed or to provide reasons for a textual choice where they were right but omitted to do so.

§ 74. Some at least of the divergences between the Athlone and the present text will therefore be traceable to differences in applying what is in effect the same method, e.g. in order to establish the 'harder' of two readings. A good example is at VIII 30 *And bete brugges aboute þat to-broke were* in which, out of the seven variants attested, *bete* (preferred by all other editors) is rejected by Kane for *bynde* 'on lexicographical grounds'. As this reading is discussed in the *Textual Notes*, it need only be said here that *bete* is also found in **Z** and that **B** paraphrases it as *do boote to*, for which *amende* at parallel C IX 33 is transparently an elucidatory synonym. The **C** reading is anticipated in the **A** copy M, where the word it appears as a scribal gloss on must be *bete*, the reading of H³ and most probably of the family original **m**. This example shows the risk involved when the 'direct' method is used without taking due account of the other versions or, in this case, of the genealogical evidence provided by the **m** witness H³'s agreement in reading *bete* with the *r²* copies VKN. Here, it may however be affirmed, it is not the method but Kane's application of the method that is at fault. For it is not disputed that in itself the d group variant *bynde* is lexically a 'difficult original' (see MED s.v. *binden* v.3 (d)). But the *sense* presumed for the adopted reading *bete brugges aboute* 'do repairs to bridges in the vicinity' cannot convincingly be called 'easier' than the sense 'reenforce by attaching lateral beams' of Kane's preferred *bynde*. The conclusion that emerges, paradoxical as it may seem, is that two competing readings, one of them perforce to be identified as scribal, may both be 'difficult,' one lexically and the other semantically, and the greater 'hardness' of either be indemonstrable. Unless, therefore, the remote assumption of laterally introduced 'author's variants' at the sub-archetypal stage is countenanced, the *lectio difficilior*, while usually a necessary, can never be a sufficient condition for determining originality in the text. (On the wider limitations that attend the concept, see further IV, §§ 15, 28).

§ 75. No less vexatious than the cases where one reading is to be identified as the harder or hardest of the available variants are five Kane himself distinguishes in which 'readings are of equivalent value and the support of the manuscripts is fairly divided' (p. 153), of which two may be examined here. At VII 20 *Chesiblis for chapelleynis chirches to honoure* Kane prefers *chapellis* as in the base-manuscript, while dismissing the support for *chapelleynis* from *r²*, **m** and one of the *r¹* copies Ch as well as from **B** and **C** (to which may be added **Z**). Before genetic evidence of such weight, *chapellis* could be preferred only for its 'hardness' and superior sense; but if it is not archetypal, its originality would have to be due to correction of T from a hypothetical superior lost manuscript (an entity about which scepticism is never amiss). This example highlights the weaknesses of the direct method as Kane himself sometimes practises it. The only explanation for his (to the present editor erroneous) decision is that, failing to make adequate 'application of genetic information' (p. 152) and to take into account the evidence of the parallel versions, he has mistakenly judged the competing readings as 'of equivalent value.' At X 86 *And þerof seiþ þe sauter, þi seluen þou miȝt rede* Kane prefers the *r¹* variant *þe salme* to *þi seluen*, the *r²*m reading accepted by Skeat, K–F and the present editor. With no parallel evidence and the decision to be made wholly on intrinsic grounds, Kane finds *þi seluen* 'the more emphatic expression, and therefore somewhat likelier to be of scribal origin' (p. 153). But even if this were granted, *þe salme* displays the greater 'explicitness' Kane likewise sees as 'scribal'. Now in this instance, genetic evidence in the form of support by two independent groups indicates that *þi seluen* and not *r¹*'s variant is more likely to be archetypal. So Kane's adherence to a base-manuscript reading he recognises as that of a 'probably genetic group' cannot be justified as it might be if the disagreement cut randomly across all three groups, or if the contested reading were of slight semantic import, like those to be considered next.

§ 76. Reservations about Kane's practice of the direct method in relation to major variants affecting the sense and metre of a line apply *a fortiori* to minor ones involving grammatical words or relatively insignificant differences in word-order and phrasing. The issue is candidly recognised in his conclusion that 'where...readings see[m] of equal value' and genetic information does not help, if neither meaning nor style is affected 'there is no choice but to let the text of the basic manuscript stand' (p. 152).[142] But from the twenty-five examples Kane gives, the following four, illustrating variations in tense, number and word-order, may be selected as controverting his claim that 'determination of originality is impossible because of the balance of representation and the equivalence of the readings' (ibid). What they show, on the contrary, is a near or absolute consensus of the other branches of the **A** tradition with some or all of the other versions. Firstly in III 3 Kane's preferred present-tense *calliþ*, where the r^1 group d is accompanied by two r^2 copies, should be rejected for past-tense *callid,* the reading of r^2, **m** and **ZBC**. Next at IV 38 singular *harm* tvE has the plural against it in the majority of **A** copies and **ZB**, just as in V 130 the singular *spynstere* of r^1 and K is opposed by the plural of r^2, **m** and **BC**. Finally in XI 4, against r^1's *sterneliche staringe Dame Studie* the preferred word-order *staringe Dame Studie sterneliche* is directly upheld by r^2 and **BC** and indirectly by **m** (whose substantively erroneous *scornynge* appears a corrupt reflex of the correct *staringe* in the same position). What these examples demonstrate is, firstly, that for minor readings the direct method proves a frail support without help from genetic and other-version evidence; secondly, that the expedient of relying on the copy-text is not the sole alternative, and is indeed a failure of the rationalism Kane's method embodies. In all these cases the truth is directly opposite to the Dreamer's assertion in B XVII 37–8 that *The gome þat gooþ wiþ o staf - he semeþ in gretter heele / Than he þat [teeþ] wiþ two staues, to sighte of vs alle.*[143]

§ 77. Conjectural emendation is, after the direct analysis of variation, the second main resort of a rationalist editor. Kane uses it only sparingly to correct archetypal corruptions, retaining lines 'of doubtful originality' (p. 156) if he finds the evidence too uncertain to justify intervention. A somewhat surprising case is XI 67 where Kane, though suspecting an original verb with *w* for archetypal *begiled*, does not print his conjecture *(be)wiled* (any more than does Ka^2), despite the persuasive 'lexicographical grounds'[144] by which he sometimes sets such store (see on *bynde* at § 74). This decision sits uneasily with adoption elsewhere of (closely similar) dialectal variants on metrical grounds. Examples are the convincing *heo* for *she* at X 141 or *ȝerne* for *renne* at II 201, which he calls 'an obsolescent form of restricted currency' discernible for that reason as 'the harder reading' (p. 161). Kane explicitly disavows K–F's recognition of the **B** Version as attesting 'another branch of the **A** genealogy' (p. 157), no doubt understandably, given that in principle revision cannot be excluded at points where a **(B)C** reading might look superior to a suspect archetypal reading in **A**. But in only a few cases does he let the later versions even serve as 'guides to conjecture' (ibid.). One such is in VI 92 *And weue vp þe wyket þat þe wy shette,* where Kane argues for emending *wy* to *wif* (pp. 445–46) but cites in support only the Latin quoted at B V 603*a* and not the obviously relevant *womman* at parallel B V 602.[145] (This emendation deserves serious consideration, though it has not been accepted in the present edition).[146] A second instance is *comsiþ* for *beginneþ* at V 59, on which Kane's critical note (pp. 440–41) again makes no reference to parallel **B** or to the pertinent situation of I 139, where the **B** archetype at parallel I 165 reads the unmetrical *bigynneþ* for an original **comseþ* conjectured in the light of agreed **AC** (and again **Z**). Bracingly ascetic as is Kane's self-restriction to direct **A** evidence, his editorial stringency here verges on suffocation. Again, though logically justified in not using agreed **BC** readings to emend Ax errors, he overlooks the implication of **AC** agreement here against **B**. For the case of *comsiþ* and *beginneþ* indicates that identical errors could arise in the **A** and **B** archetypal traditions, and for the same reasons. This said, Kane's balance and sobriety command respect, and to the present editor far from prove his early 'ideal of conservative editing' the 'delusion' he came to judge it after editing **B**.[147]

§ 78. The supplement ('Retrospect') to Kane's Second Edition of **A**, which appeared midway between the Athlone **B** and **C**, makes good several deficencies of the first, particularly in drawing on **m** to emend errors in his mainly r^{l} text. But it does not openly acknowledge the wider import of these changes; and a few remaining inconsistencies display something rather less than the 'better' metrical understanding Kane now professes (cf. p. 460). This understanding is endorsed at III 21, where his convincing preference of *coppis* to *pecis* takes 'full account' of **B** and **C** (p. 460) and cites W (but not **Z**, which also has it), though without identifying W's variant as an 'enlightened correction' (p. 463) or a contamination from **C** (a frequent feature of this copy noted at III, *A Version* § 17). But an emendation of this type should for clearness be distinguished from one like that of **r**'s *seke* at V 256 [254] to *go to,* a variant cited from EAMH[3] and K (and one supported by both **Z** and **C**). For while K's reading, like W's in the previous case, may well come from **C** (III, *A Version* § 21), **m**'s is almost certainly genetic. Further, since the **m** group shows no contamination from **C** and cannot derive from Bx (which is here corrupt), it is almost as certainly archetypal. The lack of perspicuity in the 1988 'Retrospect' contrasts with the lucidity of Kane's original critical notes, such as that on V 200 [198] *He [þr]umblide on þe þreshhewold and þrew to þe erþe,* which describes *þrumblide* in his text as 'taken from the corresponding line of the **C** Version...rather than on the authority of V' (the **A** copy in question presumably being judged contaminated from **C**). Similarly confusing is Ka^{2}'s non-acceptance of Kane-Donaldson's emendation of *olde* to *yolde* at parallel B IX 163 [166], which leaves A X 187 unmetrical. Kane's tortuous notion that the poet's having overlooked these defective lines once or even twice 'gives them a kind of sanction' (p. 463) scarcely strengthens his rationale of emendation; for the direct method assumes that scribal and authorial readings are demonstrably different. And as it happens, such a case offers slender evidence that the revising poet *did* 'overlook' mistakes in his postulated scribal copy, given that so easy a substitution-error in the **A** archetype could have recurred in the archetype of **B**. Another line that Kane leaves unmetrical is VIII 136 [135], where a 'guide to conjecture' lay to hand in **BC**'s *book bible,* if not in ms M's *book of þe bible,* which may be an intelligent scribal guess. A third such line, XI 161, could have been emended by simple inversion of *nigromancie* and *perimansie* to scan *ax / ax.* This 'minimal' pattern Kane does not acknowledge as authentic, though he accepts an 'enriched' variant of it (*ab / ab*) at VII 233 *Contemplatif lif oþer actif lif Crist wolde it alse* on the evidence of **m** and **B**.[148] The last example highlights both Kane's inconsistency in applying his own criteria and the defectiveness of a metrical theory not founded on the evidence of the core-text.[149] The emendation of VII 233 in Ka^{2} is also incongruous with the inclusion (p. 463) of V 14 among 'scribally corrupted' lines that 'would not be hard to emend conjecturally' (the sign of its 'corruption' presumably being again the *ax / ax* scansion). For by empirical criteria, V 14 is one of the securest lines in the poem, unvaryingly attested in the **ABC** tradition (and in **Z**). This instance points to an underlying incoherence in Kane's rationale of metrical emendation that will disable Kane-Donaldson's treatment of the archetypal text of **B** (see § 101 below).

§ 79. The preceding critique of Kane's A-Text has been in places severe; but it is this work that introduces into the editing of *Piers Plowman* principles that were to be applied, often with 'challengeable' outcomes, in the Athlone editions of the longer versions. Comparison with the present text will show how far it differs from Kane's, especially in its handling of minor variants, where archetypal readings with solid other-version support have seldom been rejected for those of the base-manuscript. By way of summary and conclusion, it may be said that the 1960 Athlone edition (and to some extent that of 1988) suffers from three main defects. Kane overestimates the value of r^1, fails to acknowledge the genetic significance of the r^2**m** agreements, even after accepting the continuous relevance of the parallel-text evidence, and relies on a demonstrably faulty metrical theory. In consequence he prints a text that, though little emended, is measurably further (to the present editor's judgement) than Knott-Fowler's from what Langland probably wrote. These defects, apart from the one concerning metre, differ somewhat from those of the collaboratively-edited B-Text, where speculative emendation is rife but the sub-archetypal traditions are clearly distinguished and fruitfully exploited. However, in some eighty cases, nearly sixty of them major, counting those added in Ka^2, Kane's discriminated readings and emendations (many established independently by the present editor before the appearance of Ka^2)[150] are endorsed in the parallel text of the **A** Version. Most impressive in Kane's edition are its rigorous presentation, full documentation and candid exposition, which establish a standard of accuracy and thoroughness no editor is likely to surpass. Kane's Introduction spells out exhaustively what textual rationalism may accomplish; if it also contains a warning, its combination of theoretical boldness with practical judiciousness sets a noble example.

viii. *The Athlone Editions:* Kane and Donaldson's *Edition of the* B-Text

§ 80. The *B Version* edited by George Kane and E. T. Donaldson (hereafter K–D for the editors, *K–D* for the work) appeared in 1975.[151] But although **B** is thrice the length of **A**, the volume is only half as long again as *Ka*. This is a measure of how far Kane's editorial theories are taken by K–D as largely settled.[152] A proportionately sized section of Critical Notes like those in **A** might have added a hundred pages, but now all textual problems are treated in an Introduction only a fifth longer than Kane's. As the presentation of Text and Apparatus follows *Ka* closely, the commendations and minor criticisms made above again apply. In the second volume, the exact number of agreements between pairs of manuscripts is stated (pp. 20–1), but those between three or more usually not. This caution may reflect a realistic sense of how easy it is to miscount: thus 250 agreements of CBmBoCot (p. 46) should be 263, while those of $GYOC^2CB$ (the group called 'g' at §§ 17–21 below) are some 230, as against K–D's stated 'more than 190' (p. 52). More significant are some omissions (pp. 67–9) from the list of lines found in WHmCrGYOC²CBLMH but absent from RF.[153] As most of these occur in Passus XIX, where R is defective, they could in principle have been present in the common source of RF and should have been listed here as having been lost for the same probably mechanical reasons invoked to account for the others.[154] This section has recently attracted intense critical scrutiny from proponents of a different explanation of the relationship between the two **B** families.[155]

§ 81. The Kane-Donaldson edition of **B** has proved both influential and controversial, its rigour and radicalism impressing even readers who question its use of **A** and **C** to correct archetypal errors and of bold conjecture where other-version evidence for reconstruction is lacking.[156] The

Athlone editors follow Kane's model in their lucid and thorough classification of the witnesses, from which the diagrammatic representation of manuscript relationships in the present edition substantially derives (see *B Version* § 10). However, like Russell and Kane later for **C**, but unlike Kane for **A**, they recognise for **B** a dual line of descent. As with the groups of witnesses in the **A** tradition, those in **B** do not allow the construction of a stemma that could decisively establish the archetype; for with one exception, no extant copy derives from another, nor does any group derive from a postulated ancestor of another group. The exception is the trio of manuscripts *BL Additional 10574* (Bm), *Bodley 814* (Bo, = Skeat's B) and *BL Cotton Caligula A XI* (Cot), to which K–D give the joint sigil B (adopted in the present edition). The close relationships within this genetic group recognised by Skeat (*B-Text*, xxv–xxvii) are analysed with notable economy and clarity (*K–D* pp. 40–2).

§ 82. In Athlone **B** the powerful techniques of Kane's direct method (cf. §§ 66–7 above) are concentrated on identifying some 750 readings as scribal errors in the archetypal text (called 'Bx' hereafter). An assumption fundamental to K–D's analysis is the traditional **A** > **B** > **C** sequence, supported from literary features and not from the external and internal evidence for dating, which may be insufficient to settle the issue finally (see *Intro.* V iii below). A definitive future case for re-ordering the versions would therefore gravely compromise their rationale of emendation, which appeals to the readings of **A** and **C** (severally or agreeing) for correcting presumed errors in Bx. No such case has been made, and in the present editor's view is unlikely to be made.[157] But this consideration brings out how Athlone **B** (and the present edition so far as it shares its presuppositions) resembles a 'scientific' hypothesis open to the test of 'falsification' by new discoveries. Whether the hypothesis is also able to *predict* specific data will be explored further below in relation to **Z**, a text that the Athlone editors ignore. This explicitly 'hypothetical' character differentiates *K–D* from *Ka*, which remained 'logically positivist' to the extent that it adhered to the readings of Ax, r^1 or even, in minor cases, the copy-text T. For *Ka* was 'rationalist' chiefly for its preferring editorial reasoning to genetic evidence in determining the direction of variation, not for its readiness to correct archetypal errors from other-version evidence or by conjecture. *Ka*'s residual 'conservatism' (to the present editor a virtue) is something that K–D declare 'mistaken' (cf. § 77).

§ 83. In its place K–D propound, in perhaps their most significant sentence, the fundamental editorial conviction that

> determination of originality in any version must include consideration in the first
> instance of *all* differences between versions and in the second particularly of those
> differences not evidently or probably resulting from authorial revision (p.75).

The Athlone editors here openly embrace the 'parallelistic principle,' though in respect of **A** they must perforce apply it retrospectively. This is because only with Ka^2 can the Athlone text adopt the **A** readings that K–D conclude are original after comparing it with **B** and **C** (see p. 75 n. 15). For recognising and correcting errors in the archetypal text of **B**, K–D rely on two central editorial pillars, the joint witness of **A** and **C** and that of either **A** or **C** alone. Recognising in the former 'the determinant circumstance in the editing of the **B** Version' (p. 76), K–D declare reasonably enough that unless the agreed text of **AC** is here 'itself unoriginal,' disagreement of **B** indicates either that the poet changed his mind in **C** and revised back to **A** or that the **B** archetype is corrupt. Given the character of the **B** readings and the number of **AC** agreements against **B**, they comprehensively prefer the latter interpretation. Two interconnected assumptions here bring out the character of their edition as a massive textual 'hypothesis'. One is that revision was linear and never reverted to an earlier form. Antecedently probable or not, this assumption may count as 'scientific' in being challengeable by specific examples and 'falsifiable' by the future discovery of dated holograph texts (such a discovery's improbability ensures the continuing viability of their hypothesis). The second is that the direct method, together with appeal to **AC** agreement, permits a 'compelling assessment of the quality of th[e] archetypal text' (p. 76). Both assumptions have survived the present 'parallelistic' analysis of all the versions undertaken in preparing this edition. But the possibility that the poet sometimes returned to an earlier reading must be countenanced.[158] For though the mere existence of **B** implies dissatisfaction with **A**, in principle Langland could at any point have restored in **C** what he first wrote in **A**: in response to readers' comments on **B**, for instance, he might have decided to say something again in the way he *first* said it (see further IV § 22 below).

§ 84. The second 'pillar' of K–D's edition, the witness of **A** or **C** alone for the discernment of archetypal error in **B**, is, however, less stable. Here, relying on a text of **A** established *without* consulting other-version evidence, they yet hold that 'if the possibility of revision were absent' some 300 readings (listed on pp. 84–9) would be less readily ascribable to ill-judged re-writing or to Langland's own 'scribal' error (p. 83) than to unconscious or deliberate 'scribal tendencies of variation.' Such readings they characterise as 'easier', 'more explicit' or 'more emphatic'; as arising from the copyist's conscious stylistic 'improvement' or censorship; or as evincing 'inferior' verse-technique. None of these categories is unproblematic, though in principle the third should be rigorously testable by reference to criteria founded on the poem's core-lines. In fact, most of the last group's 23 examples do display patterns that fail to meet such criteria. But as IX 32, 121 [123] and X 186 [189] scan *ax / ax*, emendation of these to read with **A** fails to convince; for the two-stave 'minimal' pattern (classed as 'Type IIIa' at IV §§ 39–43 below) is amply instanced in the core-lines and must therefore be accepted as authenticated empirically.[159] K–D's note on IX 32 *For þoruȝ þe word þat he spak woxen forþ beestes* identifies a scribal 'unconscious substitution of the prose term [*spak*] or stylistic preference' (the latter presumably *not* unconscious) and invites comparison with an earlier use of *warp*. But the fact that the Bx scribe had no difficulty with *warp* at V 363 weakens K–D's case, as does their overlooking in parallel A V 206 the 'prose term' *spak* diagnosed later as scribal. It may be therefore that in IX 32 the author simply wished to avoid over-using a somewhat 'poetic' locution that appears only once elsewhere in **A** and **B** (in different places) and nowhere in **C**.[160] In relation to the second example *Conceyued ben in ȝuel tyme* K–D observe that *ȝuel* is 'more explicit' than *cursed*. But while *ȝuel* is more general, the two terms are virtually synonyms in the period, and any stylistic preference could have been the poet's, since he also replaces *cursid* at IX 123 when revising A X 155. Finally, in *A ful leþi þyng it were* at X 186, Bx *leþi* can scarcely be 'easier' as well as 'more emphatic' than K–D's preferred *lewed*, since by ordinary lexical criteria it is much the rarer word.[161] Whether or not a sense of the doubtful contextual suitability of *lewed* in **A** prompted the revising poet to prefer *leþi*, a scribe cannot plausibly be credited with substituting a uniquely-occurring word for one that Langland used over sixty times.[162] The 'intuitional' subjectivity of K–D's remarks, underpinned by a defective metrical theory, weakens confidence in such far-reaching changes to the archetypal text of **B**. It should not be surprising, therefore, that for their 'more than 300' (actually about 275) emendations of Bx on the basis of **A** alone, the present text has only about a dozen.[163]

§ 85. Although some of these criticisms have involved metrical issues, much of K–D's account of Langland's versification (pp. 131–40) is confirmed by the present editor's analysis of each line's metrical structure.[164] This account forms an important support for their rationale of emendation, since it is certain that 'establishment of the poet's verse technique is inseparable from the process of editing.' But K–D's conclusion contains a warning for the unwary; for to presume a line 'not to be evidence for that technique because for...discrete editorial reasons it appears to be scribal' and to treat 'the verse pattern it exemplifies...in other lines...as evidence of scribal corruption' is not only, as they concede, 'precarious,' it risks becoming circular. Nor is this presumption's *a priori* character sufficiently guarded against 'by the existence of controlled situations where the effects of unmistakable scribal corruption on the versification can be observed' (pp. 140–41). For much depends on 'observing' without mistake, and the only 'controlled situation' that can truly test K–D's contention is one where the verse must satisfy empirical criteria derived from the poem's core-text. But as has already been re-iterated, lines scanning ax / ax do occur in this core-text; and some are even admitted by Ka^2 as 'sanctioned' by the poet's 'overlooking' them.[165] The chief reason why the Athlone editors' 'observation' sometimes misidentifies corruptions is that their notion of a 'controlled situation' is flawed.

§ 86. Against K–D's use of **C** alone to emend Bx may be brought similar objections to those against their use of **A** alone. As in the comparison of **A** with **B**, the direction of variation can in principle be established almost as if both texts were witnessing to a single unknown hypothesised original. But an editor must be prepared to recognise (as Russell-Kane later do) that a revision may incorporate features of the text judged corrupt. Such recognition is logically less hazardous here to the extent that K–D are not antecedently committed to a text of **B** as they are to Kane's text of **A** (subject to the qualification noted at § 83). For during the course of analysis, the text of **B** is itself in process of being established, partly (and from Passus XI solely) in the light of **C**. Nonetheless, K–D detect 'similar differences with similar effects' (p. 91) and their 230 **C**-based emendations to Bx add up to about twice as many as in the present edition.[166] It is not necessary here to re-state the categories under which these are grouped (see § 69 above). Though some of their emendations immediately convince, many more than in **A** arouse scepticism by their subjectivity or ambiguity. Some measure of this is that the emendations from **C** in the present edition amount to about two-thirds of those in K–D's *final category alone*, which corresponds to the one discussed in connexion with **A** at § 84 above. This disproportion, much smaller than in relation to **A**, reflects the fact that many of the present editor's overlap with K–D's final group in diagnosing the presence of a corruption, if not always in adopting **C** to emend it. But K–D sometimes 'correct' a minimally-staved line[167] even where the reading they believe corrupt may be strongly defended. In two instances they in any case misanalyse the verse-structure; for XVII 80 [82] will readily scan if the stress is shifted from the first to the second syllable in *Ierúsalemward,* as will XIV 270 *Moore for coueitise of good þan kynde loue of boþe* after registering the existence of 'cognative' alliteration[168] on voiced and unvoiced palatal stops (k / g), a licence abandoned here in the **C** revision.[169] Of K–D's sixteen examples, the only two accepted here are V 497 *þerafter*] *after* and XX 54 *it tid*] *it*, the first on grounds of **C**'s superior sense rather than its metre, the second also because of the mechanical ease of the error (haplography).[170]

§ 87. Even more controversial than K–D's assessment, following Blackman (note 8 above), of Bx as corrupt is their conclusion that the poet's revision-manuscript of **B**, though better than

Bx, was significantly defective. The first evidence adduced is some hundred readings 'not manifestly created by authorial revision' but differing from the 'original preserved in the **A** tradition' and revealing 'a scribal reflex' of it in the reading of **BC** (pp. 98–9). It may not be solely the out-and-out positivist who will find their position questionable; for to common sense, a Bx reading retained in **C** has been confirmed by **C** and so, even if from *some* standpoint it may appear 'unsatisfactory', it should be accepted. The principle involved here is the 'canon of ratification,' which is fully discussed later (IV, *Editing the Text* § 22 below). This canon does admit of a handful of exceptions where the reading demonstrably fails to meet the core-text criteria.[171] But because alteration of ratified readings is also generally incongruous with the postulate of linearity that antecedently favours agreed **AC** against suspect Bx, it must always and only be done for compelling reasons. K–D's painstaking argument nonetheless demands careful examination, and their general view of Langland's revision-copy seems to the present editor to deserve assent, even if it prompts them to some unconvincing emendations. But it is the pre-eminent status accorded to **A** that has the least acceptable editorial implications, as late even as the Athlone edition of **C**.

§ 88. As evidence that Langland used a corrupt revision-copy of **B** in composing **C**, K–D adduce a hundred **BC** readings which they find on comparison with **A** have originated in mechanical errors, are more explicit, emphatic or easy, or exhibit other acknowledged 'scribal' features. These could in principle be revisions, the poet's own transcriptional errors or coincidentally-produced **BC** archetypal substitutions for an original identical with **A**. But the explanation K–D prefer is that these readings reflect corruptions present in a manuscript from a pre-archetypal stage in **B** that Langland allowed to stand 'for whatever reason' (p. 103). Support for their case lies in a type of situation where **A** appears original, the **B** archetype on comparison scribal, **C** a revision to a reading of such a kind that Bx cannot derive from it but must derive from **A**, and **C** finally a reflection of Bx and not of the putative **AB** original (p.104). K–D's carefully-analysed examples, though invariably of great interest, may often fail to persuade; but no diffidence qualifies their robust editorial rationalism. Now, when they refer to the 'A tradition' both as 'presumably' original and as the 'putative original' shared with **B**, K–D necessarily mean Kane's A-Text. But they make no distinction between this text, established *without* consulting the parallel-version evidence, and its form as revised after a 'more rigorously logical editing' (*Ka²* p. 159, n. 78). This is, of course, because that 'editing' was subsequent to and consequent upon the outcome of editing the **B** Version, not simultaneous and co-dependent with it. The serious implications of these facts make themselves felt at IV 14 in K–D's replacement of *ryt ryȝt* (echoed in *rood forth* **C**) by *riȝt renneþ*, a *Ka* reading retained in *Ka²* though supported only by the *r¹* sub-family and not by the sub-family *r²* and the other family **m**, which are identical with **B**. But there is also a wider theoretical difficulty to be faced here. If, by the linear postulate (which the present editor accepts), **AC** agreement against Bx implies lack of revision in the middle version, **BC** agreements against **A** correspondingly *indicate* revision. This K–D apparently do not accept, though such is the basis on which they propose for credence the complex 'situation' described at the beginning of this paragraph. But contrary to what they suppose, agreed **BC** readings do not require proof (whatever form that might take) of being 'manifestly created by authorial revision' (cf. § 87). For, being empirically secure, they must be treated as authentic unless they breach the core-text criteria. This 'canon of ratification' K–D ignore because they are convinced that on intrinsic grounds, and even in minor readings, they can reliably tell scribal from authorial characteristics. Intuitional certitude may be necessary at times if a readable text is to be produced at all; but no editor should invoke it without apprehension.

§ 89. There is space here for only a few examples to bring out the full dimensions of K–D's approach. They are at their strongest when **C** keeps the **A** reading they prefer, if only as part of a revision echoing a suspect Bx reading, because this case comes nearer to the criterially firmer category of an **AC** agreement against the archetypal text of **B**. Thus at I 191 parallel *hardere* found in A I 165 appears at C I 186 and Bx *Auarouser* is reflected in C 187, which begins with *Auerous*.[172] Also persuasive is their argument on grounds of superior sense for re-ordering I 98–103 to accord with **A** rather than **C**, though not that in favour of rejecting **BC** *siluer* 103/100 for **A**'s *ʒeftis*, since the lines' dislocation and the (possibly authorial) lexical substitution are not necessarily connected. Similarly at X 458, although *clerkes most knowyng in konnyng* in parallel C XI 295 echoes Bx's *konnynge clerkes þat knowe manye bokes*, the word *konnynge* in the latter need not be questioned as a revision of **A**'s *kete*, a term absent from the later versions perhaps because it had been found difficult (cf. § 70 above). Here K–D virtually constrain the poet to restore an earlier expression that they prefer, something imaginable in an early reader but out of place in a modern editor.

§ 90. Various objections to specific unconvincing readings arouse wider unease about the Athlone procedure. In one instance (pp. 108–9) K–D reject Bx VI 223 *That nedy ben and noʒty help hem wiþ þi goodes*, which scans *aa / xx*, for the two-line **A** form, finding in **C**'s revised VIII 233 *In meschief or in mal-ese and thow mowe hem helpe* evidence that even the revision-copy of **B** had unmetrical *help* in its b-half. While possible, this is insufficient grounds for believing that the **B** original was identical with **A**. For it is hardly more improbable that the Bx scribe substituted *help* for some harder word[173] the poet finally replaced with a more familiar one than that *help* stood in his revision-manuscript, which like Bx was based on the first scribal copy of the holograph (as will be shown at III, *B Version* §§ 2–4). The comparative **BC** evidence here is too weak for specification either of the revision-manuscript's reading or of the 'putative' **AB** reading. While perhaps justified therefore in conjecturing that the undoubted damage to metre was caused by Bx's alteration of a single 'harder reading,' an editor cannot ignore the wider signs of revision in the environs of B VI 224–27. These indicate that the author deliberately reduced A VII 209–10 to **B**'s single line 223; and in doing so, he replaced **A**'s circumstantial account of the object and means of the recommended charity with an affirmation that the moral problem of undeserving recipients is a matter for God, man's business being to obey God, not judge other men. Rejecting K–D's text here amounts to seeing it as an 'editorial interpolation' of **A** lines which, while (obviously) 'authentic', need never have formed part of **B**. In the second example, at X 19 *Whoso can contreue deceites*, K–D substitute from A XI 19 *construe* 'construct' for Bx *contreue* 'devise'[174] and observe that **C**'s *Ho can caste and contreue* 'reflects a line with the archetypal **B** reading' (p. 110). Here there is little to choose between their conclusion and acceptance that the poet revised a word open to misconstruction. In absolute terms *construe* is 'harder'; but as the senses of both words are very close, an editor should refrain from finding in **C**'s *contreue* a 'reflection' of a (possibly) scribal reading that it does not at the same time ratify. For even if Langland did not originally write *contreue* in **B**, the revised **C** line implies his final acceptance of it. In here abandoning a satisfactory archetypal reading for that of **A**, K–D (without quite dictating what Langland should have written) ignore the 'custodial' dimension of editorial responsibility. In their remaining examples the present editor, who does not, is similarly unable to follow them.

§ 91. For the belief, however, that in revising **B** the poet did not use his own holograph copy there is solid evidence in the last two passūs, where the near-identical archetypal texts severally contain some disjunctive errors. This situation is most economically explained if **C**'s text substantially represents that of Langland's revision-copy (though K–D's view of this text as wholly unrevised is disputed at III, *B Version* §§ 71–4). But a major, much-discussed instance from earlier in the poem where revision has certainly occurred does, in the present editor's view, support their general case, and it has important implications for the emendation of Bx. The passage XV 53–68 has the same order in **C** and Bx, but this, as K–D argue on grounds of sense, is because it was dislocated mechanically at a pre-archetypal stage. In the terms of the hypothetical history of the text outlined in part III below, this took place in Bx's source, the second scribal copy 'B-Øa'.[175] But K–D's judgement that C XXI–XXII ('B²') share with Bx an exclusive common ancestor (p. 116) is unacceptable; for B²'s *immediate* source ('B¹') can be shown to be based directly on the *first* scribal copy B-Ø (see III, *B Version* §§ 1–6, especially § 5). This divergence apart, the present editor accepts with K–D that in several other cases the archetypal texts of **B** and **C** indeed share a corrupt reading inherited from their *ultimate* common source, B-Ø. One is at I 160/155 *And a meene as þe mair is betwene þe kyng and þe commune.* Either scansion of this line, *aa / bb* or *aa / xa* (K–D), is inauthentic, and the Athlone editors plausibly reconstruct by transposing the b-half nouns to give the stress-pattern *commúne*.[176] Unlike the large-scale transposition in XV for which they provide a detailed explanation (pp. 176–78), I 160 does not definitively indicate corruption at this point, as such an error could have been coincidentally introduced by the scribe of the archetypal C-manuscript (Cx).[177] Likewise, of the twenty-five supposedly unmetrical lines listed on pp. 112–13, some at least must be discounted as scanning acceptably by the empirical 'core-line' criteria, which contradict the 'ideal' metrical norms K–D invoke.[178] But while most of the others are convincingly diagnosed as sharing a scribal error, the emendation adopted here does not always follow K–D.[179]

§ 92. Kane-Donaldson end their searching analysis with the important question of why the poet retained 'so many of the unoriginal readings present in the scribal manuscript' (p. 124). They suggest by way of answer that the apparent lack of revision in the last two passūs, and its non-systematic and non-consecutive nature earlier, indicate a process 'almost certainly never completed' (p. 126). Thus, while allowing that Langland might have eventually managed to remove these residual errors, they conclude that the draft **C** Version was 'seen through the scriptorium by a literary executor' (p. 127), a hypothesis elaborated in the third Athlone volume (see ix below). But one might favour this explanation without necessarily sharing K–D's estimate of the number of scribal readings 'let stand,' the degree of **C**'s incompleteness, or the likely manner of its composition. While K–D are surely right that in textual criticism 'assessments of probability' depend not on 'numerical criteria' but on 'an editorial sense developed through experience,' their own 'demonstration' cannot be accepted as 'almost wholly empirical' (p. 123). On the contrary, it is seriously *un*-empirical in relation to their use of metrical criteria, into which the 'numerical' component they disparage must of necessity enter; in their rejection of **BC** agreement as tacit ratification of a reading; and in their judgement of some revisions as responses to corruption Langland perceived in his copy.[180] Although there is undeniably a place in textual criticism for such speculation, K–D's 'almost' needs heavy emphasis. For the impossibility of knowing why supposed scribal errors were 'allowed to stand' severely limits identification of **BC** agreements as containing or reflecting errors introduced in the archetype or the poet's revision manuscript. The present editor's own understanding, after editing **C**, is that this text is less a revision of **B** than a fresh 'version' of the poem that began at the beginning, where the writer immediately introduced striking new material. If **C** was never submitted complete for professional copying, it could well retain some readings that Langland might ultimately have corrected. But that is an argument for, not against, a fairly conservative approach to editing the text. Except in the last two passūs, therefore, it seems safer to emend **C** only sparingly on the basis of **B**, and scarcely at all on the sole basis of **A**.

§ 93. Kane and Donaldson's magisterial chapter on the text recognises three main stages in the work of editing. These are the recovery of the archetype, comparison of it with those of **A** and **C**, and an 'absolute' scrutiny of all the versions. The archetypal text of **B**, they maintain, is subject to scrutiny and control on comparison not only with **A**, **C**, **AC** and revised **C** but also in itself 'in terms of the results of the first four comparisons.' There is little here to dissent from except their rejection of 'conservative presentation of a reconstructed archetype' as inimical to recovery of 'the historical truth of the poem' and their full-blooded preference of 'foolhardiness to caution' when emending textual corruptions from extant textual evidence, or by conjecture. K–D unobjectionably describe their methods as 'a more extended application of the reasoning set out in Vol I,' principally in 'the use of evidence from the other versions.' But there is a price for 'extending' the application of 'reasoning' as a primary analytical tool. This is a subordination of the editor's custodial responsibility to the textual critic's speculative prerogative that permits a hypothesis about the lost original, as it crystallises into an edited text, to dissolve the substance of the archetype. K–D, notwithstanding, salute another tradition in laying claim to the textual criteria developed by nineteenth and early twentieth-century editors of the classics, the New Testament and Dante, and describing themselves as 'radical only in the greater degree to which they allow the logical force' of these criteria. Unconstrained by the consensus of witnesses or of previous editors, to whom they hardly refer, they consider *their* practice to exemplify a 'traditional' method. In a sense this is true, though it has been more generally thought of as a decisive break with the positivist approach previously dominant in the editing of medieval vernacular texts. K–D however believe that *Piers Plowman* has more in common with the works they mention, because it survives in abundant manuscripts subjected to active scribal intervention. They accordingly judge irrelevant to their task similar situations in other Middle English poems of comparable scope and find that 'the *Piers Plowman* problem is evidently *sui generis*' (p. 123).

§ 94. Kane and Donaldson's fundamental editorial assumption is the clear difference between the typical *usus scribendi* of scribes and that of the poet (p. 130), which they distinguish as 'vigorous, nervous, flexible and relatively compressed.' One may assent to each element here without being certain whether in any particular line it is always or evidently thus. For such a description might apply equally well to Wordsworth's *Prelude* or Eliot's *Four Quartets*, but not to all passages or at every point in any particular passage (and these are texts free from all scribal interference). Langland's 'sense' the editors not unreasonably claim to make out on the basis of their general familiarity with the poem's content and historical meaning. His metre they establish from their analysis of thousands of lines that 'presumably illustrate the alliterative principles the poet set himself and observed' because their 'originality is not in question or is confidently determinable' (p. 132). Such lines, they claim, may be contrasted with those that are identifiable as corrupt 'for discrete reasons' and reveal a scribal character in metrical deviance from these principles. An important feature of their argument, however, is that failures in style and sense usually co-occur with defects in alliteration, so that emendation *sola metri causa* tends to be relatively rare.

§ 95. K–D's acute analysis (pp. 133–40), recognising a wider range of metrical practices than Skeat's (though narrower than Knott-Fowler's),[181] forms the basis of their rationale for the discrimination of authentic lines, and it is accepted here, with certain important modifications. But K–D do not make sufficiently clear whether their 'thousands' of lines are adopted because they conform with an *idea* of the poet's style as 'vigorous, nervous etc' and his sense as 'a component of the whole meaning of the poem' (p. 131). If so, authentically 'Langlandian' lines will simply be those that meet the Athlone editors' requirements for being 'Langlandian'. There is thus an *a priori* feel to the features of sense, style and versification supposed to distinguish 'original' from scribal work. A truly empirical rationale is certainly implied by their appeal to 'evidence from other versions' (p. 129). But their notion of *usus scribendi* may be criticised for failing to meet three conditions imposed by criteria such as those on which the present edition is based. Firstly, there must be a body of irrefragable textual evidence (such as the core-text provides). Secondly, the 'confidence' this evidence gives in determining authenticity remains proportional to the degree of extrinsic support available (from four > three > two versions). Thirdly, such confidence is subject to the joint constraints of the 'linear postulate' and the canon of ratification (so that, save exceptionally, agreement of **AB** or of **BC** earns a reading authorial status). K–D contend in concluding that their case is not open to 'theoretical' objection and their text must be assessed 'in its detail' and 'by the quality of the arguments' supporting that detail and the appropriateness of their readings. This is because 'an edited text is essentially a hypothesis...' and 'its individual readings...elements of the hypothesis' (140, n. 48). True as this is, K–D's case *is* open to theoretical objection, specifically to the way in which its notion of metre defies falsification by empirical evidence. The Athlone editors may well have examined 'thousands of lines'; but the lines that are criterial for such an examination are those uniformly attested by two or more versions of the poem. There is indeed an editorial alternative to aprioristic rationalism: appeal to norms derived inductively from the core-text data. These, moreover, have applicability over a wider range than that of metrical practice; for while obviously not as strongly diagnostic in other areas, they do provide reliable guidelines concerning all aspects of the poet's sense and style (see IV §§ 1–13).

§ 96. The editorial criteria that K–D, for their part, consider as determined 'empirically' they apply through the three main processes of discrimination, reconstruction and conjecture. The discrimination of original variants where only **B** is present provides the textual situation that they call the 'simplest' (p. 141). But this is not (it should be stressed) necessarily the easiest, for in the absence of what they call 'distracting considerations' [*sc.* without any control from a parallel-version source], ascertaining the direction of variation may become a very subjective business indeed. After describing the process in detail, K–D consider cases where the texts 'lineally correspond' (p. 149), the comparison also uncovering errors in the archetypes of **A** and **C** (p. 159). Among their most striking 'extensions' of the principles pioneered in **A** is the importance they attach to convergent variation in undermining manuscript attestation as an indicator of authenticity. In consequence, K–D are ready to recognise that original readings may be preserved in one particular copy[182] (the copy in question being the 'formerly scorned' Corpus 201 [F]), even at points where it is otherwise corrupt or sophisticated. They isolate for consideration a group of cases (pp. 169–72) other than those where F may simply preserve the reading of its ancestral source ['α'] and where Rawlinson (R), the only other α copy, coincides in error with the other family ['β']. These readings K–D ascribe (pp. 171–72) to correction 'in the immediate tradition of F' [i.e. between the copying of α and that of manuscript F] from a manuscript superior at points to

Langland's revision-copy and 'intrinsically more authoritative' at those points where **B** is unique and cannot be compared with **A** or **C** (in terms of the present edition's stemma this would be the copy 'B-Øa' mentioned at § 91 above). But all of these readings unattributable to α can, it will be shown, be explained as due to contamination from **A**; and some that K–D judge 'intrinsically more authoritative' are in any case unconvincing.[183] The present edition makes occasional, and indeed unavoidable use of manuscript F. But it rejects the Athlone editors' high valuation of it and their account of F's good readings as due to correction from a superior lost **B** source, which fails to meet the principle of economy of explanation.[184]

§ 97. K–D's second main editorial process, the reconstruction of readings not instanced in any extant witness, is in essence speculative; but in using positive manuscript evidence it is distinguishable from pure conjecture. With impressive clarity and decisiveness, they arrange their reconstructions according to the types of situation exemplified, using in particular the evidence of **A** and **C**. This last procedure seems to the present editor indispensable for preparing a critical edition of **B**, and Skeat's failure to use it left his text marred by many easily remediable corruptions.[185] Nonetheless, K–D for their part sometimes reject adequate archetypal readings because of a particular interpretation of their sense, style and form, severally or in combination, which may be challenged. Thus in VII 30 they reconstruct Bx *Pouere peple and prisons, fynden hem hir foode* as *Pouere peple [bedredene] and prisons [in stokkes] / Fynden [swiche] hir foode [for oure lordes loue of heuene]* (pp. 173–74). Now, that K–D's lines sound 'Langlandian' is unsurprising, since they conflate C IX 34 with A VIII 34. But despite the Athlone editors' thoughtful argument, it is hard to see how, by their own criteria, they find the Bx line unacceptable. For in the absence of other metrical or stylistic faults, the survival of elements from **A** into the **C** Version does not in itself indicate the corruptness of the **B** archetype. What is observed here may instead be a (rare) case of 'non-linear' revision in **C**. But even if it is, the 'linear postulate' does not forfeit its status as generally trustworthy because of the occasional exception. There is, of course, no *a priori* reason why the poet should not have had access to **A** or have simply remembered what he first wrote (cf. *Intro.* V §§ 29–32). The **C** form already 'reconstructs,' using two lines, returning to the word-order of **A** at the beginning of IX 35 and 36, and echoing A VIII 34b in the second lift of its line 35. But along with **C**'s remoulding of earlier material goes its telescoping of the thought in **AB** 34/31 into a single half-line and its retention of **B**'s distinctive *prisons* in 34b. Most telling of all in the sequence of revisions are the prior survival of A 33a into B 30b and the rarity of the metrical pattern of B VII 30 (*aaa / bb*), virtually restricted to Langland and never found in an archetypal line suspect on other grounds. These points not only form a powerful objection to K–D's emendation, they encourage wider scepticism towards the textual rationalism it exemplifies. For the same arguments that identify an unusual metrical structure (*aaa / bb*) as authentic cannot be inverted or ignored to prove a line scribal, when on grounds of sense the case is fragile and on grounds of style non-existent.

§ 98. Despite these reservations, a number of K–D's 'simple' reconstructions of the archetype are convincing.[186] One example is the 'lexical re-interpretation' at V 440 *yarn] ran* in the light of // C VII 53. Here, though, it must be said in qualification that the **C** line, while 'evidently a revision of a corrupt **B** line' (p. 183), cannot strictly illustrate reconstruction from '**B** evidence alone', since the initial |j| of *yarn* is collaterally confirmed by **C**'s new verb *yede*. The Athlone editors can be triumphantly right in their corrections of palæographic error, as in their salvage of Bx *juel* from R's *euel* at XI 184, a variant that provoked a scandalised '(!)' from Skeat but is greatly superior to the flavourless β *heele* that he accepted. (One of several, however, that do not seem justified, since the archetype's sense is satisfactory, is XII 74 *were she*] *wher* K–D). A more controversial emendation that does have an identical **C** parallel is of *pisseris longe knyues* at XX 219, the 'extreme lexical difficulty' of which (p. 184) draws from K–D an emendation [*purses and*] *longe knyues* that is both metrically clumsy and semantically easier.[187] Of these supposedly 'simple' instances, many that have far-reaching implications are, in the present editor's view, too readily adopted. Thus K–D's notion that their reconstruction of *yet* V 400 as *so þe I* on the basis of F's *soþly* could be 'automatic' reveals insouciance towards the editorial obligation to justify major emendation. A similar change, *ynome* for *name* at XVI 161, which obliterates a significant emphasis on the name of Jesus with 'Crowleyan' assurance (cf. § 26), is rebutted in the *Textual Notes*. Among K–D's most radical suggestions (p. 186) is *a bouste* for *aboute* at XIII 153, the product of failing to read the allegory properly, which the present editor unwisely adopted in the first Everyman edition but now rejects (*Textual Notes ad loc*; *Sch²*, p. 391). Another such is *here-beyng* XIV 141, misanalysed as a 'random type-variant' that supposedly points to a 'polysyllabic original' *herberwyng* (p. 186). This emendation offends both against the rationalist editor's key criterion of *durior lectio*, since archetypal *here-beyng* (possibly Langland's coinage) is lexically much harder, and against the canon of ratification, since it is also the reading of // C XVI 9.[188] While this section of K–D's Introduction contains several instances of shrewd common sense[189] such as *Haukyns wil* at XIV 28 (where the oddity of Bx *Haukyns wif* escaped Skeat), it also illustrates their method at its most seductive, as one who has succumbed to it is bound to record.

§ 99. K–D's third and most controversial editorial process is the proposal of a hypothetical reading as the source of an archetypal reading diagnosed as unoriginal. Conjectural emendation, which they distinguish perhaps too sharply from reconstruction, is explicitly acknowledged as the most unsure, though an 'obligatory' part of the editorial process. One valuable control on conjecture is offered indirectly in the revised or pre-revised texts of **C** and **A** respectively. But the poem's very length, K–D believe, provides enough material to enable confident discrimination between scribal and authorial *usus scribendi*, and often deduction from the scribal reading of 'the authorial reading likely to have generated it' (p. 191).[190] This phase may be thought of as corresponding to that in which a scientific hypothesis predicts a particular outcome that is open to empirical falsification, until which point the account 'deduced' from the known data may function as a provisional theory of the text. (The empirical 'test' here would have to be the discovery of new manuscript evidence of an authoritative kind). The procedure's claim to acceptance, as K–D grant, necessarily varies in strength from case to case, and their success in identifying archetypal corruption must be gauged not only from the validity of their editorial criteria but also from their skill in applying them. Grounds for hesitation have been indicated; but no critical editor can deny the need for such a procedure, if aiding the reader's understanding is the aim of the enterprise. Proposing lost original readings, however, remains a speculative act, and their acceptability must depend largely, as K–D state, on 'the accuracy of the affective data and the informed reasoning applied to them' (p. 192).

§ 100. Like reconstruction, conjecture operates in relation to style, sense and verse-technique. K–D's exclusions of certain whole lines as spurious on the basis of style are endorsed here, except for V 233, 277, 282, XIV 34 and XIX 254. Emendations on grounds of sense, as K–D rightly aver, test total editorial understanding of the work's 'historical truth and meaning' and not just contextual grasp of the poet's local intentions. An example is at VII 121, where their reading *werche* for *slepe* appears 'plausible' enough, though it does not impose itself in place of a Bx reading convincingly shown to be corrupt. Also questionable is their substitution of *Grekes* for *Iewes* at XV 389 and 500 notwithstanding the witness of // C XVII 156 and 252, a case where 'informed reasoning' upon the 'affective data' induces a strained (and *im*plausible) defiance of the canon of ratification. Most of K–D's diagnoses of defective alliteration prove acceptable where the metrical pattern instanced is (by reliable core-text criteria) recognisably deviant, such as *aa / xa*; and a further few are attractive if not inevitable, e.g. *barm* for *lappe* at XVII 71 and (less attractively) *maugree* for *ayein* at XVIII 351. Among these, moreover, some of the boldest accord felicitously with the poem's prevailing texture and tone, illustrating how for an editor of Langland there is in this phase no necessary correlation between cautiousness and persuasiveness. Examples are *biggyng*] *dwellyng* at V 128 [130]; *Tynynge*] *Lesynge* at IX 99 [101]; and *preynte*] *wynked* at XIII 86 (the last without acknowledging its proposer, Skeat). But others fall foul of the core-text norms,[191] e.g. *vndignely*] *vnworþily* XV 243 and *diuyse*] *discryue* XVI 66 where, even if the archetypal lexemes are granted to be 'contextually easier' than those conjectured, both lines scan acceptably as *ax / ax*. In a number of cases that introduce a wholly new idea (though a satisfactory line is achievable by less radical means like simple transposition), conjecture 'involving actual addition...must seem… especially adventurous' (p. 197), as at IX 91 [93] where they read *luged wiþ* for *wors*. But that they feel no pressure to avoid conjecture is a measure of the Athlone editors' confidence in their grasp of the poet's *usus scribendi,* despite the apparent demurral. For K–D are not as anxious to save the archetypal text from their own 'adventurousness' as from that of the scribes.

§ 101. Where **B** is not open to comparison with other versions, and the main indicator of unoriginality is therefore Bx's defective metre, K–D admit to less assurance in their conjectures. In this situation, though they often pinpoint error with impressive accuracy, as at V 165 [167] and X 279 [285], their diagnosis of its causation can be less compelling and their emendation needlessly drastic. Thus at Pr 159 they read *salue* for *help* although the b-verse can be easily reconstructed from the 'split' variants preserved in β and α, and it is arguable that the archetype was not corrupt at all.[192] Similarly extreme is *purchace* for *haue* at IX 77 [79], where K–D do not recognise the 'cognative' alliteration on *p / b*, proved authentic by the core-text criteria (IV § 46), which obviates any need for emendation. (Of many such instances, most of those not mentioned in the *Textual Notes* have been considered in the Everyman editions of **B**). Among emendations that K–D judge neither certain nor likely but only possible come those in which 'the element of subjectivity is largest'. A major example is at X 242 [248], where they propose *man and his make* instead of *mankynde* as 'the least violent emendation' of an original 'also liable to be corrupted for emphasis to the archetypal reading.' But it may be objected that if *mankynde* is 'emphatic' (which is doubtful), *man and his make* is more explicit (which is not doubtful); so the emendation *is* more 'violent' than needful, adding a new idea (*make*) for which no textual evidence exists. By contrast, the emendation *animales*] *bestes* here preferred at least keeps the a-half intact, while offering in the b-half a difficult and rare synonym of the type more than once corrupted by the Bx scribe.[193]

§ 102. How far towards wholesale re-writing K–D's suspicion of the archetypal text can carry them is illustrated by a line scanning *ax / ax*, XV 313 *For we ben Goddes foweles and abiden alwey* for which they substitute *For we [by] goddes [behestes] abiden alwey.* Their justification of this emendation (p. 202) is a palmary instance of 'informed reasoning' upon 'affective data,' though with its appeal to 'two stages of substitution,' 'associational links,' 'homœography' and 'smoothing,' perhaps not of logical economy. Now, complex textual situations could have arisen for which complicated textual explanations might well be fitting. But this example reveals what can happen when rationalism gratuitously ousts a reading satisfactory in sense, style and metre so as to obscure a major thematic point, and the meddling editorial intellect wantonly misshapes a beauteous form. Into K–D's final category of 'complex textual restoration' falls another dire alteration at XII 288 [291] // C XIV 213, where for *And wher it worþ or worþ noȝt, þe bileue is gret of truþe* they read *And wheiþer it worþ* [*of truþe*] *or noȝt, þe*] *worþ* [*of*] *bileue is gret*. This fails by the canons of acceptability and of ratification, substituting for a line of good if not obvious meaning (and verbally identical with its **C** parallel) one that is doctrinally dubious and metrically inferior (in its having the masculine line-ending never found in Langland). Such 'prosthetic' emendation lops off a healthy limb and replaces it with a new one screwed in at the wrong angle. This particular intrusion (answered earlier and again here in the textual note *ad loc*) is wisely not adopted by Russell-Kane into their text of **C**; but it holds its place in *K–D²*, a re-issued volume virtually unmarked by a 'retrospective' ripple. This last example illustrates the confusion that afflicts textual rationalism when its sight-lines dip over the horizon of common sense.

§ 103. The above discussion has dealt with the main structure of Kane-Donaldson's theoretical argument and with some specific effects of their editorial approach on the text itself. But the full extent of their active intervention, signalised usually by the presence of square brackets, is not immediately obvious to the extent that it affects minor readings, as where comparison with **A** and **C** induces them to omit small words or phrases. Here, only a minute collation of their text, first with *Ka* and then with Russell and Kane's C-Text, would suffice to bring out how far K–D depart from the readings of the archetype. If, then, their *Piers Plowman* (which so little resembles any text available to medieval readers outside the poet's immediate circle) may nonetheless be thought to do honour (if not justice) to the poet, this is not because it closely approaches the original at all points, but because it takes the quest for that original with unprecedented seriousness. Many of K–D's discriminations, however, some of their reconstructions, and a few of their conjectures have been gratefully adopted here, even if more have been rejected and some rebutted (occasionally at length). In spite of these strictures, the text of **B** in the present edition, like its Everyman predecessor, recognises a sizeable debt to the methods pioneered by Kane and whole-heartedly applied by K–D. If it often arrives at different conclusions, this comes less from reluctance to pursue 'informed reasoning' to its limit than from a refusal to treat the archetype as corrupt when it cannot be shown as overwhelmingly likely to be so. With reconstructions, probability regarding the error diagnosed and the solution adopted often suffices; but conjectures demand a stricter standard of demonstration. Archetypal readings are, therefore, to be presumed authentic if they conform to the 'core-text' criteria. But it should be remembered that those criteria are applied in the present edition with an understanding of Langland's mind and art in many ways unlike that of the Athlone editors. The present B-Text is therefore, perhaps expectedly, even more different from *K–D* than the present A-Text is from *Ka*.

§ 104. In spite of these major qualifications, Athlone **B** must be saluted as a remarkable achievement. Numerous corruptions in the archetypal text are, as has been said, securely identified and successfully corrected. K–D's editing cuts much deeper than Skeat's into the substance of Langland's poetry, because their readings have been established with such expenditure of critical labour. A solid corpus of indispensable scholarly material, comprehensive and accurate, is contained in its apparatus and the less speculative portions of its Introduction. And the latter provides an enlightening initiation into textual criticism for the reader unintimidated by its lofty tone and hieratic manner. The edition as a whole, which for intellectual power stands out amongst the editorial enterprises of our time, has greatly stimulated thought about the nature of *Piers Plowman* and other texts over the last quarter of the twentieth century, and will doubtless continue to do so.[194] The main unhappy effect of its use as the normal citation-text during this period is one for which K–D themselves are not to blame. But spiriting away the multitudinous brackets around their emendations, as is regularly done by critics who do not fully grasp their implications (cf. § 57 above), is an irresponsible practice at odds with the tenor of what the Athlone editors call

> a theoretical structure...a complex hypothesis designed to account for a body of phenomena...governed by a presumption of the quality of Langland's art and... information about the effects of manuscript copying on...texts (p. 212).

K–D themselves disclaim absolute authority for their edition; but a complementary (and not unseemly) assurance marks their admonitory challenge (p. 220) to would-be future editors: 'Whether we have carried out our task efficiently must be assessed by reenacting it' (a labour that, perhaps unsurprisingly, has been carried out only once). K–D's term 'efficiency' does not adequately acknowledge their imaginative editorial boldness; but it is all the same a quality in which they stand unequalled.

ix. *The Athlone Editions:* Russell and Kane's *Edition of the* C-Text

§ 105. Appearing in 1997, and the longest in making of the three, the Athlone Edition of the C-Text edited by Russell and Kane ('R–K' hereafter) closely resembles its immediate predecessor. A full and clear description of the manuscripts is followed by their classification, and an examination of this is instructive. R–K begin with pairs having not less than 40 agreements, and of these five emerge as especially persistent: VA with 443, followed by RM and PE with around 270, and then by TH^2 with just under 200 and UD at about 130 (on these sigla see *Intro*. III, *C Version* §§ 5–13). As in the earlier editions, no distinction is made between major and minor readings; so while the sheer bulk of agreements at the upper end strongly suggests genetic relationship, the true significance of the twenty-one variational groups clustering at 45 to 100 agreements (p. 21) is not easy to grasp. To illustrate: though totalling about the same, PE has only 70 *major* agreements (26%) to RM's 120 (43%), some 17% less. Thus, despite the quantitative impressiveness of PE's total, the Athlone editors' refusal of any qualitative distinction at the initial stage can be potentially misleading. That is because, as they acknowledge, many minor agreements could arise by coincidence, and the main indication that these are genetic is their co-presence with a substantial body of major ones (a recognition tacitly conceding the latter's criterial character). This comes out clearly from a comparison of PE with AV; for of AV's 443 only 100 (22%) are major, a figure lower than that of PE's major agreements, although absolutely AV contains 38% more shared readings than PE. To estimate the true *weight* of shared readings it is therefore essential to distinguish major from minor agreements. Now it is an insufficient objection that this introduces a subjective element into the classification process, for a degree of 'subjectivity' is involved in identifying *all* agreements, and careful criteria for separating the two categories can be formulated and followed (cf. *Intro*. IV, § 28). This said, the results of R–K's classification, which prove uncontroversial, need not be further pursued here. With two main qualifications, it corresponds to that given in the analytical account at III, *C Version* §§ 5–13, the basis of the C-Text printed in Volume I.

§ 106. The first qualification concerns the position of **t**, the ancestor of the three conjoint copies TH^{2}Ch, which in their **A** portion also form a genetic group.[195] R–K see t as a member of **x** and express its relationship horizontally as $\{<[XYJP^2(UD)]D^2> <(TH^2)Ch>\}$. The prior part of this sequence accords with the one at III, *C Version* § 13 below except for the position of D^2, which is there placed with y (though the manuscript's restricted attestation makes this grouping only probable, not certain). R–K's analysis of **p** as expressed in the sequence $\{<[(PE)(VA)RM]$ $[Q(SF)ZW]> <K(GN)>\}$ is also broadly compatible with the diagram of manuscript relationships given there.[196] But they take no account of the **tp** agreements in error, ascribed at III, *C Version* § 38 to descent from a common ancestor x^2 and giving (when horizontally expressed) the relation $\{<x^1> <x^2[\mathbf{p}][t]>\}$'. As it happens, the effect of this difference upon R–K's concrete textual decisions is relatively small, since to editors relying on the direct method, **tp** agreements in error merely imply that the harder **x** reading was in those cases preserved only by the branch of that family here designated x^1. A second, more significant qualification concerns R–K's interpretation of manuscript NLW 733B (N^2) as containing corrections from a source superior to the archetypal C-Text (Cx hereafter). This judgement, which is rejected at III, *C Version* §§ 39–40 below, highlights the persisting influence of the textual rationalism challenged in the critique of Athlone **B** at §§ 93–102 above. For as with the lost source hypothesised for K–D's preferred readings from the **B** ms Corpus 201, N^2's superior variants, save a handful attributable to scribal inventiveness, can be shown to be due to other-version contamination, specifically from the β family of **B**.

§ 107. R–K speak habitually of 'the *revisions* of the **C** Version' rather than 'the **C** revision' and while they acknowledge the C-Text as 'a marvellous event of the creative imagination' (p. 64), they apparently regard it as a vigorously corrected form of **B** rather than (as it seems to the present editor) a work conceived afresh, though incorporating much of its 'source' with only small alterations. More significantly, they believe that errors in the poet's **B** copy were what provoked specific changes to the text. They also recognise in the unfinished nature of the work a major factor affecting both their treatment of Bx corruptions surviving into Cx and their identification of 'a number of **C** passages as uncompleted revisions' (p. 63). R–K are thus constantly on the watch for differences between Bx and Cx that may be due to **C**'s archetypal scribe 'or, in the unfinished state of the revision, editorial' (p. 63). This possibility 'derives initially from accumulated impressions' (influenced by the editors' prior experiences and general critical judgement) 'of distinctive shape and detail' (though evidently not so gross as to have made Skeat think of **C** as unfinished). R–K are further convinced that they can uncover the 'physical aspect of the revision and its editorial implications.' The 'physical processes of revision' that they discern are relocations of old text; supplemental insertions of new text with or without larger modification where Bx was corrupt; exclusion of (un)corrupted **B** material; re-writing of **B** where Bx was (un)corrupt; and contextual accommodation of **B** material following a major transposition.

§ 108. Now these 'eight broad classes of change' seem to the present editor undeniable, despite any disagreements as to just where they occur. More arguable is the precise sense of 'physical', as is most obvious in regard to a significant transference of material like that from B XIII to C V–VII. Since R–K acknowledge that Langland's exact motives for revision are a matter of speculation (p. 66) and that the circumstances of each alteration are 'largely unrecoverable,' these changes can be confidently judged 'physical' only in the trivial sense that 'matter' is now located at a different place in the text. But just how this was accomplished depends on the nature of the revision-copy, about which only informed guesswork is possible. If it was made up of bound manuscript leaves written on both sides, changes could have been effected *in situ* as R–K suppose, the poet indicating where they should be re-sited and inserting fresh material on separate sheets. But in the absence of any visible witness to such interventions (like that in the unique codex of *Beowulf*),[197] R–K's 'physical' is a misnomer, and the whole conception risks misleading if made too definite. For it is at best only probable (and to the present editor, no more than possible) that the revision proceeded as R–K envisage. Langland could just as well have planned his structural and verbal alterations in rough working papers and then re-drafted the new text one or more times as he progressed towards a fair copy. Alternatively, the text could have been written out afresh and a fair copy made by an amanuensis who might understand the poet's intentions. Indeed, it may be that the whole poem was produced in this way, with only rare passages such as the Ophni-Phineas lines in Pr 95–124 (and not necessarily even these) remaining in enough of a draft state to lend credence to the Athlone editors' postulated 'physical processes of revision.'

§ 109. None of this implies that R–K's account lacks foundation in the available evidence; but it is, all the same, largely inferential. To the present editor, impartial examination of their forty-odd cases of 'relocation' (pp. 65–6) as readily favours the alternative hypothesis outlined above. And, although the matter cannot be spelled out in detail here, the same holds broadly true of their seven other (sub)-classes and carries similar 'editorial implications'. R–K's disarming observation that 'literary speculation about particular instances does not belong in this edition' (p. 67) therefore fails to re-assure, since their whole notion of Langlandian 'revision' involves such speculation. This is clear from their claim that the poet's failure to check his **B** manuscript systematically 'must appear from the number of scribal errors that survived his revision' (p. 67). Such a statement can escape circularity only if those errors can be shown to exist in some abundance. Yet by the canon of ratification, Bx readings that 'survive' into **C** should not be suspected as scribal at all, unless they demonstrably breach the core-text criteria on which a valid test of authenticity depends (and to which the Athlone editors are oblivious). To regard as unoriginal any reading confirmed by **C** is nothing if not 'literary speculation,' as may be illustrated by one example from the supposedly corrupt Bx readings altered with 'additions of one to three lines.' Thus archetypal C Pr 37–8 now reads *Fyndeth out foule fantasyes and foles hem maketh, / And hath wytt at wille to worche yf þei wolde*, the new verb *Fyndeth out* having the tense of Bx *Feynen hem* but being lexically identical with // **A** *Fonden hem*. Such *prima facie* evidence may justify K–D's emendation of **B** to read with **A** and thus lend colour to the 'physical' hypothesis of the revision process, since the poet could easily 'so to speak pen in hand' (p. 67) have deleted the first *e* of *Feynen* and inserted a *d* before the second, struck out *hem* and added *out foule*. But closer inspection raises doubts; for the new phrasal verb *fynden out* means 'discover by mental effort' while **A**'s verb with reflexive pronoun means 'devise (a means of doing),' of which Bx *feynen* is virtually a synonym.[198] In other words, **C** here neither simply restores **A** nor ratifies **B**; what it does is to re-compose **B**'s a-half afresh, and then only after introducing a new line 36 *Wolleth neyther swynke ne swete, bote sweren grete othes*, from which *foule* develops naturally (in part perhaps to link annominatively with *foles* in the b-half). This example is thus far neutral as between the two competing notions of the revision process described at § 108; but the balance tips against the

Athlone editors' interpretation by 38b, which retains Bx, except for replacing *sholde* with *wolde* to make the line closer in texture to 37, with its four full staves.[199] Although the foregoing account has itself involved two examples of 'literary speculation,' it is not the superiority of these but the logical force of the canon of ratification that here renders emendation otiose.

§ 110. In this instance, judging that the poet let a corrupt reading stand has had no effect on R–K, who leave Pr 37–8 alone. But the 'editorial implications' of believing that Langland read his text 'with variable degree of critical attention' (p. 67) are more pressing in II 11 *And crouned with a croune*, where R–K find evidence against Bx in both **C** families and read *in* for *with* as in Athlone **A** and **B** (which follows **A**). This decision may not obviously infringe the canon of ratification, but it leaves unclear whether they regard *with* as a Bx corruption overlooked by the poet through lack of 'critical attention' or one that Cx introduced (like Bx) as supposedly easier than the common original attested in **A**. A further difficulty here is that the Athlone **A** reading, found in only five **r**-family copies, is not securely archetypal like that at Pr 37–8, though evidently judged so by Kane for its intrinsic hardness. In a sense, this last consideration is irrelevant, since the 'rationalism' seen in R–K's choice for **A** is still more obvious in the case of **C**. For while support for *in* and *with* divides significantly across both families (*in* p^1 + IP[2]; *with* p^2 + XUD), *with* is the only variant to ratify the archetypal reading of a preceding version. Such instances of 'rationalism' conflicting with an 'empiricist' approach to the text fairly illustrate the continuity of R–K's practice with that of K–D; so the objections made to the earlier Athlone editions hold good.

§ 111. This remains true notwithstanding that R–K, in this unlike the editors of **B**, disclaim authority to correct Bx errors 'that survived into the fair copy of C Pr–XX' (p. 90). Their statement is important for its distinction between the pre-archetypal ('editorial') text they posit as having been prepared from Langland's working papers, which could be called, in line with earlier terminology, 'C-Ø' (see § 91 above), and the archetypal text recoverable from the manuscript tradition (Cx). The distinction usefully allows scope for emendation where the Cx tradition appears corrupt but remediable, and R–K's extensive and radical alterations indicate a very qualified regard for that tradition. An example is I 112 (*R–K* 113) *Luppen alofte in þe north syde* where they offer the imaginative 'literary speculation' *in lateribus Aquilonis* for the unmetrical b-half. Here, though they attribute the origin of the Cx reading to 'an intruded marginal or interlinear gloss' (p. 169), R–K do not make clear that, if the posited gloss *north* stood in the text itself, it must have been introduced in C-Ø. This might be plausible as an explanation; but the process of error-generation diagnosed is complicated, and its correction extreme. For the simpler, one-word emendation *lefte* proposed in the present edition also explains the error in the archetype, but on a more economical assumption: that its scribe, working from the author's fair copy, substituted a non-alliterating 'synonym' for an expression he found contextually difficult through failure to grasp Langland's 'directional' symbolism.[200] This example shows that, far from reverting to **A**'s relatively positivist procedure, the rationalism of Athlone **C** is well on the way towards radical intuitionism.

§ 112. R–K's definition of their editorial objective (p. 90) as 'to recover or restore' the readings of the pre-archetype leaves them ample room both 'to diagnose what went wrong' in its making and 'to guess plausibly what the poet had in mind' (p. 90). To call Cx's source (whether proximate or ultimate) the 'pre-archetype' for short doubtless oversimplifies their position. But there is actually little solid evidence for the 'indeterminate number of stages' R–K postulate between the early 'clean copy' of the poet's revision (call it 'C-Ø') and 'the exclusive common ancestor of the surviving **C** manuscripts' (Cx), though the notion releases heady possibilities for correcting 'scribal corruption' in the latter (p. 94). What mainly acts as a brake on such correction is R–K's decidedly non-rationalist decision to let stand 'archetypal **B** errors which the poet did not correct' (p. 90). Yet 'radical' is nonetheless how R–K describe their 'deliberate retention of confidently identifiable scribal readings' (p. 94) such as those K–D often emended by reference to individual **B** copies like manuscripts F and G. Their explanation of this paradoxical stance is that the presumed 'scribal substitution[s]...occurred in the first phase of transmission of the **B** Version' (p. 93), from which derived the copy Langland used in revising to **C**.[201] One example is the important line I 39 (= B I 40, A I 39) *And þat seeth þe* [*þi* R–K] *soule and sayth hit the in herte*, which in K–D's elaborate reconstruction from archetypal **A** and the **B** copy G reads *And þat* [*shendeþ*] *þi soule*; [*set*] *it in þin herte*. Now it is hard to see how Langland overlooked an early scribal alteration of his posited original **B** line, both because agreed BxCx differ substantially in sense from Ax and K–D's conjectured form, and because C I 40 completely revises a **B** line very probably identical with its source in **A**. Such an authorial oversight in 39 must, it seems, be logically presupposed, since anything else implies tacit approval. But while in principle possible, it strains belief to the limit; for **C**'s ratification of Bx more realistically suggests that Ax was in this case corrupt.[202] There is no want of candour or consistency in R–K's position here, as a parallel-text presentation of the three Athlone texts would bear out. But the persuasiveness of their account assumes prior endorsement of the **A** reading with which their emended **B** is made to accord. And even if Ax were original, the canon of ratification provides antecedent grounds for thinking **B** a revision, since in sense, style and metre the text is unexceptionable. But even if Ax is rejected as scribal, Bx, whether a revision or a restoration of original **A**, could not be questioned as inauthentic.

§ 113. In their discussion of the last two passūs, R–K recognise four possible interpretations, all four treating XXI–XXII as unrevised. The one they favour sees in this section a B-Text descended, like Bx, from a single source (designated 'B-Ø' at III, *B Version* § 2), but also containing some thirty errors introduced by the scribe of Cx. R–K accordingly incorporate K–D's emendations of Bx to present a text of these passūs that is substantively identical with the Athlone text of **B**. Although they allow as 'not inconceivable' (p. 91) that XXI–XXII were revised but unavailable to the copyist of 'C-Ø' (§ 111 above), they exclude a fifth possibility, that Langland's revision here was light but has left some traces in the extant archetypal text. This is because R–K identify all the 100-odd differences between Cx and Bx as scribal, whereas to the present editor enough appear likely to be authorial for a total harmonisation of the texts to be unjustified. In consequence of R–K's comparative examination of the two archetypes, the Athlone edition of **C** thus emerges as in effect an editorial 'conjoint text', though by their reckoning there neither can nor need be any critically-edited parallel text of the final passūs. However, while antecedent probability may not favour either account over the other, the extensive revision in XX, displaying Langland's art in unabated vigour, contrasts so strongly with the minimal changes in XXI–XXII as to lend *prima facie* support to R–K's understanding of the revision-process as terminated at XX by the poet's illness or death. Recognition in these final passūs of authentic changes, if minor and even perhaps preliminary, is of course not incompatible with such an interpretation. Yet it neither presupposes it nor rules out Langland's having been more or less satisfied here with what he had written, as he evidently was with other (if less extended) passages earlier in the poem.[203] From one point of view, the present edition's treatment is in this instance less 'economical' than the Athlone's; but its product is not a new conjoint text. The Cx form of these passūs is here several times emended from Bx, and *e converso*; but not all its right readings are assumed to be merely preservations of B-Ø necessarily to be adopted into **B**. The critically-edited parallel texts of XXI–XXII are therefore at once near-identical for the most part and recognisably independent versions.

§ 114. In total contrast, R–K's handling of the text up to XX postulates extensive, but sporadic and incomplete acts of revision. Their numerous emendations of the archetypal C-Text are accordingly based on identifying specific readings as scribal on comparison with their parallels in **B** or **AB**. Very few such find an echo in the present text; for although in these cases R–K do not breach the canon of ratification, they often ignore what seems to this editor a strong antecedent probability of revision. (In practice, therefore, R–K's diagnoses of presumed error are seldom shared; where space permits, they are refuted, inevitably by recourse to the same direct method, if to reach a contrary conclusion). However, it should be stressed that in this edition the Cx text is retained not on 'positivistic' but on 'critically empirical' grounds, and is found acceptable always and only if it conforms with the core-line criteria (a concept fully explained at IV §§ 1–13 below). As before, the Athlone editors divide their suspect archetypal readings 'according to the grounds for identifying them as scribal' (p. 95). Some of these may be briefly considered to illustrate how the present edition differs from theirs.[204] They fall into six categories: mechanical errors; misreadings, whether visual errors or 'miscomprehension' (p. 97); (un)conscious easier readings; deliberate variations (such as smoothings or lexical substitutions); and accidental omissions. Major and minor instances are not separated by R–K, though the distinction seems crucial to the present editor, so it is mainly in major ones that the *Textual Notes* deal with their objections, and then only if it seems there is a case to answer.

§ 115. In a few instances of the first type, the analysis is wholly convincing, as at VI 223–24, where Cx misdivides and omits *owene* in 224. The likelihood of both errors being mechanical is reinforced by the recurrence of the first in the **m** family of **A** and of the second in members of **m** and *r²*, although the family originals in the latter case were presumably both correct. This example serves to illustrate the critical value of the 'parallel' approach to editing Langland's text. Firstly, the agreed **AB** reading *tests* the 'linear postulate' against the canon of acceptability based on the core-text criteria: while in itself obviously not an argument against revision, it here persuasively proposes an original **C** reading from which Cx's unmetrical a-verse will have been generated, and it further confirms the line-division after *quarter*.[205] But secondly, **AC** agreement in *when Y* at 224b // against Bx *whoso* also *endorses* the postulate's value for assaying the authenticity of Cx readings not suspect as scribal by core-text criteria. Of these two 'Athlone' readings, the first was initially discriminated by Kane in preference to K–F's and Skeat's unmetrical Vernon manuscript reading, while the second is a K–D conjecture questioning a Bx reading printed by Skeat. Another possibly mechanical error also rightly corrected is Cx's omission (through eyeskip) of *dum scit mens est* from the Isidorean list of Liberum Arbitrium's names at XVI 199a. But in most of the 90-odd cases of this type (pp. 95–6), the Athlone editors are rather less persuasive in judging the Cx reading a scribal reflex rather than a revision. An example is I 70, where for *wente* R–K read *yede* of // **ZAB**, tracing the supposed error to alliterative inducement from the following line. However, as the line is one of four (68–71) with running alliteration on *w* and the second in this sequence to alliterate translinearly,[206] authorial substitution of a commoner advancing synonym for stylistic reasons cannot be ruled out. The editor, bound by the linear postulate to the canon of acceptability, should here firmly resist the siren-song of *durior lectio*. The case for recognising revision is further strengthened by the replacement of **ZAB** *faire* with a new fourth stave *and tauhte* in 71, a Cx reading R–K also emend (though the reasoning behind their second intervention will be hard to locate for assessment).[207]

§ 116. When introducing the next class of suspect Cx readings, R–K specify as an 'easier' reading 'the one that differs less from a grammatically or an otherwise contextually postulable norm, or requires less attention or thought, than another' (p. 97). However, since Langland could sometimes have wished to accord with such a norm, R–K must be defining 'easy' not *simpliciter* but *secundum quid,* that is, by testing two or more variants in relation to one another. But once again, after allowing room for disagreement over particular cases, a more general problem arises in R–K's list of Cx readings judged 'easier' than their parallels in **B** (p. 98): its insufficient regard for the linear postulate. For while the direct method may often operate straightforwardly as between competing family variants in one archetypal tradition (or at a lower level in the stemma), matters are less simple when comparing successive versions. This is because the revising poet must be allowed to express himself at times in a manner *closer* to the 'postulable norm' than to his *usus scribendi* as specified by K–D in their edition of **B**.[208] Desire for greater clarity of statement, a recognised feature of the **C** Version, could even have been a main motive for revision. This reservation obviously applies to the 'minor' type of reading; but it holds particularly for major instances, where Langland may have consciously aimed to avoid obscurity or ambiguity if those qualities served no artistic purpose in the context.

§ 117. Three examples may illustrate this last point. At XX 78 *For he was knyht and kynges sone, Kynde forȝaf þat tyme* Cx substitutes *tyme* for Bx *prowe* in the otherwise unchanged line. A special feature here is that the indication of probability by the linear postulate is somewhat weakened by the fact of an earlier occurrence of *tyme* in the **B** family β. There can be little question that the α variant *prowe* is the harder, and so likelier to be authentic in **B**, or that the same judgement would obtain were these variants directly competing within the archetypal **C** tradition. Since they are not, however, a conflict arises between 'rationalist' regard for *durior lectio* and 'empiricist' acceptance of Cx readings that (whether or not they agree with a particular **B** variant) do not breach the canon of acceptability. But Cx *tyme* must be either a revision for the sake of clarity or a scribal substitution of a more for a lexically less common original. And lateral support for deciding against emendation is found in the immediately following line *That hadde no boie hardynesse hym to touche in deynge* which R–K, it should be noted, accept as revised. The b-half is totally re-written and the a-half substitutes *boie* (already used at 77) for **B**'s *harlot*. Here Langland's careful retention of the source-line's vowel-alliteration is balanced by the repetition of *boie*, no longer in stave-position but present perhaps for the *lexical* purpose of clarification, the point being the social status rather than the moral character of the person.[209] A few lines later, at XX 86 // B XVIII 84, where Cx's *To touchen hym or to trinen hym or to taken hym down and grauen hym* replaces **B**'s second verb *tasten* and the whole of its last lift *of roode*, R–K once more 'restore' both. But here Langland might have had a stylistic as well as a lexical motive for revision: to eliminate this particular end-rhyme and to avoid the unseemly ambiguity of *tasten*.[210] The latter verb is used elsewhere, at XIX 124 = B XVII 148 and earlier at VI 179 = B XIII 346, the survival unchanged of both **B** lines implying that neither occasioned the Cx scribe particular difficulty. But perhaps a more significant argument against R–K is that *trinen* is lexically much the harder, being virtually confined to Langland in this period.[211] Given these considerations, there seems little reason for thinking the new last lift unoriginal, since neither sense nor metre is objectionable. Finally, **B**'s *modicum* is replaced in Cx by *moreyne* at XX 224 *For til moreyne mete with vs.* If this were a straight comparison of stave-words within the Cx tradition, *modicum* would surely count as harder; but that is not what is at issue here. One reason for revising could be the relative obscurity of **B**'s macaronic stave; another, a wish to stress the religious significance of plague or (if *moreyne*'s contextual sense is 'mortality') of the *deth of kynde* mentioned at 219 (an idea explicitly linked with the plague among Kynde's *forageres* at B XX 85). Not one of these three cases plausibly indicates that the Cx readings are 'scribal substitutions for an original like that in the archetypal **B** text because they are easier' (p. 98). Emendations of this kind that use the direct method without regard for the linear postulate and the acceptability canon bring out vividly the limitations of the procedure they exemplify.

§ 118. While R–K's discussion of their cases of more emphatic scribal readings or smoothing cannot be examined here in detail, it should be noted that their account of **B** lines they believe were accidentally left out of Cx at least acknowledges that these might have been excluded in revision. In some like B XIV 105, already adopted in the present edition (= C XV 285), both the mechanical ease of omission and the case for inclusion on grounds of sense seem unarguable.[212] But instances like B Pr 115 *For to counseillen þe Kyng and þe Commune saue* are more problematic. R–K may be right to suspect its mechanical loss through visual attraction from *Kynde Wytt* 141 to the same phrase at the same line-position in C Pr 142. But omission of **B**'s point about the political rôle of the clergy could have been deliberate, given that 140 has been radically revised to make the knightly order and not the commons the source of the king's executive authority. Here the Athlone editors risk misrepresenting the poet's latest thought on a topic presumably at the forefront of his mind when revising. Rather less is at stake in their inclusion of *Si ius nudatur, nudo de iure metatur* from the Angel's speech at B Pr 137, a case which recalls *dum scit mens est* at XVI 199a (§ 115 above). This verse has, however, an undeniably minatory tone, and a further motive for omitting it might have been to join the last line of the speech with B Pr 136 so as to extend the sowing metaphor across two lines. Conceivably, this change was accompanied by a visual direction to place B Pr 137 after 135 (= C Pr 155), a speculation at all events consonant with R–K's 'physical' notion of the revision process and its material product. However, they place the line not after 155 but as in **B**, overlooking the evidence for its possible excision in the immediately following passage, which drops a Latin couplet and a single line originally found in **B**.

§ 119. Where R–K consider the text of Cx scribal on comparison with a Bx reading also found in one or more **C** witnessses, they rightly admit (p. 102) the possibility of coincident variation or of 'correction,' whether memorial or by consultation of another copy ('contamination', qualified as 'benign' where appropriate, would perhaps better cover both forms of the latter process). Particularly is this so with respect to manuscript N^2 in which, heavily sophisticated as it is, R–K profess to discern authoritative corrections from a lost source independent of the archetype (p. 102, n. 23). On a superficial view, one editor's 'correction' may look like another's 'contamination'; but the matter admits of more exact formulation. For as will be shown below (III, *C Version* § 40), apart from about five instances the N^2 variants should be ascribed to a **B** source, since some are peculiar to β where this family is in error and the presumptive Bx reading is that of α agreeing with Cx. In a wide range of instances R–K find the archetype unoriginal in its defective alliteration, omissions, and easier or more emphatic readings. But it must suffice here to single out two examples of lexical substitution and two of imperfect metre, both to vindicate the doubt already voiced concerning their judgements in these areas and also to affirm a measure of agreement with them. To begin with two of the latter, R–K, like the present editor, insert *leode* as the first lift in X 7. Here, the word's mechanical loss before *longed* is plausible, it is needed for sense as well as metre and, as the assured reading of **AB**, its insertion counts as a 'restoration'.[213] The linear postulate may therefore be set aside in this instance as there is little likelihood that the Cx reading, clearly defective by the core-text criteria, represents what the poet intended.[214] Similarly acceptable is R–K's adoption of N^2's *grettore* for *wyddore* at XX 400, whether the Cx error be due to anticipation of copy, as they suppose (p. 104), or unconsciously induced by a common collocation. In this case, though both editions formally cite N^2 as source, the true authority for the emendation is the **B** Version, from which that **C** copy derives it (cf. the case of *prumblide* in the Vernon copy of **A** discussed at § 78 above).

§ 120. Altogether different in character, however, is X 70 '*What art thow,*' *quod Y,* '*þat thow my name knowest*?' where R–K add the presumed **AC** reading *þo* after *Y* from one **C** copy, F. But the intruded adverb is not strictly needed for the sense and, more important, is unlikely to have been in Ax, as it is attested only by group t and manuscript J but not by **m** or the remaining members of both **r** sub-families. That Bx had *þo* is itself doubtful because, though present in β and ms F, its absence from R suggests that it was not in α. The metrical objection to Cx also falls once the line is seen to conform with the Type IIIa variant-pattern *ax / ax* illustrated by the core-text.[215] A case where R–K do detect contamination, but assign it differently from the present editor, is Pr 1[89] *And yf hym wratheth, ben war and his way roume.* Here they judge Cx *roume* a memorial contamination from 18[1][216] and 'correct' from the **x** family group b, a source demonstrably contaminated from the **B** Version.[217] But the 'stylistic' answer to R–K's stylistic objection is to recognise deliberate *repetitio* in Cx's second use of this verb (there are no grounds of sense for rejecting it). The same rhetorical device, much favoured in Langland's late phase, is evident at XV 10[3] *And take wittenesse at a trinite, and take his felowe to witnesse.* Here in the a-half R–K substitute *And þanne shal he testifie of a trinite* from **B**; but what they fail to observe in Cx is a real sense-difference between the two occurrences of *witnesse*,[218] the phrasal constructions being semantically distinct while lexically unified in their doubling of both verb and noun.

§ 121. The Athlone editors' rejections of several Cx readings as more explicit, easier or more emphatic than those of corresponding **B** include some where the present or an earlier edition anticipates them. At XX 226 *Forthy God, of his goednesse, þe furste gome Adam,* they are probably right in their implied judgement of t's alliterating synonym which, whether felicitous guess or memorial contamination, is most probably a scribal improvement of non-alliterating Cx *man*, not the preservation of an authentic reading by pure descent. Another example is VII 106 *And fithele the, withoute flaterynge, of God Friday þe geste,* where manuscript F has *geste,* a presumptively original reading answering in sense to **B**'s *storye,* for archetypal *feste*. This particular Cx substitution R–K class as that of an 'easier' reading, though it is one probably due to unconscious suggestion from the context of *festes* (97 above).[219] In a third case, at XVII 268 *And baptisede and bissheinede with þe bloed of his herte,* they rightly view the second verb in the corresponding (not strictly parallel) B XV 516 as harder than *bisshopid*. But they misidentify the latter as archetypal, though the Cx reading may be more credibly discerned as that of all x^1 witnesses but one and *bisshopid* better interpreted stemmatically as a criterial x^2 reading preserved in **pt** and inserted in P² by contamination from **p**.[220] The manuscript P² is also the sole **C** copy to read **B**'s *foulest* at XX 156 *For of alle fretynge venymes the vilest is the scorpioun.* But in this fourth case, where R–K identify Cx *vilest* as 'easier,' they ignore the antecedent likelihood of a change in a context that shows signs of extensive revision. For between 154–62 only three lines (157 and 159–60) escape some alteration, and **C** strengthens 156 by replacing its non-lexical first stave *For* with *fretynge*. It is in any case less than clear that *vilest* is easier than *foulest*; for the two lexemes overlapped semantically, as is indicated by the overt play on their aural affinity earlier at VI 432.[221] Most of the other readings in this section are minor, and in them R–K's grounds for preferring **B** to Cx become proportionately more subjective and more tenuous.

§ 122. The strengths and limitations of the Athlone editors' use of the parallel method appear in their account of the type of situation where one competing variant within the Cx tradition (usually **p** against **x**) is confirmed by a secure Bx reading. These include uncontroversial instances of palæographic errors and inadvertent omissions (pp. 106–7); but among twenty rejected as unmetrical, two misclassifications of probable Cx readings as of 'X and its associates' deserve attention for their wider implications. In XVI 279 (281) most manuscripts have *churche,* a formal substitution common at all levels of the tradition (including the archetypal),[222] but YDChN² attest *kirke,* giving a normative Type I line. As R–K plausibly find this form original, but without stating whether they consider it archetypal, they apparently rule out memorial contamination from **B**, though it would seem better to leave the issue open (the alternative explanation being correction, independently or from a lost source). But *kirke* seems unlikely, from the manuscript evidence, to have been archetypal, and *churche* is not emended in the present text as this is metrically unnecessary. In another example, at IX 23 *Ac [no a] pena et a culpa Treuthe nolde hem graunte,* it is obscure why R–K consider the **x** variant they reject to have 'anormative alliteration' since satisfactory scansion is obtainable by reading *no treuthe* or *nolde* in the b-half[223] (the present edition prefers *nolde,* but R–K adopt neither). Here they both misclassify the line (p. 106) and print a form of it with no staves at all, failing to see the revision process as a whole or to note that while **A** and **B** scan on *p* (as does **Z**), **C**'s replacement of *pope* with *treuthe* requires a new key-stave on *n* (*nolde*).

§ 123. Among many cases diagnosed of inadvertent substitutions by **x**, few provoke dissent, though a couple deserve closer study for the light they throw on the Athlone procedure. At X 71 *'That wost þou, Wille,' quod he, 'and no wyht bettre'*, R–K find *Wille* induced by *name* at 70 and accordingly emend to *wel* as in one **x** copy D, five **p** copies EQZKN and parallel **B**. But this is a bold change, given the manuscript indication that *Wille* is archetypal and so, since not deficient by the canon of acceptability, presumptively original (by the linear postulate). R–K's judgement is in any case dubious, since at 60 Thought has called the dreamer by his *kynde name* (so that the reader half expects to hear what this is) and the narrator has already been addressed as *Wille* by Holy Church after use of a similar phrase *calde me by name* (I 5). This earlier reading they do not emend, though the **B** parallel *sone* is attested within the **C** tradition by both manuscript I and group b, on which they rely at Pr 189 (see § 16 above). The two cases are hardly identical, since the earlier is not even partly diagnosable as mechanical; but this should not rule out the possibility that on each occasion the name may have been deliberately inserted as a kind of signature.[224] In both cases, the copies that read with **B** are suspect of contamination from the one earlier version likely to have been familiar.

§ 124. Of the numerous 'variants in this situation, attested by X and other copies' (p. 110) that R–K find scribal because more explicit or more emphatic, *Hit were to tore for to telle of the tenþe dole*; but a few notable major examples from the 'easier' category may be selected. In XIX 253 it is admittedly puzzling why Langland eliminated **B**'s *þe contrarie*; but since there is no mechanical reason for the loss, Cx is not clearly easier than **B** (though it is less explicit), and the line meets the acceptability canon, R–K are not justified in emending it. Less problematic is Pr 72 *bulles,* where again the **AB** reading *breuet* that R–K favour is attested by I and group b, now accompanied by M (and by P² marginally after deletion of its exemplar's *bulles*). But this appears another case of rhetorical *repetitio,* like that at Pr 189 discussed at § 120 above. Again, at XVI 185 the Cx reading *mens thouhte* (also that of the **B** family α) may seem 'easier' if read as a transla-tion 'man's thought', but not if analysed as a Latin name followed by an 'internal' gloss. Scribal failure to grasp this might sufficiently account for the loss of *thouhte* from the **C** group u (as it would in β), though in the case of N², contamination from a β-type **B** copy seems more likely. But however the relative 'easiness' of the two variants is assessed, terminal *mens* would be ruled out by core-text metrical standards as producing the excluded masculine line-ending. Another type of case, where the rejected reading scarcely seems easier by normal lexical criteria, is instanced at XIX 143 *For þe paume hath power to pulte out þe ioyntes,* in which support for *pulte* and *putte* divides across, not just between, the families. Here R–K are unwise to assume that Bx read *putte,* since R's *pult* may preserve the reading of α (and hence of Bx), and as support is split in both archetypal traditions, the likelier original must be sought by establishing the direction of varia-tion on intrinsic grounds. But the lexical evidence overwhelmingly supports *pulte* as harder in the context;[225] and R–K's argument may be refuted by applying their own method, here again so as to reach a different conclusion.

§ 125. In a still more complex situation, a range of readings appears in two or even all three canonical traditions, but none of the archetypes is certainly authentic (p. 112), so that the direct method is placed under the greatest pressure in seeking to isolate 'one variant...as the likely origi-nal of all the others.' An important instance is at XX 199 *Yf that thei touched þat [a QF] tre and of þe fruyt eten,* where R–K adopt *a* QF**B** and follow K–D's insertion (from Huntington 128) of *trees* before *fruyt.* The identification of Hm's variant as 'the likely original' of both versions rather than as the intelligent guess of a scribe aiming to improve the metre is bold, but its likelihood must be remote. There is a case for *a* instead of *þat,* as it effectively signalises the uniqueness of the tree of the Fall by stressing a non-lexical word in a line to be understood as scanning on vowels rather than on *t.* But *þat* can as plausibly be attributed to the author's wishing to clarify this point by eliminating the ambiguity of *a,* which (taken as the numeral) denotes 'one particu-lar tree' but (taken as the indefinite article) may misleadingly signify 'any tree.' The Cx reading could arguably have been occasioned by scribal objection to repeated *tree*; but the closeness of the two archetypal texts suggests, in this context of ongoing changes (e.g. at 196b), revision by **C** as the likelier explanation. R–K's retention of the Athlone **B** emendation is therefore unjustifiable on grounds of sense. In fact they class the case as one of 'anormative alliteration' (p. 112); but while this is strictly correct, it is not equivalent to 'unoriginal', as becomes clear once Langland's metrical variant-types are properly recognised. As it stands in Cx, this line is classifiable as the 'reduced' Type IIIb with an extended a-half, a supplemental vowel-stave in final position, and counterpoint on *t,* giving the authentic scansion *abb / aa.*[226]

§ 126. The cases where readings of the base-ms X, more often than not presumed archetypal, are attested in other **A** and **B** copies include a number of varying interest and significance that R–K correct, as does the present edition. But at VII 131 they do not make clear that, since G, the single **C** copy with *siht* for *liht,* is unlikely to have substituted a harder reading independently, this is better interpreted as a 'benign' contamination from parallel B V 492. Here, the likeliest causes of the error in Cx and in six **B** copies will have been the visual similarity of the letter-forms *l* and long *s* and the presence of *liht* in the next line. Superficially similar but more problematic is a reading in a single **C** copy which is not that of archetypal **B**. This is Chaderton's *mery* at XX 181, which R–K (p. 115) prefer to Cx *mercy,* objecting to its sense on grounds external to the text. But here they make too little of the fact that Bx is identical with Cx, that the metre is correct and the meaning adequate, and that Ch's reading could be a visual error or a contextually induced aberration (of a kind not uncommon in this manuscript). R–K's analysis here is unsatisfactory and omits any reference to the acute discussion in *K–D* pp. 208–9. Somewhat enigmatic, too, is their inclusion (p. 115) among 'less interesting' variants of *reik* at Pr 201, a notable crux discussed at length in the present edition.[227] Among this group, moreover, the mere listing of **B** or **AB** parallels does not help the reader find where in the earlier Athlone editions the grounds for discriminating the variant preferred are set out. With a case like *close* for Cx *clanse* at VIII 65, by contrast, previous discussion can be easily located in *Ka*'s Critical Notes, a valuable feature unhappily abandoned in subsequent volumes.

§ 127. The significant distinction to be drawn between *close*] *clanse* and *mery*] *mercy* does not emerge with sufficient sharpness from the data as presented by R–K. Both their emendations are rejected here because they conflict with the canon of ratification, which prohibits alteration of an assured Bx reading retained in **C** unless it demonstrably infringes the core-text criteria, and both are decided simply on grounds of sense. But R–K do not make clear that whereas *mery* is found in only one copy of either version, *close* (attested in **C** solely in the group RM), as the reading of the *r*[l] sub-family of **A**, has some claim to be archetypal (neither case is in fact treated as archetypal in the present edition).[229] The point here is that the textual weight of the competing variants is hard to measure when they are lumped together to illustrate 'variation of X supported by other copies which appears easier than an alternative' (p.114). The problem with Athlone's way of systematically grouping readings for discussion is that it discourages a comparison of them in the context of their relative strength of attestation in the several versions. For without any cross-referencing, the stronger arguments for a particular textual choice (where these exist) cannot easily be found: vexatious fatigue for the reader trying to assess the editors' decisions is the cost exacted by their use of a 'categorial' rather than a 'sequential' format. The most helpful parts of R–K's Introduction are accordingly those examining individual readings in a detailed manner that combines the benefits of Athlone **A**'s Critical Notes with the fullness allowed by a discursive presentation. The concluding portion (pp. 118–136) on problems in XXI–XXII, where the text of **B** is comprehensively relevant as 'a factor in its determination,' is particularly forthcoming in its willingness to engage with contrary arguments in the Everyman first edition of the B-Text. The appearance of Athlone **C** between that of the present edition's volumes I and II has conversely made it possible to take full account here of R–K's replies to those arguments. Between them, therefore, these pages and the corresponding sections of the present *Textual Notes* provide a fairly full study of the main difficulties in the text of **C**. Though restrictions of space here rule out answering every one of the Athlone editors' points, the reader who wishes to compare the textual approaches of the two editions could do worse than turn to these sections of the respective volumes.

§ 128. R–K's textual arguments are nearly always penetrating and provocative; but two recurring sources of dissatisfaction are their treatment of Langland's metre and their negative attitude to the Z-Text. The first, by now familiar, may be illustrated from their rejection of Cx XXII 155 *And to forȝete ȝowthe and ȝeue nat of synne* and adoption instead of their emended parallel **B** reading *And [so] forȝete [sorwe] and [of synne ȝeue nouht]*, which has *sorwe* for *ȝowthe* but in Bx the two-stave metrical pattern *ab / ab* (p. 132). Their elaborate explanation finds in Cx a memorial contamination from XII 12 or 'metrical repair on that model.' But the change could more plausibly evince the deliberate re-writing of a **B** line that contained the seed of the new idea in **C**, since the referent of **B**'s *sorwe* is clearly 'sorrow for sins past' and that of *ȝowthe* is (metonymically) '(the sins of) one's youthful life.' R–K's alteration not only flouts the acceptability canon, but their dual-purpose emendation, replacing *to* with *so* and retaining the (now metricly normative) **B** line for **C**, does not afford superior sense. For while it is clear how forgetting contrition for sin might result from banishing fear of death and age, **C** makes the subtler point that Life's behaving like a stereotypical Youth is a way of 'forgetting' his own misspent youth. R–K's metrical argument is inconsistent with their acceptance elsewhere of Type III core-lines like V 116; but graver faults are their consigning to oblivion of an acceptable archetypal line in each version, alteration of Langland's meaning, and concealment of an interesting revision. The second point, concerning **Z**, is now of mainly historical interest, since the Everyman first edition's emendation of *alle kynne* to *alleskynnes* in XX 373 so as to provide an internal *s* stave proves otiose in the light of the present editor's improved understanding of the poet's metre.[230] However, it is worth commenting on R–K's objection (p. 130, n. 49) to this conjectured form as unlikely to be Langlandian because found 'in only one *Piers* manuscript, as a morphological variant in H[3] at A X 27.' This sounds definitive in its assured use of the Apparatus evidence but, like an earlier observation of the Athlone **A** editor (noted at § 61 above), is wrong. The form in question occurs at Z III 172; and whatever else Bodley 851 may be, it is 'a *Piers* manuscript.'

§ 129. In dealing with new or revised matter in the text where no particular reference is made to **B**, R–K distinguish comparison of the two main family traditions so as to discern the original reading, and diagnosis, which involves 'an absolute comparison between actual readings and abstractions.' These important 'abstractions' could be thought of as the ideal forms from which archetypal lines found defective in metre or in 'the understood grammar of the poet's style' may be hypothesised to derive. And in this crucial (but potentially controversial) stage of the editorial process, while R–K acknowledge the risk of being 'arbitrarily subjective,' they take comfort from the 'handsome third' of such lines where they identify, in one or a few manuscripts, a variant of which they judge Cx a corruption (p. 138). That privileged reading, when it shows itself, they take to have come in by correction from 'a superior **C** copy' (ibid. n. 3); but they nonetheless recognise that scribes might have gone in for 'independent editorial adventurism' like that discoverable in the Corpus 201 copy of **B**. It has already been noted that the handy notion of 'a lost manuscript of superior quality to the archetype' infringes the canon of economy. It should now be emphasised that there is almost nothing in the **C** copies yielding the few readings admittedly superior to Cx's that cannot be ascribed to intelligent scribal guesswork or felicitous chance. In the 'unhandsome' remaining two-thirds, R–K must naturally have 'recourse to conjecture in full understanding of its implications.'

§ 130. Given how far-reaching these implications are, it is not surprising that Athlone **C** also becomes (in K–D's words cited at § 104 above) 'a theoretical structure...a complex hypothesis designed to account for a body of phenomena.' But its radical character is not evident at once from R–K's opening account of 'the more elementary unconscious errors' in X and its family ancestor, such as omissions and the usual easier and more emphatic readings that they confidently distinguish. Their observations are often plausible, as at XIX 100 *And Hope afturward of o God more me toelde,* where they offer both mechanical and interpretative reasons for preferring the x^2 reading *god* to x^1's *o god* (p. 149), and this section (pp. 143–75) contains some of R–K's most rewarding as well as most controversial arguments. But these need no further specification here, as they may be compared almost point for point with those in the *Textual Notes*.[231] At the other end of the scale, an example of invasive editing that induces deeper misgivings about the Athlone procedure is R–K's gratuitously elaborate 're-arrangement' of III 139–44 from the divergent texts attested in **x** and **p** 'which, if original, would account for the shape of both' (p. 159):

> godes forb[o]de eny more
> Thow tene me and treuthe: and thow mowe be atake
> In the Castel of Corf y shal do close the,
> Or in a wel wors, wo[ne ther as an ancre,
> And marre þe with myschef], be seynte mary my lady.
> That alle [women, wantowen], shal [be] war [by] þe one.

Apart from the archetypal inversion to prose order in the second line that R–K 'radically' leave with the inauthentic pattern *aa / xa* (cf. § 112 above), there is little in the **p** variants they favour that cannot be ascribed to this family's well-established tendency to pad out the terse original convincingly preserved by **x**, as noted by Carnegy (1934:12–13) and printed in the present text. But given the drastic treatment, it is hard to see why they also leave their third line with a masculine ending, unless they imagine that Langland wrote such lines (the core-text confirms the massive evidence of the separate archetypes that he did not).

§ 131. R–K finally discuss metrical and stylistic corruptions and claim to discern in one or a few individual copies original harder readings, some of which raise important issues of principle. One such is IX 26[2] *The tarre is vntydy þat to þe shep bylongeth,* where they prefer manuscript F's *tripe* to Cx *shep* (p. 164). The Athlone editors are doubtless right about the general unlikelihood of a scribe's substituting what would appear an 'intrinsically' harder word; but they here overestimate the power of the direct method's central editorial criterion. For if *tripe* is not a piece of 'scribal adventurism', it must be a correction from a lost superior source. Yet the Cx line possesses in the grammatical word *to* the mute key-stave that is almost a hallmark of this poet's practice (see Appendix I § 4). Now, where the *durior lectio* criterion clashes with the canons of economy and acceptability, the case for avoiding emendation should, on logical grounds, be held the stronger (see IV, §§ 27ff, esp. § 29 below). A wider implication of this analysis that should be highlighted is that, in some circumstances, a reading that is lexically harder in itself may nonetheless be judged scribal if the context provides a likely motive for substitution. Here such a motive is at hand in the failure of an otherwise intelligent scribe[232] to grasp a peculiar feature of Langland's versification, his consequent perception of the line as metrically defective, and his subsequent 'adventurous' emendation.

§ 132. The final textual situation R–K consider is one where no extant copy has a variant from which the Cx reading identified as scribal can have derived, so that emendation must rely on conjecture. One typical example of a conjecture that is not unreasonable in itself but is based on tortuous reasoning occurs among some seven cases where simple re-arrangement of word-order would render normative a line with the inauthentic alliterative pattern *aa / xa*. At VIII 30 R–K observe (p. 168, n. 26) that the **B** source-line in an archetypally corrupt form was what Langland 'received' in his revision copy: that is, a reading presumed identically corrupt in Bx and B^1 must already have been corrupt in B-Ø, the common source of both. B VI 31 *And go affaite þi faucons wilde foweles to kille* is emended in *K–D* to read as **A**; yet its sense, metre and style are unexceptionable and the reading is fully acceptable as a revision of A VII 33. What makes R–K's decision unsatisfactory is not its final product (identical in the present edition) but the faulty reasoning that underlies it. For if they believe that **B** originally read like **A**, then this line must be one of those 'overlooked' by the poet because of the conditions of his revision. From one point of view, therefore, their approach to the text is deeply conservative, despite what they appear to regard as the conjectural character of their emendation (cf. § 112 above). For the reading they print is not one uninstanced elsewhere but, if it is accepted that this underwent in Cx a simple transposition to prose order in the b-half, one that will require no more than a straightforward 'restoration' (III, *B Version* § 61) to the archetypal form of the preceding version. Yet its adoption in Athlone **C** is at odds with its rejection in Athlone **B**. From this, it emerges that any approach to editing *Piers Plowman* that is not 'parallelist' from the beginning risks ending in contradiction.

§ 133. It is, however, in the area of conjectural emendations on grounds of sense that the Athlone C-Text (like its predecessor) arouses most disquiet. For since metrical and stylistic objections are now absent, R–K must show by 'absolute comparison' why their 'abstraction' is preferable to the 'actual' reading. Here the stakes are high, since they risk destroying the author's sense and substituting their own. A striking example occurs at XVIII 236 *So is God Goddes Sone, in three persones the Trinite,* which the Athlone editors find 'very strange theology' (p. 175). But the strangeness disappears if *sone* is seen as the subject and the b-half read as an ellipsis, with *and* and *is* to be understood respectively before *in* and *the*. In R–K's *So i[n] god [and] goddes sone i[s] three persones, the trinite,* introducing the same two words understood in the proposed ellipsis, it is hard to connect the credal formula *qui procedit ab utroque* that they invoke in relation to 231 with the precise form of their emended line, which is strained in phrasing and disconcerting in sense. This is one instance where the archetypal text, however odd its conjunction of ideas, is not nonsense and may well be what Langland wrote, so that intervention is inadvisable. Again, at XVII 126 R–K alter the archetype's definition of Charity as *Lief and loue and leutee, in o byleue a lawe* to read *[Lif in] loue and leutee in o byleue [and] lawe*. Unfortunately, as cited on p. 174 the line they find 'hard to make sense of' reads *a leutee* for *and leutee*, making no sense at all. But assuming only a misprint here, the actual Cx reading may be defended as meaningful and, with its closeness in phrasal structure to the previous example, as redolent of authentic Langlandian idiom. Charity is being defined by two phrases in apposition, the first giving its components, the second a parallel statement about moral unanimity on the basis of unity in faith. R–K, whether as part of or independently of their larger emendation, alter the spelling of X's *Lief* to *Lif* as in **p** and the **x**-group u; but they are perhaps mistaken to do so, since Langland may intend a pun on 'life' and 'faith,' while group y's unusual spelling is indirectly confirmed by *leue* in the unrelated t. All this suggests the triad 'faith, love, hope' as the constituents of the comprehensive *charite* informing a distinctively 'mystical' late-Langlandian conception of 'the Church.' The passage, which shows the poet thinking at high pressure, may not be wholly lucid, but its drift is not in doubt. R–K's interference with an archetypal text that makes good sense is thus imprudent, even if it is not their quoted form that underlies their interpretation. But in XVII 131 *God lereth no lyf to louye withouten lele cause* their alteration of *louye* to *leue* for supposedly lacking contextual sense borders on *rechelesnesse*, as consultation of the following lines 136–139 on wrong or lawless 'loves' will bear out. For it is only 'love' that makes contextual sense, Langland's point being that what God wants from man is a rational or 'right' love based on orthodox belief and the morality that should arise from it. This notion, very close to that of XVII 126, again illustrates the unbreakable theological triad so prominent in the later Langland's thought. The received text is clear, sound and arresting, but as re-written by R–K nearly unintelligible. In all these instances, loss of an archetypal reading is not outweighed by the gain of any vivid new possibility. It is otherwise with R–K's 'adventurous' emendation *in lateribus Aquilonis* for *in þe north syde* at I 11[3]. This does not persuade the present editor to forsake the simpler and more economical *in þe [lefte] syde* but is, if not what Langland wrote, worthy of him.

§ 134. R–K's view of the history of the **C** Version and their treatment of its text are in most ways as radical as those of K–D. Particularly challenging are their high valuation of the sub-archetypal **p** tradition, consonant with their refusal to judge it secondary (as it is argued to be at III, *C Version* § 10), and their relatively low esteem for the archetypal text, in which they detect a host of 'errors' that baffle the present editor's most earnest scrutiny. R–K's arguments nonetheless expand and sharpen the reader's attentiveness to the details of Langland's art and meaning. If their Introduction lacks the urgency of Kane's and the penetration of Kane-Donaldson's, its 'theoretical structure' is built upon as solid and accurate a 'body of phenomena' as its predecessors'. The three Athlone volumes carry the rationalist understanding of Langland's text to its limits, and a good deal further than the present editor would be prepared to go; but they constitute, by any standards, a formidable achievement.

x. Rigg and Brewer's *Edition of the* Z-Text

§ 135. Fifteen years earlier, the edition of the Z-Text by George Rigg and Charlotte Brewer (*R–B* hereafter)[233] was published, halfway between the Everyman and York editions of **B** and **C** (1978) and the second edition of the Athlone text of **A** (1988). Kane in his 'Retrospect' was therefore obliged to take cognisance of Bodley 851, but merely dismissed it as 'useless for editing, if not actually misleading' (*Ka*[2] p. 459) with a reference to the footnote discussion in the Athlone *B Version* and his long review of R–B's edition.[234] Since the Athlone editors nowhere envisage **Z** as a substantive version of *Piers Plowman*, their verdict presumably relates to the manuscript only as evidence for the text of **A**. This verdict has already been shown to be mistaken (see § 64 above), even if Bodley 851 is taken as no more than a wayward **A** copy similar to F of the **B** Version and N[2] of **C**. R–B, however, argue for **Z** not simply as an independent **A** witness but as an authentic version anterior to **A**. Their claim, if substantiated, has important implications, immediately for the text of **A** and more generally for the work as a whole. Like the other versions, **Z** is considered fully in Part III of this *Introduction*; but here *R–B* will be examined as a pioneering contribution to the editorial tradition.

§ 136. In appearance, the edition resembles those of the EETS, but as there is only one copy of this 'version' its footnote 'apparatus' has no variant readings. Instead, at one level it records the **A** lines to which the **Z** lines correspond and supplements this with a useful ten-page Concordance

Table to the three other versions. A second level gives Critical Notes like those of the EETS and Athlone **A** editions on textual points, parallels, linguistic matters and problems of local meaning. Like Skeat, R–B mark expansions and keep the manuscript's idiosyncratic spellings, though not its word-divisions, record its (intermittent) paraph marks, and employ modern punctuation. Additionally, they place vertical lines in the margin to indicate **Z**'s differences in word-order from **A** and at a few points obeli to mark 'corrupt, unemended passages' (p. 34).[235] Otherwise their text's peculiar feature is the use of bold type for **Z**'s unique readings, which vary in length from single words to a 30-line passage at the end of Passus III.[236] (This feature, despite its obvious utility, has no place in the present edition; for as a putative 'version', **Z** is not treated differently from **A**, **B** and **C**, each of which contains distinctive material). Emendations, 'positivist' in scale, are limited to correction of mechanical errors and potentially misleading spelling mistakes, supply of missing letters, and provision of words deemed necessary for the sense.[237] R–B's final analytical section identifies the manuscript's archaic and South West Midland linguistic features as original and its non-Western forms as scribal, concluding that 'the linguistic appearance of **Z** suggests that it was copied from a text exactly answering to our suppositions about Langland's origins' (p. 127). Such 'traditional' philological interest is of a piece with their judgement that 'a unique copy of a unique version of the poem' (ibid.) should receive a conservative treatment of its text and accidentals alike. This judgement is accepted in the present edition which, however, goes beyond correcting a few more mechanical errors[238] to venture some reconstructions and conjectural emendations.[239]

§ 137. The physical features of MS Bodley 851 have proved a focus for disagreements with R–B's claims on behalf of its text. But that the codicological and textual issues can be disentangled is clear from the separate introductions to the same editors' subsequent *Facsimile* of **Z**.[240] Here the structure of the codex is analysed by Rigg at greater length and the text by Brewer, who takes account of the reception of their edition and more recent work on **Z** and its relations to **A**.[241] But the editors' two basic claims remain: first, that the *Piers Plowman* text up to VIII 92 (**Z**), forming Part III (a) of the manuscript, is by a single scribe, Hand X, who also wrote three of the Latin pieces in Part I (*Facsimile*, p. 25); second, that this scribe was John Wells, the Benedictine of Ramsey Abbey whose beautifully-drawn book-plate appears on fol. 6v. Rigg ascribes the book-plate inscription *Iste liber constat Fratri Iohanni de Wellis Monacho Rameseye* to Hand X and identifies the owner with the noted anti-Wycliffite monk who had been a student at Gloucester College, the Benedictine house at Oxford, before 1376, was *prior studentium* there in 1381, and died at Perugia in 1388. On the evidence of the handwriting and the Oxford associations of the manuscript, R–B accordingly date the Z-Text between 1376 (or earlier) and 1388, and locate its copying in Oxford (*R–B*, p. 5; *Facs.*, pp. 29–30). The manuscript's **C** portion of *Piers* (= C-ms Z) and nearly a hundred **A** lines linking **Z** to **C** they assign to a single scribe (Q) of the early fifteenth century. This account has been criticised by Ralph Hanna, who doubts that the book-plate inscription is by the scribe of **Z** and claims that the latter cannot be shown to be the Ramsey monk in the absence of any surviving autograph by Wells.[242] Hanna supports his preference for a date *c.* 1400 by noting that what he considers echoes of **C**, e.g. VI 309 and V 23–5 in Z V 124 and 142–4 (p. 18), rule out Wells as the scribe of **Z**, if C V is not earlier than 1388.

§ 138. The dating of **C** will be discussed below (see III, *C Version* § 1; V § 11); but with no independent external testimony about the latter, **Z**'s position in the sequence must depend on interpretation of the literary evidence, which necessarily lacks finality. This being so, Wells's death in 1388 cannot decisively exclude him as the copyist of Bodley 851, since **C** 'echoes' in **Z** could in principle reflect his acquaintance with the late version as a work in progress (something also possible in the case of Thomas Usk, who died a year before Wells in 1387).[243] Conversely, while certainty that **Z** was copied in the 1370s would confirm that its supposed **C(B)** 'echoes' were actually 'pre-echoes' or anticipations, this could not by itself prove **Z** 'a coherent and self-sufficient version' (*R–B*, p. 12) *anterior* to **A** that probably belongs between 1365 and 1370. Establishing an early date for the surviving copy of **Z** is therefore not crucial for settling either its nature or the period of composition of its text. Similarly, the internal consistency of the language and its recognised nearness to the author's likely dialect cannot demonstrate, though it may support, the text's originality.[244] **Z**'s claim to 'versional' status, in other words, must be tested in the same way as competing traditions of the canonical versions such as the α and β texts of **B**, the authenticity of which has never been in doubt. R–B's textual hypothesis should therefore be disengaged from too close a connection with the particularities of Bodley 851 and its scribes. For the text's credibility, as its first editors recognise, depends on critical assessment of its intrinsic character. They therefore begin by arguing that material believed by Kane to be evidence of **BC** conflation or contamination was instead 'integral to the original draft of the poem' but was 'omitted by manuscripts of the **A** tradition' (p. 10). Apart from three obelised passages where they associate the error in question with the text's draft form in the manuscript (I 101, V 124, VII 6), R–B judge all other corruptions to be 'of a simple mechanical kind.' But while they convincingly deny conflation, they do not consider whether the suspected echoes of **BC** may have been introduced by scribe X or the copyist of his exemplar. This suggestion would complicate matters; it is also incompatible with R–B's main hypothesis that such readings were original to **Z** and, after **Z** had been altered by **A**, were restored in **B** or **C**. But it perhaps merits fuller treatment than they provide; for these readings are not just 'clearly germane to the textual status of **Z**' (p. 36), they constitute a potential objection to its authenticity (III, *Z Version* §§ 26–7).

§ 139. R–B's literary argument, which may appear the more subjective, is nonetheless of equal importance, since the Bodley 851 text could hardly challenge consideration as a 'version' for its unique 'shape' without containing writing worthy of the poet of **A**, **B** and **C**. Their case that **Z** lacks signs of 'cobbling' and that its peculiar passages are beyond the capacity of a literate scribe 'able to write tolerable long lines' (*K–D*, p. 15, n. 95) does not seem overstated to the present writer. For the best **Z** lines contain thoughts and images at once suggesting the poet of the other versions and not obviously derived from these. They include Robert the Robber's macaronic couplet at V 142–3, which both 'integrates the Latin into the alliterative pattern' (p. 15) and employs the *f* / *v* alliteration of such characteristic lines as B XV 60 (see Appendix I, § 2 ii) and its revised **C** form; the 'word-wind' passage at V 34–40; and the lines on Truth's powers at VI 68–78. None would look spurious if found in **A** at these points, though reasons for their removal in revision are not far to seek.[245] R–B sensitively examine **Z**'s distinctive material (pp. 15–17); but in concluding that its Langlandian authorship 'cannot be proved one way or the other' (p. 15) they if anything understate their case. It is true that without substantial new external evidence there can be no 'proof' in such a matter; but what must and can be ascertained is whether or not these passages evince characteristics recognised as 'scribal' in the **ABC** traditions from the archetypal level downwards. One way of doing this is to compare **Z**'s unique material with known spurious passages such as those from Harley 875 (H) printed in Skeat's edition of **A**. Another way is to undertake R–K's 'absolute comparison,' not, however, with the Athlone editors' 'abstractions' but with the empirically-established core-text. There is no objection in principle to the latter exercise, since much of **Z**'s special material has no real parallel in **A**. But both comparisons would serve to counteract the subjectivity of the 'impression' on which an *initial* hypothesis of the text's originality is inevitably based. **Z**'s inclusion in the present edition is due to its having survived such comparative scrutiny; for its unique passages satisfy the core-text criteria and even illustrate metrical features exclusive to Langland.[246]

§ 140. R–B attribute **Z**'s 'few inconsistencies' to its being a draft or 'a partial revision of the earliest version of the poem' (p. 13) and see **A** as 'an authorial expansion of the shorter [**Z**]' rather than **Z** as 'an authorial (or scribal) abridgement of the longer [**A**].' The four or five local inconsistencies they examine do not, in their view, tell against the text's overall coherence. That its passus-divisions are 'quite acceptable' (though less satisfactory than **A**'s) and that no sophisticating scribe would have altered **A**'s to **Z**'s are claims that gain strength from a comparison with what such a scribe actually did in the case of the **B** manuscript Corpus 201.[247] R–B's conclusion, that the **A** passages Kane believed **Z** omitted had not yet been composed, is supported by the absence of inconsequentiality at points where these omissions supposedly took place. Finally, Kane's contention that 'some of the groups of "new" lines occur where approximate multiples of 20 or 40 lines are wanting (i.e. the presumptive contents of sides or leaves)' (*K–D*, p. 14, n. 95) has, as Brewer later remarks, 'been authoritatively demolished by Green.'[248]

§ 141. In considering the stylistic and metrical evidence for the text's draft status, R–B confine their comparison to **A**, though concisely noting both the relative inferiority of particular **Z** lines and the 'progressive elimination of a theme from one version to another' (p. 16). The 'draft' part of their hypothesis should perhaps not be invoked too readily to account for weaker lines explicable on the assumption of scribal carelessness, unless the larger context convincingly suggests incompleteness. But R–B (somewhat confusingly) resort to it even in the section of A-Text by Hand Q that links **Z** proper to Passus X of **C**, finding it 'arguable' that VIII 113–14 *And but yf Luk lye, he lernit vs anothir be foulys, þat we ne scholde / To besy be aboute to make the wombe joye* 'preserves Langland's original draft' (p. 111, note). But here (as shown in the *Textual Notes* on these lines) the substantive error of scribes in the sub-archetypal traditions of both **A** and **B** was to misidentify the referent of the noun *folis* in line 113 ('fools'), which was correctly preserved in the **m** and α traditions but misunderstood in both **r** and β as *foulys* 'birds', with subsequent smoothing and mislineation. It should also be acknowledged that features like defective metre, which are ambiguously interpretable as either scribal or draft work, cannot by themselves (dis) prove the authenticity of **Z**. To some extent, however, the impression of **Z** as a work in progress, which arises partly from specific 'oral' features that will be examined later (III, *Z Version* §§ 8–9), can be tested by comparing it with other Langlandian material that may also have come down in a draft state, C Pr 95–124 and Passus XII of **A**.[249]

§ 142. In many lines, however, the 'draft' thesis is not needed to account for what R–B call 'mere padding', which may be authorial in origin. For if the authenticity of these lines cannot be demonstrated, doubts about them may nonetheless be reduced by showing their conformity with uncontested lines in the other versions. For example, at II 177 *For eny mercy of Mede, by Marye of heuene*, it is not obvious that (taken in context) the a-verse *is* otiose, while supposed 'padding' like the b-half oath is instanced at C IV 139 *Ne thorw mede do mercy, by Marie of heuene*. If anything, comparison of these two lines might more immediately suggest **C** contamination in **Z**; but as they are not identical, no reason appears why scribe X (or his exemplar) should have interpolated a variant of the **C** line at this point. It is easier to suppose that the poet might have *removed* the line in **A** because a phrase recalling II 177a occurs at Z IV 140 (to which C IV 139 corresponds), a line unchanged in both **A** and parallel **B**. In this situation, some **ZC** correspondences may be better interpreted not as scribal contaminations but as instancing late authorial re-use of very early material. For though evidence exists that Langland lacked his original fair copy of **B** when composing **C**, there is no reason to think that he did not have access to other *Piers Plowman* materials, such as his working draft of **Z** (see V, *The Poem in Time*, §§ 29–30 below). Such a manuscript, moreover, is *ex hypothesi* unlikely to have been available to a *scribe* until after the poet's death, when renewed demand for *Piers Plowman* texts led to the production of the unique conjunction of the earliest and latest versions now to be found in Bodley 851 (see V §§ 14–15).

§ 143. Among a handful of possible 'pre-echoes' of **C** and **B** listed below,[250] perhaps the most notable suggesting scribal contamination from **C** is at V 124, where R–B print †*Quod ye nan* † *yelde ayeyn yf Y so myche haue*. Their astute note suggests that the meaningless obelised phrase may conceal either *Qwat I nam, the apparent α and possible **m** reading, or *Quodque mnam, a conjecture that is tentatively adopted in the present edition.[251] Kane's interpretation (1985:919–20) of the manuscript reading as *yeuan* (not *ye nan*) leads him to identify the line as a direct echo of C VI 309, which introduces the Welshman Evan. But although his conclusion is not accepted here, the problem hardly admits of a straightforward solution, and it is not an easy matter to eschew the positivism of R–B, who adopt neither solution that they recognise. The example deserves mention here as one of a very few where the present edition has preferred a reconstructed *durior lectio*, 'abstraction' though it may be, against the probable joint witness of two sub-archetypal variants (α and **m**), each of which may preserve the archetype of its respective version.[252] The main (if not the sole) justification for such privileging of conjectural reasoning is the exceptional ambiguity of the stemmatic indications in these cases (see the *Textual Notes* and cf. I 86).

§ 144. In relation to its immediate successor, **Z** is found unsurprisingly by R–B (p. 18) to have 'a bearing on several major cruces of the A-Text (sometimes affecting **B** and **C** also).' Thus at Pr 129, where *And that seuth thy soule* provides a basis for correcting the archetypal **A** line, although this could indicate **B** or **C** contamination, a more economical explanation is that Ax was here corrupt. The reason for thinking so is less the **ZBC** agreement in itself than the ease with which the inferior Ax reading may be derived from the posited original. Here the direct method and the weight of manuscript evidence happily lead to the same outcome. At I 86, by contrast, despite impressive support from the **m** family and Bx, R–B's wider claim for **Z**'s *plente of pes* as being also the true **AB** reading does not carry conviction. For since (as they recognise) *o* could have easily been misread as *e* if those versions had *plonte* (as **C** does), their preference of *plente* must both presume **C** a late revision introducing the 'plant' idea for the first time and ignore the context of **B**, where *plonte* fits better with the image elaborated in B 152–58. Here however it is better to retain the manuscript reading for **Z**, because it makes adequate sense, while not judging **m**'s *plente* intrinsically harder than **r**'s *plante* for **A**, a version in which the metaphor as yet lacks the development it is to receive in **B**. For *plante* (in contention as the reading of Ax) seems to contain the whole figure *in parvo* and would thus represent an evolving state transitional between

Z and **B**. In II 94, on the other hand, **ZB** *Dignus est operarius hys huyre to haue* can rightly be defended 'as the earlier, if not the superior reading' (*R–B*, p. 19). It is both, but also, more importantly, the near-certain reading of **m** (and thus, like **r**'s *plante* earlier, potentially that of Ax), while the longer form, with its unmetrical second line, looks like **r**'s corruption of a terse macaronic original. Given that R–B make these points in a note to the line (pp. 55–6), their Introduction clouds the issue by allowing that **Z** may here be contaminated from **B** (a point that would otherwise be of interest).

§ 145. The last example is another where Kane's 1988 Retrospect overlooks the confirmatory significance of **Z** in its suspecting parallel A II 87 as a place 'where revision in **B** indicates the corruption of an unmetrical **A** line' (p. 463); for the 'corruption' need only be that found in the family original of **r**.[253] This is something that *Ka²* correctly recognises (p. 461) in a parallel case at A VI 71, where **ZBC**'s a-half is attested against **r** by family **m**. At VII 5 **Z** is again associated with **m** in possessing the a-verse found in parallel **BC** but omitted from **r** (and replaced in sub-group t by a filler-phrase *so me god helpe*). In this third instance, however, *Ka²* retains **r**'s Ø-reading, although on grounds of sense it is **m**'s variant that looks original. For R–B, by contrast (p. 19), '**Z**'s support indicates that the line is genuine and that the loss of the second half must have taken place in the ancestor of the other **A** manuscripts' [i. e. in **r**]. This seems plausible enough; but though authenticity and archetypal character are usually related, they are in principle distinct. So while, by the canon of ratification, the presence of VII 5b in **B** and **C** may imply its genuineness, certainty that the **mZ** reading was in Ax and not borrowed from **B** would require definitively excluding contamination by a later version; and that is impossible. For to prove **Z** uncontaminated it is not *sufficient* that it should have a superior reading where one sub-archetype of Ax errs, as here; it is *necessary* that both sub-archetypes err and the favoured reading be unattested by **B** and **C**. In other words, since to be judged original against its Ax equivalent, a **Z** reading must be unique, demonstration of originality can proceed *only* from direct assessment of its intrinsic character. And this can go little beyond probability, though it may approach moral certainty if the readings in question meet the core-text criteria.

§ 146. An example of a hypothetical lost **A** reading (R–K's 'abstraction') occurs at VII 60 *Shal haue leue, by Oure Lord, to lese here in heruest*, where **Z**'s agreement with **B** is confirmed by the synonym *glene* in revised **C** but Ax's sub-archetypes are severally wrong. The probability of **to lesyn* as the original of **A** is recognised in *Ka²* (p. 447) but not adopted; yet the **m** variant *to leuyn* is barely interpretable as other than a corrupt reflex of Ax, which is likely therefore to have read like **B**. The contribution of **Z** here is only to corroborate, not to prove, a point that R–B may not highlight clearly enough. But the evidence for **Z**'s primary character that their hypothesis requires is at hand in a line such as I 58 *Ant was the louelokest of lyght after Oure Lord syluen*. Here, since M has the metrically necessary word *syluen*, this **Z** reading could descend from **m** and thence from Ax; but **Z**'s unique *lyght*, superior on grounds both of metre and harder sense, cannot. So if Bodley 851 is regarded as just an eccentric **A** witness, *lyght* must descend from **A** independently of the Ax tradition. If it derives from the **B** Version, this can only be *via* a lost **B** copy superior to the Bx tradition, from which the entire line appears to have been mechanically omitted.[254] But if, as it is more economical to suppose, **B** is not the source, **Z** will indeed be the earliest version as claimed by R–B and its unique right reading will therefore have been present in **A** but corrupted in Ax (though to prefer the second alternative obviously requires explaining satisfactorily all other readings that suggest contamination from within the Bx tradition).[255] A similar example is *tyleth* at VI 66, which both gives better metre than the (admittedly acceptable) Ax reading *to* and instances a lexically unfamiliar verb vulnerable to scribal substitution of *is*. No more than at I 58 is *tylith* likely to be a scribal 'improvement', even if its being what **A** read is a little less likely than for *lyght*. This second variant is ignored by *Ka²* which, though adopting the first (p. 462), also ignores its presence in **Z**. While the implications of these readings are understandably (if not excusably) lost on Kane, they also (surprisingly) pass unnoticed by R–B. Yet such examples are the strongest counter-evidence to the objection that **Z** readings superior to Ax must be due to contamination from one or other later version.

§ 147. The latter objection, which the **Z** editors do not answer, they nonetheless deny. But they also countenance an unnecessarily complicated theory of the well-attested agreements between **Z**, the **A** family **m** and **B**: that there may have been *two* authorial redactions of the **A** Version. In the first of these, represented by family **m**, some of **Z**'s readings will have been preserved, but in the second, **r**, eliminated, though afterwards reinstated in **B** (p. 25, n. 73). This explanation is sufficient to account for the presence in **r** (and **B**) of readings and passages not in **m**, since it posits **r** as subsequent to **m**; but it is not *necessary* in order to explain their *absence* from **m** (and **Z**). For no more than in the case of the α and β traditions of **B** or the x^1 and x^2 branches of **C** is the postulate of a two-stage tradition logically indispensable. This is because **r** and **m** (as similarly argued below in relation to the two longer versions) are more economically to be explained as severally defective descendants of a single archetypal text of **A**. Despite this last reservation about R–B's wider view of the early phases of the poem's composition, their work would be valuable were Bodley 851 only an **A** witness comparable to the **B** manuscript F. But if **Z** is accepted as an independent version, it becomes the most important addition to our knowledge of Langland since Price's discovery of the version now called **A**.

Conclusion

§ 148. Our analytical survey of the editorial tradition of *Piers Plowman* is now complete. It has shown that, whether or not printing in parallel is the best format in which to read the poem, parallel *editing* is the most satisfactory way to produce a truly critical text. In order not to pine for what is not, the editor of Langland must look before and after, even when the poet did not do so. For as most of Skeat's successors have recognised, each version contains some securely identifiable errors that can be emended only by recourse to securely identified right readings in the others (including sometimes **Z**). And as will be later argued (IV, *Editing the Text*, § 3), the most secure readings in any one version are those shared by one or more other versions. The usefulness and limitations of both the recensional and the direct methods of treating the versions of a major medieval work attested in multiple copies have been frankly but, it is hoped, fairly scrutinised, and the need for a correspondingly restrained (if not wholly non-interventionist) handling of the unique copy **Z** acknowledged. In the course of this account, support has been given at various points to three main 'conservative' editorial principles and one 'liberal' procedure. But it has been implied throughout that a 'critical' form of empiricism need not be equated with positivism, whether in its simpler or its subtler guises.[256] Instead, to arrest the tendency of editorial rationalism to slide towards a radical intuitionism, three fundamental canons of conformity, acceptability and ratification have been proposed. If the arguments used at IV § 3 below are valid, the 'custodial' force of these in relation to the text should be recognised even by the rationalists' most 'positive' opponents. For the methodological rules arising from these principles (all based on a more general principle of economy) favour textual explanations that make the fewest assumptions; and (save in exceptional circumstances) *their* tendency is to confirm, not to question archetypal readings found in one or more successive versions. At the same time, in acknowledgement of the force of the linear postulate, Kane and Donaldson's appeal to the agreed witness of **AC** for correcting Bx has been found a valuable editorial resort, though one not without some problematic aspects.[257] So against the varyingly rigid non-intervention of Skeat and Knott-Fowler, the Athlone editors' boldness and candour in emending archetypal errors has been welcomed as a valuable (indeed inevitable) part of the editorial process. For an edition of *Piers Plowman* to be 'truly critical', the textual evidence must be weighed, not only measured: as well as looking before and after, an editor needs to open windows on all sides, including occasionally the roof, to let in light from every possible quarter.

§ 149. Of the three editorial canons mentioned, the most important and fundamental is the first, which both expects the final text to conform with metrical and stylistic criteria derived from analysis of the poem's core-text and allows all lines that do so to be adopted in the text as authentic. Though implied to differing degrees in the practice of most editors since Skeat, this principle has not been explicitly formulated by any. Yet it is the most powerful of the three, because it sets a condition for 'originality' that is both sufficient and necessary, and because the empirically established core-lines supporting it are unchallengeable. The core-text criterion (based on attestation of the text by two or more witnesses) stands out as uniquely significant for determining authenticity at every level of transmission, and so for validating emendations. It accordingly forms the foundation of the editorial theory and practice that will be fully explained in Part IV of this *Introduction*. The above pages have shown that previous editors did not succeed in developing a coherent theory of the text; but any pretension to have done so here is bound to appear hazardous. The present editor leaves the matter to the reader and prefers to stress what he owes to a study of the strengths and weaknesses of so many dedicated predecessors, without whose efforts the synthesis attempted here would have been impossible. So whatever its shortcomings, the present enterprise should be seen not as an attempt to abandon the earlier tradition but to fulfil its promises. Reflection on this tradition suggests that an approach that *did* break with it in pursuing radically novel solutions to the problems of Langland's text would be destined to miscarry.[258]

§ 150. The third part of this *Introduction* will set out in detail the evidence for the text of *Piers Plowman*, beginning with the three accepted versions in the traditional order and ending with the most recently identified, **Z**, which is here recognised as the earliest, though as yet not widely acknowledged as authentic. The treatment of **A**, **B** and **C** follows a closely similar pattern; but in order to avoid repetition, the rationale of emendation applicable in each version is described only once (*A Version*, section vii, § 56). The discussion in part III is intended mainly for the specialist; so although the argument forms a whole, a reader less interested in the textual minutiae could omit sections iii and iv on each version and go on to section v, or proceed directly to parts IV and V. These cover the editorial treatment of the text, the wider issues of the poem's date, authorship and audience, the order of the versions, and the poem's reception and influence from the manuscript period to the first printed edition.

THE EDITORIAL TRADITION: NOTES

1 Walter W. Skeat, ed., *Piers the Plowman in Three Parallel Texts* (2 Vols., Oxford 1886).

2 J. A .W. Bennett, ed., *Piers Plowman: the Prologue and Passus I–VII of the B-Text* (Oxford, 1972).

3 George Kane and E. Talbot Donaldson, eds., *Will's Visions of Piers Plowman, Do-Well, Do-Better and Do-Best* (London, 1975; 2nd edn. 1988).

4 The first of these, by George Kane, was of the **A** Version (London, 1960; 2nd edn. 1988); the latest is the **C** version by George Russell and George Kane (London and Berkeley, 1997).

5 A foretaste of what may be expected is provided by Hanna in 'Annotating *PP*,' (1994), to which Fowler provides a response (1997) in the same journal. The enterprise is now being published by the University of Pennsylvania Press under the title of *The Penn Commentary on* Piers Plowman. At the time of writing, volumes 1and 5, edited by Andrew Galloway and Stephen Barney respectively, have appeared.

6 W. W. Skeat, ed., *The Vision of William concerning Piers Plowman. In Four Parts.* Early English Text Society (London, 1869–85) (hereafter *Sk*).

7 *Sk* I, 138.

8 Elsie Blackman, 'Notes on the B-Text MSS of *PP*', 503–4.

9 *The Vision of Piers Plowman: A Complete Edition of the B-Text* (Dent, Everyman: London, 1978; 2nd edn. 1995) (hereafter 'Everyman edition').

10 Kane, *A Version*, 2nd edn. 1988, p. 460.

11 Derek Pearsall in *Speculum* 72:517.

12 The lack has been made good through the industry of Peter Barney (*YLS* 7:97–114 [**A** and **B**], 12:159–73 [**C**]).

13 No. 20 in *Introduction* I, *The Manuscripts*; see further *Sk* II vi–x on this ms.

14 Most of them are also in the Oxford MS Corpus Christi 201 (no. 23 below), which Skeat examined without apparently noticing this fact.

15 See *Sk* II xi–xiii.

16 See B. A. Windeatt, 'The Scribes as Chaucer's Early Critics', *SAC* I:119–41; idem, ed., *Troilus and Criseyde* (London, 1984), Intro., 'The Scribal Medium' pp. 25–35; David Benson and Lynne S. Blanchfield, *The Manuscripts of PP: the B Version*, pp. 9–13; reviewed *Medium Ævum* 68:322–33.

17 Charlotte Brewer and A. G. Rigg, eds., *A Facsimile of the Z-Text* (Cambridge, 1994); and see the review in *Medium Aevum* 64: 314–15.

18 Derek Pearsall and Kathleen Scott, eds., *PP:A Facsimile of Bodleian Library, Oxford, MS Douce 104* (Cambridge, 1992); reviewed *Medium Ævum* 63:128–30.

19 Benson and Blanchfield, pp. 9–11.

20 Hoyt N. Duggan et al., *The PP Electronic Archive*, Mosaic (World Wide Web) 1994.

21 The story is told in detail by Charlotte Brewer, *Editing 'Piers Plowman': The evolution of the text* (Cambridge, 1996), pp. 181–342, a study to which this *Introduction* is much indebted.

22 See note 4 above.

23 Thomas A. Knott and David C. Fowler, *PP: A Critical Edition of the A Version* (Baltimore, 1952). See further §§ 50–4 below.

24 Kane, *A Version*, pp. 53–61.

25 Knott-Fowler, *A Version*, pp 26–7.

26 A contrast between the Athlone and the present editions is that whereas Kane later recognised the need to use **B** and **C** in editing **A** in an *appendix* of altered readings to his second edition of **A**, study of the four versions necessitated a *complete revision* of Everyman **B** as a central part of editing all the versions 'in parallel.' For although working from the outset with an eye on **A** and **C**, the present writer had neither edited them nor had any acquaintance with the **Z** Version.

27 See Russell-Kane, *C Version*, pp. 112 ff.

28 Here too the present volume returns to something like the practice of Skeat.

29 Elizabeth Salter and Derek Pearsall, eds., *Piers Plowman* (London, 1967).

30 G. Economou, *The C Version. A Verse Translation* (Philadelphia, 1996).

31 *Piers Plowman: the Z Version,* edited by A. G. Rigg and C. Brewer (Toronto, 1983). The Z-Text will be considered again below and the case for its authenticity as a separate version fully in *Intro*. III, *Z Version*, §§ 1–12.

32 See *Introduction* III, *B Version*, §§ 46 below.

33 Paul Maas, *Textual Criticism* (Oxford, 1956), p. 1.

34 Considerations of sheer economy might favour such a procedure in a single-volume reader's edition that printed **A, B** and **C** in succession, not in parallel.

35 See Brewer, *Editing 'PP'*, pp. 219–302.

36 Crowley's three impressions are briefly discussed by Skeat, *B-Text* pp. xxxi–xxxvi, Kane-Donaldson pp. 6–7, and more fully by Crawford (1957), King (1976) and Brewer (1996). They are currently being surveyed by Carter Hailey as part of the *PP* Electronic Project (ed. Duggan).

37 Printed in full by Skeat, *B-Text* pp. xxxii–xxxiv.

38 *A Discourse of English Poetrie* (1586), in Smith, ed., *Elizabethan Critical Essays* (Oxford, 1904) I, p. 242.

39 *B-Text*, p. xxxvii, n. **2**.

40 *B-Text*, p. 409.

41 *B-Text*, p. 415.

42 Brewer, *Editing 'PP'*, p. 18.

43 King, 'Crowley's Editions of *PP*', pp. 351–2.

44 Brewer, *Editing 'PP'*, p. 18, citing King, *English Reformation Literature* (Princeton, 1982), pp. 22, 332.

45 *The Canterbury Tales of Chaucer* (1775–8), pp. 74–5, n. 57.

46 Benson & Blanchfield, *The Manuscripts of PP: the B Version*, Preface.

47 No. 45 in Introduction, I, *Manuscripts*, sigil Cot.

48 Intro. I, *Manuscripts*, respectively nos. 30 (P), 35 (M) and 41 (N).

49 These are respectively manuscripts nos. 5 and 47, sigils H and H².

50 Skeat, *Text A*, pp. xiii–xiv; Brewer, *Editing 'PP'*, p. 49.

51 Oriel College, Oxford MS 79; no. 17 in the list of mss, sigil O.

52 Subsequently Phillips 8252, now Huntington 114; *Manuscripts*, no. 53, sigil Ht.

53 *Sk*, III, pp. li–lxiii; Brewer, *Editing 'PP'* pp. 37–45.

54 *Sk* III, pp. lxii–lxiii.

55 See *Introduction*, V, *The Poem in Time*, §§ 13–22 below on the order of the texts.

56 See B Pr 125–31 and C III 206.

57 See III, *B Version*, §§ 13–16.

58 The reading is actually that of only two **A** manuscripts, T and Ch, and is quite unlikely to be archetypal in the **A** Version; see the *Textual Notes* on the line.

59 Described in detail by Brewer, *Editing 'PP'*, pp. 91–178.

60 I, *Manuscripts*, no. 4, Bodleian MS English Poetry a. 1 (V).

61 *Parallel Extracts from 29 MSS of 'Piers Plowman'* (1866).

62 I, *Manuscripts* nos. 9 (A), 42 (H³) and 46 (T).

63 I, *Manuscripts* nos 8 (E) and 10 (M).

64 Called **m** at III, *A Version*, § 24f below.

65 *A-Text*, pp. xvi, xvii. They are Harley 875 (H), Trinity College Cambridge R.3.14 (T) and University College Oxford 45 (U) throughout; Bodleian, Douce 323 and BL Harley 6041 (in part); Bodl. Ashmole 1468 in Passus XI; see I, *Manuscripts* nos. 5, 46, 3, 1 and 47 respectively.

66 These are Oxford, Bodleian Laud Misc. 581, Trinity, Cambridge B.15.17 and Bodl. Rawlinson Poetry 38 for **B**; Huntington 143 and 137, Trinity, Dublin 212, C.U.L. Dd. 3.13 and Bodl. Digby 171 for **C**.

67 This could be so with one **C** copy, Dd. 3. 13, possibly as early as the 1390s.

68 Examples are Pr 14 *triȝely*] *wonderliche* VH; the whole of 34, 50–1, 109 (*om* V).

69 See Sk *A-Text* I 176–77, II 34, 182, III 98, 234, VI 1 (all unmetrical); II 31, 118, 135–43 (rambling expansion); III 19–20, 66, 91–4; VI 2; VII 26.

70 I, *Manuscripts*, no. 3; see *A-Text*, Critical Notes, pp. 154–55.

71 See *Textual Notes* on A XII 98 and *Intro.*, III, *A Version* §§ 67–8.

72 Now Pierpont Morgan MS 18 (J); I, *Manuscripts* no. 6.

73 In a section (Index VII) revising and supplementing the original pamphlet of Parallel Extracts, with J now numbered as XLV (*Sk* IV. ii. 856–59).

74 *A-Text*, p. 145.

75 A possibility rejected in this edition; see *Textual Notes* on C VI 408–13, where the lines are seen as a case of 'farcing' from **B**.

76 *C-Text*, p. xxx.

77 See I 4, 103; VI 70; VII 23; VIII 101, 108, 124*a*; X 157, 159, 179; XI 148, 197, 212, 254, 260, 291, 292; XII 9,

12, 14, 22*a*, 41, 46, 49, 50, 52, 65, 67, 72, 86, 91, 92, 93. Of these VIII 125*a* and X 157, where the archetype is in error, are the only conjectural emendations; both are commonsense corrections.

78 The main exception has been Bennett (see § 1f. above), and Laud has now appeared, with emendations from Kane and Donaldson's edition of B, in the Norton Critical Edition by Robertson and Shepherd (New York, 2006). *K–D* and *Sch* have preferred Trinity Cambridge B.15.17 (I, *Manuscripts*, no. 11) for its good grammar and regular spelling.

79 I, *Manuscripts*, no. 14; now Takamiya 23 (S).

80 *A-Text*, p. xxiii, where it is no. IX; see I, *Manuscripts*, no. 42.

81 See *Introduction* III, *B Version*, §§ 30–2.

82 I, *Manuscripts*, no. 22.

83 I, *Manuscripts*, nos. 15, 16, 17, 18, 19, 43–5.

84 Now superseded by Davis, 'Rationale for a Copy'.

85 Brewer, *Editing 'PP'*, p. 147; see Sk, *B-Text*, p. 213.

86 See Taylor, 'Lost Revision of *PP* B', answered in III, *B Version* §§ 52–4.

87 *B Version*, p. 66; a view questioned by Hanna 'Studies in the MSS of *PP*' and less radically by Adams in 'The R/F MSS of *PP*', who argues however that the scribes of both the α and β traditions incorporated authorial corrections made to the archetypal B-Text. Skeat's account is hardly more tortuous than that of Warner in his essay on 'The *Ur*-B *Piers Plowman*'; but see further Warner's extensively argued 'Ending, and End, of *PP* B', which appeared too late to be taken into account in the above discussion.

88 Brewer, *Editing 'PP'*, p. 143.

89 An opinion supported by Thorne and Uhart, 'Robert Crowley's *PP*', pp. 248–54.

90 *The Vision of William Concerning Piers the Plowman* (Oxford, 1869).

91 Exceptional is T. P. Dunning's *'PP': An Interpretation of the A-Text* (1937; 2nd edn Oxford, 1980).

92 Everyman first edition (1978), p. xi.

93 *The Vision of William...Part III* (1873), pp. cvii ff, p. cxxiv.

94 See H. Barr, *The Piers Plowman Tradition* (London, 1993), pp. 14ff.

95 I, *Manuscripts*, no. 18; see §§ 36, 38 above.

96 *C-Text*, pp. cxiii–xv. See Appendix I § 2.

97 *C-Text* (1959), Note on the 1959 Reprint.

98 I, *Manuscripts*, nos. 26, 25, 27, 29, 44, 45, 43, 46, 47, 49. They are given their current sigils, which occasionally differ from Skeat's.

99 I, *Manuscripts*, nos. 24 and 28.

100 I, *Manuscripts*, nos. 30, 31, 33, 34, 35, 37, 38, 39, 40, 41, 52, 50.

101 Followed (without acknowledgement) by Russell-Kane, *C Version*, Pr 72.

102 See § 9 above.

103 Analysis shows there to have been no perceptible contamination from **B** at the sub-archetypal level (i.e. in the recoverable text of either **x** or **p**).

104 As, e.g., at III 140–41 (where Russell and Kane choose to follow Skeat), 304; V 115; VII 204; and X 217.

105 One exception is his emendation *wyrdes* for *wordes* at XIV 32 (from KS).

106 Brewer, *Editing 'PP'*, p. 165. Skeat's *C-Text* is examined on pp. 159–78.

107 Russell, 'Some Aspects of...Revision', pp. 28–9, judged it a superior text to that found in the received version, and 'not a merely editorial attempt at repair', but abandoned this view (cf. Russell-Kane, *C Version*, p. 87. n. 36).

108 Brewer, ibid., p. 166. See III, *C Version* §§ 20–2 and *Textual Notes* on C IX 71–161.

109 *The Vision of William...*, Part IV, section I: Notes to Texts A, B and C (1877); Section II: Prefaces and Glossary (London, 1884).

110 *The Vision of William...in Three parallel Texts together with Richard the Redeless,* Vol. I: Text; Vol. II: Introduction, Notes and Glossary (Oxford, 1886).

111 'The Text of *PP*', *MLR* 4 (1908), pp. 359–89. Though published under their joint names, its argument is mainly Chambers's (Brewer, *Editing 'PP'*, p. 197, n. 38)

112 Art. cit., p. 384.

113 Brewer observes (*Editing 'PP'*, p. 203), that Chambers was indebted, as he later acknowledged, to the theory and practice of B. F. Westcott and F. J. Hort in their edition of *The New Testament* (2 vols, Cambridge, 1881 and 1882).

114 'An Essay Toward the Critical Text of the A Version of "PP",' *MP* 12 (1915) pp. 129–61.

115 Art. cit., p. 131.

116 I, *Manuscripts*, nos. 51, 48 and 10. N became known in 1915, M in 1922 and Ch only as late as 1943.

117 *A Version*, pp. 5–6.

118 E. T. Donaldson, *PP: the C-Text and its Poet* (New Haven, 1949) or D. W. Robertson Jr and B. F. Huppé, *PP and Scriptural Tradition* (Princeton, 1951).

119 In the York C-Text and the Everyman B-Text (§§ 18–19).

120 *A Version*, pp. 1–5.

121 As well as those listed in the next note the major ones occur at Pr 63, 100; I 47, 135; II 96, 161; III 193, 208, 237; IV 53, 119; V 113, 158, 252; VI 1, 68[1, 2], 92, 98; VII 57, 95, 178, 210, 238; VIII 74; IX 57; X 199; XI 177, 201, 232, 246, 263, 291, 301.

122 They are (*with* **m**): III 13, 122, 260; IV 24; V 55; VI 28; VII 128, 183, 201 (+ U); 210; X 189, 208; XI 5, 121, 211, 243–44, 250, 251, 268, 293; (*alone*): II 83; III 95; IV 19, 47, 141; V 16, 17; VI 6; 67 (+ D); VII 187 (from **B** after V), 238 (+ U); VIII 112 (+ Ch); X 193 (+ H[3]).

123 They nonetheless print its reading at XI 244/45 [= *K–F* 238/9].

124 Reasons for preferring *fayteden* are given in the *Textual Notes*.

125 *PP: the Evidence for Authorship* (London, 1965).

126 *A Version*, 2nd edn (London, 1988), p. 460. The fullest discussion of Kane is in Brewer's *Editing 'PP'*, pp. 343–79 and her two articles 'Textual Principles' and 'Processes of Revision'.

127 Kane and Donaldson, *B Version*, pp. 137–39.

128 See below, III *B Version* §§ 72–5, *C Version* §§ 4–5.

129 On α and β see III, *B Version* §§ 7–10 and on **x** and **p** *C Version* §§ 62–4 below.

130 See III, *A Version*, § 47 below.

131 They are Pr 11; II 91; III 164; IV 12; V 14, 171 [169], 239 [237]; X 187; XI 67. Only Pr 11, X 187 and XI 67 need emending; but see the note also on V 239. At X 187 and XI 67 *Ka*[2] incongruously forgoes *K–D*'s emendations at // B IX 163 [166], X 108 [109], the second a convincing dialectal conjecture accepted here.

132 These are X 187 and XI 67. On the special features of Pr 11 (also in **Z** and **B**) see the *Textual Notes*.

133 See VIII 61, 136, XI 1 and at XI 161, 191, 197 (see the *Textual Notes*). Other **m** readings superior to Kane's are at I 46 and II 154, both supported by **B** (and **Z**).

134 An apt parallel to this example is the conjecture *prescit* at C XI 208 (Schmidt 1980:107), later found to be the reading of Douce 104 and adopted (as by the Athlone editors) as unquestionably original. The case presumably would not support a judgement of ms D as 'useless for editing.'

135 This edition has come in for severe and in part justified criticism from Kane in *Editing Chaucer: the Great Tradition*, ed. Ruggiers (Norman, Okl.), pp. 207–30.

136 Kane and Donaldson's *B Version* does not make this mistake, since the two rejected mss (Huntington 114 and Sion) are both described and taken into account in the section on classification.

137 Kane's quotation is from Greg, *The Calculus of Variants* (Oxford, 1929), p. 20, n. 1.

138 See e.g. III, *A Version* § 12 (on T's agreements with Ch) and § 20 (on J's agreements with M). Both show about the same proportion of major agreements judged coincidental (25–27%); but while this qualifies the certainty of the postulated genetic groups <TH[2]>Ch and <EA(MH[3])>, it is not enough to undermine it.

139 *K–F*, p. 28.

140 See III, *A Version*, § 54 below.

141 For example, those of H[3] with M should be 73 not 60, those of A with E 35 not 30, and those of E with M 90 not 80; see also III, *A Version*, Notes 8 and 9.

142 In this he cites the support of Greg, 'The Rationale of Copy-Text', p. 31.

143 Or, one might add, *three* staves, a number not strictly necessary for scanning Langland's lines but indispensable for editing his text.

144 See MED s.v. *biwilen* v., aptly illustrated from Laʒamon and the *Gawain*-poet; later adopted by Kane and Donaldson at parallel B X 108 as a 'conjecture', though its difference from 'reconstructions' like *liʒt* at A I 110 is not clear (*K–D* p. 205 and n. 154; cf. *Ka*[2] p. 463).

145 Or, if it needs saying, the unique *wenche* at Z VI 88.

146 Among reasons given in the *Textual Notes* is the possibility that *wy* is being used with a rare feminine referent (see OED s.v. *Wye*[1], 3; MED s.v. *wie* n. (a) lacks an example).

147 Introduction to the Athlone *B Version* (p. 205, n. 154).

148 Similar unmetrical lines left without comment are X 68, 154 and XI 191, 197.

149 See *Intro.* IV §§ 39–42 and Schmidt, *The Clerkly Maker* (Cambridge, 1987), p. 33.

150 The major ones occur at Pr 73, 107; I 1, 37, 48, 122, 165; II 51; III 20, 62, 65, 201, 209, 258, 259, 269; V 1, 35, 59, 85, 87, 90, 132, 142, 243; VI 2; VII 29, 83, 128; VIII 102–03, 105, 136–37, 172; X 53, 89, 141, 215; XI 67, 75, 192, 195, 245, 308; XII 4, 12, 47, 74–6. *Ka²* adds I 110; III 21, 234; V 256; VI 71; VII 233, 270; VIII 179; IX 55; XI 266.

151 *Piers Plowman: the B Version* (London, 1975).

152 The discussion of **B** likewise assumes that the Athlone principles need not be rehearsed again and eschews detail, as the Everyman first edition's textual commentary offers something like an extended critique of *K–D*.

153 They are called respectively β and α at III, *B Version* §§ 7–9 below.

154 An example is at XIX 205–07, omitted from F through eyeskip occasioned by homoteleuton (*hem alle* 203... *hem alle* 207), a feature K–D note at Pr 171–2 and XVI 27b, 28b. As with **A**, all line-references are to the present edition; the *K–D* numbering is given in brackets if discrepancies of more than two lines occur.

155 See below at III, *B Version* §§ 51–6 for discussion and references.

156 See the reviews by David Fowler and Eric Stanley.

157 See Jill Mann, 'Reassessment of the Relation between A and B' and Lawler 'Reply', Kane, 'Letter'; also below at *Introduction* V, §§ 16–17.

158 See the *Textual Notes* on C IX 34–5 and *Intro.* V §§ 31–2.

159 See *Intro.* IV *Editing the Text*, §§ 1–14. It is also found in lines peculiar to **A**, e. g. at XI 117, 178 and to **C**, e.g. at III 342, XII 66, XIII 63.

160 See B V 86 and A IV 142.

161 K–D in fact replace not just the word but the whole line with A XI 141, whereas the reconstruction in the present edition is restricted to the b-half. See the *Textual Notes ad loc* and IV, *Editing the Text* §§ 26ff.

162 See the *Indexical Glossary* s.v. *lewed* and *lepi*, and MED s.v. *lethi* adj., (c)

163 See *Intro.* III, *B Version*, § 60 (I 98–9, 100–03; III 223/4; V 338) and § 62 (I 191; III 71, 224; V 591. VI 272; VIII 44, 100).

164 See *The Clerkly Maker*, ch. 2 and *Appendix I* on Language and Metre.

165 See *Ka²*, p. 463, on lines like A V 14, one of the most securely attested in the poem.

166 See *Intro.* III, *B Version*, §§ 62–2.

167 Described as Type IIIa in *Intro.* IV, §§ 39, 41–2.

168 On 'cognative alliteration' see *The Clerkly Maker*, pp. 40–1.

169 Another example of such a change is C VI 218.

170 The other twelve are III 296, 341; V 183 [185], 194 [196], 275 [276], 509 [508]; X 472 [478]; XI 355, 373 [374]; XV 237; XVIII 308 [309]; XX 163.

171 Such examples would be Pr 11, IV 91 (**ZAB**); III 260 (**AB**); and V 171 (**BC**), which all fail to meet the core-text metrical criteria and are conjecturally emended against the successive witness of two or three versions. See IV § 18.

172 For discussion of this emendation (accepted in the present edition) with what is hoped is appropriate diffidence, see *Introduction* IV § 30.

173 Such as *norisse*, conjectured at B VI 223; see *Textual Notes* on C VIII 234.

174 See the *Textual Notes* on C XI 15–16 for lexical details.

175 For detailed examination of this question see below, III, *B Version* §§ 71–4.

176 The emendation is unaccountably not adopted by *R–K* for **C**.

177 For another analysis and solution of the problem see the *Textual Notes ad loc.*

178 See IX 182 [185] / X 289; IX 200 / X 205; X 313 / V 165; XI 14 / 173; XII 101, 162 / XIV 46, 106; XVII 31 [33] / XIX 34.

179 Examples appear at V 441 / VII 54; X 301 [307] / V 154.

180 It can be shown to occur in **B** specifically in the line's b-half, where (presumably unconscious) transposition to prose order is common.

181 *Vision of...PP*, IV, ii, pp. xlviii–li; Knott-Fowler, *A Version*, pp. 15–17. Both, however, accept the existence of occasional lines without alliteration in the b-half.

182 Something not evidenced in Kane's edition of **A** but repeated in Russell-Kane's **C** in relation to the manuscript N² (NLW 733B).

183 See *B Version* §§ 44–6 below and the *Textual Notes* at these points.

184 As will Russell and Kane's similar assumption for N² in their edition of **C**.

185 See e.g. V 330 (*Sk* B 336) and XVIII 159–61.

186 Strictly they should exclude those from 'split variation' where α and β have 'complementary corruptions,' since these are not *of* but *to* Bx, which is unknowable and may not have been corrupt. See § 101 below.

187 R–K (p. 135) subsequently defend it against these objections, which are elaborated and sustained in the *Textual Notes ad loc.*

188 R–K nonetheless retain this unjustified change in their edition of **C**.

189 Most of these are recorded below in III, *B Version* §§ 63, 64. See the *Textual Notes* for discussion of objections to this emendation.

190 A main reservation here is that it is not either of these considerations in isolation but their co-presence in a body of hierarchically-arranged core-text that must provide the required empirical 'control.'

191 These are the empirically-based norms with power to predict that all and only lines of this type are authentic.

192 See the *Textual Notes ad loc* and cf. n. 186 above.

193 For some possible examples cf. VI 138, X 246, XI 438, XVII 38 and XIX 90.

194 See for discussions Patterson, 'Logic of Textual Criticism' in *Negotiating the Past* (Madison, 1987), pp. 77–113 and Brewer, *Editing 'PP'* pp. 380–408.

195 See III, *A Version* §§ 11–13 below.

196 Their arrangement of q is to be preferred; but that of p^2 is contested at III, *C Version* §§ 52 and 56 respectively below.

197 K. Kiernan, *'Beowulf' and the Beowulf Manuscript* (Ann Arbor, 1996).

198 See MED s.v. *finden* 18 (a), *finden out*; ibid. s.v. 22 (a); ibid. s.v. I (a).

199 It is metrically an 'enriched' Type Ib; see IV §§ 41–2 below.

200 See the *Textual Notes ad loc.*

201 This is called 'B^1' at III, *B Version* § 2 below.

202 Bx is here, as it happens, supported by **Z**.

203 See, e.g., XIV 155–312 // C XVI 10–147 and most of B XVII // C XIX 204.

204 It hardly needs saying that as Volume One of this edition appeared two years before the Athlone, its disagreements with their decisions did not evolve in response to these, as did the texts of **B** and to a less extent **A**. However, it may not be immediately obvious to the reader that all *R–K* and *Sch* agreements in discriminated **C** readings are coincidental. For while R–K (pp. 119–21) answer some arguments concerning points in the last two passūs made in the Everyman first edition, they appear unaware that, for example, their conjecture *prescit* at XI 20[8] (p. 151) was proposed in Schmidt 1980 p. 107.

205 Loss of *owene* would be better ascribed to initial haplography than to a desire to shorten the line after misdivision; see *Textual Notes ad loc.*

206 On these stylistic devices see Appendix I §§ 7 and 8, *Clerkly Maker* pp. 52–9.

207 It is given on p. 95 of the edition.

208 Cf. II, § 94 above.

209 See MED s.v. *boie* n. (1), 2 (a); *harlot* n.

210 See MED s.v. *tasten* v. 2 (b) and 3 (a).

211 See MED s.v. *trinen* v. (1).

212 So also XIII 126b (= B XI 313b) but not XVI 92 (// B XIV 252–3), where metre and sense are satisfactory.

213 For a definition of these terms see below at III, *B Version* § 61.

214 Amongst R–K's seven other examples this is likewise true of XIX 28 (for the different conjecture *lich* preferred here, see *Textual Notes ad loc*), XX 22[6], 400 and, with slightly less certainty, of XI 9[2] (*man*).

215 This is Type IIIa, the 'minimal' type; see the evidence in IV, §§ 41–2.

216 This is R–K's 183, which they incorrectly refer to as 180 (p. 103).

217 See III, *C Version* § 27 below.

218 See *Indexical Glossary* and cf. OED s.v. *Witness* sb., 2a and 4a, MED s.v. 2 (a), 4 (a).

219 R–K typically fail to note that Skeat had already made the emendation.

220 As shown in detail below at III, *C Version* §§ 24–5. On x^2 see § 2 above and III, *C Version* § 35.

221 See *Glossary* and MED s.vv. *foul* adj. Id, (b) and (c); *vile* adj. I (c), 2 (c).

222 See e.g. XXI 445, XXII 120 and cf. III, *C Version* § 65 below on x^2.

223 Both editions reconstruct Cx's a-half from the split variants in **x** and **p**.

224 Cf. Chaucer's use of 'Geffrey' in *The House of Fame*, l. 729.

225 See MED s.v. *pilten* v., esp. under 1 (c), citation from *Southern Legendary, Inf. Chr.* 725.

226 See IV § 38 below and *The Clerkly Maker*, p. 63.

227 See the *Textual Notes ad loc.*

228 See Kane, *A Version*, p. 447.

229   An important instance where RM are argued in the *Textual Notes* to preserve such a reading uniquely is XVII 116, a line that R–K reject.

230   The line is an extended Type III with double counterpoint (*abb / ab*).

231   Similar examples at III 15[3] *maide*] *mede*, VIII 216 *fial*] *filial*, IX 2[59] *wriþen*] *wroken* (pp. 150–1); III 381 *londes*] *lordes* (p. 153); XIX 23[6] *hymsulue*] *on hymsulue* (p. 157); *manliche*] *nameliche* VIII 51 (pp. 169–70) are all cases where the present editor could adopt the Athlone reading without too much hesitation.

232   That the scribe of F was intelligent is shown by his substitution of *geste* for Cx *feste* at VII 106, though this may have been prompted by recollection of *storye* in B XIII 447. The criticism of R–K here is not contradicted by the present editor's own rejection of *to* for *tyliþ* at A VI 79, since the latter verb is the reading of **Z**, which is here understood as a version, not a single witness in a sub-family group. See further IV §§ 35–6.

233   *PP: The Z Version* (Toronto, 1983).

234   See *Ka²*, p. 459; *B Version* pp. 14–5 (n. 95); for Kane's review, *Speculum* 60 (1985) pp. 910–30.

235   I 101, V 124 (an important crux) and VII 6 are all conjecturally emended in the present edition. Empty square brackets used at IV 63 are not needed.

236   Omissions include I 91 *myleliche*, 114 *Ant eke, other*; II 49 *montayne heye*. Mistaken inclusions are VI 76, 79, 80 (but for the last lift).

237   See *woman* at I 14 (*women*); *bought vs* at II 6 (*boughtes*); *kyn* I 114; *gyue* II 117; *man that* IV 88 and *the* V 135 (haplographic omissions supplied for the sense). The **BC** emendation *none* at V 155 (*om* **Z**) is less simple than *nas* for *was*.

238   R–B's conservatism is seen in their retention of **Z**'s reading at V 18, whereas *we* is introduced in the present text after **AB**; at 127 *Than* (though the sense is forced), and several where they do not actually adopt the reading they favour: VI 56 *no*; VI 99 *yclecated* for the obviously wrong *yclecaked*; VII 22 *wyghtliche* for *wytliche*; *to dyne a-day* for *today* VII 312; VIII 23 *ant* for *ac*, 91 *a* for *at*. For other restorations in the present edition see I 29, 71, 79–80, 101/2, 113, 129, 131; II 141, 163, 171, 192, 199; III 163; IV 34, 54, 63, 117; V 27, 89, 147; VI 35, 87/8; VII 6, 50, 113; VIII 33.

239   For restorations see Pr 67, 129; for reconstructions, II 165/6; V 25, 155; for conjectures, Pr 12, V 124 (after *R–B*), 152; VI 15; VII 162. On the distinctions between the three types of emendation see III, *A Version* § 55 below.

240   *PP: A Facsimile of the Z-Text*, introduced by Charlotte Brewer and A. G. Rigg.

241   They include Kane's *Speculum* review but do not mention Brewer's important article on 'Z and the A-, B- and C-Texts of *PP*' in *Medium Aevum* 53.

242   Hanna, 'Manuscripts of *PP*', p. 17.

243   See III, *C Version* § 1 below and note 8.

244   Cf. Samuels, 'Langland's Dialect', p. 247, n.77.

245   See III, *Z Version* § 12 below and Schmidt, 'Visions and Revisions,' p. 17.

246   These include the 'T-type' lines at II 118, III 158, VII 38, 245 (*Intro.* IV §§ 40–4; Schmidt, 'Authenticity of Z-Text', pp. 297–8) and 'homolexical' translineation at IV 125/6 (*Intro.* IV § 48 and Appendix I, 8. v).

247   See III, *B Version* § 46, n. 28 below.

248   *Facsimile*, p. 19, n. 37. R. F. Green, 'Lost Exemplar,' adequately answers Kane's argument that the absent **A** lines were on folios lost from **Z**'s exemplar.

249   A XII's authenticity is considered at *Introduction* III, *A Version* §§ 67–71, **Z**'s possible draft status at III, *Z Version* § 6 below.

250   See III, *Z*, § 24 below. They include C Pr 5, 35, III 19 (= B III 18), 32–33 and B Pr 223, II 12, all of which are discussed in the *Textual Notes*.

251   The problem is considered at length in the *Textual Notes* on C VI 308–12.

252   Another is at Z Pr 12, where all three archetypes are emended identically.

253   Kane's note referring to the latter as the reading of the archetype (p. 436) ignores the true significance of M, which may be safely presumed to preserve **m**.

254   R–B's note to I 58 mistakenly records *lyght* as supported by 'some **B** MSS', but the line is absent from all **B** copies.

255   See the discussion at III, *Z Version* §§ 26–7 below.

256   As it is by Patterson, 'Logic', pp. 112–13. The previous argument has made clear that the present writer's idea of 'empirical' support for a textual argument differs from that of Kane and Donaldson, which Patterson shares. A different misunderstanding of the term 'empiricism' is shown by Benson (*Public PP* [Pennsylvania, 2004] p. 8), who seems to think it means 'common sense judgement without need for evidence'.

257   See III, *Z* § 26 below.

258 The possibility of a critical edition is precluded by two seemingly opposed approaches to the problem of L's texts. One is the type of radical scepticism about distinguishing the authorial from the scribal revealed in Brewer, 'Authorial vs Scribal Re-writing' and, in less moderate form, in Machan, 'Late ME Texts'. The other is the type of radical historicising found in Hanna 'MS Bodley 851', Adams 'The R/F MSS of *PP* ' and Warner 'The *Ur*-B *PP* ', which in varying degrees cuts up the textual tradition into a bevy of wriggling worms (Warner develops his arguments at length in a study *The Lost History of* PP: *The Earliest Transmission of Langland's Work* not available at the time of this revision). But perhaps the true positive 'antithesis' to the rational 'thesis' represented by the work of Chambers and Grattan a century ago is to be found in the initial stage of the Electronic *Piers Plowman* project, in which the modern reader denied Langland's text in editorial dress is invited to put on medieval undress to read it. At a later stage, it is promised, a 'critical' ghost will emerge from the technological machine.

III. THE TEXT OF THE A, B, C AND Z VERSIONS

The A Version

i. *The Manuscript Tradition*

§ 1. The A-Text is the earliest version of *Piers Plowman* to survive in multiple copies; but most of the manuscripts date from 1420–50, and its tradition was probably the last of the three to be generated.[1] Interest in the poem is likely to have been aroused by the success of the B- and C-Texts, which were already receiving the tribute of imitation by the late 1390s.[2] A growing desire to read the 'whole' work in any available form may be inferred from the number of 'conjoint' copies extant (one-third of all **A** manuscripts), a sign that the A-Text's incompleteness was recognised by early fifteenth-century compilers aware that longer versions existed. It remains uncertain whether Langland himself 'published' the **A** Version, in the sense of releasing it for copying by professional scribes at the request of potential purchasers. But it seems reasonable to suppose that he showed a copy of the poem (here designated 'A-Ø') in its Pr–XI shape to personal acquaintances who formed his immediate 'circle' of readers. Either this or, most probably, a second copy made from it, was the archetypal text from which the surviving **A** manuscripts derive (**Ax** hereafter). From Ax two further copies, here called **r** and **m**, were produced. Passus XII, by contrast, which is incomplete and probably in draft form, descends from another exemplar. Its restricted attestation suggests that it never passed beyond the poet's 'circle' and may have been copied from his working papers after his death, in a manner similar to that later to be proposed for the Z-Text (see § 74 below, and *Z Version* § 6). For although the three extant Passus XII witnesses (RU; J) preserve in Pr–XI two distinct lines of transmission from Ax, both lines stem from copies belonging to only one family original, **r**, and the other **A** family, **m**, is not represented at all.

§ 2. The lost archetypal manuscript of the **A** Version was, it seems likely, not the poet's holograph. For as reconstructed, it can be shown to have contained about 80 substantive errors, some 35 of which are major ones that affect meaning or metre or both (see §§ 55–9). However, for a poem of some 2447 lines, Ax was not particularly corrupt, as emerges clearly when it is compared with the archetypal text of the **B** Version (**Bx** hereafter). For where **A** and **B** overlap, Bx has about three times as many major errors as Ax. However Ax (like Bx) can be directly or inferentially established in at most about 75% of the poem; for the remainder, the text of **A** is only of variable certainty. Thus in about 7%, it has to be constituted from either **r** or **m**, and where even this is not possible, from a number of readings that cut across both families. For it is a feature of the **A** tradition, one presumably connected with its lateness, that scribal corruption is not only widespread but wayward. And this is true both in the groups comprising each family and in the manuscripts constituting these groups. It is thus often necessary, in order to discriminate amongst competing variants within and across families and groups, to consult the witness of the other versions, and especially **B**. In other words, to be edited 'critically', **A** must be edited in parallel.

ii. *The two families of* **A** *manuscripts*

§ 3. The two independent copies made from Ax, **r** and **m**, both in turn introduced a number of errors; but where they can be satisfactorily compared, **r** preserves the archetypal reading about two-and-a-half times as often as **m**. In the case of major readings specifically, it does so three times as often (see §§ 23 and 45 below). Additionally, since eight complete **r** mss of Pr–XI survive but only one complete copy of an **m** witness, an edition of **A** must inevitably be based on a manuscript of family **r**.[3] The hypothetical family original **m**, though not derived from **r**, was copied later, and after the B-Text had been composed, as is indicated by its greater lexical modernisation and by its occasional inclusion from **B** of Bx readings that seem inauthentic. A few **B** readings also occur in individual **r** mss, whether by collation with an **m** source or by contamination from **B**, but none were present in **r** itself.[4]

§ 4. At least two, but possibly three further copies of **m** seem to have been made (here called *e*, *m*, and *y*). From these descend respectively two pairs and a single further manuscript that attest the readings of this family (EA; MH[3]; W). Two early copies are likewise presumed to have been made of **r**, which are here called r^1 and r^2. Another two were made of r^1 (*u* and *d*) and at least six of r^2 (*v, j, l, k, w, z*), and from one or other of the latter all the extant **r** manuscripts descend. Neither r^1 nor r^2 is derived from the other or influenced by **m**; but a comparison of these two *sub-families* of **r** shows r^1 to have introduced about four times more major errors than r^2. The independent value of r^1 is therefore limited, though it cannot be eliminated from consideration in establishing the text, as it uniquely preserves at least nine major correct readings. Moreover, only in a manuscript belonging to this family throughout Pr–XI, *Rawlinson 137* (R), does Passus XII survive entire. Lastly, the most complete r^2 copy, *Morgan 818* (J), is half a century later in date than the earliest r^1 copy, *Trinity, Cambridge R. 3. 14* (T), and so is linguistically less suitable than T as a basis for the **A** Version. The present text, therefore, is substantively of r^2 type, corrected for the most part from **m** when its witness to Ax errs. But it is presented in the language of its base-manuscript, the r^1 copy T, and for Passus XII in that of R. This is not wholly satisfactory, since R (like J) was copied half a century later than T and its language is correspondingly further from the author's. But if XII descends from a separate archetype (§ 1 above), there is little justification for altering its accidentals to conform with T's. The present edition accordingly resembles those of Knott-Fowler and Kane, which also use T as copy-text, and more particularly Ka^2 in correcting **r**'s family errors from **m**. But it differs from both in occasionally drawing on the other versions, including **Z**, when Ax is in need of emendation.

§ 5. The relationships between the extant **A** manuscripts and their postulated ancestors in Pr–XI may be diagrammatically represented as follows:[5]

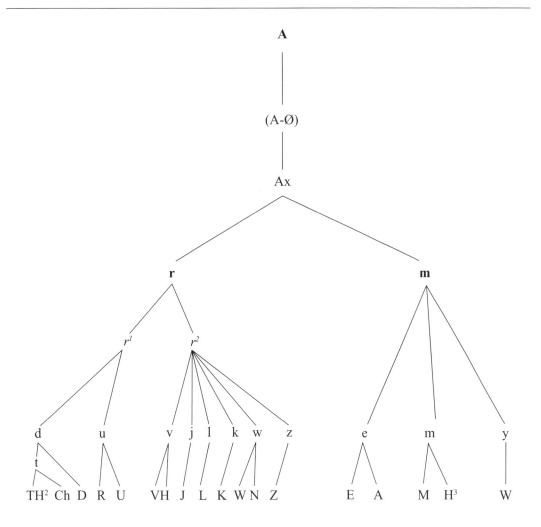

iii. *The **r** family of **A** manuscripts*

(a) *sub-family **r**¹*

§ 6. The two **r** sub-families consist respectively of manuscripts **TH²ChDRU** and **VHJLKWN**. Although preserved in about the same number of copies, *r¹* and *r²* differ greatly in weight of attested readings, since only three members of *r²* (JKW) survive complete. But to counterbalance the disproportion, TH²ChD and RU each have an exclusive common ancestor (here called respectively 'd' and 'u'). This means that from *r¹* there are only two independent lines of transmission. By contrast, *r²* with two pairs VH (< v) and WN (< w), plus the unrelated J, L, K (and Z), yields six lines of descent. However, not only do H and L give out before the end of Passus VIII (while Z is the mere 73 lines of VIII 93–185), *r²*'s individual members exhibit the capriciousness characteristic of all extant **A** copies. Thus their combined attestation of the sub-family ancestor's readings remains uncertain as well as imperfect.

§ 7. The distinctive variants of the *sub-family* r^1 are constituted firstly by the 41 major agreements in error of both its component groups. In the following list of these, a minus sign before a sigil denotes a manuscript that diverges from r^1 in containing the reading judged correct (for reasons of space, only line-references are given).

I 153 -U. II 83, 163 -D. III 243 -R. 253 -U. 268 -D. 269. IV 4, 19 -D, 71 -H^2, 113, 127, 54. V 16, 17, 34, 91–2, 109, 114, 178, 244. VI 39 -H^2. VII 18, 20 -Ch, 25, 183, 227 -U. VIII 2 -U, 13 -R, 101 -U, 119. IX 6, 14, 17, 36. X 48, 86, 168 -U. XI 47, 250, 251.

Secondly, in another 17 instances, r^1 has a major error which is shared by one member of r^2 or of **m**:

V: XI 121. *K*: IV 29. V 159. X 103. XI 239. *L*: V 244. VII 306. *E*: V 161, VII 211. *A*: X 154, XI 268. *M:* III 132. V 131. X 104, 161. *H^3*: XI 211. *W*: X 34.

The sub-family is characterised, thirdly, by at least 24 minor errors where all members present agree:

III 139. IV 42, 48, 89. V 110, 143, 219. VI 94. VII 31, 185, 212*a*/213, 217/218. IX 44, 76. X 40, 198. XI 4, 78, 134, 159, 194/196, 236, 243/244, 244.

Half a dozen unique major right readings are, however, severally preserved in u, d and t (TH^{2}Ch). These may derive from r^1 rather than another **r** source (see §§ 8, 9, 13 below). In addition, r^1 certainly contained six such readings:

Major: XI 19 construe] conterfeteþ. 67 wy] man r^2**m**. 245 suche] seyth / syke J / K; *om* **m**. **Minor**: VII 282 poret] *pl.* r^2**m**. VIII 33 oure] þe / Ø r^2**m**. XI 241 cristene] cr. men / þei r^2 **m**.

It therefore cannot be eliminated.

§ 8. The *two groups* into which r^1 divides consist of four and two manuscripts respectively, **d** (TH^{2}ChD) and **u** (RU). Neither member of u can derive from the other, U because it is a generation earlier in date and R because it lacks U's distinctive major errors, such as the extra lines after V 200. The group **u** is a genetic pair defined by 219 agreements, about half of them major.[6] Most are not recorded in the apparatus, but the following 30 appear where the variants are diverse enough to merit complete listing:

Pr 102. I 1. II 42, 58, 168. III 13, 171, 234, 262, 268. IV 24, 47, 60. V 93, 102, 113, 114, 179, 216. VI 67, 92, 123. VIII 21. X 40, 199. XI 134, 156, 209, 281, 291.

Group u cannot be eliminated, as it contains three major variants (I 103, III 29–30, IX 57) that appear in the light of parallel (**Z**)**BC** to preserve original readings by direct descent (< r^1 < **r** < Ax). Additionally, in Passus XII its two members jointly attest lines 1–19, and from 89–end R is the unique witness to the text. R is a relatively late copy, but its completeness qualifies it to serve as the *citation-source* for correcting individual errors of the copy-text T (as later will L for the B-Text; see *B Version* § 39, and IV § 56 below).

§ 9. The other r^1 group, **d**, consists of two *sub-groups*, **D** and <**TH^{2}Ch**>. The second of these (here called **t**) is further differentiated into *TH^2* and *Ch*. Neither D nor t derives from the other, because t's oldest member T is three generations earlier than D, while D lacks t's roughly 50 distinctive errors. But on the basis of their 94 agreements, 54 major and 40 minor (all recorded in the Apparatus), D and t may be regarded as a single genetic group. In the list of these, bracketed references indicate minor divergences from one recognisable substantive error:

Major I 171. II 51, 123. III 83, 102, 118, 171, 241, 257. IV 24, 114, 126, 148. V 16, 56, 93, 113, [119], 238, 253. VI 85, 92, 109, 125. VII 75, 95, 116, 164, 175, 178, 196, 222, 282, 304. VIII 26, 30, [70], 117, 141, 153, 154, 171, 172. IX 17, 30. X 64. XI 44, 124, 145, 192, 232, 235, 263, 298. **Minor** II 82, 86, 166. III 165, 206. IV 47, 58, 106, 135, 143, 145. V 114/115, 157, 193, 253. VI 69. VII 144, 172, 189, 277, 306. VIII 36, 46, 126, 164, 176. IX 15, 75, 84. X 84, 88, 181, 202. XI 3, 46, 129, 134/135, 195, 227, 280.

In two further major and five minor instances, one member of the group, Ch, has the right reading. In two minor ones another, H^2, is right where d appears to err:

Major *Ch*: III 208. XI 60. **Minor** II 95. IV 60, 95. X 201. XI 67. H^2: VIII 157. IX 54.

In the major cases particularly Ch may show correction from another source, probably of **r** type. Finally, in five major cases d shares an error with another **r** manuscript (of r^2 type) and in one with the **m** copy E:

V 161 and X 53 +V. II 94 +L. XI 186 +K. VIII 44 +W. VII 71 +E.

But seven instances (five accompanied by a single and one by two other copies), where t does not err, may represent d readings corrupted in manuscript D. Group d further attests four unique right readings and three more with the support of one other manuscript:

Major: III 27. X 30. **Minor**: VII 296 +N. XI 5 +J, 122, 195, 277 +J.

It therefore cannot be eliminated.

§ 10. The group's *singleton*, **D**, has individual major errors at I 159, III 268, IV 23, V 119, VI 29, VIII 134, 159, 170, IX 85, X 17, 208, 212, XI 80 and 246. But it also lacks a number of minor r^1 errors, perhaps as a result of correction from an r^2 source (though coincidental variation might account for them). They are Pr 75, II 88, VI 64, IX 56, 98, 111, X 172 and XI 264. However, as D contains *no* unique right readings, it could in principle be eliminated.

§ 11. The other *sub-group*, **t**, is attested by all its members **TH^{2}Ch** in some 48 major and as many minor agreements that indicate an exclusive common ancestor:

Major I 110, 159. III 72, 95, 268. IV 23, 61, 119. V 17, 119, 198, 234, 252. VI 29, 53, 68, 107. VII 5, 30, 210. VIII 32 (1,2), 45, 129, 134, 159, 160 (1,2), 170. IX 85. X 4, 12, 17, 47, 78, 176, 208, 210, 212. XI 2, 55, 56, 80, 183, 211, 246, 260, 301. **Minor** I 59, 78, 101, 135. II 59, 131, 142. III 79, 109, 139, 251, 259. IV 61, 73, 112, 129. V 25, 57, 60, 81, 93, 98, 132, 179. VI 22, 37, 48, 52. VII 32, 196. VIII 7, 8, 61, 73, 100, 122. IX 7, 74, 109, 113. X 178, 180. XI 19, 71, 77, 81, 82, 110.

About another 50, 19 of them major, show agreement of T and H^2 where Ch has a different error or is right, presumably by faithful retention of d, as in these 15 cases:

Major III 92, 258. V 7, 29. VI 6. IX 39, 70, 79. X 191 (? *by intelligent guess*). XI 293. **Minor** VIII 21. X 39, 190. XI 229, 266.

§ 12. The consequently implied relationship <TH^2>Ch is, however, challenged by some 25 readings, six of them major, where TCh agree but H^2 has a different error or, as in the following six major cases, is correct:

Pr 86 poundes] poynteþ. I 4 clyf] kiþ. II 96 a maiden of goode] of maides engendrit. III 193 *L. om*. IV 71–2 *Ll. om*. V 10 *L. om*.

Except for V 10 (where the ease of loss by homoteleuton is shown by agreement of the unrelated r^2 copies HN), these TCh errors seem too striking to be coincidental. It therefore seems likely that what H^2 shows is correction of the t readings of its exemplar rather than retention of d readings preserved in t but lost by TCh (as proposed for Ch at § 11 above). But this can only have come from an r^2 or **m** copy since, of the other r^1 witnesses, both D and u omit IV 72a and the whole of line IV 71.[7] With allowance, then, for a phase of correction, H^2 may be accepted as forming a genetic pair with T. The latter manuscript has no readings by correction, a feature it shares with the key **m** witness M.

§ 13. The sub-group t also agrees in a dozen almost certainly random errors with seven manuscripts from both families, and in one major instance with the other family disjunctively:

Major I 82 +J. VII 280 + **m**. X 193 +H^3 (*synonym-substitution*). VIII 75 +K (*censorship*). **Minor** VII 236. VIII 89 +R. III 271 +H. IX 19, 63 +J. IV 88 +W. V 46 +E. IX 13 +A.

But it also provides seven right readings, one unique, five shared with one other manuscript, and one shared with two other manuscripts from both families.

Major V 36 +M. VII 210 +VE. **Minor** I 25 (*partly*) +U. III 242 +A. IV 77 +L. X 100, 205 +V.

All of these right readings in t, like those in u considered at § 9 above, may be presumed to be present by direct descent ($< d < r^1 < \mathbf{r} < Ax$). This sub-group, therefore, could not be eliminated even if a manuscript other than T were chosen as copy-text.

§ 14. In conclusion, the sub-family r^1 remains essential for editing the **A** Version because some fifteen of its actual or probable variants, nine of them major, uniquely preserve from **r** an Ax reading lost by r^2 and **m.**

(b) *The sub-family r^2*

§ 15. This branch consists of **VHJLKWN**, which attest **r**-type readings distinguishing it from **m**, while it lacks the 65 clear agreements in error that establish r^1 (see § 7). The manuscripts divide into the genetic pairs **VH** and **WN**, and the individual copies **J**, **L** and **K**. Because three of its members H, L, N are incomplete and its representatives dwindle to only three in Passus X–XI (where W becomes an **m** witness), r^2 is much more sparsely attested than r^1, so the case for an exclusive common ancestor is largely inferential. The sigil r^2 is therefore used here mainly for convenience in differentiating the seven manuscripts' readings from those of r^1 on the one hand and **m** on the other (despite frequent agreement with **m** where r^1 errs). As the account of the individual r^2 copies below will indicate, none derives from any other. And though at least two genetic pairs appear, neither depends upon or is the source of any other member of r^2. In the list that follows, a minus before a sigil indicates that the r^2 member does not share the postulated sub-family variant, whether it has the right or a different wrong reading.

Major V 71 ouhte] miȝte -J [*right with r^1*] and -W [*wrong with* **m**]. VII 12 elles] ony -W [*right with* **m**]. VII 178 *Line-division and expansion* -LKW. X 214 schrewe] same. XI 19 conterfeteþ] can construe -K. 134 conterfetyd] contreuide -K [*right with* d**m**]. *Accompanied by one other MS:* VII 128 crowen] cowes -W, +M. 282 -W, +M. wolden] þouȝte +A. **Minor** XI 217 þo] þese. *With one or two other MSS:* VII 160 + MH^3 *Word-order.* IX 18 as me] me -J+M.

§ 16. The first of the r^2 pairs is **v**, made up of V and H, with V its sole representative after VIII 143. These have some 245 agreements in error,[8] the most important being the missing lines Pr 50–1, 99–100, 109, II 28–9 and IV 119. About a fifth of the other major errors are recorded where the lemma has a set of complex variants:

I 4, 39, 93, 135, 137, 139; II 9, 51, 87; III 14, 146, 193, 197, 208; IV 19, 24, 53, 61; V 129, 160; VI 6;VII 95, 183.

V cannot derive from H because it is half a century earlier, nor H from V because it lacks such errors as V's missing lines at Pr 34, I 149b–150a, 176–83, II 106–21, 129. The group v (or V alone, inferentially representing it) contains four unique right readings and another three accompanied by one r^2 copy. In the list of these, other-version support is indicated.

Major +**BC** V 159 warinar] weuer/ waffrer/ bereward. (V *only,* +**C**) V 200 þrompelde] stumblide. (V *only,* +**BC**) VII 187 hurde] erþe / ȝerd / hous / lond. **Minor** +**BC** Ac] And / *om.*

Group v therefore cannot be eliminated.

§ 17. The second r^2 pair, **w**, consists of the conjoint **A/C** copies W and N (*Manuscripts*, nos. 12 and 13), which are both present from I 76 to the end of VIII. After this w's sole representative in the **A** portion is W, but only as far as Passus IX; for at this point W ceases to be an r^2 witness and becomes a member of **m** in X–XI, apparently following a change of exemplar. The group is defined by 140 agreements in error,[9] about 35 major, the most important being:

(a) 4 *omitted lines*: I 131. III 206 +U, 208, 257. (b) 33–5 *added lines from* **C** *between* I *and* III: *after* I 129, 132, 152, 161; II 20, 45 (5 *added in* W, 7 *in* N), 56, 65 (12 *lines*), 131 (4 *lines in its place*), 194 (6 *lines*); III 33 (2 *lines*), 141 (*Latin*).

N adds a further 110 lines and two Latin lines taken from **C**, W another 59 and one of Latin from **B**, mainly in IV. After K (see § 21 below), these manuscripts are the most heavily conflated from the C-Text. Of the pair, **W** had the more complex history. Thus it lacks two key indicative errors of r^2 at VII 12 and at VII 128, where it agrees with r^1EH^3 but has those at VII 160, 282 and at IX 18, where r^2 is accompanied by one **m** copy. Though generally grouping with **m** in X–XI, W could conceivably reflect collation with an **r** copy at XI 19; but this explanation is rejected at § 28 below. The five *earlier* major agreements with **m**, however, more plausibly suggest sporadic consultation of an **m** manuscript after W's initial copying from w. W reveals extensive recourse to **C**, the version it continues with, and also to **B**.

§ 18. Each member of group w uniquely preserves major right readings, W having four and N two:

W: I 48 +**ZB** ylik] lik. III 21 +**ZBC** coppis] pecis / other gyfteȝ. VI 2 +**ZC** baches. 52 he (*basis of emended* *hy). XI 308 + K; (*cf.* **BC**) kete] grete. *N*: V 189 +J vm] sum. 142 so þike] soþly / so mote I the / (*basis of the emendation*).

All but one of these apparent corrections to Ax errors seem likely to result from collation with copies of **B** and **C**. The exception is XI 308 (where K alone might have preserved r^2) and W, which is of **m** character in these passūs, could have consulted such a copy. At any rate, both *baches* (which is in **C**) and *kete* (which is not) seem too difficult to be scribal substitutions for the easier readings in their presumed exemplar. Group w therefore cannot be eliminated.

§ 19. The three remaining manuscripts, **J**, **L** and **K**, derive from r^2 through at most one intermediate source not shared substantially with any other. Of these **J** has, however, some 40 agreements in error with the r^1 copy U. The four major ones are:

I 122 troniþ hem] tryeste of. III 213 go] metyn. VIII 130 metelis] mater m. (matere U). VIII 132 Peris loue þe Plouȝman ful pensif] P. lyf pl. petusly.

Thc last is a noteworthy complex variant that differs in four particulars from the Ax reading and cannot be coincidental. It may be due to the U scribe's consulting the r^2 copy that was J's postulated intermediate source (**j**). U's five other major agreements with r^2, at I 153, VII 201, VIII 2, 101 and the Latin at XI 296, are compatible with this explanation. A sixth major agreement of U and r^2 at V 196, where J (like K and r^1) has lost 196b, could be accounted for as a mechanical error rather than as a faithful reflex of j. J groups, secondly, with the **m** copy A in three major readings:

III 19 merciede] myrthed. V 143 chaffare] crafte. XI 56 kete] cowrte.

These striking agreements are hard to explain as coincidental, for though each is a substitution for a more difficult word, none is the obvious one (as *thankede* for *merciede* might have been). If they are readings of source j, it is possible that A consulted J or that A's source consulted j; for on grounds of date J cannot have got them from A, which is at least a generation younger. Finally, J has 26 agreements with another **m** copy, M. Though seven are major, all are of such a kind as possibly to be coincidental substitutions:

III 141 barnes] childeryn. V 96 wiȝt] man [*more modern synonyms*]. IV 13 þe frek] consciens. VII 9 shedyng] spyllyng [*contextually more familiar term*]. VII 245 ete] ȝit [*visual mis-resolution of* *y-ete *prompted by misunderstanding of context*; AH[3] ȝet *suggests that this was in fact the reading of* **m**]. XI 170 þe gode wyf] stody [*more explicit referent*]. XI 282 hadde he saluacioun] was [he] sauyd [*simpler expression*].

In conclusion, J's only significant relations with another manuscript are with U and possibly with the source of A, but these appear not to be genetic. Although it is the most complete representative of r^2, J is never the sole witness of a right reading in Pr–XI. But as one of the two surviving sources of lines 20–88 in XII, where it alone preserves the right reading in 22 out of 44 contested instances, J ranks with R and M among the three most important **A** copies to survive.

§ 20. The manuscript **L** is present in only four of the lines containing indicative sub-family readings (VII 12, 128, 160, 282), but it has all of these. It also shares some 16 errors with one member of the v group, H, two of which appear major, and two major ones with the **m** copy E:

H: I 1 merke] deope. III 164 gret] most [*adopted by* K–D *for //* III 177 *in* **B** *but not by* Ka[2] *for* **A**]. *E*: I 25 driȝeþ] thyrstes. VI 8 ampollis] saumples.

All of these, however, may be explained as easy coincidental errors. The first with H is both conventionally motivated and an unconscious echo of the actual phrase instanced in Pr 15. The second, an obvious use of a close synonym to 'regularise' alliteration, yields its claim to be the original in face of **ZBC** agreement with Ax. The first agreement with E is in a more explicit expression and the second is probably a visual error part-induced by the *s*-alliteration of the fourth lift with that of the next line. In the absence of any real evidence of relation with another **A** copy, L may therefore be taken as descending from r^2 through at most one intermediate source (*l*), postulated to account for some of its individual errors. Such a conclusion is not contradicted by L's two unique right readings (supported by **ZBC**), at VII 189 and 253. These are minor but rule out its elimination.

§ 21. The manuscript **K** is potentially important as one of three in the sub-family that is complete in Pr–XI. But its value is reduced by its extensive conflation with **C** (and in one instance **B**), exceeding that of WN (see § 17) and extending to over 400 lines:

C *lines introduced after* Pr 4, 12 (4 *ll.*), 14, 102 (140 *ll.*); I 31; III 45 (5 *ll.*); V 42, 219 (C VI 422–VII 61 *with omissions*), 252 (C VII 69–153 *with omissions*); VI 109 (2 *ll.*), 126 (C VII 291–305 *with additions*); *for* VI 20–95 *the passage* C VII 176–259; *after* V 39 *four lines* B V 50–1, 48–9).

All but one of these form no part of **A**. But after V 42, where Ax may have smoothed an original *hem* to *ʒow*, the reading from C V 200 (paralleled in **Z** and **B** in different forms) fills a sense-gap, and there may be a case for adopting it.[10] Also in Pr–IX **K** agrees with the w member W[11] in some 45 readings, 17 of them major:

Pr 44 knaues] hewyn (hyne W). V 126 Brochide] Prycked; 129 made] worched (wroght W) [*synonym-substitutes*]. VII 168 defendite] fett [*a misunderstanding, paralleled in* **Z**; *see* Textual Note]. II 80 bokes] chekes; VIII 55 bigge] sell; 155 lettres] seles W [(*canc. for* letturs K) *attempts to strengthen the sense*]. IX 27 stande] stomble [*the same, with possible contamination from* C X 35]. Pr 63 hy] charite; V 146 shrifte] chirche [*more explicit readings prompted by* Pr 61 *and* V 147 *respectively*]. VII 114 cunne] done; 196 ʒif þou wistest] of the [*substitutions of easier and smoother readings (as in* **B**, *here possibly an archetypal error)*]. IX 26 watir] wawes [*conventional association or attempt to avoid repeating* 25]. Pr 34 synneles] gylefully K; gylously W [*rejection of favourable original epithet and attempt to normalise allitera-tive pattern*]. VII 224 L. om. [*perhaps by eyeskip from* nam 223 > nam 225]. X 159 sed] seth [*visual error induced by preceding* seth].

All these agreements, however, reveal types of motivation that weaken the likelihood of a genetic link between K and W. That they derive from collation of K's medieval ancestor with W or a lost copy of w is therefore not very probable, as K has no disjunctive agreements with w or even with N. It is therefore better placed as separately descended from r^2, with one intermediary stage, its source, at which contamination might have occurred. But K uniquely preserves three major read-ings that seem original and shares a fourth such with W:

II 144 +**B**(**ZC**) fobbars] *five variants*. VI 1 +**B**(**C**)**Z** wight none] nane / fewe men. XI 80 +**B** whyys] *four variants*. XI 308 +W kete] grete Ax.

It therefore cannot be eliminated.

§ 22. From the above it emerges that 15 major readings judged authentic are severally pre-served in six extant copies or in postulated group-ancestors of the manuscripts comprising r^2. The only individual copy that could in principle be eliminated is H, which has no unique right read-ings. The group r^2 exclusively attests 34 right readings (14 of them major), totalling over three times as many as r^1 (cf. § 14 above). In the following list of these, dissident members are denoted by a minus sign.

Major X -KW 159 sed] *om.* XI -J 56 kete] grete. +**ZBC**: I 127 kennyn me bettur] me bet k. / better to lere. II -vW 83 mendis] frendis. III -v 135 sixe] seue. VII 174 potful] potel. +**Z**(**B**)**C**: -vJw 17 segges] seyþ god / I say. +**BC**: IV -Vw 47 for hym vneth] vnn. on hym for / for hym to wynke ne. V -v 16 puffyd] put / passchet. VIII 142 diuinede] demide. +**B**: IV -H 154 leete] loue. X 202 vn-] no / my. XI -VJ 80 whyys] weyes / werkes / priuytes. +**C**: III B†; -vK 209 kenne clerkes] ben cl. / techyn chyldryn. IV -Vw 47 for hym vneth] vnn. on hym for / for hym to wynke ne.
Minor +**C** V 109–10 (*l. div.*). +**ZB** V 143. +**BC**-WK VI 95. +**ZBC** VI 101. +**BC** -L VI 115, 120. +**ZC** (*cf.* **B**) VII 171. +**ZBC**-LK VIII 38 (1). +**BC** VIII 168. +**BC** IX 56, 67, 74. +**B** IX 96. -K X 123–25 (*l. div.*). +**BC** X 172. +**B** X 188 (1,2). +**BC** IX 193. XI 4; +**B** XI 9; 75–6, 163 (*l. div.*).

If the 15 readings of its individual members are taken as also preserving r^2, this sub-family will stand as the sole source of about 50 right readings, some 30 of them major. As most have other-version support, they may be inferred to preserve readings lost from Ax directly by **m** and indi-rectly by r^1 from **r**. Thus r^2 cannot be eliminated.

(c) The **r** *family: conclusions*

§ 23. The evidence for **r** as the exclusive common ancestor of the two sub-families is the 108 agreements in error (some 50 major) of r^1 and r^2. That these *are* errors may be established by comparing them both with the variants of the **m** family of **A** and with the parallel text of **Z**, **B** and **C** where present. The following list therefore divides readings not only into *major* and *minor* but also according to the *other-version support* for those adopted. The lemmata from the edited text are the readings of **m** unless otherwise specified; the variants are those of **r**, given in full for major instances, by reference only for minor ones. A plus sign accompanies **m** or **r** manuscripts having the rejected **r** or the adopted **m** reading in question.

Readings with other-version support

Major

+**Z**: I 110 seluyn] *om* +E. II 94 feytles] feythles / feyntles / faylere &c. VII 128 +KN Cacche] Chase +E. cowes] A; crowen *r²*m; gees *r¹*EH³. 270 plante colis] *trs.* VIII 54 þe Sautir witnessiþ] seiþ þe s. 61 leiȝe I ouȝt trowe ȝe] ȝe wyten ȝif I leiȝe. +**ZB**: I 106 mene] *om.* 112 felawshipe] felawis. II 87 *as two ll.* +E. VII 15 comaundiþ] wille. VII 60 (*emendation*). +**ZC**: V 249 coupe] gilt +MH³. +**ZBC**: II 124 bad hem] *om.* 146 þise men] þe men. 154 cacche miȝte] *trs.* III 146 hym þe gate] hem ofte / hem euere / þe treuþe / so faste. V 243 *reddere*] red non. 256 +K go to] seke. VI 9 Sise] Synay. 13 first] H³ (*om* E; fast AMW); faire **r**. 71 In no manere ellis] Loke þat þou leiȝe. 82–4 *Ll. om.* VII 5 and sowen it aftir] *om.* 60 leue] *om.* 86 masse] mynde +E. 230 +Ch hym bereuen] be hym bereuid (H³). 233 Contemplatiſ; actiſ] *trs.* [*Comparable with* **ZBC**: VII 59 hewe wiþ þe hatchet] any þing swynke. 294 +W or ybake] or rostid **m**; *om* **r**. + **B**: 87 +W L. om. VIII 54a] *om* +**Z**. 100 þe deuil shal haue þi soule] to helle shalt þou wende. 101 +W atweyne] assondir. 111 +wZ *Line-div.*; be folis] anoþer. X 32 shafte] shap. + **BC**: V 116 wayte] loke. 126 bat] pakke. 163; 167 +vN *Ll. om.* VII 61 þermyd maugree] wiþ þe corn. 68 hoten] holden. VIII 136 book bible] b. of þe b. M; bible **r**+AH³. X 22 +Ch fyue] sixe **r**+A.

Minor

+**ZBC**: I 49, 161. II 75, +W 177. III 5, 67, 129. IV 21, 106. V +W 40. VI 57 +wL, 86, +v 91–2, 103. VII 145] **r**+EAH³, +UV 158, 275. VIII 27] **r**+AH³, 84. +**ZB**: I 46, 69. IV 31, 33. VI 33 +N] **r** +EM; +w 73. VII 19. +**ZC**: II 1. +**Z**: II 137. VII 12, 16. +**B**: II 86 +HWH²] *om* (+**Z**). III 230. V +KW 80, +KW 90. VI 47. VIII 109, 111, 112. X 200. XI +J 162, 171, +J 205, 264. +**BC**: I 149. VI +LN 110, +VW 112, +VK 116. VII 73, 97 +E, 106 +EZ. VIII +v 87, 127, +v 132, +H²1 36–7, 175, +KZ 185. XI +K 5] **r**+AW; +R 305.

Readings with no other-version parallel

Major

V 79 (+J; *cf.* **B**) men] hym. VIII 105 (*cf.* **B**) belyue] liflode +A. XI 154 shewide] seide. 182 (+Ch; *cf.* **B**) he] she. 194–6 *Line-div.* 194 Dredles] God wot; wot þe soþe] *om;* 195 ben in office] benefices. 245 shewiþ..aftir] *om.*

iv. *The* **m** *family of* **A** *manuscripts*

§ 24. The second family, **m**, consists of five manuscripts. But of these only four at most appear at any one time together, **EAMH³** and **AMH³W**, because E ceases at VII 213 and W (following a presumed change of exemplar) does not decisively become an **m** copy until Passus X. They constitute a *family* because their postulated source, like **r**, descends independently from the archetype. This judgement is based first on **m**'s possession, with other-version support, of about 100 right readings (some 35 of them major) where **r** is in error. Even more important, in that it cannot be due to contamination from **B** or **C**, is **m**'s unique preservation of eight major readings with *no* other-version parallel which, if accepted as authentic on intrinsic grounds, can only be part of the original A-Text (see § 23, end). As collateral (or negatively 'criterial') readings, they will be mentioned again when the two families are compared at § 47 below. But it must first be shown that the two overlapping sets of four manuscripts form a genetic group deriving from a single exclusive ancestor, **m**.

§ 25. Of the five members of **m** only M is both complete and free of contamination from the other family (like T of *r¹* at § 12 above). While a solid link between the two sets of four is provided by **AMH³** as their common core, difficulty arises even here on account of incomplete attestation and contamination in all three. Thus *A* has large omissions in Pr–II and briefly in VII and VIII. *H³*, more significantly, becomes an **A** copy only after V 104, before which it is the **B** manuscript H. *E* has had about a fifth of its **m** readings altered by reference to an **r** copy of identifiable type. Conversely, *W* has adopted a few sporadic **m** readings earlier in the text than Passus X. Finally, both *A* and *H³* show what look like corrections from an **r** copy rather than retentions of presumed **m** readings lost by the other members. In the account that follows, therefore, the certainty of the **m** readings lessens to mere possibility where the number of witnesses falls below three, breaking the unanimity of the 'core-group' AMH³.

(a) *The manuscript-group* **EAMH³**

§ 26. This group exhibits 44 isolative agreements (32 major) between V 109–VI 103 and VII 115–186. In the following list of them, the lemma is the reading of **r** unless noted otherwise. A minus sign before a sigil denotes an **m** manuscript with the correct reading; a plus sign, an **r** copy sharing the rejected reading of **m**.

Major V 109 *as 2 ll.* eiȝen] eyn as a blynde hagge (*so* Bx). 110 lollide] lokyd (likerd wer E). *Hereafter* B V 191–92 *added* MH³, 192 *added* E, *subst. for* 111 A. 115 Symme...Noke] synne it þouth me mery. 117 Ferst] -E; *l. om* A. 132 dede] *om*; -E, *corrupt* H³. 142 so þe Ik] so mote I the. 146 for to go to shrifte] to go on his wey. 147 hym to *kirkeward*] to chirche. 153 he] herry -E. 172 hitte] caste +ChH-E. 179 acorden] a. welle *trs* M; -H³; *l. om* A. 190 *After this* B V 341 *added.* 229 And...I²] Qwat euer I namm; And euerche man M; *l. om* A; -E. VI 20 callen] clepyn -E. 31 sewide] folwde +H. 37 oþerwhile] sumtyme -E. 44 swere] s. fast +L. 65 half] hand -M. 81 þing] *om*. VII 35 conseyuede] rehersede -E; *def.* A. 40 presauntis and] *om*. 139 to wraþen hym] *om*; -E. 142 pilide] pyned -E. 157 houpide] wyschid / clepid / wepyd AMH³;-E. 171 Faitours...fer] For ferd þese f. 176 ditte] holdyn +W; driuen EChu. 187 erde] lond; ȝerd EJu. 193 blody] *om*; bodely E. 222 mouþiþ] mevith. 235 here] *om*; +H. 280 ete] hente +t.

Minor V 117 -E; *l. om* A. 143 -E. 228 +H. 242 +J. VI 26 -M+Ch. 28 -E+DR. 39 -A+VJ. 42. 48. VII 122 -E. 190 -E.

EAMH³ also attest some 25 unique right readings. These, which presumably here preserve **m**, have been given in full among the lemmata at § 23 above; the major ones are V 116 (*l. om* E), 126, 243, [256 +K]; VI 9 (†H³), 71, 82–4, 91/2. The group therefore cannot be eliminated.

(b) *The manuscript-group* **AMH³W**

§ 27. This group is instanced mainly in Passūs X–XI, where there are 27 isolative errors, 24 of them major, and also in V–VII, where there are nine, one major.

Major VII 176 ditte] holdyn. X 53 going] good dede. 69 owyng] holde (+ChK; -H³). helpe] kepe. 70 folies] falsnesse & f.(-nesse) -ed A). 88 self] soule. 168 hem] hem brymme. 186 vncomely] vnkende*ly*. 215 L. *om.* XI 5 staring] scorn*yng.* 13 werkis] wordis. 18–19 *mis-division.* as...deseites] *om* (and deseaytes W). 21 conne] can do (*trs* AW). 22 seruid] sewit (folweþ;-A). 100 *As 2 ll. expanded.* 145 scole] lore. 146 I...Catoun] in c. þu may rede. 151 enemys] fomen. 164 Foundid...formest] formest Hem f. in feth. 228 lordis] londis. 239 any man] a *man* þat is. 245 suche] *om.* 284 L. *om.* 311 Souteris] Saweris.

Minor V 116 And] I (+N; *l. om* E). VI 74 -E. 109 -E. 125. VII 115. 143 +L. 157 þat] he -E. 213 wolde not] nolde (n. nouth H³W). XI 61. 144 Leue] L. now (*trs* A). 153. 213.

AMH³W uniquely attest six right readings, four major (XI 154, 194, 195, 245), that are accepted as preserving Ax through **m** and, like the right readings of EAMH³, listed in full at § 23. This group likewise cannot be eliminated.

§ 28. The most economical account of these two four-member groups with their shared 'core' of three manuscripts is that they are one in origin, E ceasing late in Passus VII and W joining AMH³ in X after change of its *r²*-type exemplar for one of **m**-type. W's eight minor **m** readings before Passus X may all be accounted for as coincidental. The one significant case (VII 176 *ditte out*] *holdyn out*) is of a type where convergent substitution may be invoked without seriously contradicting the general presumption that major shared errors are likely to be genetic in origin. For in this instance the phrasal verb in question is rare and the scribal variant an evident gloss.[12]

(c) **AMH³** *and the other four groups of three*

§ 29. Between Passus V and XI, the three manuscripts forming the 'common core' of the two sets have 22 isolative agreements in error, 15 of them major:

Major (a) V 153 he] her*ry.* 159 warinar] bereward. VI 3 longe] to l. 37 oþerwhile] sumtyme. VII 139 to wraþen] *om.* 142 pilide] pyned. 187 erd] lond. 193 blody] *om.* **(b)** 235 here] *om* +H. 237 *pur*...konne] þat þu kenne me woldyst (k. me] me techin MH³). VIII 18 passe] partyn. **(c)** X 19 hende] thride [*inadvertently omitted from Apparatus*]. 101 comsist] gynnyst. XI 19a] *om.* 94 mele] spekyn.
Minor (a) VII 122 and] *om.* 171 Faitours...fer] For ferd þese f. 190 I wot; wel] *trs.* **(b)** VIII 20 hadde] han. **(c)** X 18 haþ] hadde. XI 170. *With an r MS:* V 116 And] I + w. IX 102 ac] and + u.

The category (a) and (c) variants given here have already been included with those of EAMH³ and AMH³W respectively at § 23 above as representing the presumed readings of **m**. In (a) the E variants at V 159 and VI 3 seem to derive from AMH³ (= **m**); at VII 139 E agrees in error decisively with **r** and in 187 with an **r** group-variant. Together, these features indicate that E's remaining three divergences, which are agreements with **r** in right readings, are due to its correction from **r** rather than to its faithful retention of **m** where the others have erred. The **r** copy used by E or its exemplar was specifically of u type, as may be deduced from the parallel presence in E of 49 errors, some 20 of them major, shared exclusively with RU (listed in *Ka* pp. 86–7).[13] In category (c), on the other hand, while W too may have been corrected from **r**, it could equally retain **m** from *y* where A, M and H³ have lost it severally. Thus X 101 and XI 94 (where the Apparatus should record 'rW' for 'r') are of a type explicable as randomly convergent substitutions in each of the three copies and need not presuppose a common source. The same could also be true at X 19 (where W again reads with **r**), if **m** read **ende* (for *hende*) and each found it seemingly nonsensical. Likewise at XI 19, the survival in W of the single word *deseites* from 19a is better explained as a reflex of its **m**-type exemplar than as due to collation with an **r** copy. For whereas an attempted correction would presumably have been more complete, the subsequential smoothing with intruded *and* is plausibly attributable to W itself. On that supposition AMH³ may correspondingly be held to have smoothed, but here by deletion of **m**'s postulated *deseites*. These last two examples might favour an immediate common ancestor between AMH³ and the source they share with W and E; but as independent substitution / smoothing by each member here is not improbable, the evidence for a relation (E[<AMH³>W]) remains slight.

§ 30. The core-group is not therefore proposed as disjunctive so much as representing **m** 'reduced' by the late and early absence of E and W respectively. As such, however, it appears challenged by three further sets of three manuscripts. Thus **AMW** has nine agreements:

Major II 161 tresour] þing. 168 preyour] thyng. VI 117 ingang] in. XI 33 neuere] neþer. 257 make] lette. 277 wende to] wynne me. **Minor** V 45 hire] *om.* XI 47 Is] Is þer. 61 &] ʒif þat.

In the first two, H³ is absent and could have read with AMW. In XI 277 H³'s *wonyn in* looks a possible visual error for the AMW variant. In VI 117 *ingate* H³, shared with uEK, may be an attempted correction of an **m** reading *in*, and *neuere* XI 33 a similar (and successful) attempt. Only XI 257 is problematic; but if *lette*, shared by the B-Text, is *right* (as it may be), H³'s agreement with **r** could be explained as an alliteratively-induced synonym-substitution. In the first minor variant, H³ is absent; the other two are trivial and could easily be coincidental (as may W's agreement with AM in an isolated right reading at V 40).

§ 31. The next group **AH³W** contains ten minor readings:

VI 3 þat] *om.* 74. VII 229 And] *om.* VIII 21 non] *om.* X 119. XI 82 to] *om.* 86. 120 Til] Whan. 136. 291.

The only comment required here is on the last two, both of which may be safely presumed to preserve **m** where now M has introduced an individual error; 136 is especially clear.

§ 32. The third set **MH³W** is identified by seven major and eight minor readings:

Major X 202 vntyme] no tyme. 204 also] lyuende. XI 21 yclepid] called. 22 serue] sewit (folweþ) W). 126 bible] bille. 132 garte] made. 149 techiþ] tellit. **Minor** V 245. VII 29 þat] *om.* 285 to] on. XI 87 And] But. 119. 175. 193 singe] and s. 217.

In the first two, A is absent and could have read the same. XI 22 and 126 look like visual errors in **m** that were noticed and independently corrected in A. XI 21, 119 and 149 could be coincidental substitutions, the last two obviously so. XI 87 and 175 are both absent in A and 193 is an easy case of addition in **m** (under influence from the Latin) and of omission in A (through alliterative attraction). Taken together, these three sub-groupings do not seriously question AMH³ as effectively representative of **m**. The core-group's status is collaterally confirmed by the 67 major agreements evidenced in its persistence throughout EAMH³ and AMH³W.

§ 33. By way of conclusion, there is a fourth set of three, **EAM**, which qualifies as deriving from a single ancestor distinct from **r** or either of its sub-families. But this does not decisively challenge AMH³ either, for it is instanced only before the conjoint H³ appears as an A-Text at V 105. Where all three witnesses agree in Pr–V, EAM may therefore be taken to represent, if with diminished certainty, the same postulated source **m** as do AMH³.[14] This identification is logically economical and (at least negatively) empirical. Since there are no other members of the complete family in this section, it would seem justified to employ the sigil **m** also to signify EAM (and EM, when A is defective). This group has about 45 agreements in error, some 30 major. A minus sign before a sigil indicates that the copy here has the correct reading, usually that of **r**:

Major I 143 -E pyne] tene. 145 pite] *om* (*added* E). 151 mete...ellis] to oþer (men) metyn. 152 ȝe; þerwiþ] *om*; vnto you. 157 in...houres] of heuenriche blys. 160 fet] fewte. 180 siȝte of] *om.* II 5 Loke...&] *om.* 6 -E hise...many] here f. many vnfeythful*ly* to knowe. 16 haþ...me] *a*t me hase grevyd. III 11 merþe &] **r**; moche; good W. 21 coppis of siluer] other gyfteȝ mony. 22 -A *L. om.* 23 -A. *L. om.* 33 *L. om.* 74 -A on] *om.* 99 -A beȝonde] b. see. 273 leute] luve. IV 50–1 *L. div.* 50 -A manye] *om.* 67 euere] *om.* 82 pees...pur] pennys *for pes* & pecys of. 84 wile¹] *om.* 96 more] better. 129 wedde] gyff þe. 146 be...it] *to me* to bryng þaim togeder. 147 ledis] landes. 157 -E he faille] elles. V 39 ȝe...betere] þai be storyd wele E; ȝoure stor better; *l. om* A. 46 lord] *om.* 64 -A leyn] ben. 69 Venym] Weriues *or* Wermes (And seyde w. M). 70 Walewiþ] walkes. 74–5 -E *Ll. om.* 78 gode happis] godnes. 90 Awey] (And) also. 95 werse] (wel) w. *be dom* of my selfe. **Minor** I 164 ac...is] & ch. II 156 wolde] shuld. 158 +H neuere] no. 161 To] For to. 193 him] he. 197 fere] ferde. III 61 -E in] in ȝoure. 76 heo] hase. 78 Or] A*l*s. 105 -A Conscience...kyng] before þe kyng con. 265 +H hem; ȝou A. V 48 +N þere] þer*in*.

§ 34. The instances, four major and one minor, where E has the right reading may derive from the **r** copy it appears to have been collated with throughout its length. Nevertheless, E's retention of **m** family errors both here and after V 105, when H^3 joins the group, tends to confirm its proposed descent from **m**. Similarly, the six readings (five major and one minor) where A is right may be attributed to correction. The most striking of these, III 22 and 23, are unlikely to have been lost coincidentally from **m** by E and M, since no obvious mechanical reason appears. Throughout V 105–VII 213, where EAM constitute part of EAMH^3, there is almost no sign (in the shape of divergences by H^3) of a distinct genetic sub-group <EAM>. For only twice with other-version support (VII 80 and 186, both minor) does H^3 have the right reading against E(A)M, and both may be coincidental.

§ 35. The relation between **AMH^3** and its new partner W in Passus X–XI is, however, somewhat different. For while W's ultimate descent from **m** seems established by its 46 agreements in error (over half major) with the other three members of the set, it departs from the core-group AMH^3 in sharing six right readings with **r** (major: XI 52, 56, 94; minor: XI 70, 231, 255). However the minor readings here could be coincidental and in XI 52 the diverging M and H^3 variants might have simple causes (motivated and mechanical respectively), the agreement of each with another **r** witness tending to indicate their non-genetic character. In XI 56 W preserves a difficult **m** reading, here presumed archetypal, for which M, H^3 and A all have recognisably easier substitutions. The sole instance, therefore, which could seriously suggest an exclusive group-original for AMH^3 is 94 (where W should be recorded in the apparatus as agreeing with **r**). But as noted at § 29 above, coincidental substitution of a modernising synonym is here very likely. With so little support, the case for a relation <AMH^3>W, like that for <EAM>H^3, may be safely dismissed.

§ 36. From the evidence so far, it would seem reasonable to assume, firstly, that two sets of four manuscripts, EAMH^3 and AMH^{3}W, qualify as potentially genetic groups. Secondly, the persistence of AMH^3 as the common core of both groups is congruent with the descent of both from a single source, **m**. For despite the absence of E in VIII–XI and W's membership of **r** in Pr–IX, the groups reveal themselves *prima facie* not as two but as one, though only intermittently attested as a result of these absences and other losses in its constituent members. Thus, although AMH^3 does not have an exclusive common ancestor, it remains recognisably the core of what proves on analysis to be a manuscript family (cf. § 25 above). Its integrity survives challenge from the three sets of three manuscripts judged non-genetic above and is unaffected by the existence of the one other which appears genetic. For the latter, EAM, may without further argument be taken as standing for **m** before the point in Passus V where H^3 begins, just as AMH^3 stands for **m** after E ceases and before the group is joined in Passus X by W.

(d) *Six groups of paired manuscripts*

§ 37. Some further subdivisions are discernible within the postulated groups of four (in their full) and three (in their reduced) forms, EAM(H^3) and AMH^3(W). There are *five conflicting pairs* within EAM and EAMH^3 (denoted below by (a) and (b) respectively). Among these, **EA** has some 30 agreements in error (about 18 major), of which 22 appear in the apparatus among complex sets of variants:

Major (a) I 179. II 9 Ip.] Puryd. III 91 as s.] *om.* ?262. IV 23. 24. 38 gade-] gos-. V 17. 77 tunge] talys. 95. 102 +H^2. **(b)**

164 dykere] Drynkere. 166 *L. om.* 190. VI 2. ?68. VII 15. 99 Dik-] Digg-. **Minor (a)** I 165 ben au.] *trs.* II 15. III 51 wr.] þerin wr. IV 21. 98. V 94 wepe] wepyd. **(b)** VI 66 And] *om.* 94 þe[2]] þat. VII 31. 103 to pl.] pleasyd.

It should be noted that M has the right reading in about half the major cases where EA err, doubtless because it preserves **m** faithfully. In the remainder it has either a different individual error or, after V 105, the same error as H[3] (at VI 2). On this evidence, EA could be a genetic group; but it cannot be eliminated, as it preserves one right reading (minor) at III 230.

§ 38. The status of EA is challenged by disjunctive agreements of both its members with M. The first of these pairs, **EM**, presents an initially impressive agreement in some 85 (over 50 of them major), which is nearly three times as many as EA. In the following list of them, brackets denote cases of only approximate agreement:

Major (a) Pr 81. 84. 95 cuntre] peple. 96–7 *misplaced after* 89. I (35 þat lef is] lesse M; no blysse E). 39. 44. 69 wyt] hert. 86. (93). 98. 99 fyue score] fyftene. 118[1,2]. 119. 123. (127). 133. 138. 139. 141. II 23 forgid] fangid. 24 begon...so] ben for*th*gang*er*. 32. 38. 46. 47. 48 +U. 51[1,2] (1 + v). 52. 53. (56) 65. 81. 103 his] *om.* 117 þi...wyf] weddyt (wendyd M). 118 +U. 121. III 146. 147. 158. 170 +Ch. 174. 206[1,2]. 211. 212 Alle kyn] *om.* (214). V 39 ʒe...betere] þai be storyd wele E; ʒoure stor b. M. **(b)** III 22 *L. om.* 35. 74. IV 50. V 64 leyn] ben. VI 106 aʒen] *om. With one or two* **r** *MSS:* **(a)** I 119[2] +RL. 137 +RK. II 48 +U. 51[1] +v. 118 +U. **(b)** III 129 +JK. 170 +Ch. 23 +v. **Minor (a)** I 37. 41. 57. 94. 102. 127 haue I] *trs.* II 29. 36. 101. 131. III 99. 105. 144 Barouns...br.] Offt sho br. b. & b. 159. 178. 201. 209. 216. IV 155. **(b)** IV 124 me God] *trs.* V 179. VI 83. VII 101 þer w.] *trs* (†H[3]). 195 hem[2]] þai (†A).

Most of these agreements appear where E and M are the only **m** witnesses; but no more than six major errors (or eight, if two where U agrees are counted in) occur in division (b) where A / AH[3] are also available. Of these, the important omission of III 22–3, which are in A, could result from visual confusion caused by *gold* (at the caesura in 21 and the end of 23) and by *manye* at the end of 22 and *mayne* after the caesura in 23 (the latter the probable cause of loss of 23 in v). A's reading in 35 arguably reflects its scribe's judgement of **m mylde-* as repeating *softely* 36. In 74 E and M may have coincidentally deleted *on* through mistaking it as a (contextually illogical) privative prefix. In IV 50 misdivision could have led to convergent omission by E and M of a word judged metrically superfluous. V 64 looks like a simple visual error and in VI 106 coincidental loss through alliterative attraction (*geten > grace*) and homoteleuton (*-en,-en*) would account for the EM agreement. In three major cases other-family concurrence with the agreements tends to confirm the likelihood of coincidental error (in 129 through alliterative inducement and echo of 128a). The minor cases all appear trivial. This suggests that, in the absence of A and H[3], it is not more likely that EM are a genetic pair than that they simply preserve what the former two manuscripts would have read had they not proved defective. An argument from silence has little force, but here the positive case for <EM> appears on analysis too weak to rule out that for <EA>. EM, however, uniquely preserves fifteen right readings (five of them major) between I 46 and II 137 (see § 24 above), all presumptively those of their ancestor **m**. The group therefore cannot be eliminated.

§ 39. The possibility that three other pairs involving A could be genetic will be considered after examination of **MH[3]**, which appears in both of the sets of four. This pair have some 75 agreements (33 of them recorded in the apparatus), but only 46 major and 22 minor readings unquestionably classifiable as errors are listed below. Here '(a)' signifies that all members of EAMH[3] are present (but for one omission of 25 lines by E and two of 50 lines by A, in VII and VIII respectively); '(b)' that E is absent and only AMH[3] can represent **m**; '(c)' that AMH[3]W are all present. An * signifies a noteworthy disjunctive error; a minus, that the copy has the right reading; brackets, only approximate agreement.

Major (a) V 108 (A *a corrupt version of* MH³; *E). 117 -E; *l. om* A. 147. (229)(*l. om* A). VI 2. 20 (*so* A, *different word-order*; -E). 28 -A; *om* E. 47 wilneþ] þenkyn. 120 Wyte] I vowe to. VII 35 -E; *def.* A. 60. 61. 99 balkis] Rotes -EA. 142 (A *a version of* MH³;-E). 171 (A *a version of* MH³; -E). **(b)** 223 vsen] wis(s)e -A. 235 of...hondis] *om*; -A. 237. 275 *l. om* A. 285 gart] getyn *A. VIII 38 *L. om* (A *def.*). 41 (A *def.*). 575 Þise...ben] For þe tresouris ben oure aldiris (a.] thralles þat is H³; A *def*). 80 +**Z**. 110 lelly] treuly. **(c)** IX 118 -A. X 13 -AW. 17 -AW. 25 calle] clepe -AW. 89 neuere] al woie *AW. 93 gynnest] *AW. 122 fruyt] frend -AW. 139-AW. 146. 175 Out-] but -AW. 205 -W; *l. om* A. XI 48 *AW. 56 -W; *A). 57 mene] fewe. 77 lelly] treuliche *W; *l. om* A. 130. 173. 182. 213. 238. 268. **Minor (a)** V 127 hem²] hym -EA. 179 -E; *l. om* A. 235 þe] *om*;-A; of E. VII 19. 26 -EA. 61² (EA *def.*). 89 my²] here -EA. **(b)** 233 Crist] (as) cr. himself (cr. oure lord A). VIII 23 God; m. hem] *trs*; -A. 32 w. not be; w.] *trs* (A *def.*). 73 (A *def.*). 110 Þat] (For) he þ. **(c)** IX 111 ne] no -AW. X 68. 104. XI 32 More] & m. 47 ne] & -A; *om* W. 100 whanne] wh. þat. 111 -A; *om* W. 115 Boþe; and] b. in; & in -AW. 151 And] He -AW. 252 To] Neiþer to -AW.

§ 40. This body of variants, even allowing that four major ones may be faithful reflexes of wrong **m** readings where A varies slightly, indicates that MH³ is likely to be a genetic group. It is attested with uniform persistency throughout the text and the fourfold recurrence of *treu*(*liche*) for *lel*(*liche*) is striking. The group, however, uniquely preserves six major right readings and one constituent member, M, has one uniquely:

Major VII 15 comaundiþ. 59 hewe with þe hatchet. 61 þermyd maugree. VIII 54 þe sauter witnessit (M). 54*a*. 61 leiȝe I out trowe ȝe (M). X 32 shatte.
Minor I 49 (M). VIII 84 in here.

All of these, like those attested by EM (§ 39 above), are likely to preserve **m** where the other family members are absent or err, and they are similarly judged archetypal and adopted. In addition one member, H³, contains half of a reading reconstructed at V 229. The group therefore cannot be eliminated.

§ 41. A fourth challenge to both EA and MH³, the two pairs so far judged likely to be genetic, comes from **AM**. This is attested in 47 readings (some 30 of them major), of which 24 are recorded in the apparatus as part of a lemma's complex variants. In the list below '(a)' denotes the section with EAM(H³) present, '(b)' that with only AMH³ and '(c)' that with AMH³W. A minus sign, asterisk and brackets signify as at § 39 above:

Major (a) I 143 -E. I 147 -ful] -i -E. II 6 -E. 193 likiþ] wolde (list EH). III (50 -E). 56 *E. 235 -E. 264 -E. IV 82 *E. 157 -E. V 24 *E. 49 affaiten] afeyntyn (*frete E). 74–5 -E. 95 *E. dryue] drawe -E. VII 95 pote] staf (-H³; *om* E +u -E). **(b)** VIII 3 & a] *om*;-H³. IX 28. 36. 60². 64 (H³ *def.* 28–64). **(c)** X 35 -H³W. (52-. 73 -H³W. 91 -H³W. XI 12 -H³W. 247 heiȝly] hol(l)y(che) -H³W. **Minor (a)** III 6 þat] *om*;-E. 61. 244 þe] to þe -E. 260. IV 129 þou] *om*; -E. V 30 He] And (*And als he E). 203 he] hym -E. VI 33 and] *om*;-E. VII 213 wolde not] nolde. **(b)** IX 3. 7 þis] þat. 20 alwey; at hom] *trs*. 47 wile suffre] sufferith. 50 þe] þe to. 82 haþ] *om*. 85 (H³ *def.* 3–85). **(c)** X 58 -H³W. XI 14 erþe] erde -H³W. 18, 257 if] ȝif it -H³W. 53 þe] here -H³; *om* W. 280 wiþ] in -H³W.

§ 42. It would appear likely that E's divergences, which create the impression of a possible sub-group <AM>, are due to its 'correction' from an **r** source in some 13 cases (it has individual errors in another six). That E's right readings do not simply preserve **m** against AM is shown by its omission at VII 95 of the group-variant presumed as that of AM (accurately corrected in H³). This is one of nearly 50 wrong readings throughout Pr–VII that E shares with the **r** manuscript U, its probable source for 'correction'. In the case of H³, since this copy is defective in IX, all the eleven readings in question could in principle have been identical with those of AM. Again, this is an argument from silence, but if the supposition is correct, as constituting further readings of the core-group AMH³, they could have there preserved the text of **m**. The matter would seem incapable of demonstration either way; but there are five important test cases in X and XI that might suggest a genetic group <AM>. Of these, however, X 35 could be a coincidental substitution suggested by *man...lik* in 32; *clense* 73 the replacement of a harder word, perhaps following visual confusion; *acordith* 91 the result of misidentification as an imperative through inducement from *wilneþ* 89 and *loke* 92; XI 12 an obviously easier synonym-substitution; and 247 (in any case not certainly identical in A and M) a possible visual error suggested by the contextual sense and the form of preceding *holde*. Of the two instances where H^3 is right against AM, its correction need not be inferred; for VIII 3 is a simple case of haplography (pen*a & a*), while at XI 53, W's zero-reading may be a true reflex of **m**, with AM convergently inserting *here* and H^3 independently *þe*. The six examples in (c) are all trivial, 18 and 257 illustrating the at times strikingly non-indicative character of this type of variant. All in all, a relation E<AM>H^3 would therefore seem unlikely, and so the earlier established groups EA and MH^3 may stand. AM cannot be eliminated, however, because it uniquely preserves (with other-version support) three readings that may be taken as transmitting **m** and, through it, Ax.

Major IV 136 mekenes. **Minor** VIII 127 I þoruȝ here wordis. 175 And how.

§ 43. The fifth pair **AH^3** is attested by 33 agreements in error, about a dozen of them major, between V and XI. In the list of these '(a)' denotes the section where E is present and **m** therefore = EAMH^3, '(b)' that where E has ended but before W joins, and '(c)' that after W has joined the core-group, so that AMH^{3}W now = **m**. Unless specially noted, the other copies are right where AH^3 err.

Major (a) V 137. 153 he] herry (Heruy M; -E). VI 21 wy] wyte. 77–8 *L. div.* (no...louȝnesse *om* M). 92 weue] weyn (wynne M; out E). VII 121 sone] *om*. 178. 187. 243 wilnest] woldis hauen. **(b)** VIII 97. **(c)** XI 153 hotiþ] biddyth. 159 many] *om*. **Minor (a)** V 106 ne...me] may not. 200 He] And. VI 11 for] þat. 113 is] be. VII 11 it] *om*. 112 And] *om*. 187 him] *om* (+**Z**). **(b)** 300 (*M). VIII 20 hadde] han (þey han M). 92 al] *om*. **(c)** X 74 for] and. it] *om*. XI 15 rentis] *sg*. 89 to] *om*. 91 wile] schal. 93 þat] *om*. 157. 183 it is] *trs*. 190 hem^2] *om*. 207 þe^1] *om*. 304 for] in +**BC**.

Of the above variants, six could simply retain the family reading: V 137 (where E and M have each an individual error), 153; VI 77–8 (where M's error is a clear consequence of a misdivision ascribable to **m**), 92; VII 187 and VIII 97 (where M is lacking). The same may be true of VIII 20 and XI 190 (where M has only *h*). Convergent agreement is again possible in VI 21. In VII 178 *bedrede* has come in from 177 to replace the repeat-word *blynde*. XI 153 appears an easy synonym-substitution and 159 the result of haplography. VII 243 on its own seems an explicit expansion that could be coincidental. The minor variants, where not trivial, admit of easy mechanical explanations, e.g. at VII 161 (repeating *so* from 160) and XI 207 (eyeskip from *f > f*). Two readings have other-version support. VII 187 is a coincidence with the same error or with an original lacking the reflexive. The other, XI 304, is a substitution probably motivated by understanding *sermoun* as 'sermon-address' or 'discourse' rather than 'sermon-text' (a sense evidently preferred in the revision to **B**). Taken together, these variants have little weight and the group's claim to be genetic may be dismissed. AH^3, however, cannot be eliminated as they alone preserve one harder reading at VIII 109, which in the light of **B** may be judged that of **m** and thence of Ax.

§ 44. The sixth and final pair to question the status of EA and MH^3 as the only genetic groups within **m** is **AW**, which has 42 agreements, some 20 of them major. About half occur in X and XI, where the second set of four (AMH^{3}W) is strongly attested. The density here is probably best ascribed to W's change from its *r^2* exemplar to one derived from **m** but distinct from the exclusive common ancestors of <EA>, <MH³>, called 'y' in the diagram at § 5. It is in these passūs that W joins AMH³ as a fourth witness to **m**, with some 32 agreements in error, although some signs of W's collation with an **m** copy have appeared earlier in the text (see § 18 above on W). In the following list '(a)' denotes the section where two or more of EAMH³ are present, '(b)' that after E ceases and AMH³W becomes theoretically possible, a minus and * as at § 41 above. Unless otherwise noted, EM / MH³ have the right reading where AW err.

Major (a) II 168 Er he be put] Put hym (Set hem M; Bot sett E). IV 2 sau3te] acorde -EM. 111 robberis] robbyng -EM. V 88 Crist] god -EM. VI 66 hei3] holly *E*M. 75 kirnelis] corneris -EM. **(b)** VIII 107 *L. om.* IX 105 þre] *om.* X 88 clene] *om* -MH³. 89 Wilne...neuere] Whil...wonyst / art (*M*H³). 97 counseilliþ] techiþ -MH³. 117 porcioun] possessioun -MH³. 218 þat is] his. XI 21 conne] do can (can do MH³). 48 hunsen] hold (*MH³). 85 þou] he. 181 siþen] *om.* 191 and... oþere] *om* (*M*H³). 270 wrou3te] wretyn -H³;*M. 272 werkis] clerkis -MH³. **Minor (a)** III 271 robe] *pl.* VI 94 For] *om.* 103 þe] 3ou. VII 91 to bedde; 3ede] *trs.* 131 me God] *trs.* 181 to kepe] and kepte. 183 Al] *om.* **(b)** 235 hondis] *sg.* 298 curse] Thay c. VIII 23 for] *om.* 144. how] of (þat M). IX 33 here on] of þis. 117 in] in þis. X 20 a] *om.* 30 of(2)] *om.* 94 so] *om.* XI 6 wittis] *sg.* 38 lewid] l. men. 158 þat] þis (*om* M). 200 and] in. 264, 275 And] *om.*

Of the major readings here, II 168 and XI 21 may be accurate reflexes of **m**, as may VI 66, from which E and M diversely vary (*it is þe way*; *fro morew*) in evident response to finding *hei3* difficult. VI 75 and X 117 could be coincidental visual errors leading to misexpansions. At XI 191 major divergent corruptions in M and H³ suggest that the b-half was lacking in **m**. The readings at IV 2, V 88, X 97 and XI 272 could all be coincidental substitutions, that at XI 272 dittography before -*ere* twice, the omissions mechanical, and such transpositions as VII 91 and 231 induced by the force of common usage. Finally, the singular / plural alternations should be treated as non-indicative of genetic origin since they are largely unconscious and can move in both directions, as at III 271 contrasted with VII 235 and XI 6. Perhaps most telling are the lexical variant at XI 48 (by no means an obvious substitution) and the phrasal one at X 89 (which is not, however, exact). Taken together, these readings fall short of establishing a genetic group, but in principle W's postulated **m**-type exemplar in X–XI could have been the same immediate source used by A. This is because most of the agreements occur after E has ceased and there is no grouping H³W to conflict with MH³, the firmest genetic pair.[15] Lastly, the three major readings IV 2, 111 and V 88 do not seriously question the other likely genetic pair EA, while the minor readings within the limits of E's presence do not question it at all. A and W cannot be eliminated, however, since both include at V 95 the substantive basis for reconstruction, while W uniquely preserves four right readings (see § 18).

(e) *The* **m** *family: conclusions*

§ 45. It emerges, then, that within the first set of four **m** manuscripts a relation (<EA> <MH³>) is probable and within the second a relation (<AW> <MH³>) possible. The pair <AW> however does not seem sure enough to warrant either accommodation in the diagram of hypothetical descent or, within the list of sigils, any disruption of the well-established core-group AMH³. W is thus perhaps best regarded as a belated addition to the family in X and XI and its immediate exemplar as directly derived from **m**. The most economical explanation of the two sets of four is, as already indicated (§ 28 above), that they are a single intermittently attested genetic group and constitute, on comparison with **r**, an independent family. Collateral support for this conclusion is found in the body of right readings **m** provides where **r** is unquestionably in error. These have already been listed with their other-version support at § 23 above but will be referred to again at § 47 below when the two families are briefly compared.

§ 46. It remains to list in full the substantive agreements in error which provide evidence for the family in eleven combinations of its five component copies. The preceding discussion has brought out that, while **m** is minimally attested throughout the poem almost without break, even its one complete member M is too corrupt to function as a 'representative' copy, as do R for **r** or L for the **B** family β. The main virtue of M is therefore a negative one: like the **r** manuscript T it is the sole **m** copy free of contamination from the other family. Nevertheless, despite the gaps in transmission that have made such detailed specification necessary, the 260 errors recorded below may be ascribed with fair certainty to the postulated family-original. The arrangement follows that adopted for **r** at § 23 but takes due account of the often reduced attestation of **m** and therefore sub-divides the variants according to the presence or absence of individual members. However, so as not to obscure the true order in which the variable groupings of **m** witnesses appear, these sub-divisions are denoted as follows: (a) = EM; (b) = EAM; (c) = EAMH³; (d) = AMH³; (e) = AM; (f) = MH³; (g) = AMH³W. In the case of (g), agreements of AW with **r** against MH³ are taken to indicate that AW here probably = **m** and the <MH³> variant is therefore an exclusive group error. Readings are categorised as major or minor to highlight the qualitative differences that are crucial in determining manuscript relations. The sequence, as for **r**, records other-version support available for the accepted reading, so as to facilitate comparative evaluation of the two families.[16] A minus sign indicates that the **m** copy specified has the reading adopted in the text, a plus sign that a member of the other family (or, rarely, another version) shares the rejected variant, an * an important corruption. The lemma is usually from **r**, but where **r** is wrong, its reading is given as a second variant after that of **m**.

§ 47. Readings with other-version support

(i) Major

+**Z**: **(a)** I 119 word] werke. 138 yedde] syng. II 32 coueitise] þing. 38 hous] bour. 46 þe writ] þai write. 48 fastnid] fef-fyd +U. 51 at his bode] *om* +v. 53 And...wille] In witnes of Simony & siuille his brother. 56 gredeþ wel heiȝe] crye (þe chartre). 58 feffe] fastne -E. **(b)** IV 67 euere] *om*. 96 more] better. 142 warpen] carpe +ChL. **(c)** VI 81 þing] *om*. VII 176 ditte] holdyn *E; +W. **(d)** VIII 18 passe] partyn. 38 *L. om.* **(f)** 41 graiþ] heye. 57 Þise...ben] For þe tresour*is* ben oure aldiris / thralles þat is. 60 resceyueþ] reseruit (*l. om* H³). +**ZB**: **(a)** I 86 telliþ] trow þou. 99 fyue score] fiftene. 119 writ] kirke +RL. 123 siȝte...textis] þe text. 128 compsiþ] coueitid (*l. om* E). III 154 þat...men] maynteners of hir. **(b)** IV 46 he... liþ] bad me thare to lye / had myn wyf badde me gon (*l. om* A). 50 manye] *om* (-A). 58 mede] I. 157 he faille] elles (-E). V 23 cumside] bygan (for) +HJ. **(c)** VII 171 Faitours...fer] For ferd þese f. -E. **(d)** 222 mouþiþ] mevith. +**ZC**: **(b)** III 130 harmede] h. hire M; harm dide E +HB. V 39 ȝe...betere] Þai be storyd wele E; ȝoure stor better (*l. om* A). +**ZBC**: **(a)** Pr 81 parissh] kirkes. I 35 þat...is] no blysse E; lesse M. 39 and...herte] be war with þair wyles. 69 wyt] herte. 117 wenden... shuln] shal aftir hym wend / w. sh. after. 118 After...day] To þat Pyne endles; dwelle won. 127 kenne me bettre] better to lere / lerne bettre. 133 I...treuþe] is trouth for soþe. 139 a miȝte] al myrth +R. 141 wiþ loue] kyndely. **(b)** 145 pite] *om* (*added* E). 151 mete...ellis] to oþer (men) metyn. 152 ȝe; þerwiþ] *om*; vnto you. 157 in...houres] of heuenriche blys. 160 fet] fewte. 180 siȝte...tixtes] þe text (*pl.* A). II 5 Loke...and] *om*. 6 manye] m. vnfeythful*ly* to knowe. 16 haþ...me] *at* me hase grevyd. **(a)** II 81 weddyng] werkis. 117 þi...wyf] weddytt (wendyd M). 118 mery] faire +U. 125 wiþ hem] *om* +w; al E. **(b)** 147 tom] tong +ChU. III 11 merþe and] moche ?+W (good W). 21 coppis of siluer] other gyfteȝ mony; pecis of s. r. 22–3 *Ll. om* (-A). 33 *L. om.* 99 beȝonde] b. see -A. **(a)** 146 leiþ] alegges. 147 floreynes go] gold goys. 158 *L. om.* 170 þe] me +Ch. 174 kilde] gylyde. IV 82 Pees] pennys for p./ in (to) presen*s*. 146 be...it] (to me) to bryng (þaim) togeder. 147 ledis] lordis. V 46 lord] *om.* 74–5 *Ll. om*; -E. **(c)** VI 81 callen] clepyn -E. 31 sewide] folwde +H. 37 oþerwhile] sumtyme. VII 40 presauntis and] *om* (*def.* A). to wraþen hym] arise rE; *om* **m**. 193 blody] *om*; ?-E. **(d)** 280 ete] hente +t. +**B**: **(b)** I 143 pyne] tene -E. V 64 leyn] ben -A. **(a)** II 121 for euere] togeder. III 206 here bidding] mede. 210–11 *L. div. wrong.* **(c)** V 95 werse] w. *be* dom of my selfe. 115 symme...nok] synne it þouth me mer*y*. 142 so þe Ik] so mote I the. **(g)** X 186 vncomely] vnkendely. 202 vn-] no (*l. om* A). XI 21 conne] can do (*trs* AW). yclepid] called -A. 29 lessoun] sermoun. 100 *As 2 ll.* knele] gon and knelid to ground. 119 half] hande -A. 146 I...Catoun] in c. þou may rede. 149 techiþ] tellit -A. 151 enemys] fomen. 162 þerewith] with hem +V. 163–64 *misdivided.* 164 Founded...formest] f. Hem fou. in feth. 228

lordis] londis. 311 Souteris] Saweris. +**BC**: (**a**) Pr 84 houuis of silke] silkyn h. +**L**. I 98 apertly] *om*; +**Z**. III 129 teiȝeþ] fetteres +JK. 212 Alle kyn] *om*. (**b**) III 74 on] *om*; -A. (**c**) V 146 for...shrifte] to go on his wey. 147 hym to kirkeward] to kirke. 172 hitte] caste ?-E+ChH. VI 44 swere] s. fast +*L*. (**f**) 60 resceyueþ] reseruit (*l. om* H[3]). lyuen] leden (**d**) VIII 97 no...fynde] non oþer pardoun. (**e**) IX 16 as a clerk] þo -A. 28 stif] fast. 57 liþen] lystyn +K. 64 wiȝt] man. 71 mylde] meke. (**g**) X 19 hende] thride -W. XI 18b–19a] *om*. 284 *L. om*. +**C**: (**a**) I 137 plante] plente +RK. (**c**) V 109 eiȝen] e. as a blynd hagge +Bx. VII 35 conseyuede] rehersede -E; *def*. A. *Cf*. **C**: III 211 alse] at þe male tyme +Bx.

Extra lines added in **m**: B V 341 after V 190; B V 352–7 after V 200 +U.

(ii) Minor

+**Z**: (**a**) II 33. 36. 60. (**b**) 161. III 112. 145 -E. 187 +w. VI 74 +W. (**c**) VII 115. 143 (+**BC**). +**ZB**: (**a**) I 57. 183. II 29. 101[1,2]. 116. III 143. (**b**) V 23 How] when. (**c**) VI 39 -A+VJ. (**d**) VII 254 +H. +**ZC**: (**b**) 65 +**B**. (**f**) VIII 73. +**ZBC**: (**a**) I 81. 94 taken] t. alle. 164 ac; is] & (+N); *om* -A. II 103 his] *om*. 106. 156. (**b**) 158. 193. 197[1,2] (1 -E). III 105. (**a**) 150. 157 +H[2]W. 159 Þe king] And (he). (**b**) IV 60 +w. 84. 92. 130. V 48. (**c**) VI 3. 28 +DR. 42. 48. 55 +uW. VII 80 (-H[3]; *def*. A). 157 þat] he (-E+W. (**d**) VII 286. 300 +H[2]. VIII 20 hadde] han. +**B**: (**b**) III 61 -E. 178 +LZ. 180 +UHKZ. V 79. 90[1,2]. (**c**) 116 (*l. om* E, +w). 131 (+L). 152 -M+N. 186 +uV. (**e**) IX 47 wile suffre] sufferith. 85. (**g**) XI 15. 86 -M. 105 +u. 111 -A. 153. 167 -H[3]. 170 -W. 175 (*l. om* A). 213. 217 -A. 255 W+J. +**BC**: (**a**) III 201. (**b**) V 24 +**Z**; *om* E. 36 +HWZ. (**c**) (228 +H. VI 109[1]+U;[2]+W. 123 +t. 125 +W. VII 62 (*def*. EA). 122 -E. (**e**) IX 3. 64 +D. (**d**) 102[1] +U;[2] -iþ] -id. 107. (**g**) X 11 +R. 18 haþ] had -W. +**C**: (**b**) III 76 (+**B**). 265 *A;+Bx. (**g**) XI 134 (+**B**. 138 (+**B**).

Readings with no other-version parallel

(**i**) **Major** (**a**) Pr 95 cuntre] peple. II 47 feffid] sesyd (+**Z**). 51 boun] buxoum +uJ; at his bode] *om*; +v. fulfille] do. 65 delites] likyng. III 35 meke-] mylde-. (**b**) III 56 ?*om*. 62 gyue] dele +J. 273 leute] loue. (**c**) VII 142 pilide] pyned -E. (**d**) VII 235 here] o*M*; +H. (**g**) IX 36 watris] wawis. X 53 going] good dede. 69 helpe] kepe. 70 folies]; falsed & f. 80 douten] dredyn +V. 88 self] soule. 89 wy] *om*; +DV. 101 comsist] gynny*st* -W. 168 hem] hem brymme. 204 also] lyuende (*l. om* A). XI 22 serue] sewit -A. deuil] deuylis lore. 94 mele] spekyn -W. 145 scole] lore. suche] *om*. 257 -H+**B**. 277 wende to] wynne me.

(**ii**) **Minor** (**e**) II 197. (**e**) VIII 152 +W. IX 95 +U. (**g**) X 88. 103 +J. 160. 163 +U. XI 23 -M;+V. 24. 82 -H[3];+u. 184 +K. 193 singe] and s. -A. 217 -A. 231 -W+u.

§ 48. These 260 separative errors in **m**, about 155 of them major, add up to more than twice the total and more than three times the major errors in **r**. The number could well have been larger but for imperfect attestation in, and further individual variation between, the extant **m** manuscripts, two factors that require excluding several further probable **m** errors (e.g. those at III 214 and X 48). There can therefore be little question that a text of **A** should be based on an **r** copy, as all previous editors have agreed. But even so, the analysis given above indicates how far neglect of **m** by Skeat and Knott-Fowler serves to weaken the usefulness of their editions. Kane's belated recognition of **m**'s value greatly improves the text of his second edition. But he ignores its serious implications for his classification of the variants, and the form his recognition takes, an appended list of corrected readings, conceals rather than signals the **m** family's full textual significance. For, as Brewer was the first to realise,[17] **m** is an independent tradition essential for reconstituting the archetype, not merely a subsidiary resource for solving occasional local difficulties. This emerges with particular clarity when **A** is edited in parallel with **Z**, **B** and **C**; for the other-version testimony compels recognition of the probable authenticity of numerous **m** readings on comparison with those of **r**. Moreover, as well as the 100-odd variants discriminated as original on the showing of **Z**, **B** and **C** (though never on their sole basis), **m** uniquely preserves seven major right readings where *no* parallel material exists. These, not strictly criterial for **m** as a family, afford collateral support for its existence. They appear at § 23 above as the lemmata in the final section of the list. As already said, **r** has three times as many sole-version readings that are correct (§ 46 above); but the significance of **m**'s contribution to the text of **A** is further substantiated by the material in the next section.

v. *Towards the Archetype*: *the agreed readings of* r^2 *and* **m**.

§ 49. A transition from analysis of the two **A** families to that of the archetypal text is provided by first considering the agreed readings of **m** with the r^2 branch of family **r**. In about 135 instances (some 55 of them major), **m** and r^2 together preserve against r^1 what is likely to be the text of the archetypal manuscript (Ax). These 'collateral' right readings are presented here in the framework employed earlier for categorising the erroneous ('criterial') readings of both families. The adopted readings are categorised according to their other-version support; where other versions attest the rejected variant, this is recorded after the latter. Lower-case bracketed letters denote the same variations in the attestation of **m** as in the list of **m** errors given above. The lemma is here the reading of r^2**m** and is taken from the first r^2 copy to attest it, in the sequence VHJLKWN; the variant in each case is the reading of r^1. A plus sign denotes agreement of an r^2**m** copy with the rejected variant, a minus, agreement of an r^1 copy with the lemma.

Readings of r^2m with other-version support

(i) Major

+**Z**: **(b)** IV 29 myle] myle wey +K;*E. 63 nomen] tok +JWEBC. **(c)** VII 123 holde] olde +WH³**B**. 183 cacche] chase. +**ZB**: **(b)** IV 57 þi-] my +KNA. 154 le*ete* þe I nulle] loue þe I wile +E. **(d)** VII 227 herde] hadde -U. +**ZBC**: **(a)** Pr 42 Fayteden] Flite þan +E. **(b)** I 153 For þei₃ ₃e] For þi -U. **(a)** II 105 besitte] besette (†E). soure] sore +vE. 163 gurdeþ] gederiþ -D. **(b)** III 132 cotiþ] cloþiþ +M. 171 menske] mylde / auaunce. IV 71–2 *Ll. om*; -H². V 43 ran Repentaunce and] Rep. 55 his soule] hym +HJ. **(c)** 216 þe veil] (þer) while / wille +E. 241 worþe] werche +EA. VI 39 with-] ne -H². 100 forþ]] (þe) for. VII 18 longe] louely. 20 chapelleynis] chapellis -Ch. 201 benes] bones -U+vK. **(d)** 306 faille] falle -R+L. VIII 2 tilien þe erþe] his erþe tilien. +**B**: **(b)** V 127 pyned] pynned +VwC. **(c)** VII 96 clense] close +vwEH³. **(d)** VIII 101 pure] *om*; -U. **(e)** IX 6 wente] wene. 14 menours] maistris. 57 foulis] briddes. **(g)** X 48 þe...In.] In. is þe grettest. 161 suche wordis; seide] *trs*. 186 me þinkeþ] I wene. 189 barne bere] bere child. XI 47 noye] anguyssh. 121 liþer] li₃eris. 211 romere] rennere +H³. 251 hethyn] hem. +**BC**: **(a)** I 1 myrk] derke +VKN. **(b)** III 260 I] In +K. wit] it +KE. 268 to trouþe] trewely. a₃eyn his wille] a. ry₃th / ony þyng / to þe wrong. 269 Leaute] His wykkide l. IV 4 Crist] god. **(c)** V 109 betil-] bittir-. 114–15. *Line-div. wrong*. 114 ben...caitif] ylouid coueitise q. he al my lif tyme. 161 Hugh] hogge / hobbe. nedelere] +E. 177 aparte] apertly -D. 196–97 *Line-div. wrong*. 196 like...bicche] *om*; -U+JK. 200 þreuh] fel +AMH³. VI 111 peple] folk +JL. **(e)** VIII 137 Daniel] Dauid -H²Ch+J. IX 17 synneþ] falliþ. 36 walwen] wawen. X 136 martires] nonnes. XI 296 *reges et*] *om*; -U.

(ii) Minor

+**Z**: **(d)** VII 227 -U+HLW. 240 -U+W. **(f)** VIII 54 -U+K. +**ZB**: **(b)** IV 91. **(c)** VII 37 +VJ. +**ZC**: VII 185. +**ZBC**: **(a)** Pr 44. I 25 -H². II 88 -D. III 139. **(b)** III 15. IV 42. 84. 89. 147. 35 +VJLNE. **(c)** V 219. VI 13 -U+JNM. 46 +W. 64 -D+W. 69 -Ch. 94. 100 +MW. VII 29–30. 31². 76¹ -U+E;² +W. 84 +E. 114 +WE. 141 +LKA. 143 +H. 190 +JLK. **(d)** 254 -U+K. 280 -U+KM. VIII 3 +M. 6¹·²-U. 36 +L. +**B**: **(b)** I 169 -Ch+HZ. **(a)** III 208 -U+LW. **(b)** V 66 -Ch. 78. 91. 104 +LW. 209 -Ch+Z. **(c)** VI 28 +E. **(e)** VIII 141 -Ch+JLW. IX 44 -D+M. 86 +A. **(g)** X 40. 151 +A. 185 -U. 188¹ -Ch+KH³;² +KAH³. 189 +JM. 198. XI 71 +V. 75–6 +K. 78. 108. 143 -Ch+AW. 173 -ChR+MH³. 205 +W. 226 +AH³. 229 -ChD+AM. 236. +**BC**: **(c)** V 110. 130. 178–9 VII 31. **(e)** VIII 154 -UZ. IX 67 +K. **(g)** X 168 -D+M. XI 5. 13 +JM. 129 +KMH³. 134, 134/5. 277 +M. +**C**: IX 100.

Readings with no other-version parallel

(i) Major (b) III 243] *L. om*; -R. **(c)** VII 210 be þe betere] *om* / at ese. 211] *L. om*; +E. **(e)** IX 98 here] his -D+H³. **(g)** X 86 þi seluen] þe salme. 154 kynde] kyn +A. 208 werche þat werk] do þat w./ wirche (208a *om* M). XI 293 ferþer] for (soþe) / Ø +M.

(ii) Minor (b) III 57] +D-N. **(c)** VII 212 Make] lat / And m. 212a–13] *Line-div. wrong*. **(g)** XI 159.

§ 50. Some comment is required here, particularly on the contribution of individual **r** and **m** copies to the postulated archetypal consensus signified by 'r^2**m**.'[18] It is noteworthy, first, that the accuracy of six of the seven r^2 copies in their presumptive preservation of **r** (and thence of Ax) is closely similar, despite the variable amounts of text attested. None exceeds 12% in defections from the sub-family reading where this can be firmly established. Thus major-reading divergencies are (in descending order): J:9; K:8; W:6; V, L:4; H:3; N:2. From this, even allowing for its lack of about four passūs, it is obvious how much greater N's textual value would have been, had its **A** portion been complete.

§ 51. All the r^1 copies except for T occasionally depart from their ancestral reading to join r^2**m**. The most frequent is U, with six major readings out of a total of fourteen. These point to a likely phase of correction in the course of U's descent from its group-original u. And that this was by reference not to an r^2 but to an **m**-type copy is suggested by U's lack of r^2's isolative errors (except at IV 129, VIII 151, IV 129 and VIII 38, the last two trivial) and by its possession of the lines on Glutton (= B V 352–7) found in **m** after V 200.[19] Of the major r^2**m** right readings found in other r^1 witnesses, Ch has three (out of a total of 14), H[2] and D two each (out of totals of four and ten respectively) and R one (out of a total of six). From among the 14 major r^2**m** readings in these five r^1 copies, one (*Daniel*] *Dauid* VIII 137) shared by H[2]ChU, is of a kind that could be due to independent scribal intervention, as R's correction here by another hand graphically suggests. Two other important borrowings from r^2**m** occur at IV 71–2 (added by H[2] to its defective source) and III 243 (added by R to its defective u exemplar). In contrast to these, the major variants in Ch and D do not suggest correction from another copy. Two probably identifiable as commonsense scribal conjectures are *chapelleynis* VII 20 (Ch) and *gurdeþ* II 163 (D). The three right readings Ch shares only with r^2 are explicable in the same way: *ʒour*] *his* VIII 38; *ʒe*] *þou* VIII 68; *wel þe*] *wele* X 188. So also are D's *at*] *om* at X 172, *it be*] *on* XI 264 and Pr 75, VI 64 and IX 56. One D agreement at IX 92 is so significant politically as to suggest deliberate correction, but it could be just a scribal response to perceived incoherence in the syntax. On balance, then, the case for seeing correction of U, R and H[2] from an r^2 (or, in the case of U, an **m**) source would seem strong, that for Ch and D weak. The remaining r^1 copy T, as already remarked, is uninfluenced by r^2 or **m**.[20]

§ 52. The **m** witnesses display about the same proportional fidelity to their family ancestor as do the r^2 copies discussed above. Manuscript A fails in two out of fifteen major readings, a low figure, given its relative completeness, E in three out of six (over eight passūs), H[3] in four out of eleven (over seven passūs) and W in one out of seven (over its two passūs as an **m** copy). The average level of defections from the postulated **m** reading is thus about 8%. But this, which is somewhat less than for r^2, is probably attributable to the defective character of E, H[3] and W. For the one complete **m** copy M lacks some 12% of the family readings and this is the exact figure for the r^2 sub-family taken as a whole (see § 50).

§ 53. It goes without saying that the substantial agreements of r^2 and **m** in right readings do not indicate derivation from an exclusive common ancestor lower than the archetype. All they imply, on the most economical assumption, is faithful preservation of Ax at these points: by r^2 through **r** (where r^1 has gone astray) and by **m** directly.[21] However, r^2's agreement with **m** in major *error* would clearly question its linear descent from **r** and would point to a shared source intermediate between r^2**m** and Ax. It is therefore significant that only in six instances where r^1 has the right reading do r^2**m** in fact err jointly:

Major (a) r^1 *entire*: XI 67 wy] man + U, Bx. **(b)** r^1 = d *and* u *is wrong*: X 30 +C?B lisse] blysse + u. **(c)** r^1 = t: X 100 isent þe] *trs*; + u; sente D.
Minor (a) VII 282. XI 241. **(b)** VII 277.

Here the minor errors are trivial and X 100 looks like a felicitous t (or perhaps d) variant of what would have been an easy archetypal transposition. In X 30, although the **C** reading should help to discriminate the **AB** original, it is precluded by the linear postulate from being decisive. For not only is *blysse* acceptable in sense and metre, coincidental substitution in r^2 and **m** (through contextual suggestion) would have been easy, a possibility underlined by the fact that the r^1 manuscript U shares the variant. Finally, the word involved in XI 67 is one notoriously subject to synonym-substitution, as shown by the witness both of one r^1 member and of Bx.[22] Taken as a whole, the evidence for an r^2**m** source appears nugatory and so the relationships in the diagram at § 5 may be accepted as likely to be close to the historical situation.

§ 54. Added to some 250 readings preserved by **r** and some 100 by **m** (with or without other-version support), these 135 readings of r^2**m** produce nearly 500 that are very likely to be archetypal. The supporting testimony of the assured **Z**, **B** and **C** readings severally or combined is significant here, as in the many instances left out of the above categories where cross-family conflict of witnesses makes even the constituent groups hard to establish. The most important readings are examined in the *Textual Notes*, but limitations of space rule out particular consideration here. However, nothing like a majority of **A** lines should be regarded as seriously uncertain, despite difficulties at many points, especially where no other-version evidence is available. This will become clear from the next section, which shows how, in at least 60% of the poem, an archetypal text is attested with near-unanimity and in most doubtful cases the 'parallel' evidence proves virtually decisive between alternative readings otherwise of equal weight on intrinsic grounds. Ax itself is not free of corruptions; but the same comparative analysis that exposes them usually suffices for emending them.

vi. *The Archetypal Text of the* **A** *Version*

§ 55. The above sections complete the examination of the respective claims of **r**, **m** and r^2**m** to represent Ax. These have been set out in full with their other-version support where this exists. It remains to consider the body of presumed archetypal text preserved with little uncertainty in all the manuscripts, in a majority of them or, where there is random variation across families, in a few individual witnesses supported by one or more other version(s). The following list therefore contains lines judged to preserve the archetype (*a*) where there is (near)-unanimous support from both **r** and **m**; (*b*) where the text is attested by at least two manuscripts of both families; and (*c*) where direct analysis finds in not fewer than two unrelated copies a harder reading identifiable as the one from which the other variants are likely to have been generated (these are given in square brackets). On the basis of their intrinsic quality and in the light of the parallel **Z/B/C** text (where available), all lines listed are judged to preserve the original text, except that wrong line-division producing no substantive error has been ignored. Other-version support is recorded here only for the 47 category (*b*) and (*c*) readings. For the rest it may be easily found by consulting the text in Vol. I, where the location of lines not immediately parallel is noted in small type at the relevant points. Excluded from the list are lines with readings correctly attested (*a*) solely by one family, even when they appear original (and so presumptively archetypal) on intrinsic grounds, and have clear other-version support; (*b*) by r^2**m** (those given at § 49 above); and (*c*) all particular right readings judged after analysis as likely to have entered individual manuscripts by felicitous conjecture, coincidence or contamination. These last, as in effect 'editorially' introduced by a scribe, are noted instead amongst the emended readings, and many are discussed at §§ 60–6. Cases where the Ax reading itself appears undecidable are in brackets. Those that are certain but have been judged corrupt and corrected in the text by restoration, reconstruction or conjecture, are listed (according to the category of emendation) in §§ 55–9 and are discussed in the *Textual Notes*.

Pr 1. 3. 5–6. 8–10. 12–21. 23–6. 28–30. 32–3. 35–41. 43. 45–55. 57–62. 64–8. 70–2. 74–9. 82. 85. 87–8. 90–5. 97–9. 101. 103–6. +**BC** 107. 108–9.

I 2–3. 5–10. 13–24. 26–30. 32–6. (37). 38. 40–3. 45. 47. 50–6. 59–62. 64–8. (69). 70–3. 75–6. 80. 82–5. 88–9. 91–2. (93). 95–6. +**Z** 97. 99–101. 107–9. 111. 113. 115. 117. 120. 124–5. 129. 131–2. 134–6. 140. 142. 144. 147. 150. 154. 156. 158. 160–3. 165–8. (169). 170–3. 175–8. 181.

II 2. 4. 10–13. 17. 19–20. 22. 24–8. 30–1. 34. 39–42. 45. 50. 54–5. *59. (63). 64. 66–7. 69. 71–4. 76. 78–80. 82. +**B** 84. 85. 89–93. 95. +**BC** 96. 97–100. 102–3. 108–9. 111–14. 117. 119. +**B** 120. 123. 126. [+**ZBC** 128].129. 132–4. 136. 139. 141. 143. 145. +**ZBC** 149. 150. 153. 157. 160. 162. 164–7. +**B** 169. 170–3. 175–8. [+**BC** 180]. 183–4. (185). 186. 188. (189). 190–2. 194–6.

III 1–4. 6–7. 9–10. 14. 16–17. +**ZBC** 18. 20. (21). 24–6. (28). 30. 32. 34. +**B** 36. 38–46. +**BC** 48. 49. 51. 54. 58–60. 63–4. (65). 66. 68. 70. 72–3. (74). 75. 77. 79. 80–2. 84–5. 87. 90. 92. +**B** 93. (95). 98. +**ZBC** 99. 100 01. 103–4. 107–11. +**ZBC** 113–16. +**ZBC** 119–20. 123. [+**ZBC** 124]. +**BC** 126. +**ZBC** 127–8. 131. 133. 136–7. [+**ZBC** 138]. 140–42. +**Z** 148. 149. 152–3. 156. 160–64. 168. 172–3. 175–7.179. 181–4. (185). 188–9. 191. 193–4. [+**ZB** 195]. 197. (198). 199–200. +**B** 203. 204–5. 207. 212–13. 215. 217–18. 220–1. 221a. 224–5. 227–8. 231–3a. (234). 236–8. 240–2. 244–52. 254–5. 257. 261. 263. 267. 270–2. 275–6.

IV 2–3. 6–9. 15. 17–18. 20. 22. 25–8. 30. 32. (33). 34–9. 41. 45. 48–9. 51–4. 56. 59. 62. 64. 68–70. 73–6. 79–80. 86–8. 90. 101–5. +**Z** 107. 108–10. 112. 115–23. 135. 137–40. 144–5. +**ZBC** 148. 151. 153. (155). 157–8.

V 1–4. 6–9. 11–15. 18–20. +**ZBC** 21. 22. 25–7. 29–30. 32–3. +**ZBC** 35. 37–8. 41. 44–7. 49–54. 56–8. *59. 60–5. 68–9. 72–3. 76–7. 81–6. 88–9. (90). 92. (93). 94. (95). 96–100. 102. 105. 107. 111. 118–25. 128. 133–4. +**BC** 135. 136. 138–40. [+**C** 141]. 144–5. 149–50. 154. 157. (160). 162. 164–6. (168). 169–71. 173–5. 180–2. 184–5. 187–8. *189. 191–5. 197–9. 204–6. 210–15. 220. 223. 225. 227. (229). 230–2. 234. (237). 238–40. 247. 251–5.

VI 4–5. 8. 10–12. 14–19. 22–5. 27. 29–30. 34. (35). 36. 38. 40. 43. 49–51. 53–4. 56. 58–61. 66. [+**ZBC** 67]. (68). 70. 75–8. 80. 85. 87. 89–90. 93. [+**BC** 95]. (96). 97. 99. 102. 104–8. 114. 118–19. 121. (122). 124. 126.

VII 1. 3–4. 6–9. 11. 16–17. 21. 23–4. *(25). 26–8. 30. 32–4. 36. 38–9. 41–2. 44–55. 57–8. 63–7. 70–72. +**B** 73. 75. 77–8. (85). 87–8. 90–4. 102–5. 107–13. 116–21. 124–7. 129. 132–8. 140. 144–54. *155. 156. 159–62. 164. 167. 169–70. 172–3. 175. 177. 180–2. 184. 186. 191–2. 196–200. 202–6. 208–9. 213–21. 223–5. 228–9. 232. 234. 238–9. 241–4. 246. (247). 248–51. 255–7. 260–5. 267–8. 269. 271–4. 276–9. 281. 287–90. 292–3. 296–9. 302–5. 307.

VIII 1. 4–5. 7–12. 14–17. 20–7. 29. 34–5. 37. 39–40. 42–43. 46–53. 55–6. 58–9. 62–71. (72). 74–9. 81–3. +**ZB** 85. 86. 89–96. 98–9. 102–3. 106. [+**B** 108]. 113–18. 120–25. 126. 128–31. 133–4. 138–40. 143. 145–50. 153. 155–60. 162–71. 173–4. (177). 178. 180–4.

IX 1–2. 4–5. 8–13. 15–16. 19–27. 29–35. 37–43. 45–6. 48–9. 51–4. *55. 56. 58–9. 61. +**BC** 62. 63. 65–6. 68–70. 72. 75. 77–8. 80–3. 87–91. 94. 97. 99. 101. 103. 105. 108–18.

X 1–5. 8–9. [+**BC** 10]. 12–21. 24. 26–9. 31. 33. 35–8. 41–7. 49–52. 54–67. 70–9. 81–3. 85. 87. 91–2. 96. 98–9. (100). 102. 105–6. 108–9. (110). 111–14. 116–20. 122–29. 131–2. 134–5. 137–40. (141). 142–50. 152–3. 155. 158. 162. 164–7. 169–71. 173–5. 177–8. 180–1. 183–4. 190–92. +**BC** 193. 197. 199. 201. 203. 206–7. 209. 211. 213–14. 216–18.

XI 1–3. 6–8. 12. 14. 16–17. 20. (24). 25–8. 31–3. 35. 37–40. +**BC** 41. 42–6. 49–51. 54–5. 57–60. 62–6. 69–70. 72–4. *(75). 76–7. 79. (80). 81. 83. 85. 87–93. 95–9. 101–4. 106–7. 109–11. 113–18. 120. 122–31. 133. +**BC** 135. 137–9. 142. 147–8. 150. 152. 155–7. +**B** 159. 160. 165–6. 168–70. 172. 174. 176. (177). 178–9. 183. 185–90. 192–3. 196. 198. 200–04. 206–10. 213–16. 218–19. 221–24 +**B** 225. 229–30. 232–5. 238. 243. 246–7. 252–6. 259–63. 265. 267–71. 273–6. 278–83. 285–6. 288–90. 292. 294–304. +**BC** 305. 306–7. 309–10. 312–13.

vii. *Emendation of Errors in the Archetypal A-Text*

§ 56. On direct examination and, in most cases, comparison with one or more other version(s), Ax reveals some 53 errors of sense, style or metre. As will be found later with the archetypal texts of **B** and **C**, these errors are capable of being emended by three procedures that are broadly distinguishable from each other, the first more sharply than the second and third. They are (i) restoration, whereby a superior other-version reading is adopted as the probable original of which Ax is judged to be a corrupted form; (ii) reconstruction, using other-version evidence to produce a reading not actually attested elsewhere; (iii) conjecture, a further stage of reconstruction where little or no direct evidence exists. About half the emendations are introduced wholly or partly on metrical grounds and all simple cases of metre damaged by transposition are placed under (ii). Non-archetypal readings in one or more **A** manuscripts that are considered likely to be original on intrinsic grounds are recorded with those in (i) if they appear due to coincidence or contamination, but with those in (iii) if reasonably attributable to scribal guesswork. Only one example of (iii) is listed here, but single- or two-copy variants judged original are listed at § 59 below and will be found above in the sections on each sub-family and its groups. Emendations on metrical grounds are marked ^. Instances where, because of conflict between families or absence of one family, the Ax reading is undecidable and so not classifiable as certainly corrupt, are in brackets.

§ 57 (*i*) *Restored readings*

Some 34 archetypal errors, all but one certain, are corrected by restoration. Ten of these emendations are taken from **B** and **C**, and as they could in principle be products of revision, they are necessarily less secure than the rest (in no case does serious doubt arise).

ZBC: I 94 II 59, 142. III 167. V 28 +J. VI 21. VII 22 +VM.; ^29 +NE; 89; 130 +KL; (^139); 163; 189, 253 +L. **ZB**: I ^48 +W. 116. VII 100–01 +W. **ZC**: VI 52. **BC**: VI ^1 +K. VIII ^136 (+M). IX ^55. XI ^266. **Z**: I ^110. III 155. VI ^79. VII ^25. VIII 13. **B**: V ^59. 148. 189 +N. VIII 125*a*. XI 75. **C**:III 30.

(*ii*) *Reconstructed readings*

Seven certain and one probable Ax error are emended by reconstruction:

VII ^155, XI ^161 *trs.* IX (^106), XI ^191, ^197, ^248 [*word-form*]. X 157 [*proper name*]. XI (239) [*synonym-substitution*].

(*iii*) *Conjectural readings*

Twelve errors are emended by conjecture, seven being adopted also for the parallel line(s). The last example could be a scribal guess but since it occurs in one *r²* and one **m** copy, it might in theory be archetypal:

Pr ^11. ^III 239. ^IV 78. VII ^165, ^266. X 187. XI 67 [*parallel conjectures*]. VII ^236. X ^23, ^68, ^154. ? XI 308 (KW).

§ 58. Among the above, several illustrate mechanical errors of the kind common both in the sub-archetypes and the groups. They include haplography, as at III 239, IV 78, VII 236 (where Ax is uncertain); omission of a prefix, as at IV 157 (Ax uncertain); loss of a small stave-word (VII 266, XI 191) or of a letter needed for the metre (X 187); and substitution of a non-alliterating dialectal variant, as at IV 63, XI 67, 197 and 248. Some errors may be due to misreading the exemplar, as at I 110; II 59; V 142; VI 21; VII 165; VIII 13 (followed by smoothing) and 125*a*; or to mistaking the word-order, as at III 185 (Ax uncertain), VII 155, IX 55 (inversion to prose order) and XI 161 (promotion of a more familiar term). Errors likely to be deliberate are the substitution of a commoner non-alliterating synonym at X 23 and 154, an Anglicised equivalent of a Latin stave-word at I 94 and II 142, a more familiar proper name at V 160 (Ax uncertain), or a contextually easier term at VII 89. Cases of words that the archetypal scribe found 'hard' are III 167, VI 79, X 23, 68 and VII 60² (where Ax may have read as emended).

§ 59. In some twenty further instances the suggested editorial emendation of a major Ax error has been happily anticipated in a single manuscript. These are *V* at V 200 and VII 187; *J* at V 28; *K* at II 144 and XI 80; *W* at I 48, III 21, VI 2 and VII 100–01; *N* at III 95 and V 31, 131; *E* at II 137; *A* at VII 128; and *M* at II 94, 107, 124, 181 and VII 145. In some the reading could come by pure descent from Ax (as at VII 128) or as a result of consultation with another version (as at III 21 or VII 100–01). In a few other cases *two* copies, related or unrelated, contain the correct reading against a probable Ax error, e.g. RD at II 180, <RU> at IX 57, KL at VII 130 and KW at XI 308.

§ 60. Errors traceable to split variation are emended on the basis of available **A** manuscript evidence. Examples are at III 234 and VII 139, 294 or, less straightforwardly, V 112, 229 and XI 67 (the latter two receiving 'parallel' reconstruction in **Z** and **B**). More complex, and involving a greater degree of speculation, are IV 61 and VII 236, where Ax remains uncertain. Emendations of individual words start with near-certain examples where a parallel version furnishes the lexical item, as at II 59, III 167 and VII 89 (**ZBC**); VII 60 (**ZB**); V 142 (**B**, which N may echo); I 110; and VI 79 (**Z**). They go on to cases where a mechanical cause may explain the error, as at XI 191 and at III 239, IV 78, VII 165 and X 187 (the last four 'parallel' emendations). Finally come cruces resolved by pure conjecture, as at X 23, 68 and 154, which involve a current word presumed to have been supplanted by a commoner non-metrical synonym.

viii. *Readings of Indeterminable Origin*

§ 61. The text identified as certainly or inferentially archetypal adds up to nearly four-fifths of the whole. The remaining readings (not separately listed here) cut across families and display the characteristic random variation due to unconscious error or to deliberate intervention by individual copyists. This tendency appears mostly amongst minor readings and has no effect on metre and little on style or sense. Instanced at the very outset of the Prologue, it can only be addressed, as in the case of the major ones, through identifying the likely direction of variation as that from a harder (more probably original) to an easier (more probably scribal) reading. The direct method is not only necessary when the alternatives in **r** and **m** are being compared, it proves indispensable at every stage of the editorial process, including the final one where the versional archetypes are critically evaluated. This is evident from the first four entries in the apparatus to the **A** Prologue, which show how the method works most effectively where the other versions are present to serve as a control on editorial reasoning. The first, *shroudes* in line 2, attested in only four out of fourteen manuscripts, is initially recommended on grounds of sense and the support of **ZB** and the **x** family of **C**. On comparison, the singular *shroud* attested by *r¹* and **m** copies alike looks suspect as a scribal attempt (perhaps under inducement from singular *abite* in line 3) to insist on *one* garment for the dreamer. The JK variant shows the same misunderstanding of the verb *shop* that accounts for *shrobbis* in the **p** family of **C**. On purely lexical grounds, the hardest reading here might appear *shregges* (see MED s.v. *shragge* n.); but this must be simply one of the Chaderton scribe's typical aberrations, as the sense 'rag' is over-emphatic and contextually inappropriate. Secondly, in line 4 the reading with the subject-pronoun could be archetypal; but its recurrence in family **p** of **C** (accompanied by the **x**-family manuscripts U and D) points to it as syntactically the easier alternative, with *Wente* being confirmed by **ZB** and the y group in **C** family **x**. In line 7 the minority variant *ofwandrit* is favoured by **ZC** agreement and the uniqueness of the form. It is moreover quite probably what Ax read, as a scribe would not have replaced *for*- with the little-used intensive prefix *of-*. In line 8, which has no **C** parallel, *bourne* is preferable to *bournis* since the uninflected possessive is arguably harder, and it is confirmed by **Z**. This judgement recognises the modernising revision in **B** (or possibly in Bx) shared by three *r¹* copies and one **m** copy (all later in date than **B**). But that Ax was uninflected seems indicated by J, despite its variant being substantively wrong.[23]

§ 62. The fifth example on this same page of text, [*me*] *mete* 11, differs radically, since here the joint witness of two other versions **ZB** is *rejected* in favour of an emendation made on metrical grounds and the indirect evidence of the revised **C** line. As it is fully discussed in the *Textual Notes* (and see IV, § 18 below), further detail may be omitted here. But this case marks the extreme limit of the direct method of editing; for the reading judged likeliest to have generated an identical error in two archetypes and a unique copy with archetypal status is an editorial conjecture, not a variant found in a copy of any version. Such a judgement may be subjective, but it cannot be called arbitrary, as could the decision over the relatively indifferent *bournes*. And while hard cases are rightly thought to make bad law, it is also true that the exception proves the rule; so the fact that line 11 is one of only two instances (the other is at A IV 78 //) where the testimony of three versions is set aside may support a plea in mitigation. Not every reader will find *me meten* justified, but to the present editor it has seemed better to conjecture what the poet might have written than to retain a reading that appears inauthentic when examined in the light of the core-text criteria. This early archetypal crux deserves attention because it illustrates the essential difference between major and minor readings that is stressed throughout this edition, and highlights the importance of focussing editorial effort upon the former.

ix. *Possible* **B** *Contamination in the* **A** *Version*

§ 63. It was mentioned above (§ 59) that a few individual **A** copies contain corrections apparently taken from other versions ('benign contamination'). It is now necessary to consider the problem (also to be encountered in **Z**, **B** and **C**) of *lines* from another version having been present by inference in one of the sub-archetypes, in this case **m**. Thus at V 87 **m**, here joined by one *r²* copy W, has a line seemingly lost from **r** (as a result of repetition of the phrase *for þe peple* 86a at 87b). Also in this passus **m**, this time accompanied by the three *r²* copies VHN, completes the roster of tavern rogues with two lines, 163 and 167, that could have been borrowed by **m** from a **B** copy. As this supposition is strengthened by **m**'s earlier evidencing a *corrupt* archetypal **B** reading at V 109,[24] it might be further inferred that v and N have them by lateral transmission from a copy of **m**. However, those manuscripts do not share **m**'s error at 109, so it is at least possible that both lines were originally also in **r** but were omitted from its other constituent groups, 163 through deliberate censorship and 167 through visual error (*chepe...rop-...hep...chiere*).[25] Later in the description of Glutton there occurs after V 190 a line corresponding to B V 341; and after line 200 appear six lines corresponding to B V 352–7, the latter shared by the *r¹* copy U. The single line could have been lost by eyeskip from *gille* to *while*; but the six dealing with Clement the Cobbler look like a **B** addition borrowed by **m** because of its obvious liveliness and humour. U may have added the line from either **m** or **B** (as at 196, where it corrects an *r¹* error retained by its genetic twin R). Both the single line and the set of six are excluded from the text, though there is a case for seeing at least the first as part of **A** (see the *Textual Notes*).

§ 64. More problematic are the two pairs of lines found in **m** after IV 17 (= BC IV 18–19) and V 31 (= B V 32–3), which are shared respectively by the r^2 copies W and J. The presence of these lines in **Z** might, if that version is regarded as authentic, argue for their acceptance. But there are reasons for believing that they were first set aside in the revision to **A** and only later restored in **B**, from whence **m** could have derived them. In the first pair, the reason is the form of **Z**, in which the lines correspond effectively to A IV 17 after the verb *cald,* suggesting that *Catoun* replaced *Tomme Trewe-tonge* in the initial revision. In the second pair, the lines on Bette and his wife could have seemed to repeat too closely those on Thom Stowe and Felis (even if one wife is being chastised for shrewishness and the other for sloth). Given no obvious breach in sense after either IV 17 or V 31, the case for including both pairs is thus not compelling. In strong contrast are the three lines at VI 82–4. Here **m** has the **ZC** wording in 83; but 82 is not in the later versions at all and **m** gives a different final lift from **Z**. In 84, where the b-half is that of **Z** not **BC**, **m** again has a distinctive reading in the last lift. But the omission of Z 77–8 may be taken to illustrate **A**'s typical pruning of **Z**'s circumstantial detail (*Z Version* § 14 below, *passim*). As 82–4 can hardly derive from **Z**, they may therefore be accepted as part of the **A** Version. Nothing in the lines' sense suggests a motive for deliberate omission, so it could be that their loss in **r** was through a mechanical cause, the similar endings of 81/82 and 85/86.

§ 65. Of the seventeen lines shared by **m** with one or more other versions, six are retained. Only three have been included in previous editions, V 87 in Kane and V 163 and 167 in Knott-Fowler. In two other cases, **B** lines are attested by some but not all **m** copies present, one supported by two members of **r**. The more significant appears after V 42, where EM (but not A) and the r^2 copies KW have B V 59. As it stands in **r**A, line 42 reads more abruptly than either **Z**'s four-line parallel, with its evident translation-expansion of the Latin formula, or the terser **BC** reading, which simply provides an object for the verb *byfalle*. The text adopted is interpreted as representing **A**'s attempt to abbreviate **Z**, and **B** is understood as having ultimately restored (from the earliest version) the phrase now composing 59a (cf. *Z Version* § 25 below). Thus the expanded form of Reason's last sentence as found in EMKW, while deserving careful consideration, is here tentatively rejected as a **B** reading borrowed by the scribes of these copies severally to fill what was perceived as a gap in the thought. In the second and less important instance, after V 110, the ancestor of MH³ (copies accepted at § 39 as a genetic pair) inserts the lines on Coueitise's chin and beard, E adds also that on his beard, while A omits them, here perhaps following the original reading of **m**. As this material has no parallel in **Z**, its claim as a possible part of the **A** Version is correspondingly weakened. Finally, after VIII 54 MH³ (here the only **m** witnesses, as A is defective) include a Latin quotation absent from both the **r** family and **Z**. In principle, this citation-line could be a borrowing from B VII 51*a*, similar to those in H³ after VII 74 [B XI 90], XI 152 [C V 58*a*] and 229 [B XIV 212*a*]. But in practice this would seem unlikely; for whereas the latter three illustrate memorial contamination from unrelated parts of the text, the quotation at VIII 54*a* correctly rounds off the sense of 54, which reads as incomplete in **r** and **Z**.

§ 66. In conclusion, it appears that one sub-archetype, **m** (in this respect quite unlike **r**), is likely to have been contaminated at points from a post-archetypal copy of a later version. But at least some of its **B**-type lines were arguably present in Ax, and by inference in its source, and so are included in this edition.

x. *Passus XII*

§ 67. The above completes our examination of the archetypal text of Pr–XI as attested, to varying degrees of completeness, in eighteen manuscripts. The continuation of **A** here called 'Passus XII' is entitled 'Passus Third of Dowel' in the only three copies that contain it. This designation acknowledges the inner sequential numbering of Dowel recorded in the colophon of VIII, which is a kind of Prologue to the *Dowel* section. The archetypal rubrics before XII are as likely as not authorial (see Appendix Two) but that of XII looks like a scribal attempt to integrate it with the preceding body of text. For as Fowler maintained, Passus XII, whether or not original, almost certainly did not form part of Ax. There is no trace of it in the r^1 group d nor in K and W, the only other members of r^2 which survive to the end of Passus XI. And while in the case of the conjoint copies, XII 'might have been suppressed by someone engaged in grafting the C-continuation to the A-Text,'[26] this could not be true for D, one of the four **r** copies with no C-Text following. More significantly, XII is not in M, the one complete descendant of **m**, the family original which there is no reason to doubt was directly copied from Ax. Thus, although Passus XII happens to survive in manuscripts that in Pr–XI are members respectively of r^1 (RU) and r^2 (J), it probably descends from a manuscript distinct from the source of Ax. This manuscript is unlikely to have been Langland's draft, though the coda by the writer who names himself John But in line 106 could no doubt have been added to a holograph obtained after the poet's death.

§ 68. At first sight Passus XII appears to have two distinct sources, since R and U (as earlier) share an exclusive ancestor (u) neither based on nor used by j, the presumed exemplar of J. Unfortunately, only in the first nineteen lines are all three copies available for comparison, as U lacks the rest of XII through loss of a leaf. In this portion, however, RU have five agreements in error, whereas J has none with either R or U; and each of these also has five individual errors, but J none. The implied superiority of j to u here continues in 20–88, where only R and J remain. For while both copies have about the same total of errors, J omits only one line (55) to R's five (65, 74–6, 78). This proportion is unlike that displayed in Pr–XI,[27] where r^2 (the sub-family to which J belongs) is right about four times more often than r^1. It seems unlikely therefore that in Passus XII u and j derived from sources forming parts of r^1 and r^2 respectively, these in turn from **r**, and **r** from Ax. Against the hypothesis of two sources (u and j), however, it must be noted that of the four cases where R and J have wrong readings (32, 34, 48, 88), one (32) shows what appears to be the same error. This could admittedly be a coincidental substitution, and it may not even be a scribal error if the exemplar was an authorial draft (cf. § 74 below). But slight as this evidence is, it may be just enough to suggest a common original for u and j. For the main counter-argument, that either witness omits *differing* sets of lines, fails if these lines can be shown to have been lost for mechanical reasons. R could easily have omitted 65 by eyeskip from *weye* 64 to *dayes* 66, and 74–6 by eyeskip from *For* 73 to *For* 76. The absence of 55 from J is harder to account for, but eyeskip from *I* 54 to *I* as initial word in 56 is a possible explanation. The most economical explanation of the origin of Passus XII may therefore be that a copy of the poet's manuscript became available to the scribes of u and j well after the archetypal copy of Pr–XI had been made and after the generation both of **r** and its immediate descendants r^1 and r^2. There is little difficulty in presuming that this copy came complete with John But's Appendix (ll. 99–117), written after Langland's death but before that of Richard II (who is referred to in l. 113 as still king); for both R and J were copied not less than fifty years later.

§ 69. The authenticity of Passus XII logically needs examining in relation to metre, style and thought before the question of emending any of its apparently corrupt readings can be addressed, though the two issues are unavoidably connected. John But's addition has here been taken as starting at line 99 and only from that point to the end has the text been treated as an 'Appendix'. This heading Knott-Fowler and Kane apply to the whole of XII. Skeat, by contrast, sees Langland's work as extending to line 105 (100), and it is certainly not beyond belief that the poet 'killed himself off, by way of finishing his poem.'[28] However, while Langland did indeed 'live to re-write it' (ibid.), he did not resort to killing himself off as a way of ending either **B** or **C**. Moreover, a reference by the *author* to 'other works...of Piers the Plowman' in 101–02 would have meant little to readers at this stage in the poem's likely evolution. Lines 99–105 are therefore better seen as part of John But's attempt to honour the dead poet's achievement (which would now have included the **B** and **C** Versions), in addition to wishing well to his soul.

§ 70. Examination of the authenticity of XII 1–98 may begin with the metre, which often appears defective by the norms derived from the poem's primary core-text.[29] Examples are lines 32, which scans *aa / xx*; 36, with a masculine ending; and 62, which is excessively long or, if divided before *welcome,* lacks a lift in the new a-half. But of these, the first admits of easy emendation, while 62 would scan vocalically with the first stave in *on* and the third in *whom* or, if divided, with a conjectural second stave **wye*. The awkward quality of lines such as 17 or 63, moreover, lessens once they are seen as examples of authentic metrical modifications. Others, with 'cognative' alliteration on voiced and unvoiced consonants, like 88 on *k / g* or 50 on *p / b*, present no problem in the light of such **B** lines as Pr 143 or V 208. Finally, features typical of Langland but seldom found in other alliterative poets are the rare line-types IIa at 38 and IIIa at 78, 90; the macaronic at 28; the mute staves at 24 and 56; and the liaisonal staves at 45 and 85 (for explanation of all these terms, see *Intro.* IV §§ 39, 43, 45).

§ 71. Weaknesses of style and expression also appear; yet the rhythm and phrasing of line 5, for instance, are very like those of I 180 and its b-half is not much flatter than those of C XIX 5 or B XVI 60. Among the poet's stylistic idiosyncrasies, the most striking evidenced in XII is the formally-scanning macaronic line with Latin staves composed of scriptural phrases. Examples occur at 28, which is reminiscent of C X 258 // and at 50–2, which splits the Pauline injunction in a manner suggesting B III 339–43. Another such device is wordplay, as at line 30 or in the macaronic 28, where it operates translinguistically across the caesura. A third is the compound name of an allegorical character, as at 82, which resembles that of Piers's wife at VII 70 (and is paralleled outside the canonical versions in Z VII 64–8).[30] A fourth is the citation of a Latin proof-text followed by its translation-paraphrase, as at 19*a*–21 and 22*a*–24, a feature illustrated notably at VIII 95–100. Finally, the passus has several examples of Langland's best manner, like the tersely epigrammatic line 6, the sardonic 85 or the lyrical 96, which anticipates B XVIII 327b in its pararhyming a-half. Throughout, there occur echoes of words and phrases found elsewhere in **A**, or 'pre-echoes' of the later versions. One such is 61, which evokes both IV 143 of **A** and its **Z** parallel. While these could in principle be attributed to an accomplished imitator, they exceed in quality anything found outside the *Piers Plowman* tradition and are more economically explained as authorial.

§ 72. The thought in Passus XII is generally Langlandian in character, though at times not coherent with that found elsewhere in **A**. Two examples are the notions of Wit as a cardinal (15) and of Kynde Wit as a confessor and Scripture's cousin (43). However, the latter character has little to do in **A**, and this Passus XII appearance may have been intended to create a rôle for him. In retrospect, it looks like a transitional step towards **B**, where Kynde Wit is closely associated with Conscience (as at III 284 and XIX 364) but remains a somewhat shadowy figure. Similarly anticipatory of later developments are the handling of the *Omnia-probate* text at 50–2 and the conception of Death and Life at 63–6 as hostile antitypes who prefigure the personages in Passus XX of **B**. But probably the strongest hint of a new direction occurs in the speech of Fever, Death's 'messenger' (as he will later become Kynde's 'forager' in B XX 81), which expands the thought further in lines 81–7.

§ 73. The broader autobiographical situation in Passus XII (which accords with Ymaginatif's allusion to *angres* at B XII 11), unless it is only a dramatic fiction, could reflect circumstances in the author's life that account for both cessation of work on **A** and this first effort to re-commence the poem. The latter was to prove abortive, but it would seem typical of Langland that he should try to conclude Passus XII in a way that deliberately echoes A I 119–21 as well as X 218 and XI 275–8, with a pregnant reference to 'working the word.' While, therefore, lines 99–105 remain arguably of a quality to be what Skeat thought them, 104 is probably better seen as John But's happy compression of B XX 100–05. These lines do not provide as satisfying an end to the passus as do 96–8; but given the uncertainty, they should perhaps be allowed an 'indeterminate' status somewhere between the authorial and the scribal, the authentic and the imitative. They seem good enough to be Langland's, but not too distinctive to be beyond the capacity of But's 'meddling' hand.

§ 74. There remains the further possibility that XII, even if it is the beginning of a formal continuation, might be only a draft and not a 'finished fragment'.[31] Such a presumption would help to explain why it formed no part of Ax's exemplar. For it may be that a copy of XII was preserved by one of the poet's associates after he himself, having shown it to them in its present form, abandoned the continuation in order to start afresh on what became the **B** Version. This is not to deny that, as a piece of authentic Langland, the lines deserve to be published, and under no obviously better heading than that of the final passus of **A**. But a reader unburdened by editorial concerns might reasonably judge the uncompromising last lines of Passus XI effective enough to 'make a good ende' to the version known as **A**: abrupt, but not much more so than those of **B** and **C**.[32]

Conclusion

§ 75. The above account of the text of **A** has begun to demonstrate the extent to which any one version cannot be edited adequately without reference to the others. These versions prove important both for discriminating between competing readings below the archetypal level and for diagnosing and correcting errors in the archetype. And they properly include not only the earlier **Z** (on which see *Z Version* §§ 13–19 below) but also the later **B** and **C**. This is because it is possible that the archetypal traditions of **B** and perhaps even of **C** preceded the generation of Ax and its sub-archetypes, among which **m** at least shows traces of influence from **B**. This possibility will be strengthened at the end of the next section, which deals with the only version of the poem that has for the last half-century been generally regarded as complete.

THE A VERSION: NOTES

1 The view of **A**'s publication taken here, developed in Adams 'Editing *PP* B', pp. 59–63, is adumbrated in Chambers and Grattan 'The Text of *PP*', p. 10; see further Sargent 'Patterns of Transmission', pp. 221–28.

2 Notably in *Pierce the Ploughman's Crede* (late 1390s), *Richard the Redeless* (*c*. 1400) and *Mum and the Sothsegger* (*c*. 1410); cf. *Intro* V § 14 below. One copy of *Pierce* precedes the poem in ms R of **C**, another is appended to ms T of **A**. See Helen Barr, *The Piers Plowman Tradition* for annotated texts and discussion of all three.

3 Skeat's is based on the Vernon ms, those of Knott-Fowler, Kane and the present editor on the Trinity College, Cambridge copy.

4 See § 61 below.

5 Passus XII is discussed separately in §§ 67–74 below.

6 Kane, *A Version*, p. 78; he lists only 210 agreements.

7 Cf. the discussion at § 7 above.

8 Not 230 as in Kane, p. 73.

9 Not 130 as in Kane, p. 77.

10 See *Textual Notes* to C 199–200 for full discussion of the arguments.

11 This supports K–F's recognition (p.26) of a relation (WN)K.

12 See MED s.v. *ditten* v. 3(b)

13 Of these the Apparatus records only Pr 42, III 260 and VII 177, 195 as parts of sets of complex variants.

14 This situation recurs yet more strongly where A fails, and only E and M represent **m**.

15 A conclusion not invalidated by instances *before* Passus X of W agreeing in error with **m**, since none contradict the hypothetical 'inner' grouping AW.

16 This method will be adopted below in discussing the **B** and the **C** traditions.

17 The present editor is much indebted to Charlotte Brewer for pointing out the importance of the **m** group in her unpublished D. Phil thesis 'Some Implications of the Z-Text' and for arguing it with force and acumen in 'Processes of Revision', pp. 71–92.

18 To simplify matters, in what follows reference is made only to major readings.

19 See Appendix, where the numbering should read not '204^a–209^a' but '200^a–205^a'.

20 However d, the postulated group ancestor of TH^{2}ChD, shares eleven errors (five major) with six r^2 mss. Of these notably X 53 (V), II 94 (L), XI 186 (K) and VIII 44 (W) may suggest consultation of one or more r^2 copies, though none is the likely reading of r^2 itself.

21 The relation of r^2 and **m** is thus quite unlike that between the **C** traditions **p** and **t**, which each preserve exclusive right readings but also share a body of separative agreements in error; see *C Version* §§ 37–8.

22 For the difficulty scribes found with *wy*, see the variants at X 89.

23 This is also the form of the **B** mss CrGHF and should doubtless have been recorded in the Apparatus; but the matter is in principle almost undecidable and in practice of no consequence.

24 Though it should be observed that at VIII 61 **m**, represented only by M, has what seems (on the showing of **Z**) the *right* reading, against the unmetrical reading in **r** and the totally corrupt one of Bx.

25 Mechanical explanation would also readily account for the similar loss of VII 211 from r^1 (*make....þe...Make...þe*).

26 Knott-Fowler, *A Version*, p. 149.

27 Cf. § 4 above.

28 *A-Text*, p. 141*.

29 See *Introduction* IV i below and *Appendix I* on the Language and Metre.

30 See III, *Z Version* § 21 below.

31 This is a question to be raised again in connection with **Z** as a whole, and with Pr 95–124 of **C**, which in different ways look like texts awaiting further work.

32 For a balanced discussion see Vaughan 'The Ending(s) of *PP* A', pp. 211–41.

The B Version

i. *The Manuscript Tradition*

§ 1. The **B** Version of *Piers Plowman*, the only one that can be confidently regarded as 'published' by the poet, does not merely continue from where the **A** Version ceased at the end of Passus XI. Langland attempted this in Passus XII of **A** but broke off, for whatever reason (*A Version* §§ 67–74). When he resumed at some time after 1370 it was to write the poem afresh, beginning from line 87 of the Prologue, if not earlier.[1] What the conclusion of B X achieves is to integrate the last lines of A XI by adding a dozen admonitory lines comparing clerks to reeves and then to embark on a new passus (B XI) beginning with the first of **B**'s two 'inner dreams'. This takes up some material from A XII, notably the 'scornful' Scripture whose rebuke precipitates the inner dream. But the formal structure is so novel as to suggest that A XII was put aside in draft (see *A Version* §§ 73–4 above). It is unknown whether Langland took up here rather than at the beginning, but there are two indications that he did so. One is that the revised Prologue preserves nearly every line of **A** with few changes, the other that it doubles **A**'s length not by expanding the text but by adding the wholly new 'Coronation' Scene and the Rat Fable. This latter circumstance makes it at least possible that B Pr 112–210, which must date from after 1376,[2] were inserted later; so there is no need to suppose as many as five years to have elapsed between Langland's abandoning A XII and commencing the **B** Version. On the other hand, there are structural reasons for regarding the new Prologue, which now appears a seamless whole, as planned in its entirety and executed according to plan. For its cautious opening treatment of kingly responsibility, within what appears an allegorised presentation of Richard II's coronation, is to be ironically recalled many passūs later in the sober handling of the theme of royal power at the end of Passus XIX. Any 'naturalistic' discrepancy due to **B**'s King in II–IV being still identifiable as Edward III (as in **A** and **Z**) evidently caused the poet little concern.

§ 2. Given the equally probable allusions to the Papal Wars of 1379 in XIX 431–32 and 445–51, **B** must have been completed no later than about 1380 (see *Intro.* V §§ 7–10, 15). For unless **A** was formally 'released' in an unfinished state, it is likely to be the longer version that the peasant rebel leaders alluded to in 1381, earning the poem a unique place in the political history of the age.[3] And unless Langland was himself one of John Ball's acquaintances, *Piers Plowman* must be supposed to have been made available to a readership wider than the poet's immediate circle. But for such 'publication' to occur, a copy would have had to be made from his corrected holograph as a basis for further such copies. It was this first scribal product (here called '**B-Ø**'), or an early descendant of it ('**B¹**'), and not the holograph, that Langland later used when composing the **C** Version (for supporting evidence see § 5 below). Passūs XXI–XXII of the **C** archetype

('**Cx**') are in fact regarded by the Athlone editors as a pure text of B XIX–XX. If they are right, this portion could have been independently added to the completed revision of C Pr–XX by an 'editor' who prepared the authorial manuscript of **C** for copying after the poet's death. On the other hand (as preferred by the present editor), its divergences from the main B-Text tradition may reflect preliminary touching-up of minor details in B^1. If so, there is no reason why Langland himself should not have positioned these two passūs after the fully-reworked C XX, where they now stand. Either way, they may be taken as in effect the last portion of the **B** manuscript he had worked from throughout his final revision. On this supposition, the second scribal copy, B^1, may be most economically identified as the direct basis of C XXI–XXII, into which some further corruptions will have been introduced by the scribe of Cx. Notwithstanding these, the concluding section is a unique dual source for the end of the **B** and the **C** Versions. To help keep this special feature in mind, the *substantive content* of the text in the last two passūs of the **C** tradition may be designated '**B^2**.'

§ 3. The third early scribal copy that must be posited was the manuscript from which all the extant copies of **B** ultimately descend. This archetypal text, referred to hereafter as **Bx**, is derived, like B^1, at one or at most two removes from the holograph. The reality of all three copies so far postulated is not open to serious doubt, as will be briefly argued here (and more fully in §§ 70ff below) from a comparison of Bx in the final two passūs with the C-Text form of them, B^2. To begin with, the existence of the first scribal copy, B-Ø, is proved by the twelve major and three minor errors shared by Bx and B^2, which must both descend from it, B^2 immediately from B^1. Secondly, that Bx was not derived from B^1 is shown by its freedom from B^2's six major and three minor errors. Finally, that B^2 was not derived from Bx is clear from its lacking the latter's twenty-two certain errors (all major). On the evidence of these two passūs alone, it seems that Langland's revision-manuscript B^1 will have been about twice as accurate as Bx. In principle, most of the disjunctive errors here ascribed to B^1 (as already recognised at §2) could have been introduced by the copyist of Cx; for B^1's character can only be inferred from what the **C** tradition preserves as B^2. But the wrong readings shared by Bx and B^2 support the simpler (and the only logically necessary) explanation: that when Langland was working on **C**, he had access neither to his holograph of **B** nor to B-Ø but only to a copy containing at least the recognised B^1 errors.[4]

§ 4. A brief comparative analysis of C XXI–XXII and B XIX–XX (given in more detail at §§ 72–4 below) reveals that the postulated first scribal copy B-Ø, assuming it lacked the individual errors of B^1 and Bx, will have possessed only about one wrong reading in every 58 lines. It must therefore have been produced by a more accurate scribe than those who made either of the other early copies of *Piers Plowman* that are directly or indirectly accessible. For B^1 appears to have made about one error in every 35 lines and Bx one in roughly every 20. Even taking into account the shared B^{1}Bx errors that must derive from B-Ø, this last figure, confirmed by the general showing of the preceding Pr–XVIII, indicates how badly the text was corrupted during its initial stages of transmission (Bx's average error-rate over the whole poem is about one in twelve lines). This is important, because Bx is the only text to which analysis of a 'logically positive' type (see II, §§ 12–13) can attain. For the editor prepared to rely on the linear postulate, it becomes possible to recover some 60 of B^1's probable readings in the passūs up to // C XI (if only partially, because of revision) through examining the joint witness of **C** and **A** in this section. But in the approximately 3200 lines of **B** from where **A** ends to where the B^2 witness begins (B XIX / C XXI), correction of Bx's errors must take the form either of simple preference for a **C** reading unsupported by **A**, or of emendation, mild or drastic. If it is quite possible that B[1], and even perhaps B-Ø, was not thoroughly checked by Langland against his holograph, it seems overwhelmingly likely that Bx did not receive systematic authorial checking,[5] with or without reference to either of these.

§ 5. That the immediate exemplar of the archetype may not have been B-Ø is suggested by the high incidence of corruption in Bx by comparison with that in Ax and Cx, which points to a stage of copying between it and B-Ø. This presumption is not invalidated by two unusual facts about Bx's production. Firstly, while in Pr–X the error-rate is about one in every eight or nine lines, in XI–XX (and omitting for the moment Passus XVI) it falls to about one in seventeen. This discrepancy suggests *prima facie* that two scribes were responsible for copying the text, the later being nearly twice as accurate as the earlier. Secondly, the excepted passus, XVI, has only two certain archetypal errors in the entire course of its 275 lines, a figure representing an eightfold superiority to the work of the better of the two postulated scribes. Two explanations of this latter feature come to mind. One is that XVI was produced by a third archetypal copyist, something that seems antecedently improbable because of the level of accuracy it evinces. A second is that the passus was corrected by the poet, though why he checked a specimen of the scribe's work from so late a stage in the poem or why the 'better' Bx scribe did not take its lesson to heart remain unclear. However, if the latter was identical with the scribe of Pr–X, and he *did*, the relative superiority of XI–XX would be a measure of his improved accuracy. For it is notable that nearly all Bx's spurious lines occur in the section by the less accurate first scribe (whether the same man or not), although one more (exactly similar) such line appears in the postulated second scribe's portion, at XIX 373. It is therefore possible that the originator of the spurious lines was not the 'careless' first copyist but the scribe of another, earlier manuscript intermediate between Bx and B-Ø, which may be called **B-Øa**. If this explanation is right, the authorial corrections to Passus XVI would have been made in B-Øa and incorporated from it into Bx by the second scribe. In any event, the spurious lines, including the pair at XIX 373, are unparalleled in Cx; so none of them can have been present in B-Ø (the logically inferred common source of Bx and B[1]), unless they were all afterwards removed in **C**.

§ 6. From circumstances like these arise the major textual problems of the **B** Version, and some of those found in **C** as well. Langland's holograph must have passed out of his hands for copying; and when he began work on **C**, neither it nor B-Ø was available to him for revision, or to scribes in the archetypal and sub-archetypal traditions for correction of their copies. Access by some scribes to just such a superior lost source as B-Ø is, however, posited by the Athlone editors to account for individual readings in manuscripts like F and G that they and (in some cases) the present editor judge superior on comparison with Bx. But as argued below (§§ 28 and 46), such readings are better explained as due to contamination from one or more of the other versions of the poem that had become available by the time these copies' ancestors were produced. At any rate, nothing superior to B[1], a manuscript more accurate than Bx but still disfigured by probably not fewer than sixty errors,[6] seems to have been to hand when Langland began revising the poem for the last time. But whatever its exact pre-history, for Pr–XVIII Bx alone is directly accessible, through the agreed readings of its eighteen surviving descendants, or indirectly through critical reconstruction from them. And it is the high rate of error in Bx that forms the main challenge for the editor of the **B** Version.

125

ii. *The two families of* **B** *manuscripts*

§ 7. The Bx readings are (near)-unanimously preserved in some 70% of the poem (= 5126 out of 7276 lines).[7] In another 1700 lines (about 23% of the whole) two strongly contrasted traditions emerge, here called α and β, which descend independently from the archetypal manuscript, as Kane and Donaldson have argued.[8] In these lines, the Bx reading may usually be discriminated with tolerable certainty in either α or β, often with guidance from the parallel text of **A**, **C** and **Z**, severally or in agreement. In the remaining 450 lines, about 7% of the total work, where individual manuscript readings cut across both families, Bx may still be recoverable, though with lessened certainty, in the light of the parallel texts or, where these are not available, by tracing the probable direction of scribal variation.

§ 8. As with the **A** Version, the two families of **B** are very disproportionately represented. Only two witnesses to the α tradition survive, R and F, and while neither derives from the other, both in their different ways are seriously wanting. R is physically defective for about 10% of the whole poem, while F is sophisticated throughout and shows contamination from **A** and possibly also **C** (see § 46 below). Thus, though its internal structure is simpler than that of **m** in the **A** tradition, α offers a special problem in being the *sole* witness to about 187 lines of **B**, some of which have no other-version parallel. Similarly, β preserves some 200 lines lacking from the other family; but by contrast with α it has, like the **r** family of **A**, a complex internal structure. Thus at least four independent copies of β were made; these are represented by the sub-family here called γ (consisting of the twelve manuscripts WHmCrGYOC²CBmBoCotS) and by three unrelated copies L, M and H. Of the former, the mid-sixteenth century witness S, which is substantively very corrupt and modernised throughout, has not been collated and will not be further referred to in the main text. The remaining eleven γ manuscripts, with BmBoCot denoted by the sigil B for their exclusive common ancestor, fall into two groups, neither of which derives from the other. These are WHmCr and GYOC²CB, signified respectively by the group sigils w and g. There is solid evidence that one member of the latter group, G, derives directly from g by a separate line of descent and the remaining five from an intermediary copy of g, here called y (§§ 11–39 below).

§ 9. Owing to their independent character, none of the four main lines of transmission from the β family-original can be eliminated, as each contains some readings which may represent β and thence Bx. The source γ is likely to have been copied directly from β, but in the case of L, M and H an intermediary stage, here denoted by the lower-case form of each manuscript's sigil (*l, m, h*), may be posited (§§ 30–39 below). Of these individual copies, L is both complete and substantively the best, as Skeat recognised; but its relative lack of grammatical regularity and linguistic consistency renders it unsuitable as a basis for the text. Superior in these respects is W, the soundest γ representative, which was used by Wright and K–D and is adopted here. The present edition of **B** thus resembles that of **A** in taking as its base a copy from the larger manuscript family (β). Its errors are corrected by reference to the smaller (α) where this seems to preserve Bx, by restoration from the parallel texts in the other versions, and by reconstruction and conjecture when more direct evidence is lacking. The text is thus presented in the language of the earliest 'complete' B-Text copy to survive. As in the Athlone edition, the α and β traditions are understood as forming two partial and imperfect witnesses to a unitary **B** Version of *Piers Plowman* intermediate between **A** and **C**.[9] The present edition does not revert to Skeat's minimal interventionism; but while acknowledging its indebtedness to the methods and conclusions of Chambers, Blackman and Kane-Donaldson, often differs from them in its approach both to identifying originality and to emending archetypal corruptions.

§ 10. In the light of the above discussion, the inferential relationships between the collated **B** manuscripts and their hypothetical lost originals may be expressed in the form of the following diagram, which slightly modifies the one given on p. lvii of *Sch²* (an early, significantly different stemma is offered by Blackman, and a recent, closely similar one by Adams).[10]

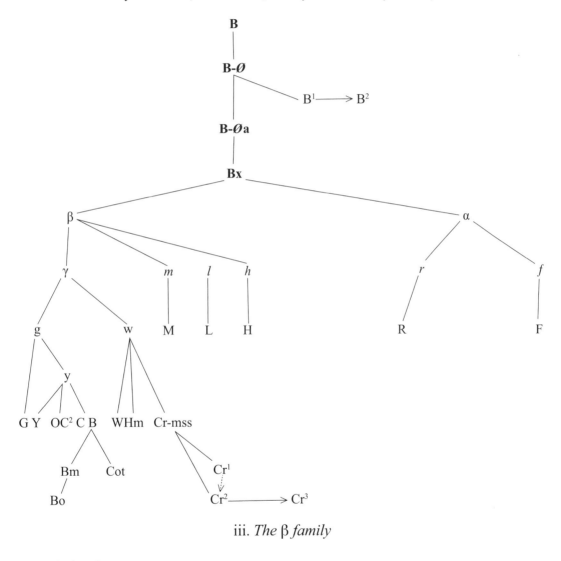

iii. *The β family*

(a) *sub-family γ*

§ 11. The two divisions of β are γ and the three manuscripts L, M and H, which do not share an exclusive common ancestor. The eleven collated members of γ may be thought of as a 'sub-family' rather than a 'group' because, first, they divide in turn into two distinct groups, **w** and **g**; and second, within g may be identified a further five-member group, *y,* itself containing at least two sub-groups, OC^2 and CB. The members of γ are virtually complete except for O, which lacks a quarter of Passus XVII, and B, the three constituents of which attest in Pr–II a C-Text linked by 110 lines of A-Text to the B-Text that follows from III 1. The sub-family γ is thus even more firmly attested than r^I of **A**, although, unlike u and d of **A**, its two major constituent groups w and g begin to be decisively differentiated only about a third of the way into Passus V.

§ 12. The distinctive variants of γ are made up first of the agreed readings of its component groups in some 38 instances, fourteen of them major, and two important (marked *). A further 25, of which 12 are major, are also found in one other β witness M,[11] the main exemplar of which was not a γ copy. In the following list of readings, a minus sign before a sigil indicates that a member manuscript diverges from γ in possessing the presumed β reading, which is judged correct unless otherwise noted.

Major II 162. V 203, 501, 542. VI 227, 326. VII 114. XV 63. XVI 8. *XVII 184b–85a, *286 *om;*-Cr, 304. XVIII 349. XX 8 -Cr; β in *error. With* M: V 351 (*over erasure*). VI 326 (*alt. to read with* L). IX 98a. XII 245 (*over eras.*). *XIII 283b–84a *om.* XIV 1, 239. XV 398, 506. XVI 50. XVIII 198. XX 287. **Minor** IV 54. V 210, 228, 446, 596, 631, 635 -Cr. VI 77, 145 -Cr, 248 -Y. VII 16, 71, 73a, 101. VIII 21, 28, 90. XI 48. XII 144. XIII 223, 374 -C. XV 91, 452. XVIII 354. *With* M: VIII 127 (*by erasure*). IX 190. XIV 146. XV 36, 396, 494. XVI 27, 60, 214 -W. XVII 15, 104 -Cr, 166 -Hm. XVIII 354.

On the assumption that the non-exclusive readings have entered M through collation with a w-type source (§§ 33–5 below), γ may thus be considered established by a total of 63 agreements in error, 26 of them major. It also has a major right reading at V 261 (in M added over erasure) and five minor right readings at V 446 (-B), ?VI 8 (*om* CB), XII 148, XIII 191 (-CB+F) and XIV 106 (added in M). Additionally, several such others appear, whether preserved by pure descent from γ or by correction, in one or other of its constituent groups w and g. A few appear in only some of their members, and in the case of G, OC^2, C and B this is almost certainly by correction from another version. The sub-family therefore cannot be eliminated.

Group **w**

§ 13. The first of the γ groups, **w**, contains the base-manuscript of this edition and (as earlier with group t of the **A** Version) accordingly receives an extended treatment here. The original of w cannot have derived from any member of the other γ group g, since W is older than all of these; or from g itself, since it is free of the latter's modernisations. Although half a dozen disjunctive variants appear before Passus VII, w's agreement with g in all major readings indicates that it preserved γ pretty faithfully up to that point. This may suggest that a second scribe was responsible for the text from there on (a situation similar to that posited for Bx at § 5 above). The group w is established by some 90 exclusive agreements in error, about 35 of them major and three important. This total includes twelve shared by M, which may nonetheless also be accepted as criterial for w since most of them have visibly entered this copy by alteration, addition or erasure, from a source very like the lost w-type manuscript used by Crowley.

Major VII 97. X 210, *246a *om*, 415, 437. XI 20, 130, 257, 339. XII 21, 47, *103 *om*, 209, 252. XIII 36, 49, 81, 96, 134, 352. XIV 23. XV 96, 152, 330, *373 *om*. XIX 78. XX 260. *With* M: VI 200 +?G. X 61. XI 398 -Cr+Bm. XIII 411. XIV 179, 300. XV 200, 224, 502. XVI 125 +F. XVIII 85, 109, 299.

Minor Pr 21. I 124. II 40. IV 29, 131, 189. V 81. VII 189. VIII 100, 128. IX 155. X 52, 205, 251, 252, 264*a*, 395, 433, 443. XI 80, 87, 150, 184, 219, 253, 298, 315, 332. XII 78, 204, 239. XIII 39, 73, 156, 205, 355, 395, 429. XIV 123, 226, 319. XV 549. XVI 43. XVII 229. XIX 276. XX 260. *With* M: I 6 +G. X 177. XV 8, 157, 455. XVIII 347.[12]

It is very probable also that in eight readings convergence of group w with the α manuscript F is coincidental: X 261, XIII 94, XVI 125 (major), X 450, XV 67, XVI 213, 255, XIX 391 (minor). The same holds of two readings shared respectively with Y (V 631) and with Cot (XI 323).

§ 14. Within w a further relation (WHm)Cr may be discerned on the basis of 55 exclusive agreements of W and Hm, some 18 of them major:[13]

Major III 36. XI 412. XV 223, 424 (*over erasure* Hm), 604 (Grekes] Iewis). XVII 20, 133, 167, 176, *210 (*l. om*), 231. XVIII 158, 224, 425. XIX 216. XX 114, 191, 235. **Minor** I 70. V 17, 31. VI 124. VII 97. X 260*a*, 268. XI 181. XII 132, 191, 239. XIII 93, 328. XV 82. XVI 78, 209. XVII 25, 120. XVIII 105, 172, 203, 208, 216, 331, 332. XIX 117, 124, 146, 169, 186, 187, 212, 292, 379, 383, 471. XX 234.

This group is not seriously questioned by the 20 agreements of *HmCr* (listed in *K–D*, p. 39). All are trivial save two, VIII 63 *wilde*] *wyde* (possibly a visual error) and XVI 22 *top*] *crop* (a synonym-substitute unconsciously suggested by 42 below), both probably coincidental.

§ 15. More challenging to WHm is the group *WCr* based on some 50 agreements, 15 of them major:[14]

Major V 195. IX 118 +M, *corr.*, 144. X 27. XIV 171, 267–8. XV 15, 107, 156, 410, 552 +M *added*. XVI 87, 204. XVIII 258. XIX 186. **Minor** Pr 77. I 126. III 222. IV 175. V 9, 248 +M *over* erasure, F, 560, 598. VI 65. IX 79. XI 82, 246, 348. XII 187. XIII 179 +M *over erasure*, 230, 241 +M *added*, 283, 284. XIV 288 +M, 308, 309, 317 +M *added*. XV 133, 139, 209, 396/7, 413, 601. XVI 159, 211. XVII 167, 241[1,2]. XVIII 74, 85 +M, 266, 312. XX 255 +F.

Of the minor agreements here, several illustrate common coincidental errors. These include spelling in XVI 159, XVII 167 and the substitution of a synonym (*mid* XV 139, XVII 241, both possible w readings from which Hm has varied) or of a contextually commoner expression (XVIII 74, 312), and all could be coincidental. Amongst the major examples IX 144 illustrates haplographic loss of *fore-* by *for > fer-* attraction, XVI 87 dittography and 204 unconscious syntactical variation occasioned by failure to grasp the metrical structure, while XVIII 258 is a visual error (a misexpanded contraction). XIV 267–68 results from smoothing of unusual word-order and XV 156 seems the unconscious replacement of a less familiar term in this collocation. In XV 410 the form of Hm suggests that w could have read as WCr, while in the most indicative instance XIV 171, *hem greue* could have been intelligently or inadvertently omitted by Hm. Thus, although slight doubt remains, it seems likely that WCr, despite its size, is not a genetic group like WHm. In the case of M's agreements, however, a direct relation must be accepted at least for the half-dozen by visible correction, a conclusion congruent with M's other agreements with w (= γ) recorded in § 12 (see also § 35 on M). The general situation regarding w may be contrasted with that of the **A** manuscripts TCh discussed at *A Version* § 12, where (unlike Hm here) H[2], the dissident member of t's postulated genetic TH[2] sub-group, must have been corrected from a copy of another (sub)-family. In the present case, the corrected member of w seems to be Cr, not a partner in a genetic pair *WCr but a copy free of several presumed w errors retained in WHm, which are such a pair.[15]

§ 16. The group cannot be eliminated, however; for w or its component copies, severally or in pairs and sometimes with other-version support, attest solely some 10 readings that seem original and a further 17 (in square brackets here) where it is accompanied by one other manuscript or α.

Major w: [V 423 +GC]. X 57 +**AC**. XI 144 +**C**. WHm: XI 287 +**C**. XIX 321 +Cr³**C**. [XX 117 +F**C**]. W: XV 461; [III 283 +GC] (*both by felicitous conjecture*). I 54 +**ZAC**. Cr: I 152 (? *by correction from* **C**). [III 342 +GC]. Cr³: XII 270 (? *by conjecture*; *no // in* **C**). **Minor** w: II 90 +**C**. [VI 201 +GC]. [XIII 334 (+M *corr.*, F**C**)]. WHm: Pr 59 +**AC**. [XII 182 +F**C**]. [XVII 137 +α**C**]. [XIX 9 +L**C**]. WCr: [XIV 257 +Mα]. [XIX 437 (+F**C**)]. W: XV 552 +**C**. [V 638 +GA**C**. XVIII 234 +R**C**]. XIX 111 +**C**: *not adopted but possibly original*. Cr: [I 176 +GZA**C**. II 35 +Y**C**. IV 94 +H**C**. XIII 223 +FM (*by erasure*) **C**].

All the agreed readings of w are recorded in the main Apparatus and those of WHm, WCr and W that are not included there are given in the Appendix in Vol. I.

Group **g**

§ 17. The second γ group, **g**, is a more complex unit having two lines of transmission from its postulated original. One is represented by **G**, its most important member, the other by a postulated source **y** from which the other seven manuscripts YOC²CBmBoCot exclusively descend, with further units formed within them. Neither g nor its sub-group y uniquely preserve an original reading by pure descent from the archetype or by other-version correction. Instead, they illustrate how rapidly the text was corrupted in the generation after the poem was composed.[16] In the discussion, greatest attention will be given to G, whose medieval ancestor adopted from an other-version source (**A**) some unique readings with a good claim to be original.

§ 18. The group **g** is established by some 230 agreements, about 100 of them major. Though strict reckoning yields around 210, this exceeds K–D's 'more than 190' (p. 52), even excluding readings where one member is absent through individual divergence or defect in the manuscript. In some 30 more instances, g's agreement with one other witness (of either family) seems coincidental, not genetic. In the list below, square brackets mark these, but not its 21 agreements with Cr²³. This is because Cr¹ was the source of Cr² (on which Cr³ is based), and the copy that Cr² was collated with was probably later than g itself. The group reads near-uniformly with w up to about V 234 (see § 13), a fact suggesting that γ itself or an accurate copy furnished the earlier part of w and g before two new sources were used that produced the distinctive text of each.

§ 19. The main characteristics of g are of a kind found in the sub-archetypes and the archetype as well as in its descendant y. These are, firstly, the omission of some 16 whole and four half-lines from γ and the insertion of four spurious lines. Next, g tends to simplify the style by omitting words, e.g. adjectives (XI 212, XVI 185, XVIII 36), adverbs (VIII 127, XII 143, XIII 131–32 [twice]), and especially 're-inforcing' pronouns (V 572, VI 50, 150, VIII 114 and XV 71). Signs of hasty copying are the repeated truncation of the stave-phrase, as at IX 75 and XVII 285, and the re-writing, virtually as prose, of IX 95–6. A tendency to modernise occasions substitution of *he* for *wye* at V 533, *barne* for *burn* at XI 361, XVI 180 and 263, *sweuene* for *metels* at XI 6 (with which compare the misunderstanding of this noun's number at XI 86), and *make* for β *macche* (itself an error for the rare and archaic *mette*). The g scribe often attempts to make the text more explicit, e.g. at X 159, 194, 467; XIV 2; XV 314; XX 163, 178 and 256) and sometimes changes the sense in seeking greater emphasis, e.g. at X 248; XI 49 and XIII 43, while not hesitating to remove characteristic rhetorical repetitions, as at X 287 and XVII 322. These features, taken together with g's omissions and spurious lines, indicate a group-original later than w, though not derived from it, since it contains, for instance, two lines w omits (XII 103 and XV 373) that were presumably in g. The manuscript is unlikely to have been much older than its earliest descendants, Bm and Bo, which date from *c*.1400.

§ 20. In the following list of line-references for all g variants,[17] a minus sign denotes agreement of a member with the other β copies wLM, a plus sign agreement of a non-member with g (these readings are in square brackets):

Major [V 255 +F], 433 -B. VI 23. IX 25, 41, 92*a*, 95–6, 97, [181 +Cr^{23}]. [X 23 +Cr^{23}], 47 -CB, 89, 194, 205 (Oure Lord] god), 219, 248, [251 (helþe) sake; +Cr^{23})], 257, 287, 337^{1,2}, *403, 438, 456^{1,2,3}, [466 +W], 467. XI 5, [6 +M], [47 +Cr^{23}], [49^{1,2} +Cr^{23}], [82 +Cr], 212, 291 -B, [339 +M], 358, [361 +Cr]. XII 16, 34, 50, [74 +Cr], 143, 154 (*spur. l. foll.*), 192. XIII 6, 15, 43, 52, 56, 132, 153 (*different. error* Y), 187 -Y, 279, 317, 343. XIV 2, 3, [70 +F], 111, [120 +Cr^{23}; *diff. error* CB], 277, [286 +Cr^{23}], [329 +F]. XV [23 +Hm], 66, [71 +Cr^{23}], 229 (*spur. l. foll.*), 253–4, 314, 316, [556 +Hm], 587 (knewe] knowe). XVI 30 -Y, 81 (CB *def.*), 126, 180, 182 (*om* OC^{2}), 185, *210. XVII 123–4 (O *def.*), [285 +F], 322, 351. XVIII [9 +Cr^{23}], 11, 24, 221, 259 (*spur. l. foll.*), *279 (*spur. l. foll.*), 294 (*spur. l. foll.*). XIX *3–4, *5, 149 (hym] it), 167, *219b–27a *ll. om*, 228, [239 +Cr^{23}], *255, *287 (*def.* O), *340. XX [48 -C^{2}+R], *95–6, 163, [182 +Cr^{23}], 191, 236 (-B; *diff. error*), 236 (siþen] seyen), 256, 346. **Minor** V [393 +Cr^{23}], [256 +F], 572. VI 50 -B, [51 +Cr^{23}], 81, 143, 150, [167 +Cr^{3}], 183, 273. VII [152 +Hm]. VIII 50, 54, [97 þat] the +Cr^{23}], 114. IX 41 seide] seith, [91 +Cr^{23}], [154 +Cr^{23}], 204. X [18 +a], 25*a*, 34, 88*a*, 94 (Nouȝt] And n.), 97, 159, 188^{1}, 188^{2} (neuere] no), 198, 206, 246, 309, 320 (wiþ] &), [327*a* +M], [355 +Cr], [376 +F]. XI 32, 46, 74, 87 (hem] *om*), 134, 146, [141 +F], 187, [199 +F], 209, 231, 252, 262, 321, 340, 378, 417. XII 49 (may] myght), 92, 102, 139, 159, 200, 226, [256 +F], 268, [273 +Cr^{23}]. XIII 34, 47, 79, 95, 120, [131 +M], [239 +R], 301, 308, [334 +L], 375. XIV 4, 14, 21, 46 (*diff. error* CB), 55, 86, [93 +Cr^{23}], 96, 111, 162, 191, 201, 244, 269, 293 (wiþ] *om*), 331. XV 50, 87, 118 -Y, 124, 130, 160, 195, 200, 252, 271, [327^{1} +F], 327^{2} (ise] þe), 370, 376^{1,2}, 402, 509, 554, 581, 582, 604. XVI 69 (CB *def.*), 176, [181 +Cr^{23}], 186, 212, 248, 264. XVII 45, 46, 315. XVIII 35, 36, 83, [86 +Cr], 109, 145, [171 +Cr^{23}], 179, 2559, 364 (hast] *om*), 386. XIX 66, [121 +Cr^{23}], 135, 206, 318 (*def.* O), 320 (*def.*O), 364, [462 +Cr^{23}], [460 +Cr, *def.* B]. XX 18, 178 -O, 305.

§ 21. Group g cannot be eliminated; for though the whole unequivocally attests no unique right readings, such are preserved severally by individual members and sub-groups, whether directly or through correction from outside the **B** tradition (see §§ 22ff below). In the following list of eight where g is accompanied by one manuscript or α, a *plus* denotes support from outside g or from another version:

Major X 124 +M**A**. XI 130 +MR**C**. **Minor** V 533 +F**ZAC**, 552 +α**ZAC**. IX 11 -CB+F. XI 81*a* +Hm. XIX 15 +Hm**C**. XX 366 +Cr**FC**.

Sub-group **y**

§ 22. The first large sub-division of g consists of YOC^{2}CB(=BmBoCot). These seven manuscripts descend from **y**, an early copy of g postulated on the basis of 75 agreements in error not found in the remaining member G, which shares its 155 other distinctive variants. There are 28 major and 48 minor readings, tabulated here as for g above, and eight more (two of them major) where y is randomly accompanied by one or two other manuscripts.

Major V [111 -C+MCr^{23}], 166 (hele] holde), 254, [*268 (*spur. l. foll.*, +Cr^{23}], 283, 296^{1,2} [*spur. l. foll.*, +Ht], [331 (*spur. l. foll.* +Cr^{23}Ht], 397 (fourty] fifty), 416, 437, [540 +Cr^{23}], [557 +F], 560 (*spur. l. foll.*) VI 47*a* (*spur. l. foll.*), 66, 129^{1,2}, 151, 216, 287, 288 (Lammesse] herueste), 294, 298, *307–8 (-CB, *ll. om*), *312. VII 30, 119^{1,2}. XV 593. XVII 17, 179 (-C^{2}, O *def.*). **Minor** Pr 141 (-B, *def.*). II [92 +L-B *def.*]. III 209 (a^{2}] the). V 131 (to^{2}] *om*), 132 (þoruȝ] by), [142 +a], 156 (of] with). 176, 234, 256, 262, 290, 294, 335, [367 +Cr^{23}], 395, 481, [538 +Cr^{23}], 587, 593, 594, 629 (any] the). VI 45, [48 +Cr^{23}], 50, 55 (s. þe k.] *trs*), 57, 67, [147 +Cr^{3}], 189, 200, 236, 257, 265, [306 +F-CB (*l. om*)], 309, [315 +F**C**], 317. VII 11, 44, [56 +Hm], 58, 69, 83, 123. VIII 81. X [85 -C+R], [205 +M], 439. XII 132, 176. XIII 77, 191. XV 7, 78. XVI [182 +Cr^{23}]. XVII 29, 200 (+**C**, *def.* O). XVIII 11. XIX 267.

It seems likely from the eight agreements of Cr^{23} with y, together with the 21 listed under g, that Cr^2 was collated at some stage with a manuscript of the y branch (see below). The sub-group y contains a unique minor right reading at VII 56 (-C+C) and two others (also minor) with F accompanying, at II 120 and VI 152. In addition, some members have right readings in two major instances, YOC^2Cr^{23} at IV 10 and GYC^2 at XVIII 160, both by presumed correction severally from **C**. Finally, there are about a dozen instances (noted below) where constituent members or pairs preserve an apparently superior reading. The sub-group therefore cannot be eliminated.

§ 23. A further division of y is into $<Y(OC^2)>$ and $<CB>$, each of which has an exclusive ancestor. K–D's judgement (p. 45) that YOC^2 probably form a genetic group is acceptable on balance; but it is noteworthy that amongst the 33 variants supporting it, only three appear significant. Of these, VI 307–08 may be reasonably inferred to represent y (CB missing the lines). In V 111 agreement of Y with OC^2 in *myn herte akeþ* could be a coincidental alteration to prose order of CB's ancestral reading *⁎akeþ myn herte* (with which M coincides), while C substitutes a synonym *werkes* for the verb. Of Y's other agreements with OC^2 (listed in *K–D*, pp 44–5) the most impressive is XX 63 *siþ...was] than...to be* (so likewise Cr^{23}). Taken with the important corrected reading at IV 10 (also shared by Cr^{23}), this may indicate that the $<Y(OC^2)>$ ancestor was the very y-type manuscript consulted by Cr^2. But other OC^2Cr^{23} agreements, such as their omission of line XVI 202, suggest rather that this copy will have been the immediate ancestor only of the pair $<OC^2>$.[18] The individual manuscript **Y** cannot be eliminated, as it attests, possibly by contamination from **C**, one major right reading at Pr 171 and a minor one at VI 207 (confirmed by **ZAC**), a minor reading at II 35 shared by Cr, and a major one at XVIII 160 shared by GC^2.

§ 24. The two copies associated with Y form the most substantially attested pair after the α manuscripts R and F (§ 44 below), with some 330 agreements, 78 of them major. This is despite O's being seriously defective in XVII and XIX. OC^2 seem to have had as their exclusive common ancestor an inaccurate transcript of the same manuscript from which Y was copied. Its main features are a spurious line instead of XV 122, two added Latin lines after Pr 39 and XI 277 (the latter = VII 87) and sixteen omitted lines: I 31, 135; II 66; V 174; ⁎VII 174–81 (on the Papal power, possibly censored); VIII 7, 24; XI 264 and XVI 171. Major errors of OC^2 are found in Cr^{23} at XVI 202 (a line probably lost coincidentally through homœoteleuton) and in Cr^3 at VI 219 (*false men] fawti man*) and 226 (*god] go*). Since the OC^2 readings are of little interest, only a few are cited incidentally in the Apparatus as part of the complex variants of a lemma.

Pr 34, 67, 152. I 31, 37, 155, 206. II 80 +H. III 258, 284. V 181. VI 77, 198. VII 138, ⁎174–81. X 50, 441. XI 49, 150, 284*a*, 402, 419. XII 17, 42, 60, 192. XIII 50, 135, 139, 223, 265. XIV 52, 171. XV 122, 126–7, 374, 528. XVI 110, 182*a*. C^2 *only*: II 3. IV 145, 193 (+M). V 179. VIII 101. X 153 (*a.h.*). XIV 101. XV 39. XVIII 12, 172. XIX 113–14. XX 256, 260, 261. *Individual* C^2 *readings cited at* X 139, 348 *show contamination from* **A**.

The sub-group OC^2 cannot be eliminated, however, as it or one member contains (mostly by benign contamination) seven unique right readings, four in which it is accompanied by one other g manuscript and eight supported by α:

Major IX 4 +**AC**. XI 398 +α. XIII [411 +B; *corrected from* C]. **Minor** Pr 159. VI 284 +**ZAC**. X 28 +**C**. [XV 577 +Cr]. *With* α: V 186 +**AC**. VI 80 +**C**. VII 93 +**ZAC**. XIII 50 +C, [255*a* +CotC]. XIV 41 +C, 131*a*. O *only*: **Major** XIX 181 +**C**. **Minor** [XV 317*a* +αC]. [XIX 46 +HmC]. C^2 *only*: **Major** I 200 +**ZAC**. [XVII 198*a* +CrC]. XVIII 160 +**C**.

Here there is a notable incidence of agreement with α and further agreement with it *in error* at XIII

97, 125, 135, 313 (+C), XIV 306 (+B), XV 319 (+G). OC²'s collation with a copy from the other family in the area of XIII–XIV, though antecedently not very likely, therefore cannot be ruled out.

§ 25. The other large sub-group in y is <CB>, made up of **C** and the three closely-related manuscripts BmBoCot, represented only in III–XX, which is given the group-sigil **B** by K–D. The genetic nature of <CB> is not seriously challenged by the existence of 87 agreements between B and a member of the α family, F. All but a half dozen of these K–D adequately account for as coincidental; but it is hard to agree with them that, had the errors of <CB> been significantly fewer in number, its genetic character might well have seemed less clear than that of BF, a group they (rightly) consider random. For they ignore the character of these errors which, even if reduced to the number of BF (i.e. by about two thirds), would still contain over thirty major examples, five times as many as those in BF. This example shows the importance of considering the quality and not just the quantity of readings when seeking to determine the genetic relationships of the manuscripts. For it is these agreements that will have been least credibly produced by 'convergent and specifically coincident variation' (*K–D*, p. 48). The group <CB> is established by some 263 agreements, of which about 100 are major. Its original would therefore appear to have been copied by a very careless scribe, who omitted 77 lines and 18 half-lines, his irresponsibility towards the exemplar being shown by the unusually large proportion of major errors. The readings of <CB> have even less intrinsic interest than OC²'s and are only occasionally cited as part of complex sets of variants.

III 154, 205. IV 33, 57, 67. V 422. VI 8, 280, 300, 303, 307. VII 27. IX 129, 130. X 124, 125, 353a. XI 370. XIII 415. XIV 101, 120, 141. XVI 30, 56–91. XVIII 161, 348, 389, 390. XIX 94.

But <CB>'s members severally contain seven unique right readings; and the group attests two supported by the other family and six more with support from one or two other manuscripts of both families:

Major [VIII 127 +α]. **C** *only*: XIX 391 +**C**. B *only*: [III 6 +αZA**C**]. [X 172 +Hm?G**AC**]. XIII 2 (+**C**-Cot; *from* Bo, *over erasure* Bm), [411 +OC²**C**]. XX 378 (+**C**-Bo; Bm *def.*). **Minor** [VI 128 +Cr**ZAC**; *def.* Cot]. [VIII 83 +α]. [XIV 198 +R]. B *only*) [III 3 +H**C**], [11 -BoCot+R**ZAC**], 12 +**ZAC**, [251 +HR], 322 -BoCot+**C**. VI 257 +**ZAC**, [277 +GF**ZAC**]. XIII 2 -Cot+**C**. **C** *only*: [II 113 +HmH**ZAC**].

It therefore cannot be eliminated.

§ 26. Among the two major components of this sub-group of y, the single manuscript C is cited only in the following instances as part of a complex set of variants:

Pr 29, 46. II 115, [130 +H]. III 150. IX 149, 169. XI 84, 125, 374. XII 228, 234. XV 69. XVI 252. XVII 214, 337a. XVIII 109.

§ 27. The other (composite) 'member' of this sub-group is **B**, of which the three constituent manuscripts (**Bm**, **Bo** and **Cot**) share over 800 agreements in error and may be safely taken to descend from a single exclusive ancestor. In the Apparatus 'B' is thus the sigil which follows readings where all three manuscripts agree, but it is preceded by a query sign when one or two diverge. Within the grouping, *BmBo* have 123 agreements, some 22 of them major, and *BoCot* 130, about 34 major, but *BmCot* only five, all minor. On grounds of date, Bm and Bo cannot derive from Cot; and while the former two are roughly coæval, there are codicological reasons for thinking Bo 'an incomplete copy of Bm'.[19] The latter appears to have been produced in a professional workshop from a specially prepared exemplar, using text from both **A** and **C** to meet the requirement presumably of a 'complete' *Piers Plowman*. For the three descendants of B are, like Bodley 851 (Z), the only 'conjoint texts' to have their two discrete versions linked by material from a *third*. Their **C** portion (which is given the **C** group-sigil b in this edition) runs from Pr 1 to II 128 and continues, after no visible break, with A II 86–198 (the end of A II). It now seems probable that the **B** Version proper begins around III 29, the first 28 lines of III being taken from an **A** copy of the same textual character as II 86–198.[20] The likelihood that this copy was descended from **A**-family r is shown by the variant *carien* at II 126; that it was of r^1-type, by *besette...sore* 105, *foolys* 144; and that its sub-group within r^1 was t, by the variants *trotten* 144 (Ch) and *quentely* 130 (H^2). Finally, that B's **A** source was H^2 or its exemplar seems suggested by the major agreement at II 190 *half...dayes*] *wit hem terme of here lyues* and the spurious line following (as noted in *K–D*, 1, n. 3).[21] There are also signs of contamination from **C** in B at XIII 2, XV 289, 549 (all by alteration in Bm); in Bm alone at III 322 (by alteration); and in Cot at XX 378 (where Bo preserves Bx, and Bm is defective). Correspondingly, contamination from the **B** Version appears in the **C** portion after Pr 133, where it adds B Pr 106; at Pr 231 *Reule*] *ryne*; at I 160 *comseth a myhte*] *a myȝte bygynneþ*; and at II 112 *and...manye*] *of Rutland sokene*. B's many variants are cited separately, or with one other manuscript, only a few times, as part of complex variants:

[V 494 +G]. VI 223, [318 +F]. VII 1. X 425, 429*a*, 461. XII 194 -Bm. XIV 52 -Bm, 73, [117 +G], 129 -Bm. XV [103 +α, 264 +α,] 280, [330 +F]. XVI 45 -Cot. [XVIII 2 +W, 431 +F]. XX 13 -Cot, 236 -Cot. Cot *only*: IV 86. XIII 119, 378. XVI 30. XX 236.

The right readings in B that prevent its elimination are given in the list at § 25 above.

Manuscript **G**

§ 28. A second line of transmission from the group-original is represented by **G**, a sixteenth-century copy whose medieval ancestor underwent extensive contamination from **A** (on which see further § 67). The independent descent of G's lost source from g is demonstrated by its freedom from the 75 group errors of y listed in § 22 above.[22] But the majority of its unique right readings are unlikely to preserve from γ readings corrupted severally by w, L, M and also α. In principle, these could be corrections from a **B** copy superior to Bx at certain points. But if so, that lost manuscript inexplicably failed to supply G's ancestor with the many other right readings solely preserved by α, which *ex hypothesi* it should have contained. For the one agreement with α, at XIII 195 (an unusually long Type IIa line inviting easy loss of the first stave), could be a rare case where G alone has accurately preserved γ. There is thus no logical necessity for positing such a lost source, as will become clear. Instead, G's corrections may be more economically attributed to 'benign contamination' from the other versions, particularly **A**. G cannot be eliminated, however, because it uniquely attests 15 right readings (12 of them with other-version support). It also has another 28 such where it is accompanied by one or two copies of both families, with other-version support in 24.

Major I 191 +**ZAC**. II 8 +**AC**. *With one other* MS: III 283 +W**C**. I 187, 206 +H**ZAC**. *With two* MSS: X 172 +HmB**AC**. XIII 195 +a. XVIII 160 +YC^2**C**. **Minor** +**ZAC**: Pr 231. I 37, 125, 174. III 124. V 583; *with one* MS I 176 +Cr. I 191; III 160 +F. IV 99 +M, 105 +H; *with two* MSS I 199, II 75 +HF; VI 277 +BF. +**AC**: Pr 67. VII 109, 146; *with one* MS V 628 +F, 638 +W; VIII 38, X 70, 420 +F; *with two* MSS VII 194 +α; X 172 +HmB. +**C**: Pr 182; *with* R XIII 424; *with* α Pr 205; XI 129. +**Z**,-**A**: *with* LR V 382. *With no other-version support*: VI 161, XVII 86 (*both* +α).

Of these, only in Pr 182 is G supported solely by **C** (there being no **ZA** parallel) and here, given the line's 'T-type' metrical structure,[23] haplography could well account for coincidental loss of *þo* in w, y, L, M, H and α, thus obviating the need to presume *ad hoc* correction from a copy of **C**. For it is noteworthy that in the other listed cases[24] G's ancestor could in principle have derived all its correct readings from an **A** manuscript. This possibility is indirectly strengthened by half a dozen more where G has a reading that has been accepted in the edited text for **A** or **C** but is here rejected for **B**, or has an **A** reading judged erroneous for that version. In some 15 of the errors listed below, G is accompanied by one of the other manuscripts extensively contaminated from **A**:

Major Pr 62 +F**A**, 82 +**A**-MSS uH**K**. I 8 +H**A**, 41 +*A*-?du**J**, 96 +A**x**. IV 107 +*A*-U, 141 +**A**. VIII 81 +F (*so A*-MSS ChRUW: *visual error or induced by contextual suggestion*). **Minor** Pr 34 +H**A**. I 48 +H**A**, 109 +**A**. III 3 +F; (*so A*-ChVE). 46 +H**A**, 109 +H**A**, 115 +H**A**, 293 +**A**. IV 137 +**A**, 193 (*so A*-wE). V 481 +F**C**. 634 +F**A**. VI 56 +**A**, 204 +**A**-*r¹*JLK. VII 56 +F**C**, 147 +F**C**, 180 +F**A**. X 180 +F**A**, 420 +**A**.

Of the remaining errors that G shares disjunctively with the two other manuscripts showing **A** contamination elsewhere (in all about 140 with F and 40 with H), the following few are recorded as part of a set of complex variants:

F: **Major** I 38 *L. om* (*probably homoarchy*). 136. **Minor** Pr 57. III 264. V 257, 628 (*cf. A*C). VI 94 (*cf.* **Z**A**C**). 196. VII 69, 177 (*cf.* **C**). VIII 93. H: **Major** I 186.

But despite their large numbers, G's agreements with both H and F are nearly all minor, and most are trivial.

§ 29. Finally, of G's numerous individual errors 76 are in the Apparatus amongst the complex variants of certain readings, major ones being asterisked:

Pr 42, 61, 76, 96, 212. I 139, 182, 196, 209. II 20, 166, 219. III 36, 118 +**ZAC**. IV 36, *155 , 190. V 84, 179, *283, 305, *469, 565, 609. VI 9, 124 +**ZAC**, *151, 180, 241, 318. VII 92, 152, 189. VIII 48. IX 149, 158. X 337, 342, 391, *459. XI 60, 79, 86, 138, 149, 178, *435. XII 138, 176, 202, 210, 212*a*, 288. XIII 3, 39, 96, 119, 300, 343, 394. XIV *89, 253, 267. XV 53, 78, *116, *443, 593. XVI 274. XVII 282, 295. XVIII 147, *423. XX 45.

Extensive contamination from **A** has given G not only several readings here rejected for **B** but also a number preferred as likely to correspond to an original corrupted in Bx. These suffice to make it the most significant γ witness (see further §§ 67–8 below).

(b) Three Individual Manuscripts

Manuscript **H**

§ 30. Outside the complex sub-family γ, manuscripts L, M and H each merit group status, since none descends from the others or from γ. **H** is a conjoint text made up of B Pr–V 125 followed by an A-text of the **m** family designated H³ (*A Version* §§ 28–9 above). Notwithstanding K–D's hesitancy,[25] there is little doubt that H descends from β or that its right readings are indeed 'by correction'. As with G, on the most economical hypothesis these come not from a lost **B** source but from **A**. In its **B** portion H shares all the β family's major wrong readings except for those listed in § 31 below. Four individual errors are derivatives from β (I 70, III 32, IV 94 and V 15) and a fifth (V 76), while it could be a reflex of the reading preserved in α, is probably also a more explicit form of β. H cannot derive from L or M, as it lacks their distinctive errors; the only γ witness it accompanies is G, with which it has about 40 exclusive agreements in error; and its closest associate is F, with which it has some 90 agreements. Most striking of all, however, is the extensive contamination from **A** shown in H's individual errors and in those shared with F and G. This probably accounts also for its 26 right readings, some found in one α or β copy (§ 32, end), a marked feature explicitly noted below. H's postulated **A** source is shown by II 123 to have been of the r^l type; Pr 10 and possibly 213 agree with the r^l sub-group u; and V 15 with U, a member of this pair. Other agreements at Pr 7 and II 159 *segges*] *men* (with **A** manuscript V), and at Pr 225 and I 186 (with **A** manuscript M), seem to contradict H's r^l affinities. But on balance these contaminations, presumably present in its immediate source (*h*) and perhaps partly memorial in character, may be taken to come from an A-Text close to u (see further § 67 below). This conclusion is consistent with its date, a generation later than U.

§ 31. H shares some 90 errors with F, and in the following list of major agreements, ten omitted in the Apparatus have been added:

Major Pr 7 +Cr, AvW, 44 +**A**, 46 +AHW, 74 +ARUEH, 163, 213 +Au. I 1 merke] derke +**A**-duVK, 91, 123 garte] made, 162 +CF. II 159 segges] men +**A**V, 163. III 69–72 *ll. om*, 166 now] oure +AuChvM, 225 kynne] manere of +AH, CAG, 265. IV 16 to ryde] *om*. 189 Erles] Lordes. V 37 dide] seyde. 78 discryue] discry3e +AuChLJEAM, 114 dedly] euere.

Of the remaining 70, which are minor, 21 are listed in the Apparatus:

Minor Pr 23, 31, 42, 44 +**A**, 62, 73, 78 +**A**tuHE, 85, 107, 116, 124, 212 +**A**UK. I 183, 202, 209. II 29, 40, 149. III 94, 162, 265.

None of these, however, is of such a kind that it could not be coincidental. The most significant, omission of III 69–72, could have been mechanically caused by the repetition of 65 at 70 or be due to clerical censorship of an injunction to noblemen that was judged imprudent. No immediate reason appears for loss of I 91, unless this too was censorship provoked by taking the statement over-literally (the phrasing being uncomfortably close to that of C I 110). A genetic relationship between H and F would, then, seem unlikely.

§ 32. H also shares over 40 errors with G (*K–D*, p. 60), which are fewer and (more important) little more impressive in quality than those with F (cf. § 25 above). A dozen are given in the Apparatus, the parallel agreement of seven with **A** possibly explaining the link with G, which was similarly contaminated from **A** (§ 28 above):

Major Pr 34 +**A**. I 8 +**A**, 186² [*coinciding gloss of hard word*]. **Minor** Pr 111, 173. I 48 +**A**, 51 +**A**. II 5, 45. III 46 +**A**, 109 +**A**, 115 +**A**.

Finally, H has ten exclusive agreements with all or some **A** copies:

Major Pr 63. I 186 (= M). II 123 (= rE), 163, 197 *leeste*] *beste* (= **A**-TDuJWM). IV 160. V 15 (= U). **Minor** Pr 225 (= M). I 59. III 73.

H is the sole authority for no **B** readings without other-version support; but despite its brevity it remains a significant witness that cannot be eliminated, because it preserves, *with* other-version support, 26 readings that appear intrinsically superior to those of Bx. Of these it attests 15 alone and another 11 along with one or two copies of either family. Pr 99 may be a felicitous guess, a borrowing from α (R is defective here) or an echo of **C**; but the rest could all come from **A** (see § 67 below):

Major +**ZAC**: Pr 41, 59 (*here closest to Ar*), 76. I 11 (*so A*-uHE). 187 +G, 206 +G. IV 105 +G, 145 (*almost right; so Z*), 190. +**AC**: II 9 +F ?= α). III 41, 48. **Minor** +**ZAC**: II 75 +GF, 216 +αG. III 3 +B, 114 +G, 132 +G. IV 47, 90, 94 +Cr. +**AC**: III 226. +**A**: I 11 (*almost right; closest to A*uE), 186 (*almost right; so A*M). III 41 (*almost right*), 251 +R. +**C**: Pr 99 (α *absent*).

Of H's individual variants, all are recorded where a lemma is given for a line.

Manuscript **M**

§ 33. **M** is of less value than H, even though present for the whole text. Its affinities with L and H include probable loss of Pr 39b in its exemplar, for which it inserts a Latin half-line. But M cannot derive from either, being a generation earlier than H and lacking such major errors of L as the omission of I 37b–38a. This latter instance exemplifies M's extensive correction (at more than one stage) from γ sources; but it cannot derive directly from γ either, since it lacks the 40 γ errors (§ 12 above). M's immediate ancestor *m* is postulated in order to account for both its first-stage γ variants and for its handful of unique right readings. That *m* was a fairly accurate copy of β is suggested by four minor cases more probably due to accurate transmission of the family original than to collation with a manuscript of the α family: VII 20, XII 16, XV 121 and 196. Before M was copied, its source *m* received, at certain points, good corrections of two kinds. Perhaps the result of intelligent scribal conjecture are those at X 60, XI 41 and XII 245 (the right reading at VI 119, on the other hand, is visibly by addition in M itself). Others probably came from collation with a γ source, such as the three at I 31, XIV 106 and XVIII 31, those at XII 161 and XIII 191, one also found in g at X 124 (possibly coincidental) and two in w at Pr 2 and 31. Four further readings, agreeing with g and α at I 37 and X 124, with Crg and α at I 38, and with w and α at XX 306, may also be due to collation or, just as probably, transmit *m*'s correct β reading where L has corrupted it. By way of contrast, in VI 326 a later hand has restored a likely β (and Bx) reading earlier wrongly adapted to that of γ. At least seven other such alterations are to the right reading. Those at III 284, XIII 223 and XIX 117 erase, and that at VI 119 adds to a probable Bx reading by looking to **A** or **C**. That at XVII 184–85 corrects (from the same source as Cr) the same mechanical error found in the reading of γ.

§ 34. M's transmission history was thus more complex than those of H or L. But unfortunately its borrowings from γ, whether made in *m* or after M was copied, mostly corrupted a manuscript that had begun as a reliable representative of β. The following 74 M variants (30 major) from the early stage of mistaken 'correction' are divided according to the γ branch sharing them and include in square brackets 18 where one other β copy or α accompanies. Readings omitted from the Apparatus are given in full:

Major γ: II 148. VI 326. XIII 283–4. XIV 1. XV 398, 506. XVI 50, 60. [XVII 339 +L]. XVIII 198, 390. g: V 166 -CB. XI 6.[26] [XIV 167 -Y+F]. w: X 61. [XI 398 -Cr+Bm]. XIII 411 (*a substitution for the senseless* Bx *reading properly corrected by* OC²B *from* C). XIV 179, [300 +L]. Cr: V 533 dwelleþ] wonyeth. XVII 304. XVIII 383. XIX 4 +F, [321 +L], 380, 399. XX 260. **Minor** g: V 210. [VIII 30 +F]. XIV 146. XV 36. XVI 27.[27] 221. XVII 11, 15, 104 -Cr, 166 -Hm. XVIII 354. g: VI 305. IX 130, 200. XI 233, 339, 372, 377, 416. XII [197 +Hm], 202, [211 +Cr, 289 +Cr]. XIII 131, [134 +Cr]. XIV [46 +F], 215. XV [22 +Hm], 353. [XVII 95 +Cr]. [XVIII 420 (+Hm)]. w: X 177. XIII 411. XV 455, 502. XVIII 84, 347. WCr: [XIII 203 (+G)]. [XV 207 +L]. XVIII 85. Cr: VI 213 (bi-] *om*.). VII 3 (hym] *om*). XVI 110a. XIX 77.

The incongruence between M's agreement with both w or its components and with g requires explanation, since w and g are separate branches of γ (§ 11 above). Possibly *m* was collated early with exemplars of both w and g types, or all the agreements with either g (25) or w (26) at this phase may result from random variation. Given, however, that M has three times as many *major* agreements with w as with g and that the second phase of visible 'correction' is from a w source (§ 34), it seems likelier that the agreements with g are the random ones. The striking failure of M's source to agree with Cr at I 37 would then have to be ascribed to a particular form of homoteleuton in Cr (one shared by H) and not to the presence of the error in Cr's ancestor (the likeliest source for M's visible correction in I 38). The other three major cases could also be coincidental: the phrase-loss in V 166 due to the unusual line-length, the synonym in XI 6 to obvious substitution of a commoner term and the misunderstanding in XIV 167 to ambiguous spelling in the exemplar.

§ 35. At a second phase of correction, itself carried out in more than one stage, M was altered by erasures, insertions and over-writing in accordance with a copy of w-type. A notable case is XVII 184–85, where M has corrected its γ-type reading from an exemplar which was obviously not L. But since M's visibly altered readings also include at least six major errors shared with Cr and none with any other copy, it would be economic to identify that exemplar with Cr's manuscript original, in which the correction came from outside the γ tradition. No distinction is drawn between these stages of correction in the following list of 34 agreements (20 major), set out as in § 33 above. They include in square brackets six where M is accompanied by one or two other manuscripts:

Major γ: V 208. IX 98*a*. XII 245. XV 63. w: [Pr 149 +GH]. [VI 200 +?G]. XV 224. [XVI 125 +F]. XVIII 299. WCr: [V 492 +YOC²]. IX 118. XIV 317. XV 410. XIX 186. Cr: V 184, 185 me] hym (*both*). IX 101. 127. XVI 110*a*. XVII 160. XIX 76. **Minor** γ: V 441. XII 245. g: XIII 355. w: [III 267 +GHF. 351 +GH]. XV 200. WCr: V 248. 364. XIII 179. XIV 248, 288. Cr XI 288 (take] toke). XIII 413 (dedes *over erasure*). XIV 148 alle] yow a., yow +M).

§ 36. M also has some 35 agreements with F, all minor and most of them trivial. Its dozen agreements with L are rightly dismissed as very slight by K–D (p. 38) and the major instance they identify (*walweþ* VIII 41) is not accepted here as an error. More important is the presumed gap at Pr 39b in *m* which an enterprising later corrector has filled with a Latin version of the half-line, in a manner recalling another intelligent alteration at X 366. As this omission is shared with L and H, it may well be the reflex of a Ø-reading or of &*c* either in β or in a common source intermediate between <LMH> and β; for it is hard to see how each individual witness lost the English b-half independently. On the former supposition, γ can only have filled out the line here from **A**. Unfortunately, the exact α reading is unknowable, but if F's omission of the line is accurate, it may be that Bx was defective or contained only the first word and that the four branches of β each attempted to repair the gap independently. Of M's individual errors some 20 only are recorded, as part of a set of complex variants:

Pr 39. IV 20. V 410. 424. VI 9 +**ZA**. 204. IX 135. X 50. 366 (*over erasure; so* **A**-ms H³). 377. XIII 270. 284. XIV 316–17*a*. XV 92. XVI 90. XVII 1. 349. XIX 408. XX 271.

M's interest is less textual than bibliographical, in its pointing to activity at a possible single centre of copying responsible for w and its descendants, including perhaps also M. But it contains four unique right readings (III 284, VI 119, XI 41, XII 245), the first three implying knowledge of **A** or **C**, which show signs of an intelligent scribe at work. M therefore cannot be eliminated.

Manuscript **L**

§ 37. If the main interest of H is its felicitous contamination from **A** and that of M its infelicitous 'internal' contamination from γ, that of **L** is its preservation of a complete β text with neither kind of contamination. L has only a few major individual errors of omission, such as the second half of the Latin XVIII 410 and the English b-half of Pr 39 discussed at § 36 above (the first acceptably but the second mistakenly abbreviated to &*c*). Its only significant pairing is with R; there are no separative LF errors. The dozen agreements of L and α (congruent with those with R) might seem to point to an exclusive ancestor between < Lα > and Bx. But some of the minor ones are probably coincidental and the major examples more economically explained as preserving by pure descent readings where Bx itself was in error and γ corrected from another version (as suggested for Pr 39 at § 36).

Major *With* RF: V 261 (*possibly original and altered in γ on comparison with* C). XVIII 31 (*perhaps a coincidental misresolution of* *liȝþ). *With* R: IV 28 (*need not* = Bx: *possibly coincidental through eyeskip from* fol- > for (*a) hadde). V 351 (*?smoothing of* Bx *trumbled*). X 271 (*most probably visual confusion of* l *and* b). **Minor** *With* RF: [I 31 +G]. *With* R: X 425. XIII 338. XIV 106 (?Bx = Ø). XVII 296 (*eyeskip from* sory > so). XVIII 39 (*possibly* Bx *over-explicitness, coincidentally levelled in* F).

§ 38. L's independent descent (< *l* < β < Bx) is, however, collaterally indicated by the more than 50 right readings it shares exclusively with α. In the following list of these, other-version agreement is noted as confirming their probable archetypal character. Agreements with one or two other β copies are in square brackets.

Major *With* RF: V 208 +**AC**, 209 +**A**, -**C**. XIII 158 (L *alt. to* g). XIII 283–84 +**C**. XIV 1, 239 +**C**. XV 398, 506 +**C**. XVI 50 +**C**. XVII 304 +**C**. XVIII 390 +**C**. *With* R: VI 200 +**ZAC**, 225. IX 98*a*. XII 245. XIII 270. XV 63, 494. XX 287. *With* F (R *def.*): XIX 190 +**C**, 217 +**C**. **Minor** *With* RF: II 148 +**ZAC**. VI 326. [XIV 85 +Cr]. XV 36 +**C**, 200. XVI 60, 221 +**C**. XVII 11 +**C**, 15 +**C**, [104 +Cr], 162. XVIII 349 +**C**, 354 +**C**. XX 6. *With* R: Pr 140, [143 +C]. V [383 +**BZAC**], [424 +Hm], 441 (= Bx; *a nearly right reading given parallel emendation in* C). VIII 30 +**AC**, 43 - γMA *and* FC. IX 64. X 435 (F *def.*), [461 +Cr¹]. XII 196 +**C**. XIII 150, 300, 301, 355. XIV 258 +**C**. XV 187. XVII 81 -**C**. *With* F (R *def.*): XIX 47 +**C**, 94 +**C**, 309 +**C**. *Possible agreements where* L *has mechanical error*: VIII 127 (no] *om* L; +CB). XI 339 (*if* ȝe *not an exclamation*). XIX 457 (*if* sowe *not p.t. of* sen).

Among these, one reading shared with RF (XIII 158) shows L visibly altering its exemplar to agree with γ, in a manner recalling M (§ 35 above) and is a case of coincidental error that tests the direct method to its limit. For if the reading *sen* is 'easier,' *deme* may equally be judged 'more explicit', so that, by two well-tried criteria for unoriginality, *either* could be of scribal origin and choice between them is evenly balanced. On the general assumption, however, that L in most cases = β, the complete Lα / ?α agreements specified here may be taken effectively as = Bx. They will therefore be included later among the archetypal readings given at § 57 below, without comment but with other-version support given where available.

§ 39. In conclusion, there are seven instances where L uniquely preserves what on intrinsic grounds has the best claim to be the original reading. In the major cases this may be that of β and thence of Bx; but contamination from **C** remains possible.

Major +**C**: XV 611; XVIII 198 (α *def.*); XIX 38. **Minor** XIV 181. 253 (α *def.*). +**C** XVI 27 (α *def.*); XX 6.

These alone would preclude L's elimination; but the examples in § 38 incidentally illustrate L's general reliability. Thus, though containing no unique material from β (as do both R and F from α), L is indeed what Skeat thought it, the best of the B-Text manuscripts. Its position somewhat resembles that of *r²* in the **A** tradition; but although L's agreements with α are only some two-fifths of those that *r²* has with **m**, this is enough to earn it the status of a group. With due allowance, then, for its necessary incompleteness, this edition accordingly treats L (like manuscript R in the **A** tradition) as the primary citation-source for the Bx lemma at all points where β is right but the copy-text W is in error (see IV § 56 below).

(c) *The β family: conclusions*

§ 40. The above survey of the structure of the β family has shown the groups and their constituent manuscripts severally to contain something like 116 variants (about 40 of them major) that, on intrinsic grounds and on comparison with the other versions, may be judged original. Some must preserve Bx by direct descent through β, but others appear to have come in by contamination from manuscripts of **A** or **C**. As none of the witnesses except Hm (which has no unique right readings but some interesting variants) can therefore be eliminated, all have been collated. The evidence for the postulated family manuscript β as the common source of γ, *h*, *m* and *l* is the body of 685 wrong readings, 248 of them major, shared by all four branches (three after H ceases). In about 515 of these, α with other-version support, and in another 110 α standing alone, has been preferred to the certain or likely β reading. The numbers of α variants adopted rise to 618 with other-version support and to 142 without it, if those also attested by some β witnesses are added (all are included in the list). But in about a dozen major examples of these, the text of β cannot be regarded as certain. It is interesting therefore that, in marked contrast, ten times as many of the *minor* α variants adopted into the text are readings shared by one or more other β manuscripts. In principle, therefore, perhaps only about three-quarters of the total minor category could be securely taken as representing the exclusive family reading of β.[26] Secondly, where consensus is lacking, direct analysis of the competing variants must be used to discriminate the probable family reading within the four branches, severally or in combination. Certainty as to what β reads here is thus effectively half of that which obtains for the α family, where only two representatives survive.

§ 41. That all the β variants in question are indeed agreements in error is clear when they are compared with α and the available **Z**, **A** and **C** parallels.[27] This situation closely resembles what we find in the **A** Version; so, allowing for occasional non-unanimous attestation, the secure evidence for β may be set out below in the form earlier used for the two families of **A** (see *A Version* §§ 23, 47 above). It thus divides both by major and minor instances and according to the other-version support for the readings adopted. The lemmata are from α unless noted otherwise, the variants from β. As with **A**, for reasons of space only major readings are given in full (the most important with *) and the minor ones by reference. A minus sign indicates agreement of R or F with the rejected β variant; a plus, agreement of another β witness with the lemma.

§ 42. Readings with other-version support

(i) Major

(a) *Both* **R** *and* **F** *present*
+**ZA:** I 70 +G bitrayed arn] bitrayeþ he (*cf.* **C**). 113 Til] But for. IV 194 he (þou F)] it. VI 103 -pote] -foot.
+**ZAC:** I 73 -R halsede] asked (haskede R). II 183 fobberes (fobbes **ZC**)] Freres. 210 -R feeris] felawes. III 6 +B world] moolde. 140 +H trewþe] þe trewe. IV 94 meken] ?mengen. V 15 pride] pure p. 469 +Cr knowe] owe. 521 Syse] Synay. 550 of hym] *om.* 557 peril (*om* F)] helþe. VI 30 bukkes (boores F)] brokkes.
+**A:** V 97 -F mayne] manye. 113 men (hem F)] *om.* VII 125 be fooles] by foweles. VIII 46 canon (þe comoun F)] Chanon. 50 -F self] soule. X 154 -F wel] it. 223 þe goode wif †F] Studie. 422 dide] *om.*
+**AC:** II 236 fere] drede. III 63 see] seye. V 84 wryngyede...fust †F] wryngynge he yede. 215 -F barly] b. malt. 326 Tho] Two. 588 -F þat] man. VI 76 -F aske] take. VIII 64 abide me made] brouʒte me aslepe. *X 291–302 *Ll. om.*
+**C:** II 200 Go] To. III 32 +Cr clerke] leode +**A**. 67 -F god] crist. 214 yerne] renne +**A**. V 76 shrewe (shryve F) shewe. 126 euere] *om* +**A**. 181 speche] riʒt. 238 a...Iewes †F] and I. a lesson. 370 and hise sydes] *om.* 495 it (*om* F)] was. VI 39 men] hem. VII 193 -F fyue] foure. X 78–9 *Ll. om.* 314 pure] *om.* *410–12 *Ll. om.* 429a +Cr[23] Sunt] *Siue.* XI 7 For] That. 8 -F and loue] allone. 41 graiþly] gretly. 59 -F dide] wrouʒte. *110 *L. om.* 121 saue] safly. 131b–32a *om.* 134 -F riʒt] *om.* 138 may al] al to. *159–69 *Ll. om.* 208 children] breþeren. 238 -F for sooþ] *om.* 265 segge] man. *382–91 *Ll. om.* 427b–29a *om.* 433 by my soule] *om.* XII *55–7a *om.* 104 lereþ] ledeþ. *116–25a *Ll. om.* 151–52 *Ll. om.* 218–21 *Ll. misord.* 229 kynde] *om.* 282 Ac] For. 287 trewe. (†F] *om.* XIII 35, 47 mette(s)] macche(s). 50 he; lif] I; as I lyue. 80 and] he. 103 best] wel. 104 drank after] took þe cuppe and d. *165–72a *Ll. om.* *293–99 *Ll. om.* 350 lef] wel. 394

(+BmBo) here (*om* F)] hire. *400–09 *Ll. om.* *437–54 *Ll. om.* XIV 204 þo ribaudes] þat ribaude. 217 Or; or] Arst; þan. *228–38 *Ll. om.* 273 neyȝ is pouerte] to hise seintes. 275 pacience (*om* F)] wiþ p. 292 poore riȝt] any p. 309 þat] and. 316 lered] lettred. XV 25 þouȝte (ofte F)] *om*.p 1116 wolueliche (foxly F)] vnloueliche. 188 .seche] speke.i *244–48 *Ll. om.* *303–04 *Ll. om.* *510–27 *Ll. om.* 528 And nauȝt to] That. 530 -F amonges romaynes] in Romayne; in greete roome F. *572b–75a *Ll. om.* XVI 121 iesus (crist F)] ich. 136 -F arne] was. 140 cene] maundee. 142 so(m)] oon. 199 alle] *om.* 220 pure †F] *om.* 250 buyrn] barn. 262 +HmGC wiþ] mid. wye] man. XVII brynge] bigynne. *69 *L. om.* 86 +G gome] groom. 103 outlawe is] Outlawes. 176 -F pulte] putte. *177b–79a *om.* 179 and] at. 196 he seyde] me þynkeþ. 207 warm] hoot. *218–44 *Ll. om.* 246 tache] tow. 290 semed] were. *309–10 *Ll. om.* 325 smerteþ] smyteþ in. 336 ouȝte] ofte. XVIII] 8 +HmB orgene] Organye. 14 -R on] or. 28 Feiþ…deye] he þe foule fend and fals doom to deeþ. 35 -F forbite] forbete. 87 Iesu (crist F)] hym. 101 deeþ…yvenquisshed] his d. worþ avenged. 129 kynde] kynnes. 156 vertue] venym. 193 -R of] *om.* 202 preie] preue. 269 Laȝar is] hym likeþ. 274 þis lord] hym. 283 I…iseised] siþen I seised. 295 he wente aboute] haþ he gon. 312b–13a *om.* 399 kyn] kynde. 410a (+g) *clarior...amor*] *om.* 411 sharpest] sharpe. XX *37 *L. om.* 38 Philosophres] Wise men. 39 wel elengely] in wildernesse. 55 made] *om.* 62 gladdere] leuere. 63 +HmCr[1]B leute] lente. 67 gile] any while. 102 lefte] leet. 117 -R+WHm brode] blody. 120 +Cr kirke] chirche. 126 -F suede] sente. 191 wange] *om.* 211 Weede; mete] *trs.* 249 lakke] faille. 253 telle] teche. 256 hem] *om.* 260 taken hem wages] hem paie. 263 parisshe] place. 291 shul] wol. 311 +Cr in þe sege] þe segg. 337 frere] segge. 351 here so] so it. 360 -F ben] biten.

(b) *With only* **R** *present*

(*Cf.* **C**): *XIII 170, 172 *Ll. om.*

(c) *With only* **F** *present*

+**ZA**: II 9 +H pureste on] fyneste vpon.

+**AC**: VIII 109b–10a *om.* +**C**: XVIII 426 carolden] dauncede. XIX 43 his] *om.* *56–9 *Ll. om.* 60 yeueþ] yaf. 68 wilnen] willen. 73 riȝt] *om.* 76 Ensense] *om.* 94 Erþeliche] Thre yliche. 117 +CrM oonly] holy. 118 fauntekyn] faunt fyn. 130 and...herde] to here & dombe speke he made. *152b *om.* 173 +CrCot *Dominus*] *Deus.* *237b–38a *om.* 250 +Hm pacience] penaunce. 269 yit...Piers] Grace gaf P. of his goodnesse. 275 aiþes] harewes. 276 Piers greynes] greynes þe. 285 meschief] muchel drynke. 286 out] ne scolde out. *337 *L. om.* 398 Or] That. 411 be...fode] þe comune fede. 457 sowne] seiȝe. 467 toke] seke. XX 7 lyue by] þi bilyue.

(ii) Minor

(a) *Both* **R** *and* **F** *present*

+**Z**: Pr 223. +**ZA**: II 122 +GYH, 171. III 12 +BGMH. IV 142 +HmCrH. V 545. VI 237, 285 +B. VII 62, 96. +**ZAC**: I 45[1], 80 +HmGM, 182, 199 +GH. II 131, 138 +GH, 216 +GH, 226. III 19[2] +CrB, 128, 130–1 +H, 162[1]. IV 103, 141. V 19[1,2], 35, 573 +G, 596. VI 42, 89, 120 +HmCr, 185 +G, 216, 218, 222 +B, 292. VII 57[1,2] +y, 68, 92[1,] 93 +OC[2], 100. +**A**: II 120 +y, 159 +G. V 111, 112. VII 106, 135. VIII 66 +B. IX 53 (*not* Cx), 188. X 20[2], 60, 128, 129, 133, 137 (*not* C), 147, 209, 221[2], 369. +**AC**: Pr 20, 37[2], 215, 216, 229. II 227 +Hm (*not* Z). III 39, 49, 214[1], 229. V 186 +OC[2], 194[1] +GCot,[2], 213, 305, 321[2] -F), 359, 575 +Cot. VI 67[1,2], 95 -RZ. VII 26 +GCB (*not* Z), 181, 186 +g, 194 +G. VIII 72, 89, 116. IX 176[1,2], 194 +B. X 223[1], 377[1,2]. +**C**: Pr 93[1], 109 +H, 205 +G. I 71 +Hm. II 91. III 8, 68, 122 +HmH (*not* ZA), 155 (*not* ZA), 214[2] (*not* A), 301, 327 +G. IV 62 +H-F. V 130, 148 +Hm, 151, 192, 195 -F, 274[2], 317 (*not* A), 321[1] (*not* A), 357, 369, 370[2], 386, 394, 398 +OCB, 403 +Hm, 407, 441a +BoCot, 442, 483, 494, 496, 502, 505 +GCot, 507 +CrG, 603a, 619 (*not* A), 620 (*not* A). VI 45 +Hm (*not* ZA), 52, 80 +OC[2],105, 161 +G. VII 8 +B, 199 (*not* A). VIII 43 -F (*not* A), 57, 59 +WHm. IX 20 (*not* A), 189. X 77, 87, 147 (*not* A), 384 +GM, 391[2], 399 +WCr, 458 (*not* A). XI 7, 20, 26, 37, 43, 58a, 84, 129[2] +G, [145; *cf.* C], 147[1], 200, 204, 238[1] +BM, 262, 288 +W, 348, 350, 367 +CrCot, 401, 415 -F. XII 138 +Cr, 203, 213[1,2], 244, 285[1,2]· XIII 4 +HmG, 56, 92, 93, 112, 330, 349, 364, 398, 410, 423 -F, 426. XIV [40; *cf.* C], 41 +OC[2], 51, 52[1], 66[1,2] -F, 67 +Cr, 72 -F, 205, 239, 257[1] +WCrM, 257[2] +CB-F, 265 -F, 289[2], 292[2] -F, 295 -F, 301 -F, 307 -F, 310 -F, 313 -F. XV 5 +WCrBM, 18 -F, 20 +HmCrY, 55a, 73[1], 74 +G-F, 78, 88, 100, 115, 162a +M, 193, 256, 317a[1,2], 355, 359, 362, 494, 502, 529[1;2] +W, 531[1,2], 575[1,2], 585, 587, 591. XVI 30, 76, 83 +Cr, 88 +Cr, 115, 123, 148, 176, 254[2], 275. XVII 1, 3, 10, 13, 14a, 15 +CrG, 23, 57, 65, 74, 85, 137 +WHm, 139, 141, 166, 176[2], 181, 202, 204[1,2], 264, 299[1,2], 302, 320, 329[1,2], 330 -F, 336[1], 339 +w, 348[1,2]. XVIII 12, 35a -F, 45, 51 -F, 85, 96 +HmCrOB, 147[1], 167, 170, 181, 192 +Cr[3]C[2]B, 241 +WCrO, 248, 261, 265, 271, 276 +Cr, 277 +wCB, 280, 319, 342, 360, 364, 376[1], 380, 384. XX 35 +CrG, 36, 38[2] +GC[2], 42, 60[1,2], 78, 87, 93, 97, 114, 119, 125 +g, 136 +Hm, 138, 139, 141, 142, 147 +Cr[23]g, 150 +W, 171 -F, 183, 194, 198[1,2], 207[1,2], 208, 210, 218, 221, 277, 283[1,2], 290 +Cr, 303 +WCr[1]B, 306 +w, 321 +G, 327, 343, 349, 357, 361 -F, 364 -F, 366 +Crg-R, 383.

(b) *Only* **F** *present*

+**ZA**: II 171. +**ZAC**: I 182, 199 +GH. +**A**: VIII 102[1]. +**AC**: Pr 20, 37[2]. +**C**: Pr 93[1,] 109 +H. I 141a. XVIII 429. XIX 24,

141

48, 64 +YBoCot, 77 +G, 91, 109, 120, 140², 145^{1,2}, 149, 151, 151/2, 154, 158, 180 +GC², 209, 217, 224¹, 224² +Cr^{23}, 229, 279¹, 282², 314, 339, 384 +Y, 399 +g, 437 +WCr, 450^{1,2}, 452, 461², 483a. XX 1, 3, 9, 11, 13², 26 +G.

§ 43. Readings with no other-version parallel

(i) Major

(a) *Both* **R** *and* **F** *present*

II 91 (cf. **C**) wenynges] wedes. 176 deuoutrye] Auoutrye. V 176 (cf. **C**) wel] wyn. 270 -F quod Repentaunce] om. 410 I late] l. I passe. 420 (it) clausemele] oon clause wel. VIII 127 no man (man *om* F)] womman (man L). IX 60 wi3t] man. 96¹ drad hym] om. X 47 worþ] 3ifte / value (cf. **A**). 239 -F propre] *om.* 284 manliche (soþly F)] saufly. 303 skile and scorn but if he] scorn but if a clerk wol. *368 *L. om.* 472 kunnyng] knowyng. XI 5 til I was †F] weex I. 179² -F oure lord] god. 184 -F iuele] heele. *196 L. om. 281 wise] parfite. 396 wrou3te] dide. [398 +OC² þolieþ] þolie. 419 þe to] to be. XIII 195 +G Marie] *om.* 267 bake] om. 272 grete] good. 290 bold] badde. 323 lakkynge] laughynge. 361 wittes wyes] which wey. 391 conscience] herte. XIV 28 which is] with his. 141 two heuenes for] heuene in. *183 *L. om.* 189 pouke] pope. 212² riche] Richesse. 274 þat...preise] ye preise faste. XV 89 muche (grete R)] long. 106 au3t †F] no3t. 337 ful] *om.* *395 *L. om.* 422 fyndynge] almesse. XVI 43 brewe] breke. 50 (cf **C**) planke] plante. 119 þat] and. XVII *112a *L. om.* XVIII 76 þrowe] tyme. 109² lese] cesse. 356² þing] þo.

(b) *With only* **R** *present*

XI 339 3ede] 3e / þe. XV 460 keperes] cropers. *471–84, 489a *Ll. om.* XVII 190 ypersed] yperiss(h)ed.

(c) *With only* **F** *present*

Pr 122² lif] man. I 149 þat spice; vseþ] trs.

(ii) Minor

(a) *Both* **R** *and* **F** *present*

II 51, 229 +CrH. III 100 +H, 231, 235 +H. V 79 +BH, 219 +y, 274 -F, 279, 408, 491, 547. VI 48¹ +Hm, 132 +G, 157, 202. VII 14 +wB, 70. IX 35, 48 +W, 86², 119, 122 +Hm, 178, 190. X 114a, 218, 262a, 379, 473. XI 193¹ +g, 197, 214 +WHmC², 277 +WHmCr¹, 279 +CrM, 289 +WBM, 295 +B, 330. XII 16 +M, 30, 34, 49, 66, 73, 78. XIII 221, 229, 255a +OC²Cot, 280, 376 +WCrM, 387 -F, 424 +G, 455, 456. XIV 88 +HmCrB, 116 +Hmg, 119, 131a +OC², 135¹, 168, 182 -F, 186 +WCr, 198². XV 90 -F, 109, 121, 144, 196 +M, 147 +B, 207, 211 +W, 281, 282, 283, 323 +CrM, 342a¹, 386¹. XVI 9 +Crg, 11 +Cr^{23}g, 45 +GCot, 77, 110a, 160, 184 +y-F. XVII 166, 171². XVIII 303, 313², 345, 356¹.

(b) *With only* **F** *present* I 153.

iv. *The α family of manuscripts*: R *and* F

§ 44. The second family has only two surviving copies, **R** and **F**, neither a complete representative of the α text. R is physically defective at three points and F's exemplar might have been so at one point. Of R's two extant portions Lansdowne 398, which formed the original first quire of Rawlinson Poetry 38, has lost folios 1, 2, 7 and 8 and thus lacks Pr 1–124 and I 141–II 40. The Rawlinson portion has lost all eight folios of quire 14, which contained XVIII 413–XX 26. Otherwise the surviving part of R is almost as complete as that of L, lacking only three and a half text-lines (VIII 101–2, 104 and 105a) and one citation-line (XVII 112a). Unluckily, however, the material in the lost leaves amounts to 764 text-lines and 14 citation-lines, a quantity comparable to that absent from the Digby 102 copy that is substantively the best of the **C** witnesses (see *C Version* § 19 below). These losses are partly made good by F in all R's defective sections, though F's own omissions include about 164 text-lines and six citation-lines. The largest of these, XV 428a–91, may have been due to loss of a leaf in its exemplar (here called *f*), and is fortunately present in R. Although their closeness in date does not totally preclude it, neither copy is likely to derive from the other. Sean Taylor[28] claims on palaeographical grounds that the scribe of Corpus 201 knew Rawlinson and judges the visible alterations in R to be in his hand. His further contention, that R may have served as F's exemplar, would be more plausible if it were the case that the F scribe had access to R in its undefective state. However, very few readings where F is superior to R and to β are such that they cannot be due to consultation of an **A** or **C** copy but must be ascribed to felicitous conjecture or to correction from a **B** exemplar independent of α or from outside the Bx tradition.[29] The omitted, the spurious and even the sophisticated lines are, to be sure, compatible with F's derivation from R. But it is hard to accept that its many contaminations from **A**, some of them necessary corrections of archetypal errors, were directly introduced by the Corpus scribe, for these have left no visible traces in F. The postulated exemplar *f* must therefore have existed, and this could have been based on R. But whether or not (as would seem likely) *f* also had such features, F as it now stands is a heavily sophisticated witness, with a text re-written wholesale in places, frequently 'improving' the alliteration and altering the style (see e.g. V 276*a*, 573). Where direct comparison is possible, F emerges as about ten times less accurate than R; so in most points of difference between them, R is the only reliable witness to the text of α. Nevertheless, F does sometimes preserve α where R is defective and sometimes even correctly against R. It is, further, the sole witness to five lines and five half-lines of the B-Text, mostly in Passus XIX, which are confirmed as authentic on comparison with the B[1] material preserved by **C**. Skeat was therefore mistaken to reject the manuscript outright, and K–D deserve full credit for making use of it. But to the present editor, they over-estimate F's value and sometimes misinterpret the nature of its distinctive readings.

§ 45. The intrinsic worth of manuscript **R** was, on the other hand, recognised by Skeat, who discovered it, and is much greater than that of F. For R is specifically the sole source of some eighteen lines of text and also a far more faithful general witness to α. Particularly important are XV 471–84, where F is defective, and without which the text of the **B** Version would be incomplete. R does not group significantly with any β manuscript except L, and these agreements, as already argued at §§ 37–8 above, seem due not to descent from an exclusive common ancestor but to each copy's independently preserving at these points its ancestral reading and thence that of Bx. Like L, R in the present editor's judgement preserves a pure B-Text uncontaminated from any other version (see § 39). Its many agreements with **C** against β may be interpreted as signifying that α often accurately transmitted Bx where β corrupted it. Finally, R contains no spurious material of its own, since the half-line after the corrupt form of XVII 8 and the three-line substitution for the presumably lost III 51–62 may both be inferred to have been present in α.

§ 46. By contrast **F**, as already noted, groups extensively with two β manuscripts, G and H, in about 140 and 90 readings respectively. However, where these agreements are not minor and probably coincidental, what they seem to indicate is common influence from **A** in all three copies (§§ 29–30 and 66–8). F is characterised first by contamination from **A**, benign at VIII 109b–10a, where the sense requires two half-lines presumed lost by Bx but possessing a slightly revised **C** parallel. In five instances elsewhere, the material does not belong in the B-Text: after Pr 94, F adds A Pr 95, and it inserts corrupt reflexes of parallel **A** lines in VIII after 49, 80, 101 and 102 (= A IX 45, 71, 93 and 95). The absence of these **A** lines from **C** (in contrast to VIII 109–10 cited above) indicates that they had been removed in the revision to **B**. It may be surmised that all of them, including the latter, were added in *f* before F was copied. The confused character of the presumptive α text round about 99–108, reflected in omission and misordering in both witnesses, might indeed have been what prompted *f*'s scribe to consult another copy of the poem. The line inserted after Pr 94 shows that he already knew the **A** Version, and it seems that he went on to adopt further readings from it at VIII 105b and 106b. For comparison of the latter with C X 104–05, a slightly revised form of the text in βR, reveals it to be not the original B-Text but that of A IX 98b and 99b. F also omits 164 text-lines and six citation-lines.

Pr 3, 33b–34a, 39, 41, 50–4, 98 (*spur. l. instead.*), 99. I 119, 157. II 11. III *69–72, 350. IV 52, 67, 193. V 275 (4 *spur. ll. inst.*), 296, 369, 471, 547, 583–84, 605. VI 161. VII 100, 176a. VIII 21, 99–100. IX 142, 221. X 21, 221, 279–80, 353a, 355, 397a, 435. XI 5 (6 *spur. ll. instead.*), 50, 247, *337–39, 414. XII 61, 167. XIII 170, 172, 301. XIV 22 (2 *spur. ll. instead.*), 41, 201, 212a, 215, 304. XV 218, 353, *428–91, 508. XVI 186, 248. XVII 186b–91a. XVIII 319a, 423. XIX 88b–89a, 161a–62, 205–07, 247, 439–40. XX 301.

Finally, F inserts some 50 spurious lines at 25 points (to the list in *K–D* 222–23 should be added its substitute for Pr 98). Like its contaminations and omissions, these evince less 'typical' scribal negligence than complete unconcern for fidelity to the original. Assuming the presence of these lines in *f*, it might thus seem more likely that this was produced by an amateur making over the text according to his own lights than by a professional scribe required to provide as accurate a copy as possible of his exemplar. A similar engagement with the poem's internal structure may underlie the manuscript's idiosyncratic passus-divisions.[30] Despite these deficiencies, however, F cannot be eliminated. Where R is absent, it attests against β some 90 right readings, 35 of them major, recorded in §§ 42 and 43 as potentially the readings of α. And where R is present but errs with β, F is right in at least the 21 instances listed, whether these are ascribed (as at V 23) to α or (as in VIII 109–10 and most cases) to contamination:

Major I 73. II 210. V 23. VII 174/5 (*l. div.*). VIII 109b–110a. XVIII 14, 193. **Minor** I 43, 45, [57 +Cr²³H]. II 51, [120 +y]. III 145. IV 15. V 32, 597. VI 95. VII 113. [VIII 83 +CB]. [XIII 223 +Cr]. XV 89.

§ 47. The special features of the α family are four. The first is the presence, among 625 exclusive right readings, of some 170 authentic lines and 15 half-lines not found in β. These have already appeared as lemmata at §§ 42–3, but for convenience they will be given together in a group at § 58 below. The second is the absence of some 203 lines and 18 half-lines found in the other family at 85 separate locations; these will be listed together at § 56. The third is some nine spurious lines occurring at three points where α lacks material present in β: III 51–62, IX 170–72 and XVI 270–73 (a tenth line after XVII 8 that K–D accept as authentic is also treated here as spurious; see the *Textual Notes ad loc*). The fourth feature is a body of some 411 other errors, about 255 of them major. In 245 of these (213 major) the α variant has been rejected for a β reading with other-version support, in the remaining 166 (41 of them major) for a β variant with no other-version support. Additionally, there is a body of readings where, as against the adopted β variant, α may possibly have been preserved in its one extant witness. In some 150 of these (85 major) there is other-version support for the β reading, but in 66 (about 20 major) none. Of the roughly 190 readings attested by F alone, it appears antecedently unlikely that more than about 10% preserve α, whereas of the 25 readings in R alone, most may be reliably held to do so. In this judgement, qualitative evaluation of specific readings is guided in part by the general character of F as a witness to α.

§ 48. **Readings with other-version support**

The evidence for α is set out in the same way as that for β at §§ 42–3 above. Unless specified otherwise, the lemmata represent β and the variants are from R as the presumed readings of α. A minus sign indicates agreement of R or F with the lemma, a plus sign that the β ms / other version denoted shares the rejected α reading, a slash / square brackets that R and F have divergent errors and so α cannot be reliably discerned:

(i) Major

(a) (*Both* **R** *and* **F** *present*)

+**Z**: VI 103² atwo] at / awey (*cf.* **A**).

+**ZA**: I 44 holdeþ] kepeth +**C**, *82 *L. om.* 134 si3te of] *om.* II 108 which] þis +**HC**. 111 Rutland] rokeland. III 127 (*and cf.* **C**) false] faire. IV 118 an hyne] nau3te / vanyte. VI 238 mnam] man +**BoCot**. VII 31 som] *om.* *41*a L. om.*

+**ZAC**: Pr 213 poundes] poudres / pownded. I 133 and troneþ] for to saue. 138 yet mote ye kenne me] I mote lerne. III 5 sooþ-] couth- / sotil-. *149b–50a *om* (*spur.* 149b F). 187 kyng] kni3t. 205 blood] lond. IV 55 hewen] hennes. 65 my lord] *om* +**CrH**. 90 moore] be. V 41 preide] preued. 70 al] *om.* 73 þe Saterday] on þe day. 519 bolle] bulle. 552 hewe... euen] men þat þei ne haue it anone. 611 forþ] *om.* VI 86–8 *mis-div.* 88 defende it (*trs* b)] Ikepid it. for...bileue] *om.* *217 *L. om.* 245 wel] for. 301 wolde wastour] ne wolde no w. 307 no3t] *om.* *309b–10a *om.* VII 37 marchaunt3 murie manye] manye marchaunt3 þat. 39–40 *mis-div. with padding*: mede] m. for þat craft is schrewed.

+**ZC**: I 41 seeþ] sueth.

+**A**: Pr 225 þe longe day] þe fayre d. F; here dayes here R (*cf.* **C**). III 219 biddynge] beggyng. VI 113 To] And 3eed to. VII 133 þe Abbesse] *om.* 156 cleyme] reue. 182 renkes] thenke. VIII 51 sleuþe] soule +**Hm**. *103 *L. om.* IX 162 crist] Ihesus. X 14 on erþe] here. 72 tyme] *om* +**C**. 135 bolde] *om.* 167 speche] berynge. 185 sotile] sau3tele. 189 Loke] loue. þee likeþ] þow thenke. 192 *simu-*] *simi-*(+**Cr²³CotL**). 217 founded] (by)fond. 376 witnesseþ] telleth.

+**AC**: III *51–62 *Three ll. like* A III 50–1. 63 of youre house] to 3ow alle. 277 ende] endede +**Hm**. V 316 dysshere] dissheres dou3ter. 344 þat herde] *om.* VI 230 þee] god. 276 be þow] yow yow / þe. VII 125 he] or. 191 didest] dost. IX 2 kynnes] maner. 29 lisse] blisse +**CrGBM**. 135 ywasshen] Iwasted. 169 cheeste; choppes] iangelynge; gaying. *170–72 *Three spur. ll.* *200–03 *Ll. om.* X 1 hote] called. *424 *L. om.* +**C**: Pr 135 *ius*] *vis*. 171–72 *Ll. om.* I 119 *et...altissimo*] &*c.* II 85 cheste] gestes. III 91 loue] lord. 310 spille] lese. IV 26 Mede...erþe] on e. m. þe mayde maketh. 40 Reson] *om.* 104 (*cf.* **C**) crist] god (*cf.* **ZA**). 173 wiþ; loked] *om*; loke. V 261 heires] vssue +**L**. 406 feble] seke. 505 ruþe] mercy. VI 48 cherles] clerkes. IX *160–61 *Ll. om.* *166 *L. om.* *179–85 *Ll. om.* X 250 merite] mercy. XI 4 wo] sorwe. 6 mette me þanne] me tydde to dreme. *46 *L. om.* 58 *pecuniosus*] pecunious +**B**. 60 yarn] ran +**Hm** (3eede F). 108 if; it knewe] *om*; it knowe. 125 reneye] receyue. 129 rome] renne +**Cr**. 130 a reneyed] he renneth. 255 folwe] wolde / welde. 356 brou3ten] brynge (bredde R). 434 þyng] *om* (man F). 435 euery man shonyeth] no man loueth. XII 59 gras] grace. 99 ei3en] si3te. 107 witted] wedded. 131 (*cf.* **C**) marke] make (+**Cr**). 135 bro3t] bou3te. *140–47a *Ll. om.* 159 what manere] whanere (ensample F). *169 *L. om.* 178 keuereth] kenneth. *185 *L. om.* 186 to book sette] sette to scole. 212a *Quia reddit*] And *reddite*. 215 assoille] telle. 233 iogele] iangele. 260 pureliche] priueliche. 266 logik] glosing. XIII *14–20 *Ll. om.* 45 and wepe] (with) many. 80 no3t] *om* (yt F). 331a *Et alibi...acutus om.* 373b–74a *om.* XIV 52 gyues] feytoures. 59 bettre] leuere. *157–59 *Ll. om.* 212 hei3e] ri3t +**G**. 213 preesseth] precheth. *252–3 *Ll. om.* 263 lond] lorde. 276a, 306 *sollici-*] *soli-* +**OC²B**. 288b *om.* 293 wi3tes] wittes. XV 42 *-itanus*] *-anus*. *72 *L. om.* 107 vn-] *om* +**WCrG**. 111 dongehill] dongoun. 118 *-greditur*; *-tum*; *-docium*; *-andum*] *-cedit*, *-ta*, *-dos*, *-atum*. 156 saueour] god +**Cr²³**. 293 soden] eeten. 297 manye longe yeres] amonges wilde bestes. 317a *brutorum...sufficiat*] *om.* 503 and...bileueþ] to on persone to helpe. 528 mennes] *om* +**Hm**. *532–68 *Ll. om.* 584 men] it hem. XVI 27b–28a *om.* 198 children] barnes. 252 sei3] seyde. *264 *L. om.* 270–73 *Three spur. ll. inst.* XVII 7b *om.* 8 Luciferis lordshipe] sathanas power. *A spurious half-line after.* *37–47 *Ll. om.* 95 he] *om.* 107 seigh] seith (+**GC²**). 109 vnhardy þat] vn-. *113²24 *Ll. om.* 140 loued] leued. 148 at] and. 152 an hand] a fust. 160 -inne] *om.* *218–44 *Ll. om.* 254 *ingratus...kynde*] ingrat...kynne. 296 now] nou3t. 300 þoru3] to. 312 nounpower] nounper. *316 *L. om.* 340 cause] resoun. XVIII 31 lieþ] likth +**L**. 41 Iewes] *om.* 62 depe] here. 83 stode] stede. 86 vnspered] opned. 93 for] hem for. 109a *cessabit vnxio vestra*] *om.* 147 I] *om.* 157 fordo] do. *179 *L. om.* 182 my suster] *om.* *198 *L. om.* 216 yno3] nou3te. 218 murþe] ioye. 226 lisse] blisse +**GY**. 233 wise of] men in. 246 see] mone. 251 leue] ?leese (*om* R). *252–53 *Ll. om.* 276 he robbeþ] & robbe. 296 tyme] *om.* 363 widder] grettere. 383 iu-] *om* +**YOCBL**. XX 48 bide] bydde +g. 62 wel] *om* +**G**. 65 were] we. 91 Confort a] *om* (a komely F). 132 bright] rede. 151 kille] calle. 152 lepte aside] seith *occide*. 158 wo] *om.* 174 dyas] dayes. 202 me] my lif. 214 Conscience] *om.* 233 for] for no. *238–39 *Ll. om.* 256 newe and] *trs.* 265 Hir ordre and] heraude. 269 out of] of / ouer on(y).

(b) *With only* **R** *present*

+**A**: X 221 wightly] mi3teliche. +**C**: VIII 21 sooþly] *om.* 100 oon] and. to...boþe] *om. No o-v.*: XV 218 The] To. 443 garte] and grete +**B**.

(c) *With only* **F** *present*

+**ZA**: Pr 27. I 145 be] is good. 146 after] soone. +**ZAC**: *Pr 3 *L. om.* 8 Vnder] Vpon. 9 watre*s*] wawys. 22 *L. mispl.* 42 Faiteden] & fele f. 43 to bedde] togydre. 46 pli3ten] pyght*y*n (+H). *53–4 *Ll. om.* 60 good] selue. I 175 ru*þ*e] mercy. 184 no man] alle men. 186 feet] fewte. 196 no3t] *om.* 201 deele] d. with. II 5 lo] se. *11 *L. om.* 28 kam...bettre] am...b. roote. +**AC**: Pr 37 han] welden. 39 *L. om.* 62 Manye] Fele. freres] *om* +G. 71 -hede] o*þ*is. auowes] fele a. 74 bonched] blessid +H. 75 rau3te] lawhte. 77 lene*þ* it] beleven on. 78 bisshop yblessed and] blessynge bisshop. 82 peple] men; poraille b. 83 parisshe preestes] vikerys. +**A**: Pr 33b–34a *om.* 205 also...heuene] it ys *þ*e. gr. g. *þ*at good into blisse. 208 *þ*at...bet-tre] tak it if *þ*ou lyke. +**C** Pr 88 in tokene] to knowe. *94 *After this* A Pr 95. 96 sitten] *þ*ey Iuggyn. *98 *Spur. l. instead* *99 *L. om.* 103 alle vertues] hevene. 112 hym] he. I 155 *þ*is fold] manhode. *157 *L. om.* 162 taxe*þ*] aske*þ* (+H). 202 *þ*at(1)] date. II 12 *þ*ereon rede] set abowhte with. 22 bilowen h*y*m] she is lowly. 24 is a] bore. XVIII *423a *Iusticia... sunt*] *om.* XIX 3 holly] holyly. 4 yede] wente +CrM. 5 eftsoones; me mette] *om*; y drempte. 8 Iesu] hymselue. 15 called] named. *88b–89a *om.* 90 And...riche*l*s] For it shal turne tresoun. 133 *Fili Dauid*; *Ihesus*] *trs* +g. 135 The burdes *þ*o] *þ*erfore men. 151 songen] konyngly s. 153 he yede] wente. *161a–62 *Ll. om.* *205–07 *Ll. om.* 239 thecche] *þ*resche. 247 *L. om.* 282 That] For he. 306 *þ*e...falle] *þ*ey men falle ageyn *þ*e kyng. 318 kynde] *om.* 320 Grace] g. *þ*at *þ*y frut. 329 watlede...and(2)] he peyntede *þ*e wallis with *þ*e woundis of. 340 alle cristene] cristendom. 342 Surquidous his sergeaunt] surquidores were sergawntys. 343 spye; oon] *pl.*; &. 345 tyne *þ*ei sholde] *þ*ey wolde stroye. 357 on wikked kepynge] wikkednesse he meynti*þ*. 377 as...of] I s. of toforehond. 381 wellede] walmede. 412 *þ*ei ben] *þ*ou art. 416 or an hennes] *om.* *439–40 *Ll. om.* 445 som] *om.* XX 23 fer to] fore.

(ii) Minor

(a) *Both* **R** *and* **F** *present*

+**Z**: V 74 +HmC[2]CAC. +**ZA**: II 161. III 23. IV 56. V 25. VI 234. VII 48, 92 +Cot. +**ZAC**: I 87, 88, 129. II 115, 143, 149, 155. III 19, 33, 36, 133. V 582. VI 130[1], 155, 168 +Hm, 171 +G, 203 +Y, 320. VII 19[1,2,3], 24. +**A**: I 78. II 237[1]. III 80, 82. V 80 +H, 109, 118, 566, 627. VII 125, 136 +G, 138. VIII 35 +HmC[2], 36. IX 10 +CrC[2]C, [28 (*om* R)], 51, [175], 206. X 20, 66, 176 (*so* C). +**C**: Pr 153, 165, 175, 185. I 136 +G. II 68, 83. III 63 (*so* A), 328. IV [36], 161 +Hm. V 40, 154 †F, 250, 275 †F, 404 +w, 433, 540. VI 50, 193. VIII 92. IX [14], 110. X 75, 86, 88a +GC[2]M, 243 +L, 246, 246a, 248 +GOC[2], 391, 408. XI 21, 101, 124 +G, 147, [151], [153], 157, 210, 220[1,2] +GCot, 245, 393, 402, 422[2]. XII 137 +B, 138, 148, 153, 165 +HmCrGCotM, 176 +L, [181], 221, 227, 258, 265, 272, 284[1]; [2] +CrL. XIII 41, 74[1] +G; [2] †F, 76, 84, 109, 116, 174, 257, [258], 427a. XIV 18 +?gL, 47, 47a, 48, 49 +HmCr, 60, 207, 216, 256 +B, 267, 289, 293, 299. XV 8, 14 +g, 53[1] +Cr; [2], 61 +Hm, 73, 81, 95, 103 +B, 121[1,2], 154, 160, 162, 170 +Y, 172, 175, 181, 404, 603, 610. XVI 89, 103, [141], 152, 200 +Cr, 209, 252[2,3], 254. XVII 9, 29 +GC[2], 50, 58, 96, 171, 245, 266 +Y, 290, 327. XVIII 22 +HmCrB, 30 +W, 50, [69], 73, 84 +Cr, 121, 189, 204, 213, 215 +HmGYOB, 220, 261a / 262, 269, 290, 298 +Cr, 302[1,2], 320, 322, 323 +WHm, 348 +Cr, 350 +g, 354, 376[2,3], 391 +G, 396, 403 +Cr[23]GC[2]. XX 45, 163 +BoCot, 166, 199, 212, 240[1,2], 242, 249, 289, 379.

(b) *With only* **R** *present*

+**AC**: V 605 +wgZ. +**C**: V 275. IX 142. XI 247. XII 61. XVIII 319a / 320.

(c) *With only* **F** *present*

+**ZA**: Pr 14, 15, 23 +HC, 24, 60 +GC, 61 +GH, 73[1] +**C**. I 146, 152[1], 204, 209 +H. +**ZC**: Pr 44 +HA. +**ZAC**: Pr 4 +H, 5, 6, 31, 42, 48, 71, 72, 76. I 142, 166, 177, 180, 181, 183 +H, 186[3] +G, 187, 190, 191, 192, 201, 203, 207. +**A**: Pr 15, 16, 66 +C, 69 +ZC. I 144. +**AC**: Pr 20 +GZ, 59 +GZ, 67, 77 (*cf.* Z), 78 +HZ, 82. I 175, 189. +**C**: Pr 73[2] +HZA, 102, 105 +WHm, 108[1], [108[2] +C)], 110 +WCr[23]H, 117[1]. I 152[2], 160[1]; [2] +CrOC[2], 162, 202 +H. XVIII 422 +wg. XIX 9 +CrgM, 11, 30, 63, 64, 78, 108 / 09, 110 +?g, 113, 114 +WHm, 140[1,3], 146 (risen] vp r.), 152[1] +Cot, 153, 231[1,2], 246 +Cr[23], 251, 279, 294, 321, 322 +Cot, 350 +W, 403, 404, 408, 414 +C[2]B, 419, 421, 454, 483 +CrO. XX 7, 8, 10 +CrYOC[2]M, 19.

§ 49. Readings with no other-version parallel

(i) Major

(a) *Both* **R** *and* **F** *present*

Pr *144 *L. om.* 208 For*þ*i] For. III 243 tru*þ*e] trewe. 352 mede] me. IV 181[2] wel] *om* (+CrGH). V 131 chaffare] ware. 139 abrood] *om.* 144 freres] *om.* 248 here] *þ*ere. 437 manye] myn (fele F). 639 knowe *þ*ere] welcome. VI 26 labours] laboreres (+Hm). VII 80 For] Forthi. VIII 100 oon] and (F *def.*). 101 That if] For if *þ*at (R *def.*) *103 *L. om.* IX 74 of *þ*at] *om.* 83 mebles] nobles (mone F) +Hm. 96 drede] loue. doo*þ* *þ*erfore] to do. 101 si*þ*þe] seche (all swiche F). *114b–17a *Ll. om.* 192 *propter fornicacionem*] *om.* X 69 kynnes] *om* +G. 204 suwen] scheweth +G. 219 to knowe what is] for to k.

255*a vel*] *aut*. 286 or to greue] *om*. 394 dide...oþere] and other dede. 395 holy writ seiþ] h. w. (s. þe book F). XI *47–9 *Ll. om.* 106 laude] lakke. 255 folwe] wolde / welde. 278 wille] wille With eny wel or wo (w. to suffre wo for welthe F). 279*a inpossibile*] *difficile*. 284 dide] *om*. 322 wondres] wordis (+B; worchynge F). 374 sewest] schewest (makst F). mysfeet] misfeith +BoCot; myschef F. 422 þi] in þi. to suwe] efte to sitte. XII 11 pestilences] penaunce(s). *13–13*a Ll. om.* 48 baddenesse she] badd vse. *76 *L. om.* XIII 143 þow lere þe] to lere and. 214 confermen] confourmen +G. 268 wole] wel. 343 it] I (he F). XIV 14 word] thouȝt. 101 driȝte] lord (god F). 129 to lyue] to þe / of lif. 139 noȝt] *om* (ryght soo þe same F). 142 moore] huire. 143 hire] heuene. 152 rew-] riȝt. 144*a transire*] *ascendere*. 155–6 *Ll. om.* 174 lord] lore (lyȝn F). 190 He] Ho (We F). 198 But] And. 320 þe actif man þo] *om* (þanne F). 323 seweþ] scheweth. XV 254*a L. om.* 264 ne] þe (+B). 280 mylde] meke. 285 fond] fedde. 317 rule] ordre. 337 fressh] ful. 341 feeste] fede. 342*a Item*[2]... *rapis*] om. 386 suffiseþ] *sufficit*. 423 goode] lele. XVI 25 witen] kepen. 48 whan] what. 51 pureliche] priueliche. 189 The. light of al þat lif haþ] þat alle þe liȝt of þe lif. 192 knowe] *om* (owiþ F). XVII 163 is] *om* +HmGCB. 192 shullen] swolle +HmCr[23]M.

(b) *With only* **R** *present*
XV 218 The] To. 443 garte] and grete +B. here and] and to +g. 447 faste] *om*. 461 mynnen] take +C.

(c) *With only* **F** *present*
Pr *50–2 *Ll. om.* 62 Manye] Fele. freres] *om* (+GA; *cf*. C). 89 signe; sholden] charge; sh. at hom. 91 Liggen] & nowht l. 120 tilie; lif] swynke; skyl. I 204 selue] in heuene. II 14 enuenymes] enemyes. 22 bilowen h*ym*] she is lowly. 32 loue] honowre. 36 How...kyng] See how dauid meneþ. 38 bereþ witnesse] ȝow techeþ. VIII 101 That if] For if þat. *102 A IX 95 *after it*. XX 387.

(ii) Minor

(a) *Both* **R** *and* **F** *present*
Pr 135[2], 143, 197 (*om* F), 210. II 98[1,2]. III 109, 236 +Cot, 324, 351 †F. IV 125, 156 +Cr[23], 181 +CrGH. V 142 +y, 254, 257, 272*a* +Cr, 277, 421, 426 +B. VI 196 (*om* F), 249. VII 74, 77[1,2]. IX 66, 76, 81, 86, 88, 107, 126, 149 +Hm, 158. X 26*a*, 94, 205 +Cr, 230, 254, 256, 263, 265, 274, 436, 468, 471. XI 81, 151, 179, 220[1,2], 245, 268, 397, 424. XII 21, 22, 23, 29, 29*a* +Cr[23], 38, 63, 69, 82 +HmB, 88, 192 (+M, *om* F), 273. XIII 123, 158[1,2], 187, 193, 203, 209, 210, 236, 239 +g, 240, 250, 279, 289 +Cr, 302, 312, 317 +GOC[2], 323, 344 +Hmg, 383. XIV 4 +Cr[23], 12, 14 +Cr[3]g, 19, 29, 47*a*, 97, 120 +HmY, 135, 139, 143[1], 144*a*, 187, 197. XV [85], 93, 121, [154], 162, 170 +Y, 263, 278, 284, 286, 294, 319 +GOC[2], 345, 417, 420, 421, 424 +HmCrCot, 426, 498, 501. XVI 4, 12, 17, 38, [59]. XVII 100, 104, 134, 307. XVIII [109], 109*a*, 255, [351].

(b) *With only* **R** *present*
XI 247. XII 61. XIV 76*a*. XV 430, 435, 454 +Hm, 461 +G, 467, 486, 491, 508.

(c) *With only* **F** *present*
Pr 36, 90[1,2], 106, 108, 111, 113[1,2], 115, 116[1];[2]+MH, 119[1] +HmGMH,[2], 121[1,2,3]+Cr, 123, 124[1,2]+H. I 150[1,2], 151, 153[2], 154, 158, 159, 160[1,3]. II 13[1,2,3], 16, 37. XX 13 +Cr.

v. *Comparison of the* α *and* β *families*

§ 50. It is now necessary to consider the relationship and comparative textual worth of the two separate lines of transmission of the B-Text that have been established. Skeat first recognised the α tradition as part of **B**; but as well as ignoring F he identified R as a 'transition stage' between **A** and **C**, 'the B-Text *with later improvements and after-thoughts*' (II, xii). Skeat based his view on R's additions and ascribed most of its omissions to carelessness. This last conclusion is acceptable, but not his judgement that R's 'mere *variations* are but few'. For there are at least 1725 cases where the Bx reading is in clear contestation between the α variant and that of β, the tradition from which all editors since Crowley have selected their copy-text. If the unique lines (individually or grouped) are counted as single readings, about 650 may be classed as major. In some 250 of these, together with about 370 of the minor ones, α alone appears to preserve Bx. Only about 38% of the readings adopted in this edition are therefore taken from α. But for a fairer estimate of the relative value of the two traditions it needs to be remembered that F, at points the only witness present, is significantly less reliable as an α source than is R (§ 44 above). Where both R and F are to hand, comparison will show the two families to attest a more closely similar number of right readings (675 for β and 625 for α). By contrast, over the roughly 780 lines with only F to represent α, the proportion of right readings is 155 to F's 37, over 4 to 1 in favour of β. Where β is absent, comparison of the two α sources over some 175 lines shows R (as already noted) to be about ten times more accurate than F. This proportion is borne out over the bulk of the poem, where both R and F can be systematically compared with β. In the light of these considerations, it is safe to suppose that if R had survived entire, the critical B-Text might have contained more nearly equal numbers of α and β readings and R even have proved suitable as the base-text, since its language is closer than W's to Langland's probable dialect.

§ 51. That R's omissions were due to scribal carelessness is the conclusion of K–D's account identifying various forms of 'eyeskip' as the main cause (pp. 67–9). But unlike Skeat, they consider the unique lines of R (and F) to be not additions to an earlier β form but part of the common source of both families that were omitted by β in the same largely unconscious ways as were the lines lost from α. This explanation has the advantage of simplicity, even if the operation of the suggested mechanisms is not always equally decisive or straightforward. Thus, it would seem unarguable that β left out XI 382–91 through homoœarchy: '*Holy writ...wye wisseþ* followed by Latin 38[2], *wise...witty...wroot bible* followed by Latin 39[2]' (*K–D* p. 66). By contrast, α's omission of XVII 113–24 through 'resumption at a wrong point' (ibid., p. 68) induced by a series of recurring key-words (*feiþ* four times, *felawe* three times, *folwen* twice) is more open to doubt. For despite the recurrence of such a situation at XVII 281–44, K–D's analysis will not satisfy a positivist editor as will one ascribable to mechanical causes. Questioning some of the mechanical explanations has led to a revival of Skeat's notion that R's text is an intermediate stage between β and **C**.[31] Ralph Hanna, for example, tries to accommodate K–D's ascription to β's scribe of its losses from the archetypal source with viewing some α passages, particularly in XI–XV, as revisions. He further urges the significance of thematic factors ignored by K–D, maintaining how XIII 400–09 and XIV 228–38 both deal with Gluttony and Sloth and appear to fill in 'gaps' in β's discussion of the deadly sins. K–D's ascription of the first of these losses to 'notional homœoteleuton (*grace...helpes* 39[9]; *mercy amenden* 40[9]' is indeed a little tenuous taken by itself. But it is much strengthened when *helpes* 399 is seen to be echoed by *helpe it* 408 (the penultimate line of the omitted passage), while the recall of *mynde...moore* 398 in *mercy amenden* 409 looks rather more like the 'verbal and notional homœoteleuton' of which K–D later speak (see § 52). Both the shape of the words and the likeness of the ideas might thus have contributed to the omission, and though this case is not classically simple, instances of eyeskip frequently fail to be. In the second instance, moreover, the first two lines omitted do not relate to the account of Gluttony and Sloth but to that of Wrath, of which they form the conclusion. So since these at least cannot have formed part of a postulated α addition, 'thematic' factors lose relevance. K–D propose 'resumption at a wrong point induced by homœoteleuton (*cheueþ* 227, -*chief* 238)', together with various 'internal correspondences' of recurring connective particles. Their explanation seems to the present editor to gain persuasiveness after observing that at the start of 239, where β resumes, α apparently read *And þouȝ,* i. e. lacked the repeated *if* which might have made a hasty scribe believe he had copied the intervening 230–38 and the two lines before them.

§ 52. There is of course no reason in principle to restrict the enquiry to unconscious scribal loss. For between 'copyist's inattention' and 'author's revision' lies a third possibility, that of 'deliberate scribal intervention'. Thus, fourteen lines after this passage, α has an omission of two lines about brothels that K–D put down to homœoarchy (*A...stuwes* 252, *A...suwe* 254). But scribal censorship on prudential grounds could be the cause here, as in other passages dealing with similar topics. Examples of this are III 51–62, a loss K–D diagnose as due to 'verbal and notional homœo-teleuton', and IX 179–85, which they attribute to homœoarchy but which ends with a Latin allusion to brothels. (Comparable to this are α's omission of the phrase *propter fornicacionem* from the Pauline quotation at IX 192 and β's mention of prostitutes receiving mercy at XIV 183, which could however be mechanical). 'Notional correspondence amounting to homœoarchy' (*K–D*, p. 68) may account for loss of XII 185 from α; but so may scribal unease with Imaginatif's uncompromising attitude to the uneducated. Censorship, now for religious reasons rather than moral or 'political' correctness, may also be at work elsewhere. Examples are in α at XII 193 and XV 72 (if the latter is not mechanical), XVI 264 (possibly superstitious objection to an unlucky word) and XVII 316, and in β at XVII 309–10. The very first β loss, at X 78–9, is seen by K–D as due to homoarchy (*That* 77, 79); but it is interpreted by Taylor, a supporter of Skeat's view of R, as a topical addition in 1382 alluding to the plague of August 1381, which particularly affected children.[32] Here, however, it is not hard to suspect a scribal deletion of lines that might have seemed blasphemous to some readers. Indirectly favouring this view is the Bx scribe's censorship of a no less outspoken expression at line 53 of the same passus. Similar, if more remotely, is the poet's own removal of A XI 161, as perhaps open to various misinterpretations.[33]

§ 53. Proponents of the hypothesis of 'revision within the **B** tradition' also find in some passages an incoherence indicative of continuing authorial involvement at a post-archetypal stage of transmission. An example is XV 528, cited by Justice[34] as well as Taylor, who deems the later insertion of 510–27 in α responsible for syntactic nonsense at 528:

> He is a forbisene to alle bisshopes and a briȝt myrour,
> And souereynliche to swiche þat of Surrye bereþ þe name,
> *And nauȝt to* huppe aboute in Engelond to halwe mennes auteres...

For the italicised phrase β has *That*, which K–D understand as a scribal smoothing after omission of 510–27. But four successive relative clauses introduced by *that* (as in the β form of this passage)[35] are very uncharacteristic of Langland's syntax. Moreover, the supposed confusion in α's reading will disappear once the sentence's elliptical structure is grasped. For the sense here is: 'St Thomas sets a shining example [of faithful duty] to all bishops, [especially to those *in partibus infidelium*], and [he did] not [set an example] of gadding about the country where they have no business to be'. It is hard to credit that the poet, if he had caused a syntactical 'mess' or 'hash'[36] through hasty intervention, would not have put it right in the **C** revision, which generally aims at greater clarity and explicitness. And yet the line, except for a transposition of the verb and the adverbial phrase, remains unaltered at C XVII 279 (see p. 605 of Vol. I). As so often with Langland, the confusion lies not in what the poet wrote but in the minds of his readers. Taylor's objections to the Kane-Donaldson shift of XV 503–09, 528–31 and 532–68, which is accepted in the present edition, lose their force once the intelligibility of 528 has been demonstrated.

§ 54. Supporters of what may be called the 'revisionary' hypothesis further argue that more than one α passage could be removed without disrupting the sequence of thought as found in β.

An example is that on Saul and the Ark at XII 116–25*a*. Yet here Taylor's claim that the preceding line 115 'lead[s] quite logically' into 12[6][37] need not count against the contextual coherence of the α lines but in favour of that of the passage as a whole (114–30). For while Langland's reference to Saul undoubtedly amplifies his warning against interference with the priestly prerogative even by the highest in the land, mention of *his sones also* at 117 is making a pointed contrast with *preestes sone* at 115, the line before the α passage commences. Similarly, the allusion to priestly anointing of a knight at 126, the line *after* the passage ends, acquires sharper focus if seen as originally following *christos meos* 125*a*. This is because what the anointed clergy 'keep' is not only the sacraments but also 'sacramentals' such as the oils of anointing. Thus, if Taylor were right about XII 116–25*a*, its incorporation into the β text would actually exhibit a carefulness incompatible with its being an 'anomalous addition' made in response to events after the Rebellion of 1381.[38] It is a weakness of Taylor's analyses that they arise from a mistaken quest for topical allusion. But this is something Langland seems to have employed only if a more general moral significance could be drawn from a particular historical event. The classic case is the great wind of 1362, which is retained unaltered from **Z** through to **C**.[39]

§ 55. The 'revision hypothesis' also requires a complicated genetic scheme to account for the α passages apparently lacking from β without adequate mechanical explanation. Hanna's argument[40] is that from Langland's original (*O*) was made a copy (*O¹*), and from this another (*O²*), which omitted about 20 of the 37 unique α passages (and which corresponds to the source here called β). At a second stage, the <rf> passages were copied into O; from O thus augmented, into O¹; and from O¹ into both the copy used for revision to **C** (= 'B¹') and into O², from whence the RF source (= 'α') acquired them. Historically speaking, such a manuscript evolution is no more improbable than the simpler one preferred here; but it seems to the present editor analytically less persuasive. For since all the evidence lies within the text, the main issue would appear to be logical rather than historical: whether a two-stage authorial manuscript and one vertical axis of transmission or a one-stage original and two-branch vertical axis better explain the data. Hanna is no doubt right to hesitate over some of K–D's homœographic explanations (which may however be susceptible of further refinement) and also to maintain that, on distributional grounds, purely mechanical losses are unlikely to have occurred only from Passus X onwards. But this is not a decisive objection to the hypothesis of a 'unitary' **B** tradition,[41] given the demonstrable existence of such losses amongst β's omissions in XI–XX and α's in Pr–IX. For the first half of β could have been produced by a more careful scribe than the one who produced the second half (the converse situation to that hypothesised for the copying of the archetypal manuscript at § 5). What seems clear is that the idea that some α passages do not 'fit' holds up in none of the cases adduced.

§ 56. Even more unconvincing is Hanna's conception of Langland's attitude to his poem as that of someone who 'felt uncompelled to ensure the accuracy of his text' but 'placed his credence in a copyist, whose work he shows no sign of having supervised and corrected.'[42] The first assertion here conflicts with the poet's strictures in XI 305–06 upon the scribal *goky* who *parcelles ouerskippe[þ]*. The second is contradicted by the singular accuracy of the archetypal text in Passus XVI (see § 5 above), which can scarcely be explained except by authorial correction. But it is not hard to envisage circumstances that might have prevented Langland from exercising continuous supervision of the scribal efforts. Further, some **C** revisions could be, as K–D believe, direct responses to uncorrected B[1] errors. But if they are, these logically endorse rather than question the *a priori* likelihood of the poet's wanting a carefully copied text of his carefully written poem. Hanna's notion might once have seemed plausible, with only Skeat's text to rely on and before Langland's poetic technique had been explored. But it rests on the incoherent assumption that the author of so 'fine a literary document' had a 'general lack of interest in local textual detail' and a 'relative lack of interest in the text.'[43] Complementing Taylor's and Justice's notion of Langland's 'syntactical confusion', which has been shown to be mistaken, Hanna's comments reveal the imprudence of generalising on no firmer a basis than 800 lines from 'widely-scattered passages', which he confidently proceeds to 're-edit.'[44] For the many changes made throughout the **C** revision, especially in the b-verses, argue strongly against his view of Langland and show both the extent and the minuteness of the poet's concern with matters of 'local textual detail' affecting vocabulary, metre, style and expression. Without comparative scrutiny of the text in all versions, such sweeping statements about the poet's 'compulsions' are vain. For both editing the text and correctly interpreting its details demand a vigilant sense of the whole when dealing with any part.[45]

§ 57. It will have emerged from the above discussion that the notion of a *Piers Plowman* that never achieved or even aimed at a final form, but remained continuously subject to 'rolling revision', is unacceptable. It is a notion that confuses authorial composition with the quite distinct process of scribal transmission; and it arises out of a misunderstanding of the nature of Langland's poetic art and his entire undertaking seen in the context of the similar enterprises of his major contemporaries Chaucer, Gower and the *Gawain*-poet. To the present editor, the textual evidence affords no firmer grounds for belief in a two-phase B-Text represented by α and β than in a two-phase A-Text with earlier and later forms represented by **r** and **m** respectively. In each of the three universally accepted versions of the poem, three conclusions seem highly probable. First, the line of transmission has divided into two independent post-archetypal branches, between which there was no reciprocal interaction. Second, the subsequent variations attested, from individual minor readings to lines and passages, were not introduced into either sub-archetype by the author.[46] Third, none of the readings that appear original on intrinsic grounds have come in from a lost source superior to Bx. Since B[1] existed for Langland's use in revising to **C**, it could in principle have provided some of those superior readings for post-archetypal scribes who had access to it. But as has been argued above (§§ 25, 28, 32 and 46), all such preferred readings may be more economically ascribed to contamination from **A** or **C** (see also §§ 62 and 71 below). After analysis, the disjunctive readings listed in §§ 41–48, which massively differentiate two competing textual traditions, suggest only one cause: scribal intervention, conscious, partly conscious or unconscious, during the copying of a long and often provocative piece of 'making'. For in most major and in many minor instances of conflicting readings, clear grounds exist for judging that one variant is derived from a source represented by the other and consequently that in each case either α *or* β is likely to preserve the archetypal text. The **B** Version of *Piers Plowman* possessed a distinctive *telos* which its poet set out to realise as scrupulously as Chaucer did in his *Troilus*, however scurvily Langland's *scriueynes* fell short of being *trewe* (see *Intro.* V §§ 23–5 below). Before examining (in §§ 60–5) the damage they wrought, it will be convenient to complete this section by tabulating here the unique lines of α and β, which Skeat recognised as part of **B** and K–D first identified as partial witnesses to a single text.

§ 58. (*i*) The β family is the sole witness of six citation-lines and some 200 text-lines, consisting of 191 whole and 17 half-lines. (The presence or absence of other-version support for these is found in §§ 42–3 above).

Pr 3. 33b–34a. 50–4. 144. 171. I 82. 157. II 11. III 51–62 [3 *semi-spurious ll. in* a]. 149b–50a. IV *none*. V 474. VI 88b. 217. 309b–10a. VII 41a. VIII 14–17. 100b. 103. IX 114b–17a. 160–61. 166. 170–72 [3 *spur. ll.* a]. 179–85 [*citation ll. at* 183a]. 200–03. X 424. XI 46–9. XII 13–13a. XIII 14–20. 373b–74a. XIV 155–59. 252–53. 288b. 309a. XV 72. 254a. 402–03. 532–68. XVI 27b–28a. 264. 270–73 [3 *spur. ll.* a]. XVII 7b. 34–47. 113–24. 218–44. 316. XVIII 179. 198. 252–53. 423. XIX 88b–89a. 161a–162. 204–07. 211b–13. 247. 439–40. XX 238–39.

(*ii*) The α family is the sole witness of five citation-lines and some 187 text-lines, consisting of 167 whole and fifteen half-lines, nine spurious lines and three (enclosed in square brackets) here treated as a scribal confection from authentic **A** material.

(*a*) *In* RF: Pr–IX *none*. X 78–9. 291–302. 368. 380. 410–12. XI 110. 131b–32a. 159–69 (167 *om* F). 196. 382–91. 427b–29a. XII 55–7a. 116–25a. 151–52. XIII 165–72a (170, 172 *om* F). 293–99. 400–09. 437–54. XIV 183, 228–38. XV 244–48. 303 04. 395. 510–27. 572b–75a. XVI *none*. XVII [8]. 69. 112a. 177b–79a. 309–10. XVIII 312b–13a. XIX *none*. XX 37. [*Spurious*: three *ll. at* III 51 (*like* A III 50–1); *for* IX 170–72; *for* XVI 270–73].
(*b*) *In* R *only*: XI 167. XIII 170, 172. XV 471–84. 489a.
(*c*) *In* F *only*: VIII 109b–110a. XIX 56–9. 152b. 237b–38a. 337.

As stated at § 57, on the hypothesis that α and β are sub-archetypes of Bx, the readings that either attests in the other's absence are, when correct, presumed to be those of the archetype; when not, they are of necessity only possibly so.

vi. *The Archetypal Text of the* **B** *Version*

§ 59. In the two lists of family readings at §§ 42–3 and 48–9, the selected lemma has been tacitly understood to represent Bx, and the rejected variant a scribal corruption of the latter in one or other sub-archetype. The more important examples will be found discussed in detail in the *Textual Notes*. But the minor ones, too numerous for individual consideration, are mostly so similar that systematic notice here would add little to what is already familiar from the Athlone editions (some typical examples will be cited at the end of § 65 below). In the following list, lines are identified as certainly or probably archetypal where (*a*) α and β agree; (*b*) β agrees with R *or* F understood as preserving α; (*c*) of the constituent branches of β (§§ 9–10 above), one or more (usually L) agree with α, or with R / F understood as = α , a '?' indicating uncertainty due to absence of other-version support (these are already listed at § 38 above). Two unadopted Lα agreements which may be archetypal and are conceivably original appear marked '‡'. Otherwise the list includes all and only the archetypal lines judged correct, ignoring wrong line-division where no substantive error results. It excludes (*a*) readings attested by only one family even if, from intrinsic character and other-version support, they appear original and so presumptively archetypal; (*b*) readings judged correct but resulting from possible coincidence or other-version contamination. The latter category embraces most of the 116 right readings noted in the foregoing discussions of the β subgroups, which will be recorded in § 62 as equivalent to editorially emended readings, the 'editor' in such cases having been the scribe. Details of available other-version support are provided only for the readings in category (*c*). As those and most major archetypal errors corrected in the text are discussed in the *Textual Notes*, except where the rationale of emendation seems self-evident, only a few are singled out for mention in §§ 65–7 below. Because of the defectiveness of both α witnesses, it is clearly stated which manuscripts are present to attest this family at any point.

Square brackets denote readings where Bx has been editorially reconstituted from split variants. A plus indicates agreement with the adopted, a minus agreement with the rejected reading.

Pr (α = F): 1–2. 12–13. 18. 20. 23. 25–6. 30. 35–6. 44–5. 47. 49. 56. 63. 69–70. [77]. 79. 85–6. 92. 94–5. 100–01. 104–05. 123. (α = RF): 125–34. 136–9. ? 140. 141–42. 145–47. 149–58. 160–70. 173–78. 180–81. 183–4. 186–88. 193–96. 198–99. 201. 203–04. 207. 211–12. 214–15. 217–22. 224. 226. 230–31.

I 1–3. 5–10. 12–30. +**ZAC** 31. 32–6.36. 38–40. 48–53. 55–6. 58–9. 61–3. 65–9. 72. 74–6. 79–81. 83–6. 89–97. 100–03. 105–09. 111. 114–18. 120. 122. 124. 126. 128. 130–32. 135. 137. 139–40. (α = F): 143. 148. 156. 159. 161. 163–64. 167–73. 178–79. 183. 188. 195. ?199.

II 2–3. 6. 15. 17–18. 27. 33–4. 39. (α = RF): 42. 44–6. 48–50. 52–4. 56–67. 69–74. 76–82. 86–8. 90. 92–7. 99–100. 102–07. 109–10. 112. 114–19. 123–30. 132–37. 139–42. 144. [145]. 146–7. +**ZAC** 148. 149–53. 156–58. 160. 162–79. 182. 184–97. 199. 204–09. 211–21. 223–25. 228. 230–35.

III 1–2. 4. 7. 9–10. 13–14. 16–18. 20–31. 34–5. 37–8. 40. 42–7. 50. 64–6. 69–70. 72–4. 76–9. 81. 83–5. 88–90. 92–7. 99. 101–03. 105–08. 110–11. 115–16. 118–21. 123. 125–26. 129. 134–39. 142–44. 146. 148. 152–54. 156–59. 161. 163–74. 176–77. 179–81. [182]. 184–86. 188–204. 206–09. 211–13. 215–18. 220–21. 223. 225. 227–28. 230. 232–34. 237–42. 244–50. +**A** ?251. 252–54. 256–57. 259. 261–64. 266–76. 278–80. 282. 285–88. 290–91. 293–94. 296–97. 299–300. 302–09. 311–15. 317–18. 320–21. 323–26. 329–35. 337–41. 343. 347–50. 353.

IV 1–3. 5–6. 8–9. 11. 13–14. 16–25. 28–31. 33–5. 37. 39. 41–6. 48–54. 57–61. 63–4. 66–85. 87–9. 92–3. 95–8. 100–02. 107–08. 110–16. 119–35. 137–40. 142–44. 146–55. 157. 159–60. 162–72. 174–80. 182–83. 185–89. 191–93.

V 1–6. 9–14. 16. 18. 20–2. 24. 27–8. 30. ?31. 33. 36–9. 42–6. 49–69. 71–2. 74–5. 77–8. 81–3. 85–96. 98–108. 110. 114–17. 119–25. 127. 129. 132–38. 140–41. 143. 145–47. 149–50. 152–53. 155. 157–59. 161–64. 166–70. 173. 177–78. 180. 182–85. 187. 189–91. 196–207. +**AC** 208. +**A-C** 209. 210–11. 216–20. 224–37. 239–47. 249. 251–52. 255–56. 258. 260. +**C** ‡261. 262–64. 266–69. 271–73. 276. 278. 280–81. 283. 285–99. 301–03. 306–09. 311–12. 314–15. 319–20. 322. 324–25. 329. 331–37. 339–43. 345–50. ‡351. 352–56. 358. 360–63. 365–68. 371–74. 377. 379–82. +**ZAC** 383. 384–85. 387. 389–93. 395–99. 401–03. 411. 413–14. 416–19. 422. +**C** 424. 425. 427–32. 434–36. 438–39. 442–45. 447–50. 452–55. 457–62. 464–65. 467. 470. 472. 475–76. 478–82. 484–86. 488–90. 492–93. 498–501. 503–04. 506. 508–11. 513. 515–18. 520. 523–25. 527–31. 534–35. 537–39. 541–44. 546. 548–49. 551. 553–54. 556. 558–64. 568–72. 574. 577–80. 584–87. 589–90. 592–95. 598. 600–08. 612. 614–16. 618. 620–26. 629–31. 633–37. 640–42.

VI 1. 3–7. 9–25. 27–29. 31–2. 35–8. 40–1. 43–4. 46–7. 49. 51. 53–8. 62–4. 68–73. 75. 77–9. 81–2. 84. 90–1. 93. 96–7. 99–102. 104. 106–12. 114–18. 121–22. 124–27. 129. 131. 133–35. 137. 139–47. 149. 151. 153. 156. 158–60. 163–67. 169–70. 172–74. 176–78. 180–84. 186–92. 195. 197. 199. 204. 206. 208–09. 211. 213–14. 220. 224. ?225. 226–29. 231–33. 235–36. 239–41. 243–44. 246–48. 250–56. 258–70. 273–76. 279–80. 282–83. 286–89. 291. 293–300. 302–04. 306–08. 311. 313–19. 322–23. ?326. 327–28.

VII 2–6. 9–16. 18. 22–3. 27–30. 32. 35–6. 38. 40–4. 47. 50–5. 58. 60–1. 63–7. 69. 71–3. 75–6. 78–9. 81–7. 90–1. 97–9. 101–03. 105. 108. 110–19. 121–24. 126–32. 134–35. 137. 139–42. 144–45. 147–55. 157–67. 169–74. 176–80. 183–90. 192. 195–98. 200–01.

VIII 1–3. 5. 7–8. 10–11. 13. 18–20. 22–4. 26–7. 29. +**AC** 30. 32–4. 37. 39–40. 42. -**A** ?43. 45–7. 49. 52–6. 58. 60–2. 67–8. 71. 73. 75–6. 79–82. 84–8. 90–1. 94. 96. 98. 106. 111–15. 117–18. 120–24. 126. ?127. 128.

IX 1. 3. 5–6. 8–9. 12–13. 18–19. 21. 23. 25. ?26. 27. 30. 32. 34. 36–7. 40. 43–7. 49–50. 52. 54. 56–9. 61–3. ?64. 65. 67–73. 75. 77–80. 82. 84–5. 89–90. 92–5. 97–8. 100. 102–06. 108–09. 111–12. ?113. 120–25. 127–34. 136–40. 143–48. 150–53. 156–57. 164–65. 167. 173–74. 177. 186. 191. 195–97. 199. 205. 207.

X 2–13. 15–7. 19. 22–7. 29–35. 37–45. 48–9. 51–2. 56. 58–9. 61–5. 67. 73–4. 76. 80–5. 88–9. 91–3. 95–107. 109–23. 125–27. 130. 132. 134. 136. 138. 148–53. 155. 157–61. 164–66. 168–70. 174–75. 177–84. 187–88. 191–203. 206–08. 210–16. 220. 222. 224–29. 231–38. 240–41. 244–45. 247. 249. 252–53. 255. 257–64. 266–70. ?271. 272. 275–78. 280–83. 285. 287–90. 305–06. 308–13. 315–19. 321–22. 324–36. 338–41. 343–66. 370–75. 381–83. 386. 388–90. 392. 396–407. 414–20. 423. 425–33. ?435. 437–45. 447–48. 450–57. 459–60. +**A** 461. 462–65. 467. 469–70. 474–5.

XI 1–3. 9–20. 22–5. 27–36. 38–40. 42. 44–5. 50–7. 61–6. 68–80. 83. 85. 87–100. 102–05. 109. 111–20. 122–23. 126. 128. ?133. 135–37. 139–43. 146. 148–50. 152. 154–56. 158. 170–78. 180. 182–83. 185–92. 194–95. 198–99. 201. 203. 205–07. 209. 211–19. 221–37. 240–44. 246. 248–54. 256–61. 263–64. 266–67. 269–76. ?277. 279–80. 282–83. 285–87. 290–94. 296–300. 302–21. 323–24. 326–29. 331–38. ?339. 340–42. [343]. 344–47. 349. 351–54. 357–66. 368–69. 373. 375–81. 392. 394–95. 399–400. 403–14. 416–18. 421. 425–26. 431–32. 436–37.

XII 1–3. 5–10. 12. 14–5. 17–20. 26–8. 31–3. 35–7. 39–47. 50–4. 58. 62. 64–5. 67–8. 70–2. 74–5. 79–81. 83–7. 89–90. 92–4. 96–8. 100–03. 105–06. 108–10. 112–15. 128. 132–34. 139. 149–50. 154–58. 160–64. 166–68. 170–75. 177. 179–80. 182. 187–91. 194–95. +**C** 196. 197–201. [202]. 204–07. 209. 211–12. 216–20. 222–26. 228–39. 241–43. 245–57. 259–64. 267–69. 271. 274–81. 283. 286. 288. 291–94.

XIII 1. 3. 5–7. 9–10. 12–13. 12–13. 21–34. 36–40. 42–4. 46. 48–9. 51. 53. 54–5. 57–9. 61. 64–9. 71–3. 75. 77–9. 81. 83–4. 87–90. 94. 97–102. 105–11. 113–15. 117–19. [120]. 121–22. 124–34. 137–42. 144–49. 151–57. ?158. 159–64. 173. 176–86. 188–92. 194. 196–208. 211–13. 215–20. 222. 224–28. 230–32. 234–35. 237–38. 241–49. 251–54. 256. 259. 261–66. 269. ?270. 271. 273–75. 277–78. 281–82. +**C** 283–84. 285–88. 291–92. ?301. 303–11. 313–16. 318–22. 324–25. 327–29. 331–33. 335–40. 342. 345–48. 351–53. ?355. 356–60. 362–63. 365–66. 368–72. 375–82. 384–86. 388–90. 392–97. 413–22. 425. 427–36. 457–60.

XIV ?1. 2–3. 5–6. 10–11. 13. 15–17. 20. 22. 24–7. 30–5. 37–9. 42–6. 50. 53–5. 57–8. 62–5. 68–71. 73–84. ?85. 86–96. 98–9. 102–05. 107–15. 117–18. 121–22. 124–28. 130–31. 136–38. 140. 145–51. 160–73. 175–76. [177]. 178–80. 184–85. 188. 191–95. 199–203. 206. 208. 210–11. 214–15. 218–22. 224–27. +**C** 239. 240–51. 254–55. 258–59. 261–62. 264. 266. 268–72. 276. [277]. 278–83. 286–87. 294. 296–98. 302–03. 305. 308. 312. 314–15. 317–19. 321–22. 324–28. 330–32.

XV 1–4. 6–7. 9–11. 13. 15–17. 19–24. 26–35. +**C** 36. 37–41. 43–52. 54–6. 58–60. 62. ?63 (-**C**). 64–9. 71. 75–7. 79–80. 82–4. 86–7. 91–2. 94. 96–9. 101–02. 104–05. 108. 110. 112–14. 117. 119–20. 122. 124–25. 128–32. 134. 137. 139–43. 145–46. 148–53. 155. 157–59. 161. 163–69. 171. 173–74. 176–79. 182–86. ?187. 189–92. 194–95. 197–99. ?200. 201–05. 208–17. 219–23. 225–43. 249–54. 255. 257–62. 265–77. 279. 287–92. 295–96. 298–302. 305–11. 313. 315–16. 318. 323–36. 338. 340. 343–44. 346–51. 353–54. 356–58. 360–61. 363–69. 371–76. 378–85. 387–92. 396–7. ?+**C** 398. 399–401. 405–06. 408–16. 418–19. 425. 427–29. 431–34. 436–42. 445–46. 448–49. 451–53. 455–59. 462–66. 468–69. 487–89. 490. 492–93. ?+**C** 494. 495–97. 499–500. 505–05. +**C** 506. 509. 569–70. 576–78. 580–83. 586. 588–90. 592. 594–98. 600–02. 604–09.

XVI 1–3. 5–11. 13–16. 18–24. 26. 29. 31–37. 39–42. 44. 46–7. 49. +**C** 50. 52–8. ?+**C** 60. 61–75. 79–82. 84–8. 90–2. 94. 96. 102. 104–10. 111–14. 116–18. 120. 122. 124–35. 137–39. 143–47. 149–51. 153–57. 159. 161–75. 177–88. 190–91. 194–97. 202–08. 210. 212–19. +**C** 221. 222–49. 251. 253. 255–61. 263. 265–69. 274.

XVII 2. 5–6. +**C** 11. 12. 14. +**C** 15. 16–22. 24–28. 30. 32–6. 48–9. 51–6. 59–64. 66–8. 70–3. 75–7. 79–80. -**C** ?81. [82]. 83–4. 87–9. 91. 93–4. 97–99. 101–02. ?104. 105–06. 108. 110–12. 125–33. 135–36. 142–47. 149–51. 153. 155–59. 161. ?162. 165. 167–70. 172–75. 180. 182–89. 191. 193–95. 197–98. 200–01. 203. 205–06. 208–13. 215–17. 247–53. 255–63. 265. 267–89. 291–93. 295. 297–98. 301. +**C** 304. 305–06. 308. 310–11. 313–14. 315. 317–19. 321–24. 328. 331–35. 337. 338. ?339. 341–43. 345–47. 349–52.

XVIII 1–7. 9–10. 13. 15–21. 23–7. 29. 32–4. 36–8. [39]. 42–4. 46–9. 52–3. 55–8. 60–1. 63–8. 70–2. 74–5. 77–81. 88–92. 94–5. 97–100. 102–08. 110–18. 120. 122–23. 125–28. 130–6. 148–50. 152–53. 155. 158. 162–64. 166. 168–69. 171–72. 176–78. 180. 183–88. 190–91. 194–97. 199–201. 203. 205–12. 214. 217. 219. 221–25. 227–32. 235–45. 247. 249–50. 254. 256–60. 262–64. 266–68. 270. 272–73. 275. 277–79. 284–89. 291–94. 297. 299–301. 304–05. 307–11. 314–15. 321. 324–41. 345–47. +**C** 349. 352–53. +**C** 354. 355. 357–59. 361–62. 365–75. 377–79. 381–82. 385–89. +**C** 390. 392. 393–95. 397–98. 400–01. 404–05. 407–10. 412. (**a** = F): 413–15. 418–21. 424. 427–28. 432–33.

XIX 2. 17. 33. 37. +**C** 47. 53–5. 61–2. 65–67. 69–70. 74. 84. 86. 95. 100. 104. 106. 107. 112. 115. 121–23. 129. 144. 147. 163. 166–67. 171. 178. +**C** 190. 193. 201. 208. 220–21. 226. 228. 235. 242–43. 257–58. 261. 266. 278. 291. 295–96. 300. 303. 305. +**C** 309. 331. 336. 338. 344. 358. 362–66. 368. 370–71. 383. 388. 393. 399. 410. 427. 438. 443. 447–49. +**C** ?457. 460. 462. 464. 475–76. 478–80.

XX +**C** 6. 12. 15–16. 18. 20. (α = RF): 28–33. 40–1. 43–4. 46–7. 49–53. 56–9. 61. 64. 66. 68–77. 79–86. 88–90. 92. 94. 96. 98–101. 103. 105. 107–13. 115–16. 118. 121–24. ?125. 128–31. 133–35. 137. 140. 143–49. 153–57. 159–62. 164–65. 167–70. 172–73. 175–82. 184–90. 192–93. 195–97. 200–01. 203–06. 209. 213. 215–17. 219–20. 222–32. 234–37. 241. 243–48. 250–52. 254–55. 257. 259. 262. 264. 266–68. 270–76. 278. 280–82. 285–88. 294–300. 302. ?303. 304–05. 307–08. 310. 313–20. 322–26. 328. 330–36. 338–42. 344–48. 350. 352–56. 358–59. 362–63. 365. 368–76. 381–82. 384–86.

vii. *Emendation of Errors in the Archetypal B-Text*

§ 60. The archetypal B-Text contains some 600 major and minor errors (six times as many as Cx and proportionally four times as many as Ax). To save space, they are referenced only by line-number, since all of the major ones will be found discussed in the *Textual Notes*. They are divided into whole-line and intralinear errors. About 55 major errors involve whole lines: two dozen misdivided, of which five are followed by scribal misexpansion or omission (denoted by *); a dozen misplaced; nine omitted; and fifteen spurious, in a dozen separate instances. Other-version evidence for emendation is indicated where available and emended readings are listed again below in the categories to which they belong. Half a dozen cases where absence of one family renders Bx undecidable are in square brackets.

(i) *Misdivided Lines*

III 223/24* (*em. from* **A**). V 149/50 *as* 3 *ll*. (*em. after* Cr[23]; *cf.* **C**). 188* *as* 2 *ll*. (*em. from* **AC**). VII 69/70. ?174/75 (*correct* F; *so* **AC**). IX 41/2. X [297/8 *only in* α; *em. from* **AC**]. 446/47. XI 148/49. 204* *as* 2 *ll*; *em. from* **C**. 346/47 (*em. from* **C**). 371/72; *em. after* **C**. XII 129/30*; *rec. after* **C**. 183/4 (*em. after* **C**). 251/2. XIII 53a/4. 56/6a. 255* *as* 2 *ll*; *em. after* **C**. 330/31; *em. from* **C**. XIV 316–17a (*em. from* **C**). XVIII 32/3; *em. from* **C**. XIX 305–06 *as* 3 *ll*; *em. from* **C**. 317/18; *em. from* **C**. 345/46; *em. from* **C**. XX 33a/5 *as* 2 *ll*; *em. from* **C**. 62/3; *em. from* **C**.

(ii) *Misplaced Lines*

Pr 189–92 *after* 197. I 98–9, 100–03 *trs*; *em. after* **ZA**. II 203 *after* 205; *em. after* **ZAC**. VI 275, 276 *trs*; *em. after* **ZAC**. [IX 166 (*only in* β) *after* 168; *em. after* **AC**]. XIII 52, 53 *trs*. XIV 286, 286a *trs*. 304a, 306 *trs*. [XV 503–09, 528–31 *after* 532–68 b; *here in* α. 532–68 *after* 502a β; *om* α]*. XVIII 6–8 *after* 9.

(iii) *Omitted Lines*

I 112 (*supplied from* **Z**). [IV 10: *in* YOC[2]Cr[23]; ? *from* **A** *or* **C**]. V 328 (*from* **C**). 338 (*from* **A**). XI 371b. XII 129b. XVIII 161. XIX 441. XX 261 (*from* **C**).

(iv) *Spurious Lines*

After: IV 38. V 39a, 54, 193, 556. VI 17, 182. VII 59 (2 *ll*). X 266. XI 67. *In place of*: XVIII 82 (*suppl. from* **C**). XIX 373 (2 *ll*; *em. from* **C**).

§ 61. Some 550 instances (about 70% major) of wrong readings within lines involve individual words, phrases or half-lines; where more than one occurs in a line they are numbered by their position in the Apparatus. They are divided as corrected by restoration, reconstruction or conjecture (see *A Version* § 56 above). Superior non-archetypal readings that appear original and are also found in one or more **B** manuscripts are included with (i) if convincingly attributable to contamination, with (iii) if attributable to scribal guesswork. (These have already been listed above in the sections on each sub-family and its groups). Lines found defective on metrical grounds are marked ^. A plus sign denotes manuscripts containing the reading adopted in the text. Instances where through conflict between families or absence of one family the Bx reading is undecidable, and so cannot be judged certainly corrupt, are in square brackets.

§ 62. (i) *Restored readings*

Some 320 archetypal errors, of which nearly 155 are major, have been emended by restoration on the basis of secure readings in one or more of the other three versions. About 15% are made chiefly on metrical grounds; in the rest, for various reasons of sense, style or expression as well as metre. Around 119 corrections, 33 being major, are based on the agreed **ZAC** reading. The next highest number is 93 taken from **AC** (half of them major) and 90 from **C** (58 major and 32 minor). There are also some 24 cases where Bx seems undecidable, but some may be archetypal, including several in Passus XIX where F is the only α witness. Just over 20 are from **ZA**, **ZC**, **Z** and **A**. About 113 of the adopted readings are *also* attested in one or more extant **B** witnesses. Of these, some 83 are minor, and most could have arisen through felicitous coincidental variation. Among the 30 major ones, many are ascribable to contamination. Those in G, H, and F come from an **A** source (see §§ 28, 32, 46 above) and those in OC[2] from **C** (§ 24). But those from L or R are, on the general showing of these manuscripts, antecedently likely to represent β and α respectively, and thence by inference Bx (see §§ 36–7).

From **ZAC**: **Major** Pr 41[1];[2]+H. 59[2](*cf.* H). [76[4] +H]. I ^165. 186 (*cf.* H). 187 +GH. 191[2] +G.^200. ^206 +GH. II 47. 180. 181. ^200. 210 +F. III 124. 132. IV 10 +YOC[2]Cr[23]. 109. V ^47. 468. [474]. 512. 514. ^557. 617. VI 179. 198. 200. 215. 221. 312. VII ^7. ^104. **Minor** Pr 29. 231 +G. I 4. 37 +G. 54 +W. 88. 104. 125 +G. 136. 142. 174 +G. 176 +CrG. 191[1]

+GF. II ^28. 75 +GHF. 89. 113 +HmCH. 198. 201. 202. 222. III 3 +BH. 12 +B. 113. 114 +H; *added* G. 117. 124¹ +G;² +F. 132 +GH. 141. 160 +GF. IV 32. 47 +H. 94 +CrH. 105 +GH. 106. 117 +HmHF. 136. 184. 190 +H. V 17. 26. 35. 463. 473 +CrGF. 512. 533 +gF. 536 +y. 567. 575. 576. 583 +G. 588. 597. 609. 610. 613. VI 2. 8 +WHmYOC². 34. 59–60–61. 65 +WCrC²CBoCot. 88. 92. 94. 119 +M *added*. 128 +BCr. 152 +yF. 205. 207¹,*cf.* YOC²;² +Y. 210. 216 +M. 257 +B. 277 +GBF. 284 +OC². 324. VII 33 +HmF. 48. 88–9. 93¹,². 94. 95.

From **ZA**: **Major** I 127 (*cf.* **C**). VI ^285. VII 49. **Minor** Pr 7. I 199. II 75 +GHF. III 15. IV 99 +GM.

From **ZC**: **Minor** I 64.

From **Z**: **Major** I 112. V 555.

From **AC**: **Major** Pr ^82. I 152 +Cr. II 8 +G. 9 +F=?a. III ^98. 151. 222. 281. IV 145 (*cf.* H**Z**). V 126. 188 *misexpanded* Bx. 193. 195. 214. 221. 223. 304¹ *misexp.* 310. 526 (*cf.* **Z**). VI +**Z** 271, 305. VII +**Z** 24. 109. 175. VIII 12. 25, 28 +F. ^31. ^93. 95. 107. 108. 119. IX 4 +OC². 7. 17. 22. X 36. 53. 68. 171. ^173. 378. 385. 421. **Minor** Pr 59¹ +WHm. 67 +G. I 200¹ +C²;². II 229. III 41 (*cf.* H). 48 +H. 87. 147. 183. 210. *24. 226 +H. 265. 284 +M *corr.* 289. 295. V 34. 209. 304². 318. 451. 466 +Hm. 471. 532. 628 (*cf.* GF). 638 +WG. VI 74. +**Z** 278, 321. VII 109 +G. 146 +G. 168. VIII 38 +GF. 70. 74. IX 169. 187. 193. X 21¹,². 54. 55. 57 +w. 70 +FG. 71. 156. 172 +HmB?G. *From* **A**: **Major** III ^71. 224. V 591. VI ^272. VIII 44. (100). X 124 +gM. **Minor** I 191⁴. II 120 +yF; *not* **Z**, *but cf.* **C**. III 251 +BHR =? α. VIII 78 +F. X 60 +M.

From **C**: **Major** [Pr 171 +Y]. I 11 (*cf.* H). II [22]. 84. 143. III 283 +WG. 292. 316. 322 +Bm. 342 +GCr. IV 90 +H. V 179. 330. 351. IX ^16. XI 110. 144 +w. ^287. [429]. XII ^129. XIII 2 +B. ^8. 96 +OC²Cot. ^175. 223 +CrF; *by erasure* M. ^341. 411 +OC²B. ^424. ^444. 454. XIV ^304. XV ^115. [^545. ^547. ^550. ^554]. 611 [+L = ?β]. XVI 27 +L. (136). XVII 234. ^316. ^326. XVIII 40. 54. 154. 160¹ +C²;² +YGC². 198 +L. ^402. ^406. XIX 38 [+L =?β]. [56]. [57]. 97 [^152]. [154]. [181 +O]. [183]. ^252. 304. ^317. 333. [337]. ^346. [367]. 433. [468]. [^483]. XX ^34. ^54. 67. 104. 106. 117 +WHmF. ^309. ^377. **Minor** Pr [99 +H]. 148. 182 +G. II 35 +YCr. 90 +w. III 226 +H. IV 90 +H. V 172. 176. 423 +wG. 441. 495. 497. 565. VI 201 +wG. VII 56 +y. X 297. XI ^127. ^287 +WHm. 325. XII 56a. [25]. XIII 45a +g. XIV 181 [+L = ?β]. 291a +Cot. XV 552 +W. XVI 27 [+L = ?β]. [142]. XVII 198a +CrC². 199. 222 +CrGC. XVIII [151]. 231. ?234 +WR. XIX [9 +WHmL]. 46 +HmO. 83 +LCB. 181 +L. 297. 376. 391 +C. 432 +CB. 434. XX 6 +L = ?β. 8. 14. 19¹ +YC²M;². 127 +CrM. 284.

§ 63. (ii) *Reconstructed readings*

Some 140 errors (all but about ten major) are identified from deficiencies of sense, metre and style. These, often on comparison with (near)-parallels in the other versions, may be securely reconstructed. As with restoration and reconstruction, the distinction between a 'reconstruction' and a 'conjecture' can be a fine one. Thus, in III 260 or V 171 a mechanical explanation of the metrical defect is at hand (here haplography). In IV 86, by contrast, the error is linguistic and stylistic (substitution of a commoner synonym causing damage to metre). The 'reconstruction' of the second of these seems hard to distinguish from the 'conjecture' at IV 91 (*wiþseide*] *seide*). But on closer inspection the latter will be seen to be more speculative than the former. For it competes with **C**, which arguably preserves (as K–D believe) a harder **B** reading supplanted by Bx; it assumes an unparalleled usage of the proposed word; and that word is presumed so unusual as to have prompted the same substitution from the **Z** as from the Ax and Bx scribes. Since editorial judgements inevitably differ about how to identify, categorise and rectify errors, archetypal readings judged corrupt will be examined in detail in the *Textual Notes*. Some fifteen reconstructions are not of a presumed original from the demonstrably faulty archetype but of the presumed archetype, where one sub-archetype is absent or both divergently defective, as in the 'split variation' at Pr 159 or V 456. These are placed in square brackets and not reckoned in the total of sure Bx errors. In others where a reconstructed Bx reading appears unoriginal, it can be emended only by conjecture; but all such instances (marked ‡) are nonetheless included here as reconstructions when based on direct manuscript evidence. Some 90 emendations (just over 60%) made wholly or partly on metrical grounds are preceded by ^. Of these, about 50 are further specified *trs* if corrected by intralinear transposition (in all but two cases in the b-half). About 60 are marked *v* (*f*) *s* / *a* / *o* where they involve verbal (formal) substitution / addition / omission, and four are by re-lineation (*rl*).

Major Pr ^117*vs* (*after* **C**). [^159]. I ^123*trs*. II ^43*vs*. III ^75*trs*. [^255*va* (*so for* // **A**)]. ^260*va*. ^344*trs*. ^345*trs*. IV 38*vs*. ^158*va*. V ^23*trs* (*after* F). ^149/50*rl* (*so* Cr²³). ^165*vs* (*after* Cr) 171*va*. 174*trs*. 194*va*. ^253*trs*. ^259*vs*. ^282*vs*. ^284*vs*. ^300*trs*. 364. 375. 405. ^412*vs*. ^415*vs*. ^441*trs;vs*. [456]. 487*vo*. VI ^123*vs*. ^242*vs*. VIII 44 (*after* **A**). ^69*trs*. ^99*trs*. IX ^33*va*. 38. ^39*vs*. 41/2. 42. ^55*vs*. ^87*trs*. ^91*trs*. 113*vs*. ^154*trs*. [155]. ^163 (*so* // **A**). ^188*vs*. X ^50*vs*. ^90*vs*. ^108¹ (*so* // **A**);² *vs*. ^131. 186*va*. ^204*trs*. ^274*vs*. [^301*vs* (*in* α *only*; *so* // **C**)]. 304*vs*. ^307*vs*. 320*vs,o*. ^323*trs*. ^337*vo*. ^367*vs*. ^411*vsf*. ^446*vs*. XI ^67*trs*. ^82*trs*. ^86*trs*. [^184]. [196; *in* α *only*]. ^239*trs*. 325. ^343‡*vs*. 385; 386; [388 (*in* a *only*)]. ^420*trs*. ^435. XII ^24*trs*. ^95*trs*. ^203*vs*. 210‡. ^251/52*rl*. 270 (*so* Cr³). 290*trs*. XIII ^63*trs*. ^82*trs*. 96*vsf*. 407; [442 (*in* a *only*)]. XIV ^8*vs*. [36]. ^61*va*. [^123*trs* (*in* β*only*)]. [131*a*]. ^260*trs*. ^311*va*. XV ^111*trs*. [126–27]. ^314*trs*. ^320*va*. ^377*trs*. ^421*va*. [480 (R= α *only*)]. 504. ^551*trs*. XVI [142]. [158]. XVII ^78*trs*. [82]. ^164*trs*. ^294*trs*. XVIII ^281*va*. ^282*va*. 283‡. 306*trs*. ^343*trs*. XIX 90*vs,o*; 186; ^230*va*; 236*trs* (*so in* // **C**). 252*vs*. 317/18*rl*. ^348*trs*; ^446*trs*; XX 366*va*. 367*va*. **Minor** XI 148/49. [XIV 299]. [XV 520, 521 (*in* α *only*)]. XVIII [170].

After **K–D**: V 195. ^440*vs*. X 273*trs*. XI [^184]. 205/05*rl*. XII 183/84*rl*. XIII 299*vs*. ^326*trs*. XIV ^9*trs*. ^223*vs*. ^304*vs*. 316–17*rl*. XV ^138*trs*. ^352*vs*. ^394*trs*. [471*vs*. (R *only*)]. XVI ^192*trs* (*so in* // **C**). XVII ^116*trs*. XVIII ^32/3*rl*. ^165*vsf* (*so in* // **C**). 316–18*rl*. ^343*trs*. 423*vsf*. XX 301*vs* (*so in* // **C**). ^380*vs*. **Minor** V 420. VII 69/70. XI 202. [XIX 434].

§ 64. (*iii*) *Conjectural readings*

In nearly 90 instances where direct textual evidence is slight or completely lacking, intralinear errors have been emended by conjecture, 70 of them largely on metrical grounds. One follows Skeat and about fifteen K–D; the rest are new. The degree of confidence they command depends on six factors: the existence or otherwise of parallel usages in **B** or the other versions, the strength of lexical support within the poem and / or the period, the context of the emendation, its complexity, its implications for the neighbouring text, and the calibre of competing proposals. No attempt is made to sub-divide the emendations according to such features; but in the *Textual Notes* they receive detailed consideration, and in some important cases alternatives are examined. As all these readings are major and this section contains the most arguable textual decisions, the conjectured lemma and the rejected archetypal reading are given in full. In the list an * indicates a word not found elsewhere in Langland. As in (i) and (ii), square brackets indicate an uncertain Bx reading, and these entries, too, are not counted in the total.

^Pr 11 me] I. ^206 so] to. I ^121 for] *om*. ^160 inmiddes] bitwene (*so in* // **C**). III ^260 (*haplography*) fel fel] fel. ^298 lordeþ] ruleþ. ^319 moot] wole. ^346 tidy] good. IV ^86 suffre] lete. ^91 wiþseide] seide (*so in* // **ZA**). V 111 liþeþ] likeþ. ^171 (*haplography*) faste faste] faste. ^282 his] goddes. ^378 it] *om*. ^400 siþenes] yet. ^412 mengen I of] go to. VI ^138 *garisoun] amendement. ^148 receyue] haue. ^150 putte] make. ^223 norisse] help. ^281 ek] *om* (*so in* // **A**). ^325 merke] se. VII ^34 drede] fere yow. ^45 preue] leue. IX ^15 biddeþ] ruleþ. ^39 welde] hadde. X ^90 loke] rule. 190 kennyng] kynne. ^242 *animales] beestes. ^246 *Gospelleres] Euaungelistes. ^251 Siþþe] Thanne. ^301 *querele] chide. [320 biyeten] biten / beten hem]. ^393 men] þei. ^446 wiþ] and. XI 49 of þe leste] if þe leste. ^181 principally] souereynly. 301 at] and. ^430 noye] doute. ^438 *rauȝte] folwed. 439 craued] preyde. kenne] telle. XII ^60 gomes lowe] lowe. ^127 Com] Was. ^131 Olde lyueris] Lyueris. XIII ^85 preue] telle. ^136 by so] so. (245 alle is] alle; *so* M). ^300 go telle] telle. XIV 7 me was looþ] looþ . 23 *myte] myste. 196 wroȝten] writen. 284–85 and Ioye / Is to þe body] is to þe body / And ioye also to þe soule. [300 lowe] ?*lawde*]. ^311 so wel] wel. XV ^123 ech haþ] haþ. [126–27 his...haue²] seruice to saue / haue]. ^312 haþ ben] was. ^393 Lede] persone. ^421 Bernard boþe] Bernard. ^470 mowen] don. XVI ^201 leodes] persones. XVII ^38 *teeþ] gooþ . ^214 þat lowe] þat. ^392 clene wasshen] wasshen. XIX [12 hise] Piers / cristis; 90 *richels] riche gold. 186 To hym] Hym. 241 of noumbres] noumbres ^244 wel er] er. 255 þat...Grace] alle quod Grace þat grace. 306 any kynnes gilte] gilt or in trespas. ^372 right saue] saue. ^409 Saue] But. ^413 leode] man. XX ^292 pleyen] make. ^293 renkes] men. 367 and my] my. 377 come for] for (*so all in* // **C**).

After **K–D**: II ^36 caccheþ] takeþ. V ^128 *biggyng] dwellyng. ^165 purueiede] ordeyned. ^415 telle I vp gesse] vp g. shryue me. VII ^59 if I lye witeþ Mathew] holdeþ þis for truþe / That if þat I lye M. is to blame. IX ^99 Tynynge] Lesynge. X ^279 barnes] folk. XII ^4 mynne] þynke. ^193 graiþ is hem euere] and he is euer redy. 270 wisshen (*after* Cr³)] wissen vs. XIV 28 Haukyn wil] Haukyns wif. XV [^224 stille] tyl / so]. ^450 fourmed] seide. XVII 90 segge] man. XIX ^230 Somme wyes] Somme. XX ^378 adreynt and dremeþ] and d. (*both so em. in* // **C**).

After **Sk**: XIII ^86 preynte] wynked.

§ 65. As in the case of the **A** archetype (*A Version* § 57), these Bx readings include mechanical errors: simple visual slips at V 111 and XI 30, 49, followed by smoothing in XIV 28 and XIX 90 (the latter presumably reflecting B-Ø); haplography at III 260 and V 171; unconscious substitutions of easier, non-alliterating synonyms (V 400, XIV 196); and losses of a small stave-word (V 378, XIII 136, XV 123) or a prefix (IV 91). But the incidence of seemingly deliberate alterations of the exemplar reading is heavier in Bx than in Ax; and it indicates a scribe determined to clarify the sense of the text, where he found it difficult, with scant regard for the resulting damage to the metre. The second half-line, in particular the key-stave, was especially vulnerable, and some at least of **C**'s revisions seem motivated by recognition of corruptions here, as at X 90, XI 430 and XII 193. At times the Bx error diagnosed has required treatment by conjecturing a word not paralleled in the author but difficult enough to have occasioned the archetypal substitution: examples are at V 138, X 242 and XVII 38. Less drastic are cases where the proposed expression is a part of the poet's recognised vocabulary that has been supplanted more than once. Examples are the verb *rulen* for three harder conjectured synonyms (III 298, IX 15, X 90) and the noun *persone* for *leode* in reference to God at XV 393 and XVI 201. The claims of emendations like the second here are strengthened by evidence elsewhere of the Bx scribe's aversion to lexically-restricted alliterating synonyms for 'man', as at XVII 90 and XX 293. But the main justification for such editorial changes to the archetypal text lies in the 85% of securer restorations and reconstructions in §§ 59–60 above. Without that evidence, the 15% in § 64 would have been adopted more hesitantly, and in some cases not at all.

viii. *Readings of Indeterminable Origin*

§ 66. Like that of **A**, the **B** tradition also contains readings that are not evidently or inferentially archetypal or sub-archetypal but randomly distributed across both families. In these, often minor instances, the direction of variation must be ascertained mainly from their intrinsic character, something most reliably done with other-version evidence as a control. This is particularly necessary where R is defective; for the Bx reading can be certain only when R is present. A good example is I 127, in which the adopted harder variant *pult* LR (understood as = β and α respectively) is also attested by one member of the γ sub-family Cr and by **Z**. The reading of the remaining γ copies and F (*putte*) is, however, supported by Ax. For *pulte* to be original, therefore, an error in Ax must have been repeated coincidentally by g, by the immediate ancestor of <WHm> and by F, or (if Cr is understood as having been corrected), by γ and F together. The mistake could have arisen from misunderstanding the sense, which seems clear enough in **Z, C** (revised) and an **A** witness W that is contaminated from **C** (*A Version* § 18 above). The error's first stage was Bx's replacement of accusative *hym* with nominative *he* so as to generate *he pult*, a possible but contextually unusual reading. Its emendation has been classed as a 'restoration' at § 60 above, since *pokede* **C** appears the reviser's response to an exemplar with *pult* rather than *putte*. But it could arguably be considered a 'reconstruction', as the full adopted reading *hym pult* is not unequivocally instanced in either **Z** or **C**. At Pr 186 L, three y mss (YOC) and R have *cracchy*, which is both in **C** and is harder than the majority *cacchen*. Here F's participation in the error suggests that it was not γ but w and three g-group members that substituted the more obvious verb, under inducement from 189 and the general context. The agreement of the latter witnesses should therefore be seen not as genetic but as due to random convergence.

158

§ 67. Often, however, because so much new material is added in **B**, no parallel evidence from **A** or **C** is available, and the 'direct' method must operate virtually in a textual vacuum. An example is the fairly minor Pr 140, where L and R (again taken as = β and α respectively) read *answeres* against γF *answerede*. The direction of variation from present to past may be diagnosed as revealing a scribal attempt to balance *greued* in 139. But F and γ may have departed from their respective α and β exemplars because Bx's actual reading was not *answeres* but a tense-ambiguous **answeryt* (for *answeryth*) that has left divergent reflexes in both sub-archetypes (see Appendix One, § 2 (b)). Acceptance here of LR's resolution as accurate will therefore depend on judging the mixed-tense form of 139–40 at once harder than the unmixed and demonstrably characteristic of the poet's practice. Such examples are frequent, but limitations of space restrict consideration in the *Textual Notes* to only the more important ones

ix. *Possible* **A** *and* **C** *Contamination in the* **B** *Version*

§ 68. The manuscripts showing most contamination from the **A** Version are (as observed at §§ 28, 30–1 and 46 above) H, G and especially F. The close links of *H* with **A** may relate to its being (uniquely) a conjoint **BA** text. For it seems reasonable to assume that if the available **B** passūs of H's postulated source *h* recommended themselves to its scribe as a 'fuller' form, he might then have been led to collate it with the corresponding **A** portion at points where the former's text seemed unsatisfactory. This would account for the presence of desirable corrections like *her wombys*] *hemselue* (Pr 59), *nayle*] *tree* (I 186), *erdyn* [for *erende*] (III 41). All of H's 'good' readings are in fact in **A** except for *hys*] *om* Pr 99, which is only in **C**. But this, the sole reading that might support for H a claim to descent distinct from β, could be a felicitous scribal guess prompted by the context. What confirms contamination as the source of these readings in H is the presence of sixteen major **A** tradition errors like *sweuenyd*] *sweyed* Pr 10 and *pountyd*] *poundes* Pr 213 (both close to group u at A Pr 10, 86). Of *G*'s unique right readings, none are shared with **A** alone; but (like H) G has significant disjunctive agreements in error with **A**, and these two factors together prove contamination. Major errors are those with Ax at I 96 (and at III 46, where H accompanies), while others are with particular **A** groupings, as at Pr 82 (with uHK) and I 41 (with *r¹*J). Minor ones occur at IV 193 (with wE) and at VI 204 (with *r¹*).

§ 69. Amongst these contaminations is an editorially challenging category in which, despite **A**'s soundness, the variant in question has been held to 'correct' mistakenly a Bx reading here judged a revision. Thus, H variants rejected include *mete* at Pr 63, a correct **A** reading but one understood as revised in **B** to *marchen*, which is retained in accordance with the canon of ratification (it is confirmed by **C**). Like some of H's minor errors, many of them shared with G and F, this one could have arisen (semi-)memorially. So might *wersse þan nouth* at Pr 186 which, while recalling the ending of a stock phrase, replaces the 'harder' stave-word *feblere* with a (non-scanning) synonym. In G a major example is III 46 *brocour*] *baud* and a minor one III 293 *ayein*] *to*, both of which K–D print.[47] Another major instance from G (where the reading is also that of **Z**) is IV 141 *helpe*] *saue*. This too is adopted by K–D but its metrical form suggests revision, since Bx here uses the rarer Type IIb (see *Intro.* IV, §§ 39–41). The general principle this case illustrates is that a reading (even when authorial in character) which is diagnosed as present by contamination is *not* to be accepted unless that of Bx is demonstrably unsatisfactory. For while originality in the source-version is a necessary, it can never be a sufficient condition for preferring **A** to a Bx reading that is by 'intrinsic' standards relatively less good but satisfies the core-text criteria.

§ 70. The same proviso applies with particular stringency to F, the copy that draws on the earlier version most openly (and often to greatest advantage). The phenomenon has been discussed in detail at § 46 above, but its causes remain open to speculation. What seems clear is that it fits better with the principle of economy to judge F's specific superior readings not (as do K–D) corrections 'from a manuscript of the **B** Version' but contaminations 'severally from manuscripts of **A** and **C**.' For the Athlone editors' hypothesis of a lost **B** copy as the source of F's 'authoritative' readings becomes proportionally more tenuous as one questions the originality of many such instances 'where **B**'s text is unique' and others for which K–D claim the F reading's 'superiority to those of the archetypal **C** tradition' (*K–D* p. 172).[48] But there is nothing tenuous about the evidence of borrowing from **A** in F, and a phase of collation of its α exemplar with an **A** copy may be securely ascribed to its postulated source *f*. The latter explanation may be defended against the charge of multiplying entities needlessly, because Corpus 201 itself (unlike M and, less extensively, Bm or Cot) does not reveal visible correction by the main or other hands (see § 34 above). One striking example is the line A Pr 95 added after Pr 94, which doubtless left no residue in the **C** Version because it was in fact removed in the extensive **B** revision of **A**'s Prologue. The plain evidence of contamination here must raise a presumption that several of F's other (real or supposed) corrections to the readings of β and R have a similar origin. Some of this **A** contamination may be semi-conscious, but if a corrupt form of **A** appears, deliberate substitution may be involved. An example is at VIII 49, where the rhetorically more emphatic *fowle flesh3* replaces the theologically more exact *flesshis wil*. But for the one **A** contamination found in either sub-archetype, the three lines that in α replace β's twelve at III 51–62, a memorial explanation will suffice (*K–D* p. 67). This example, taken with the family's numerous other missing passages, offers solid evidence that α was directly based on Bx and lost these lines mechanically, as K–D suppose (see §§ 50–1). But it could equally be that censorship on grounds of propriety has operated here (as suggested at § 52 above) and that the α scribe inserted some imperfectly recollected **A** lines to fill a too-obvious gap.

§ 71. Likewise restricted to a few manuscripts are the contaminations from **C**, which occur mainly in two γ sub-groups (§§ 24, 27 above). Firstly <OC^2> has six such readings (one major), and its constituent members O and C^2 each have three (respectively one and all major). The explanation of these lies less readily to hand than for those in the trio of conjoint **BC** copies that make up B. But in at least XIII 411 (shared with B), OC^2's source may have been trying to make sense of Bx's near-nonsensical *hys woman*] *is whan a man*, which γ, L and R seem to have despaired of. A similar enterprise is displayed by C^2 and O at XVIII 160 and XIX 181, in which *al* and *seest* are required respectively for the sense and for the metre; but neither presupposes direct scribal access to **C**. Such access was evidently absent at XX 261, where C^2's scribe has filled a perceived sense-gap either by half-recalling the lost **C** line or, more probably, by intelligently guessing its likely content. Felicitous conjecture may also explain **C**'s right reading *Mighte* at XIX 391, and at XIII 100 F's *gan rodye* and Hm's *ruddud*. The latter, adopted by K–D (and *Sch*[1]), is here rejected as a possible scribal recalling of **C**'s graphic revision of a syntactically difficult original. In the case of B, however, direct resort to a **C** copy seems a fair presumption; for this postulated group-original must have been a **B** Version with a defective beginning which was 'patched' from a copy of **C** (§ 27 above). The latter might well have been consulted additionally to make good a few readings that failed to give sense, such as XIII 2, even if more straightforward metrical corrections like III 6 need not presuppose this. But that the **C** Version was familiar to the scribes who copied B's extant descendants is indicated by such 'good' corrections in Cot as *adreynt* at XX 378 and such erroneous 'corrections' as *mercede* for *mercy* at XIX 76. K–D use the first in a reconstruction of the line followed here for both versions. They also (p. 160) accept the second as original, R–K duly following in their edition of **C**. This is rejected here; for while the word in question is undeniably what K–D call a 'Langlandian expression', very probably a coinage, its threefold occurrence is restricted to III 290–332, and it is not recorded anywhere else. The likelihood that Cot's scribe altered his exemplar to *mercede* after consulting a lost **B** copy superior to both Bx and B¹ (rather than through recalling its memorable introduction at C III 290) therefore seems remote. Correction from **A** or **C** is not restricted to OC²B, remaining at least possible in one other group-source, w, at X 57 *guttes fullen*] *gutte(s) been / is fulle*, and at XI 287 *lynnen ne wollen*] *trs*. Neither of these examples, however, seems beyond the capacity of the limited number of copyists of the extant **B** manuscripts. For these were predominantly London scribes who could have known the poem in one or more of its other versions, too.

x. Passūs XIX–XX *of* **B** *and* Passūs XXI–XXII *of* **C**

§ 72. It remains to consider Passūs XIX–XX of the **B** Version, with their unique body of supplementary attestation in the near-identical archetypal text of **C**. The following analysis fills out the brief account in §§ 2–4 above and will provide a transition to the next section dealing with the **C** Version. Firstly, in the poem's final two passūs it is clear that both Bx and B¹ (the basis of B² = Cx), descend from the same source, B-Ø. This is proved by fifteen shared errors, twelve of which are major. In the following list of these, the lemma is in all but four cases the editorially emended reading, and the variant the agreed reading of Bx and B². Where two variants appear, the first is Bx, the second Cx; and if the latter is uncertain, both contending sub-archetypal readings are given. In XIX, where R is absent, an F reading only doubtfully that of α is disregarded if Cx and β agree.

B XIX (**C** XXI) 12 hise] Piers β; cristis F(= ? α)Cx. 76 Encense F] *om* βCx (Rechels *C*-R). 90 richels] riche gold. 186 To hym] Hym (and ȝaf hym *C*-**p**). 236 buggynge and sellynge *C*-N²] *trs*. 241 of noumbres] noumbres. 305/06 *So div. C*-Y; *as* 3 *ll*. 348 caples tweyne] two caples. 372 right saue] saue. 409 Saue] But. 413 leode *C*-N²] man. 446 þe Pope; amende] *trs*. **B** XX (**C** XXII) 292 pleyen] maken. 293 renkes] men. 366 alle hem] al Bx; hem Cx. 367 and my Lady] my lady. 378 adreynt and dremeþ] and dremeþ Bx (adreynt Cot); adreint Cx.

Of the above, five require brief comment. In XIX, 12 could be another B¹ reading if F here = α and α = Bx. In 76 F's *Encense*, not supported by Cx, is taken to be (like the **C** witness R's *rechels*) a happy scribal guess and not the reading of α (< Bx). Both 236 and 413 are here judged similarly felicitous scribal improvements of B¹'s defective metre and not, as R–K believe, 'correction[s] from a pre-archetypal **C** copy.'⁴⁹ Finally, at XX 378 Cot's *adreynt* is interpreted as either a recollection of **C** or an attempt to correct a reading found faulty in sense by substituting that of the **C** manuscript posited as available for collation when Cot was produced (about a decade later than Bm).⁵⁰

§ 73. As stated in § 3 above, it is clear that Bx does not derive from B¹, since it lacks nine certain or probable B¹ errors (six of them major) that are retained in B². There is no proof (as already noted) that these were not introduced by the scribe of Cx, who obviously cannot be held incapable of error. But since B^1 is in effect known only through B^2, an attempt to distinguish further between B^2 and Cx (assuming it feasible) would hardly affect the issue of Bx's independent descent from B-Ø. In the list of Cx errors below, the lemma is an emendation, unless specified as the reading of Bx.

B XIX (**C** XXI) 242 craftily Bx] *om*. 306 any kynnes gilte] gilt or in trespas Bx; Cx *uncertain*: þynge gulty *C*-**p**; agulte *C*-**x**. 342 Bx *uncertain*: Surquidous β] Surquidours Cx?α. 377 Bx; *line om* Cx. **B** XX (**C** XXII) 13 Bx *uncertain*: noon β] þat F; Cx *uncertain*: ?þat non. 120 kirke] α = Bx; churche Cxβ. 301 hij] he Bx; they Cx. 366 alle hem] al Bx; hem Cx. 378 adreynt and dremeþ] and dremeþ Bx; adreint Cx.

Of these, too, five require brief comment. XX 366 and 378 are listed again because these emended readings are based on what appear to be 'split' variants, each partially containing the reconstructed form presumed for B-Ø. XIX 342 may be a B^1 error for the reading which β has felicitously corrected (see *Textual Notes*). In XIX 377 and XX 120 alone can it be certain that Bx retains the exact form of the common original.

§ 74. The third point made at § 3 above was that B^2 is not derived from Bx, since it lacks the latter's 25 errors. These are now listed in full below:

B XIX (**C** XXI) 12 hise] Piers β*C*-N²; Cristes CxF. 56–8 Bx *uncertain*. 56 toek Lucifer þe loþly] Cx; þanne took he lotthly lucifer F; *l. om* β. 57 hym as he is bounde] Cx; his as his bondeman F; *l. om* β. 58 he (1)] he þat F. 59 lawe] Cx; lawes F. 97 comsede] Cx; gan to Bx. 154 Bx *uncertain*: and preide þo] and bisouȝte þe; al þo propre F. 181 seste] Cx*B*-0; doost Bx. 183 þouȝte] Cx; Bx *uncertain*: tauȝte β; took sone F. 230 wyes] *om* Bx; men Cx. 244 wel er] er Bx; ?*C revised*. 252 be] Cx; were Bx. 255 þat alle craftes quod Grace] alle quod Grace þat grace Bx; **C** *revised*. 297 plete] plede Cx; Bx *uncertain*: he pletede F; pleieþ β. 301 euene] Cx; euere Bx. 306 any kynnes gilte] Cx *uncertain*: any þynge gulty *C*-**p**; agulte *C*-**x**; gilt or in trespas Bx. 317/18 *So div*. Cx; Bx *uncertain*: *div. after* worþi β; *after* vertues F. 317 forþi] worþi ?Bx. 333 home Piers] Cx?Bx (hoom F = ?α; Piers = ?β). 337 lond; þe] Cx; Bx *uncertain*: loore; & þe F; *l. om* β. 346 Sire Piers sew] Cx; Bx *uncertain*: P. plowhman seew all F; P. þere hadde ysowen β. 367 in holynesse] Cx; Bx *uncertain*: in vnitee β; strong F. 373 a sisour and a somonour] Cx; And false men flatereris vsurers and þeuis / Lyeris and questemongeris Bx. 433 soudeþ] Cx; sendeþ Bx. 441 *So* Cx; *l. om* Bx. 468 wole he nel he] Cx; Bx *uncertain*: I wole β; to presoun F. 482 That þou haue þyn askyng] Cx; Bx *uncertain*: þat þou þyn lykyng have F; Take þow may in resoun β.
B XX (**C** XXII) 8 Was] Cx?Bx (& þat was F; As β. 14 cacche] Bx *uncertain*: cauȝte β; caste F. 19 deide for þurste] Cx; *trs* Bx. 34 God] Cx; and Bx. 54 it tid] Cx; it Bx. 62/3 *So div*. ?Cx; *after* lyue Bx. 67 hir] Cx; hem Bx. hir lemmans] Cx; lemmans of Bx. 126 suede] Cx?α; sente βF. 198 heo] Cx?a; she βF. 261 *In* Cx; *l. om* Bx. 309 pardon] Cx; *om* Bx. 366 alle hem] al Bx; hem Cx. 377 come] Cx; *om* Bx. 380 hij] þei Bx; ?**C** *revised*.

Despite the many uncertain readings here, especially in XIX, the proof afforded by XX 261 is (as at § 73 above) decisive. It is therefore inferentially probable that two copies of B-Ø were made, one (B-Øa) the immediate source of Bx, and the other (B^1) used in the revision to **C**. It remains possible in theory that some scribes had access to B-Øa down to the level of individual extant manuscripts such as O, C^2 and B, and found in that early copy (which would fill the rôle of K–D's 'lost superior **B** manuscript') the correct readings they now preserve where Bx is in error. But a more economical explanation, for which reasons have been given, is that all such readings have come in by contamination from copies of the **C** Version. After their generation, it seems to the present editor likely that the two traditions of Bx and B^1 never made any direct contact.

Conclusion

§ 75. From the above account it is clear that an edition of **B** must depend even more than one of **A** (and, as will emerge, of **C**) upon other-version evidence, here from both the prior and the subsequent texts. This assumption was implicit in the practice of Skeat (I, §§ 34, 37) but was fully developed only by Kane and Donaldson. The present edition takes the assumption to its logical conclusion, by attempting to establish the text of **B** in parallel with that of all the others, including **Z**. Consideration of the latter version will be kept until after discussion of **C**, to which the next section is devoted.

THE B VERSION: NOTES

1 Ll. 49–51, which are hesitantly retained, add little and are somewhat clumsily written (see *Textual Notes*).

2 See section on date at *Introduction*, V §§ 14–18 below. If the Ophni-Phineas passage in C Pr is in draft form, it may be a late addition, perhaps suggesting that Langland saw the Prologue as an appropriate location for material of topical interest.

3 This fact Langland would moreover have had to take into account in his final revision, which was presumably made available entire only after his death. See Schmidt, 'L's Visions and Revisions', esp. p. 7.

4 Other possible signs of this in **C** that K–D profess to identify (*B Version,* pp. 103ff) seem insufficiently demonstrable to figure in the present discussion.

5 An exception is the case of Passus XVI, on which see below at § 5.

6 The hypothetical projected figure represents a sixth of the total at the error-rate of the better Bx scribe.

7 The estimate here is less strict than in the Everyman *B-Text* p. lxi, since it includes marginal cases, lines attested by only one tradition, and citation lines.

8 *B Version*, pp. 62–9.

9 Recent revivals of Skeat's view that α represents a phase of the **B** tradition intermediate between β and **C** are examined and rejected at §§ 50–55 below.

10 See Blackman 'Some Notes', p. 517 and Adams 'Evidence for Stemma', p. 274. Though Blackman's ω corresponds to γ in the present diagram, she identifies β not as a sub-archetype but as what is here called Bx, and judges α a **B** tradition contaminated from **A** and **C**. Adams sees Cr^1 as descended from $β^1$, a derivate of β on the same level of transmission as LM, which was collated with M; WHm as descended from $β^2$, a derivate of $β^1$; B as descended from $β^4$, a derivate of $β^3$ (= γ); and C^2 as descended from O.

11 These readings are discussed under both w and M at §§ 13 and 34–6 below.

12 In most of these, w is accompanied by the rejected manuscript S, which derives from the same immediate ancestor as WHmCr and will be disregarded after the next note.

13 The number rises to 58 if four shared with S are added: X 155, XIX 286 (major); XIX 452, XX 234 (minor). K–D's figure of 43 (table, p. 21) is incorrect.

14 K–D's figure of 17 (p. 21) is thus seriously out.

15 Cr's one major right reading at I 152, unless it is an inspired scribal conjecture, is probably the result of collation with a **C** copy.

16 The complex changes of exemplar within y are discussed by K–D, pp. 44–8, 51–4.

17 Readings inadvertently omitted from the Apparatus will be given here in full.

18 Though ease of loss by homœoteleuton in this instance must be acknowledged.

19 Davis 'The Rationale for a Copy of a Text', p. 144.

20 Davis, 'Rationale', p. 149.

21 The *trotten* agreement with Ch at 144 would accordingly have to be dismissed as coincidental. It may be significant in this context that H^2 and its companions TCh are also conjoint manuscripts, although (unlike BmBoCot) their **A** and **C** portions have not been linked by material from the third version, here **B**.

22 Blackman, 'Some Notes', pp. 314–15, recognises both G's contamination and its independent value.

23 See *Intro*. IV *Editing the Text* § 40.

24 To these could arguably be added III 118 and VI 124, supported by **ZA(C)**, but not adopted for **B**, as Bx is not in these instances clearly inferior.

25 *B Version*, p. 61

26 This is an indication that major agreements are much likelier than minor ones to be genetic in origin; for in most of the 120 cases of the latter, agreement of a β-ms with α appears coincidental.

27 See §§ 42–3 below for a list of β's errors.

28 In 'The F Scribe and the R MS of *PP*', pp. 530–48.

29 Examples are V 23, XII 49, XV 89 and XVIII 14.

30 See *Introduction* I, *The Manuscripts*, no. 23, for references.

31 Hanna, 'On the Versions of *PP*', in *Pursuing History,* pp. 221–22. The position is also argued by Warner in 'The *Ur-B PP*', pp. 20–21.

32 'The Lost Revision of *PP* B', p. 119.

33 See *Textual Notes ad loc.*

34 'Introduction' to *Written Work*, ed. Justice & Kerby-Fulton, pp. 5–8.

35 See *Sk* II, 283 n. Skeat's reconstructed sequence is probably that of Bx (see *TN* to C XVII 187–251); for the likely β form of 506–09, 528–29 see Justice, p. 6

36 The culinary figures are respectively from Justice, p. 6 and Taylor, p. 116. Warner aptly points out that the 'supposed hash' is also found in B I 100–1, XIV 138–9//.

37 'Lost Revision', p. 120.

38 Ibid., p. 119.

39 Z V 32–47; AB V 14–20; C V 116–22.

40 'Versions', pp. 223–29.

41 Cf. J. H. Newman: 'Now the test of an admissible hypothesis will be its incorporating without force the whole circle of statements of which it takes cognizance. Some of these may be *prima facie* adverse, and the difficulty may be reasonably solved; some may be at least accounted for, and their objective force suspended; others, it may be, cannot be explained, and must not be explained away' (*An Essay on the Development of Christian Doctrine* (1845) III, v, 5). The most radical account of the genesis of the **B** tradition, which speculatively reconstructs the transmission-history of α and β in the light of ms NLW 733, is Warner's, for which the author's term 'scenario' ('*Ur-B*' p. 23) might seem a better description than 'hypothesis'.

42 Hanna, 'Versions', pp. 219–21. Fletcher's objection ('Essential WL' pp. 62–3n4) that **L**, 'though taking trouble over his composition', might have tolerated scribal inaccuracy (over vernacular poetry as opposed to legal documents) 'within a certain latitude of reason' seems to the present writer not just 'paradoxical', as its author describes it, but self-contradictory.

43 Ibid., p. 226; an opinion succinctly described by Kane (in Alford, *Companion* p. 196) as 'pure nonsense'. Warner's similar notion of this poet's 'most distinctive trait' as a 'compulsion to tinker' ('*Ur-B*' 12) reveals basic misunderstanding of the nature of **L**'s art as a *makere* and of his activity as a scrupulous reviser. For demonstration of Langland's intense interest in the minute particulars of language and versification, see *The Clerkly Maker*, and the *Commentary* in this edition, both *passim*.

44 Ibid., p. 229.

45 'Re-editing' the **B** Version, as one who has done so might without impertinence suggest, resembles a medieval pilgrimage from Dover to Jerusalem more than one from Southwark to Canterbury.

46 An argument that accepts the integrity of the **B** Version but holds that **L** intervened in the tradition after the copying of the archetypal manuscript has been made by Adams in his important recent article 'The R/F MSS of *PP*'. For Adams, Bx was corrected, particularly in the second half of the poem, with loosely-inserted slips in the manner envisaged by R–K for the composition of **C** (see *Intro*. II §§ 107–9 above). Some of these additions were accordingly unavailable to α and others to β in what Adams discerns as a pattern of 'complementary' loss / inclusion. A unitary **B** Version is still proposed, though with Bx now seen not as a scribal fair-copy but as an authorially-altered manuscript evincing a kind of 'rolling revision' (though not the same kind as that proposed by disintegrationists like Taylor).

47 Reasons for retaining Bx in the former are given in the *Textual Notes ad loc.*

48 Among those discussed in the *Textual Notes*, see the note on B XIX / C XXI 76.

49 *C Version*, p. 102. R–K, it should be said, do not include these two particular N^2 readings in their list of such corrections.

50 K–D, *B Version*, p. 5; Davis, 'Rationale'. p. 143.

The C Version

i. *The Manuscript Tradition*

§ 1. It is unknown when and why Langland began his final re-writing of *Piers Plowman*.[1] This is unlikely to have been soon after the completion of **B**, as the notion of 'rolling revision' (rejected at *B Version* § 57 above) would allow. Time was required for the work to be read, 'received' and make the impact to which John Ball's famous allusion testifies.[2] The Peasants' Revolt of 1381 thus readily suggests a *terminus a quo*, an occasion and a motive. It cannot have been, as with **A**, the poem's imperfect state that prompted recomposition, since **B** is complete. Moreover, the low incidence of **C** contamination in the earliest **B** copies[3] argues against wide familiarity with **C** in the author's lifetime and accords with the general opinion that Langland did not finish it. The scale of **C** contamination in the **A** copies K and W, and the supplementation of **Z** and **A** by **C** rather than **B** in seven of the eleven 'conjoint' versions,[4] need not conflict with that supposition. For the relatively late date of the **A** manuscripts,[5] themselves witnesses to an unfinished version, is consistent with their having been produced to meet demand for a copy of the poem in any shape or form. This interest could have been aroused by the fame of **B**, possibly assisted by the posthumous release of **C**. The *terminus ad quem* of the final version is more unsure. Its unfinished condition, which was not remarked by Skeat, is commonly ascribed to the poet's death after completing the revision of B XVIII as C XX. But this event is dateable only from two literary sources outside the poem. One is the reference to it in the conclusion to A XII by John But, identified as the King's Messenger who died in 1386; the other, corroborating this, is the echoes of **C** in *The Testament of Love* by Thomas Usk, who was executed in March 1388.[6] More recently, a case for Langland's being still active in 1388 has been argued from supposed allusions to the Statute of Labourers of that year in the opening of Passus V, a passage thus judged to be the last-completed portion of the poem.[7] The case seems to the present editor unproven; but to accept those allusions, discount Usk's testimony or ascribe it to acquaintance with a work in progress, and attribute the A XII reference to another John But, would leave the year of the poet's death completely uncertain.[8] The only remaining downward constraint would be the date of the earliest **C** manuscripts, such as Trinity College, Dublin 212 (V), the copy containing the note about Langland's paternity. This is assigned to the end of the fourteenth century but stands textually at seven removes from the original,[9] a fact that implies strong interest in the work during the decade after the poet's death.

§ 2. As with **A** and **B**, internal evidence for dating is scanty and ambiguous. A new passage (III 200–09) criticising scandalous royal tolerance of wrongdoing suggests, as Skeat believed, Richard II's growing unpopularity in the 1390s; but it is not incompatible with earlier unease about the young king's behaviour in the mid-1380s. The lines need not be pressed too hard, as little of substance hangs on establishing the date of the author's death. For exactly how 'unfinished' the **C** Version is, and whether the last two passūs were deliberately left untouched, underwent minor revision, or were posthumously annexed as an ending because the author's working papers were too 'foul' to be copied, remain matters of literary judgement, about which major disagreement is possible. Positive knowledge of the manuscript tradition terminates in the archetypal source of the surviving witnesses. This was a copy either authorised by the poet or based on his papers as arranged by a 'literary executor' who was the work's first 'editor.' Russell and Kane's analysis of the archetype leads them to think of the poet's holograph not as a fair copy awaiting only a final touching-up in places but as made up of working drafts (*C Version*, p. 89). Consequently, for someone copying what they see as a heavily-altered B-Text interleaved with new material, there was far more chance of error than had been the case for the scribe of B-Ø, who presumably worked from the author's fair copy. Such an interpretation allows the Athlone editors an ample licence to intervene. But while it is naturally difficult to be uninfluenced in the process of editing by one's general sense of the probable process of revision, the richness of manuscript attestation in **C** and the relatively uncorrupt state of the archetype (compared with that of **B**) encourage editorial caution rather than boldness in its treatment.

§ 3. How and when the archetypal **C** manuscript (**Cx** hereafter) was generated remain uncertain. But in the case of two groups of the earlier manuscripts, linguistic evidence indicates copying in or near the poet's presumed place of origin, and within a period of at most fifty years. The first group belongs to one sub-archetypal family x^1, (from South-West Worcestershire). The second, p^2 (from adjacent South-East Herefordshire), includes all three witnesses of what may be the elder branch of **p**, a sub-division of the other family x^2.[10] Some members of p^1, the larger and probably younger branch of **p**, show linguistic features that relate them to other central south-midland counties, Gloucestershire and Oxfordshire.[11] In marked contrast with most manuscripts of **B**, those of **C** show no particular London connections. But whatever this might imply about Langland's place of residence when finishing **C**, the text itself reveals even more strongly than **B** what Pearsall calls a 'casual intimacy of London reference.'[12] Moreover, while **C** abounds in close observation of the life of the urban poor and refers in the Passus V 'Autobiographical Prelude' to the Dreamer's domicile in Cornhill and to 'lollers' dwelling in the capital, it shows no regional concerns, but retains its predecessor's national and universal outlook.

§ 4. To return to the manuscript tradition: by contrast with **B**, for Prologue to XX of **C** only one initial scribal copy of the authorial manuscript need be assumed as the source of all the thirty extant witnesses. For XXI–XXII the most economical supposition is that Cx was directly based on the last two passūs in the poet's revision copy, 'B^1' (*B Version* §§ 2–3, 71–3). The text of this could have been untouched, or lightly revised in places, the interpretation preferred here. In Pr–XX, Cx as now recoverable stands at two removes from the authorial revision-copy of **B**. But it has already been found valuably to supplement Bx in the the task of establishing **B**'s original form; and in XXI–XXII it is even illuminated by Bx where the latter lacks errors that Cx inherited from B^1. The final two passūs of **C** (where the substantive content of Cx is called 'B^2') accordingly attest some of the securest text in the whole poem. That they nonetheless contain proportionately twice as many errors as the earlier passūs may be due to their largely unrevised condition. This feature lends support to the opinion favoured here that the holograph of Pr–XX was nearer a fair copy than a working draft. But those passūs have to be edited mainly from **C** manuscript evidence alone, for all their differences from the earlier versions may be due to revision. The operation of the 'linear postulate' naturally remains subject at all times to the 'core-text' criteria relied on for assessing the authenticity of **A** and **B**. But much of **C**, particularly from the part corresponding to the middle of B XI onwards, has little or no close textual equivalent. Allowance has further to be made for lexical and rhetorical developments in Langland's style of a kind paralleled in the 'last periods' of his major contemporary Chaucer, later writers like Shakespeare and Milton, and 'revising' poets like Wordsworth, Yeats and Auden. These developments may be generally expected not to contradict the core-text criteria, themselves based in part upon the C-Text (in its *un*revised portions). But devices like *repetitio* are much commoner in new and revised **C** than in **B**, which in turn differs markedly from **A** in its more complex syntax and macaronic style. Such considerations have a part to play in the process of establishing the text of the final version.

ii. *The two families of* **C** *manuscripts*

§ 5. The archetypal readings of **C**'s 7354 text-lines are preserved uniformly or with fair certainty in only some 4350, about 60% of the whole.[13] In the remaining 3004, the Cx reading must be established firstly by comparing the testimony of traditions that originate from the two independent copies of Cx here called x^1 and x^2. In some 1180 of these readings, secondly, the text of each of these copies cannot be distinguished with complete security for such comparison, because of cross-family differences between their constituent witnesses. This problem arises largely with minor instances, in which the Cx reading must be sought amongst the competing alternatives by the direct method, with or without help from other versions. The archetypal text that emerges is still, to the present editor's judgement, much less faulty than it seems to Russell and Kane (R–K hereafter). For it has only 108 errors that demand emendation, about 1 in every 68 lines, or less than 1.5 %. This may be higher than the 1 in 58 (or 0.78) inferentially estimated for B-Ø, where this can be reconstructed in the last two passūs. But it is more than four times better than Bx's average error-rate of one in 16 (or over 8.5 %) of its firmly attested lines. These comparative figures give no reason to think that Cx was other than a direct copy of the holograph.

§ 6. The distribution of Cx's errors, with the readily explained increase occurring in the little-revised XXI–XXII, points to the work of a single scribe, by contrast with the two scribes detectable in the archetypal phase of **B** (*B Version* §§ 4–5 above). Unlike Bx (but again expectedly, given the likeliest assumptions as to how it was produced), no individual passus or passage appears virtually error-free like B XVI, which seems to have been corrected by the poet (*B Version* § 5). Cx's typical errors (discussed at §§ 67–72 below) are mechanical or broadly unconscious. A few may reflect imperfectly-finished material, such as the half-dozen in Pr 108–23 and the single line XVII 73, unless this is spurious, as tentatively judged here (see the textual note). Emendation of **C**, however, is more speculative than in **B**, since only about 40 of the Cx errors diagnosed (fewer than half) occur where parallel material is at hand. Moreover, the **C** tradition reveals a surprisingly low proportion of assured archetypal lines, something that results from the tendency of the sub-archetypes attesting its readings to introduce variants on a wider scale than do α and β of **B**. The problem is exacerbated by the unavailability of a major x^2 group witness in Pr–XI, where **t**'s extant representatives TH²Ch preserve an A-Text. The archetypal character of agreed x^1t readings in the section from XII–XXII (usually also implying agreement of x^1 and x^2) is thus necessarily more secure than that of readings in Pr–XI supported only by x^1 or by **p**. Certainty about the character of x^2 in the earlier portion is therefore unattainable; but it seems likely that the ancestral manuscripts of x^1 and x^2, which have texts of comparable quality, were near-cœval products of copying in closely related centres. For their typical errors (and particularly x^1's) are 'negative', early-stage faults of omission due to carelessness and haste. By contrast, **p** not only has these (and shares them at times with t),[14] it also displays 'positive' scribal features like deliberate substitution, re-writing and padding-out that suggest prior acquaintance with the text.

§ 7. What seems fairly sure is that, as in the case of Bx, two early copies were made from Cx. The first, x^1, is clearly attested and has a simpler history, if one as complex as that of **r** in the **A** tradition. Its eleven extant representatives are the six single-version copies XYIP^{2}UD, the four conjoint copies D^{2}BOL and the fragment H. From the second family-original x^2, which has certain seemingly contradictory features, derive the remaining seventeen. These are the twelve single-version copies PEAVRMQFSGKN, the five conjoint copies TH^{2}ChWZ, the fragment Ca and the **C** interpolations here designated K^2. The x^1 manuscripts fall into three groups, each with its own ancestor deriving independently from the family original. Thus XYIHP^{2}D^2 descend exclusively from a single copy of x^1 (**y**) and BOL from one closely related to y (**b**). Both y and b may also possess an exclusive common ancestor (**i**) that would satisfactorily account for their shared errors; but the amount of text available for comparison is too small for this to be certain. UD descend from a third copy of x^1 (**u**), which is independent of y and b, and also of i. Three separate lines of transmission from x^1 are thus shown in the diagram at § 13 below. The unusual manuscript N^2 could derive from a fourth copy of x^1; but it is heavily contaminated from the **p** branch of x^2, and its anomalous position in the list of sigla is intended to indicate as much.[15]

§ 8. The line of descent from x^2 divides into two strongly contrasted branches with separate ancestors deriving independently from their common sub-archetypal source. The first, **t**, is preserved in the three conjoint manuscripts TH^2 and Ch, which descend from t via two intermediate sources.[16] The second branch **p** comprises the fourteen copies PEAVRMQWFSZGKN, but despite its large size and complex structure is to all appearances a sub-family like t. That is, **p** is less like β than like γ in the **B** tradition, since its ancestral manuscript seems not to have been immediately copied from Cx. It falls however into two further sub-divisions with major group-status, the exclusive originals of which derived immediately from **p**. These are p^2, represented by GKN, and p^1, consisting of PEAVRMQWFSZ. The eleven p^1 copies form two further distinct sub-groups: **m** containing three pairs PE, AV and RM, and **q** comprising Q, F and S, which are joined after Passus IX by Z (in its earlier portion the Z-Text) and after Passus XI by W (up to that point an A-Text). The readings of group p^2 are closer than p^1's to those of x^1 in Pr–XI and to those of x^1t in Passūs XII–XXII. This feature could result from inter-family contamination, but it is more economically ascribed to p^2's greater fidelity to **p**'s presumed original text. The appellation 'p^2' is thus not intended to signal the group's textually secondary character but only its numerically smaller attestation by three manuscripts (one seriously defective), in contrast to p^1's eleven. For if the numerical proportions had been reversed, GKN would stand in the line of sigla just after the x^1t copies that they are more closely related to. Both branches of **p** could have been cœval, though they were generated in different locations. But with the exception of one p^1 copy (A), neither is linguistically as near as family x^1 to the archetype's presumed place of origin. This, from the evidence of the more primitive x^1 copies, was SW Worcestershire around Malvern.

§ 9. Although the ancestor of the x^2 family was not descended from or influenced by x^1, one branch t, despite its limited attestation, reads so closely with x^1 that the Athlone editors treat both t and x^1 as belonging to a single family. Agreement of t with x^1 is admittedly about eight times more frequent than with **p**. But while 80 errors t shares with x^1 seem to imply an exclusive common ancestor, even the 25 of these that could be called major may be attributable to coincidence. The dependence of t on **p** is ruled out since it lacks **p**'s 400 errors (140 of them major) in this section. But by contrast with x^1, the sixteen major errors amongst the 55 that t shares with **p** do appear, after analysis, of such a kind as to suggest an exclusive common ancestor. This is most economically identified as the direct copy of Cx here designated x^2.

§ 10. In transmitting the ancestral text, t was nonetheless much the more accurate of the two postulated x^2 branches. This may be the reason why t's readings, even after allowing for its subfamily errors, are so much closer to x^1's than are those of **p**. It is therefore convenient to denote the x^1t readings in XII–XXII by the joint sigil **x** but to forgo 'x^2' in the apparatus for the agreed readings of **pt**. If t had been present as a C-Text in Pr–XI, it might have been preferable to use the sigils x^1 and x^2 throughout; but there is no way of knowing whether t shared more errors with **p** than with x^1 in those passūs where the t copies now preserve only the **A** portion of their conjoint text. This is purely a matter of procedure, therefore, which has as its corollary the use of '**x**' rather than 'x^1' for the readings of XYIP^{2}UD in Pr–XI. It implies neither doubt that x^2 existed nor belief that t would have agreed preponderantly with x^1 had it been present. Its practical purpose is that of highlighting the clearly observable contrast between **p** and **x** throughout the text, where both traditions may be compared on the basis of numerous complete witnesses. This contrast brings out the dual character of **p** as independent (in preserving through x^2 archetypal readings lost by x^1 and sometimes by t) but also as subordinate (in often corrupting x^2 at points after XII, where t's greater reliability can be confirmed by x^1). There is another reason for keeping the separate sigil **p** even when its agreements with t presumably attest their common x^2 source. This is that **p** is the only faithful witness to x^2 (and thence by inference to Cx) in nearly 300 instances (about 80 of them major) where it is x^1 that errs and another 80 (about 25 of them major) where t shares x^1's error. Thus in Pr–XI, where t is absent, **p** in effect earns the status of a manuscript 'family'. For where it is right against x^1, **p** must be judged to preserve the reading of x^2, the family original it is presumed to share with t. But **p**'s errors in this section may or may not have been present in x^2; for this can be known only from Passus XII on, when the degree of **p**'s accuracy can be gauged through comparison with t. The evidence from here on reveals **p** to be as proportionally corrupt as its showing against x^1 in Pr–XI would give reason to expect. Yet since **p** also preserves 300 right readings, it remains an indispensable authority for the text throughout. In contrast with the **B** family α's relation to β, then, **p** emerges as secondary in importance even in Pr–XI, where the competing variant is attested by x^1 alone; but its value is relatively higher than that of the **m** family of **A** in comparison with **r**.

§ 11. In conclusion, there are two direct lines of transmission from the archetype, x^1 and x^2. From x^1, y and b descend, perhaps through a shared intermediary source, i, and u immediately. Another three lines correspondingly derive from x^2, t perhaps immediately, p^1 and p^2 through their intermediate source **p**.[17] Although p^1 seldom and p^2 never uniquely preserves Cx, neither branch can be eliminated. For constituent pairs or individual members of each appear at times to be the sole faithful witness to their ancestral text **p**. The readings of **p** are accordingly registered in the Apparatus throughout. As with the sub-archetypes, however, the complex subsequent history of their further group-traditions, involving many intermittent losses, restricts the number of group-sigils it is convenient to cite. Thus 'm' and 'q', which appear in the diagram below, are not employed in the Apparatus. Conversely, among the p^1 groups, e, because persistently instanced by four witnesses, is the only one to be used or to have its variants frequently included. Of the x^1 branches, the briefly attested but closely knit three-member group b is recorded wherever **x** is seriously in doubt, since in its few hundred lines as a C-Text it is a co-witness to the hypothetical sub-family ancestor i that it may share with y. For if b had been present throughout, a sub-family i might have emerged that rivalled **p** in frequency of citation. Next t, because entitled to sub-family status like **p**'s, is cited wherever Cx is not virtually certain from the agreement of x^1 and **p**. But to save space, t's many (and often eccentric) individual variants are ignored where an Apparatus entry is not otherwise needed. Among the two-member groups, only u is cited to any extent, as it is an independent witness to the correct x^1 reading when y errs. By contrast r, though guaranteed independent by its unique preservation of one apparently authentic line,[18] is noticed only as part of a list of complex variants.

§ 12. As the parent-group of the chosen base-manuscript, y's readings are recorded where certainly or probably recoverable. Its most complete representative, *Hm 143* (X), has been favoured by all editors since its discovery in 1924 (II § 41). But while its one serious rival *BL Addl. 35157* (U) is of closely similar date and linguistic character, there is little reason to prefer it. The present edition thus takes X as the copy-text for a reconstruction of Cx on the basis of x^1 corrected from the x^2 tradition preserved initially in **p** and, from XII onwards, in **p** and t together. In something over 100 instances, corruptions traceable to Cx, the common source of both traditions, have been emended by restoration on the authority of individual witnesses or that of the parallel B-Text, especially in XXI–XXII, by reconstruction, or by conjecture where little or no direct evidence is available. The text is thus presented in the language of a manuscript dateable to within a decade of the archetype, with grammar and orthography fairly close to that reliably presumed for the original (see Appendix I §§ 1–2).

§ 13. On the basis of the foregoing account, the inferred relationships between the extant **C** copies and their hypothetical group- and family-ancestors may be diagrammatically expressed as follows:

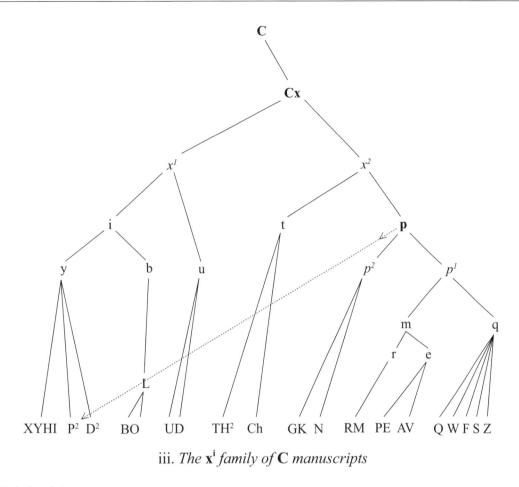

iii. *The* **x**^{i} *family of* **C** *manuscripts*

Sub-family **i**

§ 14. The hypothetical sub-family **i** comprises **XYIP^{2}D^{2}BOL** and fragment *H* (which, from the scanty evidence available, belongs immediately after X).[19] It is described as a sub-family rather than a group because, like γ in the Bx tradition, it has two distinct branches containing several manuscripts. One, **b**, was the immediate source of BOL; but a combination of losses, re-arrangement and contamination make it uncertain whether further sub-divisions exist within the other, **y**, one possible arrangement being [{(XHYI)P^2}D^2]. The sub-family i is recognisable initially on the basis of six agreements in error between y and b. The exact relation of these groups is hard to specify with certainty because of b's brevity, the absence of YD^2 over the portion attested by b, I's partial absence in the Prologue and P^2's contamination from **p**, a feature indicated by broken lines. (N^2's position is too unclear to allow its inclusion in the diagram; see § 39 below). The character of the first three readings listed indicates, however, that the relation of y and b was close.

Major Pr 28, 183 +K^2. II 9 (*corr. a.h.* O). **Minor** I 152 (*so* I, *but* -P^2), [174 +AVS]. II 66^2.

The postulate of a common source i presupposes that neither constituent group derives from the other. The <BOL> ancestor's *lack* of y's errors at Pr 107, I 102 and 192 need in itself imply only that b was at these points a more accurate copy of y than its other extant representatives, XIP^2. But more is indicated by b's unique right readings at Pr 224 and particularly at 216. Were *reik* at 216 only a brilliant scribal conjecture, b's descent from y would not be worth doubting; if original, however, it must be due either to correction from a superior pre-archetypal copy or to pure descent from Cx through x^1, the more economical explanation preferred here. For its part, y lacks b's major errors at Pr 133 and II 112, and this fact can be reconciled with the errors y shares with b only by positing an immediate common ancestor that contained both. These may seem slender grounds for positing i; but as b is present for less than 8% of **C**, they might in principle have been much strengthened had b preserved the whole text. The position of i in the diagram at § 13 above takes account of the clearly non-secondary character of y, both in Pr–II 128 and the rest of the poem (on the term 'secondary' cf. § 62). Whatever its defects, i must have been uncontaminated from **p** and other versions. For such is the case with its descendant y, though two y copies D^2 and P^2 exhibit this feature, the latter massively, and members of b are contaminated from **B** (see §§ 24–5, § 27).

a. *Group* y

§ 15. The first group includes the base-manuscript of this edition and so (as with groups w of **B** and t of **A**) receives extended treatment. Since i, the original of **y**, does not descend from b, and since X itself is earlier than L, the oldest of b's three members, y and b may be assumed to have been coæval. Apart from X the group includes three more single-version copies, one complete but damaged (P^2) and two with major losses (Y at the beginning, I in the beginning, middle and end); one conjoint copy of late date (D^2); and a fragment of 100 lines from between Passus I and III (H). The members of y cannot be ordered with precision because of substantial gaps in Y and I; but P^2 and to a less extent D^2 differ from XYIH in being contaminated from **p**. Nonetheless, after discounting D^2's absence from about half the poem, the five main witnesses can be reliably accepted as a genetic group on the basis of some 26 isolative errors, sixteen of them major. In 60 further readings, 30 major, one or two members lack the group error, or y is joined, seemingly at random, by one to three other copies. The group is imperfectly represented: (a) from II 157–XII 19 by $XYIP^2$ (joined by H for III 123–74); (b) from XII 20–XXI 79 by $XYIP^2D^2$; and (c) from XXI 80 to XXII by XYP^2D^2. Prior to II 157 there are four members XIP^2H, from I 199 to II 44. Before I 199 there are only three XIP^2, with I absent from the Prologue before 91 and after 157, a stretch in which no exclusive errors of those present are found. In the following list of y's agreements, a minus sign indicates that one member lacks the denoted error, a plus that a manuscript not a member of y shares it, the latter references being in square brackets.

Major (a) II 240. III 449, 451. IV 139, [158 +F], 178 -I. V 118^1, [118^2 -P^2+EA], [133 -I+G.] ?VII 300. VIII 20, 166, 315, 333. IX 38 [*def.* I, +AVG]. [265 +EK], 270. [XI 268 -Y+U].
(b) XII [35 +N^2], 140–41 -Y. XIII 112 -D^2, 123*a* -Y. XIV ?48 -Y, 125 -YP^2+N^2, 155 -Y. XV 144 [+EQWN], -Y, 242 [-P^2+U,] 283 [-Y+DQ]. XVI [128 -P^2+VR], 232^1 -Y, 315 -Y. XVII 210 -Y, 239 -Y. XVIII 33 -D^2, [60 -Y+U], 75 (*different error* Y), [139 *def.* I; -Y+D], 244 (*diff. error* D^2). XIX 174 -D^2; *om* X, 240, 245 (*diff. error* P^2), 297 [+DM.] XX [75 +N^2], 307, [389 -P^2+F]. XXI 48, 58 -D^2, ?113 (*om* IP^2D^2), 317, 350/51.
(c) XXI [312 +N^2W,] [320 +N], *om* D^2, [347 +N^2N,] 3[49 +S,] XXII 13^3, 186 -D^2.
Minor (a) II 217^2, 238 -P^2. III 5, 205, 342 -P^2, 447. IV 4, [132 -P^2+U.] V 160. VI 376. VII 108, 239 -P^2, [281 +K]. VIII 87 (*om* I), 148 -P^2. IX 313 -P^2, *om* I. [XI 271/2 +N^2].
(b) [XV 37 +SWN, 167 -Y+U]. XVII 173 -Y, [263 -Y+F]. XVIII [97 -Y+Z], 207. XIX 8, 138 -P^2, 187 -P^2, [227 +N], 290 -D^2, *om* P^2. XX 270 †P^2; †D^2, [441 -I+PN], [457 +N (*see Textual Note*)]. XXI 57 [-P^2+DT], 82 [-P^2+?t], 86 -D^2, 225 [+D].

§ 16. In this list the copies outside the y group that share its variant (those in square brackets) lack persistence, so they do not disconfirm the evidence of the criterial readings. On the other hand, attention is due to three copies significantly free from the postulated group-error: Y, especially in the (b) section (in 17 cases, 13 major); P^2 (in 13, four major); and D^2 (in six, four major). P^2's right readings, which are here regarded as resulting from its collation with a **p** copy (§§ 24–5 below), are congruent with its also including several **p** errors. The D^2 evidence, which may be similarly explained, is too small for certainty, but the number of instances is proportionally high. The right readings of Y, though they could derive from a source such as u, may simply be more accurate reflexes of the group-original than those of the other members.[20] But major deficiencies in Y, I and D^2, and the indeterminate character of many variants, make it hard to be sure whether y's members should be ordered as given or as $[(XHIP^2D^2)Y]$. There is a case for treating b as part of y since their agreements in b's small attested portion, if sustained over the whole poem, might have outweighed the evidence of its unique right readings. But on the available data, these favour the arrangement $[(XYHIP^2D^2)BOL]$, denoting independent derivation of y and b from i, which was an immediate copy of x^1 (§§ 13–14). Such an explanation fits with b's origin as a defective **B** copy supplemented from a **C** copy that has left echoes in the manuscript's **B** portion (*B Version* § 27; and § 27 below).

§ 17. Despite its errors, y is the soundest identifiable Cx group. Its hypothesised parent manuscript i, presumably one of the earliest generated, thus warrants a place on the same level of transmission as the x^2 sub-families t and **p**. Group y cannot be eliminated, as it contains some 30 right readings that are unique, eight of them major, and eight more (given in square brackets) shared by one or two other manuscripts. In addition, some of its members uniquely possess right readings not derived from another version. These must therefore be present by pure descent, by intelligent scribal conjecture or by correction from outside the Cx tradition.[21] In the following list of y's correct readings, a minus sign before a sigil indicates a y copy's agreement in error with **p** or **pu**, a plus sign agreement with y of a **p** copy, U, or another version.

Major -P^2 II 191. V 14, 35. VI 382, 410. XVI 183 (+ α of **B**). XXI -P^2D^2 449. -P^2 470.
Minor [Pr -P^2+b 13]. III 118, 316, [+FS 334]. V 90, -P^2 161, -P^2 190. VI 59[1], 82, 90, 381. VIII -YP^2 159[2], [-I+Q; *om* P^2 196,] 264[2], 282, 331. IX -IP^2 157, [+U 260]. X 189, -Y 229. XI 145. XVI 255, [-P^2+WN[2] 347]. XVII -Y 67, -P^2D^2 77. XIX -P^2D^2 168, [+TW 233]. XX 328, [-P^2D^2+W 464]. XII +WN 25.

§ 18. The only complete member of y is **X**, chosen as the copy-text though substantively less good than Y, which is ruled out because it is defective before II 157. While X is comparatively somewhat less sound a descendant of its original than its counterpart W for the **B** Version, its x^1 text is intrinsically preferable for the half of the poem where x^2's only representative is **p**, and it shows no contamination from the other versions. The language of manuscript X is close to the poet's presumed SWM dialect. Its handwriting places it among the half-dozen oldest copies of **C**, and the many corrections by a second hand (except for one over erasure at III 176) do not seem to have involved collation with an exemplar from a different family, as was the case with P^2 (§§ 24–5 below). X is remarkable for its systematic erasures of the name *Peres*, which begin at VI 366 (fol. 28*v*), where the referent is not actually the eponymous ploughman. Their presence is unexplained, but is more likely to have had some precautionary political aim than to be a scribe's preparation for rubrication.[22] For reasons of space, they are not recorded in the Apparatus, and except where substantive issues arise over the exact reading, as at V 31, all small alterations by the corrector's hand are ignored (for these the Athlone apparatus should be consulted). The bulk of X's individual variants are removed to the Appendix in Vol I so as not to distract attention from the family and group readings that the main Apparatus seeks to record, though the facts of insertion or erasure are noted where relevant.[23] X suffers from the mislineation common in most copies of the longer versions, but its significant omissions are few and there are no losses of lines larger than of two at the most. It wants only Pr 232 and VII 304 in addition to the two lines and eight half-lines absent from its family ancestor x^1 and the one apparently missing from i at Pr 183. It contains one minor unique right reading at XI 295 and no distinctive spurious matter.

§ 19. Manuscript **Y** resembles R of the **B** Version in that it is potentially the best copy of **C** but for lacking, through loss of leaves, the first 590 lines (as R lacks 750). Carefully written in a clear script and set out as if prose, Y has no corrections or alterations by another hand and appears, from readings like XIX 59, a fairly sound descendant of the group-original. Thus it lacks the major errors found in the other y copies at XII 140–41, XVII 173, 239, and minor ones at XV 167, 283 and XVII 210a, 263. Collation of its immediate exemplar with an x^2 copy cannot be ruled out to explain this; but the four readings free from the x^1 error that suggest that possibility could be due to intelligent scribal conjecture (VI 51, XVI 76/7, 232 and XVII 78). This interpretation is confirmed by Y's careful spellings at III 492 (shared with P^2U) and VIII 184, which preserve exact sense, and its unique correct lineation at XXI 304/05.[24]

§ 20. By contrast with the neglected Y, manuscript **I** has had its fair share of attention. Skeat thought the I form of passages corresponding to IX 128–40 and 203–79 in some respects superior to the 'received text' as found in his base-manuscript P. Just as he had judged Rawlinson Poetry 38 a later stage of **B** than that in Laud 581, he saw Ilchester as an earlier draft of **C** with readings that sometimes '*point back* to the B-Text.' An example Skeat cites is XVII 94, where 'I alone keeps the right reading *Wederwise*, found also in the B-Text.'[25] But Skeat failed to notice that this is the reading of the whole family as attested by the four x^1 copies available to him, and the error *Wonderwyse* is a major piece of evidence for the postulated common origin of **p** and t.[26] Russell, too, formerly believed I's Pr 104–24 'a superior survival of an original...deformed in the version preserved by the other manuscripts' [i.e. the archetypal text].[27] This opinion, though abandoned, glimmers spectrally in R–K's speculation (p. 194) that the Prologue's weaving of discrete passages on hermits and bishops into 'an integral discourse on a distinct topic' suggests I's access to 'surviving loose revision material' (presumably Langland's drafts).

§ 21. It will be appropriate to consider I further here in its relationship to the conflated **ABC** copy **Ht**. For in Ht the interpolation of IX 66–279 and Pr 91–127 after B VI 158 has been seen by Wendy Scase as evidence for the existence of a 'second textual tradition' of **C** distinct from that of the archetype.[28] Observing the close similarity in the two copies' linking lines and pattern of omissions,[29] Scase takes their substantial agreements in error to indicate that manuscript I was an 'improvement' of 'something close to the Ht text,' noting that Ht and I lack the 'B-Text lines interlineated with this material in the C-Text' (pp. 458–9). These passages, she argues, were not excerpts from the received C-Text but were generated in the process of incorporating the new material into the poem. The lines on false hermits circulated in a form 'cued for insertion but not edited into the C-Text revision'; but it is less clear that the Ophni-Phineas passage did so, since in I it continues as a C-Text, whereas in Ht it ends with C Pr 125–7. The passages' imperfect alliteration, clichés, lack of amplification, and possible metrical experiment all point to an unfin-ished condition.[30] Finding support in the 'autobiographical passage' of C V (esp. 1–5) for 'early, separate circulation, and subsequent re-thinking and revision,'[31] she concludes that the IHt text should be taken into account in editing **C**.

§ 22. One unexpected editorial consequence of Scase's claim is that the received text's imper-fectly alliterating Pr 105–24 would have to be seen as itself the product of a scribe's redaction 'from memory or from what [he] could decipher' (in Skeat's words) of an accidentally-defaced original copy.[32] This opinion is echoed in Brewer's statement that the 'chaotic state of the manuscripts' may reflect the process of the work's composition as much as that of its transmission.[33] But no such wide-ranging speculative inferences need be drawn from the evidence of the hermits / bishops pas-sages in manuscript I. For the whole notion of I's text as an 'improvement' of a lost IHt original is over-elaborate and arbitrary and, as Pearsall has shown, both copies contain little that cannot be attributed to an enterprising scribe bent on 'alliterative embellishment.'[34] As now printed entire in the Athlone Appendix, the Ilchester Prologue reveals its true character as what R–K call a 'compila-tion' of 'passages from C IX...set within a conveniently simple frame of the **A** Prologue, with a little filling out from that of **C**.'[35] The I text itself shows typical scribal substitutions for words that lack alliteration in the Cx form, such as *peres* for *folk* at 116 and 118, with its unLanglandian contextual sense.[36] Such 'improvements,' like those in the **B** manuscript F, may in principle be distinguishable from a hypothetical earlier and other creation underlying them. But the prospects for its recovery are slight and its textual usefulness, as all editors except Skeat have eventually agreed, is minimal. There thus seems little reason to question Pearsall's conclusion that the I Prologue is in shape and substance a wholly scribal product. All that ms I yields of value here is one correct reading at 127 (shared with K^{2}'s **C** interpolation), a felicitous conflation of seemingly 'split' **x** and **p** variants that may be what Cx actually read. And at VI 149, I uniquely attests one major variant judged original, so it cannot be eliminated. It is also the only x^{1} copy with the correct reading at X 275.

§ 23. For the rest, ms I stands firmly in the y group, on the basis of all but four of the 26 agree-ments noted at § 15 above. More specifically, it has 22 disjunctive agreements with X (*R–K* p. 44) where Y is also present, of which three are major, VI 223[1], VII 148 and X 197. This grouping is not challenged by I's 17 such agreements with Y (*R–K*, p. 44), most of which are trivial spelling-variants. The one exception is *a pes*] *an ase* at VIII 166; but this is almost certainly a y-group reading, since *a mase* X is a derived individual variant and P^{2} has altered *as* in another ink over erasure. The XI pairing is little more effectively challenged by the 38 agreements of XY (*R–K*, p. 44), since these are again largely of spellings. Perhaps no more than three where I is present are major (VII 8, XIX 91 and XXI 36), as are another three where it is absent (XVIII 147, XXI 135 and 249). So comparable a closeness between X and each of its partners permits, without impos-ing, the relation [(XY)I]; so R–K's explanation of 'sporadic consultation and "correction" in a single copying centre' (p. 44) might seem plausible. Persuasive reasons for doubting the existence of such centres have been advanced (Doyle and Parkes 1978; Horobin 2010), but the explanation appears consistent with both the orthographic and the textual evidence, e.g. the spelling *ou* for the diphthong |ɔi| in III 64 *cloustre* XY and XVII 224 *apousened* XI [in App. *read* 'XI' *for* 'X], which suggests a common exemplar, 'regularised' by I in the first case and by Y in the second.[37] These somewhat indeterminate data suggest that **XYI** (to which H should be added) are less like BOL (since no one member is based on either of the others) than like AMH[3] in the **A** family **m** (*A*

Version § 25). For within y these three copies effectively form a 'core-group' on the basis of some 18 agreements, half of them major. The reason for the great discrepancy between this figure and the 33 agreements estimated by R–K (p. 43) is that many of the variants they judge errors are not so regarded here. Moreover, half a dozen they include were shared by P^2 before its (visible) correction, so these are cited at § 15 above as evidence for y rather than for <XYI>. In other words, P^2's descent from y looks to be direct and not through any one of the three 'core' copies, their immediate exemplars, or their group original, if there was one. The same holds for D^2 which, as a conjoint text, necessarily shares many fewer readings with the core-group.

Major IV 21^1 (*corr. a.h.* X). VI 167. IX 125 haue] *om*, + *a.h.* X. IX 331. XII 237. XIX 145 him] U&r; *om* XYI, 290. XX 197, 241. **Minor** II 238. III 447. IV 4, 21^2. V 160, 190. XVII 206. ?XX 239, 270.

These variants, few and unpersistent, are not incompatible with P^2's and D^2's membership of y (§ 15 above); for the ascription of their correct readings to exemplars collated with **p** copies is confirmed by their having several indicative **p** errors (§§ 24–6 below). The grouping XYI is questioned by some 20 agreements of XYU (*R–K* p. 45); but all of these save three are minor, and most are trivial, including the simple visual error at XX 240 (*h* for *b*). In the major crux at XI 124, the reading *mette* IP^{2}D is more probably a coincidental 'correction' of a phrase rendered difficult by prior corruption of the verb than a preservation (from y and u respectively) of the true x^1 form lost by XYU (see *Textual Notes*). The IP^{2}D variant cannot be archetypal, since *ouet* XYU is a mere spelling-variant of *out* **p**, which must therefore have been the reading of Cx. At Passus XI 218 the reading of XYU is once more that of x^1 concealed by further variation in P^{2}D; and in XXI 466 the same is true, except that D here corrects from its regular secondary **p** source. The challenge from XYU can thus be safely set aside.

§ 24. Among the members of y, **P^2** underwent most contamination from **p**, first in its immediate exemplar and then by visible insertion and alteration in the manuscript. The first phase reveals nearly 100 agreements in error, some 35 major. Most could be from either **p** branch, but whereas there are no exclusive agreements with p^2 some 19, of which four are major (II 126, III 54, X 275^2 and XIX 165), indicate collation with a p^1 copy. More specific pointers to P^2's conflation-source appear in minor readings and are correspondingly less reliable. XVII 228 suggests the p^1 group m and some 70 more (*R–K* p. 27) specifically manuscript M, a copy early enough to have been used by the scribe of P^2's exemplar. A dozen readings categorisable as major by the single criterion of affecting a line's scansion are of kinds sometimes caused by random convergence. These are the *kyrke*] *churche* substitutions at III 397, V 103, VIII 26, 53, IX 9, XI 246, 250, XV 11 and XVI 255; the inverse *ch*-] *c*- at II 89; and the apparently visual errors at XVI 266 and XVII 162. In the following list of P^2**p** agreements, those shared by up to three x^1 copies and, in one case, two aberrant members of t, are denoted by a *plus* sign. Illustrating the types of readings (including 14 major ones) where coincidental variation may have occurred, they are recorded here solely to furnish a yardstick of comparison with the exclusive agreements adduced as potentially genetic. Of P^2's many additions in a later hand, the few cited in the Apparatus are placed in square brackets here. While these prove collation with a manuscript of a different tradition, they say nothing about the character of P^2's main exemplar, so most are omitted.

Major Pr 230. II 89 +ID, 126. III 54, 223, 276, 357 +U, 415 +D. V 35^1 +u, [35^2], 66, 104, 105, 122. VI 55, 68, 149, 298^1, 436. VII 176, 247. VIII 26, 167, 220, 258, 322. IX 9, 202, 338^{1,2}. X 275^2 (=p^1K). XI 246 +D, 250, 270. XII 10 +D^{2}u. XIII 195. XIV 28 +t. XV 290. XVI 105 +DH^2, 183, 255 +D^{2}uCh, 266 +UG, 302 +Ch. XVII 136, 139, 162 +uCh. XIX 165 +D^{2}N^2. XX 34*a*, [140 (= p^1)], 203 +t. XX 471. XXI 453. XXII 323 +DTH^2.

Minor Pr 13 +u. [81]. I 99, 177. II 27a^2 +b, 73, 86, 136 p^1+U, 139 +D, 159$^{1.3}$. III 14, 61, 109 +D, 191^2, 247, 305 +u, 324 (p^l). IV 37, 55 +D, 90^2, 105, 127. V 14 +u, 18, 51, [66], 78 +D, 192. VI 42^2 +I, 136, 235, 252, 269 +ID, 271, 275 (p^lN), 278, 280^2, 317, 367, 394, 414. VII 22, 58, 61^1, 97, 115 +D, 144 +D, 147, 182, 223, 245$^{1.2}$, 252, 255 +D, 257 +D, 286. VIII 30, 53 +u, 68 +D. 91, 111 (p^l+N), 115 (p^l), 139, 148 +u, 159, 175 (= p^l) +D, 190, 227, 244, 301, 304^1 (p^l). IX 8 +u, 60, 105 +U, 153, 207, 230 (= p^lG), 247, 299, [345]. X 38 +D, 50 +X, 130 +ID, 175 (= p^lN) +D, 178, 268 +DN^2, 292. XI 171, 201 +DN^2, 210 (= p^l), 266, 316 +H^{2}Ch. XII 80 +D^{2}UN^2, 113 +N^2, 185 (= p^l)+Gu, 217 +T. XIII 89 +D^{2}ut, 107 (= p^l) +NN^2, 119, 136^2, 186 +D^{2}Dt, 236. XIV 39 +D^{2}t, 56 +u, 194 (= p^l). XV 12 (= p^l) +D^2, 47 +Ch, 70 (= p^l or ?eRM), 151, 165, 214 +Ch, 243 +D, 250 +D, 257 +N^2. XVI 39 (?= e), 78 +Dt, 101 +N^2, 230 +D^{2}UTCh, 360 +tN^2. XVII 10 +D^{2}D, 28 +D^{2}DCh, 77 +D^{2}ut, 228 (= eRM). XVIII 271 +D^2. XIX 63, 65 (= p^l +U), 327. XX 8^2 +I, 82 +ChN^2, 106 +N^2, 112, 174, 229 +N^2, 231 +D^2, 320 +Ch, 354 +DChN^2, 395 +D^{2}Ch, 399 +U. XXI 11 +D^2, 13 +D^2, 42 +YD, 321 +Dt, 348 +D^{2}N^{2}t, 433 +Ch. XXII 95 +U, 245 +t, 266 +D^{2}Dt.

§ 25. From its **p**-type source, P^2 also took good readings such as the striking one at XXI 435, acquired at the visible second stage of correction (the same process appears in D^2 and D). But some 38 (six major), distributed fairly evenly through the text, must belong to the first stage and are therefore unlikely to preserve the reading of i. For the errors P^2 corrects are shared by the other y witnesses with u and so must have been in x^l, while attribution of its right readings to a **p** source correct at those points is congruent with the 100 errors P^2 shares with **p** (listed at § 24). In a further 35 cases, other x^l copies with the *right* reading have also been specified, not as evidence for **p** contamination in P^2 but to illustrate the frequency of random convergent variation. Where t concurs with them, the **p** reading in P^2 may be descended from x^2; but where D^2 and D concur, it is more probable that their exemplars were (like P^2's) collated with a **p** copy, as both (unlike t) also contain errors of this sub-family (see §§ 26 and 29).

Major Pr 20. VI 148, 359^2. IX 137. XI 266 +D. XIV 138. XVI 128 +uCh. XIX 301, 332 (*partial*). XX 389 +ut. XXI 247 +D^{2}t, [435] +D^{2}D, 480 +D^{2}t. XXII 51 +D^{2}Dt.

Minor Pr 33, 172, 208, 210. I 35, 46, 181, 182. II 60. III 262, 494. IV 15, 38, 56, 62. V 134, 151, 160. VI 6^2, 51^2 +Y, 59^3, 95, 104 +D, 312 +D, 320. VII 5 +D, 71 +D, 164 +D, 184 (*add in App.*), 240^2, 281 +Iu. VIII 42^2+D, 85, 303 +U, 314. IX [345^1]. X 45 +u, 136 +IDN^2. XI 55, 184^2 +N^2. XIII 173 +t. XIV 97 +Iut, 128 +Dt. XV 21 +t, 66 +D^{2}uN^{2}t, 261, 263a +D^{2}Ch, 296^1 +Ch. XVI 84, 330 +D^{2}t. XVII 117 +t, 261 +D^{2}DN^{2}t. XVIII 46 +IDt. XIX 187 +ut. XX 323^3 +D^{2}Dt, 373 +N^{2}t, 382 +Dt, 413 +U. XXI 82 +uN^2, 162 +D^{2}t, 246 +t, 287 +Dt, 381 +t. XXII 307 +D^{2}Dt.

These many correct(ed) readings give P^2 no special importance, but they illuminate the activity of scribes interested by the numerous differences between the two textual traditions. P^2 cannot be eliminated, since it has (probably by felicitous conjecture) the best verb-form at IX 311 and unique right readings at III 6 and XVII 147.

§ 26. The final member of y is the sixteenth-century conjoint text **D^2**. It is more loosely related to the 'core-group' than is P^2, which it resembles in that its lost exemplar also seems to have been collated with a copy of **p**. D^2's descent from y is indicated by 40 errors, some 30 major, shared with all or most of the group (see § 15). In seven cases (five major) where it lacks the y-group error, it is presumed corrected from an x^2 source. This conclusion is supported directly by its twelve x^l family errors (five disjunctive and seven more shared by other x^l copies in brackets): [XIII 186 +P^{2}D; XIV 39 +P^2]; XVII 84; XIX 41, [143 +u]; [XX 464 +P^{2}u; XXI 73 +P^{2}D, 185 +D]; and XXII 31 (to which should be added in the Apparatus [XII 88 +D], XVI 81^1, XIX 27), and collaterally by some 20 readings free from x^l family errors (see § 33). That the former's source was t rather than **p** is indicated only by the wrong line-division at XXI 241/2 and by two other (non-exclusive) major errors, at XVII 125 (+I) and XXII 449 (+P^{2}u), onc an obvious substitution of an easier synonym, the other an omission, but both perhaps coincidental. This interpretation is challenged by one major omission error (XIX 165) and two minor ones shared exclusively with **p** (XII 10, 176); but a link with t is collaterally indicated by the two major right readings at XXI 401 +N^2 and XXII 110. D^2 cannot be eliminated, as it has a unique right reading at XXI 410, possibly by happy scribal correction of an obvious gap in the sense.

b. *Group* **b**

§ 27. The major x^i group **b** comprises the three conjoint manuscripts **BOL**, which share some 50 isolative agreements, about 20 of them major. So large a number of errors in only 560 lines (about 7.5 % of the poem) confirms R–K's view that b's **C** source was a poor manuscript.[38] It was also one contaminated from **B** at Pr 72, 133 (after which b has B Pr 106), 231 and I 5 (this last shared with I), while at 160 its error *a myȝte bygynneþ*] *comseth a myhte* is significantly that of Bx. This feature is unsurprising, given the circumstances of its origin (*B Version* § 27). Most of b's readings are not recorded except when part of a larger variant entry, as at Pr 183, II 84, 112 (major) and Pr 171, 192 (minor). But b cannot be eliminated, because of its unique major right reading at Pr 216.

c. *Group* **u**

§ 28. The third constituent group of x^1 is **u**, consisting of **U** and **D**. Arguably it should be treated as a sub-family on a line with i in direct descent from the family ancestor. But though perhaps as early as y, u is unlikely to precede i; for it shows signs of collation with an x^2 copy at Pr 181–83, where x^1 seems to have been defective, and possibly at XV 80–3, where only u and t have correct lineation. The group is established from 130 agreements in error, about a fifth of them major (listed in full *R–K*, pp 30–1). Only the following appear in Vol I, as part of a larger apparatus entry.

Major Pr 181, 183. II 9. III 479. **Minor** [I 133 +S]. IV 134. VI 376.

Group u's identity is collaterally confirmed by its unique attestation of eight right readings, which preclude its elimination. In three of these the group-reading is inferentially that of only one member, the other having erred with y. D's freedom from several x^1 errors, however, is better attributed to correction from an x^2 source, because it also shares some x^2 errors (see § 30 below).

Major VI 163. XI 208 (D), 269/70 (U), [306 +YN^2]. [VII 36 (D,+VQK)]. VIII 77–8*a*. XIX 255/56. **Minor** II [159 +QF], 217. VIII 135 (D), 247/48.

That u derives from x^1 is shown by its sharing 360 presumptive family errors with y (see §§ 33–4 on x^1 below). But it cannot descend from y, as it is free of the 86 certain or probable y-group errors listed at § 15, or from the postulated source of y and b, since it lacks the six i errors (§ 14). Of u's two constituents, **U** is a complete, early and uncontaminated x^1 witness and could if required have furnished the copy-text in the absence of X. U cannot be derived from D, which is both later and free from three of its errors where all other copies are also wrong. It does not group with any other copy than D, and when lacking the right readings preserved solely by D, it may be presumed to have erred from their exclusive common ancestor. U's one unique major right reading precludes its elimination, but as it otherwise requires no further notice except when supporting other witnesses as part of a longer apparatus entry, only a few of its individual variants are recorded, as at VII 276.

§ 29. Unlike U, **D** has substantial agreements with other copies: 45 with M (*R–K*, p.28), all minor and most trivial; 68 with P^2; and 60 with N, which R–K (p. 31) convincingly judge random. Of the last, one worth notice is X 275 *lely*] *trewly*, where D's exemplar probably replaced the contextually obscure x^1 reading *leix* with *lely* from a **p** source and D then substituted an obvious modernising synonym that happens to coincide with the p^2 copy N (as again at XX 307). The high number of D's readings cited is partly due to its frequent divergence from U when the latter appears as the citation-source for u:

Pr 216. II 217. IV 180. VIII 349. X 7. XI 218, 288, XII 98^2. XIII 125^1. XIV 150. XV 8 (cf. **p**), 89 (*after erasure*), 131 (*ins.*), 167. XVII 207–10. XVIII 75^2. XIX 290^2. XX 13, 107 $+N^2$, 114, 140, 177, 337, 413. XXII 215, 236, 282.

Like P^2 of y, D's immediate exemplar seems to have been collated with a copy of x^2, as shown by its sharing nine / ten x^2 errors:

Major XV 89 $+D^2$, *after erasure*; 106 $+D^2$. XXII 13. **Minor** XII 88 $+D^2$. XVI 328. XVII 82 $+D^2$. XXI 73 $+P^2D^2$, 185 $+P^2D^2$, 321. [XII 236].

This conclusion is supported collaterally by D's 17 agreements with x^2 in a right reading:

Major XI 44 (+ *a.h.*). XIII 39/40. XXI 365, 466. XXII 240 $+D^2$. **Minor** XII 37. XIV 47, 128 $+P^2$, 193. XVI 362. XVII 104 $+D^2$, 155^1. XVIII 46 $+IP^2$, 240 $+IP^2D^2$, 248 $+IP^2D^2$, 323^3 $+P^2D^2$, 382$+P^2$.

While in principle these may merely indicate accurate preservation of u where U erred, D's persistent co-occurrence with P^2D^2 strengthens the likelihood that its exemplar was similarly corrected from an x^2 source (see §§ 25–6 above). Two major instances, IV 180 and XV 89, prove a second stage of correction in D itself, like that in P^2 (§ 24 above), but also paralleled in D^2.[39]

§ 30. Of necessity, these errors are clearly attributable to x^2 only from Passus XII onwards, where t is also present; for any earlier agreements may go back only to x^2's descendant **p**. But the repeated specific agreement with either group p^1 or p^2 that would decisively confirm the latter interpretation is not found; so the exact origin of D's five agreements in error with **p** before Passus XII remains uncertain:

Major II 185 (= PMS $+P^2$). IV 180 (*over erasure*). **Minor** II 101, 174. VII 255 $+P^2$.

The same holds true in the dozen instances where D is free of the u-group and x^1 family error and where, for its right readings, an x^2 source must be presumed:

Major VI 125, 148. VII 36 (= VQK), 164 $+P^2$, 177. XI 56. XIII 125^3. **Minor** II 187, 198 (= PEF, $+P^2$), VII 173, 201 $+P^2$, 213. VIII 42 $+P^2$.

Of these, at least XIII 125 confirms that D's x^2 source cannot have been t, which is here wrong; and that conclusion is to some extent supported by XX 321, where D's error is with **p** against x^1t. But this is minor and, like XXII 386, where conversely D's agreement in a right reading is with H^2Ch (=?t), could be coincidental. D is chiefly of interest as, like P^2, illustrating inter-family contact between an x^1 member and x^2 (probably in the form of a **p** copy). But it cannot be eliminated, as it has four unique right readings, Pr 138 and XI 56 (perhaps scribal conjectures), and two recorded at § 28 as representing u.

d. *The* $\mathbf{x^1}$ *family: conclusions*

§ 31. The above survey of the structure of x^1 has shown its groups and individual members to contain nearly 50 variants (about 20 of them major) which appear original on intrinsic grounds and on comparison with the parallel text in one or more other versions. These readings, as in the case of the α and β families in **B**, include some that may preserve the archetype by direct descent through x^1 and others that may have come in from a source belonging to the family x^2. There are a few probable contaminations from **B** in individual x^1 copies; but none of these is drawn upon to emend the text. Since all the extant x^1 witnesses contain one or more unique right readings, none can be eliminated; so all have been collated, though to save space they are cited only selectively. But the readings of group y are recorded entire in the Apparatus and those of X either there or in the Appendix. The evidence for x^1, the exclusive common ancestor of y, b and u, is the body of 380 wrong readings, some 130 of them major, shared exclusively by all three branches. The variant preferred to x^1 in the list below is presumed to be the reading of x^2, as represented by **pt** in about 60 cases; by **p** alone in another 315; and by group t in some six where x^1 seems to have varied from Cx and **p** from the presumed reading of x^2. By contrast with what may be observed in the **B** tradition, which has no inter-familial contamination, in 180 instances of x^1 errors (about 30 of them major), the reading judged correct is shared by between one and four x^1 witnesses. The secure total of crite-rial x^1 readings is strictly therefore only 200, about half of them major. But it is quickly apparent that the copies containing most of the 180 right readings (P^2, D, D^2 and N^2) are all certain to have been corrected from an x^2 source (on N^2, see §§ 39–40 below). As few as about 20 such readings appear in manuscripts other than those four, and these may be explained as due to coincidental con-vergence. I's large number may perhaps result from memorial contamination; b's may either result from contamination or preserve an authentic x^1 reading lost by y and u (after b ceases at II 128, x^1 in effect denotes only yu). Except for a few cases, such as those where U and D are uniquely error-free (listed at § 28), right readings in individual members of y or u are therefore judged likely to have come in from an x^2 source. Discounting these, agreement of the uncontaminated copies XYI (the 'core-group' of y) and U (the older member of u) indicates the probable reading of x^1. Where this is lacking, direct analysis is needed to discriminate the family reading from amongst the three (after II 128, two) branches. But these cases are few and, as will appear later, uncertainty is much less than in **p**, which has twice as many fully attested groups as x^1.

§ 32. As with the α and β readings in **B**, judgement that all the rejected x^1 variants represent agreements in error has been made after comparison with not only the readings of the other family but also the available other-version parallels. Such comparison, however, is subject to one sig-nificant consideration that did not apply in the examination of **B**: that **C** may in principle embody a new authorial reading at any given point. On the postulate that revision was 'linear', **A** and **B** readings, and even agreements of **B** and its predecessor(s) against **C**, can therefore never do more than suggest possible correction of a 'suspect' reading. And it follows *a fortiori* by the canon of ratification (see *Intro.* IV § 22) that **B** readings retained in **C** are not to be emended (the Athlone edition suffers from frequently overriding both the postulate and the canon).[40] Otherwise, with allowance for non-unanimous or defective attestation (specified no further here), the secure evi-dence for x^1 may be set out in near-identical form as for **A** and **B** (see *A Version* § 23, *B Version* § 42). It is similarly divided by major and minor instances (the former given in full, the latter by reference only) and according to available other-version support for the readings adopted. Except in a few emended lines, the lemmata understood to represent the readings of x^2 are in Pr–XI taken from **p**, thereafter from **pt** or from **p** alone, a t agreement in error with x^1 being indicated by '-t'. The variants are the readings of x^1. A minus indicates agreement of an x^2 group-member (**p** or t) with the rejected x^1 variant; a plus, agreement of one or more x^1 witnesses with the lemma; 'so', agreement of another version with x^1.

§ 33. Readings with other-version support

(i) Major

(a) *With* y, b *and* u *present*

+**ZAB**: Pr 20 +P^2 ryche] pore. I 133 trone] tour. 179 wham...desireþ] when no man here couayteth.

+**ZB**: I 39 -Ax +?N.

+**AB**: Pr 184 lewed] l. thyng.

+**B**: Pr 61 marchen] maken. 141b–42a -AVS] *om.* 145 to þe puple] *om.* 182 *L. om.* 187 hym] vs. 191 +P^{2}B ybought] ybroughte. 192 +O non raton] *om* / (n)on. I 145 for] to abate. II 66 as] *om.*

(b) *With* y *and* u *present*

+**ZAB**: II 154 -RN soure] sore. 191^2 +P^{2}D of] and. IV 1 Cesseth] Sethe. 7 fecche] seche. 75 gat ich] was gyue me. 107 reson] Mede. 134 +?D it] (it) nat. 146 þat...confesours] *om.* VI 328 penaunce his] Repentaunce is. VII 177 +D the way] today. 180^1 ar] but. 224^3 nat] *om.* VIII 211 þow] hunger. 236 God] *om.*

+**AB**: II 158 -MSN go] to. III +D 280 go] *om.* 431 hated hym] *om.* VI 233 hath] hadde. 359 +P^2 dayes] d. y bouhte it. 401 wexed] wasche. 407 He] And. VII 164 +P^{2}D seten] sette. 170 sepulcre] s. of oure lord (*so* Z), 239 (*so* Z), +IP^{2}D 260 (*so* Z). VIII 18 wihtliche] wittiliche. 307 say] sayde. IX 24 techeþ] hem hoteth. 175 men] *om.* X 56 knowyng...Y] knowlechyng. 154 þat...hadde] bygynnynge h. he. XI 44 yn] *om.* 278 comended] comaunded.

+**B**: III 66 do] *om.* 70b–71 -EG *om.* 129 -MN Corteisliche] Fol c. 421/2 *misdiv.* 421 Mebles] That dwelleth in Amalek m. 456 Moises] The which M. 479 myddell] ? Ø (*see Textual Note*). 481 shullen] and. 482 For] *Quia.* V 163 +ID here] *om.* VI 125 +D-R spiritualte] spirituale. VII 35 ouht] hit. 133 -E fresshe] flesch and. VIII 46 fro] or. IX 67 to gyuen] *om.* XI 164 me] *om.* 218 techen men] *trs.* XII 87 -t+D^{2}D masses] mo m. XIV 138 -t+P^2 so] *om.* XV 221 -t eir] *om.* XVI 260 -tN^2 men] *om.* XVII 254 -t turne] *om.* XVIII 169 -t+D^{2}D that ribaud; he] the ribaudes; they. XIX 291 -Gt Drede] Som d.; awey]. 301 +P^2-Wt on] *om.* 332 +D^{2}D-NTH^2 that his lyf] that is lyue and. XXI 161*a* oportet] *om.* 269 -Wt to harwen] to harwed. 344/45 -TH^2 *misdiv.* 365 +D and diche] a dich. -t+N^2 al] *om.*

+**A**: VII 170 sepulcre] s. of oure lord +Z?**B**.

+**Z**: VI 321 me] *om.*

(ii) Minor

(a) *With* y, b *and* u *present*

+**ZAB**: Pr 21, 33^{1,2}. I 24, 41, -N 62. II 6, 19, +P^{2}D-M 21, +b 111, 116. +**AB**: Pr -S 56 (*so* Z), 78, +b 82. I +u-N 49 (*corr. App.*), +P^2 181 (*so* Z). II -p^2 10 (*so* Z). +**B**: Pr +P^2 172, +P^2 191, -F 214. I +D-AVM 31, +P^{2}D 35 (*so* Z). II +P^{2}D 53, +I 59, -MF 60.

(b) *With* y *and* u *present*

+**ZAB**: II 163, -M 229, -GRM 231. III +P^{2}D 190, 191, 198^2, 262. IV 15, 56, +IP^2 62^2, 70^2, +D 128^1, -p^2+Y 128^2 (*corr. App.*), 129, 135. V -GM 116. VI +P^{2}D 312. VII 58, -RF+P^2 64, -K 166, 168, -G+D 173, +P^{2}D 201, 247. VIII -PAVQ+P^{2}D 42, 58, 97, 131, -p^2 153^2 (*in App. for* p *read* p^1, *for* x *read* xp^2), +IP^{2}U 180, +P^2 314, 323, 345.

+**AB**: II 145. III +P^2 173 (*so* Z), 178 (*so* Z). IV 126 (*so* Z). V -M 126 (*so* Z), -N 151. VI +I 93, +YI 219, 228 þe] *Ac* þe (*add to* App.), 319, +P^2 359, +IU 378, 383, -S 399, 417, 437^1 (*so* Z). VII 157, -K+IP^2 225, 260, +D 270, 285^2. VIII 83, 231 (*so* Z), 305, +ID 313^2. IX +D 62, 284, +P^{2}D 328. X 78, +D 81^2, -K 108^2, 108^3, 109, 111, 120, -Z+DN^2 146, +N^2 282, 284^1. XI -ZK 38, 51*a*, 53^1 (*in App. del.* G, *and for* KN *read* p^2), 106, +N^2 108, +N^2 119.

+**B**: III +P^2 59, +I 137, -M 474, 478, 483. IV +D 160, +ID 173. VI -AVRQG 36, +Y 59, +I-N 234, -R 248^1, -MSG 266, -AVM 344, 409, +U 416. VII +P^{2}D 5, 9, +P^{2}D 14, +I 70, 123, +P^2 184. VIII 208. IX +D-K 54. X +U-M 38^1 (*so* A), +DN^2-Q 234, +P^2 284. XI -F 159, +P^{2}N^2-K 184^2, +DN^2 280, 283, +N^2 296^3, +N^2 300. XII +N^2 83, +N^2 146^2. XV +D^2, -T 41^2, +D 165^2, 216, 226*a*. XVI -EQN 14, +P^{2}D^{2}D 46^2, 54*a*, 90, 102, +DN^2-TH^2 104, -R 115/15*a*, +N^2-tZWN 261, +Y-tVRZGN 271, +N^2-t 332, -t 334. XVII 20, 224, +D^2 278^1, 309. XVIII -G 131^1, +IN^2 258. XIX +P^2-N 112, +D^{2}D-TH^2 164^2, -t 189, +D-t 200, +D^{2}N^2 293^2. XX 12, -TH^2 13, +D-TH^2 69^1, -tAVWM 69^2, +N^2 85, 91, +YN^2-TH^2 158^1, +DN^2-?t 267, +P^{2}U 413. XXI -W 91, +N^2 159, +P^{2}D^2-N 162^2, -TH^{2}F 162^3, +D^{2}N^2 194, 212, +P^{2}D 287, +D-TH^2 378, +D^{2}N^2-tG 411. XXII -W 334 (*read* pt *for* p, x^1 *for* x).

§ 34. Readings with no other-version parallel

(i) Major

(a) *With* y, b *and* u *present*

I 88 thus] hit is thus (þys **p**). 148 hit^2] hit first. II 90^1 he] and.

(b) *With* y *and* u *present*

III 95² sendeþ] sende. 316 +D ys] *om.* 319 -RMQSN douwe] do. 347 with] þat. 351 hol] holy. 366² sirename] name. 375³ fecche] seche. 387 relatifs] relac*o*ynes. 395 mene] nempne. 417 +D-QF bone] loue. 429¹ +D-EGN his] is. VI 51² +YP² y] a. 60¹, 148 +D-AVMGK wrathe] w*a*rthe. 173 +D loue] moder loue. 304¹ +D what] *om.* 307² by...made] *om.* 334 +D fonk] flonke. VII 145/46 *misdiv.* 172 and in Damaskle] y haue be in bothe. 207 as] *om.* 259 be] *om.* VIII 269 grone] greue. 283 ʒif power] ʒif thow pouer. IX 23 Treuthe nolde] no t. wolde. 71–9 *mislin.* 137 +P²-M lollares] lorelles. X 39¹ +DN² as] *om.* 202 hit] hym. XI 153¹ syre] fader. 155 ʒe...bokes] *om.* 160 Thus; leaute] Thus in; lel. 177 Clergies lore] clerkes techyng. 266² +P²D deuyned] deuyed. 273/74 *misdiv.* 287 -QFSZK wihtnesse] witnesse. XII 215 after] *om;* hertely t. XIII 231 For; and] *om;* or. XV 213 +Ch one] *om.* XVI 22 on...deydest] on vs alle; on þi renkis alle t. 273 Vnkynde] Vnkunnynge. XVII [116 *in* RM; *l. om; see Textual Note*]. 190–91 sethe...name; *Ite...mundum*] *trs.* XIX 147 Be he] Bote he be. XX 61 +DN²-H²M two] to. 293 mangonel] mangrel. 294 encloye] and cloye. XXII 240 +D²D felicite] felice.

(ii) Minor

(a) *With* y, b *and* u *present*
Pr -M 115. I 25. II 106.

(b) *With* y *and* u *present*
II +D 187. III +I 86, 87¹, 89¹, +D 91², 118¹, 375¹, +P²D 399, 496¹, +D 496². IV +P² 132¹, +P²D 132², 163. V +Y 96, +P² 97², 170. VI 15, +P² 95, +P²D 104², +U 137². VII 207, 231¹, 251¹. VIII 67, +P² 85, 166². IX 141², +I-*p*² 161², +D 197, -N 277, +P² 345. XI +P² 55, +I 77, +D 82, 200, 272¹. XV -t 154, +IP²D 242. XVI -tF 34. XVII +D²-TH² 145. XIX +D 19, -TH²+N² 134, 291, +D²-RW 332¹. XX -TH² 13, +N² 65, +N² 98, 105, +N² 112*a*, +D 176, -WG+N² 200², 203², +P²N² 373, +P²D 382. XXI +P²D²-N 162¹, +D²-PEAVZ 235, +P²-H² 246¹, +D²-*p*²QWFSZ 354, +D² 359, +D 365¹, +P² 381, +P²D²-*p*² 457. XXII 56 (*del.* D), +D² 91, -F 231, +D² 243, +P²D²D-EQ 307².

Among the minor variants in this list, among which some convergent agreement is to be expected, freedom from the family error is persistently attested only by P² (44 instances), D (46), and D² (18). For D², with allowance made for its absence in Pr–XI, the evidence of x^2 contamination is comparable to that for P² and D, but less than in N² (§§ 39–40 below), which has only some 23 minor right readings against x^1 and has been provisionally placed with it.

iv. *The* **x²** *family of* **C** *manuscripts*

(a) *Sub-family* **t**

§ 35. The second sub-archetypal family is x^2, the postulated ancestor of **p** and t. The sub-family **t** begins at XI 300*a*, where it takes up after A XI 313. As in their **A** portion, its members TH²Ch continue as an assured genetic group in XI 301–XXII on the basis of some 400 agreements in error (*R–K* pp. 38–9), about 175 of them major. The most important of these is the omission of 18 whole lines as well as three half-lines lost after misdivision (see below). Despite its status as a sub-family, t's individual variants, being notably aberrant, are not given entire in the Apparatus. The 80 recorded (usually as part of a longer list of variants) include the most striking instances. In the following list, 15 more are added in square brackets, where t is joined by one to three other copies. Though not criterial, these too are probably group errors, but of the type in which coincidental variation has also operated.

Major XII 4, 37, 41, 71², 74, 114², 176, 221, 226, 239–43 *Ll. om.* XIII 7, 10, 12, 124 *L. om.*, [125 +N²], 203. XIV 23 *L. om*, 26, 29, 55, 62, 68, 108, 121/3, 122b *om*, 150, 158 *L. om*, [195 +K], 211. XV 6, 41, 58, 158. XVI 22, 92. XVII 21, 63–4 *Ll. om*, 74, 103, [108 +P²], 126, [139 +WN²], 157, 190, 251, 256, 259. XVIII [10 +N²], 33 *L. om*, [50+Z], 52, 217². XIX 21b–23a *Ll. om*, 28, 59, [171 +QFN *L. om*], 237², 253. XX 55, 98, 122 *L. om*, + *a.h.* T, 263. XXI 178 *L. om*, 228, [+D² 241, 242], 366, 389, 415, 429, 438–40 *Ll. om*, 482. XXII ?18, 174, 200, 231 *L. om*, [+XD²W 270], 332, 360, 378, 380.

Minor XI 302. XII 18², 28. XIII 155, 179. XIV 99. 181². [XV 286 +N²]. XVI [4 +N²], 308. XVII [309 +WN²]. XIX [15 +W], 104, 251. XX 106, 323, 460. XXI 31, [338 +W], [349 +WG], 410. XXII [12 +P²].

It is unknown whether t's text of Pr–XI was lost and the present conjoint structure an attempt to make good its loss, or whether XII–XXII was 'cannibalised' from an x^2 copy to 'complete' A Pr–XI. If t had the earlier part of **C**, a proportionate number of exclusive errors might well have confirmed it as the most persistent of all the groups.

§ 36. Within t, the pairing TH² found in the **A** portion reappears in nearly 200 agreements, about 40 major. These are challenged by some 80 agreements of TCh, about 25 major, and some 40 of H²Ch, perhaps six major (*R–K*, pp 28–9). The latter are too unpersistent (and minor) to be likely to be other than coincidental. Of the former, all save 25 occur where H² is defective, notably in XIV–XVI (as R–K note), and could otherwise have been further evidence for the <TH²Ch> relation. Further, some TCh agreements where H² is present could easily be random, e.g (quasi)-orthographical variation, as at XII 134 *of riche*] *in liche* (*yliche* H²), 198 *counteth*] *countede* (*counte* H²), XVI 304, XX 68 *wyhte*] *wiʒ* XX 432 *ille*] *euele*; and non-significant registration of a quotation-form, e.g. *&c* mistakenly added after *carnis* at XI 312. In one seemingly major example at XVIII 289 *renne*] *þanne*, H² has altered what could have been *þan* to *cam*. In another, at XX 338, a different hand has inserted *men*, and at XXII 23 *is*, where the exemplar may well have read Ø with TCh. At XIX 226 *blowynge*] *bowynge* (*vowynge*) and at XXII 378 *adreint*] *& dryueliþ* (*& trayliþ*), the H² variant is identifiable as an individual departure from a shared t reading of obviously poor sense. Finally, in XX 86 *trinen*] *trien* the right reading (not so accepted in *R–K*) is retained by H² where TCh have a coincidental visual error. TH² may therefore be ascribed an exclusive common ancestor that was a moderately accurate copy of t. They remain necessary for the text as the joint witness to t in the unique right reading at XV 211. The more faulty third member Ch descends independently from t and lacks five further lines (XV 7, XVII 259, XX 122, XXI 82 and XXII 301). Its striking variant *mynne*] *make* at XXII 367 forms the basis of R–K's implausible conjecture *make...memoria*. But with the best lineation of a macaronic line and its supplement at XV 61–61*a*, as well as a unique right reading at XVI 123, Ch cannot be eliminated.

§ 37. The ancestral manuscript t seems to have been a very defective witness to its family original x^2, notably in its many line-losses. The cause of these is usually mechanical, as in the homoteleuton at XVII 62–4 (*charite*) and the homoarchy at XIV 23–4 (*Ac grace*); but censorship may have operated at XIII 124. A notable feature of t is its re-writing of whole phrases, e.g. *spouse to be byknowe*] *spousehod to beknowe* at XIII 11; *foleuiles*] *felouns* at XXI 247; *That*] *Trewþe wile þat* at XXI 482; and *dyas*] *dyetis* at XXII 174. Some of these could have appeared difficult, but others are not problematic, e.g. at XIV 15 (*man shulde* for *suche be*); at XIV 26, which alters the theology; or at XVII 21, with its humorously incongruous pragmatism. Elsewhere t will normalise alliteration, as at XIII 212, where *kyndely* inserted before *therwith* after misdivision turns a correct macaronic stave-phrase into an appended Latin quotation. Other examples are XV 41, where the line and its parallel are either two-stave or scan cognatively on *p / b*, and XIX 253, where *kid* is clearly scribal (Cx's possible corruption here is considered in the *Textual Notes ad loc*). Although this tendency can felicitously generate the reading that might have been conjectured (e.g. *lede*] *wyht* at XIII 59), t's independent value is small by comparison with **p**. But since **p**'s unique right readings occur mostly where t is defective, as presumptive x^2 readings they might well have supported it. Half a dozen that t uniquely preserves prevent its elimination:

Major XIII 59. XV 211. XVI 123 (Ch). XX 444. XXI 401^1, [401^2 +D^{2}N^2]. XXII 13^3. **Minor** XII 5. [XXII 110 +D^2-Ch].

§ 38. The claim at §§ 6–7 above that t and **p** have an exclusive common ancestor x^2 is supported by 37 disjunctive agreements in error. Additionally listed here are another 40 (strictly non-criterial) readings in which **pt** are joined by one to three x^1 copies. That these are most often the usual suspects D^2 (20), P^2 (15) and D (10), confirms the earlier view of them as contaminated from **p**. As before, major readings are given in full, minor ones by reference. The lemma is the reading of x^1; a plus denotes agreement of an x^1 copy with x^2; a minus, agreement of an x^2 copy with x^1; round brackets, approximate agreement.

Major XII 88 +D^{2}D as] and, 213 +D^2-ChGS foel] foul. XIII 64 wyten] w. wel. XIV 28 +P^2 also] of (*om* VMQWSZK), 39 +P^{2}D^2-AVZ kyrke] churche, 209^2 +D^2 his] þe. XV 27 vp; and^2] *om*; for, 34 -RCh Ilyk] y. to, 51*a et orationes*] *om*, 89 +D^2 compacience] to pacience, 103 +D^2 (*om* Ch) a] þe, 106 -ECh+D(1 *added* D^2) take] talke, 156 to] *om*, 308 -ECh er] here XVI 81 +D^2 wel] *om*, (149 here] Ø **p** / he t), 183 +P^2 Mens] mannys, 219 -AVRMWZ wel] wol. XVII 82 +D^{2}D-N ʒe] þe, 84 +D^2 ʒe] þei, 94 Weder] Wonder, 136 +P^2 aloueth] loueþ, 268 +P^2 bıssheinede] bisshopid. XVIII 38 werkes; wormes] *trs*. XIX 6 -EAVZG thy] þe, 100 o] *om*, 276 charite] leel c. XX 67 her] *om*, 96/8 -Ch *L. div.*, 272 +N^2 *Principes*] Princes. XXI 114 +UN^2 Bothe] *om*, 460 For] *om*. XXII 13^2 +D wyht] wot, 33 a /6 *L.d.*, 48 -AZ byde] bydde, (103 þat euere sturcd] sterede neuere (*trs* t)), 227 -RQWFSZ holynesse] holychurche, 236 cheytyftee] chaitife, 338 do bothe] done; bothe x^1.

Minor XII 6^2, -p^2+N^2 22, -QWFSZ 151, +N^2 192. XIII -M 41, +N^2 83, 98^2, +DN^2 171, +P^{2}D^{2}DN^2 186. XIV -AMSK 13, -K 213. XV -AVRM 83, 98, -W 101, +D^2 120^1, 146, 169. XVI +P^{2}D^{2}U 230, +N^2 318, -W 325, +D 328, 360 -G+P^2. XVII 35/6, 48, ?110, 179, 193. XVIII +P^{2}D 57. XIX +D^2 27, +D^2 36^2, -W+D^2 41, (+P^{2}D^2 241), (302), -RG+D^2 311, -F+D^2 331, 188, +UN^2 241, 396. XXI -RMFZ+P^{2}D^{2}D 73, -G 158, +D^{2}D 185, -MNZ+U 190, +P^{2}D 321^2, +P^{2}D^{2}N^2-p^2 348^2, 378, -ChSG+P^2 395, 476^2. XXII +D^2 31, 60, +U 77, +P^2 245, +D^2 290.

The readings cited as evidence for x^2 are collaterally supported by others where, on intrinsic grounds and in the light of other-version evidence, **pt** is judged to be right. In themselves these need imply no more than **pt**'s accurate preservation of Cx where x^1 erred but are congruent with the hypothesis of a single family ancestor containing both (see § 64 below).[41]

(b) A transitional manuscript: N^2

§ 39. Before proceeding to sub-family **p**, it is worth examining the unusual manuscript NLW 733B, **N^2**. Though closest to x^1 (as seen on comparing its readings with x^1's at §§ 33–4 above), N^2 has been conflated with **p**, contaminated from **B** and extensively sophisticated, so as to be almost unclassifiable. But it has a few superior readings that may be original. The only conjoint **AC** copy to become a C-Text at the end of the *Visio* not the *Vita de Dowel*, and with its Passus X's first 13 lines still of **A** type,[42] N^2 runs on to XXI 428 before becoming illegible. Several omissions between X and XIII of non-mechanical origin may be due to moral or theological censorship. N^2's substantial agreements with five witnesses include some 90 each with the **p** copies W and F, some 50 with P^2 (*R–K* pp. 32–3) and several with groups of both families.[43] Although the **A** portion of NLW 733B, N, forms a genetic pair with the **A** manuscript W, a qualitative scrutiny of the readings R–K list confirms their view that no such relation holds for the **C** portions of the two copies. The same is true of N^2's agreements with F, so both must presumably be due to convergent variation. As N^2 pairs indifferently in minor variants with copies of the other family, only major readings have been noted, of which some, but not all, are recorded in the Apparatus.

i With x^1: X 154. XI 44, 151^1, 273/4, 278. XII 5. XIII 39/40. XIV 46. XV 97. XVI 76/7. XIX 115. XX 34^1, 347/8. XXI 366.

ii With x^1+t: XV 221. ?XIX 147, 332^1. XXI 344/5.

iii With **p** only: X 39, 113. XI 164. XII 87. ?XIII 172. [XV 132 +Ch]. XVIII 169. XIX 301, ?332^2. XX 294, 470. ?XXI 161a, 269 (to) sholde), 365. With p^1: XIII 392. XIV 63. XIX 165. XX 114.

iv With **pt**: XVII 217, 262^2. XVIII 60. XIX 118, 261. XX 103^1, 260^2, 272, 293.

Amongst these 40 major agreements across half the poem, the proportions are very nearly balanced (x^1 14, **p** 16, x^1t 4, **pt** 9), so that it is hard to be sure whether N^2's exemplar was of x^1 or x^2 type or whether its scribe produced a conflated text by selecting readings now from one and now from the other. That N^2 does not derive from x^2 is indicated by its freedom from the major **pt** error at XV 89 (a crux where D, by contrast, shows visible collation with an x^2 copy). But that its exemplar was textually close to x^1 is indicated by its Ø-variant in the crux at XVIII 75, where the other four disjunctive errors strongly imply such a reading for the x^1 family original (though interestingly N^2 is accompanied here by the **p** copy W, its companion in the text's **A** portion). Against this, N^2 is both free of x^1's major omissions at XIX 261, 290^2 (the latter with D^2) and shares the important **p** error at XV 132. Its omission of XIV 63 may result from independent censorship; but its 14 agreements with p^1, four major (§ 42 below) and its many pairings with W and F, p^1 copies of a single genetic sub-group q (see §§ 51–3 below) need explanation. N^2 may therefore be most economically seen as deriving from an x^1 manuscript that was compared at the point of production with a p^1 copy (of q-type) and also, as argued below, a manuscript of **B**.

§ 40. With many lines omitted and others garbled, N^2 is a ready candidate for rejection; but it is retained for occasional collation on account of five major readings that answer to the conjectural form of the original:

XI 161 That doth] Doþ N^2; That maketh X&r. XX 94 haue ruthe] rewe N^2; haue mercy X&r. 400 gretter] N^2; wyddore X&r. XXI 236 buggynge; sullyng] N^2; *trs* X&r. 412 lede] N^2; man X&r.

These and some 40 more readings listed below convince R–K, who adopt all save XXI 236, that N^2's source was authoritatively corrected from a **C** copy superior to Cx. But in comparing this situation to that of the **B** manuscript F,[44] they presuppose a textual entity no more necessary here than the one they invoke to account for F's good readings. For like those, which evince contamination from **A**,[45] the 40 N^2 readings R–K list are better understood to be contaminations from **B**.[46] That the **B** manuscript consulted by N^2 was of the β family emerges from examination of ten examples in list (b), taken from those R–K find 'available as a control' where the Cx reading 'appears a scribal derivative of that of **B**.'[47] Most in list (a) are Bx readings R–K prefer to Cx readings that they judge unoriginal. But these, though acceptable, have no place in **C** and should be dismissed. In the list below, the variants are from N^2 and the line-number of parallel **B** is in brackets.

(a) X/IX [300 +M] goed^2] *om*; 308 Ac] *om* (202). XI/X 84 Wittes] his (141); 189 Elde] he (XI 28). XIII/XI 125 for] *om* (312); 199 amys standeth] mystandit (380). XIV/XII 96 to þe] to (152); 152 as] *om*; 198 as lewede men] lewde *only* B-Cr^{23}g (273). XVI/XIV 85 Pouerte] þe pore (245); 154 al] al goed (318); 168 heuene] þe (XV 19). XVII/XV 197 here] *om* (535), 199 pees; plente] *trs* (537); 219 dede and] *om* (537); 220 his] *om* (556); 225 myhte] may (561), 226 and] *om*. XVIII/XVI 289 And] I (272). XIX/XVII 90 þat] þe (98); 176 fyn] *om* (208); 188 eny] no (222); 232 and] *om* (265); 299 Ac] *om* (317). XX/XVIII 95 fouely] felly (92); 97 was a] *om* (94); 130 þerof] *om* (127); 138 ouer-] *om* (135); 229 ther-thorw] *om* (220); 256 Lo] *om* (247); 364 alle] *om* (322); 400 (363); 421 eny felones] a f. (380); 422 hy; tretours] he; a t.(381).

Additionally, R–K include as representing **B** ten β readings rejected in the present edition's B-Text in favour of α:

(b) XII/XI 74 þat heo ne may al] al to (138); 83 þe] *om* (147). XIII/XI 162 mony] how m. (350). XV/XIII 102 penantes] a p. (93); 121 ful] *om* (112); 255 And] *om* (XIV 52). XVI/XIV 4 deyeth] d. he (135); 127 his] *om* (292); 151 lered[2]] letred (316). XVIII/XVI 129 and] *om* (95).

If all these agreements were decisively with the archetypal text of **B**, there might be at least *prima facie* grounds for thinking some of N[2]'s 'superior' readings to originate outside the archetypal tradition of **C**. But list (b) indicates that N[2] was contaminated specifically from a sub-archetypal B-Text of β type. For α's agreement with Cx against β in these ten examples tends to confirm the antecedent probability that the reading they share is original (the alternative possibility that α is contaminated from **C** has nothing to commend it). Further argument, if needed, would stress that, as there is no intrinsic objection to the adopted readings in list (a), the differences between Bx and Cx may be properly ascribed to revision, and R–K's claim for N[2]'s special authority rejected. N[2]'s few unique (nearly)-right readings are thus better seen, like those in certain other copies of both families, as products of happy scribal guesswork. For in each case, as shown in the relevant *Textual Notes*, the origin of the Cx error is readily explainable. Like P[2] earlier, N[2] indicates both strong interest in the text of the **C** Version and the relative ease of access in the early fifteenth century to x^1 and x^2 manuscripts at or around a single centre of copying. Whichever family it started from, N[2] is now to be reckoned a conflation of both, as well illustrated by XIII 39/40, where it has x^1's wrong line-division but in 39 p^1's omission of initial *Ther*. For this reason, and because of its widespread corruption, N[2] is only selectively cited.

v. *The sub-family* **p**

§ 41. The 14 manuscripts **PEAVRMQWFSZGKN** derive from a single ancestor **p**, which is directly descended from x^2. It is characterised by some 1440 agreements in error, 275 major and 1165 minor. The manuscripts divide into two main groups, p^1 consisting of PEAVRMQWFSZ and p^2 of GKN. Neither derives from the other, so both must descend independently from **p**. They are differentiated by nearly 400 readings, about 75 of them major, which fall into two sets. In the first, either p^1 or p^2 is antecedently likely to represent **p** because it also agrees with x^1(t). In the second, either could preserve **p** but both differ from x^1(t) and both are wrong. When p^2 errs with p^1, it will reflect a **p** error here; when p^2 is right in its agreement with p^1, the **p** reading attested has presumably preserved Cx through x^2. In 220 instances, p^2 is right with **x** but almost never right against p^1 and **x** in combination. For this reason, **p**'s two distinct branches are treated first and the sub-family as a whole is discussed at the end of this section rather than at the beginning (as was done for γ in the **B** tradition). These **x**p^2 readings form the lemmata in the list of p^1 errors at § 42; p^2's half-dozen divergences from **x** are italicised and will be separately listed at § 61. The similarly few minor cases of **x** and p^2 agreeing in a *wrong* reading are considered at § 44.

a. *Branch* p[1]

§ 42. The branch p^1 resembles the eight-member group g of the **B** sub-family γ (*B Version* §§ 17–21); but its structure is more complex and its distinctive variants much more abundant. It falls into two groups **m** and **q**, m dividing further into **e** and **r**, e into the two genetic pairs PE and AV, and r yielding one genetic pair RM, while no clear sub-division emerges within q. Seven members of p^1 have major omissions: *AV* VII 236–83, XXII 88–end; *M* XVI 4–157, XVIII 244–XIX 32; *F* VII 264–IX 181, XIII 93–XV 179; *S* VIII 267–X 95, XV 82–157, XVI–XX, XXI 8–323; and

WZ are conjoined with **A/Z** to XI/IX respectively. Thus, although no sub-division of p^1 appears whole throughout, each is represented by at least one (near)-complete early manuscript, m by **P** (for e) and **M** (for r), q by **Q**. Between them these three copies, supplemented by R where M has gaps and by F where Q is damaged between V and VII, are indispensable. Given, therefore, that the p^1 tradition is distinguished within **p** by its contrast with p^2, and that the relative certainty of a p^2 reading depends on the degree of its three constituents' availability, the 224 readings below have been divided according to fullness of attestation in the latter. In the list, a minus sign before a sigil indicates a member's divergence from the presumed group reading; a plus, agreement of a p^2 or x^1(t) member with the rejected reading. Italicised numbers denote those readings where p^2 also differs from the lemma.

Major

(a) *Where GKN are present* (II 218–XIII 225; XIV 41–XV 66)[48]

III 54 -M+P^2. V 97^1. VI *40*, 338, 340, 388 and *390* +N (*over erasure*), 394^2. VII 232. VIII 98–9 *Ll. om, 337*. IX 97 +D, 187 -Q *L. om*. X 274^2 -QZ, 275^2 +KP^2. XI 34, 96, 224. XIII (*ll. om* G: 39^2 +N^2, 40, 62, 63); 66 +D^2Ch. XIV 43, 62, 63 +N^2, $157^{1,2}$.

(b) *Only GN are present* (Pr 154–II 217; XV 67–XXII 40)

Pr 195 -M, 226. I 40, 92, 165 -M. II 121^2 -M, 122 -M, 160 -M. XVI 75, 108, 266 +GP^2U [*L. om through homoteleuton*], 323^2, 326^1 (*l. om* G), 371 +G. XVII 72, 151^1 -Z, 162 -QZ+uCh [*coincidental visual error*], 283. XVIII 244. XIX 10, 89, *94*, 165 +$P^2D^2N^2$. XX 73^1, 114 +ChN^2, 140 +P^2N (*alt.*), 200^1, 201, 390^2, 419, 430 -Z, 461 (*l. om*). XXI 110, 319^3, 340^2 (+P^2 *alt. a.h.*), 427, 447, 482 +GDt. XXII 6.

(c) *Only KN present* (XIII 226–XIV 40)

XIV 37 (*l. om* K).

Minor

(a) *Where GKN are present* (II 218–XIII 225; XIV 41–XV 66)

III 14 +M, 360^1, 368. IV 10, 156, 190. V *152*, 168. VI 29 +N, 32 +G, 72, 99, 122 +G, *141*, 156, 177, 248^2, 251, 271 +P^2D (*l. om* G), 275 +P^2N, 382^2, VII $2^{1,2}$, 18 +G, 20 +DG-MS, 48 +P^2-RM, ?95, 101 +N, 191, 196 -AV+N, 256, 291, 294. VIII $48^{1,2}$, 73, 83 +N, $107^{1,2}$, 112, 115 +P^2, 171, 175 +P^2D, 179, 192 -M, 216^1 -M, 246, 304^1 +P^2, 308, 313 +KN, 323^1 +N, 323^3, 324^1, 328, 332. IX 8^2+P^2u, 78 +K, 101^1 +U, 117 +N, 133 +N, 150, 153^2, 161^1, 162^2 -Q (=?q), 166, 167, 180, 188, 199, 200^2, 203, 218 +G, 246, 247^2, $254^{1,2}$, 258 -M, 261 -Q+P^2, 262 -RQ+P^2D, 279, 297 -Q, 310. X 6 -Z, 68 -F+I, 99, 118, 133, 165 +N^2, 175 +NP^2D, 184 +GN^2, 264. XI 210^1, 210^2 +P^2, 269, 287^1, 304. XII 13 -F+N^2, 22 +N^2, 63^1, 64 -FW+t, 86 +N^2, 152 +YChN, 163, 164, 173, 204 +N^2, 212 +N^2. XIII 25, 103 +N, 107 +$NP^2H^2N^2$, 134, 136, 151, 177 +Ch, 185, 202 +D^2, 210, 223^1, 224. XIV 90^3, 91^2, 118 -S, 124, 150^2, 157^2 +H^2, 165, 194 +P^2, 198, 207, 212 (*l. om* G). XV 3 +D^2Ch, 12 +P^2D^2, 17 +N^2, 26, 33^2 +Ch, 46^1, 48, 58^1, 62.

(b) *Only GN are present* (Pr 154–II 217; XV 67–XXII 40)

Pr 212, 231 -M. I 66 -M, 76 -M, 98 -MF, 190 -M. II 12 -M, 38 -M, 40 -M, 55 -M, 70 -M, 79^1 -M, 136 +P^2U, 138 -M. XV 70^1 -MW, 70^2 -QSZ+P^2N^2, *76a*, 92. XVI 57, 122, 182 -M+D^2, 281-QZ+TH^2, 316^2 +G, 341 -MW+YGN^2, 355 +ut. XVII $14^{1,2}$ +N, 61 +ND^2, 70 -WF, 82 +GD^2Dt [*coincidental visual error*], 171 -F, 184 -F+N, 193 -W+t, 251, 311 -W. XIX 37, 63^1, 65^1 +P^2U, 104 +G, 298 -WZ+D^2DCh, 311 +ND^2t, 334 +DChN^2. XX 4, 8^1, 20, 96^1 +N, 108, 112^1 +GP^2, 144 -M, 151, 198^2, 206, 208^2, 214^1 +D, 214^2 +N^2 (*a. h.* P^2), 287^1, 353 +DN, 365 +NCh, 390^1 -W+G, 457^1. XXI 186^2, 229 -F+P^2, 252, 289, 316, 319^1, 333 -F, 364 +N^2, 456^2 +X, 474 (*l. om* G). XXII 6.

(c) *Only KN present* (XIII 226–XIV 400). XIV 7^2.

(d) *Only N present* (Pr 1–154, XV 288–XVI 40, XXII 41–end) *None*.

§ 43. In this list p^1 is distinguished by some 200 exclusive readings, 40 of them major, supported by another 83, all but 12 of them minor, where it is joined by one p^2 and one to three **x** manuscripts. Most agreements with an **x** copy are likely to be random but the 21 with P^2 (six of them major) and 15 with N^2 (four major) may be ascribable to collation of these copies' x^1 exemplars with a manuscript of p^1 type (see §§ 24, 39–40 above). Conversely significant are 27 cases, six major, in which the p^1 copy M is free of the group error. Chiefly in Pr–II, these suggest close (if limited) consultation of an **x** or p^2 copy, similar to what occurs in P^2 in relation to **p** (§ 24 above and § 56 below). Also worth remarking are specific agreements with p^1 of individual p^2 copies: N (15, two major), G (10, two major) and K (one major). Most of these could be coincidental, but not N's two major instances at VI 390 and XX 140, which show visible alteration like that found at points in P^2, D^2 and D. What no p^1 copy reveals is any clear x^1 contamination in the form of definitely erroneous readings (see below).

§ 44. All in all, p^1 appears to have been a relatively poor copy of its original **p** and, as will emerge (§ 55 below), inferior to p^2. It lacked five lines: XX 461 for no evident reason, VIII 98–9 and XVI 266 through homoteleuton, IX 187 possibly through censorship. Otherwise, its only notable features are a tendency towards greater explicitness in expression and a preference for *noþer* over Cx's double negative *ne no* (e.g. XX 108, XXI 252, 289). But p^1 cannot be eliminated, since it contains a handful of unique apparently right readings, as well as those preserved in constituent members, some of which may go back to Cx through **p**.[49] The former, though minor and probably due to chance, require further attention because each contradicts **x** as well as p^2:

VII 253 in^2] *om* **x**p^2EMFS. XI 53 hym] *om* **x**p^2. 115^3 my] *many* **x**$p2$. XVI 362 þe] *om* x^1p^2. XXI 354 queyntise] *pl.* x^1p^2 +QFSZ.

The first example is a case of coincidental mechanical omission. In the second and fourth, the sense is arguably complete without the pronoun / article, which p^1 may have inserted for explicitness. In the third the rejected reading is acceptable and may even be original, echoing *many* in // B X 169. In the last the plural may have come in coincidentally under inducement from preceding *colours* (found also, after amendment of the Apparatus, in q). Together these instances, like the correction of the Latin at VIII 246*a*, XVI 54*a*, 115*a*, hardly raise serious doubt that when p^2 agrees with x^1t (or with x^1t before XII), the reading attested is probably that of Cx. There are two exceptions. One occurs at Pr 7, where the Cx reading is doubtful and must be reconstructed from the split variants preserved in p^1 and **x**, but where **x** is substantively, though not formally, supported by the sole p^2 witness N (see the *Textual Notes*). The more important case, in RM at XVII 116, will be discussed at § 49 below.

The p^1 *groups*

i Group **m**: *a. Sub-group* **e**

§ 45. The sub-division of p^1 called *group e* consists of **PEAV**, which with **RM** ('r'), make up a larger genetic group **m** characterised by some 75 agreements (see § 50 below). Before examining its structure, e's relationship to m may be illustrated by three examples. One occurs at VII 61 *no gult so greet*, where **p** transposed the first phrase to *gult non*, m next dropped *gult*, <AV> retained the noun-Ø nonsense-reading (< e < m), a later hand adding *gult* in V, and the others smoothed by inserting *synne*, <RM> after *non* and <PE> after *grete*. Secondly, at X 19, where **p** had preserved Cx, e retained m's omission of *euere^2*, while r smoothed by inserting *ȝet*. Here r may have substituted a synonym and only e omitted; but it is more economical to suppose that m read Ø, having shed the adverb through eyeskip (*euere* > *here*) or deliberately through stylistic objection. Finally at XX 287^2, though Cx was again correctly preserved in **p** (>p^2 and q), m lost *oure* by near-haplography after *oute* and e faithfully followed its exemplar, but the more enterprising r plausibly substituted *thy*. To these three e readings may be added another 14, of which these six are major.

II 237 ones] one. III 45 man] frere. VII 180 *Extra Latin line*. XVIII 173 kissyng] cossyns, 176 wille] *om*, 219 And] As.

Of these, the Latin line *Hic primo comparet Petrus Plouhman* looks less like a textual than an *ordinatio* feature of its postulated group-exemplar. Together with the three instances examined, it questions R–K's judgement that these agreements are 'not strong support' [for a PEAV grouping]; for with no 'significant conflicting evidence' (*R–K*, p. 48) in the form of a group <PERM>, they are enough to endorse the sequence PEAVRM in preference to R–K's order PERMVA.

§ 46. The four copies deriving from e form two genetic pairs. The first <**PE**> has 270 agreements (listed in *R–K* pp. 24–5), 70 of them major. Among the most important are two additional lines of Latin, one completing the Scriptural quotation at IX 326*a*, the second (after VII 203) another *ordinatio*-like feature perhaps lost from its e-source by <AV>. Eleven lines are omitted: III 420, V 158, VI 204–5, VII 186 [?lost through eyeskip],[50] VIII 275, X 168, XII 138, 180 and XVII 135, 260. Most of these omissions are mechanical, though the first and last may be due to clerical censorship. The second group <AV> shows 'absolutely persistent agreement in 443 [*recte* 435] readings' (*R–K*, p. 22). About 100 of these are major, including the loss of the rest of Passus XXII after l. 87, where the common exemplar was defective, and of another 73 lines, 9 half-lines and 8 citation-lines.

Possibly through loss of leaf: VII 236–83; *homoteleuton*: Pr 188–89, III 391–92, IV 87–9, XIX 122–24, XX 5, 430–32, XXII 26, [*at mid-line*] VIII 130b–31a, XIII 108b–09a; *homoarchy*: VI 134 [*?or censorship*], XI 312b–15a; *eyeskip*: III 6b–7a (*man > men*), XXI 88b–90a (*Resones...Resoun*); ? XX 35b. *Citation-lines*: III 189*a*, XVI 54*a*, 357*a*, XVII 235*a*, 280*a*, XIX 319*a* XX 164*a*, 270*a*.

The source of neither <PE> nor <AV> appears to have derived from the other; but since V is one of the earliest extant copies (not later than *c*. 1400), the date of e might have been within a decade of the poem's composition. AV could be eliminated, as it contains no unique right readings, and e be represented by PE, which attest the best reading at II 190 (together with N, corrected over erasure).

Group m: *b. Sub-group* **r**

§ 47. As noted at § 45, e forms part of a six-member group m with **r**, the exclusive ancestor of <**RM**>. This pair's early member **M** lacks a further 235 lines through loss of leaves (XVI 4–157, XVIII 244–XIX 32). It also misplaces XVII 188–257 (the Mahomet passage) after 286, copying XVII 286 after 186 but following it with XVII 259–85*a*. Its order intriguingly recalls that adopted in the reconstructed text of **B** (see Vol I pp 602–3); but the notion that M might reflect knowledge of a pre-archetypal form of **B** begs too many questions to be useful. **R**'s immediate exemplar, to judge by the errors it shares with e, was a faithful copy of r, whereas M's underwent extensive lateral influence from x^1 or p^2 (§ 43 above). That the pair have an exclusive ancestor is indicated by persistent agreement in some 275 readings (roughly the same number as <PE>'s), about 120 major. The most important are the omission of eight text-lines, two half-lines and two citation-lines, and the inclusion of two spurious lines:

Lost through homœoteleuton: III 239–41 (letten / leten), V 30 (hacches / churches), VI 60 (sounede / semede **p**). *Homoarchy*: VII 225. VIII 44a, XIX 134a [*both at end of* 44, 134 *in* e, ? *possibly in margin* r]. XVIII 162 [*eyeskip from* lewes 162 *beginning* > lewes 164 *end*]. XX 293b–4a [*eyeskip from* and > en-]. XVI 183 [*visual distraction*: mens ...mone...mem-]. *Two spurious ll. after* VII 217 (*R–K*, p. 185) [*the second a memorial reconstruction of omitted* VII 225].

Some 16 RM readings appear in the Apparatus as part of a larger entry:

Major VI 316, 384. VII 111, 152*a*. VIII 111. X 160. XVII 285 +Ch. XVIII 229. **Minor** VI 419. VII 138. X 197, 217. XII 164. XVII 107, 108. XIX 36.

§ 48. The genetic status of <RM> is not seriously challenged by the 70-odd errors M shares with F of p^1, N of p^2, and P[2] of the x^1 family. Among the few major ones with F *herte* for *thouhte* in VII 20 was probably induced coincidentally by *herte* at 17, while *god wot* for *tho gomus* at Pr 44 suggests parallel contamination from B Pr 43. Of the seemingly more impressive agreements with N, most major ones seem easy coincidences. Some are synonym-substitutions such as *Large* for *Grete* at Pr 53, *clepede* for *calde* at I 4, *thankede* for *merciede* at III 21, *dude* for *wrouhte* at VI 211 and *man* for *segg* at XII 163. Others are visual errors, like *gracioust* for *grathest* at I 199 (paralleled in the **A** tradition) and *cleymyng* for *cleuynge* at XVII 128. The striking *grace* for *Lukes* at VIII 109 may result from failure in both M and N to grasp the referent. The seven major errors shared with P[2] include synonyms like *legge* for *wedde* at IV 143, *liue* for *regne* at IV 171, *kuind* for *connynge* at XV 18 (induced by preceding *Kynd*) and *hurteþ* for *smyteth* at XX 385 (induced by 384). But as R–K note (p. 28), M's partner R does not pair significantly otherwise and only about 18 times with each of F, N and P[2]. Conversely, while M joins the latter thrice more frequently than does R, it pairs with R in total four times more often than with any of them and in major agreements sixteen times more often than with all three together.

§ 49. The above brief account does not wholly exhaust the interest of r, which in some 25 variants agrees with **x**, in 20 exclusively, against a wrong reading not only of p^1 but of **p** (bracketed agreements are approximate):

Major Pr 49. IV 171. V 55. VII 34 +FN. VIII 257/8, 258[2]. X 80. XV 284. XX 1 +WF. **Minor**: Pr 137. III 211 +F. VI 113, 129, 133[2], 181, 365. (VII 95). IX 52, (254), 281[3], (327). XIII 84 +G. XV 83 +AV. XVIII 70. XXI 11. XXII 331.

In the absence of agreements in error with **x** these, like M's at § 43 above, may simply be readings where r alone accurately preserved **p** ($< m < p^1$). But this cannot easily account for the presence of r's unique line XVII 116, which by every criterion, including comparison with the corresponding **B** lines, appears genuine in metre, style and sense (in contrast with, say, r's patently scribal pair after VII 217). It is also, unlike less obviously inauthentic lines such as M's after XII 249 and XX 98, the sole **C** line with no exact other-version parallel that is necessary for the sense. In principle, r's scribe could have confected 116a from the sense of 382b and 116b from that of 382a in parallel B XV. But this notion is harder to credit than that XVII 116 is authorial. Rejected by R–K alone among editors, the line is adopted here as the best solution to a major crux (see the *Textual Notes*). Either it stood in the group-ancestor m or was introduced into r from a source independent of Cx, an uneconomical hypothesis that generates more problems than it solves.

Group m: *c. agreed readings of* **e** *and* **r**

§ 50. It seems probable, therefore, that <RM> descend from a manuscript r more accurate at some points than any other in the x^2 tradition, and at one point than any in *either* tradition. That r nonetheless shares with e an exclusive common ancestor m is shown from the two groups' agreement in 45 errors, some 15 major. These are supplemented by 30, perhaps a third of them major, where M is free of the postulated group error (*R–K*, p. 47). In some, M's different error suggests merely random individual divergence, as at III 435, in which *oftest* echoes m's presumed superlative. But elsewhere intermittent recourse to or recollection of p^2 or of the other family occurs, as in M's word-order in the b-half of the same line. Because of these discrepancies, the Apparatus does not use the group-sigil r, but it records among larger variant-entries some 40 eRM readings, including (as indirectly confirmatory though not criterial) a dozen where one or two other manuscripts accompany m:

III 305, 370, 484, 490. IV 124. V 88. VI 280, 297. VII 153, 284, 306. VIII 47 +D, 246 (= ?p^1), 337. IX 5, 24, 50, 162, 186 +N, 241, 299. XI 54 +Y [? *censorship*], 72, 183. XII 147. XIII 43, 187. XIV 84. XV 111, 176 +DW, 177, 303 +FN, 304. XVII 188, 228 +P². XVIII 2 +N², 14, 131. XIX 53 +F, 58, 65. XX 7 +W, (10), 50, 256 (+N *ins.*), 302 +N. XXI 20, 96, 286, 459, 468 +W. *Where* M *lacks the* m *error or has a different one*: III 435. IX 20 +N. XVI 31 (M *def.*), 140. XXI 152 +NT.

The group m cannot be eliminated because, apart from XVII 116 (in theory possibly of non-group origin), it has at IV 35 what seems the right word-order in the light of // **B**.

ii Group **q**

§ 51. The next group **q**, less solidly attested than m, is represented throughout by only one copy **Q** and contains two possible genetic pairs <**QF**> and <**WZ**>. As R–K note (pp. 49–50), **QWFSZ** are actually present together only in Passus XII–XXII; so where one or more members are defective, the 'group' reading is inferential, though there are good grounds for thinking the inference reliable. As with m, this restricted and intermittent attestation does not favour use of the sigil q in the Apparatus, which records its variants only occasionally in a larger entry, as at XIII 59 and XVI 31. Group q is defined by 56 major agreements, seven with all members present and unanimous; minor ones (*R–K*, 49–51) are disregarded because of the witnesses' extensive defectiveness. In the list, a minus = 'manuscript free of group error', '‡' = 'different error'.

(a) QWFSZ *present*: XII 93 louye...Lordes] for ȝoure lordus loue to. 96 [*L. om through eyeskip to* 98, *but without loss of* 97]. 193 mowe] dure m. 232 ariste] wexuþ. XIII 28 ben] ben ful. 59 *As* 2 *ll.* 72 -W semeth] were. XXI 326 made] hadde. 385 ylette] bete. XXII 47 ful soure] some. XXII -WZ 228 or] for.

(b) W *absent*: X 114 -F vppon] for; 189 we] *om*; 241 synne] gult; 306b–307a -F and...lene *om*. XI 5 to Wyt] *om*. 160 -S Thus] Þis; 253 -F as] to make as; 286 ‡F many] my.

(c) F *absent*: XIII 201 -W so...profit] of felawe so fayre ne of profyt neuer þe mo. XIV 6 -Z defended] dystuted (-ted) -dyed S). 193 *Five spur. ll. added.*

(d) S *absent*: XVI 31 ‡F. 144 -F treuth-] reson-. -F 247b–48a leues...nat] *om* [*homoteleuton at caesura*: bereth...bereth]. 362 -F commissarie] consayle & c. XVII 76 follynge] prente; 215 ȝow for] *om*. 258 -W in a fayth] mafay. 298 ȝut] *om*. 302 Tho] Lo. 312 oþer] and. XVIII 50 the pouke] *om* [?*censorship*]. 58 he sayde] quaþ he. 84 ‡W this] þi. 158, [159 +G], 161: *extra Lat. ll. after* (159 = B XVI 135a), 167 Fryday] f. nyȝt; 177 *Lat. l. added*. 246 age] gate. XIX 80 faste aftur] fast (*trs* W). XX 230 Adames] (a) man(nus). XXI 20 -F noen] *om*. 247 ‡F He] Hit.

(e) WF *absent* XIII 163 egges] nestus & e.

(f) WZ *absent*: I 4 castel] clif. 95 lordene] inordine (disordeyned F). III 138 þis] þi. 276 therfore] here. VI 46 fetures] feþerus. 364 Hewe] heruey. 428 nones] onus. VII 103 foul sage] falsage.

(g) WFZ *absent*: VIII 243–6a om.

§ 52. This list reveals a p^1 'core-group' <**QFS**> (somewhat like the x^1 core-group XYI noted at § 23) which, allowing for significant absences, is attested throughout. Since all the major cases at (f) and (g) occur before WZ appear, they could all in principle be group-readings of q; but within the core-group a genetic pairing <**QF**> is strongly indicated by some 95 agreements, the 35 major ones including the loss of XVII 151 and XXII 103 (*R–K*, p. 36). This is not contradicted by the 30 agreements of **QZ** in X–XXI (*R–K*, p. 37), which are all minor and could be coincidental.[51] Rather more challenging to <**QF**> are the 65 agreements of **QS**; but of the twenty major ones ten, including the important omission of VIII 243–6a, occur where F is absent and are thus potential 'core' readings. The remaining ten wither away on closer scrutiny. Four that may be mechanically induced are II 64 *menye* for *eny* (by word-initial *me-* in *Mede, men, me*); X 245 *graye* for *grayth* (haplography after *y / þ* confusion); XII 18 *hond* for *hed* (smoothing after *e / o* confusion or deliberate correction);[52] and XXII 174 *drenges* for *drogges* (unconscious confusion with *drinkes*). Among the six non-mechanical cases, in III 125 *brown* for unusual *blew* may be a coincidental substitution like that of *blake* by both AV and GN (pairs belonging to separate divisions of **p**) as, at VII 115, may *liken* for similarly uncommon *litheth*. In VII 82, *falsages* for *foel-sages* is very probably the q group-reading from which F's *fele fals folk* further varies by way of smoothing. At VII 259, *lond* for *loue* may also be a smoothing after misreading of *loue* as *lone* (here inappropriate). In XI 212 *goed aftur*] g. *auntur aftur* the third word may have been mechanically lost by F through haplography. The most striking example of all is the one most easily explained. At VII 106 Cx *feste* is evidently wrong, q's *beste* an unsuccessful attempt to correct it and F's *geste* a happy scribal guess prompted by recollection of *storye* at // B XIII 447. The preceding analysis may be taken to confirm the grouping <(QF)S>. The 52 agreements of **WZ** in XII–XXII, over half major, are 'relatively persistent' (*R–K* p. 37);[53] so if this pair is genetic, a better ordering of q's components than the present edition's QWFSZ will be *R–K*'s QFSWZ. Group q is nowhere the sole source of a p^1 right reading against error in both **x** and p^2; but it is a valuable supplementary p^1 witness both where **p** is uniquely right (§ 44 above) and where m has further diverged. Its member F contains at VII 106 an indispensable major right reading.

§ 53. As with m (§ 42 above), some members of q appear to have been corrected from an **x** or p^2 source. This is indicated by Q's possession of a line (IX 187) that p^1 seems to have lacked. This might have been coincidentally omitted in both m and F, by eyeskip or through censorship, but Q's other right readings *serk*] *sherte* at I 99 and the Latin *sciunt*] *sapiunt* at XI 165 favour lateral transmission to explain its presence in Q. The same explanation need not necessarily apply to W in four instances, to F in six, and to Z in one (see § 51). For in each, if the correction came from a copy of the other p^1 group m, it might nonetheless have been Q alone that turned to p^2 or **x**. But which of these alternatives is true cannot be established, since Q does not elsewhere agree in error with the latter. Little can therefore be inferred from these features except that the source of Q, the earliest member, like that of the slightly earlier m manuscript M, may have had access to copies outside the p^1 tradition, and also that such access became progressively restricted. But certainly striking is the absence of solid evidence for resort to manuscripts of the other family. Thus, even if shared dialectal features suggest two early copying centres in Worcestershire (for x^1 and x^2), the origin of p^1 is likely to have been at a more central Midland location. This contrasts with the next major group, which was generated further to the west.[54]

b. *Branch* p^2

§ 54. The second branch of **p** consists of three descendants of an original produced in SE Herefordshire, just south of the poet's probable dialectal area. That p^2 was coæval with the other branch is suggested by the early date of its oldest member **G**, which is close to that of p^1's V and within perhaps a dozen years from Langland's presumed obit. G's value is, however, much reduced by its lacking over 600 lines through loss of leaves and another 100 through omissions, singly or in groups. The second early copy **K** is a mere torso, wanting the first 650 lines through loss of leaves and about the last 2900, perhaps because the exemplar was already imperfect. The only complete

p^2 copy is thus **N**, the latest. The sequential representation of <**GKN**>, indicated analytically at §
42 above, is: Pr 1–153 N; Pr 154–II 216 GN; II 217–XIII 225 GKN; XIII 225*a*–XIV 40 KN; XIV
41–XV 66 GKN; XV 67–287 GN; XV 288–XVI 40 N; XVI 41–XXII 39 GN; XXII 40–387 N.
Thus p^2 is fully instanced in about 25 agreements in error, nine major, across some 3730 lines or
just over 50% of the poem.[55] A minus sign here indicates freedom from the group error.

Major V 125. VI 40. VII 1 -slob-] -slot-. 6 A...bolk] belkynge he b. 261 in thyn h.; sytteth] *trs*. VIII 50 with] *om*. 171.
337. XII 70 And...ere] And rewarde.

Minor IV 15 hym] *om*. 133 ens.] *sg*., 190. V 30 in] at. 44 vp] upon. 66 and] *om*. 152 to þe] to. 159 places] *sg*. VI 438 in]
on. VIII 14 the] *om*. 133 of] for. IX 308 And] *om*. 325 into] in. XIII 54 þat] þe. 119 is] is he. 190 day; nyhte] *trs*.

Secondly, in some 60 readings across nearly 3500 lines (just above 40% of the poem) where K is
absent, **GN** could in principle represent p^2. The following ten are major:[56]

Pr 172 cloches] clawes. 189 roume] renne. II 13 rede] ryche. XV 188 Sobrete] Sobernesse. XVI 149 here] *om*. XVII 118
nat(1)] *om*. XVIII 17 sithe] saide. 104 and] he. XXI 151 songen] swettely s. 246 vnrihtfulliche] wiþ wrong.

Finally, for 560 lines (some 7% of the poem), N alone may attest p^2, e.g. in Pr 110 and XXII 110,
198^2 and 212 (although each of these could be an individual error).

§ 55. Because of the defectiveness in the data establishing p^2, where one of the three copies
is absent, collateral evidence may be looked for in the support of **x**. For when agreeing with **x** in
a right reading, unless contamination is posited, p^2 inferentially preserves **p** and p^1 has erred. By
extension, when the right reading appears in any one or two of its three members, unless this too
is to be ascribed to contamination from **x**, it again may be judged to preserve p^2. The 270-odd
instances listed at § 42 above where GKN join **x** to furnish the lemma imply that p^2 was a far more
accurate copy of **p** than was p^1 (see § 44 above). If these may be interpreted as the presumed read-
ings of their source-manuscript, it should be permissible to go on to identify the single or paired
agreements of G, K and N with **x** in right readings as likewise representing the likely text of p^2.
In the following list of some 40 a minus denotes a p^2 (and, where such occurs, an **x**) copy sharing
the p^1 error; a plus, a p^1 copy with the right reading:

Major

(a) GKN *present*: VI 388 -N (*alt*.). 390 -N (*alt*.). VII 20 -G+M [*unconscious substitution of near-synonym*]. X 275^2 -KP^2.
(b) GN *present* XVI 266 -GP^2U [*l. lost through homoteleuton*]. 371 -G [*visual error foll. by smoothing*]. XVII $14^{1,2}$ -N,
82 -GD^2Dt [ʒ / þ *confusion*]. XX 140 -N (*alt*.) +P^2. 256 -N (*ins*.). 353 -N [*eyeskip from her > erthe*]. 365 -NCh. 418
-NDN^2. XXI 482 -G+Dt [*unconscious substitution of contextually commoner word*]. (c) *Only* N *present* XVI 31^2.

Minor

(a) GKN *present*: VI 29 -N, 32 -G, 122 -G, 71 -N. IX 218 -G, 230 -GP^2. X 117 -GY, 184 -GN^2. XI 109 ‡N. XII 185 -GP^2u.
(b) GN *present* II 148 -N+R. XVI 259, 319 -GD^2, 341 -GY+MW. XVII 61 -N, 184 -N+F. XIX 234 -Gt+R. XX 96 -N, 112
-GP^2, 390 -G. XXI 190 -G+MZ, 390. XXII 25 -Gut+W. (c) *Only* N *present* Pr 10, 36, 58. XXII 63 +W.

Among the 43 instances listed here, G contains some twenty and N some dozen (eight major),
which diverge from the presumed group-reading to share the p^1 error. If the minor cases are dis-
counted as probably coincidental, G's remaining major ones all appear likely on analysis to have
mechanical causes. K's single example at X 275 could be a coincidence prompted by *louye* in
274; for K, though defective, is generally very accurate. Only N seems to owe four major changes
of its p^2 text to consultation of a p^1 copy. Four others may reflect earlier alteration in N's exem-
plar, but this looks likely only for XVII 14. The early G and K are thus pure examples of the p^2
tradition and only the late N seems aware of p^1. This need not imply that the relatively greater
corruption of p^1 is due to its original's relative lateness, for an initial faultiness could have been
compounded through successive copying by m, e and r, the group-ancestors of the extant copies.

But the more 'primary' character of the p^2 witnesses may well be associated with the simplicity of their generation.

§ 56. None of the three copies derives directly from either of the others and only N need have had an immediate ancestor between it and p^2. As well as being much older than N, G possesses VIII 275b–76a (which K lacks); K, as early as G, has many lines G omits, e.g. V 21, XIII 39, 63, XIV 63, 212; but N cannot derive from K, as it too has VIII 275b–76, nor from G, since it has nearly all of G's missing lines. On the basis of some 100 agreements, about a dozen major, R–K find a genetic relation between G and N (p. 35). But while they acknowledge (n. 19) that 'an indeterminate number' *after* XV 66, where K breaks off, could also be evidence for the group KGN, they fail to note that K's absence *before* II 217 also entails ignoring in the number half a dozen GN agreements between Pr 154, where G begins, and II 216. As three of these are major (Pr 172 *cloches*] *clawes*, 189 *roume*] *renne*, II 13 *rede*] *ryche*), the total reduces to about 40, of which barely half a dozen can be called major. Further, perhaps 25 minor ones (e. g. II 15 *atyer*] *tyr*, IV 116 *reclused*] *reclosed*, VI 40 *enchesoun*] *chesoun*) are simply spelling-variants that should not count as substantive agreements. The genetic character of GN, in any case uncertain because of K's massive absences, is questioned firstly by 45 agreements of GK, some ten of them major (*R–K*, pp 40–1). But since K is present for comparison with G in less than half as many lines as N, a qualitative scrutiny of their shared variants is essential. What this reveals is that GK, as well as omitting III 172 and XIII 86, have at least one reading unattributable to chance, V 10 *inwitt*] *duite* (*vnite* p^1N ? = **p**). A second challenge to GN is the 19 agreements of KN, perhaps nine of them major. The most striking include the Latin form *rectis* for *rect* at III 333 and 35 (these, paralleled in M's *rectes*, may be evidence that M used a p^2 and not an **x** copy for its run of corrections in Pr–II, as suggested at § 43 above). Others include *kyssyng*] *cursyng* VI 187, *elde*] *colde* VI 200 and *hunte*] *oute* VIII 28. Given the logical difficulty of ascribing both GN and KN to convergent variation, simple acceptance of <GN> as genetic should perhaps yield to R–K's 'alternative explanation' of 'consultation in a single copying centre' (cf. § 23 above). In the case of N, this implicitly signifies not Harley 2376 itself, which is a generation later in date than G, but its postulated exemplar. All in all, there would thus seem little reason for preferring a genetic to a chronological arrangement of the sequence of sigils in p^2. The group cannot be eliminated since it has a unique right reading at XIII 120 (where the Apparatus should read 'GK' before '*trs*' and 'p^1N' for '**p**') and a few superior single-member variants due perhaps to felicitous accident:

Major G: VII 131 syʒt] liht X&r (?Cx), 306 wel] ful (?Cx).
Minor G: VIII 148 what þat] what y; þat ?þu. IX 63 hi] he / they. N: I 187 +S hy] þei [*the metrically requisite pronoun-form*]; III 175 fle; XXII 329 come [*the superior past subjunctive verb-form*].[57]

Finally, p^2 valuably represents **p** where p^1 is absent or in error (see § 42 above).

§ 57. This discussion has shown that the principal groups p^1 and p^2 and their constituent manuscripts between them preserve some thirteen readings, eight of them major, which appear original on intrinsic grounds and from comparison with the parallel text of the other version(s) where available. These are mostly to be judged happy scribal conjectures, except for the whole line XVII 116 (§ 49 and *Textual Notes*). There are no signs in **p** or its members (except M) of contamination from any earlier version, though occasional readings like G's at VII 131 or F's at VII 106 may reflect their scribes' knowledge of **B**. Several members of both branches could be eliminated as lacking unique right readings, e.g. E, A, V, Z and K, and **p** might be adequately represented by PRMQFGN. But since ten of its fourteen members (including four of the latter seven) are defective, collating all the witnesses increases the firmness with which sub-group, group and sub-family readings can be established. This is of consequence for the text of Pr–XII, where **p** is the sole representative of x^2, its readings often preserving the archetypal text and providing the lemma for x^1's defining variants at §§ 33–4 above. But since the certain evidence for **p** itself is the agreed readings of p^1 and p^2, a control must be sought where p^1 is *un*certain because its constituent groups conflict. This is found firstly in p^2, which can aid in discriminating the likely reading of p^1 as between groups m and q; secondly, in t and (before XII) in x^1.

§ 58. As with the earlier accounts (*A Version* § 45; *B Version* § 41), all the 1445 **p** variants listed below have of course been identified as agreements in error. Against the inescapable sub-jectivity of such a judgement the main defence lies in the comparative x^1 evidence, the available parallels in **Z**, **A** and, above all, **B**. But in cases of conflict between **C** families, especially in rela-tion to minor readings, the logic of the linear postulate is here regarded as overriding the joint witness of earlier versions. Thus, when **AZ**'s support for **p** is made to rank after **B**'s for **x**, a **Z** reading ratified by **A** is understood as a reading revised in **B**, not one retained in **C** from B^1 but corrupted in Bx. At other times, the presumption that **C** could be revised may endorse an intrinsi-cally harder (or simply acceptable) **x** reading even when **p** enjoys all the other-version support.[58] In the list below, the readings identified as shared errors of **p** and t are not given again, since these will be found at § 38 above, where they are cited as joint evidence for the readings of x^2. Unsup-ported **p** variants before XII, however, may be inferred to preserve x^2 only when they are judged authentic on their own merits, because any errors in this portion might be simply **p** divergences from the sub-archetypal source. Allowing, then, for occasional non-unanimous attestation, the full evidence for **p** is set out as earlier for x^1, divided according to major and minor readings and other-version support. There are 145 major and 634 minor instances where the adopted variant has such support, 130 major and 536 minor ones where it does not. The lemmata before Passus XII, unless indicated otherwise, are from x^1, denoted simply by **x** as in the Apparatus; but from XII to XXII the same sigil denotes *joint* readings of x^1 and t. As earlier, for reasons of space, minor readings are given by reference only, but the major ones in full. This is because **p**, as in principle representing x^2 in Pr–XII where t is absent, in effect acquires family status (unlike γ in **B**, which is never the *sole* witness to β). For the sake of completeness and convenience, **p**'s readings therefore continue to be recorded in full even after XII, when agreed x^1t is denoted by **x**. Round brackets signify a near but non-identical reading; square brackets one where, despite other-version support, **p** is still rejected. A minus sign before a sigil denotes agreement of an **x** witness / other version with the rejected **p** variant; a plus sign, agreement of a **p** member with the lemma; 'so', other-version agreement with **p**.

§ 59. **Readings with other-version support**

(i) Major

+**ZAB**: Pr 2 shroudes] shrobbis. shep] shepherde. I 33 yerne] wilne. 36 ʒut mote ʒe] ʒe mote. 197 carefole] cristine. II 72 standeth] stod. 73 vnfoldeth] vnfeeld; hath] hadde. III 6 were leuest haue] w. l. to h. P^2; is l. h. **p**; l. hadde **x**. 25 man] *om.* 165 and²] alle. 181 +VM ones] one. 223 +F knowestou] knoweþ. IV 43 +M sulue] *om.* 61 +MF otes] oþer twelue. V 115 synne] s. to punyshe þe puple. 119 segges] to syggen ous. 137 forwanyen] forwene. VI 316 swythe] ful. VII 176 -P^2 calleth] clepeþ. 195 -AxP²+P hewe] hyne. 204 way theder] (heye) w. þyderwarde wyteþ wel þe soþe. 229 se] *om.* 247 -P^2+G Biddeth] Rydeth to. VIII (25 tho thow louest] þe while þou lyuest). 93 this] *om.* 257/8 +RM *L. div.* 257 +RM shal] he shal. 258¹ -P^2+RM wel] *om.* 258² +RM bireue] b. for hus rechelesnesse. 322 -P^2 neyh] *om.* IX 41 many] somme.

+ZB: II 191 -Ax, u *fornicatores*] fornicators. III 17 [-Ax, *om*] +R wedde] wende. 29 þou myhte] we mowe.

+Z: III 225 weye] wyterly.

+AB: Pr 49 +RM wyse] vnwyse. 72 bounchede] blessed. 74 -P²D gyue] ȝeueþ. 229 *til* hem] a tast for nouht. III 67 +MF se] (se and) seye. 70 An auntur] Leste. 73 +M lordes] l. loue. VI 197 Sire] *om*. 209 leef] lesyng. 382 -u Tho] Two. 393 louryng] lakeryng. 436 -P² lyf] lyuyng. IX 311 for defaute we shulle] we shulleþ for d. 338¹ dome] day of d. X 113 we] togederes we. 304 -U here] *om*. XI 21 gentele] g. and wys. 92 -XIP²N² man] *om*. 107 wo] muche wo. 217 (ho tauhte men bettre] hij t. men boþe). 264 -N² Then] Also. 270 -P² to dethe] *om*.

+B: Pr 140 Myght] The muche m. III 269 ȝerne] renne. V 141 -ZA ȝe; ȝow] hij; hem. VI 55 -P² Y lye wenen] ȝe wene ich lye. 68 -P² chalengynge] l021anglynge. 160 at euen] *om*. 163 cough] cowede. 228 -A ale] *om*. 248³ his] *om*. 284 in a doute] *om*. 426 Godes; his] þy; þy. VII 41 So with] Þat with so. 43 his] *om*. 134 lup] lemed. 137 dame] moder. [138 so] *om*; *so* **B**]. VIII 197 proud] ful p. X 66 mouthes] murye m. 84 alle] herteliche a. 95 +K-u pulte] putte. XI 68 wynneth; hath] *trs*. 76 now] *om*. 148 Austin...bokes] Herof a. þe olde made bokes and b. 220 wisest] wise. 232 goed] worldliche g. XII 20² welde] wedde. 57 for...breste] of hus breste sauete for synne. 70 (And) for his (rechelesnes) rewarden hym þere] Rewardynge hym þer for hus r. XIII 161 made...moche] þerto m. a molde / With alle here wyse castes. XIV 66 -YDN² at] a. 103 yse] ich seye. 121/3 *mislin*. XV 106 +E-D²DT take] talke. 249 oute of his poke; hente] *trs*. 258 +W etynge] ondyng. 282 -D rihtfullyche] do ryghtful. 284 +RM rychesse] riche. 299 somtyme sum] tyme of som. XVI 3 -D Hewen] Thei. 4 selde] shulle nat. 42 -F Cristene] cr. men. noon coueytous for] no couetise to. 58 haueth] shewith. 92 nat] nat ful longe. 114 Pacience] pacient. 120 by] quaþ. 246 in somur tyme; on trees] *trs*. 329 ȝerneth he into ȝouthe] he ȝ. into þouht. 356 recomendeth] comendeþ. XVII 220 +VZ-uH²Ch kirke] churche. 254 ho so] þat. 305 studeden] fondeden. XVIII 209 alle] *om*. 286 Lollyng] Longynge. XIX 50 ȝeden] wente. 196 the...Trinite; 197 Melteth...mercy] *trs*. XX 34*a* -P² *morsus*] *om*. 96/8 *L. div*. 96 for euere] *om*. 105 lordeyns] lordynges. 255 soffre] s. deþ. 272¹ -tN² *Principes*] Princes. 272² place] palys. 276 Care] Colde c. 332 trolled] troiled and trauailed / In hus tyme. 393/4 *L. div*. 470 -N² caroled] daunsede. 471 -P² riht] *om*. XXI 28 knele; to hym] *trs*. 45 lyf] þe lykyng lyf. 60 ȝeueth] ȝaue. 127 folk] fele f. 181 me] *om*. 191 men] *om*. 401 while] t; *om x¹*; for. 444 þat¹] hem þat. 449 olde Lawe and þe newe Lawe] l. boþe old and newe. 459 -D alle] *om*. 463 of my reue; to take] *trs*. XXII 17 anoenriht nymeth hym vnder] nymeþ hym anon vnder his. 18 +F yf] ȝeueþ. 37 fele nedes] for neode. 70 hit baer] bar þat baner. 95 -P²U he] *om*. 136 ȝede] hyede. 143 lowh] l. lowde. 156 his lemman; fortune] *trs*. 183 aftur] hastede a. 198² forbete] afeynted and f. 200 ney] and neihede. 208 othere] o. þynges. (293 remenaunt] r. of þe good). 297 Consience; assailede] *trs*. 323 -P²DTH² sayde] quod.

(ii) Minor

+ZAB: Pr 4. -u 10. 28. 43. (50). 58. I -b 20. [-L 37 (*so* ZAB)]. 43. 79. +MF-U 84. [82 (*so* ZAB)]. 88. +F 101. [128 (*so* ZAB)]. 136. 160¹. 161. -D 167. 174¹. 182¹˒³. 189. II +R 73¹. 73². 79². [93 (*so* Bx)]. -P² 126. -P²+E 159¹. +F 165¹. 165². -U 169. 179¹. 191¹. +M 192. +MF 202¹˒². 210. [+M 212 (*so* Bx)]. +M 216. (+F 220). 221. 223¹. 228. 229². 235. III (6). 7. -D 12. [16¹ (*so* ZAB); +AVM 16²]. 27. 133. +P²D 145. 152. +F 174. 179. 198¹. 199. 215. 227. 259. 260. [+F 262³ (*so* ZAB)]. IV 21. 27. 46. +MF 62. 79. 82¹. +F 82. 84. 87. 90¹. -D 102. 103. 126. 177. V 130. VI 4. 438. VII 57. 58¹. -P² 58³. -D 60. -P² 61¹˒². 64¹. 68. 164. 171. 180². -P² 182. 192. 194. -D 205. (214). 217. -P² 223. 228. 233. VIII 1. (25). 39. 41¹. 93. (+M; †Bx 101). 109¹. 112. 113. -D 143. (†Ax 149). 150. 156. 164. -D 172. -P²+M 227. 257. +M 294. 312. -P² 322. 325¹˒². 334. 346¹. -D 347.

+ZA: VIII 17. -B+S 18.

+ZB: II -DA+RSG 174. IV -A+MG 90. -UA+M 110. V -A 109. +FS; *l. om* 134. VII -IP²A 245¹. VIII -A 219. -A+G 313.

+Z: Pr +N 36.

+AB: Pr -Z 25. 64. -OU 75 hit] hit to. 83. [84 *so* AB]. 161. 164. [221 *so* AB]. I 174¹ (*so* Z). -U 178 (*so* Z). 188 (*so* Z). II 252. III 21. [48 (*so* AB)]. 70. -U 448. IV -ZP² 105. VI 215. 357. 358. 363. +RM 365. 380. 387. +M 391. +F 403. +Q-P² 414. VII 155 (*so* Z). 269. 285¹. -P² 286. VIII 16 (*so* Z). 27 (*so* Z). 50. 56. +S-P² 68. 76¹. +MS 76². +G 83. 229². IX 177 (*so* Z). 281¹. [+AVF-AB 281²]. +RM 281³. -D 282. 290. 293. 297. -P² 299. 302. 304. 305¹. 309. +D 313. 330. 331¹. 338². +M 343². X -ZN 11. 19. 29. 36. -P²D 38². 38³. 46. 64. 73. 77. 81¹. 108¹˒⁴. +S-D 130.¹, +N-P²D 130². -N² 143. +G 230. 235. 277. 295. XI -U+R 3. 6. -N² 15. -I 39. +S 87¹. (87²). -Y 93. 115. -N² 116, 119. 138¹, 222, 264. -P² 266¹. 271¹. -N² 293. +F 296¹˒⁴.

+B: Pr 79. 89. 91. [+M-B 136]. +RM 137. 176–7. -b 190². I 78 And also kenne] Also to k. 139. 153. 159. [II -B 14]. 35. 52. 71¹. 86². +R-P² 89. +M 94. 99. -P²bD 108. -AD 141. III +F 31. 457. 477. IV -ZA 45. 111. -ZA 122. (127). -ZAU+MSN 159. V -P²u 161. 165. 167¹. VI 41. 56. -D 57. 58¹. [-Bu 59; **p** *may be right here*]. +M 70. 72¹. -M 75. 77¹. -u 82. +F 88. -u 90. 94. +RM 129. +AF 133¹. 151. 156². 165. 178. 179. 201. 238. 245. -u 246². +PEM 249¹. 276. -P² 278, 280. 282. 285. 327. 341. 347. 361, 379 (*so* A). +E 397. 427¹˒². VII 1. 4. 6. +M 7. 9¹. 16. 22. +S 26. +P² 28. 29. 35¹. 38. 39. 40. 45. +I 47. 49. 72². 78. 80. 90. +F 92. +G 94. +MS-P² 97. 111². 112. 124¹. +M 124². -AZ 235, 236¹, 245². +K-uA 271.

VIII -**ZA** 3. 35. 37. 139. 154. -P^2**ZA** 301. IX -P^2 8^1. [-**B** 39]. -Y 42. -**A** 349. X $62^{1,2}$. 66^2. +N-**DA** 105. XI 26. 28. 74. 157.
166. +N-**D** 167. 168. 169^1. -N^2 170. +S-P^2 171. 184. 186. 189. -N^2 190. +QM-N^2 192. -N^2 215. 236. 240. -N^2 244. 285^1.
+F 285^2. 300^1. XII 23, 26. -N^2 33. 38. 69. 70. 71^1. 74^2. -$P^2D^2UN^2$ 80. -N^2 111^2. -P^2 113^2. 121. -D 129. 130. 131. 142^1. -N^2
146^1. [-**B** 150]. XIII 110 -P^2 $119^{1,2}$. 121. 127. 158. 162. 176^1. 178. 212^2. -P^2 226. XIV 53. -P^2u 56. 66. 78. -N^2 87. 90. 108.
149. 151. 152. 156. +M-YU 209^1. XV +G 2. 11^1. 19^1. 69. +MWS 72^1. +G 84. 90. [-P^2**DB** 105]. -D^2Ch 135. -P^2 165. 166.
173^2. +MWS-Ch 209. 224. $228^{1,2}$. 240. 252. -P^2 257^1. 257^2. +S 267^1. -Ch 269. 270. +SN-Yu 274. 292. +QSN-D 293. XVI
4^3. [+QF-**B** 38]. 39. +F 42. -D^2U 45. 48. +WF 49. 56. 73. +F 76. 79. +F 80. 85. 91. 93. 101. 102^1. 111. 128^1. 130. +G-Ch
144. 167. 186. 194. 205. +QWZ 207. +G 224. +M 234. +MF 264. $321^{1,2}$. 328. [+EVRF-**B** 330^2]. +MWN-Y 341. $345^{1,2}$.
356. XVII +W 112^1, 113. XVIII $35^{1,2}$. [-**B** 45]. XIX +M 50. +MW-P^2 63. +FN 66. +FG 68. -P^2 69. +G 70. -D^2DH^{2}Ch
76. 84. [-**B** 148]. 153. 164. 171. 192. 204^2. 224. 252. 255. 285. 286. +G 310. 317. 319. +N-D^2Ch 325. -P^2 327. XX -Ch
52. 56. 71. 77. [-P^2**B**]. +G 96. 112^2. 125. +WN-I 126. -P^2 162. [-**B** 163]. 171. +EWF 208. 210. -Ch 215. 220. +F 227. -P^2
228, 229^2. -P^2D^2 231. 234. 254. 260. +W 270. [-**B** 273]. +MG 281. [-**B** 299]. 302^2. 321. 337. -ICh 362. 393. -P^2D^2Ch 395.
+MQ-P^2U 399. 404. 413. 462. 474. XXI 3. +RM-P^2 11. -P^2D^2 13. 14. 21. +F 30^1. 30^2. 31. -ChN^2 44. 47. 63^1. [-**B** 63^2]. 76.
87. +F 114^2. 132. 137. 168. 188. 195. 208. 214. 220. 222. 224. 232. 233. 235^2. -D^2 259. 265. 278. 340^1. 342. 346. 348.
356. 380. 386. 389. +W 433. -P^2 437. 440. -D^2 471. 472. XXII 3. 7. 13. 15. 17. 35. 36. 42. 45. 46. 50. +W 55. +RW 60^1.
$60^{2,3}$. 65. 67. 71. 80. 95. -P^2 129. 136^1. 140. -ID^{2}DH^{2}Ch 151. 152. -D 172. 192. 196. +PE-Ch 212^1. 212^2. 215. 220. 222.
232. 235. -P^2D^2DCh 266. +F 290. +W 322. 327. +RM 331. -D^2Ch 337. +P 343. 346. 353. 364. 370^2. 374.

§ 60. Readings with no other-version parallel

(i) Major

Pr 46 also] synful. 50 aftir] *om.* I 67 and his lore] *om.* 99 fyghte and fende] feithfullich defende and fyȝte for. 110 That]
He; þat was] god. II 68 hit were so] þer to. 78 Mede] And me. 83 þat hath a] hath with. 184 *rectores*] rectours. 191 -u
fornicatores] fornicators. III 89 grayeth] grete. 153 Mede] maide. 255 *As two ll.* kyng] k. ycoroned by marye. 274 Bothe]
om. 287 +AV sayth] sheweþ. 290 +F(M) and] a. 304 *As two ll.* dette] d. for þe doynge. 316 (+M) and to] *om.* 356 -P^2U
kyrke] churche. 367 am] *om.* $369^{2)}$ alle] *om.* 376 to his lawe] þus to hym. 382 now] *om.* 385 Such...resoun] Al r. reproueþ
such imparfit peple. $397^{2)}$ -P^2 kyrke] churche. 412 Ruth] reweþ. -P^2D derfly] delfulliche. 423/4 myhte / Spille hit] myhte
spille. 427 and warnede hym by] by warning of. $499^{2)}$ recheth] recetteþ. IV 30 þe comune] þei couthen. 123 be] for. 125
ruyflares] robbers (*so* **B**). 140 *Nullum malum*; man] *trs.* V 14 -P^2u mywen] mowen. 21 They...fynden] Hem þat bedreden
be bylyue to f. $44^{1,2)}$ so] *om*; opelond] on londone. 48 This Y segge] Thus y synge. 103 +AFN-P^2 louable] lowable. 104,
105 +VRF-P^2 kyrke] churche. 125 to heuene] ryght for (and hou) to lyuen. $167^{2)}$ +RM so] *om.* VI 29 +F clerk] lered.
39 -D couent] couetyse. 42 -IP^2 clerkysh] clerkes. 65 -P^2 corse-men] corsement. 67 -I pissede] passede. 147 heo$^{2)}$] ich.
258 weyhtes] wittes. VII 255 +M-P^2D payne] pyne. ?295 graytheliche] grettliche. VIII 53^2 -P^2u kyrke] churche. 74
lele] for l. 216 filial] ?fial. 349 schaef] shaft. viii vm. IX 19 suche] sitthen. 71 Ac þat most neden] The most nedy.
195 Noyther] *om.* 259 ar wroken] ben broke. X 37 so] *om.* 98 Sholde...to] That no bisshop sholde here byddinge. 100
demede] diuinide. $196^{2)}$] on rode] *om.* 217 *As two ll.* engendrede] e. and a gome vnryghtful. 249 makynge] of mankynde.
251 -N^2 seth$^{2)}$] sitthen. XI 68 wynneth; hath] *trs.* 76 now] *om.* 78 þat loueth] lyuen. 178 manere] wyse. 203 sihte] sete.
208 -P^2N^2 *prescite*] prechen. 246 -P^2D kyrke] churche. 250 -P^2N^2 kyrke] churche. 286 ȝe] ich. XII 93 oure] ȝoure. 106
hou beste to] how he may. 169 ȝut] Thus. 176 Ennedy] Ouidius. 186 grace] grete g. 217 lete] leue. XIII 9 *As two ll.* his
hosewyf] hym ys h. and heeld here hymself. 42 fayre] *om.* 69 rychesse] grete r. 92 So þe pore] The porter. 148 ferddede]
herdeyed. 200 soffre alle] *trs.* XIV 26 worcheth God sulue] g. hymself w. $45^{2)}$ come] be. 179 pennes] feþeres. XV 8
-P^2 lotes] lockes. 72 eny] heuene. 80–3 *Mislin.* 82 mendynantz] m. and made eny sarmon. 126 +W techeth] telleþ. 132
-ChN^2 palmare ȝent] plouhman. 142–5 *Mislin.* 143 helpe] Hertely þou hym h. 232 Plente] Pure p. 238 helpe] heye h. 240
neuere was here] was þer neuere (*cf.* **B**). 248 quod Actyf; ay] *trs.* 290/1 *Misdiv.* 290 -P^2 puyre] *om.* XVI 31/2 *Misdiv.* 31
quyteth] soueraynliche q. 273 +QW curatours] creatures. 327 Worth; hit] Ys; wel. XVII 39 haue we] ȝe h. 124 letynge]
lengthynge. 125 chere] *om.* 132 and gentel Sarresines] gentiles and s. 139 -P^2 lyue] louen. 241 mannes] *om.* 247 -H^2 hy]
om. 247^2 -D^2 descendet] descendede. XVIII 80 *Actiua...hit*] lettred men in here langage *actiua* lif. 83 *Actiua*] That is
a.; *Contemplatiua Vita*] *trs.* 98 hey heuene is priveoste] heuene buth most pryue. 155 *As two ll.* bere] Broke brede to b.
156 vnkunnynge] vnknowing. 200 leue] looke þow l. 247 when tyme cometh] what t. XIX 128 *As two ll.* And] Al. he]
graythly he. hit] þat þat he gripeþ. 239 and a nythynge] *om.* 293 helpe thenne] hem h. XX 98 the dede] hym þat was d.
181 shal] shullen. 355 belyen] bygylie. 444 Þo ledis] t; Tho x^l. Alle þo.

(ii) Minor

Pr -P^2u 13. 67. 101^2. 103. 108. 123. I 19. 23. 55. 64. 75. 103. 104. 110. 111. 113. 114. $121^{1,2}$. 122. 124. 125. 142. $149^{1,2}$.

175. II 7. 22. 28. -D 29. 33. +S 44. 57. 68. 78. +F 90. 107. 121. 123. +M 125. 129. 130. 135. -P^2D 139. +MF 169. 172.
176. 179^2. 198. 218. III 44. 61. 77. 91. 93. 96. +N 97. -P^2 100. -I 108. -P^2D 109. 128. 132. 134. +M 144. -P^2 191. -D
200. 208. +F 209. 210. +RMF 211. 213. +MN 233. 240. +FS-P^2 241. -I 244^1. +F 246. -I 251. 252^1. 254. +FS-u 334. 338.
-IP^2 346. 358. 366. 369^1. +M 372. -IP^2U 380^3. 388. 392. 394^2. 400. +R-D 409. 420. 444. 491. 494^1. 499^1. V 23. 37. 54.
$55^{1,2}$. +FSG 66^1. 66^2. +M 68. $95^{1,2}$. 97^1. 121. 157. 164. 166. +F-D 187. +M 188. V +A 1. 16. +M-P^2 18^1. 24. 35^2. +F 40.
-P^2 51^1. 51^2. 54. +RM 55. 56. 60. 66. 67. 77. +AVR-P^2D 78. +MFN 83. 88^2. +S 90^3. +EAM 95^1. 95^2. 105^2. 114. -P^2 122.
192. VI 1. 14. 18. 42^1. 49^1. 51^1. 60^2. +D 84. 107. -F 116. 126. -u 137^1. -MFS 143^2. 147^1. -P^2 149^1. +RM 181. +M 186.
187. 188. 190. 192. 204. -P^2D 252. +M 255. 256. 257. 290. 291. 292. $298^{1,2}$. 303. -P^2 317. 332. 337. 381^1. -u 381^2. 409^2.
+M 421. 425. 427^2. 429. 433. VII 23^1. -P^2u 23^2. 74. 75^1. 115. 118. -P^2D 144. -P^2u 147. 148. 153. +FS 202. -P^2 252. -P^2D
257. 271. +K-u 297. 302. VIII 49. 57. -P^2 91. 160 -P^2 167. 178. -P^2 190. 197. 214. -P^2 220. 237. -P^2 244. 259. 264^1. -u
264^2. +M 271. 278. 282. 284. IX 16. 17. -P^2 56, 60. 67^1. 71. +G 74. 77. -IP^2D 87, 90. $93^{1,2,3}$. -I 104. -P^2U 105. 106. 109.
113. 120. 124. 130. -U 141. -P^2 153. 159. -P^2 162. 174. +MN 182. 193^1. 195. 200. 201^2. -P^2 202. -P^2 207. 208. 213. 214.
217. 221. -U 222. -P^2 225. 236. +N 246^2. -P^2 247. +N 249. 260. 266. 268. 270^2. 306. $307^{1,2}$. +G-P^2 343^1. +M-P^2 345^2.
X 24. 25. -N^2 37. 38^4. -u 39^2. 41. 42. -XP^2 50. 51. +M 52. +F 54. 97. 110. 127. 161. 170. 171. +K-N^2 171^2. +FN-P^2N^2
178. -u 189^1. 189^2. 196^1. 197. -N^2 199. 206. 207. +S 208. 212. 213. 225. -u+N^2 229. 242. 245. -N^2 251, 262. 263^1. 265^2.
-IU 267. 268^1. -P^2DN^2 268^2. 291. -P^2 292. 296. +G 301. 311^1. XI +M 12/13. 16. 27. 33. +SN 45. 50. -D 64. 80. -N^2 95.
109^2. -IP^2N^2 138^2. 144. -u 145. 187. 154. +QMN-D 157. 163. +MS-N^2 187. -P^2N^2 201. 238. 263. 271^2. +MF-P^2 272^2. -u
272^3. 274. 275 pyne xPN; payne pYU. 283^1. XII 18. -WS 20^1. +Y 28. 100. -N^2 122. 127. 180. -N^2 186. $191^{1,2}$. 195. 225.
227. 234. +M 236. -DCh 238. -N^2D^2 241. +MW 248. XIII 8. 12^2. 14. 15. 19. 23. 24. +W-D 37. +F 51, 58. -D^2 60. 68^1.
72. 74. 76. 77. +RMG 84. 96. 98^1 -P^2 98^3. 99. -N^2 105. 114^2. 120. 122. 170. 172^1. 175^1. +M-D 175^2. 190. 201. -Ch 209.
+S-D^2 217. XIV 7^1. $8^{1,2}$. 10. 30. +AVS 34. 76. 134. 142. +M 160. 162. 182. XV +W-D 23. 28. -P^2Ch 47. $52^{1,2}$. 68. 71. 81.
+MW-P^2 151. 157. 158. 167^1. +MW 171. 186. 205. -P^2Ch 214. 219. +WS 222. +SZ 225. +F 234. -P^2D 243, 250. 295.
+QZ-D 297. 308. XVI +F $36^{1,2}$. 63. 117. 141. 160. 164. $228^{1,2}$. 293. 304. 308. 311. 312. 313. 323. 329^1. 363. 370. XVII
+N 4^1. 4^2. +M 7. -P^2 10. -P^2D^2DCh 28. 39^1. +G 61. 74^1. 75. +M 76. 81. +F $88^{1,2}$. 93. -ID^2DCh 118. 140. 148. 153. -D 164.
168. 246. 254^2. 260^2. $292^{1,2}$. XVIII +MW 17. $18^{1,2}$. 21. 26. 47. 49. 50. 58. 63^1. +RM 70. 73. $75^{1,3}$. 81. 84. 87. 94. 96. 106.
$108^{1,2}$. 122^2. $135^{1,2}$. 141. 142. +F 152. 163. 175. 181. 193. +PG-YD^2Ch 197. 217. 222. -Ch 256. 269. XIX 18. 36. 64^1. -P^2
64^2. 77. XX 63. 79. 93. 174. 229^1. 272^3. 336. +G-N 353. 358. 405. 420. XXI 175.

§ 61. A few features of these lists deserve brief comment. Among the contaminated x^1 copies, N^2, D^2 and D have 32, 20 and 41 agreements respectively with **p**. These are significant numbers when N^2's absence in Pr–X and XXII is noted, even if coincidence could explain many of the minor ones. Easily most striking is P^2 which, out of 207 **p** agreements attested by one or more x^1 copies (some 32 of them major), has 24 major and 96 minor, or 58%, and shares about 8% of the total 1445 for **p**. On the other side, no **p** copy lacks sub-family errors on this scale, though F is free of 50 minor and seven major errors, some 4% of the whole and M does even better, lacking 70 minor and twelve major errors, or 5.75%. Though these figures do not imply certain collation of F's and M's exemplars with an **x** or x^1-type source, they may point to the involvement of scribes who had already copied such manuscripts and sometimes preferred the verbal form or substance of remembered readings. Also worth remarking are the 20 rejected readings where **x** or x^1 stands alone but the **p** variants are shared by **B**. Any or all of these could (and for consistency arguably should) be preferred. But as noted at § 58 above, in this situation it is logically defensible to subordinate other-version support to the presumption of linearity, provided that the readings adopted meet the acceptability canon (see *Intro.* IV § 16 below). Since they do, and most of the instances are minor, any agreements of **p** with **B** (like those with **A** or **Z**, but where **B** confirms **x**) may be deemed coincidental. For without t to support their claim as potential readings of x^2, the case for thinking such **p** variants archetypal lacks weight.

vi. *Comparison of* **x** *and* **p** *and of* x^1 *and* **p**t.

§ 62. Straightforward comparison of the two sub-archetypal traditions is excluded because of the absence of full evidence for x^2 from the first half of the poem. What is possible throughout the text is to compare x^1 and **p**, with the constant recognition that in Pr–XI wrong **p** readings do not necessarily imply errors in its x^2 source, which might have agreed with x^1 had t been present. Analysis of the traditions thus requires three stages. First **p** is compared with x^1; then with x^1 and t agreeing; finally **p**t (taken as representing x^2) are compared with x^1. That x^1 and t are not a single family in simple contrast with another family **p** has already been argued (at § 38) on the basis that the errors shared by **p** and t indicate an exclusive common ancestor. But even with allowance made for the number of good **p**t readings in XII–XXII (not evidence for that ancestor), it seems unlikely that x^2 could have been superior overall to x^1. As matters stand, x^1 is easily preferable, though subject to frequent correction from x^2 as preserved in **p**t / **p**. The account of **p**t favoured here is regrettably less economical than one recognising only two sub-archetypal traditions for **C**, as for **A** and **B**. It depends, too, on the correctness of identifying the **p**t errors in XII–XXII as genetic. Their secondary character (first observed in relation to **p** by Carnegy 1934) shows through on a comparison of **p**t's divergences from Cx's presumed text with those of x^1, which appear more primitive and elementary. Thus both **p** and t are characterised by over-elaboration, sophistication, and occasional failure to understand the poet's vocabulary, thought and (particularly in the case of **p**) metre. These features are best explained if both **p** and t were copied not directly from the archetype but from an intermediate source, x^2 (which is what 'secondary' is intended to signify). The conclusion drawn is therefore that **p** and t arose independently from a sub-archetypal copy x^2, parallel in generation to x^1 (the common original of y, b and u) and in places free from its errors and omissions. This is as simple an interpretation of the text's early history as that of R–K, who accept only two families, **x** (= x^1t) and **p**. But it directly accounts for the observed nature of **p**t's joint errors and it indirectly explains why, taken severally, the latter also appear 'secondary' when compared with those of x^1 and even some of those preserved severally by its three descendants, y, b and u.

§ 63. Comparison first of x^1 with **p** in Pr–XI brings out their typical differences in respect of omitted or expanded material. Thus x^1 has mechanically lost Pr 141–42 (through eyeskip from *Kynde Wit* > *Kynde Wit*) and III 71b–72a (through eyeskip from *con-* > *cou-*).[59] Very similar factors explain omission of the relative clause in IV 146a (with consequential mislineation) and XI 155a, through eyeskip or phrasal haplography (*bokes...bokes*).[60] The reason for the loss of Pr 182 and probably also 183 (which u inaccurately supplies) is less clear; but there could have been visual distraction from *belle...beygh* in 180 or else some damage in the exemplar. For its part **p**, as in III 140–41, tends to expand two lines to three[61] or, more typically, a single line to two. Examples are III 304, VII 204 and X 217, and another five such occur later, after t appears, at XIII 161, XVI 92,[62] XVIII 155, XIX 128 and XX 332. These suggest that the inertness of the three earlier instances is not inherited from x^2 but specific to the scribe of **p**. The same cast of mind shows in several major and minor readings listed at §§ 59–60, ranging from the prosiness of Pr 2 *Y shop me into shrobbis as y a shepherde were* to the timidity at XX 470 of *daunsede* for *caroled*. Lesser idiosyncrasies throughout **p** include omission of the line-initial connective *And*, substitution of a participle for a relative clause and alteration of *ne* to *nother*. Many of these features are neutral in themselves;[63] but the looseness and inaccuracy of **p** arc borne out by the figures: in Pr–XI x^1 has 280 errors (104 major) to **p**'s nearly 900 (of which 196 are major). However, the most notable discrepancy is between the relative proportions of the different types of error. For whereas in the major instances $\mathbf{p}$ is less than twice as inaccurate as x^1, in the minor, at 700:176 $\mathbf{p}$ is four times more inaccurate than x^1. This fact is attributable to the practices noted above and is confirmed by the figures given in § 64. Nonetheless $\mathbf{p}$ attests, for most of x^1's 280 wrong readings, an x^2 text that seems to preserve the archetype.

§ 64. The 'secondary' quality of $\mathbf{p}$'s errors, even more pronounced than that of $\mathbf{p}t$, remains in evidence from XII onwards. The second stage of the comparison is that of $\mathbf{p}$'s readings with x^1's (§ 38 above) where both x^1 and t are present. This reveals, however, only one distinctive feature $\mathbf{p}$ shares with t that could be a relict of x^2, the substitution of *ch-* for metrically necessary *k-* in *kyrke*. In this section, the error-ratio of $\mathbf{p}$ to x^1 is 80:26 for major, and 470:75 for minor readings. The figure for minor variants here is significantly higher, with about six times more $\mathbf{p}$ errors (as opposed to four in Pr–XI); but it is proportionately the same, relative to the major errors (three times as opposed to twice those of x^1 in Pr–XI). Neither the absolute increase nor the proportional consistency is likely to be connected with the presence here of t; for *ex hypothesi* t's agreement with x^1 merely implies faithful preservation of Cx by $\mathbf{p}t$'s postulated source x^2. What the comparison brings out is, instead, that $\mathbf{p}$ was generally much more inaccurate than t in transmitting x^2. That this is a correct interpretation of the relationship between $\mathbf{p}$ and t is borne out by the third stage of the comparison, that between $\mathbf{p}t$ and x^1. Here, to begin with, there are ten major and 65 minor $\mathbf{p}t$ agreements that appear correct where x^1 has erred. It is, of course, not these but the agreements in error that provide evidence for their exclusive common ancestor; but they offer indirect support for $\mathbf{p}$'s claim *before* XII to be in places an accurate witness to x^2 and, through it, to Cx. That claim itself is directly founded on the 335 instances, 120 of them major, where $\mathbf{p}$ alone possesses the right reading. These include *after* XII some 55, about 15 of them major, in which t's convergences in error with x^1 must therefore necessarily be judged coincidental (as argued above at § 38). As the unique witness to eight half-lines and two whole lines (one in RM only)[64] that are not found in x^1 *or* in t, $\mathbf{p}$'s importance for the text of $\mathbf{C}$ is clearly beyond dispute. But among a total of some 1840 instances (affecting about 45% of the poem) where unambiguous family variants are in open contestation, $\mathbf{p}$ gives the right reading in only about 21%. It must follow then that even the best surviving representative of the $\mathbf{p}$ tradition, which is manuscript P, cannot serve as a copy-text for the final version of the poem. This analysis indicates that Skeat might have done better to adopt Y (supplemented where defective by D and I) in preference to the comely, complete but substantively defective P.

vii. *The agreed readings of* $\mathbf{x}$ *and* p^2.

§ 65. Because of the bi-partite structure of the $\mathbf{p}$ sub-family, the archetypal readings of $\mathbf{C}$ cannot be considered immediately, as was possible with the $\mathbf{B}$ Version. The situation instead resembles that of the $r^2\mathbf{m}$ agreements in $\mathbf{A}$ (*A Version* §§ 48–53). For there exists a body of 150 readings in which one branch of one family, here p^2 of $\mathbf{p}$, agrees with $\mathbf{x}$ against the other branch in attesting what appear on intrinsic grounds the readings of the archetype. These already provide the lemmata in the list of p^1's distinctive readings at § 42 above. But it is convenient to document in this section (as earlier for $\mathbf{A}$) the evidence that points to p^2 as the older and more faithful branch. Some half-dozen minor instances where $\mathbf{B}$ happens to support the rejected reading are here attributable to coincidence.

Readings with other-version support

Major +ZAB: VIII 341. **+ZB**: -Ax I 92. **+B**: Pr 226 -ZA. XIV 63 -GN^2. 207. XVI 266 -GP^{2}U. XX 200. 201. 461. XXI 110. 427.

Minor +ZAB: VIII 175. 179. 192 +M. 308. 328. 332. **+AB**: X 115 -N. 117 -YG. 133. **+B**: IV 179. V 116. VI 251. 271. [392 **-B**]. VII 2. VIII 73. 141. 146. IX [310 **-B**]. X 68 -I. 274 +SZ. XI 210. 269. 315. XII 13 +F-N^2. 22 -N^2. [86 -N^2**B**]. XIII [103 -N**B**]. 107 -NP^{2}N^2. 177. XIV 124. 157. 165. 194. 212. XV 3 -D^{2}Ch. [12 -P^{2}D^2**B**]. 17 þat] *om*. 26. 48. 58. 100 +ZW. XVI 57. 75. 182 +M-D^2. 199. 354 +MQF. 355 -u. XVII 171 +F. 311 +W. XIX 89. [133 -**B**Ch]. 334 -DCh. XX 4. 108. 144 +M. 206. XXI 229 +F. 263. 275 +MW. 289. 316. 333 +F. 364 -N^2. 392. 447. 455 +M-ut. 474. XXII 6. 63 +W.

Readings with no other-version parallel

Major III 205. XIII 40. 62. XIV 43. XVI 108. 326. 371 -G. XVII 162 +QZ -P^{2}uCh. 283.

Minor I 40. 66, 76 +M. 98 +MF. II 12 +M. VII 232. VIII 48. 246. IX 78. 97. 117-N. 133 -N. 150. 155. 161. 166. 180. 188. 196. 199. 203. 218 -G. 246. 248. 254. 258 +M. 261 +Q. 262 +RQ. 279. X 6 +Z. 99. 160 -IU. 175 -NP^{2}D. 181. 184 -GN^2. 264. XI 96. 301. 304. XII 163. 173. 204 -N^2. 212. XIII 25. 66 -D^{2}Ch. 134. 185. XV 62. 70. 92. XVI 122. 281 +QZ. 360 -NP^2. XVII 70 +WF. 72. XVIII 144 +RM-G. XIX 10. 37. 65. 104 -G. 106 -t. XX 20. 73.

In these readings, of which some 20 (or about 2% of the text) are major, agreement of x^1 with p^2 (and t usually, p^2 t here jointly representing x^2) is taken to indicate Cx. Lines attested on the basis of **p** and t are not similarly listed, since these have been identified not as separate families but as sub-divisions of the one family x^2.

viii. *The Archetypal Text of the* **C** *Version*

§ 66. After this consideration of the divergent post-archetypal lines of descent, the next section records some 4350 lines that reveal no certain divisions between families or sub-families. As with the **A** and **B** Versions, the selected lemma in the two main lists of family readings at §§ 33–4 and 59–60, unless otherwise stated, has been tacitly understood to preserve the archetype, and the rejected reading to be a corruption of it variously by x^1, **p** or **p**t. But in some 4320 of the poem's 7354 text-lines, just under 60%, Cx is certainly or probably attested, with little or no divergence from individual copies. In the 30 lines marked √, where the **x** and **p** readings remain unsure because of conflicts across family boundaries due to coincidence or contamination, Cx may be recoverable by immediate analysis of the direction of variation. All lines listed are accepted as original, except that incorrect line-division producing no major or minor substantive error has been ignored. The lines here included as archetypal are therefore those (*a*) where x^1 agrees with **p** / **p**t (= x^2); (*b*) where x^1 or an x^1 (sub)-group agrees with one or more branches of **p** identified as preserving the sub-family reading; (*c*) where up to three unrelated members of x^1 join a single two- or three-copy sub-group of **p** (with or without t) in an intrinsically harder reading from which the other variants appear to have been generated. Details of other-version support are not given here except for readings of category (*c*), where genetic character is hardest to determine; but most of these are discussed in the *Textual Notes*. Excluded from the list are (a) the 1825 readings in contestation between the two families, even where on intrinsic and other-version evidence x^1 or **p** (whether or not supported by t) seem original (and so presumptively archetypal); and (*b*) particular right readings (noted in the accounts of the **x** and **p** sub-groups at §§ 31 and 57 above) which may have entered individual members of one family from another version, through felicitous conjecture or coincidence. The latter are noticed at §§ 73–4 and accorded the textual status of 'readings editorially emended by a scribe'. Archetypal text-lines judged to contain errors are examined in §§ 67–70 below.

Pr 1. 3. 5–6. 8–9. √10. 11–12. 14–19. 23–4. 29–32. 34–5. 38. 39–42. 44–5. 47–9. 51–5. 57. 59–60. 62–3. 65–7. 70. 73–7. 81. 85–8. 90. 92. 96–100. 102. 104–6. 109. 114. 116. 119. 121–2. 124–6. 128–35. 137–9. 147–60. 162–3. 165–8. 173–5. 178–80. 184–6. 188. 193–200. 203–7. 208–9. 211–13. 215. 217–20. 222–3. 225–8. 232.

I 1–2. √4. 6–7. √8. 10–18. 21–2. 25–30. 32. 34. 36. 38. 42. 44–7. 50–4. √56. 57–60. 61. 63. 65. 68–75. 77. 80–3. 85–6. 89–91. 93–7. 100. √102. 105–8. 115–20. 123. 126–7. 130–2. 134. 138. 140–1. 143–4. 146. 150. 152–4. 157–8. 163. 165–6. 168–9. 171. 173. 176. 180. 183. 185–6. 191–2. 194–5. 198–9.

II 1–4. 8. 13. 15–18. 20. 23–7. 30–2. 34–6. 38. 40–3. 46–51. 53. 58. 61–5. √67. 69–70. 74–5. 77. 80–2. 85. 87–8. 91. 96–8. 100. 102–5. 109–10. 112–15. 117–20. 122. 124. 127–8. 131–4. 136–8. 140. 142–4. 146–7. 149. 150–2. 155–7. 160–2. 164. 167–8. 170–1. 173. 175. 177. 178. 180–3. 188–9. 193–5. √196?. 197. 199–201. 203–9. 211. 213–15. 219. 222. 224–7. 230. 232–4. 236–9. 241–51.

III 1–4. 8–13. 15. 17–18. 20. 22–4. 26. 28. 30. 32–9. 41–3. 45–7. 49–58. 60. 62–5. 68. 74–76. 78–84. 88. 90. 92. 94. 97–9. 102–7. 110–17. 119–26. 130–1. 135–6. 138. 142–3. 146–51. 154–64. 166–7. 169–72. 177. 180. 182–89. 192–7. 201–2. √203. 206–7. 216–22. 224. 226. 228–32. 233. 234. 236–9. 243. 246. 248–50. 253. 256–8. 261. (262). 263–5. 267–8. 270. 273. 275. 277–8. 281–2. 284–6. 288–9. 291–303. 306–15. 317–18. 320. 322–7. 330–3. 336–7. 339–41. √342. 343–5. 348. 350. 352–5. 357. 359. √360. 361–3. 365. 368. 370–1. 373–4. 377–8. 383–4. 386. 389–91. 393. 396. 398. 401–2. √403. 404–6. 408. 410–11. 413–14. 416. 418–19. 425–6. 428. 430. 432–43. 445–6. 450. √451. 452–5. 458–60. 461–73. 475. 480. 484–9. ?492. 497–8.

IV 2–3. 6. 8–14. 17–20. 22. 24. 26. 28–9. 31–4. 40–2. 44. 47–51. 53. 57–60. 63–5. 67. 69. 71–2. 74. 77–8. 80–1. 83–6. 88–9. 91–4. 98–101. 104. 106. 108–9. 112–14. 116–9. 124. 130. 133. 136–9. 142–5. 148–9. 151–6. 161–2. 165. 168–70. 172. 176. 178. 181–5. 191–6.

V 2–9. 11. 13. 15. 17. 19–20. 22–3. 25–32. 33–4. 36–9. 41. 43. 45–7. 49–50. 52–3. 57–9. 61–5. 68. 70–6. 80–2. 84–7. 89. 92–4. 99. 100–2. 106. 108. 111–13. 117. 120–1. 123–4. 127–9. 131–2. 136. 139–40. 142–7. 149–50. 153. 155–60. 162. 164. 169. 171–4. 176. 178. 180–1. 183. 185–9. 191. 193–9.

VI 2–3. 5. 7–13. 16–17. 19–28. 30–5. 37–8. 43–8. 50. 52. 54. 61–4. 66. 69. 74. 76. 78. 81. 83. 85–7. 89. 91. √96. 97–8. 101–3. 105–6. 108–12. 114–15. 117–24. 127–8. 130–2. 138–9. 142. 145–6. 150. 152. 157–8. 161. 166–72. 174–7. 180. 182–5. 191. 193. 196. 198–200. 202–3. 206–8. 210–14. 217. 221. 225–6. 229–32. 236–7. 240–4. 247. 259–65. 267–8. 272. 277. 286–9. 293–6. 299–300. 302. 305–6. 308–10. 313–15. 318. 322–4. 326. 329–31. 333. 338–40. 343. 345–6. 348–56. 360. 362. 364. 366. 368. 371. 373–5. 377. 385–6. 389. 396. 398. 400. 402. 404–6. 411–12. 415. 419–20. 422–4. 428. 430–2. 434.

VII 10. 12–13. 15. 17–21. 24–5. 27. 30–3. 37. 42. 44. 46. 48. 50–3. 56. 59. 62–3. 65–7. 69. 73. 76–7. 79. 81–3. 84–9. 91. 93. 96. 98–105. 109–10. 113–14. 116–17. 119–21. 126–7. 129–30. 132. 135–6. 139. 141–3. 149–52. 154. 158–63. 165. 167. 169. 174–5. 179. 181. 183. 185–91. 193. 195–8. 200. 203. 206. 208–12. 215. 218–22. 226–7. 230. 234. 237–8. 241–4. 246. 248. 250. 254. 256. 258. 261–2. 264–8. 272. 273–80. 282–3. 287–9. 291–8. 301. 303–5.

VIII 2. 4–9. 11–14. 19. 21–4. 28–9. 31. 33–4. 36. 38. 40. 42–5. 47. 54–5. 59–63. 64 (+**B**). 65–6. 69–72. 75. 77. 79–82. 86. 88–9. 92. 94–6. 98. 100. 102–8. 110. 114. 116–17. 119–21. 123–30. 132–4. 136–8. 140. 142. 144–5. 147. 151–2. 155. 157–8. 161–3. 165. 168–71. 173–4. 176. 181–3. 185–9. 198–206. 209–10. 212–13. 215. 217–18. 222–6. 228. 230. 233–5. 238–43. 245. 247. 249–56. 260–3. 265–6. 268. 270. 272–4. 276–7. 279–81. 285–93. 295–8. 300. 304. 306. 309–11. 316–21. 338. 342. 348. 350–2.

IX 1–7. 10–15. 18. 20–2. 25. 26–7. 28–37. 43–51. 53. 55. 58–9. 61. 64–6. 68–9. 72–3. 75–6. 79–86. 88–9. 91–2. 94. 99–103. 107–8. 110–12. 114–16. 117. 118–19. 121–3. 125. 126–9. 131. 135–6. 138–40. 142–9. 151–2. 154. 155. 156. 158. 163–5. 168–9. 171–2. 176. 178–9. 181. 183–7. 189–92. 194. 198. 204–5. 206. 209–11. 215–16. 219–20. 223–4. 226–9. 231–5. 237–45. 250. 253. 255–6. 262. 263. 264. 267. 269. 271–6. 278. 280. 283. 286–9. 291–2. 294–6. 298. 300–01. 303. 308. 312. 314–15. 317–18. 320–6. 329. 332–7. 339–42. 344. 346–8. 350–1.

X 1–5. 8–10. 12–18. 20–1. 23. 26–8. 30–5. 40. 43–4. 47–9. 53. 55. 57–61. 63. 65. 72. 74–6. 79. 82–3. 85–6. 89. 91–3. 96. 101–3. 106–7. 112. 114. 116. 118. 119. 121. 123–6. 128–9. 131–2. 134–5. 137. 139–42. 144–5. 147–50. 152–3. 155–9. √163. 166. 168–9. 173–4. 176–7. 179–80. 182. 183. 186–8. 190–5. 198. 200–01. 204–5. 209–11. 214–16. 218–24. 226–8. 231–3. 236–40. 241. 243–4. 246–7. 248. 250. 252–4. 256. 259–61. 266. 269–73. 276. 278–81. 283. 285–7. 289–90. 293. 298–9. 302–3. 305. 308–10.

XI 1–2. 4–5. 7–10. 14. 18–20. 22–5. 29–32. 35–7. 41–3. 46–9. 52. 54. 57–60. 61. 62–3. 65–7. 69. 71. 73. 75. 79. 81. 83–6. 88–91. 94. 98–9. 101. 103–5. 110–14. 117–18. 120–5. 127–37. 139–42. 146. 149–52. 156. 158. 162. 172–6. 179–82. 185. 188. 191. 193–9. 204–7. 209. 211–14. 219. 221. 223. 225–30. 237. 239. 241–3. 245. 247–8. 252–62. 265. 267. 275–7. 279. 281–2. 284. 290. 294. 297–9. 302. 305. 307–11. 314.

XII 1. 3. 7–9. 11. 14–15. 19. 27. 31–2. 34. 36. 39–40. 42–5. 46. 48–56. 58–62. 65–8. 72–3. 75–9. 81–2. 84–5. 89–92. 94–6. 99–105. 107–10. 112. 115–17. 119. 123–6. 132–8. 140–1. 143–5. 147. 149. √151. 153–6. 158–62. 164. 165–7.

√168. 170–2. 174–5. 177–9. 181–4. 187–9. 193–4. 196–203. 205. 207. 209–10. √211. 213. 216. 218–20. 222–4. 228–33. 237. 242–7.

XIII 1–4. 10–11. 16. 18. 21. 26–7. 29–36. 38. 43–50. 57–61. 65. 67. 70–1. 73. 75. 80–2. 85–8. 90–1. 93–5. 97. 100–02. 104. 106. 108–9. 111. 113. 115–18. 128–9. 131–2. 135. 137–40. 142–3. 145–6. 149–50. 152–7. 160. 165–9. 174. 184. 187–9. 193–6. 198–9. 202. 205. 207–8. 210–11. 213–16. 218–20. 222. 224–5. 227–9. 232–3. 235–7. 239–46. 248.

XIV 1. 3–6. 11–21. 25. 27. 29. 31. 32. 33. 35–6. 40–2. 44. 49–52. 54–5. 57–9. 61. 64–5. 67. 70. 72–5. 77. 79–81. 83. 85–6. 89. 92–3. ?94. 95–6. 98–102. 104–6. 109–13. 115–17. 119–20. 125–7. 129–33. 135. 137. 139–41. 143. 145–8. 150. 154. 155. 158–9. 161. 163–4. 166–7. 169–78. 180. 183. 187. 191. 192. 195–7. 200–06. 208. 210. ?211. 214–17.

XV 1. 4–6. 9–10. 13–16. 18. 20. 22. 24–5. 29–30. 32. 35–6. √38. 40–5. 49–51. 53–6. 59–60. 63–5. 73. 75. 77–9. 88. 93–6. 99. 102. 104. 108–10. 111. 112–14. 116–17. 119. 121–4. 128–30. 133–4. 136–42. 147–50. 152–3. 155. 159–64. 170. 172. 175. 177–85. 187–9. 190–204. 206–7. √208. 210. 217–18. 223. 227. 229–33. 235–7. 239. 241. 244–6. 247. 251. 253. 255–6. 260. 262–5. 268. 271–2. 275–81. 285. 287–9. 291. 293–4. 298. 301–2. 304–7. 309–11.

XVI 1–2. 5–13. 15–21. 23–30. 32–3. 35. 37–8. 39–41. 44. 47. 50–5. 59–62. 66–72. 77. 82–3. 86–9. 94–100. 103. 106–7. 109–10. 113. 115. 119. 124. 136–7. 129–33. 135–9. 143. 145–8. 150–3. 155–9. 161–3. 168–9. 171–2. 174–6. 179–81. 184–5. 187–93. 195–8. 200–04. 206–27. 229. 231. 233. 235. 237–45. 247–53. 256–8. 262–3. 265. 267–70. 272. 274–80. 282–92. 294–301. 303. 305. 310. 314. 317. 320. 322. 324. 331. 333. 335–44. 346. 348–53. 357–9. 361. 364–9.

XVII 1–3. 5–6. 8–9. 11. 13. 16–19. 21–3. 25–7. 29–38. 40–7. 49–52. 54–60. 62–6. 67. 68–9. 71. 79–80. 83. 85–6. 89–91. √95. 96–7. 100. 102. 105–6. 109. 111. 114 *?116. 119–23. 126–31. 133–5. 137–8. 141–4. 146. 149–50. 152. 154. 156–61. 163. 166–7. 169–70. 172. 174–5. 177–8. 180–1. 183. 185. 187–9. 192. 194–7. 199–202. 204–5. 208. 211–17. 221–3. 226–7. 229–38. 242–5. 248–50. 252–3. 257–8. 260. √267. 270. 273–5. 277. 279–82. 284. 286–91. 293–6. 298– 304. 306–8. 312–14. 316–19.

XVIII 1. 3–9. 11–13. 15–16. 19–20. 22–3. 27–9. 31. 34. 36–7. 42. 44. 48. 51. 53. 54. 56. 59. 61–2. 64–9. 71–2. 74. 76–9. 82. 85–6. 88–93. 100–01. 103. 105. 107. 109–21. 124–5. 128. 132–3. 136–8. 140. 143. 145–51. 153–4. 157–62. 165–8. 170–4. 176–7. 179–80. 182–9. √190. 191–2. 194–6. 198–9. 203. 206. 208. 210–16. 218–21. 223–31. 232. 234–40. 242–3. 245–6. 248–55. 257. 259–68. √271. 272–3. 275–85. 287–8. 290–2.

XIX 1–9. 11–12. 14–15. 20–6. 29–31. 33. 38–40. 42–9. 51–8. 60–2. 67. 71–5. 78–83. 85–8. 90. 92–3. 95–9. 101–03. 107–11. 114. 116–7. 119–27. 129–32. 135–7. 139–42. 144–6. 149–52. 154–63. 166–7. 169–70. 172–3. 175–86. 187. √190. 191. 193–5. 198–9. 201–3. 215–19. 221–3. 225–6. 228–32. 235. 236. 237–8. 243–4. 247. 249–50. 253–4. 258. 259–60. 262–75. 277–84. 286. 288–9. 291. 292. 294–6. 298–300. 303–04. 306. 308–09. 312–16. 318. 320–4. 326. 328–30. 333.

XX 2–3. 5–7. 10–11. 14–19. 21–33. 35–6. √37. 38–49. 51. 53. √55. 57. √58. 59–60. √61. 62. 64. 66. 68. 70. 72. 74. 76. 78. 80–1. 83. 86–90. 92. 95. 99–102. 104. 107. 109–11. 113. 123–4. 127–31. 132. 133–7. 139. 141. 145–8. 150. 152–5. 157. 159–61. 164–7. 169–70. 172. 175. 177. 178–80. 183. 185–7. 189–99. 203. 207. 212–14. 216–17. 219. 221–5. 232–3. 235–40. 242–53. 256. 257. 258–9. 261–6. 268–9. 271. 274–5. 277–80. 282–3. 286–7. 289–92. 295–8. 300–01. 303–6. 308–10. 312–19. 322–5. 326. 327. 329–31. 333–5. 338–40. 342–6. 349–52. 356. 357. 360–1. 363–4. 366–8. 370–2. 374–8. 363–8. 392. 394. 396. 397–8. 401–03. 406–11. 414–17. 421. 423–43. 445–59. 463. 465. 467–9. 472–3. 475–8.

XXI 1. 4–10. 15–20. 22–7. 29. 32–8. 40–1. 43. 46. 49–57. 59. 61. 64–72. √73. 75. 77–81. 83–5. 88–9. 92–4. 96–109. 111–12. √113. 114–26. 128–31. 133–6. 138–57. 160–1. 163–7. 169–74. 176–80. 182–4. √185. 187. 189. √190. 192–3. 196–207. 209. 211. 213. 215–19. 221. 223. 225–8. 231. 234. 237–40. 243–5. 247–51. √252. 253–8. 260–2. 264. 266–8. 270–4. 276–86. 288. 290–5. 297–304. 306–7. 309–11. 313–15. 318. √319. 320–32. 334–9. 341. 343–5. 349. 350–3. √354. 355. 357–8. 360–1. 363. √366. 367–70. 372–5. 377. 379. 382–5. 387–8. 391. 393. √395. 396–400. 402–06. 409. 413. 415–17. √418. 424–6. 430. 432. 434. 436. 438–9. 441–3. 446. 448. 452. 454. 458. 461–2. 464–5. 467–9. 473. 475. 477–9. 481. 483–4.

XXII 1–2. 4–5. 8–9. 11–12. 14. 16. 20–2. 24. 27. 29. 32–4. 38–40. 43–4. 49. 52–3. 57–9. 61. 64. 66. 68. 72–6. 78–9. 81–4. 86–90. 92–4. 96–102. 104–6. √107. 108–9. 111–19. 121–8. 130. 132–5. 137–9. 141–2. 144–50. 153–5. 157–61. 163. 165–9. √170. √171. 173. 176–82. 184–5. 188–91. 193–5. 197. 199. 202–7. 209–11. 213–14. 216–19. 221. 223–30. 233–4. 237–9. 241–2. 244. 246–62. 264–5. 267–75. 277–81. 283–9. 291. 294–6. 298–9. 302–21. 324–6. 328. 330–1. 333. 335–6. 339–42. 344–5. 347–52. 354–63. 365. 369. 372–3. 375–7. 379–85. 387.

ix. *Emendation of Errors in the Archetypal C-Text*

§ 67. There now follows a list of some 90 certain and 23 possible archetypal errors in the C-Text, amounting to between one in every 65 and one in every 80 lines. They are referenced by line-number only, set out in the same form as for **B** (*B Version* § 60 above) and divided into errors of whole lines and errors within lines. Amongst twelve instances of whole-line errors, seven are misdivided, of which three are followed by scribal misexpansion or omission (denoted by ‡); two and two halves are omitted; and one is judged spurious. Available other-version evidence used for emendation is indicated in brackets, and restored or reconstructed readings are listed again under those headings. Examples where the Cx reading is uncertain because both families are wrong or one is absent are given in square brackets and not counted amongst the total.

(i) *Misdivided Lines*
[I 97–100 *div. after* ordre, poynt, faste y; *as* 5 *ll. after* knyghtes, knyghthed, serk, treuthe **p**u]. V [114/15 (*em. after* **ZAB**)]. VI 223/4 (*em. after* **AB**). VIII ‡221/2 (*em. after* **ZAB**). [XI ‡312/13] (*em. after* **B**). [XIV 121–3] (*em. after* **B**). XX 54/5 (*em. after* **B**).
(ii) *Omitted Lines*
XI 312b, XIII 126b, XV 285, XXI 376 (*all added from* **B**).
(iii) *Spurious Line*
After XVII 73.

§ 68. (*i*) *Restored readings*

Some 30 certain and six possible intralinear archetypal errors, all but one major, have been identi-fied and emended by restoration[65] of a secure other-version reading accepted as the likely **C** origi-nal from which Cx has departed. Of these, 26 are made on the basis of **B** and ten of (**Z**)**AB**. Eight emended solely for metrical reasons are marked with the sign ^. Seven cases where Cx itself is undecidable from the split family variants are placed in square brackets. Six emended readings also appear in a single **C** witness, whether by felicitous accident or guess.

Major *From* **ZAB** VII 247. [IX 23]. *From* **AB** III 429. VI ^224. ^273. X [^7]. ^172. ^301. [XI 11]. *From* **B** I ^151. III 490. VII [111]. 131 G. VIII 77–8*a*. XI 56 D. 218. 312. XIII 126. XIV 121–3. XV ^273. 285. XVI 43. 199*a*. XVIII 94 *cf.* N². XIX 13. XX 400 N². 412. 422 N. XXI 76. ^242 *cf.* F. 376. XXII [13]. 120. 329 N. [338]. **Minor** *From* **ZAB** [IX 23].

§ 69. (*ii*) *Reconstructed readings*

Some 30 certain and 16 possible errors, all but four major, are diagnosed in as many lines that appear defective in sense, style or metre. These are corrected through reconstruction of a hypo-thetical original reading on the basis of extant manuscript evidence and comparison with other-version parallels where available. Square brackets denote reconstructions not of the original from a corrupt archetype but of a presumed archetypal reading from the diversely defective sub-archetypes: an example is the 'split variation' in the very first emended reading at Pr 7. Such reconstructed Cx readings, when still judged inauthentic, are nonetheless included here if further proposed correction is founded on direct other-version evidence. Some 25 emendations on metri-cal grounds are marked ^. As with **B**, intralinear transpositions are marked '*trs*', relineations '*rl*', and verbal (formal) substitution / addition / omission by '*v (f) s / a / o*'.

Major [Pr 7 *after* **ZAB**]. ^108 *trs*. ^113 *trs*. ^116, ^118 *vs*. ^120 *trs*. 123 *vs*. ^138 D. I [88] *vo*. 97–100 *rl*. [113] *fs*. [122] *va*. III [6; *cf*. P²F]. ^139 *trs*. [321] *vs*. IV [175]. VI [205] *va*. [220] *vf*. VIII [90²] *fs*. 221/2 *va*; *after* **ZAB**. IX [316] *vs*. X ^22 *trs*. ^164 *trs*. ^267 *vs*. ^301 *vs*. XI ^143 *trs*. ^161 *vs*; *cf*. N². XII 206. XIII ^5,^6 *trs*. XIV ^23 *trs*. [68] *fs*. XV [120] *fs*. ^212 *fs*. XVI ^64 *fs* EWN. XVII [108] *fs*. [^190–1] *fs*. XIX ^91 *trs*. 94 N² *vs*. 138. XXI ^347 *trs*, *fs*. ^445 *trs*. XXII ^301 *fs*. 378 *va*; *after* **B**. **Minor** Pr 127 VIII [90¹] *fs*. XX 91 *fs*. ^173 *fs*. [260] *va*.

§ 70. (*iii*) *Conjectural readings*

In 32 certain and one possible instance where there is little or no direct supporting evidence, intralinear errors have been conjecturally emended, 24 largely on metrical grounds (marked ^). The general factors governing the degree of confidence they can be expected to command have been already described above (*A Version* § 55). Since all of them are major, both the lemma and the rejected archetypal or presumed archetypal readings have been given in full. Square brackets indicate that Cx remains uncertain.

I ^109 luther] fals. ^112 lefte] north. ^155 inmiddes] bitwene (*so // B*). III ^272 salarie] mede. ^329 cesar. V ^154 querele] chyde (*so // B*). ^182 ryht] al. VI ^155 faste²] *om* (*so // B*). ^336 myd] with. VII ^54 be] for. VIII 90 wordynge] worchynge (*so* Pe). XI ^17 leel] *om*. ^126 leide] caste. ^161 doth] maketh (*after* N²). XII 190 -sette] *om*. 208 Worthen] Then. XV [52 was as] as / Ø]. ^220 but] *om*. XVII 147 more] *om* (*so* P²). ^190–1 sethe...name; *Ite...mundum*] *trs*. XVIII ^202 his owne myhte to shewe] to se his o. m. XIX [^28 lich] body (lif t)]. XX [288 the carnel] the car / oure catel]. *So // B*): XXI 90 richeles] riche gold 230 wyes] men (*so* K–D). ^236 buggynge; sullyng] N²; *trs*. ^241 of] *om*. ^408 Saue] Bote. XXII ^292 pleyen] maken. ^293 renkes] men. ^301 hy] they. 366 alle hem] hem. 367 and] *om*.

§ 71. The archetypal errors and their emendations are fully discussed in the *Textual Notes*, so they require only brief general notice here. As in **A** and **B**, they will be found to illustrate both unconscious and deliberate scribal variation from the presumed original. Examples of smaller unconscious visual errors occur at III 90, VI 155, 224, VII 131 and VIII 90 (by anticipation). After XV 284 a whole line has been lost through confusion occasioned by word-initial similarities during the sequence *rede...rychesse...ende : renke...rychesse...rekene*. In the uncertain area between unconscious and deliberate errors belong the replacement of *k-* in *kirke* by *ch-* at Pr 138 (a frequent feature likewise of both **p** and t) and of *myd* by *with* in VI 336. So also do at least some examples of variation to prose order, as at III 139, X 22, XI 143, twice in close succession at XIII 5 and 6, at XVIII 202 (with further smoothing of the verb) and at XIX 91. Split variation of the kind also encountered in the sub-archetypes (e. g. at I 122) occurs in Cx at Pr 7 and IV 175. Very possibly deliberate scribal changes include substitutions of more familiar, non-alliterating synonyms as at Pr 116, I 108, III 272, V 154 and XIX 28. Attempts to identify a less than obvious referent or to puzzle out its sense appear at IX 23 and XI 11 respectively. Censorship was not a feature of the archetypal scribe, despite the forthright **C** Version attacks on royal and clerical abuses that might have provoked it. But a possible exception is XXI 376 (unless the poet himself struck this through as morally presumptuous). The archetype was also free of the spurious lines that afflicted Bx: even the one such example after XVII 73 could arguably be let stand after emendation (though its syntactical link with 73 is weak and it appears suggested by the last phrase of that line).

§ 72. As to the possible presence of material in draft condition, the only passage of any length that might seriously be thought to lack its final finish is Pr 95–124. Since the apparent failure in scribal accuracy here is ten times the average rate for the whole poem, and this could be more charitably attributed not to the scribe but to the rough character of his copy-text, the matter clearly deserves further comment. The errors diagnosed include three inversions to prose order at 108, 113 and 120; two substitutions of the same contextually more expected term at 116 and 118; and one failure to understand the referent at 123 (a line which is not certainly archetypal). All of these features, however, are fairly typical of the Cx scribe's performance in the rest of the work (§ 71 above). Generally speaking, therefore, while the presence of draft material here remains a possibility, the wider notion favoured by R–K of Cx's entire copy-text as an interleaved **B** manuscript with extensive insertions and deletions does not seem convincingly borne out by analysis of the evidence.[66] An essential factor for the Athlone editors, their judgement that the final passūs are a wholly unrevised B-Text, is also rejected here. Their opinion that Cx's source in XXI–XXII was the scribal **B** manuscript B[1] is, however, accepted, but with the modification that some small (possibly preliminary) changes had been inserted by the poet. This is consistent with seeing the source of Cx's Pr–XX not as a working draft but as an authorial fair copy that perhaps still required attention in a few places. As a consequence of this rather different understanding of the archetypal scribe's exemplar, nothing like R–K's practice of combining frequent transpositions and corrections of Cx with the retention of metrically imperfect lines has been permitted in the present edition. Nor have the numerous changes to Cx's minor details of wording and phrasing that R–K make on the basis of their (sometimes emended) texts of the **A** and / or **B** Versions. As already stated (§ 58 above), in the treatment of **C** the linear postulate must act with special force as a brake on editorial intervention. Alterations to the archetypal text have accordingly been restricted mainly to major instances, where the likelihood of corruption has seemed barely open to argument. **C** is thus treated, like **B**, as a work largely embodying its author's final intentions. Where readings only doubtfully archetypal are allowed to stand in the edited text, they are attributed not to presumed error in the archetype but to corruption in the course of sub-archetypal transmission. Only rarely do such readings receive emendation, as at XII 206–08, which is perhaps the most speculative example in this edition.[67]

x. *Readings of Indeterminable Origin*

§ 73. The **C** tradition has relatively few readings that look intrinsically authentic but are randomly distributed across both families and so are not evidently or inferentially archetypal. Much more common are cases where a single group or manuscript from either family contains a major right reading.[68] Thus in two cases of important group-variants, *reik* b at Pr 216 and *while Y can* t at XXI 401, the presumption of descent from Cx through i and x^2 respectively would seem to be tolerably secure. Many individual copies may be taken as uniquely preserving their group readings and thence those of their family and of the archetype, e.g. ms X at VI 382, Y at XXI 304/5 (< y) and D at XI 208 (< u). But in others, singular retention of a group-original is altogether harder to credit. Such readings can only arise (a) by contamination, (b) by felicitous accident, (c) by scribal conjecture or (d) by correction from a lost **C** manuscript superior to Cx. Among possible examples of (b) are *clawes* at VI 149, attested only by I; *more* at XVII 147 in P^2; *be thy comune fode* at XXI 410 in D^2; *craftily* at XXI 242 in F; and *siht* at VII 131 in G.[69] A second important F reading *geste* at VII 106 may belong to (a), (b), (c) or (d), and a third, *ne* at XX 462, could be simply a commonsense response, though again the scribe's awareness of **B** cannot be excluded. N^2 shares the latter correction; but in the light of the evidence given in §§ 39–40 above, contamination probably accounts for this (and for other good N^2 variants like *grettore* at XX 400).

§ 74. Explanation (d), which R–K favour for the 45 N^2 readings they adopt into the text,[70] has been discussed and rejected at § 40. Instead, to account for N^2's four unique right readings with no other-version parallel, (c) is here preferred. The reading *ledis* in t at XX 444 is likewise not beyond an enterprising scribe, to judge by an identical N^2 instance at XXI 412 which, as parallel **B** makes clear, cannot have been the reading of B-Ø, the source of both traditions in these passūs.[71] The most noteworthy possible scribal conjecture occurs not in a single extant manuscript but in the genetic pair <RM> at XVII 116, which from the point of view of its origin is the most challenging crux in the whole text. If R–K's hypothesis of a 'lost pre-archetypal **C** manuscript' found support anywhere, it would be here. However, if the explanation of this line as present in Cx but mechanically lost is accepted,[72] grounds for belief in that source disappear. As with the **B** Version, it thus seems virtually certain that no copy underived from the archetype has left any trace in the manuscript tradition of **C**.

Conclusion

§ 75. Editing **C** has at many points required taking into account the evidence of the other versions. This is clear in particular from the lists at §§ 33 and 59 above, where discrimination of the Cx reading in contestation between the two families has been guided by the archetypal texts of **A** and / or **B**. But the use made of such evidence has been subject to an important constraint. Whereas **AC** unanimity creates a presumption that **B** was unaltered, the linear postulate keeps open the possibility at all points of revision in **C**. So any agreement not of Cx but of one or other sub-archetype with **A** and / or **B** as potentially confirmation of a reading's originality should be viewed very cautiously. For in this situation, every choice in effect requires use of the direct method; and while rigorous attention to the core-text criteria may mitigate, it cannot eliminate the *a priori* element in this procedure (see *Introduction* IV § 27). As a result, solving textual cruces in the final version is in some ways less straightforward than in **B**, especially when the material is entirely new. In compensation, the archetypal **C** tradition proves to be nearly six times less corrupt than that of **B**. And because minor readings are by nature hard to establish as certain errors, few such Cx readings ask to be emended simply because they seem intrinsically less good than those of parallel **B** and / or **A**. To that extent, the present edition of **C**, on comparison with the Athlone, will appear relatively more conservative than those of **A** and **B**. This is explained largely by its very different assessment of the quality of the available textual evidence, itself the product of differences sometimes in applying the same editorial principles, sometimes in the principles themselves. These differences, as will now appear, become acute in relation to the version to be considered next.

THE C VERSION: NOTES

1 For a fuller consideration of the question, see *Intro.* V below §§ 7–11.

2 See ibid. § 10.

3 Except for OC^2 and for B and its constituent members, on which see *B Version* § 71 above.

4 See above *A Version* §§ 17, 21 and *Intro.* I, *Manuscripts* 43–52. The **B** copies BmBoCot (nos. 43–5) are also completed by a **C** beginning before an **A** link.

5 Only one **A** manuscript, the Vernon copy (no. 4), is as early as 1400.

6 Donaldson, *C-Text*, pp. 18–19.

7 See Anne Middleton, 'Acts of Vagrancy...', p. 208.

8 J. Bowers's judgement ('*PP*'s William Langland') that these facts and the frequent surprising agreement of **AC** against **B** point to **C** as the form chronologically closer to **A** has nothing to recommend it. Whether the completion of **A** copies from **C** implies informed contemporary recognition of **C** as the final version or is purely opportunistic remains

a matter of speculation. Bowers, in further taking John But to refer to Will's death while working on **A**, fails to see that the antecedent of *þis werk* A XII 103 can be read as inclusive of *þat here is writen and oper werkes boþe* of 101. The undeveloped nature of A Pr–XI and the uncertain, sketch-like quality of A XII are incongruent with its being later than **B** or **C**.

9 I, *Manuscripts* no. 33; see Kane, *Authorship*, pp. 26–33, *Introduction* V, § 4, and the diagram at § 13.

10 I, *Manuscripts*, nos. 24–28 (x^1; cf. 32, 52); nos. 39–41 (p^2; cf. also 38).

11 *Ibid.*, nos. 30, 36 and nos. 31, 37 (p^1).

12 'Langland's London', in Justice and Kirby-Fulton, eds., *Written Work*, p. 191. The view expressed in the opening of §3 needs to be modified in the light of Horobin 2005[1] and 2010, who demonstrates the London origin of the early x^1 copies and ascribes their SWM dialectal features to faithful preservation of the textual character of their exemplars rather than copying in the SWM area. Such a situation is compatible with **L**'s residence in London until his death and consequently with the genesis of the **C** archetype and sub-archetypes in the capital.

13 This compares with about 70% for **B** and 75% for **A**.

14 Unfortunately for the critical history of **C**, Skeat, like Whitaker, based his edition on a **p** manuscript, P (*Introduction* II, § 41). This was no doubt inevitable, since the two best complete x^1 copies, X and U, had not come to light, and the substantively superior Y was less than ideal, because lacking the first 590 lines. But consultation of Digby 102 and Douce 104 (D), the companion of Additional 35157 (U), in addition to I, might at the least have improved Skeat's text and forestalled the misconception he inadvertently made current of Langland's final phase as one of decline.

15 R–K by contrast place N^2 last in their list of the **p** family's witnesses. But its **p** readings could result from early comparison with a **p** copy in its immediate exemplar. They further propose (p. 102, n. 23) 'a pre-archetypal **C** copy' as the source of some of N^2's 'authoritative corrections'. But these, the only evidence for such a copy, can be explained as either contaminations from **B** or, in a half-dozen cases, enlightened scribal conjectures, as argued at § 40 below. The importance of N^2 is urged by Warner, '*Ur*-B'.

16 Were t extant for Pr–XII and ms T in contention to furnish the base-text, **C** might (like **A** and **B**) have been represented by a third Trinity, Cambridge manuscript in the same East Midland language as the other two. But better than such an appearance of Chaucer-like uniformity is the presentation of at least one of the longer versions in a dialectal form close to that inferred for the author.

17 The two families thus display a symmetrical relationship with each other at the upper level of their descent; see the diagram at § 13 below.

18 The line is XVII 116; see the *Textual Notes*.

19 H was examined and collated when the first edition of Vol I was prepared; but permission to print its readings in the Apparatus was witheld by the then owner. Its substantive variants, consequently now recorded in the Apparatus by kind permission of the present owner, will be seen to be close to those of X (see *R–K* p. 46 n).

20 This explanation does not contradict what is said of b at § 14 above, because Y's one unique right reading (XXI 304/05) is in fact a minor one.

21 E.g. Y at XXI 304/5, I at VI 149, P^2 at XVII 147, D^2 at XXI 410. The first explanation (direct descent) is preferred here as the more economical and probable.

22 See Bowers, '*PP* and the Police', p. 26; idem, 'L's *PP* in Hm 143', pp. 160–66; Calabrese, 'Corrections…in Hm 143', pp. 195–99.

23 For a full list of 323 errors apparently introduced by the scribe of X see *R–K*, p. 176, n. 32.

24 An interpretation strengthened by readings like XVII 78 and XIV 125 (so P^2).

25 *SkC*, p. xxxvii.

26 Skeat also adopted I's additional line after XI 79; his filled-out form of its extra half-line after XII 207 is accepted by Pearsall.

27 'Aspects of Revision', p. 29. For the passage see Appendix in Vol. I p. 743.

28 Wendy Scase, 'Two *PP* C-Text Interpolations'.

29 I. e. IX 85–95, 99, 113–14, 151–2, 161, 163–87, 211, 225, 275–6.

30 R–K, p. 194, agree that IHt have a common ancestor and that neither is a copy of the other.

31 Scase, p. 452. C V 5 in particular might well allude to a passage already known 'outside' the still-developing revision-text and obviously not present in **B**. But it scarcely strains belief that Langland should proleptically mention matter that appears only four passūs later (even if his earlier practice, as at B X 117, is stricter). The discrepancy may tacitly support Middleton's opinion that V 1–108 is the latest written portion of the text (see § 1 above); but that is not in itself proof of **C**'s unfinished state. For further comment on the HtI form, see Middleton ibid. 315n.

32 *SkC*, p. 450.

33 *Editing 'PP'*, p. 351; cf. p. 166. Compare the comment at *B Version* § 57 above.

34 'The "Ilchester" Manuscript of *PP*', p. 191; *R–K*, p. 194.

35 *R–K*, p. 192. The passages are C IX 75–254, A Pr 55–83, C IX 255–79, A Pr 84–95, C Pr 91–157 and A Pr 96–109.

36 Pearsall, '"Ilchester" MS', p. 191 and n. 50.

37 The first is retained as a possible true form influenced by Latin *claustrum*.

38 *C Version,* p. 40, where the agreements are listed.

39 Other examples are Pr 216 and IV 180. In D^2 at XV 106 an *l* has been inserted in *take,* the presumed exemplar-reading, evidently found difficult by the copyist.

40 This point is made again apropos of **p** at § 61 below. R–K, by contrast, emend extensively from **A**, **B** or **AB** in combination.

41 These agreements need not be listed here, since they have already appeared in the lemmata at the conclusion of iii above (§§ 33–4). See further §§ 62, 64.

42 The right reading *leode* at X 7 has accordingly not been included in list (a) below, as it occurs among lines not here regarded as a C-Text. The unique **ZC** copy Bodley 851 makes the juncture at the same point (see *Z Version* § 32 below).

43 For its agreements with *p^1* against *p^2* and **x**, see § 67. N^2 also groups with specific *x^1* copies: XID^2 at XIV 125; UD at XVI 183; D at XX 107; XP^2+M at XI 169.

44 *R–K*, p. 102 n. 23.

45 See *B Version*, § 46 above.

46 See, for example, XI 287 and XIV 138 (with *om*).

47 *R–K*, p. 102 n. 23, end. The interpretation of N^2 given here is rejected by Warner, who views the manuscript as partly attesting 'the first edition of the C Version' ('*Ur*-B *PP*', pp.7, 11); but his argument mainly concerns the relation of N^2 to the sub-archetypal traditions of **B**, not those of **C**. Readers are invited to consider whether the account in paragraphs 39–41 of this section or the article expounding Warner's remarkable thesis better deserves the description 'tortuously complicated' (ibid. 10).

48 In G, lines are lacking at XIII 39, 40, 62, 63 and XIV 62, 63.

49 Examples are the dialectal stave-word *mid* at III 252 preserved by e, Q, K (but lost in **x** and the other **p** copies) and <RM>'s unique line at XVII 116.

50 The error is shared by the C-Text interpolation in Digby 145 (K^2), which may derive from <PE>'s common source.

51 Two that are potentially major require comment. First, in *is*] *is ful ofte* XVII 76 F could have eliminated *ofte* because it seemed metrically over-weighted (W lacks the error entirely). Second, at XVI 148 *swettore*] *sofly ys s.*, though more striking, could have been induced by *sothly* at 146 preceding.

52 This does not strictly belong in R–K's list as an exclusive QS agreement, since it is in substance shared by W (*hande*) and is therefore probably a q error independently corrected by F after recognition of its inferior contextual sense.

53 One of the most striking, the omission of XV 288 after 293, can hardly have occurred except in a common ancestor.

54 See I, *Manuscripts* 30–5, 36–8, 39–41.

55 See *R–K* p. 40, who reckon 32; but among variants they count are such as *leret* for *lereth* at III 212, which are better treated as non-substantive. Those omitted from the Apparatus are given here in full.

56 They do not contribute to determining the reading of Cx but have now been included.

57 The minor exceptions in N at III 175, XXII 329 and in G at VIII 148, IX 63 are probably felicitous scribal corrections *vp gesse*.

58 In these instances, mostly minor, logical consistency has yielded to the recognition of possible revision in **C** and **p**'s coincidental convergence with (an)other version(s). Thus, an **x** reading may be adopted if it appears the harder, as at I 128; but it remains possible that **p** here preserves Cx, as at I 37 and 82.

59 The purely mechanical nature of these errors is underlined by their recurrence respectively in the **p** copies <AV>S and the unrelated EG. This point is accurately noted by Carnegy 'C-Text of *PP*', p. 15.

60 R–K's emendation (eliminating *bokes* / *ȝe*), though elegant, is otiose.

61 Both versions of the line are rejected by R–K in a reconstruction that leaves an inauthentic masculine ending in 14[0] and alters the sense of 14[2].

62 This also undergoes major emendation by R–K, who reject both traditions for the reading of K–D's B-Text, a reconstruction based partially on evidence from **C**.

63 For an earlier comparison of **p** and **x** (requiring some modification in the light of the present examination), see Schmidt, 'C Version'.

64 It is understood here both that XVII 116 is authentic and that it was not inserted in the ancestor of <RM> from a source outside the archetypal tradition.

65 For details of the three main processes of emendation, see *A Version* § 56.

66 See *R–K*, p. 89. For further consideration of the status of the Ophni-Phineas passage see *Z Version* § 6 below.

67 See the *Textual Notes ad loc*.

68 Minor readings are ignored here since, as has been amply demonstrated in this *Introduction*, most of these could in principle be due to coincidence.

69 Examples where two or three unrelated copies agree in a right reading are *hy* SN at I 187, *cople* <PE> + N (by correction) at II 190 and *ben* EWN at XVI 64.

70 *R–K*, p. 102, n. 23.

71 As this source, *B-Ø*, has already been analysed (at the end of *B Version* §§ 72–4 above), no further comparison of B XIX–XX and C XXI–XXII is necessary here.

72 See the *Textual Notes* for an account of the possible mechanism of loss.

The Z Version

i. *The* Z-Text *as a draft version or work in progress*

§ 1. An uncontroversial claim could be made for noticing the version of Pr–VIII in manuscript Bodley 851 (**Z**), which was dismissed by Skeat and ignored by Kane (*Introduction* II § 35). This is that **Z** is simply an **A** copy that lacks about 40% of the text but has some worthwhile variants suggesting possible descent from a non-archetypal **A** source. However, as stated above (*Intro.* II § 147), its peculiar qualities seem to the present editor to justify Rigg and Brewer's identification of **Z** as a separate version of the poem, earlier than **A**. A convincing demonstration of their claim that the text is not a finished work but a draft would create a presumption (though it could not prove) that it is also by Langland. An investigation might thus profitably begin with this question, because there are available for comparison with **Z** two other portions of text in what may be an unfinished state, C Pr 95–124 and A XII 1–98. It has already been argued (*C Version* § 72 above) that the Ophni-Phineas addition does not certainly reflect an unfinished original, because it displays typical characteristics of the archetypal scribe (even if concentrated to an unusual degree). So any examination of the issue should make explicit at the outset that inferior scribal work and authorial draft text are not always easy to tell apart. While application of the direct method has earlier favoured a 'scribal' interpretation of the state of this passage, the 'authorial draft' interpretation can be defended on the grounds that the level of transmission-error present is statistically improbable.[1] Given the uncertainty, therefore, comparison is also worth making with a second possible draft sequence, Passus XII of **A**, which is here accepted as authentic up to line 98 (*A Version* §§ 69–75). In relation to assessing the status of **Z**, this **A** continuation is arguably more relevant than C Pr 95–124; for it is some twenty years nearer in time to Bodley 851's hypothesised original and, like some of **Z**, attests material that the poet did not re-use (see § 6).

§ 2. The initial evidence that Rigg-Brewer ('R–B' hereafter) adduce for **Z**'s provisional character (pp. 13–14) is its internal inconsistencies. One such is its failure to mention at Pr 15 the dungeon that will be referred to 85 lines later. Here, though the text does not necessarily imply that the dreamer must have noticed the dungeon, the unprepared reference seems clumsy. It has perhaps only one major parallel ascribable to lack of final revision, the Dreamer's waking in **C** at XIX 334 without apparently having first fallen asleep at XVIII 180. The fact that no dungeon is referred to in **C** (*R–B* p. 13, n. 45) might even lead to suspicion of influence from the later version. However, comparison with C Pr 87–8 shows that **Z** differs completely from **C** in focussing not on the dale's diabolic inhabitants but on its weather. To turn from an 'inconsistency' to a redundancy: the phrase *as dym as a cloude* at Z 16b is reminiscent of A III 180 but also appears in **Z** at its proper place. Here it would seem less likely that this is an echo of **A** than that **A** eliminated an earlier use of the phrase in **Z** in order to avoid repetition, and inserted a dungeon reference to prepare for Holy Church's later mention. This example, though not proving the Bodley 851 text a draft, indicates its priority and possible originality. For since Z Pr 16b–17 do not derive from the **AB** or **C** forms of these lines, if they are scribal they must be what R–B call an 'unmotivated imitation' (p. 15).

§ 3. More cogent evidence of **Z**'s probable draft character is found in IV 122–30, lines that are absent from **A** at this point but recur as Z V 1–9 and correspond to A IV 140–49. R–B persuasively judge the first occurrence to be an earlier-written passage that was left uncancelled after the later one was composed, and for that reason was found in Bodley 851's immediate exemplar or in that exemplar's holograph source. Supplementary evidence for this conclusion is the three lines immediately before it (IV 119–21), which were presumably intended to be deleted as part of the larger transposition of this passage. These appear genuine in content and expression, for they make good sense, are in the poet's best manner and fit well with the preceding list of *impossibilia*. Moreover, the metrical form of 120 (Type IIa) and the cross-caesural wordplay on *manere* and *manes* in 121 are established Langlandian 'fingerprints' (see *Intro.* IV *Editing the Text* § 41 and Appendix I § 6. iii below). Also genuine in feel is line 124, and though part of its sense is found in A IV 143b, it can hardly derive from the latter. For A IV 143b looks like a reversion to **Z** IV 124 rather than to its re-written form at Z V 3, which compares the dumbstruck villains to a stone, not to a sluggish horse. The lines hypothetically deleted in **A** from the dialogue at Z IV 130–32 also exhibit authenticating features like the internally-rhymed b-verse of Type Ic at 131, which resembles such half-lines as B XIX 338 //. But one noteworthy sign of specifically draft character here is the grammatical ambiguity of 132. Another is the metrical awkwardness of 126, which must scan as *ab / ba* unless *seyden* is treated as an 'onset' or anacrusis and the stresses are placed on *Resoun* and *ryghtfullyche* to give a Type IIIa line. The passage as a whole would therefore seem to indicate re-working at two successive stages; and even on its second occurrence, at Z V 1–9, it has still not reached the form finally achieved in A IV 141–50. For **A**, as already noted, introduces new changes: at 143b, 149b–150a and, most importantly, 145a, where the needed stave-word finally replaces *seyde* at the metrically still defective // Z V 5. To assign these **Z** variants to a careless copyist of the **A** Version requires assuming that, though he had no problem at IV 124 with a rare dialectal word (*stuty*, recorded only here by MED), he twice substituted *seyde* for the familar *reherside*. For the latter is a lexically easy word used over a dozen times in like circumstances, as at Z Pr 113, V 76 and, in close association with *Resoun* and *seyde*, at B XI 413 //. It is much more credible, therefore, that the poet *first* wrote the obvious *seyde* but later replaced it with a suitable alliterating synonym (MED s.v. *rehersen* 4 (a)) in order to normalise the metre (even though finally he omitted the line in revising to **B**).[2]

§ 4. A similar situation suggestive of a still fluid text is found in the statement at III 1 that Lady Mede was alone, although at II 214 earlier it was said that Favel stayed with her. As R–B point out, the chance that this was scribally produced is slight, whereas a draft might well have contained such an 'uncancelled inconsistency.' The line-and-a-half here considered to have been revised in **A** are unlikely to be a scribal derivate from the **A** form, since the first has normative scansion and the second a 'small-word' stave (*to*) that is typical of Langland's practice from his earliest period (IV § 47 below). What the four **A** lines apparently do is to modify an original in which Favel was intended to be present throughout Mede's interview with the King. The exact point of Langland's changed conception can be located at the beginning of Z III. Here the first ten lines remain untouched in **A** except for line 10, the redundant b-half of which might have called for alteration. This line, of the rare variant-type IIa, has now been replaced by one of Type IIIa that again has a grammatical monosyllable (*be*) as its first stave.

§ 5. R–B's third separate example involves I 100–02, which they suspect may be a draft (note *ad loc*). But they are right also to obelise line 101, which appears a slip by the Bodley 815 scribe induced by taking *other alles* as conjunctive rather than adverbial and misconnecting it with the threat in 102. As relineated and emended here by insertion of *ye,* the line now corresponds exactly to its **A** equivalent. But **A**'s posited cancellation of the injunction to mildness in Z 100 removes a line of the Type IIa which, with its typically Langlandian structure, may be presumed authentic. The uncommon compound *loue-lawes* employed here is found in *Piers Plowman* only once again, in the singular, at C XVII 130. But the **Z** use is very unlikely to be a scribal recollection of that passage (on which see I § 133 above), as it differs completely from it in both context and referent (cf. § 2 above). The foregoing interpretation assumes *wo* 102, which gives poor sense in context, to be a visual error for *weye*. In the *Indexical Glossary* therefore the attested form has been conservatively glossed 'wretched', as in its other appearance at V 21 //; but it could be an aphetic spelling of the variant *wowon* recorded for the verb's past participle (MED s.v. *weien* v.), allowing a homophonic pun (as, perhaps, it also does at C IX 271, where the copy-text reads the standard *weye*). Alternatively, the lines in their manuscript shape could betoken a provisional phase at which the poet had not yet decided how to complete the b-verse of I 101. This explanation leaves them anacoluthic; but although this is an occasional Langlandian feature, scribal mislineation here could be just as likely. A final possible draft instance is VII 6, where the repetition of *heye weye* from 4 may have been eliminated in **A** as weak, though it looks like scribal dittography (*R–B*, note *ad loc*). These last two examples illustrate the point made at § 1 above about how hard it can be to tell faulty copying from authorial first thoughts. But the fact that in most of them unique **Z** lines that meet the core-text criteria appear *within* presumptive draft passages strengthens the likelihood that those lines are original.

§ 6. The total of **Z** material qualifying for direct comparison with **A** and **C** draft passages is nonetheless small. Apart from the lines showing inversions to prose order (II 141b and V 147b), the most impressive candidate for draft status is the complex at IV 122ff / V 1–10, and especially the repeated IV 126 / V 5, the particular metrical defectiveness of which does not look scribal. These lines somewhat resemble C Pr 116 and 118 where, if *men* in both b-verses had been expuncted in the exemplar and *folk* inserted marginally or supralinearly by the 'editor', the Cx scribe could have mistakenly copied the commoner word and thereby damaged the metre. Another suggestive similarity is the rhythmical parallelism between C Pr 124 *For ʒoure shréwed sóffraunce and ʒóure oune sínne* and Z VI 38 *That [yé] lóueyen hym léuere than yóure oune hértes,* which both also use contrapuntal alliteration in their a-verse (*abb / ax: abb / ab*). Somewhat more ambiguous are the inversions to prose order in Z II 141 and V 147, which recall those in C Pr 108, 113 and 120 but at the same time illustrate a more widely documented tendency of scribes when copying the b-verses (see *B Version* § 65 above). To turn now to a comparison with A XII, line 21 of the latter, unless read as a very rough Type IIIa, finds a parallel in Z V 152. For in both, a stave-word on *w* (*wikkednesse*) would normalise the metre (as effectively, in the latter case, as the more difficult original *wandedes* actually conjectured). But, as so often, it is hard to distinguish authorial from scribal 'meddling.' Much the same is true at 32, where the b-half again fails to alliterate. Lines 49–50 are passably lineated in manuscript J, and they have been so printed in the text. But if it is actually R not J that here preserves the <(RU)J> archetypal text, the original division might have come after the Latin, with the present 50b forming part of a new line that was never completed. Somewhat more compelling is line 62, which is at the limits of tolerable scansion and should perhaps be divided after *answered*, with insertion of *wye* after *welcome*. But here too the lineation could be either the result of scribal incompetence or the faithful reflex of a prose line waiting to be shaped into verse. All in all, a neutral verdict may have to be brought in; for A XII evinces few potential draft-lines as arresting as C Pr 108–15 though, like the **C** passage as a whole, it has many in acceptably finished form (*A Version* §§ 67–74).

§ 7. Some doubts, therefore, surround the question. But if the case for **Z**'s draft character could be sustained in relation to larger structural features (like those discussed in §§ 8 and 19 below), the local co-presence of unfinished with unimpugnable finished lines in **Z**'s unique passages would raise a strong presumption of its integral originality. For while even a proven draft text might be non-Langlandian, one with such lines could almost certainly not. However, acceptance of **Z** as a 'work in progress' need not rely exclusively on the evidence of instances like those examined. There are also the lines hypothetically removed in **A** that are not strictly identifiable as 'draft' work but resemble other (finished) lines rejected for assignable reasons during the process of re-composition. These have features that, without being conspicuously superfluous, may have made them seem otiose. One is II 40's reference to the notaries, along with Simony and Civil, which re-appears little altered at II 119 (retained in **A**), after a line on the latter as recipients of bribes (excised in **A**). A second possibly over-subtle example is Pr 53–6, which Langland might have feared would look odd in a passage satirising clerks if it failed to be read as ironic. Another is Pr 70–3 on justices, less liable to miss the mark but weak after the preceding shot at barristers. Thirdly, there are some lines evidently designed to effect a transition from one stage of the vision to the next. One is Pr 94, the point where **A**'s Passus I begins. Now in **ABC** the *mountain* ('hill' in **Z**) yields its symbolic significance to the *tower*; but **Z** mentions the 'hill' again at 99, the first of two lines removed and replaced in **A**. Together, these references may well seem to suggest the writer's initial uncertainty about the relative importance of the (high) hill: (deep) dale / tower: dungeon antinomies. This motivic issue is resolved only in **B**'s restoration of **Z**'s *castel,* but it reaches an intermediate stage with **A**'s *clyf* at I 4.

§ 8. Finally, three further passages suggest fluid first thoughts awaiting development or possible removal. One is II 1–3, which summarises what precedes and forecasts what is to follow. Another is II 163–70, noted *ad loc* by R–B, who find the uneven syntax an indication of the passage's draft character (as may be the mislineation of 165–66, if it is not scribal). A third is IV 157–59, some transitional lines connected with **Z**'s original passus-division after Reason's final speech. These become redundant with **A**'s new passus-division; but they in any case 'conflict with what follows', as R–B note *ad loc*, since the vision of Reason and the King in fact continues. Such larger passages of transition-marking material cannot easily be explained as scribal in origin. But they would fit well with a context where the poet was trying out his work-in-progress on an 'audience' unfamiliar with it, and so very different from that of his final version.[3]

§ 9. The lines discussed above sit at the boundaries of reasonably identifiable 'draft material.' Others might seem to tell against the draft-hypothesis, because they expand an idea in a way resembling known instances of enthusiastic scribal embellishment.[4] Their genuineness is, however, suggested by their both meeting the core-text criteria and containing in themselves sufficient reason for their later excision. Thus in Pr 57–8, after the passage discussed at § 7 above occurs an attack on religious provisors, coupled with a defence of poor unbeneficed clerks. The second line anticipates IV 118, which is paralleled in **ABC**. But the first line's lack of any echo in later versions may imply that Langland came to think the abuse not notorious enough to justify attacking (whereas the criticism of religious, absent from **A**, appears in a more moderate and traditional guise at B IV 120 // C 116). Another passage, II 163–70 (mentioned at § 8 above), strikes R–B as 'noticeably weak' and as a 'pastiche of earlier lines' (p. 15). But if the repetition of 164 at 168 suggests its 'half-written character,' the misdivision at 165/6 may be otherwise explained (see the *Textual Notes*). The revising poet could well have judged it 'not needed', as R–B say; but its original presence may have been due to his composing it for a primary audience of listeners, who would benefit from some reminder of what had happened. The passage is also defensible as building up to an effective rhetorical climax in the *t*-alliterating 169–70, with their characteristic polysemantic wordplay on two senses of *tene* (MED s.v. *tenen* v. 4 (a), 1). While these lines are thus not definitely proved a draft, they do have a provisional 'feel' which may be connected with their function in oral performance. This is something also suggested by I 86 // A 137, which was removed in **B**, a version apparently aimed at a reading audience.[5] The passage on words and wind at V 34–40 is also very good in itself[6] but could likewise have been excised as a narratorial digression that weakened the moral impact of Reason's sermon. Once again, anticipating an oral audience would account for **Z**'s tone of combined intimacy and urgency, a surmise supported by the use of the pronoun *vs* at line 43 (the line was presumably deleted in **A** as over-explicit and discrepant with *ye* at 41). Much the same seems true of II 1–3, whether this is taken as coming from the narrator or from Holy Church.

§ 10. The passage at VI 68–75 on Truth's elemental powers, by contrast, illustrates not *digressio* but *amplificatio*.[7] Its presumed rejection from **A** appears to initiate a larger process of *abbreviatio* continued in **B**, which names the intercessor-figures Grace and Amendment but not Truth, and even eliminates the residual mention of the tower at A VI 79. Coupled with this passage is the pair of lines on the Windsor masons at 77–8, which may have seemed too locally specific to suit the cosmic context of Truth's activities in 66–74. Here light is thrown on the **A** revision from the vantage point of **B**, which perceptibly heightens the tension by cancelling the 'lack-of-time' trope, a semi-oral feature still remaining vestigially in **A**.[8] But perhaps the chief reason for the passage's removal is its containing a quasi-contradiction that persists in **A** and is cleared up only in **B**. This is the notion of Truth as dwelling both in the heart and in heaven after death. The basic idea is already present in Z VI 92–3 as part of a passage left unaltered by **A**. But as the revision-sequence reveals a maturing conception of divine reality as apprehensible through spiritual conversion *in via,* this would render overt reference to the transcendent domain less appropriate here. Thus in successive stages the love and law of ZA VI 92–3/96–7 are superseded by the submissive charity of B V 607–08 and finally transfigured in the mystical ecclesiology of C VII 256–57. These signs of increasing theological refinement may not prove the originality of the more 'exterior' allegory in Z VI 68–73, but they highlight its 'primitive' character. Given, further, that these lines satisfy the editorial canon of intrinsic acceptability (IV, § 16 below), their independence of the version immediately following emerges clearly. This instance illustrates well how reading all four texts 'synoptically' can bring out a development of key ideas that is much less apparent when they are taken in separation.

§ 11. As noted above (II § 139), the three unique lines in Robert the Robber's speech at V 142–4 are hard to dismiss as scribal, so typical are they of the poet's characteristic modes of thought and expression.[9] Here, perhaps the most likely reason for **A**'s rejecting them might be the implausibility of so adroit a scriptural allusion in the speaker's mouth. For Robert the Robber is conceived both as a type of spiritual extremity and as a contemporary thief begging clemency from his saviour King 'mounted' on the 'palfrey' of the cross.[10] In A V 246, the **Z** lines may therefore have been replaced by one expressing a more generalised notion better fitted to the emblematic aspect of this character's compound identity. As macaronic verses with no later reflex, they invite particular comparison with A XII 50–7, which involve four occurrences of the same two Pauline phrases. The 'signpost allegory' in which those **A** lines occur was abandoned at that point in **B**; but they were recalled for other service in B III 339–44, a passage already in **A** at this point as part of what would be a postulated 80-line addition to the text of **Z**. However, the A XII line meriting closest comparison with Z V 142–4 is 28, which has no **B** parallel, and which cannot have been abandoned by **B** because its cited texts had been used in the Reason-Mede dispute.

§ 12. The longest of these apparent excisions in **A** is the satire on physicians at Z VII 260–78. Although this change is in itself not difficult to account for, the passage has one problematic feature that would seem to question **Z**'s authenticity at this point. This is that in the rhyming lines 258–59 just before it, 259b's last lift attests not the text of parallel **AC** but of a form of **B** here held to be suspect of archetypal corruption. However, if this is a rare exception to the operation of the linear postulate, it could possibly be **B** that restored a pre-**A** reading, and **C** that returned to **A**, not the **Z** scribe who substituted a (corrupt) Bx reading for one originally identical with **AC**. The textual consequence of that conclusion would of course be to support retention of the Bx form of the line as authentic. But as this example is one of several such cases, it will be more conveniently considered with the others at §§ 23–6 below. The main point here is that the passage as a whole seems to accord satisfactorily with the core-text criteria. There is, moreover, a resonance of Langlandian lexis at 276b in the phrase *medecynes shapeth*, which resembles *shop salue* at B XX 307, and a significant hint of the lines' provisional character in the repetition of 262a as 276a. One likely reason for the removal of 265–78 in **A** might be the later use of 271–72 at Z VIII 48, with reference now to lawyers, and preceded by the full psalm-verse earlier quoted in part as 270a (*R–B*, note *ad loc*). These lines, which are revised in **B** and are finally omitted in **C**, stand unchanged in parallel **A**; but it is very hard to imagine any 'scribal author' borrowing them from **A** for insertion at this earlier point. A second possible reason for the postulated cut is that **A**'s argument, which is made to concentrate on the benefits of moderate diet and the dangers of over-indulgence succeeded by ineffective physic, ignores the issue of payment for medical treatment so prominent in **Z**. The stress on doctors' mendacity in the subsequent versions is at odds with **Z**'s open-minded contrast between the *science trewe* and the *leches lyares*; but this need hardly presuppose more than a hardening of Langland's opinion on the topic. What seems beyond dispute is that 277–78 are both underived from any other extant lines of *Piers Plowman* and worthy of its poet. Their essence is kept in A VII 258, which remains unaltered through **B** and **C** despite successive changes to the a-half of the preceding line (Z 264/ A 257/ B 272/ C 296).[11]

ii. *The Content of* **Z** *compared with* **A**

§ 13. This analysis of the evidence for **Z**'s status as a work in process of composition pro-
duces on balance a positive result and opens the serious possibility that the text comes from Lang-
land's hand. It will now be helpful to set out its substantive content by way of a comparison with
A, the version of which **Z**, if it is not original, would have to be a deviant form. Since R–B (pp.
129–137) present these details in their running and tabular concordances, an analytical layout is
adopted here that will supplement rather than duplicate theirs. **Z** is some 40% shorter than **A**, con-
taining 1515 text-lines and three citation-lines to **A**'s 2545 text-lines and 50 citation-lines (count-
ing in Passus XII). The passus-divisions of **Z** and **A** correspond, except at three points: where Z
Pr 94–145 becomes A I 1–55; where V 1–18 becomes A IV 151–58 and V 19–154 is made A V
1–256; and where V 155–66 becomes A VI 1–12 and VI 1–102 becomes A VI 13–106. Otherwise
A Pr 1–109 = Z Pr 1–93; A II 1–198 = Z II 1–215; A III 1–276 = Z III 1–176; A IV 1–140 = Z IV
1–159; A VII 1–307 = Z VII 1–328 and A VIII 1–88 = Z VIII 1–92. Despite these differences,
the **Z** divisions do not betray the palpably scribal character of the passus-ordering in the **B** copy
Corpus 201 (*B Version* § 46 above); rather, they tend to confirm the impression of priority and
provisionality conveyed by the 'draft' passages examined in section i. The other main differences
between the texts, here taken as due to revision of **Z** by **A**, have been arranged under the headings
of omissions, alterations and additions. Major ones are asterisked and possible reasons for the
changes are suggested.

§ 14. (*i*) About 155 of **Z**'s unique lines are omitted by **A** without replacement, 122 in *groups*
of two or more:

Pr 35–6 replaced by one line 34; 53–8 (bishops and religious: see §§ 7–8 above, and with 54b cf. B VI 180b); 70–3
(justices: see § 7). II 1–3 (summarising 'oral' lines: see § 9); 40–2 (40 re-used later at 119 = **ABC**); 163–70 (summarising
lines). III 122–4 (the lady doth protest too much; 122b is almost repeated at IV 59 and with 124b cf. Z II 173 / A 156);
*147–76 (early conception of Conscience, superseded). IV 119–21 ('apodosis' of the 'impossible conditions': deleted as
over-explicit); [122–30] (?uncancelled first draft of V 1–9: see § 3 above); 157–9 (?uncancelled superfluous transitional
lines). V 34–40 (digression: with 39 cf. B XI 163, XVIII 322); 59–60;[12] 73–4 (needless elaboration of 72a; 74b used as
A IX 51b); 142–4 replaced by single new line. VI 68–72 and 74–5 (excision of cosmic details); 77–8 (topical details).
VII 107–8 (circumstantial details); 196–201 (unnecessary details; 197 repeats 175–6); 230–2 (digression: 230a repeats
V 48a; but 230 re-used entire as B IX 72); 260–2; 265–70; 274–8 (detailed attack on doctors: see § 12 above). VIII 75–6
(circumstantial details removed).

Some 34 more *individual lines* are omitted:

Z Pr 36, 64 replaced by a new line; 90 (?lost from **A** but restored in **B**; with 90a cf. VIII 64a //); 145. I 18 (tone perhaps
wrong); 23 (redundant); 39 (too general); 65 (inappropriate imagery); 100 (too indulgent: see § 5). II 10 (cf. 34); 45
(elimination of this characte's rôle); 47 (otiose detail); 100 (over-specific); 118 (redundant); 177 (potentially misleading,
mercy being the king's prerogative); 189 (too detailed here: but re-used at C III 78). III 96 (circumstantial detail). IV 50
(cf. II 45); 152 partly repeats III 92. V 43 (too explicit); 45, 70, 98, 101 (cf. B V 242), 130 (all too circumstantial). VII 31
(echoed in B VI 36); 49 repeats II 208, but changed attitude to minstrels also relevant; 59 (circumstantial detail); 64–8
replaced by 3 ll.; 170 (too circumstantial); 245 (as one l.); 263–4 taken up as A 257–8 (*abbreviatio*); 316 (over-emphatic
repetition; cf. 245 above). VIII 69 (qualified judgement dropped).

Lastly, there are also omitted 16 (half-)lines with identical or recognisable *parallels* in **B** / **C**:

II 16 almost = B 12 (but cf. C 13); 148 (148a = B 174a); 188 almost = B 207; Pr 5 (Pr 5a = C Pr 5a); 35; 189 almost =
C III 78 (discursive lines only part-restored in **B** but not here in **C**). III 18 = **BC** (see § 23 and note 30 below); 28b cf.
B 28 / C 29; 32a = C 33a, 33 = C 32 (details restored in revised form in **C**). IV 17–18 = **BC**. V 59–60; 75a = **BC**; 104a
= B 380a.

§ 15. (*ii*) Some 200 lines receive *revision* in **A**, for which possible reasons are again suggested. First, nearly 40 lines are variously *transposed* (line-references are to the corresponding line-position in **Z**).

Pr 47–8 → after 52, 49–52 → after 42; 59–60 → before 86; 61–3 → after 85; 74–81 → after Z 46 = A Pr 64 (after inserting 6 new ll.). I 116 → before 112. II 68–9 trs; 97 → after 99. III 71–2 trs.; 95 → after 99, 99 → before 95. IV 132–31 → V 1–9. V 139 → after 136. VI 47 → 53.

§ 16. Next, 70 lines and 37 half-lines undergo *total replacement* or *extensive re-writing*.

Pr 16b (repeated at III 131); 63b–64 (too circumstantial); 65 reduced to 2 lines; 89; 94 (see § 7); 98b; 99–100 as 3 lines (see § 7). I 21–3 as 2 ll. (with 23 cf. A III 108, C III 417, XVI 63); 104b; 121a (repeats ref. to Trinity of I 71). II 16; 56b; 60 as 2 ll.; 70–2 (70a and final lift, 71a retained in B 86); 80b (change of referent);[13] 85b (so **BC**: the b-verse of **A** is re-used at C II 156); 97; 99a (removes obscure word); 104 (repeats legal point about Meed's legitimacy already made at 90); 146 and 147b (improve metre); 148 (a-half = B 174a)*; 158b (replaces vacuous last lift); 160 (replaces lexically obscure line); 190a; 214–15 expanded as 4 ll. III 10 (redundant b-half); 28b (strengthens promise: cf **BC**); 39b (heightens dramatic irony). IV 20 (clarifies allegory); 24b (half-line repeated at 31); 62b–63a (the simple **Z** form unlikely to be derived from **A**, which is corrupt in Ax and may have read likewise: see *Textual Notes*); 78b (more exact); 85 (vocalic alliteration or else possibly a draft line with [A] *seyde* intended to stand after *me*); 100b (improves psychological allegory); 125; *130–2 (130 = V 9 ‾ A IV 149; 131 = V 13 = A V 153, 132 = V 15 = A IV 117 / V 154): draft lines. V 3b (a version of Z IV 124 with added wordplay); 24b; 27; 54b (adds new idea); *91–103 replaced by 58–208, a major amplification adding 140 ll: with 96 cf. C XIX 276; 97a = A 107a; 99 = 100; 102–3 = A 142–5; 100 (more general); *124a (major crux: see *Textual Notes*); 129a (removes title to generalise sense); 136b; 140b rewritten; 142–4 replaced by 246. VI 16 (improves sense); 32 transposes line-halves and introduces reinforcing statement; 38 improves metre: for pattern cf. C Pr 124; 44 modifies Biblical sense; 62–3 makes allegory more theologicaly accurate; 65b replaced with richer content but re-used in new line at A 108; 101b (lechery rather than self-love; cf 88 above). VII 6b; 38b (more realistic promise); 48–9 (as 3 ll. strengthening criticism: with 49a cf. II 208); 52a; 54b–55 removes archaic word in 54b; 58 (dissatisfaction with this b-half shown in threefold revision); 61; 64–68 (as 3 ll.); 76–7 replaced by one line; 82b widens reference; 87b repeats 83; 88b changes metre; 91 (circumstantial detail: re-used at B XIX 315; and cf. A 103); 98b repeats 93b; 152b (cf. **B** which retains adv.); 163b avoids anticipation;[14] 165b; 166b; 193b; 234; 238 as A 236; 259b* (= Bx); 263–4 = A 257–8; 271–3 used as VIII 47–9; 286 removes wordplay; 287b; 302b; 310b* (= Bx); 311 (witty rephrasing); 325b (repetition: phrase re-used in B XIII 268a); as new line: 61, 76–7, 91 (b-verse used in A 103 revising Z 98b). VIII 32b (more exact balance); 61 removes obscure macaronic stave; 74 (criticism strengthened); 89b–90 (order changed).

§ 17. A further 107 are revised more selectively by expansion and / or substitution / deletion of a *single word / phrase*. (Non-lexical instances are ignored, and cross-references are given for lines not immediately parallel).

Pr 9a (less specific); 48b (less ambiguous); 50a (less explicit; normalises metre); 61b = A 90 (less mild); 80a = A 71 adds detail and normalises metre; 83b = A 74 (less obvious word); 96a, b (b less specific). I 7b (theologically more exact); 36b (less specific);[15] 56a (more familiar form); 69 gives needed contrast with *word* in 68; 91a and 92b give desired rhetorical repetition often preferred in **AB**; 127a and 128a (theologically more exact). II 7a (fuller phrase); 18b removes jingling rhyme; 49 (interesting re-phrasing with repetition of *myd*); 54b (different referent); 92a (more apt); 107b–8a (transposed for better distinction); 125; 130 (tautological); 132 (= C); 136a (not superfluous). b (2) = **B** (unspecific but apparently restored); 138 (liaisonal stave replaced by lexical verb); 143b and 183a (less limiting); 206b (less vague). III 13b moderates the criticism;[16] 34 improves metre; 36b (less broad);[17] 39b (less restricted); 48b (Ax perhaps in error); 54a (closer to wedding service); 76b removes inappropriate animal associations; 87a (less weak); 90b removes ambiguity;[18] 108b (neutral term contextually more apt); 115a = **C**;[19] 120a (sense more appropriate).[20] IV 4b (synonym provides rhetorical *repetitio* in **ABC**); 10 (perhaps not a revision if *wyl* is a spelling variant of *wel* as at IV 89); 51a alters chagrin to fear; 53a adds disambiguating word (later dropped in C); 71b (preposition typical of C); 76b (more exact: cf.135b; rhetorically repeated verb reduces over-strong possibility); 99 (explicit); 103 (strengthens condition); 141b (better balance of nouns); 143b (more precise); 144a normalises alliteration and gives paronomasia; 146a (less limited reference). V 5a improves metre; 7 (emphasis); 9b (stronger); 10a gives the repetition of verb; 14b (stronger synonym); 31a generalises the warning; 52a = B 25 (formal change); 58 (more explicit); 63b and 77a (lexically recessive synonyms,[21] the latter not favoured by L. elsewhere); 87a (type in place of personification: **C** reverts to **Z**); 104b (less general or spiritual); 109a (more logical); 111a (more economic); 113b replaces difficult archaic word; 118b (less general); 123b (more dramatic); 132a (better rhythm); 136b clarifies sense; 137a (restored in **C**); 149b (neutral, but avoids rhyme with *lay* 150);[22] 152b improves metre, but copy perhaps here corrupt: see *Textual Notes*); 154a (grammatically more explicit); 158b (general term more correct; but cf VI 11). VI 2b tightens metre and avoids obvious (cf. Bx); 3b improves metre; 41b (more specific); 46b strengthens warning; 50a (formal injunction for direct command); 53 (neutral synonym);[23] 56a (cf. 50a); 80b (more comprehensive physical and religious sense);[24] 85 reduces emphasis that **B** restores; 88b raises tone.[25] VII 3b removes unusual collocation;[26] 26a (the converse of the preceding); 45a (more concise); 46a (phrasing more polite); 53b (part of re-written 53–4); 70a distinguishes two acts; 75 alters viewpoint on judgement; 132b (more precise); 134b (synonym);[27] *139b = **C** (see *Textual Notes*); 166b (precise: removes redundant phrase); 176a and 179b (more exact); 182b drops idiolectal variant;[28] 202a (more emphatic); 208a improves metre; 212b strengthens oath; 219b (more exact); 240b (more intimate tone); 241a improves stress-pattern; 253a highlights different vice; 254b = **B** (perhaps revised for play on *longe* at A 247: see *Textual Notes*); 255b; 279b (sharper sense); 281b (cf. Z IV 135); 282a strengthens assertion; 283a (synonym); 298 adds idea; 308a; *310b = Bx (see *Textual Notes*); 313a (synonym replaced perhaps to avoid rhyme); 317 and 321 (same word replaced by stronger);[29] 323a; 326b replaces non-naturalised borrowing. VIII 22 (canonically more definite); *26a = Bx (see *Textual Notes*); 37b (changed metre strengthens rhetoric); 62b (more emphatic); 63a improves phrasing; 64–7 (original past tenses altered: uniformity restored in **B**); 70b (new idea); 91a (concrete for abstract).

Between them, these three categories cover the main cases where revision of **Z** by **A** may be postulated.[30]

§ 18. (*iii*) Some 343 lines of new material with no antecedent in **Z** are *added* in **A**.

Pr 35–9 *after* Z Pr 34 expand attack on false minstrels; 52–4 *after* Z 48 also expand attack on false minstrels; 59–64 *after* Z 46 and 77–9 *after* Z 85 expand criticism of friars and modify criticism of bishops; 96–7 *after* 85; 104–8 *after* 92 add London food-sellers. I 29 *after* Z Pr 119 explains 119; 40 *after* Z Pr 129 rounds off admonition; 162 *after* Z I 111 initiates rhetorical *repetitio*.[31] III 34–89 *after* Z III 36 introduce Meed's corrupt confession and the attack on simony; 196–276 *after* Z III 146 (*amplificatio* on benefits of meed and Conscience's *responsio*). IV 17 (practical wisdom as aid to reason). V 58–106 *after* Z V 91, 108–41 *after* Z 98 and 146–208 *after* Z 104 (amplification of Envy, Greed and Gluttony). VI 61 expands commandment from Bible; 107–126 *after* Z VI 102 (expansion on necessity of virtue as well as grace). VII 53 *after* Z VII 52, 62–9 *after* Z 61, 208–12a *after* Z 211 extend religious argument for charity. VIII 54a *after* Z VIII 55 (new Latin citation).

Finally **A**, although deleting four / five macaronic lines / staves at V 124, 142–3, VII 267 and VIII 69, introduces five new macaronic lines at III 54, 238, 258, V 191 and VII 67, as well as eight more citation-lines at VII 68a, VIII 54a and (amongst the new passages) at III 64a, 85, 221a, 228, 233a and VII 212a.[32]

§ 19. The way in which these hypothetical **A** revisions have been carried out seems to support the case for **Z**'s authenticity, because it is very like what occurs in the canonical revised versions. Although this assertion cannot be illustrated at length here, one example may be given of the 'direction of revision' revealed by the comparison.

> And broughtest me borwes my byddyng to *holde*,
> Wil thy lif lasted to loue me oure alle,
> And eke to be buxum my byddyng to *wyrche*.

A I 75–6 would seem to reduce Z I 21–3 to two lines by replacing *holde* with *wyrche* (so rendering the rest of line 23 redundant) and re-writing 22 with no change of sense. This closely resembles the **C** revision of B II 110–11:

> Bette þe Bedel of Bokynghamshire
> Reynald þe Reue of Rutland sokene

where the new material in C II 112b *and redyng-kynges manye* has been accommodated by trans-ferring B 110b to C 111 and running together **B**'s two b-verses into a single new stave-phrase on *b, Bannebury sokene*. In the postulated revision of Z II 214–15 to A II 195–98 (a passage already touched on at § 4 above), it seems likelier that the earlier text should be the briefer one. For it is in **Z** that 'two' are said to be present and both to 'tremble' on arrest, whereas in the (identical) **ABC** parallel Mede is alone and the extra circumstantial detail (198a) is achieved only at the price of repeating *fere* (197b) and using a filler-phrase (197a). This example, however, recalls A II 51–2:

> And heo be *boun at his bode* his bidding to fulfille,
> *At bedde and at boord* buxum and hende

which a redactor could arguably have reduced to

> And to be boun at ys bede at bord ant at bedde

at Z II 60 by running together the two a-verses. It is thus conceivable that in Z II 214–15 such a redactor similarly condensed four **A** lines into two. What is hard to credit, though, is that he would have changed the plot so as to leave Mede with Favel as her companion and both in a state of fright-ened apprehension.[33] So if deliberate *abbreviatio* is in question at all, it is much more likely to have been authorial and the 'direction of revision' to run from **A → Z**. But this would reveal the poet not as uncertain what to write but as forgetting what he had written (cf. *Intro.* V § 17 below); for at the opening of the immediately following Passus III, Mede is found alone in **Z**, as in **A**. Thus, given the evidence of idiosyncratically Langlandian versification in Z II 215 (see § 4), the likeliest conclu-sion for an unprejudiced reader is that **Z** represents, as R–B argued, an authentic work in process of composition, with the dramatic situation of Passus II as yet undetermined in all its details.

iii. *Authenticating Features of Language, Metre and Style*

§ 20. After due allowance made for their occasional draft character, the **Z** lines that **A** omits or revises (with few exceptions) conform to the core-line criteria in language, style and metre. Bodley 851's linguistic coherence may not be in itself an argument for the authenticity of this (as it never can be for any Middle English) text. But its congruence with the poet's presumed original dialect, that of the South-West Midlands around Malvern, counts as a positive more than a neutral indicator.[34] Nor is the grammatical evidence contradicted by the nature of **Z**'s unique vocabulary. This, however, deserves analysis, as it contains (a) some 50 lexical words absent from **A**, **B** and **C**; (b) six words with senses not instanced elsewhere in *PP*; and (c) eight infrequent words found only once in the canonical versions:

(a) *annueles* Pr 63; *apropre* Pr 58; *asentaunt* III 152; *assch* [tree] V 45; **bewsoun* III 158; *bornet, blanket* III 159; *birch* Pr 9; *boten* v¹ III 158; *bourly* III 159; *caucyon* V 143; *cleken* III 36 (?= *clokken*); *clumse* VII 54 (cf. *claumsen* XV 254); *dekne* VII 231; *delys* III 161; *dollen* IV 124; **feym* VII 326; *fichen* II 160; *Flemmyng* VII 278; *helm* [tree] V 45; *lesewe* II 47; *lewdelyche* III 164; *logge* II 47; *lower* VII 270; *messe* V 37; *morgagen* III 96; *morthrare* VII 263; *nysot* II 99; *quellen* VII 263; *reyken* IV 158; *Schyr Thorsday* VIII 76; (*eny / som*) *skynes* II 180, VIII 34; *smethe* VI 80; *sowsen* II 100; *spanne* VI 78; *stat* Pr 55; *stemen* VI 75; *stowlyche* III 158; *stryuore* VII 196; **stuty* IV 124; *tetheren* III 76; *thondren* Pr 17; *tylen* VI 66; *to-bersten* V 39; *trental* Pr 65; *vnschryuen* VIII 76; *veile* VII 56; *ward* Pr 99; VIII 75; *worsted* V 100.

(b) *beten* VII 170; *foundur* III 176; *glorie* II 72; *multeplyen* III 120; *wellen* VII 286, *witen* VII 59.

(c) *apostata* I 65; *cammok* VII 91; *digneliche* Pr 54; *forsslewthen* VII 65; *pelour* I 65; *pyuysche* VII 139; *provendre* III 33; *staleword* VII 196.

Many of these terms are in keeping with the legal and ecclesiastical registers of Langland's lexis and the few archaic or regional ones are not at odds with it. Among a handful of the most uncommon, three instanced nowhere else[35] fit well enough with the generally recognised features of his usage. *Feym* is a borrowing from French; *bewsoun* is a mongrel form of the French *beau fitz* used at A VIII 146 //, resembling the anglicised (but rare) *beaupere* recorded only once before its appearances at B XVIII 230 and C IX 248;[36] and *stuty* is a restricted dialectal item. One other, *cammok*, occurs in *cammokes ant wedus*[37] at B XIX 315 which, despite a similar context, seems unlikely to have prompted a scribal substitution here, since the **Z** line is locally coherent and **A**'s so far revised as to keep from its source only one stave-word, *colter*.

§ 21. The unique **Z** lines share four stylistic features with the core-text of the canonical versions. One is their juxtaposition of clerkly and colloquial motifs, often involving typically abrupt shifts of idea and image, as at V 34–40 and VI 65–80. Related to this is the use of macaronic lines that weld Latin and English elements into a semantic and syntactical unity, as at V 142–44 or VIII 61 (the former excised, the latter replaced by its native equivalent in **A**). Third, **Z** gives Piers's son at VII 64–8 an allegorical 'command-name' (a device apparently confined to Langland) at once too unlike parallel A VII 72–4 to derive from it and too well fitted to the constraints of the long line to come from an imitator's hand. Fourth, and even more striking, is a special type of homophonic wordplay on grammatical lexemes functioning as stave-words, e.g. *for* at VII 231 and *to* in Pr 64, which closely resembles B XVIII 148. It is hard to imagine these features (especially the last) appearing at all, let alone together, in the work of a scribal redactor.

§ 22. The metrical quality of **Z**'s unique lines is, finally, perhaps their most telling feature, because amongst editorial criteria it is metre that draws on the widest possible range of evidence.[38] These lines not only observe the verse-norms of the relevant core-text (the agreed readings of **ABC**),[39] they also illustrate eight specific features of verse-practice either restricted to or highly distinctive of Langland. These are 'microlexical' or 'small-word' staves; 'transitional', Type II and Type III lines; one- or two-word b-verses with clashed stresses; cognative staves; rhyme; and elastic line-length (on the presence of these in the core-text, see IV §37–9). The first is typically a monosyllabic modal verb, grammatical lexeme or bound morpheme forming a 'full' or, more commonly, 'mute' stave right after the caesura in a standard line. Examples are *be-* at IV 159, *by* at II 97, *for* at VII 231, 260 and *to* at Pr 145. The second exploits a mute key-stave to generate the unique 'transitional' or 'T-type' line scanning *aa[a] / bb*. Examples are II 118, VII 38, 245, 279 and possibly III 158.[40] The third and fourth illustrate unusual variant line-types: IIa (*aaa / xx*) at I 100, III 10, 165, IIb at VII 76 and possibly IV 120; Type III (*ax / ax*) at Pr 50, IV 144 and VIII 74 (all made standard in **A**), and also at IV 126 and V 96 (both possibly in draft form).[41] Fifth, there are examples of the 'monolexical half-line' (*Intro.* IV § 38), with a single word carrying the two final stresses, the first a full stave (*as déstréres* II 146), and of the 'duolexical half-line', with clashing stresses also in a trisyllabic final lift-pair (*tyl they bé thére* II 147).[42] Sixth, 'allophonic' staves appear (IV § 46), including *s / sh* at II 189, III 122, 152, IV 152 and *f / v* in V 142. Seventh, internal rhyme is used at IV 131, final at II 17/18, ?VI 80/1, VII 258/9, 262/3, 324/5, and identical at IV 49/50. Lastly, line-length varies in a manner typical of Langland, from the seventeen syllables of VIII 75 to the nine of VII 170 (the latter not necessarily, as R–B opine *ad loc*, 'an experiment, intended for expansion').[43]

iv. *Objections to the Authenticity of* **Z**

§ 23. The cumulative evidence of language, style and versification set out above creates a presumption that the text in Bodley 851 is a copy, perhaps at one remove, of a Langlandian text-in-progress (though not necessarily a *first* draft). Content, structure and thought are consonant with seeing in it a version more primitive than **A**, which has hitherto been thought the earliest. In its own terms, **Z** may even be 'complete', though obviously not 'finished'.[44] The text ends acceptably (if abruptly) with the sending of Truth's pardon, but before its dramatic tearing by Piers. In **A** this event both forms the climax of the *Visio* and initiates the *Vita*'s quest for Dowel (**Z** has no *Vita*). The one potentially serious objection to this view of **Z** is the presence in it of some readings that in principle could arise from other-version contamination and thus imply its secondary and inauthentic character. Given the weight attached to this process in such **C** manuscripts as N^2 (*C Version* § 40 above), the objection obviously needs to be addressed. Of the 45 possible examples, 18 are substantially attested in the **m** family of **A**, some 27 in **B** and / or **C**. All receive detailed treatment in the *Textual Notes*, but the major ones have been listed together here for convenience. The most important are three in which the Bodley 851 text agrees with archetypal B-Text readings that arguably show as unoriginal on comparison with the joint readings of **A** and **C** (*ii*, nos. 10–12 below).

(i) **Z** *readings found in the* **m** *family of* **A**[45]
(a) *Whole lines*: 1. Z V 59–60 // B V 32–3, C V 134–35. 2, 3. VI 76 (= A VI 82), 79–80 (= A VI 83–4) // B V 592–93, C VII 239–40.
(b) *Half-lines and phrases*: 1. Z I 54 (= A I 106) mene] *om*. 2. I 92 (= A I 143) tene] pyne **AB** (*so* **C**; *not adopted*).[46] 3. II 56 (= A II 47) sesed] feffid (*not adopted*).[47] 4. II 130 (= A II 120 // B) togeder] for euere (*not adopted*).[48] 5. II 155 (= A II 146 // BC) thys men] þis mene. 6. III 93 (= A III 146 // **BC**) hem the gate] ? hem / þe treuþe ofte. 7. IV 151 (= A IV 136 // **BC**) mekenesse] resoun. 8. VI 58 (= A VI 71 // **AB**) in no manere elles nat] loke þat þou leiʒe nouʒt (+ms A). 9. VII 60 leue] *om*. 10. VII 81 (= A VII 86 // **BC**) masse] mynde. 11. VII 165 (= A VII 168) Furst the fycycyan] *trs*. 12. VIII 84 leden] lyuen (*not adopted*).[49]

(ii) **Z** *readings found in* **B**
(a) *Whole lines*: 1. Pr 90 = B Pr 223 (*om* AC). 2. II 148 = B 174 (cf. A II 139). 3. II 188 = B 207 (om **A**).
(b) *Half-lines and phrases*: 1. II 16 = B II 12 // C II 13. 2. II 125 // A II 116 syre. 3. II 136 // A II 127 ynowe. 4. III 87 // A III 140 = B III 151 habbe. 5. V 10 // A IV 150 = B IV 187 ye bidde. 6. V 52 // A 25 = B 25 here wastyng. 7. V 104a // A 209a = B 380a Gloton. 8. VII 152 // A 155 = B VI 170 to mysdon hym eftsones. 9. VII 254 // A 251 = B VI 266 afyngred. 10. VII 259 // A 256, C VIII 294 = B VI 271 for lyflode ys swete. 11. VII 310 // A 290, C VIII 329 = B VI 305 in borw ys to. 12. VIII 26 // A 26, C IX 28 = B VII 24 that they scholde.

(iii) **Z** *readings found in* **C**
(a) *Whole lines*: 1. Pr 35 = C Pr 36. 2. II 189 = C III 78. 3. III 18 = C III 19 (B 18).
(b) *Half-lines and phrases*: 1. Pr 5a = C Pr 5a Ant sey many sellys. 2. I 92 = C 164 tene (see i (a) above). 3. V 124 Quod ye nan / yeuan = C VI 309.[50] 4. VII 139 = C VIII 151 pyuysche. 5. VII 202 = C VIII 223 herke. 6. VII 227 = C VIII 256 hym licuth] þere nede is / þere it nedeþ **AB**.

§ 24. In (i) above the situation is relatively straightforward. Agreements of **m** and **Z**, whether or not with other-version support, may be interpreted as archetypal **A** readings that underwent corruption in **r**. In the case of (b) *2, 3, 4* and *12*, reasons are given in the *Textual Notes* for their not being adopted in the text, and need not be repeated here. More extended comment is required for iii. Thus (a) *1* is judged on balance unlikely to be an echo, despite expressing the hostile attitude to minstrels of **C** (which excises **AB**'s distinction of 'true' minstrels from *iaperes*), because it is one of a syntactically-linked pair, of which the unique second is not clearly inauthentic. (For

2, see comment on ii (a) *3* below). Example *3* may be a case where Ax has lost the line through homoarchy. Under (b), *1* is a line which could have been excluded from **A** (followed in this by **B**) and later part-restored in **C**, where the b-half differs completely.[51] (On *2*, see i (a) above, and on the crux at *3*, note 50). Examples *4* and *5* could both be original first-thoughts revised (the former twice, differently) before final restoration in **C**.[52] Finally, in *6* the **C** reading has gone back from **AB**'s parsimonious to **Z**'s more generous treatment of industrious workmen, further heightening the contrast with that of the slothful by adding 252–53 and *ʒut* in 257. This particular reversion recalls the similarly comprehensive change of attitude noted in (a) *1* above.

§ 25. These examples may be accommodated without too much strain within a view of the revision-process as basically linear, but with occasional restorations of the text's earliest form. They are therefore not compelling evidence that **Z**, whether in its genesis or at its first or present copying, was contaminated from either the **A** Version or from **C**. Much the same appears to hold good for (ii), with only three exceptions which require special attention. One is the case of (a) *1*, where the line's absence from **C** signifies little since the preceding line in the source at B 222, which is in **A** and (in early form) in **Z**, has also been deleted in **C**'s revision. Possibly it was lost in Ax through attention-skip from *manye opere craftes* to *As dikeris* (see the *Textual Notes*). Next, in *2* the **Z** line could somewhat more plausibly be construed as a contamination from **B**; but this occurs as part of 144–47, which already reveal major reconstruction in **A**, with **Z**'s a-half being retrieved for use in B 174 and the replacement **A** line retained, after revision, as B 178. Lastly, in *3* the elements of 188 are (not dissimilarly) re-arranged to form B 207, and those of 189, at a later stage still, fused with B III 77b to produce C III 78. In (b) *1*, the second half-line is closer to **B**, of which 12b is revised in **C** to incorporate *ryche* from Z 16a. It could have been scribally intruded in place of one like A 12; but quite possibly the latter was meant to follow Z 16, which it may have lost mechanically, by eyeskip from *rede...glede* → *red...golde* (though the closeness of *derrest pris* to *pureste perreʒe* points to B 13–14 as here developing the thought of the clearly genuine A 12). In *2, syre* may be conjectured to have been originally present in **A** but haplographically omitted before *certis* and afterwards restored by **B** in later position. In *3* the Ax reading, with its 'strong' (trisyllabic) pre-final dip, could be a scribal substitution or a revision later retracted as over-emphatic (see *Textual Notes*). In *4*, revision of an original *habbe* to *holde* and then back to *haue* in **B** is credible; but this instance remains one where 'first draft' is not easily distinguishable from 'scribal substitution', and in the text the **AC** reading has been preferred for **B** as the stronger. In the case of *5*, the **A** line looks unchallengeable; but **B** could well be 'second thoughts' endorsing the 'first thoughts' in **Z** (cf. VII 254, VIII 26 below). In *6* the verb-phrase *pat he wastide* may be authorial revision or scribal substitution; but as it involves no difference of sense or style, it is retained. In *7* it would seem more probable that **B** is a fusion of **Z**'s a- and **A**'s b-half than that **Z** is an echo of **B**.[53] In *8* Ax is clearly corrupt and its unmetrical *next metten* needs emendation, perhaps even more radically to *mette eftsoone* as in **B**.[54] In *9* the **A** reading, though not easy, might (if scribal) be due to Ax's missing the irony in *afyngred* and replacing it with *alongid* as contextually more appropriate. Alternatively, if the latter was the poet's own 'second thoughts', **B** may here be a 'reversion to first thoughts', as at IV 187 and VII 24.

§ 26. In examples *10–12*, however, although **AC** has (as in (b) *4*) been preferred in the text as 'superior', the present editor, if allowed such second thoughts, might well acknowledge the existence of alternative readings between which the poet himself hesitated and, in all three cases, let Bx stand as what Langland had written in **B**. Thus in *10* the rhyming half-line *for lyflode ys swete* may be defended as having a genuinely Langlandian ring (cf. A Pr 83 //, not in **Z**); *11* on the grounds that its sense is not obviously scribal (though, as no reason for the substitution appears, it could be a coincidental visual error); and *12* as semantically and metrically neutral. These three examples illustrate that the direct method, even when aided by dual-version consensus and controlled by the core-text criteria, cannot distinguish with finality between the scribal and the authentic. Their actual treatment in the present text may nonetheless appear somewhat paradoxical in the light of these observations; but this is the inevitable result of acknowledging both the claims of the analytical criteria and the complexity of the possible historical situation (see further IV § 19). For (unattractively complex as this account appears) the actual copy of **Z** on which Bodley 851 is based, though substantially original, could have been contaminated from a post-archetypal **B** manuscript with readings different from those of agreed **AC**.

§ 27. The editorial uncertainty here acknowledged about those readings is at variance with the earlier largely positive assessment of **Z**. But on closer examination, it need not prove seriously damaging to the latter. For it will be realised that judgement of the authenticity of the text of Bx, although made in the light of the parallel **AC** readings, has had of necessity to be reached independently of a decision on the originality of **Z**. And this originality it is logically essential not to presuppose when attempting to resolve contradictions between the canonical versions that may question the postulate of linear revision (see IV, § 2). Now, since a decision as to the scribal character of Bx in these instances depends solely upon immediate analysis, it runs the risk (like all reconstructions) of being wrong, because the direct method is by nature hypothetico-deductive, rather than purely inductive. The possibility of a mistaken editorial decision therefore obviously cannot be excluded; for while a rigorously 'parallelist' procedure may yield relative certainty, it is not indefectible. All three Bx readings may therefore preserve revisions that the author later reversed, and should arguably not be altered to agree with **A** and **C**. But except where (as here) direct support comes from **Z**, their particular challenges to the general validity of the linear postulate do not seem decisive. For a weighty consideration to be borne in mind is the volume of Bx readings with no **Z** parallel to complicate matters that are convincingly identifiable as defective in sense, style or metre. And it is such general certitude about the scribal origin of their defectiveness that justifies general confidence in the linear postulate. Finally, the pervasive authenticating features analysed in §§ 1–12, 20–22 together point to a linear development in thought and expression from $\mathbf{Z} \rightarrow \mathbf{A} \rightarrow \mathbf{B} \rightarrow \mathbf{C}$,[55] if with occasional reversions (for reasons that may evade surmise) to an earlier condition of the text. On that deliberate but undogmatic note, it should now be permissible to close the enquiry into **Z**'s implications for the other versions, which has arisen in examining the issue of its own authenticity. The next issue to address is the question of presumed errors in **Z** and the best procedure for their editorial treatment.

v. *Emendation of Errors in the Z-Text*

§ 28. It has already been stated (II § 136) that the right way to present the text of **Z** is with minimal alteration to its language and substantive readings. For if Bodley 851 is a unique witness to a distinct version, it ought to be treated as would the archetypal **A**, **B** and **C** manuscripts, had these survived, since like them it is a copy of the original at no more than two removes. But **Z** requires even greater editorial caution because, unlike the canonical versions, it appears to be a draft of the poem in its first known form. Any differences between **Z** and **A** may thus be due to **A**'s revision of its (provisional) text rather than to scribal interference. That said, it will not be surprising, that in a manuscript based on a transcript of the holograph, scribal mistakes occur. But as already shown, these are not easy to distinguish from draft imperfections when only one exemplar survives. The present edition therefore aims to present not a 'reconstruction' of Scribe X's *source* but a readable form of the text in Bodley 851, conservatively corrected in the light of its immediate successor **A** and, where relevant, the later versions. How 'conservative' the treatment of **Z** is may be gauged from the fact that even agreements with Bx readings that are emended in the edited text of **B** are kept in **Z**, since they meet the core-text criteria and may in principle have been revised in **A** (see § 26).

§ 29. Amongst the mechanical slips in Bodley 851, those recognised by its first editors are corrected here, along with some 55 more. Other rejected readings of the copy-text occupy indeterminate ground between possible scribal errors and draft lines faithfully transcribed but unsatisfactory in sense or form or both. The general issue involved has been touched on at § 5; but these instances have been assembled in full at this point for convenience of comparison with similar examples in the three canonical versions (cf. *A Version* §§ 56–8 above). Finally, there are cases where a presumptively authorial text seems to have been altered, perhaps deliberately. Beyond this, only four major conjectures have been adopted, on the assumption that Scribe X or his exemplar substituted an easier reading for a plainly difficult original. Such changes to **Z**'s readings touch the limits of legitimate editorial intervention. But in order to present a text of **Z** that allows for the peculiar character of this version but also meets the 'core-text' criteria, these emendations have been regarded as defensible.[56]

§ 30. The readings given here, like those diagnosed in the archetypal A-text (*A Version* §§ 55–7), illustrate the commoner types of unconscious scribal error. The Z-Text nowhere omits or misplaces lines and so any such divergences from **A** are regarded as due to revision (see § 14). But it has half a dozen misdivided lines: at I 90/1, 95/6, with omission of the last lift at I 79/80 and with damage to metre also at I 101/2, II 165/6, III 133/4 and VI 87. Whether occasioned by ambiguity in the source-manuscript (see § 31) or of purely mechanical origin, this group perhaps overlaps with the final category, since division of long-lines may not have been marked with exactness in the manuscript at the composition stage. Amongst mistakes of visual origin is letter-confusion, as of *e / o* (common in Bodley 851): Pr 113; I 14 *woman*] *women* (?visual error for *womon*); IV 149 *renkes*] *ronkes*; VI 3 *-hem*]*-hom*, 81 *sothe*] *sethe*; of *l* and long *s* at VI 40 *wolt*] *wost*;[57] of *u / n* (common in all traditions) at II 199 *yhouted*] *yhonted*; and of ʒ / þ at III 111 *ye*] *the* and VII 113 *be ye*] *bethe*. Non-specific visual errors occur at Pr 67 *nat*] *om* (confusion after *ant* I 13); I 13 *is*] *as* (?or relict of original *is as*), 29 *seynt*] *senne*.[58] Others perhaps due to simple misreading of the exemplar include at I 123 *For thise arn*] *Foryth* and the somewhat similar *troneth*] *tronen* (pl. for sg.) at I 71; *take hyt*] *taken* at I 131; *vp*] *vn* at II 50 (suggested by following -(o) *un*); *lost*] *?loft* at III 163; *me*] *one* at V 83 and *nas*] *was* at V 155. Dittography is fairly common, as at III 133 *pyte*] *thow pyte*; V 72 *filio*]*filij*; VII 148 *that y*] *thay y*. Haplography is even more frequent, involving omission of a single letter at Pr 112 *non*] *no*,[59] II 133 *bown*] *bow* and IV 141 *nullum*] *nllum*; of a word at Pr 129 *hit* (needed for sense), I 81 *thow*, 101 *ye* (cf. *ye* 100, 102), 114 *kyn*, 129 *Y*, II 192 *go*] (after *to*), III 109 *the*] (after *-eth*; cf. III 17), IV 117 *yt* (?or *yf yt*)] *yf* (cf. VII 12), V 18 *we* after *lib*be, VI 15 *kynde*, 35 *ant*; or of a whole phrase, as at IV 88 *man that*] *om.* and VII 312 *dyne a-*] *om* after *deyn-*. Several cases of eyeskip are illustrated, as at II 171 *the*] *om* → *tho* (or possibly haplography after preceding original **qua*th); III 108 *the*] *om* (→ *thow*); IV 92 *mede*] *me* (→ *ma*de); VI 56 *no*] *om* (*Ploke* → *plonte*) and VII 35 *to my*] *om* → *co-*, *cro-*. Eyeskip sometimes also occurs through alliterative inducement and with omission of a whole phrase, as at II 117 *go gyue*] (after *gyle* → *gold* attraction). The two processes operate together at IV 32 *kyng thenne*, caused by *the* → *thenne* attraction or haplography after *the kynge* 31; at V 27 *thenne*, *y* (attraction to *then* and to *y* 28); at V 89 *that*] *om* after *wyth* and → to *a* and at VI 100 *thou*] *the* (attraction to following *efft*). A recurring omission with a visual and / or *auditory* origin is of the (pre)-final preterite morpheme *-ed-*, as at I 51 *knigted*] *knigten*, 97 *honged*] *hongen* (?for *hongeden*); III 144 *-edest*] *-est* and IV 34 *wordeden*] *worden*, 54 *pleyneden*] *pleynen*. Probably auditory are *bought vs*] *boughtes* at II 6, *ofsent hire*] *ofsentare* at III 38, *my by-*] *by my* at V 25 (unconscious consonantal transposition), *-ted*] *-ked* at VI 99, *he* after *yf* at VI 112, *wyght-*] *wyt-* at VII 22 and the substitution of *to* for *tho* at IV 149 and V 151.

§ 31. A smaller group of about a dozen errors could relate to the draft condition of **Z**'s exemplar. Pr 84 *blyssed*] *om* may arise from a gap in the copy (since eyeskip seems unlikely here) or be a sign of a work-in-progress, but is satisfactorily emendable from **A**. II 87 could be an expuncted authorial first thought (cf. **C**, which restores it with appropriate change in the last lift); 163 *to*] *to that* has anacoluthon; II 141b and V 147 have prose order, so are possibly scribal (cf. the Ophni-Phineas passage in C Pr 105–24 discussed at § 6 above). In VI 37 and 38 *ye* omitted without apparent mechanical reason, and in 77 *ne*] *om* after *-re*, are perhaps errors of haste, whether of a scribe or of the composing poet. In VII 6 *Ich wol*] *Ant schal* is possibly due to unconscious suggestion from *ant* 5, but the draft text may have wanted the pronoun and auxiliary. Other ambiguous cases are VII 50 *seide*] *quad*: ?unconscious substitution; 162 *boȝede] *a yede*: perhaps not certainly an error (see note); VIII 33 *oure*] *om* (?or haplography after *for*); 44 *copiede*] *copede*: possibly auditory error; 68 *beggeres*] *beggaueres*: ?the false form a scribal or authorial slip; 71 *a*] *at*: caused by visual attraction to following *that* and 91 *For*] *Ful*: ?an auditory error induced by following *loue*. All these examples again illustrate the difficulty of telling authorial undecidedness from scribal inaccuracy. But in the light of the other versions, correction would seem to be relatively straightforward, except at VII 162, where the need for a parallel emendation in **A** doubles rather than halving the uncertainty.

§ 32. Finally, a handful of errors may be due in part to conscious scribal intervention. The simplest *þou*] *y* IV 132 perhaps arises from misconstruing the larger contextual sense, though conceivably from simple ȝ / þ confusion. Similarly *wil*] *wel* VI 61 may be motivated partly by a failure to grasp the allegory. Either deliberate or automatic is the substitution of the non-alliterating dialectal variant of a pronominal form at I 113, an error repeated in the archetypes of the other versions.[60] Perhaps the only controversial emendations are four where the sense is acceptable but the metre defective: Pr 12 *me*] *I* (*xa* / *ax*; so AxBx); IV 80 *withseyde*] *seyde* (*aa* / *bb*; so AxBx); V 152 *wandedes*] *mysdedes* (*aa* / *xx*); V 124 *Quodque mnam*] *Quod ye nan* / *yeuan* (possibly a mistranscription following a misunderstanding).[61] As the rationale of these conjectures is given in the *Textual Notes*, brief comment may suffice here. The first two exemplify 'simultaneous' emendation of metrically defective **AB** lines that the **C** parallel shows Langland to have eventually re-written as normative, but with use of the same stave-sounds. The third may well seem as 'adventurous' as the Athlone editors' reconstruction *purses and* at C XXII 219 // and the fourth as otiose as their Latin conjecture *in lateribus Aquilonis* at C I 112b, both rejected (the first in the *Textual Notes,* the second also at II § 111). Probably the best that can be said by way of defence (or apology) is that each of these conjectures aspires to what Russell and Kane call 'an absolute comparison between actual readings and abstractions' (II § 219 above). To follow where angels have not feared to tread is to act, like R–K, in the belief that it is better to have guessed and erred than never to have guessed at all.

vi. §§ 33–5 *Conclusion*

§ 33. Four authentic versions of the poem, only one of them likely to have been completely finished and 'published', have now been described and the sources of their texts analysed in such detail as the scope of this edition permits. To the **A**, **B** and **C** Versions accepted since Skeat has been added the work-in-progress that Langland put aside (but never wholly forgot) after embarking on **A**. Nothing is at present known as to how **Z** became accessible; but it is a fair presumption that interest in *Piers Plowman* was renewed by the release of a second long version soon after the poet's death. This could have stimulated the creation of the various conjoint **AC** manuscripts and thereby led to the discovery and copying of the present Z-Text's lost source. A contemporary reader encountering the latter might well have thought it (as do the Athlone editors) a truncated form of the shorter version **A**, which also now surfaced and circulated. This would explain why, as in the case of **A**, a text of the **C** *Vita* should have been annexed to **Z**; for it is revealing that at least one of the conjoint copies, NLW 733B, adds C X–XXII to its **A** portion at the same point (the end of the second Vision) as does Bodley 851.[62] But before doing so, the Q scribe of **Z** introduced the 100-line linking-passage (= A VIII 82–185) that R–B call 'Q¹'. This ends with a spurious couplet and a colophon that, spurious or not, is inaccurately positioned here.[63]

§ 34. R–B (pp. 28–30) favour seeing Q¹ as based on a second exemplar, distinct from **Z**'s source and textually affiliated with the **A** copies J and U, but not with the **m** family, the relation of which to **Z** is recorded at § 23 (*i*) above. This seems highly probable, and Q¹'s addition may imply its scribe's awareness of the scene with which the Second Vision ended in the most familiar version **B** (as it does in **A**), the tearing of Truth's pardon, followed by a coda on the validity of dreams, pardons and dowel. R–B nonetheless find it 'arguable' that in lines 113–14 (= A VIII 111–12) '*Q* preserves Langland's original draft' because 'the hypermetrical 113 and the non-alliterating 114 would have been enough cause for scribes to rewrite the line' (p. 111, n.). But even if the Q¹ lines were the reflex of a draft, there would be no reason to suppose that they remained such in **A**; for except in Passus XII, **A** does not contain any draft lines. Moreover, as argued in the *Textual Notes* to A VIII 111–12, the **m** tradition has these lines correctly divided, and their substantive readings are supported by α of **B**. The aberrant Q form is thus recognisable as a variant of the corrupt **r** reading, not a reflection of an authorial draft.

§ 35. If this conclusion is correct, there is no obstacle to accepting R–B's wider judgement concerning the whole text, that 'the logic of the second vision is complete' (p. 29) and that **Z** finishes at VIII 91–2:

> [For] loue of here lownesse, Oure Lord hem hath graunted
> Here penaunce ant here purgatorye vpon thys puyr erthe.

What remains of the earliest version thus appears to end on a positive note. This, as subsequent developments prove, was not Langland's last word on the theme, and it may not have been his intended last word even at this early stage. But as it stands, **Z** could fittingly be followed by the colophon that Q^1 affixed to his continuation from **A**: *Explicit vita et visio Petri Plowman*. There, it is obviously wrong , but after VIII 92 would make very good sense.

THE Z VERSION: NOTES

1 See *C Version* § 72 above. In virtue of its possible draft character, the passage has a better claim to be a late addition than does the 'autobiographical' opening of C V, in which Middleton detects allusions to the 1388 Statute of Labourers ('C Version "Autobiography,"') but which shows no comparable stylistic or metrical deficiency.

2 Substitution of *seyde* for *reherside* is instanced in W and N (see *Ka* Apparatus to A IV 145); but the same phenomenon in **Z** requires another interpretation because of differences in the wider context and the double appearance at two locations. However, the case reveals how hard it is to tell scribal prosification from authorial first thoughts in (semi)-prose. (For a parallel, cf. the rhythmically smoother line produced by replacing *haued* at Z V 132 with the less easy *was*). The presence of *quad* in Z VII 50b is taken here as a scribal error, but it could be a first-thought revised to the less usual *seide* at A VII 50 (see § 30 below).

3 An audience that would include many familiar with the B-Text.

4 An example is the lines printed by Skeat from Harley 875 as A II 136 9, 141 3.

5 Despite occasional 'oral' features (e.g. *ye men þat ben murye* at B Pr 209). Other lines suggestive of such a situation include II 1–3 and 10.

6 Discussed in detail in Schmidt, 'Visions and Revisions', pp. 17–18.

7 Similar examples are III 122–24, V 142–44 and VII 196–201, 265–69. Amplification also occurs in shorter doses at I 18, 39, 64; II 10, 47; III 96; IV 50, 152; V 43, 45, 70, 73–4, 130; VII 59, 77, 107–08, 245, 316 and VIII 69, 75–6.

8 From these the moon, the wind and fire have already been omitted.

9 To these may be added *erit* at Z IV 141, which makes good macaronic syntax and is unlikely to be a scribal substitution for **A**'s *with*.

10 See the lyric in Gray, *Religious Lyrics* no. 28, ll. 13–14.

11 The Bx form must be conjectured from the split variants in α and β (*TN ad loc*).

12 These lines, found in **m**, could have been lost from **r**; but see *TN* to C V 134–5.

13 Similar thrice-repeated linear revision (mostly of the b-verses) is seen also at III 28, IV 100, V 9, VI 16, 65, 88, VII 38, 58, 287. Twofold revision is about twice as common: I 21, 69, 104, 127; II 92, 97, 146, 158; III 10; VI 41, 80; VII 3, 6, 25, 54, 87; in the cases of I 128 and VII 139, **C** harks back to **Z**.

14 The half-line better fits the effect of barley-bread and beans (see the *TN*).

15 See MED s.v. *bede* n. 1(c); cf. 2. 60 // A *bode*.

16 This is to take *somme* as 'some', not as a spelling variant of the adv. *same* 'together'; but the revision may imply both.

17 R–B (note *ad loc*) see it as a possible form of *clakken* 'chatter foolishly' (OED s.v. *Clack*); but more probably *e* is an error for *o*, as often in this manuscript.

18 I.e. *fallen* is presumably a West Midland spelling of *fellen* and *ryght* is a noun, not an adverb; the secondary sense works, but is distracting.

19 Possibly original in **A** and replaced by *Conscience* to avoid an internal rhyme here after Ax had corrupted *gabbe* to *leiʒe*.

20 The sense of the verb is presumably intended to be as in MED s.v. Ib (a) 'augment' (not 3, as at B VI 326), and of the noun as in MED s.v. *manhede* 2 (a) 'dignity' (not the scantly-attested 3 (f) 'manpower'). Meed would find little favour with the king if she were offering the proposed bridegegroom a private army.

21 The former is not used by **L** elsewhere; *made* in **A** and **C** may be archetypal substitutions.

22 The phrase is found at Pr 118 // and III 87 //.

23 There is no semantic or metrical difference; the reading could also have been *hand* in the intermediate versions (cf. C III 75 //).

24 See MED s.v. *clene* adj. 2 (a), 4 (b).

25 The text is not unproblematic, since **A** might be expected to read *wyf*, as conjectured by Kane after **B** (pp. 445–46); but see *TN* to C VII 249.

26 Paul's association with Rome is correct but unexpected; the **A** revision is, like **BC**, more conventional.

27 The word itself is typical of **L**'s lexis; for the semantic overlap see MED s.v. *haunten* v. 4 (a), illustrated at C XV 198, which links them as synonyms. It seems inconceivable that a scribe would have substituted *haunten*.

28 For the verb's overlap in sense with *putte*, see MED s.v. *pilten* v. 2 (a).

29 Though *gruche* is eliminated from **A**, its return at B VI 314 and C 337 suggests the word's initial presence in the first version, since neither appearance in **Z** would seem to derive from these (wholly new) lines.

30 A handful of cases where **A** diverges from **Z** do not count as revisions but probably indicate an error in Ax, which is emended here from **Z**: A I 39, 94, 110*, 116, 183 (so **B**; perhaps emend **A**?); II 59, 142; III 18 (so **BC**; possibly lost in **A** through homoarchy and should perhaps be inserted in **A**), 101b (?possibly dittography), 116; IV 63; V 155 (so **BC**), 156 (so **C**); VI 30 (**Z** right; not clear whether Ax was corrupt, as it is unknowable), 66 (possibly revised out as obscure); VII 25b (Ax uncertain; cf. **BC**), 89, 90b (so **B**), ?139a, 160b (so **BC**), ?314 (so **BC**); VIII 13, 22. Others may be archetypal but are attested only in **m**, e.g. IV 17–18, which may belong in **A**, though on balance it is rejected here (see *TN*).

31 The line Z I 117, repeated in A 162 to introduce the 'avaricious parsons' sequence, is retained in **BC**, but **C** (like **Z**) uses it only once.

32 Most of the new citations are introduced in the three passūs of the **A** *Vita*.

33 Similarly, a scribe is unlikely to have turned A VI 75–6 into the theologically less exact Z VI 62–3: although baptism consoles, it is not consolation that saves.

34 The apparent counter-indication at I 113 is paralleled in the **AB** archetypes and is here understood in all cases as a scribal error. The form presumed original is attested in two **A** copies, J and N.

35 See MED s.v. *fame* n. (2), recorded *c.* 1425, *stuti* adj; *bewsoun* is not in MED.

36 Ibid. s.v. *beau* adj. 2 (d), (f).

37 Ibid. s.v *cammok* n.; MED's other citations are from encyclopaedias and herbals.

38 All lines have been classified and the results summarised in *Intro.* IV §§ 37–48 and Appendix I; see also Schmidt, *Clerkly Maker* ch. 2 and 'Z-Text: a Metrical Examination'.

39 See *Intro.* IV, 'Core-Text' § 11 (a). Obviously the primary core-text (= **ZABC**) cannot logically be invoked in this connection.

40 For discussion of these terms see *Intro.* IV §§ 37–49 and Schmidt, 'Metrical Examination' pp. 296–9.

41 It may be that *loue and* was originally present or intended to be present before *charite*; see *Textual Notes* for discussion.

42 With the first, cf. XIX / XXI 332(1) *déuísede*, 351/350 *Cóntrícioun*; with the second, cf. *cán súlle* at BC XIX / XXI 402[1].

43 For short lines of similar sound, cf. A XI 83–4 / B X 127–28; several lines of seventeen syllables or more are found in the core-text (e.g. A I 98 // BC 100/97).

44 The Dreamer's awaking and some reflection on his dream (in the manner of A VIII 131ff) could have been envisaged; but without the dramatic quarrel between Piers and the Priest to wake him, something more perfunctory might have sufficed.

45 These are considered in detail by R–B, pp. 23–4. As the strength of attestation for **m** readings obviously fluctuates, only those supported by the 'core-group' AMH[3] are treated as securely preserving **m**, and variations in members present are noted. On this see *A Version* §§ 25, 29.

46 See *TN* on C I 164 for full discussion of this problem.

47 See *TN* on A 47.

48 See *TN* on C II 170.

49 See *TN* on C IX 173.

50 See discussion in *TN* to C VII 309–10.

51 Unlike **A** ms K, which inserts the **C** form of the whole line.

52 See *TN* on C VIII 151 and C VIII 223. **L.** uses *herke* only once.

53 R–B's remark on V 104 ('similar to B V 379; om **A**') is confusing. **Z**'s a-half = **B**'s a-half, but **B**'s b-half = **A**'s.

54 On the synonymity of the adverbs, see MED s.v. *eft-sone(s* adv. 2 (a).

55 For straightforward examples of linear three-stage revision see note 13 above. The postulated existence of Langland's 'repertorium' of half-lines (see Appendix III) may explain some of the exceptions to the general operation of the linear postulate.

56 The issues are fully discussed in the *TN ad loc*.

57 Unless *wost* is a possible abbreviation of *woldest*.

58 Or it could be a misreading as 'hold sin hard' (but the idiom is unattested).

59 Inadvertently omitted from the Apparatus.

60 JN of **A** alone preserve *hy*; but only in **Z** is it in fact metrically essential.

61 The emendation **boȝede] a yede* at VII 163 may also belong here; but possibly the text is not an error (see *TN*).

62 See *Intro*. I, *Manuscripts*, nos 46–51; NLW 733B is no. 51.

63 See *TN* to Z VIII 92 (under C IX 185).

IV. EDITING THE TEXT

i. *The Core-text of* Piers Plowman

(a) *Nature of the Core-text*

§ 1. The principles and procedures adopted in this edition have been frequently mentioned earlier in the *Introduction*; there now follows a direct examination of the theoretical and practical problems of editing the poem. Four independent versions have been accepted, and in the last section, in order to justify recognition of **Z** as a work by the author of **A**, **B** and **C**, the Bodley 851 text has been examined in the light of criteria derived from the poem's 'core-lines'. That these criteria are editorially relevant for much more than the authentication of **Z** (III, *Z Version* §§ 20–22) is clear from their use in relation to Passus XII of **A** (III, *A Version* §§ 69–71); but that they provide an empirical test of originality in all the versions makes them crucial to the idea of a parallel-text. Further, since each textual tradition shows corruption at every level of transmission, these criteria are almost as important for editing any one version on its own. The discussion therefore begins with the concept underlying the basis of the entire enterprise: that of the 'core' lines attested in common by two or more versions.

§ 2. If the 'originality' of a unique reading is certain only when it conforms with the core-text criteria, it would follow that *Piers Plowman* should ideally be edited 'in parallel'.[1] But since parallel-editing depends on the authoritativeness of these criteria, the lines that **Z** shares with the canonical versions can be considered to be part of the core-text only if **Z**'s authenticity is settled without reference to these lines. To escape circularity here, it would strictly be necessary to include in the core-text only those in **A**, **B** and **C**. However, there is at present no 'other' evidence that could prove **Z**'s authenticity; so if this is to be tested, it would seem reasonable to employ, provisionally, the portion of text in which **Z** attests lines shared with other versions, as part of a 'heuristic' procedure for discovering the status of its unique lines (for it is chiefly in lines unique to each version that authenticity becomes a major issue). The most important of these groups is **ZABC**; and from a purely logical standpoint, **Z**'s presence in this group may be discounted, the lines in question being regarded as part of a group[2] **ABC** that **Z** happens to join with. But from a procedural point of view, **Z**'s inclusion helps to distinguish, at the outset, lines attested by four independent sources from lines attested by three or two, without forgetting that the hypothesis does not presuppose **Z**'s authenticity. The **ZABC** lines have therefore been listed below at the beginning rather than the end of the core-text repertory. What they suggest is that the revision-process was 'linear' or uni-directional. That is to say, whether Langland added, omitted or altered, he rarely restored his poem to the form it had in the text prior to the one he was revising. For example, **C** very rarely 'revises back' to **A**, or **B** to **Z**.[3] This 'postulate of linearity', which acts as a control on emendation of the text by appeal to another version, is *a priori* in character to the extent that it relies on antecedent probability (see III, *Z Version* §§ 26–7 above); but like the postulate of the core-text, it can be empirically justified. Careful study of the versions as they evolve moves this probability close to virtual certainty.

§ 3. Now, if **Z** lines agreeing with either **A** or **B** or **C** are (provisionally) admitted into the corpus of core-text, those **Z** lines agreeing with all three, the largest possible number of versional witnesses (see § 5), will serve to constitute its 'primary' division. If after enquiry **Z** is not accepted as genuine, and its status in relation to disputed single-version readings becomes that of an unclassified **A** witness (important simply because not descended from Ax), the criterial value of the **ABC** common lines (§ 11 (a) below) will remain unaffected. In any case, the inclusion or exclusion of **Z** does not affect the ascription of special authority to unanimity between versions, since the text becomes increasingly securer where two or more agree. This assertion is not itself *a priori* as applied to any two versions that stand in immediate sequence; but it partly presumes their order determinable on grounds other than their sharing lines located in versions at different stages of development. However, the assumption that revision was linear is strengthened when unique lines are compared in the light of the common lines seen in their several contexts. What the core-text generates is the axiom that 'a line's textual authority is proportional to its versional attestation'. This is the 'principle of unanimity'; and from it arises a 'principle of acceptability' that certifies unique archetypal readings as authentic, without further argument, if they conform to the core-text criteria. These principles furnish the canons of guidance or 'methodological rules'[4] for editing that will be elaborated at §§ 16ff below. But first the rationale of the core-text needs to be explained and fully documented.

§ 4. To determine each version's archetypal text when the pairs of family witnesses disagree, to diagnose errors in that text and (where possible) to emend them, all demand an objective standard of reference as a counter-weight to inevitable editorial bias. But as is generally recognised, the high incidence of random variation at every stage in the traditions rules out systematic reliance on the most objective (because most impersonal) editorial technique, recension. 'Immediate' analysis accordingly proves indispensable in many cases as a means to ascertain the direction of scribal variation (see II §§ 66–7). But the 'direct method' is in essence a hypothetico-deductive procedure; and its key notion of the *lectio difficilior,* though rational in principle, is always partly intuitive in application. Moreover, this important traditional criterion (as those who have used it know) may fall short in practice even of the qualified degree of objectivity[5] to be expected when the text being analysed is a poem. And it is chiefly as a way of minimising the criterion's arbitrariness that the editor needs to look to the norms of language, style and versification that can be derived from the core-text. To qualify for the core-text, lines must ideally show no verbal or syntactic differences that affect sense or metre. But in this area it is possible for the textual critic to be rigorous without becoming rigid, e.g. in acknowledging a line's substantive identity across versions even when a near-synonymous lexical word may have been introduced in a metrical dip. And, after recognition that revision has occurred, common identity may be accorded to two parallel lines even when revision introduces a new stave-word (but without causing change of meaning) into the line's final lift, which is always metrically 'neutral'.[6]

§ 5. In the light of these observations and qualifications, a 'basic core-text' can be recognised in some 4140 lines preserved by two or more versions, of which 2680 (64·5% of this number) are wholly identical.[7] Its primary category **ZABC** is instanced in 530 lines (12·5%); a secondary category in the four three-version groupings **ABC**, **ZAB**, **ZAC** and **ZBC** (some 598 lines or 14·5 %); and a tertiary category in the six two-version groups **ZA**, **ZB**, **ZC**, **AB**, **AC** and **BC** (some 3020 lines or 73%). Of these, **BC** (even when Passūs XXI–XXII are omitted as possibly representing only one version) stands out, with some 41·5% of the common text and 24% of the fully identical lines. In the lists below these eleven groups have, however, been ordered according to the number not of lines but of versions that they represent. For this better indicates a group's relative weight as evidence for authenticity, given that the strength of textual testimony is proportional to its independence (see § 3). But since the manuscripts in each of the **ABC** traditions derive from a common archetype, each version constitutes only one independent witness to the 'common' inter-versional text. It follows that, if **Z** is shown to be authentic (III *Z Version* § 19), the lines of highest authority will be those in **ZABC**, which will have passed a threefold authorial scrutiny and attest an initial version retained to the end, while those in group **ABC** will rank next. On the supposition that **Z** is prior, the group **ZAB** will be of almost equal weight as manifesting a like unbroken linear continuity, again with one (here the final) revision to follow (**B** > **C**). The lines of group **BC**, where not newly added in either version, will witness to one re-working if **A** here retained **Z**, to two if **A** had already revised or added to **Z**. Those of **AB** will be lines revised either twice (**Z** > **A**; **B** > **C**) or, if not present initially in **Z** or finally in **C**, only once. The other large two-member group, also linear, is **ZA**.

§ 6. The remaining five groups ostensibly suggest an absence of linear continuity; but on analysis the discrepant member in each case will be found to disclose archetypal corruption, not to be a genuine revision later reversed.[8] The eight-line **ZBC** group, listed separately below for clarity, is actually part of **ZABC**, though this is concealed by archetypal corruptions in Ax. In the slightly larger **AC** (28 lines) and **ZAC** (20 lines), the fifty or so deviations of **B** may be similarly attributed to corruptions in Bx. In principle, **B** in all these instances could have revised, and **C** could then have reverted to the **A**(**Z**) reading. For even a high antecedent probability of linearity allows that the poet (who seems to have kept a topicalised 'repertory' of (half)-lines for use in different situations)[9] may have re-called or consulted earlier forms of his work. This is what happens at C X 60, which echoes A IX 52; at C X 184, which is nearer to A X 58 than to revised B IX 67; and at C XIX 134b, which corresponds to A X 28b. Of course, the conclusion that most **B** lines diverging from (**Z**)**AC** show not **B** revision but Bx corruption is bound to contain an element of 'subjectivity' arising from the method of direct analysis that diagnoses the corruption; but this can be reduced significantly under the guidance of the core-text norms.[10] Amongst the other two 'non-linear' groups, the **ZC** agreements (few of them perfect) could again be instances of **Z** readings abandoned in **A** and **B** but finally reinstated in **C**.[11] Similarly, **ZB** agreements could be readings removed from **A** and restored in **B**, only to be again rejected in **C**. But though the existence of both groups must qualify the absoluteness of the linear postulate, it does not undermine its general validity. Further, on the (admittedly more complicated) supposition advanced at III *Z Version* § 26, **ZC** and **ZB** breaches of linearity may even evince scribal contamination from **B** or **C** introduced by the copyist of **Z**'s exemplar. That explanation continues to remain possible since the **Z** manuscript Bodley 851 is not a holograph and could have been made by someone who read **C** while it was in progress or soon after its release; but it obviously does not impose itself.

The challenging readings of these small non-linear groups, which represent a mere 0·5% of the core-text, are therefore statistically of limited evidential value. This said, their problematic nature merits the detailed attention that they will receive in the *Textual Notes*.

§ 7. The numerically significant groups, by contrast, are the linear **ZABC**, **ABC**, **ZAB**, **ZA**, **AB** and **BC**. These add up to some 4074 lines that, with the non-linear groups' 66, give a basic core-text of 4140 lines, nearly twice the number of lines in **A** and some 22% of the four versions' total of 19,000. Two further classes of 'auxiliary' lines are also available to augment the core-text. The first is that in which one version diverges from its group in a single lift, most often the last, where a change has least metrical impact (cf. note 6 above) or, in a few cases, within a dip, where metre is again unaffected. A second class consists of half-lines that persist through two, three or four versions. These are illustrated only selectively at § 13, since the main corpus is large enough to satisfy its criterial function. The basic core-text is of fundamental importance for specifying the poet's linguistic and metrical practice in the way needed to provide a strong test of authenticity over the poem's stages of development. It is a convenient resource, in that it consists of whole lines accessible through the parallel-text format even where transposed (since all larger instances are printed twice). It is logically coherent, in recognising lines with multiple attestation as 'original' not *a priori* but on the basis of all and only those features exemplified in the corpus. And it is empirical, in that its analytic postulate of 'Langland' as 'the author of the lines recorded in the corpus' is validated by all and only those lines. The core-text norms, which are both permissive and stipulative, obviously cannot be applied mechanically. But they constitute the most reliable editorial guide for authenticating lines found in only one version, and for identifying those that are spurious or corrupt.

§ 8. The theoretical demands of 'parallel-editing' have now been indicated, and the aims and principles of this edition will be set out in detail in section ii below. But it may be helpful here to summarise them in relation to the core-text norms that provide their basis. The four editorial goals kept in mind have been: to determine and discriminate between competing family-variants in the received versions; to establish the archetypal texts; where essential, to emend them; and to test the **Z** text's claim to originality. For achieving these, appeal is made to criteria based on the 'Langlandian core-text'. The principle of *unanimity* derived from this corpus provides the necessary and sufficient basis for the two main tasks of the 'critical' editor. These are: to test the acceptability of the syntax, lexis, style and versification of unique lines in terms of their conformity with the core-text criteria; and to use these criteria in correcting the errors thus revealed in the archetypal texts of **A**, **B**, **C** and (allowing for the restraints imposed by its draft character) in **Z**. Such a method can never be sufficiently *a posteriori* to satisfy the positivist; for it presumes *a priori* that unanimous attestation is equivalent to unitary authorship of all four versions (or, if only the 'secondary' core-text is in question, the 'canonical' three). But though this presumption cannot be proved on internal evidence alone, it can be defended as a heuristic hypothesis with great potential for discovering whatever data are needed to confirm it. Moreover, conclusions reached by this method count as 'empirical', since they remain open to being falsified by possible future discovery of external evidence that **Z**, **A**, **B** or **C** is not from the hand of the author of the other two / three versions. The approach described, which may for convenience be described as 'critical empiricism', adopts a less simple notion of the substantive text than does the 'positivist' in any of its varieties. But its aim is to formulate criteria of comparable definiteness (see §§ 14–36) that retain the strengths of the recensional and the 'direct' methods, while remaining free of the main weaknesses of all three.

(b) *Repertory of the Basic Core-text*

§ 9. In the corpus of 4140 lines forming the eleven core-text groups, where one or two versions diverge, their sigil is recorded in brackets so as to acknowledge the possibility of revision. 'Ax', 'Bx' and 'Cx' (or '?Z') in brackets imply probable corruption in the respective archetype / exemplar, so such instances are not counted in the total. Lines marked + (or ++) are those where one or more versions display one / two variation(s) in (usually) minor lexical words that have little effect on sense or metre. Small differences in grammatical words or in word-order are not noted. Lines wholly unchanged are in italics and their numbers in brackets after each total; in categorising them, metrically neutral non-lexical variants (such as *a* for *on* or *he*) have been ignored. Line-references are keyed to the versions present in the order **CBAZ**.

§ 10. The *primary* core-text consists of some 530 (247) **ZABC** lines attested in Prologue–Passus IX (references to passus- and line-number are keyed to **C**). The list includes twenty given at § 11 (c), as cases where Bx was probably corrupt, and eight given at § 11 (d), where Ax was corrupt; but these are not counted in the total here.

Pr *1–3*. 6. *19*. 20. *21*. 22–5. 27. *30*. 31. *32*. 33. *34–5*. 41. 42 (Bx). 43. *47*. 49 (Bx). *51*. 66. 67. 68. *69*. 71. 73. 74 (Bx). *76*. 77. *162–63*. 232+ (**Z**). **I** *3*. *10*. 12. *13*. *20*. 30. 33–5. *36*. [*39*(1: Bx; 2:Ax)]. *41*. 45. 48–9. *50–1*. 52. *53*. 54. *57*. 58–9. *61–2*. 63. *68–9*. 70+. 71. *72*. 78. *79–83*. 85. 88. *89–93*. 98+. 101–02. *105*. 126. *127*. [*128–29* **C** *differs in lift* 2]. 134 (Bx). 136. *138*. 140 (?**Z**). 143. 161. 162. *165*. *166–8*. *169* +(Bx). *170*. *171*+ (Bx). *172*. 174. *176*. 177. *178*. 179–80. 182+ (Bx). 188–89. ++190. 191. 194+ (1:Bx;**Z**; 2: Bx). *195*. 196+. 197. 200 (Bx). *201*. **II** 1 (?Bx). *2*. *3*. *5*. *8*. 10. *19*. *23*. *30* (Bx). 47 (?Bx; *see* Textual Notes [*TN*]). *72*. *79*. *93*. 108–09. *113*. 114+ (Bx). 115 (?Ax). *116*. 118. 147. *151*. *153*. 154. *155*. 157. 158 (**Z**). 159. *160*. *162*. 168. *173*. 191 (Bx). *192–93*. 194. *195–96*. *202–03*. 204. *208–10*. 211 (1:**ZA**; 2: Bx). 212 (Bx). *214–16*. *220–30*. 231 (Bx). *232–33*. (234). 238 (?**ZB**x). 240–41. **III** *1*. *2*. *3–5*. 8+. 9+. *12*. 13++. 14+. 15. *17*. 18 (**Z**). *20–22*. 23. *25*. 27. *28*. *34*. 36–7. *127*. 133. 137. 145–46. 147 (?Ax). 150. 151–52. 154. *155–56*. 157–58. 159 (Bx). *160*. 161. 163. *164–65*. 166. 167 (Bx). 170–71. 173. *174–84*. 185+. 187 (Bx). *188–90*. 191. *192–95*. *197–99*. 214–17. *219–24*. 226–31. 258–61. **IV** *2–3*. *5–9*. *10* (Bx; *see TN*). *11*. ++12. 16. 20. +42 (**Z**). 57–8. 59–61. *63–4*. 74. *75*. 78. *79–80*. 81. *88–91*. 94. *96*. 97. 100+. *101–03*. 105. 107. *108*. 109+ (**Z**). 110. 111–12. 124+. 133+. 135. *136–37*. *144*. *146*. 157. *158*. *179*. **V** 115. *116–17*. 118. 119. 121–22. *123*. 128 (Bx). 130–33. 136. *137*. 141. *143–44*. 145 (Bx). 197. 199. **VI** 1+. 2+. *3*. 5–6. 7. *8* (**Z**). *310*. 311. *312*. 316+. *318–19*. 321 (Bx). *326*. 327 (1: Bx; 2: ?**Z**). 328–29. 438–39. 440+. **VII** 56–61. 62 ++. 64 (Bx). *65*. 66. *67*. *154*. 155. 156 (1:**Z**; 2:Bx) 157. 158 (AxBx). 159. *161*. *164–69*. 174–76. 178–82. 185–87. *188*. 192. *193*. 194. 201. 210. *213–14*. *218–19*. 222–5. *226–7*. 228. *229*. 230+ (**C**). 231. 236. 239. *242–3*. 244. 245. 246+ (**C**). 251. *253* (?**Z**). *261–3*. 264. 265+ (**C**). 266. 268 (Bx). **VIII** *2*. 3. 5. *6*. *15*. 16. *18* (**Z**). *20*. 24. 26. 28–9. 32 (Bx; **Z**). *33*. 35. 36. *39*. 40. 42. *62*. *80*. 81. *92*. 94. *95*. 97. *100* (Ax). 101. 102. 103. 105. 106 (Ax). 107. *108*. *113–14*. *116* (Ax). *117*. *119–20*. 121. 123. 125–27. 129++ (**C**). 133. 134. 141. *142*. *149* (?Ax [*uncertain*]). 153. 154. 156. *161–2*. 164. *165*. 171. *172*. 173. *174*. 175 (Ax). 176 (Bx). *180–1*. *183*. 188. 204 (Bx). 207 (Bx). 210 (Ax). 211. *212*. 217 (Bx). *218*. 223. *224*. 226 (Bx). 227. *228*. 231 (Bx). 238+ (**C**). 257+ (**C**). 258 (?**Z**). 273. 274. *276*. +277. 291 (Ax). *293*. [?*294* (**Z**;Bx); *see TN*]. 301–02. 304. 312. *314–15*. 316. *317*. 318. 322. 326. 327++. *328*. 329 (**ZB**x). 331 (**Z**). 333 (Ax). 334. 336+ (Bx). *343*. 346. 347. **IX** *1–3*. *5*. 7 (Bx). 22. 25. 27. 28 (**Z**;Bx). 29. *36*. 37. 41. 46. 58. 61. 63. 167 (Bx). 170. *176*. 177. 185 (Bx).

§ 11. The *secondary* core-text of 588 lines consists of:

(a) Some 320 (272) **ABC** lines attested in Pr–XI; again keyed to **C**.

Pr 48. 53. *54*. 55+. *56*. 57 (Bx). *58*. *62*. *63*. 65. 78. 79. 80 (Bx). *82*. 84. 159. *160*. **I** *1*. 2. 7. **II** *145*. *215–16*. 235. *249–51*. 252+. **III** 31. *38*. 40++. *42*. 45. *47*. 50. *51*. *79*. 80. *82–4*. 85. *115–16*. 127. 249. 264+. 265 (Bx). *266*. 267. *268*. 269 (Ax). *273*. 279. 280. *283*. *312–13*. *428*. 429 (Cx). *431–33*. *436–39*. *441*. *443*. *446–47*. *452*. **IV** *1*. *5*. *92*. *109*. *140*. *142*. *145*. **V**

120. 140. 149. **VI** *63.* 94 (**A**). *196–97.* 198 (Bx). *199.* 203 (Bx). *205–06. 208–10.* 212. *213–17.* 219. *220.* 223. 224 (Bx; Cx). *227. 229.* 231 (Bx). *232.* 233 (Bx). *349–50. 354. 356–60.* 363 (Bx). *364–66. 371. 373–76. 378–79. 383. 387–93. 395–96. 398–400. 403–06.* 407 (AxBx). *414–15. 417.* 438–40. **VII** 220. 267. 269–74. 278. 280–87. 289–90. **VIII** 68–71. 75–9. 82–3. 110. *232.* **IX** *62.* 166+ (Bx). *293. 295.* 296 (Bx). *297–99.* 304 (Ax). *308–09. 311–14. 319–20.* 324. 325 (Bx). *327–39.* 342–44. *346.* 348–50. 352+. **X** *1–5.* 7 (Cx). *8–11.* 12 (Bx). *19–20. 27–33.* 34 (Bx). *44–7. 57–8. 63* (Ax). *64. 68–70. 72–3. 77. 81.* 82++. *83.* 87++. *88–9. 103. 106–07. 113–21. 123–24. 128–40. 143–47.* 151. *155–56. 172. 228. 230–31. 273.* 276 (Bx). *277–81. 295.* 298. **XI** *1. 3. 4. 7–9. 31.* 37 (Bx). 38–41. 47–8. 53–4. *85. 88. 90. 92. 102–03.* +116 (Bx). *117–24. 128–29. 210–11.* 222++. *255. 257. 259–60.* 264 (Bx) *278. 294.*

(b) Some 240 (120) **ZAB** lines attested in B Pr–VII = ZA Pr–VIII; keyed to **B**.

Pr *4. 7. 12–14.* 24. *26. 220.* **I** 14. 16. *17–19. 23.* 24–6. *27–8.* 30. 34. *39.* 48+ (?Bx). *50.* 51. 59. *68. 73.* 76. 80. *82.* 103+. 104 (Bx). 105. 107–09. 110+. *111.* 112 om Bx]. 127 (Ax;Bx). *128–29. 132–33.* 134 (?**Z**). *135. 139. 143.* 144. *146.* 191+ (Bx;**Z**). 199+. 202+. 209+ (Ax). **II** 6. (9). 19. 45. 46. 54. 55. 74. *75.* 102. *105.* 110. 111. *118–19.* 120. 122–4. *125.* 126. *129. 131.* 133. 136 (**A**). 137. 139. *148. 150–51.* 152–54. 156. 158 (?Ax). 159. 161 (?Ax). 162. *164.* 165 (?**Z**). 167. 168 (**Z**). *171–72.* 180 (Bx). *187.* 189. 194. *195. 202. 227–28.* 233. **III** 6. 7. *15.* 23. 25. 29. 102++. 104. 105. 108. 165. 168. *187–91.* 192–93. +194. 195. *196–97.* 198–200. *201. 206–08.* **IV** 13. *14.* ++23. 27. *28–30.* 45. 46 (**Z**?Ax). 49. *51–2.* 59. *64.* +65. *66. 68–70.* +71. *72.* 73. *81.* 87. 91 (**Z**AxBx; *see* Textual Notes). 99 (**Z**). 118. *126. 128. 131. 142.* 191+. *192.* 193. 194. **V** *1.* 10+. *22.* 24. *57. 63.* 72. 73. 224+. *226.* 227+. 381. 382. *460.* 528. 533 (Ax). *552–3.* 556. 560+. *561. 565. 586.* 587+. **VI** *10. 15.* 44. 50+ (**Z**). 51. 55 (?**Z**). 56. *62. 66* (?**A**). 87. 108–9 (Ax). 124. 130. 153. *158. 160.* 166+ (**B**). 169+ (**B**). 183+ (**B**). *186.* 214. *220. 231–4.* 235++ (**Z**;**B**). 236 (**B**). 237. *239–40.* 246. 249. 252. +257. *258.* 269. 275. 285 (Bx). 293++ (**Z**). 299. 315++ (**B**). *318.* 322. **VII** *4.* 9. *10.* 17. *19.* 26+ (**B**). 27. 29. 31+ (**B**). *47.* 50. 61–2+ (**Z**). 96–7+ (**Z**). *98.*

(c) Some 20 (3) **ZAC** lines, keyed to **C**. This list includes lines also given at § 10 on the presumption that in original **B** these lines read as **ZAC** and that in all but II 146 Bx was certainly corrupt.

Pr 42. 49. 57. 74. **I** *50.* 84. **II** 146. 190. 191. **V** 145. **VI** 321. 327. **VII** 156. [158(Ax)]. **VIII** *176.* 204. 217. 226. 336. **IX** 7+. *185.*

(d) Some 8 (3) **ZBC** lines, keyed to **C**. These also appear under the 'primary' category on the assumption that Ax is here corrupt.

I *92.* **III** 19 (?Ax). 225 (?Ax**B**). **V** *130* (Ax). **VII** 157 (Ax uncertain). **VIII** 175 (Ax). 210 (Ax). *291* (Ax).

§ 12. The *tertiary* core-text of 3023 lines consists of:

(a) 130 (60) **ZA** lines attested in Pr–VIII 80; these are keyed to **A**. In four cases Ax and in three cases ms Z are presumed corrupt.

Pr *45. 100.* **I** 101. 110 (Ax). 111. *119–20.* 136. 137+. 138. 169. **II** *22–3.* 24–6. *30–2.* 35. *36–8. 39.* 40+. *41–2.* 43–4. *46.* 48. 49. *50.* 53. *58.* 59 (Ax). *60.* 66. *70–1. 80. 107. 130. 133.* 140. *186.* **IV** *28–30. 53.* 63 (Ax). *66. 73. 89. 91. 107. 133. 136.* 137. 138. *140.* 147. *158* (**Z**). **V** 2. *11–12.* 53. 241. 242+. 254 (**Z**). **VI** *46.* 79 (Ax). 80. *81. 93.* 97. **VII** 10–12. 21. 26+. 30. 33. 43. 109. 115. 124. *125.* 127–28. 130. *131–4. 136.* 137+. 138. *141.* 148. 176. 223. 230. 232++. *227.* **VIII** 11. 12. 14. *15.* 16. *17–18.* 28+. 29–30. 33 (**Z**). 38+. 39–40. 41. 43–6. 47–8. 51. 55–9. 60. 61+. 62+. *74–5.* 78.

(b) 8/9 (1) **ZB** lines (keyed to **B**). In most of these cases the evidence that Ax may be corrupt is not decisive.

Pr 223 (? *l. om* Ax). **I** *36,* 79 (against **AC**; see *TN*). 127. **II** 136 (see *TN*), 163 (see *TN*). [*207; see* Textual Notes]. **III** 168. **V** 25.

(c) 3/4 **ZC** lines (keyed to **C**).

Pr 36 (*l. not in* **AB**). **II** 217 (*against* **AB**). **III** 32–3 (*ll. om* **AB**), 78. **IV** 69. *See* Textual Notes *on all.*

(d) Some 303 (156) **AB** lines; keyed to **B**.

Pr *16.* 35. 36+. 38+. *39. 66.* 222. **I** *30–1.* 64. 180. 198. 205. *208.* **II** *121.* (127). 128. *150–51. 157. 170.* 184. *188.* 190.

210. 234. **III** 10. *37.* 39+. *50.* 63. *73.* 76–7. *80–1.* 82. *89–92.* *94–5.* 99. 103. *216–21.* 222 (Bx). *223.* 224 (Bx). *227.* *229–31.* +232. 233. *234.* 246. *247–49.* +250. *251–53.* 255 (?Ax; Bx). *256.* *259.* 260 (AxBx). *262–63.* *288.* 293. **IV** 111. 137. *146.* **V** *9.* 77.78–9. *80.* 83. *85.* *93.* 94–6. 99–100. 103–05. 106–07. 108 (Ax). 109. 110. 111 (AxBx). 112. +113. *115.* 117. +118. *122.* *124.* 220. 224. 225+. *226–27.* *299.* *302.* *314–15.* *325.* *362.* 456 (?AxBx). +461. 468 (Bx). *562.* *566.* 575 (Bx). *627.* **VI** 50. +58. 59–60 (Bx). *218.* 243. 272 (?Bx). 281 (AxBx). **VII** 80. *106.* *114–18.* +119. *120.* +122. 123. +124. *125.* 127–8. ++129. *130–32.* 133. +134. +135. *137–9.* *153.* +154. *156–57.* +159. 168. +172. 173. ++197. **VIII** *6.* +13. +32. 34–5. *36.* +37. +38. +45. *46.* ++47. *48.* 49–50. +57. *66.* *73.* 81–2. 84. 89. 93 (Bx). +94. 95 (Bx). *98.* *101.* *102.* ++103. *104.* +109. 110. **IX** *28.* *31.* 48–51. *52.* +54. 59. *119.* ++124. +129. *131.* *136.* *156.* 157–8+. 159+. *162.* 163 (AxBx). 164. *165.* *167.* *174–6.* *186.* ++187 (Bx). *198.* +199. +204. *206.* **X** *5–7.* 8+. *12.* *14–16.* 20. ++21. 33–5. 36 (Bx). 46. +47. 48. *49.* 51–2. +59. *60.* +65. 66–7. *72.* +104. *107.* 108 (AxBx). +110. *115.* +116. *119–22.* +123. *124.* *126–29.* *132–33.* *135–6.* +140. *141.* *143.* *150.* +152. *154.* +162. *164–68.* 169. 170. 187. 197+. *198.* +200. 201. 209–10. 212. *215.* 217. *220–21.* 222. *223.* +224. 225. +227. +228. *229.* 293. 295. 331. 332+. *333.* *346.* +347 (?Bx). *348.* 349. 350 (?Ax). +362. +363. *368.* 369. 414. 424. 452–53. 462.

(e) 28 (13) **AC** lines; keyed to **C**. These are also listed in 11 (a) above and are there judged **B** lines that were corrupted in Bx.

Pr 80. **I** 76 (*see* Textual Notes). **III** 124 (*see TN*). 276. **IV** 142. **VI** 198. 203. 205. 224. *233.* *357.* **VII** 170 (*see TN*). **VIII** *207.* 294 (*see TN*). *329* (*see TN*). **IX** 28 (*see TN*). 284. 325. **X** *12.* *34.* 106. *107.* *134.* *143.* **XI** 37. 116. *118.* 211.

(f) 2551 (1804) **BC** lines; keyed to **C**.

Pr *85–6.* *89–92.* +94. +125. *126.* +127. *128–29.* +131. *132.* +134–35. 136. *139.* *141.* +143 (Bx). *148.* +149. *150.* 166. 167. *168.* 169. *173.* *180.* 182. 183. *184.* 185. *186–8.* *190–93.* 194. *195–200.* 202. 203–5. *207–8.* 209–10. *213.* 217. **I** *31.* +139. *150.* 151–4. 155 (BxCx; *see TN*). *156–9.* **II** *24.* 49. 50. 51. *53.* 58. *59–62.* 64. +66. *67.* 69. 71. *84–7.* 89. *92–4.* 96. *97–9.* +103. 211 (Bx). **III** *35.* +56. 57–9. *60.* 61–2. *63.* +64. +66. 69. *70–1.* 72. 422. 424. *425.* 434. +435. *453.* 454. *459–60.* 461. 465. *467.* 468 (Bx). 469. *472.* *474.* 476. 477. *478–9.* 481–2. 486. 487–90. 492 (Bx). +494. *495.* **IV** *25.* *86.* ++114. +119. *130.* ++148. +151. *160.* 169. *171–2.* 173–4. **V** 138. *152.* *153.* 154 (BxCx). *160.* +161. *163–5.* 167. *169.* 170–1. *180.* *191.* **VI** +36–7. 43. *55.* +56. *57–8.* *69.* ++70–2. *73–4.* *77–82.* *85–8.* 90. 94. ++95. *97.* 103. 125. *128–33.* 134 (Cx). *135.* *152.* 153. *154.* 155 (BxCx). 156 (Bx). *157.* 160 (Bx). *161.* 163 (Bx). 164. *165–6.* 168. +178–180. *183.* +184–5. 200. 202. 228. *234–5.* 236. 239. *240–2.* 245. 248–9. *250.* 251. 254. +260–1. *262.* *264–6.* 268. 269. *270–2.* 273 (Cx). +274. *275.* 276. *277–9.* 280. *281.* 282. *283–4.* 288. *294.* *296–7.* *339.* *341–3.* 343–5. 346–7. *408–9.* *411–13.* 425. **VII** *1.* *3–4.* 5. *6.* 8. *10.* 11–14. *16.* +17. *18–19.* 24. 26. 28. 30. 31. 32. *35.* 36–8. *39–40.* +41. *42.* 43. *44–8.* 54 (Bx Cx). *55.* 69. 71–2. 72. *76–8.* *80–2.* 83 (Bx). 84. *85.* 86–7. *88.* 90. *92–7.* +98. *99–103.* 104. *105.* +106. *107–14.* +115. *116.* 120–3. *124.* 125–6. *131–2.* 134. *137.* +138. 139. 141–2. 149. *151–2.* **VIII** *12.* 38. 72. 73. *192.* +197. *270.* 351. *353.* **IX** 13. 52. *53.* 54. 171. 310. **X** 14. *15–17.* 61. *62.* 66. *74–5.* *86.* 104–5. *122.* *141.* 142 (Bx). *233.* +234. *236.* 237. 257. +258. 286. ++287–8. 305. 308–9. **XI** *14–15.* *21.* 51 (Bx). *164–5.* *168–9.* +170. 171. *172.* +173. *174–5.* *179–86.* 188. +189. *190–97.* 205. *210.* +212. +214. ++218 (Cx). 223. 229–32. *239–40.* +245. 249. 252. 258. *281.* 284–5. 296. *308–09.* 312 (Cx). 313–15. **XII** *1.* +3. *7.* 9. *10–14.* 15. 19.*21.* 31. 33–5. *36.* *42–44.* 45 (?Bx). *48–59.* 61–5 (63 (Bx)). *67–9.* *73.*76. ++77. *82–3.* +86. *87.* *91.* 110. *111–12.* 113. *114–16.* *119.* *121.* *124–5.* *128.* +130. *136–9.* *143.* +144. *145–9.* 150. *153.* 155–5*a.* **XIII** 100–05. *107–10.* 111–12. *116–21.* ++122. *124.* 125. 126 (Cx). *127.* *135–41.* 142. 143–5. *147.* 149. +150. *156–8.* *160.* +161. +162. +163. +166. *173–4.* *177–9.* *198.* +199. [204–5 French]. +209. 211. *212–13.* *214–15.* +221. 222–6. +228. ++229. *235–7.* *242–3.* +246. **XIV** *1.* 17. *18.* 44. *46–52.* 53–4. 56. *57–61.* +64. *65–7.* +68. *77–86.* +87. 89. *92–6.* *98–100.* +101. *103–4.* +105. 106–8. ++109. 110. *111–15.* 116. *117.* 118–19. *120–22.* ++125. *126–28.* 129. *130.* +131. 135–9. +140. 141–2. +144. *145–7.* 148. *149.* 150. *151.* 152. *153.* +154–5. *156.* ++158. *170–1.* +185. *187.* +190. 191. *192.* *194.* +195. *196–7.* ++198. *199–200.* 202–7. +208. 209–10. +211. 212–13. **XV** *1–3.* ++4. *5.* *9.* + 10 (Bx). +12. *15–17.* *31–2.* +39. *41.* +42. *43–5.* +47. *48–51.* +56. *57–8.* ++64–6. 67. *69.* ++83. *84–5.* 88. 90. *93.* 96–7. 99–100. *101–2.* 104 (Bx). 105. *106.* +107. ++108. *110.* +111. *112.* 113. 121–2. +123. *124.* +129. 136. +144. *148–9.* *159–60.* ++165–6. +172. *173.* 174. 176. *180–1.* *187–90.* +191. *192–3.* *203.* 204. *205.* ++206. *207–8.* +209. *210.* 226–9. +230. *231.* 239. +240. 241. *244–5.* +253. *254–5.* 256. *257–8.* ++259–61. *262.* 263. ++265. +266. *267–70.* 272. *273* (Cx). 274. ++282. *283–4.* 289. +290. *291–94.* 295. *298–9.* *301.* 302. **XVI** *1–2.* +3. 4. +5. 7. 8. ?*9* (*see TN*). 10. *11.* 13–14. 15. +38. *39–52.* 54–5. +56. *57–62.* 64 (Bx). *66–68.* +69. *71–5.* +76. 77. *80–3.* 84. +85. *86–7.* +88–9. ++90. 91. *93.* *95–8.* *100–04.* +107. +108. *110.* *115.* 119. 122. +123. *124–9.* *131–32.* +134. *137–8.* *142.* +143. *144–5.* +146. 147–8. *151.* ++154–5. 164. *165–7.* +168. 181. 182–3. +184. *185–90.* *193–4.* *196–213.* +214. 215–17. 220. +221. 222. +223. ++232. 233. +234. *236.* 237. +241. 244. *245–6.* +247. 250–2. +253. *254.* 257. 260. +261. *262.* 265. ++266. *267.* ++268. *274.*++275. 276. 277. 278. +279. +291. *292.* 295. *297–8.* *316.* 321–2. 329–30. 332. +334. 337. 341. *344–6.* *348–53.* ++354. +355. *356.* +358. 359. *361.* 362.

++363. 370. **XVII** *13*. 14. *17*. +18. +19. *20*. 21. 28. ++55. *56*. ++77. +94. *96*. *100–01*. 102. 104. *105–7*. *109*. +111. *113*. *120–1*. 171. +182. 187. *188*. 189. *192*. *195–6*. 197. *198*. 199. *200*. 201. *203–7*. 208 (Bx).+209. 210 (Bx). *211*. *213*. 214. ++215. *216*. 217. 218. +219. *220–6*. 229. +232. 252. *253*. 254. *255*. +256. 257–9. +260. 262. *263–9*. 270. +271. ++276. *277–8*. 279. *280–2*. 297–9. +300. 302. 305–6. 310. *311*. 315–16. *318–19*. 320. **XVIII** *31*. 33. +34. 35. +36. *37*. 38. +40. *43–4*. *109*. 110. *112–17*. +120. *124–7*. 129. *131–4*. *137*. 155. 161. *164*. 167. 169. *177*. *182–3*. 185. *202* (BxCx; *see TN*). 203–06. 207. *208–9*. 241. +243. *244*. +252. *253*. 254. 255. +257. +258. +259. *266*. +267. 270. +271. 272. 273. +274. 275. *276–79*. 280–1. *282–3*. +284. 285–6. *287–8*. 289–92. **XIX** *1–2*. 6. *11–16*. *19–22*. 25. +27–8. *29*. +30. *32*. 34. +36. *46*. 47. +49. *50–1*. 52. 56. *57–8*. 59–60. *61–2*. *66*. 67. *68–9*. 73. 78. ++83. 84. *85*. 90. 96. +97. *99*. *112*. +116. *117*. +118. *119*. 121. *123–5*. *141–4*. +145. 148–9. +150. *153–7*. *162–4*. 165–6. *167*. 168. *169–70*. 171. *172–3*. +175–9. +180. 181–2. *183–6*. 187–9. *190*. 192. 193. *194–6*. 197. *198–9*. 200. *201–5*. *207–220*. +221. *222–28*. 230. 232. *233*. 249. 250. +251. 252. +253. *254–62*. *264–7*. +268. *269–73*. *277–85*. +287. ++288. *291–2*. 293–4. *295–6*.+298. ++299–300. *301–4*. +305. *306*. *308* (Bx). *309–13*.314. *315–18*. *320–31*. 332. *333–4*. **XX** *1*. 3–4. 5. *6–11*. 12. *13–19*. 21. 22. 23. *25–7*. 28–30. *31–4*. 34. *35–7*. 39 (Bx). *40–4*. 47. +49. 51. 52. 56. *57–60*. 64. *65–7*. 68. *69–70*. 72. 73. +75. 76. 77. *81–3*. +84. *87–9*. *91*. 92. 94 (Cx). *96*. 99. 101. *102*. *104–06*. 108. *113*. 115. *117*. 119. 120. 122 (Bx). 123–9. 130. *131–3*. 135. *136*. 137. +138. 139. +140. *141–6*. 147. *148–9*. +150. *152–3*. 157 (Bx). *159*. 160. 163. *165–70*. *173*. ++175. *176*. 178. *179–80*. *182–4*. 185. *190–1*. 192. *193–4* *199–201*. 203. ++204. *205–11*. 214. *219–23*. 225. 226. 227. 228. ++229. *230–4*. 236. *237–40*. 241. *242–7*. 248. *249*. *251–5*. 256. 257. *258–9*. 264. *265–6*. *268–70*. ++273. *274–80*. *295–8*. 299. *300–01*. 302. *313*. 321. *322*. 323. 325. *329*. *330–1*. *335*. 337. 341 (Bx). *342*. +344. *362–3*. 364. *365–6*. +367. 368. 372. *373–5*. *377–8*. 388. +389. +390. *391*. +393. 395–396. *397–8*. 399. 400 (Cx). *401–3*. *408*. 412 (Cx). 413. *414–15*. 417–18. *419*. 421–3. +424. *425*. 426. *427–8*. +429. 430–1. *438*. 439. 441. *443*. 444 (Bx). *445–6*, +447. 448 (Bx). 450. +451. *455–7*. 460–74. 476–8. **Passus XXI–XXII**: *these are assumed identical unless noted otherwise*. **XXI** 12 (BxCx). 21. 39. 43. 56–7 (Bx). 63. 76 (Cx). 90 (BxCx). 97 (Bx). 111. 134. 140. 164. 183 (?Bx). 186 (BxCx). 187. 206. 230 (BxCx). 236, 241 (BxCx). 242. [244b]. [252: *two changes*]. [254: *two changes*]. 256. 272. [281 *first lift*]. 286. 297 (?Bx). 303 (Bx). 305 [*both differently*]. 316 (Bx). 336 (?Bx). 345 (Bx). 347 (BxCx).360. 365. 366 (?Bx). 376 (Cx). 378–9. 384. 389. 402. 403. 408 (BxCx). 411. 413 (Bx). 429. 441 (Bx). 445 (BxCx). 467 (?Bx).482 (?Bx). **XXII** 8 (Bx). 13 (Cx). 14, 19, 34, 54 (Bx). 62. 97. 130. 167. 261 (Bx). 292–3 (BxCx).301 (Cx). 309 [*lift 4*]. 312.338 (Cx). 366 [*both*]. 367 (BxCx). 378 [*both*].

Auxiliary Core-text

§ 13. As noted at § 7, there is an auxiliary body of lines where two or more versions differ in only one lift-phrase, yet cannot be considered even substantively identical since the revision involves a major lexical change. For purely illustrative purposes, some 150 examples are given here from the portion of text (= C Pr–IX 186 //) where all four versions are present. Line-references are to the target version in the order **ZABC**.

(a) Differences occur most commonly in the *fourth lift* of a standard line:

From **Z** → **A**: I 4. 75. 120. 143. II 14 (*removing rhyme*). 121. 187. III 13. 27 (*with change from* Type Ia *to* T-type; *reversed in* **B**: cf. Z III 30). 160. IV 76.98. 120. 149. V 18. 223. 251. VI 53. 58. 82. VII 3. 135 (*changes* Ie *to* T-type). 169. 245. 252. 278. 296.

From **A** → **B**: Pr 37. I 103. III 39. 42. 102. IV 111. 186. V 10. 116. 197. 225. 229. 449. VI 24. VII 122, 124. 134 (Type I *to* T-type). VIII 33. 45. 111. IX 153. X 125. 130, 335 (*metrical change to* T-type). 138. 153. 197. 226. 294. 332. 343. 370. 459.

From **B** → **C**: Pr 130. 133. 165. 171. 174 (*internal rhyme*). 175 (Type Ia → Ib). 189. 218. I 145. 148. II 63. 65. 148. III 475. VII 70 (*by deletion of last lift in a* Type Ic, *giving* 'clashed' *b-verse*).

They occur much less commonly in the other stave-positions:

(b) in the first lift:

Z → **A**: III 172. VIII 72 (Type IIIa *to* Ia). **B** → **C** Pr 172.

(c) in the second:

Z → **A**: IV 131 (*changing* Ib *to* Id). VIII 62. **A** → **B**: III 41. IV 80. V 216. **B** → **C**: Pr 140. 178. 201. 216. III 76.

238

(d) in the third lift of an extended line:

A III 167 (← Z III 115) → B III 180.

(e) at the key-stave position in a standard line:

Z → **A**: Pr 51. II 8. 99. III 129. VI 92. VII 184. 259 (*changing* T-type *to* Ia). VIII 68. **A** → **B**: Pr 63. I 8. III 32.

The rare lexical changes in the dips usually occur in the a-verse:

Z → **A**: V 31a. 53a. VII 178a. 181b. 262a. 268a. **A** → **B**: III 299a. IV 71b. VI 169a. VII 167a. **B** → **C**: I 147a.

But identical half-lines are abundantly instanced, the changes being mostly in the b-verse. Significant metrical consequences are noticed:

Z → **A**: Pr 16. 82. II 51. II 137 (*clashing* b-verse *changed to* Type I *with removal of rhyme*). 149 (*changing keystave noun to verb*). III 92. 143. IV 23. V 6. 27. VI 78 (*re-written as* Type IIa). 105. VII 37. 55. 59. 82. 92. 93 (*changes* IIIb *to* IIIa). 103. 155. 166. 168. 194. 282. 304. VIII 22. 32. 86. **A** → **B**: III 36. 98 (Type Ia *to* IIb). 100 (Type I *to* Type IIa). IV 160. VI 28. **B** → **C**: Pr 137. 170. 179. 181. 214–15. I 149. II 88. 103a. IV 35–6.

ii. *Editorial Principles and Procedures*

(a) *The canons of unanimity and conformity*

§ 14. The above completes the corpus of evidence in support of the principle that agreed lines in two or more versions are to be understood as constituting 'what Langland wrote.'[12] The *unanimity principle*, as it has been called, makes only a 'minimal' assertion; for Langland as clearly, if not as surely, wrote in its surviving form much more of the material than just the core-text. But its positive substance (the core-lines are textual 'facts') and its analytic form (it covers all and only these facts) give the core-text the secure empirical character necessary for an edited text that seeks to win wide assent. Moreover, since the principle acknowledges the legitimate claims of the 'positivist' conception of the text, it is a fit starting-point for a work aimed at scholars with very different approaches to editing. Ascertainment of 'unanimity' cannot, of course, be absolute, since the poet did more in revising than simply add, subtract or transpose lines and passages. He altered the text in so massive and detailed a way as to make the successive versions appear (to some readers) more as stages in a process than as finished products. The appearance of 'process' is most striking in **Z** and (to a less extent) in A XII and C Pr 95–124. But while the parallel-text's juxtaposition of closely similar lines highlights *Piers Plowman*'s evolution as a 'life's work' with true spiritual unity, it should not be allowed to obscure how each text embodies a separate and distinct artistic intention. That this claim is not universally accepted of even the one completed version is shown by recent 'provisionalist' studies that question how finished and final the **B** Version is. But whereas these arguments have already, it is hoped, been adequately rebutted (III, *B Version* §§ 52–7), it is not being contended here that **C**, let alone **A** or **Z**, can be satisfactorily read in isolation. What is being urged is the recognition at successive stages of an implied will to completion, notwithstanding that this 'will' was expressed through acts of (re)composition that produced **A**, **B** and **C**. As the enterprise lasted more than twenty-five years, it generated distinctive material at each stage. The effort to discover what Langland 'intended' at *any* stage therefore demands a firm empirical basis. This, it is argued, only the core-text can provide. For as all accept, the circumstances of copying prompted at *every* stage deliberate scribal intervention in response to the poem's content, form and language. So for nearly 40% of the **ABC** text, correcting transmission-errors involves direct analysis in order to find the archetypal reading that lies behind the extant variants.[13] By way of compensation, an editor can 'control' his analysis in the light of the scribal variation evidenced by reference to almost four times as many lines than the core-text itself contains. The core-text can, in turn, furnish an understanding of the poet's idiom reliable enough to justify emending the archetype when it too is suspected of error. But this 'rational' method of discerning the direction of scribal variation, though a vital editorial procedure, cannot be treated as a canon, even if its central *durior lectio* criterion may aspire to the rigour of a principle. For the irreducibly *a priori* element in this method is clear from the disagreements its particular applications can arouse. But if it is to remain the *primary* procedure, its criteria for judging a reading 'harder' must conform to the data of the core-text.

§ 15. Now 'difficulty', as stated at II § 74 above, can never suffice the editor as a means of discriminating the reading of the archetype among the conflicting sub-archetypal, group or individual variants. This reservation applies *a fortiori* when the archetype is suspected of having corrupted a 'harder' original, and a wholly conjectural emendation is proposed (cf. II § 77). For a criterion that is neither entirely logical nor entirely empirical can obviously never entail emendation. Accordingly, even an editor who relies on the core-text's authority cannot readily allow a procedure that is analytic ('rational') to risk becoming speculative ('radical'). Instead he should try where possible to preserve the reading of the archetype, on account of its 'logically positive' character. This is because 'editorial conservatism' is the only way to safeguard the reader's textual rights. And such conservatism should not be objected to as uncritical, let alone irrational, because the canon of economy that governs it is wholly rational (see § 19). In practice this means that if non-paralleled archetypal readings conform to the core-criteria, it is more logically economical to retain them, unless an overwhelming case for rejecting them can be made. When it is not necessary to emend, it is necessary not to emend;[14] an axiom that demands resistance to the lavish 'correction' of minor archetypal readings of rationalist editors like Kane-Donaldson and Russell-Kane. But conversely, conservatism of this kind does not imply concurrence with positivists of varying stripe like Skeat, Knott-Fowler and Pearsall, who restrict their interventions to choice of the 'best' readings but offer no arguments for believing that these are what the poet wrote. Excessive editorial confidence, whether in one's chosen base-manuscript, literary taste or sense of Langland's *usus scribendi*, tends to frustrate the reader's legitimate expectations from a critical edition. For while even a secure archetypal text is not beyond criticism, it should never be abandoned without misgiving.

§ 16. The second major editorial canon is the *principle of acceptability* of readings that meet the core-text norms. This is arrived at after analysing the unique as well as the common lines in the received versions and **Z**, and it admits few exceptions (see § 18). On its positive side, the canon presumes that unshared lines claiming authenticity will conform to the core-text criteria. Though this is not a logical stipulation, it is a presumption the strength of which will be clear from the extent of the tertiary core-group (f) of **BC** lines and the proportionally large size of both the secondary core-group (a) of **ABC** lines and the tertiary core-group (d) of **AB** lines (see §§ 11 and 12 above). For these groups show that the common lines' main features persisted unchanged from the poem's earliest accepted form, **A**, to its latest, **C**. And since this persistence increases if a primary core-group **ZABC** is provisionally recognised (and **Z** placed first in the group), the presumption of conformity is also favoured by the principle of economy (see § 19 below): i.e. the poet wrote the same types of line from beginning to end of his work on *Piers Plowman*. Now, not impossibly a Langlandian line could breach the core-criteria and still be authentic. As Shakespeare's late plays include lines with more than the ten syllables of his early ones, **C** might have introduced a new metrical type not found in **A** (none in fact appears). But this canon's permissive power is less restricted than its stipulative: for it allows as authentic all unique lines that conform to the core-criteria. If any of these lines were in fact proved inauthentic, it would follow that a scribe who wrote lines exactly like 'Langland' (the poem) would be, from an editorial standpoint, indistinguishable from 'Langland' (the poet). But the *principle of economy* raises the presumption that these lines (with few exceptions) are original, to near-certainty. On its negative side, failing the core-criteria will render such lines correspondingly likely to be corrupt. But as the canon of acceptabilty / conformity remains 'falsifiable' (by discovery of a holograph or externally authenticated text), it qualifies as 'critically empirical'.

§ 17. The acceptability canon is thus foundational for a parallel-text edition. Firstly, although not as analytic as the unanimity principle, it is derivable from the purely rational principle of economy (described below). For it must be more economical to hold that all 'acceptable' lines are likely to be authentic than that some are not. This is not to say that 'acceptable' lines defy scrutiny; but where they have no parallel, an editor should not be in haste to question them. Secondly, the criteria of acceptability envisaged here have been deduced not from an 'idea' of how the poet might have expressed himself (R–K's 'abstractions') but from a body of evidence even more 'logically positive' than that of a single versional archetype, namely the 'core-text'. This protects against the error of insisting that the poet conform at all points to his specific practice at *some* points; the present edition does not aim to be, in the Athlone editors' sense, an 'ideal' text (cf. *K–D* p.213). Further, since the acceptability canon formally authorises rejection of unparalleled lines that fail to observe the core-text norms, it is more fundamental for editing than the *durior lectio* criterion. For that criterion by definition operates rigorously only where there are two or more archetypal readings to compare; whereas a critical edition must both authenticate lines unique to each version and exclude spurious lines and corrupt readings.[15] This second canon, which is for the present editor what the concept of *usus scribendi* is for Kane and his collaborators, is thus stronger and more rigorous than the Athlonean standard. Its permissive power also exceeds that of the canon of unanimity; for it permits rejection even of lines *within* the core-text. At first glance this may appear a logical contradiction, since 'acceptable' lines are precisely those that meet the core-text norms. The paradox may be resolved as follows. Since some kinds of scribal error (especially mechanical ones) are liable to be made repeatedly at the sub-archetypal level, they might even occur in the core-text (as it is here maintained they do). But such cases of repeated archetypal error should be very few in number; and if each apparent exception can be adequately explained, the concept of 'core-text norms' will not be falsified but confirmed (see § 18). Nor is the anticipated objection that 'hard cases make bad law' apposite here, since the guilty party in these cases is not the poet but his scribes. As no lines that conflict with these norms in fact occur in the primary division of the core-text, it will be argued below that the few found in the other divisions do not undermine the theory's general soundness.[16]

§ 18. Now, of the thirteen examples of apparently corrupt core-text lines, the five that demand immediate attention occur in the secondary division.[17] In group **ZAB** are two, both revised in **C**, where a fairly complex process of successive archetypal corruptions must be posited. At Pr 11 // [*me*] *meten*] *I meten*, mechanical error in the form of haplography seems to have played an important contributory part. In the case of IV 91 // a thrice-repeated scribal substitution of *seide* for original *wiþseide has been supposed (though other 'harder' originals could explain the line's breach of the core-text metrical norms). At VI 407 *He thromblede at the thresfold and threw to þe erthe,* where **AB** appear corrupt on the showing of **C**, the Bx reading could have been *trembled,* a different error from the g-group's *stumbled,* or else both could be easier scribal reflexes of an archetypal (and original) *thrumbled,* which is here adopted on the showing of **C** (whence *A*-V has derived its correct reading). At III 225 *weye* **AB** (severally) and at VIII 329 *brewestares* **ZB** (jointly) conflict with **ZC** and **AC** respectively. But while both examples challenge the linear postulate, they do not undermine the validity of the core-text norms, because in all versions the acceptability criterion is satisfied. In III 225 no emendation is made, and there is almost as strong a case for so leaving VIII 329, which *is* tentatively emended, but not without some misgiving (see the *Textual Notes* and cf. § 15). The other eight cases appear in the tertiary division. Group **AB** has at III 260 an instance of presumed haplography (exactly paralleled at C VI 155) and two of specific visual error, at V 111 *liþeþ* (where there is *ȝ / þ* confusion) and at IX 163 *any* (which seems to show loss of -y through attraction to preceding *yong* or following *any*). At VI 281 *and [ek] an hauer cake,* the line's metrical defectiveness is ascribed to visually-induced loss of a grammatical word functioning as a mute liaisonal stave (K–D's restoration *a cake of otes* from parallel **C** ascribes the error to lexical substitution). At X 108 *bigiled,* a verb widely instanced in the text, is diagnosed as having ousted a less common variant-form *biwiled.* In group **BC** at I 155 the lexically easier *bitwene* is understood to have supplanted the rare preposition *inmiddes.* Finally, haplography is taken to account for the unanimity of the archetypes' faulty metre at VI 155 *faste [faste] for faste* and at VII 54 *(for* substituted for *be).*[18] The total of lines to be ascribed to convergent substitutions amounts to a mere 0·3% of the whole. So it does not seem excessive to claim that, since the validity of the core-criteria is unchallenged over 4140 lines, their general applicability for the remaining four-fifths is massively endorsed.

(b) *The principle of economy*

§ 19. The third editorial principle (mentioned at § 16 above), which is also foundational, is in theory conceptually prior; and it is not peculiar to works in several versions, but equally relevant for editing any text. The principle of *simplicity or economy* insists on employing the fewest assumptions that will adequately explain the available data. Obviously, the 'simplest' account of a textual tradition may not be the historically true one; for if some necessary evidence is unavailable, what is explained 'adequately' may be less significant than lost material that could be reasonably postulated.[19] Further, the possibility of a conflict between 'historical' and 'analytical' approaches may well prompt the wider question: whether to edit 'critically' means to deduce the original text from the evidence of the surviving witnesses or to reconstruct from bibliographical history the stages of its generation and corruption. These alternatives are somewhat artificial, however; for to avoid fancifulness, the analytical critic must know how medieval texts were written, reproduced and disseminated, and to escape triviality, the historical bibliographer needs to understand what a literary text is. The issue is too large to explore in detail here, but one negative proposition needs emphasis at this point. This is that the antecedent probability on which historical reasoning is based cannot achieve the certainty required by an editorial principle: it is thus unarguably more 'economical' to stick to the data and refrain wherever possible from speculation.[20] However, editing still remains at bottom a 'discipline' without self-evident first principles. For while it may aim to be empirical, to the extent that it is 'critical' it is also 'hypothetico-deductive'; so it cannot operate without some (indemonstrable) assumptions. And when account is taken of its lexical and contextual aspects, which are not successive steps in an experiment but interwoven threads in a fabric of interpretation, editing Langland properly cannot seek to be other than 'historically' informed throughout. The reader is invited to discover from the *Textual Notes* and *Commentary* how successfully this edition has balanced the historical and the analytical in establishing the text and interpreting its meaning.

§ 20. The key importance of the canon of economy emerges nowhere more vividly than in relation to one major textual issue that divides the Athlone editors from the present editor. Though it may seem phantasmal to the 'strict' positivist dealing non-critically with facts rather than explanations, it should engage the attention of rationalist and empiricist alike. The issue concerns the true authority of readings that appear, without other-version support, in individual copies or in the postulated source of an established genetic pair: readings found by 'direct' analysis superior to those of the archetype, but judged too good to be scribal conjectures. The most notable of these is C XVII 116, which is omitted from all copies except the RM group of family **p**:[21]

> Bote they fayle in philosophie - and philosoferes lyuede
> *And wolde wel examene hem - wonder me thynketh!*

The 'eclectic positivist' editors[22] of **C** happily include it; but Skeat, referring to parallel B XV 376 [382], observes only that his other collated copies 'leave the sentence incomplete' (*SkC*, note), while Pearsall asserts (incorrectly) that it is 'supplied from P'. If this line is considered non-archetypal yet essential, it could be explained as a correction from a 'superior lost **C** manuscript', though only at the cost of breaching the canon of economy. The present edition also admits XVII 116, on grounds of sense, but supports it only with a genealogical argument. This argument is not 'simple' in itself but is conceptually more economical than recourse to a second explanatory assumption; and by tacitly acknowledging a complex 'historical' situation behind the reading, it invites scrutiny of its 'analytic' claim in the light of the textual situation as a whole.[23]

§ 21. This particular case is one where the Athlone editors do not invoke a hypothetical lost source, because they omit the line without comment and leave the reader to conclude (as presumably they do) that the sentence at issue is not 'incomplete.' But they do hypothesise such sources for 'good corrections' in the **B** manuscript F[24] and the **C** manuscript N^2.[25] And since in both sets of instances their interpretations have been rejected, the situation again raises the spectre of a conflict between 'historical' and 'analytical' understandings of the nature and origin of some important readings. Now the present editor has earlier countenanced what appears to be a hypothetical 'lost source' in the form of **C**'s revision copy (B^1), as well as a primary scribal **B** manuscript ('B-Ø') prior to both this and to Bx (III, *B Version*, § 2 above). But it needs to be stressed that 'B-Ø' has not been postulated as an antecedently probable cause of the agreements between Bx and B^1; it has been inferred as the logically necessary reason for those agreements. Thus, to affirm the existence of B-Ø as the source of Bx and B^1 while denying that it is the immediate or proximate correction-source of F is only to underline the axiom that simple deduction is always preferable to complex speculation. For while the cited analyses of certain superior F and N^2 readings suggest intelligent guesswork in the case of N^2's five instances, they demonstrate contamination in the case of F. Moreover, as both of these scribal phenomena are abundantly instanced in the **ABC** traditions, there is no call for a further editorial assumption (like the supplementary Ptolemaic epicycles) to explain the aberrant orbits of 'rogue' manuscripts. This may seem much ado, if not quite about nothing, then about textual trifles light as air; yet there is more at stake here than a theoretical point. For what the Athlone editors hypothesise is unnecessary entities to account for readings that they prefer on intrinsic grounds. But a more economic explanation is at hand; for analysis shows that F borrowed from an A-text and that N^2, besides making some felicitous conjectures, drew on a B-text, and one identifiably of β type. These instances undeniably confirm the value of the 'direct method' in discerning the superior originality of some of these readings; but the method falls short of explaining the origin of either set. It remains an indispensable 'critical' procedure; and its subjective element is virtually eliminated by 'historical' appeal to other-version contamination as explanation for the 'superior' readings in these two witnesses.

(c) *The linear postulate and the canon of ratification*

§ 22. As should now be clear, the economy principle underlies the canon of conformity / acceptability, making agreement with the norms generated by the unanimity principle the formally sufficient and virtually necessary criterion of authenticity. One special feature of its application that differentiates the present from the Athlone text is that the latter's editors often prefer the reading of an earlier versional archetype (**A** for **B**, or **B** for **C**) to a later one that they believe corrupt. They sometimes even adopt the minority reading in a later version if it agrees with the archetypal text of an earlier one that they consider superior. This edition agrees with theirs in sometimes choosing for **B** an **A** reading confirmed by **C** (assuming always that the core-text norms are satisfied). But such emendations are authorised primarily by the linear postulate and only secondarily by the *durior lectio* criterion. In this way the principles of economy and acceptability are both preserved; for though a lost **B** original *is* hypothesised to account for the readings preferred, only one reading is assumed for **A**, **B** and **C**. And since in these cases Bx is rejected only when it fails to conform to the core-text norms, neither the linear postulate as confirmed by the **AC** agreement nor the intrinsic 'hardness' of the adopted reading is being treated as sufficient justification for that decision. By the same token, no Bx reading that meets the core-criteria is set aside for an apparently superior **A** reading. This is because the same postulate that presumes **B** unrevised when **A** and **C** agree presumes it revised when **B** differs from **A** but **A** is not confirmed by **C**. And that conclusion obviously holds *a fortiori* when **B** is confirmed by **C**. For though the 'methodological rule' here called the 'linear postulate' cannot qualify (any more than the *durior lectio* criterion) as a 'principle', its congruence with the canon of economy allows the deduction of a third rule that does possess the stipulative and permissive force of a principle. This is the *canon of ratification*, which affirms that all readings retained by a subsequent version are implicitly ratified by it. Such readings may therefore be rejected as unoriginal only if they breach the core-text criteria, something confined to the rare instances of B Pr 11 and B IV 91//.

iii. *Specification of the core-text criteria*

(a) *Linguistic and stylistic aspects*

§ 23. These criteria it is obviously desirable to specify as fully as possible, just as the Athlone editors describe their notion of Langland's *usus scribendi* on the basis of their total experience of editing the text. But how convincingly this can be done for a poem composed over at least as many years as Shakespeare's entire *oeuvre* is debatable. For there must exist an antecedent likelihood of some stylistic change between **A** and **C** (as is indeed borne out by examination of each version's distinctive material). It is therefore necessary to recall that 'core-text' norms derive by definition from the common features, those that remained constant. But the conformity canon does not so much stipulate all authentic features of each version as proclaim authentic only those features common to two or more versions. The details of how it does may be found by referring to the earlier discussions of such features in **Z** and in Passus XII of **A** (III, *Z Version* §§ 20–2; *A Version* §§ 69–71). In the present editor's judgement, the most secure aspect of any 'specification' is the versification. And the **ABC** core-text amply furnishes metrical criteria for assaying the originality of lines that lack other-version support, including those in **Z**. Lexical, syntactic and stylistic norms admit of less precision. And while appeal to the *durior lectio* helps to sharpen certainty, opinions can differ sharply as to what constitutes a 'harder reading'.[26] Consequently that criterion, even when guided by the core-text norms, cannot rule out the possibility that an 'easier' reading may come from the revising author and not a scribe. This caveat does not imply an automatic reluctance to accept non-archetypal harder readings. But regard for the economy principle as expressed in the acceptability canon dictates great caution when preferring them.

§ 24. It will be no surprise, therefore, that while the present edition sometimes emends, it remains in general much closer than the Athlone to the preserved or reconstructed archetypal forms of each version. This is because to establish the archetype from conflicting variants is not a purely analytical matter of applying the *durior lectio* criterion; for if the acceptability and economy principles are followed, it is to a significant extent an empirical matter. That is, it gives due weight to the genealogical implications even of non-straightforward variants. But to emend a preserved or reconstructed archetype, even by 'low-level' restoration of **B** from **AC**, must increase the subjective element, inasmuch as the linear postulate itself rests on an *a priori* assumption. For any rejection of an archetypal reading must occur along a continuum of relative *un*certainty. Every restoration, however well founded, qualifies the authority of the final text; every reconstruction, however prudent, lessens it; every conjecture, however brilliant, weakens it. This said, even an editor who prefers positive data to imaginative hypotheses, and demonstration to persuasion, will (if he also feels a dual obligation to his poet and readers alike) with difficulty avoid occasional resort to both. A 'definitive edition' of Langland, however desirable, therefore remains unattainable. And on that sober note, this account of editorial principles and procedure may conclude by summing up the main aim of the present work in a single word: economy. This amounts in practice to printing the recoverable archetypal texts of each version with the minimum of necessary emendation. And it has meant steering a course between the positivist rock and the rationalist gulf, keeping both ears open to the siren-song of the 'ideal text', but remaining bound by the core-lines' four-ply cable.

Minor readings

§ 25. The area of the text where for the most part the archetypal form has been retained without much difficulty, even where some divergent witnesses find support in one or more other versions, is that of minor readings. Here study of the entire tradition leads the present editor to reject the Athlone view of scribal and authorial characteristics as distinct enough to enable confident recognition of one minor reading as easier or harder than another. For as comparison with a text of comparable length such as Chaucer's *Troilus* readily brings out, the flexibility of word-order and word-choice allowed by the unrhymed alliterative long-line tempted scribes to far greater verbal liberties than when they copied rhyming stanzas made up of lines with fixed syllabic length. And that even apparently problematic cases can be dealt with satisfactorily if the canons of economy and acceptability are observed may be illustrated from an example of syntax relating to the juxta-position of clauses without any co-ordinating conjunction at C I 161–2 //:

> And þat falleth to þe fader þat formede vs alle,
> Lokede on vs with loue and let his sone deye.

Since all four versions here have no *And* before *Lokede*, the 'primary core-text' consensus points to this less common (and so 'harder') asyndetic usage as probably authorial. **Z**'s further omission of *and* before *let,* in therefore conforming with the strongest core-text criteria, will both count as acceptable and may even seem (relatively) 'harder' than the **ABC-p** reading *and let*. But it does not follow that the zero-form *let* in the **x** tradition of **C** must therefore be preferred to *and let* in **p**. For while it is undecidable which sub-archetypal variant preserves Cx, the **AB** support for **p**'s similarly acceptable if (relatively) 'easier' reading allows that **C** might here have been unrevised. This example is called minor because it does not affect sense, metre or style. But if, as is simplest to suppose, **p** preserves Cx and Cx the original, then **C**'s non-revision may be taken to ratify the archetypal reading *and let* in **A** and **B**. The linear postulate, because it deals in probability and not certainty, cannot by itself prove non-revision; but the economy principle it too embodies will in such instances favour it.

§ 26. At I 182, an example involving grammatical number, the Athlone editors prefer the singular *dede* as harder than the plural:

> And as ded as a dorenayl but yf þe dedes folowe:
> *Fides sine operibus mortua est.*

Here the textual evidence is divided across the traditions, with *dede* supported by *C*-**p**, *B*-*G* and *A*-**r**, *dedes* by *C*-**x**, Bx, *A*-**m** and **Z**. But while the plural may be preferred as closer to the Latin, the direction of variation cannot be convincingly demonstrated. The only basis for decision is therefore the weight of the genetic evidence: two archetypes and two sub-archetypes against two sub-archetypes and a contaminated individual copy, G. This clear situation contrasts with the less clear one of almost exact archetypal equipollence at II 223 *And byschytten hym in here* shoppes (Ax?Cx against **Z**?Bx), where there would arguably be a case for keeping the archetype in **ZAC** but adopting the base-manuscript's reading (supported by F) for **B** on the grounds that Bx is uncertain. However, in the comparable *weddyng(es)* at II 118 (Bx**Z** pl. against ?AxCx sg.), it would seem better to accept the lack of linear uniformity. For here the sub-archetypal readings of Ax are ambiguous, **m**'s substantive error perhaps concealing an Ax plural, whereas **C**, which revises the entire line, determines the number by using the indefinite article. On a surface exami-nation, this case seems to suggest a paradoxical conflict between two arguments both supported by the economy principle: one in favour of adopting *weddyng* in all four versions, the other of keeping the discernible archetypal form in each. But a deeper analysis reveals that in minor read-ings of this type it is not possible to distinguish decisively between the authorial and the scribal. The more economical course is therefore to prefer the archetype, because this makes it unneces-sary to emend **Z** and adopt a minority (GC^2) reading for **B**, while the difference of sense, though not trivial, is still minor. A parallel case where superficially it seems that the direct method *can* distinguish originality between competing minor readings is *Here myhtow se ensaumples in hym-*

self one at I 167, in which *C*-**x**?Bx**Z***A*-**r** stand against *C*-**p***A*-**m**. But on closer study this instance proves not to be a minor reading at all, as it involves a significant difference of meaning (see the *Textual Notes*). What the two previous sub-archetypal conflicts nevertheless indicate is that, since scribes apparently substituted a singular for no discernible reason, they might well have done the same in similar cases elsewhere. It is not being assumed, of course, that the major / minor distinction invoked here is always a hard and fast one, and there are borderline cases. Yet even where doubt exists, if the principle of economy is observed in relation to minor variants, it has been found to support the archetypal reading against that of a group or an individual copy.[27]

Major readings

§ 27. Matters are quite otherwise with respect to indisputably major readings, where the direct method plays a much more important part. At the lower end of significance, where only a metrical aspect is affected, is C VII 170: *'Fro Sinoye', he sayde, 'and fro þe* sepulcre' in which *of Oure Lord* is added at the line-end by **Z**, archetypal **B**, the **x** family of **C** and the A copies A, H[3] and K. Here the rejected variant is not in conflict with the core-text's metrical norms. But it is judged 'easier' because it is (and here very obviously) more 'explicit'; and the one judged harder has a b-verse with a double lift in a single word (*sepúlcre*) exemplifying a rare 'monolexical' stress-pattern confirmed as 'Langlandian' by the core-text.[28] What gives the *durior lectio* criterion its power here is that one of the two variants is so much more compressed, elliptical and metrically idio-syncratic that it can reasonably be claimed as the source of the other. In theory, *of oure lord* could have been removed in **A** and so, on grounds of intrinsic acceptability, should be kept for **Z** (as it is in the present text). But though the **C** traditions again divide, the **p** variant may here be defended as likelier to represent Cx, in part because the resultant agreement of **AC** will make it easier to interpret Bx and **x** as 'explicitation-glosses'.[29] In this instance the linear postulate is logically not strong enough to decide the outcome, since if AH[3]K preserved Ax, and **x** preserved Cx, then **AC** agreement would support the *rejected* reading. So here the *durior lectio* criterion acts valuably as a *schoriare to schuyuen hit vp*, and the decision is reached mainly by 'rational' analysis.

§ 28. In the case of major readings, most particular textual situations display special features; but leaving these out of account, it is possible to generalise the issue roughly as follows. In the contested variants of a major reading the (non-metrical) features that may be described as 'harder' or 'easier' include its style, lexis, meaning or syntax. Thus a word may be uncommon, or its local sense unusual, or the patterning of the entire phrase unexpected. These are not, of course, the sole areas in which scribal substitutions are found to occur, though they are the most typical; and more could be said about how the 'difficulty' of variants is to be assessed. But it must be recognised at the same time that, while major errors are antecedently unlikely to be unconscious, there may be factors to consider distinct from the lexico-syntactic character of the reading, for example censorship. What the example in § 27 does not imply is that a sub-archetypal *durior lectio* within one version should be always adopted when its rejected competitor forms the secure archetypal reading in another. For an archetypal reading is in effect the 'logical' *residue and remenaunt* of the 'positive' text. The same caution is therefore needed when it is rejected for a superior other-version reading as when no parallel exists and choice is between two sub-archetypal variants in a single version. For if, as seems likely, scribes who copied *Piers Plowman* could have half-consciously picked up features of Langland's idiom (something easily overlooked by a rationalist editor), discriminating originality becomes a delicate, even a hazardous business. So much seems evident from C Pr 216 *For hadde ȝe ratones ȝoure* reik *ȝe couthe nat reule ȝowseluen,* a classic case where a truly circumspect editor would probably not favour group b's minority variant *reik* against the majority (and potentially archetypal) reading *reed.* The main justification for preferring *reik* is that in this case **C**'s changing **B**'s source-line from the rarer Type IIIa to the normative Type Ia (as scribes like the *B*-F redactor frequently did) is identifiable not as a scribe's but as the author's choice of a second full stave, insasmuch as its sense closely answers to archetypal *wille* in **B**. On balance (and the *Textual Notes* spell out how fine the balance is), the lexically harder *reik* may be adopted for **C**. But while the semantic equivalence noted allows the possibility that **B** also read *reik,* this cannot justify emending Bx to accord with the critical reading of **C**. In doing so, therefore, K–D elevate the *durior lectio* criterion over the canons of economy and acceptability, which forbid unnecessary emendation. And that the emendation is unnecessary is shown by the fact that the core-text evidence authenticates the scansion pattern *ax / ax,* which the Athlone editors (mistakenly believing it scribal) use as metrical grounds for 'correcting' the archetypal text of **B**.

§ 29. The admonition against adopting *reik* for **B** may nonetheless appear at odds with the resolution of the crux at A I 110 as *And was þe louelokest of* [*l*]*iȝt aftir Oure Lord seluen,* where **Z** is used to emend Ax and the line in its **Z** form subsequently adopted into **B**, which omits it. The detailed rationale of this complex reconstruction is given in the *Textual Notes,* but it will be worthwhile here to draw out some of its wider implications. To the Athlone editors, who first adopted the [*l*]*iȝt* emendation (*Ka^2,* p. 462; *K–D,* p. 205n), **Z**'s reading would have to be a happy scribal guess by an otherwise aberrant **A** witness, or else a correction from some 'lost **A** source superior to Ax'[30] (though, as already noted at I § 64, in overlooking **Z** they necessarily forgo both possibilities and emend by straight conjecture). The theoretical question is this: if retention of *siȝt* would yield a passable Type III line, how can the emendation *liȝt* be justified both in **A** and in the line as then restored in **B**? For the same principle of economy invoked against adopting *reik* for the text of B Pr 201 argues against emending Ax here. If Ax's form is acceptable, the unemended line should also (by the linear postulate) be preferred in the reconstructed **B**, on the supposition that it is likelier to have been retained in **B** than revised back to the form of **Z** ('When it is not necessary to emend, it is necessary not to emend'). In defence of the decision, *liȝt* has been judged 'superior' to *siȝt* in part as lexically harder but in part on 'positive' grounds; for the rejected Ax reading can be shown with near-certainty to be a visual error. But this makes its emendation from **Z** less a conjecture or a reconstruction than a 'restoration'. And this, being the class of correction that makes fewest assumptions about what cannot be proven, is least vulnerable to positivist objections. On a less superficial scrutiny, the 'rationalist' emendation can be claimed not to breach the 'positivist' principle of economy but to endorse it. For the emended line, now identical in all three versions, both explains the rejected form of Ax and fills the undoubted sense-gap in Bx. The example thus differs from that of C Pr 216 more than resembling it. For as the latter shows no mechanical reason why *reik* should have been supplanted, it must be less economical to read *reik* in **B**, when the rationale for rejection of Bx *wille* is largely (and mistakenly) metrical. But in **C**, as stated above, the main reason for preferring *reik* to *reed* is that its sense corresponds more closely to *wille.* Far from proving *wille* a non-alliterating scribal substitution for the same original, *reik* may simply illustrate **C**'s (well-documented) tendency to normalise the 'metrically harder' Type III lines of **B**.

§ 30. In the above cases it has been argued that the subjective element in the 'direct' approach to editing can be to a great extent controlled by appeal to self-consistent 'methodological rules'. But it must be conceded that an editorial 'reason' more closely approximates the soft-edged *ratio decidendi* of the law-court than the hard-edged conclusiveness of the laboratory. A case in point involves the word *hardere* itself, which has been preferred to archetypal *auarouser* in B I 191 *Are non* hardere *þan hij whan [hij] ben auaunced.* As the textual evidence here is both the agreed **ZA** reading and **C**'s revised *Aren none* hardore *ne hungriore then men of Holy Churche,* the grounds for decision will be partly antecedent (the linear postulate) and partly analytic (the canon of ratification). However, the rejected Bx reading *auarouser* cannot be deemed intrinsically unacceptable and, if annominative wordplay on *auaunced* is discerned, may even merit adoption. Likewise, its echo in C 187 Auerous *and euel-willed whan hy ben auansed,* which completes the line's re-writing, could imply not that *hardere* stood in original **B** but that the **C** Version is a new synthesis of **B** and **A** incorporating both words. As **C** would thus in part be confirming the reading while revising it, to reject *auarouser* as an over-explicit substitution by B-Ø's scribe would require a complicated explanation defying both the canon of ratification and the principle of economy. These 'positive' objections to the reconstruction adopted need answering, since any single abandonment of editorial principles requires defence, especially where the reading has a representative character (as this one has). What is relied on here to provide an answer is, it must be granted, not pure logic, but something analogous to the accumulated practical wisdom of the experienced judge: a broader (if less formulable) contextual understanding of Langland's probable train of thought that would justify challenging the credibility of the Bx witness. Thus in **ZAC** the speaker connects 'hardness' with the sin of *pride*, since it is clerks promoted to higher-paid posts who are being said to resist calls on their generosity. But this point is more telling if mention of *greed* (meaning both *coueitise* 'desire to get' and *auarice* 'desire to keep') is deferred until the metaphorical lines B I 196–7 //:

> Thei ben acombred wiþ coueitise, þei konne noȝt out crepe,
> So harde haþ auarice yhasped hem togideres.

If this argument from 'antecedent poetic probability' is reinforced by recalling the oral dimension postulated for the earliest text **Z** (*Z Version*, §§ 8–9 above), the more narrowly logical counter-case (which must be very carefully weighed) may be judged weaker than the one that is less formally rigorous. It should, however, be acknowledged that **C** abandons the 'deferral' noted and, like Bx, names the clerics' greed straight after declaring their want of charity. The matter, as said in the last paragraph, can be very uncertain; and so complete consistency, not to say 'definitiveness' (§ 24), is in such complex cases well nigh unattainable.

§ 31. In the last example, the archetypal reading at B I 191 was concluded to be scribal on the showing of agreed **ZA**, despite its echo in the two-line form of **C**. In another type of case, as at II 95 (= B II 91) *In* woldes *and in weschynges and with ydel thouhtes,* there is no **ZA** evidence to hand. Here the **C** reading is thus not a clear (if ambiguously interpretable) reflex of **B**. Instead, both archetypes must be determined on the basis of three substantive sub-archetypal variants, of which *wedes] woldes* appears in both traditions (in *B*-β and in *C*-**p**). On the one hand, the principle of economy as embodied in the canon of ratification would recommend *wedes*, which also satisfies the canon of conformity. But direct analysis identifies as harder *C*-**x** woldes which, though not identical with *B*-α *wenynges* (in K–D's attractive reconstruction, **wenes*), is close to it in sense. What the recurrence of *wedes* reveals is that scribes in both traditions sometimes responded to readings that they found difficult by means of convergent substitutions for what were discrete originals. As is brought out in the *Textual Notes*, the α reading of which revised **C** appears a reflex is (as in the similar case of *reik] wille* at § 28) lexically harder than that of the β family. So here, though the contention is less straightforward than if it were between two agreed sub-archetypal variants from each version, the plea of *durior lectio* will perforce carry great weight.

§ 32. Any notion, however, that a reading's 'hardness' can pass beyond the 'suasive' to the 'demonstrative' needs further elaboration. For it is not enough for a *lectio* that is *durior* in one of the ways described at § 28 to provide the best available reading in the context. It should also account for the other variants and, if possible, be supported by the linear postulate or the canon of ratification, or both. An example where a reading that may be lexically the hardest does *not* satisfy these other requirements is at A X 136 *Boþe maidenis and* martires*, monkis and ancris*. Here *r¹* reads *nonnes* for *martires* but the dissident t copy Ch has *mynchons*, which expresses *r¹*'s sense but produces a normatively alliterating line (and is, partly for that reason, adopted by Kane). However, to see *mynchons* as archetypal requires presuming, first, that *nonnes* was coincidentally substituted for it by the ancestors of TH², D and u, and a collocatively commoner stave-word *martires* substituted by both *r²* and **m**; second, that Langland used an *r²***m** revision-copy of **A** and allowed this corruption to stand in **B**. Now, the presence of *martires* in **B¹** and perhaps also in B-Ø (like that of *auarouser* in Bx at B I 191) is suggested by its reflex in C X 206b *confessours and martres*; but by contrast with the B I 191 case (§ 30 above), there is here no semantic or other ground for objection to *martires*. By the canons of acceptability and ratification it should therefore be retained in both **A** and **B**. What this example indicates is that even so powerful a critical procedure as the *durior lectio* must be a less dependable resource than a basic principle. Serious methodological difficulties can thus arise from over-reliance on it. Firstly, Kane's complicated explanation of the textual evidence fails to satisfy the principle of economy. Secondly, Kane-Donaldson's retention of *martres* in **B** contradicts Kane's decision for **A**. Thirdly, there arises in consequence Kane's awkward notion that the poet's 'passing over' of scribal errors in his revision copy lends 'a kind of sanction' to **A** readings that he identifies as corrupt on intrinsic grounds (*Ka²*, p. 463). But if *martres* is read in both **A** and **B**, the canon of ratification can be followed and the principle of economy preserved.

§ 33. Kane's discussion of the other Ch readings he adopts (pp. 161–2) highlights what may be singled out as the central weakness of the 'Athlone' method. The reading *mynchons*, Kane holds, is harder than the alternatives, so can only be rejected outright if it is judged a 'brilliant scribal emendation'. And doing this 'seems to make nonsense of the basis of textual criticism by assuming a scribe capable of improving on the poet's work'. But Kane's assertion that the lexically harder reading is an improvement is open to question. For if, as he claims, *martires* could have been scribally substituted 'because of the suggestion of the common phrase of liturgy and ecclesiastical calendar', it could no less have been what the poet wrote, since it is contextually appropriate and conforms with the core-text criteria. Further, whereas martyrs *are* thematically important in Langland, nuns are not; *martires* offers a second distinct category, whereas *mynchons* comes close to repeating *maidenis*; and the unusual *mynchons* appears nowhere else in the corpus. Secondly, it is no less questionable that 'brilliant scribal emendations' are virtually impossible; for the Athlone editors themselves helpfully demonstrate that they occur. One such emendation that they adopt in place of the archetypal reading is *tripe* from manuscript F (CUL

Ff. 5. 35) at C IX 262 *The tarre is vntydy þat to þe* shep *bylongeth*. Here, though R–K (p. 164) recognise that Cx's key-stave could be *to*, they judge it unlikely that the relatively uncommon *tripe* 'small flock' would have been put in place of *shep*. The word is rare (see MED s.v. *trippe* n. 2), but this might not be sufficient reason why an enterprising scribe could not have substituted it. For that such things occurred is shown by the example of C VII 106 *And fithele the, withoute flaterynge, of God Friday þe geste*. Here Cx reads the inappropriate *feste* but F has *geste*; and if *geste* is not a 'brilliant scribal emendation' (prompted in part by recalling **B**'s contextually apt synonym *storye*), it can only be a 'correction from a superior lost MS', an explanation that (as always) violates the canon of economy. However, in VII 106, by contrast with *shep* at IX 262, the archetypal **C** reading fails of originality by the criterion of sense, and should be emended to the F scribe's reading on the grounds that the latter cannot be bettered by any editorial conjecture.[31] But if *geste* is not derived from a superior lost **C** copy and could be a 'brilliant scribal emendation', so might *tripe* (though the requirement of sense will not compel its adoption). Kane's third suspect claim is that the *durior lectio* criterion forms 'the basis of textual criticism' and that the notion of a scribal variant being other than 'easier' would make 'nonsense' of it. But the foregoing analysis has shown this conclusion to be mistaken. For the criterion of the harder reading is not a basic principle; however valuable, it is only a procedure (§ 21). And as examples like this must indicate to its most hardened advocates, it is a procedure that is by no means universally applicable.

§ 34. Kane is of course right to contend all the same that 'the editor must at the outset allow the possibility of originality to these readings' (p. 162). But it is one thing to take theoretical cognisance of possibly authoritative manuscript corrections 'at the outset', and quite another to reject archetypal readings that are confirmed by a later version. The Athlone editors regularly confuse the possible with the probable, because they do not appreciate the force of the canon of ratification (they appear wholly innocent of that concept as elaborated at § 22). Now *martires* is an example where both **B** and **C** confirm the majority and probably archetypal reading of **A**, whereas in the case of *shep* there is no comparative material because the line is unique to **C**. But there is massive evidence in the core-text to show that Langland used *to* and similar grammatical words as mute key-staves (see § 47 below), an idiosyncratic practice that might be overlooked by a scribe who formed his notion of 'correct' metre on more conventional alliterative writers. In the case of VII 106, by contrast, which has a parallel in **B**, F's *geste* is just what an editor might propose for **C** on the basis of the form of Cx *feste* and the sense of Bx *storye*. Further favouring such a 'conjectural restoration'[32] is the fact that *geste*, unlike *mynchons* or *tripe*, is a word instanced in the **BC** core-text (at XI 21 and XV 200) in the sense required of '(sacred) narrative'. The contextual suitability that licenses emendation of Cx *feste* is thus supported by antecedent lexical probability, since *geste* demonstrably figured in the poet's word-stock.

§ 35. Now in fairness to the Athlone editors whose methods and conclusions have been criticised, the present editor must confess to rejecting the very same small-word stave as R–K at C IX 262 in favour of a comparable 'conjectural restoration' at A VI 79. In *The tour þere Treupe is hymself [tyliþ] vp to þe sonne*, Ax reads *is vp to* for *tyliþ vp to* and, by core-text metrical criteria, scans 'acceptably' on *to*. The crux of the argument for nonetheless emending is that (in contrast with C IX 262) *to* is here unlikely to be the intended stave-word. For in its one other appearance elsewhere as a 'full' stave, it is in a context where the repetition of two discrete homophones has a clear rhetorical purpose, pointed up by the emphatic paronomasia. This is B XVI 148 *The whiche tokne* to *þis day* to *muche is yvsed*, where the first *to* is the preposition of A VI 79 and C IX 262 but the second is the comparative adverb, and the line's characteristic wordplay is enhanced by the homophone's prior occurrence as the first syllable of to*kne*. In A VI 79 there is no such contextual justification for particular stress on the particle, so a full-stave *to* in the b-half would be pointless as well as clumsy. The basis of the 'conjectural restoration' offered is the parallel Z VI 66, and it is here contended that A VI 79 read likewise and the Ax scribe (not the poet) substituted *is* for a verb that was lexically unfamiliar. This example well illustrates what may be called the 'normal' processes of corruption; and its emendation presumes *tyleth* antecedently unlikely to be a scribal substitution for *is* (though the striking examples discussed above have vividly shown that such a possibility existed). There is, therefore, justification for the apprehensions of Kane, or of any editor who resorts to the direct method. If a scribe could make such a 'brilliant emendation' as *tyleth*, the entire *durior lectio* criterion might be at risk of becoming as threadbare as Coveitise's cloak and leaving barely enough room for the louse-leap of a conjecture. But by way of answer: while *tyleth* superficially resembles *mynchons* and *tripe*, two important features distinguish **Z**'s reading here from those examples. First, like *geste* earlier, *tyleth* has a parallel, at C VI 220 // AB *Til ten ʒerde other twelue* tol[led] *out threttene*, where the C-**p** spelling *tilled* for *tolled* should be especially noted. Second, it yields a reading both semantically and metrically stronger than that of Ax. Either feature by itself might be inconclusive; but together they point to **Z**'s originality and furnish a defensible rationale for emendation of **A**. What should be remembered in these situations is that the linear postulate has both a retrospective and a prospective dimension. It presumes either that a revision will not reinstate the version before the one being revised, or that if a later reading judged inferior to its predecessor is not ratified by its successor, revision cannot be assumed to have occurred.

§ 36. A theoretical objection to this argument arises that must now be answered, and it is as follows. If the linear postulate measures not certainty but only probability, however high (§ 25), it must admit exceptions. Langland might therefore have been prepared, for the sake of intelligibility, to adopt the poetically lame *is vp to* in place of the lexically obscure *tyleth*. But this possibility clashes with the antecedent probability that the purpose of revision was to improve what he had written. Thus it has been the common critical view of the changes from **A** to **B** that, though Langland (for structural or thematic reasons) omitted some passages of high quality, his direct rewriting yielded poetry that is both more profound and more precise. Cases of (perhaps regrettable) omission might include A X 118–30 and Z V 35–40,[33] examples of successful revision, the development of *plante of pes* at A I 137a into B I 152–8. But *Piers Plowman* studies have laboured under the mistaken belief (induced by Skeat's edition though largely lifted by Salter's and Pearsall's pioneering work)[34] that **C** is often poetically inferior to **B**, because it privileges the religious message over the artistic medium. It is of course arguable that not all **C**'s detailed changes are improvements, as in the case of *yʒoten hitsilue* at C I 149 compared with (*y*)*eten his fille* at B I 154.[35] But the experience of parallel-editing has brought it forcibly home to the present editor how generally **C** improves on **B** in depth of thought, exactness of language and clarity of expression as much as **B** surpasses **A** in richness of imagery, complexity of style and variety of tone. There is little sign of poetic decline up to the very last point where major alterations are detectable (C Passus XX). Such a judgement will, it is hoped, become widely accepted in time as a result of reading this critical text of all four versions in parallel. It is stated here mainly to underline that an antecedent expectation of progressive improvement is borne out by the evidence, and assists the editor in discriminating original readings from archetypal corruptions at each stage of the linear sequence of versions. Whether that expectation ever justifies emending an acceptable archetypal reading is something better left to the judgement of the reader, who may object that the principle of economy should always override the claims of the *durior lectio* criterion. The same reader is asked to remember, however, that while to alter an archetype is to offend against economy, to emend by adopting the reading of an earlier version does not multiply entities but reduce them. The case of *tyliþ* discussed at § 35 thus illustrates *in nuce* the subtle and complex lexical challenges faced by anyone attempting to edit the poem in all its extant versions.

(b) *Metrical Aspects*

§ 37. In §§ 23–36 above, selected syntactic, lexical and stylistic examples have brought out how the core-criteria assist in the work of discrimination and emendation. The theoretical demands of parallel-editing have now been sufficiently explored to place the reader in full possession of the textual principles relied upon in preparing this edition. The section will conclude with a formal account of the metre. This, though summary and illustrated mainly from the core-text, is based not on a representative sampling but on a complete analysis of the poem's 19,000 lines, one already cited selectively in an earlier study.[36] But as the confines of an edition do not allow for the listing of every line under its metrical type, the account below will mention only the lines of 'variant' type, the 87% not listed being of the *aa / ax* form rightly regarded as 'normative'. The aim of the following discussion is to 'fingerprint' the versification of all and only the lines of core-text, so as to provide a firm basis for recognising originality in singly-attested lines and a secure rationale for emending readings judged corrupt on metrical grounds.

Langland's Versification

§ 38. *Piers Plowman* is composed in accentual long-lines, which may be end-stopped or 'run-on' (enjambed),[37] and are divided into two halves ('a' and 'b') by a medial pause. The a-half may contain two or three stressed syllables (lifts) but the b-half must contain only two. Any lift may be followed, and the first lift in either half may be preceded, by a weak or a strong dip (of one or more than one unstressed syllables respectively). Rhyme and pararhyme of various kinds are used as ornamental or expressive devices, and their density exceeds that found in other alliterative makers; but as they are not unique, they cannot qualify as textually criterial (in Appendix One, §§ 5–6, it will be proposed that *identical* rhyme and *full-word* cross-caesural pararhyme are potentially criterial). The metre's main formal principle is the use of structural alliteration to heighten or reinforce the stressed syllables and so give the line its characteristic metrical shape. But contrary to the claim of Hoyt Duggan's 'Metrical Rule II' (unfortunately ambiguous in its formulation) that 'Alliteration always falls on a stressed syllable',[38] Langland sometimes alliterates syllables without stress and stresses syllables without alliteration (see § 39 below). Langland's lines vary much more in length than those of such contemporaries as the authors of *Purity* or *Wynnere and Wastoure*, of whom the first seems to have read and the second to have been read by him. Thus they range from ten syllables (as at B X 127–8 // A, Z VII 170) to almost twenty (C XV 226 // B), the majority falling between these extremes, with an increase in length between **A** and **B** proportionally continued in **C**. Such elasticity could induce scribal mislineation at all levels of transmission;[39] but it is what allows the poet to adhere to the natural stress-patterns of ordinary speech or prose and so achieve both tense and relaxed utterance at will. This capacity for expansion or contraction, which makes possible the poem's fluid movement and flexible tone, depends on the number of slack syllables (varying from one to four) in the dips that separate the lifts in each half-line. 'Zero-dips' or clashing stresses can occur in the b-verse, either 'duolexically', in two words (*cán súlle* XXI 402 // B, *póynt ménes* Z VII 232) or 'monolexically', within a single word (*sépúlcre* VII 170 // A?B,[40] *bihéstes* XX 320, *déuísede* XXI 331 // B, *cóntrícioun* XXI 350 //, *Iústície* XXI 400, 477 //; *vítáilles* B V 437, *décéites* B XII 130)[41]. Since the duolexical type is to be found elsewhere,[42] it is the monolexical variety of half-line that is criterial for authenticity. The lifts usually number four in the *standard line* of Types Ia and b, but augmentation of the a-verse by an extra lift gives the Type I variants Ic–e and Types IIa and b. The first lift always carries alliteration and is a 'full stave'. But in the commonest *extended* variant, Type Ie (as at IV 64 // ZAB),[43] the extra lift, whether analysed as occupying the second or third stave-position, may be 'blank' (unalliterated) or 'counterpointed' by a matching stave-sound in the second lift of the b-half (§ 39, end).

§ 39. The metrical term 'staves' has been customarily applied only to alliterating lifts; but Langland's practice over 19,000 lines requires formal recognition of three distinct types of stave. These are the traditional 'full' stave with stress and alliteration, the 'blank' stave with stress but no alliteration, and the 'mute' stave with alliteration but no stress. The blank stave appears not only in the extended Type Ie (scanning *aax / ax* or *axa / ax*) but in the 'reduced' Type IIIa (*ax / ax*), as at III 222 // ZAB.[44] In Types I and III, full staves stand in both halves of the line, but Type II is unusual in having them in the first half only, giving the 'clustered' scansion-pattern *aaa / xx*, as in II 227 //. All three Types may be alliteratively 'enriched' if a normally blank stave is made full. In Type I this decorative stave is the fourth, giving Type Ib (*aa / aa*), as at Pr 1 //; the third, giving Ic (*aaa / ax*), as at I 3 //; or the third and fifth together, giving Type Id (*aaa / aa*), as at III 174. In Type III the enriched lift may also be the fourth, giving Type IIIb (*ax / aa*), as at IV 12. But Types II and III yield two further enriched variants with a second repeated stave-sound. One of these is Type IIIc (*ab / ab*), as at VI 229 // where, despite the cross-caesural linkage, the alliteration is 'antiphonal', since the *a* and *b* staves have equal 'thematic' prominence and independence. This Type is very rare before the longer versions and is therefore not found in the primary core-text. The other enriched variant is the even rarer IIb (*aaa / bb*), as at IX 6 // B and B III 50 // A, in which the *a* and *b* groups also relate 'antiphonally' (not 'contrapuntally'), because the *lettres* or 'stavesounds' are not *loken* or 'interwoven'. Type IIb, in which no mute staves feature, is the only one of the main line-types that is strictly criterial.

§ 40. The distribution of staves found in one enriched variant of Type Ie (*aab / ab*) produces a pattern of 'contrapuntal' staves that could be described as ornamental or decorative (as at X 150 //AB). But that found in Types IIb and IIIc establishes new structural types, because the primary and secondary staves (with their ratios 3:2 and 2:2 respectively) achieve (near-)equal prominence. Now in over 400 lines, both common or singly attested, the first lift of the b-verse, the 'key-stave', is unstressed ('mute'), as in *with* at Pr 24 //. But when by way of compensation the two lifts following this muted stave introduce a second stave-sound, a new pattern results, as at VI 322 //. This special type of *transitional* line ('T-type' for short), which shares features of the muted Type Ie and of Ib, is apparently unique to Langland and so strongly criterial. It is given a special notation *aa / [a]bb*, the brackets signifying that the key-stave is mute. Despite a superficial likeness to Type Ie, these *a*- and *b*- staves are not thematic and contrapuntal respectively (§ 39). But because the first of the b-staves carries part of the key-stave's function of stress (lost after muting), it is more than ornamental. Structurally, it may be thought of as forming with the second b-stave a sort of alliterative 'cauda', and this new pattern should be recognised as a separate category. Some thirty examples appear in the core-text, and the T-type is also abundantly illustrated in the non-paralleled lines of the poem's canonical versions. But since it is virtually confined to Langland, its occurrence in the unique Z III 158 and VII 38 serves to give the T-type line a significant part in the metrical case for **Z**'s authenticity.

Variant Line-Types

§ 41. As the patterns briefly analysed above provide firm guidelines for establishing the acceptability of lines attested severally in each version, their representation in the core-text is worth setting out here in full. Of lines that scan in one or other of the *ten anormative types* (non-*aa / ax*), the primary division of core-text yields some 60 or about 11.3% of its 530 lines; the secondary division of 598 lines, some 70 (= 11.7%); and the tertiary (totalling 2150 with the 870 of C XXI–XXII // excluded), some 286 (= 13.3%). Of the 3280 lines strictly qualifying (i.e. the total 4140 *minus* Passus XXI–XXII), some 416 or 12.6% are therefore 'variant'; so at some 87.4% of the core-text, the 'normative' lines can be seen fully to deserve their name. In illustrating the variant types, estimates have been conservative, no ambiguous examples or lines capable of normative scansion being admitted (a query recognises the possibility of alternative scansions). It will be observed that the degree of homogeneity displayed is very striking, **BC** indicating only a *marginal* increase in departures from the norm, while the small non-linear groups **ZB**, **ZC** and **AC** yield no variant lines. For ease of reference, the data have been set out by type, indicating the relative degree of representation in each core-text division. An '*' denotes counterpoint in extended lines, a '+' enrichment or supplementation in lines of Type II or III, 'm' = macaronic. Line-references observe the sequence **CBAZ**.

Type Ib *aa / aa* **ZABC**: Pr 1. I 61, 68, 190. II 220. III 166, 179, 194. IV 88–9. VII 59, 214, 225. VIII 2, 94, 153. IX 61. **ABC**: Pr 55, 84. III 50, 431. VI 196, 400, 414. VII 280, 289. VIII 78. X 19, 44, 77, 118, 134, 139. XI 4, 128. **ZAB**: Pr 12. I 17, 68, 209. II 123. III 108. IV 13, 118, 126. V 382. VI 165, 214, 246. VII 4. **ZA**: V 53. VII 12, 125. VIII 17. **ZB**, **ZC**, **AC**: 0. **AB**: III 217, 262. V 108. VIII 47, 101. IX 52. X 110, 119, 126, 167, 170, 333. **BC**: Pr 131, 217. II 84, 97. III 465. VI 58, 74, 260, 270. VII 18, 94. X 86, 309. X1 180, 181. XII 119. XIII 100, 173. XIV 8, 48, 51, 54, 60, 65, 77, 120, 138, 145, 185. XVI 4, 125, 148. XVII 105, 182, 216, 270, 281. XVIII 34, 183, 284. XIX 32, 57, 192, 230, 251, 261, 310, 330, 334. XX 145, 169, 180, 364, 375, 419, 447, 455, 473, 476. *Total*: 122 = 29.3%.

Type Ic *aaa / ax* **ZABC**: Pr 19. I 3. II 3, ?30, ?157, 202, 212. III 3, 23, 127, 176, 195. IV 16, 20, 91, 97. VI 8. VII 161, 268. VIII 123, 129, 164, 165, 224, 294, 318, 333. **ABC**: Pr 65. VI 63, 390, 417. VII 281. X 130, 155. XI 41, 47. **ZAB**: I 34, 105. II 129, 161. V 63. VII 62. **ZA**: II 22. IV 137. VII 128, 176. VIII 15. **AB**: Pr 16. VII 172. X 36, 295. **BC**: Pr 148, 183, 195. I 139. III 478. V 160. VI 56, 249, 277. VII 13, 48. 77, 80, *83, 98, 138. IX 54. X 15, 141. XI 190, 212, 314. XII 10, 15, 121. XIII 111, 137, 211. XIV 94, 97, 103, 171. XV 5, 260, 293. XVI 143, 144, 214, 257. XVIII 31, 292. XIX 193. XX 4, 36, 56, 59, 210, 225, 374, 431, 474. *Total*: 100 = 24.0%.

Type Id *aaa / aa* **ZABC**: III 174. VIII 207. **ABC**, **ZAB**: 0. **AB**: VII 156. **BC**: Pr 149. VI 262. *Total*: 5 = 1.2%.

Type Ie *aax / ax* etc. **ZABC**: I 82. III 18. IV 64, 74, 79 (*axa / ax*). *V 130 (*aba / ab*). VIII 317, 322, 347 (*aax / aa*). **ABC**: III 267. V 120. VI 395. VIII 76, 77. X 120, 135, *144. XI 38. **ZAB**: I 73. II *122, 202. V 227. VI *87. **ZA**: II 42. **AB**: V 83. VII 80. VIII *50. IX 54, 136, 204. X *66, 215. **BC**: Pr 90. II 49. III 422, 487. VI 69, 157, 236, 250, *275, 297. VII 19, 42, 71, 116. VIII *270. XI 165, 194, 196. 229, 239. XII 11, 49, 110, 111, 115, 136, 144. XIII 103, *104, 110, 119. XIV 18, *85, 104, 106, 121, 142, 194. XV 39, 43, 136 (m), 144, 203, 227, 231, 253, 263. XVI 3, 8, 66, 85, 90, *93, *96, 108, 110, 128, 130, 147, 168, 184, 194, 217, 348. XVII 13, 94, 100, 265, 316. XVIII 274. XIX 16, 46, *59, 83, 85, *142, 145, *223, 255, 267, 294, 298, 311, 312, 316, 332. XX 12, 42, 47, *49, 57, 94, 137, 143, 171, 176, *179, *185, 231, 245, 246, *254, 257, 268, 270, 342, 362, 388, 412, 425, 430, 472. *Total* 143 = 34.3%.

Type IIa *aaa / xx* **ZABC** II 227. IV 107. VII 97, 331. **ABC**: Pr 80. VIII 110. X 68. **ZAB**: V 72. **ZA**: VII 131. **AB**: †III 255. VIII 32, 36. X 47. **BC**: †VI 155. VII 47 (*enriched*), 151 (m). XII 114, 137. XIV 58, 213. XVII 120. [XVIII 124 (m)]. XIX 165, 279. 299. XX 68, 122, †157, 236, 398, 424, 466. *Total* 31 = 6.9%.

Type IIb *aaa / bb* **ZABC, ZAB**: 0. **ABC**: IV 145. X 72. **ZA**: VI 81n. VIII 78. **AB**: III 50. V †456. **BC**: XV 96. XVI 82, 182. XVII 203, 318. XX 229. *Total* 11 = 2.6%.

Type IIIa *ax / ax* **ZABC**: III 222. V 116. VI 319 (*axx / ax*). VII 178, 179. **ABC**: VI 199, 229, 376. VII 220. IX 289, 320, 335n. X 70. **ZAB**: II 105. IV 59. VI 248. **ZA**: VI 46. **AB**: II 127. III 10, 229. V 9 (*ext.*)n. X 162. **BC**: Pr 166. VI 345. [XII 12 (m)]. †XIII 126, 127, 198. XIV 99, 204. XV 41. XVI 210. [XVII 203, 318]. [XVIII 124.] XIX 34, 190, 299. *Total* 38 = 8.5%.

Type IIIb *ax / aa* **ZABC** IV 12. **ABC**: IX 309. **ZAB, ZA, AB**: 0. **BC**: XVI 223. *Total* 3 = 0.7%.

Type IIIc *ab / ab* **ZABC**: 0. **ABC**: VI 229. **ZAB**: 0. **ZA**: VIII 14. **AB**: V 627. X 201. **BC**: XI 46, 175. XII 3. XIX 190. *Total* 8 = 1.6%.

'T'-type *aa / [a]bb* **ZABC**: I 41. (V 135 ?†Ax). VI 322. IX 170. **ABC**: X 146. XI 124. **ZAB**: I 22. (?108). †IV 91. 194. **AB**: Pr 218 (cf. // C). **BC**: Pr 196. †I 155. VI 180. VII 36, 95. X 14, ?122. XII 34, 52, 70, 147. 192. XVI 51, 185. XVII 215. XVIII 287. XIX 15. XX 27, 132, 160, 408. *Total* 29 = 7%.

These lists show that (after the composite 'T-type') Types II and III, at about 10% each, are the rarest and Type Ie the most favoured variant, closely followed by Type Ib.

§ 42. The ten variant types are also exemplified in the unique lines of **B** and **C**, all but the very rare IIb in **A** and all but Id, IIb and IIIc in **Z**, which has, it should be noted, only about 200 non-paralleled lines (or 13% of its text). As supporting the common authorship of all four texts, this evidence is illustrated with one example per passus where possible. But because of its special importance for the authentication of A XII and **Z**, the data for these are given in full.

Type Ib C: Pr 175. I 27, 202–3. II 104. III 94. IV 65. V 7. VI 54. VII 148. VIII 178. IX 174. X 100. XI 74. XII 215. XIII 30. XIV 60. XV 98. XVI 23. XVII 127. XVIII 22. XIX 3. XX 196. **B**: Pr 50. II 18. III 306. IV 43. V 108. VI 46. VII 35. VIII 92. IX 44. X 24–5. XI 217. XII 41. XIII 6. XIV 11. XV 241. XVI 177. XVII 70. XVIII 252. **A**: II 137. III 31. IV 149. V 70, 97. VII 3. VIII 37. X 28. 45. 114. 137. 160. XI 81, 177, 183, 257, 272, 295. XII 23, 27, 34 (*s / sh*), 79, 80, 94. **Z**: Pr 57, 83, 100. II 60, 143. IV 146. V 3, 24, 39, 45, 140. VII 53, 58, 198.

Type Ic C: Pr 30, 37. II 41. III 351, 356. IV 195. VI 101, 118. 301. VII 13. VIII 89. IX 207, 273. X 79. XI 298. XII 88. XIII 29, 65, 187. XIV 21. 38. XV 122. XVI 17. XVII 67. XVIII 10. XIX 242. XX 317. **B**: Pr 45. II 107. IV 195. V 429. VII 36. IX 106, 178. X 329, 340. XI 63, 159, 172, 183, 227. XII 5, 20, 68. XIII 125, 224, 237. XIV 1, 18. XV 297, 348. XVI 20, 117. XVII 82. XVIII 95. **A**: X 75, 99, 152, 158, 159. XI 188, 222, 310. XII 20, 59, 61, 70. **Z**: Pr 94. I 116. II 167. III 150, 151. IV 1, 131. V VII 323. 74, 93. VI 74.

Type Id C: Pr 88. I 94. III 404 (m), 480 (m). X 77. XI 18. XII 119. XVII 126. XVIII 246. XX 112. **B**: III 72. X 95. XII 228. XV 433. XVII 139, 345. **A**: V 97. **Z**: O.

Type Ie C: Pr 96. I 103. II 18. III *96, 100. IV 170. V 68. VI 169. VII 204. VIII 41. IX 35. X 174. XI 67. XII *161. XIII 1. XIV 134. XV 119. XVI 8. XVII 32. XVIII 1. XIX 72. XX *98. **B**: Pr 129. I 115. II 36. III 245. V 131, 141, 242. VI 140. VII 53. IX 54, 67, 73. X 284. XI 26. XII 17. XIII 21. XIV 44. XV 66. XVI 6. XVII 37. XVIII 55. **A**: I 178. VI 27. IX 45. XI 252. **Z**: Pr *54, 99. I 113. II 91. III 54, 169. V 95. VI *70. VII 59, 286, 316.

Type IIa C: Pr 100, 117. I 113. III 122 (monolexical staves), 274. IV 62+. V 17. VI 96. VII 306. VIII 177. IX 130+. XII 233. XIII 230. XIV 31, 33. XVI 24, 160. XVII 40, 83. **B**: III 100, 265. IV 171. VIII 23. IX 70. X 302, 365. XI 153, 262. XII 51, 118. XIII 114. XIV 30. XV 3+. 250. XVI 73. XVII 43. XVIII 383 (*f / þ*). **A**: VII 235+. X 56+. **Z**: I 100. III 10, 165. IV 120. VI 3. VII 76. VIII 69.

Type IIb C: I 55. III 338. ?355 (m),494. VI 51. X 35, 215. XIII 192. XIV 161. XVIII 92, 219. **B**: Pr 95. V 370. 394 (*liaisonal*), 407. VII 30. X 274 (em.). XI 39. XII 227. XIII 32. XIV 48, 137. XV 71, 198. XVII 170. XVIII 46 (m). **A**: V 49. XI 213 (*mute 2nd st.*). **Z**: 0.

Type IIIa C: Pr 110. III 30, 342. V 53. VI *22. VIII *209. IX 261 (m). XI 109. XIII 63. XIV 4, 72. XV 158. XVI 191 (m). XVII 140. XVIII 119 (m). XIX 26. XX 20 (m). **B**: I 118. III *334, 341. IV 159. V 2, 38. VI 180. VII 73. IX 182, 200. X *98, 264. XI 50, 53. XII 30, 40. XIII 35. XIV 98. XV 117, 119. XVI 16 (m), 150. XVIII 71, 113. **A**: XI *163, 178, 254 (m). XII 28 (m), 49, 78, 83. **Z**: Pr 50. IV 144. V 96. VI 78. VIII 74.

Type IIIb C: III 335. VI 267. X 179. XI 33, 68. XV 215. XVI 270, 282. XVIII 7. XX *198. **B**: I 120. II 33. IV *36. IX 88 (or IIIa on *sh / j*). XI *7, 397. XII 146. XV 295, 444. XVII 101 (ext). **A, Z**: 0.

Type IIIc C: XIII 40. XVI 173. XVII 38. XVIII 61, 237. XIX 9. XX 216. **B**: V 101, 509. 275. VI 241. IX 71. X 438 (m). XI 52, 214, 397. XII 81. XV 69 (*Latin*). XVI 244, 257. XVIII 54, 308. **A**: IX 52. **Z**: 0.

'T'-type C: Pr 7. II 12, 27. III 296. IV 116. V 23, 111. VI 46, 180. VII 36. VIII 237. IX 180. X 56. XI 44. XII 5. XIII 245. XVI 219. XVII 291. XVIII 4, 24, 262. XIX 176, 206. XX 217. **B**: Pr 163. I 150. II 37. IV 157. V 421. VI 133, 240. IX 45, 55. X 118. XI 148. XII 16. XIII 346. XIV 274. XV 113, 484. XVI 49. XVII 107. XVIII 301. **A**: X 108, 126. **Z**: II 118. III 158. VII 38, 245, 279.

Of these ten variant-types, the eight found in other writers[45] obviously do not count as criterial. But the general showing from the four versions' typical patterns is congruent with their coming from the hand of the same poet, and the 'idiometric' (or metrically unique) Types IIb and 'T' indicate that this is likely to be the case.

§ 43. What is true of the 'straight' English line-types also holds for most of the Latin / French-English macaronic lines, as is shown by some 50 core-text examples from C Pr–XI, where **ABC** are all present:

ZABC: Pr 226 (*French*). I 48, 82, 92, 195. II 191. IV 140–1. VI 315, 320, 329. VII 56. VIII 95, 266 and 334 (*French*). IX 3, 23. **ABC**: Pr 40. III 311, 432. VI 398. VII 77. IX 311 and X 11 (*French*). X 134–5. XI 7, 51, 299. **ZAB**: II 123. V 475. VI 232. **BC**: III 463. V 171. VII 6, 116. (IX 69). X 20–1, 258. XI 165, 174, 178, 191, 249. **AB**: VII 127. IX 49. X 343, 346.

These are exactly paralleled by about 40 examples from C Pr–XI found in one version only:

C: II 185. III 299, 355–6, 405. IV 164, 188, 190. V 46, 86–8. VI 257. VII 291. IX 45, 186, 257–8, 261, 272. X 95, 175. **B**: III 350. IV 120. V 242, 276, 298, 419. VII 136, 151. X 44, 282, 320. **A**: VIII 135. X 50, 262. XI 254. XII 28, 56–7. **Z**: V 142–3. VIII 61.[46]

A mere handful of 'licensed' macaronic lines have only two full staves in the a-verse:

ZABC: V 199. **BC**: III 489, 493. VI 64, 153, 283. VII 152.

These too are paralleled in lines unique to a single version:

C VI 302. B XIII 196. A VIII 123. Z VII 267.[47]

The macaronics likewise support attribution of the canonical versions, A XII and the Z-text to one and the same hand.[48]

Stave-Types

§ 44. The variant types of line (especially IIb and 'T'), however useful for discrimination and emendation, are not the only available means to achieve a comprehensive metrical 'fingerprinting' of the poet. The core-text also illustrates twelve distinct categories of *stave*. As well as the full, mute, blank, monolexical and contrapuntal, it offers examples of the supplemental, the internal, the liaisonal, the cognative, the dialectal, the macaronic and the microlexical (or 'smallword') types of stave. Consideration has already been given to the first three, the foundation of the variant line-types (§ 39 above); to the monolexical,[49] usually featuring one full and one blank stave in a single word (§ 38); and to the contrapuntal stave that functions both decoratively (§ 39)[50] and as a structural device for creating the T-type (§ 40). No less 'idiometric' than these is the interesting minor category of the 'supplemental' fourth stave. This is sometimes found when the line's *first lift* (invariably a full stave) is a word of low semantic rank such as a bound morpheme, grammatical lexeme, modal verb or the verb *to be*.[51] Occasionally it appears also when the *key-*

stave is such a word and is muted (C VII 197, X 172 //, XV 145; B XV 244), and sometimes to strengthen the stave-pattern in the b-half of a Type III line (*B IX 87).

Core-text: IX 283 // AB *by*-[1] → *bulle*, X 172 // B *y*- → -*ynne*, XIX 165 // B *For* → *fynger*, XXI 271 // B *Gregory* → *gode* and XXII 298 // B *In* → *heeld*.
Single-version: C V 198 *seynt* → *soules*, VII 197 *where* → *woneth*, X 41 -*ful* → *fallynge*, X 108 *so* → *spede*, XI 125 *con*- → *compas*, XV 145 *with* → *wynne*, XIX 135 *al* → *euere*, XX 71 *somme* → *assaie*, XXII 298 // *In* → *heeld*. **B** II 107 (in *a*-half) *wiþ*[1] ← *while*, IX 87 *Cristes* → *kynde*, XI 70 *Ac* yet → *konnyng*, XII 147 *But* → *beste*, XIII 321 *was* → *wille*, XV 247 (with *liaised* first stave) *Ac avarice* → *kynnesmen*. **A** VII 235 *He* → *hondis*.

Latin or French staves (§ 43 above) follow the same rules as native words. So does the rare 'dialectal' stave, a South-Western variant of the standard pronominal forms *they* and *she*, of which examples are *hij* at B Pr 66 // A and *heo* at B III 29 // ZA, B IX 55 (T-type).

§ 45. Also noteworthy are two 'licences' virtually unknown outside Langland that may be regarded as criterial. One is the internal stave, a sound that must be isolated from its consonant-group to furnish the structural alliteration of a formal line-type. An example is *l* [← *cl*] in III 35 // B, replacing an *l*-alliterating Type Ib line in A III 31 that itself revises a Type IIIb in Z III 34.[52] Others are:

V 153 // B [*k* ← *sk*]. VIII 67 [*g* ← *gl*]. X 105 // B [*r* ← *thr*], 269 [*k* ← *sk*]. XI 197 // B [*t* ← *st*] and the macaronic XXI 202 // B [*p* ← *sp*], XXI 152 // [*r* ← *Chr*], 202 // [*p* ←*sp*], 303 // [*p* ← *sp*]. B IV 23 [*w* ← *tw*]. B VII 39 [*l* ← *pl*]. B XVII 3 [*r* ← *wr*].

A second licensed variety is the liaisonal stave, a device through which a preceding word's final consonant provides the needed stave-sound by liaison with the next lift's initial sound (usually a vowel).[53] Examples are:

d at B V 394 (*quod he*). *f* at B II 194 // ZA, B V 627, IX 27, XV 289, XVI 231 (all three removed at // C X 153, XVII 15, XVIII 248) and A XI 46; *f* + consonant at B I 18 // ZA (*fw, fl, fl*). *k* at B XV 247. *n* at VII 217 and VIII 40 // ZAB, VI 128 // B. *s* at C III 104 (*this haue*), V 200, B XII 22, XIII 19 (*mac.*); *s* + consonant at B X 402 (*sw, s, s*). *t* + consonant at B V 287 *it were* (cf. XX 247). *þat* B X 233 *þe articles* (+ *f*), XVII 88.

Perhaps the most striking case occurs at XX 247 // B *Tho þat wéren in héuene token stélla comáta*, where the *t* of *þat* functions as the first stave, liaising with *weren*. With its mute key-stave in [*to*] *ken* and internal supplemental stave in *stella* [*t* ← *st*], this line demonstrates how a concentration of idiometric features helps to produce the peculiarly Langlandian tone of 'vernacular clerkliness'.

§ 46. Similar to the last two 'licensed' categories are the *cognative* staves, exploited by the poet to enlarge the range of his alliterative repertoire.[54] Occurring where voiced and unvoiced consonants (such as the stops *b, d, g: p, t, k*) are alliterated together, these may be thought of as 'metrical allophones'. Like them is *s* / *sh*, widely attested in all versions including **Z** (III 122); but this is not criterial, as it is found in other alliterative works.[55] Neither, strictly, are the labial spirants, since it seems likely that the poet's dialect levelled *f* and *v* as |v|, and possible that his idiolect did the same for the pairs |f| and |θ| (= *th, þ* in lexical words), |v| and |ð| (= non-lexical *th, þ*). But *f, v* and lexical *þ* alliterating together may be an instance of 'idiometric' allophony (see Appendix One, A.§2(a)). Examples from the core-text are:

Stops. **b** / **p**: V 165 // B. XVI 67 // B, 115 // B (m). **k** / **g**: VIII 79 (*internal* 1st *stave*). XIX 279 // B. XXI 213, 323 // B. A IV 91 // Z. **t** / **d**: XX 182, 325.
Spirants. **f** / **v**: Pr 69 // AB. III 36 // ZAB. V 191 // ZAB (m). XVI 221 // B (m). XVII 109 // B. XIX 271 // B. XX 123, 154 // B. **f** / **v** / **th**: B I 23, V 382 // ZA. **s** / **sh**: Pr 221 // AB (*T-type*). II 24, 59 // B. III 429 // AB, 460 // B. VI 355 // AB.

III 460, VII 28, XIX 277 // B. **B** II 126; 159, 164, 168 // ZA [in these last three, the **C** revision alliterates only on |s|]. B V 73, VI 232 // ZA. B III 50 // A. **A** IV 28 // Z.

And examples found in the four versions severally include:

b / p in C XVI 263, 289; *d / t* in C XV 127 (cf. B XIII 117), B XVIII 379 (from liaison of *pat̲ is̲*); *f / v* at C XV 5, B Pr 190; *f / þ* at B V 410; *k / g* at C XIV 132, B V 136; *s / sh* at C Pr 13, Z III 122, 152, IV 152.

This evidence, which indicates that some kinds of metrical allophones formed a part of the poet's repertoire from the earliest stages, argues against any emendation of 'cognatively'-scanning lines on metrical grounds.

§ 47. Perhaps the most distinctive stave-type of all is the microlexical or 'small-word' stave, a grammatical morpheme that may appear in either half of the line as a full or a mute stave.[56] This type, which includes modal verbs as well as pronouns, prepositions and prefixes, was first recognised by Kane and Donaldson[57] and is best known for providing (very conspicuously) the key-stave at numerous points in the core-text and in each version severally. In itself, it is an indicative authenticating feature as well as being the structural basis of the strictly criterial T-type line (§ 40 above). Excluding such lines and equally all others with bound-morpheme prefixes like *con-*, *des-*, *en-*, *mys-*, *pro-* or *re-* occurring in Romance-derived words capable of variable stress, there are nearly two hundred mute key-staves to be found in the core-text. Where possible, one from each passus is given for illustration, reference being as usual to the 'senior' version in the grouping:

ZABC: Pr 24. I 54. II 209, 212. III 36. IV 57. V 119. VI 322. VII 56. VIII 105, 266 (*French*). IX 1, 61. **ABC:** II 252. III 283. VI 56. VIII 328. X 120. XI 1, 50, 90, 137. **BC:** Pr 85, 180. II 36, 66. III 51. VI 37. VII 4. **ZAB:** B I 23, 132. IV 28. V 25. **AB:** Pr 62. II 128. III 221, 227. X 107. **ZA:** I 120. II 30. VII 226.

Over 200 examples are also found in each version severally (for a full list of both classes see Appendix One):

C: Pr 85. I 18. II 12. III 65. IV 21. V 19. VI 16. IX 32. X 181. XI 1, 151. **B:** Pr 180. II 14. III 235. IV 34. V 86. VI 47. VII 55. IX 36. X 161. **A:** V 68. VII 236. VIII 33. X 57, 145, 206. XI 62, 64, 165, 224. XII 11, 19, 24, 567 (m). **Z:** Pr 145. II 148. IV 159. VII 59, 231, 261.

Mute staves in other than key-position include:

ZABC: I 43. III 190. IV 1.V 197. VII 187. VIII 54. **ABC:** Pr 48. VII 235. X 3, 144. **ZAB:** I 50. V 224, 200. VII 63. **BC:** VI 184. XIII 103. **AB:** V 110.

But even more striking than these mute staves are the much rarer microlexical full-staves, which contextually receive heavy stress. Like their mute counterparts, they are mainly grammatical lexemes and modals, and the same words tend to recur (*with, for*). But because their identification demands a higher interpretative element, only unambiguous examples are cited (some in non-key position are given):

ZABC: II 234 *with*. IV 50 *for*. 62 *bi*. VIII 110 *wol*. IX 167 *with*. **ABC:** Pr 78 *bi*. **BC:** X 237 *for*. XV 228 *but*. XVI 221 *emforth*. XVII 193 *so*. 268 *bi-*. XIX 164 *For*. 261 *to*. XX 70 *so*. 417 *my*. **C:** II 34, VI 26 *my*. IX 200 *by*. XI 75 *þe*. XIV 37 *with*. 91 *But*. **B:** III 353 *so*. XIII 321 *was*. XV 171 *kan*. 284 *by*. 324 *for*. 569 *by*. ?XVI 130 *so*. 148 *to* (1, 2). XVII 36 *so*. 154 *for*. 279 *to* (1). **A:** V 136 *be*.

§ 48. Close examination of this rough double-dozen of line- and stave-types suggests that, at the metrical level, the poem's textual transmission was much less unreliable than the Athlone editors suppose. The latter deserve full credit for their recognition of Langland's 'small-word' and monolexical staves and their illuminating metrical concept of 'modulation'.[58] But the unhappy textual consequences of shortcomings in their metrical theory appear in several groundless emendations of Type III lines and of cognatively, internally and liaisonally staved lines among those cited above.[59] Such mistakes can be avoided by heeding the authority of the core-text, which furnishes the editor with a broad range of metrical as well as syntactical or stylistic means for characteristing the poet's practice comprehensively and accurately.[60] But of these the *strictly* criterial features, as described and exemplified above, are five: among types of line, the IIb *aaa / bb* and 'T'-type *aa / [a]bb* pattern;[61] of half-line, the monolexical; of stave, the internal and liaisonal. To the 'intralinear' stave-types that feature at the line-level may now be added, at a level beyond that of the single line, the 'homolexical' translinear stave. This is the name for a stave formed by the same word appearing as the last lift of one line (usually blank) and the first of the next (always full). The thirty examples of this feature, which when read consecutively are so striking as to have a claim to being also criterial, are given separately here for convenience (they are included again in the complete list of translinear staves at Appendix I § 8 v).

Core-text ZABC III 2~3. 36~7. IX 62~3. **ZAB** IV [43~4]. 187. X 35~6. **BC** XI 284~5. XVI 47~8. XIX 254~5. XX 403~4. XXI 92~3. XXII 189~90.
Separate versions C VI 13~14. 62~3. 244~5. XIV 198~9. XVI 47~8. 243~4. XVII 173~4. XVIII 10~11. XIX 254~5. **B** IV 187~8. V 141~2. XII 165~6. 168~9. XIII 128~9. XIV 322~3. XVI 12~13. **A** X 52~3. **Z** IV 125~6.

One further feature unlisted above because not especially characteristic of Langland is the feminine ending required at the end of the line. The first 13 lines of the Prologue show this syllable to occur eleven times in inflexional *–e(s)*, once in *–ed* (7), and once in unstressed *hit* (11; cf. *sweuene* in // B 11). The practice is observed throughout the poem, and its editorial significance may be judged from the list of archetypal lines given in Vol. I pp 761–2 where a metrically needed final *-e* has been added to the last word in a line.[62] Although this feature is not criterial, its function as a constraint upon conjectural emendation is shown in its ruling out as acceptable any b-half emendation that does not end with a single unstressed syllable.

iv. *Presentation of the* Text *and* Editorial Matter

(a) *The Text*

§ 49. This explanation of the principles and methods used in preparing the parallel-text edition concludes with an account of the presentation of the **A**, **B**, **C** and **Z** *Texts* in Vol. I and its relation to the *Textual Notes* forming Part B of Vol. II. The treatment of the text has throughout aimed at ease of use by readers concerned with the structure and meaning of the poem. The main effort has therefore been to present for each version surviving in multiple copies the substantive readings of its reconstructed archetype, emended only where necessary, in the language of the chosen copy-text. But since each base-manuscript has been preferred less for its superior readings than for its completeness, early date and consistency of grammar and dialect, the linguistic forms have been carefully preserved and all emendations adapted to accord with them. In the case of **Z**, the object has not been to reconstruct the language of Bodley 851's exemplar, let alone of that exemplar's source, which analysis indicates was an authorial draft (III, *Z Version* § 28). For as there is only one witness for this version, except for correction of evident mechanical errors, its linguistic accidentals have been kept unaltered even where they may conceal substantive forms that were closer to the original.

§ 50. The copy-texts of the three main versions have been prepared after a full collation of each of the four manuscripts (*T, W, X* and *Z*). In preparing the selection of variants used in the Apparatus, it has fortunately been possible to consult the originals of nearly all the other manuscripts. But for a few, such as manuscript W of **C**, the former Duke of Westminster's copy, microfilms have been used. In the edited text, all manuscript contractions are silently expanded to accord with the prevailing forms of the copy in question. In Latin quotations & is printed as *et* and &c as '...'. One contraction of particular note that occurs in MS Huntington 143, the copy-text for **C**, is *ll* joined by a ligature. Though its significance is not certain, it has been interpreted as syllabic where a final -*e* is metrically required at the line-end (see § 48 above), but not in other positions. Elsewhere, when any of the copy-texts lacks such a final -*e*, it is supplied in italic (see Appendix Two in Vol. I). All exterior presentational features such as capitalisation, word-division, punctuation and paragraphing are editorial. No record is made of such features as they appear in the base-manuscripts, though they have occasionally offered interpretative guidance.[63] Skeat's Oxford Edition was inconsistent in its handling of Middle English letter-forms but preserved the manuscripts' paragraphing and medial pointing. The Athlone editions use modern punctuation but not capitals for proper names, and have no paragraphing. In contrast with both, this edition's treatment of presentational features, especially punctuation, is thoroughgoing and explicit; its basis is a conviction that the poet's meaning can be securely understood from the structure of his sentences, which shows the impress of training in Latin grammar. Although (as the present editor is aware) the author of *Piers Plowman* enjoyed wordplay, his ambiguities tend to be semantic or lexical rather than morphosyntactic. So it has seemed that this edition would best serve the reader's interests by using the resources of punctuation and paragraphing as Langland might have done had he been writing today. Those who believe that his metre and sense are better appreciated through attending to the layout of manuscripts prepared for readers close in time to the poet have the option of inspecting facsimiles of the copytexts, all of which have now been published.[64]

§ 51. The original spelling has, on the other hand, been kept, including the obsolete letters *ȝ* and *þ*.[65] Though no loss of sense would be sustained if these were replaced by their modern equivalents, as in standard editions of Chaucer (or the Everyman *B-Text*), an undesirable discrepancy would arise between the Text and the Apparatus and *Textual Notes* that could cause confusion.[66] Where particular spellings of the base-manuscripts are rejected because misleadingly ambiguous or unlikely to represent 'true' forms instanced in the period, they have been recorded in the Appendix (e.g. *selles* C Pr 5, *cussed* C Pr 95 or *bygge* C V 90). The same treatment has been given to Latin and French text, which is printed in italics even where the base-manuscript may have no rubrication, underlining or boxing. Critical readings taken from another manuscript of the version in question retain spellings where compatible with those of the copy-text or adapt them to the customary spelling of the latter (e.g. *kairen, cracchy* B Pr 29, 186). The same holds for all readings without manuscript support that are introduced as restorations, reconstructions or conjectures (e.g. *luther* C I 109 or *wiþseide* B IV 91 //). Readings 'restored' from another version have the form of the relevant version as printed in this edition, but adapted to the copy-text's spelling where appropriate (e.g. [*a*]*redy* A IV 155 or [*þr*]*umblide* A V 200). Square brackets in the text are used only around readings restored from another version (e.g. [*Til*] and [*were*] B Pr 41); reconstructed from extant evidence (e.g. *of-wa*[*ndr*]*ed* C Pr 7); or wholly conjectural (e.g. [*me*] B Pr 11 // ZA). Brackets are not placed around readings adopted from one or more extant witnesses to the version in question. When the emended reading's source is obvious from the parallel text(s), this fact is not repeated in the Apparatus, but its original proposer (where there is one) is acknowledged (e.g. 'K–D' at B Pr 76).

§ 52. The treatment of the copy-texts disregards most intralinear *ordinatio* features of the English text and larger interlinear ones like section-headings, as well as internal or marginal glosses and annotations by the main scribe, a corrector or a later hand. *Incipits* and *explicits*, however, as potentially informative, are recorded in the *Apparatus* under the manuscript form judged closest to that of the versional archetype. More often than not this is the inferential form of one or other sub-archetype. For example, in the rubric for Passus I of the **C** Version (p. 27), the wording of **x** as accurately preserved in the copy-text X is treated like a standard lemma and that of **p** as a normal variant. Significant positive variants usually appear in brackets, e.g. the divergent α rubrics at Passus III of **B** (p. 86), and major negative variants are also recorded, e.g. '*om* GC^2' at the same point. Where the archetype apparently lacked a rubric but some copies supply one, these are noted, e.g. at the end of Passus VII of **B** (p. 354). There is probably no part of the rubrics that can be regarded with certainty as original (see the discussion in Appendix Two). But as the internal organisation of the text indicates that at least the numbered passus-headings are likely to derive from the author, these are given in an equivalent English form in the text.[67]

(b) *Apparatus*

§ 53. The main function of the *Textual Apparatus* (touched on briefly at *Intro.* II, § 6) is to record information relevant for the establishment of the archetypal text when the latter is not attested by the manuscripts with actual or virtual unanimity. When no entry appears, it is to be assumed that there are no variants or that the few which exist are so corrupt as to be useless for editing.[68] For each of the three main versions, when both family readings are certain and the text is based on one or the other, the Apparatus gives one as the lemma and the other as the variant. These families are **r** and **m** for **A**, α and β for **B**, **x** and **p** (or x^1 and **pt**) for **C**.[69] For **A**, the Apparatus also records the readings of the sub-families r^1 and r^2; for **C**, the major groups y, p^1 and p^2, with a query sign if there is uncertainty. For the **B** Version, where the main α witness R is defective at beginning and end, the numerous variants of the other witness F, which are often very corrupt or sophisticated, are not recorded entire but only when deemed likely to be a true reflex of α. These economies, the aim of which is to avoid cluttering the Apparatus with information of no value for establishing the text, involve a degree of editorial judgement. But the reasons for regarding F as of limited intrinsic value will be found set forth at length at III, *B Version* § 46 above.[70] By contrast, the variant readings of R, the only reliable α copy, are all given, either in the main Apparatus or, if F agrees with β in a reading judged original, in the Appendix. Among the other variants given, group-sigils are employed for all versions wherever they appear correctly to represent the shared readings of the manuscripts in question, divergent individual copies being noted within brackets. The rejected readings of each version's base-manuscript have been relegated to the Appendix if unique or supported by up to three unrelated witnesses. But those of the constant three-member variant groups are recorded in the main Apparatus (for the **A** Version TH^{2}Ch, with the sigil t, and for the **B** Version, WHmCr, with the sigil w).

§ 54. The Apparatus uses the following conventions. *(i)* At the beginning of each passus the manuscripts collated are listed, then the opening rubrics (explicits are given at the end of each passus). *(ii)* The order of citation follows the initial list, whether manuscripts are cited individually or by their group sigils. Thus in A Pr 7, 'v' after 'TCh' indicates that 'VH' (and their inferred ancestral source) both support the reading *of-*. *(iii)* A group-sigil appearing immediately after the lemma indicates that the reading's specific manuscript-source is the first member of the group in its sigil-order as listed. Thus at C Pr 216, *reik* is cited from group b's first member, B. *(iv)* The *variants* are given in order of their degree of semantic distance from the lemma.

§ 55. *(v)* The lemma is ordinarily cited from the base-manuscript when this preserves the family reading, as at B Pr 6, where the family-sigil signifies that both lemmata are taken from β in its W form. *(vi)* When the family reading is not unanimous but is discerned in that of a group, the latter's sigil appears after the lemma, as at B Pr 2, where the group is w and the reading is being cited from W, its chief representative. *(vii)* When the adopted reading is supported by a minority of witnesses, these are listed as ordered in their respective genetic groups, with the base-manuscript first (unless it has an eccentric spelling, when another member of its group is cited). Thus in A Pr 7, the six copies supporting the prefix *of-* are cited after the lemma bracket, beginning with T. In this (fairly typical) case, 'R&r' after the rejected majority reading means that 'R and the rest of the manuscripts' read *for-*, and that this variant is cited from R. *(viii)* The abbreviation *&r* indicates that the reading of the cited source-manuscript is shared by all other copies save those for which other individual variants are specified. Thus in A Pr 2 'T&r' signifies that *a shroud* appears in all except the four copies with the adopted reading and the three with the two other discrete variants recorded.

§ 56. *(ix)* This procedure does not apply to the **Z** Version, which has no variants. For each of the other versions, a lemma or rejected family-variant not taken from the base-manuscript normally comes from a single 'citation-copy' chosen for its substantive superiority (and one otherwise qualified to serve as copy-text but for its defectiveness or inferiority in accidentals). The sigils of these manuscripts, which are R for **A**, L for **B** and Y for **C** (before C II 157, U), often precede '&r' signifying as described at § 55, e.g. at A Pr 8, B Pr 13 or C II 223[(2)]. *(x)* For **A**, ms R further functions as 'citation-copy' for the reading of its family **r** and also its sub-family r^1. But when the adopted or rejected reading is that of the other **r** sub-family r^2, the source cited is V and, after V ceases, J. When it is that of the other **A** family **m**, the citation-copy is **m**'s chief (and only complete) representative, M. *(xi)* When Ax is emended, the rejected form given after the lemma bracket is ordinarily that of the base-manuscript, T, e.g. for *I* at A Pr 11. If T diverges from Ax, R or the next manuscript in linear order is cited to represent the presumed archetypal reading. *(xii)* For **B**, ms L acts as citation-copy and provides the β lemma when W has an individual or group error. Thus at B Pr 231, a line that is missing from W and two other copies, the entry cites 'L&r', meaning that the text prints L (adapted to the spelling of W), *except* for the order of *I seiȝ*. This last follows ms G, which is cited in its exact form as the second entry, followed by 'K–D' to acknowledge the editors who first printed the adopted reading. The rejected variant is then cited in the form it has in L and the remaining copies other than G. The sequence in which the first entry records the three copies that lack line 231 follows the normal linear order of the individual sigils: after W comes Y from its sub-family γ and then F from family α.

§ 57. (*xiii*) In **C**, ms Y (and before it becomes available, U) functions like R and L earlier to represent the presumed **x** family reading when X errs or is absent. (*xiv*) For **C** the family **x** (= x^1 before Passus XII) and the group y are cited from the copy-text X, b from B, u from U and t from T. 'Family' **p**, sub-family p^1 and group e are all represented by P, and sub-family p^2 by G, K and N in that order. This may be observed at II 5, where the lemma is from **x**, and II 6, where it is from **p**. From Pr–XI the family-sigil **x** has the exclusive sense 'x^1'; for as the only 'x^2' witnesses present belong to **p**, it remains uncertain whether t would have agreed with **p** or with x^1. From Passus XII to XXII '**x**' is used inclusively for agreed readings of x^1 and t, e.g. at XII 2, where **p** cannot represent x^2. In this section, however, it becomes possible to use 'x^1', as at XII 5, where the correct reading is preserved by t**p**. But while such agreements of t and **p** in right readings might permit a sigil x^2 and such agreements in error as XVII 94 might stipulate it (see diagram in III, *C Version* § 13, and cf. III § 38), the sigil is avoided, for the reasons set out in III § 10. Instead, only '**pt**' is used for agreed readings, whether lemmas or variants, that stand in clear contrast to those of x^1, as at XVII 117 and 136 respectively. (*xv*) The order of citation of group sigils is ordinarily that of the copies comprising the groups, as at II $9^{(1)}$, where 'yb' answers to the sequence XIP^{2}BOL. One special procedure to be noted is illustrated from the same entry. At II $9^{(1,2)}$ the sigil-order '**pu**' is a deliberate acknowledgement that the readings (one a lemma, the other a variant) are supported first by a 'virtual' family,[71] then by a group of the other family. The aim of this procedure is to recognise the relative weight of attestation and to highlight the discrepant alignment between different branches of the Cx tradition.

§ 58. Three conventions of abbreviation in the *Apparatus* require comment: hyphens, italics, and query signs. A hyphen is used to indicate that in a compound word only the part immediately following the hyphen has variants among the collated copies. Thus in C Pr 7 '-wandred' indicates that the lemma's full form is as in the text and the variants' full forms are both preceded by *of*. But no hyphen appears before either variant because in the cited source both are separated from preceding *of*, the grammatical status of which is clearly different in the p^1 variant (gerund) and that of **x** (past participle). The italics in this case denote that the ending of the variant cited as 'walk*ed*' itself varies in some of the sources. If these variations are substantive, they will normally be specified after the lemma-bracket, as here in the internal entry after '**xMN**', where four copies attest a gerundial form. When no such further information is offered, it should be assumed that the other members of the family or group show a non-substantive, often merely orthographic difference from the form in the lemma or main variant, e.g. 'che*ff*ede' at Pr 33. A query sign has as its specific purpose to draw attention to evidence that may qualify the validity of the sigil immediately following the sign and to alert the reader to a problem in the text that may receive attention in the *Textual Notes*. A good example is Pr 49, an early instance raising the possibility that the RM ancestor may have been collated with an **x** copy or represent an independent line of transmission from **p** (cf. III, *C Version* § 48).

(c) *Format*

§ 59. In Vol. I (pp. xv, xiii), the basic features of the parallel-text format and the meaning of the sigla are described, and the latter more fully in the introductory sections of part III. Wherever possible, the texts have been arranged to make the parallel material start and end at points where the sense is substantially identical or closely similar. This applies also to transposed passages where the parallels are printed for a second time. Limitations of space have not always allowed such treatment for shorter passages or for the printing of both the **B** and **C** lines twice in their respective new positions. However, the location of this material has been signalled by page-references at the place where a form of it might appear. This happens particularly often with **Z**, which lacks several passages presumed added in **A** and may not resume for many pages after the point of expansion. There are similar problems, on a smaller scale, with **A**. Main entries in the *Textual Notes* therefore contain bracketed references to the related **B**, **A** and **Z** material, however close or loose the correspondence.

(d) *Textual Notes, Commentary and Indexical Glossary*

§ 60. The *Textual Notes*, like all the illustrative material in part IV, are keyed to the final version; but when lines or passages in **C**'s predecessors have been omitted in revision, reference is first to **B** and then to **A** for material confined to **A** and **Z**. Where the substance of the note has to do with **Z**, **A** or **B** but **C** possesses broadly corresponding material, the text-reference is again to the latter. The *Notes*, which have been designed to be consulted alongside the open parallel text, focus on issues concerning the establishment of the readings adopted in Vol. I. Where interpretative comments appear, these are sometimes on metrical or (mainly) lexical matters bearing on the text and involving cross-reference to the *Indexical Glossary* (e.g. XI 41). The *Commentary* and *Textual Notes* have not been combined, since (given the great length of both sections) it has seemed more convenient for the reader to keep them apart, as in the Everyman B-Text. All general interpretative information is therefore placed in the *Commentary* unless it directly relates to the resolution of textual problems (e.g. at X 294) or involves proper names (e.g. on A X 153). But by contrast with the procedure adopted in the Everyman B-Text (where textual and lexical notes formed one section), historical information on the sense and associations of glossed items, and also explanation of metrical points, is placed in the *Commentary*. The *Indexical Glossary* (the rationale of which is fully explained in its headnote) aims to be at once comprehensive and concise. It too is keyed to the **C** Version in the first instance but provides referenced glosses for all lexical items unique to each of the others. Unlike Skeat's *Glossary*, it contains only words occurring in the edited text; but variants found in the Apparatus that receive specific mention in the *Textual Notes* appear in a supplementary index of items. The *Bibliography* lists all works referred to (usually by short title) in Vol. II and a number consulted but not specifically cited in the *Introduction*, the *Commentary* and the *Textual Notes*.

IV. EDITING THE TEXT: NOTES

1 This is a matter of principle; whether the texts should also be printed in parallel is a pragmatic issue.

2 For greater clarity in examining metre, the two sets of readings are separately presented at §§ 10–11 below.

3 Although **C** does not revise a **B** line back to its **A** form, it sometimes uses **A** material omitted from **B**: e.g. A 2.166 at 2.248, A 10.125 at 13.23, A 11.306 at 3.395 and A 11.201 at 5.76. Likewise, **B** at Pr 223 may be restoring a **Z** line Pr 90 (unless this was omitted by Ax) and, at 2. 207 similarly, Z 2.188 (see further *Intro*. III, Z, § 23 (ii)).

4 In Karl Popper's phrase (*The Logic of Scientific Discovery* § 11) these 'are ...conventions...[that] might be described as the rules of the game' [*here*, of textual criticism].

5 'Objective' here answers to Popper's 'inter-subjectively testable' (op. cit. § 8).

6 It is 'neutral' even though a full stave in final position characterises the distinct metrical Types Ib and d, IIb, and IIIb and c; for these are all *variants* (of Types I, II and III respectively) and not base-forms defining the line-type in question. Examples would be *wente*] *ʒede* at C I 70 or *ouhte*] *sholde* at C VII 98.

7 Whole numbers and decimal fractions close to the decade by no more than two are rounded up or down to allow for ambiguous cases in the more numerous categories.

8 Each example is separately discussed in the *Textual Notes*.

9 For evidence of such a repertorium see *Intro*. V §§ 29–30 below and Appendix III ('Repertory').

10 The present edition therefore often follows the Athlone in correcting clear archetypal errors in **B**.

11 The most striking examples are Pr 35 and III 32–3, 78.

12 To adapt Popper (*op. cit.* § 21), the theory of the core-text is 'empirical' because it prohibits a class of 'potential falsifiers' [e.g. the metrical type *aa / xa*] and permits another class with which it is consistent [e.g. the type *ax / ax*]. This canon is obeyed in the present edition with only two exceptions where the common text of **ZAB** is conjecturally emended, B Pr 11 // and B IV 91 // (see § 18 below), both of which are discussed in full in the *Textual Notes*.

13 See *Introduction* II §§ 66f above.

14 Whether this is so in every such instance in the present edition may be open to debate; see for example § 29 below.

15 This is something that pre-Athlone editors rarely did, and Skeat included many such lines in his A-Text.

16 In the much-discussed *baches* at C VII 158 // (*Ka* p. 444, Adams '*Durior Lectio*', pp. 8–12), Bx is corrupt but Ax is *uncertain*, though it probably read as **ZC**; see *Textual Notes ad loc*.

17 All the examples cited are discussed in detail in the *Textual Notes*.

18 B V 456 cannot count here as a core-text anomaly, since both archetypes are uncertain and have to be reconstructed from sub-archetypal split variants, and Z appears corrupt.

19 This is a key difference between explanatory hypotheses in the humanities and in the natural sciences, since in principle lost documents may be unique and so permanently irrecoverable, whereas natural entities instantiate a class. Though Popper rejects the phrase 'principle of economy of thought,' his term 'simplicity' corresponds to what is meant here by economy: 'Simple statements, if knowledge is our object, are to be prized more highly than less simple ones *because they tell us more*; *because their empirical content is greater*; *and because they are better testable*' (op. cit. § 43).

20 Like that of Russell-Kane (*C Version* p. 89) and Hanna, 'Versions', pp. 236–8.

21 Discussed at *Introduction* III, *C Version* § 49 above.

22 See *Introduction* II, §§ 9, 18 above.

23 See *Textual Notes ad loc* below.

24 See *Introduction* II § 96 and III, *B Version* § 46.

25 See *C Version* § 40 above.

26 Adams, 'Editing and the Limitations of the *Durior Lectio*', p. 14 n. 3.

27 A similar position is taken by Adams, 'Editing *PP* B' pp. 40–4 and Brewer, 'Authorial vs. Scribal Writing' pp. 68–9, *Editing* 'PP', pp. 386–91.

28 Uninstanced elsewhere, this is as much of an authorial 'fingerprint' as the T-type line, and is found in the coretext as well as in each version severally (e.g. Z II 146 *déstréres*). Such a pattern is also found in the a-half, e.g. *pálmére* VII 179 // **ZAB**; but see further note 41 below.

29 For detailed discussion, see the *Textual Notes ad loc*.

30 This (theoretically possible) view of **Z** is to the present editor insufficient to explain the ensemble of **Z**'s textual features taken as a whole.

31 See the *Textual Notes ad loc*.

32 See III *A Version* § 56 above.

33 On the second of these see Schmidt 'Visions and Revisions', pp. 17–18.

34 See *Introduction* II § 18 above.

35 The Athlone editors would not agree, since they regard the Bx reading as a scribal corruption of an original identical with **C** and emend accordingly.

36 For a systematic account see *The Clerkly Maker*, ch. 2.

37 The scale of **L**'s use of enjambement can be judged from the following sample percentages from one passus in the two longer versions: C XVII 5.5%, B XV 3%.

38 See Duggan, 'Langland's Meter', p. 44. As Duggan would presumably exclude the fourth lift of a standard line of *aa / ax* type, which is by definition stressed but is also blank, his Metrical Rule II should have said 'Alliteration falls *only* on a stressed syllable'. Unfortunately, this would still not be true, as may be seen from *I myhte gete no grayn*

of Wittes grete wittes at C 11.84, where lift four (*wittes*) is 'notionally' blank but 'really' alliterates with unstressed *Wittes* before the key-stave. Duggan's earlier statement that 'Structural alliteration occurs only on stressed syllables' (1986:123n14) is unambiguous, but is also open to objection in not covering the very important category of mute staves, over 400 in total. For since these (nearly half of them in the core-text) have alliteration but not stress, they cannot be treated as 'non-structural' (see further Appendix One § 4 i). For further comment on defects in Duggan's metrical theory, in this case his 'Metrical Rule V', see at note 62 below.

39   Line XV 226 falls victim to mislineation in most **C** copies and in parallel Bx.

40   This is a line where emendation of **B** is justified on the basis of presumed linear agreement of **C** and **A** (*A*-family **m** being also 'filled out').

41   In VII 179a *pálmére* may not be a true zero-dip if the *l* is taken as syllabic.

42   See e.g. *warre sone* and *life dures* in *Wynnere and Wastoure* ll. 85, 108.

43   An extra lift occurs sometimes in an 'extended' Type IIIa, as at VI 319 //.

44   Unless specified otherwise, examples are from the primary core-text: the text-reference is to **C** and '//' = '// **ZAB**'.

45   E.g. Ib: *William of Palerne* 163, *Wynnere and Wastoure* 167, *Purity* 1; Ic: *WPal* 18, *WW* 386, *Pur.* 3; Id: *WPal* 386; Ie: *WPal* 14, *WW* 116, *Pur.* 23; IIa: *WPal* 62; IIIa: *WPal* 72, *WW* 429; IIIb: *WW* 103.

46   On the basis of this evidence Bx is conjecturally emended at VII 45.

47   In A XII 50 the first lift is blank, i.e. stressed but unalliterated.

48   Macaronic alliterative lines are found elsewhere only in poems heavily influenced by *PP*, such as *PPCr* 691, 713–14 and *MS*.

49   These are paralleled by, e.g., *couherde* and *stepchilderen* at *WPal* 4, 131, *onyʒed* 'one-eyed' at *Pur.* 102; but these are strictly compounds and so not truly monolexical like *deseites* at B XII 130 or *conqueste* at BC XXI 43. However, *manhede* at *WPal* 431 closely resembles *maleese* at B XVII 193.

50   These are rare but not unparalleled, e.g. *aab / ab* at *WPal* 429, *Pur.* 11.

51   An apparent parallel outside *PP* is in *WPal* 5536, where a grammatical morpheme stave formed by liaison with a preceding adverb is supplemented by a lexical fourth stave (*wil he* ← *lenges*): *ʒif þe lord god lif wil he in erthe lenges.*

52   An internal stave occurs in *WPal* 3150 (*p* ← *spayne*), and another possible case is 5533 (*n* ← *kn*owe); but the line could scan as Type IIIa with a quadrisyllabic onset.

53   For a possible liaisonal line elsewhere see *WPal* 5531 *edwardes douʒter.* This core-text feature provides precedent for the conjectural emendations **any olde* at B IX 163 // A and **ek an* at B VI 281 (a line with a mute key-stave and a supplemental fourth stave).

54   The rationale for this type of stave is discussed in *Clerkly Maker*, pp. 40–1. The *f / v* staves, which are dialectally indicative, are listed in Appendix One, § 2 (a).

55   For *s / sh* cf. *WPal* 76; for *k / g* likewise *WPal* at 166, 2361.

56   Mute staves are not, of course, confined to such words and frequently consist of contextually de-stressed lexical words, some as important as *God* (as at I 46 // ABC, III 427 // BC, C Pr 117, 121). For a complete list see Appendix One, § 4. i.

57   *B Version*, p. 135; see also Kane, '"Music"', p. 53.

58   See K–D, *B Version*, pp. 135, n. 20 and 139, n. 43, Kane, '"Music"'.

59   Examples of Athlone emendations of Type IIIa lines appear at III 222, VII 178, B III 229; of lines having internal staves at X 105 //; liaisonal staves at B V 394, IX 27; and cognative staves at XIX 279 // XXI 213 // (with resultant confusion of the poet's theology of creation and grace).

60   See *The Clerkly Maker*, chs. 2 and 3.

61   This type is not found in other alliterative poems that have been studied from a metrical point of view.

62   On this feature see Cable, 'ME Meter', esp. pp. 53–4, 67–8 (it is recognised by Duggan in 'L.'s Dialect and final –*e*', p. 184n61); in other positions Duggan seems to be right that final –*e* may be properly treated as subject to elision and syncope. However, Duggan's Metrical Rule V (governing the shape of the b-verse) is only partly true of **L**'s practice as instanced in the core-text and as confirmed throughout the poem's archetypal lines except for those listed in Vol. I, Appendix Two. For while **L**'s 'line terminal dip' is indeed 'always weak', the core-text, massively supported by single-version evidence, shows that it is not 'optional' (Duggan, 'L.'s Meter', p. 45). The 'Rule' as Duggan here formulates it is actually self-contradictory in claiming that 'A strong b-verse dip is a string of one to four unstressed syllables. A weak dip has one syllable'; for if the second sentence is true, the first must be false (the latter needs to delete 'strong' or replace 'one' by 'two'). Duggan corrects this error in 'L's Dialect' (p.159, with no acknowledgment of the earlier

misformulation). However, his new statement mistakenly re-affirms the optionality of the line-terminal dip and fails to note explicitly the frequency of *zero*-dips before either lift in the b-verse (more commonly the first), as in the primary core-text line 1.167. This said, Duggan's 'Rule V' is broadly borne out by the core-text data, as is his case for sounding of final *–e* in such 'historically motivated' forms as plural adjectives like *hokede* (in the core-text line Pr 51), which must be trisyllabic to meet the requirement that 'One of the dips preceding either lift must be strong' (Duggan 1987[2]:45).

63 For the **C** Version these may be found in the *Facsimile*, ed. Chambers; for **B** in Benson-Blanchfield and in the Electronic *PP* edition of Trinity, Cambridge B. 15. 17.

64 Unlike the *Confessio Amantis* and the *Canterbury Tales*, **L**'s originals have left no traces in the form of Latin *commentum* or *annotatio* that might conceivably derive from the author.

65 Except that in **B** the value |z| for *ʒ* has been denoted by *z*, a vestigial inconsistency arising from a (misguided) wish to reduce the visible differences between the present and the Everyman text (*Intro.* I § 19), the second edition of which was being prepared for press simultaneously with Vol. I.

66 Retention of the obsolete letters carries no implication that **L** belonged to a 'provincial' school of alliterative writing (whatever that might mean); for if he was a 'maker', he was a maker of the capital.

67 For a detailed account of the poem's *Rubrics* see Appendix II.

68 The numerous such variants are given in full in the Athlone Apparatus.

69 The rationale for handling the last of these, which is somewhat complicated, is described in III, *C Version* §§ 10, 62–4 and § 57 below.

70 Many of F's variants have no more claim to special attention in relation to **B** than do those of N[2] in relation to **C**.

71 On the 'virtual' family status of **p** in at least Pr–XI cf. III *C Version* §10

V. THE POEM IN TIME

i. *The Authorship of* Piers Plowman

§ 1. The quality of mystery that invests the titular hero of *Piers Plowman* extends to his creator, about whom little is known except what can be inferred from the text. This little is discounted by some scholars as either fictional or as too distorted by irony to serve in constructing the poet's biography. In Chaucer's dream-vision poems the protagonists are recognisably *personae* of the author, in the *Legend of Good Women* very clearly and closely so. But the Will of the **A** Version of *Piers* is perhaps to be better understood, like the Dreamer in *Pearl*, less as a self-portrait than as a representative figure, modelled upon the author, through whom the relation between human and divine love and between God's justice and mercy, compelling preoccupations of the age, may be dramatically articulated. Our ignorance of even the name of the Cotton Nero A. X. poet is understandable enough, because *Pearl* is extant in only one copy and cannot have been much read. But the mystery about the authorship of *Piers Plowman* is that it survives in as many manuscripts as *The Canterbury Tales* and the *Confessio Amantis*, it proved popular and controversial, and was even, arguably, the most extensively-circulated poem of its time. The paucity of our information about Langland[1] might be due to his prudent avoidance of publicity, since outspoken religious and political criticisms risked arousing conflict with both ecclesiastical and secular authorities.[2] But a more general reason could be that, whereas the English courtly poets (and before them Chrétien de Troyes, Dante, Wolfram and Machaut) named themselves as the authors of their works, the personal history of the writer of a non-courtly work, however wide its appeal, may have been regarded as of scant interest by medieval readers. Even in the case of Chaucer, though more is known of him as a poet from contemporaries, the details that make his 'literary biography' possible have been preserved largely thanks to his career as a public servant. This said, the 'Langland' *within* the poem still seems shadowy by comparison both with the 'Chaucer' who refers 'internally' to his various writings, and with the 'Gower' who declares himself as *auctor* in the Latin commentary-gloss surrounding his English text.[3] However, by way of compensation, Langland's 'self-revelation' in the Prelude to C V is more detailed than anything those writers give us. As such, it has come in for intense scrutiny, though scholars differ about how factually it is to be taken.[4]

§ 2. The Dreamer of *Piers Plowman* is named Will, a felicitous homonym of the common noun denoting in medieval psychology one of the three main *potentiae* of the soul. This is the power fundamental to the search (for Truth and Dowel) of a protagonist who is allowed to describe his experiences in the first person. The textual evidence is, even here, not free of uncertainty; for where the Dreamer is called 'Wil' by Thought at B VIII 126, that word may denote the faculty rather than a person (A IX 118); and *Wil* is changed to *oen* in C X 125, whether to conceal the author's identity or not to have it (mis)taken as a proper name. Conversely, at C I 5 'Wille' is substituted for 'Sone' of **ZAB**, though there too it is not contextually sure whether Holy Church means to name a person or a faculty, the revision allowing both.[5] On the other hand, three third-person references to the Dreamer-narrator as Will occur in the 'core-lines', the most reliable part of the text. The one at C VI 2 // ZAB once again exploits the semantic-referential ambiguity of 'Will'. That at B XI 45 alludes to the proverbial 'wit' / 'will' contrast and, in its revised form at C XII 2, generates a double pun on the senses of both the proper name ('William' / 'the will') and the common noun ('the faculty' / 'the object of desiring'). A third, found only at A VIII 43 // Z and perhaps meant to balance the first (at A V 44), effectually identifies author and protagonist. And this identification is sustained in the later versions' frequent mention of the poem's dreamer as the poem's writer (e.g. at C XXI 1 // B). Outside the core-text, references to Will (apart from the unique one at C I 5) occur in portions of text that not all scholars accept as original. The two at A XII 51, within the part of that passus here judged authentic, seem to be no less equivocally 'personal' and 'faculty' denominatives than at any other point. The use of 'Wil' purely as a generic personal name is evident at VI 70–1 // B, where any ambiguity is between two referents rather than between a sense and a reference. A complementary univocal use of *Wil* for the faculty is at C VII 233 // ZAB, which provides the proverbial basis for equivoques like that at B VIII 126 // A.

§ 3. 'Will' is, then, meant to be understood at once as the shortened form of 'William' and as a pregnant 'nature-name' proclaiming the Dreamer's embodiment of 'volition' and 'desire' (MED s.v. *wille* n. 1 (a), (a)). That this appellation is persistently punning is clear from its use at B XV 152 *'I haue lyued in londe,' quod I, 'my name is Longe Wille'* (removed in revision), where at one and the same time 'tallness' is ascribed to the 'Will'-persona and 'patient perseverance' to the faculty he embodies.[6] The line was noted by a late C15th hand in the margin of *B*-ms Laud Misc 581 as giving 'the name of thauctour'; and this early reader's equation of Dreamer-persona with poet accords with both the reconstructed archetypal colophon of C IX and the established practice in the late work of Chaucer and Gower. That the author's name was Will is also asserted in John But's conclusion to A XII, which claims knowledge both of his 'other works concerning Piers Plowman' (presumably the other versions) and of his death (A XII 101–5). Whatever the precise relationship between the poet's biography and its reflection in the poem, contemporaries are likely to have understood the Dreamer's Christian name 'Will' to be the writer's. But the conclusion that B XV 152 also puns on the surname 'Langland' depends on information external to the text.

§ 4. Early traditions that attribute *Piers Plowman* to 'Robert Langland', as Skeat noted (*B-Text* xxviii), are likely to have originated in the corrupt reading of B VIII 1 *yrobed* as *y Robert* found in *B*-ms F (and also in *A*-ms M). An early 16th ascription on a pastedown in the *B*-ms Hm 128, like other ascriptions associated with the antiquary John Bale, expresses uncertainty as to whether 'Robert or william langland made pers plow[man]'.[7] But none attends the statement about the poet's paternity written in an early C15th hand on fol. 89v of the *C*-ms TCD 212 (reproduced as pl. 1 in Kane 1965):

> Memorandum quod Stacy de Rokayle pater willielmi de Langlond qui stacius fuit
> generosus & morabatur in Schiptoun vnder whicwode tenens domini le Spenser in
> comitatu Oxoniensi qui predictus willielmus fecit librum qui vocatur Perys ploughman.

> ['It is worthy of record that Stacy de Rokayle was the father of William de Langlond.
> This Stacy was of gentle birth and lived in Shipton-under-Wychwood, a tenant of the
> Lord Despenser in the county of Oxfordshire. The aforesaid William made the book
> that is called *Piers Plowman* '].

This note appears to be of independent authority, and its language and the type of interest it displays suggest a person involved in the legal profession.[8] It is unlikely to be an inference from B XV 152 (see § 3), since successful detection of an anagrammatised name would presuppose knowledge that the poet was called Langland. But as the correctness of the Dublin inscription is corroborated by B XV 152, acceptance of it reciprocally confirms the presence of an anagram in that line (and supports the case for finding the name also in A XI 118). A problem arises here as to whether the surname 'Langland' was the poet's; for if he was the son of Stacy de Rokayle, he ought by rights to have borne his father's surname (a matter, interestingly, accorded special importance by Conscience at C III 366). But the questions whether the poet did not call himself 'William Rokayle' because he may have been illegitimate or because (his work being too 'inflammatory' for him to risk using his family name) he adopted the *nom de plume* 'Langland', as maintained by John Bowers,[9] must remain unanswered in our present state of knowledge. A second, more circumstantial challenge comes from a rubric-reference (possibly archetypal) to 'Willelmi .W.' in the explicit to C IX (Vol I, p. 355). Kane (*Evidence for Authorship*, pp. 35–7) suggests that this '.W.' could be a scribal error occasioned by preoccupation with rubricating the letter or (more plausibly) may signify another surname beginning with *W* (e.g. 'Wychwood').[10] The use of an abbreviated form '.W.' would tend to suggest, however, that the author's actual name was common knowledge; yet none beginning with *W* has been found associated with *Piers Plowman*. Neither objection to the presumptive accuracy of the TCD ascription therefore holds much force; so, failing discovery of a 'William Rokayle' who could be shown to have written under an assumed name, it seems safest to accept 'William L.' (rather than 'Robert L.' or 'William W.') as the name of the author. How many versions the TCD ascription's 'liber' denotes remains disputed, as it was in the early twentieth century, when multiple authorship of those known (a theory going back to Hearne and Ritson in the eighteenth) was advocated by Manly and opposed by Jusserand, Chambers and others. But there now seems a consensus (arising perhaps more from indifference than conviction) that the **A**, **B** and **C** Versions, whatever their order or state of completeness, are the work of one poet, whom it is convenient to call William Langland.[11]

§ 5. In the absence of documentary evidence of Langland's relations with his family, all biographical inferences must depend on the text of the poem. But though as an allegorical dream-vision it is obviously a work of fiction, not everything in it need be 'fictitious'. In parts it more closely relates to the realities of the time than do comparable works such as *The Parliament of Fowls* or *Pearl*, which describe imagined worlds based on books and reflection.[12] For *Piers Plowman* mentions historically-recorded natural catastrophes like pestilences and storms, political and religious events like the French Wars and the Schism, and public figures like John Chichester, whose mayoral office helps to date the B-Text. Such factors predispose towards our taking WILL as an accurate depiction, if somewhat 'fictionalised' according to the dream-vision genre's conventions,[13] of the poet as an unbeneficed clerk in minor orders surviving precariously in the manner described in the Prelude to C V. Even more important than these outward details is what the poem conveys of its author's quality of mind and deepest concerns. His choice of an archaic (if 'reviving') metre need not in itself signify a deliberate effort of dissociation from the metropolitan cultural world. Alliterative verse, though provincial and regarded as alien to the South by Chaucer's Parson (*CT* X 42–3), was not restricted to one region, but was found in the South- and North-West Midlands, in Lincolnshire and in Yorkshire. It was used in heroic poems like the *Morte Arthure* and romances like *Sir Gawain and the Green Knight*, where the bedroom scene of

Fitt III is tonally much closer to the courtly sophistication of *Troilus* Book III than to the clerkly bluntness of *Piers* XXII 189–98. But whether Langland knew works belonging to this variegated tradition or only those with broadly 'moral' themes like *Winner and Waster*, he differs from his predecessors and followers in one striking respect. This is his fusion of immediate observation of contemporary social and economic life with an intensely individual re-imagining of 'holy writ' in his extended sense of Biblical, patristic and other religious and devotional writings (the figure of Piers most memorably exemplifies such a 'fusion'). It is at present unknown whether moral and religious poetry was all Langland wrote, or whether he commenced 'maker' in a more conventional way (as did Chaucer with the *Roman de la Rose*) by translating from a work in French. In this regard, David Lawton's speculation that Langland might have been the 'William' who translated *William of Palerne* (*WPal* 5521–6) deserves to be carefully examined, as the lexical and metrical evidence of affinity from all four versions is very suggestive.[14] In the case of *Piers Plowman* itself, however, even the rudimentary and tentative **Z** Version owes little to known vernacular or learned models. The poem's original language, as far as it can be ascertained, is consistent with its 'locating' the first vision on the Malvern Hills.[15] But in **B** and even more in **C**, the work comes across as decidedly not a 'regional' but a 'London' poem, from Haukyn's mention of the missing Stratford bread-carts at B XIII 266–7 to the Dreamer's at V 1–2 of his cottage in Cornhill, 'a narrow east-west street in the middle of a city of lanes'.[16]

§ 6. There is no evidence in *Piers Plowman* to indicate that its author ever belonged to a religious order, but some that he had studied Arts at a higher-level institution, and had attended lectures on the Bible, perhaps in preparation for the priesthood. Though wholly internal to the text, this evidence is more reliable than may at first be thought. In theory, the educational experiences that the Third Vision describes, leading through the trivium and quadrivium to the beginning of theology or canon law, need not have been the poet's own. But several passages show an understanding of syllogistic procedure (not paralleled in his poetic contemporaries) that can only have been acquired in a university or *studium generale*. Instances of this understanding, the most extended being WILL's disputation with the Minorites (C X 20ff //), support interpretation of the *laudes scolae* at B X 303–4 as recalling first-hand acquaintance. But the latter are linked with equally warm praise of the *cloistre*, and *Piers Plowman* shows more sympathy with what Morton Bloomfield called 'monastic philosophy'[17] than with formal scholastic theology, of which Langland seems suspicious. This circumstance may point to his association with a monastic house (possibly Little Malvern Priory) during his early years; and Bowers's suggestion that Langland had been a secular student at the Benedictine cathedral school at Worcester would be attractive did it not mistake the contextual sense of *scole* in C V 36 and fail to see the significance of the poet's familiarity with dialectic.[18] However, Langland's concern with the condition of 'English clerks' (B XV 414) is in no way confined to the religious orders but extends generally to the spiritual mission of the clergy, and specifically to the secular priesthood's pastoral rôle and its contemporary shortcomings. The whole text tacitly supports what the C V Prelude expressly states: that the creator of the Dreamer-persona was a 'clerk' who, whether owing to his marriage or some other reason, had a secure place in no canonical order within the Church. Langland himself may well have confronted at some point a crucial choice between the mendicant and the monastic ways of religious life, with their differing valuations of the place of thought, prayer and evangelisation. But while his poem might be defensibly read as the dramatised reflex of some such crisis, we can only speculate as to the extent of the spiritual autobiography it contains.

ii. *Audience, Date and Early Reception*

§ 7. If the poet cannot be disentangled from his poem, neither can the poem from its audience. This is because it is virtually certain that *Piers Plowman* was known to the leaders of the Peasants' Uprising and even seems to have been re-worked partly in response to its reception by them. In speaking of the poem's audience, a distinction needs to be made between the 'outer' audience of actual readers and the 'inner' audience implied by its content, language, form and occasional direct address, which Anne Middleton calls its 'public'.[19] By the time of **C**, Langland's final outer audience, some of whom had doubtless formed judgements about the author's intentions, might have had to be taken account of when constructing the new 'public' or 'internal' audience of the revision. About Langland's very first readers nothing is known;[20] but it seems a reasonable assumption that the audience of **A** and *a fortiori* of **Z** would have been his immediate acquaintances. *Piers Plowman* does not seem to have been commissioned but to have been a personal enterprise, perhaps stimulated by Langland's 'prophetic' response to growing social instability following the first Statute of Labourers (1351) and by such memorably 'apocalyptic' events of the 1360s as the plague, tempest and war described as early as **Z**. It has been maintained by Anne Hudson that **A** was the version known to the leaders of the 1381 Revolt.[21] If she is right, Langland could be imagined at an early stage of his career as writing for a 'primary audience' of reform-minded lower clergy. This would have included at its 'centre' men with views as relatively moderate as those of the later author of *Pierce the Ploughman's Crede*,[22] at its 'outer edges' as radical as those of John Ball (see §§ 9 and 10 below). But apart from the Vernon and Trinity copies dated *c.* 1400 there are no surviving **A** manuscripts from before the first quarter of the C15th; and given this version's unfinished state, it seems doubtful whether circulation of **A** could have been extensive enough for the allusions to the Plowman and the Triad in Ball's letter to the Essex insurgents to have been readily grasped (see *Intro*. III, *A*, § 1). Admittedly, interpretation of Piers as a 'peasant hero' challenging the authority of the Church (and perhaps by implication of the state) might be more easily encouraged by **A** than by **B**, with its simultaneously disconcerting and re-assuring transformation of Piers into a *figura* of Christ. But the completed and presumably 'published' **B** was a substantial work, of which the earliest extant copies were made in London, and this seems more likely to have been the version that achieved wide circulation. Its archetypal manuscript was presumably generated only a couple of years before the Rising, which some of its ideas and images may have unintentionally inspired (see *Intro*. III, *B*, §§ 1–3). It is of course quite possible that both versions were known to the rebel leaders, who took from **B** what they had already found in **A** and ignored the later, enigmatic evolution of the Plowman as 'something to their purpose nothing'. But there are no convincing reasons for thinking that they did not know **B** in summer 1381 because it was as yet unwritten.

§ 8. The 'implied' first audience of *Piers Plowman*, however, seems (on the same sort of internal grounds appealed to at § 6) to have been one of educated people like Langland. For from the earliest version to the last, this is indicated by its macaronic lines and quotations, many untranslated, which presuppose *litterati,* readers competent in Latin.[23] These need not have been clergy in the narrower sense, since there was a growing number of 'Latin-literate' laymen (Chaucer and Gower among them) who could have understood the poem without difficulty.[24] But what the texts suggest, progressively, is that wholly 'non-literate' readers were being 'headed off'. Thus, hazardous ignorance of the learned tongue is implicitly warned against in the *commune*'s capping of the Goliard's response to the Angel at B Pr 145, and more explicitly in the aside ('authorly' in its use of *write*) at B XIII 71–2:

> Holi Writ bit men be war - I wol noȝt write it here
> In Englissh, on auenture it sholde be rehersed to ofte,
> And greue þerwiþ þat goode men ben - ac gramariens shul rede:
> *Vnusquisque a fratre se custodiat...*

The B-Text's projected 'public' is one of *gramariens* who know Latin and are intellectually mature enough to 'place' the work's strong criticisms of the clergy. The *lettred lordes* of III 124, by contrast, are doubtless so called ironically, since for them the Latin Biblical warning *is* translated. And at C III 340–42 the King himself amusingly voices to Conscience a need to have him explain his learned *mede / mercede* analogy that might have been shared by non-grammarians ('for En-glisch was it neuere'). It would have been only realistic for Langland to anticipate that a poem on the universal theme of salvation might reach a wider 'mixed' readership (including the *lewede* men addressed at XIII 25), and to allow for this at different points. Thus at B VII 59–9*a*, for example, the passage cited for the *legistres and lawieres* is left in the Latin, no doubt on the assumption that they can read it. From the **Z** Version to **C**, the poem may be said to assume a primary internal audience of the 'literate' in the accepted late-medieval sense.

§ 9. The internal audience is reflected in the 'external' one to the extent that recorded owners of *Piers Plowman* texts in the next half-century were in the first instance ordinary clerics, and secondly, educated laymen of modest background. This conclusion emerges from studies of wills bequeathing copies of the poem. The earliest wills include those of Walter de Brugge, Canon of York Minster, who died in Trim in 1396 and left his copy to John Wormyngton, an English priest in Ireland, and William Palmere, parish-priest of St Alphage, Cripplegate, who died in 1400 and left his to Agnes Eggesfield.[25] Moreover, the dominant classes in the 1381 Revolt, who were upper-rank agricultural workers and town-tradespeople (many of them literate in English) with lower clergy among their leadership, are thought by Anne Hudson to be recalled 'with fair congruity' by 'the kinds of men associated with copies of *PP*'.[26] Among identified contemporary non-clerical readers are writers like the A-Text epiloguist John But,[27] and Thomas Usk, who wrote *The Testament of Love*.[28] But the authors of the works that the poem most deeply affected, all of them written *c*.1395–1410, remain anonymous, and their status obscure. *Richard the Redeless*, *Mum and the Sothsegger* and *Pierce the Ploughman's Crede* are all composed in Langlandian metre and idiom and belong loosely to the tradition of social and political debate initiated by *Winner and Waster* nearly a half-century before.[29] Authorship of the *Crede* is claimed by the writer of *The Plowman's Tale*, a poem in rhymed stanzas assignable to the same twenty-year period:

> Of freres I have told before
> In a makyng of a 'Crede',
> And yet I coud tell worse and more,
> But men wold werien it to rede (1065–9).[30]

Yet of Langland's two imitators in the 1390s, the *Richard the Redeless*-poet inspired by his social / political concerns and the *Crede*-poet by his religious, only the former could be called close to Langland in spirit and outlook. Judging from these works by 'followers', and others such as *Patience*, *Purity* and *St Erkenwald* by contemporaries, Langland's influence was largely confined to the 'non-Chaucerian' writers (though if *The Plowman's Tale* is by the *Crede*-poet, it in a sense bridges the two traditions in its attempt to foist the poem off on Chaucer's pilgrim-Plowman).[31] In the manuscripts, however, *Piers* keeps company with a wide variety of prose and verse compositions, from *Mandeville's Travels* and *Troilus* (no. 53 in the list of *Manuscripts*) to the *Lay Folks' Mass Book* (no. 16) and Richard Rolle's *Form of Living* (no. 11). It is never found exclusively with alliterative pieces, and this may give some notion of the range of the poem's appeal.[32] It is, as it happens, mainly the later codices that include *Piers* with other works; and apart from the Vernon A-Text, the Trinity B-Text, the Digby 102 C-Text and the unique Bodley Z-Text (nos. 4, 11, 25 and 52), the important **ABC** manuscripts preserve the poem by itself.[33] These and other, later copies, with their annotations and signs of provenance and ownership, yield interesting information about what *Piers Plowman* continued to mean to its readers from within a decade of Langland's death to the period of Crowley's printed editions.[34] But since the audience they reveal is not the immediate one the poem may have been written for, what they illuminate is its transmission and reception, rather than its genesis.[35] Unfortunately, except for that of the Rebels, no closely contemporary reactions survive that might suggest motives, beyond the obvious one of improving the poem's quality, for Langland's continuing to work at it; so these motives can only be surmised from the nature of his revisions.[36] Since some of the poet's attitudes to the state of the Church resemble those of John Wycliffe, its most important fourteenth-century critic, it is not surprising that *Piers* should have interested and provoked imitation from Lollard writers.[37] But it is noteworthy that while those immediate responses that draw the poem into the fold of history are mainly responses to its perceived political attitudes, the author of the chief of these, John Ball, was (rightly or wrongly) also regarded as a disciple of Wycliffe by monastic writers like Walsingham and Knighton, who calls him Wycliffe's *premeditator* 'intellectual forerunner', and by the compilers of the *Fasciculi Zizaniorum*.[38]

§ 10. John Ball's letter to the commons of Essex in 1381 (given below from BL MS Royal 13 E.ix, f. 287) contains in the phrases italicised unmistakable allusions to names and ideas that appear in the poem:

> Iohon Schep, somtyme Seynte Marie prest of ʒork, and now of Colchestre, greteth wel Iohan Nameles, and Iohan þe Mullere, and Iohon Cartere, and biddeþ hem þat þei bee war of gyle in borugh, and stondeth togidre in Godes name, and biddeþ *Peres Plouʒman* go to his werk, and chastise wel *Hobbe þe Robbere*, and takeþ with ʒou Iohan Trewman, and alle hiis felawes, and no mo, and loke shappe ʒou to on heued, and no mo.
>
> > Iohan þe Mullere haþ ygrounde smal, smal, smal;
> > *þe kynges sone of heuene* schal paye for al.
> > Be ye war or þe [? *for* ye] be wo;
> > Knoweþ ʒour freend fro ʒour foo;
> > Haueth ynow and seith 'Hoo';
> > And *do wel and bettre* and fleth synne,
> > And sekeþ pees and hold ʒou þerinne;
> And so biddeþ Iohan Trewman and alle his felawes

So does a letter purporting to come from 'Jack Carter,' which is included in *Knighton's Chronicle* (from BL ms Cot. Tib. C.VII):

> Jakke Carter prayes ʒowe alle that *ʒe make a gode ende of that ʒe hane begunnen*, and *do wele and ay bettur and bettur*, for at the even men heryth the day. For if the ende be wele, than is alle wele. Lat *Peres the Plowman* my brother duelle at home and dyʒt us corne, and I will go with ʒowe that y may to dyʒte oure mete and oure drynke, *that ʒe none fayle*; lokke that *Hobbe Robbyoure* be wele chastysed for lesyng of ʒoure grace for ʒe have gret nede to take God with ʒowe in alle ʒoure dedes. For nowe is tyme to be war.[39]

These allusions are hard to explain except on the assumption that *Piers Plowman* was familiar to the leaders of the uprising. In both letters, the rhyming name 'Hobbe the Robber' recalls 'Robert the Robber' in B 5.462 //, Hobbe (MED s.v. *Hobbe* n.) being a familiar form of Robert. The context excludes any notion of an allusion to Sir Robert Hales, the unpopular treasurer killed by the rebels on 14 June 1381; and in the Carter letter, the phrase *for lesyng of youre grace* 'in order not to forfeit the divine favour [your cause deserves]' is evidently warning the peasants against indiscriminate looting. The 'do well and better' phrase echoes the first two stages of Langland's Triad (though in *Piers* the double-comparative form *better* occurs usually only in *non*-Triad references [cf. *IG* s.v. *bettere* av]). In the Ball letter, 'The king's son of heaven' is a characteristic group-genitive phrase little instanced outside the poem (B 18.321 //), and its conjunction here with the idea of 'paying for all' will recall the argument of B 18.341–2. In the Carter letter, the 'good end' phrase echoes B 18.160. A non-verbal 'echo' of a Langlandian thought is detectable in the 'even / end / well' collocation, which is reminiscent of B 14.134–9; the phrase 'ay bettur and bettur' recalls one of the sub-archetypal forms of B 18.363b; and 'heryn the day', which seems to mean 'hear what work was done that day and reckon the payment due for it' (MED s.v. *heren* v. 4d(b)) evokes B 5.421. Now, except for 'that ye none fayle' (echoing B 2.146 // ZAC), the absence of these phrases from **A** tells against Hudson's case (§ 7), pointing instead to **B** as the version the rebels knew. By making Piers Plowman his 'brother' (perhaps an allusion to B 6.207 // ZAC), 'Jack Carter' enlists in the rebels' cause a peasant hero who famously tore up an 'official' document *for pure tene* (B 7.115 // A), and thereby 'appropriates' the poem. Whether its author might have been more troubled than pleased by such 'appropriations', they obliquely illuminate changes in **C** that imply intense reconsideration of his poem in the light of the 1381 events and their aftermath.[40]

§ 11. Neither the TCD ascription nor the insurgents' allusions, however, give any firm indication of Langland's dates. His obit is indicated (somewhat uncertainly) by the third primary source, the reference in A XII 99–105, as not later than 1387, if what it says is correct and if its author was the John But noted as dead by April of that year.[41] This conclusion accords with at least one clear echo of **C** in Thomas Usk's *Testament of Love*, which was completed a year or two before his execution in March 1388. As this could in principle reflect Usk's knowledge of the final version while it was in progress (see *Commentary* on 6.21–6 and 18.60), it does not firmly establish Langland's own death-date as 1387 at the latest. The question has been thoroughly examined by John Bowers, who rightly objects that most of the Usk parallels with **C** observed by Skeat are also in **B** (though Usk could conceivably have known *both* versions). However, while Bowers places a genuine query over the indebtedness of *TL* III v 1–5 to *PP* 18.6, his dismissal of the echo of C 6.22–6 in *TL* I v 117–20 is not persuasive. For here 'wening his own wit more excellent than other' clearly recalls 'Wene Y were witty and wiser then another' (C VI 24). And a little less obviously, Usk's phrase 'scorning al maner devyse' looks to be derived from the poem's '*Scorner* and vnskilful to hem that *skil* shewede, / In *alle manere* maners my name to be yknowe', where in addition to the two verbal echoes, *skil*, though not the identical word, closely answers in sense to Usk's *devyse*.[42] Recent studies have argued, on the other hand, that Langland was alive in 1388, on the grounds that the C V Prelude reveals acquaintance with specific provisions of the Statute of Labourers enacted by the Cambridge Parliament in September of that year.[43] If this were correct, the statement in A XII 103–5 would be fictitious or, if factually true, have to come from another John But than the king's messenger. Its further consequence would be to leave the poet's date of death lying at some point between 1388 and the earliest assignable date of any extant manuscript. This could be as early as 1390 (see § 12 below) but not later than about 1409, the probable date of *MS*, which directly echoes the **C** Version (commonly assumed to have been left unfinished because Langland had died).[44] Accepting *c*.1388 as the earliest time for the cessation of work on **C** (to allow for copying of the text through its successive stages) might therefore favour 1389 as the 'notional' year of Langland's obit. And since that of Usk does not exclude this (if he read **C** in draft), Skeat's proposal of *c*.1393 for the C-Text cannot at present be ruled out. But the case for 1388 as an earliest limit is, though attractive, a matter of interpretation. By contrast, the A XII evidence offers a positive statement (with the same authentic ring as the TCD ascription) that cannot be lightly set aside, and the most plausible John But still seems to the present writer the one identified by Rickert. On balance, then, 1386/1387 is to be preferred as the likely date of Langland's death.

§ 12. For the poet's date of birth no external evidence has been found, and the best hope for it lies in the future discovery of certain documentary reference to a son of Stacy de Rokayle named William. Internal references to the Dreamer's age may, if we follow the accepted dream-vision convention of broad correspondence between author and first-person narrator, be cautiously drawn on to construct the 'biography' of the poet (that their oneness is intended is clear from XXI 1, with its distinction between *wrot* and *dremed*). Thus at B XI 47, Lust of the Eyes is said to follow Will forty-five years; so, taking the date of **B** as 1378–9 (see § 16 below), on the straightforward — if somewhat disconcerting — supposition that the poet was afflicted by greed 'from the time of his birth' rather than (more charitably) 'from the time of puberty or adolescence', he would have been born *c*.1333. Langland would thus have been old enough to witness the social and moral effects of the Great Plague (1348–9), which he touches on at various points.[45] About his upbringing and education, the C V Prelude offers details in no way contradicted by the solid internal evidence of the work's thought and expression considered at § 6. Moreover, because of its gratuitousness, this passage is antecedently less likely to be pure invention than what Donaldson called in his pioneering study an *apologia* for the author's known (and troublingly ambiguous) manner of life. But the Prelude remains 'generic' in character, nonetheless. Will informs his interlocutors in this waking episode that his father and family paid for his education up to what may be interpreted as the beginning of the theology course at a university or else at a cathedral or mendicant school in the capital (35–9) which 'provided training equivalent to that acquired at a university'.[46] But he does not say what sort of people they were, nor why, though he still wears clerical garb (41), he was not ordained. How closely this evocation of an amphibian persona moving between lay and clerical estates answers to historical 'reality' remains uncertain. The Langland whose 'represented life' has been recently re-told by Ralph Hanna may have deliberately chosen to depict himself *in persona alterius* (the greatest of portraitists, Rembrandt, sometimes painted himself *in many kynne gyse* — as St Paul, in oriental garb, and even as a friar). And even if this 'brilliant portrait of the personality of a man who knew himself well'[47] is no more 'truthful' than Rembrandt's self-depictions, then it has a great deal of value to tell us about the author. Unfortunately, as Langland (unlike Chaucer writing to Bukton and Scogan) nowhere addresses a named acquaintance through whom we might locate him in a specific social context, his immediate 'circle' remains a subject for conjecture. All, however, is not left in deepest shadow. For the poet's wider 'milieu' has recently been shown, through controlled 'historicising' speculation from the evidence of the text and manuscripts, to encompass a London readership with a taste for serious vernacular literature. This readership would have been made up of scribes and civil-servants, progressive clergy and religiously earnest members of the knightly class somewhat on the lines of the well-known 'Lollard knight' Sir John Clanvowe.[48] And it requires little effort to see the sort of audience who might have been attracted by Gower's 'In Praise of Peace' or Chaucer's Boethian Ballade 'Truth' being drawn to a longer work that makes God's first 'nature-name' *Treuthe* and concludes Christ's victory over Satan with a harmonious colloquy between God's Daughters 'Peace' and 'Truth'.

iii. *Sequence of the Versions*

§ 13. If the questions of authorship and audience cannot be wholly separated, neither can those of the date and sequence of the versions. It has been seen that 'The Book of Piers Plowman' has been traditionally ascribed only to an author called Langland. The notion, based upon supposedly major differences between the versions, that **A**, **B** and **C** are by more than one author, was much discussed in the last century; but it finds almost no support today. The **B** Version is ascribed to John Trevisa by David Fowler;[49] but Donaldson[50] tellingly cites C V 92–101 as evidence for single authorship of the three (or as the present editor contends, four) versions of the poem. And George Kane shows how the 'signature-line' B XV 152 is further evidence that one man wrote all the versions.[51] It has been maintained above (III, *Z Version*, §§ 20–2; IV §§ 1–8) that single authorship of the canonical versions **A**, **B** and **C** is indicated by the common linguistic, stylistic and metrical qualities that distinguish them from the work of the other alliterative makers, and that the presence of these qualities in the contested **Z** Version argues for its authenticity. The question of the sequence of **Z**, **A**, **B** and **C** ought ideally, of course, to be settled by appeal to external evidence for their date. But such evidence is not common in the period, and is hardly more forthcoming in the case of Chaucer, a public figure of some celebrity. At best, the four versions present a second kind of internal evidence, that of virtually certain allusions to dateable events; and these, when combined with the aforementioned features of language, form and expression, create a 'moral' certainty as to their order. That conclusion has been recently challenged, and the case for reconsidering the sequence must accordingly be examined. At this point, suffice it to say that if the received order for **ABC** is confirmed, and if **Z** is judged authentic on grounds of its intrinsic quality and assured 'core-text' characteristics, then its content and structure allow it only one possible place in the sequence. This is at the beginning, as the earliest (and in all probability draft) form of a more or less complete version of *Piers Plowman*. It will then follow that **A** revised and expanded **Z**; that it was abortively continued in Passus XII; and that it was then abandoned for the new start represented by **B**, which was completed and 'published.' This version, at least partly in response to its reception, was revised and reached its intended final shape **C**, in all but a few places, by the time of Langland's death.

§ 14. Before considering the objections to this account, it is necessary to look at the internal evidence for dating all four versions. As already noted, the date of each and the sequence of all cannot be separated; but they are in principle two distinct questions (see *Intro*. II, §§ 137–8). Failing other positive external evidence, the latest date of composition of a medieval text will be that of the earliest manuscript in which it survives, a matter that can now often be established with some precision. The period of 1390–1400 has been proposed for two copies of **C**, no. 33, TCD 212 (V), containing the Latin memorandum (in a much later hand) on the poet and his father, and no. 39, CUL Dd. 3.13 (G).[52] If *c.*1390 is correct, these copies come very close to the presumed obit of Langland, which is not later than 1387 (on the basis of John But's testimony) or earlier than 1388 (on that deduced from supposed echoes of the Cambridge Statute of Labourers in C V). Their very early date naturally argues a rapid process of generation (and degeneration) of the text of **C** (*Intro*. III, *C*, § 1). But if the date is tilted to the end of the decade, these manuscripts take their place as coævals with a dozen other important witnesses of approximately 1400: nos. 4 (V of **A**); nos. 11, 20, 22, 23 (W, L, R and F of **B**); nos. 24, 26, 28, 30, 31, 40 and fragment iii (X, I, U, P, E, K and H of **C**); no. 46 (the conjoint ms T of **AC**); and perhaps no. 52 (**Z**). With the addition of nos. 2 and 10 (R and M of **A**), these include most of the manuscripts essential for editing *Piers Plowman.* Considered together with the Langland-influenced poems *PPCr, RRe* and *MS*, which belong between the mid-1390s and 1410, this clustering indicates a marked interest in the poem during the last ten years of the fourteenth and the first ten of the fifteenth century. It is only a guess that the poet's death and the release of **C** provoked this interest; but the fact that copies of all versions were then produced, and the presence of at least one conjoint text, strongly suggest as much. The date of the earliest **C** manuscripts and the internal evidence that **C** was written after and partly in response to the Peasants' Revolt thus help to fix its composition within the decade 1381–1390.

§ 15. Desire to read the poem (in whatever form) at the turn of the century also best accounts for the production about then of the one early single-version copy of **A**.[53] But that **A** was early recognised as an 'incomplete' representation of *Piers Plowman* is implied by its having been supplemented from another version over the next two decades in at least six of the surviving copies (nos. 43–5, 47–8, 51). Now, if the A-Text was not circulated widely till after 1400, and if the version that Ball's letter alludes to is **B** (as seems likeliest from § 10 above), some time would have had to elapse between the 'publication' of the latter and its becoming well-known to the rebel leaders. This probable necessity accords well with the internal evidence. For though no early copy of **B** survives to provide a limiting latest date of composition, this is provided by the internal evidence of allusions in its final passūs to the Papal Wars. These are best understood as the campaigns of April 1379 that immediately followed the Great Schism (see *Commentary* on 21/19.430 ff and cf. C 22/20.127, which appears to be a revision). Kane's relation of these lines to *pre*-Schism papal conflicts in the 1360s and 1377 seems to the present writer implausible.[54] So too does the claim of Anne Hudson, who places **B** firmly after the Rising and judges that 'the simplest understanding' of these papal wars is as referring to the Despenser Crusade of 1383.[55] But her argument that, as the earlier territorial wars of the papacy did not involve England, they were unlikely to have struck Langland or his readers sufficiently to justify such an allusive reference (ibid. p.100n18) does not persuade; for the first hostilities between Urban and his opponents in April 1379 will have caused far the greater moral shock and are better reconcilable with the completion of **B** in that year, and well before the Revolt, of which this version has no convincing echoes (Hudson's comment on B 15.566=C 17.232 is answered in the *Commentary*). Finally, that B 15.525–7 refers 'almost certainly' to Archbishop Sudbury, who was murdered by the insurgents in June 1381, as maintained by Fowler (1962:174–5), has no evidence to support it. For the text shows the reference as plainly to Thomas Becket, to a generic category of bishops and to the sub-category of those *in partibus infidelium*.[56] (Sean Taylor's similar arguments for regarding **B** as post-1381[57] have been considered and rejected at *Intro*. III, §§ 52–4 above). On the other side, the extensive internal evidence for a *post*-1381 date for **C** indicates that **B** must have been completed well before that date.[58] The Rat Fable in B Pr 176–208 is commonly understood to refer allegorically to the Good Parliament of 1376, perhaps as seen from the standpoint of 1377 (when the boy Richard II became king) and B Pr 123–45 have been connected with the coronation celebrations in July of that year.[59] But since in principle both these sets of lines could have been inserted in the Prologue at any point before 1379 (the date of the Schism), only the *earliest* possible date for **B** can be securely established from a piece of solid internal evidence: the unusually exact reference at B 13.265–71 to the dearth of 1370 and John Chichester's mayoralty. That this 'long-to-be-thought-upon' event was 'not long passed' (268, 265) does not, unfortunately, help to establish when Langland began work on **B**. But this version's length and complexity suggest that it could have occupied him for much of the decade.

§ 16. The date of **A** has no such firm evidence as Chichester's mayoralty to fix on. Bennett argued on the basis of various allusions for *c.*1370, but some of these now seem insecure. One such is that in A III 185 to the death of Edward III's Queen Philippa in 1369; for the critical text (see *TN*) makes the 'mourning' here not the king's for his wife but that of the English army over their reverses (and the line is already in **Z**). That the phrase 'Rome-renneres' at A IV 111 would be an 'appropriate' use in the period 1367–70 (because the Pope was away from Avignon) is a more plausible point, but this detail is again in **Z**. The best evidence for 1370 is Lady Mede's description as an allusion to Alice Perrers, as proposed by Huppé, but this one is a matter of interpretation.[60] Certainly, **A** cannot come before 1362, because A V 14 mentions the great wind of Saturday 15 January of that year (see *Commentary* on C V 114–17); but since its latest possible date is only that of the oldest **A** copy (the Vernon MS of *c.*1400), there is no external proof that **A** is early. Internal evidence of a more subjective kind must therefore be cited in this version: its simplicity of outline and its stressing social and political rather than religious and spiritual issues more than does **B** (if less than **Z**), are features that have traditionally been taken to indicate its priority. For **B** reveals expansion of as well as addition to **A**, an increased complexity of thought on political and religious themes, and greater richness of style. All these indicate considerable development since the composition of **A** and a date for the latter in the early rather than mid-1370s.

§ 17. Recently **A**'s special features have been ascribed by Jill Mann to its being an abbreviated version, subsequent to **B** and **C**, prepared by Langland or someone else for a particular, less sophisticated audience of, perhaps, young people and women. The notion of **A** as an abridgement for a non-clerical audience, first proposed by Howard Meroney, seems counter-intuitive and unparalleled in the major writers of the period.[61] Thus, even without considering the positive internal evidence for lateness, the difference in depth and subtlety between the Short and Long versions of his younger contemporary Julian of Norwich's *Showings* (which *prima facie* resemble the case of Langland's A- and B-Texts) shows every sign of being due to revision over (or after) a long period rather than to the aim of addressing a different audience, which could be made to support a later date for the Short Version. Mann argues that the **A** Version lacks many of the Latin lines of **B** and **C**, but unfortunately for her case **A** also possesses Latin quotations and macaronic lines not found in the later versions; and while some of its unique quotations are translated (e.g. X 94*a*, at 93), others are not (e.g. VIII 123, X 41*a*, 90).[62] It is puzzling indeed to understand why in some copies **A** should have supplemented its text from **C**, 'the abridged text being preferred as far as it went' (p. 47). For this begs the question of whether **A** *was* an abridgement (incomplete, at that) and not simply the early version that was all the compilers could lay their hands on. It is *a fortiori* even harder to accept Mann's ascription of the **BC** echoes in **Z** to *its* being an abridgement made after both **B** and **C** had been written (p. 45), since **Z** like **A** contains unique Latin lines, translated or untranslated as may be (VII 271; V 142–3, VII 267). But more generally, it would be a strange 'abridgement' that not only restricted itself to the first two visions of **B** (where **A** had covered the first three) but revealed a fundamentally different conception of the second vision's action to that of **A**. For **Z** lacks the tearing of the pardon (so does **C**, but it retains Piers's *consequential* quarrel with the priest). Whatever the undertaking imagined by Mann might be, it could not credibly have had Langland's approval, implying as that would a poet with no idea of how he wanted to be understood, successively uttering contradictory deliverances in various states of development. Now, a negative judgement of **Z** as an enthusiastic but misguided scribe-author's memorial reconstruction of **A** (widely straying at some points, uncannily accurate at others) is less unintelligible than this argument, if no more persuasive. But it would envisage a very different entity from the authorial or, at best, authorised abridgement that Mann proposes the **A** Version to be. For **Z** (III, *Z Version*, §§ 1–12) reads not like the reduced form of a finished long poem but like the first draft of a new work with no antecedent, such as **C** has in **B**. Further, as well as lacking the clarity and assurance of **A** (which no one has ever claimed to be a draft), **Z** displays tentativeness, redundancy and repetition. It also contains unique material that it is scarcely possible to see being added in an 'abridgement'.[63] Mann's case for revising the order of the versions, which rests mainly on **A**'s supposed omission of Latin quotations, 'sexual' material, passages critical of the clergy and nobility, and metaphor, has been forcefully answered by Traugott Lawler and George Kane.[64] To the present writer, it defies credence that a version of *Piers Plowman* not merely shorter but concluded with challenging abruptness could ever have been produced for an audience deemed incapable of grappling with the demands of **B**.[65] For despite Mann's arguments to the contrary, there is very little sign of **A**'s having been purged of the characteristic difficulties of **B**. A vigorous and impressive poem as far as it goes, the **A** Version arguably offers in Passus XI a kind of 'ending', if not a true conclusion. But while it makes good sense as the first completed phase of Langland's life-work, it makes none as a simplification of that work after its completion.

§ 18. From the above it will have emerged, however, that even with the traditional sequence of the versions still in place, dating them with certainty is not possible at present. A set of 'ideal' dates would perhaps be 1365 for **Z**; 1370 for **A**; 1379 for **B**; and 1387 for **C**. But over-precision must yield to the obligation not to over-value the meagre external evidence or the inferences to be drawn from internal evidence. What can be asserted about the Ball, But and Usk testimonies, the order of the texts and the authenticity of **Z** has now been summarised. It hardly needs saying that varying weight will be attached to arguments for dating based on metre, language, style and structure, which are interpretative to a greater or less extent. It has been the purpose of this section, however, to refrain as far as possible from speculative reconstruction of the poet's life and milieu, which some scholars today would regard as a form of 'myth-making'.[66] This is not to deny that the poem's fictions mediate 'truths' about the poet. But there are self-validating truths and truths depending on antecedent readiness to believe; likewise, there are two kinds of inferences that may be drawn from them. That the poet (as in Donaldson's 'biography' and Hanna's 'represented life') was an educated psalter-clerk, or that his having a wife and daughter impeded his advance in the Church, is a possible truth of the second kind: a 'myth' that explains what it does not prove (as myths by their nature cannot). But that Langland's understanding of syllogism-structure implies that he had studied at university or equivalent level is a likelihood that it behoves the demythologiser to *dis*prove. However, in the present instance, while this probability does not strengthen, neither does it serve to challenge the larger 'myth', a consideration that will hearten those less eager to investigate Langland's way with words than his way of life.

iv. *Later Reception of the Poem*

§ 19. Langland's supposed relations with Wycliffe and his followers are a subject that currently attracts attention, if only because much more is known about those who might have read the poem than about the poet himself. And here lies scope for a further myth: that *Piers Plowman* was an inspiration to the Lollards *c*.1390 as it had been for the Rebels *c*.1380. If, however, the 'Lollard myth' is well-grounded, its origin (as in the case of the insurgents before them) is less likely to be what the poem says than the Wycliffites' antecedent readiness to believe that the poet was of their number, if not of their name. This would have found expression in those selective interpretations to which the poem's 'dialogic' procedure renders it vulnerable. Such Langlandian '(mis) reading-circles' might have elected to ignore, for example, the poet's uniformly attested vision of Christendom as a sacramental society where an authoritative priesthood is of the essence. More specifically, as has been observed, Lollard readers would have had to forget that Langland, though strongly criticising the fraternal orders, does not seek their abolition.[67] The influence of *Piers Plowman* on religious dissenting movements that persisted through the fifteenth century and resurfaced as Protestant reformation in the sixteenth has been amply surveyed by recent writers; so there is no need to recapitulate here what in fact belongs to the work's afterlife.[68] Langland's social as much as his religious ideas, in his own time and up to the Tudor age, were exploited for their own purposes by radical reformers from John Ball to Robert Crowley. And though his writing was misinterpreted, anyone who set out to compose an ambitious poem on the theme of religious salvation (as surely as one on the value of earthly love) was bound to run such a risk. The 'ideas' in question, moreover, were not being communicated as straightforward polemic, whether in verse or prose, like *The Simonie* or the 'Jack Upland' tracts.[69] Instead, they were embodied in a work of creative imagination as complex and original as the *Troilus* of Chaucer who, after being misunderstood by his (courtly) readers, supposedly recanted his supposed attack on love and women.

§ 20. It is not unreasonable, then, to envisage Langland's C-Text as a kind of 'response' to his readers. For it significantly modifies the B-Text's treatment of the relations between the individual and the religious authority that taught him to be a citizen of the heavenly kingdom, and those between the individual and the secular authority that told him how to behave as a subject of the king of England. It may well be that the Rising of 1381 and the condemnation of Wycliffe's teachings at the Blackfriars Council in 1382 gave Langland occasions to ponder his poem's potential for being misinterpreted. And it would not be difficult to agree with Anne Hudson that the 'actuality' and the 'aftermath' of the Revolt, together with its 'implication of his own poem in its course,' might have given him 'the spur to compose'. But on the other hand, it is not easy to agree either that the **B** Version expresses 'evidently very mixed feelings about the revolt' or that **C** constitutes 'a hasty, sometimes panicky, sometimes overingenious response to a text its author at times appears to disown'. The **C** Version indeed shows signs of urgent and deep reconsideration; one passage (C Pr 95–127) is unfinished (though that is not itself a sign of haste); and the *mede / mercede* distinction in III 332–406 is 'overingenious'. But how this connects with the poet's 'unease about his own responsibilities to the rebels'[70] is not clear, and the statement may suggest a misconception about what *Piers Plowman* is. To all who have edited it (and the present writer is no exception), *Piers Plowman* is above all a great literary work. Rather than speaking about Langland's responsibilities to the rebels (about which the poem says nothing), it might be better to speak of his responsibility for his poetry and to his poem (which he mentions first in B XII 20–22a and later, as the lines seem patient of interpretation, in C V 92–101).[71]

§ 21. For it could be argued without too much difficulty that Langland remained politically and theologically what Elizabeth Kirk calls a 'radical conservative'.[72] All the versions show, as Pamela Raabe recognises,[73] that what he 'evidently' desired was repentance for sin, the restoration of the divine image in man through sacramental grace and, to make these things possible, the renewal of social and (first and foremost) religious institutions by restoring them *ad pristinum statum.* Drawing his exemplars from *The Golden Legend* and Arthurian romance, Langland ends by evoking for his 'ideal bishop' the image of a martyr, and for his 'ideal king' (perhaps more surprisingly) that of a knightly hero. Proof of this appears in a passage added at XVII 283–92 that shows not 'panicky haste' but full-blooded re-commitment to his earliest principles:

> Euery bisshope bi þe lawe sholde buxumliche walke
> And pacientliche thorw his prouynce and to his peple hym shewe,
> Feden hem and follen hem and fere hem fro synne...
> And enchaunten hem to charite, on Holy Churche to bileue.
> For as þe kynde is of a knyhte or for a kynge to be take
> And amonges here enemyes in mortel batayles
> To be culd and ouercome the comune to defende,
> So is þe kynde of a curatour for Cristes loue to preche,
> And deye for his dere childrene to destruye dedly synne.

It was, however, precisely over how to define and attain this *status pristinus* that the similarities and differences between Langland and both rebels and Lollards would have required 'negotiation' when he was composing **C**. And while this negotiation ultimately led him to emphasise submission to authority so that 'the plant of peace' might flourish, his final revision neither renounced its critique of those entrusted with authority nor, to any degree, the 'option for the poor' that marked his outlook from **Z** onwards.[74]

§ 22. Inevitably, Langland would have had almost no control over the 'responses' of contemporary readers. The most significant of these readers were perhaps those who wrote poems modelled on his, like the author of the *Crede*, the centrepiece in what is known (not without irony) as 'the *Piers Plowman* tradition'. As an impassioned *dialogus* that articulates opposing 'positions' with equal vehemence, through visionary satire at once cerebral and demotic, sublime and coarse, *Piers Plowman* threw down a challenge to those 'strong' misreadings to which major poems seem susceptible.[75] The fate of Langland's work in his time (which is all that concerns the present discussion) suggests that the authorities regarded his 'vernacular theology' neither with hostility nor with favour, but with indifference. Archbishop Arundel's Oxford Council of 1408 did not condemn the poem along with works of heterodox theology (as the Bishop of Paris in 1277 had denounced the *Roman de la Rose* in company with the writings of the Latin Averroists); 'trial material', in Anne Hudson's words, 'produces no evidence of the confiscation of *Piers Plowman* copies from suspected heretics.'[76] But neither did they appreciate the fundamental orthodoxy of a work that some of the dissenting wing had made their own.[77] The defeat of Lollardy in 1415 and (perhaps even more important) the triumph of the 'Chaucerian' poetic line in the fifteenth century helped to push *Piers Plowman* to the margins of its culture. And for the next fifty years the centre ground was dominated by a supreme literary 'entrepreneur', the *un*radical conservative John Lydgate, who was in many ways Langland's antithesis in method and motivation and who shows no interest in Chaucer's great contemporary. Many of the paradoxes and contradictions that doubtless exercised readers of *Piers Plowman* in its time have continued to energise critical interest in ours, often at the expense of its literary qualities. The main danger for *our* time is not of *Piers* being 'misread' as of its not being, as a poem, read at all; and this may be the worst form of misreading. Elizabeth Salter's declaration that 'the most important reason for reading *Piers Plowman* is...that it contains a wider variety of fine poetry than any other work from the English Middle Ages' is, if true, one that deserves to be hung above every Langland scholar's desk, but with 'reading' emended to 'reading and writing about'.[78]

v. *The Composition and Revision of* Piers Plowman

§ 23. If the main postulates of this *Introduction*'s argument have proved acceptable, it should now be possible to give a concise account of Langland's methods of composition and revision and, for want of a better word, his 'sources'.[79] To the reader who doubts the authenticity of **Z**, the versions' traditional authorship and sequence, the poet's clarity of purpose, his seriousness about the details of his art and his concern with the accurate transmission of his text, what follows may draw only qualified assent. From the beginning of the present enterprise, however, all but the first of these assumptions have been embraced as the necessary basis for a parallel-text. And as it has been argued that editing in parallel validates these assumptions, including the first, the supporting evidence (set out in *Intro.* IV above) need not be recapitulated here. Volume I provides in a convenient form the primary materials for studying a work preserved in successive stages of completeness. But although contingently co-present as 'alternative' textual possibilities, the versions representing these stages (it may be assumed) were not intended by the author to exist essentially as such (in this they are unlike the 'states' of an etching, which the engraver, using a medium open to progressive — if irreversible — alteration, may approve as variant interpretations of his subject).[80] That this is true the conflicting scribal readings in the archetypal traditions amply bear out. These 'variants' were the price Langland had to pay if his poem was to be disseminated at all under the limitations of a manuscript culture, for 'l'écriture médiévale ne produit pas de variantes, elle est variance'.[81] But as contended earlier in this *Introduction*, it is the major 'variations' of *non*-scribal origin that distinguish one 'version' from another.

§ 24. This is not to deny that two versions of *Piers Plowman* might have been 'in competition' during the decade after **B** was put forth for copying, probably the last of the poet's life. For it would be unlikely that Langland lacked readers for **A** in the decade *before* he completed **B**. Possibly even, to hazard more (unavoidable) speculation, their mixed 'responses' to the circulated text 'spurred' his composition of **B**. As readers typically do, they may have admired and criticised, inquired of Langland if and how he intended to go on, and urged him to do so (with good effect, since *his* 'response' was an original masterpiece). But it is also hard to believe that Langland could have seen **A** as a viable alternative or have sanctioned its continued circulation after realising his project in the form of **B**: at which stage, comparison would show **A** as superseded by its expanded, extended and completed successor. For an important difference between **B**'s relation to **A** and **C**'s to **B** is that **B** was from the start a new venture. Carefully planned and executed, it is from Passus XI onwards not a revision at all, since there is no antecedent material in **A**. By contrast, **C** is a critical re-construction, comparable in length, of a completed poem that in places no longer said what Langland wanted to, or did so in a way he was no longer disposed to say it. **C**'s excisions and additions are made in reaction to a pre-existing text that is in a real sense its 'source', as **A** (after Passus XI) never was a source for **B**. That difference noted, the nature of the 'revision' nonetheless compels us to regard the C-Text as a poem in its own right. This poem Langland doubtless meant as the last word on his life-long theme of justice and salvation. But he could hardly have been unaware that it would be fated to 'compete' (in a way that **A** never could have) with the text that had made his reputation, if not his 'name'. For the situation in the later 1380s was significantly altered from the early 1370s, when Langland might have 'shown' **A** to an immediate 'circle'. The fact of **B**'s 'publication' with his approval (attested both by its completeness and his checking of the archetypal text)[82] would have imparted urgency to his rewriting: the 'responses' of some readers (after the 'reactions' of others) will have been sharper than in the case of **A**. So, even if 'fools' approval' did not sting Langland into re-writing so much as his own 'exasperated spirit', it cannot have been a negligible factor.

§ 25. It will be clear from what has been said so far that editorial experience, fortified by a modest measure of speculation, provides little ground for supporting any 'indeterminist' theories of composition. To the present writer the four texts of *Piers Plowman* do not declare themselves as 'photographs that caught a static image of a living organism at a given but not necessarily significant moment of time',[83] with the author impulsively altering the **r** form of **A** by adding or removing lines and phrases so as to create the **m** redaction for a particular group of readers; dangling before his interpellatory audience now the β and now the α text of **B**; and, during his massive re-construction of **B**, appeasing them with bleeding chunks of 'London' satire to make 'lollers' rage and cottars laugh through their tears.[84] On the other hand, it does not strain credulity that during his final labours Langland should have allowed (or even invited) certain *acutiores* to 'read' completed parts of his new version, if it was their criticisms that had 'spurred' him to attempt it (and these might have included Usk, Wells or But, though no evidence like Chaucer's 'Envoy to Bukton' lends substance to the speculation). For the **Z**, **A**, **B** and **C** Versions make much less sense as points of stasis in an 'endless' process of 'rolling revision' than as purposeful, if painful, steps (*passūs*) towards realising a grand and noble design. And that this was Langland's aim seems clear from his confident transformation of the **A** Prologue into that of **B**. Since the structural coherence of individual visions is now widely accepted (that of the Second Vision in **B** was demonstrated long ago, and an analysis of the Sixth Vision's intricate organisation will be found in the *Commentary*),[85] it would seem reasonable to assume that what Langland sought in the parts he aimed at in the whole. This was *unity* (neither the word nor the idea strikes as unLanglandian). But 'Langlandian unity' is not the same as the boldly foregrounded formal architecture seen in *The Parliament of Fowls* or *Sir Gawain*, works retaining a residue of 'Ricardian' ambiguity to 'saffron with' their tentatively affirmative endings. Had the **B** Version fallen silent after the Easter mass-bells, its likeness to the major Ricardian pieces would not have passed unremarked. Particularly noteworthy would have seemed its closeness to the most 'through-composed' of these poems, *Pearl*. For B XVIII 475–6 and *Pearl* 1208–10 both envisage the reception of Communion as the 'eschatological' symbolic act of *fratres habitantes in unum* (Ps 132:1 = B XVIII 425a), whereas now *Pearl* concludes virtually with an 'answer' to what is Langland's actual final passus. Indeed, that **B** may have ended at Passus XVIII, and that XIX and XX were *added* in the **C** revision, has been mooted by Warner as a 'startling possibility'.[86] Too startling, one may feel, to be really probable; for the building of Unity and the immediate attack on it would seem (to most readers) thematically indispensable if **B**'s conception of Grace's activity in time is to be completed and 'salvation history' shown as continuing into the present. Conversely, had Langland wished the poem to end at C XX, our sense of this version as a 'revision' would demand matchingly drastic revision. But those are possibilities to be pursued no further here; **C** offers the same disconcertingly dramatic end as **B**.

§ 26. In what is commonly acknowledged as the greatest religious allegory of the period, the *Divina Commedia,* Dante created a poem with its end potentially present in its beginning, and capable of accommodating a mass of historical material within its intricate *post-mortem* architectonic. By contrast, the recalcitrance of Langland's resolutely *in via* theme, and his lack of any guide or model, offered daunting challenges to the realisation of his enterprise. Most readers tend to agree that the sense of effort and striving conveyed by *Piers Plowman* is refracted rather than contained by the formal structures of its eight main visions. Langland has no envelope of eternity to restrict the energies of his poetry from flooding into the real world of late-medieval English society. His poem may well strike readers familiar with the *Commedia* as being carried forward through its revisions on an ever more rapidly-flowing stream of historical time, even as being 'about' the process of the Christian experience in time, or what is called 'the drama of salvation history'. However, the recent critical notion that will be rejected in the next two paragraphs is not that the poem's composition was other than a 'process' (and obviously, given the conditions, a protracted one) but that process could ever have been what Langland aimed at. 'Post-modern' interpreters, laudably eager to win friends for *Piers Plowman*, its time, and its culture, should be wary of projecting onto the life-work of a fourteenth-century *makere* the ambivalences of decentred pluralism.[87] Medieval religious allegories mirror the epoch's common understanding of history, personal and universal, as a linear movement with its *ende* (both 'purpose' and 'conclusion') in death and judgement. The 'death' is that of the author *whan þis werk was wrouȝt* (A XII 103), the 'judgement' not that of 'times to come' but of the Judge of all times. Thus C V 94–101 would make little psychological (not to say spiritual) sense unless Langland's 'end' was to get 'this work' finally 'wrought'.[88] Nor would John But have prayed for WILL's soul unless he believed the poet had reached his 'end', in death. Even Chaucer's *Canterbury Tales*, which seems to point down the road of indeterminacy with the author's invitation to 'turn over the leaf and chose another tale' (I 3177), finds itself sharply re-aligned with the age's central paradigm when the pilgrims arrive at their destination, the Parson reminds them that life is a journey to judgement, and the maker takes his leave of his book and of his readers. And to instance a piece of possibly unfinished work, the abrupt end of A XI should not be thought to imply that the author espoused a poetic of fragmentation, any more than does the more obviously 'broken-off' Book III of *The House of Fame* (Ricardian poets sometimes know they should leave off if they do not know how to go on). Though it may be granted that 'perfection of the work' was, for Langland, not disjoined from but co-extensive with 'perfection of the life', his poem attests what was a lifelong struggle for the humility to accept imperfection. But an aesthetic of 'accepted imperfection' is not the same as an aesthetic of indeterminacy. Despite its modern-seeming plasticity, *Piers Plowman* rests on the same late-Gothic structural principles as *Troilus, St Erkenwald, Pearl* and the *Confessio Amantis*. Nor does there seem much reason to believe that Langland's artistic principles were at odds with those of the Ricardian masters who wrote these poems.[89]

§ 27. The situation with regard to Langland's texts is nonetheless singular enough, and our knowledge of his compositional practices sufficiently meagre, to baulk further speculation (the present writer has exceeded his licence already). But by way of conclusion, it is perhaps worth saying that for even the one more recent work that is 'semblable somdeel to *Piers þe Plowman*', Wordsworth's *Prelude*, it was not a 'process' but a product that its author kept constantly in view. Langland's poem is admittedly in many ways less like that work than *The Recluse*, the unachieved larger work on 'nature, man, and society' to which Wordsworth's enquiry into the growth of the poet's mind was a 'prelude'. The versions of *Piers Plowman* that survive may be read today, according to taste, in some historically 'authentic' manuscript text, or in the form of 'critically' reconstructed archetypes. But the poem they transmit seems too publicly engaged, right from its opening scene in a 'field ful of folk', ever to have existed as the sequence of re-copied holographs that Wordsworth's (never-published) *Prelude* constitutes.[90] Langland may have praised, but there is little sign that he practised, the reclusive life; his represented isolation is an inward condition, not (like the later poet's) a deliberate rural seclusion. He left the Malvern Hills, instead of lingering there; *clerk þou3 he were*, he stands out in his time as the critical celebrant of *ertheliche honeste thynges*, 'active' to his inky fingertips. And in all this he is essentially *of* his time, which may have tolerated, even on occasion admired, but generally did not foster solitariness.

§ 28. Langland may therefore be envisaged as a thoroughly social, even a public writer,[91] showing or reading his work to friends from whom he received (and perhaps solicited) comments and suggestions. All poetry, insofar as it *is* poetry (and including even didactic religious writing), is meant to give people pleasure. And if the poet's own quarters proved too cramped for this purpose, he presumably knew people (they need not be called 'patrons') with space to offer, encouragement and refreshment.[92] His activity was also, from A VIII 89–XII 98, and from B XI until the crisis that provoked renewed work, one of composition rather than revision. Thus **Z** preserves a draft (not a first, it seems probable, but a second or later draft) of a work that was completed but not 'finished'; fit to be read out, but not to be read 'in'. This version Langland turned into **A** by adding the extraordinary Tearing of the Pardon after its closing 'beatitude' words on the poor. Our sole manuscript copy of **Z**, it may be surmised, is most probably the posthumous product of a time when interest in *any* form of *Piers Plowman* was strongest, and when Langland's literary remains were being preserved for and distributed to those who had supported him during life. These remains, it may be assumed, would not have included rough papers that showed his composing hand at work. For medieval aesthetics was not concerned with the preparatory stages of 'masterworks'; and the 'aesthetic of imperfection' mentioned above must be understood not in terms of the later idea of the inspired fragment, but of St Gregory's idea of 'perfection in imperfection'.[93] This notion betokens acceptance that no human work can be perfect (though man should nonetheless strive to make it so) and not the Romantics' acknowledgement (nourished by belief in the mysteriousness of poetic inspiration) of the *opus imperfectum* as a legitimate artistic category. Nor is the poet himself likely to have parted with the early draft texts, as opposed to finished portions, of any version. If **C** was known to Usk, this might simply imply that it *was* (like **Z**) virtually 'complete', though not 'finished', when Langland died (see § 11 above).

§ 29. It seems a fair assumption therefore that Langland might have kept his draft materials with him, notwithstanding that he would have had to give up his final manuscript of **B** for copying and that the C-Text unquestionably reflects errors present in the text of **B** he worked from, which must therefore have been a scribal product. But there is no real evidence for thinking that he used a scribal manuscript in revising from **A** to **B**. And since **A** (by contrast with **B**) is likely to have undergone only limited scribal copying in the poet's lifetime, he could well have held on to his own fair copy or a pre-final draft. Quite possibly, if they contained anything of potential future value, he also kept working-papers of **A** (and later **B**) too extensively written-over to be of use as scribal copy-text. It is of course more than possible that, in the highly mnemonic culture of his time, Langland composed long passages of the poem in his head before writing them down (even in the age of print, Milton and Wordsworth did as much), and could subsequently recall the material he needed at will. But supposition aside, there is evidence recoverable through analysis of the text that he did indeed possess a 'repertorium' or 'poetic bank' of lines and half-lines, ready to be drawn upon in different situations.

§ 30. This document could have been alphabetically arranged for convenience like the Biblical and preaching concordances of the day, and it would not be hard to reconstruct it from the material given below in Appendix Three. From this it appears that some 65 lines and 250 half-lines (37% of the latter b-verses) are used more than once, whether in the same version or in a later one (not all are verbally identical, and where a small difference is found this has been duly noted). It is admittedly not usual to think of Langland as to any degree a 'formulaic' poet (although his use of rhetorical *repetitio* is well known).[94] But even according to the flexible rules of versification that he employed, he could hardly have composed nearly 19,000 lines without re-using units of verse-structure. What is surprising is not that Langland sometimes resorted to metrical set-phrases, but that he did so very rarely. With only the half-lines counted as properly formulaic (whole-lines belonging more to rhetorical *repetitio*), they amount to only 0.70% of the whole. The 65 full lines are, at 0.33%, an even smaller proportion, though their impact is necessarily greater. These figures explain why the style of *Piers Plowman* does not strike as 'formulaic', even though some half-lines are repeated as many as sixteen times.[95] For though Langland no more than Chaucer or Gower avoids common phrases and idioms in constructing half-lines, he relatively seldom repeats them, so that his style comes across as colloquial without being prosaic. By definition, most of these non-parallel *repeated* half-lines do not belong to the core-text, though a small number occur more than once in more than one version. But 'repeat-verses' distinguishable from parallel-lines are also to be found outside passages that (even after repositioning) appear parallel when compared with the relevant displaced material.

§ 31. Most studies of Langland's revisions have understandably focussed on the four larger procedures of omitting, adding, transposing and re-writing material from the immediately antecedent version. Useful analyses of **A**, **B** and **C** appear in the Athlone editions (Kane 19–24; Kane-Donaldson 72–8; Russell-Kane 63–4), and Malcolm Godden's pioneering study covers all four included in this edition.[96] A full examination of the revision-process would, however, require a separate volume, and none is attempted here, though the most important changes are discussed *ad loc* in Sections B and C of the present volume. But while it has been maintained that the poet's acts of revision were essentially 'linear' (IV § 22 above), analysis of repeated **C** half-lines shows that Langland felt free to restore what he had previously written if he so wished. For there is no reason to doubt that he had access to these earlier forms, and not only in the 'repertorium' form hypothesised. A representative example is the line 'And is to mene in oure mouth more ne mynne' (III 395), a somewhat 'formulaic' addition in a new passage of **C**. Here Langland was taking up **A** XI 306 'And is to mene in oure mouþ more ne *lesse*', the second and fourth lifts of which he had revised in parallel **B** X 456 to 'And is to mene *to Englissh men* more ne *lesse*'. But in **C** he both changed *lesse* to *mynne* in the b-half to make up a Type Ib line *and* he remembered to alter the b-half lift in parallel C XI 293 to read 'And is to mene no more to men *that beth lewed*', where only lift four contains a new idea. This is evidence that Langland re-composed with the texts of both **A** and **B** to hand (or, less credibly, in his head), since he was clearly taking into account the implications of re-using elements from a version anterior to the one directly under revision. Even more striking is a line from a part of the poem corresponding only to the B-Text, 'So is he fader and formeour, þe furste of alle thynges' (C XIX 134), which repeats A X 28 except for adding the onset-phrase. At B IX 27 he had revised the b-half of this line to *of al þat euere was maked*, presumably to avoid repeating the previous line's 'of alle kynnes *þynges*', and now he altered this b-half to 'of al þat *forth groweth*'. These lines suggest not recourse to a repertory-concordance but eye-access to the full A-Text. By contrast, C Pr 88b, which appears to repeat A II 45a, is more likely to be drawn from the repertory, as it is a formulaic half-line used a dozen times in **C** and three times in **B**, half of these falling in the b-verse.

§ 32. Another example that may point to similar access to **Z** when Langland was writing **B** and **C** is B IX 72 'Of þis matere I miȝte make a long tale', which is deleted in **C**, is absent from **A** but is first encountered in the earliest version as VII 230. To a sceptic of the authenticity of **Z**, this might seem evidence that the substantive text in Bodley 851 post-dates **B**. But the line's presence in **B** could also be explained by its having been in Langland's repertorium, not wanted in **A**, but re-activated later for use in **B**. For it is a transition-forming quasi-filler, repeated at B XV 89 except for substitution of *muche bible* for *long tale*. Again, in **C**, in a passage without parallel in **Z**, Langland picked up III 78 'Bothe schyreues and seriauntes *and suche as* kepeth *lawes*' from Z II 189 'As seriauntes and scheryues that schyres han to kepe', altering the last two lifts, the word-order and the sense. The strongest evidence that this might indeed be a 'repertory' line is that it does not appear in **A** or **B** and can scarcely have been inserted in **Z** by a compiler working with more than one text, because it is not present *at that point* in **C** (i.e. in the 'Drede' scene at C II 217–19). On a simpler explanation, Langland could have picked the line out directly from his copy of **Z**, which (as said at § 29 above) he is antecedently unlikely to have given away for keeping, let alone copying, to an acquaintance. But the 'repertorium' explanation here better accords with the other evidence produced so far. The widely disjunct appearance of **B** lines in **C** (i.e. in non-parallel positions both earlier and later than the **B** occurrences) also provides support-ing evidence for the existence of the repertorium. Thus B 2.187 // ZC appears as late as C XVII 249, III 193a (modified) at C XIII 56, IV 32 at XV 37, XV 486 at C XVII 230; while X 121b appears in an *earlier* position at C X 104, XIV 182 at C XIII 57, and XV 120 at C III 228b. In all these cases, Langland is careful to make modifications to the corresponding passage in the later text, presumably so as to avoid unintended repetition. With these fitful but illuminating glimpses into the shadowy interior of Langland's 'cave of making', we may turn to the broader and vaguer question of the maker's 'sources.'

vi. *The Sources of* Piers Plowman

§ 33. To find a dream-poem framework as the setting for his vision in the Prologue, Langland need have looked no further than the opening of one of the few earlier alliterative works that he certainly knew, *Winner and Waster*. But apart from a delayed echo of that poem's symphony of birdsong in the transitional waking-sequence before the Third Vision (X 61–7 //), and the detail of running water in B Pr 8–10 // ZA (= *WW* 33, 44), the earliest version **Z** immediately strikes out independently to evoke a symbolic landscape that owes everything to the Bible and nothing to the *Winner*-poet (see *Commentary* on Pr 14–21). Langland's second major departure from his English predecessor's example was to construct two self-contained dream-visions, and make the first lead naturally on to the second. This was required so that he could answer WILL's great question to Holy Church, 'How can I save my soul?' The answer was, 'All who live a "true" life in their appointed state in our corrupt society will be certain to receive a pardon from TRUTH, and the patient poor of this world will receive the greatest pardon of all'. This 'answer' sums up the 'meaning' of the first version of *Piers Plowman*, and it takes two dreams to convey. Langland is thought to have got the structural device of multiple visions, as well as various aspects of his later treatment of the life of Christ, from a source not in English but in French, the 'vernacular of clerks'. This is the tri-partite corpus of dream-visions by Guillaume de Deguileville, the *Pèlerinages de Vie Humaine, de l'Ame* and *de Jhesucrist* (*c.*1330–60), a work noticed by a number of earlier scholars and most recently examined by John Burrow.[97] However, apart from these and Robert Grosseteste's *Chateau d'Amour*, which he seems to echo in IX 234ff, 269ff (see *Commentary*), Langland displays relatively little interest in the Continental dream-allegory tradition. He is indifferent to its *fons et origo* the *Roman de la Rose*, in strong contrast to Chaucer, who started his career by translating that work and found the *Roman* a life-long inspiration, or even the alliterative peer who adapted some lines of 'Clopyngnel' in so wittily 'Langlandian' a fashion in *Purity* 1057–64 (but see the *Commentary* on I 6). The language of 'French men and free men' (B XI 384) was apparently for him no more than an assumed accomplishment. Unlike Chaucer, Langland (who gives no sign of having travelled to France) shows little susceptibility to its siren-song, which he perhaps associ-ated with the ostentatiousness of decadent knighthood and the luxury of papal Avignon. Langland obviously wanted this 'richest realm' left in peace and left to itself, and the throwaway insult of X 135 may obliquely hint at a reason why. His antagonism to France (if it is really that) seems to be based not on a sense of cultural inferiority but on suspicion of the exterior 'Gallic' polish that the spirit of *mondanité* could cunningly exploit in order to entrap a *cœur simple*. But if Lang-land's own poetry is not unsophisticated, it may be fairly described as *anti*-sophisticated. Thus even *courtoisie*, the emblem of French civilisation for his contemporaries, never simply 'means good' in *Piers Plowman*, which struggles to wrench this ambiguous token-term from the keeping of Lady Mede and enlist it in the lexicon of grace.[98] During Richard II's later years, Langland is no more likely to have approved *Troilus and Criseyde's* painstaking endeavour to 'redeem' *fin' amour* than *Sir Gawain's* painful transvaluations of 'chivalry' and 'courtesy'. For those central values of the time his defiant exemplar is a saviour 'without spurs or spear' in ploughman's garb.

§ 34. For all medieval poets 'social man' living in community formed the real, the principal artistic subject. So even when WILL has a vision of Nature from the mountain of Middle-Earth, he quickly turns his gaze from the blameless beasts to focus (with whatever chagrin) on the troubled world of fallen men and women. But typically, in an age without romanticism, Langland (unlike Wordsworth) shows no nostalgia for a lost childhood of visionary innocence. His quest is not for the rusty gate of Eden but the well-oiled drawbridge of the City of God. And this (following the dual model of 'Jerusalem' as bride and city in Apoc 21:2) is the 'spiritual organism' manifested to the Dreamer first as HOLY CHURCH and finally as UNITY. But the 'drawbridge' to be crossed is the 'material organisation' in which that organism had become historically compacted. For ines-capably, the spiritual reality to which Christian learning and worship were held to grant access finds itself summoned into the poetry through the insistent citations from *holiwrit* that sound Langland's most distinctive note. These *tixtes* provide him a handhold on the attention of his more cultured and presumably influential readers; they are what might have impressed Wycliffe if that stern *doctour* ever read *Piers Plowman*. Together with the macaronic lines, which usually embed morsels of larger quotations, they stand in tension with the de-provincialised vernacular through which Langland probes a domain of discourse where it had no recognised rights, feeling with its fingers the fleshly heart of *clergye*. Highlighted in the manuscripts of the poem by underlining and rubrication, the Latin quotations conversely serve to 'prove' Langland's metropolitanised English. But to the reader today, as doubtless then, they resemble a door (whether locked or open) into the work's innermost recesses. For to Langland, 'þe Engelisch of oure eldres' is not in itself an alternative mode of access to religious truth; because salvation, to his thinking, lies in 'þe cofre of Cristes tresor,' to which 'clerkes kepe þe keyes' (B XII 108–9). So immediate, indeed, is Langland's sense of Christianity's 'Roman' lineage that he treats its arrival in England as a thing but of yesterday. He makes vivid to himself how the compassionate intercessor for the pagan Emperor Trajan was the same champion of the heathen English who with a legendary pun on his lips[99] resolved to send Augustine to Canterbury. He sees Christianity as a Latin 'thing', the *res Latina* as the *res Christiana*. Against this rooted conviction is set, to be sure, the other pole of the cultural dialectic, the simple faith of simple folk, 'pore peple as plouȝmen, and pastours of bestes'. Yet even this faith, we cannot fail to notice, must be formulated in the phrase *sola fides*; even these folk have no choice but to 'Percen *with a Paternoster* þe paleis of heuene' (A XI 310–12). For Langland never calls the Lord's Prayer the 'Our Father'; and he never recognises 'true' knowledge of religion without *clergye*.[100]

§ 35. 'Vernacular theology' may in some sense describe parts of *Piers Plowman*, even if to think of the poem as a 'theological' work risks the irrelevance that arises from generic misclassification.[101] But Langland seems to have employed 'þe Engelisch of oure eldres' because it was appropriate to *makyng*, not because he thought it able (as did Reginald Pecock a century later) to capture the Queen of the Sciences for the mother tongue. Thus, unlike the Lollards he does not even desiderate 'þe Bible in English' in order to 'expoune' Scripture, as one Wycliffite writer has it, 'myche openliere and shortliere...and myche sharpliere and groundliere' for the benefit of 'a symple man'. And this because for Langland, *clerkes kepe þe keyes*. Rather, his work resembles what David Lawton calls (in reference to Rolle) 'a limited form of functional bilingualism, enabling devotional and liturgical recognition of familiar text'.[102] *Piers Plowman* is not (as is *Patience*) a work of *translatio*, however 'free'; for somewhat like the anonymous author of *The Cloud of Unknowing* as Nicholas Watson describes him, Langland 'acts not simply as a clerical translator of learned material but as a fierce vernacular *critic* of the academic world from which his learning derives'.[103] These formulations may help to situate Langland in relation to certain aspects of his wider intellectual milieu. To the student of *Piers Plowman*, tension between the learned and the vernacular, foregrounded by a unique style forged in revising, is its fundamental dynamic and merits the close attention of all who approach it as a poem.[104]

§ 36. The Latin quotations mentioned above remind us that, whereas study of the medieval poet's method of composition tends to start with 'sources', Langland does not strictly seem to have any.[105] John Alford has argued, however, that he '*began* with the quotations, and from them, using the standard aids of a medieval preacher, derived the substance of the poem'. And his view finds support in Judson Allen's claim that 'the text of the poem obeys no logic of its own, but occurs as commentary on a development of an array of themes already defined elsewhere as an ordered set — usually by the Bible.'[106] But even allowing, as Allen does, that Langland might have come across major compilation-sources such as Hugh of St Cher's Psalter Commentary only *after* writing **Z** (which has barely more than a dozen quotations), both comments are surely much exaggerated. An unprejudiced reader of the poem in the sequence **ZABC** will not be quickly moved to abandon the traditional view of the Latin quotations as designed to reinforce and illustrate the sense of the English text, which is primary. They provide the germinal idea of particular thematic structures, suggest developments, create networks of allusion and broaden contextual meaning.[107] In this way, the quotations can resemble conventional 'sources', as when the Latin is translated or paraphrased before or after being given.[108] But textually speaking, they figure as the chief element of a cultural matrix furnished by the *Biblia glossata* and 'aids' to its study such as incipits, concordances and dictionaries. They provide a horizon of transcendental reference and ensure that the 'meaning' of the 'earthly honest things' of English 'experience' that form the poem's foreground is not lost.

§ 37. As a psalter-clerk, Langland will have been involved to some degree in the communal prayer by which monastic and other religious clergy 'sacralised' the hours of day and night. But even more important than the complete Divine Office for widening access to the words of Scripture beyond the circles of the *litterati* was the circumambient 'text' of *masse and houres* in which the people at large were able to participate and which (as Sr Mary Davlin puts it)

> exist[s] not to be read or heard passively, but to be participated in, played out, worked and played with over and over; their purpose...experience, both aesthetic and religious, [through which] they release an increasing fullness of connotative meaning.[109]

Langland evidently assumed, for example, that observance of the Sunday obligation implied attendance not only at Mass but also at the 'hours' of Matins and Evensong.[110] And while the exact meaning of the Missal or Breviary readings might have been lost on all but the few, in a broader sense the Church's daily worship formed a shared 'possession' of layman and clerk alike. The Latin of the liturgy was perceived less as a 'learned' than as a 'sacred' language, consecrated to a special purpose that elevated it above the mundane vernacular. In particular, the ceremonies of the Easter Triduum, a recurring communal 'immersion' in the most moving and dramatic texts of the New Testament, constituted a solemn rite of collective spiritual renewal. Preceded by Lenten sermons, and followed by the miracle plays of midsummer, the central days of the Church's year offered a religious experience of high intensity, at an emotional rather than an intellectual plane.[111] Langland could therefore expect the Passion narrative of B XVIII to be appreciated by an audience wider than the formally 'literate'; but understood, of course, at more than one level. It is not so much that (as the comments of Alford and Allen propose) the 'substance' of his greatest Passus is 'derived' from the fifty Latin quotations that vein its English text as that this substance, embodied in an 'earthly honest' fourteenth-century South-West Midland vernacular, is nourished by a flow of regionally and temporally unrestricted 'sacred' speech. This language is marked in the written text by rubrication, and invites (when read aloud) a change of pitch and tone. The pinnacle of Langland's 'clerkly making', Passus XVIII offers a model for comprehending the entire question of his 'sources', or what might better (if more loosely) be called his 'inspiration'. The resonant textuality that sustains this passus, together with the quieter reflectiveness of the one that follows it, furnish our widest perspective on his enterprise.[112] Langland, it clearly emerges, was inspired by the same sources as the community of believers whose corporate experience of sacred 'timelessness' he alone of his contemporaries managed to articulate 'in time'. English speech and Latin liturgy joined to give Langland an *os magna sonaturum,* a voice of great compass with unique expressive and communicative power.

§ 38. A distinction should perhaps be recognised, then, between the poet's sources in this broader sense and his reading as such. But Passus XVIII not only draws deeply on 'enacted scripture', the shared words of a rite of *anamnesis*; it also uses a text that the poet had presumably 'read', not 'heard sung or recited', the account of the Harrowing of Hell in the Apocryphal *Gospel of Nicodemus.* This Langland certainly knew in the Latin, probably also in the C13th English translation, and possibly through a dramatisation in the Corpus Christi plays that were taking shape in his early years (though Latin para-liturgical dramas had been composed since the thirteenth century and vernacular cycles were known by the last quarter of the fourteenth, the individual pageant-themes were probably in formation not earlier than *c.*1350).[113] Once again, to contrast Langland with his great contemporary, whereas Chaucer's personal discovery *Il Filostrato* was a narrative source that he could conceal from his audience under the fictitious name of 'Lollius', the *Harrowing* that Langland used was common cultural property. This story had no part in the formal Easter service, but popular tradition had made the *Descensus* narrative familiar enough to toll reminiscent bells through the measures of Langland's resonant verse, and invite attention to what was new and unexpected in its presentation. And unlike the more *recherché* Debate of the Four Daughters of God that precedes it, the *Harrowing* story worked with motifs that were widely known in the visual art of the time.[114] That Langland himself found this episode a continuing artistic challenge is clear from the significant changes he made to his treatment of it in Passus XX, the last fully revised part of **C**.

§ 39. Connected in principle (though not always in practice) with the liturgy and 'paraliturgy' (processions and devotions) was another public auditory experience, that of the preaching-sermon. A typical Sunday homily from the local *persone* might offer little to feed the poet's imagination; but London in his time had outstanding preachers, often mendicants, who could be heard in their own great churches or at St Paul's Cross (where the Gluttonous Doctor was heard to preach on fasting a few days before WILL met him in Conscience's house). The impress of sermon-like features is detectable throughout *Piers Plowman*, though modern readers may be less apt to see the poem (like G. R. Owst, the pioneer in this field) as 'the fine product of English medieval preaching'[115] or the sermon as the origin of its attitudes, images and ideas so much as something that encouraged the poet to express all these in particular well-known ways. Elizabeth Salter accordingly turned from Owst's concentration on thematic content to study the formal influence of the *ars predicandi* on Langland's poetic procedures. And A. C. Spearing followed her, arguing that the preacher's organisation by 'division' of the 'theme' provides the poem's main ordering principle, and offering an analysis of Reason's address to the Folk of the Field (V 125ff).[116] While this *sermo prelati ad status* is probably the only formal sermon in the poem, other longer discourses like those of Anima and Holy Church are similarly constructed. But as Siegfried Wenzel observes, though the structure of Holy Church's speech resembles that of a Middle English sermon he examines, 'its *mode of progression* and development' are uncharacteristic of fourteenth-century sermons and more reminiscent of devotional writings like the *Ancrene Wisse*.[117] This needs saying, since the influence on Langland of English and especially of Latin devotional prose, such as that of the Bernardine-Bonaventuran tradition, is easy to underestimate.

But sermons, it should also be noted, are not always accepted in *Piers Plowman* as authoritative instruction. Sometimes dubious characters are seen preaching, such as an unlicensed pardoner (Pr 66) and troublous mendicants (XI 54, 207). And even Mahomet is shown to exploit, as a means to deceive the gullible, the combination of oratory and personality that successful preachers depend on. Langland often voices suspicion of practised sermonists who 'prechen and preue hit nat' (XVI 262, XVII 383–4); and at B XV 448 he proclaims his preference for miracle-working over eloquence as a means of evangelisation. The cynical might not marvel if this should prove in shorter supply; but what Langland is really asking for is preaching valorised by holiness of life, as witness one of his best macaronic outbursts:

> '*Beatus*,' seiþ Seint Bernard, '*qui scripturas legit*
> *Et verba vertit in opera* fulliche to his power' (XV 60–1).

This exhortation is meant to apply to all who study the Bible, but *a fortiori* to those who make sermons on problematic texts, as do (ten lines later) the 'Freres and fele oþere maistres þat to þe lewed *prechen*' (B XV 70). As so often, the poet's key concern in highlighting the ambiguous relationship between Latin as the language of *holy loore* and English as that of *kynde understondyng* is the responsibility of the *lered* to the *lewed*.

§ 40. This said, Langland is by no means always the earnest moralist. Nearer to Dickens in some ways than to Milton, he can be humorously sceptical about the readiness of religious experts to leap up and preach, as witness Dame Scripture mounting her pulpit two steps at a time (XII 42). And the Z-Text Dreamer's wry response to Hunger's exposition of the 'theme' *servus nequam*, that 'hit fallet nat for me, for Y am no dekne / To preche the peple what that poynt menes' (Z VII 231–2) seems consciously ambiguous as to which response is invited: 'What a pity!' or 'And a good thing too!' None of this is meant to question that some of Langland's poetic figures of speech owe a genuine debt to the rich homiletic culture of the time, and Wenzel is probably right that investigation of unread Latin sermons may 'bear fruit for *Piers Plowman* scholarship'.[118] But while one may hope, one hesitates; for though Langland uses *sarmon* in the sense both of 'discourse' and 'preaching-sermon', it is the former that he seems most to have profited from. Indeed, his one favourable reference to the latter, in the line 'Patriarkes and prophetes, precheours of Goddes wordes' (VII 87), seems to envisage not churchmen but august scriptural personages like Jeremiah and John the Baptist. He had probably heard enough sermons to have reservations about them as a force for good, if what they taught was contradicted (as it doubtless often was) by the lives of those who preached them. And one suspects that though Langland scorned *idiotes preestes* who mangled the liturgy, his conviction that *sola fides sufficit* guaranteed a limit on the harm that *overskipperis* could do to the *lewed*. In regard to sermons, by contrast, for preachers to urge self-denial while living like epicures brought clerks, *clergye* and *the feith* into disrepute. On the whole, then, the tradition of interpretation stemming from Owst may have overstated the direct influence of the pulpit upon the poet's creative processes. For if participation in the Church's liturgy provided the *lewed* a comforting spiritual shawl, exposure to preaching could prove like standing in a cold east wind. The poet preferred the shawl to the wind.

§ 41. Sustaining what may be thought of as Langland's broadly communal 'inspiration' was, however, a select body of Latin writings that helped him to refine his understanding of the central Christian 'mysteries' as the medieval Church received them. These mysteries were the Incarnation, the Trinity, and the operation of Grace through time in the lives of the Saints whose memorial feasts formed a 'sanctoral' cycle intertwined with the 'temporal' cycle of the Church's Calendar. The terseness of the Gospel narratives, moreover, prompted in this period the writing of 'lives' of Christ that filled it out and 'pointed' it with colourful detail. Taking example from the impassioned eloquence of St Bernard, these attempts by (largely) Mendicant writers to arouse devotion among the laity readily found their way into the vernacular. The most influential was the *Vita Christi* of the fourteenth-century Carthusian Ludolf of Saxony, which is drawn upon in the C revision.[119] But one that might have had a special appeal to Langland was the *Philomena* of the thirteenth-century Yorkshireman John of Howden, a lyrical-epic Passion-meditation in rhyming quatrains of almost 'Metaphysical' pointedness and complexity that call Langland's methods to mind:

> *Scribe corde, quod lingua proferam:*
> *Scissae carnis loricam laceram,*
> *Seminatam in fronte literam,*
> *Quam cum lego, da corpus deseram* (*Philom.* XIX 61).

The 'unmeasurable' mystery of the Trinity, which some modern interpreters have seen as an organising structural principle of *Piers Plowman*, had received its fullest treatment in the 'books and books' of Augustine's *De Trinitate*.[120] But an unexplored further possible source is the *De Trinitate* of the twelfth-century mystic Richard of St Victor, whose strikingly original presentation of the divine nature as 'shared love harmoniously in community...fused into one affection by the flame of love' (III. xix)[121] furnishes an image that underlies passages such as XIX 169–71. For *seintes lyues redyng* Langland turned to the *Legenda Aurea* of the Dominican master James of Voragine, a favourite book that he mentions three times by name.[122] Such writings offered a key enabling him to 'decode' the text of salvation inscribed on the body of Christ in its 'mystical' extension through historical time, the Church. In a more general way, the entire range of man's moral life Langland found treated in another major authority that he refers to by name. This is the *Moralia in Job* written by the one of 'Peres foure stottes' he twice calls (among eight several mentions) 'Gregory the grete clerk', whose thought and theory pervade the entire poem. Such lofty doctrine, finally, he supplements with the *oother science* of Cato's thrifty couplets, a repository of everyday prudence.[123]

§ 42. The 'natures of things' also seem to have fascinated Langland, whether it was the way that birds and mammals copulate or the paradoxical means by which scorpion-bites are supposedly cured (XIII 143–66; XX 154–59). So did the natures of words, as revealed in his insistence on the etymologies of *loller* and *hethen* (IX 213–14, B XV 458–60.[124] But Langland is especially fascinated by the relationship between words and things, espousing not the 'conventionalist' theory standard among students of language in our day but (like the medieval *modistae*, who were 'Realists') a form of 'lexical Platonism', which posits substantive affinities between the referents of homophonous lexemes.[125] And in the same general tradition of metaphysical Realism, he embraces the 'sacramental' understanding of language and the world of the twelfth-century poet-theologian Alan of Lille, which goes back to the Augustine of *On Christian Doctrine*. More particularly, Langland's vision of creation as thrown into disorder by human sin owes much to Alan's *De Planctu Naturae* (a work Chaucer cites in *The Parliament of Fowls* 316), where the poet's encounter with Nature (not seen in a dream-vision but decidedly visionary) follows upon his anguished questionings in the opening elegiacs:

Heu! quo naturae secessit gratia? morum
Forma, pudicitiae norma, pudoris amor?...
Sed male naturae munus pro munere donat,
Cum sexum lucri vendit amore suum.

Other traces of Alan's ideas surface in the poem's sombre vision of how 'man and mankynde.../
Resoun reulede hem nat, noþer ryche ne pore' (XIII 181–2) but also, in a more hopeful vein, in
its positive valuation of 'ertheliche honeste thynges' (XXI 94) as the *liber, pictura, speculum* and
fidele signaculum of mankind's 'life, and death, and state and fate' (*Omnis mundi creatura*).[126]

§ 43. It has been shown by a number of scholars[127] that the 'monastic philosophy' of the
twelfth and thirteenth centuries, especially the Bernardine tradition of interior self-understanding,
becomes after the turning-point of the first inner dream the guide that directs the Dreamer's
spiritual 'journey' through the *Vita*. This journey records his progress from preoccupation with
intellectual knowledge (*scientia*) in the Third Vision to a fervent embrace of spiritual wisdom
(*sapientia*) in the Fourth and Fifth. It may have been essentially a prolonged reflection on the
'nature' of his most original creation, Piers, that inspired the poet's transformation of WILL from
a fiercely contentious 'knight' of Pride to a silently attentive servant of Humility. Yet Langland's
selective but impassioned reading may be allowed to have played a part in this. Whether or not a
fresh discovery in the pseudo-Bernardine *Cogitationes piissimae* that *Multi multa sciunt et seip-*
sos nesciunt prompted his return to the 'affective' monastic tradition after a period under the spell
of scholastic training, the Dreamer's attitude to the theology of the schools appears throughout
the poem negative if not hostile, marked by the anguish of one who has 'ay loste and loste' (V 95).
It is a matter of speculation whether this 'represented' disillusion is to be connected with a crisis
in the author's life in which he turned from the disputes of the mendicant theologians *in scole*
to seek relief in the wisdom of the *cloistre*, perhaps first encountered in youth on the Malvern
Hills. Certainly, since Bloomfield, students of Langland's 'philosophy' (the present writer among
them) have found the ascription of specific scholastic sources harder to establish than those from
monastic tradition.[128] Langland criticises both mendicant and secular *maistres* for propounding
'materes vnmesurable to tellen of the Trinite' (B XV 71). But on this awesome subject the only
authority he *quotes* is Augustine, 'highest of the four' (and fount of monastic sapience), recoiling
from the schoolmen's obsession with 'insolibles and falaes' (XVI 229) and naming 'Coveytyse to
conne and to knowe sciences' (XVI 222), the purpose for which in a sense the Schools existed, as
the sin that drove man out of Eden.

§ 44. The strain of vehement anti-intellectualism voiced through WILL need not, of course,
convey Langland's own conviction. But it figures as the dialectical antithesis of a reverential awe
before the majesty of REASON, God's Law at work in nature and in the structures of human society,
including those of government and justice. Only a clerk, perhaps, could excoriate clerkish wrong-
headedness, greed and mendacity with such force. But only a 'genuine poet' (see § 45 below)
could adequately imagine the reckless viciousness and sordor of sublunary existence, see it, and
'in time' learn to suffer it. And it is not the least strength of *Piers Plowman* to escape at so many
points (though not always) the 'immodest tone' of the indignant preacher. Partly he manages this
through his other flexible and original creation WILL, the wincing butt of those stern instructresses
Holy Church, Study and Scripture, partly by articulating his punitive spleen through the voices
of several variously authoritative protagonists, from Reason and Piers to Anima and Conscience.

But one particular clerkly poetic tradition it seems Langland also learned from is that of 'goliar-dic' Latin complaint, which lies behind some of his most memorable satire, as in the scenes of Glutton's Confession and the dinner at Conscience's house. In this same body of writing Lang-land could have satisfied his evident taste for puzzles, riddles, enigmas and pseudo-prophecies, none of which are prominent features of vernacular verse. The tradition of clever, coarse railing, not without a dash of *turpiloquium*, is loosely associated with the twelfth-century Archdeacon of Oxford, Walter Map. The latter's works appear in such manuscripts of monastic origin as Bodley 851 (bound up with the Z-Text), and have been aptly labelled 'interclerical', because they are 'written by clerics for clerics, targeting different clerical communities'.[129] Langland's 'translation' of this variety of learned vituperation involves a measure of softening to accommodate it to the ears of laypeople among his audience. But his lines on Glutton's excesses:

> A pissede a potel in a *Paternoster*-whyle
> And blew his rownd ruet at his rygebones ende,
> That alle þat herde þe horne helde here nose after
> And wesched hit hadde be wexed with a weps of breres (VI 398–401)

are perfectly in the spirit of goliardic writing. For the cream of the jest here is that the same image of the 'horn' recurs some 200 lines later, after Repentance's lofty prayer 'God þat of Thi good-nesse' at C VII 122ff:

> Thenne hente Hope an horn of *Deus, tu conuersus viuificabis nos*,
> And blewe hit with *Beati quorum remisse sunt iniquitates* (VII 151–2)

— lines that come from the Introit of the Mass. This contraposition of the sublime with what is customarily (if inaccurately) called the grotesque, the spotless eucharistic table and the tavern-floor slippery with urine and vomit, is characteristic and original. But it is still short of the perfect fusion of the *Philomena* and *Golias* modes that will form the true 'Langlandian grotesque' and that represents his supreme achievement as a clerkly maker. This unique kind of poetry is best illustrated (like much else that is best in the poem) in the great scene of the Harrowing of Hell. For here the chaotic quarrelling of the Devils (mirroring and magnifying that of the Daughters) is astonishingly transformed in the revised lines of C XX 275–94, where battle-poetry that would be at home in the *Morte Arthure* is embedded in a context that undermines even as it elevates:

> 'Ac arise vp, Ragamoffyn, and areche me alle þe barres,
> That Belial thy beelsyre beet with thy dame,
> And Y shal lette this loerd and his liht stoppe.
> Ar we thorw brihtnesse be blente, go barre we þe ʒates!' (XX 281–84).

§ 45. This last reference to another great alliterative poem of the period, of uncertain date but almost certainly later than Langland, brings us back full circle to the 'mystery' with which the discussion in this section began. Now, however, this is the mystery not of who Langland the Man was, but of where Langland the Maker 'came from'. What is known about this was first made explicit in a seminal study by Derek Pearsall: that the South-West Midlands were the original place where the alliterative tradition mysteriously *rekeuerede and lyuede*, yielding in time a rich harvest of longer poems, at least half a dozen of them masterpieces.[130] But a century of research has not dispersed the mist that hangs over the 'sources' and 'origins' of the Ricardian age's most controversial poet. How much is tradition and how much individual talent remains disputed, and there is still much to be done and discovered. Perhaps the most significant point is that Langland managed, apparently without help from any known predecessor, to produce what Wordsworth called in the penultimate sentence of his 'Preface' to the *Lyrical Ballads*

> a species of poetry...which is genuine poetry...in its nature well adapted to interest mankind permanently, and likewise important in the multiplicity and quality of its moral relations.[131]

There is evidence enough that *Piers Plowman* 'interested' readers in its time, for reasons about which it is difficult now to be completely clear. But if it continues 'to interest mankind permanently', it is perhaps most likely to be for the reason Wordsworth mentions: 'the multiplicity and quality of its moral relations'.

THE POEM IN TIME: NOTES

1 For a valuable overview of the documents, see Hanna, *William Langland* (*WL*), now updated in Hanna 'Emendations', whence they are cited.

2 As argued by Kerby-Fulton in Justice & Kerby-Fulton, *Written Work* pp. 69–70. Kane 'Labour and Authorship', p. 422, rightly maintains that the *PP* texts do not support her arguments.

3 See *The Legend of Good Women*, G Prol 255–66l; *Confessio Amantis*, side-note to Bk I, l. 60.

4 The passage is examined by Middleton in a volume of essays that find in its 'apparent self-portraiture' what their editor calls 'an opening...into the character of vernacular authorship in Ricardian England' (*Written Work*, p. 2). The fullest account of the 'myth' of Langland is in Benson, *Public 'PP,'* pp. 3–41.

5 Scribal objection to a proper name is registered in the C-b variant *sone*, the product of contamination. For acute discussion of the referent of 'WILL' see Simpson 'Authorial Naming' in Hewett-Smith, *WL's 'PP,'* pp. 145–65.

6 MED s.v. *wille* 6 (a), citing the *MP Psalter* of 1350: 'Our Lord is...of *longe wille* and michel merciable'.

7 The Bale inscriptions are given in full in Hanna, *WL* pp. 158–9; on Bale (1495–1563) see Simpson, *Reform and Cultural Revolution*, pp. 17–31.

8 The note, with the annals it accompanies, has been placed by Lister Matheson and M. T. Tavormina, in Abergavenny *c.* 1415 (unpublished paper cited in Hanna, 'Emendations', p. 186). The Rokayle records collected in Moore 'Studies' (1914), pp. 44–5 are reprinted in Hanna, *WL,* p. 158, and the discovery of new information on Stacy's father Peter (**L**'s putative grandfather) and his associates is mentioned by Matheson in his review of this work (p. 194). That the author of *PP* was called William de la Rokele was first proposed by Cargill, 'Langland Myth' (1935). Hanna, 'Emendations', p. 186, notes Matheson's discovery (reported in an unpublished paper) of a William Rokayle ordained to the first tonsure [i.e. to a stage preparatory to the first canonical grade] by Bishop Wolstan de Bransford of Worcester, possibly at Bredon near Hanley Castle in 1339 (Wolstan's Calendar # 1021, 199b). Further documentary evidence that Stacy had a son William, and that he had received minor orders, would create a strong possibility that Matheson's Rokayle was the poet.

9 Bowers, 'Editing the Text, Writing the Author's Life', p. 80.

10 Kane, *Evidence for Authorship*, pp. 35–7.

11 See the useful bibliographical summary in Pearsall, *Annotated Bibliography,* pp. 45–64.

12 A specific social setting for *PF* has long been the subject of speculation, and Bowers ('Royal Setting') intriguingly locates *Pearl* in the context of Ricardian cultural-political conflicts of the mid-1390s. But the landscapes of both works are countries of the dreaming mind, Alanian or Johannine, and their air is that of neither the Malvern Hills nor Cornhill.

13 See Kane, *Autobiographical Fallacy*; Burrow, *Fictions*, pp. 83–9.

14 Lawton in Alford, *Companion* (AlfC), p. 245. See further in the *Commentary* the notes on C VI.46, X.289, XIII.148, XIV.295, XV.40, 205, XVI.174, XX.6, 395, 455, 463, 478, XXI.70, XXII.303; B X.268, 334, 360, XIX.82; A III.251, XII.73; Z III.158, 159, 160. For the most recent discussion see Warner, 'L. and the Problem of *WPal*'.

15 See Samuels in AlfC, p. 201, Samuels, 'L.'s Dialect', p. 234, and Appendix I on Language and Metre. That the Malvern Hills have symbolic rather than personal significance is plausibly maintained by Benson, *Public 'PP'*, pp. 203–6; but the choice of locale is unlikely to have been arbitrary.

16 Du Boulay, *England of PP*, p. 61; medieval Cornhill is vividly described in Benson, *Public 'PP'*, pp. 206–33. The poem has some thirty mentions of London and particular places within or near it; see further the *Commentary* on Pr

83, 89, 91; II.148, 169, 174; 5.1, 4, 44, VI.83, 96, 365, 367; XI.65; XV.71; XVI.286; B V.317; X.46; XIII.264; Z VII.274. On the 'London' aspect generally see Barron, 'London Poet', Simpson, '"After Craftes Counseil"', and Pearsall, 'L.'s London', and Hanna, *London Literature*..

17 The term used by Bloomfield (*Fourteenth Century Apocalypse,* pp. 68–97) for patristic and neo-patristic Biblically-based writings on moral and psychological topics, a field profitably harvested in Bourquin's pioneering *PP:Etudes*. The stress in this 'philosophy' (perhaps better called 'theology') on the importance of self-knowledge, and hence on 'moral psychology', is brought out in Wittig's important study of the 'Inward Journey' of the Dreamer. On the thought of the Cistercians and Victorines see Stiegman in Evans, ed. *Medieval Theologians*, pp. 129–55.

18 Bowers, *Crisis of WILL,* pp. 18–22; but against this cf. the *Commentary* note on V.37. See further the *Commentary* on X.21–9 and also on XIV.202–17, XV.263–5 and B X.343–6. For the C14th university arts course, see Courtenay, *Schools and Scholars*, pp. 30–6, and on the theology course ibid. pp. 41–3. A significant allusion to contemporary preoccupation with logic *in scole* (on which see ibid. pp. 221–40) occurs in the criticism of mendicants' applications of dialectic to theology; see *Commentary* on XVI.228–30.

19 For Middleton's distinction see her 'Audience and Public' in Lawton, ed. *Alliterative Poetry*; the present distinction between internal and external audience follows that of Dieter Mehl, 'Audience of Chaucer's *Troilus*'. For further consideration of the complexities involved, and the position of the author as reader of his own work, see Schmidt, 'Visions & Revisions', pp. 10–13.

20 By comparison with the specificity of a commissioned poem such as *William of Palerne*, 5521–40, the **A** Version's 'public' exists as a conventional construct at some remove from its real 'audience': cf. 'preche it in þin harpe / Þer þou art mery at mete, ȝif men bidde þe ȝedde' at A I. 137–8.

21 '*PP* and the Peasants' Revolt', pp. 87–8.

22 For a balanced estimate of this work as a deceptive link between **L** and the Wyciffites, from whom he stands distinct, cf. Von Nolcken, 'Wycliffites', esp. p. 85, and for a judicious and sensitive consideration of the whole question Pearsall, 'L. and Lollardy'. Cole argues that **L**. does not use *lollere* to mean 'Wycliffite' (with its necessary implication of doctrinal heresy) but to refer to 'a specifically lay oriented version of virtuous poverty and Christian discipleship' ('WL's Lollardy', p. 28).

23 See for instance Z V. 142–3; A X. 86*a*, 94*a*, XI. 154*a*.

24 See Parkes, 'The Literacy of the Laity' in Parkes, *Scribes*, pp. 275–97. On the poem's projected lay audience see Somerset, *Clerical Discourse and Lay Audience*, ch. 2.

25 For the wills see Burrow 1957, repr. 1984 with postscript. On Walter de Brugge, see Cargill, 'Langland Myth' pp. 36–9, Davies, 'Life and Travels', pp. 49–50, 56n20; for another clerical Yorkshire owner *c.*1410 J. Hughes, *Pastors and Visionaries*, p. 205; and on Palmere, see Wood, 'C14th Owner', pp. 85, 88n21. Their copies, like most of those mentioned in bequests, are not extant; but one ms Douce 104 (no. 29) is probably from Ireland (Pearsall, *Facsimile* pp. xii–xiii), where Brugge had worked.

26 Hudson, 'Revolt', p. 91.

27 The whole of the passus is ascribed to him by Middleton in her very full 1988 discussion, but he is taken by the present editor as author only of the A XII Appendix. Materials on the recorded John Buts are assembled in Hanna, *WL,* pp. 160–3, who favours ('Emendations', p. 187) another But than the traditional one on the strength of the arguments in Scase, 'John But's *PP* ', which seem to the present writer unconvincing. 'But' is argued to be a coterie code-name (like 'Longlond') by Kerby-Fulton and Justice (1997:73).

28 Usk, who was executed in March 1388, wrote the *Testament c.*1385–7.

29 The questioning of the traditional early dating of *WW* in the mid-1350s by Salter, 'Timeliness' and Trigg, ed. *WW,* does not seem persuasive to the present writer. The most recent editor of *RRe* and *MS* (following Kane, 'Some C14th "political" poems', p. 90) takes them as earlier and later compositions (*c.*1400 and 1409 respectively) by one author, and reaffirms the traditional date of *PPCr* in the late 1390s (Barr, *PP Tradition*, p.16; for the full supporting arguments see Barr, 'Relationship'). A pioneering study of the 'Piers Plowman' tradition is Lawton, 'Lollardy' (1981), which takes *MS* as the work of 'a Lollard sympathiser' (788); and a very detailed account of the poems mentioned and of a later alliterative piece *The Crowned King* (1415) is Barr, *Signes and Sothe*.

30 Ed. Skeat, *Chaucerian and Other Pieces*, no. II, who observes that against the *Tale*-author's claim 'there cannot be adduced any argument whatever' (ed. *Crede*, pp. xiv–xv). Barr's objection on the grounds that the *Tale* is in rhymed stanzas rather than alliterative long lines (*Tradition*, p.10) lacks cogency. The two Lollard poems have many phrases in common and 'alliteration is employed in the Tale very freely' (Skeat, *Chaucerian*, pp. xxxiii–iv); so the relationship of the two pieces is not unlike that of the long-line *Sir Gawain* and the stanzaic, rhymed and alliterative *Pearl*, poems accepted without difficulty today as by the same author.

31 This personage, together with the conception of the structural plan of the *General Prologue*, represent Chaucer's recognisable debt to Langland (*Sk* IV.ii p. 863; Cooper, 'L's & Chaucer's Prologues'). But it is also tempting to see in the dramatised encounter of the *Troilus*-poet with two questioners in *LGW Pr* (G 234–545) echoes of the *Piers Plowman*-poet's examination by Reason and Conscience in the 'Prelude' to C Passus V. Welsh writers of the 14th and 15th c. have been plausibly claimed to have read *PP* (Breeze 1990, 1993). Some influence on Hoccleve has been detected by Kerby-Fulton (in Wallace, ed., *Cambridge History of Medieval Literature* [*CHMEL*], p. 537), and later there are John Audelay in 'Solomon and Marcol' = Whiting no. 2 (*c.*1426), discussed in Simpson, *Reform,* pp. 378–80, and Skelton, especially the figure of Drede in *The Bowge of Court* (*c.*1498). For the *Erkenwald*-poet's debt to Langland see Schmidt, 'Courtesy', pp. 153–6 (noticed by Morse, *St Erkenwald*, pp. 27–8) and for the *Purity*-poet's ibid. and Schmidt, '*Kynde Craft,*' p. 123n63. Hanna's conclusion from his belief that 'some passages unique to **Z** depend for their intelligibility on the reader's knowledge of other versions' seems to the present writer untrue. But given that he finds **Z** 'often logically disruptive to the sense of a passage', his judgement that the author of the Z-Text was 'an imitator, "editing" with a *Piers* reading circle in mind' (*CHMEL* p. 519) seems hard to credit.

32 Those it appears with include *Joseph of Arimathea* (see *Intro*. I, *The Manuscripts*, no. 4), *Susannah* (no. 6), *The Wars of Alexander* (no. 8), *The Siege of Jerusalem* (nos. 12, 31), *Richard the Redeless* (no. 18) and *Pierce the Ploughman's Crede* (no. 34). On the Vernon grouping see Lawton in *CHMEL* pp. 480–1. Langland is interestingly compared with Mandeville (and with Margery Kempe) in Benson, *Public 'PP'*, pp. 113–56

33 They are R, U and M of **A** (I, *Manuscripts*, nos. 2, 3, 10); L, R and F of **B** (nos. 20, 22, 23); and X, I, U and P of **C** (nos. 24, 26, 28 and 30).

34 See for the annotations on the mss of **B**, Benson & Blanchfield, *MSS of PP*: *B Version* and on **C**, Russell, 'Early Responses' and '"As They Read It"'. For what can be learned of **L**'s early readers see Middleton, 'Making a Good End', Scase, *New Anticlericalism*, Hanna, *WL*, Kerby-Fulton, 'Bibliographic Ego', Davies, 'Life, Travels and Library', and Kerby-Fulton and Justice, 'Langlandian Reading-Circles'.

35 Whereas, by comparison, *William of Palerne* is stated by its poet to have been written at the behest of Humphrey Earl of Hereford (*WPal* 164–8); cf. however Justice, 'Langlandian Reading Circles.'

36 See especially the *Commentary* on Pr 138, 140; I.75, 94–100; II.243–end; III.200–01; IV.174–5; V.181–3, 186–8, 195–6; XIII.25; XIV.35–7; XV.13–14; XVI. 22; XIX. 231–48*a*; XX.350–8; XXI.251–5.

37 See the *Commentary* on XVI.320, 338; and cf. Gradon, 'Ideology' and Hudson, 'Legacy' in Alf*C*, p. 261.

38 See Hudson in Alf*C*, pp. 66–8, Hanna *WL*, pp. 164–5. For Knighton's phrase, see his *Chronicle*, ed. Martin, p. 276.

39 The texts are given from Hanna, *WL*, pp. 165–6 (in the Carter text in the most recent edition by G. H. Martin, the phrase *for lesynge of* is mistranslated). Other accounts of the poem's real or supposed relations with the Rising are Bowers, 'PP and the Police', Green, 'John Ball's Letters' (who compares them with *PPCr* and prints them in an appendix), and Rydzeski, *Radical Nostalgia*. The letters and other documents connecting *PP* with the 1381 Rising are carefully examined by Hudson, '*PP* and Peasants' Revolt', pp. 85–106; but her conclusions that **B** is a response to the Revolt and that **C** represents a hasty re-writing strike the present editor as implausible (see further n. 47).

40 For a judicious analysis of Ball's response to *PP* see Barr, *Signes and Sothe*, pp. 10–133, and for a detailed if at times tendentious account of the rebels' attitudes to the poem see Justice, *Writing and Rebellion*, pp. 102–39, 231–54.

41 See Rickert, 'John But'; among the materials concerning the known John Buts in Hanna, *WL* pp. 28–31 see esp. 5 (g). Hanna criticises Rickert's identification, though the evidence he cites for But's contact with the Despenser family (9. n. 18) tells for, not against it. He is right, however, that Rickert's interpretation of *duk* and *dedes* in A XII 87 as respectively 'king' and 'documents licensing an arrest' is unconvincing; but if Langland wrote XII 98 (as argued in *Intro*. III, *A Version*, §§ 68–70), it is also irrelevant. From within the poem itself, the circumstantial and favourable comparison of the *pore pacyent* to a messenger (C XIII 32–91) would have appealed to the John But of the traditional identification. Kerby-Fulton and Justice ('Langlandian Reading Circles', pp. 71–3) deduce from A XII that 'But' (the name being possibly assumed) was a member of a circle of scriveners and civil servants, probably with legal connections, who took an active interest in the poem. Bowers more specifically speculates ('Editing the Text', pp. 87–9) that But may be the man recorded as controller of customs at Bristol in 1399 (and a candidate for authorship of *RRe* and *MS*). But this presupposes acceptance of Jill Mann's re-ordering of the versions ('Power of the Alphabet') to make **A** the last, which is rejected below.

42 Bowers, 'Dating *PP*'. See also Lewis 1995, who presents non-Langlandian sources for Usk's tree-image.

43 Echoes are detected by Baldwin, *Theme of Government*, pp. 59, 101n9; Coleman, *PP and Moderni*, pp. 41, 66; Godden, *Making of PP*, pp. 171–2; and at adequate length by Middleton, 'Acts of Vagrancy'. Relevant extracts from the text of the Statute, with comment, are in Hanna, *WL*, pp. 163–5.

44 See the *Textual Notes* on 11.126 and *MS* 348; the echo is noted in Barr, *Signes,* p. 14n65. Coleman's view that C belongs to the 1390s (*Moderni,* pp. 41–20) has little to recommend it.

45 For **L**'s judgement of the Plague's effect on marriage, religious belief, sexual behaviour and the upbringing of children, see the *Commentary* on respectively X.273–5; XI.59–64, XV.219–25; XXII.98–120; B V.35–6.

46 Courtenay, *Schools,* p. 99. A comprehensive sketch of **L**'s likely course of education deduced from the text (and subject to the necessary reservations) is provided in Orme, 'L. and Education'.

47 See Donaldson, *C-Text and its Poet,* pp. 199–226.

48 Kerby-Fulton, 'Bibliographic Ego', pp. 116–7. Clanvowe's religious treatise *The Two Ways* is an isolated work; but readers might have found this knight's tone reminiscent of Langland's Knight Conscience in B XIII.180–211.

49 Fowler, *Literary Relations of the A and B Texts,* pp. 185–205.

50 Donaldson, *C-Text,* p. 226.

51 *Evidence for Authorship,* p. 70.

52 Doyle, 'Surviving MSS', pp. 42–3. A similarly early date has been proposed for no. 52 (the hand-X portion of **Z**), which Rigg-Brewer would place between 1376 and 1388, but Hanna (following Doyle) around 1400. See *Intro.* II § 137 and n. 242.

53 Cf. Adams, 'Editing *PP* B'; Hanna, 'Studies', pp. 19–20.

54 Kane, in AlfC, p. 185.

55 'Peasants' Revolt', p. 100.

56 Fowler, *Relations,* pp. 174–5.

57 Taylor, 'Lost Revision of *PP* B', p. 119.

58 See note 36 above.

59 See Huppé, 'Date of B-Text'; Bennett 'Date of B-Text', and the *Commentary* on Pr 152–7, B Pr 128.

60 See Bennett, 'Date of A-Text'; Huppé, 'A-Text and Norman Wars'.

61 See J. Mann, 'Alphabet'; Meroney, 'Life and Death of Longe Wille', pp. 22–3.

62 Cf. also A X.108, 111*a,* 120*a* (paraphrased); A X. 81*a,* translated at preceding 79–80, which is also in B IX. 94*a* but *not* translated there.

63 See Z V. 91–101 for 'draft' features; Z III. 147–76, Z V. 33–40 (the complicated but coherent argument of which is examined in Schmidt 'Visions', pp. 21–2).

64 Lawler, 'Reply', deals very fully with short passages, long passages, and 'characteristic **B** ideas'. Kane's 'Open Letter', which is decisive, adopts an uncharacteristically courteous tone towards Mann's (uncharacteristically implausible) piece that contrasts with that of his review of Rigg and Brewer's serious case for the authenticity of **Z**.

65 It is unknown which version William Palmere bequeathed to Agnes Eggesfield, as the copy in question is not identified among those extant.

66 *Public* '*PP*', pp. 3–107. Benson's notion of 'myth' does not tally with that of the present writer.

67 Hudson, *Premature Reformation,* p. 22; Barr, *Socio-literary Practice in the C14th* p. 151.

68 See Lawton 'Lollardy'; Jansen 'Politics, Protest'; Barr *PP Tradition*; and especially Hudson *Reformation,* pp. 398–408.

69 Salter, '*PP* and *The Simonie*'; *Jack Upland,* ed. Heyworth.

70 Hudson, 'Peasants' Revolt', p. 102. If one agrees with Hudson that the version the rebels knew was **A** (ibid. pp. 88, 90), it becomes slightly less easy to claim that they had misinterpreted Langland's Piers as challenging traditional notions of authority in society and the Church (Astell, *Political Allegory* ch. 2 claims that they had not misunderstood **L** at all). Hudson places **B** after the Revolt partly because she interprets B XIX.446–9 'as alluding to the 1383 Despenser crusade' (ibid. p. 100 and n. 17); but reasons have been given (see note § 15 above) for finding this unconvincing.

71 See Schmidt, *Clerkly Maker,* pp. 142–3, 'Visions and Revisions', pp. 22–6.

72 Kirk, *Dream Thought of Piers Plowman,* p. 9.

73 Raabe, *Imitating God: the Allegory of Faith in* PP.

74 Acceptance of spiritual authority for the sake of unity within the Church is stressed by Conscience in a notable new line at Pr 138; serious criticism of ecclesiastical abuses at Pr 95–127, and of misuse of civic and royal power at III.200–14; deep sympathy for the plight of honest poor people in IX.71–98. See the *Commentary* on all these passages.

75 The concept of a 'strong' or creative misreading was introduced by Harold Bloom in his seminal study *Poetry and Repression*; see further Schmidt 'Visions and Revisions', pp. 10–11.

76 'Legacy of *PP*', p. 255.

77 Lawton's pithy formulation 'The issue is really that Lollards had Langlandian sympathies' ('Lollardy', p. 793) has

been sharply challenged by Simpson, *Reform and Cultural Revolution,* pp. 371–2. A judicious summary of **L**'s relations with Wyclif and his followers is given in Hudson 'Legacy', pp. 398–408 and most recently 'L. and Lollardy?', pp. 93–105.

78 Salter, *PP: an Introduction*, p. 1. The pioneering appreciations of *PP* as poetry by Coghill, Lawlor and Salter (all published in 1962) and by Spearing (1963 and 1964) were followed after a decade by book-length critiques (Kirk 1972, Carruthers 1973, Aers 1975, Schmidt 1987, Davlin 1989, Godden 1990, Simpson 1990, and Burrow 1993). But over the 1990s the growing body of specialised studies has concentrated on the text, context, background, and theological and political ideas, rather than the poem's qualities as a great work of medieval literature, the assumption on which the Athlone and the present edition are predicated. Two encouraging recent exceptions have been Rogers, *Interpretation in PP* and (in the Salter tradition) Davlin, *The Place of God in PP.*

79 An account of the poem's structure, themes and literary art has not been attempted in this *Introduction*. What is possible within the limits of editions for the student and the general reader may be found in Schmidt, *Vision of PP,* pp. xxx–liv and *PP: a new translation,* pp. xi–xl.

80 The four versions of Rembrandt's masterpiece *The Three Crosses* (1653–1660) will aptly illustrate this point; see Boon, *Rembrandt: Complete Etchings* pls. 244–5.

81 Cerquiglini, *Eloge de la variante*, p. 111.

82 The basis of this inference is the virtual absence of scribal errors in Passus XVI; see *Intro.* III, *B*, § 5.

83 Donaldson, 'MSS R and F', p. 211.

84 Against Scase's claim that a passage of *C* circulated independently, see the arguments in the *Intro.* III, *C*, §§ 21–2, and notes 33, 35.

85 See Burrow 'Action of L.'s Second Vision' and the analytical headnote to the *Commentary* on C XX.

86 Warner, '*Ur-B PP*', p. 24.

87 One recent such critic is Rogers (*Interpretation in PP*), in many ways a judicious exponent of a lucid 'post-modern' hermeneutics (see the present writer's review in *RES* 55 [2004], pp. 446–7).

88 Cf. the discussion of these lines in Schmidt, 'Visions and Revisions', pp. 23–5.

89 A study conscious of **L**'s 'Ricardian' sense of human limitedness and 'Gregorian' awareness of imperfection in perfection is Nolan, *Visionary Perspective,* pp. 205–58. Another showing a firm conviction (not always well-articulated) of **L**'s artistic control and coherence of purpose is Raabe, *Imitating God.*

90 *The Prelude* achieved two-book form in 1799 as 'a limitedly private autobiography' (Stephen Gill, *Wordsworth*, p. 231) and five-book form in 1804; was completed in thirteen books in 1805; revised in 1832; then brought to its fourteen-book form in 1839, the version printed after the poet's death in 1850 (see the Norton edition, ed. Wordsworth et al.). To Gill, 'Wordsworth's greatest poem encompasses and unifies many genres. Satire and narrative, description and meditation, the visionary and the deliberately banal — all are exploited in...the flexible blank verse he made his characteristic instrument...As an autobiography...it was written not only to present a self-image to posterity but to assist the writer to understand his own life so that the rest of it might be lived more purposefully and in accordance with truths perceived in the act of writing the poem' (ibid. 1–2). But Gill's claim that the poet could not bear the idea of finality is convincingly disputed by Leader, who maintains that Wordsworth 'held to the goal of mastery or perfection, or the attempt to come as close to it as possible' (*Revision*, p. 35). The analogy with Langland and his critics will not escape notice (for direct comparison of both poets as revisers, see Wordsworth, 'Revision as Making').

91 Following the pioneering work of Middleton, 'The Idea of Public Poetry', Benson has developed this notion as the central argument of *Public PP.*

92 The convention of soliciting a drink still mimicked in *WW* is avoided, as is the fiction of an audience 'present and *reacting*,' except at Pr 217 after **B**'s 'Rat Fable' addition, which might have provoked laughter.

93 'Quo se ipse imperfectum respicit, inde ad humilitatis culmen perfectior assurgat' (*Moralia* 5. 4.5). See the illuminating discussion in Straw, *Gregory the Great*, pp. 188–9.

94 For examples of *repetitio* see the *Commentary* on Pr 28; I.12, 20–1; II.11–12; III.94–100; VI.162–3; VII.111–15, 264–5; VIII.139; IX.44–5; X.18–20; XI.16–18, 235–8; XII.108; XIII.156–60; XIV.94; XV.18; XVI.120; XX.207; XXII.35–50. On B XI.218–26 see Schmidt, *Clerkly Maker*, pp. 55–7.

95 The phrase *al my (his / hir) lyf-tyme* (Appendix Three, C Pr 50b) is a stock expression not confined to literary use like *as the world askes*, which occurs only once but is also found in *SGGK* 530.

96 *The Making of 'Piers Plowman'*, the first study to do so.

97 See Jusserand, *PP,* p. 173; Owen *PP: A Comparison*; Bourquin, *Etudes,* pp. 780–98 and Burrow, *L.'s Fictions,* pp. 113–18. For other French sources and analogues see Gaffney 'Allegory' (Nicole de Bozon), Cornelius '*Roman de Fauvel*' and Nolan, *Visionary Perspective* (Huon de Méri, Raoul de Houdenc and Rutebeuf).

98 See the very revealing French proverb quoted at XVII.163–4; and cf. *IG* s.v. *cortesye* for the 'redeemed' uses of the term beginning as early as I.20.

99 See B XV.442–3, C XII.82–9, and Schmidt, *Clerkly Maker*, p. 108 for discussion.

100 The limiting cases of Trajan and Dismas 'prove' this contention in the sense of showing it to be *generally* true, though admitting extraordinary exceptions under the principle *misericordia eius super omnia*; see the *Commentary* on XII 76.

101 The phrase, taken from Bernard McGinn, is explained and defended in Watson, 'Censorship and Cultural Change', p. 823n4. That **L**'s 'entire enterprise looks like' the 'vernacular theologizing' prosecuted by the ecclesiastical authorities is nonetheless urged by Middleton 1997:291; but if it does, the resemblance seems to have evaded record (see § 22 and note 77 above). On Langland's 'theology' see Hort, *Contemporary Religious Thought*, pp. 28–59; Coleman, *Moderni*; Harwood, *Problem of Belief*; and for a general survey Adams in AlfC, pp. 87–114 (with the caveats noted by Schmidt in *JEGP* 89 [1990] p. 214). It may nonetheless be better to speak of 'the use of theological ideas in *PP*' than of '**L**'s theology'.

102 Lawton, 'Englishing the Bible' in *CHMEL*, pp. 470–1 (the Wycliffite claim is cited by him from Hudson, *Selections* p. 69). Rolle's 'amphibian' negotiation of vernacular and Latin adumbrates Langland, who may have known some of his writings (see Schmidt, 'Treatment of the Passion', pp. 174–6).

103 'The Middle English Mystics', in *CHMEL*, p.553.

104 A contribution was made by the present writer in *The Clerkly Maker*, pp. 81–107. The fundamental work in this area was Sullivan, *Insertions*.

105 A good guide to **L**'s 'sources' is Pearsall, *Critical Bibliography*, pp. 74–110. The classic instance of the importance of source-study is Chaucer's *Troilus* as edited, with the Italian original *en face*, by Windeatt. *Patience* (based on Jonah) is another example, as is one of the earliest works of the Alliterative Revival, *William of Palerne*.

106 See Alford, 'Role of Quotations', p. 82l; Allen, *Ethical Poetic*, p. 275.

107 See the *Commentary* on Pr 40, 108; I.82110a, 121a, and *passim*.

108 See for example A X.80–81a; B IX.130–30a; C X.230–41.

109 Davlin, *Game of Heuene*, p.5. The specific contexts of **L**'s quotations in the *Breviary*, first noted by Skeat, emphasised by Hort (but see for criticisms Adams 'Liturgy Revisited') and highlighted in the notes to *Pe*, are amply documented in AlfQ, *passim*.

110 Although 'hearing matins and mass' is regarded by **L**'s Sloth as proper for monks (VII.65–60), but for him an act of special penance, the implication of other passages is that it should be normal practice for the laity (see C IX.227–9).

111 For an accessible account of the Holy Week ceremonies as performed in this period, see Duffy, *Stripping*, pp. 22–37; and on the contextual heightening imparted to the quotations in B XVIII see Barr, 'Use of Latin Quotations', pp. 440–8. The importance of the liturgy in shaping the structure of the last passūs is shown by Saint-Jacques, 'Conscience's Final Pilgrimage'; and for a persuasive argument that the Glutton scene is a satiric parody of the liturgy of the Easter Triduum see Wilcockson 1998.

112 This point is properly emphasised by Vaughan, 'Liturgical Perspectives', building on the germinal studies of St-Jacques (1967, 1969, 1970), and serves to counter the text-based approach to **L**'s Biblical sources in Robertson and Huppé's pioneering *PP and Scriptural Tradition*. The structural significance of 'enacted scripture', though not confined to B XVIII / C XX, especially centres on the services of *þe Saterday þat sette first þe kalender* (see for example the *Commentary* on VII.119–53a, which closely relates in 'pitch and tonality' to that passus). **L** seems fully aware that every Mass is interpretable as an epitome of the Easter Triduum.

113 See Kolve, *Play Called Corpus Christi*, ch. 10. **L**'s mediation between disparate sources and contemporary modes of interpreting this theme is examined by Taylor, 'Harrowing Hell's Half-acre'.

114 Because so much medieval art was destroyed by Reformers and Puritans, examples in England are few; but one from North Cove church, Suffolk is given as pl. 8B in Benson, *Public PP*, p. 180. For the relation of **L**'s poetry to late Gothic art, see Salter, '*PP* and the Visual Arts' in her *English and International*, pp. 56–66; Davlin, *Place of God in PP and Medieval Art*.

115 Owst, '"Angel" and "Goliardeys"', p. 271; the subject is treated in detail in Owst, *Literature and Pulpit*, pp. 548–75. A balanced and accurate formulation of the 'diffuse and widely dispersed influence' of sermons is furnished by Wenzel in 'Medieval Sermons and Study of Literature' and in his chapter on medieval sermons in AlfC.

116 See Salter, *Introduction*, pp. 24–30; Spearing, 'Verbal Repetition' and *Criticism* [rev. ed. 1972], pp. 107–34.

117 See Wenzel in AlfC, pp. 168–9, and the *Commentary* on XVI.264–5.

118 Wenzel, ibid. p. 161. See the *Commentary* on V.136–9, VI.337a, VIII.46, B Pr 145.

119 As noted by Pearsall (see *Commentary* on II.32); on Ludolf see Conway, '*Vita Christi*'.

120 Cf. the *Commentary* on XI.148. For the poem's structural embodiment of Trinitarian ideas, see especially Clopper 'L.'s Trinitarian Analogies' and 'Contemplative Matrix'; and for expansion of the 'trinity' idea more widely, Fletcher, 'Social Trinity' and Galloway, 'Intellectual Pregnancy'.

121 In *PL* 196:1–1378; tr. Zinn, *Richard of St Victor*, p. 292.

122 See 17.157, B 15.269, and *Commentary* on B 11.160.

123 On 'Cato', the name of an unknown C4th Latin writer who is quoted five times (cf. *Commentary* on 4.17), see Galloway, 'Two Notes on L.'s Cato'.

124 See the *Commentary* on these passages, in which the *kynde* meaning of words is emphasised.

125 See Schmidt, *Clerkly Maker,* p. 90, referring to Mann, 'Satiric Subject', who builds on Jolivet, 'Quelques cas de "platonisme grammatical"'. For a selection of examples see the *Commentary* on Pr 5; I.20–1, 35–6; II.235; III.403, 476, 495; V.134–5, 142; VI.87; VII.36–7; VIII.133–4; X.54; XI.128; XIII.67; XIV.136; XVII.10; XVIII.25; XX.266; XXI.86. This type of clerkly wordplay extends to proper names (X.251, XII.2) and across the Latin-English linguistic boundary (VIII.77, XV.50, 57; XVII.66–6*a*).

126 See *PL* 210:579.

127 Notably Bloomfield, *C14th Apocalypse*; Davlin '*Kynde Knowynge*'; Bourquin, *Etudes*; Wittig 'Inward Journey'; and Simpson, 'From Reason to Affective Knowledge'.

128 See Schmidt 'L. and Scholastic Philosophy'. **L**'s general familiarity with scholastic ideas and arguments is nonetheless demonstrated in Coleman, *Moderni* and cogently argued in Harwood, *Problem of Belief.*

129 Kerby-Fulton in *CHMEL* p. 531. For the possible influence of Map, see the *Commentary* on 15.100.

130 See Pearsall, 'Origins' and Lawton, 'Diversity'. The argument is challenged by Hanna in *CHMEL* pp. 488–512.

131 Owen & Smyser, eds., *Prose Works of Wordsworth*, p. 159.

B. TEXTUAL NOTES

Reference is in the first place to the **C** Version; where **C** has no text, citation is from **B**. The other versions are denoted in brackets, ordinarily in the sequence **ZAB**. Lines with no corresponding material in **C** are discussed as near as possible to the point where they stand printed in parallel to the text of **C**. Notes on these, where they exceed a single entry, are indented for ease of reference. A few additions and corrections to the Text and Apparatus are included here if relevant to the discussion, but they are collected together for convenience at the end of this Volume. Abbreviations in the form '*A*-M', '*C*-**x**' etc signify a ms or family / group of the version specified in *italic*. Bold **L** = 'Langland'; *&r* 'and the rest'; Ø = zero-reading; ⊗ = 'contamination'; '⇒' = 'substitution'; ↔ = 'transposed'; < = 'deriving from'. For explanation of the ms and group sigla used see Vol. I, p. xiii, and *Introduction* II–III.

Title

The poem has no title *within* the text. All titles must therefore be presumed part of the extrinsic format (*forma tractatûs*) of any given ms. Although variously named *tractatus*, *dialogus* and *liber*, the work is most commonly called *visio*, as in *C*-ms P, a text with elaborate scribal layout. A title incorporating the Dreamer's / Author's name and the poem's chief subject must have been familiar in a form such as '*Visio Willelmi de Petro Plouhman*,' followed (as at **p** Passus XI = X in **x**) by '*Visio eiusdem Willelmi de Do-wel*,' at **p** XVIII [**x** XVII] by '*V. e. W. de Do-bet*,' and at **p** XXII [**x** XXI] by '*V. e. W. de Do-best*.' The rubrics in **B**, the only version certainly completed, are argued by Adams (1985) to be scribal rather than authorial, a view extended more tentatively to **C** in Adams 1995:51–84. They are nonetheless the most important element of the *forma tractatûs* and deserve to be recorded in an edition (as by *Sk* but not Athlone after **A**; see Appendix Two). Crowley entitled his first printing (1550) *The Vision of Piers Plowman*, and although both *Sk* and *K–D* have included 'Dowel, Dobet and Dobest' in their full titles, most explicits typically read '*Explicit (liber) de petro ploughman*.' Such a title, omitting reference to 'Do-wel', etc., accords with John But's reference to Will's 'werkes.../ Of Peres þe Plowman and mechel puple also' (A 12.102). Early wills of 1396 and 1400 speak of 'my / a book (called) Piers Plowman' (Davies 1999:49; Wood 1984). And while contemporary readers might have known the poem as 'The Book of Piers Plowman' (cf. Chaucer's 'Book of Troilus'), the only early reference outside a testamentary context (the inscription in TCD ms 212 of *c.* 1400) names it *Perys ploughman*. Outside the explicits and incipits, no other titles survive from between the presumed date of **L**'s death (*c.* 1387/8) and the earliest critical mention, by Puttenham (1589) following Crowley or Rogers (1561), who also calls the poem *Piers Plowman*.

Prologue

RUBRIC The heading *Prologue* appears only in *A*-ms R, in the form *Hic incipit liber qui uocatur pers plowman. Prologus*. This scribal contribution agrees with the (presumably authorial) numbering of passūs in **A**, **B** and **C**-family **x**, where *passus primus* prefaces the section immediately following the Prologue. Whereas the wording of the incipits and explicits varies somewhat, the number and order of passus-divisions in all versions seems secure, the most deviant copies being Corpus 201 (F of **B**), and to a less extent Bodley 851 (**Z**), on which see *Introduction* I, *Manuscripts*, nos. 23 and 52. In Pr the important mss of **A** are fully represented, but Y is defective for **C** and R for **B**.

2 (ZAB 2) *shroudes*: the corrupt variant *shrobbis*, in the **A** mss JK presumably by contamination ('⊗' hereafter) from a copy of the **C** family **p** (and also in *B*-Cr), will have resulted from mistaking *shope* 'dressed myself' (MED s.v. *shapen* v. 5) for 'betook myself' (ib. 6). *A*-Ch has an idiosyncratic near-synonym. The plural form seems assured from the **BC** readings, correct and corrupt; *C*-BOL *a shrowde* (so R–K) may have been induced by the singular nouns with indefinite article in 2b and 3a. *B*-H (sg.) may show ⊗ from an *A*-source here, as so often later (e.g. at 42, 74). Possibly **A** read *shroude*, a form that might have invited addition of an art. or a pl. ending; *A*-W's *a shrowedes* can only be a slip; **Z**'s witness here favours the plural. *shep*: 'sheep' not 'shepherd', which finds no lexical support; **p**'s variant will be by ⊗, a scribal substitution ('⇒' hereafter) after failure to grasp the point of the comparison.

    Z 5 The a-half could be by ⊗ from **C** 5; but the b-half's characteristic semantic pun ('say' / 'see') does not look scribal, resembling but not imitating **C**'s *adnominatio* on *sel-* and *sel-*. The line would fit satisfactorily in both **A** and **B** at this point, but no reason for its loss appears, unless perhaps visual distraction due to homœoarchy / homœoteleuton (*many sellys...alle* /*...May...Hylles*).

6 (Z 6, AB 5) *But*: a revision of **Z** or an error in the **A** archetype (Ax), and in *B*-H by ⊗ from an **A** ms; emendation is unnecessary, since the sense is identical. **7 (Z 8, AB 7)** *of-wandred*: the **A** reading is confirmed by **Z**, several **A** mss showing a further smoothing to the form found in *B*-HF and Cr (? by ⊗ respectively from **A** and **C**). **B**'s *for-* may be a revision, since the *of-* form is very rare, although it could have been scribally altered as in *A*-R&r and later restored in **C**. The *-yng* variants in *C*-**p** show the same scribal smoothing as in *A*-DvWE, and the archaic construction with *of* + verbal noun in **x** may thus be identified as original. But the substantive reading is still likely to be **p**'s, since the moral implications of 'wandering' are lost in *walked* (cf. Bx *walke* for *wandre* **A**, a reading confirmed by **C**, at B 5.195 below). Against this, *walken* replaces *wandriþ* A 8.79 at B 7.95, C 9.172; but here the sense is neutral and **L** may have wished to *avoid* a moral implication

BA 10–12, Z 11–12 *sweyed* (MED s.v. *sweien* v. (1)) *or* its homonym *sweien* v. (2)) goes better with *murye*, and *sweyued* (MED s.v *sweiven* v.'whirl, sweep') could have been visually induced from *sweuene* 11, as presumably was *A*-RV *sweuenede*. *me (to) meten*: tentatively emending an unmetrical line in AxBxZ (*xa / ax*). The revised equivalent C 9 points to the solution, along with such instances of preference for the impersonal construction with *meten* (MED s.v. v. (3), sense 2) as C 10.67 (B 8.68, A 9.59); C 21.481 (B 19.485). A clue to the source of the **ZAxBx** error may be the reading of VJM *mette I me* for *mette me* (*mette I* A) at A IX 59. Whether or not preserving the Ax form split into those of A and of T&r, this later variant suggests how *gan I meten* could derive from an original **gan me meten* that had lost *me* through haplography before *meten* and with subsequent ⇒ in AxBx of a necessary pronoun (*I*). The likelihood of repeated error in the **Z** copy and successive archetypes is to be countenanced here, since *gan* with impersonal *meten* is not found elsewhere (Kane 1996:319) and could therefore have presented difficulty to scribes.

14 (Z 14, AB 13) In the light of **Z**'s Ø (so also *A*-HWM), **K–D**'s emendation *Ac* for **B** is rejected as unsure. *And* **B**-WCMH is a scribal intrusion; but *Ac* **A** may be a revision later dropped or else an Ax attempt to ease the transition. **Z 16b–17** are unique, 16b anticipating the *dymme cloude* of Z III 131 below. **20 (Z 19, AB 18)** *ryche*: although *pore* **x** makes sense if *mene* means 'of middle condition' (MED s.v. *mene* adj. (2)), it seems likelier that *alle* should imply reference to the whole range. Terms denoting the poles would be apter, *mene* thus signifying 'of poor or low status' (MED s.v. adj. (1), sense 2). The formula recurs at 219, clearly with the latter sense. **24 (Z 23, AB 22)** Support from **Z** points to *wonne þat* as the probable reading of Ax. *A*-M may here represent the common original of the family **m** or, like KUW, show correction of an **r**-type reading from a **B** or **C** source. Presumably **r**'s ambiguous **wonn* was mistaken for the

relative pronoun *w(h)om*, further smoothed or levelled in later descendants. *B*-F *þese* could here (in the absence of R) represent its family original α or else be derived from **A** or **C**. Its omission from **Z**, as from *B*-β, may be due to visual attraction from *wonnen* to *wastours*. **26 (Z 25, AB 24)** *of clothyng*: the expression caused little difficulty to the **AB** scribes and both **C** families support *of*. **Z**, which appears to distinguish face and dress, if not original, could show influence from a **C** source like PE. **27 (Z 26, AB 25)** *penaunces* **CZ** against *penaunce* **AB**: whether revision or scribal ⇒ is involved seems undecidable on intrinsic grounds. **28 (Z 27, AB 26)** *ful*: adopted as the **C** reading in the light of **ZAB** and the likelihood that the common original of *C*-yb (= **i**) substituted a synonym to avoid repeating *ful* in 22 and (with *harde* again) at 23 above. *harde*: repeating 23, though insufficient grounds appear for judging it scribal with *R–K* (29 is also revised). **31 (Z 30, AB 29)** Whether showing asyndeton after preceding *holde(th)*, or a suppressed relative pronoun, **ZAC** suggests that Bx *And* here is scribal. **33 (Z 32, AB 31)** A preterite for both verbs is preferable on stylistic grounds, conforming with the preceding past tenses and balancing the two present tenses in 34. The variation in the second verb here (as in other instances to be noted and discussed as they occur) could reflect an ambiguously-spelled original 3rd person sg. / pl. ending in *-yt*, a form capable of resolution as *-id* (*-ed*) or *-eth* (*-en*). **36 (Z 35, AB 34)** The **C** revision of **AB** could be a reversion to a first thought, or else **Z** here show ⊗ from **C**. But the following **Z** line 36 looks authentic (see *Commentary*). In **AB**, notwithstanding previous editorial consensus, *synnelees* is retained, giving a line of Type IIa, or of Type IIb in **B** (*B*-GH *trowe* for *leeue* shows possible ⊗ from A). Scribes variously aimed at conforming the alliterative pattern to Type Ic (*giltles*, *gyleles*); at doing this and also making a negative criticism (*gylefully* K, *gylously* W); or at the latter simply (*synfulliche* H²). But though not found elsewhere in *PP*, *giltles* was not uncommon (see MED s.v. 2 (b)) and would not readily have invited ⇒. **40 (AB 39)** *is...hyne*: absence of *B*-F here makes Bx indeterminable, the LMH readings suggesting the b-half's absence from β and its insertion from an **A** source in γ or severally in the ancestors of WHm, G, YOC² and B. Alternatively but less probably, γ here preserves β and LMH have a common ancestor that lacked the half-line. Its retention (revised) in **C** indicates its presence in **B**. **42 (Z 38, AB 41)** *bretful*: securely attested in **ZAC**, *breed ful* Bx being identifiable as smoothing of an ambiguous original *bred ful* (a spelling attested by H). The form of Bx's a-half is irrecoverable in the absence of α, but *Wiþ* (whether < Bx or not) is part of the smoothing process consequential upon misidentifying the sense of *bred*. The H reading, half-way between **ZAC** and ?Bx, could be the result of ⊗ from **A** in the b-half. *was* **ZC**: presumably original (with immediate antecedent thought of as subject); but *were* **A** may be kept and provide the standard form for **B**. **43 (Z 39, AB 42)** *Fayteden*: certain in **ZBC**, but in the **A** tradition conflict of variants for the first main verb cuts across both families (M against E). Despite *Ka* (p. 160), *K–F* are right here, since *faiten* was the rarer verb, little instanced outside *PP* (see MED s.vv.) and *flite* could have been a ⇒ to avoid repeating a word perhaps mistakenly understood as *fiȝten* (for the ambiguous variant spelling *feytyn* see MED s.v. *fighten* v. 1a (a)). On grounds of contextual sense, the beggars might have been less likely to *flite* after eating to repletion than to exercise deception as a general habit. **ZC** agreement in *and* may not be significant, as the conjunction could have been added independently in ms Z, as in *B*-HF, or be original and later omitted (cf. 67). *R–K*'s deletion of both is unwarranted. **45 (Z 41, AB 44)** *vp B*-HF: either coincidental or showing ⊗ from **A**. **46 (Z 42, AB 45)** *also* **x**: weak, as *synful* **p** is over-emphatic, though closer to **B**. *R–K* omit, but it is unlikely that **C** ever read as **AZ**. *suche*: M's *hem* perhaps echoes **B**. **49 (Z 51, A 48, B 49)** An intrusive pronoun in β may be recognised as scribal in the light of **ZAC**. The correct reading could have been in α, since F's *&* may be ⇒ for Ø rather than *They*. The reading *on* **xZ** is rejected by *R–K* for *in* **p** agreeing with A*B*-β; at 15.186 **p** has Ø (so *R–K*) while **x** divides between *in* / *on* (with the sense unaffected either way). **50b** reads in M as **ZAB** (so *R–K*), but this is likelier to be recollection of a familiar line than correction from a superior lost **C** copy (cf. 46).

B 50–2 are not in **AC** and were either omitted in revising **B** or are spurious (their metre correct if awkward, the clustering of Type Ib lines untypical). They begin five lines unattested by the sole α witness F and, while 53–4 are authenticated on **ZAC** evidence, 50–2 could potentially be a scribal interpolation in β. However, the metaphor appears at B 14.309 and the implied association of mendacious pilgrims with 'bad' minstrels through the image of 'tuning' sounds authorial.

55 (A 54, B 57) Emendation of Ax *ermytes* by adding the (etymologically correct) central *-e* presumes scansion of *And...hem* as the three- or four-syllable prelude-dip of a Type IIIb line in **AB** rather than of *hem* by itself as the first stave-word. The smoother form of revised **C** allows *hemself* to be the first lift, easing the line's scansion to Type Ib. *R–K*'s emendation to **AB** *shopen hem* is groundless. **56–77, 81–4** Manuscript **I** is present here as a corrupt text made up of **A** lines interspersed with text from **C**; only the **C** lines 91–157 are fully collated. *R–K* (pp. 186–194) print the I *Prologue* in its entirety, with discussion. **57 (Z 44, A 56, B 59)** Agreement on **AC** as the probable original reading in all versions seems fairly secure. The participial form in WHm is by correction in their immediate ancestor and Bx will have read as L&*r*, having perhaps misconstrued a pr. pple

spelled *prechend* (a form attested in *A*-J) as the past pl. *precheden*. The source of the error could have been the unexpectedness of a participle in a sequence of preterites and the awkwardness of the transition. The easy reading *hemselue* in the b-half appears scribal in the light of **ZAC**; H's nearly correct variant may be derived from an **A** copy. **61 (A 60, B 63)** **A** and revised **BC** are very close in meaning: *meten* 'touch' (MED s.v., v. (4), 5(a)), *marchen* 'be in tandem'(MED s.v. v. (1), sense (c), with deliberate play on sense (a) 'adjoin'). Attempts to substitute a similar idea are *maken* 'mate' *C*-**x** (*macchen C*-O) *B*-Hm*A*-M. *B*-H shows ⊗ from an **A** source, *C*-M an attempt to replace one metaphor by another, although the homophony across the caesura already allows it.

Z 53–8 are unique and unexceptionable on grounds of metre, style and sense. 53–5 anticipate Z 8.13–15. The specific criticism of provisors in 57–8 is not repeated here in other versions, though it is made later in 4.125–30 //. 57b anticipates B Pr 146a, 2.62. **Z 63b–4** do not appear scribal so much as an early form of A 82–3; the *adnominatio* of *-to, to* in 64 is characteristic of **L** (cf. B 16.148). **63 (A 62, B 65)** The **A** line is virtually repeated at A 12.58. **64 (A 63, B 66)** *And* C**F** / Ø A*β*: Bx is uncertain in the absence of R, but with little difference of sense involved. *hy*: the recessive Southern (S) pl. pronominal form (confirmed by **B**) and the Ax reading behind the **A** variants except for KW, which show influence from **C**, and *biginne* v, which perhaps misread *hi* as *bi* and smoothed by deletion of preceding *and*. **65 (A 64, B 67)** *vp*: in the light of **AC** the presumed **B** reading; but Bx is irrecoverable, and *vp* G is likelier to be due to ⊗ from **A** than to be a reflex of **g** (cf. also *falsnes* at 71, where β's *falsehede* is acceptable). **67 (Z 75, A 66, B 69)** *And* **ZC** / Ø **AB**: the conflict here that ostensibly argues against linear revision (or for **C** influence on **Z**) may be non-significant, as at 43 above, also involving *and* (cf. the reverse situation at 68 //, where **C** omits the conjunction, and see *Intro*. IV §25). **69** Here and in 72 the Apparatus records an I reading of interest as indicating its **A** character in the section 56–90. **70 (Z 78, A 69, B 72)** *wordes* **ZBC**: *A*-M's variant may be ⊗ from **B** or an accurate reflex of **m** (*A*-E here showing an **r** character); but no reason appears for seeing **A** as here having revised **Z**. **72 (Z 80, A 71, B 74)** The rare *bounchede*, not instanced in the C14th outside *PP* (MED s.v. *bonchen*), is presumed original as the harder and apter reading; *blessed* **p** was perhaps induced from 76 and occurs as a variant in all versions except **Z**. *B*-HF may show ⊗ from an **A** source of RUE-type (which have *blessed*) or a **C** source like **p**. The support of **Z**, in what seems an earlier form of the line, is conclusive for this reading. *bulles*: illustrating the *repetitio* common in **C**; so, despite the agreement of *C*-b and M, representing respectively **x** and **p** types, *breuet* (adopted *R–K*) should be rejected as ⊗ from **B**. **74 (Z 82, A 73, B 76)** *ȝe; ȝoure*:

discrimination of the 2nd person as the correct form in **A** is guided by **C** supported by **Z**, and *K–D*'s emendation of **B** is accepted on that basis. Bx might have read Ø for *ʒe* and *hire* for *ʒoure*, to judge by the variants. *geven A*-E: adopted as the **A** reading in the light of **Z**B**C**-**x** and the metrical requirement of a palatal stop (Ax presumably read *ʒeuen*). *helpe*: H's variant, whether derived from an independent **B** tradition or (as here judged) the result of ⊗ from **A**, appears right from **ZAC** agreement, *kepe* an arguably over-emphatic ⇒ by the Bx scribe. **76 (Z 84, A 75, B 78)** *yblessed*: supplied in **Z** for both sense and metre. **80 (A 79, B 82)** is clearly of the rare Type IIa in A**C**; *K–D*'s emendation may be safely accepted for **B**. Loss of one *p* stave, *peple* in Bx (so *A*-RH) and *poore* in *C*-X, was doubtless occasioned by eyeskip from *por-* to *par-*. The **B** variants *pouere, poraille, pore men* could all be reflexes of ?Bx *por :::*le*. **84 (A 83, B 86)** *so* / Ø: revision here in **C** is uncertain, *swete* giving better rhythm (so *R–K*) but *so* being explicable as a consequence of revising *for* to *while*.

A 84–102 In ms *A*-K (see *Ka* pp. 36–7) appears here an A-Text conflated with **C** readings, of **x** type in the sequence C 85–232 except at 164 (individual readings are recorded at 183, 216, 224). For notes on these lines see at 159 below (Vol. I, p. 19).

B 94 The extra F line could have been in α (< Bx), but its absence from **C** points to ⊗ here from **A**, as is common in F (see on 8.49, 80, 101, 102, *Intro*. III *B* § 46). **91–157** appear on fols. 5r–6r of ms I immediately preceded by A 84–95 and followed by A 96–109 (end of A Pr; see *R–K* 186–92). The present editor agrees with *Pe* (1981) that it is a skilful scribe's work. The Cx text cannot be described as 'not in any recognisable alliterative form' (Donaldson 1949:246f) except at a few points, nor its sense as 'dubious' (Russell 1969:29, who in *R–K* 87 n.36 abandons his judgement of the I passage as much closer to the original). But since it recalls uneven work such as A XII and Z 4.129–59, 5.1–18, it could possibly derive from a late insertion that **L**'s death prevented from receiving its final form (see *Intro*. III *Z* § 6). Against this, some errors needing emendation for the metre are of a usual scribal type: variation to prose order at 108, 113, 120; ⇒ of similar but commoner idiom at 123; and of more familiar words at 114, 116–8. Only their relative density and the high number of Type III lines (some ten) suggest a provisional or draft character for Cx's source. *R–K* 87–8 see the passage as the content of a single-leaf draft misplaced by the 'editor' who prepared copy for Cx, leaving it unemended as 'the roughest of **L**'s drafts.' Why an 'editor' should have placed it here is unclear; but the *poet* may have done so because he wished to link the prelates attacked in 101ff with those of 85ff through the familiar Biblical association of greed with idolatry (e.g. Col 3: 5, Eph 5:5). The one-line addition at 138, support-

ing the authority of reforming cardinals and Pope so as to counterbalance the critique of avaricious prelates, favours the positioning of 95–124 as authorial. So does direct address adopted at 125 to make these lines fit in with the mode of 96ff. The I form of 105–24, the most textually distinctive portion, is given in Vol I, p. 743 (Appendix) but not drawn on in emending the text here. Scase (1987) holds that the Ophni-Phineas passage in I and the conflated ms Ht may have circulated in a form distinct from that in the Cx tradition, discerning in I and Ht a shared shape and content, with many substantive agreements in error. The argument, though of interest, is unpersuasive (see further Hanna 1989; *R–K* 193–4; *Intro*. III *C* §§ 21–2; Galloway 1999:72–80). **95** *cused*: the aphetic form, the likely Cx reading underlying both the **p** and the (contextually unacceptable) **x** variant. **107** *For Offinies synne*: the sense requiring *synne, sone* is explicable as a visual error for *sunne (with *u* = |y|) in the immediate source (so b). The trisyllabic form of *Offinies* is preferred as providing the second (or first) stave in a line of Type Ia (or IIIa) and a characteristic chime with *Fines,* also to be scanned as trisyllabic *finees* as P suggests (cf. 123 below, where the stress is on *Óffni* and // B 10.281, where it is possibly though not certainly on *Offýn*). **108** scans as Type IIIa on *d* as emended or as Type I, reading *batáyle* with cognative second stave. The b-half in Cx shows presumed scribal inversion to prose order. *Dei* **p** is preferred after B 10.282 (so Vulgate). **111** scans as Type IIa on vowels (*as, it, hym*), with a vocalic 'supplemental' stave (*Intro*. IV § 44) on *Ísrael* (for consonantal Type IIa see 117). **112** scans like reconstructed 108. **113** The Cx line shows variation to prose order in the b-half. F's attempt to correct the metre is clearly scribal padding. **114** scans either on vowels, with rhetorical stresses on the pronominals, or on lexical keywords, with two liaisonal staves *his_chayere, his_nekke* (although *ch-* could have been sounded |ʃ| to alliterate as a metrical allophone of *s* (so *Sk* III, n.); for further *s* / *sh* alliteration cf. 119b (and on this type see *Intro*. IV § 46). F's ⇒ ignores **L**'s idiosyncratic consonantal approximations. **115** scans as extended Type IIIa on vowels with counterpoint (*abb / ax*) or (with muted key-stave *þat*) as Type Ia on |v| / |f|. **116; 118** lack in Cx a satisfactory key-stave. As here emended, they scan on |v|, |f| and have a closely parallel rhetorical structure (*for þei were prestis.../ Forthy Y sey, ʒe prestes*). Cx's replacement of *folk* by *men* may have been induced by the phrase's greater commonness (though **L**'s use of the conjectured expression at B 15.384 occasioned no difficulty for the scribe of Bx). 116 now scans as Ie, if both *for* and *þei* are full staves, as the sense seems to require, 118 as extended Type IIIa. Reading *segges* for 118 would yield a Type IIIa line with an arguably superior stress-pattern; but the collocation is unparalleled. A third possibility is to make *Hóly* the key-stave in both lines, with *hy* for *þei* in

116; but the stress-pattern produced is uncharacteristic. **119** scans on *s / sh,* the key-stave being *-schípe.* Wrenching of stress from root syllable to suffix is not elsewhere instanced in this word (unless perhaps at B 1.48), but parallels are *afterwárdes* B 10.224 and *welcómed* 15.31, 37, 16.170, 22.60. **120** could scan as Type IIIc on *here* and *hem,* but such unusual emphasis would seem forced here, and the emendation adopted presumes scribal inversion to prose order. **121; 122** scan as Type IIIa, the first on *sh / s,* the second on vowels (*hardere; on*), with rhetorical parallelism and cross-line variation of stress from *suche* to *on.* **123** scans after emendation as Type IIb on vowels and *f / v.* Both traditions show corruption, but the sense is largely preserved in **x,** while **p**'s *or on here* looks like a smoothing of the awkward *here,* a pl. possessive referring back to *both* men ('Ophni and Fineas their father' = 'O's and F's father'). *R–K*'s acceptance of **p** destroys the parallel between Christian bishop and Jewish High Priest emphasised by the rich rhyme through including the sons as objects of the punishment. However, the threat to the prelates is not defeat in battle but dislodgement from their 'chairs'. The error in **x** will have resulted from the awkward caesura, which separates Fineas from Ophni. **124** scans as a double-counterpointed line *abb / ab* on *3, s / sh.* A more conventional structure might come from emending the b-half to *synne of 3oure oune,* but this is much less effective rhetorically. **127 (B 99)** *his:* accepted on grounds of sense and supported by **C,** from which *B*-H does not elsewhere show ⊗; it could also have been the α reading, for which no witness remains. *Con(si)storie*: here used metaphorically (contrast *kyngdom* B 105, where there is no possessive in // C 133 but WHmF have incorrectly inserted one). In the b-half **x** has the right order but the wrong pronoun, **p** the wrong order and the right pronoun, with rhythm that appears suspect on comparison with **B.** I has both right, perhaps by lucky correction, as also has the **x**-type source of K^2, if that was not I. **133 (B 105)** *C*-b and also U here show ⊗ from **B,** as in the next line (cf. also *here* at 125 and *shonye* at 189). **135 (B 108)** *presumen*: if *B*-F preserves α, **B** could have been a present and β a mis-resolution of tense-ambiguous Bx **presumyt.* But since 134–37 are revised in detail, they may be here, and F be a coincidental agreement with **C.** **138** could be of Type IIa in ?Cx with *quod* as second stave; but more probably ⇒ for *Kirke* of the commoner *chirche,* which affects the metre of the b-half (as at 22.120, B 10.411), goes back to Cx. D's *kerk* (if < u) may preserve **x** or else be a felicitous scribal correction (cf. on 16.279). The form *kirke* is nearly always used as a stave-word (see *IG* s.v.), the exceptions being 17.276 and **B** 15.197, 545, 19.446 (*chirche* in // B 15.525, C 16.337, 17.202, 21.445 [no // for B 15.384]). **140** *men*: another hand in P^2 adds the controversial *mene* of I. **141–42** Loss of two half-lines in **x** (as also in **p**-AVS) will have been by eyeskip

from *wytt* 141 > *wit* 142. After 141 *R–K* unconvincingly insert B 115; but **C** must be understood as reducing Clergy's political rôle by replacing him with Kynde Wit in 142. **143 (B 117)** The Bx b-half is metrically defective, and reconstruction from // **C** presumes ⇒ occasioned by objection to the punning *repetitio* or else by desire to widen the scope of the *fyndyng.* **145 (B 119)** *to þe puple*: required on grounds of sense and confirmed by // **B,** though **x** will scan as Type IIIa; loss will have been by eyeskip from *-able* to *pupl*e. **B 122** *lif*: adopted as providing an adequate stave-word; but if F's reading was prompted by *lif* 120, α itself (< Bx) might have read *lede,* of which *man* β is an exact synonym (cf. N^2's happy conjecture *leode* for *man* Cx at 21.412).

> **B 125** *Hereafter the sigil α denotes the family reading understood as preserved in **R,** unless indication is given to the contrary. **F**'s numerous sophisticated variants, recorded only if judged possibly to represent α, will be found in full in the Apparatus to K–D.*

148 *Kynge*: an unceremonious address, modified in M (and in P^2 marginally *a.h.*) by prefixing *sire,* which *R–K* adopt. This is here judged an echo of **B,** not a correction from a superior **C** source. **149 (B 126)** *leue / lene*: the *B*-CrF readings are either ⊗ from **C** or visual errors for Bx *lene.* Arguably Cx *leue* is itself such an error (*R–K* interpret the mss as *lene*). On grounds of sense, Christ might be more plausibly asked to 'grant' than to 'permit'; but a cooler tone towards the 'King' would be in keeping with omission of *sire* in 148 (and see 156). **154 (B 134)** From this point until 2.216, when they are joined by K, *p*^{2} has *two* representatives, G and N. **156 (B 136)** Cx's omission of B 137 enables the sowing image to continue without interruption from images of stripping and measuring as in **B** and contains a warning to the King not present in the remaining lines (B 139–45, with their dialectical opposition of minatory and submissive political viewpoints, have been correspondingly dropped in the careful revision of this passage). *R–K*'s inclusion of it is accordingly unacceptable.

B 140 *answeres*: the present-tense form of L (? = β)R(? = α), perhaps a resolution of tense-ambiguous **answeryt* Bx, is here adopted as slightly harder in context; cf. on 135 and pr. t. *serueth* in C 160, which is p.t. in **ZAB** (*C*-P^{2}DG *serued* is adopted by *R–K*). **B 143** scans 'cognatively' on |g| and |k| (cf. B 18.48, *Intro.* IV § 46) and needs no emendation as in *Sch* (*can*) and *K–D* (*comsed*). **159–64** occur earlier at Z 65–9 / A 84–9 (Vol I, pp. 12–13) and later at B 211–16 (ibid., p. 24). The 'lawyers' passage' was evidently a highly mobile portion of the Pr. **159 (Z 65, A 84, B 211)** *selke*: final *-e* is added in both **A** and **B** to provide the necessary feminine ending; this type of formal emendation will not be noticed hereafter (all examples are listed in Vol I pp. 761–2). Z 65 forms the basis of **A**'s expanded 84–5. **161 (Z 66, A 86, B 213)** *poundes*: certain in **C** and perhaps the reading of all earlier versions, or else a revision of a difficult expression in **AB**. The form *poundes* could be noun or verb; if a verb, either *pounen 'expound' (not recorded) or *pounen* 'pulverise' (MED s.v. v. 1(a)), with a possible pun on both senses. If *pounen, it would be an unknown aphetic form of the verb *expoun(d)en* instanced at B 14.278 (the verb-form in MED s.v. *pounden* v. is cited from this passage in **A** only). Unless *poundes*, therefore, were an *ad hoc* Northern form, it could only be tentatively regarded as a present-tense verb; but though *poundyt* A-u*Ka*, B-F?H (*pountyd*), *K–DSch¹*, would fit well with the tense-sequence of all preceding verbs in **AB**, direct lexical evidence for *poun(d)en* 'expound' is lacking. Preferable would be either main sense of *pounen*, 'pulverise' or 'beat': the advocates 'mince' the law for their clients' money or 'belabour it' on their clients' behalf. Interpretation as the former is suggested by *B*-R's corrupt *poudres*, either an attempt to make explicit the metaphorical idea of 'pounding' to dust or a pr. t. (Northern) form of *poudren* (MED s.v. 3c (fig.) 'season'), which would be not unapt in context. Much depends on whether *B*-FH transmit respectively the true α and β readings or show ⊗ from an **A**-type source. In the light of **C** and **Z** (the latest and the earliest reading), *poundes* in all its ambiguity is here accepted as punning on one or possibly two verbs and the noun. The main notion is that the greedy lawyers work only for money (164), whether the sums be small or large. Variants of the penny / pound collocation occur at 2.232 and 16.297; so, all in all, *R*–*K*'s emendation of **C** to *pounded* should be rejected. **162 (Z 67, A 87, B 214)** *nat*: Ø **Z**, perhaps expressing 'an incredulous aposiopesis' (*R*–*B*), to which 68 would be an answer; but more probably the negative particle has been inadvertently omitted through distraction from *Ant* preceding. *Vnlose*: adopted for **B** as the form favoured by *ZAC*, though *vnlese* L (< β)R(< α) may represent Bx; both forms are cited from this passage by MED s.v. *unloosen* v. 2(a), *unleesen* v. 2 (the earliest for the former). **164 (Z 69, A 89, B 216)** *er* / *til*: contextually intersubstitutable adverbial conjunctions evenly attested in the **ABC** traditions. But the sequence **Z**B-α**C**-**x** supports *er* as more probably primary in **L**'s dialect and as the original reading of **A** (cf. also 173). **166 (B 147)** scans either as Type IIIa or IIIc on *m* and *þ* (from liaison of *with_hem*) or else as Ia with an internal *m* stave (*smale*). In either case, *myd* of *B*-W (so *K–D, R–K*) is as needless a scribal correction of the metre as *C*-M's ⇒ of *among* for *with*. **167 (B 148)** *Comen*: *K–D*'s emendation of Bx's mistaken *And* is accepted in the light of **C**, since the number describes the whole gathering, not just one part of it, as *And* would require. **170 (B 151)** *somme*: more precise here, and a possible revision, *hem* (agreeing with **B**) being ⇒ of a more expected word.

B 152 *dredes*: 'something inspiring fear' (MED s.v. *drede* n. 5a; with special reference to the Rolle quotation). With no real tautology after *doute* 'fear', *K–D*'s preference for OC²'s feeble *dedes* is to be rejected.

171 (B 153) *sorre*: the hardest reading and the likeliest to have generated the competing variant, the comparative adverb meaning 'all the more grievously [*sc.* if they complain]'. Found in the early G and in M, it could easily have been adapted to the advancing comparative *sorrer* in most **p** copies or corrupted to the positive as in **x**.

B 159 *Sayde*: if with an absolute sense 'spoke' or 'narrated a story' (MED s.v. *seien* v. 6(a); 11 (a)), this needs a semi-colon after *alle;* if not, *quod he* 160 becomes pleonastic, though not perforce scribal. *hemseluen alle*: neither β nor α is metrical (*aa / xa*; *aa / bb*). The line here reconstructed as Type Ie with 'standard' counterpoint (*aab / ab*) presumes 'split variants', rendering superfluous such conjectural stave-words as *salue* (*K–D*, *Sch*) for *help*. **181 (B 166)** *here way roume*: *K–D*'s questioning of Bx *awey renne* does not seem justified, though *R*-β at 171 shows that confusion of *renn*- and *rom*- was easy enough (and lost α could in principle have read as **C**). Cx is hard to reconstruct securely in the absence of a clear **x** reading, but **p** is acceptable on grounds of sense and unlikely to derive from a **B** source, since 189 sounds like the deliberate *repetitio* typical of **C**. The group-original of b read *way briȝt siluer*, O having substituted *knowe* over an erasure after *way*. If b here preserves x^1 through i, the lacunae will have affected the last two words of 181, plus all 182, and 183 minus the last two words (K^2 in omitting all three lines clearly belongs with x^1). The basis for thinking this right is the discreteness of the attempted corrections. Thus u and P^2 (which originally read as b) offer what seems the reading of B 174; but absence of 182 from u renders it unlikely that *way shonye* could represent what x^1 read, while 183 in u looks like an intelligent scribal attempt to fill out the imperfect x^1 source-line from the context. X first erased *way* and substituted *war,* then inserted *beyȝ* (a poorly spelled ?*be y-*), the sense intended being presumably '(hereby) be aware'. **185–87 (B 170–72)** The lines B 171–72 will have been lost by α through eyeskip from *mowen* 170 → *mowen* 172, and *pleye* 171 → *pleye likeþ* 173. G and sub-group w may have lost 170 through anticipation of 172. In B 171 Y's *rometh*, direct from g or by felicitous correction, is apter on grounds of sense and looks secure in the light of **C**. Confusion of *rem*- / *ren*- occurs at 20.103 in some **p** and **x** copies (and possibly at // Bx), as does *e / o* confusion, so an error-sequence *rom* → *rem* → *ren*- seems not improbable. But whether the error was in Bx remains unknown in the absence of α. **189 (B 174)** *ben*: an infinitive dependent on *mowe* understood (187), the **x** and **p** variants severally making explicit the sense OLU have corrected, perhaps by reference to a **B** source. *R–K*'s adoption of *shonye* b (like 133, another echo of **B**) has no warrant. **194** *R–K* add B 180 hereafter; but no reason for its loss appears, omission could have been intentional and there is no obvious gap in sense. **196 (B 182)** Whether or not the line is scanned as T-Type on |m| and |θ| / |ð|, *tho* improves the metre and could have been easily lost from Bx by haplography / homoarchy before the verb. *B*-G may have it from **C**, from a superior lost **B** copy (*K–D*) or by felicitous conjecture (*Intro.* II, *B Version* § 28). **202 (B 188)** *be we*: b and F are here taken to preserve the correct reading, by reference to **B** or by felicitous variation, as against the *x¹* error (shared by *B*-H). The pronoun will probably have been lost through *be* > < *ne-* attraction.

B 189–92 occur after 197 in Bx and presumably had that order in *B¹*, the poet's revision-copy of **B** (*Intro.* II, *B Version* § 2), since **C** 203 stands immediately *after* the equivalent **B** line (188), following these lines' removal in revision. *K–D* (p. 176) argue persuasively, on grounds of inconsequence in the argument, that they were misordered in Bx and (more speculatively) that their deletion in **C** was a sign of *L*'s dissatisfaction with the text he was revising. But if the lines' position in B¹ was as here re-ordered, and they were retained in **C**, it becomes at least possible that Cx lost them mechanically through homœoteleuton (*shewe...sh(e)rewe*).

211 (B 206) *so*: the key-stave in revised **C** is here conjectured as the **B** original for which the expected particle *to* is a Bx ⇒, producing a line of pattern *aa / xx*. *B*-F's *slen* (adopted by *K–D*), a metrical 'improvement' characteristic of this ms, should be rejected as giving poor sense. For the mouse cannot be arguing that the cat be allowed to *kill* them at will (cf. 189 above), rather that if they do not vex the cat by some constraint, he might stick to *conynges* and not kill rats and mice. **216 (B 201)** *reik*: a conjecture of Onions in 1908 accepted by all subsequent editors, though its 'intrinsic merits' (Mitchell 1939) require support from the ms evidence and the reading of **B**. For b's *reik* 'way', D's meaningless *roife* over erasure may represent an exemplar spelled *roike*. X's *ryot* (*a.h.*) over erased *reed* is perhaps a reversed spelling for *royt*, a variant of *royke* recorded only in *Promptorium Parvulorum* (MED s.vv. *raike*; *roit*). Of this, U's *rued*, despite its 'unusual' spelling (Mitchell), can hardly be a reflex, MED giving it as a spelling-variant of *red* (though only of n. (3) 'reed' not of n. (1) 'counsel'). In the light of X's erased reading, P² and the **p**-family, it is thus possible that Cx read *reed*. On the other hand, *reik* b may be an **x** reading corrupted in D and perhaps contaminated from **p** in P². The appropriateness of its sense 'way, preferred option' is supported by that of Bx *wille* (also attested, perhaps as a synonymsubstitute, by the **C** interpolation in K²). But *reed* 'way of proceeding, course of action' (MED s.v. n. (1), sense 3a) would be almost as suitable, especially if taken as ironic. The mouse's notion is of the rats' wilful behav-

iour as a *reed* that is *reedlees* (a 'plan' without 'counsel'), playing on closely-related co-polysemes in characteristic late-Langlandian manner. In **B**, the sense of *wille*, closer to *reik* than to *reed*, may indicate that Bx (and K²) substituted an easier near-synonym (so *K–DSch¹*); but since the Bx line scans as Type IIIa, and preference for Type Ia is a marked feature of the **C** revision, the case for emending Bx has little force (see *Intro.* IV § 28). **220 (Z 59, A 96, B 217)** Agreed **BC** *bondemen* may be seen as a revision, anticipated in some **A** mss, to a more readily intelligible word. The harder reading *bondage* of **A** is supported by **Z** and is unlikely to be scribal in either. **224** *of* / *þe*: split variants of the form attested in b.

B 223 (Z 90) is a line possibly lost from Ax, since it effects a better transition to A 102, *dikeris and delueris* being indeed *laborers,* not practitioners of *craftis*. **226 (Z 92, A 103, B 225)** No clear reason appears for the variants *longe* γA, *dere* B-L, *fayre* B-F, *here* B-R, Ø B-H (cf. *A*-M); but the closeness of *B*-R to **C** is evident despite the second (adverbial) *here.* If β had read Ø (as does H), *þe longe day* could have come into *B*-γM from an **A** source, in which case R could stand for α (< Bx), with L *dere* a visual error for this, and be preferred. The *B*-γ reading also appears in *C*-M, presumably by ⊗ from such a source. **232 (Z 93, A 109, B 231)** *Y say*: in the light of *ZAC* agreement, the order of *B*-G is to be preferred as original, whether by pure descent from g, ⊗ from **A**, or felicitous chance variation.

Passus I

RUBRICS In **B** the archetypal rubric's confirmation of this as Passus One may be regarded as also correct for the other versions, where one family omits (*A*-m) and one misnumbers through taking Pr as Passus One (*C*-p). The full form naming 'Piers Plowman' may go back to an authorial heading in **B** that was retained in **C**.

1 (AB 1, Z Pr 94) *the* / *þis*: either **B** is a revision of **A** reversed in **C**, or a more explicit Bx ⇒, or else **A** read *þis* and **C** is a new revision. **3** *lere*: the variant *lore* appears a contextually prompted misresolution of a presumed original **leore.* **4 (Z Pr 96, AB 4)** *þe*: Bx's *a* appears a scribal ⇒ that misses the reference back to the *tour* of B Pr 14. *castel*: Ax evidently had *clyf* 'steep slope' (MED s.v. 1 (b)). *ZBC* agreement on *castel* suggests possible damage in Ax's exemplar after initial *c-*, and the variants indicate scribal dissatisfaction with the sense. The presence of *clif* in *C*-q may be due to memorial ⊗; it has no claim to represent Cx. **5 (Z Pr 97, AB 5)** *Wille*: a revision following the change of *faire* to *by name* in 4; *sone* C-Ib appears memorial ⊗ from **B** (as earlier in both at Pr 72).

Z Pr 98–100 The thought in 98b is echoed at Z 125 and perhaps for that reason removed in revision to **A**. These unique **Z** lines seem authentic in both sense and metre: 99 is Type Ie with lift 2 blank, and 100 is Type Ib. **9 (AB 9)** *thei halde*: a word-order less usual in such a construction, so likelier to be original here, by revision. **11 (Z Pr 102, AB 11)** *may...mene*: **Z**Ax**B**x have inauthentic *aa / xa*. If their exemplars had lacked *be* from a presumed original with the **C** form, the **Z**Ax scribes could have produced the attested wording with *is þis to* by ⇒ of *is*. *A*-RUHE and *B*-H, the latter perhaps by ⊗ from an **A** source (*Intro.* III *B* § 30), will then have corrected the metre by conjecturing *bemene* 'signify', a verb-form certainly used at Pr 217 // (line not in **Z**A) and 1.56. Bx either duplicates the **Z**Ax error or retains **B**, with the error overlooked by **L** in a presumed scribal copy of **A** used in revision. *B*-H may preserve **B** and γLMα all have varied from Bx; but this seems unlikely, and *is this to mene / may this bemene* are perhaps best seen as split variants of a common original later restored in **C**, the more explicit form of which seems to have been Bx's at 60 below. The **C** tradition, being free from uncertainty, is accordingly adopted for all versions. The unsupported reading *bemene* in *C*-D is more probably an echo of Pr 217 than a correction from a superior lost **C** source (as *R–K* judge in adopting it). 15 is either Type IIIa or Type I with two staves in *fayful*. **21 (Z Pr 112, AB 21)** *thre*: omitted by *C*-MF, probably by haplography (*tho, thre*). The numeral gives the a-half a falling rhythm like that of 19a and the *repetitio* of 20 does not suggest unoriginality (as *R–K* hold), since it is common in **C** (e.g. *drynke* in 24, 25).

BA 24–5 (Z Pr 115–16) *And*: Ax *þat oþer* may be scribal over-explicitness designed to avoid repeating *And*; but a revision later reversed in **B** cannot be excluded. *þow driest*: favouring the originality of *þe driзeþ A*-t as a more archaic impersonal construction modernised in **B** (and anticipated in most **A** copies) is the support of **Z** (cf. also *the* for *þou* AB 26 in // Z).

25 (Z Pr 118, AB 27) *Lo*: in the light of *For* **ZAB** to be judged the Cx reading lost in **x** by haplography before L*oot;* for the idiom, cf. 12.90, 221. The interjection forms a prelude-dip in a Type Ia or, if stressed, transforms the line to a Type Ic. **30a** *Genesis*: omitted by DS. **L** does not cite sources in the earlier texts, but comparison of 16.141*a* with // **B** leaves it uncertain whether both references or neither may be due to the scribe of Cx. **34 (Z Pr 124, A 34, B 36)** *Al is nat / Hit ys nat al*: in the conflict of **Z**B and A**C**, the latter have the slightly harder reading, and **Z** may show ⊗ from a post-Bx source or coincidental agreement with **B**. But as the sense is identical, emendation of so minor a variant is not justified (see *Intro.* IV §§ 25–6). **35–6 (Z Pr 125–26, A 35–6, B 37–8)** The **B** half-lines 37b, 38a have been lost severally in *B*-(WHm) CL, doubtless through eyeskip from *likame* to *liere*. Loss of 37 by *B*-CrH may result from haplography of the pre-caesural lift. **37 (Z Pr 127, A 37, B 39)** *Which*: the less usual relative form, so likelier to be a revision than a

scribal ⇒ (see *MES* 196). *wolde þe*: the Ø-relative **ZBC** form must underlie the reading of *A*-m, and attempted smoothing in **r** destroys the metre in the b-half. **39 (Z Pr 129, A 39, B 41)** **Z**'s verbal inflexion explains the origin of the ?Ax a-half *And þat shent þi soule*, where *s(h)ent* is a visual error for **seuth*, easily made if its immediate exemplar had *sh-* for *s-* (cf. *C*-X's *schenth* over erasure and *shende* in *C*-L's rewritten line *For thei wolde shende thi soule...*) and / or *-t* for *-eth* (*seut*). The probable *B*-β reading (in γM) elicited puzzled responses from L and Y, perhaps because spelled *seit* or *sees*; *B*-α shows the same orthographic or lexical error (*-ue* for *-eu*) found in **x** and one **p** witness N, while *C*-PG appear to reflect a hypothetical Cx form **seuth* (actually that of **Z**). *Sk* translates 'And that [i.e. *Mesure* 33] looks after the soul and speaks to you in your heart'. More naturally taken, *þat* is not the subject but the object of the verb: 'and the soul sees that [alliance of the devil, world and flesh against man] and speaks to you of it in your heart' (implying a distinction between rational and voluntary powers). In **Z** *hit* is presumed lost by haplography following *seyth*. In the b-half, only H²K of the **A** witnesses preserve what appears from **ZBC** the correct reading. If **m** is taken as a piece of scribal re-writing, the reading *set* looks like scribal smoothing after ⇒ of *shent* for *seeþ*, perhaps prompted by **r**'s having spelled it **seyt* (cf. *B*-C's ambiguous spelling *setth*). *B*-G's agreement here with *A*-**r** can now be explained (against *K–DSch¹*) as ⊗ from an **A** source, *B*-F seeming also to echo this tradition in its sophisticating b-half. The error *sleth B*-Hm*C*-M can be seen (in Hm visibly) as convergent ⇒ for a difficult original, the posited Cx **seuth*, which has left a reflex in the back-spelled **sueþ-* forms (cf. *B*-α). Bx *This and* for *And* appears an attempt to find a pl. prn object for the verb (*B*-F taking the process a step further with *þese three*). Apart from this last error, Bx seems to have had the right reading as in **Z** and **C**. The latter adds in revision a line with *wysseth* (40) making clear that, as with both verbs in 39, there is only one subject. In the light of the preceding, *Sk*'s identification of this as *mesure* is unacceptable. For acute discussion of this crux in all versions see further Galloway 1999:79–82. **40 (A 40, B 42)** scans awkwardly in AxBx as Type IIIa on *þou, þe*, unless *war* belongs before *shuldist*. **42 (Z Pr 131, A 42, B 44)** *holdeth / kepeth*: a plausible genetic explanation is lacking for the clash *holdeth* **Z**Aβ / *kepeth* α**C**; but no major issue of sense being involved, β is kept for **B**. Either α may represent a phase of the B-Text intermediary between β and **C** (an interpretation rejected in *Intro.* III *B* §§ 51–5), or it may show ⊗ from **C**, or be an easy coincidental ⇒ of a reading later adopted in revision (contrast 66 below). **43 (Z Pr 132, A 43, B 45)** *to wham*: Bx adds *madame*, which is rejected on the agreement of **ZAC** as scribal interpolation. F may show influence here from **A** or **C**, or have omitted independently, substituting a pronoun in the a-half (*3e*).

A 46 (Z Pr 135, B 48) The **m**-variant, with *Wheder* given here in the contracted form of **Z**, indicates for **A** likewise a Type IIa line scanning on *w* rather than a Ia line with wrenched stress on -*shipe* scanning cognatively on *sh / s* as at Pr 119 discussed above and as in *KaK–F* (Bx may, but need not, be scanned so as to give a 'T'-type line). The reading of GH is presumably from an **A** copy (see *Intro.* III *B* §§ 28–32 on ⊗ in these mss).

B 50 (Z Pr 137, A 48) Ax lacked the participial pro-clitic *i-*, which appears on the showing of **ZB** to form a mute stave two in a Type Ia line.

47 (Z Pr 138, A 49, B 51) *hym / Ø*: the rhythm of **ZA** in the b-half is smoother than that of ?Bx, but *hym* could be a revision to strengthen the sense and GH may have deleted by reference to a copy of **A**. **48 (Z Pr 139, A 50, B 52)** is revised from Type IIIa to Type Ia with muted second stave and from a double to a single macaronic (*R–K*'s *cesari* for *Cesar* is unwarranted). **50 (Z Pr 141, A 52, B 54)** *ri3tfulliche*: confirmed for **B** by **ZAC** and its correctness recognized by *B-W* in felicitously altering Bx. **55 (Z I 2, A 57, B 59)** *That* Bx: perhaps scribal over-emphasis induced by *That* 61, as suggested by *The* in **ZA**B-H (which shows the usual influence from **A**) and parallel (revised) **C**; but emendation is unnecessary. **56** The variants indicate difficulty sensed in the AxBx traditions over the form of *bymene*. The genetically-unconnected **A** copies R, HJK and M point to an Ax spelling **be mene*, and if Bx's exemplar had read the same this might have invited smoothing to *be to meene* (the reading accepted for **B** at 11 above on the showing of // **C**). *B-GFH* may all show influence from an **A** and C²Cr³ from a **C** source. But *bemeene* is here accepted for **B** on the evidence of **C** and probable Ax as well as the contextual appropriateness of the sense 'signify' (applied to the *dale*). **59** *þat... name*: 'whose name is Wrong'; on genitival *that* + possessive for 'whose' see MED s.v. *that* rel. pron. 1c. (b). *R–K*'s adoption of *is yhote* after MU, which show ⊗ from **B**, is unwarranted, as 58–60 are all revised. **60 (Z 7, A 62, B 64)** *fond*: agreement of **ZC** and the characteristic asyndeton suggest that Bx *and* is a scribal smoothing, whether of *a* (= *he*), as in **A**, or of a Ø-relative (HmF may show ⊗ from **A**). *hit*: perhaps lost in **Z** through attraction to *hymsylfe*. **63 (Z 10, A 65, B 67)** *byiapede*: agreement with **C** against *iapide* **AB** need not here indicate ⊗ in **Z**, since both forms were in free variation; *A-M* has the prefix and MED s.v. *japen, bijapen* records **L**'s as the first use of both verbs. **66 (Z 13, A 68, B 70)** *he...sonest*: **C** is (? coincidentally) closer to β, while α, here joined by β-G (presumably by ⊗, but not from an α source), is identical with **A**'s revised form of **Z** (the reverse of the situation at 42). *B-H*'s unmetrical synonym reflects β. In **Z** *is* emends what is either a mechanical error or a partial reflex of **is*

as. **68 (Z 14, A 69, B 71)** *heo*: adopted for **A** on the showing of agreed **Z**(**B**)**C** as the AxBx form of which **mα** is a correct reflex and **rβ** *it* a scribal corruption. **70 (Z 16, A 71, B 73)** *halsede*: judged the original **B** reading on the grounds of intrinsic superiority and **ZAC** agreement. F will presumably have here corrected its α (< Bx) source *f* by reference to a **C** or more probably **A** copy. For (*pace K–D* p. 168) *hasked* R is likelier to be a spelling variant of *asked* than a corruption of *halsede*, the heavy incidence of unetymological *h* in **Z** (as in *hasked* Pr 136) indicating a relict of a possibly idiolectal feature. *wente*: found as a ⇒ in *B-F* but in **C** probably revision of a lexically recessive form to give a verb alliterating translinearly with 71, so that *R–K*'s emendation to *3ede* is unwarranted.

Z 18 appears original, with characteristic translinear alliteration from 17; but its omission in **A** (as superfluous, and to avoid anticipation of *fayth* at A 74) is no loss. **73 (Z 20, A 74, B 76)** The simple form *þi feiþ* is adopted for **A** on the showing of **Z** and **B**'s *þe*, which is less probably the pronoun than the article (in the latter sense the phrase makes up B 15.447b). The form of *A-JM* (*þe þi f.*) is also found in *B-G* (? by ⊗) and this or the vKW order may be original, though **C**'s revision of the b-half in the sense of *fre* found in B XIX 39 reduces certainty. **74 (Z 21, A 75, B 77)** *Thow / And*: **AC**'s pronoun gives the most satisfactory reading, *B-GHF* perhaps taking it from an **A**, *B-Cr* from an **A** or **C** source (cf. on 56 above). It is accordingly adopted for **B**; but a verb-form without pronoun (found e.g. at 20.379, also 2 p. pret.) may be the true **B**, as it is the **Z** reading (*B-HmOC²* more probably reflect smoothing of the latter than an original split into *And* and *thou*).

Z 21–3 show probable 'draft' redundancy after 21, the three lines being adequately contracted into two by **A**. **76 (Z 24, A 77, B 79)** *knelede / courbed*: agreement of **ZB** against **AC** may suggest scribal efforts to avoid the pleonasm of *knelide...knees*, *courbed* in itself being lexically harder (MED s.v. gives no other C14th use). If so, **Z** could be echoing **B**, the reading then belonging to the scribal layer of the **Z** manuscript's descent. However, in contrast Z 2.4 below is *with* **AC** against Bx, and the possibility of successive changes from **Z** to **A**, then back to **Z** in **B**, and finally back to **A** in **C**, though challenging the linear postulate, must argue for caution here in emending **B**. *B-H* shows ⊗ from **A**, its reversed word-order also appearing in *A-vJ*.

B 82 (Z 27, A 80) is omitted from *B-α* for no apparent reason, but from **C** presumably as a revision. *manne*: inflected dative for the required feminine ending. **80 (Z 29, A 82, B 84)** *saynt art yholde*: a sense 'that hold sin firmly' is possible for **Z**'s *senne hard yholde*, but contextually not apt. More probably *senne* is a bad **Z** spelling for *seynt* (cf. *sent* 2.80, *seyn* 5.69) and *hard* for *art*, as *R–B* note. HC is being referred to as she named herself at Z 19, and such specific reference to her power over sin (alluding to Mt 18:18) would be premature. **81 (Z 30, A 83, B 85)** *quod she*: possibly a Bx attempt to avoid running HC's answer into Will's question, or else an authorial explicitness deleted in C. **84 (Z 33, A 86, B 88)** *For*: required by the sense, and restored as the probable **B** reading on the showing of **ZAC**; no reason for mechanical loss in Bx appears. *who* **CZ**: possibly the original in **B** also if *B-R He* (smoothed further in F) is a visual error. **87 (Z 36, A 89, B 91)** *also*: a (characteristic) C synonym for *ek* (which is replaced by it at 2.252, 21.429 and dropped at 8.311, and which could have been lost by Bx through eyeskip to following *ylik*). **88 (Z 37, A 90, B 92)** *Þe*: possibly over-specific but clearly attested in Bx, less clearly in Ax, and perhaps deliberately dropped in revision to C. *B-H*'s reading may be by ⊗ from an A source like ChRVH(J). *thus / þys*: choice of reading is difficult since **x** seems to incorporate an element of **ZA** (*hit*) and an echo of **B** (*þis*), while **p** is identical with **B** (where *B-H* again follows **A**) yet too simple to have generated **x**. The reading adopted accounts for the form of **p** and instances a use of *thus* sufficiently uncommon to have prompted **x**'s expansion.

Z 39 Arguably lacking in appositeness here, the line seems to have been omitted as otiose in **A**. That *Treuthe* is valued by all has already been stated (38).

91 (Z 41, A 93, B 95) Initial *And* is either the Ax reading or added in **r** (the **m** mss are here variously corrupt), and is omitted from the text in the light of **ZBC**. **92 (Z 42, A 94, B 96)** *transgressores*: the exemplars of Ax and C-*p¹* have replaced the Latin with an exact English equivalent (see *Commentary*), possibly as a marginal or intralinear gloss suggested by *trespas* 93. If **Z** is here not an echo of **B** or **C** it must be judged, as a harder reading not in the Ax tradition, a pointer to the original reading of **A**, and may be brought in as evidence for **Z**'s priority to **A**. *B-G*'s error shows ⊗ more probably from an **A** source than from **C**. The Anglicised form in P²b suggests the word's early currency, though MED has no prior record. **97–101** The first instance in **C** of long lines misdivided in the archetype of **x** and **p**. The division is correct in **p** for 97–8 but wrong for 99, where the b-half has been expanded. *R–K* adopt **p**'s lineation and adverb, reading *serk* (with the masculine line ending **L** avoided) and *thei* as first stave. But its inauthentic character appears on comparison with 15.226–27, where *pureliche* achieves the same padding-out as *feithfullich* here. In the Apparatus for **p** in place of *def.* read *defende and fyȝte for*. **98 (Z 50, A 102, B 104)** *passeth*: Bx's incorrect tense may result from a visual error in resolving its exemplar's **passyt*, a form actually instanced in A-ms J (cf. on Pr 33, B 140). *þe ordre* **ZB**: arguably also to be read in **A**, since Ax may have had Ø (so **m**) and **r** have supplied an appropriate modifier. **101–02 (Z 44–5, A 96–7, B 98–9)**. On grounds of incon-

sequence in the argument *K–D* (p. 104) convincingly give the lines the order they have in **ZA**. That **C** has them in Bx's order is due to a mechanical error going back to B-Ø, the source of Bx and **L**'s revision-ms B¹. **104 (Z 51, A 103, B 105)** *knigted* **Z**: the ms form *knigten* may be an incorrect reflex, induced by preceding *kynggen*, of an exemplar reading **kniȝteden. tene*: clearly disyllabic in **ZAC**, so **B** is given a final *-e* for the necessary feminine ending. **105 (Z 52, A 104, B 106)** The uniformity of this **ZABC** 'core' line argues against making *Cherubyn and* a prelude-dip and giving *Seraphyn* two lifts. Rather, a |ʃ| pronunciation may be presumed for *Ch-*, a 'metrical allophone' of |s|, giving a standard line.

B 108 (Z 54, A 106) *me(e)ne*: *A-m* contains the stave-word missing in **r**, which could easily have lost it through haplography if *mayne* had been spelled *mene*. *B-G*'s omission, if not coincidental, suggests collation with an **A** source of **r** type.

Z 58 (A 110, [B 112], C 106) The line, absent from Bx, is metrically faulty in *A-***r**, which wants the key-stave and has a defective last lift. The lack of a second full stave was evidently seen as a deficiency, which group **t**'s reading seems an attempt to remedy (adopted by *Sch¹* in ignorance of **Z**). For *siȝt* can be understood as an Ax misreading of original *liȝt* caused by confusion of long *s* with *l* (the converse error occurs in *Pearl* 1050 [BL Cotton Nero A. x]; for a case of the same in *PP*, cf. App. at B 5.492). *Ka²* so concludes, following a conjecture of *K–D* for B 1.112, in unawareness that *lyght* is attested by **Z** at 1.58. But since *no* ms in the Ax tradition reads thus and the line was (inadvertently) omitted from Bx, **Z** must derive from an **A** or **B** source superior to Ax or Bx, or be a brilliant scribal guess, or be the original reading of a version prior to **A** (the interpretation favoured here as the likeliest). That **Z**'s *lord syluen* is shared by M does not argue against this conclusion, since M also reads *siȝt* with the other **A** copies and its *seluyn* may represent the family original without **m** having to be posited as the origin of **Z**. The loss of *seluen* in **r** will probably have been due to homoteleuton (the word occurring again at the end of 111) and that of the whole line in Bx to homœoteleuton (*he*uene, *sel*uen).

B 116 A Type III line like B Pr 147; *B-W* alone hypercorrects *wiþ* to *myd*.

109 lacks a key-stave with *l*. A possible original underlying unmetrical *fals* is *lyeres*, given the association of Lucifer's fall with lying in parallel B 1.118 and later in C XX 350ff. But *luther*, the conjecture preferred here, is another word favoured by **L**, though not otherwise common. It is applied to Lucifer at B 18.355 with special associations of deceitfulness and has the contextually synonymous sense 'false' at 19.246, while here it suggests treachery, as at 3.317 (see further *lu(y)ther* in *IG*). **111–13** are here taken as part of HC's speech,

R–K's ascription of it to Will being scarcely credible if their emendation of 112 is accepted (see below) and unnecessary in any case; HC is speculating rhetorically on the mysterious origin of evil. **112** The Cx line scans *aa / xx* and evidently lacks a key stave on *l.* The word conjectured here may have been supplanted by inducement from *northerne* 114 and (possibly) a marginal or interlinear gloss in the exemplar, although it could also have been visually mistaken as *lofte* and so replaced by an apt direction-word. It is the strangeness of the expression, given the aerial perspective of the description, that will presumably have prompted the hypothetical gloss. The reference to the quarter of sunrise in 113 anticipates HC's direction to look on the left (i.e. towards the north) at 2.5, where the speaker is standing in the east. *R–K*'s ingenious conjecture *in lateribus Aquilonis* for the whole of 112b (p. 169), diagnosing *north* as an intruded gloss upon a phrase drawn from Is 14:13, deserves respect; but such archetypal ⇒ for the Latin half of a macaronic has no parallel. **113** *Thenne to*: reconstructed as the original of the **x** and **p** split variants. **B 121** *for*: Bx scans *aa / xx* and *for* is conjectured as unconsciously omitted through preoccupation with the sense. *K–D*'s *ful* would seem to anticipate *togideres.* **B 123** Bx scans *xa / ax* and since simple ↔ of verb and object will give a Type IIIa line, *K–D*'s elaborate reconstruction is otiose.

122 *ne meuen*: reconstructed as giving both the verb needed for metre and sense and, as a consequence of the redundant negative particle, the form likeliest to have generated the *n*-variants, which were possibly written in Cx as ambiguous **nemeuen.* **126** *summe*[3]: adopted also for **B** on the strength of **ZAC** agreement. Bx presumably inserted *and*, whilst G omitted it after collation with an **A** source. **128 (Z 64, A 116, B 127)** The Ax reading *he put out* (from which only W varies) is supported for **B** by γMHF. But L's *pult*, taken as representing β (with the support of Cr derived from another source than w), and R's *pelt* (representing α) offer the harder reading. Bx may thus be reconstructed as *he pult out* 'he displayed' (a meaning illustrated only from this instance in MED s.v. *pilten* v. 3 (b)). The *B*-γ reading, to which HF have coincidentally varied (M perhaps by ⊗ from γ), will then seem an attempt to make sense of a probably unintelligible phrase (there is no real evidence for the sense 'display'). Much harder is the sense of **Z**, which cannot derive from an **A** or **B** source but which is very close to revised **C** (see MED s.v. *pilten* 1 (a) 'thrust' and *poken* 1 (b) 'push or thrust'). If its immediate exemplar read thus, Bx, having failed to grasp that 'pride' was the verb's subject, and influenced by the commoner phrase *he putte*, will have substituted *he* for *hym* and γMHF have then levelled to the more familiar expression. Finally **C** restored the original sense, but with a verb less liable to being mistaken. Thus, although the evidence from **Z** and **C** is more inferential

than direct, it seems fairly safe to conclude that the form of the phrase in both **A** and **B** was identical with that in **Z**, and to emend accordingly. At B 8.97 the verb *pulte* again caused difficulties, though there LR agreement (pointing to Bx) is supported by OC[2] and what appear attempted corrections in CrY of ?γ *putte*. In // C 10.95 **p** has *putte* against *pulte* **x**, as do *A*-DM for the difficult **A** original *pungen*, the only cited example of this sense in MED s.v. *pingen* v. **133 (Z 71, A 122, B 133)** That the key-stave of the b-half begins with *t-* (for which *c-* in the *croun-* variants would be an easy visual error) is evident from both **ZB** and revised **C**. The singular, making the Trinity the subject, gives a reading which may not be harder but is more apt. Construing the verb in **Z** and some **A** copies as plural may have been due to the influence of a series of pl. verbs after *þo* A 119 and to the ambiguous number of the *-iþ* ending. In **C** choice is evenly divided between *tour* (which recalls Pr 15 and collocates with *heuene* 132) and *trone*, echoing **ZAB** *troneþ* and relating more figuratively to *heuene*. Either could be a misreading for the other.

B 134 (Z 72, A 123) Z's Type III line will pass but would make better sense if *Y seye as* were understood as a first lift lost through haplography as in Z 129.

134 (Z 74, A 125, B 136) *Lere*: a sg. imperative (as in **ZC**, more apt in context; but the addressee is implicitly pl. as much as sg., viz. the whole *lettred* audience of the poem. *þus*: emendation of Bx seems secure in the light of **ZBC. 135** *That*: the objection of ungrammaticality (*R–K* p. 166) is irrelevant, since the whole clause is in effect elliptical: 'That "Truth" and "true love" — no treasure is better [than these]'. *That* clearly derives from **B** and editorial 'correction' to *than* is otiose. **136 (Z 76, A 127, B 138)** In the form of the a-half **ZC** stand against **AB**, in that of the b-half Bx seems fairly certain (supported by **Z** and *C*-**x**), while in the Ax tradition one variant is that of *C*-**p** (but *ʒe mote* **p** can hardly have generated *ʒut mot ʒe* as supposed by *R–K*). The version with double *ʒet* may seem the most attractive, with its discrimination of senses ('still'; 'even more'), but no emendation of **Z** or **C** is called for. **140 (Z 79, A 130, B 142)** The ms reading as it stands makes acceptable sense, and emendation of 79 could be avoided. Divided after *louy*, **Z** 80 will scan as a Type IIIa line on *þ* as the original draft reading. This would become a smoother Type Ia, reading [*Lord*] *God*; but the reconstruction of **Z** from **ABC** favoured here presumes that *in thyn herte* was accidentally omitted (perhaps through having been written in the exemplar's margin). **142 (Z 81, A 132, B 144)** The second *thow* will have been easily lost by haplography in copying **Z**. The prose order of **Z**'s a-half may reflect the draft stage of composition (for examples of prose order that could be either scribal in origin or due to the draft character of the text, see C Pr 108, 113). **145 (B 148)** The sub-archetypal readings *for* and *to abate* could be split variants of **for* to *abate* which, like **x**, would give a Type Ic line with an impossible b-half; but the form of // **B** reliably guides choice of **p** as representing Cx here. **147 (Z 86, A 137, B 152)** The reading *plente* stood in *A*-**m** and **Z**, probably in *B*-β (but H is absent) and possibly in *B*-α (but R is defective), *plante* in *A*-**r** and **C**. The latter is preferable on grounds of sense (see further Adams 1991:12–13) and its difficult referent may have prompted scribal ⇒ of a word often accompanying *pees* in common usage (see 17.93, 199 and cf. 13.170). More simply, *plente* could have resulted from *o / e* confusion (as in *C*-AR). But *plonte* was clearly the reading of **C** and quite probably of **A**, from one of which sources *B*-Cr will have derived its correction. *B*-Y's *planetes*, if not a simple misspelling, may have been induced by the association of one of them (e.g. Venus, Chaucer's 'wel-willy planete') with peace. **149 (B 154)** *eten* **B**: though α is uncertain without R, β seems to be *y-eten*, so that F's *h* may more plausibly be taken as an intruded aspirate (as in the **Z**-ms passim) not the indication of a spirant. Mechanically, however, *yeten* could be a reflex of *yȝeten*, a spelling variant of **C**'s substantive reading, with *his fille* to be seen as a Bx smoothing after misconstruction of the 'beget' verb as 'eat'. But *K–D*'s interpretation of Cr as a correction from a superior lost *B*-ms is an unnecessary hypothesis, since the reading is **C**'s, from which Cr shows occasional ⊗ (as at 147). The Bx form, though bold, is metaphorically coherent in itself and with later development of this image as the Tree of Charity (B 16.3ff), while avoiding anticipation of the incarnational statement in 155 and strengthening the pregnant figure of heavenly love drawing sustenance from human nature. **C**'s figure, more theologically explicit, is better seen as a new idea than as the **B** original underlying Bx. The pervasiveness of revision in this passage argues against *R–K*'s replacement of *As* 151, *Tho was hit* 152 by *And* and re-ordering of 150–51 to accord with the sequence in **B**. **151 (B 155)** *þis*: if a Type IIa structure with vocalic 'small-word' stave (theoretically possible) is excluded, the stave-word needed will have |v| or |f|, most probably *þis*, the metrical significance of which could have been missed by the Cx-scribe. The ease of *þe* ⇒ for *þis* appears from the identical error in *B*-OC² (and cf. Bx at 206, A 180). In Bx and Cx the 5-syllable prelude-dip is awkwardly long and both lines would be improved metrically by reading *tho* for *when*.

155 (B 160) If a vowel / *k* Type IIb structure is disallowed (cf. note on 151) and the lexical words are stressed as they seem to require, unoriginal *aa / bb* results. *K–D* emend by transposing the two b-half staves and finding the needed *m*-stave on *-múne*, but *R–K* adopt Cx. While variation to the commoner *order* of words in the phrase could well have occurred in both archetypes, the emendation proposed here presumes instead scribal ⇒ of a commoner *word*, viz. *bitwene* for original *inmiddes*. The latter had an

adverbial sense 'between' (see MED s.v. 2) but the sense here conjectured is rather 'in a mid-position (between)'. The resulting scansion, which manages to avoid *K–D*'s wrenching of stress, gives a 'T'-type line: *aa / [a]bb*.

160 (Z 88, A 139, B 165) *comseth a myhte*: Bx's b-half suggests scribal variation to prose-order and ⇒ of a commoner synonym for the verb. In principle, Bx would scan 'cognatively' with G's simple ↔ ; but in the light of **ZAC** agreement, it seems safe to emend. In **ZAB** the (normally monosyllabic) nominative is emended to a disyllabic form (by analogy with the inflected dative form, as in **C**) to provide the required feminine ending. **164 (Z 92, A 143, B 169)** *tene* **ZC** / *pyne* **AB**: perhaps due to **Z**'s ⊗ from **C** or *A*-**m** during scribal copying of the draft, with *pyne* then being also the presumed original reading of **Z**, retained in **AB** and not revised until **C**. Alternatively, *tene* could be a **Z** original revised to *pyne* in **A** or (if ?**m** *tene* – **A**) in **B**, on the possible basis of a revision ms of **r** type, **C**'s being then a restored reading, not a revision of B¹. On intrinsic grounds, *tene* may be judged both contextually harder (as ambiguous) and stylistically superior (as avoiding anticipation of *paynede* 166 //). There would thus be a case for adopting *tene* in both **A** and **B** and rejecting *pyne* as scribal in both *A*-**r** and Bx. Finally, though, despite lack of signs of major changes in 1.154–74, *tene* may indeed be a **C** revision back to an earlier form and *peyne* a reading **L** found acceptable for **B**, even if originating in a supposed scribal **A** copy. Retention of *pyne* for **AB** in the face of *A*-**m**'s witness is not very satisfactory; but emendation of the (unexceptionable) *p(e)yne* hardly more so. Definitely unacceptable is to adopt *peyne* in **C** as do *R–K*, rejecting a Cx reading to which there is no intrinsic objection. **167 (Z 95, A 146, B 172)** *ensaumples*: the pl. to be preferred in all versions as harder and more exact, referring to the dual examples of power (shown in mercy) and humility specified in 168 //, and closely echoed in 171 //. **169 (Z 97, A 148, B 174)** *hengen...hye*: clearly preterite in tense, either strong or weak forms being suitable for emending **Z**'s (doubtless mechanical) error (for *e / o* confusion in **Z** see on 147 above). The adverb *hye* is clearly attested in the b-half, and *A*-**r**'s *by* a visual error for *hy*. Agreement of **ZAC** indicates that **B** is also likely to have read as in *B*-G, which presumably shows ⊗ from an **A** source such as v (itself more likely to have *heiȝe* by good correction from an **m**-type or **C** copy than to preserve **r** against all other members of the family). **170 (Z 98, A 149, B 175)** *ȝow*: the *A*-**r** error *þe* seems a misreading through ȝ / þ confusion of **ȝe*, which is found in two copies and may have been in Ax as it is in **Z**. But the *A*-**m** reading is clearer, is that of **BC**, and specifies *haue* as imperative pl. and not infinitive or subjunctive. **171 (Z 99, A 150, B 176)** *myhty*: apparently the original form of the adjective, Bx *myȝtful* probably anticipating B 173 (where it is securely attested in all versions). G presumably shows ⊗

from an **A**, Cr more probably from a **C** source. **172–73 (Z 101–02, A 151–52, B 177–78***)* *R–B* suggest that Z 102 may follow directly from 100 (with 101 parenthetic) and offer a possible translation for the ms form: 'or else you will be sorry for it when you go hence'. But as it stands, 101 is unmetrical and the lines are better taken as meaning the same as **A** but as having suffered misdivision. The adverb *therewyth* must here have the sense 'as a consequence' (MED s.v. adv. 5(f)). The earliest thought, like the latest, is that of commensurability, for good as well as for evil; but though *wo* seems less fitting than what replaced it, the case for emending to *weiʒe* is not strong. *ʒe*: necessary for the sense and possibly lost in **Z** through distraction from *Ye...ye* in 102. **177 (Z 106, A 156, B 182)** *ʒow*: in the light of **ZBC** perhaps to be judged omitted from Ax's exemplar; but no emendation on grounds of sense and metre is needed. *goodliche*: with disyllabic suffix, since this is a core-text line, in contradiction to Duggan's claim (1990:179) that it is never so, since otherwise the b-verse will not fulfil the requirement of his Metrical Rule V that 'One of the dips preceding either lift must be strong' (Duggan 1987:45); cf. 18.58 and B 16.78 (neither a core-line) where *-liche* must also be disyllabic, for the same reason. **180 (Z 109, A 159, B 185)** *iugeth* **ZC?A-m**: perhaps present-tense in all versions since (while neither is clearly harder) both may be conflicting resolutions of a tense-ambiguous original ending in *-yt* (see note on 98). What does not seem in doubt is that the verb is 'judge'. *Ka*'s claims (p. 435) that *ioynide* 'is more pregnant, implying both judgement and injunction' lacks lexicographical support (see MED s.v. *joinen* v.(2)) and that '*iuggid* can scarcely have produced...its own unmetrical synonym *demys*' is incomprehensible. But the *A-t* reading may be only a scribal attempt to make sense of a word in which *u / n* confusion could have easily occurred. *R–K* sensibly abandon this notion, opting for *iuged* after MFN. **181 (Z 110, A 160, B 186)** *feet*: a word so spelled as to be interpretable as either 'deed' or 'feet', thereby allowing a pun on *folowe* in 182. *A-***m**'s variant, which is also that of *B-F* (perhaps by ⊗ from **A**), is influenced by *feiþ* and is an attempt to make sense of a contextually difficult word. The article is here omitted on the basis of **ABC-p** against **ZC-x**, which is less vivid. *feblore*: in the b-half, Bx seems to have attempted to 'improve' the rationality of the original, and *B-H* is presumably based on a partially recalled **A** source; but emendation in the light of **ZAC** agreement seems secure. *nautht*: no final *-e* is added since the diphthong could have been realised disyllabically, as at 9.112. **182 (Z 111, A 161, B 187)** *dedes*: nearer the Latin, while *dede* corresponds more closely to the number and sense of *fait* and to the form of the adjective *ded* (see *Intro.* IV § 26); but revision of **Z** by **A** looks unlikely (*B-G* may show influence from an *A-r* source). **183 (A 162, B 188)** There seems little logical justification for Bx *Forþi* in a

strong sense and it could be caught up from the (justified) connective at 175. But if it has a weaker sense 'accordingly' (MED s.v. *for-thi* adv. & conj.), omission of it as scribal will be needless. **186 (Z 113, A 165, B 191)** *hardore*: judged the likeliest reading for **B** on the showing of **ZAC**, *Auarouser* looking like Bx over-explicitness, perhaps unconsciously motivated by the collocation of the positive forms of the two words at B197. G's *herder* is presumably by ⊗ from an **A** source. **187** *hy*: the older vocalic form of the pl. prn would seem metrically preferable for **ZB** in the light of **C**. Though revised, C 186 also alliterates on vowels, but 187b seems to have suffered from the same ⇒ in Cx, and *C*-SN to have corrected the metre independently (like *A*-J?V). The line will scan as Type IIa in all three archetypes (but not **Z**, which as here emended is a Type Ie). *R–K* retain Cx in 187, presumably finding the key-stave in *aváunsed* (a credible Langlandian scansion); but reading *hy* here and emending to this form in **ZAB** enables the pronoun to function as a full stave, giving better balance with the a-half. For further discussion see *Intro.* IV § 30. **188 (Z 114, A 166, B 192)** *kyn*: the line may scan on |k|, with *Cristéne* containing two lifts or, more probably, on vowels, with the privative prefix and the strongly contrasted *here, alle* bearing full sentence-stress and alliteration. **Z**'s Ø-reading is just possible, but the nominal use of a pl. possessive is unidiomatic (contrast the sg. at 13.7) and loss through distraction from preceding *vnkynde* likely.

    A 169 (Z 118, B 195) *For ʒe*: reconstructed in the light of **Z** taken as the original of which *ʒe* and *For* are split variants (A's an attempted smoothing of the postulated **m** reading).

190 (Z 119, A 170, B 196) *out crepe*: perhaps the original word-order in **Z** as well, though emendation can be avoided by adding a final *-e* for the required feminine ending (see MED s.v. *out* (*e*) adv). **194 (Z 123, A 174, B 200)** Agreement of **AC** in the a-half guides emendation of both Bx (where H has been influenced from an **A** source) and **Z**. For the latter *R–B*'s explanation of *Foryth* as *forgyt*, governed by *trecherye*, is possible but strained. More probably, it is a confused reflex of **For thy(se)*, with accidental omission of *arn*). In the b-half, agreement of **ZBC** furnishes an emendation of Bx's unmetrical synonym (for a case of a possible converse ⇒ cf. B 10.246). The line scans on |w|. **199** Here the **C** *fragment* H begins. In Passus I it attests 199–end and belongs with y (see *Intro.* III *C* §§ 15–17). **200 (Z 129, A 180, B 206)** *siht of*: seemingly part of the text in all versions, though a line without the phrase will scan as a vocalic Type IIa or a counterpointed Type Ie. Its omission in both Bx and *A-m* could suggest ⊗ of the latter from a **B** source or that the revision to **B** was made from a scribal **A** ms of **m** type. But no mechanical reason for the loss appears, other than distraction from preceding *seiȝe...seide*. B-GH have presumably corrected here from an **A** source of **r** type, as has *A*-E in its copying of this line for a second time (for full details see *Ka* Apparatus *ad loc*). The presence of the phrase in **Z** indicates the latter's textual independence here: it cannot be derived from a **B** source or from an **A** source of **m** type, while the preceding 127–28 show no other affinities with one of **r** type. *Y*: presumed lost in **Z** by haplography after *Forthy*.

Z 131–2 *take hyt*: MS *taken* is possible, but inferior in sense to the conjectured form of the original, one which could have been easily corrupted through unconscious ⇒ of *yn* for *hyt* under inducement from *in*, th*yn*. **Z 132 (A 182–3, B 208–9)** *the wyth* **Z**: perhaps a case of ⊗ from a **B** source, or else lost from Ax. The sense does not strictly require it, and in the absence of confirmatory evidence from **C** it is not adopted in the text of **A**. The final lift *Lord* may be realised as a disyllable without needing to sound the medial fricative historically found in *lauerd* (cf. on *nauht* at 181 above).

Passus II

Collation Fragment **H** continues to 44 and reads with **y** unless otherwise noted.

Z 1–3 are unique to **Z** save that 2b and 1b were retained at A 1.2, 182 respectively (**Z** has a different half-line for A 1.182 and omits A 1.2). Z 1a substantially repeats the first phrase of Z 1.131, the phrasing of 2b recurs at Z 5.145 // **A** and that of line 3 looks forward to C 8.229 //. Metrically correct, these lines exhibit the redundancy typical of a draft (as likewise at 10). They are probably to be assigned to the narrator-poet since HC has given a farewell blessing at 1.132, but they may have been intended for her if the original plan was that she should leave at a later stage. These are further symptoms of **Z**'s draft-character here.

1 (Z 4, AB 1) *courbed* **B** could be a Bx ⇒ for *knelide* or else a revision finally rejected in **C** for the earlier reading. **A** has dropped **Z**'s *For*, presumably after omitting the summarising transition Z 1–3. **3 (Z 6, AB 3)** *blissed / blisful*: the reading of Ax remains uncertain, neither variant being contextually the harder (*blisful* 2(b) = *blessed* 3(a); see MED s.vv). *B*-C² may show ⊗ from a **C** source here; unless **Z** has ⊗ from **B** at the scribal level, it serves to confirm *blisful* for **A**. The **C** revision is anticipated in seven **A** witnesses, while *blisful* is read by the five **C** mss ILDMN. *bought vs* **Z**: the obvious emendation for what here appears a possible aural error. Z 7 scans a little awkwardly as Type IIIc on *f* and *k*, unless there has been scribal ↔ of verb and object in the b-half. A 4 moves the stresses to lexical words and sharpens the sense of the a-half, both signs of a revising hand.

9 (Z 12, AB 8) *wonderly*: the majority **p** variant *wonderlich riche* is apparently an error for Cx *wonderliche*. The *B*-G reading adopted for **B** in the light of **AC** may be a ⊗ from an **A** source. However, Bx is uncertain since R is absent and F sophisticated. If it read as *B*-β and **Z**, the latter must be either an original form rejected in **A** and restored in **B** or else a **Z**-copy echo of a post-archetypal **B** source (as *A*-M may also be). The *worthely* variant could have arisen from *n / r* confusion induced by anticipation of B 19 (Z 19); the converse occurs at A 15, where uvN have *wonderly* for *worpily* (*Ka* App.) **10 (Z 13, AB 9)** *pe pureste*: preferred for **B** as metrically necessary, supported by **ZA** and confirmed by partially revised **C**. F's correct reading could represent α here or be (as H probably is) by ⊗ from an **A** source. That *pureste* was found hard is indicated by the three **A** variants, one of them (J) that of β. **13 (Z 16, AB 12)** The **Z** line could be echoing **B** in the b-half or else be a first form partially restored in revised **B** after being earlier replaced in **A** (perhaps to bring in a topical allusion to Alice Perrers). **20–1 (B 21–2)** *ylow; lakked*: transposed needlessly by *R–K* after **B**, though Cx's sense is acceptable and the new line at 22 indicates active revision at this point. *Leutee; hym*: masculine contextually even without reference to **C**. *B*-β's *hire* may stem from recalling the grammatical gender of this noun-type in French and Latin and suggestion from the local abundance of feminine pronouns (20, 23, 24). If F's Ø-reading = α and α = Bx, β's error becomes the easier to account for.

A 19 *she*: emended by *K*–FKa to *heo* to obtain a Type IIIa line scanning on vowels (a type now not recognised by Ka) or Type Ia with liaisonal third stave (*was hire*) scanning on *s / sh*. De-stressing of *Wrong* can be avoided if the line is scanned as Type IIa with 'supplemental' fourth stave (*aaa / xa*). B 24 revises to a smoother Type Ia, while retaining *s / sh* 'cognative' alliteration.

23, 30 (Z 22, 25; A 18, 21; B 23, 28) In the case of **C** the base-ms representation of the feminine pronoun is corrected to the unambiguous standard SWM form. That of **Z** is left unemended in keeping with the treatment of its manuscript spelling throughout. In **B**, emendation is unnecessary in the first and, strictly, in the second instance; but a better stress-pattern results if 30 // is treated as an extended line of Type Ic with mute keystave. Cases involving only spelling-emendation of the base-ms are not discussed henceforth unless they affect sense or metre. **27 (B 27)** **C** re-writes as T-type a Type Ib line with an awkward five-syllable onset and a (probably) mute key-stave (*as*). **B** would read more smoothly with ↔ of *after, hym* to give a liaisonal stave (*hym_after*) and a Type IIa line; but **C**'s retention of the word-order in its unrevised a-half cautions against emendation. **27a** *Talis...filia*: to be preferred as an authentic adaptation of the phrase influenced by the passage in Ezech 16:44 that is the probable source (see *Commentary*). **30 (Z 25, A**

21, B 28) *a* **Z** may be an error for *of* (so *R–B*) or for *of a,* but the sense of the ms-reading will just pass.

Z 28 (A 24) *here*[2]: **Z** is revised in **A** to give sharper sense; in **Z** 'their' refers to both Fauel and Gyle.

B 33 scans awkwardly on vowels as *ax / aa* and would be smoother if pleonastic **He* were presumed lost before *shal* or **leef me* after *lord* (by eyeskip to *leef*).

34 *That what man*: '[with the consequence] that whatever man'; preferable to **p**'s abrupt form, which lacks any link with 33. **37 (B 35)** *lippe*: preferred for **B** as the harder reading to which YCr vary (perhaps by ⊗ from **C**) and for which Bx substituted a more familiar form, as did *C-p*.

B 36 *cacchep*: conjectured for the needed stave-word in the b-half as a less usual term for which Bx substituted a non-alliterating synonym. It is instanced at B 11.173 in a similar context, with which cf. also the metaphorical use at B 13.299.

44 (Z 29, A 25, B 43) The Bx line scans as Type Ie with counterpoint in the a-half but has an awkward stress on *is* in the b-half, the conjectured prn form *heo* furnishing a better stress-pattern. However, the stave-sound in **A** is |l| and it may be that Bx missed the irony in original *lady* (the key-stave in // **C**) and substituted *she* for it. *this*: Cx could have read as in P[2], with *that* and *this* as split variants in the two sub-archetypes. **ZAB** have the conjunction, but **L** commonly omits it (36 above). **47 (Z 33, A 29, B 47)** Emendation of Bx's b-half as evident scribal ⇒ seems justified in the light of // **ZA** and revised **C**. The error may be the result of conscious objection to repeated *alle* 45 and partially induced by the thought in B 48a below. **C**'s revision manages to eliminate the repetition in re-writing B 45b.

A 32 (Z 36) will scan cognatively on |k| and |g| as Type Ia or Ie.

53 *aslepe*: the **x** reading *as aslepe* could be original, suggesting a comparison in parallel with 54b. But while the vision may be 'as it were' in dream, the sleep is a fact and *as* probably a sub-archetypal dittography induced by *as it were.*

A 35 (Z 39) *ofsent*: preferred as giving better sense and corresponding to a line in parallel with *sompned* in Z 42 (deleted in revision); the verb recurs at B 3.102.

Z 39–50. 39–44 are reduced to A 35–7. Z 40 recurs as Z 119 and is retained as A 110. **45** This anticipation of 159 is removed in **A** as otiose, with deletion of the following connective. **47** An authentic-sounding line dropped perhaps as superfluous amplification. **50** *vp*: mechanical error perhaps through eyeskip to *panel*oun.

A 42 (Z 51) *telid*: a rarer form of the same verb (*tylen*) instanced at Z 6.66 (see also *tollen* at 6.220) and more probably original, with sense 'spread out' as opposed to 'pitched' (*teldit*); see MED s.v. *tillen* v. (2) (c), *telden* v. (a). **A 47 (Z 56)** *feffid / sesed*: either is a possible visual error for the other. The former could have

been induced by co-occurrence of *feffe* with *mariage* at 37; but since the error (if any) would be mechanical, there is no strong reason to adopt **m** for **A**, despite the support of **Z**. The ⇒ of *feffyd* for *fastnid* by **m** at 48 may even be smoothing after recognition of the prior ⇒.

66 *R–K* unwarrantably omit *forth* and transpose 66b to accord with **B**; but the revision begun in 65 continues. **72 (Z 62, A 54, B 72)** *Thenne*: perhaps lost from **A** before *stondip* (its position in **Z**) or *Symonye* (**BC**) but not needed for sense or metre.

79 (Z 65, A 57, B 75) Either the jussive subjunctive or the imperative is apt; but the linear sequence **ZAB** with alteration in **C** seems the most likely, the subjunctive in most *A*-r copies being scribal anticipation of the revision in **C**. *erthe*: original in the light of **ZAC** agreement, with *pis* a Bx intrusion of the same kind as *C-p* here. GHF presumably reflect collation with an **A** source. **84 (Z 67, A 59, B 80)** *prynses* **ZBC** is conjectured as having been corrupted to *present* in Ax through visual error, giving weaker sense and losing the anticipation of 'the Prince of this World' at A 10.8. **88 (Z 69, A 60, B 84)** *Yre* could be a revision and Bx could scan (weakly) as standard with *and* as a mute key-stave. But emendation here is probably justified, as *wrape* is quite likely to be a scribal ⇒ of the more familiar word for 'anger' used throughout Passus V. *Ire* does not otherwise occur in **B** but once in **Z** at 5.91 and twice elsewhere in **C**, at 20.435 and (problematically) at 11.110 (see note). **90 (Z 70, A 62, B 86)** appears in four distinct forms, **Z**'s b-half resembling **B**. The whole 'charter' section has undergone extensive revision. **91 (Z 71, A 63, B 87)** The form of the a-half is closely similar in **ZBC**, which lack **A**'s 'isle' metaphor; all four b-halves differ. In **A** *pe faste,* the hardest of the six variants, appears likeliest to have generated *laste* and *false,* which resemble it in shape. **L**'s characteristic view of this vice as 'gripping tightly' occurs at 1.191 //, with which compare 16.87//. A contextually apt sense 'hard-hearted, ?niggardly' (MED s.v. *fast* adj. 7(d)) appears to have been obsolete. **93 (Z 68, A 61, B 89)** *With*: in the light of **ZBC**, unconscious ⇒ of *And* in Bx is presumed, perhaps through eyeskip to 91.

Z 71–2 are lines apparently not derived from any of the other versions, 72 being unique, while 71a is closer to **BC**, 71b to **C**, than to **A**.

95 (B 91) *woldes*: the variant *wedes* *C-p*B-β is plausible enough in context and its (relative) unexpectedness, together with inducement from *wille wolde* 96 might have invited ⇒ in *B*-α and *C*-**x** of a word connected with thoughts and desires. But as *K–D* conjecture, the rare *wenes* 'hopes, expectations' (MED s.v. *wene* n. (b)), would explain the form of *wedes,* the form and sense of *wenynges* and the sense of *woldes.* The two attested variants are, however, not inferior in sense to *wenes,* though *woldes* is the less difficult, given the common collocation with *wisshes* (e.g. Gower, *CA* VI 923). The form of *B*-α could have been *wendynges, or else F, here accepted as having the right sense, may preserve α correctly (*wenynge* is securely attested at 22.33). That of H (*wendys*) might suggest likewise that β had a form *wendes (? an analogical verbal noun from a preterite, like *woldes*) which might have baffled scribes and invited the 'correction' *wedes*. Here it is assumed that **C** has revised **B**, though **p**'s ⇒ for *woldes* is harder to explain than if Cx read *wenynges*. R–K, notwithstanding *K–D*, read with **p**; while both **B** and **C** remain uncertain, emendation is necessary in neither. **101** *in...spene*: the second *speke* is here taken as a verb, though it could be a spelling variant of *speche* **p**u (to which IL*P²* should be added, emending the apparatus entry). Since OB share X's *speke*, and this is the harder reading, it is possible that two members of y (I and *P²*) and one of b (L) have severally varied from the group reading through interpreting *speke* as a noun (when the comma after *ydelnesse* would stand after *speke*). On the other hand, *speke²* as a repeated verb, closely coupled with another (*spene*) that requires a slightly different sense of *in vayne*, is a rhetorically effective *repetitio* with good claim to be original. **105** R–K remove the line to stand after 101, making *This lyf* the direct object of *spene*; but such re-writing cannot be justified. **106 (B 103)** *a dwelling*: the variants *a* / *þay* perhaps point to an ambiguously-spelled *a dwellyn Cx, in which *x¹* wrongly took *a* as the pronoun and *x²* (> **p**) rightly as the article, a reading supported by // B 103. **109 (Z 79, A 72, B 108)** *þis*: unusually for **C** giving a Type IIIc for a Type Ia line, unless *þis* is a Cx error for *which*, as *B*-α (here supported by H) could be for *which* ?Bx (> β, supported by **AZ**). In α's case, the ⇒ could have been induced by *þis* at 105 (a line deleted in **C**). **114–15 (Z 84–5, A 77–8, B 113–14)** If these lines are indirect speech, they would involve a (not unusual) tense-change from 109; if direct, would require that Simony or Civil or both be speaking in the third person about themselves. The present tense favours direct speech, most probably from the speaker of 74. Theology's rejoinder is to Civil (as last speaker) in **AB**, to Simony in **C** and (originally it appears) also in **Z**, though the latter alters to what is presumably intended to be Civil (*Cyuynye* ms). The form of the verb as third person passive is assured in **C** and **Z** and was probably that of Ax; but Bx seems to have had *I assele*, a reading arguably harder and, if original, a revision. The form of 85b in **Z** is identical with that of **BC**, from one of which it could derive; but if **Z** is original here, **B** will have reverted to a **Z** form later abandoned in **A** or retained in **A** and replaced by Ax with a (contextually-apt) reference to notaries. A's b-half here is used by **C** at 156 below, which may also preserve the **B** original. **118 (Z 88, A 81, B 117)** *weddyng*(*es*): the sg. without article is arguably harder, but the pl. provides a contrast between the gen-

eral category and the particular example furnished by *þis weddyng* (118), so Bx may stand as one revision (reverting to **Z**), and **C** as another (reverting to **A** with addition of the article). **120 (Z 90, A 83, B 119)** *engendred* **B**: the -*th* spelling of *B*-YCLR perhaps pointing to that of Bx, paralleled in the -*t* endings of **ZA** (not in **C**), and indicating a past participle form (cf. B 120). **125 (Z 91, A 94, B 120)** *graunte*: the variation in tenses may derive from a tense-ambiguous *grauntyt* in the archetypes and the exemplar of **Z**, capable of resolution as present or preterite (cf. note on 1.180). In revised **C** the verb-form is again ambiguous, though a past tense is preferable following *plyhte*124: *graunte* **C**-**x** may be an assimilated present (<*graunteþ*) or preterite (<*grauntede*), with *were* meaning 'should be', or even a jussive subjunctive. The latter is possible, given the Ø-preterite variants in **A** (and see MED s.v.); but while the sense of B 120 is now contained in 124, 125 could refer to future events (*were* 128 balancing 125). The **x** form allows both.

B 123 (Z 94, A 87) In the absence of the *A*-ms A, the sole **m** witness is here taken as preserving the group-original (E here deriving from an **r**-type source), to be identified in the light of **ZB** as = Ax. Alternatively, **m** could here show ⊗ from a **B** source and **Z** derive from **m** or **B**. The line in **r** could scan on *is, his* as Type IIIb (a variation not acknowledged by *Ka*, who nonetheless accepts it with *K–F*; but the natural way of reading gives unmetrical *aa* / *bb*. It therefore looks like a scribal expansion-gloss and not, as *R–B* suggest, an **A** revision, while **Z**, **m** and Bx are highly unlikely to represent a contraction through omission of two half-lines. The witness of *B*-H at this point could in principle signify its distinct line of descent from **B**; but as this would have to be independent not only of β but of Bx, the reading is more economically interpreted as a case of H's ⊗ from an **A** ms of family **r**. **128** From here on, **b** (BOL) having *ceased* as a **C**-Text, the *x¹* group of **C** is represented only by XIP² and UD until 157, when ms Y begins. BOL here *continue* with a transitional passage of **A** material (2.186–98, not collated because of no textual interest) before taking up at the beginning of Passus III as a **B**-Text with the sigil B. **139 (Z 99, A 91, B 127)** Ax scans as an awkward Type IIIa line with two stresses on *nótories*, unless it has transposed an original order as found in **B**. Revision in **A** could have been prompted by the rarity and potential difficulty of **Z**'s *nysotes*, of which MED s.v. has only one earlier example, from *WW* 410 (and no citation of Z 99).

B 135–6, Z 108–9, A 99–100 Agreement of **ZB** in *lawe* does not necessitate emendation of Ax. For the **A** reading (like **Z** having both *lawe* and *leaute* but in different order) looks a transitional stage between **Z** and **B**, which does not mention *leaute* here, doubtless because of the positively moral and non-neutral character of this term as used in the later versions.

143 (Z 102, A 94, B 130) *faythles / faytles*: the hardest variant on grounds of sense may well be *feyntles* 'untiring' (so *Ka*). However, *feytles* ?'without deeds' (a sense not recorded in MED s.v. but suggested by *R–B ad loc*, referring to Z I 110 //) could be the original, revised to *feibles* **B**, which is retained in **C**. *Faytles* may, on the other hand, be only a spelling variant of the latter (*t* for the *th* ending). The **A** variants *feyth-* and *feynt-* would then be scribal attempts to resolve an orthographically unfamiliar form; those of V, R and E do not appear to be reflexes of any other. **150 (Z 109, A 101, B 137)** *iuggede* **Z**: past subjunctive, sitting awkwardly with the imperative that follows; while possible, it may be a mistaken reflex of the exemplar's **iugget = iuggyth* (see on 125). In **AB** and (revised) **C** the tense of the conditional clause is uniformly present. **154 (Z 113, A 105, B 141)** *soure*: the harder reading as well as fitting better with **L**'s thought elsewhere, as at 15.49 // and particularly B 10.359, though *sore* appears in one **A** family and in *B*-Crg (?by ⊗). **156 (Z 115, A 107, B 143)** In the **A** tradition, ms M is here identified, in the light of **Z**, as the reflex of **m** (< Ax) or else as a felicitous correction of an incomplete b-half like that of **r** (left unmetrical by *KaK–F*; the readings of E and particularly L may be by ⊗ from **C**). In Bx *seruice* clerical censorship may be operating, since the *seles* it substitutes for would presumably be a bishop's. In emending, the sg. is preferred as the line is reconstructed to accord integrally with **C**. Bx *also þe* is metrically possible, but its inconsequential character shows as scribal on comparison with **ZC**.

157 From here on, with the presence of Y, the readings of **C** group **y** are attested by XYIP²; XYIP²UD therefore now = *x¹* (representing **x**). When the readings of X are corrected from another **x** authority, this will be Y unless otherwise indicated.

158 (Z 117, A 109, B 145) *go*: the visual error *to* in *C*-**x** and in several **B** mss is one that recurs at B 2.200 in β (where **B** may be revising **A**). *Go* is preferably to be read as imperative not infinitive, if Fauel's speech is taken to run from 158–61 (and likewise in // **ZAB**). In **Z** omission of *gyue* through partial haplography after *gyle* would perhaps be more easily explained if *go* had not been present in the exemplar. But the phrase could have been lost by eyeskip from *Gyle* to *gold*, another contributory factor being misunderstanding of *bad* as meaning 'offered' not 'bade'.

Z 118 is a draft line (perhaps T-type), presumably omitted as otiose in **A**.

161 *with...speche*: a revision that *R–K* unwarrantably replace with B 148. It certainly anticipates 167 below, but such echoic *repetitio* is common in **C**. **165 (Z 125, A 116, B 152)** *syre* **ZB** has perhaps been lost from **A** by haplography (**sere* before **sertis*); but the line has satisfactory sense and metre. **166 (Z 126, A 117, B 153)** *wyt / wittes*

ZA / B: the sg. in *B*-GHF may reflect ⊗ from **A** more probably than a **B** tradition distinct from Bx. Since the pl. gives good sense, it is retained in the absence of counter-evidence from // **C**. **167 (Z 127, A 118, B 154)** *thorw*: preferred for **AB** in the light of **ZC**. Ax *wiþ* may have been visually induced from *wyt* 117, a mistake found in all members of *B*-β save H, which seems to descend separately from the family ancestor. *tonge*: *C*-M has *speche*, taken by *R–K* as a correction from a superior **C** source but here understood as probably ⊗ from **B**. **169 (Z 129, A 120, B 156)** *þat þe* **AB**: here judged the original form of which *þat* and *þe* are split variants (**C** is revised). **170 (Z 130, A 121, B 157)** *for euere* **AB**: perhaps a revision of **Z**'s *togydderes*; but the latter reading in **m** is hard to see as a coincidental ⇒ for the **r** variant supported by **B** (unless perhaps it was a modernised form of an Ax reading mistaken as **yfere*). **173 (Z 133, A 124, B 160)** *bowen*: final *-n* is added in **Z**, which has presumably lost it through haplography after *w* (or **u*). **174 (Z 134, A 125, B 161)** *hym*: the pl. *hem* occurs in at least one family in each of the later versions as well as in Ax; but in the light of **Z** and the b-half of **C** (*his*), sg. *hym* is preferable as the harder variant. Whichever is adopted, the expression in **C**'s b-half remains slightly awkward after the preceding pl. verbs *leten* and *bade*. M reads *þis* and F *þe* (so *R–K*); but both may be scribal responses to an awkwardness possibly of authorial origin. **175 (Z 135, A 126, B 162)** *cairen*: judged the original for **A** in the light of agreement between **Z** and *B*-αLM against AxB-γ. The easier *carien* has been induced by the form of preceding *caride* and contextual reference to carriage-horses. **C**'s revision (as at 4.24) reveals **L**'s awareness of the word's potential difficulty.

Z 136–8 136 (A 127, B 163) *ynowe* **Z** may show ⊗ from **B** or be an early reading restored in **B**, with *of þe beste* an Ax alteration of **A** after judging *ynowe* too close to following *al newe* or visually misconstruing it as identical with the latter. The **ZB** agreement challenges the linear postulate, but since the former phrase meets the criterion of acceptability, the case for emending it may be allowed to lapse. **138 (A 129, B 165)** scans as Type Ia with a liaisonal stave (*Fals_on*), perhaps revised in **A** (if *sat* has not been lost from ms **Z** through attraction to *that*.

A 130 (Z 139, B 166) *fetysliche*: the **A** groups VH (= v) and EM (= **m**) preserve the ostensibly harder *feyntliche* 'feignedly', which could have been the reading of Ax. H², however, may be seen as offering a synonym for *fetisliche* rather than as reflecting *feyntliche*, while Ch is an idiosyncratic ⇒ close in sense to *fetisliche*. The spelling of J and *B*-Cr (*fetelych*) suggests that the AxBx form was written with the *s* obscured or omitted. *Feyntliche* might seem to read better in context than the other variants, including **ZBx**; but the notion of 'fine words' (or of flattery) as akin to 'fair clothing' is characteristic of **L** (cf.

16.268) and intrinsically no less likely to be original. *B-G* may be a reflex, following loss of the nasal suspension, of a reading derived from an **r** source of v type or (less probably) one of **m** type, or simply a spelling-variant of *feetly*, a word closely related to the Bx form.

Z 141–8 141 (A 132, B 168) *on....goen*: in the light of **A**, the verb and adverbial phrase in **Z** appear to have been miscopied in prose order, whether at the scribal phase or in the original draft form (for parallel cases see C Pr 108, 113). The verb, here in fully expanded form, must be in final position to provide the required feminine ending. **146 (A 137)** *destreres*: not requiring to be scanned as tetrasyllabic, since the stress-pattern *déstréres* is authentic (cf. *sepúlcre* C 7.170 //), Z 147 repeating this rhythm and re-inforcing it with rhyme. **A** revises to Type Ib by adding *south dénis*. **148 (B 174) Z** here either shows memorial ⊗ from **B** or attests an early form of a line replaced in **A** by one about the Paulines, restored in **B**'s revision and omitted again from **C**. Scansion would be smoother with *hy* for *they*.

185 *vppon*: the expanded form as in 184 (conjectured or accidentally substituted by one ms, F), needed to furnish a first stave in the a-half (Cx evidently read *on*). **190 (Z 150, A 141, B 180)** *drawe*: in the light of **ZAC** agreement the probable original of **B**; Bx *lede* (perhaps anticipating 182) offers no difference of sense and will be an arbitrary or unconscious scribal ⇒. **191 (Z 151, A 142, B 181)** *oure* **ZAC**: the probable original, Bx's ⇒ attempting to avoid repetition of 180. *fornicatores* **ZBC**: while an English form (perhaps a coinage of **L**'s) could have been used in **A**, this is unlikely if **Z** was prior. A Latin term seems preferable in all versions, since the word reads as a quotation from a charge-sheet (cf. on *transgressores* at 1.92). If Ax's exemplar was unrubricated, the word could have been mistakenly understood as English (although it was not common and MED records no earlier example than this). The same error occurs in *C*-**p**, which makes a similar ⇒ for *rectores* at 184. **193 (Z 153, A 144, B 183)** *fobbes*: possibly the original form for **A** (so *Ka*), unless **Z** is a scribal echo of a **C** source. It is not clear from the **A** variants what Ax read, the *fo*- forms indicating either *fobbes* or *fobberes*, and the *-ers* forms favouring the latter, so *A*-K's reading (that of α < ?Bx) is adopted for **A**. No difference of sense is involved, and as both forms are cited by MED only from **L**, they may have alternated freely in the sequence **Z(AB)C**. The *B*-β*A*-Lw variant *freres* shows a scribal animus perhaps influenced by recollection of *Frere Faytour* of 8.73 and the collocation at 11.54 // **AB**. *rennen*: the Ax reading for the verb in the light of **ZBC**, with *iotten* (a presumed preterite of *gon*, idiosyncratically varied to *trotten* in Ch) a scribal ⇒ by group t. Despite *Ka*'s arguments (*Notes ad loc*), this seems a case where an ostensibly harder reading (if such it really is) shows from the other evidence as more probably scribal,

and *R–K* sensibly abandon it. *B-H yede* suggests ⊗ from a source of *A*-t type. Brewer's contention (1996:396) that *iotten* could be an original **A** reading rejected in favour of the 'clearer and more communicative' *rennen* is contradicted by the fact that **Z** already reads *rennes* (as noted ibid. p. 395n). It is more economical to presume scribal activity here. **195 (Z 155, A 146, B 185)** *this men*: preferred to *þis mené* 'this company' which, though *prima facie* the harder reading, is to be judged a misunderstanding of the sense through taking the presumed pl. demonstrative adjective form *þis* (clearly instanced in **ZC**) for a sg. and then smoothing with a sg. noun. *B-G* once again shows ⊗ from an **A** source of r type. *R–K*'s intrusion of *meyne* into **C** seems remarkable (cf. note on *rennen* at 193 above). **197** *sende*: read by *R–K* as *seude* (Ø-relative preterite), which is probably better.

Z 163–70 These lines of summary, to judge from the repetition of 164b at 168b, seem to be in draft form, and this would account for the anacoluthon in 163. But the misdivision of 165/6 may be due to the scribe of Bodley 851. The two lines will scan correctly as re-arranged here and *lach* is easily emended to the required disyllabic form by addition of final *-e* (for the phrase *lacchen mede* cf. C 3. 390 below).

200 The minority reading *wel* MF adopted by *R–K* is here taken as a reminiscence of **B**. The repetition (of *alle* in 201) is a characteristic feature of **C** (cf. on 161 above). **Z 171 (A 154, B 193, C 204)** *the*: omission in **Z** a scribal slip (perhaps wrongly emended as following *tho*) or reflection of the text's draft character (cf.3.17).

B 198–203 Bx makes several successive errors that may be emended in the light of **ZAC** and the context generally. In **198** *wol loke* illustrates scribal over-emphasis (here paralleled in *A*-H). In **200** *þyng* for *tresor* is a generalising idiomatic ⇒ for the agreed **ZAC** reading (in the a-half, despite the damaged state of R, the α reading can be divined in the light of **C** as that underlying F and so accepted as = Bx). In **201** the Bx inversion error, diagnosable on comparison with **ZAC-x**, is one also shared by *C*-**p**, the precipitating mechanism in both cases being attraction of the adverb to a position immediately after the verb. In **202** inserted *and* is a smoothing that reduces the immediacy of the command as recorded in **ZAC**. In **203**, misplacement of the line, which on the showing of **ZAC** belongs after 202, may have been prompted by a wish to dispatch the three named villains as a group before turning to the somewhat different treatment of Mede.

217 (Z 187, A 169, B 206) *dene / doom*: the **ZB** readings seem secure and Ax probably read *doom*, the variant *dune* VJL being explicable as memorial ⊗ from **C** (so *Ka*). Neither word is more obviously appropriate to the context: *din* was fairly rare, *doom* is perhaps contextually harder (*Ka*), if it possesses the sense 'command' cited by MED s.v. *dom* n. 3(a) (and see *R–K* 115), though the context might equally have suggested it to the Ax and Bx scribes. The *doom* reading in *C*-P² is visibly by addition, perhaps by ⊗ from a **B** source, while that in *C*-D (in App. *add* also N) could result from visual confusion of an exemplar read as *deme* and then smoothed; neither throws serious doubt on what Cx must have read. On balance, it seems best to accept that **A** and **B** could have had *doom* and **C** altered to *dene*, with subsequent revision of 218a. **Z** would then be either a first thought that was rejected in **A** or an echo of later **C** entering at the scribal stage of **Z**. The former, though challenging the linear postulate, would seem likelier if the sequence Z 188–90 is original, since this contains material used in the later versions but not in **A** (see next).

Z 188–90 are probably draft lines that anticipate rather than scribal lines that echo the later versions (188 = B 207, 189 = C 3.78). Although exhibiting the redundancy typical of scribal padding-out, they also display correct metre (with characteristic *s / sh* alliteration in 189) and syntax (with object / subject inversion in 188 as at 22.80 //). 188 could have been present in **A**, lost by Ax, and then restored in **B**. In the light of C 218a, which summarises the content of B 207–8 // Z, there is a case for inserting at least Z 188 after A 169; but since the Ax text makes adequate sense, it may be allowed to stand. **190** *fore*: probably 'beforehand' (MED s.v. *fore* adv. 1, citing *WPal* 4142), but possibly the preposition, if a following *fere*'fear' has been haplographically lost (cf. 192).

219 (Z 190, A 171, B 210) *feres*: the assured reading in the b-half of **ZAC**, Bx's ⇒ (if βR *felawes* is so taken) perhaps arising from objection to the repetition necessitated by the wordplay at 211 (cf. on B 181 above; *for fere*[1] is removed in C 219). The F reading presumed correct, while it could represent α, is more probably due to ⊗ from **C** or **A**. **221 (Z 192, A 173, B 212)** *to* **Z**: an adverb of motion with an implied verb, a misreading of *go*, or the infinitive particle (with following *go* having been lost through visual assimilation), the possibility favoured here on comparison with **ABC** (cf. on Z 190 above). **223 (Z 194, A 175, B 214)** *shoppes / shoppe*: the collective sg. is more probably original, but nothing is to be gained by rejecting the advancing form here and elsewhere (cf. *churches* at 231). **225 (Z 196, A 177, B 216)** *thenne*: the potentially ambiguous original form ('from there') preserved in **ZC**, which would explain the mistaken reflex *þanne* β and is accordingly adopted for **A** and (from α) for **B** (*B*-GH show ⊗ from *A*-r). **227 (Z 198, A 179, B 218)** In all versions this is a Type IIa line with de-aspirated *wh* in the second lift, as clearly reflected in **Z**'s spelling *nawer* (cf. *wham* 17.89, scanning on |w| and the **Z** spelling *wam* at Pr 132). **228 (Z 199, A 180, B 219)** *yhoutid*: preferable to *yhonted* (so *R–K*) on grounds of sense as well as providing a characteristic chime with *yhote*; people who shoo Liar away are not likely to 'hunt' for him

only to tell their quarry to 'pack up and be off'. The error is a visual one, but the **m**-group variants point to the true reading preserved in RD of **A**. **Z**'s error must belong to the scribal stage of copying (or it may not be one, since the manuscript reading is not certain). **231 (Z 202, A 183, B 222)** *on...seeles:* the correct order, on comparison of **B** with agreed **ZAC**. Although unobjectionable in itself, Bx seems to have anticipated through visual attraction of se*nten* to se*les. churches*: the pl. more probably original in all versions since the sg. formed part of a familiar set phrase. **233 (Z 204, A 185, B 224)** *thei*: for *thei* of // **BC**, Ax read either *hy* or *hy hym*, the form presumed to underlie **Z**, and the alternative preferred as likely to have generated the split variants *þey / hym. A*-TD show progressive corruption of *hym > he > þe*, requiring the preterite to be read as the p.p. (though the grammar remains poor). **237 (Z 208, A 189, B 228)** *Ac* **ZBC** is conjectured for **A**, though (if Ax read Ø) the other mss could have variously substituted an appropriate connective. **238 (Z 209, A 190, B 229)** *withholden / helden*: agreement of **Z**Bx against **AC** is to be explained either as due to **Z**'s ⊗ from **B** or by positing the sequence: Ø-prefix **Z** (or omission in ms Z), *wiþ-* **A**, omission **B**, *wiþ-* **C**. Haplographic omission could have been induced by *with* in Z 208, 210 (B 228, 230). *half* **ZAC**: possibly also the original in **B**; but the α form is acceptable. **249–52 (Z 214–15, A 195–98, B 234–37)** The **A** revision of **Z** is retained unaltered and is an expansion comparable to that of Z 60 at A 51–2. In **C** it comes after six extra lines, incorporating A 166, a rare case (like 3.395) of an **A** line omitted in **B** being retained in **C** (though not after C 214, the parallel passage, which reads as **B**). Either **L** deliberately restored the line because of its intrinsic importance and new appositeness, or an earlier form of what became C 243–48 was drafted for **B** but then omitted by **L** or (whether accidentally or deliberately) by Bx.

Passus III

Collation *Fragment* H is present from 123 to 173 and reads with **x** unless noted.

2 (ZAB 2) *Thorw* X&r: a small example of preference for one preposition of agency over another. *R–K* mistakenly see as archetypal ⇒, but the usage is already found at A 1.107, 6.106, B 1.32 and in C's retention at C 2.248 of A 2.166, but with replacement of *for* by *thorw*. In *C*-MF *Wiþ*, correction from a superior *C*-ms seems remote and reminiscence of **B** likelier. *Kynge*: this word, particularly prone to loss of final *-e* (see 3.215 //), could have possessed the disyllabic bye-pronunciation that spellings like *kyingus* Z 2.161 suggest (cf. also *byhyend* Z 3.36 and contrast Z 3.126 // B 3.188). But the dative inflectional *-e* is overwhelmingly probable here to provide the feminine ending. **3 (ZAB 3)** *callede*: the present-tense forms in some

A mss may be wrong reflexes of an ambiguously spelled Ax *callit*. (see 13, II 125 for parallels). *y can* ZAC is presumed original for **B** also, and Bx may have inverted through alliterative attraction to preceding *called, clerk*. **5 (ZAB 5)** *Y shal*: the **r**-variant *I wile* may represent *Ichul* (so V), a possible miscopying of Ax *Ischul* (the substantive **m** form confirmed by **ZBC**) which was mis-resolved as *i(ch) wil(e)*. **6 (ZAB 6)** Either b-half **C** variant may represent Cx, but the form reconstructed here is proposed as the likeliest to have generated both. P^2's exemplar has corrected its **x**-type original from a **p**-type ms like F, a copy that here preserves *to* from its group-original but substitutes for *is* the subjunctive verb-form required for the key-stave on *w* (now mute not full as in **B**). U has for its group original *leuest hire were*, which is close to the **ZAB** reading.

8 (ZAB 8) The random A variants *þe / þis / my / here* may reflect a Ø-reading in Ax. For **B**, α's pl. noun is preferred in the light of **C**, *þis* being a spelling variant of the pl. demonstrative (common in **C**). *þe gilt* **B**-FB may reflect an **A** source. **9 (ZAB 9)** *thenne*: omission in **Z** may be due to the Z-scribe or a sign of draft character (cf. 20). **10 (ZAB 10)** The **B** line is revised in **C** as two, the first of which scans as Type Ia on *m* while the second perhaps echoes from **AB** the grammatical word *by*, used as key-stave in following 11b. The **Z** line, of the rare Type IIa almost exclusive to **L**, contains a redundant b-half suggesting its draft character. **A** revises to Type IIIa with a (semantically unjustified) main stress on *be*, which is retained in **B**, the vowel being presumably long (= *by*) in **A** also. Ka^2 judges *brouȝte* **AB** to be scribal and emends to the harder *mened* on the strength of *B*-F's variant *mente* (omitted from Apparatus), referring to MED s.v. *menen* v. (4), a use illustrated only from C15th. This presupposes that Ax substituted *brouȝte* (thus destroying the metre), that F corrected from outside the Bx tradition, and that B^1 was also in error (**C** retaining *brouhte*). This interpretation is rejected because of its incorrect understanding of **L**'s metre and uneconomical hypothesis of a superior **B** source for F, a copy here showing its habitual tendency to 'regularise' metre. But that **L** remained content to use *by* as a full stave is clear from 11b, and once the authenticity of the Type III structure is recognised the problem becomes non-existent and the solution gratuitous. **13 (ZAB 12)** *worschipede*: the second verb's present-tense forms in **A** and **B** mss may be mistaken resolutions of archetypal spellings with *-et* (the form actually attested in A-H^2) for *-ed*. That each original had contrasted verb-tenses appears likely from the agreement of **Z** and **C**, the latter's *new* first verb (*wendeth*) still having a present tense. **15 (ZAB 14)** *dwelde*: final *-e* is added in **Z** for the required feminine ending (though the terminal *-l* may be syllabic here). Present-tense endings in the **AB** traditions may be aural reflexes of a p.t. ending with *-t*. **16 (ZAB**

15) *And*: a **C** revision or an x^1 smoothing of an archetypal Ø-reading (so *R–K*) misconstrued in **p** as the participle. In **B** the pt. pl. form conjectured is that likeliest to have been corrupted to the ambiguous *conforten* through loss of the central preterite morpheme, before being smoothed to the unambiguous infinitive in Bx (cf. the inverse situation at **Z** 26 compared with // **ABC** below). *B*-HB's smoothings accord with the tense-sequence of their respective verbs in 14 to coincide with **C**. **18 (ZAB 17)** *the*: **Z**'s omission of the article may be a scribal slip or a sign of the text's draft status (cf. Z 2.171 above). **19 (ZB 18)** The identical form of this line in ZC allows that it may be in **Z** a scribal echo of **C**; but it is better judged an original line lost by Ax through homoarchy (*For* occurring at the beginning of the lost line in a different sense) and might well be restored in **A**. If the **Z** line preserves the original, it may be Bx that has varied in the first phrase and by addition of *and*. But since its form is otherwise unexceptionable, and the sense of Ax acceptable as it stands, no emendation to either text is imperative. **20 (ZB 19, A 18)** *and*: the **A** variant *a* (also in *B*-BoCot) may be a mistaken reflex of ?Ax *or*, a substitution for *and* (the error is repeated in *B*-β). Agreement of **ZC** but chiefly superior sense ('ingenuity' and 'strength' being two separate resources) are here decisive in discriminating the **AB** variants. **23 (ZB 22, A 21)** *and* **AB** / Ø **ZC**: retention or omission of the conjunction is a matter of indifference, though the Ø-form attested by **Z** and most **C** mss of both families is arguably harder (cf. *Intro*. IV § 25 above), with *and* then to be presumed as archetypally intruded in (at least) Bx. *coppes* **ZBC**: *pecis* A-**r** could be original if it is scanned 'cognatively' as Type IIa (*k / g*) and if *A*-W is seen as showing ⊗ from **C** or **B** and *m* as a scribal attempt to avoid apparent duplication of sense. But **Z**, unless itself echoing **B** or **C**, supports *coppis* as the supplanted original, being not a 'repetition' (Ka^2) but (with short vowel) specifying small drinking cups or bowls (< OE *cuppe*) as against large, chalice-like vessels (< OF *coupe*: see MED s.v. *cuppe* n). The annominative word-play is characteristic (see Schmidt 1987: 67–75). **24–5 (ZB 23–4, A 22–3)** have been lost by *A*-EM perhaps through eyeskip (*manye > man > mayne*); but on the evidence of A, they could have been in **m**. **29 (ZB 28, A 27); 31 (ZB 30, A 29)** The lines exhibit revision, **Z**'s reading *loke* 28 being replaced by one of uniform sense though variable wording. That **Z** *deureth* 30 is a scribal echo of *dure* at **C** 29b seems unlikely, since it could be an attempt to avoid repeating *lasteth* at 33b (// C 32). On the assumption that **B** is original, **C** here would apparently attest **L**'s readiness to re-use **Z** material rejected in **A** and **B**. **30 (ZB 29, A 28)** *heo þanne*: the word-order adopted here for **A**, only possibly that of **r**, is supported by // **ZB** and gives superior rhythm. The form *heo* is retained as the probable original, making the line of standard type. **C** revision to

Type IIIa is unusual; but for **C**'s replacement of a pronoun with a proper name cf. *Lyare* at 2.234. **31 (ZB 30, A 29)** *ȝow*: adopted in **AB** as the harder reading, **Z** confirming and *B*-L, R being taken to represent respectively β and α. The abrupt transition to direct speech, involving a mixed construction, would account both for the levelling to the indirect in *B*-γMF and Ax (unless *A*-RU alone preserve Ax) and for the deferral of direct address in **C** to the next line. The infinitive *make* without *to* (attested in WN) is adopted for **A** as the form likeliest to account for both the *ȝow / hem* variants in the other **A** mss and for the form with *to* in **B** retained in **C**. **Z** 30's b-half is identical with that of AB I 78/76, where the *equivalent* Z line 22 is of completely different shape, and appears to have been removed in revision. **32–3 (Z 32–3)** A form of these lines appears after A 33 in *A*-WN, a genetic pair with ⊗ from **C**. Though the **Z** lines could also derive from **C**, they are here judged draft material rejected in revising to **A**. Either **L** resorted to his text of **Z** or retained a 'repertory' of lines and passages which he drew on when revising to **C** (see *Intro.* V §§ 29–30 and Appendix Three). *pluralite*: a striking case of the unvoiced labial stop counting as a metrical allophone of |b|. *R–K* (p. 168) adopt F's unique *here bonchef* with the sense 'the prosperity that they [*sc.* the benefices] confer'. But, given **L**'s well-attested licence of 'cognative' alliteration (*Intro.* IV § 46, this must be mistaken 'scribal repair of alliteration'. **34 (ZB 31, A 30)** *atte*: adopted as the likely AxCx reading, of which *at, at þe* appear logical reflexes, and preferred for **C** in the light of **B**. *do*: the secure **ABC** reading (of which *A*-vm may be a phonic reflex) is rejected by *KaK–D* (p. 100) but on inadequate grounds, for it gives much superior sense: Meed is able to facilitate the canon lawyers' promotion, not cause it directly (cf. 66 // below). Possibly Ax read *to don* (as in W) with *do* and *to* being split variants of *r²*, while *r¹* smoothed to Ø. **35 (Z 34, A 31, B 32)** *clerk*: in the light of **C**'s secure text preferred as the substantive Bx reading, *B*-α plural being a scribal slip induced by 34. Loss of the line in *A*-A and agreement of *A*-E with **r** leave it uncertain whether *A*-M here preserves **m** (and thence possibly Ax) or has ⊗ from a *B*-α source. If the former, *A*-**r** and *B*-β would appear scribal attempts to 'correct' *clerk* for one or other reason: failure to discern the internal |l| stave, censorship, objection to the repetition, or wrong perception of a contrast between *ledes* ('people' generally) favoured by Mede and the specific group of *clerkes* of 33 (34). But **Z**'s indefinite *hem*, perhaps echoed by *lede A*-**r**E, is another reason for accepting *lede* in **A**. In **Z** the caesura presumably comes after two-stressed *lówednésse* in a line of Type IIIb. **37 (Z 36, A 33, B 34)** The *absence* from **Z** after 36 of the 57 lines following in **A** (34–89), if due to loss of a leaf in the exemplar, would be evidence of **Z**'s status as a *scribal version* of **A**. That it does not have to result from deliberate omission seems

established from Knott's argument (1915: 393–94), cited *Ka* 56–7. However, **A**'s scene with the friar-confessor (34–52) and the didactic excursus it provokes (53–89) appear to form a self-contained piece of new material added to a source which, taken by itself, shows no obvious discontinuity. This tells not for but *against* mechanical omission of the lines and so against a scribal character for **Z**.

39 (A 35, B 36) Bx *melled þise wordes* is regarded by *K–D* (pp. 105–06) and *Sch¹* as one of several ⇒ of a censoring kind in 36–46. But despite revised **C**'s closeness to **A** in phrasing and choice of adverb, the Bx b-half is not obviously scribal, if less than strictly necessary before 37a. Likewise, **C**'s *myldeliche* could be seen as deliberate avoidance of a lexically restricted verb (see MED s.v. *melen* v.) dropped in the revision of B 3.105, a line (already present in **ZA**) that repeats B 36 entirely. Bx's supposed censorship could have been undone by restoring the verb as well as an adverbial synonym in **C**. But a more plausible motive for **B**'s revising out *loutide* could have been (as when replacing *baudekyn* at A 40) its exaggerated quality (one **C** ms, M, actually adopts *loutede* for *sayde*, doubtless in recollection of **A**). **40 (A 37, B 38)** *bothe*: the revision introduced in **B** disambiguates the scansion that in **A** requires elision: *léiȝe þe þ'ichóne*. It seems unlikely that either **A** variant *alle* or *boþe*, each apparently a dissatisfied response to the rhythmical pattern, is archetypal. **48 (A 45, B 46)** Bx *brocour* is seen by *K–D* (p. 106) as scribal censorship of a reading preserved in G by correction from a source independent of Bx. H's *on hand*, which makes poor sense, could be a visual error for **owen baud* (cf. *erdyn* at 41 above): following *after* indicates that the substantive reading was indeed that of G (and **A**). Both G and H may here, however, show ⊗ from an **A** source and *brocour* be a **B** revision making for greater obliquity of suggestion: cf. the ⇒ at B 41 of *bedeman* for *baudekyn*, a coined derivative of the word in question (see MED s.v. *baudekin* n. (2)). **48–9** transfer B 41–2 (already revised at 43–4), keeping B 42 unchanged. **48 (A 40, B 41); 51 (A 47, B 48)** *ernde; stande*: in the light of agreed **AC**, Bx *message* and *sitten* look like scribal ⇒, and so emendation to *erende* and *stonden* is justified. Unless *B*-H derives from a **B** source distinct from Bx, its right readings will be by ⊗ from an **A** copy (for a back-spelling similar to *erdyn*, cf. the variant *lenede* recorded in the App. at 13.172). **55–67 (A 50–2, B 51–63)** The **B** lines are found only in β, the three α lines corresponding to B 51–4 being unmetrical expansion of A 50–1. This is apparently the only case of either **B** family ancestor showing direct indebtedness to **A**. **66 (B 62)** *ho payede*: adopted by *Sch¹* after *K–D* as the likely **B** original but now rejected, since Bx *and paie* makes good sense and **C** may merely be continuing the detailed revision instanced in preceding 65. **67 (A 52, B 63)** *se:*

preferable on grounds of sense to *seye,* which is presumably a visual error for a similar form of the verb 'to see'. The appearance of *seye* both in sub-archetypes of Bx and Cx (coupled with *se* in C-*p¹*) and in the randomly grouped **A** mss VH, M, W indicates that it was an easy scribal ⇒, perhaps induced by preceding *segge* or the shape of *peynten, purtr*ayen in 66 (62). **70 (B 66)** *worlde:* final *-e* is added for the required feminine ending since, though *rl* could be syllabic, the oblique-case noun in line-final position is likely to have been inflected (cf. 10.48).

B 69–72 No mechanical reason appears for the loss of these lines from FH, and all are present in **A**. A possible explanation is clerical circumspection: the admonition to *alle good folk* B 64 tolerable, but that to *lordes* too provocative.

73 (A 60, B 69) *writyng(es) / werkes:* K–D (p. 81) take **AC** agreement in *writynge(s)* as indicating that Bx *werkes* is a scribal ⇒ of a more general term, the motive being perhaps to avoid a jingle with *writen* in 70. However, since **C** both removes the jingle and restores the (now necessary) reference to *writynges,* furthering a process begun in **B,** objection to Bx as scribal cannot be sustained.

B 71 (A 62) *gyue:* the Bx reading *dele* gives the inauthentic scansion *aa / bb* and suggests a scribal ⇒ of a familiar collocation, in part alliteratively induced. But that *A-m* also reads *dele* allows the possibility that this was the reading of Ax and that any archetypal corruption was rather the ⇒ of *men* for original *gomes* in the a-half of an extended line that would then have scanned as Type IIb. However, agreement of (the genetically unrelated) *A-J* with **m** points to the likelihood that *dele* is of scribal origin, and possibly influenced by awareness of the Bx tradition here. There may be a vestige of B¹ *dele* in revised C 76 *delest.*

75 (A 55, B 73) *hand:* certain for **C,** as is *half* for **B** (where H presumably again shows influence from an **A** source). The evidence for **A** is randomly divided, perhaps because scribes have variously identified the implied nominal referent of the Latin, which omits *manus.* The two terms are fully interchangeable, since *hand* is the subject (as in the Latin) of a verb of knowing (*be war, wite*) not of doing, and associated in **BC** with *syde,* which collocates equally well with either.

B 75 The Bx line's defective *xa / ax* pattern and its omission from H may point to its spuriousness. But transposition of subject and verb gives an acceptable Type IIIa line, the sense of which recalls A 64 and is echoed in revised C 74–75b. Other possible emendations are *comaundeþ* for *bit* or *gomes* for *men* (cf. on B 71 above).

A 65 (B 76) scans defectively in Ax (*aa / xa*), on the showing of **B,** through misdivision from 66. The emendation offered here (to the reading of **B,** but retaining Ax's original verb-complement order) is adopted by *Ka²* without notice.

77–83 (A 65–70, B 76–81) The **C** revision, which at 77 anticipates Mede's request of 115 (// B 87, A 76), recognises the anacoluthic character of the syntax in both earlier versions and normalises accordingly. A 69–75 / B 80–6 are effectively parenthetical, with a very idiomatic resumption of the main sentence at *mayr* A 76 (B 87) taking up *meiris* A 65 (B 76) [suggestion of J.A. Burrow to the editor]. C 78 apparently re-uses Z II 189 along with B 77b to form the new line. **95** *sendeth* **p:** ostensibly less strong than *sende* **x,** which if subjunctive and not indicative specifies the vengeance asked for; but a result-clause reads more smoothly, with *falleth* 97 in elaborative parallel, than a second purpose clause in parallel with *avenge* 93. However, *p¹* has weakened by losing the causal connection between the prayer and the divine use of punishment *on this erthe* (101) as an incentive to repent and so escape punishment *in helle.* **104** *Al this haue:* the first *s*-stave is generated by liaison of *this_háue.* **115 (A 76, B 87)** *a bisowte:* in the light of **CA-r** agreement, Bx*A*-**m** appears a plausible corruption which could have arisen through the scribes' taking the pronominal *a* as intended for *hath,* or perhaps through seeing the repeated subject as redundant and then smoothing to the form with auxiliary and past participle. The line's masculine ending betrays its scribal character and suggests the likelihood of **B** having read as **AC.**

118 (B 90) *And* **p** */ Ø* **x:** the **x**-reading either introduces asyndetically a purpose clause in indirect speech (like *Graunte* at 100 above) or forms the opening of the direct statement by Mede (so *R–K*), with 118a constituting a (dramatically) ironic self-undermining citation. But in // B 91 / A 80 her speech begins with the injunction to 'love' them, and this guides choice of the variant here.

B 95 (A 84) *tolde:* the superficially harder *tok* of *A-r¹* may reflect stylistically-motivated scribal objection to *tolde...telle.*

123 From here to 175 *fragment* H of **C** is present. **124 (A 86, B 97)** *lordes:* secure in **C** and *leodes* unobjectionable in **B.** The variant *men* in four **A** sources may indicate that some scribes found *leodes* lexically difficult or objected to a source-reading *lordes* on grounds of sense (*leodes* Bx could be similarly explained). Presumably *lordes* is meant to cover people like mayors, who would be particularly vulnerable to bribery, and *office* in B 100 may argue for preferring it in **B** too. But while **C** reversion to an **A** reading is unusual, it undoubtedly occurs (cf. note on II 249–52). Retention of Bx challenges the linear postulate (*Intro.* IV § 22), but since Bx meets the acceptability canon, alteration of it to accord with **AC** is better avoided.

A 89 (B 100) *or ȝerisȝiuys: Ka* shows the origin of the *r¹* variant *for here seruice* (retained by *K–F*) in visual confusion of *ȝ* and *s.* The other variants appear individual ⇒ of common synonyms for a harder reading.

125 (A 87, B 98) *forbrenne*: Bx has the inauthentic metrical pattern *aa / bb* and loss of the proclitic intensive, here stressed on the prefix as a stave-word in a Type IIb line, could have been through visual distraction from *fir-* to *for.* **129–30 (Z 40–1, A 93–4, B 104–05)** The tenses of one and perhaps both verbs in **AB** are in contestation. The present is here preferred as probably archetypal, though both past and present are possible resolutions of hypothetical forms spelled with final *-*it* (for *comsit* Ch, *comensit* M, *mellyt* E in the A tradition, see *Ka* Apparatus). Evidence for this spelling as possibly original appears in relict forms such as *thechet* in Z 3.61; see on 2.120 above. However, the tenses of **Z** and (revised) **C** are clearly preterite and so retained. **133 (Z 42, A 95, B 106)** *woman*: accepted in **A** on the showing of agreed **ZBC**. *Ka*'s case (p. 164) for *wy* as the difficult original does not account for all the readings (as claimed). For the presence of a Ø-variant suggests that Ax was probably defective here and that NL (the latter transposing *woman* with *vnwittily*) have corrected independently, though perhaps by reference to a **B** source. **137 (Z 43, A 96, B 107)** The line would scan more smoothly in **B** and **C** if the key-stave were identified as |w| (so **Z** and possibly **A**); but in conjunctive use *þo* is more usual, *whan* being commoner as the interrogative adverb. Both **B** and **C** will scan on |v| (< *þ* / *f*) with four-syllable prelude-dip and possible wrenched stress on *neuére* as at 12.38 (expanding the enclitic pronoun-subject to *thow*). In **C** an alternative but less satisfactory scansion is as an extended Type IIIa, with *For* as stave one. Three **B** and two **C** mss (VN) have *whan*, by ⊗ from an **A** source or by independent correction (presumably on metrical grounds). **139** *a-take þe mowe*: an emendation to correct the metre in the b-half, which has been damaged through inversion to prose order. *R–K*, despite gratuitous and implausible reconstruction of 140–41, leave Cx unemended and 140 with a masculine ending. **140–41** The original is here seen as preserved in **x**, of which 141 is the rare but authentic Type IIa, with evident rhetorical emphasis, and **p**'s *marre þe with myschef* as characteristic scribal padding-out after misdivision of an unusually long line (cf. 15.226), rather than (as *R–K* hold) an authentic half-line omitted by *x¹* with subsequential smoothing (see further *Intro.* II § 130). *as an ancre*: unconvincingly rejected as a scribal gloss by Carnegy (1934:12–13) but defended by Mitchell (1939:486–8). It is necessary on grounds of metre (the line otherwise has a masculine ending) and of sense: without the mitigation of enclosure in an *anchorhold*, there could hardly *be* a 'wel wors woen' than (imprisonment in) Corf Castle. **146 (Z 47, A 100, B 111)** *to wyue*: R (? = α) preserves what is probably also the authentic Bx form, giving good balance with *haue*, and should be preferred in the text. **147–48 (Z 48–9, A 101–02, B 112–13)** The **C** reading in 147 is certain and identical with that of **Z** and *B*-R

but conflicts with *B*-βF and Ax. Whether or not repeated *ellis* was a revision of **Z** in **A**, objection to it occurs in Bx which, however, seems secure in the light of C 148 (supported by **Z**). In 112 *B*-F may have coincidentally varied with β or show ⊗ from an **A** source, or else *B*-R may be itself an independent correction from **C**. There is no intrinsic objection to *ellis* in A 101, such cases of 'identical-rhyme' occurring elsewhere, e. g. at Z Pr 69 / 70, **B** Pr 127 / 8, 1.146 / 47, 7.36 / 7 and Appendix I, 5.ii.b). But Bx *soone* 113 is emended, despite support from one family in // A 102, since **m** (here accompanied by V) may in this case have ⊗ from a **B** source. In B 112, by contrast, it seems preferable on balance to see *B*-R as representing α and thence Bx, with β a (perhaps unconscious) variation to an associated parallel locution. **149 (Z 50, A 103, B 114)** *Thenne* **ZAC**: accepted as the probable reading for **B**, Bx having inserted *And* and GH having deleted it by reference to **A** (though G, unusually, re-inserts the connective). **152 (Z 53, A 106, B 117)** *What / To wite what*: the elliptical form of the question understood in *loutide*, here identified as original, is spelled out in **p**, Bx and variously in a few **A** mss. But the *C*-xAx reading, shared by **Z**, appears intrinsically harder. **153 (Z 54, A 107, B 118)** The **p** reading *maide* (so *R–K*) seems closer to **AB**(**Z**) *womman* (*lady*) but the tone of the unceremonious *Mede* **x** is more in keeping with the King's attitude as shown at 142–43 above. His plan is to make an honest woman of Mede by marrying her to Conscience, change of name (143) perhaps bringing change of nature. *quod þe Kyng* **B** (Ø **ZAC**): possibly a Bx intrusion, omitted in G (presumably following an **A** source); but it could have been added in **B** and deleted again in **C** as one of various (small) revisions in 153–54. **154 (Z 55, A 108, B 119)** *and*: omission in **AB** may be authorial or archetypally scribal; but **Z** need not here show ⊗ from **C**, since the intrusion could have been mechanically induced from **Z**'s *ant* (for *yf*) in 54 above. **158 (Z 59, A 112, B 123)** Of the **A** variants *She* **r** / *And* **m** either is acceptable and either may be an attempt to fill in a Ø-original. Alternatively, **m** may be a scribal reflex of Ax *a or ⊗ from a **B** source. **159 (Z 60, A 113, B 124)** *In trist; (s)he* **CZA**: identified as the likely original readings for **B**, from which Bx will have omitted *In* with subsequent smoothing (omission of *she*). G's ancestor presumably inserted *In* after **A** but left the verb as in Bx, while F's *she* (in the b-half) is only coincidentally correct, being part of a wider re-writing of a type characteristic of this ms. *teneth* **CZA**: here judged the probable **B** original replaced in Bx by a more explicit verb through alliterative suggestion from preceding stave-words in *tr-* and the general context of allusion to betrayal (esp. of a king in 127), or by memorial ⊗ from B1.70. The scribal character of Bx is indicated by its abruptness in introducing a new grammatical subject for a verb that in **ZAC** parallels one preceding and two following with Mede as subject (*B*-H is presumably ⇒ of a near-synonym for Bx *treieþ*). **161 (Z 62, A 115, B 126)** *lereth*: confusion of tense in *r¹* resulting from mis-resolution of an **r** form spelled like M's *lernyt, louet* (cf. on 129–30 above). **163 (Z 64, A 117, B 128)** The verb-tenses are clear in **Z** (present) and **C** (past; present) but contested in **AB**. Confusion may have arisen because of the variation in tenses betweeen the two verbs, correctly preserved in **C**. The past (preterite in **A**, perfect in **BC**) is preferable for the first, the present for the second: Mede once poisoned popes but continues to harm the Church. This distinction, which appears a revision of **Z**'s draft original (unless *-th* in *Poyseneth* is there meant to represent a preterite *-t*), is lost in *A-r¹*, *B-βF* but correctly preserved in *B*-R, **C** and *A-r²***m**. **165 (Z 66, A 119, B 130)** *and²*: the several attempts of *B*-FC-**p** (*alle*), and of *B*-β plus a random group of **A** mss (*in*) to correct a supposed logical error miss the general sense of the half-line: 'anywhere, even if one were to look throughout the world'. Either *and* is a co-ordinating conjunction in an ellipsis for 'between heaven and hell and [between hell and] earth' or it is being used as a separable part of the conjunctive adverbial phrase *and thogh* 'even if / even though' (MED s.v. *and* conj. 5(b) gives examples which, though C15th, have just the sense required here). If *B*-F's sophistication *þey men al erthe* is judged to show ⊗, it must have been from a **C** source of **p**-type. **167 (Z 68, A 121, B 132)** *þe*: preferred on the showing of **ZAC** as probably original against *a* Bx (GH presumably deriving from an **A** source). *knaues....alle* **ZAC**: the Bx b-half, acceptable enough in itself, seems scribal in the light of **ZAC** agreement, being over-specific in its mention of *walking* and missing the force of *alle*. **171 (Z 72, A 124, B 135)** *nere*: the contracted colloquial form giving better rhythm and likely to be original in all versions. **173 (Z 73, A 126, B 137)** *She*: presumed Ax *And* could have been a misreading of the exemplar's *A* 'She'; cf. on 181 below. *and*: presumed lost from *C*-**xZ** through alliterative attraction (cf. Z 79, 86, 105 below). **175 (Z 75, A 128, B 139)** *fle*: the Cx reading *and fle* appears also in some **A** mss and in *B*-F (possibly from an **A** or a **C** source). The prepositionless infinitive or (elliptical) 3rd person subjunctive is the hardest reading and seems the likeliest original, so Cx may be emended to read with **ZAB**. **176 (Z 76, A 129, B 140)** *And*: adopted for **A** in the light of **BC**, though both *And* **m** and *Sche* **r** may be scribal resolutions of Ax **A*, or smoothings of Ø (as in **Z**). *Treuthe*: the personified form is contextually more vivid, assigning to False's earthly opposite the same name as his heavenly one, as at 191 // below (and cf. also 14.209, 212, with similar sense). The variant *þe trewe* is perhaps induced by a wish to achieve parallelism with *þe fals* or to avoid confusion with *Treuthe* having the referent 'God'. *teieth:* the **m** variant *fetteres* gives a Type IIb line, but if **r** is not original this could be a scribal reflex of

Ax **tethereth*, as in **Z**. In the **C** tradition the correct reading is that of **p** which, unusually, appears to have been adopted into ms X from a **p**-source over an erased reading **techeth hym f[a]l[s]te*. Clearly wrong on grounds of sense, this appears a visual error also underlying D's weak attempt at correction. **177 (Z 77, A 130, B 141)** *harmede*: in the light of **ZAC** agreement, Bx *harm dide* (so *A*-EH) may be diagnosed either as a scribal ⇒ to achieve greater emphasis, or as a visual reflex of the exemplar's **harmedede* (with erroneously duplicated preterite morpheme). **180 (Z 80, A 133, B 144)** The Ax reading is clearly *as,* but **ZC** agreement might indicate that **A** also read *thus* (so *A*-JN) and Bx made the same ⇒; or *as* could be a minor revision and right for **A** and **B** (so also *C*-P²M). **181 (Z 81, A 134, B 145)** *He(o)*: **ZAC** provide a firm basis for rejecting *And* (?Bx, unless F = α) as a scribal error for the form **A* presumed in the exemplar. *ones*: 'on a single occasion (in a month)' (cf. 21.391), more arresting and more probably original than *one* 'in a single month (as compared with four months)'. See MED s.v. *ones* adv. 1(a). **183 (Z 83, A 136, B 147)** *Heo* CA is likely to represent also the **B** original, with Bx having anticipated *For* in 148 (the same mechanism accounting for **Z**). It may be, however, that both the **Z** and Bx scribes were offering an *explanation*: Mede's privy access to the Pope gives her greater power than the King's privy seal. **184 (Z 84, A 137, B 148)** *For / Sire / For Sire:* all three are acceptable and **ZC** agreement here could be coincidental. The connective may however have been lost from Ax and it improves the sense by giving a reason for the provisors' knowledge. **185 (Z 85, A 138, B 149)** *thow*: the *A*-W spelling (*þif*), showing þ / ʒ confusion, helps to explain the error *ʒif* in several **A** mss. **186 (Z 86, A 139, B 150)** *prouendreth*: clearly attested in **ZC** and the extant **B** family, and also the probable reading of Ax. The verbal form *Prouendris* in *A*-H²RHE and *B*-C could well explain how **r**'s error arose: through mistaking a verbal sg. for a form of the nominal plural. **187 (Z 87, A 140, B 151)** Agreement of **AC** in the harder reading *holde* suggests that *haue* Bx is a scribal error, perhaps the result of misreading an exemplar form *halde* as *habbe* (the actual **Z** form, which could be scribal or original here), and of unconscious suggestion from the phrase *to have and to hold*. **188 (Z 88, A 141, B 152)** *bringeth*: **ZC** agreement points to the finite form of this verb (the fourth in a succession of such verbs) as original in all versions. Ax and Bx will have then varied towards the easier sense with an infinitive (or possibly an elliptical indicative pl. with understood subject 'they'). The latter would make the priests (or their concubines) and not Mede the implied subject of the verb. But while good literal sense, this is less striking than to make Mede, herself accused of bastardy at 2.24, the metaphorical parent of the clerical bastards (the Latin C 188*a* will allow either reading, the pl.

matres perhaps favouring the former). The minority of **A** and **B** mss with *bryngeth* are less likely to preserve Ax and Bx than to be independent recognitions of the correct sense. **191 (Z 90, A 143, B 154)** *falleth ryght ofte* **Z** makes good sense; if *ryght* is an adverb, then *falleth* = 'falls'; if a noun 'justice', *falleth* = 'fells' (see MED s.vv.). **192 (Z 92, A 145, B 155)** *þe* αC / *youre* **Z?A**B-β: possibly *A*-M preserves **m** (<Ax) and thence **A**, and **Z**A-r*B*-β have each substituted a more emphatic reading. **193 (Z 93, A 146, B 156)** *hym þe gate*: the only reading commanding assent on intrinsic grounds. The seven major **A** variants (including Ø) suggest a lacuna in **r** that the group-ancestors and individual mss variously tried to fill (t possibly, U clearly from 143b); Ax will then have been preserved only in **m**, as support from **Z** also indicates. But if **m** was also defective, its gap may have been filled from a **B** source, as occasionally elsewhere. **197 (Z 95, A 149, B 160)** *mote*: the absolute use of the verb appears original from secure **ZAC** agreement. GF have presumably corrected by reference to an **A** source, Bx to have missed the construction and H to have smoothed further.

Z 96 is a unique line, apparently authentic on grounds of metre and meaning, but omitted in **A** perhaps because of redundancy. Only the b-half adds anything (and that not quite apt to a *mene man* in **L**'s sense) while the main point is made again in 98. **198 (Z 97, A 150, B 161)** *ende*: the reading also for **Z**, where *hynde* with an intruded aspirate and raised *y* for *e* is unlikely to represent the adj. *hende*. The verb's *-n* ending (after eQK) is perhaps what helped to generate the **x** error. **199 (Z 98, A 151, B 162)** *he*: the sex of 'Lawe' may be masculine or feminine. Ax could well have been the latter, and *he* is also an ambiguous spelling in the **C** tradition (as at Z 99, 100). But given the habitual association of justices and barristers with the legal process, the masculine form is preferable (cf. 4.144 below). **200 (Z 91, A 144, B 163)** *in* / *to*: in **A** perhaps split variants of Ax *into* (so **Z**). **212** *lereth*: preferable to the more obvious *ledeth* in a context concerned with the corruption of the learned (*clerkes* 210, *witt* 211, and cf. *maister* 214). **213 (Z 103, A 155, B 168)** The first *hem* seems to have been lost from Ax, but the second *hem* may be an Ax error and *þei* a scribal ⇒ of the advancing form of the (nominative) pronoun (anticipating *þei* in **B**). **Z**'s *hey* is taken to reflect a presumed original *hy*, which is adopted here for **A**.

Z 108–11 *the*: accidentally lost, in 108 for no clear reason, in 109 through assimilation to preceding *-eth. schewen*: an acceptable contextual sense is 'proclaim' (MED s.v. *sheuen* v. 7 (c)), but this seems less appropriate than 'say' since Mede has not yet replied to Conscience. **111** *ʒe*: ms **Z**'s reading presumably results from confusion of *þ* with *ʒ* in the exemplar and scribal inattention to contextual sense. **222 (Z 112, A 164, B 177)** is unmistakably of Type IIIa

in all four versions. *K–D* (p. 205n), rejecting this pattern as inauthentic, emend **B** to *most* on the basis of the **A** mss HL, which normalise to *aa / ax* (though *Ka²* inconsistently leaves **A** unemended, as do *R–K* **C**). The textual evidence the Athlone editors ignore serves to invalidate their theory of **L**'s metrical types, as their discrepant handling of **A** and **C** tacitly concedes. **225 (Z 115, A 167, B 180)** *weye*: unless **Z** here shows ⊗ from **C**, this will be a first form revised successively in **A** and **B**, to which **C** returned. Neither of the former is however suspect as scribal on the usual grounds. *gabbe*: not an especially difficult word (MED s.v. has many citations); but it may have been glossed in Ax's exemplar and the gloss copied in its place, or else *leiʒe* may be Ax ⇒ of a more explicit verb (*A*-H²'s late correction is presumably from a **B** or a **C** source). Although **Z** could be here echoing **C**, as with *weye*, there are no grounds for rejecting *gabbe* in **B** (as do *K–D*).

Z 122–24 These three unique lines appear authentic. The idiom of 122b recurs at Z 4.59 //, 124b repeats Z 2.173b (and was perhaps removed in **A** for that reason).

B 190 (Z 128, A 177) *hym*: omission in **Z** gives the verb the sense 'were ashamed', lexically possible (see MED s.v. *shamen* v.1a (a)) and so accepted by *R–B*. But the key issue in all versions seems to be the effect of the two antagonists' actions upon the King, so *hym* is supplied here as needed for the sense.

A 185–8 (Z 136–38, B 198–200) Difficulty over sg. and pl. pronoun referents begins with the contested reading at A 185, where ?**m**, if it does not itself show ⊗ from **B**, may preserve (with inversion) the true reading corrupted in **r**. The source of the error would have been *þ* / *ʒ* (or *y*) confusion in *mery(ʒ)e*, read as *merþe* in **r**. Loss of *men* in **r** would have come through assimilation to following *mer-* and smoothing of the damaged reading to *hym* would have ensued. While A 186–87 is more easily read with a sg. or a pl. throughout, the whole referring to the king or to his men, the sudden change of referent at 186 (or 185), supported by **ZB** and here adopted, is more difficult and not untypical of **L**.

241 *þe Kyng*: possibly a Cx intrusion which produces an excessively heavy (five-syllable) pre-final dip; smoother would be an elliptical original without an object or reading simply *hym* or Ø for *þe...kyng*. In any case, it might be better to omit *to*. **244** *conquered*: the past participle in agreement with the pronoun subject as the hardest may be the likeliest original. The **p** reading makes explicit while **x**, correctly resolved by D, attempts to rationalise the sense but without taking in (from *Hit* 245) that the grammatical subject's referent is the territory and not the conqueror. **252** *thermyd*: the probable original, substituted by a few **p**-group copies for Cx *therwith*, illustrating loss of the lexically recessive stave-word to the advancing (but here unmetrical) form also found elsewhere in the text (see 5.135 and Apparatus). For other instances of *thermyd* in stave-position see 9.270, B 15.316, A 2.37 and 7.212. **261 (Z 143, A 192, B 205)** *Ye* **Z**: if this and not *3a* was the Ax form of the exclamation, **r** could have lost it through quasi-haplography induced by initial *þ* / *ȝ* confusion. Unless the same error occurred in Bx, **B**'s deletion was retained in **C**. The idiom is instanced at 11.155, 314; 16.137. **262 (Z 144, A 193, B 206)** *Vnconnyngliche*: the harder reading and probably that of Cx, since shared by the sub-group *p²* (G's *Vnwisly*, to which N's *Vnconnabelyche* should be added, is evidently a reflex of it). *conseyledest*: **Z**'s omission of the preterite tense-morpheme must be scribal, since the accusation refers to an act now completed; cf. Z 4.34 for a similar case. **265 (A 197, B 210)** *men mede* **AC**: adopted for **B** as a slightly harder reading that Bx (like *A*-VH) replaces with one bringing the relative pronoun into direct conjunction with its antecedent. **266 (A 198, B 211)** *and to*: reconstructed for Ax from what appear split variants in the light of Bx*C*-**x**, presuming *and* lost by attraction of *To* > *to alle*. **267 (A 199, B 212)** *be byloued*: giving an awkwardly long four-syllable dip in the a-half when compared with **B** (the line is Type Ie). Possibly *be* is Cx dittography following *be* / *by* in its exemplar (*R*–*K* omit, after P²uP (which lack *be*). **269 (A 201, B 214)** *ȝerne* / *renne*: there is no sense-difference contextually but *B*-α's rarer form seems likelier to represent Bx than does β, which scans *aa* / *bb* like Ax. The verb-form *ȝerne* also preserved in *C*-**x** is thus to be seen as the probable **A** original, too, and *A*-M's corrupt reading *Þei desiryt* interpreted as a scribal synonym for a word misread as its homonym *ȝerne* 'desire'. **272** The Cx line scans *aa* / *xx* yet appears to reflect an attempted revision of the vapid **AB** b-half (adopted by *R*–*K*), which scans as Type Ib. The last lift sounds authentic, though the construction *mede thei asken* / *And taken mede* may suggest that the problematic third stave in 272 is unlikely to have been also *mede*. To scan, this would require a preceding liaisonal stave on *seruantes_for*, theoretically giving Type IIa, but with an inferior stress-pattern and a weak anticipation of 273a. The conjectured stave-word *salarie* occurs, significantly collocated on both occasions with *seruauntes*, at 7.39 and B 14.142 (so also at *RRe* IV 46). It was unusual enough to have invited ⇒ under inducement from the form of 275b and the many local occurrences of *mede*, one of which might well have been inserted *parentrelinarie* as a gloss. (On the lexical distribution of *salarie* see MED s.v.; the main C14th appearances are in **L**). **276 (A 209, B 222)** *kenne clerkes* **B**: the form of the a-half in Bx appears corrupt in the light of agreed **AC**. The verb *kenne* was found difficult by the *C*-**p** scribe as by some **A** scribes and *A*-M's reading very probably shows direct ⊗ from a **B** source (though in the absence of A it is not certain if this represents **m**, E reading here with *r¹*). The form of the adverb in *C*-**p** could be tentatively

reconstructed from the variants as *herfore 'for this', a form which might have been that of Cx (cf. *of hem* in // **AB**) or a ⇒ for the Cx form here accepted as preserved in **x**. **277–78 (A 210–11, B 223–24)** The form of Bx, with a Type IIa line in 223, is not obviously unoriginal (although the position of the caesura is untypical) and may seem to confirm the *A*-**m** form of 211 against *A*-**r** as the reading of Ax. However, **C** evidently agrees with **r** both in the form and in the sense of 278 (277b is revised from **B**) and this suggests that the Bx form is here scribal and that **m** may have ⊗ from a post-Bx source. The *A*-**r** form is therefore preferred here as likelier to have been also that of **B**. Having perhaps already undergone misdivision in Bx's immediate exemplar, it would have invited expansion of 224 by the Bx scribe. The new phrase *at...tymes* seems over-explicit and the rhythm of the b-half uncharacteristic. *A*-**r**'s *alse* is accepted in the light of synonymous *bothe* **C** as a likely reading for the last lift in **B**. **279 (A 212, B 225)** *prentis*: the aphetic form adopted here on the evidence of both **p** and Ax, giving a single feminine ending as in the other versions. Grammatically it is either a plural with assimilated *-es* or a collective singular. **280 (A 213, B 226)** *Marchaundise* **AC**: the probable **B** reading for which Bx will have substituted the concrete pl. noun, perhaps through visual error induced by supposing parallelism with *preestes*, *men* (223, 225); H will have its reading from an **A** source. The line could be T-type, but is better stressed on *nede* to rhyme internally with *mede* and (in **C**) anticipate internally rhyming *lede*.

B 241 scans in Bx as Type IIIa with four-syllable prelude-dip, though the a-half may have inverted noun and verb to prose order under inducement from the b-half. **311 (A 233a, B 254a)** *recipiunt*: the present-tense form, evidently that of Cx, understood as a deliberate alteration of the familiar scriptural text, to which three sources (RM) (QFS) (P²) have severally 'corrected'.

A 234 (B 255) The variants divide between *louȝ* and *lewed* in both traditions of each version, and *Ka²*'s diagnosis (p. 461) of split variation induced by virtual dittography of *low lewed* can be invoked twice just as appropriately as once. Alternatively, but less persuasively, one of the variants is right and the lost stave-word to be identified as a harder synonym of *folk* (*lede*, not instanced in any copy) or of *taken* (*lacchen*, actually substituted by the scribe of *A*-N).

319 *desauowe*: X's mistaken *desalowe* may be coincidental or result from comparison of its source with a **p**-type ms like QFS, and the same error may have been made in U before erasure and re-correction. A possible motive for X's alteration might have been scribal censorship of the notion that king, emperor or pope could break a 'vow'. **321** *hy...of*: the reflexes preserved in the readings of **p** and **x** are taken to be split variants of the Type Ic line here reconstructed as the probable reading of Cx (*hi* is the actual form of the pronoun in N). **328** *si ne*: the **p**-reading *synne*, which gives the implied sense 'without a qualifying clause "subject to not sinning"' would be acceptable, but looks like scribal smoothing of archetypal '*si* ne' (or '*sin* ne'), each a harder reading, with its elliptical use of Latin. The likeliest form of **x** is *sine* but the version in I (and probably Y and U), adopted by *Pe,* is the clearest and comes closest to the probable original, yielding the sense: '*if* you act justly [*ryhte* 324] you will enjoy divine favour'. The line scans as an extended Type IIIa with double counterpoint (*sgg / sg*) and *R–K*'s conjecture *grace* for *thing* is otiose. **329** *cesar*: the line reads unmetrically as *aa / xx* in all mss and is so left by *R–K*. But the variant *so may* YIU could preserve an archetypal form *rihte so sothly, so may,* in which each *so* had a distinct sense ('in this way' and 'also') and which would obviate the need for emendation. On the other hand, *so may* could be merely a scribal attempt to supply an extra stave-word in the a-half. The more drastic conjecture proposed here requires a form *cesar* elsewhere attested in stave-position (e.g. at B 1.51), gives superior rhythm and arguably collocates more aptly here with *pope* than does *kyng*. A reason for its loss would have been association of the *c*-form (instanced at B I 51) exclusively with the pagan ruler in the Gospels rather than the contemporary Holy Roman Emperor. The latter was usually *kayser*, as at 318, 322 above, and the form with |s| was used mainly as a titular name of the former (see MED s.v. *cesar* n). **335** *As:* seems more expected, introducing the comparison, and *ac* may have come in from a*cordaunce* 336. *Ac* is read by *R–K* as the ms and archetypal reading, giving a half-line identical with 393a, and is defended by Carlson 1991. It could arguably answer to the scholastic *Sed* '(But) now', introducing a middle premiss; but the syllogism would be left with no conclusion. So it might seem better to take **L** to have meant not the conjunction but the comparative adverb seen at 360b, since 360–1 echo, gloss and explain 335–6. **347** The undeniably awkward syntax of **x** may accurately reflect a Cx reading that was misunderstood by **p**; but a better parallel between the simile-example and the larger grammatical trope emerges if *beleueth* is read as 'remains' not as 'believes' (see MED s.v. *bileven* v. 3(b)). In 349 *To pay* is then to be read as an ellipsis, a verb '(and) expects (him)' being understood before it. **351** *hol*: the variant *holy* **x** looks like scribal over-emphasis consequent on failure to grasp that *hol herte = cor integrum*, the condition of *treuthe* in the righteous man. **364** *cause*: the context points to *cause* 'reasonable grounds' as the certain Cx reading. *Sk*'s and *R–K*'s preference for *case* is not supported by the summarising lines 370–71, which specify only two out of the three grammatical categories. **365** *and²*: evidently the reading of Cx, though possibly **C** read Ø, to which *Pe*'s emendation *to*] *and* would closely answer (cf. the simple infinitive *stande* at 245). **366** *sire²*:

presumed lost from **x** by haplography rather than added to **p** by dittography or deliberate correction. It derives from *sur* (< Lat *super*) where *syre* (n.) is from OF *seior* (< Lat *senior*). MED gives *sirename* as compound s.v. *sire* n. 3 but cites the present passage under *surname* n. (b), and the spellings here suggest that the two were probably not distinguished. **L** himself may have intended a pun while aware that *sire²* is but a spelling variant of *sur* (or *sor*) and not etymologically linked with *syre¹*. The context in any case clearly requires that it is not the father's personal or *kynde name* (10.69) but his family name that is in question. **368** *worliche*: evidently a pronunciation-spelling of a word that most copies give as *worldlich* 'human, of this world' (*Sk*) not of *worthli(ch)* 'excellent', as taken by P² and *Pe* (see OED s.v. *Worldly* a. (2), MED s.v. *worldli* a. 2(b), citing this passage). This sense is confirmed beyond doubt by 369, which refers to the bad as well as the good qualities of the speaker's natural offspring; cf. also *wordliche* 10.91, with loss of *l* but retention of the stop. **380–81** Both alternative pairs of readings make sense but *mere; lordes* seems contextually more apt than *myre; londes*. The word *mere* could mean either 'boundary' (MED s.v. 2a), such as a path or embankment, or 'lake, pool' (MED s.v. 2). Arguably an expanse of water between adjacent estates would have greater need of a single visible marker and fits better as a metaphorical image for the property to which two parties make claim. **387** *relatifs*: **x** here appears to have substituted *relacyounes* for the more apt *relatifs* under inducement from the contextually dominant set-phrase *relacyoun* (*indi*) *rect*. **394** scans very awkwardly with *in²* as key-stave, and *gendre* could be an intruded scribal gloss for *kynde*. In the text for *acordaunde* it would be preferable to read *acordaunce,* the better as it is the archetypal reading. (In C-App. for first entry *read instead*: acordaunce] Y&r (acorde E); acordaunde XP²). **396** The needed third stave on |m| is provided by wrenched stress on *wymmén*. **403** *is man*: I's variant *is he man*, adopted by *Pe*, is rejected in the light of the general sense of the passage, which refers to man, not Christ (see *Commentary* further).

 A 239 (B 260) Both archetypes lack a stave-word on |v| in the b-half. *Ka²* following *K–D* p. 205n proposes *þat* as the first stave-word on the basis of *A*-vW, to produce a line scanning as Type IIa. But no plausible reason appears for the replacement of *þat* by *þe* in the other **A** mss, and it is more natural to suppose *þat* a reflex of the phrase *whi þat* 'why'. *Þat* would then arguably be metrically non-significant, and it could hardly be a demonstrative referring emphatically to a vengeance not yet specified (the expected *þe* is what both archetypes read). The more drastic emendation here proposed is the adjective *fel* in post-nominal position, presumed lost through haplography in Ax and Bx. The play on this homophone (here also a homograph) and the mechanism of loss are of the simplest (a similar case is conjectured for the CxBx readings at 6.155 // 5.171, *q.v.*; and for a parallel cf. the omission of *beste* by C-YA from the phrase *beste bestes* at 426 below). **412** *aftur Ruth* **x**: a hard and contextually apt reading, with **p**'s *rew(e)th* is a mere spelling-variant. *R–K*'s emendation *of þe reuthe* is doubly phantasmal in this regard. **415 (A 242, B 263)** *derfly*: lexically the harder, as *delfulliche* is stylistically the more emphatic reading. The base form of the latter is collocated with *deth* at B 15.521, which **p** may here be recalling, though the phrase is quasi-formulaic.

A 243 The omission from **BC** of this line (specifying the reason for the Amalekites' punishment) is not sufficient reason for suspecting it to be a piece of scribal elaboration of *eldren* 242. However, the cause of its absence from ?r^l is not clear; presumably it will have been added to R from a ms of r^2 type, since d and ∪ do not have an exclusive common ancestor allowing R alone to represent r^l here. **417 (A 245, B 265)** *To*: adopted into **B** on the strength of **AC** agreement. Bx may have added *Thee* to its (Ø) source-reading and *B*-Hm(OC^2) have independently substituted *to*. *bone* **p**: not strictly necessary on metrical grounds, since the line could scan as Type IIa like // **B**, but obviously preferable on grounds of sense to *loue*, which could be a visual error for *lore* or for *bone*.

B 267 (A 250) *Bernes*: in the light of **B** the minority **A** reading is adopted as the honorific word for 'men', which stands at the opposite end of the scale from *bestis*. It is unlikely that a synonym for *Children* 247 would be introduced again so soon. **421** *Mebles* **p**: *That dwelleth in Amalek* appears to be a gloss on the previous line mistakenly included in the text by the scribe of x^l. **423 (B 269b, 271a)** The **C** line, which recomposes two **B** half-lines, here scans as an expanded Type IIIa with counterpoint (*abb / ab*). The somewhat awkward Bx 271, which seems to scan on grammatical words (*For*^{1,2}; *þow*) may be corrupt. If the stave-sound in original B 271 was |m|, the key-stave could have been *man*, a word vulnerable to loss through assimilation to preceding *monee*, or else one such as *moste* for *loke*; but given the uncertainty, emendation is best avoided. In C 423–24 there may be split variation from Cx, **p** correctly retaining *spille* in 423b but omitting the first lift of 424, while **x** omitted the translineating *s*-stave but kept the (presumably repeated) *Spille* in 424. Each of the Cx sub-archetypes would thus exhibit translinear haplography, and Cx might be reconstructed to read *al that thow myhte spille / Spille hit*, giving two Type Ia lines. This possibility notwithstanding, the form of Bx 272, though itself open to doubt, points to **x**'s unusual (but authentic) metrical pattern as more probably retaining the form of the revised original. *R–K* insert *fynde* after *myhte*, but this reconstruction from **B** is unnecessary. **427** *and...by*: **x**, though syntactically somewhat elliptical, is acceptable if *warnede* is taken in close conjunction with *wolde* read as a full lexical verb. It probably

preserves Cx, the syntax of **p** showing signs of smoothing here. The sense is: 'in a manner other than God wished, and other than He had warned him [to do] through S.' **429 (A 255, B 277)** *seed*: the Cx line scans *aab / ba*, an extended and counterpointed variant of the *ab / ba* form avoided by **L** (or, with a liaisonal *s*-stave, *his_for*). But insertion of *seed* is warranted on the showing of **AB**. It is unlikely to be a revision distinguishing between Saul's family and his posterity (see 431) but could easily have been lost in Cx through distraction from *sayde* in 428a above. **430 (A 256, B 278)** *Saul* Bx, which seems unnecessary for the sense and weakens the force of the clashing stresses in cross-caesural pararhyme, could be a scribal insertion; but its presence in revised C 430 cautions against emendation here. **432 (A 258, B 280)** *culorum*: presumably pronounced *clôrum* to provide a first lift without wrenching of the stress. *cas*: the three substantive and the Ø variants in the **A** tradition may be due to **r**'s having had a lacuna; but *cas* could be a conjecture in ChN and in **m** preserve Ax or be a borrowing from **B**. **433 (A 259, B 281)** The line probably scans on *n* with first stave and key-stave liaisonal (*An auntur; noen ende*), though it could equally be vocalic, with the second stave muted. Bx *men* might easily have arisen through anticipating *noon* or from misapprehension of the sense; it is clear from 434–35 // that the speaker fears danger to himself, not displeasure to his audience. Emendation is on the joint witness of **AC**. **435 (B 283)** *sothest*: the Bx reading *sothes* is acceptable in itself but weaker than that of **C**, with its ironically balanced superlatives; loss of *-t* could have been induced by *-es* > < *is* attraction. *R–K*'s adoption of **B** destroys one of **L**'s local improvements. *B*-WG's appear to be individual corrections possibly made in knowledge of **C**. **436 (A 260, B 284)** *Wit me*: though the Ax reading could have been *wit it me* or *wit me it*, of which *wit me / it me* could be diagnosed as split variants, the joint witness of *A-r*^{2} and **m** tells against this. A reading including both *wit* and *it* lies behind that of Bx; but agreement of **C** and (probably) **A** seems to justify omitting *it* also from **B**. **441 (A 265, B 289)** *vs*: the Bx reading *hem* is unacceptable on grounds of sense, unless it has the remote referent *reumes* 285, since the immediate one it repeats (288) denotes enemies. *A*-**m** could here show ⊗ from a **B** source, and agreement of *A*-**r** (? = Ax) and **C** indicates that *vs* was also in **B** and Bx a ⇒ of *hem* through inducement from preceding 288 and inattention to the sense. **444 (B 292)** *trewe men:* reconstruction of **B** in the light of **C** is needed to emend the unmetrical Bx line (*aa / xx*), into the b-half of which the familiar *trupe* has come through probable inducement from 293 (cf. C 456 below). **445 (B 293)** *treuthe*: should be capitalised as a personification (cf. 139). Its referent is implied by // **B** to be 'God', although in **C** it could be simply the quality. **446 (A 269, B 294)** *no lif*: though *A*-**m** and W could here show ⊗ from a **B** source, they may equally preserve Ax, **r** having misunderstood the line through unconscious association of *lif* with *lese* in contexts involving the administration of justice. This would have occurred more easily if Ax had read *no lif* for *and no lif*, a reading which would account for the variation *and / or* between the **A** mss. But the sense of A 270 makes clear that *lif* here = 'person' and is meant to stand in contrast with *Seriaunt*, so that there is no reason for doubting that **A** itself read the same as **BC**. **447 (A 270, B 295)** *þat:* the probable Bx reading *here* is not objectionable in itself but is rejected in the light of **A?C** *þat* as likely to be a more explicit scribal ⇒. The **C** variants may however suggest that the reading was Ø in both Bx and in B[1]. **448 (B 296)** *paueloun / cloke*: against *K–DSch*, *cloke* is not here regarded as scribal, but *paueloun* **C** is taken as an alteration of **B** from a Type IIIa into a Type Ia line, a common feature of the revision (cf. B 3.10, 229, B 4.59). **449 (A 272, B 297)** *euel*: required by the sense in **C** if an uncharacteristically flat assertion is to be avoided; it will have been lost from y through partial haplography of *euel* after *Muche*l, to the precise form of which the omission affords oblique testimony. **450 (A 273, B 298)** *lordeþ* **B**: the Bx line has the inauthentic pattern *aa / bb* and to emend it *K–D* (p. 195) propose *ledeþ* as the stave-word supplanted by *ruleþ* (so *Sch*). But *ledeþ* is not lexically difficult, as would be *lordeþ*, offered as an alternative conjecture here. This word is instanced transitively in Chaucer (*Complaint of Mars* 166) and is found in intransitive use at 11.69 //, the first recorded appearance (see MED s.v. *lorden* v.). Its rarity, together with presumed scribal objection to the adnominative repetition of *lorde(s)*, a characteristic feature, would account for the ⇒. *letteth*: a subject *a* 'she' is to be understood, with *Mede* not *euel* as the referent. **454 (B 302)** *wonder*: Bx gives the line a bumpy trisyllabic final dip, unless it is taken as the key-stave, providing wordplay with *wonder* 304a. Otherwise the word could be an intensifier induced by the latter and replacing original *wel* (= *so* in revised **C**). **456 (B 303)** *Moises*: despite an apparent parallel to **x** in 22.62a, *The which Moises* here appears to be a senseless scribal expansion of a seemingly short line when compared with **p** and // **B**, and resembles the one noted at 421 above. B 303 scans not as a T-type (*aa / [a]bb*) but as standard with a liaisonal key-stave on *m* (*come͜into*). *K–D*'s emendation *into [myddel] erþe* is quite unnecessary. **457** *briht*: a revision, of characteristically Langlandian type (cf. 20.100 for a similar phrase), which *R–K* incomprehensibly reject for *brode* **B**. **468 (B 316)** The line in Bx scans *xa / ax* unless, improbably, *commune* is two-stressed and preceded by a four-syllable anacrusis, giving an awkward and uncharacteristic Type IIIa line. Emendation from **C** seems justified here since *carke* was lexically difficult enough to be vulnerable to scribal ⇒. **471 (B 319)** *moot* **B**: Bx *wole*, giving an unmetrical

b-half, appears a scribal ⇒ for the needed stave-word in *m*. Of the two possible modal verbs, *moten* is here preferred to *mowen* as the stronger. But in the light of the **C** revision, Bx's ⇒ could perhaps have been of *truthe* for *trewe men*, as at 292, with subsequent smoothing. **476** *smethen*: an elliptical infinitive (with *shal* understood); but YIP[2]UR have the singular subjunctive *smythe*, which is closer to **B**, and Cx just as probably read the latter. **479 (B 327)** *myddel*: the first lift in **C**, to judge by // **B**; **p** presumably preserves Cx, P[2] having acquired the reading from a **p**-source. The omission in I and the insertions in X (*a.h.*) and P[2] suggest that **x** read Ø. The immediate sources of u and Y must have inserted their respective conjectures independently, since none of the substantive **x** variants alliterates or is derived from one of the others. **485–86 (B 334–35)** The **B** line scans as an extended Type III counterpointed in the a-half (*abb / ax*) with þ / v (perhaps pronounced |v|) as the 'thematic' stave sounds (see Schmidt 1987[2]:92). However, if the form of the pronoun in Bx was *hij* (as in YCLMR) the fricative stave-word would have to be *That* (1) or (2) in the a-half, producing an awkward stress-pattern. In the light of **C**, which is evidently a revision adding a third palatal lift, it might be conjectured that in **B** an archetypal *hij* was put for **ӡe* through failure to see an original *wynneþ* as 2nd pers. pl. (cf. the 3rd pers. pl. form *haueþ* adopted at 335 to account for the variants *haþ, haue, hadde*). But as so much uncertainty remains, **C** being 3rd pers. sg. (except *taketh*, which is parenthetical), this emendation is not adopted here. **489 (B 339)** *probate*: capable of being scanned with a cognative second stave in *próbáte* and a three or four-syllable metrical 'onset' (contrast 493//), unless the line is metrically anomalous because macaronic (see Schmidt 1987:101). **490 (B 340)** *lyne*: if Cx read *leef*, this could have represented a misapprehension of its exemplar's *lyue* (unconsciously induced by associations with *ende*), itself an easy visual error for original *lyne*. *Sk* (Apparatus) recognises the latter as the correct reading for **C** but prints *leef*, and the formal emendation is made by *Pe*. **491 (B 342)** The **B** line may scan vocalically with muted key-stave and contrapuntal *l*-staves or else (preferably) as Type IIIa on *l*, the theme-stave of revised **C**. **492 (B 342)** *felle*: for Bx *fele* 'many', which Cx might also have read, *felle* being a felicitous scribal correction in three **C** and two **B** mss. Since there is no // **A** here, *B*-GCr's reading (if not a scribal guess) must be from either a thus-corrected **C** or (least probably) a lost **B** source. But since *felle* is the harder, more apt and so more probably original reading, YP[2]U could well represent **x** (< Cx). The precise sense here may be the relatively unusual 'subtle, wise' (MED s.v. *fel* adj. 2(a)) rather than 'fierce, harsh' (ibid., 3 and 5), the preferred (and commoner) sense at B 5.168. However, since 'more words' are indeed to follow and those quoted *are* shrewd ones, a homophonic pun may well be intended. **493 (B 343)** The a-half would seem to lack an alliterating first lift unless *Quod bonum est* forms a four-syllable onset before two-stressed *ténéte*, which is very awkward since the first vowel is short. More probably, the a-half is permitted to be anomalous because macaronic (see Schmidt 1987²:101). In both halves, though, a 'compensatory' extra stave appears (if the mid-line pause in **C** comes after *tixst*, a standard line results).

B 344–46 344 appears as the first of three corrupt lines and may point to scribal failure of attention on approaching the end of the passus (cf. *Notes* on B 2.198–203, towards the end of Passus II). The Bx form yields the scansion *ax / xa*, and *K–D* plausibly emend *ferde* to *mysferde* to provide a standard line (so *Sch*). Less drastically, inversion of verb and noun through promotion of the more important idea may be diagnosed in the a-half here and the line emended to scan as Type IIIa. **345** The Bx form could be Type IIIb with a four- or five-syllable onset and a two-stressed *Sápiénce*. But the normal pronunciation of the latter word, as is clear from 333 above, is *Sápiènce*, and the emendation here suggested presumes only Bx inversion to prose order in the a-half, producing a smoother line, still of Type IIIb. **346** is unmetrical as it stands in Bx (*aa / xx*). *K–D* propose *trewe*, but it is hard to see *good* as a ⇒ for this. The word here conjectured, *tidy* (OED s.v. 3(a) 'good, useful', and see MED s.v. 3b) occurs at 3.474 = B 3.322; 20.332, 21.442; B 9.105). In these cases *tidy* is used only with *man*, but this may tell for not against it here, since the novel usage might have been what prompted the Bx scribe to replace it. In the comparative form at 12.189, the context suggests the sense 'useful, profitable' that is exactly right at B 3.346. **494 (B 348)** C revises to the rare Type IIb what appears to be a Type IIIb line on |v| with liaisonal first stave *if ye* or a Type Ia line with a slightly awkward key-stave on a modal verb *shul* enclosed by asymmetrical contrapuntal staves (on such 'line-type ambiguity' see Schmidt 1987:37–8). **499** *recheth* x: in context the harder reading, avoiding a pointless repetition; for though *recetteþ* **p** 'harbours' (MED s.v. *recetten* v.) is apt enough, it could have been suggested by the noun in the b-half.

Z 147–76 The unique 30-line passage that concludes Passus III in **Z** shows no specific verbal ⊗ from **BC** and only 162b has left a trace in **A** (at A 3.236). But there are echoes of its thought in one or other later version. Thus 153a is like 8.185a; 166 recalls 21.456 and 151 is reminiscent of Conscience's actions in 22.228ff. A simple account of these **Z** 'echoes' as a *scribal* response to **C** (especially its final section) is challenged by the evident authenticity of the writing in **Z**. A second possibility, that the passage is post-**BC** but still *original*, leaves unexplained the no less evident primitiveness of its conception of Conscience and of Mede's relation to him. A third interpretation would see the passage as an early form of the ending of Passus III, cut from **A** because its lengthy attack on friars seemed irrelevant at this point, but later drawn on in the **B** conclusion when describing Conscience's fatal ambivalence towards the friars as confessors. The resonances of **B** and **C** would therefore be 'pre-echoes' or anticipations of material and ideas later to be worked up and pointing to the existence of a Langlandian *repertorium* of lines and phrases. **Z 163** *a lost*: *R–B* find the sense of ms *aloft* unclear and possibly concealing a corruption. But if *f* is a visual error for long *s*, the crux could be resolved as *a lost*, with wordplay on *lust* 'pleasure' and *lost* 'loss', the ME form of the latter paralleled at 5.97 below, and presumably an original spelling. **175–6** As punctuated, the sense is that 'without Conscience's knowledge, Meed does nothing of which he is not the prime originator'; but with a semi-colon after *sothe* it would be that 'she does nothing without his knowledge, but he is not the *prime* originator [of all human acts]'. Awkward as the shift is, it is possible to read 175 as spoken to the King (about Conscience) and 176 as directly addressed to Conscience (about himself). 175 would undoubtedly read more easily if *not* were a spelling of *noght*: 'Without his being privy to it, I perform no action of which Conscience is not the source'. For an acute discussion of the problem in these lines see Brewer 1984:216n7.

Passus IV

1 (ZAB 1) *Cesseth*: **Z** *seseth²* could be a scribal insertion, but is not paralleled in extant **ABC** mss and might be a first-version original. *C-x sethe*, perhaps a verb derived from the noun meaning 'satisfaction' or 'reparation', is not to be seen as a substantive revision of **B** but a visual error induced by following *sauhtene*. **4 (ZAB 4)** *rathir*: if **Z**'s *arre* shows ⊗ it may be from a **C** source of y-type. The adverbial *arre* is not elsewhere instanced but could be the form underlying *A-r erst*. If the **B** variant *for euere* were a reflex of **er* (for *arre*), then *are* might be preferable for **C**; but no difference in sense is involved and either could be original in **BC**. Substituted *are* presumably results from stylistic objection to repeated *rather* in two successive lines. **5 (ZAB 5)** *-tyl* **ZC**: a uniquely instanced non-substantive variant of *-to*, the advancing form used in every other occurrence (see *IG*). **6 (ZAB 6)** *þe* **AB**: omission of *þe* in **ZCx** (added in *C-YP²D*) is supported by six **A** mss randomly and one **B** ms (Y). Present in AxBx, it may be original in those (or all) versions. **10 (ZAB 10)** The line was probably in **B**, though no reason, mechanical or otherwise, for its loss from Bx appears. It was presumably restored in the ancestors of Y<OC²> from **A** or **C** and in Cr²³ from **C**. **15 (ZAB 15)** *hym*; *sayde²*: apparently absent from Bx and adopted on the joint showing of **ZAC** from F, which here may be corrected from a **C** source. Bx, which has a satisfactory Type IIIa line as it stands, presumably substituted *bad* through stylistic objection to repetition of the verb (cf. on *are* at 4). **16 (ZAB 16)** *the a:* adopted on the showing of **AB** as the probable Cx reading, preserved coincidentally in *C-F* (D actually reads *þere* not *þe*), of which **p** and **x** attest split variants. **17–9 (B 17–9, Z 17–8, A 17)** Ax could have contained **BC**18–19, from which *A-*m**W** might have preserved them, W by reference to a source of **m**-type. One possibility is that **m** could here show ⊗ from **B**, as could **Z**. Alternatively, the **Z** form could attest a first draft, from which Z 17–18 were then dropped in the revision to **A** (but with retention of *And cald*) to create the present 'Cato' line A 17, only to be subsequently restored after the latter in the revision to **B**. Given the uncertainty, 18–19 are omitted as not indispensable for the sense in **A**. **21–2 (Z 20–2, A 19–21, B 21–3)** Revision is apparent in each stage from **A** to **C**. *Wyl* **Z** may be original, a spelling variant of *wel* (as at Z 89 below) or a ⊗ from C 22, which introduces an allegorised 'will'. Burrow (1990:142) supports it as the original **AB** reading corrupted to *wel* in both archetypes, a possibility all the easier if *hym* had been present as a reinforcing appositional pronoun with original *wil*. But as the half-line is confirmed by **C**, the principle of ratification cautions strongly against emendation of **AB**. *Auyseth-þe-byfore:* continuous revision is again apparent. The Ax reading is uncertain and could have been *riȝt wytful,* of which *wytful* and *riȝtful* would then be 'split and fused' variants; but more probably the latter is a contextually induced aural error for the former. **23** *with peynted wittes:* found puzzling by Burrow (1990:141–2) but allowed as acceptable by *Pe* if *with* means 'against', *peynted* then being understood figuratively as 'specious' (like *coloured* at 21.349). But though ingenious, this seems unnecessary, as the notion is plainly one of 'will' being restrained by 'wit', here plural because a more specific sense like 'reason', 'judgement' (OED s.v. sb. 13, MED 6(a)) is intended. The allegorical detail is either secondary or else *peynted* here = 'florid [eloquent]', but in an innocent sense like that at 16.321 (MED s.v. *peinten* 5 (a) rather than 6 (a) 'specious'). *Pe*'s emendation of *wittes* to *withes* 'withies' is thus otiose.

B 23 (Z 22, A 21) *he / we:* apparent revision in **B** makes it difficult to argue for the randomly-attested variant *he*] *we* as the original reading in **A**. The line scans more smoothly in both **A** and **B** with |w| as the sound of the key-stave (an internal stave in *twies* in **B**), though the sense is unaffected. The occurrence of the random variants *come* for *be* in *B-*CrGC²H) and *be* for *come* in *A-*N leave it uncertain if *be* **Z** is also original or a scribal variant, whether random or an echo of a **B** source. **25 (Z 24, A 23, B 25)** *ryt:* the majority form *ryȝt* could be that of Cx as the adverb used with an understood verb of motion. But more probably it is the contracted 3rd pers.

sg. (< *rydeth*) spelled with ȝ to indicate vowel length, but to be rejected on grounds of ambiguity (that the verb is intended seems confirmed from // **ZAB**). *swype* **A**: the six scribal variants reveal difficulty with the lexical use of the word ('quickly') though this was not uncommon (MED s.v. *swithe* adv. 3(a)). **28 (Z 26, A 25, B 28)** *for they* **ZAB**: no mechanical reason appears for loss in *B-*LR. If these two mss (as pure descendants of β and α respectively) preserve the defective reading of Bx, then γ (the source of *B-*wg) and F may merely be offering a commonsense emendation of a perceived gap in the sense, or correcting from an **A** ms (rather than another **B** copy of a tradition superior to Bx). **30** *þe comune* **x**: the **p** variant (conceivably a smoothed reflex of Cx **þe comen* misread as *þei connen*) is excluded on grounds of sense since, even if Conscience might complain to the king, there is no one for the king to complain to. **32 (Z 30, A 29, B 32)** *Ac:* on the showing of **ZAC** Bx *And* looks a scribal error for *Ac*, probably induced by initial *And* 33 (cf. C 41 below). *myle* **A**: preferable on grounds of rhythm and supported by **Z**. **35 (B 35)** The word-order of **p** is discriminated on comparison with **B** as that of Cx. **36 (B 36)** Bx scans as an extended Type IIIb with counterpoint (*abb / aa*). A better balance with 35 would arguably be obtained if, in the light of **C**, the line were taken as Type Ia with *l* as stave sound and a liaisonal key-stave provided by conjecturing *hij* for *þei* and inversion of verb and pronoun in the b-half (*wol_hij*). But the emendation is not strictly necessary and so is not adopted here. **38 (B 38)** Bx scans as Type IIIa and the unmetrical line following is rejected as scribal padding; but *K–D*'s extensive reconstruction is unnecessary. Though *chiknes* is not obviously unoriginal, the presence of *capones* in the spurious line suggests that its position in **B** was as in // **C**. **39 (B 39)** *his:* preferred as less probably scribal than the over-explicit *goddes* **x**. **41 (B 43)** *Ac:* the conjectured reading of Cx as indicated by the sense and form of the competing variants. **42 (Z 32, A 31, B 44)** *kyng thenne:* lost in **Z** through haplography (*R–B*) after 31b. *aȝen* **A**: adopted as the probable Ax reading preserved in **m** and **Z**, unless both (improbably) show ⊗ from **B**; *(in)to* **r** looks like a scribal attempt to remove a perceived ambiguity in the preposition that commonly signifies opposition (see 16.214, 20.262 and MED s.v. prep. 4(a)). **44 (Z 34, A 33, B 46)** In **A**, the word-order of **m** is adopted in the light of **ZB** but *wel* is retained as the adverb despite *ful* **Z**. Neither sense nor metre is affected and *wel / ful* seem to have been in free variation. *speke / worleden:* possibly present-tense in **Z**, but this seems unlikely given the sequence of preterites from 30 onwards and the ease of loss of the internal preterite morpheme *-ed* after *-d* and before *-en* (cf. Z 3.144, and note under 3.262). The error occurs also in *B-*C² and *A-*N (and cf. Z 54, where the syntax necessitates a preterite subjunctive). **46** *forleyen:* internal *-e* is

added to expand the participial morpheme as a full sylla-
ble (*ley-en*) for the needed feminine ending. **52** The prefix
a- is judged archetypal on the agreement of most **p** mss and
x, and *He* **p** is preferred to *And* **x** (contrast the **x**-reading at
56). It is possible that the original read **A wayteth* (so
R–K; cf. 58 below). **56 (Z 41, A 40, B 53)** On the basis of
superior metre and **ZBC** agreement, **m**'s reading with
final *neuere* is discriminated as that of Ax. Although **A**
could have been unchanged from **Z**, Ax being preserved
in **r** with inversion of the adverbs to commoner prose
order, it is more economical to adopt an *A*-family reading
that needs no emendation on metrical grounds. **58 (Z 43,
A 42, B 55)** *hewen*: certain for **A** in the light of **ZBC**
agreement, *hynen r*[1] and *hynes* **C**-DAVRMQFS probably
reflecting *n / u* confusion in copying a form spelled **hy(u)
en.* See also on A 94, 104 below. **61 (Z 46, A 45, B 58)**
otes: judged original on the showing of **ZAB**. Possibly **p**
misread the last word of the line as *other* and conjectur-
ally completed the sense while MF corrected from an **x**
copy or **B**. **62 (Z 47, A 46, B 59)** The **A** mss E and M have
corrupt attempts to fill a probable lacuna or make good a
damaged exemplar, and the **m**-group reading is likely to
have contained the contracted form *bat* (so **Z**, with
retracted vowel as in *rat* C 3.406), of which *bad* seems to
be a confused recollection. Of the two lines in *A*-E the
first may echo **C** (if *treth* = *threteth* // *manascheth* **C**), the
second (an alternative attempt to supply the line) either **B**
or another **A** source, while M corrupts further by adding
wyf. **64–6 (Z 50–2, A 48–9, B 61–3)** The unique line 50
in **Z** seems original, though of draft character (it could
have been dropped because judged redundant), as does Z
51a, forming part of a standard Type Ia line. The identical
rhyme with *tolde* 50 is exactly paralleled at A 5.9/10 and
recalled in the non-identical end-rhyme of C 65/6 // **B. 68
(Z 63, A 61, B 75)** is continuously revised, only **Z** and **C**
being metrically satisfactory as they stand. Both scan as
Type Ia on vowels and **Z** shows affinity in meaning but
no direct sign of ⊗ from **C** in its a-half. The **B** line gives
good sense, but the metre assumes somewhat awkward
scansion with lifts on *his*[1,2] against the natural expectation
of emphasis on the semantically salient nouns. *B*-F's nor-
malisation of the metre by inverting object and adverb to
prose order in the b-half is unlikely to represent α and
thence Bx, given the agreement of R with β**ZAC**. Most
probably the line's unusual pattern is due to its both echo-
ing and deliberately varying that of 64a. In the a-half
most **A** mss (the t-group excepted) attest *his / of his* with
no following verb, suggesting a lacuna here in Ax. The
conjectured verb *offride*, if miscopied from an exemplar
*offryt in the present-tense form *offres*, could have been
lost through occasioning eye-skip from *of his* to *handy*.
The source of t may have been recalling the b-half of B
64 in its attempt to repair the exemplar text; but it is
unlikely to preserve an Ax reading lost from **m** and from

most members of **r**. Although **Z** makes sense, it is argu-
able on comparison with the b-half in **ABC** that *payed*
should be seen in **Z** also not as a preterite but as a past
participle, Wrong specifying the conditions under which
he will pay, not those under which he is paying now; the
conjunction is accordingly treated as a probable scribal
intrusion. The identity of **Z**'s reading in preceding 62
with that of W at A 60 will be fortuitous rather than evi-
dence of some link between these mss, for the form of the
following line shows W's source attempting (like that of
the unrelated E) to produce sense from a presumably
damaged exemplar reading. W's adverb *fast* could thus
be explained as an attempt to complete a line which, hav-
ing lost *hym to helpe*, would have seemed defective in
both sense and metre. Not impossibly, however, *hym to
helpe* belongs in the a-half of A 61, the position occupied
by the closely parallel *And for to haue here helpe* **C. 70
(Z 54, A 52, B 66)** *pleyneden* **Z**: the preterite morpheme
added on the evidence of **ABC** and the tense-sequence of
53 (for similar omission cf. on Z 34 above). **73 (Z 65, A
63, B 77)** *nomen* **A**: the harder word adopted as the likely
A original on the showing of **Z**; *tok* will have come into
r[1] and randomly into *A*-JWE as the more modern term
(and perhaps as that familiar from parallel **BC**). The Ax
form of this line also, however, shows a case of moderni-
sation: though scanning satisfactorily as Type IIIc (*ab /
ab*), it appears (like *B*-HmGC[2]CB and*C*-xAS) to have
substituted *wiþ* for *myd*, which is accordingly adopted
though not strictly required for the metre. **80–1 (Z 73–4,
A 71–2, B 84–5)** The first line was lost in *r*[1], probably half
of the second in *r*[1] and all of it in t, while both were added
to H[2] (or its immediate ancestor) from an **A** ms of *r*[2] type.
82 (Z 75, A 73, B 86) The Bx line will scan as Type IIIa
with an awkward five-syllable anacrusis, but *lete hym
noȝt* looks doubtful in the light of **ZAC** *schal / sholde nat.*
Bx's possible reason for a paraphrastic ⇒ could have
been scribal unease at the sudden shift to direct speech.
Alternatively, **B** might have been a substantive revision
and Bx unconscious ⇒ of a (non-alliterating) synonym
for the lexical verb with *s* here conjectured. The **C** line
would then have to be seen as a wholesale revision, per-
haps prompted by defective metre in **L**'s ms (B[1]), but in
any case reverting to a combination of modal verb with
Bx's and possibly **ZA**'s (?) indirect speech (the latter has
been treated as direct speech in the edited text but need
not be). **84 (Z 77, A 75, B 88)** *do*: here taken as a revision
of **B**, though not impossibly it has come in by eyeskip to
mysdo at 86 below. *R–K* adopt *make* after *C*-F alone,
though neither metre nor sense requires it and it is better
seen not as a correction from yet another superior **C**
source but as easily induced by the common collocation
maken amendes. **86 (Z 79, A 77, B 90)** The form of the
a-half in *A*-tL may preserve an archetypal and original
reading lost in the rest of the tradition and is unlikely to

have been a scribal alteration, as it is clearly the harder. An Ax spelling of the pronoun subject as in **Z** (*a*) could have been misread as a cardinal numeral, giving the sense 'that one wrongful action', and so omitted for reasons of censorship as seeming to encourage an attitude of laxity. That *mysdede* was a verb in **A** seems indicated by the form of both **Z** and of revised **BC**. *And* **B**: preferred to *And so* on the showing of **C** and presumably accidental in *B*-H, since it cannot be by ⊗ from **A** or **C**; *so* will then be a Bx scribal intrusion, perhaps visually suggested by *-sdo*. **87 (Z 80, A 78, B 91)** All versions before **C** have the inauthentic metrical pattern *aa / bb*, though there is no objection on grounds of sense. The proposal of *K–DKa²* that **C** *witnessede* was also the original of **AB** presumes a threefold occurrence of 'substitution of the common collocation by alliterative inducement' (*Ka²*, p. 461). This could also have occurred if the word for which *seide* was substituted was in fact an exact synonym *quod* (used only before or after direct speech, and not as main verb with noun-phrase object as here). The more drastic emendation here proposed traces the error to both a mechanical cause (loss of initial *wiþ* through haplography following eyeskip after final *-wiþ* in *þerewiþ*) and also to the hardness of the stave-word, which is instanced only once in any of the four versions (see A 4.142). If the original read *wiþseide þe same*, the sense would be 'made the same point in opposition' (i.e. to the king, while agreeing with Wisdom), with *þe same* as direct object, as at 3.30, or 'objected likewise', with *þe same* used adverbially, as at 3.27, which is perhaps the more likely with this verb. The reconstructed line has the 'T'-type structure abundantly instanced in all versions. The problem of thrice-repeated loss associated with *K–D*'s conjecture also remains here, but is offset by the greater difficulty of the supplanted word (for the converse case of a conjectured loss of the second element, the lexical morpheme, in a *wiþ*-compound, see on 12.190 below). **90 (Z 83, A 81, B 94)** *Thanne*: the probable reading for **B** on the showing of **ZAC**, *And* Bx appearing a scribal intrusion perhaps induced by *And* 95; *B*-Cr will have corrected from **C**, *B*-H from **A**. *she*: a word easily lost from Ax*C*-p if its form was *he* (as in *B*-R?*C*x), through quasi-haplography before following *be-*. But as it is not necessary to the sense, it is not adopted in **A**. **91 (Z 84, A 82, B 95)** *puyre*: the (possible) *A-r* reading *purid* (so *C* -M) is acceptable in itself but on comparison with **ZBC** may look like scribal over-emphasis. **92 (Z 85, A 83, B 96)** The **Z** line scans either as Type IIIa on |ð| with stress on the possessive (paralleled in C 7.103), or vocalically as Type Ia with a mute stave in *amendy*. Loss of this stave-word in *A*-vJEM could have occurred more easily (through quasi-haplography) if Ax had read *of me man* as in *r¹* and the same omission could have affected **Z** in the copying of the ms. But in the light of the later revisions, the form with *man* in the a-half that

looks likeliest to be original in **A**, and the word-order of *A*-Aw is adopted as giving the smoother rhythm achieved in **BC**. **94 (Z 87, A 85, B 98)** The word-order of the a-halves in *A*-**r**, **m** records divergent reflexes of an **A** original presumed preserved in **ZBC**; either AxBx scribes added *to* or the ZCx scribes omitted it. **95 (Z 88, A 86, B 99)** *man that*: lost from **Z** through eyeskip (*that* > *that*) or haplography (*R–B*). *ofte*: Bx *so* is omitted (following *B*-GM) as perhaps visually induced by *so* in 97b. The metrical pattern of Bx, with a trisyllabic pre-final dip, is indeed that of the conjecturally restored A 5.130, but without the semantic justification of *so* in that instance. **97 (Z 92, A 90, B 103)** *Mede*: the Z-ms error is a mechanical slip induced by the proximity of *-de, my, me*. **99 (Z 93, A 91, B 104)** *God*: no emendation to *Crist* in **ZA** on grounds of metre is required, since the line scans 'cognatively' on |k| |k| |g|. The revision in **BC**, eliminating the 'cognative' stave, is extensive and progressive. **100 (Z 94, A 92, B 105)** *wendeþ*: the revision to *goth* in **C** alters the line-type from Id to Ia so as to throw the stress onto the adverb (see next note). If *goth* is a Cx error, no grounds for its occurrence appear, since *wendeþ* is hardly difficult. *ar* **ZAC**: on comparison Bx *erst wol I* suggests less an authorial revision finally rejected than a scribal heightening of dramatic tone or smoothing after miscopying conjunctive *er* as the adverbial *erst*. *B*-GH here are not witnessing to a better **B** tradition but ⊗ from an **A** source. **101 (Z 95, A 93, B 106)** *Lope*: preferred for **B** on the witness of **ZAC**, Bx *For* appearing a scribal attempt to ease a transition. *awey*: added in *C*-PEN (so *R–K*) as in *B*-F (presumably from **A**), but its omission in **BC** avoids ineffective repetition of *away* 100. **104 (Z 98, A 96, B 109)** *Y lyue* **CZA**: although *he lyueþ* Bx is not obviously wrong and revision in the line's b-half might sanction revision in the a-half as well, the phrase looks suspect in the light of agreed **ZAC**. The 3rd-person form may have come in through inducement from adjacent *hym, he, hym* (the same error appears in *A*-W, which has borrowed the whole line from a ms of the later version). **105 (Z 99, A 97, B 110)** *men*: either a scribal addition in *A*-**r¹**Bx*C*-**x** or else added in **A**, retained in **B** but lost in *A*-**r²m***C*-p through assimilation to the preceding plural morpheme *-(m)e* in *summe* (as judged here). **110 (Z 108, A 106, B 115)** In the absence of *A*-A, the Ax reading may be only probably and not certainly divined as that of **m**. But it is confirmed by **ZBC** and by *A*-W, though the latter may show ⊗ from **B** as at 96 (see on 104 above). The reading of **r**, requiring an awkward caesura and reducing two separate statements (generic + specific) to one, results from the recognised scribal tendency towards the simplest word-order and from anticipation of the post-nominal infinitive. The error might have occurred more easily if **A** had read as **Z**, omitting *al*. In **A** *it* (**ZBC**) is not added after *here* since not strictly needed for the sense. **113 (Z**

106, A 104, B 118) Though **C** completely revises the b-half, the **ZAB** readings are identical but for added *be* in **AB**. The figurative term for 'a thing of low value' is rendered as *heþyng* by *A*-Ch, a reading here judged a ⇒ for Ax *hyne* (cf. Ch's idiosyncratic *raike* at 153, *schregges* at Pr 2). *A*-M *heuene* is evidently an error for an exemplar-reading spelled conjecturally **hyuen* (cf. 58n above), though in part perhaps unconsciously induced by preceding *holynesse*. **124 (Z 112, A 110, B 127)** *he*: lost from **Z** for no evident mechanical reason but needed for the sense; such omissions are characteristic of the manuscript, but may reflect the exemplar's draft-status. **125 (Z 113, A 111, B 128)** *ruyflares* x: not a sub-archetypal ⇒ for a Cx reading preserved in **p** (so **ZAB**) but a striking revision inserting a word found little elsewhere outside **L** (see 6.315, and for the verb 4.54, B 5.230, 234; MED s. vv. *riflen* v., *riflere* n., and Wilcockson 1983). **127 (Z 115, A 113, B 130)** For *croune* A *Ka* finds *rⁱ coyn* 'stamp, impress' (MED s.v. *coin* n. 2a. (a)) 'harder and less obvious'; but agreement of *rⁱ*m and **Z** points to the former as the probable Ax reading. The likelihood that *koyne* at C 1.46 above bears the sense cited by *Ka* supports *coyn* here; but given the **BC** revision in the b-half, grounds for rejecting *croune* are not decisive. **129 (Z 117, A 115, B 132)** *it*: *yf* **Z** is corrected to *yf yt* as in **B** by *R–B* (diagnosing loss of *yt* by partial haplography) but here to the simpler *yt* as in **AC**.

Z 119–32 contain three groups of unique lines, all unexceptionable for sense and characteristic in metre. 120 is the very rare Type IIa; 121 may be either Type IIIa scanning translinearly from 120 on *m*, or Type Ia scanning on *n*. Z 122–23 correspond to A 141–42, and 126–30 to A 145–49; they are re-written at the opening of Z V below, 126 here having the same defective metre (*ab / ba*) as its counterpart line at Z 5.5. This duplication strongly suggests the draft character of these lines, in which neither alliterative alternative to 'say', *rehersen* and *recorden* (A 145, B 172), was yet determined, although the former was soon to be used at Z 149 below (see Intro. III *Z* § 3). In 130 and 132, where the errors have mechanical causes, emendation is desirable since 'for grammatical reasons, either *y* or *schalt* (pres. 2 sg.) must be emended... Reason is saying that the king cannot rule justly while Meed is at court' (*R–B*, p. 75, n.).

133 (Z 134, A 119, B 136) *seyen* C: a revision, with unexceptionable sense, so *R–K*'s ⇒ of *shewen* has no basis. Alteration of *schewen* at Z 3.108 to *seiȝen* in A 3.160 indicates near-synonymy of the lexemes in some contexts. *othere*: correction of Bx *ouþerwhile* to *ouþer* on grounds of both sense and metre seems justified in the light of **ZAC** agreement. *B*-R may preserve the α (< Bx) reading with correct *ouþer* and scribally added *ouþer-while*, which have been levelled convergently in β and F to a less awkward form. **139** *do*: elliptical, as part of

a revision, 'nor [shall I] grant mercy for payment'; but *y*'s Ø-reading (retained by *R–K*) could be original and is closer to **B** (so I*Pe*). **140 (Z 141, A 126, B 143)** *þe*: **ZAB** is stylistically preferable, and perhaps lost mechanically from Cx by eye-skip from 'malum' to 'man'. In **Z**, loss of *u* (or *n*) in *nullum* will be by haplography. **142 (Z 143, A 128, B 145)** *in Englische*: in the light of agreed **AC**, loss of the preposition (*on / in*) from **Z** through quasi-haplography may be diagnosed (*on, En-*). *B*-H *englys* corrects, perhaps memorially from **A**, what appears an intelligent Bx attempt to restore from a badly-spelled **onglys* what it took as an original insisting on the uncomfortable literal sense of a crucial Scriptural text. **152–53** It would be better to delete the stop after *thonkede* and place a semicolon after *speche* (*R–K*).

B 158–9 158 The Bx line scans either *aa / xa* or, if *And Wit* form the anacrusis, *ab / ab* (Type IIIc on |k|), an authentic pattern. If *Wit* forms the first lift, the simplest emendation would be transposition of *comendede* and *hise wordes* (considered and rejected by *K–D*). But their emendation *Kynde* for *And* is convincing in the light of revised **C**, for in this context the character Wit is indeed 'corrupt and venal' (*K–D*, p. 181) as at near-identical B 91, which might have unconsciously influenced the Bx scribe. **159** The Bx line scans as Type IIIa, and since there is no objection on grounds of sense and there may be a deliberate avoidance of repetition of 152, *K–D*'s emendation of *halle* to *moot-halle* is rejected.

155 (Z 151, A 136, B 160) *Mekenesse*: agreement of **ZBC** in the a-half supports *A*-**m** as representing the original and rejection of *A*-**r** as a scribal ⇒ giving inferior sense and metre. Repetition of *Resoun* is awkward, leading to the word's incorporation in a six-syllable onset and placing the caesura after *Mede*. What is at issue is whether repentance for wrongdoing or pecuniary means should procure the king's mercy: to obey *mekenes* is thus to follow Reason (cf. A 125 above). The agreement of E's reading suggests ⊗ from **r** (here preserving Ax) or ⊗ of **m** (represented by AM) from **B** (which seems improbable).

Z 152, 157–9, V 3 (A 143) 152 seems authentic but perhaps otiose. **157–9** look original but strongly suggest draft character; contradicting the opening of Passus V, they were presumably cancelled in A's revision. **V 3** The b-half in **Z** has been revised in **A** to a form that echoes the comparison (to a dumb beast not a stone) at Z 4.124, which occurs in the earlier portion of **Z** corresponding to A 141–8

B 172 (Z V 5, A 145) The line scans as Type Ia in both **A** and **B** but lacks a first |r| stave in **Z** here and at 4.126, unmetrical *seyde* (a variant in *A*-w) being either scribal in both instances or a sign of **Z**'s draft character. **A**'s stave-word *reherside* has already appeared as part of the poet's repertoire at Z 4.149 above, but its use at A 145 could be a revision, so the case for emendation is not strong. **178 (Z V 7, A 147, B 184)** *And alle*: also the reading of Ax. Of the two words one is omitted in each of the phrase's appearances in **Z**, *alle* here (so also *A*-M), *And* at 4.128 (so also *A*-UVA, Bx). Emendation of Bx is on the basis of **AC** agreement. **184 (Z V 13, A 153, B 190)** *ryden*: clearly attested from **Z** to **C**. While unconscious replacement of *ryde* by a colourless non-alliterating synonym *wende* in *A*-d is by no means improbable, ⇒ of *raike* may be identified not (as by *Ka*) as the harder original behind d but rather as an idiosyncratic choice of the Ch-scribe (see on 113), notwithstanding that this word featured in the poet's lexicon (e.g. in the draft line Z 4.158, cancelled in *A*). *hennes* **ZAC**: to be preferred as the probable reading of **B**, *fro me* Bx illustrating scribal over-emphasis here. *B*-H presumably shows ⊗ from **A**. **187 (Z V 11, A 151, B 188)** The line scans as Type IIIa in Ax and **Z**. *Ka²*, rejecting this metrical pattern as inauthentic, emends *quaþ* to *seiþ*, the reading of *A*-N. But *seiþ* could be a **B** revision, re-inforcing the key-stave with a second mute *s*-stave. **L**'s Type IIIa lines avoid a mute key-stave, and it seems that names with 'Saint' could bear stress on the title (cf. 12.100, 14.136).

A 155 (B 192, Z V 15) *aredy*: reconstructed in the light of **ZB** as the probable Ax form of which *?als* **m**, Ø **r** are reflexes.

B 194 (Z V 17, A 157) The line scans 'cognatively' on *gkg* and *ff* as a T-type (*aa / [a]bb*). Emendation by *K–DKa²* of *graunte* to *graunte gladly* after *A*-V is agratuitous adoption of a plainly scribal attempt at metrical 'correction'.

Z V 18 (A 158, B 195) *libbe* Z: taken by *R–B* as an infinitive after *graunte*; but this seems somewhat strained and (without *to*) uncharacteristic both as an idiom and as an example of **L**'s practice. In the light of **AB**, *We* is accordingly conjectured as omitted through partial haplography after '*libbe*', such omission being typical of the Z-manuscript's scribe.

Passus V (ZAB V)

10 *inwitt* **x**: *vnite* **p** is an easy visual error for *inwitte(e)*, which is required on grounds of sense ('sound of body and mind'). The collocation of *inwit and his hele* at 10.182 confirms the reading here, though the sense 'mind' (see MED s.v. *inwit* n.) puzzled copyists in the **p** tradition (and that of *P²*, who presumably found *inwit* and *vnite* in his **x**- and **p**-type exemplars respectively but rejected both). GK *duite* is striking evidence of an immediate common ancestor with readings distinct from those of N, the other representative of *p²*. *R–K* (p. 159) ingeniously suggest *unnit* 'vain idleness' (MED s.v. *unnit* n., not instanced after mid-13th century), for which the two main family variants would be scribal attempts at making sense of the word's minims. But their unawareness of 10.182 makes their conjecture, questionable on grounds of obsolescence,

superfluous. **19** scans with a mute key-stave *or*, though the line would be metrically stronger with *hogges* for *swyn* (M's *hogges* erroneously for *gees* seems unlikely to be a reflex of a Cx stave-word). The third *or* would also give better rhythm if expanded as *oþer*. **21** In this major crux the probable Cx reading is divined in the sub-archetypal variant judged harder and so less likely to be derived from the other. That *Hem þat bedreden be bylyue to fynde* looked simpler seems clear from its adoption by a later hand into *P²*, which presumably had in its main exemplar a corrupted version of the form here proposed for **x**. In reconstructing, meaningless *the by* is here seen as an **x** error for Cx **therby*, with *r* damaged or omitted; **x** could have lost *be* through eyeskip from '*be*tered' to 'ther*by*' or (if the wording was *I be betered* as in ms I) through haplography (*be-*, *bet-*). I's reading is substantively nearest the conjectured Cx form but has varied to prose order, producing inferior rhythm. X's *marginal* correction (adopted by *Pe*) yields much the same sense as I: 'does the *comune* benefit from your way of life, since it provides you with the means of life?' But X's *inserted* correction, with an active construction = *they ybetered be*, is unlikely to be original, though witnessing to the perceived difficulty of **x**'s compressed syntax. The latter would have been clearer if preceded by *That*; but the sense can be ascertained without it: '(So that) those who provide you with your living have some advantage from what you do'. Alternatively, *to* is to be understood before *be*, giving a construction like those at 6.48 (*They to wene þat Y were*) and 21.233 (*They leely to lyue*). But **p**'s reading, adopted by *R–K* with insufficient discussion, could never have been found hard enough to give rise to that of **x**. **35** *ȝong²*: could have been dittographically added in y (or perhaps to normalise) or (like *syre* at 3.366 above) haplographically omitted in **pu**, with further smoothing in **p** to fill out the line. If instead u is taken as here preserving *x¹* and thence Cx (**p** having inserted *quath ich*), the line scans as a terse Type IIIa of a kind common in **A** and **B** (and still found, though less frequently, in **C**). On the other hand, *ȝong²* is more likely to have been (deliberately) omitted from *P²*, the latter's main exemplar being a y-type ms. This may suggest that u (like **p**) omitted the word through missing its intensive force ('very young indeed'), a sense tacitly recognised by the surviving witnesses of y, none of which omits or deletes the second *ȝong*. *R–K*'s conjecture *ȝut ȝong* is in any case otiose, since either **x** or **p** will provide a metrically acceptable reading. **40** *y*: added in X in another hand but absent from YIU. **44** *opelond* **x** / *in londone* **p**: the **p** form of this line, long familiar from *Sk* (and adopted as *vp london* by *R–K*, p.154) offers attractive wordplay, and a punning allusion to the second half of the author's surname may be intended in the repetition of *lond* (cf. B 15.152 and the comparable allusion to the *first* half in 24a above). But the main point seems to be that he lives, in the manner described in 42–3, 'both in the capital and out in the country', a meaning supported by the internal 'facts' of the Dreamer's life and by the ease with which the corruption could have occurred if **p** had read *vpon londen* as in GKN (= p^2). **53** scans somewhat stiffly, as Type IIIa on *m. R–K's semeth* for *thynketh* will by their metrical criteria place the caesura before *syre*, giving a (very short) b-half with an unidiomatic stress pattern *Sýre Résoun.* But the line thus emended would also scan satisfactorily as Type IIIa (ax / ax). **61** R–K re-order, placing hereafter 67–9, 62, 63–6, with full stop after the last. This gives acceptable, perhaps superior (certainly different) sense to that of Cx. But the repetition 'God' after 'Crist' (R–K 62) does not sound right, nor does recommending lords' *kin* (rather than lords) as the object of serfs' service. It seems safer to retain the text, taking *lordes kyn* in the wider sense of 'gentlemen's children' as at 73 below. **71** *barnes*: 'children', as in 70 (with which it balances), *bastardus* being postpositive, notwithstanding *R–K* p.154, who prefer *barones* YAP^2 (o + P^2). But the gradational move from 'lawful sons (of serfs)' → bishops, to 'the illegitimate children (of anyone)' → archdeacons reads better in the context of complaint about decline. **72** *sopares*: not a difficult, if a rarely instanced word. Both *soutares* X and *schipherdes* I are linked (though not disparagingly) at B 10.461 as *lewed iuttes*, and the XI scribes might have been independently distracted through recollection of this key passage. **78–9** *refused; taken*: better read (like preceding *han be, leyde, ryden*) as past participles dependent on the causal temporal clause that introduces this eleven-line sentence, and not as linked main verbs. The departure of sanctity (80) is seen as the consequence of a series of abuses, simony being the last of them. **88** *voluntas Dei*: likelier to represent Cx than the more familiar form of the *Paternoster*-phrase (as found at 15.252, with a b-half echoing this line). The <eRM> ancestor presumably 'corrected' to the usual wording. **91** *mynstre*: 'monastery', preferable, notwithstanding its ostensibly asymmetrical relation to *prior*, since metonymic for 'abbot (of a main monastery)'; *mynistre* (perhaps only a spelling variant here) gives inferior metre, though the sense 'superior of a religious order' is acceptable (MED s.v. *ministre* 2b, but cited only from here). The line scans either as Type IIa with *But* as first stave or as Type Ia with cognative staves |b| / |b| / |p|. **98** *wordes*: contextually the aptest reading, the 'words' being those of the Gospel quotation following. The variant *wyrdes* (adopted by *R–K*) may have been prompted visually by *wynnyng* and semantically by the cognate *warth* and preceding *happed* 95. **103** *louable*: either from (1) *louen*, with internal |v| (< OE *lofian*) or (2) *(al)lowen*, with internal |u| (< OF *alouer* < Lat *allaudare*), both meaning 'praise', 'commend', or (3) *(al)lowen* (< OF *allouer* < Lat *allocare*) 'assign (credit) to'. Alf*G* 4 notes that 'L's usage frequently suggests the blending of

award and praise', as here if (2) and (3) were in question. At 17.130 *allouable* appears, of which present *louable* may be an aphetic form (MED s.vv. *loven* v. (2), *louen* v. (4), *allouen* v. 1(a)). **104** *Y wente*: R–K's emendation to imperative *ywende* provides no reason for the second command, and the formula-like reprise at 105a may be original. **107** *Syʒing*: the form adopted has a modified spelling close to that of X. Possibly the (substantively erroneous) *Schryuing* I is attempting to make sense of a y reading with initial *sch-*, while Y's *smytynge* offers a more radical ⇒ for a word found unintelligible. Occasional initial |s| as *sch* in X may derive from a linguistic stratum close to the original (at 7.300, a range of variants have been generated from a conjectural form *$s(c)hy(ʒ)$ en* in **x**) but this spelling is rejected here as potentially confusing.

    AB 2 (Z 20) scans as Type Ia in **ZA**, as IIIa in **B**. *K–D* p. 88 adopt the **A** form, claiming that in Bx 'The piety of the occasion is increased [*sc.* by a scribe] by excluding a mundane detail' [viz. *þe mete*, the key-stave in **A**]. Even if this were true, the change may well be authorial, the tone of 'piety' being heightened not diminished in the **C** revision (105–08). *K–D* also find defective metre, rejecting the pattern ax / ax (well-instanced in the core-text) as unoriginal, while scanning it incorrectly as *xaay*. **BA 7, Z 25** *my bileue*: R–B consider that *by my leue* **Z** may be a scribal slip or an authorial joke. It is judged the former here and accordingly emended. **109 (Z 27, AB 9)** The revised **C** line may scan as Type IIa or like **AB** as extended Type IIIa with counterpoint (|v|, |m|), the theme-staves being *þanne* and *byfore*. **Z** is either a (metrically imperfect) draft or has lost *thenne* through scribal eyeskip to following *then* (as here conjectured). **Z's** *fore telle* may be a draft form further corrupted by visual mistaking of *o* for *e* and *d* for *l*, with omission of *Y* through haplography. Only the latter is here restored as necessary for the sense, and the awkward (but possible) reading 'than I tell above / before this' may stand (see MED s.v. *fore adv.* 1). *K–D* judge that the earlier versions read *mette me* with **C** and not *sauʒ* I (so *Ka*^{2}), but the sequence **Z > A > B** cautions against drastic emendation. **110 (Z 28, AB 10)** The self-rhymed *tolde* in **A** may reflect an earlier form corrupted in ms **Z** (but see note above and that on Z 4.50–2 under C 4.64–6) and it seems to be echoed by the *repetitio* of the verb (*mette*) in **C** 109–10. Bx *seide* could thus arguably register a scribal objection to the repetition. But as its sense and metre are unexceptionable, it is perhaps best taken as recording a stage in the process of revision (*tolde* in *B*-H would then be a characteristic ⊗ from **A**). For another case where revision, this time from **B** to **C**, eliminates identical end-rhyme, cf. B 7.36–7=C 9.40–1. **114–15 (Z 29–31, AB 11–13)** As divided in Cx, 114 has the unoriginal pattern aa / xa and could be simply emended by transposing the preposition and noun-phrase, to leave line 115 as Type Ic. But since the form of the **ZAB** lines points to *prechede* as probably the last word of revised C 114, re-lineation is justified. The cause of the misdivision will have been the unusual length, not of 114 as a whole, but of the immediate post-caesural dip (eight syllables). *C*-**p** presents a further stage of corruption, in effect the converse of that diagnosed in Cx: shortening of 115 and addition of a half-line to create a new line that looks a model instance of scribal 'over-explicitness'. **A**'s *pestilences* seems to revise **Z**'s singular while retaining the sg. verb-form (securely attested with pl. subject for **BC**), which was doubtless what led several A-Text scribes to smooth the noun's number.

Z 34–40, 43, 45 are unique lines of acceptable metre and sense. **Z 37** *messe ant*; *the masse*: possibly dittography for the single phrase *the m(e)sse*; or an original form **the masse, the messe* (with reference to the Mass as both sacramental meal and liturgical sacrifice). For a similar doublet cf. *pays* and *pees* at 18.177.

118 (Z 44, AB 16) Either *poffed* or *possed* could, on grounds of sense, be original in one or all versions. If **Z** is authentic, so may be *possid* in *A*-EM (? = **m**, v *passched* being a spelling variant) and *C*-yEA, *puffid* **B** being either a revision discarded in **C** or a Bx ⇒ coinciding with r^2, and **p**uP^2. Either variant could be a visual error for the other (*f* for long *s* or long *s* for *f*) and given the uncertainty, it seems best to retain **Z** and prefer *poffed* for **A** and **C** in the light of Bx. Against the originality of *poste* in **Z** may be adduced the greater appropriateness of 'puffed' in the context of preceding Z 40 on the 'wind' of God's powerful word that broke down the gates of hell (39; with which compare *breeþ* B 18.322). **119 (Z 41, AB 17)** *segges*: despite scant manuscript support, worth cautiously adopting for **A** on the strength of agreed **ZC** (**C** perhaps revising *ʒe segges* **B**). The latter reading, in an ambiguous form *ʒe segge, probably underlies *A*-EA *I sey*; *A*-M *to men* (so coincidentally in v) will then be a smoothing that indicates the presence of *segge* in **m** and thus, inferentially, in Ax. The variants *seyþ* RUD and *sent* t reveal successive stages of smoothing after misreading *ʒ* (for g) as *y* / *þ* and point to the absence from r^1 of *ʒe* before the noun. The family-readings may therefore be reconstructed as *seʒʒe* **r**, *y seʒʒe* **m**, pointing to Ax *(*ʒe*) *seʒʒe* (= *ye segges* **B**). In the **A** form here offered *ʒe* is omitted as more probably a **B** revision (if it is not a Bx ⇒). The *C*-**p** variant may be seen as a final stage in the corruption, the noun *segge* becoming *to segges* in x^2 (= 'to men') and then the verb-phrase *to segge* (*ous*) 'to say to us' in **p**. *that*: adopted for **B** on the strength of **Z?AC** agreement. **122 (Z 47, AB 20)** *hem* **x**: adopted for **C** in the light of **ZAB** agreement; for while *ous* **p** would seem the more logical choice after *we* 119, *hem* here resembles **ZAB** inasmuch as the latter have it (also asymmetrically) after *ye*. The shift in address from the outer to the

inner audience, superficially the result of inadvertence in revising, could be authorially intended, and the more 'correct' logic scribal. **125 (Z 50, AB 23)** On solely metrical grounds, the forms of **x** (Type Ia) and **p** (Ic) are both acceptable; but the major **p**-variant will have arisen from misreading *heuene* as *leuen* 'live', the divergent smoothings *ryght for* / *and hou* well illustrating the dual transmission of **p** through p^1 and p^2. The **B** line has clearly been revised from **A**; the reading of Bx was probably that of ?βR, which has the inauthentic scansion *aa / xa* (unless F here preserves α). But whether or not F's correct metrical form is original, the infinitive particle is to be included in the reconstructed archetypal text as having occasioned the variation to prose order in the b-half of β-R. **126 (Z 52, AB 25)** *þat he wastide* 25 may be an Ax corruption of an original identical with that of **ZB**, or **Z** may show ⊗ from or (as here presumed) anticipation of **B**. But **C** is too extensively revised to furnish evidence for emending Ax, which is acceptable. **128 (Z 53, AB 26)** *And* **ZAB** / *He* **C**: four **B** mss have anticipated **C** by substituting *He* for archetypal *And*, perhaps through misreading the ampersand as *A. leue*: Bx *lete* is metrically and lexically unexceptional but seems pointless as a revision of **A** reversed in **C**, and so is rejected as a probable scribal ⇒. **130 (Z 55, AB 28)** *stowe*: the reading adapted for **A** from *A*-J, which was most probably derived from a **B** copy of BHF type, with *of* before *Stowe*. Ax's presumed loss of the surname, by eyeskip to *staues* at the line-end or through haplography induced by following *tauʒte*, would have been easy if the name had been spelt *staue*. **Z**, unless showing ⊗ from **B** or **C**, here points to the likely presence of a surname in **A**, since *Thomas* alone seems too formal to have been the authorial version. **133 (Z 58, AB 31)** *half*: the metre of Ax requires an awkward stress on a^1 and it may be that *half* has been omitted through auditory or visual error from an original *a half. *A*-N's variant, here judged correct, is presumably by ⊗ from a **B** or **C** source. On the strength of **ZBC** agreement, *half* may be restored without the article.

A 31 Hereafter two lines resembling C 134–35 (B 32–3) appear in **m**J. Their presence in Z 59–60 would argue for their having also been in **A**, a possible reason for their loss from **r** being eyeskip from *worþ²* at 31 to *werche* at the end of the last phrase *wolde werche* (particularly easy if *a grote* had been written in the margin of the exemplar). Against this, J's agreement with **m** here points to its r^2-type exemplar having been collated with another source, less probably an **A** ms of **m**-type than one of the **B** Version (to judge from J's likely use of a **B** source at 28 above). Since, therefore, it is not impossible that **m** (and also **Z**) have added the lines, they are omitted from **A**. A major reason for caution here is that similar signs of 'farcing' in this passus appear in the **m** tradition after 42, 110 and 190, perhaps indicating desire to represent a popular scene in its fullest form from whatever source. The theoretical possibility that **m** descends not from the same archetype as **r** but from a different *redaction* of **A** is not strong. Firstly, **m** also *omits* lines found in **r** (viz. 74–5), something better explained if it is a sub-archetype of Ax, and most of its additional lines (which also appear in **B**) are shared by one or more **r** copies (e.g. K,W and U). Manuscripts such as these are more likely to have derived the lines from **B** than from **m**, with which they affiliate no further in the many readings where **r** and **m** vary disjunctively. The behaviour of these **r** witnesses itself strengthens the assumption (intrinsically more economical) that **m** likewise resorted to a **B** source in order to amplify the descriptions of the Sins. A second factor telling against **m**'s pure descent from Ax here is that the form of the present lines is not both authentic and distinct from that of **B**. But though this comment applies also to 87, 163 and 167, there are grounds for treating those lines differently. Thus at 87, mechanical explanations of the line's loss from **r** such as homoteleuton appear, while censorship might also have operated, suggesting that **m** *is* there derived from Ax rather than by ⊗ from **B**. **136 (Z 61, A 32, B 34)** *He*: in the light of **(Z)AC** agreement, *And þanne* Bx may be omitted as a case of scribal over-explicitness. **138 (B 40)** *spryng*: expanded in the light of **B** from Cx *spryg,* which may show loss of the nasal suspension here in the **x** reading; a form *spryg* without *n* is attested in the same sense but MED s.v. *sprigge* n. (1) quotes only this example. **139a (B 39a)** The line following in Bx scans *ax / ax* (Type IIIa) but seems otiose, 'prompted by [the] Latin line and...translat[ing] it' (*K–D* p. 193). **141–42 (Z 64–5, A 35–6, B 42–4)** The two later texts (**B** securely, **C** in **x** only) make the whole utterance direct speech, **Z** and *A*-**m** make it indirect, while *A*-**r** offers a transitional form (in *C*-**p**, coincidental agreement with **A** seems to have resulted from failure to see where the direct speech begins). This might be evidence for two lines of transmission in the A revision of **Z**, one leading to **m**, the other to **r**, from a ms of which the **B** revision was made. But the fact that *A*-H and (in part) W, both **r**-group witnesses, share the variant may indicate rather that **m**'s reading here is due to mistaking *ȝe* for *þei* (35) through *þ / ȝ* confusion, with subsequential smoothing in the final pronoun and in 36. While the same explanation could be adduced for **Z**, the tense of *prechyd* in Z 64 suggests that the indirect speech-form may have been original in this version. In B 44 the spelling of the base-ms W (supported by C^2CH and possibly M, which alters the *e* to *y*) has not been changed to that of L&r (? = Bx), since it better facilitates possible wordplay on *leue* in the b-half. **145 (Z 68, A 39, B 47)** *stewed*: adopted for **B** on the strength of **ZAC** agreement, *ruled* Bx appearing as a 'substitution of a more emphatic and easier reading, possibly with deliberate elimination of the pun' (*K–D,* p.

82). The word is either the rare verb meaning 'restrain, check' (MED s.v. *steuen* v. (1)), with a homophonic pun on *steward*, or a spelling-variant, with semantic pun, of the more common *stowid* 'established (in order)' (see MED s.v. *stouen* v. 1 (c), 2 (b)). **146–79 (= A XI 204–13, B X 292–329)** For convenience, notes on the parallel **AB** passage in this first instance of *major transposition* in **C** are given here and not later. They are to be read with the Apparatus that appears in its normal place in the text of **AB** in Vol I (pp. 424–428). **149 (A XI 208, B X 296)** *lygge*: presumably also the Ax reading (< r^2**m**), for which r^1 will have substituted the adverb *longe* after misreading *dreiȝe* as the verb. T will then have smoothed the reading of its group original t (*longe*) and DH^2 have corrected to *lyggyn*, whether independently or by reference to an r^2 source. **150 (A XI 209, B X 297)** The line that follows 297 in B-α (Vol I, p. 426, Apparatus, β omitting B 10.291–302) is rightly dismissed by *K–D* (p. 193) as a scribal intrusion. Though metrically acceptable, it is best diagnosed as a piece over-emphatic padding after 297 had been rendered too long by the addition of *quod Gregorie* and subsequent misdivision. *K–D* reconstruct B 297 to accord exactly with **A**; but in the light of **C**, it seems better to make *religion* rather than *it* the subject of the two verbs in **B**. The rare *roileþ* of **A** is, however, to be preferred to *rolleþ* R (a probable visual error) and the imperfectly alliterating *trollyþ* F, perhaps an anticipatory echo of B 18.298 (all three verbs have much the same sense). **153–54 (B X 300–01)** The retention of the **B** lines apparently unchanged in **C** indicates that **L** was willing to alliterate the |k| of *cloystre* in 153 (300) with the stop within the consonant-group *sk* in *scole, skilles* (cf. 8.67, 10.269 and see *Intro.* IV § 45). In 154 (301), however, no head-rhyme is possible between the a-half stops and the b-half affricate. A simple emendation would be cognatively-alliterating *gome* for *man*, giving a Type IIa line, but this has an unidiomatic feel here. It may therefore be presumed that a difficult original invited ⇒ of a commoner word in Bx and Cx successively. The intense revision, e.g. at 151, 155, argues against **L**'s inadvertent acceptance of *chide* from his scribal **B** ms (as evidently judged by *R–K*, who retain *chyde*). Their conjectural emendation *carpe* (MED s.v. *carpen* v. 3(c)) is described by *K–D* as 'lexically adventurous' (p. 207) and so, obviously, is the rarer word *querele* proposed here (see MED s.vv. n., v.). Repeated ⇒ in Bx and Cx could have occurred the more easily if *chide* had appeared as an intralinear gloss; but this does not strictly need to have been the case. **155 (B X 302–04)** corresponds to three **B** lines, the text of which is uncertain. The form of the sole **B** witness α at 302 scans (a little awkwardly) as Type IIa with the first lift on *But*, Bx possibly having read *beþ* for *is* or had a second *but* before *to¹*. The resumption of β at 303 offers choice between its reading and that of R

(=α), F here being evidently corrupt on grounds of sense. β offers an acceptable metrical pattern like that in 300, but with the |k| stave in the b-half. However, R's variant is superior in stating both that reason prevails in a university (echoing but varying the sense of *skiles* 300), and that the clerk who refuses to learn deserves contempt. β could have missed the first point (which is not self-evident) and have supplied the needed third stave by substituting the obvious *clerk* for the indefinite *he*. In 304 the pointless Bx *loueþ* in the b-half, repeating *loue* in the a-half and plainly induced by it, appears scribal. The conjectural emendation here proposed on grounds of sense follows the rationale adduced above for preferring α at 303: that the activity of co-operative study is a *reason* why harmony and not discord should prevail amongst scholars. *K–D's* suggestion *loweþ hym to* is prompted by the sense of **C**'s revision *louhnesse* and by its closeness in form to Bx's verb. But it seems likelier that *loueþ* came in through objection to repetition of the verb here conjectured (*lere*), after the earlier repetition (in identical rhyme) of its free variant *lerne*, as a result of failure to grasp the difference in sense (here *lere* = 'teach' not 'learn'). **158** *lawedays*: R–K read *louedaies* with P²DM, but these must show ⊗ from **A** or **B**. The Cx reading, in a line and passage revised in detail, is harder and insists more strongly on the monastic regulars' entanglement in secular affairs by dint of their position as major landowners. **159 (B X 307)** revises to a standard Type Ia a Bx line with the inauthentic scansion *aa / bb*. The conjecture *vpon* for *on* provides a second stave in the a-half, giving the line a Type IIb structure very close to that of A 11.213, with its second stave found (not very satisfactorily) in the unstressed second syllable of the verb *Pópèriþ* (and the same emendation may be desirable). The ⇒ of *on* was presumably unconscious; see on 15.212 below and cf. on 2.185 above, where one **C** ms offers the required form. **165 (B X 313)** There are no metrical grounds for questioning the authenticity of the line (identical in **B** and **C**); *K–D's* conjecture *þei purely* for *hemself* is thus otiose and R–K sensibly leave **C** unaltered. No difficulty appears once 'cognative' alliteration on *p / b* is discerned, with *be* as either preposition or subjunctive verb (more probably the latter, since it stands in contrastive apposition with indicative *ben*). The line scans as Type Ia with *ben* unstressed or as Type Ic with *ben* stressed. **166 (B X 314)** *chartre*: the occurrence of the variant *charite* in **p** readily suggests how it could also have been a Bx ⇒ for *chartre* **B**, the harder **x** reading here preferred for **C**: the sense of the half-line is 'though that is their very *raison d'être*'. B-F *charge* is closer in both form and sense to *chartre* than to *charite*, allowing the possibility that α read *chartre* and that R has varied coincidentally with β, which will then have gone on to corrupt further by omitting the stave-word *pure*. But revision in **C** is quite possible, the

blunt sarcasm of *pure charite* being replaced by a graver tone. **172 (B X 320)** The Bx line does not make sense, whether *biten hem* or *beten hem* is read. The present emendation *biyeten* replaces a more complex earlier one (*Sch¹* 1978), diagnosing the α and β readings as misunderstandings of a difficult phrase *biyeten hem* 'obtain for themselves', thus enabling 321 (in Bx a Type IIIa line) to remain unemended. The sense of *biyeten* is 'acquire possession of' (MED s.v. 1(a)), its direct object being *That* 321. The pronoun *hem* could be retained as dative reflexive 'for themselves' but on balance is better omitted as a scribal smoothing after ⇒ of a verb that required a direct object. In the context, it would seem likelier that the barons should reclaim the land on behalf of their *heirs* (the *barnes* of 321). **175 (B X 323–24)** The Bx line 323 scans anomalously as *aa / xa* and emendation is on the grounds of the unusual sequence, that of colloquial speech, being what have motivated the inversion that destroyed the metre. In 324, a Type IIa line, two staves are to be found in *Grégòries*. Since the second must be mute, this is to be regarded as a licensed exception, Type IIa normally requiring three full staves (cf. the closely similar *Poperiþ* at A 11.213, noted at 159 above). But it may render otiose a conjectural stave-word in the b-half ([*gan*] *yuele despende Sch,* [*vngodly*] *despended K–D*). **179** *kirke*: the Cx line scans as Type IIIa, but emendation of *churche* to *kirke*, proposed by *Sk* (and attested by D), while not strictly required, is adopted here as according with **C**'s tendency to normalise Type IIIa lines in revising. **182** *ryht so*: proposed to restore the metre and sharpen the sense of a line that scans imperfectly in Cx as *xa / aa* (and is so left by R–K). Nobles and commons should be at one with each other *just as* the king should be with his whole people.

[*The parallel text returns to the main sequence here*]

B V 54 The line that follows in Bx lacks alliteration and is rightly judged spurious, one of those prompted by, and introducing, a line of Latin (*K–D*, p. 193).

Z 70 is unique to this version and, while conceivably a piece of enthusiastic scribal elaboration, could well be an authentic line deleted as inappropriately expansive at this point. For three earlier such examples cf. Z 2.47, 189, 3.96. **199–200 (Z 72–5, A 42, B 58–9)** Z 75 is a line that appears to be a draft version of B 59 (itself later revised as C 200) and follows two lines of authentic appearance, the second of which introduces 75 in a manner without parallel in **B** or **C**. This suggests that the line was also originally in **A**, and a version of it in fact appears in KW and in EM, the latter pair perhaps representing **m** (A lacks the line). But this attestation by some **A** copies of two unrelated families may be due to ⊗ from a **B** or **C** source in each case. The line could have been omitted with Z 73–4 in the revision to **A** and have been later restored in **B**. But since the sense in the majority of **r** witnesses is satisfactory, its restoration here, though desirable, does not seem imperative. *Qui....Filio*: line 199 // has a blank first stave but a 'compensatory' fourth stave (like the 'supplemental' type described at *Intro.* IV § 44), a metrical licence that sometimes occurs in macaronic lines. *Filio* Z: correcting a simple mechanical slip. **200** *thus endede*: with key-stave formed liaisonally (*thus_endede*), one of the clearest examples of this stave-type to be found (*Intro.* IV § 45).

Passus VI (ZAB V)

2 (Z 77, A 44, B 61) *garte* **BZ**: perhaps replaced in Ax by the regionally less-restricted *made* which, as the probable original in **C**, will be a revision (the metrical usefulness of *gart* is clear from its appearance in stave-position at C 5.146). The variant in *A*-A may be due to ⊗ from a *B*-source, whereas *B*-HF may show ⊗ from Λ and Hm from C.

    Z 83 *one*: apparently a visual error, perhaps induced by *o* in adjacent words.

16–17 The repetition in the a-halves, despite the varied word-order, will seem empty unless implying (a) 'to each parent in turn' and (b) 'over and over again'. A stronger if more obvious contrast would emerge if *vnbuxum* 17a were originally *nat buxum*. But reconstruction, by omitting *of mercy...ybe* and re-lineating, is to be resisted, as is *R–K*'s conjecture *bold* for *vnbuxum*². **22** scans as an extended Type IIIa with counterpointed a-half if the stave-sound is *sk*, as unambiguously in 25, but if vocalic, as Type 1a with onset and 'echoic' counterpoint (Schmidt 1987:65). Either alternative obviates any need to posit a lost *s* stave-word such as *swiche* in position two.

30–62 The first of several passages of **C VI** and **VII** that revise material from **B XIII** as part of a more extended treatment of the SINS (though earlier 19a already echoes B 13.282). For notes on **B** see below *ad loc.* **32** *wilnynge*: the variant *wilned* here (as at 41) may be an erroneous reflex of a participial form **wilnende* in Cx. **37** Though the reading *hym*, which seems to be that of **x**, could be an oversight in revising from B XIII (*Pe, ad loc*), this would have the effect of making a scribal reading (that of **p**) 'correct' against an authorial one. More probably it is a family error, perhaps induced by unconscious recollection of **B** (as at 59–60). **39** The **p** variant appears a scribal slip perhaps prompted by an exemplar reading *couet* with nasal suspension. D's *couetes* may suggest an ambiguously-spelled exemplar: this ms has *couent* and *couetys(e)* elsewhere and the present instance may be intended as a plural of the former word. **40** Here *p*² seems nearer to the probable form of **p** and *p*¹ a secondary smoothing of an exemplar presumably found mean-

ingless. **46** has an onset translinearly alliterated with the blank fourth lift of 45 to form a T-type, though *for* could be stressed here to give a normative line. **51 (B XIII 305)** scans as Type IIb on |v| and |s| with a wrenched stress on *neuére* providing the second lift. **B** could be Type Ie, the most likely pattern, or Ib with a 'strong' (five-syllable) second dip. **56 (B XIII 309)** The word-order of **x** is preferred in the light of // **B**, but the pl. form of **p** is more probably original. The masculine sg. *he* of **x** is now not logical after revision of **B**'s second *hym* to *here* and is most probably an erroneous reflex of the original *hy* preserved from **p** in two members of *p*² (*R–K*'s unwarranted emendation of Cx *here* to *hym* should be rejected). Accepting the (gender-indeterminate) pl. pronoun *hy* gives a Type Ic line; but the line would also scan, as Type IIa, with *þei*. **59–60 (B XIII 312–13)** *Pe*, retaining **x**, takes these implicitly as authorial comment, as in the **B** lines under revision. But it seems preferable with *Sk* to follow **p** (to which Y has corrected) in seeing them as part of Pride's speech, the present tense of *seme* 60 in **x** going better thus, while treating the free-standing Latin of 60a as authorial commentary, as in **B**. The conflicting tenses of *sounen* in **p** and **x** may be the consequence of a tense-ambiguous Cx form *sounyt* (see at III 129–30). It is resolved as past here to accord more aptly with the a-half verbs, preterite indicative and subjunctive respectively after *tolde* 47, *swor* 51 (*take* 53, *sygge* 54 are infinitives, after *wolde* understood) and with the general sequence of past-tense verbs throughout the confession.

    Z 89 *that*: necessary for the construction and securely attested in the other versions, but lost mechanically by eyeskip from the exemplar's *Wyth to a.* **Z 91–101** appear to form an early draft that was much expanded in **A** and progressively thereafter; to explain them as a garbled scribal summary of an **A** original is implausible. The collocation of Envy and Wrath in 91, though anticipating **C**'s hostile confrontation of these vices at 66, is independent, while evincing a like understanding of Envy's nature. Line 96 will scan as Type IIIa if the break is placed after *be*, though giving an uncharacteristic rhythm in the b-half, with its five-syllable final dip. Possibly a stave-word like *leel* (as conjectured at B 9.188) or the phrase *loue and* (as at 19. 276) has been omitted; but the awkwardness could be due to the draft character of the line.

64 (A 59, B 76) The direction of thought in the earlier versions is partly to be recovered from the final form of **C**. That Envy's cry is effectively a curse in **C** helps to discriminate *schrewe* as the bold **B** original, the β variant being a scribal relapse to the uncontentious **A** original and *B*-H a ⇒ nearer to the presumed form of Bx and the sense of α (F is here evidently a scribal reflex of α's verb). That *shrewe* was also the original **A** reading is undemonstrable, but not very likely if *cope* is the object. The chief problem in establishing **A** is the unusual noun that has generated the other four variants. This is distinguished by *Ka*, its hardness helping explain the revised **B** form, one more resistant to corruption by scribes. The emendation *comsiþ* in **A** is not vital on metrical grounds, as the line could scan cognatively, but seems safe enough (cf. B 1.165 // **ZAC**). **65** *corse-men*: **p**'s unique *corsement* is hard enough to be original and the form underlying D (='cursing'), and also, *pace Pe*, allegorically appropriate, because Langland's Sin is 'hostility, resentment, hatred' generally (*Invidia*), not just 'envy' in the narrower modern sense (the symbolic 'clothes' an ironically reversed counterpart of those in a passage such as Col 3:12–14). However *corse-men*, perhaps a transient personification, is even harder, and U's reflex, accepted (without conviction) by *Pe*, points to this as the probable x^1 reading behind y. **66 (A 67, B 84)** The closeness in thought and form of **C** and **A** (anger; the strong verb *writhen*) may argue in favour of *K–D*'s emendation of **B** to read with **A**. But against this, the α form preserved in R gives the same sense as **AC**, only with a weak verb of OE Type 2 and omitting the pun on anger, while the line (notwithstanding *K–D*) scans as Type IIIc or counterpointed Ie. The β corruption of the presumed Bx reading may have arisen through mistaking the preterite morpheme for the verb *yede* and subsequently smoothing with a pronoun and a participial ending to the verb stem. (In *C*-App. *add* he] **p**; *om* **x** (+ *a.h.* X)). **67** *pissede* **x** / *passede* **p**: though either act might have provoked anger, it seems likelier that **p** is toning down the original than that **x** is strengthening it (cf. also the thought at 8.151). **69** It is possible that **A**'s 74–5 were originally here in **B**, since **C**'s 69 corresponds in position to A 74; however, **C** omits A 75 with no breach in sense, and its form is not that of A 74 but of B 13.325. **B 89** scans either as an extended Type III with rhetorical stress on *his* or, preferably, as Type IIIa.

A 74–82 74–5 appear original in sense and metre and will have been lost from **m** by homoteleuton (*ofte* 73, 75) and inserted in E's ancestor from an **r** source. *K–D* (p. 84) ascribe to the same mechanism loss of these lines from Bx after 93. But the omission seems deliberate, A 5.74a being used later as B 13.325, and no echo of the unused line-and-a-half appearing in **C**. **79 (B 97)** scans vocalically in **r** with mute key-stave or a full stave on *I*, and in **m** on *m*, the stave-sound of revised **B**. The latter gives superior sense, making Wrath the cause of dissension between his neighbour's retainers and other people. By contrast, **r** has the dissension between the neighbour and his own retainers, which while acceptable is further from **B** than is **m**. The Bx reading is to be discriminated as that preserved in R, while F is close to the *A*-**r** variant. **81–2 (B 99–100)** The verb-tenses are presumed in **A** to have been non-according with those in 83–4, their later accord in **B** being (variously) anticipated by H²JWN and by T&r. But a present tense for *hate* is to be favoured in the light of **B**.

B 102 (A 84) Bx scans not *aa / bb*, an inauthentic pattern, but *aa / ax*, with stress rhetorically thrown from *woot* to *my* in the b-half. The change, which makes the threat allusive rather than explicit, is in keeping with that in 101b from A 5.83b.

A 87–90 A 87 (B 105) A mechanical reason for the loss from **r** might be the presence of *for* (...)*þe peple* in both 86a and 87b. But the presence of *aftir* at the beginning of 88 in ?**r** would suggest that **r**'s exemplar had been damaged, leaving only the final word of 87, which was subsequently taken over to begin 88. The line's presence in **m** is thus less likely to be by ⊗ from **B** than by descent from Ax, since a clear vestige of it remains in **r**. But *A*-W may well be thus derived, since it has *Aftre* at the beginning of 88 as well as at the end of 87. **90 (B 108)** scans in **r**, leaving 91 as metrically possible but very abrupt. *Ka* convincingly explains Ax loss of initial *Awey* by attraction to preceding *awey* in 89a. *Also* **m** looks like a scribal provision of a first stave, but could be a reflex of a damaged Ax, and **B** a revision. Although **B** ⊗ in **m** has been recognised (5.133 //), recourse to **B** here seems to have been avoided.

B 109–11 B 109 (A 91) *Eleyne* Bx: if original, a revision for which no reason appears. A masculine name would fit more easily here, as the F variant evidently implies (though Wrath's dual sex is later instanced at B 5.155ff). In 111, 112 *his* must therefore have a generic force and cannot refer back to *Eleyne*. Possibly the feminine name, with the α spelling *heleyne*, arose as a visual error for Bx **he heyne*, with *he* either anticipatory dittography or a pleonastic pronoun of emphasis. **B 111 (A 93)** The reading *liketh*, probably that of Bx (and one among the five substantive **A** variants) seems scarcely hard enough to have generated the other four in **A** or the inferior **B** variant *aketh*. On grounds of sense, *lighteth* would be acceptable but seems insufficiently unusual to have invited ⇒. The proposed reading *liþeþ* is instanced at A 7.180 and C 19.71, though only in a literal sense, the first of these causing difficulty to some scribes; the sense here is 'alleviate, ease' (MED s.v. *lithen* v. (2)). If the original had been spelled *litheth*, the variant *lihteth* could have been generated by metathesis (as at C 19.71 in ms X); if *liþeþ*, then *liȝteþ* could equally well have arisen through þ / ȝ confusion. The hardness of the meaning and the mechanical ease of the ⇒ described combine to recommend choice of the conjecture over any of the attested variants.

A 95 (B 113) is reconstructed in the light of **B**, the required sense of **þere þat* (the presumed original of the split variants *þere, þat*) being equivalent to *þat* 'inasmuch as, because' in **B**. The pronoun form *hy* is likely to be the Ax reading underlying the **r** variants. The metre of **B** may be of T-type, *wel* having been added to produce on *do wel* (in **A** on *do bet*) a witty 'anti-pun' (on this see Schmidt 1987:111).

69–85 (B XIII 325–42) For the Apparatus to **B** see Vol I, p. 534.
70 (B XIII 326) The b-half in Bx has evidently undergone scribal inversion to prose order, and *K–D* 's reconstruction after revised **C** restores the metre. **72 (B XIII 328)** The stresses in **C**'s b-half are either *fíkel and fàls tónge,* or *fíkel and fáls tònge* with double feminine ending, or *fíkel and fáls tónge,* which makes a lexical word part of a 'strong' penultimate dip but is preferable. **74–5 (B XIII 330–31)** *K–D*'s re-division of **B** 330–31 in the light of **C** gives a more balanced pair of lines: though Bx 330 is not unmetrical, 331 has a clumsy a-half. However, their judgement (p. 90) that on comparison with **C** the Bx b-half shows 'miscomprehension induced by preceding context' is not compelling. For whilst the repetition is a little weak, it is not obviously unoriginal, and it seems to have invited the sort of changes typical in **C** (there is also revision in following 76). **76** is syntactically linked with 75 and introduces the Latin, which is better presented as authorial comment. *R–K* treat this line and 76*a* as the speaker's, but it seems incredible that the character Envy should quote these two psalm-passages and their homiletic introductory line. **77** The sense is unexceptionable and *R–K*'s emendation *with* for *such* gratuitous. **79** *an*: lost in **x** by haplography before *angre.* **84 (B XIII 341)** Bx scans as Type IIIa, but the lack of parallelism between 340 and 341 appears suspect: for in **C** 'God' corresponds to the Soutere, his 'word' and 'grace' to the latter's 'charm'. *K–D* reconstruct **B**'s a-half as *For goddes word ne grace*; the simpler solution here presumes *God* lost through visual attraction to following *Goddes,* with resultant smoothing of *ne* to *no.* **91 (B V 124, A V 103)** *the beste*: in **m** perhaps by ⊗ from **B**, *to goode* not being evidently scribal, and the **B** reading certainly more emphatic. But **r** equally may be attempting to tone down the optimism, which B 125 will stress more strongly than **A**. **93 (A 105, B 126)** *Enuye: þat segge* Bx looks suspicious on comparision with **AC**, which repeat the Sin's name, indicating vocalic scansion with counterpoint on *s.*

From this point the **m** *family of* **A** *is represented by a* **fourth** *ms,* **H³** *(Harley 3954), hitherto a* **B** *copy* (**H**). The *group-sigil* **m** henceforth (subject to the variations recorded in the Apparatus) denotes *the agreed readings of* **EAMH³** and by inference those of their exclusive common ancestor.
94 (A 106, B 127) *K–D* (p. 102) object to Bx *megre* (retained in **C**) as scribal, because Envy was earlier described as swollen. But his lean physique is compatible with his 'swelling' through emotional turmoil, and *bolniþ* AB 99/118 does not imply 'fatness'. **96 (B 128)** The Bx line has an inauthentic pattern *aa / xx,* revised in **C** with use of a different stave-sound. *K–D* p. 195 plausibly conjecture *biggyng* 'residing' as unusual enough to have invited ⇒ of a commoner term (see MED s.v.

biggen v. 1(a)). **99** The archetypal reading (< **x**p^2) may be *þat,* or else *so* and *þat* could be split variants of the form reconstructed here, which yields a T-type line, as indeed does the p^1 reading. Arguably *and* should be omitted as a scribal insertion; Cx clearly lacked it. **105 (B 135)** The **B** line scans either vocalically as a variant of Type Ie with mute key-stave or as Type IIIa on *w,* the latter perhaps preferable in the light of **C**, which revises to Type Ia on *w* with mute key-stave.

B 136 scans as Type Ia on cognative staves (*k / g*); cf. B 18.48.
126–27 (B 149–50) Of Bx's three lines the first may be scanned as Type Ia (with liasonal *r*-stave) and the second as Type III on *I,* while the third is unmetrical. *K–D* securely adopt the corrected Cr² division, but its source is unknown. The simplest explanation is that it derives not from a **B** source superior to Bx but from collation with **C** which, though revised at this point, retains the presumed original structure of **B** clearly enough to have guided a corrector. Cr¹ could be an earlier attempt to correct from **C** and *K–D* (p. 91) may be right to omit *wikked* as over-emphatic. **128 (B 151)** *abbesse*: containing both b-half lifts without intervening dip, originally perhaps uncontracted *abbodesse.* If so, this was presumably in **B**, where the β-tradition evinces dissatisfaction with the metre by supplying *boþe* as the final lift. **134 (B 157)** *ac*: sharpening the sense and here conjectured lost in Cx by haplography before '*a c*okewolde' (so also in *B*-HmCr²³G, where *B*-Cr¹y substitute *And*).

B 165 *purueiede*: providing for Bx's missing key-stave an 'alliterating synonym with a particular contextual meaning lexically well established but not actually instanced in the poem' (*K–D* p.197). This meaning (spelling out *forwit* 164) is either 'foresaw' (taking *for* as conjunction) or, more probably, 'provided' (the actual reading of Cr), with *for* as preposition, which would be merely an extension of the literal sense instanced at B 14.29. If *provided* Cr is from a lost **B** source superior to Bx, the word it is echoing would be *purveiede,* but it is probably an intelligent guess. Like the Bx and conjectural readings, Cr has a 'monolexical' stave-pattern paralleled by 128 (cf. also 4.172, 7.170 and see *Intro.* IV § 38). The Bx reading itself could be a marginal or supralinear gloss incorporated into the text, or ⇒ of a contextually more familiar word. **147** The general sense of the passage (taken along with *Y, boþe* 148) shows that **p**'s *ich* must be wrong (though understandably so, given the shifting viewpoint of the speaker from 145 to 148). But **p**'s *hue* furnishes the needed third stave and directs emendation of **x**'s first *and,* consequentially, second *she* to *heo.* This is a major instance of a recessive pronominal form having served as a useful metrical resource. *R–K* leave the line unmetrical by their criteria (not discerning a mute key-stave). **149** The **p** reading makes as good sense as that adopted, though it is less vivid and fits less closely with 150. But the presence of *on* in the **x**-mss (altered in P²'s source and visibly in D) produces a nonsensical reading and suggests that Cx read *cloʒes*, the error having arisen through ʒ / þ confusion (cf. on B 111 and 163, 194). If *cloþes* was archetypal, I's reading would be an intelligent response to the perceived lack of sense of *on with the clopes*. The form *cloʒes* is sparsely attested and its rarity may have contributed to the error (see MED s.v. *claue* n. (1)). *R–K* p. 161 argue for *clothes* (in the sense 'coverchiefs'), but *clawes* looks like a moderate reworking of **B**'s (perhaps exaggerated) *knyues*. **155 (B 171)** The form of the line in BxCx allows barely acceptable scansion on *don*, *-dayes* and *to* (cognative and mute). *K–D* conjecture omission of *perf* as the third stave-word before *bred*, thus restoring the stresses to their natural position. But no reason appears for its loss except inducement from the common collocation, and *R–K* abandon this conjecture, leaving the line unmetrical. The reading adopted here presumes mechanical loss of the following adverb through haplography; for similar examples cf. *ʒong ʒong* 5.35, *fel* B 3.260 (and for a parallel cf. 3.426 *beste bestes*, where YA have omitted *beste*). The adverb *faste*, identical in form with the verb, will here have the sense 'severely' or 'diligently' (MED s.v. *faste* adv. 4 (c), 6 (c)). **156 (B 172)** In the light of **C**, the **B** reading is reconstructed as that presumed for α, of which R and F preserve split variants. **158 (B 174)** The Bx line will scan as Type Ie on voiced fricatives (*-þi, haue_I, þo*) and so emendation is not strictly necessary. But a better correlation of staves and significant lexical words is achieved by identifying the stave-sound as *l*, as in revised **C**. The emendation, which presupposes Bx inversion to prose order, yields a Type IIIa line with *likyng* in the same first-stave position as its synonym *luste* in **C**. **160 (B 176)** *at euen* in **C** is judged original in the light of **B**; **p** may have omitted it through seeing the line as over-weighted (as is **x** at 173b). *and whan* **B**: reconstructed in the light of **C** from the split variants *and, whan*. *wel*: preferred to *wyn* on comparison with **C**'s revised adverb *late*. **162 (B 178)** is either Type Ie scanning on vocalic theme-staves or an extended Type IIIa with *w* as contrapuntal stave. **163 (B 179)** *couʒe*: suggested by the context as the substantive lexeme; a metaphor from the preceding image of overdrinking. The spelling of *C*-y is best construed as an idiosyncratic variant of that preserved in *C*-u rather than as a preterite of *couʒen* or an approximation of *coupe*. The latter is to be rejected on grounds of poor idiom and inappropriate tense, as is the former if *wiste* 162 is conditional (as *woet* implies) and not a simple past tense as **p** takes it. **C**'s revision increases the malice of Wrath's slanders by hinting that they are not surely based, whereas **B**'s two indicatives (*woot* 178...*woot* 179) imply that they are. **170–74** These lines left virtually unchanged through **ZAB** are developed with material from B XIII into a much longer

account of Lechery. **173 (B V 73)** *loue* **p**: the reading of **x**, semantically possible but metrically inferior, may have arisen through the scribe's unconsciously taking the petition as addressed to Christ; the more natural sense of *for thy moder loue* would be 'for the love of your mother' rather than 'because of your mother(ly) love'. **174 (B V 74, Z V 90, A V 57)** *myd* **BZ** and *with* **CA**: possibly in free variation in the author's dialect; so, since the word is not in stave-position, the form used in the base ms (for **A** and **C** also that of the archetype) is retained. **198 (A 109, B 188)** In the light of **C** the correct **A** form would appear to be that of *r²*. The line's unusual length appears to have led to expansion of the b-half in both *A*-**m** and in Bx; misdivision, sometimes with expansion, being common in all versions where exceptionally long lines appear, it seems right to emend Bx to accord with **C**. The phrase *as a blynd hagge* serves to create a Type IIIa line after a preceding Type Ia, and objection to it is not on metrical grounds but because the half-line adds nothing to the sense by comparing Greed to an old woman. Bx may have introduced the error, or the poet's *A*-ms could itself have been of **m** type; but more probably **m** here shows ⊗ from the Bx tradition, similar signs of desire to expand the Sins' descriptions appearing after A 110 (with which contrast A 87 above). **200 (B 190)** alliterates on *s*, treated as a metrical allophone of ʃ in **L**'s metrical practice (cf. *Intro.* IV § 46) and *ch*, the latter perhaps sounding close to ʃ in the liaising phrase *his_chyn*. A bye-pronunciation of *cheueled* with ʃ may also have existed, since it has left a reflex in *shiver* (see MED s.v. *chiveren* v. (c)). **202** *hat*: better than *lousy hat* B 192, which anticipates B 194. **203 (A 111, B 193)** The line following in Bx is rejected as spurious since it is over-emphatic, unmetrical and stylistically alien. But its *Al torn* seems to echo a presumed original epithet in 193a (preserved in identical **AC**), which is adopted in place of *tawny*, as the poet's concern seems to be the tattered state of Coueitise's coat, not its hue. **204 (A 112, B 194)** In **A**, the form of 112b is the unmetrical *aa / xa* in **r** (ms W of this family being perhaps a scribal 'improvement' influenced by an **m** source) and in all **m** witnesses except H³. The corruption may have arisen through the presence in the b-half of two verbs of supposition, *leue* and *trowe*, one of which the **r** scribe deemed superfluous. But the probable Cx form (*hit / hit as*) seems syntactically too simple in itself to have invited alteration; so it is inadvisable to emend both **A** and **B** to accord with **C** (as do *Ka²* p. 461, *K–D* p. 93). The readings here offered are somewhat tentative reconstructions. Evidence that Ax contained the phrase *I trowe* is its presence in some members of **r** as a variant of *leue*. In Bx a syntactically intervening stave-phrase is presumed lost through homoarchy from *lepe* immediately preceding at the mid-line; *þe bettre* is retained, but could have been a scribal ⇒ if *I trowe* was judged a repetition. The Bx form as emended now seems satisfactory in both sense and metre. In the light of the majority **x** witnesses, it would seem that *hit* was present in Cx, whether or not followed by *as* (so **p**). The XD reading then is likely to be an intelligent scribal guess, though arguably superior to the *hit / hit as* form deducible as that of Cx. **205 (A 113, B 195)** *He* in **C** may be masculine or an ambiguous Cx spelling of *Heo* (as may be the case in *B*-α). In **A**, however, the feminine forms are unlikely to have arisen from *He*, and Ax may be judged to have read *Heo*. A feminine form is securely attested in *B*-β and in *C*-P² (added *a.h.* in X). In **C**, however, the pronoun has been left in the gender-ambiguous form since the sex of the louse (doubtless here the flea) was perhaps of as little consequence to the poet as it is to the reader. In all probability y had no negative particle and II either retained *nat* from **x** or added it, perhaps by reference to **p**. The double negative *ne... not* is preserved in *B*-R (? = α). **216 (A 124, B 206)** The variants *lyser* and *list* are identical in sense (see MED s.vv. *liser* II. and *liste* n. (2)). In the Bx tradition the two copies supporting *list* are suspect of ⊗ from **A**, whilst in the Ax and Cx traditions the appearance of both words in mss of each family suggests that they were in free variation. *K–D* (pp. 153–54) suspect *lyser* as a scribal variant induced by at-traction to following *lenger,* but against this, it seems to be the rarer word, and the distribution of manuscript support points to its having been archetypal in the later versions and probably also in the earliest. **218 (A 126, B 208)** All three traditions have manuscript support for a stave-word (*pak*) having *p* rather than *b*. It is attested by *B*-γ and also by *B*-M over an erasure of a word that may fairly be presumed *bat* as in α and L (and thus, quite probably, in β); the likelihood is therefore that Bx read *bat.* In **C** *pak* is attested by most **p** mss and by UD, suggesting that y (and possibly also *x¹*) read *bat.* In **A** the split is fairly clear, **r** reading *pakke* and *bat* being probably the reading of **m**. *K–D* (p. 205n) and *Ka,²* identifying the key-stave as *p*, retain *pak* as the second stave-word and emend the first (*Brochide*) to *Prochide* on the strength of *A*-U. But *Ka²* is not convincing that U finds support in KW *Pryckede*, more probably a scribal gloss on a difficult original that could have been either (cf. *Prikede* M as substitute for the *second* stave-word *bat*, the probable reading of **m**). *K–D* rightly find *prochid* 'brought together' harder in sense than *broched* 'stitched loosely'; but it can also be construed as the *A*-U scribe's attempt to 'correct' the metre rather than as a survival of the original. But *bat-nedle*, which is also harder than *pakke-nedle*, cannot well be such an attempt, since the resulting line has a *p*-stave in the second half. The simplest solution is to see both **A** and **B** as intended to scan 'cognatively' with an unvoiced labial stop for key-stave and the voiced stop in the a-half (see *Intro.* IV § 46). **C**, if *bat* is here accepted as the second stave-word, must

then have been revised to scan on *b* only, exhibiting the tendency to a more uniform metrical practice common in the latest version. **219 (A 127, B 209)** *pressour(es)* **AC**; *presse* Bx: the lexeme is likely to have been *pressour*, whether pl. or sg. in **B**. *pynned*: in the light of **AB** best taken as past tense, *bande / playted* (218) and *potte* likewise not being infinitives like *brochen* but finite preterites. *C*-YI only possibly preserve the *x¹* reading here, the other members' present tense resulting from the tense-ambiguity of the first verb. The verbal lexeme's identity is clear in **C**, but whereas in the **AB** traditions *pyned* may be no more than a bad spelling for *pynned*, its metaphorical boldness supports it on intrinsic grounds as the probable archetypal and original reading in both. **C** would then be a revision in the direction of literalism (like *yȝoten hitsulue* for *yeten his fille* at 1.149 //). **220 (A 128, B 210)** The most precise and appropriate verb-form for **C** is that attested for **AB**, *tolled* 'extended, was drawn out to' (MED s.v. *tollen* v. (1)). The two **C** family readings are perhaps orthographic variants, or that of **x** may represent the preterite of *tellen* 'amount to, reach the number of' (MED s.v. *tellen* v. 17 (h)). The **p** spelling with *i / y* is arguably authentic, given a form such as *tyleth* at Z 6.66; but that with *o* is preferable, since the probable pun on *tellen* (preterite) would be best achieved by adopting the spelling of **AB** here. **221 (A 129, B 211)** *wynstere* **A**: the probable reading of **r**, providing a characteristic punning suggestion of profiteering (with play on 'win') along with the literal sense of 'one who winds threads (of silk or wool)' (MED s.v. *windestre* n., recorded only here; OED s.v. *Windster* has post-1700 examples). The fact that *webbester* was substituted for it in six **A** mss (three from group **m**) is inadequate reason for doubting, with *K–D*, the originality of Bx *webbe*. For **B**'s occasional replacement of a rare word with one more familiar anticipates **C**'s general tendency to seek immediate intelligibility. **222 (A 130, B 212)** The reading *oute* **BC** points to *out* **m** as derived from Ax, if it is not a ⊗ from **B**; but **r** *softe* 'loosely' (MED s.v. *softe* adv. 3(b)), unless original as *Ka*–*K–D* judge, cannot easily have been generated from *oute*. Some slight evidence survives in *so softe* R and *per owt* EH³ that Ax may have had *so* before *oute*, and this would better account for *softe* **r** by smoothing and *out* AM by elimination of *per*, EH³'s (if not **m**'s) ⇒ for postulated Ax *so*. The perceived metrical awkwardness of *so oute* could have prompted the revision attested in **B** and preserved in **C**, an improvement anticipated by AM. The contextual sense of *softe* 'loosely' is approximately that of *oute* here; the reference of *so* 'in this way' would imply that the thread was to be spun in a manner suitable for racking after the cloth had been woven (see *Commentary*). **223–24 (A 131–32, B 213–14)** In the light of agreed *A*-**r**Bx, it seems that *more* ended 223 rather than beginning 224. Misdivision will have occurred through ambiguous placement of the adverb in Cx's exemplar, as in that of *A*-**m**. This may have facilitated loss of the first stave-word in 224, but the main mechanism here will have been haplography before the first syllable of aun*cer*, as in all **A** mss save JEL (the JE spelling of 'own' is significantly *awne*). Though in error, *r¹* shows awareness that the line must scan vocalically. *payede*: a potentially ambiguous spelling like *A*-J's *payȝed*, cited as the lemma for *r²*, would account for the variant *peysede* (ȝ being read as z) and its unmetrical synonym *weid*. *whan I*: judged from **AC** agreement to be the **B** reading, altered in Bx to the more emphatic *whoso*. **227 (A 135, B 217)** The ⇒ of *hem-* for *hym-* occurs randomly in copies of all three versions through misconstruing demonstrative *þat* as a relative, with *laboreres* as antecedent; but *hym*, involving semi-personification of the ale, is the harder reading. **228 (A 136, B 218)** *ale* BxC-**x**: regarded by *K–D* (p. 86) on comparison with **A** as scribal explicitness; an addition easily explained as incorporating a marginal or interlinear gloss in the exemplar. However, since the a-half is revised in **B**, the explicitness may be authorial (compare the pronoun *he / a* in **BC** at 229, not present in A 137). **231; 233 (A 139, 141; B 221, 223)** On the strength of **AC** agreement *Whan* and *þis elleuene wynter* may be confidently restored as the original text of **B**. For since both Bx readings show on comparison as unambiguous instances of 'scribal over-emphasis', the linear postulate and the *durior lectio* criterion in combination may be allowed to outweigh the canon of acceptability.

A 142 (B 224, Z 99) An Ax reading with a form such as N's *so þike* would explain both the visual error *soþly* in **r** (< **soþlike*) and the paraphrastic reflex in **m**. Restoration proceeds by resolving N's form into adverb + verb + pronoun on the model of *B*-β. The early **Z** reading (taken with B 235), confirms that a Norfolk dialectal oath is intended.

B 232 (C 238) The *B*-γ reading is the clearest, and the absence of *be* from LR and from M's exemplar could be due to Bx's having lost the verb through homoarchy (< following be*ttre*). F has independently corrected and is unlikely to represent α here; so unless Bx preserved an elliptical original, γ is to be preferred as a felicitous correction. The **C** revision incorporates *be* but the line now scans on vowels (unaspirated *h*), as Bx could have done (Type IIIa or Type Ia with mute key-stave). **242** The asymmetry in the archetype's verb-tenses has been adjusted in uRMF to the more logical sequence of **B**. But *lente* 243 shows **C** revising towards a consistent use of preterite finite forms, Greed describing what he did 'in his youth'. *R–K*'s alteration of both to infinitives is thus inadvisable. **245–46 (B 246–47)** Bx's verb-tenses are first present, then preterite, and Cx could have alternated likewise (mixture of tenses is not uncharacteristic: see on 3.13). However, the preterite attested at C 246 is

not certainly even sub-archetypal, and the revision may have deliberately held back a past-tense verb until 247 to contrast the occasional act of one of Greed's victims with his own habitual practice. Given the *repetitio* of forms of *lenen* (six times in seven lines), *R–K*'s alteration of *lene* 246 to *lede* is indefensible on grounds of sense or style.

B 253–61 B 253 The Bx line has the inauthentic metrical pattern *aa / xa*. As in C 3.139, simple transposition to prose order has occurred, with loss of the needed key-stave (here the voiced labial stop |b|). Both earlier emendations, *for pure nede* for *mote nedes* (*K–D*) and *purely mote* for *mote* (*Sch¹*), which it prompted, become otiose once 'cognative alliteration' is recognised as part of **L**'s practice. **261** *heyres*: γ+M, here accepted for **B**, although the agreement of L and (almost certainly) α suggests that Bx read *ysue*. Presumably all beneficiaries, whether bodily descendants or not, were intended, and γ's correction may have anticipated this by commonsense or in awareness of the **C** reading (cf. V 441); see MED s.v. *issue* n. 3 (a) and entries in *IG*.

258 *weyhtes*: the clearest spelling of what is, in context, almost certainly the precise sense of the original. The reversed spelling of XY (a reflex of their immediate ancestor's) and the more familiar uP² form indicate that *x¹* quite probably read *wyhtes*, an ambiguous spelling of the lexeme meaning 'weights'. The form of the **p** variants (with RFS here coinciding with uP²) would suggest that Cx likewise read thus. The contextually plausible majority **p** reading accepted by *R–K* could have been generated through the influence of a common collocation ('word and wit') and the proximity of *wit* (here 'intelligence applied to sharp practices'). But in context 'weights' is harder, more apt and avoids anticipating 261, 264, and so should be preferred. **267** scans as a Type IIIb on vowels, though it would read better with stresses on lexical words. Either the a-half could have verb and noun-phrase transposed in both archetypes or *on* could be emended to *vpon* (so *C*-F), with the break coming after *pynched*. **273–74 (B XIII 385–86)** The Cx line 273 scans *aa / xx* before and *xa / ax* after re-lineation. Both are inauthentic metrical patterns and on the showing of // **B** the parenthetical phrase *woot God* may be restored to provide the a-half's second stave, lost through eyeskip from wi*lle* to wi*tterly*, with resulting mislineation due to the wish for a line of adequate length. Following **B**, the word-order is **x**'s and the initial negative is omitted as in **p**. The line as emended forms one of 23 in succession only slightly altered from **B** (13.366–99a, with omissions). In B 385, unless coincidental, omission of *I* by L and R (possibly < β and α respectively) may indicate its absence from Bx; but the γF reading (that of **C**) is preferable. **280 (B XIII 394)** *with my*: possibly also the original reading in **B**, from which Bx could have lost *my* (like *C*-eRM). Alternatively, *with / my* β-R / F could be split variants of the same form in Bx, loss of *my* having been caused by semi-haplography before *moneie*. But the issue of sense is too slight to justify emendation.

B 266 (C 289) The form of Bx seems reasonably secure in the light of revised **C**. It contained the phrase *of þyne* before the mid-line break, so F's incoherent variant may be seen as attempting to provide a lexical *p* stave in the b-half, with consequential smoothing of the preceding phrase, which has partly determined its form. The wG reading is a (probably coincidental) levelling of the asseveration to a more familiar form. Once a mute 'cognative' stave on *bi* has been identified for the b-half as the Bx reading (< ?gLMR), conjectural emendations such as *For pyne of my soule* (K–D, p. 187) and *so God pyne my soule in helle* (Sch¹) become otiose.

290 (B 268) *Thow*: the **x**-reading with omission of the conjunctive particle seems more idiomatic and closer to the source-line. *Pe*'s stop after *wiste* and retention of ms X's inserted *ʒif* gives a logical but (in context) inappropriate meaning. **297 (B 275)** *Ys huldyng / Beeþ holden*: not different in sense, but the more colloquial variant with a sg. verb after antecedent pl. *alle* at 296 // 273 and a form of the past participle resembling the present is likelier to be original. In **B**, the clear differentiation of γ from LM in relation to the verb is blurred over choice of the participial form, only R retaining the one identified as original. In **C**, support cuts across both families as to the form of both, implying substantive equivalence.

B 276a–82 276a Between the psalm-verse cited and 277 α has a line scanning *aa / xx* (cf. 282 below) that resists emendation and adds nothing, but disrupts the flow of sense from 276a to 277. It may be an intrusion by the α scribe prompted by memorial anticipation of Piers's rôle as 'servant of Truth' in 540–50 below. F corrupts further by omitting the crucial 276a *Ecce enim in veritatem* that elucidates 276b ('wher I mene truþe'). **277** is a satisfactory Type Ib with a full rhetorical stress on *wiþ*, a word often muted in key-stave position (e.g. at B Pr 22). **282** expresses an important motif which recurs, with the same quotation following and a line about mercy preceding, at B 11.139. In principle, the *aa / xx* scansion could indicate a typical scribal addition introducing a Latin quotation. But the defective metre is easily emended by conjecturing *His* (= *eius* in the Latin) as the original supplanted by an unmetrical and obviously more explicit term (for a parallel conjecture see C 6.307 and cf. 173 above). The line will now scan as an extended Type IIIa with counterpoint (*abb / ax*). Both are rejected as spurious by K–D (p. 193) on insufficient grounds.

306–08 *Pe* suggests that the original may have consisted of 306a and 307a, the first asseveration having come in from 296b and then been amplified in **p** by addition of a second in 307b. This would certainly give a more economical line. The twofold oath must therefore be

defended as expressing Repentance's indignation at Coveitise, as the tone of 294 sufficiently implies. Metrically, 307 is an acceptable Type IIIa line scanning on |k| in **p**. But there are reasons of sense and style for preferring vocalic alliteration in this line since *arste*, whether as here spelled or more suggestively as spelled in **p**, provides sardonic wordplay on both *ers* 305 and *errant* 306. The simple emendation *Hym* (with which may be compared the conjectured readings at B 282 and the parallel case at 21.12) presumes on grounds of sense that *Cryst* is scribal. For **L** normally keeps distinct the functions of the Persons of the Trinity and, though the Creator becomes creature in another context (B 16.215), does not speak of Christ the incarnate Second Person as 'Creator' (notwithstanding 16.165, where reference is to the theological notion of 'New Creation' through Baptism).

309–10 (Z 124–25, A 229–30, B 456–57) The lines on Evan the Welshman are a revised transposition of B 456–59, a passage of uncertain form that retains a text close to **A** and possibly **Z** (see Vol I, pp. 236–7), all three earlier versions appearing corrupt at the same point. On the face of it, the a-half of B 456 // A 229 (*And yet wole I yelde ayein*) preserved in the larger families *B*-β, *A*-**r** could be accepted as satisfactory in metre (Type IIa) and sense (as main clause taking a noun-clause object represented by B 457=A 230) and as identical with C 309–10 but for the latter's first two words *Hyhte ʒeuan*. The presumptive α reading *what I nam* R, of which F's variant is a modernising reflex, could thus be dismissed as an attempt to provide an object for *yelde* after failure to construe the grammar of the Bx reading preserved in β. What questions this account is the possible support of α by *A*-**m** and **Z**. The evidence for **m** is fragmentary: only H³ preserves the posited reading, but with *euer* inserted as an intensifier after *Qwat*; A lacks the line; E reads with **r**; and M rewrites the half-line under influence from following 232a (though *euerche man* could derive from **What euer ich nam*, the error being initiated by transposing the consonants in *nam*). Agreement of **m** and α could be due to ⊗ of **m** from a B-Text of α type; such ⊗, where identified in Passus V, is in principle as likely to have been from a source later than, as from one anterior to, the generation of the **B** sub-archetypes. Support for this diagnosis may be at hand in **Z**'s apparently senseless *Quod ye nan*, resoluble as a visual error for *Quad y nam. Hanna (YLS 7:18n, following Kane 1985:919–20) reads *ye nan* in **Z** as *yeuan*, the line thus becoming a clear echo of C 6.309. On the other hand, *n / u* minim confusion is hard to settle definitively without recourse to the local context of meaning. Another objection to this interpretation is that the posited appearance of 'Evan the Welshman' in **Z** is neither prepared for as in **C** nor syntactically integrated with what precedes and follows in **Z**. Thus, if *yelde ayeyn* in **Z** is taken as part of the speaker's name as in **C**, there is no main verb; if not, it is an infinitive lacking an expected (but understood) verb of volition, such as **A** and **B** provide. If, then, the hypothetical reading underlying **Z**'s *Quod ye nan* is *Quad y nam*, and the speaker still Sloth (cf. Z 5.110), it may be explained either as an **m**-type **A** variant derived through ⊗ from an α-type **B** source, or as an authentic early reading forming, like those of **m** and α, *part* of the proposed reconstructed text of **AB** *And yet what I nam wole I yelde ayein*, with *And yet* and *what I nam* identified as split variants. The verb *yelde* will then have *two* noun-clause objects, one preceding and one following it, and the posited split will have been occasioned in both sub-archetypes by the line's length and the grammar's unexpected complexity. The **C** revision, which is textually unproblematic, now replaces the *whole* phrase *And yet what I nam* by *Hyhte 3euan* (naming a character new to the Sins-sequence who is introduced by the explanatory line 308), and not merely by *one or other* of the parts of the phrase preserved in **r**β and **m**α. There would thus be a good case for reconstructing **Z** to accord with the form now adopted for **A** and **B**. But an *alternative* interpretation is to see **Z**'s reading not as a corrupt reflex of this reconstructed form but as an early version having as the first two words of the a-half a difficult Latin phrase *Quodque mnam* (the noun perhaps ambiguously spelled *nam*). R–B (p. 83) offer this as their second explanation of the crux, detecting a reference to the text of Lk 19:11–27 cited at B 6.238ff. The form *Quodque* would result from mistaking feminine *m(i)na* as neuter. This difficult conjecture is tentatively preferred here as the form likeliest to have generated the surviving reading in ms Z, although corruption of a Latin stave-phrase is admittedly very rare in the *PP* tradition as a whole. The consequences for the textual history of the passage are accordingly as follows. **Z** is an early version, *semantically* difficult in character, which was revised to an **A** form exhibiting *metrical* and *syntactic* difficulty. Since the **Z** line is maca-ronic, its scansion could permit the licence often found in such lines, giving *xaa / bb* (*mnám, yélde, ayéyn; Ý, háue*). But a small emendation of *yf* to *yyf*, which is the **A** form (though not there strictly needed for the metre), makes the line one of Type Ia with muted key-stave and the Latin phrase now forming the anacrusis.

311 (Z 126, A 231, B 458) *my*: slightly less hard than *me* XY (supported by **Z**B-R). But whilst the reading with *my* could mean both (a) 'though I lack means to live' and (b) 'though my standard of living suffer', and that with *me* can mean only (a), both are compatible with the declaration in 313–14. **312 (Z 127, A 232, B 459)** *That*: in constructions like this often having a preclusive sense 'but that' (cf. 7.61, and K² in App; and see MED s.v. *that* conj.1 (d), with citation from Grimestone). Accordingly *shal* **p**, confirmed by **ZAB**, is to be preferred as correct. **316 (Z 132, A 236, B 463)** *And*: certain in **BC**

and presumably a revision to avoid weakening the adversative force of *Ac* in 317//. This 'improvement' is anticipated by **A** mss from both **r** groups and **m**, so need not be due to ⊗ from **B**, and *Ac* may be accepted as = Ax since it is supported by **Z**. -*wyth* **ZAC**: adopted as the **B** original, Bx being a pointless ⇒ of the contextually near-synonymous *of* (cf. the *contrast* between the two in 15.241). **317 (Z 133, A 237, B 464)** *Ac*: in A 237 assured on grounds of superior sense and support from **ZBC**; but here, by contrast, it is Ax that may have 'improved' and the VLN reflex could well show influence from **B**. **319 (Z 135, A 239, B 466)** reads identically in all three archetypes and also in **Z**, if *the* is there presumed lost by haplography. The only acceptable scansion is as extended Type IIIa (*axx / ax*) on |δ| (*Tho; the*). The *bismas* variants in *B*-R, *C*-UVK must be regarded as scribal attempts to make the line normative, not as reflexes of an original mistakenly 'corrected' by the other mss. The name of the 'Good Thief' is uniformly attested as Dismas (see *Commentary*). **321 (Z 137, A 243, B 468)** *me*: the certain reading only of **Z** but probable for **C** and possible for both **A** and for **B** (where F may have it from an **A** source, Hm more probably from **C**). **ZC** agreement need not in this instance be significant, since **p** could have supplied as a commonsense emendation a word that might have appeared omitted in Cx. *Robert*: firmly attested in **ZAC** and providing a better grammatical fit with the 1st person verb *haue* than does *Robbere* Bx, which may have been prompted through distraction from 462 above and the -*ere* ending of *Redd*ere. **322 (Z 138, A 244, B 469)** *with...knowe*: 'by means of any skill I have knowledge of', supported by **ZACB**-α, is preferable to 'that which I owe' (*sc.* the goods he has stolen). *A*-N may here show ⊗ from a **B** source of β-type. **323 (Z 141, A 245, B 470)** Ø **ZC** / *But* **AB**: presumably added in **A**, retained in **B** and then deleted again in **C** (cf. the omission of *Ac* Z 145 / A 247 at B 472 / C 326). **327 (Z 147, A 249, B 474)** *coupe*: harder than the competing variant *gilt*, which would give a cognatively-scanning line; firmly attested by **ZC**, it could well have been in *B*-α here (but the evidence is wanting). In the Ax tradition, *coupe* is likely to have been the reading of **m**, of which the genetically-related members <MH³> have varied to the **r** reading also attested by *B*-β (cf. 350, where *coupe* is secure in **BC** but subject to variation in **A**). *to...eftsones*: in **Z** the reading is as probably a scribal error as a metrically imperfect draft original; the metre of the b-half can be corrected by transposition to the **AB** order, which is confirmed for the final phrase by **C**. R–K adjust the direct and indirect objects in **C** to accord with **AB**, but revision may have occurred here (see next note). **328 (Z 148, A 250, B 475)** *penaunce* **p** (for *Penitencia* **ZAB**): only possibly archetypal, though preferable for sense to *Repentaunce* **x**, which was perhaps prompted by the appearance of this name at 330 below. In

315–29 the other four personifications have Latin names and, unless there is revision here, both **p** and **x** readings could be 'translation-splits' of a Cx reading identical with that of **ZAB** (so *R–K*), or perhaps one Englished from **C** as *penitence*, a word of quasi-technical register (see MED). *wolde* **ZC** / *sholde* **AB**: probably a non-significant clash, since **Z** here shows no ⊗ from **C**'s revised a-half. After 328 *R–K* insert B 476, presumed lost for no obvious reason, which completes but is not absolutely necessary to the sense. However, since the idea of 'walking in the right path' is taken up in *romest* 330, deliberate omission may be understood. **334 (B 284)** *fonk*: like *flonke* a rare word, each instanced only once outside **L** in the C14th, in Gower and the *Gawain*-poet (see MED s.vv. *fonk, flaunk*). D has doubtless drawn on a **p** source but P[2] has substituted an easier synonym. *inmiddes*: conjectured as the missing stave-word in Bx's unmetrical b-half on the showing of **C**'s *amydde* (with which cf. also *amed-des* 9.122). The word may have been lost because it is required to act as a full stave, whereas stressing *þe sée* in accord with sense and syntax will reduce it to a mute stave in a 7-syllable antepenultimate dip. **336–37** As divided in both **x** and **p**, 336 has the unmetrical form *aa / xx*, while 337 in **p** is Type Ie and in **x** Type IIIa. The basic **p** form of 336 is adopted since, after emendation of Cx *with* to *myd*, it provides a line with grammatically superior separation of the subject and anticipatory adverbial phrase from the three verbs that together convey a logically ordered moral sequence. (The recessive preposition *myd* as a stave is found at 4.73 and 16.180; here ⇒ of *with* in Cx may have been unconsciously induced by final *wille*.) **345** remains after revision of Type IIIc, despite replacement of *is* by *be*, the break being unlikely to fall after *beste*.

A V 148 (B 299) *Ac*: conjectured as the **m** reading underlying *Bot* EM. That of **r** was possibly Ø as in HN, the two variants in W and V appearing attempts to find an appropriate connective, whilst *And* T&r shows the obvious reading adopted by the majority under influence from preceding and following *And*.

353 (A 149, B 300) In both **C** and **A**, though occupying different halves of the line, 353a / 149b each have two full staves, **C** scanning as Type Ia, **A** as Type IIb. But to scan at all (on vowels), Bx requires that the adverb become a trisyllabic dip (as is possible but not necessary in **A**), giving an awkward rhythm and stress-pattern in the b-half. The reconstruction assumes transposition of the adverbial phrase and verb-phrase in Bx and gives a line scanning on |w| as Type IIIb, an extended variant with vocalic counterpoint in the a-half, if both verb and pronoun are stressed, as in **A**. **356 (A 152, B 303)** Although **C** deletes it in revising, *quaþ heo* is here judged to have been in **AB**, and omitted in **m** (though added in M) perhaps through eyeskip to 153 or 154. **357 (A 153, B 304)** *Hastow*: in **C** certain, in **A** almost so, on the strength of *r*[1]**m** agreement.

The shortness of the line may have prompted the needless scribal filler *ought* in several **A** mss; but the fuller and more explicit *ought in þi pors* seems due in vN to ⊗ from a **B** source, as elsewhere in Passus V (see below on 163). Bx itself appears more obviously scribal on comparison with AC, and is accordingly emended. **361 (A 158, B 308)** *Souhteres / sywestre*: either reading giving acceptable sense and metre, the former being perhaps the harder, since female shoemakers were presumably less common than seamstresses. *Sywestre* may thus be a scribal ⇒ of a more expected expression, and *B*-B (which has it) could have derived this reading from a **C**-source of **p** type, while *B*-M's *sowsteresse* is an amalgam of both variants. If Ax read *sowestre*, it will have been revised in **B**, since Bx unmistakably has *souteresse*. *A*-V's scribally explicit *souters wyf* is shared by **C**-P[2] and (with visible addition a.h.) **C**-D. **362 (A 159, B 309)** *warinar*: discriminated for **A** in the light of **BC** as the likely *r*[2] reading, itself possibly a correction (from a **B** source) of a damaged exemplar reading *we(r):::* or *wa(r):::*, variously supplemented or supplanted in *r*[1] and **m**. **363 (A 160, B 310)** *Tymme*: a name of uncertain form in all versions, the extensive *Symme* variant in **A** and **B** mss probably pointing to the vowel as having been *y*, and the *Thomme* variant to the initial consonant as *t*. In either instance, a more familiar name has been intruded in place of one found nowhere else in the poem (*Tomme* appears at 5.130 //, *Symme* at 6.207 //). *knaues*: well-established in **AC** and so presumptively in **B**, *prentices* Bx being a seemingly pointless ⇒, though neither metrically nor stylistically objectionable. **364 (A 161, B 311)** The spelling-form adopted for *Hugh* in **A** is that of **B**, which is also instanced in *A*-E.

A 163, 167 (B 313, 317, C 366, 372) It is uncertain whether these (undoubtedly authentic) lines were in **A**. The main authority is **m**, from which in principle vN may have borrowed them. As they were not in **r**, both **m** and vN could have adopted them from a **B** source which, on the evidence of vN's reading at 153 and that of **m** at 109, was post-Bx. But against this explanation A 178, an authentic line (it is also in **C**) supported by both **m** and ?*r*[2], is *absent* from Bx. If 163 was in Ax, its omission by **r** could be due to censorship; but no such reason appears for the omission of 167. This second case, and possibly also the first, may be instances of 'farcing' of Ax with lines from a section of **B** well known and popular (cf. the rejected lines in **m** and some other copies after 31, 42, 110 above and 190, 200 below). **366** *Peres*: this name is erased here in X, as very frequently in its later appearances, referring to Piers Plowman. The point is not noticed further and the reason for it (possibly precautionary) remains uncertain. **373 (A 168, B 318)** *of*: on the strength of **AC** agreement to be seen as lost from Bx (and from *A*-RUHJA) through failure to grasp the partitive genitive construction. *And* and *of* appear split variants of the Ax reading preserved in VH[3]. **382 (A 176, B 326)** *Tho*: erroneously supplanted by *Two* in one each of the **BC** sub-archetypes and four **A** copies. This is probably due to an ambiguous archetypal spelling *To* (attested e.g. in *C*-YI), the relative rareness of the pronoun (*tho* being commonest as temporal adverb / conjunction, as illustrated by the error in *B*-F), and (in the C-Text) by a contextual expectation of reference to the (two) *arbitreres* of the barter named at 381. **384 (A 178, B 328)** is securely preserved, in revised form, only in **C**. The **A** variants may point to a lacuna in Ax, **m** alone (with which H partially accords) giving a complete line. One sub-family (r^1) omits 178b and runs 178a into 179, while ?r^2 has an empty reading with *hoso* (W has its own equally vapid form). Finally, the line is lost from LK, perhaps through eyeskip from *togideris* 176, 179 (they have also lost 177). A mechanical explanation of Bx's almost certain loss of 328 would be haplography due to repetition of initial *And*; like 338, it was probably in **B**, since it is present in **C** (with revised b-half) as well as **A**; but its precise **B** form is undeterminable. Accordingly, since **m**'s reading may itself be a scribal conjecture (though a better one than r^2's), the **C** form is here adopted for **B** (contrast B 338 below). **385 (A 179, B 329)** The diverse a-half corruptions of the initial pronoun in the **A** mss may arise from Ax having read *Tho*. One variant *tweyne* suggests that **m** read *two*, an easy misconstruction of pronominal *Tho* spelled **To* in its exemplar (cf. on A 5.176). Another, *þen* d, might reflect misreading of the same word as the adverb *tho* 'then' (cf. on *B*-F's variant at B 326), with subsequent insertion of a supposedly necessary pronoun *þey*. **386 (A 180, B 330)** *þei bysouȝte*: safely reconstructed for **B**'s b-half as a revision of **A** identical with **C**. The source of Bx's error will have been ȝ / þ confusion generating the contextually nonsensical *soupe*, perhaps preceded by *Hy* [for *þey*] *by*, giving the reading **by þe southe* preserved in β. This was vulnerable to the further corruption witnessed in α following misconstruction of *soupe* as a noun, and β will then have smoothed so as to produce a half-line with at least some surface sense. (For further examples of similar ambiguous spellings cf. 163 //). **390 (A 184, B 334)** Unless contaminated from a **B** source (on which see 394), **x** may be accepted as preserving the original a-half fragmentarily attested in GK (?< p^2) and grammatically simplified in p^1, to which N has here varied (perhaps following comparison with a ms of p^1 type). **391 (A 185, B 335)** *repentede*: clearly preterite in **BC**, the present-tense forms in **A** mss (and in *C*-MK, which *R–K* adopt) probably reflecting yet again a tense-ambiguous Ax reading **repentit* or *repente* (as in **m**), each identifiable as a spelling variant of the normal past-tense form. **392 (A 186, B 336)** *of*: retained as acceptable, though *Ø* is probably original in **AB** and possibly also in **C** (to judge by the striking case at 335). **393 (A 187, B 337)** *louryng*:

the rejected *lakeryng* **p** is a uniquely instanced form, glossed by MED as 'noisy revelry', but suggested by *Sk* (*Gl.*, s.v.) as derived from **lakkeren*, an (unrecorded) frequentative form of *lakken* 'reproach'. More probably it is *likeryng*, also a hapax, which MED implies may be a gradational variant of the latter. *Sk*'s guess 'frowning' (*Gl.*, s.v.) on the basis of Sc. *lucken* 'knit the brows' is, however, attractive, making it a contextually apt synonym for *louryng* which could easily have generated the other four **p** variants. But while as an obviously harder reading it could be judged a revision, *louryng* **x** is unlikely to be a ⊗ from **B** (for the opposition of 'laughing' and 'louring' cf. also A 8.107, which has no **BC** //). **394 (A 188, B 338)** No reason appears, except possibly anticipation of the verb in 339, for Bx's loss of this line, which may be confidently restored by the joint showing of **AC** (cf. B 5.328 above). The form adopted for the b-half here is **A**'s, though there is no serious question that Cx read *þo* (lost in **p** by partial haplography) and *awake*, a convincingly original revision, for which p^1 *aryse* could be a scribal ⇒ prompted by recalling the hypothesised **B** form (cf. on 390).

A 189 (B 339, C 95) *vmwhile*: easily borrowed by the **A** copies NJ from **B** or **C** to correct the Ax reading *sumwhile*. The latter, while not obviously wrong on grounds of sense or metre, is probably a scribal synonym for a regionally restricted term, and perhaps partly induced by the line's environment of heavy *s*-alliteration. **397 (B 341)** is present in *A*-**m** and could be argued to have been lost in **r** by eyeskip from *(v)mwhile* 189 to *Paternoster-while* 191 (though in that case 190 would presumably also have been lost). It is perhaps best regarded as another example of **m**'s 'farcing' the A-Text from a **B** source, as again after A 200. **399 (A 193, B 343)** *And* **p**: syntactically preferable here to *A* **x**, despite support for the pronoun against the conjunction from *A*-J?**m** and *B*-R. The latter all read *He*, a reflex of a presumed group-original *A*, which could have been smoothed to *And* in **r** and βF or else be a visual error for original *And*.

A 196 (B 347, C 403) The b-half could have been lost from **r** by r^1 and the r^2 copies JK coincidentally, though no mechanical reason for the loss appears. Alternatively, vN may have corrected from **m** or, as elsewhere, from a **B** source, as has the r^1 ms U, which shows definite signs of **B** ⊗ after 200. **A 198 (B 349, C 405)** *leiþ*: preferred for **A** in the light of **B** (confirmed by **C**), which is unlikely to be a revision. Ax could have read a tense-ambiguous form **leit* (cf. on A 5.185 above) and vM have corrected from **B**. **407 (A 200, B 351)** *thromblede*: reliably established for Cx on the agreement of **x** and ?p^2, N (randomly joined by <PE>, M and P[2]) having independently varied to the commonplace scribal conjecture *stumblede* also attested in *B*-γ and Ax. The form of the difficult word's first syllable is reliably suggested by the *C*-R<QFS> variant. Either *trom-* or *trem-* was the probable Bx reading (> Lα, *B*-M here having visibly altered from a γ source). The origin of *A*-V's right reading is unlikely to be a copy in the Ax or Bx traditions, so it must be either a felicitous guess or correction from a good **C** ms. The hardest reading in sense and form, it is on metrical grounds the only acceptable variant attested. It was possibly even an invention of **L** (MED s.v. *thrumblen* v. gives the only other example from Malory, in a different sense).

408–13 (B 352–57) The presence of these lines in *A*-**m** is most probably due to borrowing from a **B** source; despite corruptions, they transmit a text unmistakably that of **B**, not of **C** (see Vol. I, Appendix I). Their possible presence in Ax and subsequent loss by **r** are not explained by mechanical or other features. The lines are not in vN, which elsewhere in Passus V show signs of drawing on **B**; but their presence in U reveals at least one scribe of an **r**-type ms judging it worthwhile to incorporate a vivid and (after the success of **B**) doubtless popular passage in his text. In the light of the cases of probable 'farcing' in the Sins sequence noted above, it needs little prudence to reject them as not part of the original A-Text. **410 (B 354)** *greued*: here taken as a past participle (see MED s.v. *greven* v. 3a (a)), harder than the more obvious *gronyd*, a possible visual error. *R–K*'s ⇒ of the **B** reading *grym* has no warrant on grounds of sense or metre. **419 (A 206, B 363)** *spake* **CA**: forming either lift 2 of a Type IIIa line or, less probably, part of the dip in a Type Ia line, with *was* providing the second stave-word and a |w| pronunciation posited for *who*. Agreement of **AC** against Bx here might point to *warp* as a case of scribal over-emphasis perhaps prompted by finding *was* too weak as a second full stave. But the criterion of **AC** agreement cannot be applied mechanically; occasional 'non-linear' revision could have occurred. Whilst *warp* gives better rhythm, its very hardness might have prompted a **C** revision back to the form first used in **A** (the *B*-Hm ⇒ for Bx, if not ⊗ from **C**, might also be aiming at clarity); the criterion of *durior lectio* cannot be applied mechanically either (see *Intro.* IV § 28). *Warp* in this usage occurs earlier at B 5.86, of which 5.363 could be a scribal recollection. But since that line was not in **A** and is omitted from **C**, which thus contains *no* instances of *warp*, **L**'s early and later judgement of this verb as insufficiently plain does not preclude his use of it in revising A 5.206. The word also occurs in A 4.142 and 10.33, the former not in **BC** but supported by **Z**, the latter revised in **B** to *spak* (unless this is a Bx ⇒). **420 (A 207, B 364)** is textually certain in **C**, with its wordplay, and virtually so in **A**. That the metrically-required *wytyd* was the first stave seems sure from its being the probable **m** reading (> EA) reflected in H³ *wyssyd*, a weaker idea expressed in a word of similar form unconsciously influenced by the visual likeness of *witen* 'know'. M, the other member of **m**, in this case *joins*

r in ⇒ of the advancing synonym *blamide*. V's *warnede* corrects the metre while ignoring the available alliterating synonym for *blamide* **r**. The **m** reading strongly indicates its independent descent from Ax, since ⊗ from a post-Bx source, reliably inferrable elsewhere, is ruled out here. In the b-half, Ax corresponds partly to Bx and partly to **C**, but need not be judged to derive from the latter either. On the other hand, ⊗ from **C** or **A** could explain the reading *wif* in *B*-?w (from which M has here been visibly corrected), since Bx cannot have read other than *wit*. The latter, whilst a possible **B** alteration, later incorporated by **C**, that also echoed **A** (cf. note on 419 above), is likely to be *part* of a reading that included *wif* in the a-half, loss of *wit* being due to the length of the line, which was also revised in the b-half. As here reconstructed, **B** now contains a double subject for the reproach to Glutton, the line becoming Type Ic. **421 (A 208, B 367)** The a-half of the **C** line is so much closer to **A** (especially in its *r²***m** form) than to **B** as to suggest 'non-linear' revision and direct reference back to the A-Text. However, the b-half clearly echoes the 'shriving' idea added in **B**, not that of **A**, and the **C** line now presents as a re-worked amalgam of the two earlier versions. Since no difference of sense arises, the word-order adopted is that of *r¹* supported by representatives of *r²* and **m**. **424** All copies save YIDQFS have *Y me* for *me*. The pronoun was probably in Cx, and while it could have been lost by haplography (as likewise in Bx) it is strictly redundant after earlier *Y*. **431 (B 374)** The reading of *C*-M might echo **B** or simply be offering a more familiar synonym for a harder word introduced in **C** apparently for the wordplay.

B 375–82 375 *feestyng*: the sin of *delicacye* envisaged here is contrasted with a different offence, against Church discipline, three lines later. Bx *fastyng* may be taken as a visual error for the conjectured word, partly induced by the presence of the more familiar phrase in 378. **377** scans cognatively with a mute key-stave on *to* as a T-type. No emendation is required on grounds of sense: Glutton eats in taverns for the sake of the drink (an idea echoed in // C 6.433b) as well as the scandalous gossip to be had there. **378** *it*: conjectured as the necessary stave-word (here mute) in a line with the pattern *aa* / *xx* in Bx. The idiom combines a generalising sg. subject (denoting a class of situations) with a pl. verb (following a noun-phrase complement in the plural). F's attempted 'correction' gives a line with an inauthentic pattern (*aa* / *bb*). **380 (Z 104, A 209)** has no // in **C** and is closer to **Z** than to **A** in the a-half, suggesting either reference back to **Z** in revising or an echo of **B** in **Z**, at the scribal stage of its production. The former alternative seems more probable in the light of the **C** echo of **A** at 421. But *sorwe* **Z** is not an echo of **B**, which retains *doel* from **A**. **382 (Z 106, A 211)** *faste* **ZB**; *to faste* **A**. The Ax reading eliminates the wordplay in **Z**?**B**, which would allow *faste* to be both adverb and infinitive (though *to* would be normal after *auouen*). Addition of *to* to *B*-M is presumably the result of comparison with a γ-source, the original M reading having been as L (= β) and R (= α). *for...furste*: the adopted form (**B***C*-**p**) is in contention with *for eny hunger or furste* **Z***C*-**x** as the reading for the b-half in all versions. Cross-family distribution of support amongst the **A** mss and the clear attestation of **B** may be allowed to decide. **436 (Z 105, A 210, B 381)** *lyf* **x**, which is confirmed by the witness of preceding **ZAB**, here has the sense 'living' (MED s.v. *lif* n.5(c)), which the **p** variant explicitly spells out, but at the expense of the polysemy.

Passus VII (ZA V, B V and XIII)

Collation For 176–269 the *C*-interpolations in Digby 145 (K[2]) are selectively collated after **p**. **7 (B V 392)** *romede* **x**:'roared' as in **B** where *rored* could be a visual error or deliberate ⇒. MED s.v. *romien* v. (c) records the subsidiary sense 'arouse oneself', also appropriate in context, but not 'stretched' (*Pe* Glossary). The **p** variant *remed* 'yawned' or 'cried out' (MED s.v. *remen* v. (1), (4)) is also apt here and occurs in participial form at 20.103. But the rarer *romede* is the harder and so more probably original form (P[2]'s modernising ⇒ is a gloss on one of the sub-archetypal variants). **9 (B 394)** revises the b-half to give a Type Ia line in place of the Type IIb with a liaisonal stave on *quod_he* in **B**. There is no reason for suspecting the Bx b-half of being a ⇒ for an original identical with **C**, for Sloth here expresses *wanhope* rather than terror of death as in **C**.

B 400 (C 15) The Bx reading *yet* gives the inauthentic scansion *aa / xx*. But the point seems to be not that Sloth 'furthermore' or 'until this day' lacked sorrow for sins but that he felt no continuing sorrow for them *after* confession, as he should have (in order to be deterred from future sin). The ⇒ of *yet* for conjectured *siþenes* was evidently an easy one (cf. C 7.29, Apparatus, where it replaces *thenne*) and could have been induced by *for*yete at 398. If Bx's exemplar had *sennes* or *synnes* for both the adverb (as in Z 6.16, 7.266) and the noun, it could have been mistakenly deleted as dittography (as likewise in B[1]). This would have motivated both the Bx ⇒ and **C**'s revision of a now metrically imperfect line. **17** *ten*: officiously altered (after **B**) to *two* by *R*–*K*, who overlook the change of *two* B 415 to *ten* at C 29. **20 (B 405)** *puyre selde*: emending a Bx line with inauthentic scansion *aa / xx*, that has a ⇒ of the familiar (but here unmetrical) adverb *ful* for the rarer (and more characteristic) one of **C**. As with 15 (B 400), **C** correction of Bx's metrical defectiveness in the b-half seems to have prompted further revision of the last lift, here away from the T-Type of reconstructed **B** to a standard Type Ia, probably with muted key-stave. Cf. the revision of B 407 in C 22, which

follows **B**'s IIb structure but with a different stave-sound. **27 (B 412)** *mengen I of*: conjectured to emend a ?Bx line scanning imperfectly as *aax / xx*, and needing a stave-word on *m* in the b-half. F's variant (if not a reflex of α) offers a verb with implied sense of 'motion towards' which could have easily invited ⇒ of the obvious *go*, and is used by *K*–*D* for their emendation *moste to* (so *Sch*[1]). But the verb preferred here is one echoed in the revised **C** b-half, where the sense of the latter is less likely to be 'remember [to go to]' than 'be remembered at' (MED s.v. *memorie* n. 2(a), 4(b)). Sloth is here understood to *recall* that he can safely arrive late at the Friary Church without risk of the rebuke his parish-priest would give him. Bx, on this diagnosis, will have replaced a verb of intention with a more explicit verb of motion.

B 415–20 415 (C 29) *telle I vp gesse*: the Bx b-half is the fourth non-alliterating key-stave in fifteen lines. Bx seems to have substituted a more explicit and emphatic verb *shryue* (so as to augment the gravity of the offence) and then inverted adverb and verb as part of a process of smoothing. The conjecture of *K*–*D* (p. 181) adopted provides a necessary stave-word in *t* based on the revised b-half. The C Version, as in 15 and 20 above, has revision in the last lift. **420 (C 34)** *clausemele* **B**: the harder reading (the word is found only here), which β has smoothed after mistaking the adverb for a combination of the noun and a different adverb of similar visual shape (cf. *Parcelmele* B III 81). Revised **C**'s form and redundancy of sense indicate that *it* (omitted) may be an insertion in α. **34 (B 422)** *Catoun*: **x** supported by two **p**-sources is here judged likelier to be original than *canon* (e, q, GK), despite apparent support for the latter from **B**. The **C** line is revising two **B** lines, 420 and 422, increasing Sloth the Priest's ignorance to the point where he cannot read a Latin school text let alone the Psalter or a tome of Canon Law. It is unlikely that the <RM> ancestor here has ⊗ from an **x**-source or independent ⇒ of *Catoun* but quite possibly retains the reading of **p** (< C**x**), from which e and q have each convergently varied. The likelihood of this is strengthened if N's reading (agreeing with RM) is that of *p*[2] and not an individual scribal correction, from whatever source. **35 (B 423)** *bygge*: 'buy', *ytayled* doubtless recording an act of borrowing connected with the purchase. Even if the original form of the the verb was *begge* (so *C*-XUDG, *B*-Cr[1]GR), choice of the text-spelling is dictated by need to avoid ambiguity, the phrase 'beg or borrow' being irrelevant. **36 (B 424)** Choice is between (a) vocalic scansion of the line (reading *if*) as Type Ie or as an extended IIIb with counterpoint, and (b) scansion on |j| (reading *ȝyf*) as a Type Ia line with muted key-stave (in **B**) or as a T-Type line in **C**. The alternative (b) is preferable, since this allows a more natural emphasis, throwing the a-half stresses onto lexical words. The witness of LR suggests that Bx may indeed have read *ȝif*; but Cx seems to have read *yf*.

B 440 (53) *yarn*: conjectured as the necessary first stave-word in **B**, for which the advancing verb-form appears a Bx ⇒. This preterite is found in stave-position at B 11.60, and for a parallel case see *C*-**p**, *B*-β and Ax at 3.269 // (Apparatus). In revision, *yarn* is replaced with a near-synonym less vulnerable to corruption and the b-half of the line further revised (cf. note on 20 above).

54 (B 441) *beggere...(y)be be*: both Bx and Cx have the defective scansion *aa / xx* as a result of the same presumed corruption either by haplography (*(y)be* < *be*) or by deliberate deletion of *be²* through failure to grasp its sense 'for, on account of' (MED s.v. *bi* prep. 7a), followed by ⇒ of the same non-alliterating synonym (for parallels see 5.35, 6.155). In reconstructing, the word-order of **C** (noun; past participle) is adopted, necessitating inversion (in emending **B**) of what appears the likely Bx order. The minimal form (without *haue I*) in LR is identified as archetypal, *haue I* having been added by γ (and visibly so added from a γ-source by M), whether by ⊗ from **C** or by independent anticipation of **C**'s expanded form. **58 (Z 113, A 218, B 445)** *fro*: the form preferred for **B** (against *Sch¹*) is that attested by *C*-**pu**, **Z** and probably Bx, but in contention in **A**. Discrimination of *fro* as a preposition requires *wolde* to be part of a relative clause with Ø-subject (*that* is actually inserted in *A*-**m** as in **C**) and not as introduced by the subordinating conjunction *for*. *wolde* **x**: preferred to *wol* for all versions on the clear showing of **B** + **Z***A*-**m**. **61 (B 448)** *þat...is*: an apparently logically necessary *nys* could have been lost through assimilation to preceding *-nesse*, with *is* then an archetypal ⇒. But the conjunction of *-nesse / nys* is uneuphonious, and idiomatic use of *is* following *þat* with a preclusive sense 'but that' (so actually *K²*) is attested elsewhere (cf. 6.312 //). In **A**, by contrast, choice between the two forms is influenced by the reading of **Z**, though arguably here too the negative particle should be omitted. **64 (Z 119, A 224, B 451)** *make*: Bx *lette* appears in the light of **Z**A**C** a scribal ⇒ of a more emphatic and explicit verb.

Z 124, A 229, B 456; Z 135; B 468, 474 For extended discussion of these cruces see the notes on **C** 6.309–10, 315–29 above.

70 (B XIII 411) On the evidence of GYC (? = g), L, and R (= α), the Bx reading was the nonsensical *hys woman*, a visual error based perhaps on aspirated spelling of the verb and misreading of **wan a man* as *woman* together with inaccurate recollection of Glutton's wife at B 5.358–64. The emendation by w has been borrowed by M but F's is probably independent. However the <OC²>B correction, though evidently derived from **C,** is likely to be what **B** read (cf. on B 14.28 below). **83 (B XIII 424)** *in hope*: supplied in **B** to provide a vocalic key stave-word presumed lost in Bx through semi-haplography (*liþen hem / in hope*). The line scans as an extended Type IIIa with double counterpoint (*abb / ab*). **101 (B XIII 442)**

If Bx also read *ryche*, the anacoluthic conjunction *þat* reconstructed as the form underlying the variants *at / men at* F may have been inserted by α (β is defective here); but it could be authorial. **103 (B XIII 444)** *thy*: evidently the second of two grammatical words (*for* 'in place of' being the first) that bear strong sentence-stress. The Bx reading cannot be known for certain in the absence of β, but α may have substituted *þe* through inattention to the unusual distribution of stresses. R's *þe heyȝ*, possibly an auditory error for *thye* (as *the hye*), is unacceptable on grounds of sense, since the rich man would presumably not breach decorum in this way (any more than does Conscience the knight with the poor hermit Patience and Will at 15.42). **106 (B XIII 447)** *geste*: a shrewd scribal conjecture in ms F rightly adopted on grounds of sense by *Sk*, followed by *Pe* (who misattributes it to **B**, of which it is not the reading) and by *R–K* (see further *Intro.* IV § 34 above). Cx *feste* is inappropriate as Good Friday is not strictly a feast and the precise point being made is that the 'story' of Christ's heroic suffering teaches a different message from that of the *foul sage*. An attempt to emend a damaged exemplar, inducement from the *f*-alliteration, confused anticipation of 115 or unease over the secular associations of *geste* may all have helped towards the corruption. There are no other signs of revision in C 7.96–116, so Bx *storye* could conceivably be a simplifying scribal 'gloss' for *geste*; but it is unobjectionable in itself. **111 (B XIII 452)** *liþed*: the likely reading of the sole **B** witness α, presumably that of Bx, is harder, gives good sense and should be original. In **C** the variant *leued* (or *lened*) **x** is unsuitable in context, since L's concern is not so much with 'believing in' or even 'giving to' minstrels as with 'listening to' them (cf. 115, 118) and has doubtless been suggested by immediately preceding *lyue*. *Sk*'s substantive suggestion is accepted but the tense judged preterite as in the b-half (and in the **B** source, now seen to be unrevised). This contrasts with the present in 109–10, isolating the moment of death, which provides the subject's envisaged viewpoint. **113 (B XIII 454)** *for...so*: not absolutely necessary for the metre in **B**, since the Bx line will scan as a clipped Type IIIa with two lifts in the first lexical word (*wélhópe*). But the sense is sharpened by its presence, which identifies heaven as *mede* for the right dispensing of *mede* on earth. B 450–57 are otherwise unrevised except for *loued* 456, unless that is a Bx error for *lythed* (cf.*C*-**p** at 111 above). **123 (B V 482)** *liche*: revising to a Type IIIa line what may be in **B** a Type I, if *man* falls before the caesura. This would be unusual, and more probably *man* **B** belongs in the b-half while **C**'s omission of *moost* makes the line smoother with little loss of meaning. Vocalic scansion with mute key-stave as Type I is possible but inferior. **128 (B 487)** *sone*: *and* after *sone* in Bx is to be rejected as a redundant scribal insertion resulting from misunderstanding of the sense. **129 (B 488)** *secte*: having the sense of *sute* 'guise, attire' at 16.98 (= B 14.259), so *sute* **B** is unlikely to be a scribal ⇒ for it here. *B-W's secte* is presumably a coincidental agreement with the revised line. The two words have considerable semantic overlap; see MED s.vv. *secte* n. 1(c), *sute* n. 1(a), 2(a). **131 (B 492)** *siht*: providing the necessary key-stave with *s* (though a liaisonal scansion *lees_liht* is possible). Cx ⇒ of *l* is through visual confusion with long *s*, unconscious association of sun with light and inducement from *liht* 132 as in several **B** copies, visibly in M (for the converse error in Ax, see A 1.110 and note on Z 58 //). *C-G* is presumably a felicitous correction, perhaps made in knowledge of **B**. On this more pregnant (as it is unquestionably the harder) reading, see the *Commentary*. **134 (B 495)** *The / And þe*: In **C** the construction is clear, with *lihte* as subject re-inforced pronominally (*hit*); if identical in **B**, then presumably misread in the a-half by Bx, which inserts ungrammatical *þoruȝ*, *was* being a further smoothing introduced by β. The reading with *þoruȝ* and without *it* is quite possible (with 495b parenthetical); but grammatically this would require *blewest* in 496 and contextually *liȝt* needs to be the subject of this active verb (*blewe* B 496, *brouhte* C 135), which describes a first action completed by a second (both duly realised in 20.368–69 //). **136 (B 497)** The proclitic is not strictly necessary for the metre, though the b-half reads more smoothly if *ȝedest* bears the stress and *Thow* is muted. This does not occur in Type IIIa lines, but *þer-* may function as a 'supplementary' stave in the a-half. Its loss in Bx could have been occasioned by distraction from *þ-* in preceding *þridde* and following *þow*. **138 (B 499)** *so¹ / Ø* **pB**: here **x**, now scanning as Type Id, is seen as a **C** revision that stresses the privileged way in which divine consolation is vouchsafed to sinners. *C-p* has lost the significance of *so¹* 'in this way' (echoed by *so²* in the b-half), perhaps through reading *al* and *so* as *also* and eyeskip to the following *so*lace, *so*ffredest. **152a (B 508)** *C-IU* probably preserve by chance rather than by reference to **B** the correct lineation of two macaronic lines with unusually long b-halves followed by a freestanding Latin line.

Z 151–2 (A 253–4) 151 *tho*: the temporal adverb clearly attested in **ABC** and the probable reading of **Z**, which sometimes omits / adds *h* (see e.g. 4.149, 6.95), rather than the redundant adverb *to* in a compound verb meaning 'to throng together'. **152** The **Z** form of this line has the unoriginal metrical pattern *aa / xx*, though the 'monolexical' structure of *mýsdédes* (*Intro*. IV p. 38) is authentic. **A**'s *wykkide dedis* could be a revision of a line unmetrical in the draft **Z**, or the reading for which the *Z-mysdedes* is a non-alliterating scribal synonym (though arguably the harder reading). But another possibility is that the **Z** original was more not less difficult than *mys-*

dedes while both having its metrical structure and providing the needed stave-sound in key-position. The extreme rarity of the conjectured word *wandedes* would account both for the presumed ⇒ in ms **Z** and the revision in **A** (cf. **boȝede* A 7.165 //, *tyleth* Z 6.66 //; 22.308 and notes). Though OED has *wandeidy a.* cited under the prefix *wan-*, MED cites no example under the same; but it may be that the adj. *wan* is in question, used figuratively of deeds, as in *York Plays* 36/38 (cited in MED s.v. *wan* adj. 4). Another difficult synonym in *w*, with a metrical pattern like that of **A** but not of ms **Z**, is *weðer-dedes*, a compound found in Laȝamon's *Brut*, 10521, possibly here with sense 'evil' (MED s.v. *wither* adj. (b) but cited under (a) 'ferocious, hostile', which does seem the certain sense at *Brut* 8143). **156 (Z 154, A 256, B 512)** The **ZAC** reading, agreed but for **A**'s addition of *To haue* (revision of a terse original) allows secure reconstruction of **B**, of which Bx preserved most of the a-half (omitting *to* haplographically after *go*) but substituted for the lost b-half a filler-phrase of plausible sense but defective metre (scanning *xx*). **157 (Z 155, A VI 1)** *was*: erroneous in **Z** on grounds of sense, unless a following *noon* is to be inserted, on the showing of **ABC**. But a less radical emendation is to read *nas* and see *noon* as an **A** revision, perhaps of an exemplar with the grammatically faulty reading found in ms **Z**. *wye*: on the showing (here) of **ZBC** the first stave-word, revised in **B** to the near-synonymous (and evidently commoner) *wight* or replaced in Bx by this word. Ax, now irrecoverable from the divergent witness of **r** and **m**, was probably closer to *was nane* **m** than to **r**'s milder variant, with its look of a scribal filler, perhaps generated by misreading *weye non* as *we men*. A-K may have corrected from a **B** source or by intelligent guess, but its substantive reading is here modified to agree with **ZC** as giving the likeliest form of **A**. **158 (Z 156, A VI 2, B 514)** *baches*: firmly attested in **C**, from which *A*-W may have derived it, the hardest reading, with a good claim for all versions. The **A** variant *bankes* EA may show ⊗ from a post-Bx source; though the word's shape or the wish for an alliterating word could have suggested the ⇒, the sense could not have. By contrast both *dales* (perhaps representing **m**) and *valeis* **r** preserve the correct sense of the presumed original, but at the cost of the metre in the b-half. If **Z** is here original, and not showing ⊗ from **C**, it preserves an important reading that might have been lost to our **AB** texts in the absence of any stronger evidence than that of *A*-W. There is indirect support for *baches* in what seems an echo of this phrase at 10.232 // **B**, revising **A**, where *dales* points back to the presence of its rare synonym here in 7.158. The discussion in Adams 1991: 8–12 unfortunately ignores the witness of **Z** (see esp. p. 10).

Z 160 (A VI 6, B 518, C 162) *wethewyse* 'withywise': possibly original, so loss of *-windes* **ABC** need not be presumed. *ywowden*: either an idiolectal spelling with assimilated medial consonant (cf. *Hensong* 5.123) or showing loss of *n* through haplography.

165 (Z 163, A 9, B 521) *Syse*: clearly attested in **CZ**, but causing difficulty in both the *A*-**r** and *B*-β traditions, where scribes puzzled by the aphetic form of Assisi (*asise* in *B*-R) have derived from A 14 (B 526) the name of a perhaps more famous pilgrimage destination. In the *A*-**m** tradition E and in the C**x** tradition uF preserve a corrupt reflex of the correct reading, while H³ substitutes at random. **170** *þe sepulcre*: a 'monolexical' stave-word that furnishes both lifts in the b-half. Amongst the **A** mss, K may show ⊗ from a **C** copy of **x**-type, AH³ influence from the B**x** tradition (which here however has an unmetrical form). If **Z** has ⊗, it is more probably from **C**. However, in each case where *of oure lord* has been inserted, the source may have been a marginal gloss in the immediate exemplar. The harder reading is undoubtedly *þe sepúlcre*, which is allusive and has a metrical pattern paralleled in 4.172, 7.70, 20.158, 21.331). while the expanded one gives a rhythm that is uncharacteristic. This reading is retained for **Z** alone as it may be original there; but where the sub-archetypal traditions offer a choice, it is omitted, and reconstruction of the clumsy b-half in **B** is directed by the choice made for A and C. **172 (Z VI 4, A 16, B 528)** *and in Damaskle* **p**: not an intrusive scribal ⇒ for the reading in **x**, which must be dittography of the entire 171b, but a revision that gives specificity to the vague half-line retained from **Z → B**. **174–75** make more logical sense in this order, and so R–K's inversion of them to follow **AB** is completely unwarrranted. **176 (Z VI 8, A 20, B 532)** *quod they* AC/ Ø ZB: a speech-marker phrase possibly absent from **Z**, but on the showing of **AC** judged to have been probably lost in B**x** on account of the line's unusual length. For the next 93 lines the *C-Text interpolation in A*-**K** is collated as another **p**-family witness, its exemplar having changed from the **x**-type ms used in Pr–VI and the opening of VII. **177** *wissen*: the probable original in **B**, which B**x** has expanded (deliberately, given the identical error at 304), probably under partial inducement from *auȝt* at 532. *B*-gF have felicitously omitted, possibly but not necessarily after comparison with **A** or **C**. **178–79 (Z 10–11, A 22–23, B 534–35)** Apart from the single detail of **Z**'s present tense for preterite, *both* lines in all four versions are incontestable examples of Type IIIa (see *Intro.*, IV §§ 41–2). K–D's emendation of *saw* to *ne saw* on the basis of *A*-V and *B*-B to make the line scan on *n* (p. 205n) seems little short of desperate (so *Ka²*). R–K retain this in 179 but abandon K–D's adventurous emendation of B 534 (*me...helpe*] *God glade me*). This example shows the incoherence in the Athlone texts that arises from confusion about the nature of **L**'s metre, and its serious impact on the process of editing. In 179, *pálmére* may be interpreted as a 'monolexical' stave-word with two lifts in consequence if *l* is given

full syllabic value (cf. *folowáre* 188). **181 (Z 13, A 25, B 537)** The unapocopated **CZ** form *heued* (archetypally attested in **B** at 14.233) is adopted in **AB** to provide the required feminine ending. **183 (Z 15, A 27, B 539)** The **BC** readings and that of **A** are secure and satisfactory. **Z** scans awkwardly with two stresses in *Cónscyénce* as it stands, and *kynde* in post-nominal position is accordingly conjectured as having been omitted through haplography before *kened* (**kende* being a likely spelling of the word in **Z**'s exemplar), a loss further induced by the presence of *kyndely* in 14 above. The sense is not strong, but that fact helps to explain why **A** substitutes another epithet (*clene*) in pre-nominal position and adds a second noetic figure as a guide. Persisting dissatisfaction with the half-line is attested by the further revision in **B**, retained in **C**. *A*-N is best seen as showing ⊗ from **B** or **C**, not isolated attestation of original **A**. **184 (Z 16, A 28, B 540)** The form of the a-half is secure in **C** and in **Z**, the earliest form, which cannot be derived from any of the later ones, having no factitive verb and the adverb as first lift. In **A**, the latter has been lost by *r¹* and (coincidentally) HE, presumably by eyeskip to *serue* (positing an exemplar form **sethe(n)*), but corrupted to *sothe* in M and further smoothed to *sothenesse* in H³. The form of **C** (*sykeren... sethen*) echoes both **A** and B**x**, probably indicating that **B** had both the original adverb and a new one. The latter is here taken to have occasioned the loss of the former through homoarchy (*siþþen, sikerly*), but the length and sibilance of the resultant Type Ic line may have prompted the compact re-writing of **B**'s revised a-half. **188 (Z 18, A 30, B 542)** scans either vocalically as Type IIIa (or Ia with mute second stave) or on |f| / |v|, with *folowáre* as quadrisyllabic (and so to be expanded in **ZB**, where *l* may be interpreted as a syllabic grapheme).

A 32–9 (Z 20–7) 32 *eek*: presumably lost from **r** by haplography before its exemplar's postulated **ykepide* and severally restored by UV; likewise individually lost by EA from **m** (here represented by MH³, their reading confirmed by **Z**). **35 (Z 23)** *his*: a revision, unless *þis* represents an original **A** reading. **39 (B 552, C 195)** *hewe*: to be judged the original form in **A** as in ZBC. J's unusual spelling suggests a possible A**x** form **hyȝe* to explain the majority *hyne*, a variant (perhaps induced by following *hyre*) also that of the *C*-**p** group (except P) and of P²D (over erasure).

197 (Z 29, A 41, B 554) *wy*: in the A**x** tradition, the likely original of ?**m** *wiȝt*, though the form of A**x** itself might have been a bad spelling such as *we*, that could have motivated the ⇒ *he* in the majority of **r** mss. In B**x** the key-stave is now *where*, either full or mute, and *he* could be a revision in response to a sense of *wy*'s register as perhaps inappropriate to Truth (= God) as referent, not implying that **L**'s **A** copy was corrupt at this point. In **C**, the blank stave *Treuthe* carries the b-half stress and a mute stave *where* the alliteration, an added *w*-stave providing 'supplemental' alliteration' in the last lift (see *Intro.* IV § 44). **198 (Z 30, A 42, B 555)** *wel...place*: certain in **ZC** but uncertain in the Ax tradition and suspect in Bx. The **A** readings may be identified as split variants falling into three groups, the omitted word being *way* or *wel* or *riȝt*. Reconstruction proceeds under guidance from agreed **ZC**, the adverb *wel* being taken as modifying *ryht*. Bx *witterly,* though not unmetrical, seems empty and over-emphatic in the light of **ZC** (and reconstructed **A**) through losing the important idea of *directness* on the route to Truth. The revised **C** line, with alliterating *wol* for *shal*, retains the idea while omitting the word *wey* (presumably as understood).

B 556 The Bx line that follows should be rejected as scribal padding, despite its apparent 'pre-echo' of C 204. Although its metre could be corrected by reading *wonyng* for *dwellyng*, it adds nothing to the sense, does not fit syntactically and interrupts the movement from the pilgrims' ingenuous offer to Piers' angry response.

200 (Z 32, A 44, B 557) *þe...soule*: on the showing of **ACZ** the likely reading of **B**, which has been corrupted by Bx to give *ab / ba* instead of *ab / ab*. **201 (Z 33, A 45, B 558)** *nolde*: certain in **B** and probable in **C**; in **A** *nolde / wald noght* may be split variants of a doubly negative original that read as in **Z**. **203 (Z 34, A 46, B 559)** *lasse*: a **B** revision, retained in **C**, of *wers* **ZA**, which scan satisfactorily as Type IIIa. *A*-VLN have anticipated or show ⊗ from **B**. **204 (Z 35, A 47, B 560)** *Ac* **ZBC**: also likely to be the original form in **A**. *ant* **Z** 'if': conjectured as necessary for the sense and as the form likeliest to have been lost through visual error (assimilation to preceding A*c*). **206–07 (Z 37–8, A 49–50, B 562–63)** *ȝe*[1,2] **ABC**: omitted twice in **Z** for no visible reason, unless as a result of haste in copying. In **Z** 38 the scansion appears to be vocalic (Type III), with the rhetorical stress on *him* (Truth; Christ) and *loueyen* forming part of the prelude-dip, although a Type III scanning on *l* is possible with a final pattern *oúne hèrtus*. **A**'s revision (retained in **BC**) unambiguously promotes the lexical verb to chief position as first lift. **211 (Z 40, A 52, B 565)** *wolt* **Z**: an obvious emendation on grounds of sense for scribal misreading of *l* as (long) *s*, but *wost* could be an assimilated form of *woldest* and no emendation necessary. *hij / hy*: the antecedent being pl. in all versions, Bx *he* may be seen as a scribal misresolution of *a*, the number-indeterminate pronominal form found in **Z**, but not elsewhere instanced in the Bx tradition, so best rendered here in the plainest SWM pl. form. Ax *men* is acceptable, but in the light of **ZC** also likely to be a scribal ⇒ for a vocalic pl. pronoun. **212** *R–K* (incredibly) read with **B**; but the whole line is plainly revised. **213 (Z 42, A 54, B 567)** *Forto*: firmly attested in **ZA** and acceptably so in **C**, so likely to be the **B** reading for which Bx (like C-*p*[1]) has substituted the advancing conjunction,

perhaps in response to a transitional form *Fortil* (actually instanced in *C*-ms U) in its immediate exemplar. *ford*: the unusual spelling *forþe* in three distinct **A** sources, could perhaps reflect Ax, or have come in from *forþ* in 53, but is rejected as distracting and unlikely to be original. **214 (Z 43, A 55, B 568)** *at* **ZC**: either coincidental or showing **C** ⊗ in the copying stage of ms Z; but perhaps lost from AxBx by assimilation to following *pat*. **221–22 (Z 50–1, A 62–3, B 575–76)** *þou; thyn* **CAZ**: are likely to be also the correct original readings for **B**. β and Bx respectively will have substituted plurals under influence from the preceding forms in 554–69, failing to recall the abrupt change to the singular at 570 // and the subsequent unambiguous address to each individual pilgrim severally. Plurals resume in **B** and **Z** at 597 (83); but since the // lines in **AC** have the sg., it may be that no great significance attaches to the variation, all four becoming pl. again at 247 //. It seems on balance that the pronouns would have been sg. in **B**. **226 (Z 54, A 67, B 580)** *berw*: on the strength of agreed **ZBC**, discriminated from among the five variants as the original in **A**. Their number, range and grouping suggest that Ax had a badly-spelled form that was hard to interpret and that scribes variously conjectured an appropriate stave-word, some perhaps with recollection of **B**. **227 (Z 55, A 68, B 581)** *Is*: a subjectless verb, most probably original in all versions. In the Ax tradition, neither **m**'s relative / demonstrative nor **r**'s personal pronoun (like *B*-β) is evidently a reading for which the other must be a ⇒. Ax therefore is quite likely to have kept the original Ø-relative of **A** preserved in **ZC** and in *B*-α. **228 (Z 56, A 69, B 582)** *no* **ABC**: evidently better in **Z** also, despite the different construction there, since if what Piers meant was more a threat than an admonition, *vp* would be more natural than *for*. **229 (Z 59, A 70, B 583)** *þow*: adopted for **B** on the joint witness of **ZAC**; see note on 221–22 // above for discussion of the mistaken pl. number in Bx. *B*-G is quite probably the result of collation with **A** (see *Intro.* III, *B,* §§ 28–9). **230 (Z 58, A 71, B 584)** *In...nat*: on the showing of agreed **ZBC** to be discriminated as the probable reading of **A**. The **r** variant does not alliterate with the b-half and emendation of *manis* to *ledis*. So, either **m** has here preserved Ax and **r** substituted an unmetrical half-line prompted by the sense of the preceding line or Ax was here defective, **r** representing one scribal attempt to fill the gap and **m** another, drawn from a **B** source. **233 (Z 61, A 74, B 587)** *Wil*: on the evidence of **AB** and (revised) **C** likely to be the original **Z** reading, of which ms *wel* is an orthographic not a substantive variant, i.e. not the adverb, which is syntactically and idiomatically improbable. **234 (Z 62, A 75, B 588)** *The carneles ben of* **ZAC**: reconstructed as also the original in **B**, for which Bx has substituted a construction parallel to and perhaps induced by *Botrased* 589. **237–38 (Z 65, A 78, B 591)** The revision shows **A** rewriting the b-half of **Z** after adding a third full lift in the a-half to create a Type IIa line. This process continues, though in **B** only the third lift is revised. While Bx offers acceptable sense and metre, the line's expansion into two in **C**, the b-half of 238 identical with **A**'s, suggests that the latter's final lift was lost from Bx, perhaps through the need to write it in the margin. Decision here is thus more tentative than in straightforward cases of identical **AC** witness against a Bx reading defective in both metre and sense, and non-linear revision cannot be excluded; but on balance emendation seems justified.

Z 66–75 66 (A 79) *tyleth* **Z**: probably original as the key-stave in a Type Ie line. The widely attested verb (MED s.v. *tillen* (2) (b)) occurs at A 2.42 // Z 2.51 and, in its more commonly spelled form *tollide*, at A 5.128 //, with the identical form *tylyd* in *A*-E (see *Ka* Apparatus) and with *tilleth* as the **p**-family variant in // C 6.220. The Ax line could scan on |t| with a key-stave on *to* or else vocalically, both scansions scarcely improving on the form of **Z**. The problem for the Ax scribe lay perhaps less in the word itself, which caused no difficulty on earlier appearances in its directional meaning (as at A 2.42 //), than in its contextual application to stone rather than to a fabric, as in the other two instances. But it was uncommon enough for its ⇒ by the **Z** scribe for original *is* to be improbable. The present reading thus affords lexical evidence for **Z**'s authenticity, if not necessarily its priority; for even if **Z** represents a form of the **A**-Text, it must derive from a source distinct from Ax for which no manuscript evidence exists outside **Z** (see further *Intro.* IV § 3). **68–72** show no metrical or stylistic sign of being unoriginal (see also 77–8 below, and *Commentary*). They would seem to have been deleted in **A** as part of a progressive reduction of the **Z** account of Truth's tower till it is completely removed in **B**. **68** *A may se*: for the stress-pattern using this modal cf. 2.149, 3.252. **73 (A 81)** *þing*: adopted for **A** as giving a line of (the rare but authentic) Type IIb (|d| / |θ| |f|), though **m**'s Ø form with 'monolexical' *déféndiþ* is also characteristic of **L** (as in *déserued* 4.172, *sepúlcre* 7.170). **74–5** are unique lines, with integral metre and characteristic wordplay in 75.

A 82–4 82 (Z 76) is present in **m** only and could easily have been lost from **r** through homœoteleuton (*-endiþ* / *-ondiþ*). The distinctive form of its last lift tells against **Z**'s derivation of it from an of **m**-type **A** source or, conversely, of **m** from **Z**, Ax having *had* to read like **m** so as to occasion the postulated mechanical loss in **r**. The line, not being in **B** or **C** in either form, must be either original or a scribal addition in both cases. But the latter possibility would require a direct connection between **Z** and **m** for which there is little evidence elsewhere in the form of agreements in error. **84 (Z 80)** The b-half differs completely from the **BC** form, *clene* appearing on the face of it an **A** revision of **Z** *smethe* (for *smothe*).

Z 77–8 are unique lines that make good sense and have authentic metre (78 scanning as Type IIIa); perhaps omitted in **A** as too topical and circumstantial to be appropriate in a description of an allegorical building. **77** *ne*: inserted as necessary for the sense and presumed lost through virtual haplography after -*re* in *Wyndeleso*re.

239–40 (Z 79–80, A 83–4, B 592–93) may be judged to have been lost from *A*-**r** for reasons perhaps connected with the prior, but more easily explained, loss of 82. They exhibit continuous revision from **Z** to **C**, *hatte* **C** being unusually a reversion to **A**, and the last lift in *A*-**m** a movement away from **Z**'s physical to **BC**'s completely spiritual image. Once again, the independence of **Z** and **m** from each other and from **BC** is manifest, both lines giving firm grounds for belief in **m**'s linear descent from Ax and, if **Z** 79–80 are taken with 77–8, the priority of **Z** to the latter. **239** *bydde* **BC**-**p** / *byde* **ZAC**-**x**: *byde* is presumably a bad spelling for *byd(de)*, the context favouring *bydden* in all versions; cf. the converse situation at 22.48 below. **242–44, 246 (Z 81–4, A 85–8, B 595–89)** *sothe* **Z** 81: a mechanical error, perhaps induced by *smethe* (a genuine spelling variant) at 80 above. *woot* **B** 597: the indicative (as shown by the context and the witness of **ZAC**) being the required mood for the verb, as *B*-F's synonym ⇒ tacitly recognises (the subjunctive results from failure to grasp where the direct speech commences). **247 (Z 87, A 91, B 601)** The **Z** line is re-divided after *A*-**m**, **B** and revised **C** to provide the necessary feminine ending and, if *mayster* has its normal disyllabic pronunciation, a final lift (for an identical case of misdivision in **Z**, see 1.95/6, where *onus* is again at the line-end). *Grace* **C**: corresponding to *ones* in its correct position in **B**. *hym* **ZAB**: clearly demanded in **C** on grounds of sense. The error is unlikely to have been in **B**[1] and overlooked in revision; rather Cx, distracted by *зow* preceding, will have misconstrued the imperative as introducing another direct command. **249 (A 92, Z 88, B 602)** *wy* **A**: almost certainly the Ax source of the other substantive variants; for although on comparison with **ZB** this could seem a corruption of original **wy(з)f*, that word was not difficult enough to prompt ⇒ or to need revision as was *wy*, with its more restricted and (contextually) indeterminate reference. The **C** revision ascribes the shutting of the gate to both Adam and Eve and the Ax reading here accepted may indicate **L**'s first wish to imply what is finally stated explicitly, after the more conventional assertion of **Z**. Conceivably **B**'s reading was influenced by the sense of 603*a* and (un)conscious anti-feminism. **253 (Z 91, A 95, B 605)** *in*[2]: lost through haplography in all traditions, but **Z** may be left since the need to emend on grounds of sense is not overwhelming. **260 (Z 94, A 98, B 609)** *Wrath-the (nat)*: the spellings with single or double fricative consonant alike are to be interpreted in this context not as the noun (as by R–K) but as the imperative + reflexive pronoun object. Omission of the latter by some **AB** witnesses (as by *C*-X) is due to the scribes of individual copies or lost group-ancestors; each of the archetypes and **Z** seem to have intended the verb. In **AC** it is not certain whether the imperative was negative; in **Z** it is negative, in Bx it was not, leaving original **B** uncertain. The **A** reading with *nouȝt* conforms to the pattern of negative commandments at A 57, 60, 64, as *R–B* note *ad loc*, and taken closely with the prior imperative *be war*, the underlying meaning is 'beware not to get angry', even if the (seemingly illogical) surface sense 'beware of not-getting-angry' might have invited scribal deletion of the negative particle. The probabilities are hard to ascertain, but since no significant issue is at stake, the Z-ms form, Bx's and those likeliest to represent Ax and Cx are retained. **261 (Z 95, A 99, B 610)** *For*: on the joint witness of **ZAC** lost from Bx, for no clear cause; the conjunction sharpens the sense by citing Wrath's hostility to Charity as the reason for being on guard. **264 (Z 98, A 102, B 613)** *so* **ZAC**: unlikely to have been revised to *þanne* in **B** as this would pointlessly repeat the end of 612, whence it has doubtless come into Bx by unconscious repetition. **265** *close*: an instance of *repetitio* (after 264), an important feature of **L**'s style in C that *R–K*'s unwarranted emendation to **AB** *kepe* ignores. **266 (Z 100, A 104, B 615)** *thow*: *the* for *thou* in **Z** is paralleled at A 12.91. **268 (Z 102, A 106, B 617)** The **ZAC** agreement questions the authenticity of Bx. Although metrically emendable by transposition of object and verb in the b-half, it suspiciously repeats both adverbs and the main verb of 615. This may point to scribal censorship, perhaps prompted by unease at the laxism suggested by the condition set out in the a-half. *ac*: perhaps also the reading of **A**, and adopted in reconstructed **B** on the strength of **ZC** agreement; but Ax *and* being acceptable, no emendation is strictly required. **270 (A 108, B 619)** *ouer*: possibly the original preposition in Ax, although K is here judged to reveal ⊗ from **C**. The other three variants, of which *of* also shows as that of *B*-β, could be ⇒ for the reading with the fullest and most definite sense, one implying authority, not just duty. **271 (A 109, B 620)** *Vmbletee*: to be discerned in the light of **C** as the more probably original spelling, *B*-R here representing α (< Bx), with *B*-F having varied to the advancing β form also attested in Ax. **276** *places*: U *puttes* (so *Pe*) is a scribal ⇒ (possibly suggested by the allegory and recalling *prisones in puttes* 9.72) for a Cx reading with a contextually difficult sense 'field of battle' (see MED s.v. *place* 2(c)), and cf. *Commentary*). **278 (A 114, B 626)** has the somewhat unexpected structure of an extended Type IIIa line with a-half counterpoint scanning vocalically on *He* in **AB** and on *Is* in **C**. The remote possibility that a (mute) stave *wel* was lost before *faire* in all three archetypes cannot be ruled out, but no emendation is justified. **279 (B 627)** C re-writes as Type Ia a line

of apparent Type IIIa form scanning on |v| and |s| with a (liaisonal) first stave on *if_ye* and one on rhetorically-stressed *þise*. Scansion as Type I on *s* with the caesura after *some*, a five-syllable prelude, and two lifts in *séuéne* is barely possible; but the line would yield a satisfactory Type Ib structure if *but if* were diagnosed as a ⇒ error for *saue* in AxBx (cf. 21.408 //, where this emendation is proposed for a line that would otherwise not scan). **280 (A 116, B 628)** *eny of ȝow alle*: the elliptical form attested in **AC** is likely on 'linear' grounds to have been the reading of **B**, the Bx reading showing typical scribal explicitness (the omission of *quod Piers* from GF perhaps the result of comparison with **A**). **290 (A 126, B 638)** *so*: on the witness of **AC** the probable reading in **B**, with Bx *bi* apparently induced by following *bi-*. The reading of W judged correct is presumably coincidental, though G could, as at 280, derive from comparison with **A**. **297** The third stave is liaisonal (*þat_Y*) and *R–K*'s reconstruction *this to hym* as from split variants is (though plausible) otiose. **300** *sighen*: the reading of U (and D also, if *siggen* is only a spelling error for it), the least unsatisfactory of the five available variants, but going poorly with the mood and tone of 301. The y verb *chyden* fits better, but is evidently an anticipation of *chyde* in that line; the curious *shien*[*de*] of X (with the last two letters erased and written over) could be a back-spelling of a word intended for *chyden* but with the affricate represented, as often in X, by *s(c) h*). The **p** reading *synnen* (so *SkR–K*), presumably from an exemplar spelled *synegen* (whence the vapid PE variant), is to be rejected as incompatible with the sense of 301. The difficult original underlying y (and so perhaps **x**) could conceivably be **shien*, apparently unattested in ME, but found in OE. This is still extant as *shy* (OED s.v. *Shy* v.[1]) 'to take fright', and has a more appropriate sense in the context. The rarity of the word would have made for its loss as conjectured; but given the poor lexicographical evidence, it is safer not to emend. **306 (ZA VII 1, B VI 1)** In each of **ZAB** the line appears of Type IIa structure, with *(w)hoso* apparently scanning vocalically. But in Cx it seems to have the scansion *aa / xx*. A spelling such as *wo* in **Z** implies an alternative pronunciation with |w|, which would allow the Cx line to scan as Type Ia. But the presence of *wel* in **Z** may suggest that an adverb, absent from **AB**, was later added in **C** and that this was *wel*. Cx could then have substituted for this the increasingly common intensifier, perhaps under unconscious visual suggestion from *fol-* in 307 or objection to positively collocating *wel* with *wikked* when they are normally in contrastive relation (cf. *wel or wikke* at 16.175). The less obvious variant *so* eRM is unlikely to represent **p** and has probably been induced by following *hoso*. C-G thus provides here a felicitous scribal 'correction' in the interests of the metre which is adopted as giving a line of authentic character. **307 (ZA VII 2, B VI 2)** *myhte*: on the strength of **ZAC** agreement judged the probable reading of **B**, for which Bx will have substituted another, more emphatic modal verb.

Passus VIII (ZA VII, B VI)

3 (ZAB 5) *and...aftur*: lost for no apparent reason by *A*-**r**, the terse rhythm of which is found in (rare) later lines like A 11.83–4. While the filler in *A*-**t** is evidently scribal, **r** is not to be rejected out of hand as deficient, since the completed forms in **Z** and *A*-**m** could be derived from **B** or **C** (though no other line in *PP* has fewer than ten syllables). However, on grounds of sense it seems unlikely that **L** would have had Piers set off on pilgrimage without sowing the field he had ploughed. Most probably, therefore, **r** derives from a defective exemplar and **m** may be assumed to represent Ax here. **4 (ZAB 6)** *Y wolde*: correcting the Z-ms reading, which is anacoluthic after 5, the first-person pronoun being required. *Ant schal* could be an auditory error for an original *[I]ch wol* (with vowel missing), heard as *schal* and then smoothed by inserting the conjunction. **6 (ZAB 8)** *þe*: Bx probably read *þere* (> LMα) and γ will have felicitously varied or corrected to what is on the showing of **ZAC** the likeliest reading for **B**. **10 (B 11, ZA 19)** *on*; *sowen*: as taken here, *sowen* is a jussive subjunctive (with *That*) following the direct address of 9. Possibly **C** read not *on* but *an* (representing *han*) and *sowen*, which fits well with *to sowen* in Cx (so *PeR–K*, following the B-Text); but the reading adopted gives the same sense without need for emendation. In the Ax tradition, *þat* and *ȝe* show as split variants of the reading preserved in **ZBC** and reconstructed for **A**. The imperative mood of the verb in **r** is an evident scribal smoothing. *whan tyme is*: from the evidence of the ?**r** and ?**m** variants, Ax may have read **whanne it tyme is*, but v is preferred on the agreement of **ZBC**.

ZA 12–15 12 *yt*: the Z-ms *yf* is intended for *yf yt* or for *yt*, as adopted for **A**. **15 (B 16)** *comaundiþ*: the *A*-**r** variant will yield a line scanning as Type IIa; but in the light of **B**, the MH³ reading may be discriminated as that of **m**, either by ⊗ from **B** or, on the witness of **ZB** agreement, from Ax. Like *wille* **r**, *biddes* EA may result from the scribe's objection to the corporal works of mercy being treated as 'commandments' rather than 'counsels' (see *Commentary* on 13).

B 17 After this in Bx follows a metrically defective line that could be emended by transposition of *riche* and *poore* in the b-half to give a standard line scanning 'cognatively'. But in tone and content, it appears a scribal expansion, closely comparable to those that follow in Bx at 4.38, 5.93 and 6.182.

16 Cx perhaps read Ø and **p** made a plausible correction. The **AB** article is preferred, though **Z** agrees with *C*-**p**. **18 (ZA 22, B 20)** *hym*: on the strength of **ZBC** agree-

ment the minority variant is judged the likely original in **A**. Ax will have substituted a pl. prn through identifying *wynneþ* as pl. under influence from the two preceding pl. verbs. *to* **B**: possibly inserted by Bx and, though affecting neither sense nor metre, probably better omitted. *wihtliche*: judged original in the light of agreed **AB** and on grounds of sense. The Z-ms reading is clearly a mechanical error, but *C*-**x** has smoothed further, perhaps starting from a group-reading without the spirant (P²D corrupt to *witturly*).

ZA 25 (B 23) The reading of the b-half in Ax is difficult to recover, given the number and range of variants, but perhaps the likeliest is *I wille conne erie* V. A spelling-variant of the verb *conne* (i.e. *gonne*) would explain the ?**mJ** variants *gynne / gon* and KN *comsen* (its form induced by *connen*, its sense by its synonym *gynnen*). The verb *leren* in **r** would then be an easy ⇒ of a commoner synonym for *conne,* while *eren* could have been introduced as a final lift under visual inducement from preceding *wille lere(n)*. However, this reconstruction is challenged by the agreement in the key-stave *be Cryst* of **ZBC**, each of which versions nonetheless has a distinctive *final* lift. This suggests that an oath was removed in Ax, through censorship or stylistic objection to repetition (23), leaving a lacuna that was variously filled (in L by a similar oath). **Z**'s verb looks the likely original that *assaye* **B** is replacing, while being the same as in **r**'s pre-final lift. The reconstruction furnishes a metrically and semantically satisfactory text for **A** identical with **Z**.

25 (ZA 28, B 26) *labory*: the agreed reading for **ZAC** being the verb 'to labour', the phrase *labours do* could be a Bx ⇒ with subsequent smoothing by insertion of *opere.* But since sense and metre are satisfactory, and revision in both **B** and **C** possible, no emendation is proposed here.

Z 31 is a unique line of acceptable sense and form, which **A** could have omitted either as not strictly necessary after 30 or because of the negative associations of the verb *meyntene* in such contexts. However, since B 36 has identical sense, the line has perhaps been inadvertently lost from Ax.

30 (Z 34, A 33, B 31) *wylde...culle*: an easy emendation of the Cx half-line, which scans *aa / xa*, on the basis of **ZAB**. Verb-noun ↔ to prose order may have been induced by attraction of *foules* to *diffoule* at the line-end in 31. **31 (Z 35, A 34, B 32)** *to my*: on the evidence of **ABC** and on grounds of sense presumably in **Z** and lost perhaps by attraction of *cometh* > *croft*. **32 (Z 36, A 35, B 33)** *þanne* **A**: restored on the showing of agreed **ZBC**; evidently lacking in Ax, though JE position their synonym correctly. *conseyued*: the hardest reading, clearly established only in *A*-**r**, for which the **m** and J variants appear evident scribal ⇒ in their failure to alliterate. The reading of Bx is *comsed*, as it is of three **A** mss and, in present-tense form, of a fourth and of ms Z. On intrinsic grounds, *con-*

seyuede is unlikely to be a scribal ⇒ for *comsed* which, while itself often replaced by a non-alliterating synonym (e.g. *C*-N *bygan*), was the more readily intelligible. But by that token, *comsed* could be a **B** revision, retained in **C**. The **Z** reading would then be explained as either a draft, replaced in **A** by *conseyuede*, or a mis-expansion of an exemplar reading thus, or a ⇒ by the scribe of ms Z under influence from a **B** or **C** source. Against the authenticity of *comsed* in **C** stand *C*–DM, which cannot derive from a post-Bx **B** source and are unlikely to show ⊗ from **A**. D could here represent u, as at 9.208, where its genetic partner U errs, and M likewise be the one accurate descendant of the *p¹* source it shares (immediately) with R and (indirectly) with q, e. It is improbable that *conseyuede* is a scribal correction, whether by conjecture, by ⊗ from **A**, or by reference to a lost superior **C** source. D and M together are therefore reasonably likely to be witnesses (though isolated, mutually-supporting) to **x** and **p** respectively and so, by inference, to Cx. If *conseyuede* is judged authentic, **C** will here have retained or restored a **B** original lost in Bx. With no direct evidence, its adoption in **B** is perhaps nearer a conjecture than a reconstruction, supported by **C**'s probable and **A**'s virtually certain reading. The **A** variants *rehersede* and *answeryd* suggest that the relevant meaning here was taken as 'utter' (MED s.v. *conceiven* v. (8c)) not 'grasp, understand' (MED s.v. 6(a)), its evident sense at 10.56, where neither Ax nor Bx is in doubt because the word offers no contextual difficulty. This accepted, it seems reasonable further to reject Bx *quod he* 34, on the showing of agreed **AC**, as a scribal insertion. The case for also emending **Z** is as strong as (or no weaker than) that for emending Bx; but since **A** *could* be a revision of **Z**, it seems safer on balance for the 'acceptability' criterion to outweigh that of *durior lectio* and *comseth* to stand in **Z**. **35–53 (ZA 39(38)–49, B 37–54)** The alternation of sg. and pl. pronouns in **BC** may be non-significant, or intended to suggest the dual relationship of Piers to the knight, as servant and as authority. F's alteration of the Bx reading to a consistent singular may show ⊗ from **A**. **44 (B 47)** *sitte*: PEN's variant *(y)sette* is preferred on grounds of sense and in the light of // **B** by *R–K* (p. 167); but the past-participle of *setten* should be *(y)set*, and the disyllabic form attested indicates rather (with understood auxiliary *shal*) an infinitive form of a verb with the same sense as *sitten* (see MED s.v. *setten* v. 34 (d), *sitten* v.).

Z 48–9 (A 47, B 52) has a different form of the line that becomes A 47, though its idiosyncratically spelled *holde* may be the origin of the new verb in **A**. The extra line following is reminiscent of Z 2.208, but the b-half expresses a more cordial view of a group towards whom **L**'s attitude seems to have fluctuated considerably.

51 scans weakly in **ABC** with wrenched stress and an assimilated consonant group *ml* before the first lift. *R–K* (pp. 169–70) argue persuasively for *manliche (MED s.v.

mainli adv. 2(c) meaning 'especially', a word replaced by *nameliche* in the Trevisa instance cited, which has the spelling found in ms X at 9.335, and also in XUD at 2.159. This attractive conjectural reconstruction gives much better metre; but it has to contend with the securely established archetypal reading of all three versions in all three cases (a precedent would be *me meten in ZAB Pr 12). The possibility remains, however, that the *manliche* appearances in X could be scribal ⇒ for a stave-word found too licentious, though one **L** may have tolerated. See further 9.335n. **54 (ZA 50, B 55)** *sayde*: conjectured for **Z** in the light of **ABC** as the required key-stave, for which the familiar synonym will be an (? unconscious) scribal ⇒. **58–60 (Z 53–4, A 54–6, B 59–61)** In the light of agreed **AC(Z)** the Bx reading with the 1st person and present tense for 3rd person and preterite (*He; his; heng*) may be diagnosed as scribal ⇒ followed by smoothing. It was perhaps prompted by misreading *A 59 in the exemplar as &, as at 58 in *C*-**x**, though without the consequent errors and smoothing. **63 (B 64)** *pilgrimages*: an unexpected pl. (also found in *B*-CrMF, though not likely to represent Bx) perhaps induced by *palmeres*; but its sense being acceptable, it is retained here and again at 93 // below. **64 (Z 90, A 95, B 103)** *plouh-pote*: 'plough-pusher' (a forked stick), firmly attested in **ZA**, for which *B*-β and several **C** mss substitute *ploughfoot*, the 'foot' of the plough (*plough-bat = plough-staff* is a different instrument, a long-handled spade for cleaning the cutter). *pyk-staff*: the firmly established **ABC** reading, presumably a revision of **Z** *pik* (if this is original and *staf* has not been lost by eyeskip to following *pich*). The sense of *pik* is 'point', the abbreviation being synecdochic for the whole implement, the staff tipped with a metal point used by pilgrims (see 7.179 // **ZAB** for an earlier use of *pik* alone). But the form *pyk* t is unlikely to be original in **A**, while *potent* A could be an echo of B 8.97. *pyche a-to*: clearly established in **CZ**, but *a-to* is contested by *at B*-α and (possibly) Ax. The phrasal verb's somewhat unusual sense is 'thrust asunder', the action of the plough-pusher to facilitate the vertical cutting action of the plough. The variant *at* appears to be a reflex of *ato* suggested by the sense of *pote*, but overlooking the effect of the pointed instrument in thrusting both 'through' and 'at' the encumbering roots. This detail is spelled out in Z 91, a unique line that **A** revises to focus attention on the furrows being cleared (the b-half was preserved in **L**'s 'repertory' and recurs in 21.314). The **A** variant *vp* expresses an understanding of *pyche* as equivalent to *pyke* 'dig up with a pointed instrument, hoe' as does, more remotely, *awey* (cf. C 118 // below). **65 (A 91, A 96, B 104)** *clanse*: firmly established in **B** and in **C**, and possibly the reading of Ax, although each of the six **A** mss attesting it could perhaps show ⊗ from **B**. Ka argues persuasively for *close* on grounds of sense and *R–K* concur, following *C*-RM. But while *clense* 'clear' (MED s.v. *clensen* v. 1 (d)) gives a different contextual sense, it is equally apt; and if either alternative has been generated by visual error, *close* is the likelier, as it could result from failure to register a nasal suspension in the exemplar (the presumed explanation for <RM>). The possibility that **B** *clense* is a revision of an original **A** *close* cannot be ruled out. **66 (Z 58, A 59, B 65)** The b-half shows continuous linear revision in all four versions, with **ZBC** each specifying a single action among the necessary agricultural works Piers engages in (harrowing, sowing, weeding). Only for **A** is the witness divided, *r*'s *any þing swinke* appearing a scribal ⇒ for the reading preserved in **m** (here imperfectly attested), for one like that of **Z**, or for a lacuna in Ax. But the last of these explanations seems unlikely, since the **m** form is close to that of **Z** in its double vocalic alliteration, similar phrasing and rhythm, and also specifies a concrete action as do the other three versions.

Z 59 is a unique line, of Type Ie, with no echo in **ABC**; perhaps deleted as describing a work not so immediately appropriate to the season.

67 (ZA 60, B 66) *glene*: a revision of *lese* **B** replacing with a commoner synonym a word of more restricted circulation (*B*-Cr's variant may be ⊗ from **C**). The vocalically-scanning *A-r* reading appears a scribal smoothing after omission of the first stave word (*leue*). Perhaps realising that now the sense was weak (whether *here* was adverb or noun), the *r*-scribe further expanded *þermyd* 61 to provide, as an equivalent cause for the labourer's rejoicing (a product rather than an employment), giving metre as well as sense inferior on comparison with **ZBC**. The **m** variant by contrast appears to play convincingly on the noun ('leave') and the verb ('live' or 'remain'); but again the sense is poor, since *þermyd* 61 fits with neither. The emendation adopted here proceeds from diagnosing a visual error in **m** induced by preceding *leue*. The C reading, if it is not (as *R–K* assume) a C ⇒ for *lese*, requires in *glene* an internal *l* stave (a device paralleled at e.g. 5.153: see *Intro.* IV § 45). **68 (ZA 61, B 67)** *merye þermyde maugrey*: clearly attested in **BC** (the unique **Z** equivalent of this line having been completely replaced in **A**); the **m** variant selects itself on grounds of sense, metre and confirmation by **B**. The *r* ⇒ *wiþ þe corn* leaves the line as Type IIIa, a possibility considered by *Ka* but rejected by *Ka²* for the reading of **m**. In fact, **r** could be easily emended to Type IIa by adopting *myd* for *wiþ*; but *r*'s reading reveals itself on examination as a second stage of the smoothing begun in 60 with ⇒ of *haue...more* for *haue...leue to lesyn*. *bigruchen hit*: **BC** word-order and subjunctive mood, found together in the Ax tradition only in N (presumably by coincidence), with **m** having the right mood but no pronoun, **r** the wrong mood and order. It should be noted, however, that at 155 the same verb seems indicative, unless the *-eth* ending is a fusion of original *-e* and

hit, as possibly in D. In the present instance, *bigruchen* **x** can be interpreted as an elliptical infinitive after understood *may* or *sholde*; **p**I have *bygrucche*, which should probably be preferred. **74** is a 'Janus-faced' line in which the simple **x** reading *lele* without *for* (= 'as') allows a double sense. If the subject of *holdeth* is the *lollares and losels*, it means (a) 'Whom idlers and wastrels consider honest men', if *lele men* (b) 'whom honest men consider idlers and wasters'. The friars (the immediate antecedent of *That*) come off badly either way; but only sense (a) is permitted by **p**'s variant. **76 (A 66, B 74)** *forthere*: almost certain in **C** (only RM having *fourth*) and probable for Ax, providing the basis for emending Bx's ⇒ of a loosely similar word for one meaning 'more, to a greater extant'. *B*-B may have inserted *forþ* in awareness of **C** or **A**, but on metrical grounds (and despite possible syllabic *r*) the disyllabic adverb is preferable to the word familiar from the common phrase *telle forþ*. RM's variant may be a ⊗ or, more probably, a coincidence with the rejected reading of *A*-T&r. **77 (A 67, B 75)** scans as a macaronic Type Ie (with mute *de*) and the lineation here follows that in u (omitted from the Apparatus) and **AB**. Most mss treat the Latin a-half as 'appended' rather than 'enclosed' (see Schmidt 1987: 93–102). **79 (A 69, B 77)** The metrical pattern of the line is ambiguous, as it may scan vocalically with first stave on *áscaped* or on cognative palatal stops (|k| |g|), the second of these mute and the first 'internal' (*ascáped*). **82–3 (Z 64–8, A 72–4, B 80–2)** The name of Piers's son in **Z** is much longer than its equivalent in **A**, which has been completely revised, retaining only **Z** 66b. Given the difficulty of adapting composite allegorical nomenclature to fit alliterative metre, the **Z** lines constitute *prima facie* evidence of authenticity. They make good sense, are technically perfect and owe nothing to any of the accepted versions (even if the thought of 68a is like that of B 10.39b, 42a). **90** *And by*: reconstructed from the presumed split variants *And* (lost from **p**) and *by* (replaced in **x** by *aftur*, which has come in from 91). *wordynge*: Pe's definitive emendation on grounds of sense. Cx *worchynge* is excluded by the meaning of 91 and may have been induced by the sense of synonymous *doynge* and the sense and form of immediately following *worche*. While the verbal noun itself is not instanced from before 1600, the verb was common (C 13.245, B 4.46, 10.427) and is found in participial form at B 17.48. **97 (Z 74, A 80, B 88)** *defenden...fende*: the agreed wording of **ZAC** (here in *prose* order) against which that of Bx, unobjectionable in itself, may be diagnosed as scribal (though the cause of the transposition is obscure). On the hypothesis of linear revision, Bx is accordingly emended, whereas in C 99 the same hypothesis supports *not* emending the order of the nouns in the a-half (against *R–K*, who make **C** accord with **AB**). *and* **C** / *for* **ZAB**: a **C** revision to Type IIa, unless *and* is taken as a Cx ⇒ for original *for*. **101 (Z 79,**

A 84, B 92) *my*^{2}: on the showing of agreed **ZA** and probable **C**, omission of *my*^{2} in Bx appears a scribal slip, perhaps induced by alliterative attraction (*corn > catel*). *my*^{3} **ZC** / *þe* **AB**: though **C** could be restoring a more explicit reading, there is no real ground for thinking **Z** to show ⊗ from **C** or **AB** rather than being a first version restored after revision. **106 (Z 84, A 89, B 97)** *it*: in *B*-F insertion of a pronoun (*om* RM*R*–*K*) not strictly necessary for the sense, either coincidentally or by ⊗ from **C**. *douhteres*: in itself A*x frendis* is acceptable in metre and sense, offering a Type IIIa line and a contrast between 'friends' and 'children'. But in the light of **Z**, *douȝtres* challenges consideration not as a **B** revision but as the probable original reading of **A**, rejected by A*x* for a supposedly more logical contrast. The **ZBC** reading may imply for *children* a specific sense it only acquires through coming after *douȝtres*; or else it implies no opposition, but merely appends the 'hypernym' (superordinate) to complete the sense specified by the preceding hyponym. **107 (Z 85, A 90, B 98)** *dette is*: the sg. appearing harder on grounds of sense (the 'debt' being what Piers owes to God), this is accordingly adopted for **BC**. But the A*x* reading, though inferior, is acceptable, and emendation not imperative here. **114 (Z 94, A 99, B 107)** *digged*: in the A*x* tradition, whether the verb was *deluen* or (more probably) *dyggen*, the present tense was certain, misinterpreting an ambiguously-spelled preterite **dyggyt*. In the light of **ZBC**, the felicitous NA correction is accepted as likely to correspond to the original **A** reading. **115–16 (Z 95–6, A 100–01, B 108–09)** The b-half of 115 has been revised in **C**, but 116 confirms that the adverb *ȝerne* goes with *wrouhten* as in **ZB**, necessitating that *faste* qualified the verb of B 108 // (*preised*). This is preferable on grounds of sense to the reverse order attested in A*x*, which presumably results from visual error (ms W must here have corrected from a **B** source). **126 (Z 106, A 111, B 119)** *here*: although not strictly necessary, sharpening focus and appearing likely in the light of **ZAC** to have been in **B**. Bx could have lost it through alliterative attraction of *grayn > growith*, *B*-M have added from **A** or **C**. **130 (Z 112, A 115, B 123)** *pleynt*: the Bx line scanning *aab / bx* (an inauthentic pattern), *pleynt* is here conjectured on the showing of **ZA** as the **B** original and Bx *mone* a ⇒ under inducement from the common phrase *maken mone* and suggestion from preceding *made*. The revised **C** form indicates that this reading was in B^1, where it provided the basis of a refashioned line scanning on *m*. **134 (Z 117, A 120, B 128)** *nother*: to be discerned from **ZAC** agreement as the **B** reading, with the simple negative a Bx ⇒ through failure to find terminal *-er* and confusion of *þ* with *ȝ*, followed by smoothing. The BC*r* correction will be from **C**. **135 (Z 113, A 116, B 124)** *Ne haue*: the presumed C*x* reading (actually that of D), reconstructed from the surviving split variants as a revision of **B**; *We*

haue **p** is too easy to have invited ⇒ of *Ne* **x**. *ye* **Z**: the grammatically necessary plural securely restored in the light of **AB**, the Z-scribe doubtless having mistaken *ȝ* for *þ* in copying.

Z 120–5 (A 123–8, B 131–2) 120 *holde*: in **ZA** either a spelling variant of *olde* (with redundant pre-vocalic *h*) or a separate word (MED s.v. *hold* adj. 'loyal','trusty'), an interpretation indirectly supported by C 195 below. **B** takes it in the former sense and alters 'ought' to 'commanded' (which, though not an obvious improvement, need not be scribal). **121 (A 124, B 132)** *W(h)iche*: the harder reading on grounds of sense, following more naturally from *warne* A 123 // and likelier to be original in **A**. The erratic *A*-R spelling perhaps points to the underlying ?A*x* reading from which the error *Suche* (= *Swiche*) derives. **125 (A 128)** *koes*: the hardest reading, from which *crowen* and *gees* probably come. In principle **Z** could originate from an **A** source of **m**-type, as does *A*-ms A, but since **Z** is known not to derive from A*x*, its witness here independently confirms the latter's probable reading.

B 138–50 138 (Z 129, A 132) *garisoun*: here proposed as furnishing a necessary key-stave word, Bx *amendement* being ⇒ of a non-alliterating synonym to give the unmetrical pattern *aa / xx*. The sense of the conjectured word is contextually appropriate to deliverance from both sickness and from imprisonment, the conditions specified in B 136 // above (see MED s.v. *garisoun* n. (b)), and it could have been suggested by the shape of the b-half in **A** (gare *hem to a*rise). **142** *afelde*: though *l* here could be syllabic, the inflected dative is more consonant with **L**'s practice, so final *e* is added for the necessary feminine ending. **148** *receyue*: providing the needed stave-word for which Bx seems to haue a (near-)synonym ⇒, producing a line with the inauthentic pattern *aa / xx* (the palpably scribal rewriting in F, as at 150, is characteristic of this ms). The present conjecture provides both better rhythm and a simpler explanation of the corruption than *riȝt noȝt* (*Sch*^{1}), a phrase that occurs at 151 and is unlikely to have been repeated within three lines. **150** *putte*: conjectured as the required key stave-word, for which the Bx ⇒ is the common collocation *make at ese*. The F variant adopted by *K–D*, providing a metrical b-half that could scarcely have invited ⇒ by Bx's, cannot be other than flagrant sophistication.

148 (Z 131, A 134, B 146) The line as it stands in either ?**x** (reading *what*) or ?**p** (reading *þat*) tends to yield a Type IIIa pattern with vocalic stresses (*Y*, *hem*); for there to be sufficient notional substance and metrical weight in the a-half, the caesura must be located after *hem*^{1} and the key-stave in *hem*^{2}. But reconstruction here derives *what þat* from the split variants attested in **x** and **p** and scans the line on |w| as Type I with a mute second stave in *wolle*; a reading coinciding with that G preserves by felicitous scribal conjecture. **149 (Z 136, A 139, B 152)**

to wrath hym: from **ZBC** agreement, the probable reading of **A**. The **r** variant *arise*, which E derives from an **r**-source, yields a line of Type IIIa, while that of **m** suggests a lacuna in its exemplar, and thence perhaps in Ax. The **r** reading would be an attempt to fill it, while **m** achieves some easing of the rhythm by inserting the prefix *be-* before *gan*. **151 (Z 139, A 142, B 155)** *pyuische*: a rare word not found outside **L** in the C14th (MED s.v. *peivish* adj.), the presence of which in **Z** suggests possible ⊗ from **C** at the scribal phase, or else that this was a draft reading subsequently twice-revised. None of the four readings instanced is obviously scribal in character and accordingly no emendation is proposed. Since, however, *A-***m** *pyned* could show ⊗ from **B**, while **r**'s *pilide* is arguably harder and cannot stem from it, the latter is retained for **A**. **153 (Z 140, A 143, B 156)** scans as Type IIIb except in *C*-**p**, which could be a scribal attempt to accord the line to Type I (here enriched with a fourth *w* stave as Ia) or a revision (as here judged), **x** having diverged to the more familiar version of the set phrase used in **ZAB**. **155 (Z 142, A 145, B 158)** *permyde*: the more archaic second element of this adverb, not strictly required on metrical grounds but appearing from **ZB** agreement to be the probable **m** form, is here taken to represent Ax, though preserved only in M.

B 162 (C 159) *while ilke*: adjective and noun (somewhat counter-idiomatically) ↔ to restore the metre damaged in Bx through inversion to prose order. In principle, the line could scan as an extended counterpointed Type III (*abb / ab*) but this goes against the natural tendency to stress the lexical words in both halves (for a similar error see B 13.82). F's correction shows cavalier disregard for sense.

A 151 (Z 148, B 166, C 163) *welde*: the harder **A** reading, supported by **Z**; *bere* in **B** is a revision, anticipated by *A-*t*r²*MH³.
166 (Z 152, A 155, B 170) The b-half is revised from **Z** → **A** → **B**, and in **C** the whole rejected for a new half-line replacing B 169b. The **Z** form anticipates the adverb of **B**, which preserves **A**'s verb. The Ax order *next metten* gives an unmetrical structure *aa / xa*, unless (improbably) *hy* is read for *þei* and weak vocalic scansion on non-lexical words is posited. The conjectured emendation requires simple ↔ of verb and adverb, with addition of the required final *-e* found variably in the adverb. **170 (Z 155, A 158, B 173)** The metrical structure of the **C** line is problematic. Although scansion as a Type III on voiced fricatives is possible, the earlier versions point to lexical stave-words and thus scansion on |w|; but this gives a masculine ending, unless *nat* is expanded as a disyllabic form *na-uht, na-wiht*. (cf 9.112 and note below). However, a 'licensed' breach of the feminine-ending rule may be conceivable, given the special rhetorical emphasis suggested by the sense of the revised b-half, and two

juxtaposed monosyllables in 'clashing stress' are certainly very striking. **175 (Z 160, A 163, B 178)** *gottes*: on the showing of **ZBC** and as avoiding repetition, this is judged likely to be the original **A** reading, *mawis* having come in from 159. **176 (Z 161, A 164, B 179)** *hym byleue*: on the agreed witness of **ZAC** the last lift would appear to have been replaced in Bx by a phrase more emphatic and explicit, although in its α form metrically unexceptionable.

A 165–8 (Z 162–5) 165 On the evidence of *A-r²* ?**m** the reading of Ax was *he ȝede* or *heȝede*, and this would account for the form of **Z** *a yede*, in which *he-* has been taken as the pronoun subject. The line could scan as an extended Type III with counterpoint (*abb / ax*), the vowel staves being *a* and *hem*, an acceptable pattern, or as standard with two stresses in *bétwéne*, an 'idiometric' monolexical pattern (cf. *Intro*. IV § 38). The present emendation *boȝede* likewise provides full stresses on lexical words, the rationale of the conjectured corruption being the ease of *b / h* confusion and the relative rarity of the verb, which is found at B 5.566 // **ZA** (revised in **C**; see MED s.v. *bouen* v. (1), 6 (a)). **166 (Z 163)** *permyd*: preferred in the light of **Z** as the probable form in this (revised) line, giving in **A** a characteristic homophonic play with *amydde*. **168 (Z 165)** *defendite / yfet*: the *A*-W and K reading *fette* is presumably a chance variant coinciding with **Z**, since *defendite* appears a revision, doubtless due to realisation that water taken on top of beans would cause indigestion.

178 (B 182) After 182 Bx has an unmetrical line that could be emended by reading *mened* for *preied* but appears a piece of enthusiastic scribal expansion like those after B 4.38 and 5.193 (see *Intro*. III B § 60). The revised **C** line recurs in part at 192. **179 (Z 168, A 171, B 183)** In the light of **Z** and (revised) **C**, a temporal adverb is likely to have appeared in **A** having the form *þo*. In the Ax tradition, a reflex of *þo* appears in the demonstrative *þese / þo* of **m** but has evidently been lost from **r** and restored independently in V and, correctly positioned, in JN and H (as *þen*). The **B** reading *herof* could be a revision or a Bx ⇒ for the same word. **180 (Z 169, A 172, B 184)** *flailes*: the nonsense reading *fuales* in XY (< y) and D (< u), probably that of **x**, has been independently corrected in the other **x**-family mss, in P² probably from a **p**-source.

Z 170 is a correct unique line, presumed omitted in **A** as unnecessary elaboration.

182 (Z 172, A 174, B 186) *potte ful*: firmly attested in **ZBC** and more appropriate for a serving of *cooked* peas. No reason appears for its possible ⇒ for *potel*, a word which shows no variation to *potful* at 6.398 // **AB**. *ymakid* **A**: **ZB**'s expanded past participle form authorises emendation of **A**. **184** *Spitteden*: the past pl. of *spitten* 'to dig to a spade's depth' (see MED s.v. *spitten* v. 2). The tense-ambiguous **p** form, to which u varies, results from assimilative loss of the preterite morpheme. **188 (Z 175–76, A 177–78, B 191)** *blynde*: in A 178 supported by Z; the punctuation here aims to reduce what may be judged a weakness in the repetition. *Ka*'s conjecture *blereyed* on the basis of the RUE variant for *bedrede* at 177 is unjustified on grounds of sense or style. Concerning Bx, however, K–D may be right that some material is lost after 192, for the *brokelegged* idea of **ZA** 176/178 is retained at C 188, and that of *lame men* **ZA** 178/180 at C 189. However, after the change evident in B 192, reconstruction would be hazardous; so this must remain a possible case of 'non-linear' development, with **C** re-using **A** material omitted in initial revision to **B**.

ZA 177 (179) *ote*: preferrred here to *hote* on the strength of **Z** (and cf. *hauer* at A 266 below, and the w reading in its Apparatus). Either has acceptable sense and metre, and Ax was quite possibly spelled with unetymological *h* as at **Z** 120, 130.

196 *lone*: the harder reading (MED s.v. *lone* n. (1), 1(c) 'reward') and one that gives a characteristic internal rhyme in the b-half. It doubtless represents y and thence x^l, the **x**-witnesses I and u having varied to the **p** reading for the same presumed reason that **p** diverged from Cx, visual error partly induced by mistaking the sense as 'loaf' (*SkR–K*). But in its five other uses in the sg., four in **C** and one in **Z**, the 'loaf' word is spelled *loef* or *loof*, and the present instance must involve a lexeme of wider meaning (though no doubt the *lone* included a 'loaf'). The **p** ms Q has made the converse variation from its exemplar to the reading here judged correct on grounds of sense. **197, 203 (Z 182, A 184, B 197)** correspond to one line in each of the earlier versions. 197 is closer in the a-half to the word-order of **B**, 203 to that of **ZA**, possibly suggesting that the sequence subject / verb / adverb in original **B** might have been as in **ZA**; but since neither sense nor metre is affected, there is no case for emending Bx here (cf. B 198). The second line is rejected by R–K (p. 172) as a Cx error; but the repetition has a rhetorical purpose, need not have been supplied to provide a subject for *3af* 204, and could thus be original (cf. the repetition at A 177–78 above). **204 (Z 183, A 185, B 198)** The Bx line has no obvious fault of sense or metre, and the acceptability canon ought perhaps to override the linear postulate here. But in the light of **ZAC**, scribal rewriting is strongly suggested by its caution about generosity to erstwhile feigned beggars, and the K–D restoration to accord with the other versions is consequently adopted. **207 (Z 185, A 187, B 200)** *erd*: certain in **Z**, the probable reading of *C*-**p** and, to judge by the **C** variants *erthe* and *3erd* **x** (replicated in the A and B traditions), also that of ?Bx (< L(M) = β, R = α). Of the **A** readings, four are easier reflexes and the fifth, *hurde* V, an orthographic variant of the same presumed form (the spelling is here adapted to that of ms T). *euere*: judged on

the strength of agreed **ZAC** as lost in Bx through partial haplography (*þere* < *euere*). **209 (Z 186, A 188, B 202)** **C** revises unusually to scan as a vocalic Type III or, if the caesura comes after *Hunger*, as Type Ie. **216** *filial*: recorded only here (see MED s.v. *filial* adj.), and so inevitably a cause of difficulty to the copyists. The **p**-scribe probably wrote *fial*, two of the reflexes (QS, M) suggesting that it was understood as connected with 'faith' and a third, *final*, being a desperate attempt at correction that produces virtual nonsense (D may have compared its **x** exemplar with a **p** ms here as often elsewhere). The required sense '[love] due from a child' would also have seemed odd, because the folk are not Piers's children but his brethren. But **L** may have meant '[love] due to me as a [fellow] child of Truth [i.e. as a sibling]', or, as MED s.v. glosses, 'expected of...a fellow Christian', an idea that fits well with *blody bretherne* in 217 (see further Hill 2002:67–72). The **p** reading *fial* 'trustworthy, genuine' (from OF *fiel*) defended by R–K (p. 151), though also a *hapax* in ME, is not quite as hard as *filial* contextually (and has left no trace in the language). **217 (Z 191, A 193, B 207)** *And*: on the showing of agreed **ZAC** restored to **B** as lost from Bx through visual assimilation to *And* 206, 209. If R here = α, this could be what Bx read, β and F having both levelled to the more commonly expected pronominal form, and Y(OC²) having introduced *& yet* as a further smoothing. *for* **ZAC**: the probable form of **B** (to which Y has felicitously varied), Bx having inserted an unnecessary attribution-phrase. **221–22 (Z 195, A 197, B 211)** In the light of agreed **ZAB** the Cx lines both appear scribal in form: they scan (221) as inauthentic *aa / bb* or, with some strain, as *aaa / bb* (Type IIb) on vowels, and (222) as Type Ia, but with the first lift requiring two full staves in *lyflode*. Reconstruction here presumes the **ZAB** phrase lost by eyeskip from *hem* > *hem*; correcting the damaged line, it improves the metrical structure of 222, which emerges as new and displaying translinear alliteration initiated by the (revised) last lift of 221. The sense is also superior to that of Cx, which has an unidiomatic phrase *amaystren to*.

Z 196–201 are unique and are presumed deleted in revision as yet another case of unnecessary elaboration (cf. Z 1.65, 2.47, 100, 189, 3.96, 122–24, 7.245). **223 (Z 202, A 198, B 212)** *herke(ne)* ZC / *here* AB: the small but real sense-difference suggesting a reversion to the first verb so as to heighten the urgency. The **Z** phrase, however, shares its word-order with **AB**, not C. **226 (Z 205, A 201, B 215)** *abaue*: in the light of **ZAC** identified as original **B**, a rare word inviting ⇒ of another with similar form (though different sense) that might have seemed contextually more expected (see MED s.v. *abaven* v. 4, but with no illustration of the required transitive use); in **ZAB** evidently seen as specifying the command *holde* 204 //. *Sk*'s reading of the word as *abanen* (MED s.v.

banen v., citing only this) gives an inappropriate sense ('injure'). The conjunction *And* in most **A** mss may be a mis-expansion of (perhaps detached) *A* in Ax, and in **C** a revision after alteration of the preceding line's b-half, and perhaps better omitted. **227 (Z 206, A 202, B 216)** *gromes* 'low fellows' (MED s.v. 3a), which is better in context; *R–K*'s change to *gomes* is groundless, though Bx read *gomes* and *B*-M's reading could come from either **A** or **C** (*A*-V, conversely, has *gomes*). **229 (Z 208, A 204, B 218)** *Fortune* **ZAB**-β / *Fals(hed)* / *fals men)* ?*B*-α**C**: a conflict attributable not to α's ⊗ from **C** but to anticipation of *false* in 219, the substance of which becomes otiose if α is authentic. **C**'s condensation of two lines into one eliminates reference to Fortune.

B 219–27 219 Bx as it stands is a Type IIIa line with an awkward five-syllable onset; the expanded form of the conjunction *oþer* adopted here provides an internal voiced fricative stave eliding with *any* to form the first lift (a full stave). **221 (Z 211, A 207, C 231)** *kynde wolde*: discerned on the showing of **ZAC** as indicating the probable **B** original, for which *god techeþ* Bx appears a scribal ⇒ aiming to increase Hunger's authority. The injunction, coming from this speaker, would more properly express natural than divine positive law. **223 (A 209, C 233)** *norisse*: conjectured as the required stave-word in key-position to correct a Bx line scanning imperfectly as *aa / xx*. Its unusual extended sense here (see MED s.v. *norishen* v. 4(a) 'support, sustain') might have invited ⇒ of the alliterating near-synonym *help*; no wider reconstruction is required. **225 (A 212)** *þow*: necessary as the key-stave in a line of either Type IIIa or of Type Ia (with *Theiȝ* as first stave). L and R here appear to preserve β and α respectively, and thence Bx, M having varied with γ (though not in this instance by correction). **227** *bilowe*: here judged the likely Bx reading (< LM = β, + α) against *biloue* γ. The latter is admittedly closer to the Latin and to the translation of this in // **A**, but it may have been suggested by the former. On the other hand, the wordplay of LMα seems characteristic, and the rôle of humility in winning grace recalls the teaching at B 5.620. The form, a recognised variant of *bilouen*, is more probably a coinage based on the simplex *lowen*, found at 10.306 with reflexive prn (see MED s.v. *louen* v.1 4(b)). **236 (Z 212, A 213, B 228)** *good*: on the strength of **ZBC** agreement judged the probable reading of **A**, though perhaps not that of Ax (which may here have had an ambiguously-spelled **goud*). Five unrelated witnesses have corrected a reading obviously inferior in context. **241** *swoet and*: rejected as tautological by *R–K*, who for *swetynge* adopt *swetande* to account for Cx; but as the *annominatio* is typical, the reconstruction is unjustified. **242** *oure*: needlessly emended to *ȝoure* by *R–K*, who take the verbs as imperatives, whereas they are better read as infinitives dependent on *we sholde* understood. **242a**

The **p** order (preferred by *R–K*) is more logical, but not therefore necessarily original: **x** has the order found in the macaronic parallel **ZAB**, where *swynk* = Lat. *labor*, and this may have influenced **L** in revising. **244 (Z 219, A 220, B 235)** The **ZA** lines appear to be 'licensed' macaronics with a blank first stave, and the **B** line may be of the same type unless *frigoré* has two lifts and *Piger pro* forms a dip, giving a Type IIIa line. **L**'s 'conjugate' macaronics (Schmidt 1987:98) allow both lifts of a Latin half-line to fall in a single word only if this is a lexical compound, and do not base the second lift on an inflexional ending.

247/48 (Z 221/22, A 22/–23, B 237/38) The ?**C**x form of line 248 scans awkwardly with a five-syllable prelude-dip including an important noun (*suluer*). The original of 247 as here reconstructed makes the de-stressed lexical word the verb and reduces line 248 to one with a more normal shape in the a-half. The present re-division has been anticipated by u, which may represent **x** (as at 19.255 / 6), y having therefore presumably erred here with **p**, or be an independent correction. **248** *menyng*: treated as a verbal noun by *R–K*, who read *in*] *and* after P²RM, but easily interpretable as a participial adjective in an elliptical construction ('and [he did this] intending that...').

Z 230–32 seem authentic in both metre and phrasing, with typical wordplay on *for* as preposition and conjunction in 231. 230a had been previously used at Z 5.48 // and the whole line is re-used at B 9.72, which it seems hard to imagine a scribal redactor recalling at this point. The anecdotal character of the parenthesis may have led to removal of the lines in **A** as serving no useful purpose.

255 (Z 226, A 227, B 242) As it stands, Bx will scan as a Type IIIb line with *he* its first lift. But this gives the pronoun unnaturally heavy emphasis and may be diagnosed as the consequence of Bx's ⇒ of *wiþ* for the word here conjectured, in the light of **ZA** *senes / siþen* and **C** *thenne*, as the necessary vocalic first stave (*after*). **257–58 (Z 227–29, A 228–30, B 243–45)** The line-division of **C** may be securely accepted as that supported by **ZAB**. Since *p²* here agrees with e and q, and it is thus likely that *p¹* will represent **p**, <RM>'s source may have been collated with a corrected copy of **p** (see also on 17.116; *Intro.* III C § 49) or else compared with **x** (as suggested also by their substantive reading at 10.80).

A 235–36 (Z 238, B 250–51, C 260–61) 235 is of Type IIa on vowels with a 'supplemental' fifth vocalic stave, but it would scan more effectively on lexical words in the a-half if *get* were emended to *fet*, the contracted 3 sg. of *fetten* (MED s.v. 4(a)); **B**'s *fedeþ* may be a revision-echo of this (cf. note on *garisoun* B 6.138). **236** in principle scans vocalically with a mute stave in each half, but meaning and rhythm are greatly improved by conjecturing in position two the adverb *here* to balance *here* in 235. The sense is that the faithful worker with his hands is assured of reward from God in this world in the form of his sustenance. The first *here* will have gone by haplography before *here²*, a loss all the easier had Ax read as J, with *here²* immediately following *here¹*. In seeming awareness of the gap in sense, tR supply the postulated adverb *after* the object noun.

269 (Z 242, A 240, B 255) *groneth* **p**: arguably less likely to be original than *greueth*, which corresponds more closely to *akeþ* **ZAB**; but equally, it may have been moved back to take account of the revision of B 257 at 271. One or other variant is a visual error for Cx's reading (in *C-R* an original *grewith* is altered a.h. to *Gronythe*). **271 (Z 244, A 242, B 257)** *þat*: judged the probable **B** reading in the light of agreed **ZAC**, *and* Bx having been inserted to ease the transition, with *B*-B coinciding or else showing ⊗ from **C**.

Z 245 exhibits authentic metre and is less likely to be a scribal expansion of 244 than an original line omitted as over-specific in revision to **A**. Vestigial retention of *ofte* as the last word in A 242 is indirect evidence of the authenticity of Z 245.

274 (Z 250, A 247, B 262) *til* **BC** / *forto* **ZA**: certain in **C** as in **Z**; but the pair *for* and *to* in the AxBx traditions could be split variants of the form reconstructed for **A**. Since **B** nowhere instances the word, which is little found outside **L** (see MED s.v. *forto* prep. 1(a)), while **A** does (with minority support) at 7.2, the commoner form is preferred for **B**, the rarer for **A**.

A 250 (Z 253, B 265) *Leue*: in the light of **ZB** preferred for **A** as fitting better with the secondary sense of the final phrase ('persuasive to luxury'). *Loue* (though also apt here) is presumably the consequence of *e / o* confusion.

B 266, Z 254, A 251 The **A** reading *alongid* is harder than *afyngred* and more likely to be revision of the latter than a scribal ⇒ for it. Thus if **Z** does not here show ⊗ from **B**, it must preserve an original first revised in **A** and then restored in **B** (*B*-F, which is closer in sense to **A**, is here unlikely to represent α and thence Bx but may show partial ⊗ from an **A** source).

283 *be of* **p**: necessary for the sense, and producing a line with cognative staves (|b| |p| |p|); no reason immediately appears for loss of the phrase from **x**. *R–K* take the conjunction *ʒif* as the imperative of *ʒiuen* and read [*the pore be thy*] for *be of*, but no emendation is required for either sense or metre. **284** *in thy gate* **x**: rejected by *R–K* (p. 155) as having the contextually less apt sense 'way' (MED s.v. *gate* n. (2) 2(a)), while **p** is very close to 11.42 (*at þe ʒate*). But there is no reason why *gate* here should not mean 'gateway' (MED s.v. n. (1) 1 (a)), this use of *in* is harder than *at*, and the sense 'at the gate of your house' identical. **290 (Z 255, A 252, B 267)** *eres*: firmly established for **BC**, the minority **A** variant likely to be a

revision of **Z** *eyes*, for which ?Ax *armes* may be a visual error (*eie* and *hede* seem random ⇒). **291 (Z 256, A 253, B 268)** *hodes*: in the light of agreed **ZBC** (only *C-DM* having *hode*) preferred as the probable original reading of **A**. The sg. may have been induced in Ax through the influence of *foode* in the b-half, parallelism with *cloke* 254, or judgement that a single garment was apt for a single actant (*A-L hodes* looks coincidental). **294 (Z 259, A 256, B 271)** *lest liflode him fayle* **AC**: tentatively adopted as the probable **B** reading, for which the Bx b-half seems a ⇒ conflating a word from the posited original (*liflode*) with a reminiscence of B Pr 86 (*for* [...] *is swete*). In principle, Bx could be revising the **A** form back to that of **Z**, and **C** revising **B** back to **A**. But as this would involve an unusual process of double restoration, it seems on balance preferable to see Bx as scribal, leaving the possibility that the **Z** ms reading here shows ⊗ from a post-Bx **B** source. Emendation of **Z** is however pointless, since the line gives acceptable sense and metre, and 'double restoration' cannot finally be ruled out.

Z 260–78 form a unique passage of nineteen lines, one of which (271) recurs at Z 8.47 // **AB** but is aptly deployed here between an English line introducing it and another translating it. 263–64 correspond to C 295–96 // **AB** (see esp. on **B** 272), but the rest of the digression on physicians has no parallel in the later texts. Stylistically, the lines cohere with **L**'s usual manner and the macaronic 267 seems of the 'intermediate' type (Schmidt:1987:100) found e.g. at 7.152, Z 7.219, scanning *aa / xx*. The passage's excessive length and over-particularity sufficiently explain its replacement by a pithy couplet in **AB**, only the first line of which is revised in **C**.

295 (Z 263–64, A 257, B 272) In the Bx tradition the line fails to scan both in β and in α (*aab / ba*) and to make sense in the a-half of α, unless R's *morareres* is a mere scribal slip for *morþareres*. In the light of Z 263, the substantive reading of β's a-half recommends itself as a basis for emendation; but **A**'s *mo* favours instead α's form and invites explanation of R's meaningless noun as misconstruing an α reading **mo:::eres*. (*B-F*'s *moraynerys* appears an individual attempt to make sense of a reading like R's). This is here reconstructed to accord with **A** *mo liʒeris*. **A** 257–58 may then be seen as rendering the two main ideas of Z 263–64 (that ignorant physicians are (a) murderers and (b) liars) in the reverse order, preserved in **BC**. The variant *murþereris*, β's attempt to make intelligible the problematic original attested in R (possibly a defective reading in Bx), will then be perhaps a coincidence with Z 263 (suggested by the sense of B 273) rather than a source of ⊗ in **Z** at its scribal phase. **297 (Z 279, A 259, B 274)** *Poul / Pernel*: secure readings in **Z**, **B** and **C**. The reading of **A** is likely to have been as in **Z**, since *Pernel* could hardly have been a ⇒ for *Poul*, and both **A** families attest it. The **A** variant *Poul* may reflect misreading of an abbreviated form of *Pernel* rather than showing ⊗ from a **B** source. **298–99 (Z 280–81, A 260–61, B 275–76)** In the light of agreed **ZAC**, the Bx order of these lines appears likely to be scribal, though no obvious reason for the error appears. **301 (Z 282, A 262, B 277)** *I¹*: necessary for the grammar of the sentence, and perhaps lost from Bx by distraction from *I* in 278 below. *B*-GBF may have added by collation with **A** or **C**, but the commonsense correction could have been independently made. *the* **ZC** / *God* **AB**: both acceptable, and the direction of revision uncertain. Most probably *God* is a revised form in **A**, *the* likewise in **C**, but either scribal intensification or censorship remains a possibility for *God* or *the* respectively. *ne wol* **x** / *nel* **p**: despite agreeing with **ZA**, **p** is less likely to be original, since the last two lifts are required to bear heavy emphasis so as to form the T-Type line in **B** that was retained in **C**: *ne wól I wénde*. For an exact parallel to this unique authentic metrical pattern (*Intro.* IV § 40) cf. *wél youre wórdes* Z 7.279. **302 (Z 283, A 263, B 278)** *Er* **AC** / *Til* **ZB**: the **Z** reading may show **B** influence, or **B** may have revised back to the first form, with **C** then restoring the reading adopted in **A**. But just as probably, since the two conjunctions were contextually in free variation, Bx *Til* may be unconscious scribal ⇒ of an advancing form. **305 (Z 286, A 266, B 281)** The **A** line is evidently a rewriting of **Z**, which seems original, but scans imperfectly in Ax, as in the light of revised **C** does Bx (*aa / xa*), though the last two lifts appear substantively authentic. In the emendation proposed here, the particle *ek* provides a mute key-stave in what now scans as a Type Ib line. The mechanism of loss could have been eyeskip from *an(d)* > *an* in both archetypes. K–D's adoption of *cake of otes*] *haue cake* from // C VIII 305, attractive because a reconstruction rather than a conjecture, nonetheless presupposes ⇒ of a lexically easier expression (for the word's rarity see MED s.v. *haver* n. 2, where **L**'s is the only C14th citation other than proper names). **309 (Z 290, A 270, B 285)** The b-half reading in **Z** confirms that attested in *A*-family **m**, where *plante* is the past participle with the sense 'planted out' (see MED s.v. *plaunten* v. 1(a)). The **r** ↔ to an easier reading is repeated in *B*-β, which may but does not certainly here preserve Bx. The **Z** ms could have derived from *A*-**m** but more probably retains the original form of **Z**. The *B*-α variant appears to have been an unmetrical phrase involving *herbes*, F characteristically normalising the metre with an alliterating synonym for *queynte*; but the **C** revision's a-half indicates the likely presence of *plauntes* in **B**. **315 (Z 295, A 275, B 290)** *Thanne*: on the showing of agreed **ZAC** probably the original **B** reading, Bx having inserted *And* through inducement from *And* 289. *me*: the assured reading of **ZC** and superior on grounds of sense. *B*-F here shows either unconscious influence from preceding *þi*, as presumably does *A*-**r**, or ⊗ from an **A** source of **r**-type. **316 (Z 296, A**

276, B 291) *tho*: in the light of agreed **ZBC** likely to have been present in **A** and lost by Ax, perhaps through visual assimilation to following *pe*-. The *A*-R reading may be an attempted correction in awareness of *þo*-, but misunderstanding it as the demonstrative; **w** presumably corrected independently, perhaps by reference to a **C** source. **317 (Z 297, A 277, B 292)** *lappe*: in the light of agreed **ZC** the collective singular, the older and arguably harder form, is preferred as the probable original in **B** (> Bx > α > R) and in **A**, where Ax may have read *lappes*. **321 (Z 302, A 282, B 297)** *poysen* **AB**: here presumably replacing *peyse* **Z** as part of a complete revision of the b-half. **Z**'s reading is that conjectured by *Ka* (in ignorance of **Z**) as the original of **A**; but there is no serious reason for rejecting the boldly humorous metaphor of quelling Hunger with food. A motive for **A**'s revision could have been the poor logic of **Z**'s b-half; **C**'s exhibits characteristically greater directness. *opere erbes*: a b-half with awkward rhythm due to the heavy four-syllable dip before the pre-final lift. However, if this is *cresses*, **C** may have read simply *opere* or *erbes*, either word being a Cx insertion consequent on judging the sense incomplete. **322 (Z 303, A 283, B 298)** *and*: clearly the reading of **C** and adopted here for **B** as superior to the presumed Bx reading, possibly the asyndetic original. But on the showing of **Z**, where it is in a subordinate clause (co-ordinate in **C**), it is probably better in **A** to accept *þat* (functioning as a temporal conjunction), since the Ø-reading would make *cam* into the main verb. **323** *dentiesliche* XYD: here taken as a form of *deynteuosliche* (so *p¹*), but possibly an error for *deyntifliche* IUQK (preferred by *R–K*). Both adverbs are rare and their sense is the same (see MED s.v. *deintevousliche* and *deintifliche*). **325** *wandren*: the second of three infinitives in 325–26 dependent on *wolde*; the preterite in **p** is an easy error, attested also in several copies of **A** and **B**. **329 (Z 310, A 290, B 305)** *brewestares* **AC**: here tentatively judged the probable original for which *in burgh is to* will be a smoothing after a visual error. The sense and metre of Bx are unexceptionable, and it could be a reversion to the **Z** form of the b-half, like the case at C 294 //, challenging the uniform operation of linear revision. Alternatively, as tentatively concluded here, **Z** could show ⊗ at the scribal phase from a post-Bx **B** source (for discussion of the problem see *Intro.* III **Z** §§ 23–7). **330 (Z 311, A 291, B 306)** *to lyue on but* **C**: to be discriminated as the probable original in **B** and also in **A**. The variant *but lyue on / with* attested in some **AB** mss is a simplification (though acceptable) of the boldly figurative revision, returning to the form that might have been original in **Z** (unless the **Z**-ms here shows ⊗ from an **A** or **B** source). **331 (Z 312, A 292, B 307)** *Deynede...aday*: perhaps the identical reading in all four versions, and certainly giving the best sense; but as revision is possible, emendation of **Z** must be cautious. The verb will have been preterite in

ZBC, those **A** mss with the present probably reflecting a tense-ambiguous Ax form **deynet*. The negative particle was in **AC** and may be judged omitted from *B*-α through visual error (*-en t*o) or through mistaking the verb 'to deign' for the one meaning 'to disdain' (see MED s.v. *deynen* v. (2); and cf. B 10.78). The latter could have been the intended verb in **Z**, but *not* could as well have been lost mechanically there, as it seems (on grounds of sense) that the phrase *to dyne a* was omitted through eyeskip from *Dey-* to *day*. In **AB** *dynen* is transitive 'eat' (MED s.v. *dinen* v. (2) 2 (a)), in **ZC** (with *of*) has the sense 'dine (upon)' (ib. (1)). **333 (Z 314, A 294, B 309)** *or ybake* **ZC**: supported by *B*-β and almost certain to have been the reading of **A**. Ax having read Ø / *bake*, *A*-**m** may have inserted / substituted *rostid* or have been contaminated from a **B** source (and then corrupted). The reason for the loss in *A*-**r** will have been the length of the line (Type Ic), causing misjudgement of the caesura as located after *flessh* and so of the line as of Type Ib. The sense requires *or ybake*, for the contrast is not between 'fresh meat' and 'fried fish' but between '(variously) cooked *fresh* meat or fish' (eaten hot) and 'smoked meat or fish' (eaten cold).

Z 316 is a unique line of good sense and correct metre, presumably deleted in **A** as repeating too closely the sense of Z 310, 314 (for a similar case cf. Z VII 245). **336 (Z 318, A 297, B 312)** *waryen* **ZAC**: most probably also the original reading of **B**, for which Bx may be a censoring ⇒ of a milder, less hostile term in a politically sensitive context. **340 (Z 321, A 300, B 317)** *non* **ZC**: providing the most acceptable metrical form, though that proposed for **A** (on the basis of J's variant and that of R, which here reads *her non wolde*) gives the same sense and, with elision of *wolde* and *here*, smoother metre than Bx. The latter, in having both *per* (?retained from Ax) and *of hem* (? = *here* **B**), requires muting of *wolde* and deferred stress on *noon* to avoid producing an uncharacteristically heavy four-syllable final dip. **341 (Z 322, A 301, B 318)** *his* xp^2 / *þe* p^1: the p^1 variant, supported by the majority of **A** and a couple of **B** witnesses, may be a pointed allusion to the demands of the Statute of Labourers that could have been censored in **x**, ?Bx and sundry **A** mss. But if **Z** is here original, the metaphorical sense of *statut* would appear to have been present from the outset, and it was failure to grasp this that prompted ⇒ of *þe*. The 'Statute' in question is that of Hunger, the labourers' 'master'. *so sturne* **C**: apparently an authorial transposition to prose-order so as to produce a Type Ib line with the rhythmic feel of a T-type. In the new b-half *lokede* does not now form a lift, but yields its stress to the alliterating non-lexical adverb *so*, and *R–K*'s alteration to the **AB** reading has no warrant whatever. **344 (Z 325, A 304, B 321)** *thorw* **CA**: judged likely to have been the reading of **B**. In principle, **B** could have restored the form first used in **Z**, or *wyth* could be a Z-ms ⊗ from a **B**

source, but more probably Bx is a scribal ⇒ of a synonym contextually in free variation with it. *wastours to chaste* **ABC**: **A**'s revised b-half following **Z** in its use of end-rhyme. That **Z**'s rhyme-word is different is diagnostic evidence of originality, this being a device no scribe could have imitated so closely. **346 (Z 328, A 307, B 324)** *sayth* **ZAC**: likely to have been original also in **B**, Bx's preterite being a ⇒ under influence from following *sente* and perhaps a tense-ambiguous exemplar form **seit*. The second verb *sente* is quite possibly a contracted present, rather than a preterite in a sentence referring to a current message but a past warning (since they are the same). **347 (Z 327, A 306, B 323)** *thorw*[2]: probably absent from both Ax and Bx, its presence in **Z** and in *C*-**x** (?< Cx) arguing for its inclusion in all versions, since it is more likely to have been scribally omitted as redundant than to have been added.

B 325 The Bx line has the inauthentic pattern *aab / bx* and it seems likeliest that either the verb or the noun (rather than the adverb) has been supplanted by a non-alliterating word. Against an earlier conjecture *mone* (*K–D Sch*[1]), the present suggestion posits scribal ⇒ of a commoner verb rather than the somewhat pointless replacement of one heavenly body by another, though C 350 could admittedly be interpreted as the reflex of such a reading. (The conjectured verb *merke* offers a possible emendation for *se* later at B 13.25, but the case there is less compelling).

349 (B 326) *an viii* **x**: most probably the reading of Cx on grounds of sense (however elusive). The presumed **p** reading *an vm*, and MN *a vin*, both not just enigmatic but nonsensical, reveal progressive stages of misreading of the three minims after *v*. The line appears to scan as an enriched extended Type III with counterpoint on |θ| and |ʃ| (*abb / aa*), the second fricative stave being liaisonal (*with_an*) and muted, but with a 'supplemental' |f| stave in *fólwynge*. The substantive correctness of 'viii' is indirectly confirmed by the quoted form of this line in Crowley's preface, which gives 'eight' (see *Sk*, B, xxxiv), and more directly by *eighte* in B 326, the line under revision. *R–K*'s tentative conjecture *vii* for *viii* (p. 170) should therefore be rejected. *multiplied* **B**: elliptical for 'be multiplied', and most probably the reading of Bx (< Lα), M having here unusually *added* to a reading originally the same as that of γ (see *Intro.* III *B* § 34). But agreement of L and α will adequately guarantee Bx here, if *multiplie* is judged an easier reading induced by desire for parallelism with the preceding infinitive *haue*.

Passus IX (ZA VIII, B VII)

Collation In 75–281 a second text appears in **I**, selectively cited in the Apparatus with sigil *I*.

1 (ZA VIII 1, B VII 1) *sente* **ZAC**: discriminated as the probable **B** reading, Bx having inserted an unnecessary pronoun. **7 (ZAB 7)** *manere* **ZAC**: adopted in **B** as the necessary first stave-word, Bx *ooþer* being a ⇒ of the non-alliterating near-synonym common in the phrase 'or any *x*'. **10 (ZAB 10)** *reumes*: preferred also in **A** on the strength of agreed **ZBC** and greater contextual appropriateness of the plural. **13 (ZAB 13)** *yblessed that / yf*: **Z** is closer to **BC**, though the Ax reading is not easier or objectionable in metre or style. However, its sense is less appropriate in context, since it would seem more important that the bishops should be 'holy' than that they should bestow formal blessings. While **Z**'s a-half could show ⊗ from **B** or **C**, this seems unlikely since the b-half corresponds to that of the **A** tradition and not the revised **BC** form. Ax *þat* could originate from misreading *y* as *þ* and taking *blissen* as an original perhaps spelled *blissyt, a form ambiguous between the past participle intended and the present indicative (*blissyþ*), with *and* a subsequent smoothing.

　　ZA 19 (B 17, C 21) *hey*: the right **A** reading on grounds of sense, doubtless adopted into *A*-HKM as individual corrections, perhaps in knowledge of **B**. Error could have arisen through inducement from the Ø-article form, by misidentification of the final consonant in *hiʒ* as *s* or *r*.

23 (ZA 21, B 19) *no a*: reconstructed in the light of **AB(Z)** as the probable **C** reading, of which *no* and *a* appear split variants. *C*-x *no pena* is identical with **Z**, a possible first draft, but *a* is unlikely to have been dropped in **C**, since it forms part of a formula. *nolde*: required in **C** as the key-stave in what is, after revision of the b-half, an extended Type IIIa line; either could be right in **ZAB**. **25 (ZA 23, B 21)** *and* **ABC**: adopted for **Z** on grounds of sense, as there are two oaths, not one, the Z-scribe mistaking *ant* for visually similar *ac*. **28 (ZA 26, B 24)** *And (That) bad / That they sholde*: either reading is acceptable on grounds of sense and metre, but the direct form attested in **A** and reflected in **C** indicates that Bx may here be a ⇒ of an indirect-clause construction suggested by the phrase *a lettre* in 23. If the Bx form is scribal, it is likely to be the reading present in **B**[1], the copy used in revision to **C**, since the latter's *That bad* appears to accommodate both **A** and Bx. The Z-ms reading could show influence from **B** here or be coincidental, although in principle this could be a case of non-linear revision: **Z(A)B(C)**. **29 (ZA 27, B 25)** *wynnynges* **CB**-α**Z** / *wynnyng* **B**-β**Ax**: either is acceptable, but one is likelier to be original in all versions, and Ax's singular is here judged an error caused perhaps through failure to register an abbreviated plural ending. **30 (ZA 28, B 26)** *men* **ZBC**: possibly lost from **A**, but as the sense of Ax is unexceptionable, no emendation need be made. **33 (ZA 30, B 28)** *Amende / bete(n) / do boote to*: progressively revised, but with unchanged sense ('repair'). The multiple variants in the Ax tradi-

tion suggest a difficult original, and while this could have been *bynde* d, the reading *bete* in *r*[2]?**m** (for which M *amendyn* is a synonymic ⇒) is closest to expanded **B** and revised **C**. But *aboute* could now mean 'in the region' as well as 'around their centres', as it probably does in *A*-d (see further *Intro.* II § 74). **35 (ZA 33, B 30)** again shows progressive revision (minor in **A**), with probably a 'non-linear' return in **C**'s a-half to the idea of God's love that is present in **ZA** but omitted in **B**. In **Z** *oure*, required for the sense and restored on the evidence of **A**, will have been lost by attraction of *for* > *Lordus*, as also in *A* -JWM.

　　B 33–4 (ZA 36–7, C 37–8) 33 *angel* **ZAC**: the probable original also in **B**, for which Bx (like *C*-I and *A*-M) will have substituted the more emphatic and metrically awkward *Archangel* (B-HmF's correction may show ⊗ from **C** or **A**). **34** Progressive revision (minor in **A**, from Type Ia to Ib) terminates in a **C** line of Type Ib that guides emendation of the unmetrical b-half of Bx (*aa / xa*). *drede*: the noun (close in sense to *despeyre* **C**), here conjectured as the necessary key-stave for which Bx *fere* is a non-alliterating synonymic ⇒, subsequently smoothed to a verb by addition of the pronoun *yow*. *deying*: judged also the reading of Cx on grounds of superior sense.

39 (ZA 38, B 36) The *C*-x line is preferred as having the same metrical pattern as **B** (Type Ie); **p** will have lost se*the* through homoarchy before se*nde*. **41 (ZA 42, B 37)** *wopen / wepten*: either the strong or weak preterite is acceptable, the present-tense form in some **A** mss the result of *e / o* confusion with the former. **42 (ZA 44, B 38)** *preyde for* **C**: evidently a revision, and *R–K*'s ⇒ of *preiseden* **B** has no warrant. *copiede*: conjectured on grounds of sense as the correct reading in **A** and as necessary for the same reason in **Z**. A near-homophonic pun on *copede* 'provided with clothing' (i.e. metaphorical for 'glossed', 'laundered') may be intended in the light of preceding *clopis*, which could have induced the *copede* variant. *couth / couden*: 'made a return / recompense (of)'. *Ka*'s reading (p. 450) of the phrase as a 'somewhat unusual... assimilation of *connen þonk* to *don...mede*' is unconvincing; for while in ME one may 'feel thanks', and so 'offer it' (MED s.v. *connen* v. 6(g)), it is not possible to 'feel reward' and so, by extension, offer it (the construction *coude mede* is paralleled in *kydde reward* at *Purity* 208). The verb is therefore more convincingly identified as the pt. pl. of *kithen* (MED s.v. v. 4(a)), with loss of *th* through assimilation to following *d* and with *ou* the reflex of an original rounded central vowel |y| < OE *cyþen* (cf. the nominal form *couthe* at 17.196). The variant spellings *coupe* HN, *cowthin* J, *couth* **Z** may indicate assimilation of *d* to preceding *þ*. Either way, loss of one or other consonant from an original *coupden has produced a form orthographically identical with the preterite of *connen*. **44 (ZA 45, B 39)** The identity of **C**'s a-half with **ZA** may suggest (on the 'linear' assumption) that **B** read the same;

but *pardon* in preceding C 43 indicates that the word was likely to have been present in B¹, so that this may be another case of 'non-linear' revision in **C**.

B 45 *preue*: Bx could have a 'licensed' macaronic structure (*aa / xx*), but is here judged a ⇒ of the more obvious 'believe' for a stave-word with the contextually-appropriate sense 'find [by experience]' (MED s.v. *preven* v. 4(a)).

47 (Z 51, A 50, B 41) *innócent(z)*: with wrenched stress to provide a required first stave, and bringing out the etymological sense, which each b-half further specifies; repeated in 19.270 //. The normal stress-pattern is exhibited earlier at 3.98 and B 3.242 (no //). **48 (Z 52, A 51, B 48)** *coueyteth nat here / hise*: the form of ZAC suggests that Bx, while unexceptionable in metre and sense, may have smoothed a defective b-half **coueiteth hise*; but emendation is very tentative, as non-linear revision in **C** cannot be ruled out (cf. 28, 35, 44). **49 (Z 53, A 52, B 49)** Since the a-half gives acceptable sense and metre, the whole **B** line could be rewritten and this be another case of 'non-linear' revision in **C**; but near-agreement of ZAC's a-half favours emending the over-explicit reading of Bx. *lawe...declareth (shewiþ)*: the Bx line (Type IIa with an enriched fifth stave) looks like a scribal transposition of the main idea to the a-half, with subsequential smoothing.

A 54 (Z 55, B 51, C 50) *sykirly sauf* A: the order preferred on the evidence of **Z**, making the adverb a functional intensifier, not a mere asseveration. *þe...witnessiþ*: the **m**L order and wording, supported by **Z** and by (revised) **B**.

54 (Z 61, A 60, B 58) *mede* ABC: *mercedem* **Z** produces an authentic macaronic line; but while it seems to anticipate (or echo) the thought of C 3.290 ff, the Latin here bears the simple sense 'reward' of the Biblical text cited at C 3.311, and its use is neither inconsistent with nor necessarily derived from **C**'s elaborate distinction between *mede* and *mercede*. *here (his) / Ø*: possibly (in the light of ZBC) lost from Ax; but no emendation for metre or sense seems required. **57 (Z 58, A 57, B 53)** *nedede / nediþ*: both perhaps reflexes of a tense-ambiguous Cx form **nedyt*; the past subjunctive is preferred as slightly harder (cf. 87 and 19.34).

B 59 (Z 62, A 61) The b-half appears metrically corrupt in *A*-**r** and in Bx, where it is followed first by what seems a scribal expansion of the presumed original and a spurious line. Correction of *A*-**r** is by transposition of its prose order, and it seems probable in the light of *trowe* ?**m** that the verb, whichever it was, meant 'know' or 'believe' rather than 'blame'. The **m**-variant, though based only on the one witness present (M), is preferred as having the support of **Z** (its variant *now* for *ou3t* arguing against its deriving here from **m**). In Bx, *Mathew is to blame* indicates that the Bx scribe took the verb as the

imperative plural of the homograph meaning 'blame' (MED s.v. *witen* v. (3)). As here given, the **B** line is superficially closer to *A*-**r**; but since the reconstruction borders on conjecture (see *Intro.* III *B* § 61), it is best on balance to prefer for **A** the ?**mZ** form, satisfactory in itself and attested by two independent sources. **C**'s lack of any reflex of **B** may suggest that B¹ had a highly corrupt reading.

Z 69 is a unique parenthetic line of the rare Type IIb, perhaps dropped as too grudging in tone, given the strict conditions already laid down in Z 70ff.

63 (Z 71, A 69, B 66) *he*: on the showing of **ABC**, *at* **Z** is diagnosed as an error for *a* 'he' (induced by following *that*) rather than as the vocalic (mainly NE Midl.) form of the relative pronoun. *3f* **ZBC**: omitted from Ax but independently added by RJ, and likely to have been in **A** if it bears stress and *but* is mute. *hy*: adopted for **C** as the probable Cx reading, of which *he, they* are divergent reflexes (*hi* G being a happy coincidence or survival in this very early witness). The singular (randomly attested) will have resulted from objection to the mixed number of the verb-subjects in the line. **66–7 (B 69–70)** The **B** line is re-divided so as to avoid the awkward rhythm produced by the Bx lineation, which requires in 69 either a masculine ending (*3yue þát*), an untypical final half-stress (*3yue þàt*), or else emendation by transposition of the prose order to *þat 3yue*. The re-division here leaves 70 as a Type IIIa line, with a gradation established from 'the needy', to 'the more needy', to 'the neediest'. In *B*-M, the comparative morpheme may be a reflex of the β reading, eliminated by γ and (unusually) by L, and visibly erased by M too, though the double comparative seems the harder form. *to gyuen* **p**: preferred to Ø **x** as giving a characteristic T-type line; this is unlikely to be scribal in origin, whereas the last lift could have been lost in **x** by assimilation to *gyue* at 66 above.

71–161 The first *large-scale addition* of completely new **C** material to which there is no parallel in **B**; it ends with an echo of 63, 67 above. Parts of this are inserted into the *A*-type Prologue in ms I (75–162, 188–254 after Pr 54, and 255–81 after Pr 83) and lines 66–281, with some omissions, also appear in the conflated **BC** ms Ht after B 6.158. Scase (1987) argues that their versions of the **C** lines on hermits derive from a single source, distinct from the text in the Cx tradition, that circulated independently before being incorporated into the [received] C-Text, and should be taken into account in editing. But the imperfect alliteration, clichés, lack of amplification and possible metrical experiment that Scase notes point rather to its unoriginal character as an extract transplanted by the scribes of Ht and I. The reason is adequately explained by Pearsall 1981:193 (with reference only to the scribe of I) as to promote 'matter that seemed to him of great importance to a more prominent position' (see further *Intro.* III *C* §§ 20–2). The text of the lines in Passus IX of I is collated here as *I*, and their repeated form in the Prologue as *I* (following *Sk*). In no cases do *I* variants provide distinctive readings justifying full citation in the Apparatus; they are given in full in Pearsall 1981:186–7, and *R–K* 186–94. **87** *hym*: more unexpected than *hem* since preceded and followed by a plural verb and possessive, but characteristic of **L** in focussing on both the individual and the group. ID are **x** mss that accord with **p** in making the 'fit' more logical. **101** *lorélles*: the variant *lollares*, which does not allow generation of the needed |r| stave, has come in apparently by anticipation from 103. **107** Here and at 213 the scribe of Y has written 'lollard' (Schaap 2001). **137** *lollares* **p**: preferred to *lorelles* here in part because the phrase deliberately repeats 107, and the point of altering the collocation would be obscure; ⇒ of *lorelles* was presumably to avoid repetition or the allowing of any creditable meaning to *lollare*, which could have acquired too specific associations of religious heterodoxy by *c.* 1395, when **x** was copied (see *Commentary*). **157** *han / an*: both variants representing either the contracted form of the verb or the indefinite article with intruded aspirate, the former being preferable. **161** *beggares*: better than the sg. with both *lollares* and *strikares* 59, *they* 161. **166 (Z 74, A 72, B 88)** *they* ZAC: preferable also in **B**, for which Bx gives (as in 89) the plural pronoun of direct address, a ⇒ either deliberate or due to *ȝ / þ* confusion, and followed by smoothing. *lyue*: a revision of **Z** *leuen* 'believe', unless that is a spelling variant of *lyuen*, and *in no loue* (which the sense would require) has been lost by visual assimilation to the preceding verb. *nouȝt in no* **A**: although *A*-VW agree with **BC**, a double negative seems likely in Ax, with VW, T&r having split variants of the reading preserved in MN. This might suggest that **Z** *nat* is a vestige of the same reading (see note above).

    Z 75–6 These lines on the *lollares'* failure in their religious duties are an elaboration of *lawe* 74 and could have been dropped in **A** as inappropriately mild before the serious charges to follow in Z 77–85=A 73–81. They appear stylistically and metrically authentic (*ward* 75 if stressed has an understood final *-e* or a syllabic *r*) and the elliptical phrasing of 76a is similar to that of C 15.58. **167 (Z 77, A 73, B 89)** In the light of (substantially) agreed **ZAC**, the **B** line may be reconstructed, *Manye of yow* declaring itself a scribal interference with the categorical statement attested. The Cx reading could have been as in **x**p^2, rather than as reconstructed from the posited split variants *Thei* and *Ne*, and a like reading in **B** might more readily account for Bx intrusion of *Manye of yow*. On balance, however, it seems preferable to conform the phrasing of **BC** to that of **ZA**, which have the pronoun. **173 (Z 84, A 80, B 96)** *lyueth*: *leden* **Z** could be an original revised in **A**, and the **m** variant a scribal ⇒ for a near-synonym in a set phrase.

    B 97 (Z 85, A 81) *he; was* AB / *war; they* **Z**: revised

in **A**, the word-order *war they* pointing to an original form, to which the final version reverts (C 174 *Þai*). **177 (Z 88, A 84, B 100)** *in*: lost in *A*-**r**B-β by haplography after *-brok*en. **183 (Z 89–90, A 85–6, B 101–02)** **Z**'s b-half in 89, which is syntactically and metrically coherent with following 90, shows as an original form revised in **A**. The b-half in Z 90 uses the idiom employed at Z 7.39 //, but with a different reference. This suggests its authenticity, while its implication that the humble afflicted may be *superior* to Piers could help account for its removal in the revision to **A**. In **C**, B 102 // has been revised to become the concluding line of the pardon's dispositions. **184 (Z 91, A 87, B 103)** *For*: on grounds of grammar and sense the agreed **ABC** reading is adopted for **Z**, whose scribe has anticipated the *l* of *loue*. **185 (Z 92, A 88, B 104)** *vppon this puyre*: adopted on the showing of **ZAC** as the probable reading of **B**. Amongst the sub-archetypal variants the form of ?α gives a line with a possible key-stave in *vpón* that could represent Bx; but omission of *pur* might have resulted from misunderstanding of its sense and consequent objection to its linking with *erthe*, a possibility the two substantive **A** variants confirm. Alternatively, the loss occurred through homoarchy (*pur*g*atorie* > *pur erthe*), as in the Ø variant attested in some **A** mss. ?Bx's elimination of the characteristic homophonic wordplay is thus unlikely to represent a revision that was later restored to its **A** form in **C**.

    After 92, the **Z Version** *ends*. MS Bodley 851 continues in a different hand (*Q*) as an *A-Text* to the end of Passus VIII (printed in full by *R–B*). This is collated here with the sigil 'Z' that is used later for this copy's **C** continuation. 'Z' has one unique reading *inproued* at 153 (for *inpugnid*); at 111 its variant *anoþir þe foulys þat we ne sholde* conflates the readings of **m** and **r**; and in a few instances it groups with UJ. Otherwise Z displays no striking affiliations in major readings over the course of some hundred lines; after two unmetrical lines of scribal prayer for blessing, it ends on fol. 140v with the unique colophon *Explicit vita et visio Petri Plowman* (omitted in the Apparatus). Hand *Q* continues in the next leaf with a **p**-type text of the **C** Version.

    186 (Z 90, A 86, B 102) *the* **x**β and *Peers* eRMN are unlikely, in the light of **AB** and the distribution of ms support, to be split variants of Cx *Peres the*. Rather the eRM group reading, to which N has varied, suggests an attempt to restrict the implications of what could be seen as an ambiguously generic term. **187** The presence of this line in Q suggests that it was also in q, unless added by reference to a p^2 source. Its omission from the common source of <eRM> could be due to a mechanical error caused by the presence of *ermytes* in 188 and 190; but possible scribal objection to the idea of 'holy hermits' as a category cannot be ruled out (*C*-F has presumably varied with <eRM> for one or other of these reasons). The line introduces *a second major new passage* of 92 lines that balances some 20 of material omitted from **B** 115–38*a* // **A**. **197** *here* p**D**: the logical number after *Summe* is plural (so twice in 198) but **x** could reflect **L**'s use of a distributive singular or Cx have had no possessive. **201** *they* **x**: with *holy ermytes* in apposition would appear the harder reading, and *þese* an attempt to smooth the expression to a more familiar phrase (plural *Alle* **p** must, however, be the correct form). **206** *Helden*: the contextually preferable resolution of a presumed Cx form **heolden*, of which *Holden* will be a tense-ambiguous reflex. **208** *That faytede*: a more characteristic expression, preferred here as at 71, where **p** again replaces a verb-phrase with a noun-phrase as subject. **212** *he lyueþ*: in the light of the Latin line that follows, with its general demand for observance of the law, the I-variant *of leuey*, less apt in context (*pace Pe*), shows as a scribal attempt to make intelligible an exemplar with a form such as **[Aȝen þe lawe] a liuie* (with *a* 'they' governing a plural verb). **214–18** Scase 1989:151 proposes elimination of the stop after *souneth* 216 and correlation of *As by* with *Rihte so,* a punctuation followed by *R–K* and argued for by Wittig 2001:176–7. But the translation proposed is forced, involving an unnatural comparison between a 'meaning' and a 'fact'. This does not fit well with the assigned referent of *hit* (the *word* 'lollen', not the *fact* of 'being crippled') or the meaning of Langland's habitual phrase *as by* 'according to' (see *IG* s.v. *as*). Wittig's understanding of the metaphorical sense of *lollen* 218 as 'lean idly upon [i.e. spuriously seek support in?] the belief and law of Holy Church' is accordingly unconvincing. **259** *wroken*: on the basis of two **x** variants *wriþen* P[2] and *wroþen* D, *R–K* (p. 150) argue for the sense 'insinuate themselves' (OED s.v. *Writhe* v. 10 and 11 'move sinuously / with writhing motion'), which would be apt for a wolf slipping under a fence. They see *wroken* as 'probably not even a true form but a subconscious overlay of the family ancestor's *writhen* and *broken*'. But arguably the latter variant (**p**) points to *wroken* as the Cx form and *wriþen* / *wroþen* as intelligent scribal attempts to make sense of a very difficult original. OED records under *Wreak* v. the sense 'pass' (but used only of time) and the earliest sense (in OE only, and transitive) was 'drive, press' (1.a., c). Thus *writhen* must remain a possibility, and may be right. *Shep*: *R–K* argue for *tripe*, F's unique variant. With sense 'flock' (MED s.v. *trippe* n. 3a.) this, if ever, is a case where a particular scribe has failed to discern the mute stave on *to* and substituted a synonym in *t* to provide a full stave in key-position (see *Intro.* II § 131 for discussion). Another example of the F scribe's 'normalising' of an unusual alliterative pattern is *se* for *chayere* at Pr 114. **264** *shyt*: a contracted form of the verb, here

apparently having the sense (elsewhere unattested) of the compound (MED s.v. *bishiten* v.) and signifying that the wolf 'befouls' the sheep (see 266)) with his excrement (as a sign of how near them he is). The I-variant *bischit* may represent an attempt to disambiguate the verb, which normally means 'excrete', thereby illogically referring to the consequence of an act that has not yet occurred (see MED s.v. *shiten* v., which gives no example of the sense 'befoul' for the simplex). I's *Folde* carries this process a stage further, but *wolle* (repeated at 266 and translating *lanam* 264*a*) must be right. **264*a*** The quotation, being proverbial (see *Commentary*), probably had an abbreviated form in Cx (like that at 20.453), but for convenience is given in full here. **284 (A 93, B 109)** *In*: adopted in the light of agreed **AC** as the probable reading of **B** (*B*-G may show its usual ⊗ from **A** here), *Al* appearing a piece of scribal over-emphasis in B*x*. *lettre*: evidently preferable in context on grounds of sense, *leef* being a wrong expansion of contracted *lettre* or an unintelligent alteration for greater emphasis.

B 110a–b have been inconsistently numbered in the edited text of **B** as citation-lines, but should properly be treated as 'text-lines' in all three versions.

289 (A 98, B 112) The uniformly attested **ABC** line will scan as Type IIIa if *Bote Dowel* is made the anacrusis and *haue*[1] read as the first lift; but if stressed according to the natural sense, it yields two inauthentic patterns, *xa / ax* and *aa / bb* (on *w / s*). Possibly the form *wol* lies behind *shal* in each of the archetypes; but the absence of any attempt in the sub-archetypes so to emend, and the need to posit thrice-repeated loss would stretch probability. If this, the only apparently uncorrupt line not to scan, were deliberately unmetrical, some hidden symbolic purpose might be involved, connected with its sense and hinting at the virtual impossibility of obeying the pardon's condition (a parallel case might be the imperfect fifteenth stanza-group in *Pearl*, in which the extra stanza increases the poem's total to one more than the 'perfect' number 100). **291 (A 100, B 114)** *Bote* C: revising the 'preclusive' *Þat* of **AB** to give a more modern and unambiguous expression. *þe...soule* **AB**: either variant in the Ax tradition is acceptable on grounds of sense and metre, **r** scanning as an extended Type IIIa with counterpoint (*abb / ax*). The **m** reading could show ⊗ from **B**, but more probably **r** is a scribal attempt to avoid repetition of 98b (for a similar case later, in the Cx tradition, see 10.78, 80 and Apparatus *ad loc*).

A 101–12 101–02 (B 115–16) The Ax line-division is acceptable in itself but the ease with which the misdivision could have occurred and the superior rhythm attested (randomly) in HNH[3] support the form of **B**, which makes 116 (= A 102) a quasi-macaronic scanning as Type IIIa (*ámb-, vmb-*). Line 101, with *atweyne* preferred in the light of **B**, scans as counterpointed Type Ie (*ppt / pt*) with internal half-rhyme. **105 (B 119)** *belyue* ?**m**: preferred as a harder than *liflode* and in form closer to **B**'s revision *bely ioye* (if that is not a Bx visual error for *belyue*, as K–D judge). The **r**-variant will have come in from 107, 110. **109 (B 123)** *opere manye* ?**m**: here judged original in the light of **B**, *A*-**r** having inverted to prose order (as has the Bx sub-group y). **110 (B 124)** *ful mete* A: the four variants are of dubious value and may point to an obscure reading in Ax; but the one chosen, even if a scribal conjecture, may best approach the original, and points forward to the revised **B** form without being derived from it. The sense of *mete* is either 'pleasant' (MED s.v. *mete* adj 1b) or 'sufficient' (*s.v.* 3b), with a possible play on both and a further pun on the homophonic substantive meaning 'food' (with allusion to *panes* in the Latin quotation following). The variants *mochil, more* may point to an archetypal form *meche, of which *mete* could also be a reflex (though here understood as the *correct* original that could have given rise to the postulated Ax form). **111–12 (B 125–26)** *be folis A*-**m** *B*-α: preferred as the harder and more pregnant reading, which looks forward to the idea of 'God's fools' developed at the end of the poem (22 / 20.61,74), but not without a play on *foweles* in alluding to birds' freedom from worldly cares (A 115–17, B 128–29). The difficult phrase seems to have been wrongly resolved in *B*-β while *A*-**r**, having likewise missed the correct referent, has smoothed to *anoper*. The surviving variants for A 112a may suggest that its form was not exactly as in AH³ but nearer to *Þat we be nou3t*; a conjectured archetypal form *Be nou3t would more easily account for R's *are not* and the smoothed reflex of M. However, it seems safer to retain the AH³ reading, which is identical with **B** and lucid, than to attempt reconstruction. **296 (A 130, B 143)** *a myle* AC: restored as the original of **B**, for which Bx may have had an imperfect form as in R (?=α) which was later smoothed to make syntactical sense in β. **304 (A 136, B 152)** *book Bible* BC: reconstructed as the probable reading of **A**. As Ax stands, *bible* seems to have been misunderstood as a gloss and taken as the substantive reading with subsequent omission of *book* preceding. M has corrected the metre, perhaps in awareness of **B**; but only the **BC** appositive phrase-structure will have generated the Ax reading. The presence of *for* in the line makes the syntax of 305–10 // anacoluthic; lack of revision in **C** shows this was intentional.

B 156 (A 140) *cleyme*: clearly the correct reading on grounds of sense. A Bx spelling *cleme could well have generated the ?β variant *cleue* (doubtless induced by *departed* 157). Thereafter **w** and three **g** mss will have corrected and α substituted a contextually appropriate term for one apparently meaningless. **311** *shulle*: adopted from P² as the plural form needed for the feminine ending. **316** *Israel*: convincingly proposed by *Pe* as the name given the patriarch in Gen 32:28

(presumably unfamiliar except as the name of the people) and as the likely Cx reading for which *Iacob* is a (substantively correct but unmetrical) ⇒, *Isaak* **x** a (mistaken) 'correction'. The line recalls A 3.243. **324–25 (A 158–59, B 174–75)** The line-division of **AC** is judged as that of original **B**, ?Bx having brought forward the object of the verb and F representing α or having corrected from **A** or **C**. **325** *ioye*: adopted on the showing of **AC** as the presumed **B** original for which Bx *heuene* appears a more explicit scribal ⇒, perhaps under influence from *celis* in 176a. That *ioye* is **L**'s short-hand for 'the happiness of heaven' is clear from an earlier passage such as B 7.36. **327 (A 161, B 177)** *Lord forbede* AC: Bx may be a smoothing after misreading the *e* of *forbede* as *o*; but the sense is identical. **335 (A 169, B 185)** *nam(e)liche*: a wrenched stress in all versions to provide an extraordinary first stave on |m| (the normal pronunciation, with stress on *ná-*, is instanced at 2.159 //) stretches tolerability here (see discussion of 8.51). More probably *maistres* is trisyllabic and *nameliche* forms part of a strong initial dip. X has uniquely *manliche*, which could be right (see discussion of 8.51). **343 (A 177, B 193)** *fyue*: preferred to *foure* on the strength of **C** as the (harder) **B** revision, present in Bx, which F and β seem to have 'corrected' as a supposed error.

A 179 (B 195, C 345) *þe patent of þi pardoun*: here tentatively accepted as the Ax reading from which T&r have lost *of þi pardoun*, levelling *þe* to *þi* / *3oure* by homœoarchy (*pat-* / *par*). But the DRK(A) reading could be due to memorial ⊗ from **B**: the opening dip is long enough to suggest that *3iue* could be an Ax ⇒ for *paye prompted by finding *paye* contextually inappropriate to the colloquial asseveration. The **B** term *patentes* is, perhaps significantly, absent from **C**. **351 (A 185, B 201)** *At* BCA-**m**: the inevitably correct reading in **A** since **r** gives no sense (*Þat* may have come in by visual attraction from 184). AM will here represent **m** (< Ax) and KZ have corrected independently on grounds of common sense.

Rubric The substance of the **C** *Explicit* is that the *vision* of 'Piers Plowman' has ended and that of 'Dowel' now begins. **A** concurs with the first part of **C** but declares that the *life* of 'Dowel, Dobet and Dobest' now begins. (On the unique form of the colophon in the **A** portion of ms Z, see the note at Z 92 above). The character of the **B** *Explicit* remains uncertain. It seems to have been lacking in γM, but the marginal note in L to the opening of Passus VIII suggests some indication in β that the 'vision' concluded with VII and a new section was now beginning (see note on **B** VIII Rubric; the term *inquisicio* used in M at VIII implies a common source with L, i.e. β). R's long title to VIII (see Apparatus *ad loc*) is very close in form to that of **A** and may well have stood as the general title in Bx, making clear that the new passus is the eighth of 'THE VISION OF PIERS PLOWMAN' and a beginning concerning 'Dowel, Dobet and Dobest', the content of the rest of the [same] work. It is unclear whether 'of William' formed part of the postulated Bx rubric to VIII as it does in **AC**, but this must be at least probable. The letter 'W' after 'William' in one family of the **C** tradition finds no support in either **A** or **B**. It could preserve the form of the Cx reading which **p** went on to expand into 'William', as also did **x** (but without dropping the single letter, which stood for the same name, and became redundant after expansion). If it refers to a surname, no explanation has been forthcoming. (On the rubrics generally, see Appendix Two, and on **B**, Adams 1985, on **C** Adams 1994).

Passus X (A IX, B VIII)

RUBRICS On these see the terminal notes to C IX above. Selective collation of N^2 as a **C** ms begins at 14, as 1–13 are an A-Text (see 13 note). ms Z, after some transitional **A** readings, is now a C-Text, classed as a p^1 member of the 'q' group.

6 *as I wente* **A?B** / *in þis worlde* **C**: Z here reads *as I wene* (the r^1 variant in **A**) and N^2 *as I went*, the reading of $A-r^2$**m** and of **B**. N^2 here as at 13 is clearly an A-Text and so *R–K*'s rejection of *in this worlde* Cx is unwarranted. On the other hand, in the light of *B*-F support for β and **A**, R's variant may be seen not as representing α (and thence Bx) but as coincidental ⇒ of a semi-proverbial phrase (cf. 4.136, 15.167, 19.104, 20.242). For by contrast with *as I wen(t)e,* this expression is so common that no need arises to see R as in some way transitional between **B** and **C** (see *Intro.* III *B* §§ 52–5) or suspect of ⊗ from **C**. Nor need β as well as F show ⊗ from **A**, since there is no sign of this elsewhere in its tradition. **7** *leode*: restored on the strength of the **AB** witness and the contextual and metrical need (N^2, as an A-Text, reads thus here). It was probably lost by homœoarchy before l*onged*, and if Cx read as **x**, the **p** smoothing is easily explained. **9** *witte*: with doubled *t* and final *-e* added in **A** to provide the necessary feminine ending. **12** *aboute* **AC**: restored as the probable **B** reading supplanted in Bx by a more emphatic last lift, perhaps under suggestion from adjacent verbs of motion at 11, 14 and especially 6a above, which **L** is unlikely to have repeated here. **13** *dere...me*: C-N^2 here reads *doþ me to wisse*, the reading of **A**, which *R–K* (inconsistently with their practice at 6) do not adopt. Here, as in 6, **C** is revising and N^2 would appear to have made good a deficient opening to its exemplar's Passus X from an **A** ms, in a manner like C-I earlier (see on Pr 91–157). N^2 continues as a **C** witness of basically **x**-type showing strong ⊗ from a **p**-source. **14–17** Omission by α of these lines (which are not in **A**) need not indicate that α was an earlier and β a later form of the B-Text. The cause looks to have been

eyeskip from *dwelleþ* 13a to *dwellynge* 18b occasioned by *dwelle* 17b. **18 (A 14, B 18)** shows continuous revision from **A** → **C**, and the Bx form is unexceptionable on grounds of sense and metre. *B*-F seems to have adapted the **A** reading, the first of some fourteen such instances in this passus, presumably by direct consultation of an **A** copy (see e.g. at 41, 48, B 49). The notion that these agreements of F with **A** against βR represent correction from a **B**-source of superior quality to Bx is rejected at *Intro.* III *B* § 46. A slight piece of evidence of possible scribal censorship in the source of BxB[1], recognised by **L** in revising, might be the mild asseveration *sothly* in the same position as **A**'s *Marie*. But against this, it is plain that **C** is aiming at its characteristic effects of rhetorical *repetitio* in prefacing Will's *Sothly* 21 with an earlier use of the word, which recurs 'traductively' at 22 (*sothe*). **22** Cx has varied to prose order, giving the inauthentic pattern *xa / ax*. The reconstructed line scans as Type IIIa, throwing heavy stresses on the alliteratively linked 'joy' and 'Jesus' (cf. C 21.25, B 11.184 where the conjunction of ideas recurs). *R–K* leave the line unmetrical, presumably judging it still in draft form, while Hanna (1998:184), ignoring the evidence of // **B**, drastically reconstructs by dividing 21/2 after *die* and omitting *falling* as scribal. **25 (A 18, B 23)** The Cx line scans as Type Ia with a heavy stress on the negative particle to enable the feminine ending (*nát wèl*). The Bx line (scanning satisfactorily as Type IIa) preserves from **A** *as me þynkeþ*, but omits *sertis*. Restoration of the latter in **B** here is syntactically possible but not necessary on grounds of either sense or metre. The awkwardness of Ax is due to the absence of *doþ yuele*, which is present in **B**, whether or not by addition, and is needed to give the syllogism its correct structure (see *Commentary*). The omission of the apodictic proposition in **A** could have been deliberate, so as implicitly to undermine Will's pretensions as a clerkly disputant. But the text remains doubtful here, and arguably *doþ yuele* should be in **A** and *certes* in **B**, with the caesura coming (unusually) after the latter in both texts, which would then read as identical. Though this is supported by the appearance of *certes* as the (mute) keystave in revised **C**, on balance it is safer to leave **A** and **B** unemended. **29 (A 21, B 26)** *other-* **x**: to be accepted on the showing of **AB** as the likeliest Cx reading, for which **p**'s synonymous *vm-* is a ⇒ later smoothed to unmetrical *sum-* in various copies. **31 (A 23, B 28)** Bx scans satisfactorily as a Type IIa line, and could be a revision, but in the light of **AC**'s prose order is to be judged inauthentic. F may be an independent re-writing to produce a Type I line, but is more probably ⊗ from **A** or **C**, with *tyȝde* added by the F-scribe or his exemplar. **33 (A 25, B 30)** *a* (3): one of the rare but significant instances where L (=β) and R (=α), supported by **AC**, agree in a minor reading against γ (here accompanied by F and M). See 43 below for another LR agreement, and cf. B 28 above (with M). **34 (A 26, B**

31) *wagyng of the bote* **AC**: judged also the reading of **B**, which has become unmetrical in Bx (*aa / xa*) through promotion of the noun as main referent. **37** *so* **x**: needed on grounds of syntactical coherence and giving an expressive T-type line (in preference to scansion as Ia with four-syllable pre-final dip). N^2 omits with **p**. **38** scans either with a four-syllable final dip or, more satisfactorily, with *so* as a mute stave (to avoid repeating 37) and stress on *fareth* as in 41. **41 (A 33, B 38)** *hit fareth*: to be accepted on grounds of **AC** agreement as the probable reading for **B** also, *falleþ* having perhaps come into Bx through con-textual suggestion (B 32–3); *B*-GF will here have ⊗ from an A copy. **46 (A 36, B 41)** *waleweth*: to be adopted on **AC** agreement as the probable original reading for **B** (see MED s.v. *walwen* v. 4 (a)). Presumably LM here = β but α has (untypically) varied with γ, owing either to the ease of *w / k* confusion (cf. C 10.160, App.) or the unusual nature of the verb, the *C*-P²RMN variant *walkeþ* (so *R–K*) being hard enough to be original (see MED s.v. *walken* v. (1).1). **48 (A 38, B 43)** *oure / þe / þi*: the **C** reading, which could be the source of *B*-F here, firmly established, like that of **A**. But *þi* is preferred for **B**, on the strength of L (=β) and R (=α), as a reading transitional between **A** and **C**, which has accommodated the modifier to preceding and following *þe* (M perhaps showing ⊗ from γ). *R–K*'s rejection of Cx *oure* and *þis* has no warrant. *þis* R: preferred for **B** as the reading confirmed by **C**, although β*F þe* (agreeing with **A**) could equally represent Bx here. *freel*: supported by **C** as the reading of **B**'s revision of **A** (from which F here shows ⊗). **49 (A 39, B 44)** is so revised as to offer no decisive confirmation for either **B** or **A**. But on metrical grounds **A**'s form is preferable as the likely original of **B**, although the superior rhythm of *a daye* suggests possible revision. The Bx line allows a Type Ib pattern with *a daye* as the b-half's first dip; but the uncharacteristic rhythm comes from the unidiomatic word-order caused by promoting the notion of 'every day' over that of 'seven times'.

B 49 The line that follows here in F appears a sophisticated version of A 45, added to or by its source with subsequent smoothing through insertion of *&* at the beginning of 50 as in **A**. Although it could in principle be derived from a **B** source independent of Bx (*K–D*), it finds no echo in **C**, is not necessary on grounds of sense and could as well have been deleted by **B** as omitted by Bx. **60 (A 52, B 61)** *with good ende to deye* **C**: closer to **A** than β R (? =Bx) *goode men to worþe*, and so perhaps supporting *B*-F's *good ende to make* as derived from a **B** source superior to Bx. But despite its blunter tone, Bx is not necessarily scribal here but could represent revision, and F's reading a ⊗ from **C**. The **A** line scans as Type IIIc ('crossed' *ab / ab*) and while **B** clearly revises to Type I, emendation of Ax *ʒiue* to *giue* (*Ka*) is otiose. **62 (A 54, B 63)** *wilde*: the secure archetypal reading of both **C** and **B**, emended by *R–K* from D to *wyde*, which is likely to

have come in from *wydewhare* in the previous line (if this seems implausible, their note at p. 165 on what **B** read is incomprehensible). **63 (A 55, B 64)** *abyde me made* **CB**-α: an inevitable emendation (one of the few *Sk* makes to his base text) to provide a correctly scanning b-verse. **65 (A 57, B 66)** *lythen* **CB**: the reading that clearly under-lies *lystyn* A-**m**. While *lerne* would appear to give 'hard' sense, this does not justify its adoption here, let alone *K–D*'s emendation of Bx on its basis. It is hard is to know what 'learning' the birds' lays in this context might mean; but *lythen* is in any case the more uncommon word lexi-cally. *þat þe*: preserved in *B*-α (< Bx) and here adopted as the Ax reading accidentally preserved in KA, of which *þat, þe* appear split variants.

A 60 (B 69) The **A** line, giving satisfactory sense and metre, is revised in **B** to scan on |w| and replace the obsolete *driʒt* and dubiously apt *doute*, a word difficult enough to generate four distinct variants. The r^1 variants seem to be dissatisfied scribal responses to *in doute*, but *drouth* **m** is not one such and is hard to explain if Ax read *in doute*. Anne Middleton proposes in an unpub-lished paper on 'Langland's Language' that **L** wrote *in douth* 'in [a] company' (MED s.v. *douth* n.). This semi-formulaic expression, probably obsolescent by the time Ax was generated, would partly explain the form of **m** (though not its unapt sense), and its loose general sense 'anywhere' might account for the closely similar sense of **B**'s phrase *wiʒt in world* (an almost exact parallel is Laʒa-mon's *Brut* 9857, where ms Cotton Caligula A. ix reads *on dugeðe* and the more modernised Cotton Otho C. xiii has *on worle*). But β R (< Bx) has the inauthentic metrical pattern *xa / aa*, and the transposition here provides a cor-rect if abrupt line of Type IIIb (*ax / aa*) which leaves the final lift in its **A** position. There is thus no need to emend the whole line on the basis of **A** (as *K–DSch*). F gives smoother metre, but its apposition of parenthetic and main verbs in the b-half is stylistically uncharacteristic.

69 (A 62, B 71) *kynde*: despite support for the majority **A** variant in *C*-**p**, not only the harder but the only metri-cally correct reading (*C*-I's *kynde righte* suggests that I has incorporated a gloss in its exemplar). The *A*-**m** form could have been *kende, thus easily generating the con-textually inappropriate *kene* M. **70 (A 63, B 72)** The Ax line, scanning on |ð|, seems to have a mute key-stave, and if *quaþ_I* has a liaisonal second stave, the line will be securely of Type I, not Type III. The form *quod I* **BC** may conceal the same original with internal fricative, but both have in the pronoun *þow* a full stave in the b-half (*C*-**p** has presumably lost this by haplography after *þow* in the a-half). *R–K* needlessly re-shape the line on the basis of *C*-F (which has *I þo*) to conform with *A*-tJ and *B*-βF. **71** The Cx reading *Wille* is here taken as a revision, from which six sources DEQZKN (four, if QZ = q and KN = p^2) have varied, possibly through memorial ⊗ from **B**.

The contextual appropriateness of the Dreamer's being named by his own Thought should not be doubted. **72 (A 65, B 74)** In **AC** the line scans by preference as the rare but authentic Type IIb on vowels and fricatives ($Y^{1,2}$, *art; Thouhte, thenne*). The speech-marker phrase *quod I* is thus restored in **B** as the second stave, having been lost through eyeskip (*I > I*). Bx *what þow art* appears a scribal ⇒ for the reading attested by **AC**, which in F is found presumably by ⊗ from **A** (or **C**). **78 (A 72, B 80)** After B 80, ms F has a line corresponding to A 71, its likely source (no trace of which remains in **C**). The sense of B 80a overlaps slightly with that of A 71a, a line anticipating the description of Dobet in A 77 (retained as B 85), considerations that may account for its deletion in **B**. **80 (A 74, B 82)** *and of his two handes*: a b-half perhaps suspicious since no clear reason for the repetition of 78b appears; as it could be a mechanical error in both **x** and <RM> (if e, q, p^2 here reflect **p**), the form of Cx remains undecided. The repeated half-line does not obviously improve on **AB** *takiþ but his owene* (to which *PeR–K* emend); but on the other hand, such rhetorical *repetitio* is found at 25/6 and 191/93 (cf. **B** 8.100, 105, 10.120, 127) and is a particular feature of **C** (e.g. at 262/65), while the half-lines each work to balance (with a requirement to act) two potentialities for 'truth'. Whatever the case, the **x** form of the b-verse is preferable to that of **p** which, despite a theoretically possible liaisonal stave in *halt_wel*, looks patently like a scribal attempt to *avoid* repetition. **81 (A 75, B 83)** *deynous C-***p***B-*α: preferred on the clear showing of **A** to the competing form *dedeynous*; no difference of sense is involved. **91 (A 84, B 93)** *Ʒe (wordliche) wise* **CA**: Bx lacks a first stave and *Ye wise* is conjectured lost through distraction from *vnwise*, with *and* as subsequential smoothing. **93 (A 86, B 95)** *crose* **CA**: referring to the bishop's crook-shaped crosier and not his processional cross (as at B 5.12), and contextually preferable as also the original reading for **B**. Bx will have levelled to a more familiar word, perhaps as a consequence of a spelling like that attested in **C**. **94 (A 87, B 96)** In the light of the **C** line's b-half, which echoes that of **A**, original *to gode* in **B** could be judged to have been archetypally replaced by the more emphatic *fro helle*. But the Bx line scans correctly as Type Ib, the sense is satisfactory, and any emendation lacks certainty. *ille*: the harder reading. Coincidental cross-family agreement in error of X and M, if not a deliberate alteration of the restrictive sense of *ille*, could have been visually induced by the form of *halie*. *life* A: final *-e* is added to provide the necessary feminine ending, though the scansion *goód lif* is not ruled out. **95 (A 88, B 97)** *pulte*: a revision in **B** of *pungen* **A**, with much the same sense. The **ABC-pu** variant *putte* is either a visual error or a ⇒ of an easier, more familiar near-synonym. The sense here is 'thrust' (MED s.v. *pilten* v.1(a)); cf. also notes on B 1.127 and 19.143. **100 (A 90, B 99)** *demede*

x: preferable here on grounds of sense, *diuinede* **p** being perhaps a visual error partly induced by eyeskip to 102b. *a* **x**: the harder and probably archetypal reading, the variants *and, as, at* all being attempts to clarify a difficult expression the form of which they cannot have generated. *ordeyned...amonges*: emending a Bx line with the metrical pattern *aa / xa* produced by inversion to prose order in the b-half. For a similar case likewise emended cf. *ayeines* at B 9.154 below.

B 100–10 The α family in this passage omits lines and half-lines, perhaps owing to material damage in the exemplar, which α seems to have tried to reconstruct from memory. The true state of α is presumably that reflected in R, since it contains three lines lost in F, which after 101, 102 shows recourse to another version [A], a feature instanced elsewhere in this ms. However, F's witness is valuable at 109–10 where it preserves, doubtless by reference to copies of **A** or **C**, the authentic half-lines 109b, 110a missing not only in α but also in β (and thus presumably in Bx).

101 (A 91, B 100) The **C** line scans on |k|, and β or Bx seems to have substituted *rulen*, as a more obvious and stronger way of specifying the king's function. This was perhaps by suggestion from following 106a, where *rule* follows a b-half (105) that repeats 100 with slight variation (a repetition added in **B** that C eliminates). **102 (A 92–3, B 101)** The revised **C** line may be merely amplifying the sense of B 101 (= A 92); but while the verbs of volition and admonition could reflect a **B** line lost in Bx that was close in sense to A 93 (*vnbuxum // wolde nat* **C**; *bidding // tauhte* **C**), they could equally be an echo of the latter. F inserts such a line, from either **A** or a lost **B** ms distinct from Bx. Given the corrupt state of the passage in α, as noted at B 100–10, the former explanation of F's line is favoured, since a lost 'superior' **B** source would *ex hypothesi* have been free of the omissions manifest in Bx as well as α in these lines.

B 102 (A 94–5) *sholde; prisoun*: preferred for **B** on the strength of α agreement with **A**, the superior coherence of the conditional with the tense-sequence of *dide* 101 and the more appropriate register of *prisoun* in the context. After the **A** line parallel to B 102 is one emphasising the severity of the king's justice, which is inserted here by *B-*F, presumably once again from an **A**-copy; it could have been eliminated in the revision to **B**. For while something of its harsh tone remains, C 101b is making a different point (about the king's rights rather than his attitude) and does not support the case for F's line as strictly necessary to the sequence of thought. Such instances of **B**'s *abbreviation* rather than expansion of material in **A** (as earlier by **A** of lines in **Z**) are not unprecedented (cf. B 7.30 // A 8.32–3, B 7.36 // A 8.38–9). **104 (A 98, B 105)** *to kepen vs alle* **C**: corresponding, with slight revision, to the Bx b-half. F may be presumed to have adopted the **A** form as part of sustained ⊗ attested in 100–01 motivated by desire to correct a perceived damage to the exemplar in these lines. **105 (A 99, B 106)** *here thre wittes* **C**: providing satisfactory scansion either as Type IIIa on vowels or as Type Ia (as it must in **B**), with *thre* treated as disyllabic with internal |r| stave (cf. B VII 39). Adoption of F, here showing ⊗ from **A**, or of the earlier conjecture *rede of hire wittes* (*Sch*[1]), cannot be justified. **106 (A 100, B 107)** *ne ellis nat* **AC**: to be adopted as the reading of **B**, from which Bx (scannable as Type IIIa) will have omitted as supposedly pleonastic. **107 (A 101, B 108)** *so* **AC**: preferred in **B** as the adverb for which Bx has substituted a synonym under unconscious influence from the preceding fricative monosyllables. F's sophisticated form conceals probable ⊗ from **A** or **C**. **108–09 (A 102–03, B 109–10)** On grounds of sense and metre the βR (=Bx) reading must be judged defective on the showing of **AC**. The error could have occurred through syntactic anticipation of 110. *B*-F will have inserted 109b and 110a by reference to an **A** rather than a **C** copy (*helpe, lerne* against *spede, here*); but the substance must of necessity have been present in original **B**. On comparison with *A* and Ø in C 109 / A 103, F's *For* might seem scribal; but since choice for **B** between **A** and **C** is undecidable, there is no need to emend. **111** A comma may be better after *dwelleth*, given the sense of *wole* 'is willing'. **112 (A 106, B 113)** The **C** line scans firmly on |k| and Bx is a Type IIIa with heavy stresses on *noon* and *now*. If Ax is also Type IIIa scanning on |n|, emendation of *wot* to *not* on the strength of V will seem gratuitous. But as double negation is common in **L** and there is a possible reflex of it here in the revised b-half of **C**, it could be that **A** had a standard line. The same may have been true of **B**, but the line is left unemended in the absence of ms support. **118 (A 112, B 119)** *a; speche* **AC**: adopted as the probable **B** reading for which Bx has substituted a noun suggested by the sense of the preceding half-line, with accidental omission of the article.

C X (continued); A X; B IX

RUBRICS The Ax tradition, following the colophon to VIII, seems to reflect an understanding of A IX as 'prologue' to the 'vita' of Dowel, &c., a recognition explicitly made by mss W and M. Passus X is accordingly treated in **A** as the *first* Dowel passus. But in **B**, where VIII is accounted *primus de dowel*, the present passus is made *nonus de visione* (so LMR). Attempts therefore to specify it as either about 'Dowel' (HmB) or about 'Dobet' (γ) cannot be reliably regarded as deriving from Bx.
130 (AB 3) *is it* **BC**: preferred in this Type IIa line, since one or other word is probably a full stave and the inverted order, allowing full stress to the pronoun, gives a more speech-like stress-pattern. *A*-DKW diverge coin-

cidentally from Ax under influence from the word-order normal in verb-phrases with preceding complement. **131 (AB 4)** *wittyly* **CA**: on grounds of sense the preferred reading, for which Bx is ⇒ of a more emphatic term, possibly through misreading an exemplar form **witliche* as intending a contraction of *-er* after the *t*. The ancestor of <OC[2]> has presumably corrected from a **C** source. **134 (AB 7)** *to here hath enuye*: preferred to a Bx reading not obviously scribal on grounds of sense or metre, since **C** revision back to **A** seems improbable here. The unexpected word-order and delayed noun-phrase subject may have prompted the Bx scribe to make *enuye* a subject while *hatep*, translating accurately the sense of *hath enuye*, could have been suggested by preceding *hatte*. The apparent paronomasia here seems pointless (cf. 15 below). **138 (AB 11)** *duk* **AC**: preferred also as the reading of **B**, with ?**g** and F having corrected a reading unobjectionable but unlikely to be a revision.

B 15 *biddep*: in the absence of **AC** evidence, rejection of Bx *rulep* as scribal is arguably unjustified, since the line scans vocalically as Type IIIb and gives a defensible pattern of stresses on rhetorically prominent *he* (1,2),*alle*. However, the context foregrounds the dual rôle of commanding and teaching (16), and a better stress-pattern emerges with lexical words on |b| as the staves. To this end *biddep* is conjectured in the absolute sense 'directs' to provide authentic-sounding polysemantic wordplay with *bit* 'commands' in the a-half (MED s.v. *bidden* v. 4(a), 4(b)).
141–42 (B 14–16, A 14–15) It is possible that two lines on Dobest are missing from Ax, since he is introduced at 14 along with Dowel and Dobet but without any prior account of his function. *A*-J adds here two lines: *dobest is in hir bowre & boldyth þat leuedy / and berith a batte on his honde lych a byschoppys mace*. These are not derived from either **B** or **C** though they are perhaps sufficiently Langland-like to be a reflex of a lost original, as noted in *Ka*[2] (p. 463). But not impossibly, line A 14 has a long pause at the caesura, introducing *Dobest* as a kind of afterthought not strictly governed by the logical force of the opening *Þus*. It would therefore be safer to treat the J lines as an accomplished scribal conjecture and not adopt them into the text. **142 (B 16)** The Bx line could scan *abb / ab* (stressed *his léryng*); but on the showing of revised **C** it seems rather the result of inversion to prose order, and is therefore emended. **143 (A 16, B 17)** *hem alle* **AC**: judged also the **B** original replaced by a more emphatic idea, perhaps out of stylistic objection to repeated *alle* at 18a and at 22. A vestige of the presumed **B** reading seems to remain in Bx *al*. **148 (A 21, B 22)** *Goed-fayth*: a revision that *R–K* emend without warrant to **AB** *Godefray*. *alle* **AC**: preferred as the **B** reading for which Bx substitutes an empty intensifier from probable stylistic objection to repeated *alle* (see note above). **149 (A 22, B**

23) *fyue*: the secure reading of **C** and on the showing of βR evidently that of Bx, F having altered perhaps under influence from an **A** copy of **r**-type. In the Ax tradition one **m**-ms A has also varied to the **r**-reading, perhaps through inducement from the (secondary) alliteration on |s| in lexical words and the wish to count Inwit among the castle's outer defenders. Presumably Ax itself read **v*, which could have been easily misread by **r** as *vi*. In **A** the *sones* (= 'the sense-faculties with regard to their moral orientation') are posted to protect the *castel* (the body), while the rational / moral power Inwit guards *all* (soul, body and senses). This distinction having been eliminated in **B** (see 23), it might seem more logical to read *sixe*, though the textual evidence of Bx and **C** indicates that the senses' protecting rôle is still envisaged as separate from reason's supervisory one. However, the line scans on voiced and unvoiced fricatives and Bx either stresses *þis* or treats it as a muted key-stave. In the light of **AC**, which have *for* as key-stave, and of **C**'s *Anima*, Bx *lady* may be suspected as a scribal intrusion, with a preceding *for* (as in **AC**) omitted, and subsequential smoothing. But since the evidence is inconclusive and the line will pass muster, no emendation is offered.

A 23 The Ax line, removed in revision, has the pattern *xa / ax* and could be easily emended by diagnosing in the a-half inversion to prose order from an original *þis womman to kepe* (in a Type IIIa line). The J variant *kepe wel* appears a characteristic scribal 'correction' that does not recommend itself as the likely original (as it does to *Ka²*). The conjectural reading here proposed, however, is hard enough to have invited ⇒ of a commoner term, perhaps through desire to achieve parallelism with *kepe* in 24b. Moreover *wite* is well-established in **L**'s usage, as at A 67 (and at B 7.35, 16.25), and here enables homophonic wordplay on *wit* 'wisdom' suggested by *wise* in 23b and by the constable's own name.

150 (AB 24) *kepe*: in the light of agreed **AC**, the Bx reading *saue* may be diagnosed as a scribal ⇒ alliteratively induced by *sende, selue* and by the same tendency towards parallelism, here with *saue* 23, seen in Ax at 23. In the last lift *for euere* likewise appears as ⇒ of a more emphatic expression, perhaps under inducement from *euere* in 27b. F is here presumed to have derived both readings from an **A** copy. *and*: given the agreement of **AC**, perhaps preferable to Bx *to*, but no difference of meaning arises. **153 (A 28, B 27)** The shape of **C**'s revised b-half strongly supports the authenticity of Bx as preserving a **B** revision. The *B*-F reading could derive from **A**, but with characteristic sophistication based on the sense of Bx. The Bx line scans either with a mute stave on *þat* or more probably with a liaisonal stave on *of_al*, as Type I. While the b-half could raise doubts that *euere* has been suggested by following *neuere* and desire to intensify *al*, its rhythm (with a strong pre-final dip) is exactly

matched at 40, which is not open to question, so it should be regarded as authentic. *þinges* **A**: the pl. preferred on metrical grounds as probably underlying revised B 26b. *A*-RK will have severally corrected Ax's sg., which could have come in by visual anticipation of 31 and 34. **157 (A 32, B 31)** *shafte* **AB**: the preferred reading in **A**, where **r**'s *shap* seems to form part of a simplified understanding of the phrase as signifying 'feature and form' (as at B 11.395 and 13.297). But *shafte* is meant to imply both man's appearance and his (spiritual) nature as made in the divine image, a point explicit in the new **C** line 158 (see MED s.v. *shafte* n. (1) (d)). Despite an earlier view to the contrary (*Sch¹*: 277), *shafte* is better seen as the **B** original for which CrGC, independently or influenced by an **A** source of **r**-type, have an easier ⇒ of similar form.

B 32–9 32 (A 33) *warp / spak*: the former the harder reading and evidently that of Ax. H³W have either preserved the reading of **m** or filled a lacuna by reference to another **A** ms of **r**-type, the latter being likelier, given the randomly divergent AM variants. **B** must then have been revised, unusually to a Type IIIa line. The use of *warp* with *word* is, however, earlier instanced in **B**; at 5.86 **B** has no parallel, but in the parallels to B 5.363, *spak* is archetypally attested in **AC**. If the present instance is not a case of Bx ⇒ of *spak*, it may mirror **L**'s unease at using with reference to God a verb hitherto used only in connexion with the 'word' uttered by a Deadly Sin. But the **AC** parallels to B 5.363 tell against this, unless they too are scribal ⇒. Given the uncertainty, then, it seems prudent (against *K–DSch¹*) to let the archetypal reading stand in each case (as do *R–K* at C 6.419). After 32 there follow in *B*-F two spurious lines and another which appears an ungainly rewriting of A 34 unlikely to be (as *K–D* p. 171 hold) part of the original **B**. **33 (A 35)** *man*: likely to have been part of the Bx reading, on the showing of the **A** line under revision. *Adam* was probably a gloss in β, though omitted from γ, and possibly also present in α, though omitted from R and in F integrated into the text. If the gloss was in Bx, it was presumably inserted to provide an explicit parallel with *Eue* and an antecedent for *his* in 34. If Bx read like F, the line could scan (awkwardly) as a vocalic Type IIIb; but with the supralinear gloss here understood as scribal, it requires a third stave on |m|. This is found by diagnosing the simple superlative as a Bx ⇒ (perhaps deliberate, to avoid repetition of 31a) for the composite form, adoption of which provides a Type IIb line with vocalic b-half staves, alliterating translinearly with 34. **38** *ne*: conjectured as necessary for the elaborate simile to make sense and presumed lost from Bx through misunderstanding of *and* as 'if'. **L** is saying that, even if two conditions are fulfilled (parchment, ability to write), successful letter-writing requires a *third*, the instrument (*penne*). **39** *welde*: the Bx reading *hadde* yields an extended Type IIIa with two vocalic staves (*he, hadde*) and possible counterpoint on |w| in the a-half. But the line would read more strongly if the key-stave were also on |w| and both *write* and *wel* were thematic not contrapuntal staves in the a-half. The verb *welde* is therefore conjectured as providing an apt stave-word (attested in the sense 'possess' at 11.10, 72 //, 14.18 //, 22.12 //, B 10.29, 90).

160 *schalkes*: apparently the Cx reading and clearly right on grounds of sense; the comparison of sunshine to grace is a favourite one, as at 18.72–5, 19.194. The variant *shaftes* introduces a human referent to make sense of contextually inappropriate *schawes*, a mistake for *schalkes* by easy confusion of *w* with *lk* (cf. on 46). **162** *sheweth*: possibly a visual or aural error for *seweth* induced by *shewe* at 160 (an interpretation supported by 18.72 below). Alternatively, *seweth* is the ⇒ for *sheweth* of an easier phrase. The grammar, with *suche synfole men* as direct object, would require *sheweth* to mean 'look with favour upon', i.e. grant his grace (see MED s.v. *sheuen* v. (1)). But there may also be polysemantic play on the sense 'make revelation to' (MED s.v. 9(a)), establishing a closer parallel between 162 and 160. **163** *And*: the simpler reading and one expressing clearly enough the consequence of God's withdrawal of grace. However, it could be a ⇒ for an apter and more exact conjunction that is contextually harder, whether introducing a result, = 'so that' (MED s.v. *as* conj. 5) or a simple comparison with understood relative after *somme* = 'like some (who)' (s.v. 1(a)). Arguably therefore, *as* could be judged the more likely original and is so preferred by *R–K*. **164** *yworthe lat hem*: a reconstruction presupposing that the b-half in Cx has varied to prose order with loss of the key-stave in |w| (cf. 3.139 above). In principle Cx could scan as Type IIIc on vowel and approximant (*óf, wýte; hém, ywórthe*) or as Type Ia on vowels, as *R–K* presumably judge. But this would result in de-stressing the lexical verbs *wol* and *lat*, which seem crucial to the theological point of the argument concerning God's 'will' to 'know' [= acknowledge] man.

B 41–4 41 The Bx line could in principle scan vocalically on non-lexical words. But 42 would then count as a wholly non-alliterating macaronic, something **L** generally avoids. It is possible that *þere he seide* is a Bx scribal insertion, and that **B**'s Latin line was free-standing as in **A**. The alternative analysis proposed sees the mislineation as due to the postulated line 41's unusual length. The structure is then either Type II, with three vowel lifts as in Bx, *it, hym, as* (a structure closely similar to B 11.204) or that of a vocalic Type Ia with an unusually long five-syllable pre-final dip (*þe...he*). More speculatively, *Þe Bible* is a scribal ⇒ for *scripture* and the line scans on |s| as Type I (with omission of the final phrase). **42** *Faciamus*: the Bx reading *& facta sunt* is here diagnosed as a mistaken expansion of its exemplar's posited **&c*, since the scripture being cited (Ps 148:5) appears the wrong

one, being concerned with the non-human creation. This may result from 'anticipatory recollection' of B 14.60*a*, where the psalm-verse is fittingly quoted after a line describing the creation of the animals. The correct scripture in 41*a* (as *K–D* recognise) is Gen 1:26, the one cited in F, doubtless as a consequence of ⊗ from **A**. This appropriately concerns God's creation of *man* in his image and likeness, the pervading theme of this passage.

171 (B 48) *þat* **x** / *and* **p**: possible reflexes of Cx ∅; but the pronoun is preferable in the light of **B**. *his* **B**: absent from β but preferable on grounds of sense and presumably added by W independently rather than by ⊗ from an α source. **172 (A 42, B 53)** *yclosed*: Cx, like *B*-β, apparently lacking the past-participle marker required to provide the line's key-stave, which is here mute (the fourth lift *-ynne* serves a 'supplemental' function).

B 55 (A 44) *heo*: conjectured as the metrically required form of the feminine pronoun, providing the key-stave in a T-type line. Bx *he* could well have been an incorrect reflex of a gender-indeterminate exemplar reading **a*.

176 (B 60) The **C** line revises by inverting the order of object and verb in the b-half and replacing the a-half noun-object with a pronoun *hym*. The latter is unlikely to have been the underlying Bx reading, since the line would not scan with it, whereas it will scan with either sub-archetypal variant, as Type IIa in α and Type I in β. The α reading is preferred as giving a rhetorically superior stress-pattern in both halves.

A 47–70 47 *help* Ax: somewhat weak, not in itself but in view of the repetition at 49b. On the basis of the t variant *Ka* conjectures *allie*, but *halle* is more probably a careless reflex of a group-original *halp* or possibly *hele*. With the sense '(spiritual) strength' *hele* (MED s.v. n.3(c)) would be appropriate as a difficult original for which *help* could be a scribal ⇒; but the case for emendation is not compelling (see further *Intro*. II § 71). **51** *reccheles*: little instanced as a noun (see MED s.v. 4(c)) but the hardest and most probably archetypal reading, the variants with *-nesse* being ⇒ of more familiar forms. **53** Unless there has been ↔ of subject and verb-phrase, the Ax line scans with two stresses in 'begýnnére', another example of a rare b-verse type earlier illustrated at A 6.14 // (and cf. 4.172, etc.). *going*: preferred on grounds of metre and harder sense as the probable **r** reading. The 'paternal' conception of Inwit established at A 17ff above is here developed, *good speche and going* corresponding to *Seywel* and *Go-wel* at A 19, 21. **68** scans *xa* / *ax* (thus in *Ka²*), with J's variant being a manifest attempt at scribal correction that does not account for the Ax reading *pore*. A simple emendation, giving a Type IIIa line, would be ↔ of *cateles* and *pore*, on the presumption that the more inclusive notion has been promoted by the Ax scribe with consequent damage to the metre. But *caitif* 'poor' (see

MED s.v. adj. 2(b)) is conjectured as lexically difficult and providing a stave-word with the requisite sense. It occurs as a noun at 14.90 and semi-metaphorically at C 13.109 //, while the derived noun *cheitiftee* (with internal gloss *pouertee*) is instanced at 22.236 //.

186 The scansion of the line is uncertain. If *to* is adverbial = 'in addition' (MED s.v. *to* adv. 9(a)) it could be a scribal ⇒ for original *als*, making the line of Type IIa. As it stands, it scans as Type IIIa with presumed cognative alliteration of *ch* and *sh*: cf. the spelling *chingled* in ms X at 235 (Vol. I, Appendix One). But examination of 184–85 suggests that the C lines are drawing not only on B 67–8 but also on A 69–70: compare *helpe hem and saue / Fro folies* **A** with *and fram folye kepe / And...helpe to* **C**, where there is no close verbal parallel in **B**. Possibly therefore a verb *ouht*, corresponding to *owyng* in A 69, was lost by Cx before *to* in the a-half of 186, which would then be a Type IIa line. This is one of the more striking cases of (partially) non-linear revision. A final possibility is that *And* here means 'If', requiring a semi-colon after *kepe* but thereby promoting the first word to full-stave status, and again giving a Type IIa.

B 77–91 77 will scan either as an extended Type IIIb line with vocalic theme-stave and counterpoint on |p| or (preferably) as Type Ia with a cognative key-stave *but*, or, if this is muted, then as a T-type. A possible emendation of *haue* to *preue* here (*Sch¹*) seems, by contrast with earlier B 7.45 (q.v.), insufficiently unwarranted. **87–9** The Bx form of 87 scans *aa / xa* unless *good* is taken as a cognative third stave in a Type IIb line, as it may be (leaving an uncharacteristically short b-half). The emendation here provides a Type IIIb line with *Cristes good* a unitary phrase given prominence as the key-stave (in either analysis there is a 'supplemental' fourth / third stave in *kynde*). The word-order here is such as to have easily invited inversion to the prose order evidenced in Bx. **88** scans most naturally as Type IIIa (possibly extended, if *ben* is a blank stave), with cognative alliteration between the key-stave *shame* and |tʃ| generated by liaison of *As* and *Iewes* in first position. **89** seems to scan vocalically on the morphemes *hir*, *vn-*, *I* the last mute), requiring a quadrisyllabic prelude-dip including the lexical word *commune*: the *vnkynde* Christians of 84 are being contrasted unfavourably with the *kynde* Jews of 86, whence the stress on the prefix. The alternative scansion as Type IIIa on *m* with wrenched stress in *commúne* and key-stave on *me* gives an inferior rhetorical pattern by comparison. An alternative to the above reconstructions would be to re-divide 87–8 after *Iewes* and read *aren* for *ben* in 88, scanning this line on vowels. **91** has the unmetrical pattern *xa / ax* in Bx and is here emended to a Type IIIa line by simple ↔ from prose order.

A 75–80 75 *wyt*: here taken as a spelling variant for *wyte*, which in context is more apt; *wyt* 'reason, under-

standing' may have been suggested by 71b (*wys vndirstanding*). Either way, chiming or annominative wordplay is to be discerned (see Schmidt 1987:113–16). **77** *miȝte*: final *-e* added to provide the necessary feminine ending. **80** *douten* 'fear' (MED s.v.3) not 'doubt' (MED s.v. 1); evidently the harder reading for which **m**, here independently accompanied by V, seems to have substituted an unambiguous synonym. But 82, in which Ax is uniformly attested, implicitly bears out the exact equivalence of the verbs by equating the nouns (in **B** *dreden* alone appears between 93 and 96, very possibly in order to avoid the ambiguity).

B 98a–99 98a *verbo*: unlikely to be a scribal alteration of the well-known quotation from Js 2:10, the reading preserved in L (?=β) and R (?=α) probably representing Bx, which is here judged original. M has altered its β-type reading, perhaps following γ, and F has conflated the two readings. What is clearly in question is 'custody of the lips', and while *space* 98 allows that *any* misuse of time may constitute potentially grievous sin, *speche* 101 specifies the particular kind envisaged. **99** *Tynynge*: conjectured as the required first stave for which Bx has substituted a commoner non-alliterating synonym. The verb is well instanced in the relevant sense at 5.93 and at C 14.7–8, which recalls the present passage.

A 86–90 86 *þi seluen*: preferable on grounds of sense to the pointlessly repetitive *þe salme*, a visual error induced in part by preceding *Sauter*. **89** *wy*: the inevitable emendation of a word perhaps spelled **wheye* in Ax and so misresolved in *r¹* and omitted as syntactically awkward in **m**, though necessary as the key-stave and squaring well with *hominem* in the Latin. *iudicat*: preferred on grounds of sense as the resolution of a visually ambiguous reading (for a parallel case cf. B 16.20 below); proposed by Alford (1988:74), who notes that the phrase is a legal maxim, 'the will or intention judges the man'. This gives stronger meaning than *indicat* 'reveals, manifests' and fits better with the sense of *acorde* 88, which has legal overtones (Alf*G* s.v. II), and the judgement motif of 94, which completes the argument on conscience.

197 *seth*: taken by Sk*Pe* (as by **p**) as the temporal conjunction, and providing an acceptable illustrative parallel with the envisaged loss of land and life in 194. But more probably the causal conjunction is intended, **L**'s point being that Christ's preparedness to lose his life constitutes the *reason* for expecting martyrdom from the Church's leaders: their vocation to 'do best' involves facing death in order to spread the faith and obtain peace for the world (cf. the argument of 17.264–76). In mss XI (see Vol. I Appendix One) the reading *al* for *he lees* may be a truncated reflex of **a lees* 'he lost', *a* being a probable original form of the pronoun. **203** *defaute*: like *lacke* **p** a blank stave, but on balance more likely to be the original. It is well-instanced in identical context at 15.231, 273 and *lakke* in L has the sense '(moral) fault' (13.210, B 10.262).

A 91–130 The longest passage of **A** to have been omitted in **B** with almost no sign of its use elsewhere in revised form. Most of the material is unique, though two lines echo the end of the **A** *Visio*, 129 (= A 8.87a) and 130 (= A 8.183a). **A 94a** The second part of the quotation was probably omitted from Ax but is included for convenience as the sense is incomplete without it. **110** The variants *of, þat* and *how* all appear unlikely to be original, and Ax probably read Ø here. **119** *soueraynes*: here not the pl. of the concrete noun *souerayn* but a rare form of the abstract noun (MED s.v. *soverainnesse* n., which omits this earliest example). It stands in balance with preceding *suffraunce*, with which it 'chimes' annominatively (Schmidt 1987²:113–16).

204 (A 131, B 108) The Bx line, like C 205 which partly revises it, scans as Type IIIa and no emendation is needed, that of *Sch*¹ 95, 278 (after *K–D*) producing a line with unacceptable masculine ending. **206 (A 136, B 112)** *martres*: unquestionably the reading of **BC** and more unexpected in collocation with the three contemplative categories than *nonnes*, the non-alliterating *r¹* reading. It is very improbable that *mynchons* underlies the latter (as *Ka* believes), since *martires* in the two unrelated families *r²* and **m** can hardly have been generated from it. Although lexically harder than *nonnes*, *mynchons* is not in context harder than *martires* and is best regarded as one of Ch's many idiosyncratic substitutions (here for the sake of the alliteration; see further *Intro*. IV §§ 32–3). **207 (A 137, B 111)** *cherles* **B**: possibly a scribal ⇒ suggested by the familiar 'oppositional' categorisations, the minority *clerkes* being more apt in a list of 'honourable' social orders; but BoCot and F may show influence from **A**, and *cherles* is otherwise acceptable.

B 113 *wye*: adopted as the clearest realisation of a word probably spelled in Bx as **wey(ʒ)e*, a form also attested in the Cx tradition (see *IG weye* n²). Deliberate ambiguity may here be intended, but on balance the unambiguous form seems preferable; cf. also C 18.229 below.

A 141 *heo*: convincingly conjectured as the Ax reading underlying *she* (a non-alliterating dialectal alternative) and *Eue* (a visual reflex that awkwardly repeats 140), a pair of variants randomly attested across the genetic groups.

B 121 (A 140) The Bx line scans as Type IIIc, on |k| and vowels, with a possible blank stave on *tyme* making this an extended variant of the type. *K–D*'s emendation *cursed* for *yuel* is gratuitous, since the metre and sense are acceptable. **B** appears to have replaced **A**'s *cursid* both here and at 123 (revising A 155), perhaps in order to avoid excessive use of *corsed* prior to its climactic appearances at 136 (A 170) and 138 (A 172). The restoration of *corsede* in C 215 (reinforced by the repetition at 220) represents a return to the **A**-Text, without calling in question the authenticity of **B**.

214 (A 150, B 122a) *in dolore*: clearly established in Cx, and perhaps running together Gen 3:16 with Ps 7:15 (*Pe*; see *Commentary*). The reading also appears as the β variant and could be archetypal and original in **B** too, but *dolorem* α is here preferred on the showing of **A**, as no major difference of meaning is involved. **216 (A 141, Ø B)** The **C** line corresponds to an **A** line either deliberately omitted in **B** or lost by Bx, presumably after 121. The former seems more likely since the **C** passage goes on to add a line (217) in the spirit of A 142, developing the account of Adam and Eve's intercourse after the Fall, of which no trace remains in **B**. *K–D*'s case for seeing A 141 as lost from Bx and requiring restoration is therefore not convincing.

B 124, 127 (A 153, 157, 159) The name *Seth* is clearly established in A 153 as is *Seem* in B 124, and the same referent is intended, the son of Adam (Gen 4: 26) not the son of Noah (Gen 7: 13). In A 159 it seems likely that Ax read *Sem* and that Ch, M and the source of <RU> have corrected to *Seth*, presumably in the light of 153 (as also at 179 below). At A 157 it is also probable that Ax read *Sem* and *r¹* has smoothed to *seye* perhaps on the basis of an immediate exemplar reading **seʒe* (with ʒ mistakenly for earlier þ). Since both *Seth* and *Sem* are instanced in the Ax tradition, it seems best to adopt *Seth* in all three cases so as to avoid contextual confusion with Noah's son. In the Bx tradition, however, only *Seem* is attested. At B 127 there is a possibility, realised by CrM, that *some* could be a corruption of *Sem*, and this certainly provides a closer parallel with the **A** line under revision (159). But *some* is acceptable as referring to the progeny of Seth (*þi* 126, *his* 128) and fits well with *hir* 129, so no emendation is required. The *authorial* confusion of names (if that is what it is) may be due in part to seeing the Flood as both the consequence of the sin of Seth's offspring and also as the occasion for the salvation of Noah's (of whom the most important was Sem). The error is decisively rectified in **C** at 251–55 where *Seth, Adames sone* is specified and the name twice repeated to obviate any risk of confusion. But since *Seem* in **B** could be an authorial rather than a scribal error, it is retained there.

A 154 The line could in principle scan on |k| as a Type IIIb but the resulting five- or six-syllable dip in the a-half would necessitate de-stressing the contextually prominent verb *mariede* at the expense of the meaning. The conjecture *manside* presumes ⇒ by Ax of a more familiar word under inducement immediately from *acursid* in 155b and more remotely from its earlier appearances in the vicinity (146, 148). The word occurs in an identical context in *Purity* 774 and though not instanced in **A** is found in **C**, in a non-restrictive sense, at 2.41 // and also in **B** at 4.160, 10.278, 12.84, 22.221. The edited line, scanning on |m| and |k|, is the rare Type IIb.

247a (B 152a) The grammar of the quotation in C is

correct but that of Bx seems to have run together two constructions, one with a passive verb needing a nominative subject, and another with an accusative object which would require an active verb. Although **C** has this (as has *B*-F and, with different person, g), the passive form is adopted here for **B** as clearly archetypal and the noun is given in the correct nominative sg. form from w. **249 (A 180, B 154)** *makynge* **x**: apparently redundant before *made*, as is *of mankynde* **p** before *men*. Both could be reflexes of Cx **makynde*, a participial form erroneously substituted for a verbal noun, which was later restored in **x**. Cx itself could have been attempting to restore a damaged form (*ma...de*) of an original **mansede*, which would be without the redundancy of both sub-archetypes. *R–K* p. 160, objecting to the perceived tautology, propose *maugre kynde*; but the rhetorical *repetitio* is not ineffective, and no conjecture is warranted here. *Goddes wille ayeines* **B**: tentatively adopted for its more telling rhythmic pattern, though Bx could scan as an extended counterpointed Type IIIa, with wrenched stress giving the keystave *áyeìn* and a 'supplemental' |w| stave in position five. It presumes Bx inversion to prose order with loss of the important original key-stave (*wille*) and requires expanding the preposition to its trisyllabic form to provide the necessary feminine ending. **251** *seth*[2] **x**: a form presumed authentic as punning on the name *Seth*.

B 155–163 155 (A 181) The *B*-β variant gives satisfactory sense and metre, but in the light of the b-half of the **A** line under revision the sub-archetypes may be conjectured to preserve split variants of an original containing *men, now* (as in αA) and also *þat, so* (as in β). The length of the line as reconstructed would have been the main factor occasioning the split. **163 (A 187)** *any*: conjectured as providing the necessary key-stave (by liaison of *any_olde*), the AxBx lines scanning *aa / xx* as they stand. The conjecture *yolde* (*K–D, Sch*[1]) for *olde* is attractive, the sense 'submissive' being attested in the period (MED s.v. *yelden* v.1a (c)), though the more appropriate '(sexually) exhausted' is only from a century later (OED s.v. *Yolden ppl.*, citing Dunbar; not recorded in MED). It is here presumed that *any* was twice replaced by the more expected *an*, the ⇒ being occasioned by the presence of *any* twice in 188 following (once in // **B**) and distraction from preceding |j| in *ʒiuen...ʒong*. Alternatively *olde* provides a key-stave if pronounced with a SW palatal glide (MED s.v. *old(e* adj.).

267 *ac*: conjectured as the liaisonal stave (*ac_late*), required in key position, for which Cx is presumed to have substituted the non-alliterating synonym *bute*. Emendation by inversion of *be knowe* (*R–K*) is excluded because it yields an unacceptable masculine ending. There is a 'compensatory' *k* stave in position 4. **269** Alliteration is on |k|, the first stave being internal to the consonant-group *sk* in *squier* (see *Intro.* IV §45). **273 (A 190, B**

166) On the joint showing of **AC**, where the line comes directly before 274 // (on the pestilence), it may be safely transposed to give in B 162–74 the identical sequence preserved in A 186–98, without any revision. Omission of the line from α for no evident mechanical cause may suggest its absence from Bx also and restoration in β from memory (if so, more easily at the wrong point). **275** *lely* **p**: the reading that gives both satisfactory sense and metre and also accounts for the semi-nonsensical **x** variant *leix* (?= *leiʒes*). Presumably the **x** scribe perceived a clash of sense between *lyen* and *lely* through failing to grasp the adverb's asseverative-parenthetic function (cf. the oxymoronic effect of the similar combination of *lely* with *layne* in *SGGK* 1864). The idiosyncratic spelling is explained by *R–K*'s interpretation (p. 160) of *lyen* as 'lie (physically)', which allows the sense 'fallow' for *lei*, explaining *leix* as a homœograph; but on balance it seems better not to emend here. The **x**-mss I and D have both made individual commonsense corrections, the latter coinciding with **p**-N's 'normal' ⇒ of a less paradoxical synonym, while ms I was guided by the metre or referred to a **p** source to resolve the crux. **276 (A 192, B 168)** *many*: securely conjectured on the evidence of **AC** as having been present in **B** but lost in Bx through alliterative attraction of *forþ > foule*. **277 (A 193, B 169)** *choppes*: to be safely accepted on the showing of **AC** as the probable reading of **B**. The six diverse variants, which include a form *choppyng* close to the presumed original, suggest that both α and β (and hence Bx) may have read an unintelligible word (such as *cloppyng*) that prompted a range of scribal ⇒. **283 (A 199, B 175)** *togyderes*: discriminated as the presumed **A** original in the light of **BC**; the superficially harder synonym *ysamme* may have been induced by *same* 200. **286–90a (B 179–85)** A possible reason for loss of these lines in *B*-α could have been eye-skip from *man*er 179 to *man* and wom*man* at the end of 186, followed by resumption of copying at the next line; but censorship cannot be ruled out as another possible cause (see *Intro.* III *B* § 52). The omitted material, which is all new in **B**, is preserved entirely in **C**, where two Type IIIa lines (179 and 182) are revised to respectively a Type Ia and an extended Type IIIa with counterpoint, no question of emendation on metrical grounds arising in either case. **293 (A 203, B 187)** *bedbourde*: on the showing of agreed **AC** to be accepted as the likely **B** form for which Bx is a ⇒ of a more commonplace expression. **294 (A 204, B 188)** *Clene*: in the light of **AB** perhaps better placed at the end of 293, as no reason for changing the last lift appears. But since the **C** lines scan without difficulty and the enjambment is not uncharacteristic, no emendation is demanded. *leel* **B**: conjectured in the light of **C** (and secondarily **A**) as the necessary stave-word in |l| supplanted by the more obvious non-alliterating *parfit* (an epithet often collocated with this noun). **A**'s point is that the pair be legitimately married and love each other, **C**'s both this and also that they be faithful to each other. The phrase conjectured for **B** emphasises the Christian love of the spouses as based in marital fidelity, *leel* retaining, as usually, a residual semantic link with law (here divine positive law ordaining canonical wedlock). This is emphatic and explicit in **C**'s revision of the line and of B 190, which seems to revert in part to the argument of A 206–08. The possibility that *loue* was lost before *of soule* in Bx (since it appears in both **A** and **C**) is offset by the fact that *charite* has replaced *lawe* in the b-verse. **295 (A 205, B 189)** *dede derne*: a word-order assured in **C** and, as the harder, to be discriminated as the probable original in **A**, where the adjective has been lost from **m** and a majority of *r¹* and *r²* mss have normal prose order. However, as sense and metre remain unaffected, the Bx reading may be retained. **298 (A 209, B 193)** *That*: on the agreement of **AC** adopted also as the **B** reading, Bx seemingly having inserted *And þei* to smooth the transition. **300 (A 211, B 195)** *goed* (2) **p**: offering, of the two repeated words available to form the key-stave, both better sense (the repetition of *gete* being pointless) and characteristically contrastive wordplay on *goed* in the a-half; these 'gadlings' prosper neither materially nor spiritually. **301 (A 212, B 196)** *whiche*: providing the necessary key-stave in **C**'s b-half, the Cx line scanning *aa / xx*. In the light of **B**, however, *what* may be equally judged the *w*-word in **C** that was supplanted by *þat*, and the *what*-variants in the Ax tradition to support this inference. Though the conjecture *alle whiche* is proposed as likeliest to underlie the Cx form *alle þat,* the pronoun *al-what* (MED s.v. (c) 'whatever') may be preferable as involving only a 'reconstruction'. *R–K* leave the line unmetrical. **305–09 (B 200–03)** are not in **A** and could in principle have been added in β to a text already complete in the α form as it stands. But a mechanical explanation for the loss is at hand in the form of eyeskip from *Dowel* 200 to *Dowel* 204 (cf. on B179–85 above).

Passus XI (A XI, B X)

RUBRICS Like Ax, the Cx tradition ceases continuous passus-numbering with C IX, and seems (also like Ax) to regard Passus X as the prologue to Dowel (Dowel, Dobet and Dobest in **A**). None of the archetypes had a 'Prologus' rubric at the beginning of the poem, although a Prologue is implied through each one's managing to number correctly from Passus I onwards. Of the sub-archetypes only *C*-**p** errs by taking the untitled Prologue to be I and going on to number I as II. It may be safely inferred that this opening ∅-rubric form was authorial and it is quite likely, in the light of **AC** agreement around A X / C XI, that there was only intra-sectional numbering in the **B** original, if it was not introduced by the scribe of Bx.

However, the practical convenience of continuous numbering in all versions is so great that it is adopted here and the manuscript rubrics are consigned to the Apparatus. This is not to minimise their interest; but since only the passus-divisions as such are formally cognisable as units of the text, the remaining ms nomenclature, whatever its relation to the original, cannot be easily included in the text in modified form without distortion.

7 (AB 9) *Nolite / Noli*: the pl. form, clearly established in **C** with appropriate change to a pl. addressee, is also that of the Biblical source-text. But (in the light of **B**) Ax is judged to have been made sg. to fit the local context. The pl. in *A*-**m** and the *r¹* sub-group d, may then be regarded as a scribal ⇒ of the form familiar from the Vulgate. **11 (AB 13)** *heo*: presumed the original reading from which the gender-ambiguous reflex **a* in Cx could have generated the variants *wit* **x** (misconstruing the referent) and *studie* **p** (construing it correctly). Neither is a likely ⇒ for the other. **12 (AB 14)** *a*: conjectured as the grammatically required pronoun lost in Cx perhaps through careless construing of the clause as one of relation not of result. **15–16 (AB 18–19)** The **A**-Text may here be securely accepted in the light of **BC** and on grounds of sense as that in **r**. From this passus on W derives from an **m** source but shows partial ⊗ from **r**, its source from Pr–IX. In 19 *can construe r¹* is to be preferred as the harder reading and the one partially confirmed by **BC** (*can*). The sense here is 'practise' (MED s.v. *construen* v. 5), and *Conterfeteþ ?r²* will be a scribal gloss of a difficult sense, while K's *contryven* could show ⊗ from **B** or **C**. **17 (AB 20)** *leel*: conjectured to emend the Cx line (which has the inauthentic metrical pattern *aa / xx*) on the presumption that the intensifying epithet was lost through homœoarchy (*let-* >< *lel-*) or through deliberate suppression of a qualifier supposed redundant. F's attempt to make the line scan correctly as *& lette trewþe with louedaies & begile þe leel trewe* is an intelligent scribal re-writing that may felicitously 'echo' the conjectured original. It might be simpler to take *treuthe* as an archetypal ⇒ for its synonym *lewte*; but the form of **AB** suggests that the collocation *lette treuthe* was retained in the revised **C** line. *R–K*'s conjecture [*lewed*] *treuthe* introduces a concept possibly though not necessarily implied by *peple* 19 but definitely not implied by *consayle* 18 and (even more strongly) *lordes* B 22. **18 (AB 21)** *That*; *are / ben*: in the light of **AC** agreement diagnosed as the original and Bx *is* a scribal alteration of the absolute relative pronoun to a more explicit form, with subsequential smoothing of the verb number. In the b-half, the word-order preferred for **A** is that supported by **B** and the *r¹* order may be seen as coincidental anticipation of the revised **C** form.

B 28 (C 27) As it stands, the (probable) reading of *B*-β in the b-half (<GYBL) is satisfactory in both sense and metre. But it does not account for the reading preserved

in α which, on the showing of **C**'s revised b-half, would appear to have been present in **B**. The β and α readings may be diagnosed as split variants from an exceptionally long line (though one not longer than B 13.255). In the form of Bx as reconstructed, *God* now appears twice as part of a dip (one and two), grammatically first as subject and then as object, having a parallel repetition of *good* as both key-stave and as stave one, with the verbs as staves two and three in the a-half (*Thilke þat God moost góod gyueþ, God moost gréueþ — leest góod þei déleþ*).

31 (A 24, B 32) *Ac*: in the light of agreed **BC** reasonably supposed to have been present in **A** but lost in Ax, whence both the Ø-reading of **m** and **r**'s insertion, perhaps under inducement from *And* 25, of a connective judged necessary (V's felicitous variant is unlikely to represent Ax). **34 (A 29, B 36)** *or leet herfore (by)* **CA**: a phrase judged likely to have been lost from Bx and *C-p* for similar causes, the length of the line being one. In Bx eyeskip from le*te* > le*sson* may have occasioned attraction of *loued* to (*þ*)*erfore*. Agreement of **AC** authorises restoring to **B**, here in its **A** form.

B 37–50 37 (A 30) *daunted / dauncelid*: the **B** reading may be taken as a revision of **A**, the word in the sense 'made much of' (MED s.v. *daunten* v. 3(c)) being actually rarer. However, *dauncelen* appears the probable reading of Ax, and the **A** variant *dauntid* is presumed a tK ⇒ of a synonym later adopted in revision of the whole line. There is no need to postulate either that **L**'s *A*-ms was a scribal copy containing the variant *dauntid* or that tK here show ⊗ from **B**. **50 (A 37)** *game*: conjectured on the basis of // A 37b as the original for which Bx is a non-alliterating synonymic ⇒ under unconscious inducement from 48 and 52. *B*-M *glee* is an independent attempt to correct the metre and is unlikely to be the β and thence Bx reading.

37 (A 40, B 53) *how two slowe þe thridde*: to be safely adopted on the showing of **AC** as the **B** original for which Bx has a bland if metrically correct scribal ⇒ occasioned by objection to the blasphemous character of the image (not *authorial* censorship in response to readers' objections). **38 (A 41, B 54)** *take(n)* **AC**: preferred as the original also in **B**, apposition of main clauses without a conjunction being characteristic of **L**'s practice and *and* most probably a Bx addition to ease the syntax. **39 (A 42, B 55)** *presumpcioun*: on the showing of **AC** taken as the reading of **B**, the article being a Bx intrusion that eliminates the subtle play on the word's logical and moral senses (see MED s.v. n. (1) (a) and 2 (a), under the latter of which the present instance is cited). **41 (A 44, B 57)** *gnawen...gorge*: in both **B** and **C** plainly metaphorical, = 'defame God with their words' (*Sk*; see further Stanley 1976:445–6). This is probably also the sense of **A**, which has *in* for *with*. *K–D*'s argument (p. 103) that the sense 'bite God persistently in the throat' which they see as that

of **A** 'was either missed or rejected as outrageous' and that the reading *gnawen wiþ þe gorge* 'is actually nonsense' is unconvincing, since the *with* form is retained in **C** and presumably thereby given 'a kind of sanction' (*Ka²*, p. 463). But *K–D*'s claim (103n7) that the MED gloss (s.v. *gnauen* v. 3a) as 'disparage, carp at' is the result of being misled by the variant *in here* (tK) for *in þe* is mistaken. It makes no difference whether *here* or *þe* appears, *here* simply being more explicit and not generating another idiom. What the (indubitably irreverent) laymen do 'when their guts grow full' corresponds to what the gluttonous Doctor later does, in a less blatant manner, under similar circumstances, when challenged to speak 'of a trinite' (cf. 15.111). The word *gorge* here refers to the throat primarily as an organ of speech (as at B 66) and only secondarily (but with an apt quasi-pun), as an organ involved in eating. The possibility of a meaning such as that proposed by *K–D* for **A** is remote, though it may well have been in order to avoid the possibility of such unseemly literalism that **L** altered 'in' to 'with'. *gottes fullen*: almost certainly, on the showing of **AC** and as a harder reading, the original of **B** felicitously restored by w. Bx seems to have read *gutte is fulle* as a result of misconstruing the pl. subject as sg. noun + verb and pl. verb as sg. adjective.

43 (A 46, B 59) *afyngred*; *afurst*: the past-participial form attested in **BC** may also have been the **A** original and Ax could have substituted a noun in each case and then replaced the proclitic by a (more emphatic) preposition (*for*) under influence from *for* in the b-half. But as revision is possible here, emendation is rejected, DV *of*[1,2] being adopted as the closest in form to **L**'s later idiom. **44 (A 47, B 60)** The a-half of the revised **C** line, which condenses A 47–8, B 60–1 into a T-type, corresponds closely in sense to that of **A** (*haue hym in // nymen him in*), suggesting that Bx *neer* is a scribal error for **B** *in nor*, the felicitous conjecture of *B*-ms M. The meaning 'betake himself to, go (to)' for *nymen him* (MED s.v. *nimen* (v) 4*a*) is contextually possible but involves an awkward shift of referent between *hym* in the a-half and *his* in the b-half. More probably it is a Bx smoothing of *ne* or *nor* to *neer* after *in* had been lost through assimilation to the minims of preceding *hym*. The M-form *nor*, unusual in **L**'s language, is retained as obviating the need for emendation and as likelier to have prompted the postulated Bx ⇒. **50 (A 52, B 65)** The presence of *Mony* in revised **C** may be an echo of *Manye* in **A** which, as preserved in Ax, is an extended Type Ic line. *B*-F's variant *Manye mendynauntis* is either due to ⊗ from **A** or preserves *Manye* from α where *B*-R has joined β in omitting it by haplography before men*dinaunt3*. Because of the uncertainty, however, the Ax?Bx forms are each allowed to stand. **51 (A 55, B 68)** *in Memento* **AC**: here conjectured as the probable **B** reading for which *ofte* is Bx ⇒ of a vague general phrase, perhaps through failure to grasp the precise (but not obvious) reference to Psalm 131:6, quoted in 68a //. **51a** *i.e caritatem*: perhaps intruded in Cx (it is omitted by QFSZ = q) but possibly authorial and, as accurate and illuminating, worth preserving (see *Commentary*). **52 (A 56, B 69)** *knyhtes*: evidently a necessary coupling with *clerkes* in joint contrast with the *mene men* of 53. In A *kete men* seems the hardest reading and so likeliest to have generated the three substantive variants. Bx *opere kynnes men* thus becomes suspect as a vague phrase (of the type noted above at B 68) which does not provide any such effective contrast with *meene men* 70 and may well be a censoring scribal ⇒ for a B original identical with A. However, though capable of improvement, it is metrically acceptable and not impossibly (a weak) authorial change, so emendation is here avoided. **53 (A 57, B 70)** *hym*: preferable for the sense and in the light of **AB**, though possibly inserted by p^1. *here* **AC**: preferred to Bx as unlikely to have been revised in **B**, though there is no objection to *þe* (if it was lost in Bx's immediate exemplar, the definite article could have been supplied). *B*-FG either show ⊗ from an A source or independent ⇒ of (what is here) the more explicit word. **54 (A 58, B 71)** *vp* **AC**: judged to have been omitted by Bx as redundant; it is unlikely to have been removed by **L** and then restored in **C** since *fynden vp* is an integral phrase (see MED s.v. *finden* v. 21(b)). **55 (A 59, B 72)** *pestilences*: apparently a **C** revision taking account of more than one attack of the plague (cf. 60 // below). Two **C** mss U and M add *tyme* (pl. U); but while the sense does not require *tyme* in **B**, β is preferred on the showing of **A** and α judged to have omitted the noun, perhaps as metrically and semantically redundant. **56 (B 73)** presents problems of meaning in all **C** mss except D (and also F, which here reads *þei preche*). The **x** version gives poor sense, with both *prechyng* and *enuye* having to be objects of *haen founde* 54 as a consequence of reading *and* for the required *in*, as do also two **p**-mss K and Z. Omission of the line from the common ancestor of <eRM> and individually from Y may be due to censorship, whether from objection to the specific criticism of friars or from seeing the b-half as indiscriminately attributing *enuye* to clerks as a whole. The sense of the b-verse, however, appears to be 'because of sheer ill-will *towards* the clergy', with *clerkes* here implicitly having the restrictive sense 'the secular clergy' (MED s.v. *clerk* n. 1(b)), in contrast to the friars, who are regular clergy. Some evidence to substantiate this reading is the implied opposition between friars and 'clergy' in this sense at 22.376 (with which may be contrasted the contextually ambiguous use of the word at 22.228, where *friars* answer the summons addressed to Clergy). The form of the b-half phrase as preserved in q?p^2 (here supported by D) may well be that of **p** and thence of Cx, is the only acceptable one, and is confirmed by *for* in // **B**.

In the a-half, while the Cx reading *prechyng* is grammatically possible after *haen founde*, it is inferior on grounds of sense to *prechen* **B**, for which it may be an unconscious mechanical error. This has been corrected by D alone which, unless a felicitous conjecture, must derive from **B**.

A 67 See note below on B 108.

61–2 (B 78–9) The content of these lines suggests less that they are an addition to α than that their omission from *B-β* was due to censorship. In R the extended b-half, rendering the line of Type IIb, can be convincingly identified as scribal on comparison with **C**, and could result from misconstruction of an exemplar reading **hus here* as incomplete (F, unusually, may have retained the correct α reading). **79** *forgrynt*: a verb of extreme rarity, found only here and not in OED or MED. The **C** revision *togrynt* (also rare but not unique) is recorded in MED s.v. *togrinden* v. **74 (B 90)** The Bx line will scan awkwardly as an extended Type IIIb on vowels, with all the full staves falling in non-lexical words (cf. C 75); but a more satisfactory stress-pattern is provided if the important *litel* forms one of them. In the light of revised **C**, *loke* is therefore conjectured as the key-stave for which *rule* is a Bx ⇒ of a more or less apt non-alliterating synonym under unconscious suggestion from the sense of *weldeth*. The phrase *loke hym* here means 'behave, conduct himself' (see MED s.v. *loken* v. (2) 11(b)), whereas in **C** it has its commoner sense 'pay attention (to), find out (about)', as at B 15.185 (ibid. 8(b)). **76 (B 92)** *lettred*: almost certainly the reading underlying p^2 and the p^1 mss QFZ). The ⇒ *lewed* by the <eRM> ancestor and S suggests censorship aimed at protecting the clergy. But it is presumably of spiritual as well as secular lords, not only of upper and lower ranks of the laity, that greed is here predicated, and the collocation *lord and lewid* would be most unusual. **79** After this follows an extra line in I, adopted by *Sk* and *Pe*, which could have been dropped from Cx through scribal objection to its blunt criticism of *clergie* (cf. previous note). But it is not necessary to the sense and (by contrast with the case of RM at 17.11) its origin would remain difficult to account for textually. It is thus perhaps best taken as an indignant anti-intellectual outburst by the I-scribe that echoes A 11.19 (B 10.19). It is especially worth noting that *after* 81 ms I has, instead of a form of the Cx text, five lines corresponding to A 11.6, 9–12, B 10.6, 9–12. The **AB** line that I's extra line may recall occurs soon after this passage and could easily have suggested it.

B 108–39 (A 67–95) 108 (A 67) *biwilide*: a reconstruction (proposed by *Ka*, p. 156 and adopted by *K–D* but not by Ka^2) to provide in both Ax and Bx the *w*-stave required in first position. The form posited is the rare verb of Norman-French derivation attested in *SGGK* 2425 (see MED s.v. *biwilen* v.) as that for which the commoner non-alliterating variant is an archetypal ⇒. *wye*: accepted on the showing of **A** as the original key-stave in **B** for which Bx's non-alliterating synonym is a scribal ⇒, perhaps motivated by desire for a more emphatic contrast with *womman* (for a parallel, cf. 21.230 //). **119–20 (A 75–6)** In the light of substantially identical **B**, the true form of **A** may be established with reasonable certainty, though the VJ re-lineation probably comes from **B**. The mislineation in Ax will have been caused by the excessive length of 75, which resulted from inserting a prefatory phrase to introduce a line supposedly translating the quoted Latin 74 (the line expands and illustrates the sense of Rom 12:3 rather than translating it exactly). On the evidence of the majority of its members, **r**'s form of the first phrase was *That is to seyn*, and on that of AH³W, **m**'s was probably *That is*. The latter phrase, if included, would leave 75 scanning satisfactorily but is otiose and appears a scribal attempt to ease the juncture. **124 (A 80)** *whyes*: the ms evidence indicates *weyes* as the reading of Bx and probably that of Ax too. With sense 'ways' this would be an acceptable (if commonplace) echoing of, e.g., Is 55:8–9, and *whyys A*-K, *B*-gM could be seen as scribal 'improvement' suggested by the prominence of *why* at 66 (107), 75 (119) and 82 (126). However, since *weyes* is actually a common Cx spelling for *wyes,* and could be authorial (see *IG* s.v. *weye* n²), it may also have been used by **L** to represent the homophone *whyes*. The intrinsic hardness of the sense argues for preferring *whyes* and substantival use of *why* is little instanced outside **L**. The other main use is at C 14.156 //, where the **p** family and some **x** mss (I and the t-group) make the same mistake and where **x** is presumably an intelligent scribal re-formation of Cx *weyes*. (In the case of the sg. form at 18.147, the danger of ambiguity being much smaller, no problem appears in the ms tradition). **131** *ablende*: a verb securely attested at C 20.140 // and conjectured as providing the necessary (here muted) vocalic key-stave (initial *a*- could easily have been lost by aural or visual assimilation to preceding *to*). **135 (A 91)** *For*: the syntactically more complex reading preferred here as more appropriate on grounds of sense, treating the curse as conditional on the curious enquirer's doing well rather than as a blunt rejoinder to his enquiry. The *Ø*- reading may well have been prompted by the easier syntax and the lack of any original punctuation to make the syntactical structure explicit.

139 (A 95) *deep*; *arere*: both evidently revisions, *a dore nayl* and *on syȝde* having presumably come into F and C² by ⊗ from **A** (in C² by visible correction here, as again at 153 below).

92 (A 104, B 149) *man*: on the showing of Y and u possibly present in **x** or else lost from Cx and individually restored by scribes wishing to 'regularise' the metre. Its contextual appropriateness is obvious, representing Study's acceptance of Will's offer at 88 to be her 'man'.

B 153 (A 108) scans adequately on vowels in AxBx

with *as* forming the first stave. But *Hij* for *Thei* would be better, placing emphasis on a word of higher semantic function vulnerable to replacement by the advancing pronominal form.

103 (A 111, B 156) *Gladdere*: on the showing of **AC** judged the original reading for **B**, *And* being presumed inserted by Bx under inducement from *And* 157, 158. **110** *ire*: rejected by *R–K* p. 167, who see it as an intruded marginal gloss for *enuy* (added by visible correction in V). But it is not clear why *wrothe* should have needed glossing by a *less* usual synonym (*wrathe* occurs nine times more often), and rhetorical doubling here is very possible.

A 124 (B 169) *þinges*: the majority and probably the Ax reading is confirmed by **B**. *Ka* prefers *wyttes* 'departments of knowledge' as harder in sense, but it is also the more explicit reading and could have been induced by preceding *wyt* 123. **115** *ouerseye*: ambiguously spelled *ouerse* in Cx, a form of preterite not elsewhere evidenced in the tradition. I's reading, though probably an intelligent scribal correction, furnishes both a better form and a characteristic play on preceding *sey* and should be preferred as the more likely original. *many*: agreement of **x** and *p²* here points to Cx as having read *many* (a possible reworking of B¹'s scribal reading at B 171), with *p¹* having missed the contraction sign (in C-App. *read* many] x*p²* my *p¹*; his N²). **116 (A 126, B 171)** *a / the Bible* **CA**: in the light of virtual **CA** agreement, to be preferred as the probable **B** reading, for which Bx has substituted a vaguer phrase. The motive was possibly objection to the notion that the Bible could have had any other author than God; but *wrot* implies only agency, not authorship in the proper sense. *grette*: not certainly archetypal in both later texts; but while perhaps aurally suggested by following (and in **B** preceding) *sette*, it is the less expected and harder reading. **117 (A 127, B 172)** *yglosid* **AC**: to be preferred also for **B** on grounds of sense; it is the Psalms that Scripture studies with the aid of the gloss, not the glosses for their own sake. B and Hm could have corrected independently or have been collated here with **C**. G's uncertain reading *?glosse* falls ambiguously between **AC** and Bx, presumably through ⊗ from **A**. The error could have arisen from omission of the past-participle marker and / or the preterite morpheme.

118 (A 128, B 173) *al þe Lawe aftur* **AC**: to be preferred also as the probable **B** reading for which Bx has substituted a vague generalising phrase as at 171 above. **121** *opere*: *opere mo* FN², which *R–K* follow, is unnecessary for the sense and probably by memorial ⊗ from **B**. **124 (A 134, B 179)** *here / Ø*: if **r** and not **m** here represents Ax, **AC** agreement may suggest that the possessive could also have been lost in Bx through alliterative attraction (-*tr*- > *tooles*). But since no serious issue of meaning is involved, it is not adopted here. **126 (A 136, B 181)** As it stands the Cx line scans awkwardly on |b| as Type IIIa, with both full staves in non-lexical words that lack normal sentence-stress (muting of *bothe* with consequent generation of a T-type line would be unlikely, since there is only one main stave in the a-half). A modest emendation making the line scan on |k| would be to read *ek* as the original for which the near-synonym *bothe* is a Cx ⇒. This would produce a liaisonal key-stave and thence an authentic T-type, the second |k| stave being located internally in *squire* (for an unambiguous parallel see 10.269). However, the present more radical emendation takes |l| as the stave-sound in the light of the **AB** form and proposes *leide* as having been replaced by one more familiar in connection with reckoning or construction (see MED s.v *casten* v. 20 (a), 25 (a)). This usage is paralleled in *ms* 348, which comes close to the form here proposed: *And laide leuel and lyne a-long by the squyre.* The line now scans as Type IIIb, with almost the same sound-pattern as the example of this type at 4.12. If *leide* is accepted as the original verb, it will form a phrasal construction with *ouet* 'out', which appears to be the Cx reading. IP²D *mette* (adopted by *PeR–K*) is then to be seen as an intelligent conjecture, 'cast measurements by means of the square, etc,' prompted by dissatisfaction with the phrase *caste oute*. But whereas I and P² could derive from y, D's reading is more probably an independent emendation; for if it preserves u, then U will have varied coincidentally with y. The reading is, however, unlikely to be original since it gives the line the pattern *axx / bb* or *ax / (a)bb* (so left by *R–K*, presumably as a draft). In the upshot, there is little real difference of sense: 'laying out' [foundations and elevation of a building] with these *toles* is closely related to 'casting the measurements' [of a building] by means of the same.

B 186–88 186 (A 141) The Bx line scans as Type IIIa with internal rhyme, and the sense is adequate as it stands. Yet the context requires not simply the existence of love but the explicit presence of love 'within' Theology, as insisted upon in **A**; so it may be conjectured that *perinne* has dropped out of the b-half. Arguably the adverb should be placed as the last word, this being the one most vulnerable to loss through homoteleuton, for the resulting identical *end*-rhyme would certainly be of a type well-instanced in **L**, e.g. B 1.146–47 // (and see Appendix I 5.ii). But against this, placing it pre-finally allows the main verb both the same relative position as in **A** and the Leonine internal rhyme favoured elsewhere by **L** (as at 21.325 // **B**). **188 (A 143)** *lakked*: the past tense in subjunctive function following an open-condition present, the harder reading in **A** and the one supported by both traditions of Bx. The scribal present-tense form, which aims at 'logical' uniformity, may have been suggested by a tense-ambiguous original spelled *lakkyt* (as

actually in *A*-H³); but it follows **L**'s tendency elsewhere. Thus, the easy mixture of tenses in **A** is illustrated in the four verbs of 138–39, with which contrast B 183–84, where the unified tenses seem to be the result of revision (so in // **C** 129–30).

134 (A 144, B 189) The Ax line (taking *vppon* as metrically preferable to *on*) scans as Type IIIa, without any need to conjecture a lost stave on |ð| in the a-half (as does *Ka²*, suggesting *þou*). Rhetorical stress here on *þérvppón* will appear justified because of its emphatic reference back to *loue* in 143 and the shift of full stress now to a word *(þere)* that did not carry stress in that line (contrast *þerwiþ* at A 162 // B 215 below). The **B** revision changes the action prescribed from 'believing' to 'loving'; but on stylistic grounds the plainer *Loke* β is perhaps preferable to the homonymically punning *loue* of α (though neither alternative is supported by the revised form of **C**'s a-half, which introduces a third verb *lerne*, echoing B 20.208). Both the β and α versions give acceptable scansions (Types Ic and IIa respectively) and in the b-half choice betweeen α agreeing with *þou þenke* **A** and β agreeing with *þe like* **C** is likewise evenly balanced (though *loke* at B 207 favours β here). Since no major question of meaning is at issue, β is accepted as closer to the final version.

B 190–204 190 (A 145, C 135) *kennyng*: an emendation not strictly necessary on grounds of sense or metre. But on comparison with **A** (*louis scole*) and **C** (*doctour*) the reading *kynne* seems contextually out of place, the word required being one that emphasises love's rôle as a teacher not as a relative, and this is just that of the Theology 'in which love is' (see note above and the verb *kenneþ* at 198 below). The noun *kennyng* here has the sense 'training, discipline': see MED s.v. *kenninge* ger. (b) and cf. 196 below, which contrasts Cato's *kennyng* with love's. The Bx form *kynne* could easily have been generated mechanically if the postulated reading in its exemplar had been cropped at the line-end (*kenn-*). **197** *yeme*: a revision, with Cr²³ a commoner synonymic ⇒ for the same reading in Cr¹'s lost ms source and F a ⊗ from **A**. **201 (A 153)** scans as Type IIIc, both scribal and editorial attempts to alter it to a standard (Type Ie) line being otiose. **201a–06a** revises **A** material occurring some eighty lines further on at 245a–255 (see Vol I, pp. 434–45). The whole passage on *ooþer science,* expanded in the first revision (B 191–219=A 146–65), is completely removed in the second. **201a** *habemus* β in the quotation (following the Vulgate) should arguably be *est* α, which is the reading at A 11.245a and fits better with the interpretation of the name of Piers's wife (*Dame Worch-when-tyme-is*) at 8.80 // (see *Commentary*). **204 (A 249)** *to swiche nameliche*: ↔ of indirect object and adverb to emend Bx's line scanning *xa / ax*. The adv. ('especially'), which is more restrained than **A**'s *souereynliche* 'supremely', is less likely to be an unmetrical scribal ⇒ than a revision. The stylistic motive could have been a wish to avoid undue repetition, since the adjective *souereyn* occurs in two different senses ('efficacious'; 'chief') at 208, 212, in lines newly added in **B**.

A 157–97 157 (B 211) *pre* A (*two* **B**): the 'unthrifty' *science* of **A** including astronomy, which **B** presumably excludes. While *two* could be an officious scribal correction, the awareness implied of a distinction between the practical science and judicial astrology could be authorial. **L** seems to have changed his mind about Albert in revising A 11.160 as B 214, so an altered attitude to astronomy may be plausibly maintained here. Study's less censorious tone about the natural sciences in **B** accompanies a more logical view of herself as their author, in keeping with the omission of **A**'s reference to conjuring the devil, which would seem to carry the joke too far. **159 (B 213)** *many / fele*: giving a liaisonal stave (*of_many*), unless *many* is an Ax ⇒ for the less common **B** form *fele*, which may otherwise be taken as a revision strengthening the alliteration at the key position. **161** As it stands, the Ax line has the inauthentic metrical pattern *xa / ax* (so left in *Ka²*), here emended to scan as Type IIIa. The two terms could have been transposed to give prominence to the seemingly more important word. **L**'s is the first recorded example of *pyromancy*, and the Ax scribe could have been ignorant of its exact sense 'divination by fire' and have thought it a high-sounding synonym for its more familiar partner. But it is the latter, understood pseudo-etymologically in its medieval spelling *nigromancie* as '*black* magic', that is primarily concerned with raising the *pouke*, and is therefore juxtaposed with the latter as here reconstructed. **163 (B 216)** The mislineations of *r¹* and **m** indicate scribal dissatisfaction with a line judged too short. But *r²* has preserved it in an acceptable if abrupt form, having the pattern *abb / ab* with vocalic theme staves and contrapuntal staves on |s|. *Sikir* could be a scribal filler after loss in Ax's exemplar of a b-half like that of B 216 or of a final lift **Studie* that Ax could have construed as a marginal gloss. But it resembles *sobly* at A 175 below, though 163 would scan without it, as a Type IIIa. **171 (B 224)** The form of the b-half in *B*-F is close to *A*, its inclusion of *hem* making it identical with *A*-U, and ⊗ from **A** is probable here. *bobe*: in **B** adjectival but in **A** adverbial in all mss except UVM (W has an adverbial synonym). Although *bobe* could be the adjective used pronominally if a full-stop is placed after *wyf* (as *Sk*'s medial point allows), mid-line sentence-separation is untypical of **L**. So it is better to regard **B** as a revision that by adding the co-ordinating conjunction establishes the construction anticipated by *A*-UVM. **177** *collide*: preferable contextually on grounds of sense, though the readings of H²Ch, of J and of V (presumably a synonym for *collide* in v) are most probably intelligent scribal corrections of an Ax reading

callide. **178** scans as Type Ie with muted key-stave or as Type IIIa (on *w*). **180** scans 'cognatively' on |t| |d| |d|, the first *t*-stave being either in *To*, stressing the purpose of his visit, or in the liaisonal *at_ȝów*, with stress on the instructors. As neither alternative is without awkwardness, Ax could have inverted to prose order a Type IIIa line reading in the a-half: *Dowel at ȝow to lerne.* **182** *he*: mCh, very probably a correct reflex of an ambiguous Ax form misread as *heo* (so actually V). Since the equivalent of this speech is given to Clergy in **BC**, it would be more natural for him to reply to Will's words at 179–81, as is supposed by A 12.2; so on balance it would be preferable to read *he* here and take the speaker as Clergy (see Schmidt 2004). **191** *ben*: conjectured as the necessary second stave lost in Ax by distraction from preceding *Obed-*, *bre-*, and from be*b*, *bre-* in 192. As it stands, the Ax line gives the scansion pattern *aa / xx* (so left in *Ka²*). A simpler solution of the metrical difficulty ('reconstruction' more than 'conjecture') would be to see *brethren* as having supplanted *sustren* in position two through unconscious inducement from the familiar phrasal order. **195** *ben in office* **m**: contextually superior on grounds of sense, the *office* being a bishop's and its discharge corresponding to the *facere* and *docere* in 196*a* that earn the term *magnus* (= Dobest). This reading and the correct lineation of 194–96 strikingly illustrate **m**'s independent textual value. **197** be*b*: conjectured as the required first stave in a line with Ax ⇒ of a form normal for dialects other than Southern in the singular. As it stands, the Ax line gives the imperfect pattern *xa / ax* (so left in *Ka²*). But while the RUAW transposition will yield a Type IIIa line, this requires a syntactically unconvincing caesural pause after *is*, and so emendation here seems justifiable.

141–42 (B 232–33) The scansion of B 232 is here taken to be Type IIa, though it would read better if *Chirche* were *Kirke*. 233 may have vocalic staves, but since two Type IIa lines in succession would be uncharacteristic, it is better scanned on voiced fricatives, the first being generated from elision of *be* and *articles* or liaison of *Wib* and *alle*. If both are treated as staves, the line becomes Type Ic. **143** *alyhte Goddes sone*: subject-verb ↔ providing the required key-stave in |l|. Cx has inverted to prose order (with damage to the metre) to promote the main idea to first position. *R–K*'s conjecture *loue* for *sone* may be 'elegant' (p.170), but it is also otiose.

B 242 *animáles*: conjectured as the original for which the common word *beestes* is here judged a Bx ⇒ giving the inauthentic pattern *aa / bb*. The rare synonym, with stress on the third syllable, provides the necessary key-stave in |m|. MED s.v. cites Trevisa's *Bartholomew* from *c.* 1398 as glossing *animal* 'a best'; but the Latin source-word should have been familiar enough for the term to be acceptable.

148 (B 243) *made*: despite αL agreement and the appearance of the pronoun in **C**'s second version of the half-line at 154, *he* may be omitted from **B** on the showing of immediately // **C**, as sense and metre are unaffected.

B 246 *Gospellere*: conjectured as the necessary key-stave, here scanning cognatively with the |k| staves of the a-half, for which Bx is a ⇒ of the more familiar non-alliterating synonym. An earlier conjecture *same* explaining Bx *Euaungelistes* as a marginal gloss in its exemplar misread as a correction is now abandoned mainly because scansion on |s| necessitates reduction to a prelude-dip of two important lexical words in the a-half. The same objection holds against another conjecture *so þe*] *so* (presuming *so* (2) lost by haplography), which makes the line scan on |s|. Though not elsewhere instanced in **L**, the term *gospellere* is widely attested in the period (for the converse situation, with *gospel* as scribal → for *euaungelie* in Bx, see on B 1.200).

157 (B 248) *alle* **C** / *lewed* **B**: perhaps suspect for failing to make clear like **C** that belief is a universal requirement, and so as a scribal product induced by antithetical association with *clerkes* in 247. The g reading *men* could thus be viewed as a non-alliterating reflex of Bx *ledes*, closer in sense to *alle* but capable of suggesting or being mistaken for *lewed* in four lines of transmission (LMwα). On the other hand, g could be an attempt to counter misunderstanding, later carried through by **C**. So *lewed* may be allowed to stand in **B** as a loose first thought with the elliptical meaning 'ignorant (lay) people [and we are all, where understanding the Trinity is concerned, ignorant]'. **161** Two formally acceptable scansions of Cx are (i) as Type IIIb with two lifts in *Dówél* and a four-syllable prelude-dip or (ii) as Type Ib with a cognative first stave on *to* (cf. on A 180). However, reading with a more *natural* stress-pattern yields the inauthentic metrical schemes *aab / bb* (with |m| as theme-stave and |d| as counterpoint) or *xa / aa* (on |d|). The emendation here is anticipated by N² (one of the **C** mss that most often displays both **x** and **p** readings), but the relative pronoun is retained from Cx as probably original. The resulting play on two polysemes 'act', 'make' of the lexeme *don* (MED s.v. v. 1a (a), 4 (a)) seems characteristic but, if original, could nonetheless have provoked stylistic objection from the scribe of Cx.

B 251–90 form an unusual example of a long passage added in **B** and then deleted rather than revised in **C**. Ll. 279–82 provide the germ of C Pr 105–14, a newly-composed passage (see *ad loc* above), and the thought of 287–87*a* is echoed in C 9.260. **251** *Siþþe* 'next' (MED s.v. *sitthe* adv. (d)): conjectured here to provide a necessary first stave-word for a line scanning *xa / ax* or *xxa / ax* in Bx. *Dowel* has been described, without being named, starting with *It* at 232, and 251 now introduces the second of the three Do's in its proper order. **266** There follows in Bx a line of acceptable metre (Type IIIc) that nonetheless seems suspect from its lack of logical or syntactical con-

nexion with 266 and over-emphatic listing of the ranks of higher clergy. It exemplifies the same cast of mind found in such spurious Bx lines as those after 4.38, 6.17, 182 and 19.373. **271** *lost*: superior on grounds of sense to *boste* 'idle noise', the reading of R and originally of L (but altered to *lost*). Either both mss have coincidentally made the error through visual confusion of *l* with *b* or the RL agreement testifies to the reading of α and β respectively and thence of Bx (with γ and F having corrected independently); but M has not visibly altered an L-type reading to accord with γ, so the case for L as representing β is less compelling here and *lost* would appear anyway intrinsically preferable. **273** The Bx b-half has lost the key-stave by ⇒ of the order commoner in such phrases, and is easily reconstructed; see further B 8.99. **274** *no wiȝt*: here reconstructed in the expanded phrasal form to provide the necessary third stave in this Type IIb line, for which Bx has a commoner non-alliterating ⇒. **B 279** *barnes*: conjectured as the necessary stave-word in b for which *folk* might have suggested itself as a more familiar synonym, giving a Bx line with the pattern *aa / xx*. Either *burnes* 'men' or *barnes* 'children' would suit, and scribal objection to the first will presumably have been on grounds of its restricted lexical distribution, to the second through failure to see its special Biblical sense. Both occur in **B** (at 3.267; 3.152); but reference to the **C** passage that develops these **B** lines provides convincing support for *barnes*: see C Pr 105, 111, where *children of Israel* occurs twice. **B 291–327*a* (A 202–18)** For notes, see above on C 5.146–79 *ad loc.*

XI 162–197 (B XI 1–36) For convenience, textual notes on parallel **B** are included at this point. **167 (B XI 5)** *warth*: in the light of **C** the inevitably required verb. Bx will have written *wraþe* by inducement from the noun in 4b above. **168 (B XI 7)** scans as an extended Type IIIa with standard counterpoint, the theme-stave being *f* and the contrapuntal stave *r*; or as Type IIa on *r* with liaisonal stave in *For Y*. **169 (B XI 8)** *and loue*: preferred on grounds of sense in both versions, where the same error has occurred, presumably for the same reason, i.e. mistaking the ampersand for the indefinite article and *u* for *n*, through the unfamiliarity of the notion of *þe lond of loue*. The mechanical ease of the error doubtless accounts for cross-family agreement in both traditions (*B*-F with β, *C*-M with XP²N²). It is just possible that the *C*-I reading may preserve that of group y, accounting for the levelled form of the other y mss but not for Y, which has corrected either independently or from a u-type source. Contextual and thematic arguments also support *and loue*, notably the balance between the false love of this first inner dream in **B** and the true love of the second (the *loue-dreem* in B 16.20), and the apparent echo of the phrase *longyng and loue* (C 169) at 180, *to lyue longe and ladyes to louye* (for discussion of B 16.20 see below). **177 (B XI 16)** *con-*

tinence: the Cx spelling of *contenaunce* **B** may involve a sardonic 'clerkly' pun on the homophone *continence*. M has *contynaunce* and R *countenance*, eliminating the pun. *clergies lore* **p**: preferred in the light of **B**'s *Clergie*; the T-type line generatied by reading *lore* 'compensates' for the excessively long prelude-dip. But *R–K*'s wholesale adoption of the **B** reading lacks justification. **193 (B XI 32)** scans awkwardly on fricatives with the first two staves *Couétyse of Yes*, (creating a long prelude-dip and stressing a semantically insignificant word), or on vowels, placing the caesura before *thow* and making *here* the key-stave (the latter preferable). **197 (B XI 36)** scans on *t*, the first stave being found internally in *stoupe*.

B X 337 *at nede*: *as nede techeþ* ?β / *at pure nede* α. Neither sub-archetypal reading appears to derive from the other, but both may be attempts to provide a last lift in consequence of mislocating the caesura after *nauʒt*. The reconstruction takes the line as Type IIb, with the mid-line pause coming after *it*, and *nauʒt but at nede* as an integral adverbial phrase forming the whole b-half. Thus *pure* α may be seen as an attempt to provide a fourth lift and *as...techeþ* β as a smoothing with the same aim. Both scribes evince unease with the Type IIb structure, authentic in **L** but rare elsewhere.

A 236–54 236 (B 347) The A line scans as standard, the **B** line either as extended Type IIIa with counterpoint on *s* or preferably, in the light of **A**, as Type I with *is_óure* as liaisonal key-stave. Though *þat* could be a Bx ⇒ for **A** *so*, with its characteristic wordplay ('of such a kind' / 'in such a way'), emendation is not required here. **237 (B 348)** *an*: the aptest reading in both versions on grounds of sense, one non-Christian being envisaged as at hand to baptise a dying pagan who requests it. Ax, to judge from **m** and u, could have read Ø, and ChK be a commonsense correction. But if *B-C*² gets its alteration from an A copy, it will be from one of d type. **239 (B 350)** *any man*: reconstructed on the basis of **B** as the true reading of **A**. Agreement with *r¹* of K, the only other remaining *r²* witness, may argue for the stronger theological statement as original; but generation of *an hy* from *any* is an easy visual (and even easier aural) error. J may therefore be judged to preserve one part of the Ax reading (*any*) and **m** another part (*man*), though M's *he* may suggest rather that *any* was the group reading. But the possibility of revision in **B** to tone down the original assertion cannot be securely ruled out. **240–41 (B 351–52)** scan either as Type IIIa or, preferably, as Type Ia with cognative staves |k| / |g|. *Ka²* inconsistently prefers J's *crist* to *god* in 240 on metrical grounds while accepting *degre* in 241 (on which see *lG* under *degree* n²). But J here is mistakenly attempting to correct the metre after failure to grasp the 'cognative' principle (as may KH³ with *decre* for *degre* in 241). **245** The line as reconstructed by *Ka* retains *suche* from **r** but omits *sone* from **m**, which is here

kept as there is no reason other than euphony for rejecting it. The characteristic wordplay on *shewiþ, sewiþ* (virtual homophones in **L**'s idiolect) suggests that it is not scribal padding designed to introduce the Latin of 245a (as evidently for *K–F*, who omit). So does the presence in **r** of *suche*, a hypermetric vestige of the line lost, as *Ka* notes, perhaps by inducement from *alle* in 244, 246. **245a–49** correspond to **B 201a–204** discussed earlier. **248 (B 203)** *giuen*: emending Ax *ʒiuen* as an unconscious ⇒ of the (here) unmetrical commoner form (though pointed scansion on vocalic grammatical words is possible). The line evidently proposes a characteristic polysemic play on *good*, noun and adverb, like that at B 9.160. For confirmation of the emendation, see B 203, the revised form of A 248, which has *gyuen* as key-stave, though the pun on *good* has been removed. **254 (B 366)** *Non mecaberis*: 'thou shalt not commit adultery', evidently an authorial error in both versions for 'thou shalt not kill' (*non occides* in Lk 18:20, Ex 20:13, where it comes before *non moechaberis*). *Ka*'s complicated argument (retaining *Ne* from TH²) that this is a correlative use, with '*mecaberis*....not translated by *ne sle nouʒt* but parallel to it' (p. 456) is unconvincing. For *Non* is clearly the Ax reading and is repeated in B 366, where it cannot form any part of a supposed parallel construction. Further, the sole commandment in question in the context of A 252–55 / B 364–68 is the commandment not to kill. Neither A 254 nor B 366–67 can admit any interpretation but that *sle(e) no(u)ʒt* is being offered, albeit erroneously, as the translation of *non mecaberis*. Possibly **L** was confusing this uncommon verb with *necare* and misremembering the latter as deponent. Such appears the expedient (even more desperate than the Athlone editor's) of the *B*-mss Cr²³Y and GL, the latter pair going so far as to spell the root *necha-*, while Cr¹OC² opt for the correct future form of *necare* and M for the Vulgate verb, as does one *A*-ms, H³. But for the suggestion that **L** may have associated the fifth and sixth commandments in a particular way, see the *Commentary* on this passage.

B 367–70 367 *also*: conjectured to provide the required key-stave word from which Bx appears to have omitted the second element under inducement from the common expression *al for þe beste* (found earlier at B 5.484). **368** is presumably lost from β by homoarchy (*For* 368, 369). **370 (A 257)** The possible **m** readings *misdedes, lette* could be original in **A** or reveal ⊗ here from **B**; but no serious issue of meaning is involved.

208 *prescite* 'foreknown [*sc.* to be damned]': the reading preserved in D (< u); both right on grounds of sense and of a form such as to generate the attested variants. The nearest to it, *prescient* 'foreknowing', is not recorded in **L**'s day, though *prescience* is, from the 1370s (see MED s.v.), but U's error implies that it existed. Its sense is wrong here, but it may have been known as an English word, like the familiar noun, whereas *prescite* is still half-Latin, as apparently indicated by the underlining in D. It is here treated as anglicised, however, so as to provide a better balance with the more fully English *predestinaet*, a word also (and wrongly) underlined in D. One of the earliest examples of *prescit* cited in MED s.v. (from Lydgate) collocates it with *predestinate*. But the absence of prior citations, other than one from an early C15th Wycliffite tract, suggests its C14th restriction to technical usage and **L**'s use here could well have been the first in English. The spelling *precyet* in y may indicate descent from an **x** form spelled **precit*, and *prechen* **p** then be seen as smoothing a form misconstrued as *prechyt* under inducement from *prechen* 207. **211 (A 265, B 378)** *made*: preferred on the basis of **AC** agreement as the probable **B** reading for which Bx *tau3te* is a deliberate ⇒ after taking *sapience* as the common noun 'wisdom' rather than as the title of a portion of the OT writings (see MED s.v. (a) and (f)). **215 (A 268, B 381)** *Dede* **A**: good sense in context, given that *in werk and in woord* 269 covers more actions than just Solomon's judgements (e.g., building the Temple, writing 'Sapience'). *Ka*'s emendation to *Demde* in the light of **BC** is therefore to be rejected as gratuitous. **B** is plainly a revision that saves Will's argument from appearing too obviously self-contradictory in stating both that Solomon did well and that he is damned (though what salvation requires is to *do* well). The revision of *wrou3te* A 270 below (apropos of Aristotle) to *wissede* (B 382) supports this interpretation. For like *demed* at B 381 (retained in **C** just as *wissede* **B** is through its synonym *tauhte*), this verb points to the distinction between teaching 'dowel' (the fruit of knowledge) and living virtuously (the fruit of grace) that becomes crucial in B XIII. *techiþ* **A**: the **B** reading *telleþ*, which appears in MH[3] as *tellit* (?< **m**) is either the original **A** reading or, as more likely here, ⊗ from **B** or coincidence with it. **218 (B 383)** *prechen*: in itself the **p** reading is unexceptionable; but the form of **x**, echoing **B** though wrong in repeating the verb from the a-half, prompts reconstruction of the line as (except for the order of object and adverbial phrase in the a-half) identical with **B**, which is needlessly adopted wholesale by *R–K*. The a-half form of *C*-I need not point to the presence of *prechen* in Cx but is either a guess or an echo of **B**. **221 (A 271, B 385)** *in helle*: agreement of **AC** suggests that Bx may be ⇒ of a milder phrase, perhaps through objection to the starkness of the original. **223 (A 277, B 387)** The **A** line makes sense as it stands, though the contrast between the sages' wisdom and their fate is not made as it is in **B** and **C** by the relative pronoun. Ax *And* may be ⇒ for original *That* under visual inducement from preceding *And* (twice); but the other signs of major revision in **B** here (see on 215 above) caution against emendation in this instance. In the b-half, *wonyn* H[3] may show ⊗ from a **B** source; *wynne* **m** is likely to have come

in by inducement from 276b. **224 (B 388)** *y* **x**p^2: unlikely to be ⇒ for *we* in p^1, contextually the more logical form after *we* 222; so if it is an unconscious relict of the **B**-Text under revision, perhaps original and to be retained. **233 (B 393)** *At*: following P², *R–K* read *Ac at*, which eases the transition (D has *Ac in* and RGK *Ac*); but there is no necessity for this and Cx may stand. *men* **B**: conjectured here as the required key-stave word for which Bx is ⇒ of a non-alliterating near-synonym. Possibly **B** read *hij* in an extended Type IIIa line scanning vocalically with standard counterpoint on *m* (*abb / ax*). But the stave-sound *m* in **C**'s revised b-half and the presence of two lexical words with *l* in Bx's b-half support the emendation. The line now scans as a normal T-type (*aa / [a]bb*). **251 (B 409)** *foles*: a possible spelling for *foules*, the word contextually most appropriate (cf. 242 above). But a play on the sense 'fools' is also apt, since the ark as type of the faithful remnant prefigures the *foles* of 22.61–2. The pun has been established as early as A 8.111 // B 7.125 (see the note *ad loc*). **252–54 (B 410–12)** The Bx lines have been lost from β very probably through homœoteleuton (*-ine* 409a, *-inne* 412). **253 (B 411)** *Kirke* **B**: conjectured as the necessary key-stave word, supplanted in α (and possibly Bx) by the commoner non-alliterating variant-form. In revised **C**, however, this is satisfactory, as the line scans on *w*. **262–63 (A 286, B 420)** **C**'s revision of **B** as two lines scans vocalically in 262 with strong rhetorical stresses on non-lexical words and has a secondary stave-pattern on *p*, the last lift alliterating translinearly with the first of 263. But if 262 was one of a pair scanning on *p*, Cx may have transposed the last two words to the present prose order. **264 (A 287, B 421)** *Then*: 'than' as in // **B**, but taken as 'then, next' and replaced in **p** by a synonym. *myhte do*: restored on the joint showing of **AC** as the likely **B** original for which Bx (scanning *aa / bb* or wrenching the stress in *wommán dide*) is presumed to have substituted *what womman*, perhaps under prompting from the (same mild) anti-feminism displayed towards the Magdalen by the narrator at 21.162 //. But **A** overtly and **B** tacitly establish an important contrast between possibility in 287 / 421 and actuality in 288 / 422 that depends in part on the syntactic contrast between 'mý3te do' and 'díde' (abandoned in **C**'s revision of 422). **266** *deuyned* **p**: confirmed by the context and **B** *conspired*; **x**'s *deuyed* (? or *deniyed*) being doubtless induced by *denyede* 265. **268** *lettere* **p**: apparently *leare* 'liar' in **x**; perhaps a scribal attempt to make sense of an exemplar misread to mean 'preventer' (as at 1.65), in consequence of missing the Biblical allusion and perhaps under unconscious influence from *gyle*. The YD corrections may as probably reflect independent recognitions of the allusion as recourse to a **p**-type source. **269–70 (A 289–90, B 423–4)** As it stands in **p**, the one-line version omitting *to dethe* is metrically unexceptionable. But the latter phrase, present in **AB**, weakens **x**'s b-half by de-stressing *peple* and benefits from the re-lineation actually offered by U. In **B**, 424 may have been dropped from α as a result of censorship (cf. the β omission of a comparably strong statement at B 78–9). In β, *Muche* seems inserted to fill out a line of untypical terseness (though in pattern paralleled at 127 // **A**) and may be safely omitted on the showing of **AC**. For **L**'s point is that 'even the (future) apostle was capable of *killing* Christians', not that 'he killed *many* rather than few'. **271 (A 291, B 425)** The Bx form of this revised line is metrically just satisfactory, being of Type IIIa with a five-syllable prelude-dip and two stresses in *sóueréyns*. A more regular shape closer to **A** could be obtained by diagnosing Bx loss of *so* by haplography before so*uerayns*, with subsequent smoothing to *as* (*so* seems to have been lost by the same mechanism in *A*-tH³). Alternatively, simple omission of Bx *as*, following **C**, would improve the rhythm, as would *swiche* for *þise*; but no emendation seems imperative. The **C** line, recast perhaps with direct recourse to the earliest version, reverts to the form of **A** in its b-half.

   A 293 *am I forget*: RD, J, M (? representing respectively *r¹*, *r²* and **m**); an idiom more unusual than the normal *haue I forget* preferred by *Ka* and thus unlikely to be derived from it. The meaningless TH² variant may well reflect t's visual error for *am I*, Ch the ⇒ of a familiar expression for that reading. K and H³ have made the same ⇒ for the readings of their respective group-ancestors (*r²*, **m**), which was probably that of RDJM. If a preterite of *forgeten* formed with *ben* existed, its rarity would account for its replacement by the commoner construction with *hauen* and A's levelling to *I forgat*. B 441 is arguably abrupt, and the form of C 277 may suggest that Bx lost a line at this point. *K–D* accordingly insert A 293 before B 441 (so *Sch¹*); but as evidence for reconstruction is uncertain, emendation is better avoided. The line's meaning being somewhat oblique, **L** may have preferred abruptness to obscurity in **B** but later have prepared more carefully in **C** for the introduction of the important idea in line 278.

274–75 could 'look like scribal padding-out into two lines of an original reading *Ho is worthy to [for] wele or to [for] wykkede pyne*' (Schmidt 1980:105; so *R–K*). But the punning *repetitio* characteristic of **C** seems detectable here. Thus *wele* 274 is to be read as a (deliberate) variant of the adverb *wel* (with long vowel) in an elliptical phrase 'well or wicked doing' (*Pe*), while in 275 *wele* is the noun 'happiness' (MED s.v. *wele* n.(1), 2 (a)) and *wikkede* means 'fierce, cruel' (MED s.v. *wikked* a. 2 (b)).

   B 435 *wote*: the reading of L (?< β) and R (? < α), harder in conjoining present indicative with past subjunctive than the more logically concordant γ form, so likelier to be original. The form of g suggests w, its sense that of LR.

278 (A 294, B 441) *comended* **p**: on grounds of contextual appropriateness and the support of **AB** to be preferred to *comaunded* **x**, which is not impossible but could here be no more than a bad spelling, one paralleled in *A*-KDMH³ (*Ka* Apparatus). **283 (B 446)** The Bx division of 446 from 447 is acceptable in itself but syntactically the pronoun object falls better at the end of 446, rewritten **C** providing no firm guidance. Either way, 446 has a non-authentic pattern *aa / bb*, so *wiþ* is conjectured as the required key-stave for which Bx substituted the more obvious *and* (unless its reading was Ø as in R). The line now scans as a T-type. **287 (B 450)** *wihtnesse* **p**: the more unexpected and therefore harder variant, though possibly less appropriate here since it stands for physical strength which, like mental capacity, is declared unavailing without grace. The **x** reading, to which **p** group q has varied (*add* FS after Q), may have been suggested by the implied context of examination in a court (cf. *euidences* 286). But it presumably has a sense (MED s.v. *witnesse* n. 1) answering exactly to *wisdom* in **B** (so *C*-N²). **288 (B 451)** The reading of **x** is ungrammatical and that of **p** makes poor sense. For while *grace* and *fortune* evidently form the two lifts of the b-verse, the links between each, and between both and the a-verse, are obscure. The emendation here presumes loss of *is* in Cx through haplography before *his*; in **x** assimilation of the latter to *which*; and in **p** smoothing of *which* to *with* and *of* to *and*. The sense of the reconstructed phrase *his grace of fortune* is something like 'God's grace granted for a specific occasion' (*sc.* the *meschief* of // **B**). The unconventional conjunction of two terms (*grace; fortune*) customarily contrasted with each other (as objected by *R–K* p. 155, who read *with*] *which / with his*) may well underlie the original corruption. **295 (A 308, B 458)** *kete* **A**: the Ax reading *grete* could alliterate 'cognatively' with |k| and *kete* 'distinguished' be no more than an attempt by KW to 'correct' the metre. But if a conjecture, it seems a good one, given the presence of *konnyng* in the **B** and **C** revisions and its earlier occurrence in a closely similar context A 11.56, where the same two mss, accompanied by V, preserve it (very possibly from Ax) and one of the erroneous variants is *grete* (see further *Intro*. II § 70). *in*: only in X ('**x**' is a misprint), preserving the intrinsically best reading; *and* Cx makes *konnyng* an adjective not a noun. **299** *paradys ober*: emended without warrant by *R–K* to read as **AB**, though there is no reason to doubt rewriting here. Thus B 463 is revised from A 313 and is in turn revised to C 300 so as to fuse B 463a and 464b into a single line (with minor alteration of the epithet), leaving *paradis* from B 464a to be re-used in C 299.

300a (A 313, B 465) At this point the majority of the **A-Text mss** break off, **RUJ** to be followed by Passus XII, **TH²Ch** and **K** by a C-Text of **x**-type (the Latin **300a**

is in the former). **D**^{2} joins y as a fifth member of this **C** sub-group, its readings agreeing with y unless otherwise noted. TH^{2}Ch now form a *C*-group **t**, readings of which are cited when agreeing with **p**, but only selectively when isolative. The four extant A-Text **rubrics** all appear to be scribal, the absence of an archetypal *explicit* indicating the unfinished state of this version. For convenience, notes on C 11.301–17 // B 10.469–75, 11.37–43 are given here, and notes on **A XII** after these.

306 (B 474) will scan as Type IIIa in the majority and perhaps archetypal reading. But the 'church' variant with *k* as in the **B** line under revision gives a firmer feel to it by linking the noun closely with the custodial verb *kepe* that for **L** defines the Church's providential function (cf. the shift at C 246 to *k* as key-stave sound from the vocalic stop of the **B** line it revises). **312** The **x** form of 312 will scan cognatively as Type Ib on |k| / |g| and, with two stresses on *bigýle*, 313 will scan as Type IIIa, while the **p** form has *aa / xx*. But in **x** the shortness of 313 and in **p** the uncharacteristic placing of the adverb clearly point to Cx's loss of a half-line after the macaronic a-verse of 312 and reflect sub-archetypal attempts to repair the omission by re-lineation. In the light of B 11.40, it therefore seems safe to restore *ne Coueytise of Yes* as the lost b-half and relineate accordingly. It is possible that *grettly* is a Cx error for an original *graythly*, as seems to be the case with *gretly* β in the Bx tradition. This is the reading of one *C*-ms, F, and is adopted by *R–K*; but as the Cx sense is acceptable and revision here is possible, no emendation need be made.

Passus A XII

On the authenticity of Passus XII see the *Introduction* III *A* §§ 67–74. It is here accepted as original up to l. 98; the last nineteen lines, headed *Appendix*, are to be ascribed to John But, and are given in italics. The rubric *Passus tercius de dowel* appears the product of the scribe of u and will not have been in the source of J or, presumably, in the common source of <uJ>. It could have been prompted by recognition that Clergy's opening words are a reply to Will's speech in XI 258–313. The metrical irregularities in the passus may be in part authorial if it derives from a draft (as occasionally with **Z**; see *Intro*. III *Z* § 6). But the text has been treated generally as if it were a finished fragment and emendations made on the assumption that some errors are likely to be scribal. The presence of two independent witnesses (R, J) for the first 88 lines makes comparative analysis of the readings possible, though there is no *parallel* material apart from some Latin quotations in any of the other versions. The copy-text is R, the only complete witness; for that reason, as in the case of **Z**, the ms spelling is retained. Only substantive variants are recorded in the Apparatus.

1–98 3 The <RU> line has the inauthentic pattern *xa / ax*, which could result from the u scribe's transposition to prose order of a phrase *betere don* in a Type IIIa line. J scans normatively, though with an unusually strong stress on *bene* after a six-syllable prelude-dip. This could be a scribal correction of the metre, but the fact that *don betere* would be the phrase expected supports its claim to be original. **4** *peryth* J: preferable to *put h(i)m* RU as the harder word, the verb being little instanced outside **L** (see MED s.v. *peren* v.(2)). As well as B 16.417, where it collocates with *apostles*, *peeris* (n) is linked with *aungeles* (the other category cited here) at B 16.71. **5** *seye*: presumably the preterite of *seyen* 'see' (= *seyȝ*; cf. C 11.115). The slackness of the b-half may be due to its draft character. **15** *fonte*: final *-e* is added to provide the necessary feminine ending. **17** scans as a familiar extended Type IIIa on vowels with standard counterpoint on *sk* (*abb / ax*). **21** scans very awkwardly as it stands as Type IIIa with the caesura after *ben.* But the tense-sequence of 20 suggests that the verb should be rather *were* 'should be', yielding a line of Type IIa. Alternatively, *synne* may have been substituted in the common source for *wikkednesse* under inducement from *synful* in 20a, 24b. Grounds for emendation are, however, not sufficient here. **32** scans *aa / xx* in the common source, but *lerne* may be diagnosed as a scribal ⇒ for a less expected word *cunne* 'know how to'. **34** *skele*: an inevitable emendation, R's variant perhaps an attempt to make sense of the reading attested by J rather than deliberately ⇒ for *sk(e)le*, a common word. **36** scans in J as Type IIa with the third stave *to* 'cognative' on *t*, the fourth lift *do* providing a 'supplemental' |d| stave and the b-half scanning *gó dó wèl* to give the necessary feminine ending. Less probably, *do* could form the key-stave with *wel* expanded to the disyllabic *wele*, which was mainly Northern in this period (see MED s.v. *well* adv.). **45** scans as either Type IIIa with caesura after *desyre* or as Type Ie with caesura after *him*. Both alternatives require a liaisonal stave *with_him* though in the second the key-stave becomes *for.* **48** The reconstructed form is proposed as generating the variants attested. J's inverted word-order is more probably original, though R's is exactly echoed at C 18.17; also preferable is the recessive lexeme *sypes* R, which is sometimes replaced by its advancing synonym (as in the subarchetypal **p** tradition at C 6.427). **49–50** As divided in J, the first is a Type IIIa with caesura after *me.* Final *-e* is supplied for the necessary feminine ending; but arguably *þan* should be placed before not after *a clerioun*, or *she* should read *Scripture*. Line 50 is to be read as an 'anomalous licensed' macaronic (Schmidt 1987:101) scanning either *xa / ax* cognatively or as Type I with two staves (one cognative) in *próbáte*. The apparent stress-pattern of this Latin phrase on its recurrence at 56 and its appearance in a macaronic at C III 489 // **B** argue for the former scansion of 50. **52** is either an anomalous macaronic scanning *xa / ax* on *b* or a licensed macaronic (Schmidt 1987:101) of Type IIIa with a mute key-stave on *Quod* (the latter in principle possibly a full stave). Doubtless *Sk* is right that J's spelling is an error for *borowhe*. **56** *And I*: conjectured as the original behind the split variants in J and R. **62** This sixteen-syllable line has five lifts and a caesura after *answered* and can only be scanned as a Type IIa with a 'strong' four-syllable dip before the final lift *be*. It looks to have been miscopied from two lines of Type Ib and Type Ia respectively divided after *answered*, with loss of a stave-word like*wye* after *welcome* (an error that could have arisen through scribal failure to see *I answered* as forming the whole b-verse of 62). **63** scans either as normative with a liaisonal key-stave *d* in *and_(H)unger* or like 17 as an extended Type IIIb with counterpoint on *d* (*abb / aa*). **67** *fentyse*: reconstructed from J's substantive form and R's spelling as the form of this word in 68, the one likely to underlie the two variants. The wish for internal rhyme in the b-half may have determined the precise form of the noun (cf. 74a below). **84** *house*: final *-e* is added for a feminine ending, but the stress pattern of 84b could have been *oúre hòus*, with strong internal rhyme. **85** is either Type IIIa or Ia with a liaisonal stave on *þat_oþer*. **88** is reconstructed from the split variants of R (*god wot*) and J (*quod he*), with *he* emended to *I* on grounds of contextual reference. The first three words form a prelude-dip before *Gód*, and the line scans cognatively as Type Ia (|g| |k| |g|). **90** The most natural scansion of this line is as a vocalic Type IIIa with the caesura after *lyf*; but it would doubtless read better if *l* were the stave-sound and *leue or *lede were inserted after *lyue*. **91** *Þou*: the nominative of the pronoun is obviously required by the grammar of *tomblest*. A similar slip occurs at Z 6.100. **92** *worþ*: a secure emendation, given the suitability of the sense 'will become' in connection with man's future happiness. **98** is here taken as the point where **L**'s text breaks off, in a manner that recalls A XI 313 but is no more decisive as an ending (97–8 echo A 1.119–0).

99–117 Lines 99–105 are regarded by *Sk* as probably authentic; but **L** is unlikely to have ended the A-Text in this way with a reference (in 101–02) to what were presumably the later versions of *Piers Plowman*. John But's portion may thus be reasonably seen as beginning with the shift to the third person (though this is paralleled at A 5.44 // and A 8.43 where **L** is speaking of his dreamer-persona). On metrical and stylistic grounds 99–105 are in keeping with **L**'s habitual manner, but if 104 is an echo of 22.100, 105 // (see *Intro*. III A § 68f and *Commentary*) this is evidence that But not **L** wrote it. **99** *þo wiste*: an obvious emendation on grounds of sense; the error could easily have arisen from an exemplar spelled *þoo wustt(e)*. **107** scans *aa / xx*; if *busyly* has been caught up from 106b above, the key-stave should perhaps be *soofly* or *sikerly*. **113** will scan as standard on *r* if *Kyng* and *rewme*

are transposed in the b-half; but it can also be read as extended Type IIIa with counterpoint (*abb / ab*) and *þis* as key-stave. **116–17** Two Type Ic lines in succession are unparalleled elsewhere in the poem, but would arguably be in place as a coda here. Although securely ascribable to But, they show him to have a very fair understanding of **L**'s alliterative practice.

Passus XII (B XI)

Collation From here on, the sigil **x** is used to denote the agreed readings of the y-group (now comprising XYIP²D²), the u-group (UD) and the t-group (TH²Ch). A new sub-family sigil *x¹* is used for the exclusive agreed readings of y and u. Where t and **p** agree against *x¹*, they may be taken to represent the text of their postulated common ancestor *x²* (for discussion see *Intro*. III, *C Version* §§ 5–11, 31–2, 35–8). But a new sigil *x²* is not used in the Apparatus; instead, these readings are followed by the sigils t**p** (where the lemma or variant is cited from t) or **p**t (where it is cited from **p**).

Introductory Note

The content of **B XI** is revised and expanded in **C XII** and **XIII**, the material coming together in parallel again at **C XIV = B XII**. From approximately C XII 169 to 249 (the end of XII) and then from C XIII 1–99 appears a 180-line continuous sequence of unique C-Text even longer than the 'autobiographical' passage inserted at 5.1–108. As with the revision of B Passus V, Passus XI has been divided into two in **C** after expansion. These changes largely account for the final discrepancy in the passus-numbering of the two longer versions (20 in **B**, 22 in **C**). However, from C XIV (B XII) to XXII (B XX) the passus-content, despite extensive revision as far as C XX, runs almost in tandem, any gaps being of not more than thirty lines. There is one exception: from about **B XIII 264–460** there is no direct parallel-text in **C**, as most of the Haukyn material has been shifted to the revised Confession of the Sins. These roughly 180 **C** lines are reproduced on the right hand page of the text-volume (pp. 131–43). The Apparatus of the parallel **B** material appears below the main text of **B**; for discussion, see under the textual notes to C VI and C VII.

1–89 (B XI 44–152) 3 (B XI 46–9) The *B-β* lines are accepted as authentic, since 46 is retained as C 12.3, the substance of 48 in C 11.316 and part of the sense of 49b in C 11.317; they seem to have been lost from α by homœoarchy (*Couetise...con- > Coueitise...com-*). In 49, the probable β reading *if þe leste* gives a metrically acceptable line of Type IIa; while this could be archetypal, the sense is weak and the absence both of α and of parallel **C** leaves some uncertainty. The conjecture proposed here takes *þe leste* as a nominalised adjective ('the least') that was misconstrued by β (and perhaps Bx) as the impersonal verb *þe leste* ('you like'), either after misreading preceding *of* as *if* or through smoothing that word to *if* in order to make it fit the supposed syntactical form. As reconstructed, the phrase is to be taken as referring implicitly to the three Do's, though 48 names only two; the 'least' is presumably Dowel (for the thought cf. B 10.131–36). An alternative emendation would omit *of*, making *þe leste* refer not to Dowel but to ('the least bit of') knowledge about the three, as direct object of *knowe* (*ouȝt* being adverbial 'at all'). But the form adopted here, taking *knowen of* as a phrasal verb, better accounts for the presence of *if* in β. The g variant, which also takes *l(e)ste* as a noun (though a different one *lust* < *list* 'desire'), is clearly scribal in its redundancy, which further exceeds that of LMw. **4–6 (B 53–4)** Despite misdivision of 4 from 5 after *riche* to give an unmetrical line, t already shows its textual value both in retaining 5a (present in // **B**) and in the superiority of its text there to **p**, which also has the half-line, by descent from t**p**'s postulated common-source x^2. The misdivision, with consequent loss of 5a in x^1, appears caused by the succession of long lines, each of more than fifteen syllables. Line 5 scans as a T-type, *confésse* bearing its common accentuation (as in // **B** 54) and *good* being a cognative full stave (rather than forming part of the pre-caesural dip). In // B 53 the scansion is as Type IIIb with two lifts in *cónsciénce, goode* as cognative final stave, and a four-syllable prelude-dip. Though this is metrically acceptable, the line would read more smoothly as a Type Ib if *seide* were seen as a ⇒ for *quod*, which is not normally used introductively without a subject but could perhaps have originally been placed after *conscience* (cf. *IG* s.v. *quethen*, first entry). B 54 is Type IIb with the b-half scanning cognatively on |ʃ| / |s| and the a-half having *þee* as a cognative second stave or, possibly, is Ia, with *þi* as key-stave. **10 (B 58)** *pecuniosus* **x**β: linguistically the harder and rhythmically the superior reading. For another case of **p** anglicising a Latin stave-word, cf. *trespassours p¹, transgressours p²* for *transgressores* at 1.92 above. **12 (B 60)** *forȝat*: either 'forgot, lost recollection of' (MED s.v. *foryeten* v.1a) or 'lost, gave up' (MED s.v. 4(c), citing this passage). This second sense of the word (here given in the unambiguous form *forȝat*) is illustrated with relation to a *quality* (e.g. *myght, cruelnes*) only from early C15th examples; those from **L**'s contemporaries have only a *faculty* (mind, wit) as the object of loss in this sense of the verb. The later use could have been current earlier, but possibly **L** is here playing on two polysemes of the same lexeme, 'forgetting youth' having a special metonymic implication of 'forgetting the *sins* of youth (as one runs on into age)'. That is something Ymaginatif warns against at B 12.4–8, where Will's

fernyeres are in effect the days of his youth, and this is the exact sense of the phrase in its second appearance at 22.155. *K–D* find no appropriate sense of *foryeten* here and emend to *foryede*, the preterite of *forgon* (MED s.v. v. 1b 'forsake, go from' or v. 2b 'lose, be deprived of'). Although contextually perhaps preferable, this reading is not clearly the harder, if wordplay on *forȝat* is accepted. The *C*-**x** reading *forȝet* need not (despite doubts in *Sch²*) be seen as a reflex of a lost original *foryede, since this is a well-attested spelling of the preterite of *forȝeten*. *K–D*'s emendation is thus hazardous in presuming 'corruption by visual error' (p. 111) in successive archetypes (it is rejected by *R–K*).

B 67–96 67 The Bx line scans as Type IIIa, with some awkwardness, reading two stresses in *cristnéd*. The inversion of p.p. and verb as emended here to give better rhythm presumes their ↔ to prose order in Bx (more speculatively, *man* could be seen as a Bx ⇒ for *gome* in an original Ia line, scanning cognatively). After 67 Bx has a spurious prose line transparently designed to underscore the axiom attributed to Conscience by extending it to cover a man's whole life or the part of it spent in the parish he may have moved to. **70** scans as Type IIa on |k| if a liaisonal first-stave is found on *Ac_yét*, with a 'supplemental' fourth stave on *konnyng*. *K–D*'s emendation on metrical grounds (p. 194) is otiose. **81** will scan stiffly as a Type IIIc line on |k| in *cóntricion* and a 'strong' (three or four-syllable) pre-finale dip (*to...heiȝe*). But an alternative that seems preferable here takes |t| as stave-sound and *to* as a full key-stave, making the dip disyllabic or trisyllabic. A T-type line seems excluded since the a-half has only one full stave (cf. 82). Drastic emendation of *heiȝe* to *court / kingdom of* is to be avoided. **82** *be so*: the Bx line, reading *so be*, is metrically unobjectionable; but it seems clear that the chief idea in the b-half is expressed not by *be* but by *so* 'in this way' [*sc.* by contrition alone], which should thus carry the stress, giving a true T-type line (*aa / [a]bb*). It is probably desire to give *so* rhetorical stress that has caused the presumed Bx ↔, thereby changing the metrical pattern to the inauthentic *aa / bb*. **84** *louȝ*: preferred on the showing of C 23 as giving a better contrast with *loured*. Though not unacceptable in metre and sense, Bx *loke* may well have been induced visually from *loked* 85 or by a preterite of *louȝen* spelled with a stop *k* in the exemplar (cf. conversely the palatal variant *pouhe* for *poke* at 9.342 // B 7.192). **86** The Bx line scans with an excessively long prelude-dip of seven syllables (five in revised C 27) that may result from alliterative attraction of the phrase *amonges men* to *metels* in the b-half. The ↔ of adverbial and speech-marker phrase (the latter to its position in // C 27) reduces the initial dip to one of three syllables. **87** scans as standard on cognative staves |p| |p| / |b|. **89** scans, in the light of C 31 (which omits *quod I*), on vowels and cognative labial stops (|b|,

|p|) as a free T-type line, the key-stave *and* being mute and *àllègge* accented on the first syllable. **93** The quotation appears convincingly in the light of // C 35 to be 'appended' or free-standing Latin (Schmidt1987:88–93) and so recognised by F (against Bx). Like the other two proof-texts in this sequence (93, 95 // 30, 35) but unlike 106*a* // 41*a* (a piece of Latin following the English which translates it), it deserves to be numbered as a 'text' not a 'citation-line'. **96** scans as Type IIIb on |s|, the first stave being either in *licítum* or by liaison of *is_licitum*; so there is no need to emend *segge* to *legge* (*K–D Sch*[1]).

38 (B 103) scans on voiced or voiced / unvoiced cognative staves, the first stave being in *neuéremore*, which is here taken to have 'wrenched stress' (cf. 3.320, 17.147, where it has normal alternative stress on first / third syllable). *C*-**p** and the two **B** copies HmF fail to grasp this and accordingly supply *þow* as a first stave, **p** losing *-more* in the process. **39 (B 104)** The revised **C** line has its caesura after *nat* and appears accordingly a T-type (scanning on *s* and *t*). **40 (B 105)** There is line-type ambiguity in revised **C**, which could be a Type IIIa like **B**, with cognative staves on unvoiced and voiced fricatives (*Thyng*; *thow*), or a Type Ia with cognative staves on labial stops |b| |p| / |p|. Given the rhetorical contrast between B 105 and 101, where *þyng* is respectively first lift and part of the dip, the former alternative may be preferred; but revision of *is* **B** to *wolde be* **C** supports the latter scansion. **41 (B 106)** *labbe it out* **C**: clearly a revision of **B**, which is closer to the Latin quotation. The reading of t, coinciding with the *B*-G variant, may express dissatisfaction with the failure of *labbe* to translate *lauda*, whereas G may be seen as ⇒ of a more familiar word for its β original (non-alliterating *B*-W *preise* is such another). The Gt reading offers characteristic paronomasia with *loue*, but the greater rarity of *lauden* is shown by MED, citing **L** here for its first appearance (*labbe* in // **C** is likewise so cited, s.v. *labben* v.). The *B*-α reading must remain uncertain, *lakke* R being nonsense as it stands but more probably therefore a faithful record of what prompted F to rewrite the whole a-half. Possibly α read like **C**, the R variant *lakke* being due to *k* / *b* confusion, and if so, *labbe* is in contention as the reading of Bx. But against this is the hardness of β *laude* and the ease with which α could have erred by inducement from *lakke* in the b-half as well as the presence in R of the negative particle, where *oute* would be expected after *labben* as in **C**. In sum, despite the distance in register between the two verbs, both illustrate **L**'s lexical adventurousness, and the originality of neither need be doubted. **45 (B 110)** *of Oure Lord*: restored (following *Sk* App.) as the likely **B** reading on the showing of **C**. Bx cannot be firmly established in the absence of the line from β (for which there is no obvious reason unless that the scribe misconstrued the syntax of 109 as complete). But α very probably had the ungrammatical R

reading, the result of anticipating *þat* in the b-half, which has prompted F's rewriting, in a manner similar to that at B 106. **57 (B 121)** *saue* **x**α: 'a decoction of herbs taken internally as a remedy' (MED s.v. *save* n. (1)); the harder and more appropriate reading in context (cf. *drynke* 58 //). Both *safly* β and *sauete* **p** result from failure to discern the noun in its spelling without *l* (that with *l* is found at B 17.76), which better enables paronomasia on the religious sense of *saue* (v) and *sauacioun*. *R*-*K*'s acceptance of *saue* here contradicts *K–D*'s preference (p. 152) of *sauete* in (needlessly) emending **B**. **63 (B 127)** *chatel*: required for the alliteration, the sense 'moveable goods' being that of the more familiar non-alliterating ⇒ *catel* in Bx and most **C** mss. **66** scans as Type IIIa, like the **B** line under revision, and *R*-*K*'s emendation to the reading of a single **B** source (w) is unwarranted. **74 (B 138)** *þat heo ne may al*: evidently a development, to a more explicit form, of the *B*-α reading with its characteristic Ø-relative (found at 76 // and B 152). The β variant appears a smoothing of the latter, which may be presumed the probable reading of Bx. It is adopted by *R*-*K* (p. 102) from N[2] as supposedly a correction from a superior lost **C** source, though much more likely to be by ⊗ from a **B** ms of β type (see further *Intro.* III *C* § 40). **75** The t-group and D[2] here read *beth...aboue* as in **B** for the apparent Cx reading *bothe...are aboue*. D has *beth* but includes *are*, as does P, which spells the former *beþe*. These latter mss suggest a variant spelling of *boþe* as the source of the D[2]t readings, though if t retains the reading of x^2, this could in principle represent Cx. However, the revisions from 48 on are in matters of detail and the reading of BtD[2] is not obviously superior in sense to that adopted here. **77 (B 141)** *Hiȝte* **B**: making good sense (despite *K–D Sch*[1]), the somewhat abrupt mid-line shift to direct speech in 143, though unusual, being not unparalleled (cf. 10.13 // **AB**). B-Cr here strikingly shows ⊗ from **C**. **79 (B 143)** *Gregori*: the revised **C** key-stave replacing **B**'s |k| stave-pattern, in the interests of greater precision, with compound cognative staves |kr| |kr| / |gr| (contrast 80 //, where |kr| is used in all three lifts in **C** but **B**, treating |k| as the active stave-sound, has |kl| in first position against |kr|). *R–K*'s emendation to *clerkes* **B**, like their alterations of *helle* 78 and *thenne* 80 to read with **B** have no warrant on grounds of metre or sense. **84–5 (B 148–49)** 149 in Bx scans awkwardly with a seven-syllable prelude-dip that includes the important word *grace*. Re-division after *grace* restores this to prominence, making 148 a T-type. The revised **C** lines offer some support in their syntactic parallelism. **88 (B 151)** *as*: x^1, preferable to *and* x^2 (< **p**t) if the phrase *my lawe rihtfol* means 'my own proper religion' (MED s.v. *laue* n. 4a (a); *rightful* adj. 4(b)), not 'my just administration'. **L**'s thought seems to be that 'love' was in effect (and so was effectually) Trajan's religion, even if he lacked *lele bileue* 'true Christian faith'; so *as* is less likely to be the ⇒ than is *and* (for the relevant sense of *as*, see MED s.v. *also* adv. 5d 'in the manner of' and cf. B 13.171). This interpretation is supported by **B**'s b-half; but an alternative, giving due weight to the explicitly legal *leele dome y-vsed* of 90, might associate *as* more closely with *lawe* than with *Loue* and understand the b-half 'in the form of / through the agency of my just administration (of the law)'. A play on both senses of *lawe* is not excluded here.

90ff (B 153ff) The ascription of the long speeches that follow (in **C** to 13.128, in **B** to 11.318) arouses editorial disagreement and raises larger questions of interpretation (for which see the *Commentary*). Despite difficulties about the appropriateness of some **B** lines to the Emperor Trajan, there is a strong textual signal at B 319 (*wiþ me gan* oon *dispute*) that the speech begun at 140 (*quod* oon *was broken out of helle*) is here concluded, though the only clear narratorial reference to a speaker is to Trajan at B 170. *Sk* ascribes B 170–72 to him as a quoted utterance within a long speech by Leute (153–318), making the *oon* of 319 more probably Leute (all line-numbers those of the present edition). But apart from the mention of *leautee* at 153 echoing Trajan's at 145, there is no justification for this ascription. For this is a reference not (like *quod Troianus*170) to a speaker but to a quality, one found in Trajan and as naturally to be predicated of himself in the exemplificatory third-person style as to be applied to him by Leute, who finishes speaking at 106*a* and is thus very unlikely to be the referent of *oon* in 319. *K–D* allow only 170 to Trajan, breaking the syntax to ascribe 171ff to the Dreamer, who is also given 153–169: consistent enough, apart from the abruptness of the syntactic interruption at 171, but inevitably limiting Trajan's direct part in the 'dispute' to lines 140–52 and line 170. This seems at variance with B 319, where the speaker says that the dispute was with *him*, whereas 140–52 are evidently aimed at Scripture (see 139 'oure bokes', 140 'baw for bokes') and 170 is *agreeing* with 153–69 (lines *K–D* ascribe to the Dreamer). The verb *disputen* could indeed signify 'engage in discussion, conversation, or reflection' (MED s.v. v. 2(a)), but in **L** is usually 'debate with...contradict' (ibid., 1(b) and see s.v. in *IG*), the sense indicated by Trajan's exclamation *baw* (140), an anti-clerkly equivalent of the *contra* introducing Will's earlier 'dispute' at B 8.20 //. But apparently favouring *K–D*'s interpretation is the fact that **C** ascribes its expansion of B 153–318 to *Rechelesnesse*. Earlier introduced at C 11.199 and, importantly, named at 276ff, he is specified at 13.129 as having *aresened* Clergy, and he is associated with Will by a verbal echo at 183 (*resonede*). On the other hand, it is Clergy, the object of Rechelesnesse's 'rage', who at 13.131–33 is *offered* Kynde's help (in **B** given to the Dreamer at // B 320–25), and Will who *receives* it. A major revision

has evidently transferred a speech largely by Trajan to a new speaker presumably meant to be a more suitable opponent of *clergie*. But the **C** transition from Trajan's speech to Rechelesnesse's, accepted here (with *SkPe*) as occurring at 12.90, is unfortunately little clearer, since no internal indication of the speaker is given and his naming as Rechelesnesse at 13.129 comes as a surprise (perhaps intentional). What is noteworthy is that **B**'s passage on Trajan's rescue from hell, culminating in the interjection at 170, is eliminated. (For further support of the interpretation here, see the *Commentary* on these omitted passages, B 159–69, 190–95, 211–29 and 268–72*a*.).

B 159–96 Loss of **159–69** by β may be explained as due to eyeskip from *Troianus*158a to *Troianus* 170a; but their omission from **C** is harder to account for. Possible reasons are that their suggestions of the Harrowing of Hell in 163–64 or of Trajan's having worshipped the true God (thereby seeming implicitly to identify the Natural with the Mosaic law at 167–69) were thought inapposite. The lines' authenticity is not in doubt, as 166–67 are echoed in C 98–9 and the thought of 168b in C 14.37. **167** One of three instances of individual lines (the others are 13.170, 172) where R is the sole **B** witness, F being deficient, and **C** having no parallel. **181 (C 101)** The presumed Bx line as attested in βR scans either *aa / bb* or, with *souereynly* as first lift, *xaa / bb*, neither being an authentic metrical pattern. The revised **C** *nameliche*, forming the prelude-dip in a Type Ia line, suggests that B[1] had its adverb in the same position, and the emendation proposes a word for which *souereynly* would be a non-alliterating ⇒ in Bx (and inferentially in B[1]). Both words are part of **L**'s standard lexicon, but *principalliche* is instanced in a closely similar context at B 14.195. The reconstructed B 181 now scans as Type IIb. The a-half ⇒ of F (adopted *K–D Sch*[1]), with acceptable metre and plausible sense, is here rejected as having been prompted by scribal unease at a double reference to the poor (181, 183) but no mention of one's neighbour in general. However, 182–83 merely elaborate 181 in reverse order, allotting a whole line to each half of it: **L** is here using the characteristic scriptural idea of a 'neighbour' as one's fellow-man in need (illustrated in Lk 10:30–7), which becomes for him specifically the poor (cf. esp. C 9.71). While BxB[1] were thus corrupt in at least the adverb, **C** keeps the remainder of 181 and uses B 183b to complete 101, excluding F's more commonplace notion. **184** *iuele*: understood as the harder reading for which the more obvious *heele* is a β ⇒. Cr modernises this as *helthe* and F coincides with β, doubtless after finding its α source *euel* contextually impossible, if construed as 'evil'. The βF line scans as Type IIIc, that of R as Type Ia. But the main argument for seeing R as a bad spelling for *iuel(e)* α (< Bx) is lexical, not metrical: for the sense 'a beloved person', well-illustrated from *Pearl*, see MED s.v. *jeuel* n. 2(c). **196** Loss of this line by β could have been due to eyeskip from *riche* at the caesura to *riche* at the same position in 197. With alteration of *hath* to *hadde*, the line would make grammatical sense in R; but the reconstruction interprets R's *Almiȝty* and F's *all* as split variants of an α reading with double wordplay on *Al-*, *alle* and *miȝty*, *myȝte*. The notion that God permitted inequality *for þe beste* and not through *nounpower* (B 17.312) seems characteristic of **L**.

112 (B 202) *gentel*: omission of *and* Bx, which makes the second half-line appositive rather than complementary, gives a better grammatical and semantic fit. **114 (B 204)** As divided in Bx, the two lines scan as Type Ia and Type IIIa, though the staccato structure of the second, with redundant *echone*, is untypical even of **L**'s shortest lines, such as B 10.127–28 // A 11.83–4, both of Type Ia. Parallel **C** suggests that Bx may have found the line excessively long and so divided it as two. The **C** form itself is not without metrical awkwardness, being a Type IIa with two of the three vowel-staves in non-lexical words (*Ín; ás*) and the phrase *the...telleth* required to function as a five-syllable 'strong' dip. But a parallel instance is *þe Bible telleþ þere he* at B 9.41, where the rationale of reconstruction is similar to that invoked here, though there is no // **C** line. On the other hand, B 12.73 (no C //), which has the identical a-half, scans on *l*, and it is possible that the key-stave phrase should be **ledes sonnes*, an expresion unusual enough to have suffered ⇒ of *mennes sonnes* in both archetypes. **B 217** *alle synnes*: preferred as closer to Vulgate *peccata multa*, 'many' rendering a Hebraism for '(her) many sins', i.e. all her sins. **123 (B 231)** *lome* **C**: taken as a revision of *ofte*, **B** scanning vocalically with contrastive a-half stresses on *hir*, *oure* that remain as a secondary pattern in **C**. **131 (B 239)** The revised **C** line scans either as Type Ia with caesura after *louelich* and a trisyllabic pre-final dip, or as Type IIb (*aaa / bb*), which is preferable stylistically and metrically. The order of its a-half suggests that B¹ may have read as Bx, which gives an unmetrical line (*xa / ax*). The present reconstruction corrects a presumed ↔ of adjective and verb to prose order and gives a Type IIIa line. **140–41 (B 251)** All members of **C**-y except Y omit two half-lines apparently by eyeskip from *wille* 40 to *wille* 141, both occurring at the caesura (for a similar case see on B 196). The result, though unmetrical, gives plausible sense, but the retention in 140b of *hasteliche* from B 251a supports the originality of the two-line revision. Y either preserves y by direct descent or has collated with a **p**, t or u-type source. **150–51 (B 261–62)** Revised **C** renders *penaunce and pouerte* the double subject of *Maketh* and supports α's Ø-relative in 262 understood as subject of the verb (β being an evident smoothing). The order of nouns in **x** is a local revision, **p**'s reversion to **B**'s order promoting a more purely material understanding of the terms. **154** *by day*: acceptable as a revision, and *R–K*'s rejection for

deth **B** is unwarranted. **156** *churche*: *wrytte* in **C**-ms D, a reading preferred by *R–K* p. 162, who argue for the key-stave *hoso* as conventionally alliterating on |w|. This is implausible, since the D variant is explicable as an individual scribal response to the fact that 156–61 paraphrase Christ's words, which are directly quoted at 161a. **159** *logheth*: the variants in *g(h)*, *w* and *th* (X) indicate that Cx probably read *ȝ*, a form often represented as *gh* or misread as *þ*. **B 278** The β form of this line is accepted as giving good sense and fitting well syntactically with 279. The F reflex of α makes no sense and its b-half of 278 is patent scribal padding. The R reflex, however, might be made to yield sense if *For* 'despite' is read for *With*, and it could be that the missing b-half accurately records the condition of α, and α the reading of Bx. β will then have eliminated the a-half to produce the present (in itself satisfactory) reading. The a-half preserved in R could thus, in principle, be authentic and a conjectural reconstruction, taking into account both F and C 158, might read [*For*] *any wele or wo* [*in þis worlde to suffre*]. However, any completion of the line must be largely speculative in the absence of fuller evidence from **C**, so it is best avoided here and the half-line omitted.

168–249 are new in **C** and extend through **XIII 1–99**. Textual notes on **B** 11.285ff continue with the resumption of the parallel text at p. 480 of Vol I. **169** *ȝut* **x**: 'further, still more' (MED s.v. *yet* adv. 1 (a)); the difficult and contextually more suitable meaning, since self-denial is being affirmed as a 'counsel' to *all*, not just the *perfecti* of 164. *Thus* **p** may be a scribal ⇒ after misunderstanding the sense as 'nevertheless' (MED s.v. 2(a)). **176** *Ennedy* **x**: the **p** variant *ouidius* is doubtless the result of ⇒ of a familiar (if inappropriate) name after misreading Cx **enedie* (*e* as *o*, *n* as *u*). *Eneide* (the form in u) presumably represents *Ennedy* rather than Virgil's *Aeneid*. **190** *withsette* 'resist' (see MED s.v. *withsitten* v. 2(a)): conjectured as the needed key-stave, Cx having the inauthentic pattern *aa / xx*. The verbal part of the compound could have been lost by visual assimilation to following *for*stes, assisted by inducement from the common b-half rhythmic pattern /xx/x, the occurrence of *with þe forst* in 194a, and the relative rarity of the word. The proposed verb's cognate *withsytte* is found at Pr 174, 8.202, 10.98 (preterite *withsaet* at 18.250), and that may have been the form of the word conjectured here too (the sense 'resist' is not recognised by MED before 1420, but see OED s.v. *Withsit* v.). The **p** repetition of *with* in following 191 is a further scribal corruption absent from **x**, which is thus fully compatible with the emendation in 190b, providing two further noun objects of the conjectured transitive verb. (For a parallel case of presumed corruption in a verbal compound involving *with-* cf. **wiþseide* at B 4.91 // **ZA**). A simpler emendation would be *shullen* for *mowen*, with the latter explained as having come in from 188 or 193. *R–K* p. 170 conjecture an omitted stave-phrase *in somer* after *þat* (ascribing its loss to inducement from the shape of 188) as one expressing the difference of farming procedure implicit in the context. But **L**'s point concerns not only *when* seeds are sown but what sort of 'seeds' they are: those able to endure 'winter' hardship (*soffry may penaunces*). **203–04** As here punctuated, 203 gives a multiple subject for the verb in 204; but no less acceptably, the three nouns could be objects of *soffren* as transitive verb (like its synonym in 206/7) and *Bito-keneth* have a Ø-relative subject; the sense is identical. **206–08** present a serious crux occasioned by corruption in 206 and, as here argued, in 208. The Cx reading in 206 is uncertain, though *so to* seems possible, given that a comparison of the suffering saints and the wheat-seed would be expected. This is taken as original by *R K*, who adopt *Angeles* with **p** in 208, with the consequence that Christ's words in 209 are now spoken by unannounced celestial beings. But *Then* in **x** needs to be accounted for more fully. Manuscript I attempts to resolve the crux by inserting a half-line with the comparative adverb *more* to link it with *Then* (understood as 'than'). The missing b-half plausibly conjectured by *Sk* is adopted by *Pe* who also (unlike *Sk*) accepts I's variant *owen degre* (? < **aun gre*) for Cx *anger* and emends *to seyntes* 206 to *tho seyn-tes*. But though grammatically acceptable, this is not conceptually coherent; for the saints can hardly be *more* praiseworthy than angels 'at their own level of beatitude', which is logically not that of the angels. The confusion could be put right by reading *muche* for *more* in I's added a-half and *worthy* for *worthier* in *Sk*'s conjectured b-half, as well as emending *Then* to *As*. But the resulting reconstruction is not only fragile, it is otiose; for if I's half-line and 208 variant are both rejected as scribal, the archetypal text may yield adequate sense with a simpler emendation. That text is most probably represented by **x**, since omission of **þan* in **p** could easily have occurred by partial haplography before an*gels*, an*ger*. *Then* may consequently be analysed as the cropped remnant of the required verb **worthen*. This ought to be preterite subjunctive ('would become' after *saide* 206) but could equally be present indicative 'will become'. But either way, it requires *that* to be understood after *saide* and *so to / to / to his* to be seen as smoothings of absolute *so* '(that) thus / in that way' (referring back to the 'worthy' wheat-seed of 193). The phrase **Worthen angelis* may be taken as elliptical for 'would be(come) *as* (angels)', the thought being that saints would be, in their *anger* 'affliction' the equal of angels because they show perfect *obedience* to God's will, just as the holy virgins later are *euene with angelis, and angeles pere* (18.90) because they resemble them in *purity*. The ellipsis ought not, however, to obscure the boldness of the phrase's literal sense, since the notion of man being transformed into something higher seems

latent in that of sorrow (*tristicia*) being transformed into joy (*gaudium*) in 209, a thought to be echoed in 22.47 (cf. MED s.v. *worthen* v. 4(a)). Here the Latin points to the authenticity of *anger*, lexically characteristic of **L**, hard and apt, as against the easy and inappropriate *owen (de)gre*. *Worthen* thus becomes the first of three render-ings of *vertetur*, the second and third being *turne* (210) and *chaunge* (211). **213** *foel*: in the light of *stulte* 217a, obviously the right reading. **215** *hym after* **p**: on balance the best reading in context (see *Commentary*). The ?*x¹* reading *hym* is metrically possible, but the enquiry seems directed to the audience *concerning* the fool in 215–16 (hence *he* 216), and only turns into direct address *to* the latter in 217. This parallels in reverse the shift from 2nd to 3rd person in Lk 12: 20 ff, **L**'s immediate source, which is quoted in a variant form at 217*a*, with conflation from Ps 38:7. The t reading (adopted by *Pe*) is a characteristic piece of scribal intensification comparable to that at 221. **217***a egrediatur*: the subjunctive, though unexpected, is arresting enough to be original. **L** is here paraphrasing, and there is no need to emend the probable Cx reading in the interests of greater simplicity. **232** *ariste*: a contracted form not of the third person sg. but (analogically) of the third person pl., the spelling of which was identical in **L**'s dialect. **239–43** will have been lost from t by homo-teleuton (*þat hit kepeth* 238, 243). **248** *drede*: clearly occasioning difficulty to various scribes; but the sense is not 'strained' (*Pe*, preferring *grete*) so much as punningly ironic: the *drede* 'respect' that the rich get through money is not without *drede* 'fear' of losing that money to rob-bers. **249** The M line that follows (adopted by *Sk* in *PT*) is not totally unworthy of **L**; but unless it represents pure descent from **p** (< *x²* < Cx), it is likely to be a scribal attempt to round off the Passus more decisively.

Passus XIII (B XI)

5 scans imperfectly in Cx (*axx / xa*), probably through transposition of verb and complement to prose order in the b-half. As emended, the line is an extended Type IIIa with blank second and third staves. The **p** reading, for which the lemma is taken from M (*men rat*), is pre-ferred as giving a better placement of the a-half lift. **6** Cx has the incorrect scansion *xa / ax*, here as a result of promoting to first position the dominant idea of excess. The emendation adopted yields a normal Type IIIa line. More drastically, *mesure* could be conjectured as having been supplanted by *noumbre*. But this would be difficult to account for, as the phrase in question was a common idiom that posed no difficulty of sense: see MED s.v. *mesure* n. 8(a) and 9(b) for the phrase = 'immoderately, intemperately, excessively'. It is not found elsewhere in **L**, whereas the occurrence of *out of nombre* at 22.270 // leaves no reason to doubt its authenticity here. *R–K* leave

6 and 7 unmetrical, presumably judging them not fully finished. **7** *his*: referring correctly and economically back to *mebles* in 6; *auȝte* t (so *PeR–K*) is a plausible filler, as is *al hus good* **p**, but both were doubtless prompted by the line's brevity (contrast 9, which is exceptionally long, and see on 14.211). **9** Although **p** offers in this instance two acceptable lines of standard type, it is much likelier that the Cx line's exceptional length (seventeen syllables) and the unexpected position of the caesura after *Abraham* led to misdivision followed by typical padding in **p**. **10** *spouse to be*: *spousehod to* t (so *Pe*), a smoothing, possibly after loss of *be* through haplography before *beknowe*. It gives acceptable sense and metre but looks scribal in the light of x^I**p** agreement. **12** *kynde kynge*: reconstructed as the probable Cx form of which *kynde* and *kynge* appear split variants. P^2 and N^2 and D may have consulted a **p** source, and the same could be true of YD^2, or they may have preserved y faithfully where <XI> have erred (and U by coincidence). Suspect as scribal, however, is the reading of t adopted by *Pe,* with its characteristic padding by the addition of *comely*. **20** *and*: *in here* **p** (stressing the internal virtue) may even imply that poverty in itself is bad, a reading with some support in 12.206–09 above. But the argument is that objective poverty *is* a good, as the condition if not the cause of the moral virtue of patience. **36** Even with final *-e* added to *messagere* to provide the necessary feminine ending, the line remains awkward to scan, perhaps the best of the alternatives being as a Type Ie; but it would read better if *nede* were omitted (as in 48a below). **40** shows as a clear instance of the rare Type IIIc (*ab / ab*) on vowels and *l*. **41** is an extended Type IIIa with counterpoint on *w* (*abb / ax*). **56** *mette*: likelier to be original despite the breach of tense-sequence, since such mixtures are characteristic of **L** and the 'logical' one more probably a scribal ⇒. **59** may scan with a liaisonal stave on *wole_hym* and *lede* be a felicitous conjecture by the t scribe. However, since *lede* occurs six times elsewhere in **C**, *wyht* could be a Cx ⇒ for this comparatively uncommon word meaning 'person' or 'man' (see MED s.v. *lede* n. (2) 1(a)) and the t reading may be cautiously accepted here. The QWFSZ variant here (which even in its corrupt two-line form implies *wiȝt* in **p** and thence in Cx) is the strongest individual piece of evidence for the existence of q, these five manuscripts' exclusive common ancestor. **63** *hostiele*: **p**t (=x^2), metrically preferable to x^I and, as elliptical, more likely to be original (contrast 64, where x^2 has the arguably redundant *wel*). **72** *treuthliche*: the spelling of X alone; *treuliche* in the remaining mss, which is presumably what Cx read, should preferably be adopted. **79** *ȝe*: preferred as the contextually harder reading, for which various witnesses across both families have substituted the more expected *þe* (in the text read *ȝe* for misprinted *þe*). *boþe two þe*: the presumed Cx form, of which *boþe* and *boþe two* are imperfect reflexes. X will

have read with *?y*, lost *boþe* through visual distraction from following *þe*, then neglected to add it in the space provided. Y either preserves *two* direct from y or has corrected from a u (or **p**) source. *Pe's* conjecture *bowe to þe*, anticipated by N except for the article, could be justified by positing a Cx **boȝe* miscopied as *boþe* through that commonest of single-letter errors, *ȝ / þ* confusion. But the context makes plain it is not submission to unspecified laws that is in question, but obligation (cf. *ybounde*) to the requirements of both charitable action and liturgical / penitential observance. **92** *So þe pore* **x**: *The porter* [*sc.* God] **p**, induced by unconscious suggestion from *gateward* 91 and difficulty over the sense. The question as to who 'performs the law' must relate to the poor (= the messenger), not to God.

100 *The parallel text of* B *resumes here* (XI 285)

102 (B 287) *lynnen ne wollene* **C**: the word-order presumed for **B** also, Bx having inverted to a more familiar one in which the chief fabric comes first, to give *aa / xa*. The immediate ancestor of WHm, or else each ms independently, has felicitously corrected. **104 (B 289)** *nyme*: adopted in **B** to provide the needed third stave in this Type IIa line, Bx's ⇒ of the familiar synonym being visually induced from *take* 290b.

B 299–300 are mistakenly judged by *K–D* (p. 114) to be 'untranslatable' and so in need of emendation. The text is not in doubt, and it may be that the idiosyncratic phrasing combined with the blunt explicitness of 301–02 seemed unsatisfactory to **L** and prompted omission of these lines in revision. The sense is: 'I think he has more faith in getting a benefice through [the mere fact of] his ordination than on account of his education or reputation for godly living'. **B 301** *at*: conjectured as necessary to give the phrase *wonder at* (found also at 346 // below), with *why* treated as a nominal direct object (for the appropriate sense see MED s.v. *at* prep. 7(a)). The Ø-reading of CrB makes sense but is more likely to be a correction of meaningless *and* than an accurate record of Bx, which presumably read *and*, a ⇒ for *at*, with *for* an intelligent guess at the intended meaning.

114 *shendeth*: clearly the hardest of the variants and a word strong enough to have invited scribal censorship on doctrinal grounds, whence the presumed Ø-reading of x^I required to explain those of $ID^2(X)$ (all from y) and U (from u). The x^I mss Y and D have therefore presumably corrected here from an x^2 source, of **p** or t-type. If the sense here is 'ruin' or 'damage' (MED s.v. *shenden* v.1(b)), the implication that the Mass could become invalid on account of the priest's sins would be *prima facie* unorthodox and ill accord with the authorial-sounding words of Liberum Arbitrium at 17.117–21. But the latter envisages only *lewede vnderstondynge* rather than the fault of *luyther lyuynge* adjoined here, and **L** expresses elsewhere (through Haukyn) the view that intercessory prayer may be rendered powerless on account of the sin of the petitioner, including priests (*mannes masse* B 13.259, significantly revised however to *mannes prayere* in // C 15.230). It is remotely possible that the word replaced by Cx *shendeth* (not because doctrinally objectionable but because of its coarseness in context) could have been *shiteth*, with a sense ('befoul') attested only for the rare verb *beshiten,* but possibly so used by **L**, as arguably at 9.264, where two mss have an erroneous variant *schent* (perhaps induced by an exemplar form **shet*) for *shyt*. However, there seems adequate reason for accepting *shendeth* here in a qualified sense of 'vitiate', 'spoil' or simply 'dishonour' rather than '(sacramentally) invalidate', a Wycliffite opinion even Rechelesnesse is unlikely to hold. **120 (B 307)** *is hit*: adopted on the strength of two *p²* mss (G and K) and **B** as the presumed Cx form (retaining **x**'s neuter subject and **p**'s word-order). **122** *For* **x**: needlessly emended to *To* by *R–K*; but the line is re-ordered and the sense is 'for the benefit of' (MED s.v. *for* prep. 3(a)). **125–26 (B 312–13)** In itself the **p** version of these lines could pass as acceptable in metre and sense, scanning as a cognative Type Ia followed by a Type IIIa line with two stresses in *sápiénter*. The **x** version can be re-divided after *nat*, as actually in D, with adoption of the spelling *nauht* to provide a disyllabic final lift (= *náwùht*). In discriminating between the two, therefore, **p** is to be rejected as showing in *clerkes as* a characteristic expansion of the **x** form that is supported by // **B**. But comparison with **B** also tends to suggest that the line's length led to misdivision and loss of 126b, though the precise mechanism of the loss is obscure; the b-half may thus be restored reasonably securely from **B**. The only attempt at a wholesale re-writing is by N², which reads for 125b–126: *þat can nouȝt wel her crede / þei sauoure nouȝt in sapienter to synge ne to rede.* **127 (B 314)** is a Type IIIa line with a six-syllable prelude-dip, scanning on *b*. It may be that *is* has replaced *beþ*, since sg. *beþ* 'is' occurs as a full stave at B 10.345, where the key-stave is *be* (cf. the emendation at A 11.97 above), and its adoption would give a smoother line here, of Type Ia. The rarity of the usage, *beth* being a plural form elsewhere in **L**, might account for ⇒ in both archetypes successively. Scansion as Type Ia on three non-lexical words in *n* is also possible (as presumably for *K–D, R–K*), but unlikely and unnecessary.

    B 322 *wondres*: so clearly apt in context that the ?α reading may be no more than a visual error for it, perhaps unconsciously suggested by the nearer context of discourse (*dispute* 319, *ensamples* 324 and *wit* 322). That α read as R is indirectly indicated by the shape and sense of *worchynge* F, a scribal response more probably to *wordis* than to *wondris* (the source of ms B's reading

remains uncertain since there is no // **C** and borrowing between the families is virtually uninstanced in the Bx tradition). In support of α as a harder and original reading is its possibly intended allusion to the 'book of creation', of which the 'words' would be the natural *ensamples* to be specified below (see *Commentary* further). It could then be *wondres* that was suggested by the dominance of this notion in the wider setting of the passage and the frequency of the word's appearance (at 328b, 346a and 349b) as an obvious ⇒ for the contextually obscurer *wordis* (for a parallel case, cf. at B 7.125 *foles* α, supported by *A*-**m**, against *foweles* β, again with no // **C**). **B 324** scans vocalically as an extended Type IIIa line, with counterpoint on |f| and *énsaùmples* stressed on the first syllable. *K–D* conjecture *forbisenes* as the key-stave for which Bx will have substituted *ensaumples*. In MED s.vv. sense 2 (b) of the former and 4 (a) of the latter overlap closely; but the required meaning of *forbisene* does not occur elsewhere in **L**, whereas that of *ensaumple* is instanced at 5.119 //. The emendation, which would yield a Type Ia line, should therefore be rejected.

133 (B 325) *creature*: *creature and* Bx; syntactically possible, making the two activities of 'knowing' through creation and loving God separate, the second perhaps consequential on the first. But this runs against the grain of the sense so clear from the **C** line, which is substantially identical: it is through discerning the wisdom and love manifested in the created world that man is brought to love the Creator. The error may result from the Bx scribe's taking the sense of *kynde* as '(type of) natural creation', in parallel with *creature*, not a Langlandian 'nature-name' for God, in apposition with *creatour*. **143 (B 334)** scans either as Type Ia with *sey* as first lift or as Type Ic, pronouncing *Resóun* as the first stave alliterating cognatively with unvoiced *s* following. **146 (B 337)** The **C** line alliterates as Type IIIa either on *they* or on *rótéyed* and *reste*, but awkwardly if the stem vowel is short. The former verb's rarity is clear from its being found only here, as likewise is the noun *rotey* in // **B** (see MED s.v. *rutei* n., *ruteien* v.). **C** would scan more smoothly if auxiliary and participle were judged to have been inverted to prose order in Cx, and accordingly emended. Alternatively, *anon* may have lost preceding or terminal *riȝt* through distraction caused by its belonging syntactically to the b-half but metrically to the a-half as hypothetical stave two before the caesura. It is certainly very unusual for **C** to revise a **B** line from a Type I to a Type III; but *R–K*'s adoption of **B**'s reading here cannot be justified. **147–48 (B 338–39)** *a morwenynge(s)*: satisfactory in both sense and metre, Bx and Cx differing only in number. *K–D*'s imaginative conjecture *al mornynge* 'melancholy [*post coitum*]' (adopted *Sch¹*) appears to have the (ambiguous) support of *C*-ms D and possibly that of *B*-Hm (*all mornyng*). But the first could be a spelling variant and the second suggested by the sense of B 340ff. What is sure is that **C** makes no attempt to obviate recurrence of this supposed error but revises and tightens up B 339, characteristically shifting the position of subjects and verbs (as in the handling of B 325 at 133). The revision of 339 produces a closer parallel in both syntax and content, altering to Type Ia a line which is a vocalic Type IIa, or IIb (stressing *femélles*). This metrical change, *towards* the standard, is in the usual direction (cf. note on 146 above). *ȝede*: in **B** the presumed α reading, which was also the intended reading of L (the ms being marked for correction, as *Sk* notes). If L's source *l* was an accurate reflex of β, it is probable that γ misread *ȝe* as *þe* through *ȝ / þ* confusion. This verbless phrase was faithfully preserved in M and in g, while w smoothed by adding a verb (*ben*). The relative weakness of the Bx line, while helping to explain its revision, does not justify emending it. **150 (B 341)** is lost in some C-mss by homoteleuton (*þat...hadde* in 149, 151) and/or homoarchy (*Ther ne was*) and was presumably not in *p²* (it is also absent from G and inserted a.h. in K). **154–55 (B 343–44)** *token*: a form according with the preterite plural with short vowel (not present 'rýde') and wrongly emended by *PeR–K* after P²*Sk*. *drynkyng*: a participle, preferable to the gerund as modifying the circumstances of human sexual intercourse; t's intrusive *in* implies inebriation as a separate sin, not a specific, Lot-like occasion of *lost of flesch*, the only vice with which these lines are concerned (contrast 187–90 below). *mid* **B**: conjectured as the required key-stave, Bx *wiþ* being ⇒ of the advancing non-alliterating synonym, possibly under inducement from the a-half (for a parallel case later see B 12.203). F's b-half could be due to ⊗ from C 153a or suggestion from the identical half-line at 370 and is a typical attempt to regularise α, here preserved by R. **158–59 (B 346–47)** The re-lineation of Bx may be safely adopted on the showing of **C**, which is revised only in 159b. Although Bx 347 would scan adequately as Type IIIa, 346 might have been found too short because of the staccato character of the third and fourth lifts, both nonetheless disyllabic if *wher* is expanded as in **C**. (For a similar case of scribal difficulty with the disyllabic nature of *pye*, cf. the w-variant at B 12.252). **161 (B 349)** On comparison with **B**, the **x** form reveals **p** to have divided Cx on account of its length to produce a Type IIIb line and a characteristically padded-out Type Ia. **B 353** is an awkward Type IIa, which could easily be improved by reading *hij* for *þei*. **170** scans with a liaisonal stave on *toke_Y* or as an extended Type III with double counterpoint (*abb / ab*). **172** *ledene* 'speech, song' (MED s.v. *leden* n. 2(b)) is obviously correct and *lenede* a back-spelling induced by *strenede* 171. U could have corrected by commonsense conjecture rather than from a **p** source, and P²'s variant is similarly explained. The reading of u cannot be ascertained, because of D's illegibility (*R–K*

claim to read *ledene*). **175** For *on*[1] it is arguably better to read *of* with DChRM (so *R–K*) as balancing *of* in the b-half. **180 (B 369)** C scans as Type IIIa on vowels or as Type Ia with stress on *Resóun*. **182–83 (B 371–72)** As they stand in Bx, the lines scan as respectively a Type IIIa with two lifts in *rébúkede* and as an inauthentic variant (*aa / bb*). The rewriting in F appears a scribal response, and an incompetent one, to a line of perceptible irregularity. Possibly 371a formed the b-half of 370; but in the light of C's revised lines, both of which alliterate on *r* as Type Ia, the phrase *neiþer riche ne pouere* may be fairly safely presumed to have been lost through eyeskip from *Reson*[1] to *Reson*[2]. The lines as reconstructed scan as a Type Ia and as a T-type (here retaining *-seluen,* which *K–D* omit). **186 (B 374)** *sewest* **B**: in the light of revised **C** *reuledest* it is possible that *schewest* R (? = α) is the Bx and original **B** reading. The sense would be 'teach' (MED s.v. *scheuen* v. 8(a)), which is close to that at C 13.233. But since metrical allophony of *sh / s* appears a feature of L's idiolect, the present case could be a simple spelling variant (by contrast with 10.162, where the same possible alternative is acknowledged but rejected). Here it is likely that *sewest* in Will's challenge balances *folwe* and repeats his earlier *folwede* 371, which is revised to *sewen* in // C 180 (cf. also the phrasing at B 422 and the revision at // C 233). **187** *sorfeten*: clearly archetypal and better in context than *forfeten*, the possible reading of IPEG, which *R–K* read for X and prefer, though their note (p. 148) is unpersuasive. **190–91** *oþer Bestes* **p** / *oþer bestes They* **x**: both variants possibly reflexes of Cx *oþer / Bestes þei*; but **p** is more satisfactory in its rhythm, which avoids too close a repetition of 186 and reserves the noun for contrast with *renkes* in the b-half. **192 (B 373)** As it stands in the two **x**-mss YU, this 19-syllable line is a Type IIb with an unusual strong dip after the third lift and another single-syllable dip after the caesura: *mérueileth me — for mán is móste_ylìche the // of wít*. The group original of t may be reconstructed as identical with that of <XIP²D²>, *the* having been lost through assimilation to preceding *–che* in TH² and padded out in Ch, which for *man...werkes* reads *man is most worthi / Boþe of wit and of werkes and most like to oure lorde*. Y and U may each have preserved by direct descent its respective group original (i.e. y and u), but it is just as probable that they (correctly) judged the line a single unit and copied accordingly. **193** *leueth* y: spelled *lyueþ* in **p**Yu. The words are identical (= 'live'), though the possible contextual ambiguity has been unequivocally resolved by M in the sense 'believe'. **197 (B 393)** *noli*: preferable on grounds of accord with preceding *te* and closeness to Vg. The form *noli te* is presumably a misunderstanding of the verb as reflexive: DtVRZKN have it as *nolite* (wrong here as a plural, and probably a mechanical error). **198 (B 379)** scans as Type Ia on cognative staves |g| |k| / |g| with a five-syllable prelude-dip and heavy rhetorical stress on *God*. For a parallel example of *soffrede* forming part of a strong (here four-syllable) prelude-dip cf. 3.327. **199** *amys standeth* **C**: here judged a revision, and N²'s reading *mystandit*, which *R–K* follow, ⊗ from **B**. **201–10 (B 382–91)** The **B** lines, partly retained and revised in **C**, are authentic and could have dropped from β by eyeskip from *wye wisseþ* 382 to *wise...witty* 392, where β resumes. The loss would have been facilitated by *Bible* 392 (= *Holy Writ* 382) inducing the β-scribe to believe he was resuming where he had stopped (after 381). **B 382** *wye*: preferred as the normal spelling in **B**, and to avoid the syntactical confusion that might arise from taking *weye* as 'way of living' (referring to God's *suffraunce* 378). **206 (B 385)** *þe quod* **B**: taken here as the presumptive α reading (< Bx) of which *þe* and *quod* are split variants. In **C** *þou* may be seen as part of a revision of the whole line. **207 (B 386)** *if þyn* **B**: reconstructed from *if þow* and *þyn* as giving the best sense in context after *my lif*. **209 (B 388)** *Crysten* **B**: reconstructed in the light of **C** as the likely original which Bx could have omitted, leaving a Ø-reading that merely repeated the sense of 387. This would have invited supplementation like that in R and F, which scan respectively as Type IIa and Type Ia, but each with suspicious phrasing, F anticipating 389a. The point having been made in 387 that man (like other creatures) cannot create himself, 388 now affirms, with use of deliberate wordplay on two senses of *make*, 'create' and 'render', that neither can he achieve salvation through his own powers. **B 397** scans as Type IIIb with two lifts in *creatúre,* but would undoubtedly be smoother if *bad* were seen as a Bx ⇒ for *comaunded*. **217 (B 406)** *chydde* **B**: possibly a Bx ⇒ for *sherewede*, as conjectured *Sch*¹ (cf. 6.75 // B 13.331). But if a pronunciation |ʃ| is assumed, a cognative stave for |s| may be found. At 423, 424 below the two phonemes |tʃ| and |ʃ| are kept distinct in successive lines; but **L** may have allowed them as 'metrical allophones' and so, by extension, |tʃ| as capable of alliterating with |s| (see C 7.300, Apparatus, though MED does not illustrate *chiden* spelled with *sh*). **B 420** The Bx line has anomalous scansion (*xa / ax*) or else a very awkward one with two lifts in 'líkýng' and a four-syllable dip preceding. Emendation to *no likyng hadde he* presumes Bx inversion to prose order and gives a reconstructed line of Type IIIa. **230** *of þ / Ø* **x**: either gives good sense, **x** requiring *preuete* to stand in apposition with *why* (so *R–K*). For *preuete* XIP²D² (?= y) read *preuede*; Y may here have corrected from a u- or t-type copy. **239 (B 429)** *To blame*: logically and syntactically required by the presence of *or* at the head of the α line, the phrase's restoration is inevitable, though no reason for its omission appears except eyeskip from *To bl*ame → *to b*ete. **240 (B 430)** The Bx line could in principle scan vocalically on three non-lexical words; but the stress-pattern would run counter to the flow of the sense and the evidence of **C**, the revised

b-half of which suggests that |n| was the key-stave in the original B-Text (though perhaps also corrupted in B¹). An earlier emendation *né stérue* (*Sch*¹) posits loss of *ne* before following *he* and preserves the line's *n*-alliteration, though at the price of a clumsy (if not unprecedented) stress-pattern in the final two lifts. *K–D* conjecture *for nede*] *for doute*, making the adverbial phrase modify *sterue* rather than *nymeþ* and producing wordplay similar to that at 22.20 (though the repetition has less point here). The present conjecture gives a word with appropriate sense (MED s.v. *noi* n. (b) 'affliction' or (c) 'suffering'), which overlaps with sense 4 of *doute* 'danger, peril' (see MED s.v.). The latter might have been a Bx ⇒ made to give greater emphasis or because the grammatical construction and the sense 'lest he die on account of his suffering' were missed. **B 431** *Shame*: effectively a personification on a par with Nede (and fully such in 435), so probably also to be capitalised here. **244 (B 435)** is unmetrical in both sub-archetypes, and so the reading of Bx cannot readily be recovered from them without reference to **C**. The latter, however, strongly indicates that **B**'s b-half contained the verb *shonye* together with a noun meaning 'company'. The former survives in β, but in the wrong position, giving the inauthentic pattern *aa / xa*, while the latter is preserved in α as *felachipp*, resulting in the equally inauthentic *aa / xx*. β's *euery* has the sense of **C**, while α's *no* shows as a smoothing aimed at accommodating the substituted verb *loueth*. As reconstructed, there is still some awkwardness and Cr's *ech* would undoubtedly improve the rhythm. But this could have been a revision in **C**, and *euery* β is acceptable as the (likely) Bx form. **245 (B 436)** is in both **B** and **C** decisively T-type, with mute *was* as key-stave. **247–48 (B 438–39)** **C**'s revision of B 438b and of 439 (with a different stave-sound) may well be responding to corruption in B¹ perhaps as extensive as postulated for Bx. The latter is unlikely to have read *reuerenced hym after*, since *folwed* is presumably a ⇒ for a verb not of greeting but of motion, alliterating on *r*. The form here conjectured is the preterite of *rechen*, for which see MED s.v. v. 5(a), illustrating from B 8.35 (with *to*) and from *Purity* 619 (with *after*). Line 439 in Bx fails to alliterate (unless as vocalic Type III in *óf, his*), so emendation here is wholly conjectural, **C** showing no trace of B¹'s form except for *telle*, now as the blank fourth-lift. The verb proposed as the key-stave is suggested by the evidence of |k| alliteration in the surviving stave-word *curteisie* and is illustrated elsewhere in **L**'s usage (e.g. 7.91, B 15.161), as is *craued* (8.101, B 13.165). No clear reason for the presumed corruptions appears.

Passus XIV (B XII)

1 *Ymagenatyf*: to judge from the first appearance of this name at B 10.117 (in stave-position one) to be pronounced as five-syllables, with stress on the first; but the fourth syllable may also be stressed according to metrical requirement: *Ymagenátyf*. In none of its appearances (except possibly 15.21) is it stressed on -*má*-, an indication of the word's continuing link with its substantival root *ýmàge*, so pronounced in **L** at B 1.50 (cf. also on 15.21). By contrast the verb *ymáginen*, similarly derived, may be so accented in two of its three occurrences (21.278, B 13.289) though not in its third (B 13.358). **2** *sete*: 'should sit', the preterite subjunctive (if it is not a mere spelling variant of *sit(t)e*); preferred for **C** despite the alternative variant agreeing with **B** (adopted by *Sk*). The b-half has been revised and *sete,* the evident Cx reading, is unlikely to be a ⇒ for easier *sitte*. Here its tense is governed by the force of *was* 1, not *is* 2 (cf. a similar case at 6.99). **4** scans as Type IIIa, stressing *Dowél* as keystave, though a pun may have been lost through Cx ⇒ of *fol* for original *wel*, the ChR reading adopted by *R–K* (p. 163). The Bx line less doubtfully has the inauthentic pattern *aa / xx*, from ⇒ of a non-alliterating synonym for the less familiar word in key-stave position. The conjectured verb (MED s.v. *minnen* v.1 (a) 'remember or think about, call to mind, recall') also has a contextually more exact sense, since moral reflection based on recalling past actions is in question here (it is found at B 15.461 and at C 17.210 gives the emendation for // B 15.547). Derived from ON *minna*, it is etymologically distinct from *men(e) gen* (< OE *mynegian*) 'call to mind', 'remember' (MED s.v. *mingen* v. 3(a), (b)), which also occurs at 8.104 // and is conjectured at B 5.412. **12** The Cx reading is somewhat compressed and it may be either that *he* was lost through assimilation to following *be* or *and* inserted before simple *be*. The reading with *to be* in QSN² adopted by *R–K* is smoother but unlikely to be original.

B 13–48 Loss of **13–13a** from α may have been due to construing *strike* 14 as a translation of *castigo* 12a, but without noticing how *staf...yerde* translates *virga...baculus* 13a. **16** *makynge*: 'the composition of poetry', **L**'s use running together senses 5a(a) and 5b(a) (MED s.v. *making(e* ger.); to be preferred to the plural (= 'poems'). This is the form in John But's *medleþ of makyng* A 10.109, which probably echoes the present passage, and also of the word's other occurrence at A 11.32. **18** could scan cognatively on *t* and *d*, but is perhaps most satisfactorily read as having a five-syllable onset and the caesura after *Dobet*, with the stress shifted rhetorically in the final term of the triad (*Dobést bóþe*) to give a T-type. **22** scans as Type Ia with a liaisonal stave *as_I*; but conceivably *self* has been lost after *hym*- in what would then have been a Type IIa line. **24** could scan in principle as a Type IIa

with a 'cognative' third stave on |b| and a 'supplemental' |p| stave in position five. But *to ben* belongs closely with *parfiter,* having its normal unstressed structure as part of a strong dip after the second lift of a standard a-half. The b-half's adverbial phrase is thus presumed to have been transposed to prose order in Bx. **30** scans as Type IIIa, though this entails de-stressing of the first theological virtue and would be better as an extended Type III, with **þre* read after *alle*. **40** scans as Type IIIa with two lifts in *Lúcifér* that highlight the etymological sense of the name. **42** scans as Type IIa, since to take it as Type Ia with the caesura after *Iew* would involve depriving the important adverb *deere* of stress and locating it as part of a strong pre-final dip (even if *he it* were omitted as a scribal intrusion). **48** *baddenesse* 'wickedness': first instanced here, α's more explicit ⇒ *badd vse* being possibly on account of the noun's rarity. A specifically sexual sense in this context is likely, given the associations of the adjective (MED s.v. *badde* adj. 1(b)).

17–18a (B 55–56a) The **B** lines may have been lost from β for reasons connected with repetition at 58 of *riche(sse) riȝt so* from *riche...riȝt so* 51a; but 'normal' eyeskip should also have produced loss of 52–4a. *Scientes...vapulabunt*: correcting the grammatically incorrect *C*-**x** form found also (in part) in α, the sole **B** witness. The source has a sg. reference, and to adopt *vapulabit* α and emend the participles to *sciens* and *faciens* would arguably give the most satisfactory reading (the immediate antecedent at 18 // 55 is sg. *hym*), but not perforce the original. The reading adopted in both versions is a compromise.

22 *Druyeth*: obviously superior on grounds of sense and contextual appropriateness (cf. *woky* 25), *Druyueth* being a mechanical slip producing the wrong meaning. **23 (B 60)** Both texts appear to have archetypal errors in the b-half that render the lines unmetrical. **C**'s inversion is *from* prose order (the converse of the error in **p** at 26b). In **B**, a stave-word seems to have been lost and the conjectured form, apt in sense and metre, is one easily prompting visual assimilation in Bx to preceding *amonges* if the latter were spelled aphetically in the exemplar with a nasal suspension, to yield in effect an anagrammatic form of **gomes*. **24 (B 60)** *gode-wil*: clearly indicated as the Cx reading (< *x¹* +**p**); perhaps censored on doctrinal grounds by those mss reading *god wole*. The thought parallels that of B 61–2; on the theological significance of the two readings, see the *Commentary*. **25 (B 61)** *woky*: 'moisten', a rare word (< OE *wacian* 'weaken') recorded in this sense only in **L** (MED s.v. *woken* v. 2(b)), and doubtless found difficult by scribes. The ⇒ *waky* is (loosely) apt to the context but destroys the metaphor of spiritual growth through the 'waters' of grace, which soften and break open the husk around the seed. **32** *wierdes*: 'destined (qualities)', = 'gifts of fortune' or *chaunce* (cf. 33), contrasted with God's gift of grace. The sense is not obvious and the majority variant *wordes* (that of **x** but unlikely to be archetypal, since it is inappropriate as well as easier) may be a visual error for Cx *werdes* (so Z). The N^2 synonym is presumably by ⊗ from its **p** source and not a ⇒ for an **x** form *wierdes*. (For elucidation of the wider sense and support for the reading adopted here, see *Commentary*). **37 (B 72)** *and Crist*: the elliptical harder reading, requiring an understood verb *wroet* not dependent on *witnesseth*. The key point is that two separate statements about 'writing' are being made, relating respectively to God and Christ. The p^1 source seems to have taken the b-half as necessarily governed by the main verb, its ⇒ an appropriate phrase qualifying *God wroet* and seeing 37–8 as concerned solely with the OT law written on the tablets of stone by the finger of God. As punctuated, the two statements of 37 are illustrated respectively by 38, the law of love here standing for justice (cf. B 1.151), and by 39, where the 'confirmed' law is that of grace. In the absence of GK, only one copy attests p^2; but N is unlikely here to show ⊗ from an **x** source. **42a** *Qui*: possibly *Quis* in Cx, but Vg has the (indefinite) relative *qui*, correctly rendered by *That* 41.

B 76 has presumably been lost from α by homœoteleuton, or by homoteleuton, if 75 had the form *dede* for the noun meaning 'death' (MED s.v. *ded* n.). **B 95** With normal stressing, Bx has the inauthentic pattern *xa / ax*, but with a four-syllable prelude-dip will yield a Type IIIa line. However, two lifts in *miroúrs* would be awkward (cf. *maister* at 101 below), and the conjecture offered presupposes Bx ↔ of verb and complement to prose order. The emended line scans as IIIa with stresses normally located.

46 (B 101) The structure of the **C** line is certain on the showing of both **pt** (= x^2) and **B**; presumably x^1 lost 46a through eyeskip from *bokes* 45 to *God* after *bokes* 46. *mayster*: clearly attested in final position in both archetypes, yet problematic, since two lifts plus a final dip are needed and the word is normally disyllabic in **L** (and largely elsewhere). An *ad hoc* trisyllabic pronunciation is therefore presumed (as in the well-known case of *entrance* in *Macbeth* I v 39); but it is uncertain whether the extra syllable is to be found by smoothing the diphthong or by adding an unetymological final -*e*. The genetically separate *C*-mss V and GN (< p^1 and p^2 respectively) solve the difficulty by ⇒ of the Latin form, which will better tolerate a second stress on the central syllable (monolexical macaronic b-halves occur at 2.191, 12.10, 17.309 and B 13.198). In the revised **C** form, with *here* for *þe* B, an alternative scansion of the line is available as an extended Type IIIa with vocalic theme-staves and contrapuntal staves on |m|, and not impossibly the article is a Bx ⇒ for an original possessive as in **C**. *K–D*'s ↔ of subject and complement in the b-half, giving an unacceptable masculine ending, is abandoned by *R–K*. **48 (B 103)** *þe hye*

strete: firmly established on the basis of **p**, u (< x^1) and **B**. The y reading could have retained from x^1 the erroneous metathetic *sterre*, a vestige of which remains in Y's ↔ of adjective and article, and u have corrected its x^1 exemplar from an x^2 source. But more probably the error was confined to y, and x^1 read correctly here with x^2. The erased reading in X could have been *strete* and the alteration a scribal conjecture motivated by a wish to make sense of *hye þe strete*; but since the error also appears in P^2 and D^2, which do not derive from X, it was probably in y. **55 (B 110)** The metre of Cx's b-verse is awkward, whether *lewed* or *lered* is the key-stave. That *lered* is authentic seems confirmed by the naming of both categories in 71, so *R–K* are mistaken to omit it on the basis of N^2's *lewde men*] *lewed and lered*. But it is possible that *to helpe* is a scribal insertion, since without it the syntax connects as smoothly with that of 56 as in // **B** 111, *lewed and lered* forming the indirect objects of *ʒeue* (if this was missed, 55 might have appeared incomplete in sense).

B 116–25a could have been lost by β through eyeskip from *cheste* 114b to *cheste* 125a, though the scribe nevertheless managed both to copy 115 and to omit 125a.

58 (B 113) The line is either of Type IIa, with a second vocalic stave *in* (as in the closely similar 12.114) or standard Ia, with non-lexical *hit* promoted to key-stave for its contextual importance. **60 (B 115)** *prest*: preferable on grounds of sense and the support of // **B**; *prestis* may have been induced by the genitive second stave (the other following nouns are sg., as is *man* 59, which should appear in the text after *lewede*). **62 (B 117)** *hem bytydde* **C**: on the strength of x^1 and ?p^2 agreement the reading of Cx, which t, p^1, and N^2 independently reject, perhaps to avoid the near-exact repetition (but *sorwe* is muted). The easier readings of p^1 and N^2 are perceptibly derived from the one attested by x^1. That of t, *betauʒte* 'allotted' (MED s.v. *bitechen* v. 4(b)) is hard enough to be original, though the only available subject is *Saul* (*R–K* p. 165 transcribe it as *becauʒte*, p.t. of *bicacchen* 'trap; delude; get the better of'. But it is better judged an intelligent scribal variant in the light of x^1p^2 agreement and the appropriateness of such parallelism in a solemn admonition. The repetition, with the variation *hem* for *hym* and stressed pronoun, seems deliberate, and similar end-rhyme occurs at 17.39/40, 18.237/8, B 7.36/7. **B 119** scans awkwardly on grammatical vowel-staves in the b-half and would give a smoother Type IIIa line with ↔ of the two nouns. **67** *medle we* **C**: the *B*-α reading may be reconstructed from R and F in the light of *C*. **68** *chaufen* **C**: the hardest and on contextual grounds most suitable reading, a secure basis for emending *B*-α *chasen*, which presumably resulted from misreading *f* as long *s*. The infinitive form presupposes *we sholde* understood. *to wo*: of the **x** variants, *two* seems the likeliest original of x^1 since ∅ without a sense-lacuna (as in **B**) would not have invited any ⇒, while in **C**'s b-half *and*, securely archetypal, shows revision of the syntax. The attested form *two* is here analysed as a running together of *to wo, with *to* a spelling variant of resulting *two*, which has been subsequently misinterpreted as the infinitive marker in X, smoothed in P² and further expanded in I. The t variant will have preserved the postulated noun from x^2 but have replaced the preposition with *in*. Yu present no more than a correct spelling-variant of a word (the preposition) incorrectly taken as the numeral, but point to the reading of x^1. The **p** reading appears a scribal attempt to create acceptable syntax by replacing a functionless preposition with an adverb. On grounds of sense, the numeral is inappropriate here and the isolated preposition redundant, but the conjectured Cx form *to wo* provides both the apprehended outcome of an angry act and the textual explanation of the x^1 and x^2 forms reflected in the surviving variants *t(w)o* and *in wo*.

B 127–47a 127 Bx scans *xa / ax* and a Type IIa line could be produced by reading *Nas* for *Was* (cf. in the Apparatus the rejected variant at B 138 below). However, this would place the third stress on the negative particle rather than on the substantive *knyƷt* that is alliteratively linked to the even more important key-stave *clergie* in the b-half. In the light of the parallelism in *cometh* 128, the line may be presumed to scan on |k| and *was* as the first stave to be an easy ⇒ for conjectured *Com*. **129–30** In the light of C 80 the form of Bx 129, run together with 130 to produce the inauthentic patterns *aa / xx* or *aa / bb(b)*, may be diagnosed as scribal. In principle, 129a could form the b-verse of 128 if this is scanned as Type IIb with two heavy a-half dips (*wìt; sìƷtes*). But as reconstructed here in the light of **C**, 129 provides for the line a b-half from C 80b's important generalising statement on the sources of experiential knowledge. 130 scans cognatively as Type Ia with double lifts in *décéites* (on this 'idiometric' monolexical structure see *Intro.* IV § 38). **131** *Olde*: adopted as the required vocalic first stave in a line where the key-stave is *vseden* and Bx has the inauthentic metrical pattern *xa / ax* (the completely revised **C** provides no evidence on which to emend other than by conjecture). It is not clear why the word was lost, unless because deemed redundant in merely repeating *toforn vs.* In the line as now given, *Ólde lyueris* may be treated as a (single-lift) compound or as providing two of the three lifts in the a-verse of a Type Ie line. **140–47a** The β lines, which appear authentic on intrinsic grounds and on the showing of // C 84–91, could have been lost from α by eyeskip from d*eum* to d*iuersori*um, with an aural element contributing (*apud Deum / habet diuersorium*).

88 (B 144) *and of* **p**: possibly but not necessarily the Cx reading of which *and* t and *of* x^1 are split variants, since a comma in its place would give the same sense. The 'minimal' x^1 form could be that of **x**, *clennesse* appar-

ently repeating 86, where the referent is unambiguously the Virgin Mary. The **p** reading here adopted has the advantage of avoiding the ambiguity of x^1, which requires a particular punctuation. *hexte* **B**: on the showing of LM the probable β and possible Bx form, which gives better rhythm in this strong five-syllable dip than the one with long vowel commonest in this period. **95–6 (B 151–52)** The α lines appear authentic on grounds of their intrinsic character and presence in **C**; but no mechanical reason for their omission from β appears. **99 (B 155)** scans either cognatively as Type Ia on |ð| and |f| or as Type IIIa on |t|. **105 (B 161)** *B-γ sikerer* is grammatically correct and, with elision, rhythmically as acceptable as the probable Bx *siker*, which assimilates the comparative morpheme to preceding *-er*. **106 (B 162)** is identical in both archetypes, scanning vocalically as Type Ie with 'semi-counterpoint' on |k|. It is uncertain whether the first lift after muted *and* (1) comes in *swymmen* or the auxiliary *kan* treated as a lexical verb, the latter being semantically but not rhythmically superior. The unnecessary *K–D* emendation *kan* for *haþ* is abandoned by *R–K* (inconsistently with their emendation of *han* 72 to *kan*). **109 (B 169)** Loss of the **B** line from α may have been induced visually by repetition of *swymme* 168 at the beginning of 169. **114 (B 174)** *a*: required as the subject for *knoweth* (Cx being ungrammatical) and here given the form likeliest to have generated the error under inducement from *And* 115. **121–23 (B 181–83)** The unusual length of these lines has led to misdivision in both sub-archetypes of **C**, **x**'s four lines being Type IIIa, Type IIIb, unmetrical, and Type Ia, and **p**'s three Type IIIa, Type IIIb (on vowels, after padding), and Type Ia. Reconstruction after **B** (which is identical but for the blank final lift of line 123 // 183) restores the presumed archetypal shape. The metrical structure of line 123, in its reconstructed **B** form amongst the longest in the poem, is uncertain. But if *parauntur* is pronounced according to its spelling-form in **C**, it may be mute, or else *bothe* may be the key-stave and the a-half have the three full-staves that identify it as a Type IIa. Bx also appears wrongly divided, with the important *Vnkonnynge* placed as prelude-dip in 184; redivision accords with (revised and) reconstructed **C**. This case is a paradigm instance of the value of parallel-text editing of *PP*. **125 (B 185)** The **B** line, authenticated by its retention (revised) in **C**, will have been lost from α by homœoarchy (*wo / wel*). **128 (B 188)** is a macaronic line of Type Ie, stressing *Domínus*, and with the second stave blank (*heréditátis*). **132 (B 192)** is shortened in revision, to scan cognatively on the consonant-groups |kr| |gr|, as *R–K* here tacitly (if inconsistently) recognise. **133 (B 193)** The Bx form of this line can only be conjectured, in the absence of α. Possibly it contained just the a-verse, which α omitted completely, while β filled out with the half-line attested in L&r. But the latter could reflect Bx's ⇒ of non-alliterating *redy* for harder *graiþ* and inversion to prose order with smoothing for a b-half having the form adopted here. The β form will scan vocalically as Type IIIa, but with poor syntactical connexion between the two clauses. The felicitous W emendation, understandably adopted by *Sk*, cannot be authentic, but W's pronoun *þat* (where Bx perhaps read Ø) is retained as necessary to make the construction clear. The key stave *graiþ* that *K–D* postulate is found earlier at B 1.205 //, AZ 8.41 and C 6.230 meaning 'direct' (MED s.v. *greith* adj. 2); and though the required sense 'ready' (MED s.v. 1(a)) is not instanced elsewhere in the poem, it was widely current (as at *SGGK* 448). As now given, the line scans on |g| like its revised **C** form, with stress on the conceptually significant word *grace*. **136 (B 196)** *as(s)erued*: the almost certain spelling of Cx and, on the showing of LR, the probable one of Bx. The aphetic form, although well-attested (MED s.v. *serven* v.(2) 2(b)), would be potentially ambiguous in this context. **142 (B 202)** *Seynte Iohn ne* **C**: adopted also for **B** as the reading of which β and α appear split variants (omitting respectively *ne* and *Seint*). **143 (B 203)** *mid* **B**: conjectured as the required key-stave (mute as at C 16.180), Bx scanning *aa / xx* and **C** revising the b-half to use the advancing form *with* and a new (lexical) word as key-stave. The form *mid* appears in probable stave-position at 4.73 // **ZAB** (where AxC-**x** both substitute *with*), at B 17.169 (where **C** revises to *with*) and at 16.180 (no //). The word also occurs at B 12.295, where only R (?< α < Bx) has it, βF read *with* and C 14.217 revises to *with*. **150 (B 210)** *leue* Y: established for **C** on intrinsic grounds and the support of **B**, the issue to the fore being the speaker's belief in graduated reward, not the nature of the thief's life in heaven. The t variant has presumably been influenced by the sense of preceding *telde*149 and possibly also by *y / þ* confusion in its exemplar (*lyue y* read as *lyueþ*), as may have happened in <PE> N). *þat* **C**: simpler than the form reconstructed from the **B** variants, which yields good sense. The point in **B** is not *that* the speaker believes the Thief in heaven (as he could hardly not) but *what* he believes about the Thief's status. The exact reading of Bx is uncertain but is likely to have been that preserved in β, having changed *be* from a preposition to a verb by moving it from before *þe þef* to after it. If R is an accurate reflex of α (in which *þef* had been lost by haplography), F is an attempt to produce sense by substituting *it* for pointless *þe* (a *C*-variant identical to the one reconstructed here but for the reading *of*] *be*, which is that of *p¹*). However, an alternative and arguably superior possibility is that **B** lacked *by*, giving much the same form as **C**, which remains elliptical despite the addition of *þat*: '[as Trajan did not dwell in the depths of hell...], so I hold the Good Thief [does not occupy a high position] in heaven' The reconstructed form has however been preferred for **B** as that likeliest to have given rise to

the presumed reading of Bx, though there is no case for adopting it in **C** (as do *R–K*). **152 (B 212)** *los(e)li(che)* 'loosely, insecurely', not '*losel*-like'; though the thief *was* a 'rascal' in life (see MED s.v. *losel* n., with all C14 quotations from **L**) he is now one of the blessed in heaven. The t-variant *loueliche* 'gladly' or 'humbly' rationalises, perhaps because objecting to the notion that anyone could be in heaven 'conditionally'. But though theologically rather odd, this appears to be the sense here, as preceding 142–46a // make plain. The analogy would plainly work better if the thief stood for repentant sinners *in via*, not for the narrowly-saved blessed *in patria*. **153 (B 213)** displays 'line-type ambiguity' in that it may scan either as vocalic Type Ia (with *hym* as key-stave), as vocalic Type IIa (pronouncing *úppòn*), or as Type Ie on |k|, with *cryant* as key-stave, a liaisonal first-stave in *Ac_why* and a four-syllable dip before the third lift. None is fully satisfactory, but the last is to be preferred as allowing greatest metrical weight to the conceptually significant *cryant*. The primary sense is presumably 'vanquished', this being the aphetic form of *recreaunt* attested as the *x¹* variant at 20.103 // and as archetypal in **C** and probably **B** at 132//, which the present line echoes. MED s.v. *creaunt* adj. & n. acknowledges only this sense, but *Sk*'s gloss 'believer' points to a contextually appropriate secondary sense: it is the thief's faith that saves him, and 'entrusting his faith' to Christ precisely enacts the sense of the word's etymological root *recredere* (see OED s.v. *Recray*). Given the existence of a well-attested noun *creaunce* meaning 'belief', including religious faith (MED s.v. 1), it is possible that an adjective with the sense 'believing' was in use; but none of the MED examples cited under *creaunt* will bear this interpretation. **154 (B 214)** The **C** revision improves style at the expense of metre, leaving *þat* as mute second stave. That Cx has not lost *theef* appears likely from the similar revision in 155, which omits a lexical word *skile* present in **B** (perhaps as the first b-stave in a T-type line). *R–K* needlessly insert both words to make **C** accord with **B**. *woldest*: presumably monosyllabic [*wost*] rather than [*wold*], the subjunctive form in *B*-gL. **156 (B 216)** *whyes* **x**: preferred on grounds of sense and the support of **B** to *weyes*, a word semantically induced from *come to* 157, 158 and superficial conflict between 'why' and 'how' in 156b/157a. It is possible, though, that Bx had an ambiguous spelling, as suggested from B 10.124, where the preferred reading is not archetypal.

B 217–29 217 *a rebukynge*: either article + gerund (an absolute phrase appositively qualifying the verb) or preposition + gerund (taking final *-e* as inflexional and *a* as 'on'); if the second, *a-rebukynge* should be read. MED s.v. *rebuking(e* ger.), takes *aresounen a rebukynge* as a phrasal verb meaning 'to reproach', but cites this line only. The context (with *Reson* as object) implies the sense 'I engaged in argument with Reason, reproaching him', i.e. making two separate statements, the first of which appears rational (*skile* 215) until exposed as arising from passion (*willest* 218, *likyng* 219). **218–21** The α order of these lines gives a more logical progression to Ymaginatif's case, placing immediately after *aresonedest* the critically modifying *willest* (see on 217), then arranging 'birds and beasts', 'flowers', and 'stones and stars' (animal, vegetable, mineral) in a sequence that comes full circle with repeated 'beasts and birds'. **229 (C 162)** *Kynde* **B**: adapted to the spelling of W from α *kende*, which may be a pun and reflect the spelling of Bx (explaining loss of the noun in β by haplography).

164 scans as Type IIIa, cognatively on |g| / |k|. It is also possible that the stave-sound was |w|, if *goed* was a Cx ⇒ for **wele* or if the a-half phrase shows ↔ from the less conventional order **of wykke and of goed* in Cx.

B 232–65 232 scans either as Type Ib with mute key-stave (*his*) and a strong trisyllabic pre-final dip, or Type Ie with enriched fifth lift. **B 240 (C 174–6)** Bx scans as Type IIIa on |m| with a five-syllable prelude-dip, but would read more smoothly with *he* for *þe pecok* (revised // **C** has a pronoun *þey*). **245** *taille* 'tally' (MED s.v. *taille* n. 3 (e)); the presumed Bx reading (< R = α, L = β) altered by M to that of γ, which F has independently varied. The homœograph *tail* and the influence of the dominant usage will have induced the variation; but it is better to keep the spelling distinct from the word for 'tail' (241, 248), while recognising that a punning figurative sense 'the end [of the rich]' is being evoked alongside the literal reference to their 'account' with God. The line scans as Type IIa or cognatively on |d| / |t| as Type Ic. **251–52** do not need re-division purely on grounds of metre, since 252 will scan as Type Ia (with caesura after *ere*). However, the final lift of 251 belongs syntactically with 252, *I leue* here being the main verb of the whole sentence, not parenthetic as at B 222 or semi-parenthetic as at C 166. In 251 *wille* thus requires the disyllabic oblique-case form attested in L, while in 252 the caesura may fall after *be*, giving a b-verse of near-minimal length (the w-intrusion *chiteryng* shows a scribe 'completing' a b-half judged too short) or after *ere* (resembling a 'longer' b-verse like 239). The rich man's *ledene* is being compared to the magpie's, which is *foul* like the peacock's (13.172). **255** is syntactically dependent on *leue* 254, *enuenymed* being the past participle with *shal be* understood. The γ reading, from which M shows ⊗, sits less well with 254, vouchsafing what the latter only supposes. It will have been induced through failure to grasp (as Cr does) the elliptical construction noted above, or else γ may be a wrong resolution of a β participle ending in *-yt*. **258** *witnesse(s)*: either reading could be original, that of βF being analysable as either sg. noun or present-tense verb. If the former, it recalls C 13.9; if the latter, Pr 120, with *and* in adversative sense (MED s.v. 4). **265** The Bx line scans with theme-stave

|t|, assuming pronunciation *Aristótle*, cognative semi-counterpoint in the a-half (on |g| |k|), and a 'supplemental' theme-stave in the b-half. In its other appearances, the Philosopher's name is stressed on the initial vowel (e.g. C 193 below); but a shifted stress here is plausible, since *Áristótle* is established as the standard pronunciation in Chaucerian verse (*CT* I 295). This makes the line formally an extended Type IIIb, and emendation (*K–D Sch*[1]) becomes unnecessary.

195 (B 270) *weyes*: either 'ways' or a spelling-variant of *wyes* 'men' (with a pun on the latter). The words were virtual homophones for **L** and wordplay is to be expected here (cf. note on 156 // above). *wenen*: presumably a revision of the conjectured **B** original, for which *wissen* (which gives no sense) appears a Bx ⇒ induced by its preceding occurrence, with *vs* as subsequential smoothing. Cr[3] must be a felicitous guess, not a ⊗ from **C**. The form **wisshen* might have involved a play on *wissen* if *ss* had a sound like |ʃ| in **L**'s idiolect, as their frequent metrical allophony implies (see *Intro.* IV § 46). **198** *R–K* adopt t's reading (shared by GK), which is that of **B**; but while the majority variant may be anticipating 199a, *here bokes* is more likely to be by ⊗ from **B** and could well have been eliminated in **C** to avoid repeating 196b and to retain the rhetorical *repetitio* (*tho clerkes* 198 / *thise clerkes* 199) for its more pointed contrastive function in 198 / 99 (pagan: Christian). **200** From 201 **H²** *is defective until* 16.23 and **t** is represented only by TCh. **203 (B 278)** The **C** line scans as a 'licensed' anomalous macaronic *aax / bb*, unless the verb and adverb have been transposed in Cx from the order preserved in Bx, which is a correct macaronic Type IIb with a liaisonal stave on *vix_iustus*. **204** may scan vocalically as Type Ia with a mute key-stave *and* or as Type IIIa on *s*. **207 (B 282)** *Ac*: *For* β is preferred by Burrow 1993 on interpretative grounds; but the clear support of **C** for α makes this improbable as an original **B** reading. There is no contrast between *For* and *Ac* at B 284 (C 209), rather two senses of *Ac*, '(But) now' and 'However' (see *Commentary* further). **209 (B 284)** *trauersede*: identical in meaning with *transuersede*, a spelling variant; both first instanced here and possibly introduced by L. **211 (B 286)** *wolde*: the likely reading of Cx, implying the sense made explicit in **B**. The t insertion *leue*, accepted by *Pe*, is a characteristic attempt to fill out an elliptical phrase deemed incomplete (cf. on 13.7 above). *R–K* insert *amende* from **B**; but simple *wolde* fits in context with **L**'s stress on the paramount importance of the voluntary power, and is filled out by *wille* in the b-half. **213 (B 288)** The text is secure in both versions and its meaning, though not straightforward, is not in doubt: that if one's (moral) 'fidelity' (*treuthe*) produces a just way of life, it may be deemed in effect faith in the 'true' religion (*fides implicita*). Rejecting the possibility of sense in the archetypal lines, *K–D* emend to *And* *wheþer it worþ [of truþe] or noȝt, [þe] worþ [of] bileue is gret.* This is textually unnecessary, as there is no reason to believe **L** would have left unrevised a major reading that was scribally corrupted, and it is metrically unsound (in giving the line a masculine ending). The emendation is nonetheless sturdily and acutely argued for by Whatley (1984²); but its claim that 'the intrinsic value of faith is great, whether it actually comes to be faith in the true religion or not' would necessarily commit **L** to maintaining the value of *any* religious belief, provided it is sincerely held (and this can hardly have been his purpose in focussing on Trajan). The emendation is relinquished by *R–K* with a silence that is understandable.

B 290–5 The Bx order *eternam vitam* obscures the riddle concealed in the Latin name for God, DEVS: *dans eternam vitam suis* 'giving eternal life to his own' (see *Commentary*). **B 295 (C 217)** *myd* **B**: not strictly necessary for the metre, since the line could be of Type IIa and is revised to scan on *w*; but as the new word *þerwith* in **C** bears stress on the prepositional suffix, *myd* in **B** is likely to have borne it as well.

Passus XV (B XIII)

Collation The **B** mss remain intact until XIX but both families of **C** mss have gaps. In particular, *x¹* has lost I of y, *x²* has lost H² of t, and **p** has lost K, which ends at 66, leaving *p²* represented only by GN (and for 15.288–16.40 by N alone).

2 *fay*: from the context probably the original in **B** too, ms B having doubtless corrected from **C** a reading found meaningless. If R's *fere* represents α it may be, like β *fre*, an attempt to make sense of a Bx form **fer*, a postulated miscopying of the exemplar's *fei*. The meaning here could be 'unfortunate, ill-fortuned' or even 'stricken' (MED s.v. *fei(e* adj. 3(a), (b)), given the immediate context (line 5). But the predominant sense is rather 'doomed to die' (MED s.v. 1(a)), since it is Will's thoughts of his coming end and subsequent fate that overshadow 11–15. In its only other appearance, at 16.195 (no //), the word has the related sense 1(b) 'dead' (so in comparing himself to a *mendenaunt* (3), Will appears as one destitute of earth's supports (5) and thus as incipiently dead to the world), or it may imply '(afflicted) with (a sense of) my life running out'. **6–8 (B 6)** The revised C 6 scans on |m|, unless auxiliary and infinitive in the b-half have undergone ↔ to prose order in Cx. The t variant yields a line that will scan as a T-type, but appears a re-writing after failure to grasp the parenthetical character of the conditional clause ('even if I should happen to live long') and the dependence of the elliptical *leue* 'that he would leave' upon *manaced*. The sense of *me byhynde* (7) is presumably itself elliptical, i.e. 'abandon, cast aside [my youthful state]' 'disregard me' (see MED s.v. *bihinde(n* adv. &

pred. adj., 3(h)). MED s.v. cites the present example as the first transitive use of 'vanish' (*vanishen* v. 4 (a) 'cause to disappear') but gives no other before the mid-C15th. This may be correct, or else a further ellipsis should be presumed for *vanschen* ('and [threatened me, that] all my virtues...would vanish'). *fayre lotes* 'attractive manners', as in *SGGK* 1116, cited in MED s.v. *lot(e* n. 1(a). The **p** variant *lockes* is a further corruption of the exemplar's presumed near-synonymous *lokes* (so instanced in D), the result of *t / c* confusion and possible memorial anticipation of a later passage involving Elde (22.183–84 //). **10 (B 8)** *peple*: the key-stave being clearly *pris*, the line requires a first stave on |p|. On the showing of **C**, *peple* may be securely adopted for **B** and Bx seen as ⇒ of a non-alliterating synonym through unconscious parallelism with 7b. **12 (B 10)** *byquath*: natural in this context of successive past-tense verbs, with *blqueþe* **B** presumably a spelling-variant of the preterite also attested in *p¹*. **17 (B 14)** scans either vocalically as a T-type with a mute key-stave (*in*) or (less probably) as a Type IIIb on cognative voiced and unvoiced dental stops, with the first found liaisonally (*þat_Ymaginatyf*).

B 14–20 These β lines show as authentic intrinsically and on comparison with **C**, with no mechanical reason for their loss from α unless eyskip from *Ymaginatyf* 14 → 19.

21 scans vocalically as Type Ia unless |m| is the key-stave in *Ymáginatif*, giving a Type IIIa line; the name is not stressed elsewhere on the second syllable (see *TN* on 14.1). **22–3** Both macaronic lines may be analysed as scanning normally, the second as Type IIIa, the first not as *aa / bb* but as Type Ia, with the stave-sound |dʒ| and a monolexical final lift (*iudicii*). They appear as a single line scanning *aaa / bb* in RMQS (so *R–K*), excessively unwieldy and unlikely to represent *p¹* (and thence **p**). **30 (B 25)** The revised **C** line scans as Type Ia on |m| and the **B** line could be a Type IIIa on either |m|, with two lifts in *máistèr* or on vowels, with *he* as key-stave and *I* as stave one (for a possible trisyllabic pronounciation of *maister* here cf. on 14. 46 //). Another possibility is **merkede] seiȝ*, as conjectured at B 6.325. **31 (B 27)** On the showing of **B** and the repetition of virtually the whole line at 37, the *x²* reading may be judged secure, and *x¹* to have lost *wel and* by eyeskip from *wel → wel-* (as have QZGK). The line, scanned preferably as Type Ie to facilitate the play on *wel* (1, 2) shows the second verb to have had shifting stress. **34** *Ilyk x¹*: either the adjective meaning 'like, resembling' (MED s.v. *ilich* adj.1(a)), and thus the same in sense as *pT Ylike to* (cf. 1.87 //) or else the adverb 'likewise' (MED s.v. *iliche* adv. 1(c)), the sense illustrated at B 1.50 If the latter is accepted, and *ȝent* at 132 read as 'yond', Piers is to be understood as present and to be the referent of *him* 37 and the implied subject of the Ø-relative clause *Crauede and cryede* (Kane 1994:16). This reading failed to satisfy the scribe of x^2, who made the adjectival sense explicit by adding *to*; but it explains why Piers speaks at 139 without having been earlier introduced. The half-line *Conscience knewe him wel* (37) may then be seen as dramatising, in an act of recognition, Conscience's assertion at B 13.131b, which echoes *Piers*'s own earlier claim to acquaintance with the latter in B 7.134 and reliance on his 'counsel' in C 8.13. **40 (B 34)** The Bx line will scan as standard (like C 43b) with the caesura before *and*, Patience being the subject of the verb. But arguably *Pacience* has come in too soon by anticipation of line 35, which makes clear that he is not seated at the high table. **41 (B 35)** Agreement of Bx and x^1**p** is decisive. The adverb *prestly* (so *PeR–K*) has a kind of contextual appropriateness (Conscience *knowing* that Will needs Patience as a companion); but there is no reason for its loss and every reason for seeing it as a typical t intrusion to normalise the scansion. The line is either Type Ie with a cognative key-stave |b| or, preferably, Type IIIa, with caesura after *Y*. **51a (B 45a)** *effuderitis*: the grammatically incorrect (probable) Bx form altered in the γ sub-group g and then (visibly) in two unrelated copies Hm and M. **52** *was as*: reconstructed as the original from which the verb is postulated lost by haplography (assisted by the unexpectedness of the construction, which lacks a pronoun subject). The presumed **x** form is ungrammatical; I's *was* is grammatical but gives poor sense (who should advise Reason?) while **p** (which has the right sense) must be a scribal smoothing, as it is too simple to have given rise to the reading of **x**. **57 (B 49)** *Dia*: almost certainly the archetypal form in both versions, though C-**p**, some **x** mss and a group of **B** mss have officiously corrected to the form of the Latin adverb *Diu* what was doubtless a deliberate pun on the semi-naturalised English word for 'drug' found at 22.174 //. **L**'s image is that of perseverance as the 'medicinal potion' that sustains the constant exercise of a virtue. **61–1a (B 52–6a)** The C lines are shorter and simpler but still suffer from the difficulties scribes experienced in copying text with enclosed or appended Latin. Thus only one **C** ms (Ch) has a lineation that allows 61 to be scanned as a macaronic, while leaving the rest of the quotation free-standing, though D may also bear such an interpretation. Neither **B** family manages this, ?β dividing as in Cx and α rendering 56 unmetrical but treating the whole psalm-phrase as an appended quotation. Emendation here, as in **C**, is thus effectively conjectural. In B 52–4 re-ordering follows *K–D* in finding inconsequential the Bx order of the statements in 52 and 53 (*ooper mete* presupposes that one course has already been served). The ↔ presumably occurred because both lines' first lift contained the verb-phrase *he brouȝte vs*. This is a reason for not dropping it from the text (as do *K–D*), since to have caused the mislineation diagnosed it must have been in Bx's exemplar (even if, arguably, not in the original).

The present 21-syllable macaronic line, with its seven-syllable prelude dip, is one of the the longest in the poem, but is metrically a standard Type Ia. The following line, divided after *dissh*, is completely unmetrical in Bx, a macaronic with the English in the b-half (a feature that elsewhere occurs only in macaronic lines of correct metrical structure, as at B 139). As re-divided (again after *K–D*), 53a now forms with the second half of the Latin phrase quoted an 'appended' line closely similar to 56a (// C 61a). This enables 54 to scan as a perfect T-type macaronic, with the caesura after *Dixi* and the b-staves on *Confitébor* and *tíbi*. **63 (58a)** The macaronic **C** line scans cognatively on |t| / |d| as Type IIIa (-*tritum, Déus*), as could // **B**, which may nevertheless be treated as a normal citation-line of appended Latin. **68 (B 63)** The Bx line can theoretically be scanned, but in practice the dip before the key-stave (*with*) is excessively long, with two syllables before and another five after the caesura. Most probably Bx inverted participle and adverbial phrase to prose order; ↔ produces a b-half with a mute stave on the preposition and the two important lexical words as fully-stressed blank staves. **71–2** The past conditional *soffrede* 'would have to suffer' followed by the present *coueyte* is harder than the smoothed form of **p**. **72** *eny kyne* **x**: on the face of it illogical, **p**'s *heuene* presumably being an attempt to improve the logic, and *kyne* then requiring the further smoothing evinced in the unrelated <PE>, M and N. But for **L** *ioye* means '(one of) the joy(s) of heaven' (MED s.v. *joi(e* n. 2(a)) more often than 'a feeling of happiness or pleasure' (ibid., 1(a): the two senses are effectively contrasted in the identical-rhyming B 7.36–7). Here the phrase will thus signify 'any of the joys of / any kind of happiness in heaven'. **73** *how þat...what*: smoothed in *R–K* by omitting *what, he*; but the anacoluthic expression may be original. **80–3** The various mislineations here, with addition of a spurious half-line in **p**, will be due to erroneous division of 80/81 consequent upon mislocating the caesura. The only satisfactory division is in UD (<x^1) and t, presumably an accurate reflex of x^2; while **p** (also descended from x^2) goes astray only at 82, once again after mislocating the caesura in a line structurally similar to 80. **81** Cx seems to have read *diuerse*, a rare form recorded only here in C14 (see MED s.v. *diverse* adv.) and this is more likely than *diuersely* P^2D^2PQWS to be original. **88–9 (B 79–80)** present a major crux in both versions, requiring separate solutions that leave some difficulties unexplained. In **C**, choice between x^1 and x^2 (= **p**t) is unproblematic, since *compacience* is a reading so hard that it could hardly be scribal in origin. The metaphorical sense 'compassion, sympathy' is here first instanced, though not cited by MED s.v. *compacience* n. (quoting Trevisa from the C14th only for the literal sense of 'sympathy' between physical organs). The x^2 reading may thus be diagnosed as a scribal attempt to clarify an expression found obscure, with subsequential smoothing of *and* in 89 to *he*. D, by erasing *com-* but without adding *to*, may have adopted it after comparison with a t or **p** source. Since the rejected x^2 reading is actually identical with that of Bx, it might seem better by the *durior lectio* criterion to diagnose the identical corruption in Bx and adopt the **C** reading for the presumed original of **B**, as do *K–D*. However, x^2 could here have coincided with Bx (or been influenced by it) but Bx itself attest a **B** reading (acceptable in itself) revised in **C** to the form attested by x^1 as probably original. The unusual contextual use as intransitive of the normally transitive verb is here presumably elliptical for *preueþ* [*pite* understood], the verb meaning 'demonstrate' (MED s.v. *preven* v. 9(a)), as in revised **C** (cf. the sense in the conjectural emendation at B 85 below). This Bx reading (as preserved in α), which now appears hard enough to be original and to have prompted revision to **C**'s syntactically more explicit (if lexically harder) form, may thus be accepted and the same punctuation adopted for **B** as for **C**.

B 82–6 82 (C 92) *þis ilke doctour bifore*: reconstructed as the original form of **B**, the Bx ↔ to prose order involving loss of the required key-stave (*dóctoúr* with two lifts is excluded as giving a masculine ending). **85 (C 94)** *preue*: conjectured as the required first stave in the a-half. In principle the Bx line could scan as Type IIIa with a four-syllable prelude-dip; but the verb *telle* seems weak in context, since what Will requires is for the Doctor to 'give a practical demonstration' that 'shows by example the truth' *of which he preched raþer*, not more *prechyng*. These are two senses of *preuen*, and a play on them here seems quite likely (see MED s.v. v. 9 (a) and (b), and for the association of *preue* and *preche*, 5.141 //, B 4.122). **86 (C 95)** *preynte*: the required key-stave, conjectured as having been in Bx but replaced in β by its non-alliterating synonym and in α by a word (*bad*) that alliterates cognatively but could not have generated *wynked*. The rare *prinken* is cited in MED from only two other C14th sources, recurring as a stave in a line with an identical final lift (122 // below), and in 20.19 //. **98** The construction is elliptical, *he shal* being understood (and accordingly inserted by N^2); *R–K*'s reconstruction after **B** is otiose. **104 (B 95)** *forel*: on the showing of **C** and the contextual reference to a book (*leef* 105 //) presumed the original in **B**, for which Bx substituted (or misread) perhaps under inducement from preceding references to food (a *fraiel* was a basket, especially for fruit; see MED s.v.). In its other appearance, *forellis* probably means 'boxes' (A 9.159 // B 10.213 *forceres* 'caskets'). But the sense here may be the 'bound volume' itself rather than its metonym 'a box for books', as in *ms* 1586, where the sense 'book' rather than 'book-cover' [Barr] is more appropriate. **105 (B 96)** *leef*: contextually the most appropriate word (cf. VI 209) which, especially in the variant-

spelling with voiced fricative *leue*, puns homophonically with *leue* in the b-half. *B*-g's ambiguous shape has been corrected in <OC^2>Cot either independently on grounds of commonsense or by reference to a C-Text. The readings of the other mss in this group suggest that g read *lyue* as does w, the other member of γ, and this could have been a visual error for Bx *lyne*, the reading preserved in LM (?< β) and α. That *lyue* was a variant of *leef* encountered in the *PP* tradition is suggested by the occurrence of the converse error at C 3.490, where Cx (doubtless under influence from *leues* at the *lyne ende*) apparently read *leef* for required *lyne* (see on // **B**). **106 (B 97)** *take*: 'take on, engage with', a metaphorical application of the sense classed under MED *taken* v. 5(a) 'make an attack'. The reading *talke* is weak here in conjunction with *appose* 'confront / dispute with' (MED s.v. *apposen* v. 1(a), (b)) and is unlikely to preserve x^2, despite its attestation in I, since Ch reads *take*, which is harder and therefore more likely to be the group reading of t (< x^2). The **p** ms E and the x^1 mss D and D^2 substitute independently the reading of the other family, presumably through contrasting judgements as to the appropriateness of the exemplar's reading. In the Bx tradition, α may have read as R, but F's re-writing, which substitutes the b-half's *aposen* and for the latter reads *pyttyn to* may reflect an α *take* for which *talke* could be a ⇒ in R (as in <OC^2>'s ancestor). The relatively unusual sense of *take* here involves wordplay with *take* at 103//. **107 (B 98)** *Dobest*: preferred for **C** on the showing of **B**; four individual mss and the source q correct independently, doubtless through identifying the Triad. **109 (B 100)** *rodded*: here taken as a revision of *rubbede* **B**, either a past participle (with redundant final -*e*) as in **C** or a preterite (necessitating insertion of a comma after *rose*). Though the revision is an improvement, this does not in itself call in question *rubbede* (as in *K–DSch*^{1}). *B*-Hm may thus be seen as prompted by antecedent *rody* in the a-half or as a ⊗ from a **C** copy, F as a further re-writing on the same basis. The passage running from 96–111 shows several signs of detailed revision (98b, 107b, 108a, 111b) and this may be an instance of a slightly larger one. It remains possible, however, that Bx under the influence of a sequence of preterites found the unusual *rodded* lexically difficult (see MED s.v. *ruden*, citing also *SGGK* 1695 for the p.p.) and replaced it with the simpler preterite *rubbede* (as did *C*-W). **114 (B 105)** scans on |n|, the first two staves in **B** being probably liaisonal (*noon_yuel*; *þyn_euen*-). **116–17 (B 106)** The Bx line scans as Type IIa with a liaisonal stave in *quod_I*, and there is no need to see *Dowel* as having undergone ↔ from key-stave position. Revised *saide* Y 116 and final *Dowel* 117 support both the stave-status of *quod_I* and the position of the object in the common source of BxB^1. *nouhte*: *nouthe* in three x^1 copies YIU and *now* in P^2N^2, which could be a reflex of *nouthe* y. This reading adopted by *R–K* requires *passen*117 to mean 'transgress' (MED s.v.10 (d)), whereas *nouhte* presupposes the sense 'surpass' (ib. 11a (a), as at A 12.4 or 'do' (13 (d)), the tone being sarcastic. In favour of 'not' is the presence of *noȝt* in B 106; *nouthe* may then be accounted for as a spelling error due to *ȝ / þ* confusion. **118** Y reads *louyeth* or *leuyeth* (so *R–K*) and arguably 'live' is better in context, since the Doctor's definition of Dowel at 114–15 has not mentioned 'love' as such; but positive charity seems to be implied by the quotation at 118*a*. **120 (B 110)** *But þat Dowel wol*: reconstructed as the presumed Cx reading from what appear to be the split variants *Bote dowel* in *x²* and *That dowel wol* in *x¹*. **123 (B 114)** **C** revises to Type Ie a line of Type IIa form, with normal stress shifted in the phrase *Sire doctour* in order not to mute the third stave (something **L** avoids in this position). *R–K*'s adoption of the **B** reading is thus ill-advised. **126–28 (B 116–18)** The scansion of the three **C** lines is as Type Ic (with cognative third stave on |t|), Ia (cognative key-stave on |d|), and either Ia (with cognative second stave on |t| and liaisonal third stave on *halde_hit*) or, alternatively, vocalic Type III with *halde* as key-stave and counterpoint on *d / t*. In 127 the preferred order is that of **p**, here probably representing *x²* (t having varied with *x¹* under inducement from the prose order in 128b); this provides a key-stave (*Dobet*) where *x¹*t have none (scansion of the line as Type II with *to* as second stave would seem unduly forced here). However, the indefinite article is retained from *x¹* as unlikely to be a scribal intrusion. Of the // **B** lines, 117 may be a Type Ia with a cognative first stave on |d|, although the caesura could come after *trauailleþ* and the line scan on |t| with a six-syllable prelude dip paralleling the five-syllable dip of following 118, which scans unambiguously on |s|. The latter two scansions produce lines that are not wholly satisfactory in their de-stressing of the second and third terms respectively of the triad. It may be therefore that in 118 *seiþ* is a Bx ⇒ for *techeth* intended to avoid repeating a verb that *actually* appeared in all three b-halves in succession, as in **C**. In that case 118 would also scan cognatively, with |t| in key-position. **129 (B 119)** *carpe* **C**: revising to an imperative what in **B** is an interrogative (with pronoun omitted), so emendation is unnecessary (as in *K–D Sch¹*). Cot could be an aural error or by ⊗ from **C**.

B 121 *hym*: preferred as giving better sense and as the probable reading of Bx, from α (> R) and β (> L, M). The γF variant *hem* reflects failure to grasp that the Seven Arts teach others (here Life, the referent of *hym*), not themselves.

132 (B 124) Despite its agreement with **B**, **p**'s reading *plouhman* (to which Ch and N² have varied, the latter probably by ⊗) is likely to be a scribal ⇒. The phrase *palmare ȝent* would have been found difficult because Piers has not been named as a palmer, and an epithet *ȝent*

(see MED s.v. *gent* adj. 1(a) 'noble') would have seemed unexpected in sense and spelling. Since the pronunciation (< Fr *gent*) must be with |dʒ|, *ȝent* would presumably then have been a Cx error for an original with *g*. However, Kane (1994:16) convincingly interprets it as a spelling variant of *yond* adv. 'over there' (P²'s re-spelling of the word). Thus *ȝet* YuT [correcting App. 'DTH²'] may be interpreted as a puzzled scribal response to an unusual spelling found, e.g., in the Harleian *King Horn* 68/1181 cited by MED s.v. *yond* adv. (d). The reading is to be taken with Kane's understanding of *Ilyk* at 34 as an adverb 'likewise' (OED s.v. *Ylike* adv., MED s.v. *iliche* adv.1 (c)), the required sense being found in B 1.50, where HmR omit final *-e*. This interpretation fits well with Piers' having been invited to join the company at dinner (37), so that his speech at 139–49 is now prepared for, and not wholly unexpected (see on 34).

B 128–39 128 scans unambiguously with a cognative key-stave on |t|. **136** *by*: conjectured to supply a cognative key-stave lost by *þo > < so* attraction. Bx would need to stress *displese hym* as third and fourth lifts, producing an unacceptable masculine ending. **139** scans as Type Ia with a cognative key-stave *tauȝte* (|d| |d| / |t|). **142–45 (B 137–46)** If the **p** form shows in 143 its characteristic padding after re-division and the other **x** mss' divergent mislineations variously result from judging 142 too short (XIP²D² divide 142–45 after *helpe, heued*, Dt treat 142–43 as a single line), Y's apparently correct lineation is likely to be by direct descent from *x¹* (< Cx). What seems secure is that Y's 142 corresponds closely with the form of B 137, now scanning as Type Ib but with *Deum* replacing *inimicos* (and the latter being translated in C 143a). **144** allows two alternative scansions, as Type Ie on |k| or as Type Ia on vowels, the first being preferable in treating *kynde* as (in context more appropriately) adjectival. **145 (B 146)** is Type IIa with a 'supplemental' *w* stave in both versions (cf. *Intro.* IV § 44); *with*, lost in eight **C** mss and replaced by a non-alliterating synonym in two, is metrically essential. **148 (B 147)** scans in the b-half with a normal feminine ending, as is clear if *lauhe on* is read with sounded final *-e* followed by an initial glottal stop. **154** *And*: possibly an intelligent **p** correction of an obvious error in *x²* (shared with *x¹* and thus presumably < Cx). **156** *to*: elliptical for 'to [that enterprise]', wrongly omitted by *x²* through being seen as redundant because connected with *wynnen*, a prolative infinitive dependent on *wolde*. **158** scans on *w* as a Type IIIa, t's *þe wy* for *he* (adopted by *R–K*) being a scribal attempt to adapt the less common pattern to the normative one. **162 (B 153)** The **C** revision confirms that Bx will have read *bere...aboute*, indicating that the **B** variants *abounte* and *a beaute* are mistaken scribal attempts to produce a grammatical object for the verb *bere*. That object is clearly *Dowel*; the referent of *þerinne* could be the pregnant Latin phrase of 152b (on which see *Commentary*) but is more probably the *loue* of 147, 151. *K–D*'s bold conjecture *bouste* 'box', here specifically the pyx (MED s.v. *boist(e* n.1(a)), accepted by *Sch*¹, is now rejected on grounds of contextual meaning. Patience is not in holy orders, and only a priest would be authorised to bear the Host. The revised C 164 endorses this reading decisively, since it implies that *anyone* is potentially able to carry *this abouten hym*. Here the antecedent is explicitly *pacience* (161) and the gloss *caritas* (166a), as in **B** (which deliberately leaves the former obscure as part of the riddle).

B 158 *se if*: reconstructed from L and α as the probable reading of Bx, and one of two cases where L has been visibly altered, perhaps by collation with a γ source such as W (the other is 10.271, where the original L reading is clearly an error). In the absence of // **C** it is uncertain whether *deme* is to be interpreted as a more emphatic and explicit ⇒ for *se*, or *se* as a ⇒ of the contextually more obvious verb. The reconstruction presumes the former but retains *if* against α *wher*, here virtually a synonym.

165 (B 162) *Ne nopere*: here judged the Cx source of the split variants *Ne* **x** and *neiþer* **p**. The reading is actually attested by D, perhaps correcting by reference to a **p** source, and is that of **B**. *Ne* will have been lost from **p** by assimilation to following *neiþer* and *neuere* **x** induced by aural confusion (possibly being an idiolectal homophone of *neþer) or visually from *neuere* 164a.

B 165–72a may have been lost from β through eye-skip from the Latin quotation 164a to that at 172a without noticing that they were different. **167–68 (C168–69)** Re-division of the (presumed) Bx lines after *þee* in the light of **C** is preferable in order to prevent the object-pronoun being isolated with its complement *Maister* in 168. The order of verb and pronoun in F is **C**'s, but gives the b-half an awkward five-syllable pre-final dip. The rhythm would be better with *ne* omitted, as was permissible after this 'preclusive' *þat*; but R needs no emendation. **170** The revised C 170 supports the authenticity of R's line, which is required by the syntax and will have been lost from F through misconstruing the sense of *and*169 as 'if' (MED s.v. 5 (a)), with subsequent smoothing in 171. **171** is a Type Ie line that scans on |ð| as theme-stave (*þee, þei, þee*) with |ȝ| as contrapuntal stave (*ȝyue, yemere*). **172** is lost from F but original, leaving an echo in C 171b. **174 (B 175)** *parfourme* **C**: judged also the probable **B** reading for which non-alliterating Bx *conformen* (attested in this sense at B 209) will be a ⇒ under aural inducement from preceding *Kan* (see MED s.v. *conformen* v. 4 (b) and *performen* v. 4).

B 196 scans as a 'quasi-macaronic' of irregular structure (see Schmidt 1987:100). **B 203** The β reading may be discriminated as *take conge to*, 'offer [his] farewell to', with *take* here meaning 'give' (MED s.v. *taken* v. 31a). The construction usually had *of* before the indirect

object and this is substituted by two members of w, one of g, and M. The α reading is uncertain and was either *and* R or Ø, the latter possibly the reading of Bx also, since it is substantively equivalent to that of β.

191 (B 221) The b-half of **C** is revised to give a T-type line and so does not direct choice for **B** as between α and β. Bx may have read Ø for *and* / *þei*. **193 (B 223)** *hym* (2): the Ø-reading of *B*-γ agrees with **C** which, however, appears to have shortened the whole line by omission of the adverb as well as of the pronoun (it seems that Bx read *hem telle*, with the pl. pronoun obviously redundant before *To Conscience* 224). The CrF removal of *hem* could have been an independent commonsense alteration (as with M, which erases); but F may well show ⊗ from **C**, since it also omits *first*. **200** *and*: possibly Ø in y, to judge by the four discrete variants. **208 (B 233)** *iogele*: preferred on grounds of sense for both versions. The word is first instanced here and is rare, whereas *iang(e) le* (only randomly attested in the Cx tradition) was not and will have come in by visual error aided by unconscious suggestion from its common collocation with *iape* (as at 2.99 //). **209 (B 234)** *sautrien* **C**: here taken as a revision of **B** *saute*, a near-synonym of *saille* (lexically as rare as *sautrien*). The latter has doubtless come into *B*-C (and into F with alteration of word-order) by ⊗ from **C**. **211 (B 236)** *furste to brynge*: to be judged the archetypal reading, preserved ($< x^2$) in the t form, of which x^1 and **p** present split variants. On the agreement of t and **p**, *brynge* will have been in x^2 and, on the showing of **B**, in Cx. **212** *vppon*: reconstructed in **C** as the form providing the required key-stave (here mute). Its rarity in temporal phrases would account for loss of the first syllable (but cf. a similar emendation in a purely locative phrase at B 10.307, and on C 5.159). *parsche*: preferred in the light of B 237–8 to *parscheprest* (which *R–K* read), *prest* having come in from 214. **213** *one*: either added by **p** or (as here judged) lost from T, to coincide with x^1 (it is in Ch). The line scans as Type Ic; the rejected form is either Type Ib (but with the caesura coming between the first and second of the two main lexical verbs) or Type IIa. **220 (B 253)** *but*: conjectured in **C** as the necessary first-stave lost in Cx through syntactical inducement from the construction *founde Y þat* or through ⇒ of *þat*. In principle, the line could scan vocalically on grammatical words, as B 253 probably does; but stress on these fulfils no useful semantic function. The important words are *blessynge* and *bulle*, which take up key elements from B 250, a line also drawn upon here, and so it seems justified to regard the **C** line as intended to scan on |b|. *R–K*'s major reconstruction of the b-half after B 250 is without warrant. **221 (B 254)** *luythere eir*: on grounds of sense the only acceptable reading, as papal blessings and bulls could not be expected to stop the activities of the wicked. The word *eir* has been lost by haplography after *this luyth*ere, which has been inattentively read in **x** as 'these evil men'. I spells this out but P²'s *morein* reflects its consultation of a **p**-copy. The // **B** line, which scans as Type IIIa on |l|, needs no emending, and the unidiomatic *K–D* conjecture *me thynkeþ* for *I bileue* is gratuitous. **226 (B 255)** is presumed a single line, the two-line forms being scribal products with characteristic padding in the b-verse (Bx, C-**p**). It seems likely on the showing of Y (< *x¹*) and t (< *x²*) that Cx preserved the line correctly and that I simply has a filled-out form of the misdivided y text (D² reveals consultation of a **p** copy). In Bx, the first of the two lines scans either *ax / ax* or *abb / aa*, the second *xa / ax*, the latter's b-half revealed as unoriginal on comparison with **C**. Bx *hymself* may be a scribal intrusion, as it is the only element differing from the smoother **C**, in which *Peter* is unmuted. F's omission may be due to ⊗ from **C** and is unlikely to preserve α. **231a–33** For a parallel, see B 14.75–6*a*.

B 270–460 Substantive notes on these lines that involve *direct comparison* with **C** are given under C 6.30–7.118*a*. Lines *unique* to **B** and problems separable from the // **C**-Text are considered here, as are some already discussed in part under **C**. **270** *þritty*: the correct reading, preserved in L from β and in R from α. M seems to have corrected its error from knowledge of the true date, not by reference to an L-type source; but while metrically acceptable, its reading is unlikely to be that of Bx. **271** scans formally on |w| as Type Ia, but both staves two and three are mute, and the blank staves (*gésene; Chíchestre*) alliterate in cognative counterpoint (*a[a]b / [a]bx*). **276** scans either as Type Ia or as Type Id, placing the caesura after *plot* (2) and regarding *vnbúxom* and *spéche* as cognative and internal staves respectively (the latter scansion avoids an ungainly pre-final dip containing a major lexical word). **283** The loss of 283b–284a in wg and M is almost certainly a γ error that coincidentally occurred in M, as a consequence of eyeskip from *hymself* 283 to *hymself* 284. The retention of both half-lines in L points to their presence in β; α confirms their archetypal character and (slightly revised) // **C** their originality. **293–99** are attested in α alone and no mechanical reason for their loss from β appears. That they were present in B¹ is shown by their appearance in C VI; but α must have them from Bx and not by ⊗ from C 6.42–7, which extensively revise. **299** *loos*: required for the sense and given here in the spelling found at B 11.295 and 13.449 (in the phrase *good loos*), which indicates a long vowel (see MED s.v. *los* n. (2), here in sense 2 (b) 'praise'). The correct form is obscured by R's ambiguous spelling, one nonetheless attested for this word, that may indicate a variant pronunciation with short vowel (cf. conversely the spelling *loos* for 'loss' at C 6.275). F's sophisticated re-writing appears to reflect α *loos* in *looþ*. **300** *go*: conjectured as the required key-stave, the lexical main words of the a-half scanning on |g|,

as does revised C 6.47. Loss of *go* will presumably have been by homoarchy after go*mes*. The line may be read as Type Ia or as a T-type with cognative b-staves (|t| |d|); scansion as Type Ie on vowels would place the stresses on *he* twice (or on *he, if*), whereas the sense requires that they fall on the verbs. **302** *on*: more probably lost through haplography (*ly* on) in α than added in β. **323** *lakkynge* α: in context more aptly specifying the cause of discord. **326 (C VI 70)** *to...it*: reconstructed after **C** to provide the key-stave omitted through Bx ↔ of verb and indirect object to prose order, with loss of the preposition. **330–31 (C VI 74–5)** On the showing of // **C**, the Bx lines may be securely re-divided so as to keep the adverb with its verb and prevent a metrically clumsy and semantically pointless prelude-dip in 331. The misdivision may have occurred under inducement from the apparent rhythmic parallelism between 330b and 329b preceding. **334 (C VI 77)** *swich*: adopted on the basis of unrevised **C** as the probable **B** original, *taken* here being the same verb appearing at 337 (MED s.v. *taken* v. 13 (a) 'be subjected to, suffer' rather than 14 (a) *taken with* 'submit to'). Possibly Bx read **wich*, with the *s* lost or obscured, and this was preserved in α and thence in R (corrected by F) and in β, whence it came to γ, L and M. The last altered correctly, as did w (or possibly only <WCr>, if Hm originally read *which*); but g and L seem to have taken **wich* as an error for *with* or else confused it visually with the latter. This case is unlikely to be one where w and M have referred to a **C** copy, since the passage occurs in a section of the **C** Version remote from its **B** counterpart. **341** *God ne*: see under C 6.84. **343–45 (C VI 175–78)** The α scribe wrongly rendered *it* 343 (with referent Haukyn's coat) as *I*; this was corrected by F; then α erred again in 344; finally in 345 R corrected the pronoun successfully, though F went astray this time. The initial mistake with *it* 343 could have occurred by a simple visual error (though one perhaps partly induced by the context and by confusion of *I* 342a with the *I* at 343a). **346–47 (C VI 179–80)** Both **B** lines may be T-type, though the first need not be, as is suggested by **C**'s omitting *tyme*. F's similar omission could be mechanical, the result of possible ⊗ from **C** or, less probably, an accurate reflex of α. **355–56** *of pointes his cote / Was colomy*: 'that his coat was grimy with spots of dirt' (MED s.v. *of* prep. 21 'with'). On the evidence of L, β read *his* and M has visibly added *of*, perhaps by reference to a γ-type ms. From R it appears that α also read *his* and F or its exemplar likewise inserted *of*, again through mistaking the construction as *parcey-ued of* and *Was* as a Ø-relative clause, whereas *parcey-ued* introduces a contact-clause with Ø-conjunction (*that* understood). The alteration of *his* to *þis* in w shows the latter diverging further from γ in this instance and has g. **358** scans vocalically as Type Ia or, if *ymágynede* is read here, as Type IIIc on |m| and vowels. **359** scans as an extended Type IIIa with semi-counterpoint on |m| in the a-half. Possibly Bx substituted *wiþ* for original *mid* as key-stave; but emendation is unnecessary and the counter-intuitive *K–D* conjecture *Thoruʒ* for *Wiþ* generates an a-half than cannot be scanned. **361 (C VI 258–59)** On the assumption that C 6.258–59 are a complete revision, *gyle* taking up *bigile* and *glosynge* echoing *wittes*, **B** may be established from the substantive reading underlying R. Thus F's *wit* correctly identifies the noun, R's *whitus* being a (perhaps idiolectal) variant with intrusive aspirate of the substantive *wittes*, the form given in the text. The alternative here rejected is that *whitus* is a back-spelling of *w(e)yhtes*, the substantive reading of revised C 258, for which *C*-ms X gives *whites* (*whit* in Y) and **p** substitutes *wittes*. But in that **C** line *weyhtes* is contextually the aptest and lexically the hardest reading (cf. also 16.128 //), whereas here it would be over-specific, and the more general *wittes* 'cunning devices' (MED s.v. *wit* n. 5, citing Br Pr 156) is also the more appropriate (cf. also *ymagynede* 358; *wit* 363, 366; and 21.453–58, especially the sense of *wit* 453, associated with *gyle* 458). The β reading appears a scribal smoothing after misreading as 'ways' of Bx *weys (a well-attested, possibly authorial spelling-variant of *wyes*). As it stands, the β line lacks an original stave-word (which may be conjectured to have been **w(e)yes*), presumed lost from the b-half through haplography, and yielding the sense 'ways to deceive'. But the evidence from α and **C** points rather to the form reconstructed here as the likeliest reading of **B** (see also 16.128 // B 14.293). **369** scans either as Type Ia on |b| or preferably as Type Ib on vowels with mute key-stave, in either event having both a-half staves on non-lexical monosyllables. **373–74 (C VI 269–70)** Loss of 373b and 374a, which appear authentic on intrinsic grounds and the support of unrevised **C**, will have presumably occurred in α through distraction from *rope(n)* at beginning and end of 374 and visual attraction from *neghebor(e)* to *or*. **376** scans vocalically as Type Ia with muted key-stave or, better, as Type IIIa on |b|. **391** *conscience* α: both (i) 'mind or heart as seat of thought, feeling and desire' (MED s.v. *conscience* n.1) and (ii) 'moral sense, conscience' (ibid. 2(a)), the latter being the dominant meaning in **L** (as at B 15.31–2 //). The β variant, taking up only (i) and scanning *aa / bb*, may result from objection to the use of *conscience* here in sense (ii). **400–09** appear authentic in themselves and on comparison with C 6.424–32, which retain ideas from only 402a (C 427) and 404 (C 428–29). The lines must have been in Bx, since they introduce the theme of Sloth developed in 410ff; their omission from β may have been occasioned by eyeskip from *helpes* 399 to *helpe it* 408, involving loss or subsequential deletion of 409. **407** *worþ*: the inevitable emendation of a metathetic α and possibly Bx error, exactly paralleled in Bx at 11.5; F's ⇒ was presumably suggested by *wende* in

the b-half. **437–54** are retained almost without revision (see on C 7.96–113) and could have been inserted in α at a second stage of **B**, or have been borrowed from **C**. But there is a clear gap in sense between 436 where β ends and 455 where it resumes that seems to rule out the possibility of β's constituting a distinct stage of the poem (see *Intro.* III B §§ 50–4). The passage may therefore be securely presumed lost by β, most probably through eyeskip from *wordes...amonges* (435–36) to *amonges... wordes* 454–55.

C XV cont'd; B XIV begins

B 14.1–28 are omitted in **C**; but for some material parallel to 16–22, see on C 16.25–31*a*. The ***main sequence of parallel text*** resumes at C 15.234.
1 *oon hater*: preferable on grounds of metre and sense, with *hool* best seen as a scribal intrusion. Though *hool* could have been lost from Lα by haplography, it overweights the a-half and introduces the irrelevant notion (perhaps from recollecting 13.314) of Haukyn having other coats, whereas the allegory is concerned only with his one 'coat of Christendom' (13.274). M's exemplar will have derived its reading from a γ ms of w type. **5** allows two alternative scansions, on vowels or on *l*, both giving Type Ia. **7** The grammar of the b-half is defective in βR (= Bx) and F's variant is an attempt to make sense that has led on to complete re-writing of the following line. As reconstructed here, F's (presumably conjectural) *þat* and *me was* are retained to provide the result clause required by the sense, the ↔ providing smoother metre. The precise mechanism of loss of these phrases in Bx is obscure, but doubtless includes distraction from *þat* 6b, *losse* 7a. The line now scans as Type IIIc with cognative b-staves, the fourth translineating with *God* 8. **8** *gome*: conjectured as the required third stave in a Type IIa line, *man* being presumed a Bx ⇒ for the commoner non-alliterating synonym. The Bx line could scan vocalically as Type IIIa, but this would put the semantically most significant words into the metrically weakest positions. **9** Bx scans *ax / xa* and reconstruction here gives a Type IIIa line that restores the key-stave lost through ↔ to prose order. **21–2** As found in wLMR (= ?Bx), the line has an awkward six-syllable prelude-dip; F omits the Latin and expands *Dobest* into two lines which, though metrically correct, are unnecessary to the sense if not irrelevant (the first was adopted by *Sch*[1] after *K–D* but both are now rejected as spurious). As in *Sk*, the final two words following *after* are here detached to form a new quasi-macaronic line, though tentatively, since it is anomalous in lacking alliteration. Possibly *Dobest* belonged in 21 in place of *satisfaccion*; this would enable the Latin portion of the line to stand alone and in exact parallelism with the earlier 'parts of penance' at 17*a*, 18*a*. **23** *myte*:

conjectured as more appropriate to the sense than *myst*, which elsewhere in **L** signifies 'mist', is poorly attested as 'fume or cloud of smoke' and not at all, in this period, in the sense 'mildew' (see MED s.v. *mist* n.(1), 1b. (a) and (d) respectively). The *s* in Bx could be a mistaken reflex of *ʒ*; a spelling with medial spirant (signifying vowel-length) is recorded by MED s.v. *mite* n.(1) but not in the period. Association of mites with moths as damaging fabrics is found in Chaucer (*CT,* IV 560) and the stain the insect causes would be aptly denoted by the verb *bymolen.* **28** *Haukyn wil*: a reconstruction commending itself decisively on grounds of sense (as F has realised), since Haukyn is *Activa Vita* and comparing his *wife* with other minstrels would be bizarre. Bx is nonetheless defended by Alford 1977: 86n26 in the light of B 17.330–1, an explicit piece of allegorical interpretation of no relevance to the present passage, where the dichotomy is not between 'soul' and 'flesh' but between soul restored to a state of grace after confession and soul 'defiled' with sins committed since confession. It would be nonsense to say that 'no minstrel shall be more valued than Haukin's wife' [*sc.* 'flesh'] since the flesh may 'contrary' the soul (B 17. 331) but obviously cannot in itself be morally better or worse. Conscience in saying that no one will have a better 'garment' refers to Haukyn's improved spiritual condition if he assiduously uses all three parts of the sacrament of penance, as a result of which he will also be highly valued in his society (Benson's attempt [2004:54] to support Alford's criticism of the *K–D* emendation only makes confusion worse confounded). The present error could well be due to aural / visual suggestion from following *waf-*, reinforced by confused memory of the reference to his wife at 3 (and possibly of the exegetical trope found in 17.330–1). Smoothing to *Haukyns* will have followed, although if F's form *Haukyn* accurately preserves α, Bx may have had an uninflected genitive misconstrued as a nominative. For a closely similar mistake (nonsensical *hys woman* for *is whan a man* similarly induced in part by inaccurate association) see on B 13.411, under C 7.70. *which is* α: giving better sense even as the reflex of a Bx line with corrupt a-half reading, since *his* β is in any case grammatically incongruent with *wif*. Possibly *with his* originated as a visual error for a Bx form spelled **wich hys* with an omitted and a wrongly added aspirate (cf. on B 13.334). **36** *yow eiþer*: reconstructed for α (< Bx) as semantically fuller than β, metrically superior to F and grammatically more correct than R.

240 (B 40) *here*: preserved only in XIP²D² (=?y) and accepted as a revision giving the semantically sharpest reading; but arguably it is the reading of the remaining mss, identical with the presumed reading of α (? < Bx), that is archetypal. **242 (B 42)** *þat*: adopted as giving the best grammar and sense, and as probably the reading of *x²*, to which three *x¹* mss have independently varied. The original

x¹ and could perhaps be best explained as a reflex of a Ø-relative in Cx, **the worm wonte* (unhistorical final *-e* in a contracted verb-form is common, e.g. in ms X at 21.435 *sente*). *woneth*: the reading of P² and the rest, XU having *wonte* and YID² *wond(e)*. The *wonte / wond(e)* readings have here been interpreted as spelling-variants of the assimilated 3rd pers. sg. of *wonen*. But *R–K* take them as the noun meaning 'mole', a rare word derived from OE *wand* (MED s.v. *wonte* n., citing only Trevisa in the period; OED s.v. *Want* sb.¹). This undoubtedly hard reading deserves serious consideration as possibly original. **249 (B 37)** The **C** line scans as Type IIIa with two lifts in *Páciénce* and *R–K* needlessly insert *paciently* from B 14.37. **251 (B 48)** The **B** line scans as Type IIb with the third a-stave found in the suffix of *liflóde*, either with full stress, so that *it was* becomes the pre-caesural portion of the dip before *Pacience,* or else with half-stress (*liflòde ɪt wàs*), the other half being found in the verb. This would be a special licence made acceptable because of the presence of the secondary |p| staves in the b-verse. **252 (B 49)** The **B** line is to be read either as a quasi-macaronic scanning *aa / xx* or, preferably, as a true macaronic of extended Type III with semi-counterpoint, the key-stave being the voiced fricative *voluntas* alliterating allophonically with *þanne* (*abb / ax*). **258 (B 55)** *etynge* **x**: preferable to *ondyng* **p** which, though harder lexically, is suspect as a scribal attempt to complete the listing of the senses (*heryng* MN² illustrates the same tendency). The less predictable *etynge* (unaltered from **B**) indicates an activity of the sense of *taste*, with its specific vice of 'over-delicacy' in the matter of food, and does not repeat *tonge* 257, which (as usually in **L**) refers to speech. **259 (B 56)** *Thar þe / Tharstow*: the form with *Th* is preferred in both versions as free from the semantic ambiguity of *Dar þe / Darstow*. The latter could be the reading of β and was almost certainly that of *x¹*, but the erroneous **p** *That* points to *Thar* as having been the form of Cx. The two verbs have separate origins but had become confused in usage (see MED s.vv. *durren* 2(a) and (b), *thurven* v. 2(b)). **L**'s original is indeterminable, since in this unique use the word occurs in non-stave position. **263a (B 60a)** *sunt*: adopted in **C** as the correct form of the verb; possibly Cx read Ø, **p** completing correctly, *x¹* and t incorrectly. **264 (B 61)** *boþe*: conjectured for **B** on the showing of revised **C** as a necessary second stave, the mechanism of loss being identified as *mowen* > < *men* attraction). Scansion of the Bx line as Type IIIc entails an awkward subordination of *men* to *bestes* that **C** avoids through having *bothe* as the (mute) key-stave (cf. also the metrical pattern of B 64b //). The emendation adopted counteracts this by making the nominalised numeral adjective precede the caesura, so as to anticipate the sense of *men* before the key-stave *beestes* that bears full stress. **270** The **p** variant *telden* (*tolden* in MqN) may be a different lexeme *tellen of* 'discern, find' (MED s.v. *tellen* v.16(a), (b)). **273 (B 70)** *moore*: conjectured for **C** on the evidence of **B** as the required key-stave, presumably lost from Cx by quasi-haplography after *neuere*.

B 72–98 72 *Cristes*: possibly induced by 71b; but the more obvious *cristen* is the likelier scribal ⇒ (F coinciding with β), while parallel *Cristes* 72 underscores the contrast between ideal and actuality. **89** *ynliche*: lexically harder and theologically more precise, the variant *yliche* presumably resulting from scribal loss of the nasal suspension. **91** scans as a perfect macaronic, whether Type Ia on |p| with key-stave full or muted, or Type IIIa on |k|, stressing *peccáta* as in 93.

276 scans as an extended Type IIIa on vowels with a-verse counterpoint on |p|; *R–K*'s [*properly*] *parfit* is otiose. **281 (B 101)** *God almyhty*: a **C** revision of *Oure Driʒte*, which is presumed the reading of β and so of Bx. Both *lorde* R and *god more* F are to be taken as variant ⇒ for the same original, the latter perhaps showing ⊗ from **C**. Although apparently found difficult here, *Driʒte* in its other appearance with referent 'God' (B 13.269) caused no problem to the scribes. **285 (B 105)**: supplied from **B** as necessary to the sense, its absence leaving the sentence without a main verb. The line could have been lost from Cx through visual distraction (*rede...richesse* 284 / *renke...riche was... rekene*), and a copyist who paused at 284 and resumed at 286 could easily have lost the syntactical thread. The empatic connective *Then* (*Þat / And*) need not, however, be a scribal intrusion, since the rest of the line also displays revision. **286 (B 106)** *when he*: possibly revising an original that made the verb-subject the impersonal *it*; the latter, preserved in L (< β) and R (< α), will be the reading of Bx, γ a ⇒ of *he* as subject under inducement from *he*105b, 106b, and M an alteration from a γ-type ms. Alternatively, γ (preferred as supported by **C**) preserves a reading present in Bx (and in **L**'s revision ms B¹), and *it* is a coincidental ⇒ in LR. **299** *sende* pDX (t *alt. to* d): perhaps a form of the past subjunctive (*sente* would go better with *were* 300). **300 (B 119)** *elles were hit*: the order of **p** is preferred to that of **x** as preserving 'Platonic' wordplay on *ellis wher* and *elles were* (t agrees with *x¹* by varying coincidentally to prose order from the *x²* reading it would have shared with **p**). **B 123** *riche were*: the last two words requiring ↔ to provide the line's key-stave (Bx having unconsciously inverted to prose order in a manner akin to C 13.5). **310 (B 130)** Cx scans vocalically as Type IIIa on non-lexical words. It could easily be made a T-type like the **B** line under revision by insertion of *So* before *David* (corresponding to *as* in B 130); but grounds for emending are insufficient. **311 (B 131)** The Cx line introduced by *And sayth* presents as a metrically anomalous quasi-macaronic, whereas the **B** line under revision is a true macaronic verse of Type Ib. Possibly original **C** had *And sayth Dormierunt* as the b-half, making 310 a

(long but) regular Type Ia, and the supposed anomaly has arisen through misdivision (*R–K* follow W, which divides 311 from 310 after *inuenerunt*). In **B**, the last phrase of the quotation is reconstructed from the split variants of α to include the important words *eorum ymaginem*. The Bx form *sompnum* (accusative of 'sleep', where F following Vg reads *sompnium*) is retained as supported by Cx and so as possibly original. Doubtless it is intended metonymically to signify 'dream' (but for similar loss of a vowel, cf. the spelling *Eice* for *Eiice* at B 7.138*a* and 10.264*a*).

Passus XVI (B XIV–XV)

In the reconstruction of this section, B 14.319 corresponds to the point (16.155) where **C** makes a major break after omitting 14.320–32, the lines that end this passus in **B**. **3 (B 134)** *Hewen* **x**: retained from **B**, and not lexically difficult, so *Thei* **p** may reflect an exemplar spelled *Hyen* and mistaken for *Hy*, with D either having a coincidental error or showing ⊗ from a **p** source. **4 (B 135)** *to dyne* **C**: a construction, whether anacoluthic or elliptical, unlikely to be a scribal ⇒ for the easier *þat dyneþ* t**B**. Possibly it shows Cx smoothing by insertion of *to* in an exemplar reading with Ø-relative and number-indeterminate *a* for *he* (cf. the pl. pronoun *they* in **p**). However, the 'absolute' use of *to* + infinitive in an elliptical construction is instanced at 7 (*to fonge*, retained from **B**), so the originality of *to dyne* here need not be questioned and *R–K*'s adoption of t**B** should be rejected. **9 (B 141)** *here-beynge*: the firmly attested **BC** reading, and lexically just tolerable, though *and heuene herafter* B 141b which completes the thought, was perhaps omitted by Cx and should be restored. *R–K*'s retention of *K–D*'s emendation to *herberwynge* is baffling.

B 146–59 146 Choice between *alle,* the possible reading of Bx (> β > L, > α > R) and *hem alle* is not determinable on intrinsic grounds. But its broader scope (balanced by *alle*148), which is not restricted to the poor, suggests that *hem* γ is a scribal intrusion (M here presumably having ⊗ from a γ source [w]). **152** *rewfulliche* β: 'mercifully' (MED s.v. *reufulli* adv. (c)); preferable in context to the more obvious *riʒtfullich* α (though both *ruþe* and *leaute* are specified at 145, 146) and less likely to have been the ⇒, though this is exactly what occurred at A 8.10. The point is that acting *rewfulliche* is here something not confined to the rich, whereas acting righteously could never be so thought anyway. **155–59** were probably lost by α through eyeskip from *Ac* 155 to *Ac* 160.

22 (B 168) *þat on þe rode deydest* **p**: here taken as possibly preserved (through *x²*) from Cx. Presumably the mechanism of loss in *x¹* was eyeskip from the phrase *vs alle* 22a to its repetition at 23b and loss of 23a would have been expected; but since this half-line was noticed, the only consequence was mislineation (y divides after *mercy*, U after *mercy* and *meke*, D after *vs* and *meke*). If the lacuna was also in x^2 (and therefore in Cx), editorial choice between two completions of indeterminate authority must be made solely on intrinsic quality. The t variant *on þi renkis*] *on vs* (adopted by *PeR–K*), while metrically correct, is flat and has a filler-like redundancy; but **p** not only scans correctly, it is apt in context; while it echoes a line such as 6.318, it recalls the thought instead of merely the phrasing; and its linking of Christ's death on the cross with being *meke* 'humble' (23) is of a piece with 1.68 //. **25** scans as Type IIIa with two stresses in *cóntrición*, but it would give a smoother line (of Type IIIc) if noun and verb-phrase in the a-half were judged to have been inverted to prose order by Cx. *R–K*'s conjecture [*clereliche*] *to clanse* is wholly gratuitous. **30** scans as Type IIIa with two stresses in *cónféssio* (cf. on 25); *R–K*'s conjecture [*knowlechyng and*] *shrifte* is otiose. **31** *satisfaccio*: preferred as original since the three Latin penitential formulas appear to stand both in parallel together and in contrast with their English forms at 25–7. Underlining of *satisfaccion* in X and Y probably indicates recognition of its technical status; but this was obscured by omission of the *operis* part of the formula in Cx, for which no obvious reason appears (its intrusion in <PE> will have been encouraged by the presence of the complete formula at 31*a*). It seems likely that **p** read *satisfaccio* as in the text here and that the **x** mss correcting to this form did so independently or by collation with a **p** source. In the b-half, *soueraynliche* appears typical padding in **p** after erroneous division as two lines. **34** scans vocalically with mute key-stave and counterpoint on |b|. If *oþer* is mute and the stress on *bet*, the final lift in the b-half may be taken as compensating for the extra a-half muting (cf. *Intro*. IV § 44). **36** scans as Type IIa with *þat* as the third stave; if it is semi-muted (an irregularity), *defénde* may be meant as a 'supplemental' fricative stave.

B 174–96 174 *Lord*: in parallel with preceding *God* 170 and following *Crist* 179 as part of a prayer; *lore* 'lost' ?α is possible but inferior here. **177** *wynter tyme*: reconstructed in the light of // 178 as the underlying Bx form. **181** *his*: lost from γ and M but posited here for β on the strength of L, with indirect support from R *alle his*. The latter may preserve α's reading from which F has dropped the possessive, but *alle* is not necessary for the sense. For while the Ø-reading of γM is too indefinite, it is *Christ*'s 'nobility' or 'generosity' (MED s.v. *gentris(e* n. 2 (a)) that is the issue, so L's *his* may be safely accepted as preserving Bx. **190** *He*: the certain reading of β and probably also of α, *Ho* R being presumably a misspelling. F has doubtless altered to *We* to make the subject accord with the object of the devil's malice *vs* in 189; and the deed of acquittal might well be carried by the recipient. But *this*

document could be produced for the devil only at Judgement Day, where the appropriate person to bring it would be Christ the mediator, the understood referent of the pronoun here accepted. **196** *wroȝten*: conjectured as misread by Bx under unconscious inducement from *writeþ* 199 and references in the immediate context to written documents of various kinds. The error could have arisen if the exemplar read *wroten* (for *wrohten*), a current form of the preterite pl. of *werchen*. The reading *writen* is pointless here since what is in question is actions, especially devotional, on which money and effort are expended.

39 (B 198) *welle*: convincingly attested as archetypal in both versions and providing a homophonic pun on *wille* through using a dialectal variant of the latter (Kentish) presumably familiar in the contemporary language of London. **43 (B 202)** *þat þer ben*: to be accepted as original for **C** on the strength of support from **B**, *þat* (2) Cx being redundant, given that *For* is a conjunction, not a preposition. The collocation of *þat* with *ben* 'exist' here is slightly unexpected, and this will have led both to its omission in four **B** mss and to intrusion of *þat* (2) in the b-half there and in Cx. Possibly, however, the original (in **B** at least) had a Ø-relative clause in the b-half but a main clause in the a-half, and the a-half's relative pronoun was inserted in both Bx and B^1, whence it came to **C**. **46 (B 205)** *þere þat* **p**: to be discriminated on the showing of **B** as the form of Cx, attested *þere* and *þat* being split variants. **48 (B 207)** *And*: preferred also in **B** on the showing of **C**. The line expands but does not modify the argument of 46 (B 205), so *R–K*'s emendation to *Ac* is unnecessary. **50 (B 209)** The apocopated form *way* could also have been that of Bx (> ?α) but as no difference of sense is involved, β is retained. **53 (B 212)** *riche* α: the object of the verb, preferred in the light of the revision, which shows the *hey way* as a bumpy road to a man burdened with wealth; the alteration in **C** could have been prompted by the ambiguity of **B**. **64 (B 223)** *ben*: discriminated as the required verb-form for the key-stave, and so reconstructed in **B**, *arn* being an unconscious ⇒ in Bx and Cx perhaps under influence from the vowel beginning of *eueremore* and the vowel staves of 65 (B 224). The **C** mss reading *ben* are likely to show (like *B*-F) felicitous conjecture. **67 (B 226)** scans as Type Ia with a cognative first stave on |b| or as IIIa with two |b| staves. *R–K* sensibly refrain from *K–D*'s extravagant emendation of the b-half to *þe feblere is þe poore*.

B 228–38 look authentic on intrinsic grounds and from their appearance (lightly revised) in **C**. No mechanical reason appears for their loss from β, unless visual distraction induced by alliterative likeness in 229 / 238. **78 (B 237)** *more ful* **p**t: the x^2 reading accepted as preserving Cx, x^1 having omitted both words through attraction of *neuere → mer(ye)*, with loss of the first stave on |m|. For similar (conjectured) loss of *moore* in Cx, cf. 15.273

and on 17.147. **92 (B 252–53)** In the absence of these lines from α, no reason for which appears unless censorship, Bx must remain uncertain. It seems likely, however, that despite the two-line **p** form's likeness to **B** (and *pace* Schmidt 1980:105), it is **x** that represents Cx, with *ful longe* to be seen as a scribal filler. The **p** shape is metrically acceptable, but the second line also seems to pad out the material common to **x** 92b and to B 253a, while omitting the separate idea in B 253b. In **B**, the β form is here judged to have been preserved in the L variants, M having varied to the γ reading through influence from a w-type source. L could have substituted *were* so as to avoid repetition of *stoode*, but more probably *stoode* in 253 has come into γ from 252, the repetition being pointless here. The phrase *no þyng* seems to be an attempt to spell out the sense of the elliptical *noon* ('no custom[ers]'), which **C** will make explicit as *noen haunt*. *RK*'s reconstruction after **B** is without warrant, as the *C*-**x** line is satisfactory in both sense and metre (a Type IIa). **96 (B 257)** *is*: preferred as the harder reading in both versions, specifying the nature of Poverty's *rôle*, more than his *relationship* to God. Thus *is* and *his* are here unlikely to be split variants of **is his* (the actual reading of *C*-QZ); rather, *his* is to be judged a reflex of verbal **hys*, with intruded aspirate (of the type common in the Z-Text). **99 (B 260)** *asken and cleymen* **B**: ↔ of the order of the verbs in Bx to provide the key-stave (presumably Bx inverted the order so as to promote the concept (*cleymen*) regarded as more important). The line is now an extended Type IIIa scanning on vowels with semi-counterpoint on |p| (*abb / ax*) and the second b-half verb occupies the same position as in revised **C**, which makes |p| the theme-stave and has 'running' counterpoint on vowels (Schmidt 1987:63–4). An alternative scansion is as a vocalic Type Ia, with the second a-half lift in *is*. **105 (B 266)** *paramour*: preferred as avoiding the unintended number-ambiguity of the form with final *-s*, which is attested in the period for the sg. noun (see MED s.v. *paramour(e* n., where the sense 1(b) 'husband' corresponds to *make* in **B**). **106 (B 267)** Bx scans as an extended Type IIIa on vowels, and while *hym* could be a ⇒ for *man*, the latter, not being a difficult word, is more probably a **C** revision (to Type Ie) bringing the main stresses onto lexical words. **108** *persones*: one of several **C** revisions here. *R–K* adopt *parties* **B** without warrant, a word scarcely difficult enough to invite ⇒.

B 271–4 271 (C 110) scans as Type Ie, with the first stave in *So* (the comparative adverb carrying strong initial stress), the blank stave here in position 2 (*vch*) and a 'supplemental' |s| stave (*forsáketh*) in the fifth lift (see *Intro.* IV § 440). **273 (C 112)** *so neyȝ is pouerte* α: preferred as the more probable reading of Bx in the light of **C**'s *semblable bothe*. Perhaps β substituted the logically weak and contextually unapt *to his seintes* through objecting to Bx's repetition; this is echoed in **C**'s revision

which, however, varies *syb* instead of repeating *pouerte*. **274 (C 113)** The Bx b-half *þat here faste preise* is judged to survive in R, which mistakenly replaced the adverb *here* α with a verb *huyre*, but without a subject-pronoun. F substitutes one for *þat*, providing the basis for the *K–D* reconstruction *I here yow*. The phrase is here interpreted as an elliptical mode of address: an understood *ye* was supplied by β, which smoothed by dropping *here* (thereby damaging syntax and metre) to make the line scan *aa / bb*. **115 (B 276)** scans as a macaronic Type Ib line with two cognative Latin staves in the b-half (*odibíle bónum*). The list following is taken as prose and numbered as one citation line (115*a*) as in **p**. The **x** tradition erroneously appends the first item (*Remocio curarum*) to 115, thereby obscuring the character of the latter as a true verse. **115*a* (B 276*a*)** *solicitudine*: on grounds of sense and confirmation by the Latin source the preferred reading, *solitudine* being explicable as a visual error caused by assimilation of *-ci-* to following *-tu-*. However, if the presence of *semita* unconsciously suggested *solitudo*, the error may have been in Cx (and Bx) and corrected in *p¹* (and possibly β). But while it is repeated in α at 306, it seems to have been avoided in Cx at 141*a*. **116 (B 277)** scans like **B** as a counterpointed Type Ie, but with a mute key-stave on |k| (*aab / [a]bx*), while the **B** line has a full stave at key position (*kenne*) and treats *quod Haukyn* as extra-metrical. Despite the apparent resemblance to **C** of the R form of 277, this cannot be what **B** read, since the second line is prose and the first has an untypical full key-stave *quod*. **117–18 (B 278–79)** In the revised 117, *Pacience* is a full stave in position two. B 278 is a line of vocalic Type IIa with the semantically important *hard* as stave three and *quod Pacience* forming part of a strong dip before the second stave.

B 284–86*a* give inferior sense as preserved in Bx, and in 285 defective metre (*xa / ax* unless the caesura comes after *pure*, as it cannot). The reconstruction here follows *K–D* in making Bx 285a the b-half of 284 and in transposing 286 and 286*a*. This enables the first axiom cited from 276 to stand as a summarising conclusion of the preceding English, as occurs successively at 290*a*, 291*a*, 294*a* etc; in **C**, by contrast, at 121*a* and 126*b* the first two axioms *precede* their English, so *R–K*'s elaborate re-ordering after **B** has nothing to recommend it. In 285, the final phrase of Bx *And ioye*, replaced here at 284 by *is to þe body*, becomes the onset, the adverb *also* being inserted to provide a first stave. While loss of the latter through attraction to following *soule* is easy to conjecture, the mechanism of corruption remains obscure, and the rationale of the reconstruction is a general understanding of the total argument, the coherence of which should now be clear. **128 (B 293)** *wightes*: 'weights', on grounds of sense and context the likeliest substantive reading; so *wittes* **B**-R,

C-TH² may be interpreted as a reflex of the back-spelled *whittes* attested in y (< **x**), which was also the probable reading of *B*-α (*B*-F *wyʒles* is a near-synonymous ⇒ for α *whites read as *wittes*). A parallel earlier occurs at C 6.258=B 13.361. **129 (B 294)** Since natural stressing might prefer the key-stave mute in what would otherwise be a Type IIIa line (such muting being avoided by **L**), it seems probable that *neyhebore* supplies a second stave by having stress wrenched onto its final syllable (a cognative 'compensating' final stave being provided by *paye*). However, if *but* is not here prepositional before demonstrative *pat* 'that which' but part of the conjunctive phrase *but pat* 'except, unless', it may carry both stress and alliteration. **130** *me*: the unstressed reduced indefinite pronoun (MED s.v. *me* pron. (1)), presenting no problem as the key-stave here, as it is mute. But in position 1 (always stressed) this form is not permissible. Undoubtedly the line would scan more effectively on ‖ as a Type IIa, reading *ledes* for *men* (2), and the harder synonym could have been supplanted in Cx under inducement from preceding and following *men*. If so, the reduced form *me* (1), which would then fall into the onset, would be explained and acceptable. But on balance, major emendation here does not seem justified. **135 (B 299)** *is hit*: the verb-subject inversion here is probably due to omission of the numeral (*fifte*) and its replacement by an adverb. All the other 'points' from fourth to ninth follow the pattern *hit is a*, and **B** may be presumed to have done likewise, since it has the numeral (*fifte*) in conformity with all the others. Accordingly *it is* may be conjectured as the reading of Bx, to which α added the article and from which β omitted the pronoun (as in all the other cases from fourth to ninth). **136 (B 300)** *lowe*: conjectured as providing a reading in **B** that makes good sense and explains the form of the attested variants. Of these, *lawde* is nonsense, *lewde* over-specific and inappropriate (morality is in question, not learning), *land* vague and ill-fitted to the metaphor in *leche*, while *lawe* has no contextual relevance. The revised C form, making *foule eueles* the object of the *leche*'s ministrations, may point to a stave-word in **B** such as *lupere*, which could have lost its second syllable through assimilation to following *euere* in Bx. But a form **law(e)* / *lewe in B-Ø might equally have generated a postulated Bx *lawd that would account for all four variants. The present emendation accordingly supposes the referent to have been 'the humble', since of two conjectured alternatives *luthere* and *lowe*, the second is more apt to the context: poverty promotes chastity in those whose position in society is a humble one. This affirmation may then be related to B 252–53, on the brothels, suggesting a correlation of this 'point' of poverty to the capital sin Lechery. **140 (B 304)** *liʒter*: conjectured on grounds of sense and the showing of revised C as the probable original in **B** also. While *hardier* provides tolerable sense and

metre, the Bx line being of Type Ib, repetition in *hardy man of herte* 305 is suspicious and suggests that *hardier* has come in by visual inducement from the following phrase. But *liʒter* goes better with the sense of *cantabit* in the parenthetical quotation. In **C** it is mute, so as to accommodate metrically the final adverb (though the text would be better without it). **141a (B 304a, 306)** The Bx lines provide an acceptable sequence as they stand; but if the emendation of *hardier* is accepted, the re-ordered sequence will appear preferable. Thus 304a now glosses the preceding and following English line (*liʒter // cantabit*; *peues // latrone*) and 306 sums up the argument for the sixth 'point' by quoting (in full) the axiom given in part at 276a. Each of the nine citations listed occurs in this way at the *end* of its amplificatory English passage. **144 (B 309a)** The omission of the Latin line, the seventh of the 'points' of poverty, from both α and Cx may suggest its absence from both versions, since no mechanical reason for the loss appears. However, since *all* the other points are quoted in their proper places, it would seem best to follow β in including this one too in **B**. Among the **C** copies, F places it in the margin beside 143, R at the end of 145, PQWZ at the end of 144 (so *SkR–K*), and it should arguably be included in the text. **146 (B 311)** *so wel*: conjectured in the light of *sothly* C as the possible **B** reading from which Bx could have lost the required first-stave *so* by visual distraction from following *deserue, somer*. Although the **C** lines are otherwise unrevised and *sothly* could be also what **B** read, a mechanical explanation is preferable in the absence of any adequate reason for Bx's change of that adverb. **150 (B 315)** The Bx line, just tolerable with two lifts in *sík(e)nésse*, would run better if the final phrase were transposed with *good leche*. **151 (B 316)** In the light of **C**, **B** may be re-lineated, improving the metre and removing the important name *Seint Austyn* from its (unstressed initial) position in the prelude dip of 317.

B XVI *ends here.*
C XVI *continues.* B XV *begins.*

Rubric in B The passus-heading in β is correct, R being out by one and F completely aberrant (F's rubrics are given in *Sk* II xxvii–xxx). B XV was perhaps intended to be the Prologue of *Dobet*, since the β rubrics at B XVI point to that passus (though with less than complete certainty) as being the first of *Dobet*. Similarly, the **C** rubric at XVII indicates that passus as the Prologue of *Dobet* (in **x**) but Passus I of *Dobet* in **p**, which has been one out in passus-numbering from the beginning of the poem. **165–66 (B XV 16–17)** 165b and 166b are transposed by *Pe*, following the arguments of *K–D* (pp 209–10) for such ↔ in **B** on grounds of 'contextually unsatisfactory sense'. But even if 'physically simple' (*K–D*), altering a reading identical in both archetypes needs unusually strong justification. Here the presupposition of identical error in Cx strains credence and the arguments for emendation are tenuous (*R–K* abandon it). The sense of the text is that the souls of all were created by God; some are Christian; all are 'known' in heaven (in that Christ died for all); and some (the just) will enter there, including those who receive the faith or repent of sin at the end of life (*neuere so late*). For a relevant comparison, cf. the thought at 20.418–20. **172** scans as Type Ia on |f| with a liaisonal first stave (*Of_som*) or else as Type IIIa with *fihte* as first stave; *R–K*'s emendation *fele* for *som* is otiose. **173** Either order of the nouns in the b-half would give satisfactory metre, but **x** is preferred as varying the stress-pattern of *som tyme* from the preceding line. It is either Type IIIc or (if *to* is regarded as the mute second stave) Type Ia with counterpoint. **177** scans in Cx as *aa / xa* unless, improbably, the stave-sound is identified as |ð| and a cognative liaisonal-stave found in reconstructed **qua[th]_Y*, giving a Type IIa line. The felicitous variant of *C*-ms W, adopted here, enables the stresses to fall on three lexical words in |b|. Given that 177 is an unusually long line, the error could have come about if *quod he* had been found squeezed into the margin of the exemplar and then wrongly placed in copying by the scribe of Cx. **183 (B 25)** *Mens Thouhte*: reconstructed as the *x¹* form (< Cx) on the evidence of XY's substantive reading and the u (and D²) variant, as well as the form of *B-α*, accurately preserved in R and corruptly reflected in F. The *x²* reading involves smoothing after misinterpretation of *mens* as an English genitive plural. That of u has rightly recognised it as Latin, but like *B-β* has omitted the following gloss *thouhte* (presumably judging it marginal) to leave a line with a masculine ending (N², usually grouping with y, here reflects a **B** source of β-type). As here understood, the 'gloss' is internal and authorial, not scribal; for a parallel see on 22.236 // (*chey-tyftee pouertee*), where the gloss is not on a Latin but on a rare English word. **195** *body*: a blank stave in a Type Ic line scanning *aax / ax*. The revision of *flessh* **B**, to which FCh vary by alliterative inducement (mistakenly followed by *R–K*), is doubtless intentional, since **C** stresses death where **B** ambiguously suggests asceticism. **199a (B 39a)** *dum scit Mens est*: restored on the basis of **B** as omitted by the Cx scribe, perhaps after failing to recognise *Mens* in 183 as Latin (// Bx clearly had it). It seems unlikely that **L** dropped *Mens* from the Isidorean list simply because he had added *Liberum Arbitrium*, since the faculty Thought in any case appears in 183, whether that line originally contained *Mens* (as here in the edited text) or not. **215a (B 55a)** yields the pattern *aa / xx* with internal assonance 'compensating' for the omitted stave-sound |t| in the b-half. *opprimatur*: the Cx reading, supported by that of *B-R* (< α < ?Bx); perhaps an authorial alteration of the source. *B-F* has changed to the future indicative form of

Vg, while β has rationalised by substituting the present indicative (as has *C-N²*, presumably from a β source). But **L** could have intended to make the prophecy a malediction. **223 (B 63)** scans as Type IIIb on vowels with 'echoic' counterpoint (Schmidt 1987:65) on |p| in the a-half (*Pòtte / Páradys*). *Pulte* **B**: on the evidence of L (and original M) the reading of β, on R's that of α, and to be preferred on grounds of lexical hardness and contextually appropriate sense. The word has earlier caused scribal difficulties. At B 1.127 it is attested by LR (and Cr) against *putte* γMAx and supported by **Z** (**C** is here revised). At C 10.95, where y (< *x¹*) has *pulte* and **p**u *putte*, the variant *putte* in // **B** is only randomly attested, and *pulte* would seem secure as the original of w and g (< γ) as well as of L and α. In the present instance, the **B** variants leave it unclear whether γ or w and g severally altered to *putte* (visible alteration in M does not serve to establish whether γ or only w or g read *pulte*); for the <OC²> ancestor has in *pullede* a reflex of postulated β *pulte*, though this could in principle be by correction from a ms of *l* or *m* type. Confirmation of *pult* as still part of **L**'s active vocabulary in **C** is found at 11.208, a new line that refers to God's foreknowing, where no scribal difficulty has been experienced. It appears therefore that in the three uses of a word to denote acts of divine 'expulsion' (from heaven, from paradise and from the state of grace), **L**'s characteristic choice is *pulten* (on which see MED s.v. *pilten* v. 1(a), (c)). Some grounds thus exist for seeing *potte* as a Cx ⇒ for original *pulte* and for emending accordingly; but as the sense-difference is small and revision possible, it may be let stand. **224 (B 64)** The **C** line is here accepted as a revised form that consists simply of **B**'s a-half, now scanning vocalically as Type Ia (the b-half could have been lost from Cx through inattention, as possibly at 16.9); but since the sense is complete and the following line largely revised, there is no real case for reconstruction. **227 (B 69)** B may be scanned as a Latin alliterative verse-line of Type IIIc (*ab / ab*) with an English prelude-dip *That is* (cf B 12.278 // earlier). Revised **C**, however, is a true macaronic of Type Ie in which three of the original four Latin words are again staves. Thus *sapere* (1) and (2) are full staves, *Non plus* the prelude-dip, *saide þe wyse* a phrase of the *quod he* type commonly treated as extra-metrical, *oportet* the second stave (blank), and *synne* the key-stave. An alternative scansion would make *saide þe wyse* intra-metrical and part of a strong second dip. Yet a third would have *pruyde* as key-stave, with the Latin a-half staves *plus* and *oportet* (words of high semantic prominence) and an eight-syllable dip. On balance, the first is to be preferred, since *synne of pruyde* appears an integral phrase with a full stave on the generic term, while both *oportet* and *sapere* can receive the major stress they require. The line's exceptional length, macaronic character and potentially ambiguous scansion not unexpectedly provoked mislineation. But neither of its two-line forms provides acceptable metre for both lines, and the felicitous relineation of TN²QWZ imposes itself as correct. That of D may be interpreted as a single line and is so recorded in the Apparatus; but it is perhaps better seen as another case of division after *sapere* (2), since the scribe's usual medial colon does not appear after that word but after *wyse*. Pe's division of the two lines after *wyse* leaves the first unmetrical, while *R–K*'s more drastic ↔ of the Latin and English phrases after *wyse* leaves *quam...sapere* as an isolated 'appended' line; both solutions are unsatisfactory in different ways. **228 (B 70)** *fele*: the revised **C** form suggesting that *fele* B-β derives from Bx and is not a ⇒ for a possible *manye*, and that the line is to be scanned on |f| / |v| with a cognative stave on |δ| (from *þat*, probably muted). **230 (B 72)** On the showing of revised **C**, this line was securely in Bx and may have been lost in α by eyeskip from *bileue* 72b to *bileuen* 73a. The wordplay on *bileue* noun and verb (abandoned in **C**) seems unmistakable. The *K–D* conjecture *lome* for *oftetymes* is rejected (despite its attractiveness) since based on an erroneous view of **L**'s metre as excluding Type III lines. While C 12.123 certainly has *lome* for Bx *ofte*, that line may be seen, like the present revised one, as a particular case of **C**'s generally increased preference for the Type I pattern. Where *lome* appeared in **B** (as comparative *lomere* at 20.238 //), it caused Bx no difficulty, though the scribe of ms L thought it worth a supralinear Latin gloss (*sepius*). **B 73 (C 231)** The Bx line is to be reconstructed from the evidence of both sub-archetypes as preserved in L (< β) and R (< α). The clue is the key-stave *by* 'as regards' (MED s.v. *bi* prep. 9a), which seems to have been lost by β through haplography after B*ettre*, b*ileuen*. The particle puns homophonically on the prefix *bi-*, which here carries sentence-stress, just as *bileuen* in turn puns semantically on preceding *bileue* (72). The sense of the line may be rendered: 'it would be better, in the case of several theologians, to give up that kind of teaching'. The line's metrical structure may be analysed as Type Ia, and it would be smoother if *by* were treated as a mute stave; but considerations of sense overide those of rhythm here. **232–33 (B 76–7)** *foliliche*: in the light of the **B** lines under revision, to be securely discriminated as the same adverb in both **C** lines, with neither instancing *folliche* 'entirely, utterly' (MED s.v. *fulli* adv. 1(b)). Both appearances of this variant are spelling errors for *foliliche*, caused by loss of *i* between syllabic-terminal and syllabic-initial *l*. The rhetorical figure used is *repetitio*, not *annominatio*. **234 (B 78)** *in to* **B**: here resolved as preposition + adverb in the light of *in* **C**, *B-β* offering the same reading as *into* B-α (presumably from Bx) but with an intruded conjunction. The *preposition* 'into' would be grammatically out of place after the verb *spenen* 77 and could not acceptably relate that verb to *shewynge*.

 B 84–90 84 scans awkwardly either on |s| as Type

IIa with a liaisonal stave on *as_it*, or as Type IIIa on |f| with a wrenched stress on *fórsakeþ*. **89** *muche*: adopted as the probable Bx reading preserved (unusually) in F's *mychil*, with ⇒ of one synonym (*grete*) in R and another (*long*) in β. Any of the three variants would give a Type Ia line, F one with a full stave, R and β probably one with a mute key-stave (*make*). The metrical argument is, however, weaker here than that from *durior lectio*, and the word *muche* can be cited as appearing at least once, at 21.368 //, in the relevant sense 'large' (MED s.v. *much(e* adj. 3(c)). **90 (C 240)** *ouer* ?α: preferred as the harder reading for which F, coinciding with β, has substituted *of* under visual or aural inducement from preceding *of* and *Of* 89. For a similar use see B 1.108 // **ZA** and for a case where β has *of* for α *ouer* (here confirmed by // **C**), see B 5.619.

248 revises to make explicit what is elliptically implied in *swiche* B 98 (cf. *wexe* 253 / Ø // **B**). This line could have been lost from Bx through visual distraction (*bowes...bereþ none / bowes þat bereþ nat*); but the semi-anacoluthic **C** line seems an afterthought, and the case for inclusion is not strong. **261 (B 109)** *þei* ?α: necessary for the correct sense and either lost coincidentally by F or re-introduced by R. The βF reading (Ø-relative standing for *þei þat*) is possible with a comma after *hem*, but is less close to the revised **C** form than is that of R. **263** scans as a Type IIa line with cognative alliteration (|p| / |b| |b|). **264 (B 111)** *in Latyn ypocrisie* **B**: the required ↔ restoring the first stave in what is now a Type IIIa line that scans on *l*, Bx presumably having inverted the order to give prominence to the dominant idea. In theory, Bx could scan vocalically with the initial stress on *ýpocrisie* and two mute staves (*in, is*) but in the light of **C**'s revision to a Type Ia scanning on *l*, the emendation seems justified (and cf. pronunciation of *Ypócrisye* in C 263). **266 (B 113)** Coincidental loss of the line in *p¹* and three mss from *p²*, y and u here provides a classic instance of homoteleuton. **267 (B 114)** *prélátes*: pronounced with two full stresses. **268 (B 115)** *ben* **B**: emended on the evidence of (revised) **C** to provide the needed first stave in a Type Ia line. Bx might be scanned if both words of the French phrase ended the a-half (*paroles* then being a full cognative stave), but this would give a weak b-half with a full stress on *and*. **C** adds a second |b| stave to lengthen the b-half as if to ward off possible stave-loss through scribal ⇒ of *aren* in first position. **269 (B 116)** *wolueliche* α: on grounds of sense and metre and in the light of revised **C** the only possible reading, β being a visual error and F a capricious ⇒. **270 (B 117)** *Crísostómus*: two-stressed in both versions, **B** scanning as Type IIIa and **C** as Type IIIb. *R–K* add *and prestes*, creating a 'scribal' amalgam of **B** and **C**. **271 (B 118)** *corruptum*: the neuter form preferred on grounds of sense, since the presumed referent is *sacerdocium* (the ordained clergy) not *tota ecclesia* (the

Church as a whole). The error could have been induced from the following adjective ending in -a (*marcida*).

B 120–27 120 will scan as Type IIIa on |m| or, preferably, on |w| with *was* as stave one. The word *who* in **L** appears always to be vocalic, and the other two **B**-Text examples (10.436 and 11.346) cited by *K–D* (p. 13, n. 15) of its occasional pronunciation with initial |w| are Type IIIa lines that their metrical theory mistakenly rejects. (On a possible |w| pronunciation of *wham* see at C 17.89). **121, 122** may both scan cognatively on |p| and |b|, line 121 as Type Ib and 122 as Type Ie with vocalic counterpoint or as Type IIIc. **123** *ech*: conjectured as providing a key-stave *ech_hath* alliterating (cognatively) with |dʒ| in *Iohan* and *Geffrey*. The Bx line scans *aa / xx*, but a Type IIIa pattern remains remotely possible if *Iohan* is pronounced as a Latin name (with |j|) and *girdel* has the palatal sound reflected in (rare) contemporary spellings with ʒ (but MED s.v. illustrates *ʒirdel* no later than OE). Another emendation, involving heavy (perhaps appropriately sarcastic) stress on the titles, is the ↔ of *siluer a girdel* favoured by *K–D*. **126–27** The postulated Bx line, *Hadde he neuere seruice to *saue* [*haue* R] *siluer perto, seiþ it with yuel wille*, scans as a Type Id (or Ie) but yields little sense. The thought is commonplace, the use of *perto* unidiomatic, and the expression clumsy: the meaning would be that such a priest 'never saves money to buy himself a breviary', and only says his offices with grudging ill-will. The present reconstruction clarifies the syntax and explains how Bx could have been generated, identifying *his* as the key-stave in 126 and *haue* R as the verb, so as to relate the priest's activity to the 'tool' he performs it with. In 127 *saue he haue*, with *saue* as conjunction (MED s.v. *sauf* prep. 4(a) 'except, unless'), is offered as the origin of the β verb *saue* and in turn connected (but with greater appropriateness) to the priest's wish to receive payment for saying his offices (*perto*). Loss of the postulated half-line will have been through assimilation of the second *haue* (127) to the first (126), and *haue* R (< α), *saue* (β) can now be distinguished as split variants of 127a. The reading is reconstructed only from material Bx is judged to have conflated from the proposed two-line original. Two copies respond to the perceived incoherence of Bx by adducing drink as a reason for the priest's dereliction of duty. F concocts *þat is betake to tauerne hows for ten schelyng plegge* after 125 to explain the priest's lack of a *porthors*, then re-writes 126 as *If he hadd no seruice ne siluer perto with evil will he will synge*, which corresponds in substance to 127 as reconstructed here. But the <OC²> source's b-half variant *for spending at ale* cannot be what *seiþ it with yuel wille* was generated from or anything except explicit scribal invective against priests like Sir Piers of Pridie of B 5.313//. *K–D* adopt OC² into a two-line reconstruction, matching its inventiveness with *He syngeþ seruice*

bokelees, their new a-half for 127. *yuel*: accepted on the evidence of α (recoverable from R and F) supported by L (< β), and on grounds of superior sense, as preferable to *ydel* γ, to which M (or its original *m*) has varied, no doubt by ⊗ from a w-type source.

273 *Vnkynde curatours*: the correct form of this phrase reconstructed from the split variants in **p** and **x**. Liberum Arbitrium's target here seems to be the clergy's pride and greed rather than their ignorance, and his phrase recalls Holy Church's words in I 186–88. The **x** variant could be due to recollection of the common term of criticism as used at, e.g. 15.16 //, that of **p** to mis-expansion of an abbreviated form, perhaps influenced by associations between *vnkynde* and *creature* like those at 6.294 //. **275** *oþer wyse* **C**: treated as a pronoun followed by an adjective (here a full stave) agreeing with *God*. R–K, in treating *oþerwyse* as an adverb (with inferior stress-pattern), overlook the relevance of *witty God* **B**. **279 (B 136)** *Churche*: possibly revision to a Type IIIc line or else a Cx ⇒ for *kirke* as in *B*-β, to which *C*-YDChN² have independently altered. But the new pattern being acceptable, there is no need for emendation (for another case of *churche* **C**] *kirke* **B** see 337 //).

B 138 *entreþ þe bisshop*: ↔ provides the key-stave lost through presumed inversion to prose order in Bx (*aa / xx*). The line now scans as Type Ia. **B 140** Type Ia on |n| with a liaisonal first-stave *seyen_(h)e*.

282 (B 145) C revises a Ia line scanning on |g| to a vocalic IIIb, the type with a 'supplemental' stave in fourth position. Heavy rhetorical stress falls on *here* because it anticipates syntactically relative *That* in 283, which is wholly revised. **284 (B 149)** Both lines offer several possible scansions, depending on how the key-stave is identified and the sense of the whole line interpreted. **B** is either Type IIIa, scanning on |tʃ| like // C 296, Ia on vowels with a mute key-stave *A*, or vocalic Ie with counterpoint on |tʃ|. **C** offers no clearly superior option, and is either Type IIIa scanning on vowels, with *is* as key-stave; Ia on |ð| with *þat* as key-stave and a liaisonal stave derived by reading *quath_Y* for *quod Y*; or Ia on |t| |d| / |t| with *þat_is* as liaisonal key-stave, *quod_Y* as second stave (cognative and liaisonal) and *Charité* as first stave, with stress on the final syllable. The last alternative is probably to be preferred, as it avoids the de-stressing of the most important word consequent on locating it in the onset. (At B 156 the line's key-stave is not in doubt, but in revising it, C 288 restores the word's stressed position by establishing *Charite* as a full stave). **289 (B 157)** The revision, which detaches the Latin as a citation-line, scans either cognatively on |p| |p| / |b| or vocalically with *hym* as key-stave, the former being preferable as nearer to the pattern of normal speech stresses and to its source B 156, a Type Ic with a cognative third stave. B 157 may be scanned as a Type I Latin verse-line alliterating on |n|, with English *As* the initial dip. There is a case for including in the C-Text the third clause of the Biblical quotation, which is translated in the English of 291a; the truncated form in Cx could have omitted an *&c* present in the original (as in D²Q). **305** alliterates as an extended vocalic Type III with double counterpoint on |g|; so *R–K*'s ↔ of *opere* and *ne greue* to give a Type I line is quite unnecessary. **330 (B 189)** *purtinaunces*: a revision to plural supported by the form of this expression at 2.108 //.

B 207–244 207 will scan on vowels but the stresses would fall more effectively if the stave-sound were |m| and *wiþ* a reflex of β *mid* (< Bx), the uncommon contextual sense of which might have invited ⇒ of *on* α, *yn* g (see MED s.v. *mid* prep. 6(a)). **213** Whereas easier scansion would be produced by reading *in lolleris nys he noȝt* in the a-half or *ne lyueþ* for *nys*, this will pass as Type Ie scanning on |n| with counterpoint on |l|, the (mute) key-stave being generated by elision of *ne + in*. F's *loveþ* is a characteristic scribal attempt to make the line normative. **224 (C 347)** *stille* **B**: conjectured by *K–D* as the required key-stave, *so* α being acceptable metrically but giving somewhat weak sense in context and failing to account for the form of the (equally unsatisfactory) β variant (see MED s.v. *stille* adv. 5 'continually'). It may be presumed that *tyl*, the *m*-reading altered to *for* in M by ⊗ from a w-source, was that of β, and *so* α could have resulted from mistaking the adverb for the adjective and judging the sense inappropriate here. Alternatively, *charite* had a by-pronunciation in |ʃ| furnishing a cognative stave for the |s| staves of the a-half. There is some spelling evidence of merging between *sh* and *ch* (see *TN* on 7.300), but the key-stave sound of the revised **C** line is clearly |tʃ|. On balance *stille* seems to offer the strongest sense, is seemingly echoed in *all here lyues* **C**, and could explain the form of β *tyl*. **234 (C 357)** Bx scans vocalically as a Type IIIa with strong sentence-stress on *hir* as key-stave and support in both half-lines from 'echoic' counterpoint on |w| and |l| (Schmidt 1987²:65–6); *pace K–D* and doubts in *Sch*¹, no emendation is needed. **244–48 (364–67)** The α lines seem genuine on intrinsic grounds and the showing of the (much-revised) **C** equivalent. No mechanical reason for their omission from β appears, but censorship may be suspected, since this is one of the most explicit criticisms of the hierarchy in the poem. **244** scans (after *Sk*'s inevitable relineation) either vocalically with a mute key-stave (*and*) supported by 'supplemental' fourth stave (*Holy*), or else cognatively on |b| |b| / |p|, the latter alternative perhaps preferable in the light of (much-revised) **C**. **247** scans either as Type Ib on |k|, with the first stave found liaisonally in *Ac_áuarice*, or else as a vocalic T-type line with counterpoint on |k|, the latter perhaps more likely on the showing of C 365, which scans on vowels. **254a** β: lost from α perhaps through eyeskip from *moore* 254 to *mooste* 255.

[B XV *continues*]

Passus XVII (B XV *continued*)

RUBRIC See the note on the Rubric to XVI. It would appear that the **x** tradition regards XVII, the seventh of Dowel, as in effect a Prologue to *Dobet*, since XVIII is headed the *first of Dobet* (see Rubric to XVIII). But **p** sees Passus XVII as the *first of Dobet* and proceeds accordingly.

B 268 The F variant *verred* challenges consideration against *verray* as the possible α reading for which R may be a ⇒ of the same easier word as β (so *K–D Sch*¹). MED s.v. *averren* v. 1(b) 'cite' does not instance the unapocopated form before C15¹ or record *verren* separately, though OED s.v. *Aver* v. gives *ver* itself from *Destruction of Troy* (? early C15), and the word was lexically hard enough to have puzzled the βR scribes. On the other hand, the βR syntax is hard enough to be original and to have stimulated F's source to clarify (here felicitously). For *quod he* must refer both backwards to the quoted Latin phrase, as a parenthetic statement-index, and forwards to the English of the b-half, as a transitive verb taking a direct object. The point seems to be less that *many* examples are being cited than that they are *true*.

15 (B 289) *of_Austynes* **B**: providing the key-stave by liaison, so no emendation is required. The phrase *or ellis frerys lyen* in ms B seems to echo the revised b-half of C 16. **24 (B 295)** *souel* **p**: to be preferred as the etymologically more correct spelling (< OE *sufol*: see MED s.v. *souel* n.2.), avoiding confusion with *saule(e)* (< OF *saolee*: see MED s.v. *saule* n.), which occurs at B 16.11. Whichever spelling **L** used, the pronunciation is disyllabic, *souel* better facilitating the possible semi-pun on *soule* 'soul', 'life-principle' (see 22): the sustenance of heavenly grace for the contemplative takes the place of physical food.

B 303–07 303–4 (C 29–31) appear authentic on intrinsic grounds and on the showing of revised **C**, and may be presumed lost from β by eyeskip (*yfed þat folk* 302a → *foode by foweles* 305a, *beestes* 303a → *beestes* 305b). **307 (C 34)** Bx 307 scans *réligioús* and would give better rhythm with a final plural *-es* or an inserted *men / renkes* after *religious* (cf. *holy men* in // C 34). **37–8** Division after *saide* **p** is to be rejected as giving an anomalous Type IIa with third lift on (phrasally unstressed) *was* and the semantically important *blynde* then forming a dip (*To his Wýf whén hě wás blýnde*). As lineated in **x**, 38 scans as Type IIIc with crossed alliteration on vowels and |bl|.

B 312–14 312 *haþ ben*: conjectured to provide the needed key-stave for which *was* is a Bx ⇒ of a more obvious form. The theoretically possible vocalic scansion on monosyllabic grammatical words yields an unnatural stress pattern and verb-participle ↔ in the last lift (*K–D*) is ruled out as giving a masculine ending. **313** *foweles*: not to be taken as an error for *foles* (as by Cr), despite the apparently paradoxical notion of (metaphorical) 'birds' being fed by literal birds (though the *briddes* are also symbolic). A pun on *foles* is doubtless intended, as was the converse pun on *foweles* at B 7.125; but Anima's bird-imagery here is principally and directly related to that he uses at 471–79, and only secondarily and obliquely to that of 'God's fools' in B 20.61–2 //. As no case for emending appears, *K–D*'s conjecture [*by*] *goddes* [*behestes*] for *ben Goddes foweles* must provoke wonder (cf. *Intro.* II § 102). **314** *by lyue*: particle / infinitive ↔ necessary to restore the key-stave lost through Bx's presumed inversion to prose order (cf. closely parallel phrase *þat they with deleth* in C 9.167 //).

48 *grene loue*: the reading *grene-leued* **p** is perhaps preferable on grounds of contextual appropriateness, with further support to be found in its echo of 16.248, 253, referring to the tree of the Church. But though *grene loue* **x** could be an error caused by *e / o* confusion or partly induced by the sense of following *charite*, it is the harder reading, strongly and interestingly defended in Hill 2002:72ff by appeal to Gregory's exegesis of Job 44:24, and should be adopted. **50** *Holy Churche*: the evident reading of Cx, two mss altering to the normative scansion. While *kirke* could have been the original reading of **C**, the present Type IIIa structure promotes a functional stress on *Holy* that generates ironic tension between the sense of the epithet and that of the verb *amende*. **53 (B 317a)** The Latin text in **B** has the feel of a supporting citation and is printed as prose. That in **C**, being more the quoted utterance of a speaker first named in the English of 51, is set out as verse, following the layout in ms X. *Numquam*: either an authorial error for *numquid* (the reading of *B*-Cr²³F, *C*-DW) or to be taken as part of a statement, the question proper beginning only with *Aut*. In **C** either *eis* has been omitted after *cum* (preposition) or *cum* is here the conjunction ('whereas') with *eis* understood. **55 (B 320)** *moore* **B** 'further' (MED s.v. *mor(e* adv. 1 'to a greater extent'): conjectured in the light of revised **C** as the required first stave in a Type IIa line and presumed lost through partial haplography before *amortisede*. **C** has the word in stave-position two, creating a Type Ia line, and by forming a noun phrase with *eny* removes the last lift of **B**. But **C**'s retention of *chanouns* renders *K–D*'s conjecture *monyales* superfluous. **62** scans cognatively on |k| |k| / |g| as a Type Ia, so *R–K*'s emendation of *bigynneth* to *comseth* is not required.

B 335–42a 335, 339 *robeþ*: in both cases the evidently right reading on grounds of contextual sense, Bx's error being presumably corrected by four mss severally (five in the case of 335, Y erring with the majority in 339). **342a** *Item* (2)...*rapis* β: lost from α by eyeskip from *Item* (1) → *Item* (2)...*Si autem*.

73 The archetypal line that follows scans cognatively *aa / xa* and could be emended without difficulty by ↔ to [*printe gode*] in the b-half. However, it looks suspiciously like a scribal expansion prompted by generalised ill-will against debased coinage and immediately by suggestion from the phrase *oþer worse* at the end of 73 and *printe(de)* at 75, 80). Thus the sense anticipates (and virtually repeats) that of 74–5 (*metal...nauhte = badde peny*; *printe puyr trewe = gode printe*). The thought flows better from 73–4 if the line is omitted, *Of...ygraue* elaborating the simile at 73b. Though identified as the sole spurious line in Cx, this one resembles the scribal line that follows B 5.193 (see Apparatus) and may be safely rejected from the text. **74** *moche moné*: the addition of the phrase *þat is mad* in t is a typical padding-out of a terse line doubtless felt to be too short. Instances such as this illustrate the untrustworthy character of the t-scribe's expansions (see Apparatus at 38 and 13.12). *nauhte*: 'worthless' (MED s.v. *nought* adj. (b)); the word is historically disyllabic and probably to be expanded as *ná-ùht* rather than having a diphthong + sounded final *-e* (cf. 1.181n and 9.112). **78 (B 352)** *of many of* **p**t: loss of the key-stave in *x¹* will have been caused by eyeskip from *of* (1) → *of* (2), the scribe of Y making an attempt at correction that restores the metre but at the expense of the sense. *myd* **B**: conjectured as the required key-stave for which *with* is a Bx ⇒ of the (effectively standard) synonym. This emendation leaves following 353b saying the same as 352b, and a conjectured form such as [*myd*] *synne is foule*[*d*] would remove the redundancy and offer smoother metre; but on balance minimal interference seems advisable. **85 (B 355)** *vnresonable* **B**: 'against (the) reason(able order of things)', because a disordered macrocosmic reflection of human sinfulness, as in B 5.13–20 (MED s.v. adj. 3b). The mistaken citing of this example to illustrate (uniquely) the sense 'wild, inclement' (*ibid.* 4) is perhaps due to taking it as a supposed error for *unsesonable*. But the preferred sense is supported by the whole passage B 358–70 (on nature) and 371–83 (on man and society). Neither banal ⇒, *vnstable* F nor *vnseasonable* Cr²³ (adopted *K–D*) can be seriously considered a likely original. **87** *so* **p**t (= *x²*): 'to such an extent' (MED s.v. *so* adv. 8(a)) establishes a more exact relation between the line's two clauses than does *and x¹*, even should this mean 'if' (MED s.v. *and* conj. (& adv.) 5(a)), as it probably does (the sense to be excluded is 'and'). For though this would neatly juxtapose 'unbelief' (lay) with 'wrong belief' (clerical) and challenge *so* as instancing scribal anti-clericalism, the thought recalls 16.272–73 and the preceding Latin, and is characteristic of **L**, with *erren* having a moral more than a purely intellectual sense (MED s.v. 2). **89** scans vocalically as an extended Type IIIa with a-half counterpoint on |w|, the key-stave being vocalically-pronounced *(wh)am*. It is possible that *wham* had a by-pronunciation in

|w|, but the relative pronoun is elsewhere sounded as an unaspirated vowel (see *TN* on B 15.120). **95 (B 357)** *lode-sterres* 'guiding stars' (MED s.v. *lode-sterre* n. (b)). The sg. form appears a scribal attempt to specify a particular one, the Pole Star (ibid. s.v. (a)). **99 (B 361)** *while*: preferable on grounds of sense, since **L**'s theme is decline, the variant *wel* being a probable reflex of an ambiguous Cx spelling without *h*. **101 (B 364)** *sulle myhte* **x**: on the basis of the context and the identity with **B** to be preferred as the original in **C**, **p**'s variant being doubtless the result of misreading *sulle* as *sulde* and then smoothing *myhte* to the infinitive of an appropriate verb. **103 (B 366)** *follwares*: 'retainers, (farm) servants' (MED s.v. *folwer* n. 2(a)), i.e. the *tilyares* of 100 (the referent correctly identified by the scribe of P²). The **p** variant *sowers*, which makes the line of Type IIb, may result from initial misreading of *f* as long *s*. But the (non-related) variants of P² and N² suggest that the word was found difficult in this sense. **106 (B 370)** *clymat*: '(region with respect to its) weather'; proposed for **B** on the assumption of a hypothetical Bx form **clemet* misexpanded as (meaningless) *clement* in α and then misread or rationalised to the plausible *element* in β (MED s.v. *element* n. 3 'atmospheric conditions; weather'). The latter is adopted by *K–D*, their line then scanning with two lifts in *cálcúled* but is securely to be identified as an error in the light of the lexical evidence and **C**. **108–09 (B 372–73)** Division of the lines according to **p** (as in **B**) leaves **x** lacking a second stave. This may be reconstructed from **p**'s *nouthe non* as *noon nouthe* which, in the form **non nou* in *x¹*, could easily have suffered haplographic loss of the adverb. The <RM> variant *no wye now* can be explained as a corruption of **p**'s reading, if a back-spelled form **nowhte now* is postulated (M's spelling *nowithg* may be a reflex of such a form). *Pe*, objecting to **p**'s 'padding', substitutes *of þise newe clerkes* from **B** to provide the omitted stave-phrase. But there is no justification for this, as the repetition of *nouthe* in 108a after 107b is characteristic of **L**'s late style. **110 (B 374)** *can*: necessary as the first stave in this Type IIa line and presumed lost by haplography before con*strue*. **112 (B 377)** *to fourmen hym vnder* **B**: reconstructed as an original phrasal form (partially) inverted to prose order in Bx, with consequent loss of the key-stave. F's attempt to remedy this loss results typically in altering the sense of the entire b-half. **115–16 (B 382–83)** In principle, line 115 as found in all mss except RM could make sense, if *bote* is taken not as a conjunction but as the noun meaning 'help', 'remedy' (MED s.v. *bote* n. (1)), with *and* having the sense 'and yet' (MED s.v. *and* conj. 4). But the presence in B 382b of the phrase *if swiche were apposed* and the greater completeness of the syntax with it argue for regarding line 116 as original. *Pe* follows *Sk* in printing the line but ascribes it to 'P', though it appears only in RM. It could in theory be a bril-

liant conjecture (partly inspired by **B**) on the part of the scribe of these copies' ancestral source r, since its absence from t and from the other **p** groups suggests that it was lacking in *x²* as well as *x¹*. But if the line is genuine, its loss from *p²*, e, q and t will be most simply explained as due to coincidental operation of the same mechanical factor as in *x¹*. This factor is the threefold occurrence of (near)-identical endings in the sequence of six lines of which it is the last: *maister*; *thynketh* (1); *maistres*; *-libet*; *lyuede*; *thynketh* (2). Such a lexical configuration is arguably singular enough to have occasioned an identical line-loss in five discrete sources. The metrical and semantic integrity of RM's line 116 argues against editorial scepticism based on unwillingness to accept so much convergent variation. Only one witness, F, recognises the lacuna in sense; but its distinctive b-half is probably a metrical filler borrowed from 112b rather than a partial reflex of the lost 116b, since the form incorporating the parenthesis *and...hem* gives superior sense. If it is authentic, the line's survival is most economically ascribable to independent descent of <RM> from *p¹* (< **p** < *x²* < Cx). The alternative explanation, correction of r from a 'lost superior **C** ms', entails positing a textual entity for which there is no logical necessity. **118 (B 386)** *hastite* **x**: preferred as the harder reading for which **p** and some **x** mss substituted the easier near-synonym. MED s.v. *hastite* n. does not cite this occurrence, which is earlier than those recorded except for the one from *Cursor Mundi*.

124 *letynge* **x**: preferred as both theologically bolder and contextually apter than *lengthynge* **p**; but both words are lexically rare and first cited here, the former uniquely in this sense (MED s.vv. *leting(e* ger. (b) 'leaving or relinquishing', *lengthing(e* ger. (a) 'extension of life'). Salvation *in articulo mortis* by bare profession of faith might, however, seem more relevant to the situation of heathens than conversion towards the end of a long life, the presumed implication of **p**'s reading. (The inferior spelling *lettynge* is to be emended as inviting confusion with the gerund of *letten* 'hinder'). **125** *chere* **x**: to be accepted as the second stave in this Type Ia line and doubtless lost from **p** by visual assimilation to preceding ch(e)rche and following char*ite*. While not very uncommon (see MED s.v. *cher* adj. 2(a) 'dear'), the word has in three witnesses invited ⇒ of an existing synonym (*dere*). But in the rarer sense 'solicitous' (ibid. 2(b)) at 148, it seems to have caused no difficulty to the scribes. **131** *louye*: obviously the correct reading in the light of 136ff, and *R–K*'s emendation to *leue* (p. 174) mistakenly ignores the decisive sense of 130, 136–40. **L**'s subject is 'lawful love', love based upon *leaute* or righteousness. **132** *gentel Sarresines* **x**: 'pagans', i.e. non-Christians other than Jews. The **p** reading would distinguish pagans ('gentiles') from Moslems ('Saracens'), the former category presumably being thought of as covering such as the Prussians or Lithuanians. But **L**'s concern with contemporary 'heathens' is generally (and here quite specifically) with those of monotheistic faith (see 134–35), viz. the Moslems. **136** *aloueth* x^1: 'commends' or 'sanctions' (MED s.v. *allouen* v.1(a); 3), preferred as being free from the ambiguity of *louep* x^2. If the latter is only an aphetic form of the former (MED s.v. *louen* v. (4)), then no pun on *louen* 'love' can be intended, other than perhaps a visual one. Given the concentration of references to law in the context (126, 130, 133, 136, 137, 139), the probable sense of the verb here is 'sanctions' (MED s.v. 3). That of the derived adjective at 130 will also be the legal one 'permissible' (MED s.v. *allouable* adj. (c)) rather than ibid. (a) 'praiseworthy, commendable', the sense under which this line is cited; but there is a recognised overlap of meaning. **139** *lyue* x^1: required on grounds of sense; only love that arises from a just *life* pleases God, and *louen* is interpretable as induced by preceding references to love, including the one at 136 in x^2. It might well have been the **p**-scribe's ⇒ for an original Ø-reading in x^2 (attested in t) misleadingly suggesting that the understood verb was *louyen* as at 137 and 138. The P^2 error both here and at 136 will be due to ⊗ from a **p**-type ms. **145** *the py* **p**D^2Ch: preferred as maintaining **L**'s distinction between the willing self (*animus*) and the disembodied soul (*spiritus*) presupposed by the allegorical *interpretatio* in 143–44 of *amicum* 140*a*. Failure to grasp this distinction (on which see 16.182//, 196//) has presumably led **x** to mistake the personal pronoun *pe* for the definite article and so to delete *py* as redundant. The presence of the latter in Ch (but without *pe*) could indicate that it was in t but lost thence by the immediate ancestor of <TH²> and was accordingly also in x^2. **147** *more*: present in P^2 by felicitous variation and adopted as providing the key-stave in this Type Ia line; for while vocalic scansion is theoretically possible, it is rhythmically and semantically counter-intuitive. Presumably *more* was lost from Cx's exemplar through partial haplography after *neuere*, and *eft* is a ⇒ under influence from a parallel common locution. For a similar loss of *more* after *neuere* in x^1 (where x^2 retains it), see on 16.78, and cf. also 15.273, where Cx omits without ⇒. **155** *lente*; *sente*: either preterite or, in spite of final -*e*, contracted present-tense forms of both verbs, the latter preferable on contextual grounds since *lyf* and *lyflode* alike are continuing not momentary gifts of God. Metrically, it would be better to expand the second verb as *sendep*, since disyllabic *sente* pr. sg. is a 'false form'. *R–K*'s omission of *and* but retention of *sende* (now rendered subjunctive) confuses the issue: acknowledgment of God as provider, not supplication to God to provide.

B 393–6 393 *Lede*: conjectured as the required key-stave for which Bx is judged a ⇒ of a non-alliterating synonym. The sense here (MED s.v. *led(e* n. (2) 1(a) 'person'), though also well-illustrated as applied to God

(ibid. 1(c)), could have troubled the scribe because of its accompanying epithet *almyȝty* (Cr's ⇒ of *god* suggests that even *persone* could seem to want dignity when thus collocated). That no difficulty was found in the same word at B 16.181, referring to the divine persons, may be due to its there denoting only a visual *representation* of the Trinity as human beings 'in one body'. The lost stave-word here cannot well have been *lord* (as *K–D* conclude), for this would neither have caused problems of sense or appropriateness nor have prompted *persone*, which is not a synonym of *lord* though it is of *lede*. **394** *bileuep in oon God*: inversion of verb and noun-phrase, here unusually to prose order, is required to provide the lost key-stave. Bx's diagnosed ↔, perhaps from dissatisfaction with the metrical form of the presumed original, may have been induced in part by 395b. The line as emended does not have a masculine ending, since the last lift is the semantically important numeral of *in oón Gòd* (by contrast, in the next line the stress-pattern is *oòn Gód*). **395** scans cognatively as a Type Ia line on |k| |k| / |g|; the vocalic scansion that *K–D*'s rejection of *k* / *g* stave-rime requires would both be intolerably awkward (through placing *Cristene* in the prelude-dip) and fail to achieve the b-half stress-variation from 394 (*oon* to *God*) that cognative scansion facilitates. Loss of the line from β will have been due to the simplest of mechanisms, eyeskip from Bx's identical 394 b-half to *mys*bileue in 396 (cf. 402–03). **396 (C 159)** The Bx line has two lifts in *mýsbiléue*, a well-established 'monolexical' pattern (found in 273a) justified by the extra sentence-stress on this conceptually important key-word. Possibly, however, the original line-division came after *brouȝte*, as hinted by the verb's presence as final lift in 181 // 409.

165 (B 398) *Men* x^2: the stressed form of the indefinite pronoun needed for the first lift (cf. 3.477, 4.121, where *me* is not a stave, and 9.128, where it is mute). **174–75 (B 402–03)** The **B** lines, which seem authentic on intrinsic grounds and the support of **C**, will have been lost from α by eyeskip (*ere* 401 → *ere* 403). **182 (B 410)** *leuen*: preferred on grounds of sense, syntax (*on* **x** must require 'believe' not 'live') and the clear testimony of **B**. The *B-M* reading, which substitutes *lyued* not for *leeuen* but for the two adjectives, shows visibly as adopted from a w-source (unless Hm has been corrected).

B 416–89*a* have no parallel text in **C**. 416–27*a* have been suspected of not belonging in **B** but of being clumsily inserted by a scribe at the present point in Bx while actually forming 'a draft of matter perhaps originally intended for the opening of C XVII' (Warner 2004:122). This is unconvincing, since the lines show none of the characteristics of 'draft' material as it has been identified in the **Z**, **A** and **C** versions. Moreover, they form the opening of a much longer excised section (B 416–84), the rest of which Warner does not find suspect. 418 and

423 are indeed re-worked as C 17.35–6, 48, but the lines' interruption of 'a developing discourse about evangelism, not alms' (ib.120) should not be exaggerated. The comparison of the contemplatives to the *apostles* at 417 anticipates the lines on the (apostolic) evangelisers and their successors beginning at 437, and their life of intercessory prayer for peace (426–7) is clearly part of what **L** thinks of as effectual Christian 'mission'. **418** *þat*: providing the mute cognative key-stave in a standard line. **421** *boþe*: conjectured (following *K–D*) as the required third stave in what becomes a Type IIa line, and presumably lost in Bx by assimilation of *-þe* to following *þe* and *bo-* to preceding Be*rnard*. *K–D*'s positioning of *Boþe* as the first word of the line gives only half the explanation of the loss (attraction to following *Be-*). But attributing its omission to the difficulty of the word's probable sense here ('likewise') fits better with its position *after* the proper nouns, while a purely mechanical explanation would suffice (for a parallel quasi-adverbial use, cf. 7.51 // B 5.438). **422** *fyndynge* α: preferred as a more unusual (yet also characteristic) word found in a very similar context at C 6.293 and providing a pun on *fynde* 424a (see *Commentary* further). The contextually less exact *almesse* will have come into β from its appearance at the line-end in 419. **423** scans as Type Ic in β but as the rarer (and thus arguably more authentic) Type IIb in α. Choice is finely balanced, as *lele* could well have come in from 422b, and since no major issue of sense arises, *goode* may be readily adopted. **428a–91** Because of the gap in F here, presumably due to loss of a leaf in its exemplar *f*, α is represented solely by R, which at 471–84 provides the unique witness to fourteen **B** lines with no **C** parallel. **450** *fourmed*: conjectured as the required first stave-word in a standard line, Bx being ⇒ of a commoner word less apt in the context (see MED s.v. *formen* v. 5 'instruct'). However, as this sense has been instanced at B 15.377 without troubling the scribes, the emendation is less than wholly secure. Simpler solutions would be to read *fullynge* with two staves (an unattractive prospect), insert *was* before *and*, or conjecture mechanical loss of a stave word **fullyche* before *what* or after *fullynge*. **460** *keperes* α: preferable on grounds of sense and of coherence with the terms of the simile (= the Christian clergy: see the relevant use at C 16.273, and cf. 465). The (irrelevant) *croperes* may be a rationalisation of **creperes* β, a visual or aural error with reduplicated *r* for the reading identified as that of Bx. **461** *mynnen* W: on grounds of sense and metre a good candidate for originality, if in W probably a felicitous correction of *menen* w. Although *mynnen* could have been the reading of β and *nymmen* a metathetic error or the result of minim-confusion, it is just as possible that β read *nymmen* (as an accurate reflex of Bx), since α *take* (and so coincidentally C) can only be a synonym-substitute for the latter. A rare sense 'understand' for

nimen is, however, illustrated by MED s.v. 6b (a)) where the citation from *The Wars of Alexander* gives the Ashmole ms variant *mynned* for the correctly alliterating Dublin ms reading *nomyn* (the converse of the situation here). Theoretically the (presumed Bx) line could have the caesura after *man* or be of Type IIIa with a five-syllable dip; but *mynnen* is preferable as lexically more coherent with **L**'s usage (cf. C 17.210 where //B-β substitutes *Wite*, and 19.231 (no //)). **470** *mowen*: conjectured to provide the required stave-word in position 1 where Bx ⇒ of the more obvious *don* is doubtless due to unconscious expectation of the verb that commonly follows the comparative adverb *so*. A more conservative emendation would diagnose simple ↔ of *men* and *rightfulle* to prose order in Bx. More radical is *K–D*'s *menen...after*, which finds its model in 404 and 474; but in those cases the idiom caused no difficulty to the archetypal (or to any other) **B** scribe, so their emendation corrects the error without explaining it. The present conjecture *mowen*, which gives the elliptical sense 'so may just men [be said to] desire mercy and truth', does so, since Bx *don* is no more than a simplification of that sense. **471–84** form the bulk of a coherent paragraph of text starting at 465 and constitute the first of two passages in B XV attested in only *one* sub-archetype (the other, 532–68, is in β only). There is no doubting its authenticity on grounds of thought or style, despite the lack of any **C** parallel, since it convincingly concludes a longer archetypally-attested passage (416–89a) with no reflex in **C**. As 471 begins with the first part of the fowls / calf simile and the lines in the second part are in β, the following fourteen, which elaborate the 'fowls' analogy, may be safely presumed to have been in Bx. The reason for their loss from β will most probably have been the scribe's resumption of copying at the wrong point in the text through inducement from four words or phrases at the beginning and end of the passage (*K–D* p. 67). **471** Since *understonde* is a past participle and *folk* a subject noun, the verb *is* would be expected. R's *his* is either one split variant from α **is his* (the possessive referring obliquely to God or Christ) or an idiolectal spelling of *is* with intruded *h*, as taken here. The line scans as standard with *fedde* as stave one or with a liaised cognative |δ| stave in *þe_honde*, or as vocalic Type IIIa with strong sentence-stress on *is*. **479** *wissynge*: 'instruction' or 'guidance', conjectured as providing superior sense contextually to *whistlynge*, which could be a visual error induced by homoteleuton (the identical rhyme in 478–79 does not itself indicate inauthenticity, being paralleled at, e.g., B 7.37, C 17.39–40). **480** *þe*[1]: reconstructed to provide a subject for *bymeneþ*, which is transitive; *by* has either come in through anticipation of the verbal proclitic or else a pronoun *he* (with the Evangelist as referent understood) preceded the verb in α and was lost through visual assimilation to *by*. **489a** was omitted from β perhaps through a rubricator's oversight (*K–D*) or because the quotation at the end of 489, verse 1 of Ps 131, was thought sufficient indication of what follows (though 489*a* does not in fact appear till five verses later in the psalm). In context, the pronoun has as referent not the feminine nouns of preceding vss. 4 and 5 ('sleep', 'rest') but the *arca* of following verse 8. It is thus *eam* in Vg, as in its appearance at C 11.51*a* // AB, where it is glossed '*caritatem*'. The R or α scribe may have taken its referent as *locum* (vs 5) or even *David*.

C 187–251 (B 491–568) The re-ordering of **B 503–68** is based on arguments of *K–D* (pp. 176–79) for the lines' dislocation in the archetypal text. Their content and order in Bx is uncertain because of imperfect attestation and internal incoherence. Thus, each sub-archetype has lost *part* of this sequence for mechanical reasons. β has lost 510–27 by homoteleuton (*bere...names* 509, *bereþ þe name* 527) and α has lost 532–68 through mistaking in 'adjacent passages similar or related words or notions in approximately similar positions' (*K–D* 178n). The omitted passages appear securely authentic, both in themselves and as preserved (somewhat revised) in **C**, α at 17.262–78 and β at 194–251, though **C** inserts seventeen new lines between the main portion of the β passage and its last two lines (see Vol. I, pp. 608–9). Up to the gap at 532, α has the text in the order as here reconstructed and continues correct thereafter; but β, as well as losing 510–27, displaces the seven lines before it (503–09) and the four after it (528–31) to directly after 532–68. *Sk* inserts the α passage (510–27) between 509 and 528 as here given. The exact location in Bx (and in Bx's source) of the lines missing in α is likely, on the evidence of // **C**, to have been as in β. Consequently *Sk*'s order may be safely regarded as that of Bx and, as is clear in his parallel text, its closeness to **C** shows this order as likely to have been also that of the revision-manuscript B[1]. The displacement must therefore have occurred in B-Ø, the common source of <BxB[1]> postulated as the first scribal copy of the **B** Version (see *Intro.* III *B* §§ 2–6). It might thus appear unjustified to reject **C**'s confirmation of Bx in so large a matter, when it has been regularly accepted in smaller ones; but there is a difference of principle. For what is at issue here is not a textual reading, where **C**'s retention of Bx may be said to ratify it, but a textual *sequence*, where **C** could have accepted the scribal order while modifying the text in a way that takes cognizance of the incoherence produced by that sequence. That such was the case seems probable from *K–D*'s demonstration not only of the mechanism of dislocation but of the inconsequence in the argument of the passage, as well as from three revisions apparently designed to remedy it. The inconsequence lies in the separation of **L**'s criticism of the bishops for the failure of their mission to Moslems (and also Jews) from the reinforcing argument that such a mission *should* have a good chance

of success since both groups share part of the Christian faith (belief in one God). **L**'s first revision addresses this inconsequence in BxB[1] by placing B 500–02 as C 17.252–54 and following these lines with the 'reinforcing argument' referred to (C 255–82). A second revision, less compelling evidentially but worth noting, is the insertion at C 156–58 of lines on Mahomet as false mediator that anticipate B 505–06 (533–34 in *Sk* = Bx) // C 257–58. A third, more suggestive than demonstrative, is the addition of a new passage 233–49 just before the presumed point of dislocation 'as if to smooth an awkward transition' [i.e. to the lines now relocated as B 500–09, = *Sk* 492–94*a*, 532–38]. *K–D* recognise that the deficiencies diagnosed in the Bx sequence could be authorial in origin, but defensibly maintain that 'editorial decision must finally turn on assessment of relative likelihoods'. The Kane–Donaldson shift has been challenged on the grounds that α and β may preserve separate phases of the **B** Version (see *Intro.* III *B* § 53). But the gain in clarity and force would seem to justify their 'very simple rearrangement', which is accordingly adopted.

188–257 are transposed with 258–85*a* in *C*-ms M, a feature *Sk* rightly describes as 'not easy to follow or explain' (*C-Text*, xl) and *K–D* ascribe to either 'sophistication' or 'good correction' (p. 179n). Correction, if from **B**, would presuppose recourse to a lost **B** source independent of both Bx and of B[1] (which apparently had the same order as Bx) and thus of B-Ø (see above). But while the possibility of such a source may be accepted, its availability at the post-archetypal stage of copying is antecedently improbable. If from **C**, a source independent of Cx must be postulated, since M belongs to a distinct branch of the Cx tradition at five or more removes from the archetype (see diagram in *Intro.* III *C* § 13). But there are no grounds for hypothesising such a source, the case for N[2] having corrected therefrom being unsustainable (see ibid. §§ 39–40). The order in M must accordingly be put down to mechanical causes; the dislocation of both 286 and of 259–85*b* are noted in the manuscript. Though interesting, therefore, M's witness is unlikely to have any bearing on the arguments for re-ordering B 503–68. **190–91 (B 494–95)** The emendation is based on identifying the three major **C** variants as unoriginal on comparison with the Bx line under revision. In *x[1]*, which may fairly securely be taken to represent Cx, 190 has unmetrical *xa / ax*. Of t and **p**, either may represent *x[2]*, but more probably both are independent attempts to provide a missing stave, t more obviously by translating from the Latin sentence 191 (*mundum*). While the latter, uniformly attested as the reading of Cx, might be a 'mongrel' line not governed by the verse-rules of true-bred macaronics (Schmidt 1987:100), it could result from the Latin having been entered in the margin of the authorial exemplar and then misplaced by Cx in copying. Reconstruction starts from the fact that

the b-half of the **B** line under revision (494) is a paren-
thesis placed between two parts of a single syntactic unit
wente…To be. The English b-verse of Cx's 191 is made
the b-verse of 190 and the Latin treated as a separate line
amplifying the new 190b and syntactically dependent
upon it, so that the whole phrase (190b–191) now forms
the expanded parenthesis between 190a and 192 (the lat-
ter two syntactically identical with **B** 494a–495). The
reconstruction, which eliminates the scribal phrases and
restores the metre without altering the sense, is supported
by the strikingly similar construction at 17.59–60, where
a Latin imperative stands parenthetically between *bidden*
and an infinitive.

B 500–31 *For notes see below on* **C 252–82** *in their
proper place.*

192 *prelates*: *R–K* alter to *pastors* after **B** to accord with
pastor 193*a*; but given the revision in 190ff, there is no
warrant to alter a reading satisfactory in metre and sense.
194–251 (B 532–68) On the placing of these lines in **B**,
see under **187–51**. **199** *pees and plente*: inverted by *R–K*
to accord with **B** on the basis of N^2, though they do not
follow N^2 in omitting *and* in 201. Both instances indi-
cate ⊗ from **B**, not correction from a superior **C** source.
201 (B 539) *and* **C**: a revision anticipated in WCrB; but
asyndeton is a widely-attested feature of style in **B**. **206**
The **x** variant *religiones* could be a visual error; although
religioun in personal application is recorded (MED s.v.
1(a)), **L**'s usual form is that of **B**. **208 (B 545)** *clerkes*
B: conjectured on the showing of unrevised **C** as the
required key-stave for which β (or Bx) *men* is a (no doubt
unconscious) ⇒ of a non-alliterating term very com-
monly collocated with *Holy Kirke / Churche,* as at 202b.
210 (547) *Minne* **C**: conjectured on the showing of **C** as
the first stave-word for **B** (cf. on B 461). Conceivably **C**
revised to scan on |m| a **B** line with the stave-sound |w|,
and the original key-stave was *wyes. But on balance it
seems likelier that β substituted *Wite* under inducement
from following *wise*; and since, in the absence of α, the
certain Bx reading remains unknowable, the emendation
from **C** evidence (retaining *men*) is here to be preferred.
213 (B 549) *dampnede* **C**: a revision strengthening the
restrained **B** original, as at 215 below (B 551). **B**'s variant
(with that of Bm visibly by correction) may be seen as a
⊗ from **C**, not a correction from a hypothetical superior
lost **B** source. **214 (B 550)** *come auht* **C**: adopted also for
B as the needed key-stave presumed lost in β, perhaps
through failure to grasp the line's rhythmic structure (so
that *Right* not *clerkes* was taken as first lift) together with
unconscious influence from the common phrase *er longe.*
C revises the syntax to give this and the following line a
new subject (*coueitise*), a change better in keeping with
the tone of *dampne* (**B**'s *þei* has as its referent 'Reason
and rightful doom'). **215 (B 551)** *depose youre pride* **B**:
verb-object ↔ (here to prose order, following **C**'s lightly

revised b-half phrase) provides the required key-stave.
218 (B 554) *lese…euere* **B**: reconstructed on the basis of
C to provide the required key-stave lost in β and possibly
Bx through inversion of adverbial and verb-phrases. **228**
ȝe: the reading of x^2, to which Y will have varied coinci-
dentally, unless it alone preserves x^1. Either *ȝe* or *þe* could
be a visual error for the other, but on grounds of sense *ȝe*
is harder and so likelier to be original. The unexpected
shift from one addressee (*lordes* 227) to another (*kynges*
228), though awkward, is not much more so than that
from the same addressed subject to a new verb-subject
making the *kings* potential beneficiaries of an action by
the baronage. The sg. form *kynge* in ID, though pointed,
cannot be original, as reference must be to kings gener-
ally (cf. *Alle londes* 237) or at least to the English
and French monarchs, not the King of England alone.
230 The added **C** line is of ambiguous metrical structure,
either vocalic Type Ib with a mute key-stave *and* 'sup-
plemented' by the fourth 'enriched' stave (*Intro.* IV § 44)
or more naturally as Type IIIc with alternate staves on
|ð| and vowels, the first generated by elision of *The* and
heuedes. Standard scansion is excluded because *vnder
hem* fails to provide a feminine ending (*ben* may be a
Cx error for *aren*). To read *hem* for *tho* would make for
smoother metre, but is stylistically clumsier. **231 (B 565)**
charite: undoubtedly an improvement in style and metre;
but the Bx reading with a four-syllable prelude dip is not
necessarily scribal, since the rhythmic pattern, seen in
550 or 560 above, is a common one. **239** scans either as a
vocalic Type Ie with mute key-stave and counterpoint or,
preferably, on |m| with two lifts in *Mácométh*. **240** *quyete*
x^2: preferred on grounds of sense, since acknowledging
Mahomet's political astuteness (*gyle* 242), not ascribing
Trajan-like qualities of justice to him. **247** *descendet* **x**:
the present (presumably denoted by the *-et* ending) gives
better sense, the reference being not to the single event
of Pentecost but to the permanent offer of divine grace in
response to devout prayer (specifically in the consecra-
tion at Mass).

252–82 (B 500–31) See Vol I pp. 602–05 for the text and
apparatus of the **B** passage and parallel text of the relevant
C lines. **254 (B 502)** *turne* **p**: present in the **B** line under
revision and essential for sense and metre, but lost from x^1
and t possibly through visual attraction of *sholde → hoso*.
256 (B 504) *grete holy God* **B**: reconstructed in the light
of revised **C** as the probable form of **B**, that of Bx being
not securely determinable. The α reading is metrically
acceptable but would come very abruptly after 503, the
sense of which it leaves incomplete (F's *&* is an obvious
attempt to smooth the transition). On comparison with
C, *On…greden* suggests the corruption of a hypothetical
form **On a god þe grete* in α's immediate exemplar. In
β *holy grete* may owe its metrical awkwardness to ↔ of
the two epithets through alliterative attraction of *grete* to

god; the same error occurs in *C*-N², which is probably by ⊗ from a *B*-β source (see *Intro.* III *C* § 40). In the Cx tradition, the underlying *x¹* reading may have been *grete god* as in YD²u (so *R–K*); but the form of X's *grethe* and t's added *of heuene* suggest a missing word between the first epithet and the noun, either *heuene* (in the possessive) or *hye*. The latter is preferred in the light of *B*-β and on the grounds of its contextual suitability (cf. *hy* 247, 262). **258 (B 506)** *lyueth* **C**: preferable also as the original for **B** (B*x* < L = β, + α). The source γ (to which M varies, as frequently elsewhere) will have substituted *leue* through attempting to make explicit the elliptical construction whereby *leue* is 'understood' in the b-half as 'borrowed' from the actual verb of the a-half. The latter could have had the spelling-form *leue* (see MED s.v. *liven* v (1)); but annominative chime (Schmidt 1987:113–17) rather than exact homophony may have been intended. (One *C*-ms, Ch, has *leueþ,* adopted by *R–K* with the sense 'believe'). **264 (B 512)** *by sad resoen* **C**: adopted also for **B** as providing a stronger and more characteristic sense than the reading *þat by* for *by* α (which does not necessarily represent B*x* here). The 'firm / serious ground *or* argument' in question is the literal *ensaumple* of Christ's acts of 'mercy and grace' [his healing miracles]. The *resoen* here is thus metaphorical (cf. MED s.v. *resoun* n. (2) 5(c)), whereas in α's reading it must signify 'reason' (ibid. s.v. 1a(a)). The relevance of this to the conversion of the Moslems could have prompted the variant; but 268 // and 270 // indicate that **L** has in mind 'suffering unto death' as the spiritual condition of both healing-miracles and the 'miracle' of conversion (on the linking of *ensaumple* with Christ's power, mercy and suffering see 1.167–69 //). **268 (B 516)** *bissh(e)inede x¹?α*: adopted as lexically harder, though its precise meaning in context is somewhat uncertain (*R–K* read *bisshemede* in XYI, but U has the unambiguous form *bishined* and D *bescyned*). MED has *bishinen* with only the strong preterite in all senses, of which the aptest is 2(b) 'enlighten' or 2(c) 'make illustrious' (with a metaphorical sense as of 'illuminating' a manuscript, or 'causing something to shine'); so **L** must here be using an otherwise uninstanced weak preterite. Alternatively, the word intended is **bisigned*, a (completely unrecorded) ?intensive form of *signen* 'to mark with a sign' (the actual ⇒ by F for the presumed α reading in R). Whatever the exact form of the lexeme, its extreme rarity caused difficulty. But *bisshopid x²* 'confirmed' has small claim to originality; for though also uncommon, it can hardly have generated *bissheinede* and is best judged a response to the implications of *metropolitanus* (267) as a title of Christ. The 'baptismal' significance of Christ's death on the cross was a familiar notion (see 21.325), whereas confirmation was associated with Pentecost (21.226–28 and see *Commentary*). **271 (B 519)** *enfourme*: clearly the right reading on grounds of sense (MED s.v. *enfourmen* v. 4 'teach or

spread' [the Gospel]). The variant *enferme*, perhaps no more than orthographic, might have been unconsciously induced by the contextual references to bishops (as, clearly, were *conferme* and D²B-F *ferme*). **275 (B 523)** The revised **C** line scans, like 276, on vowels, but as a Type IIIa. Four *C*-mss TVZN² severally read *kirke* for *churche*, which certainly provides effective contrast with the vocalic stress-pattern of 276. *R–K*'s adoption of this normalisation is at odds with their acceptance of Type III in 273, where the caesura is unlikely to come after *mony* and simple ↔ of the half-lines would yield a Type Ia line. **279 (B 528)** The variant *That* β for *And nat* CB-α is an attempt to achieve a juncture between 509 and 528 by borrowing the relative particle from the beginning of 509 and turning 528 into a second relative clause by reading *that* for the (now meaningless) *And nauʒt*. The sense of the **BC** line is elliptical: 'Thomas is an example to all bishops, and especially to titular bishops *in partibus*, [of martyrdom], not of wandering about England'. See further *Intro.* III *B* § 53 for fuller discussion. **B 572b–75a (285–86)** are attested by α and will have been lost from β by eyeskip (*goostly foode* (1) → (2)) but are clearly authentic on grounds of sense and metre (the 'patched' β line will scan but is defective in sense). **285 (B 572)** *follen*: 'baptise' (MED s.v. *fulwen* v.) rather than 'fill' (MED s.v. *fullen* v. (1)(b)), which is not appropriate here and will have been suggested by preceding *Feden*. The sense is not particularly apt, since baptism was specifically the parish priest's duty, and *fermen* 'confirm' might have been more exact. **286** On the order in M, see note on 186 above. **292** scans as Type Ia with a five-syllable prelude dip. **293 (B 578)** The **C** line, unless it has lost a |k| stave (whether an adverb **ek* or a first object before *haen* such as *clerkes* as in // B 580), must scan with a liaisonal stave on *Ac we*, an unusual example of revision of a Type Ia to a Type IIa. *R–K*'s conjecture *crede* for *lawe* (p. 171) anticipates *bileue* 294, obscuring the specific meaning (*lawe* = *moral* teaching).

B 583–611 583 is a 'licensed' macaronic with only one |p| stave in the a-half, the whole scanning *bba / ax*, unless it is a Type II with |dʒ| staves on *-gé* and on *Iéwen*. **584 (C 296)** is here taken to have *Messie* as key-stave (the revised line is a standard Type I). An alternative scansion on |t| would allow the α variant *it hem*; but in the light of **C** it seems better on balance to see |m| as the stave-sound. **604 (C 313)** *Grekes*: here taken as a reference to (some at least of) the pre-Christian Greeks, not to the Greek Orthodox, who were of course Christians as well as monotheists (MED s.v. *Grek* n. 1(a), not 1(c)). In spite of the revised **C** line's mentioning Jews and not Greeks, the WHm variant *Iewes* is likely not to be original but to have come in by visual error from 606, where *Sarʒens* also appears in the a-half as in 604. Possibly this happened coincidentally in WHm, and the w-group reading was correct as in Cr. **611 (C 320)** *rendren*: in the light of **C** the harder reading, preserved in L alone, and likelier to be original in **B**. Unusually α here reads with γM and, unless this is a reading of Bx which L has corrected by collation with **C**, is to be seen as a coincidental error. The mistake could have resulted from misconstruing the nasal suspension through failure to identify the correct lexeme. The precise sense is not certain here and the word's virtual restriction to **L** before 1400 suggests that it was found difficult. Thus, although the association with *recorden* 'remember' seems to favour the sense 'recite, repeat' (MED s.v. *rendren* (c)), there is room for doubt. To illustrate the only other sense of this verb acknowledged by MED 'translate' (s.v. (d)), the sole example cited is A 9.82 (= B 8.90, C 10.88), where the context suggests rather 'read aloud and expound' than 'translate'. Possibly, therefore, *rendren* here too means 'explain the meaning of', since what is in question is the progressive catechesis of adults with already-formed religious beliefs, not the instruction of infants learning by rote.

Passus XVIII (B XVI)

RUBRICS The Cx tradition (if accurately preserved in **x**) seems to make XVIII the *first* passus of *Dobet,* and XVII implicitly its Prologue. This fits with the *B-β* reading and points to the latter as representing Bx. Where *C-**p***'s numbering is one ahead, *B-R*'s is one behind and *B-F*'s completely anomalous.

25 (B 24) scans as a Type Ie line on |δ| and |θ| with mute key-stave *that* or as Type Ic with original **quath_he* for *quod he* to give a liaisonal stave on |θ|. This is not very satisfactory and it may be that Cx has substituted the commoner *bereth* for *shuyueth* to avoid too close repetition of 20.

    B 20–8 20 *loue-dreem*: preferred on grounds of contextual meaning as well as metre, notwithstanding the argument for *lone* in *Sch*[1] and Schmidt 1986:29–30. The dream is produced by the *pure ioye* of hearing a beloved name, and the first-element stress of the compound phrase (*lóue-drèem*) would not be idiomatically possible with the reading *lone*. For a similar error see *allone* β for *and loue* αC at C 11.169 // B 11.8. **25** *witen* β: preferred as providing characteristic wordplay on *wite*. For although the α line could scan as Type IIa with *wiltow* as a full stave and *kepe* appears in revised C 28b, *kepen* is likely to be a ⇒ for this lexically less familiar verb, which is found also at B 7.35, A 10.67 (see OED s.v. *Wite* v. 2 'keep (safe)', MED s.v. *witien* v.(1) 'protect'). **27–8 (C 31–2)** *B-α* has lost two half-lines 27b, 28a through homoteleuton (*wynd...wynd*) at the line's mid-point. L's conditional is preferred in the light of **C** as likely to preserve β, M having varied to the γ reading.

37 (B 33) scans as Type Ia on |s| (|ʃ| and |s| in **C**) with a

stress in *norisc(h)éth* seemingly wrenched from the root syllable to the inflexional morpheme. The identical form of the line in both versions argues against *K–D*'s conjectural emendation of the key-stave *som* to *anoþer*. The metrical difficulty it posed is registered in the attempts to regularise by *C-G*'s and *B-F*'s adding *nyce* respectively before *wordes* and in place of *tyme*. **50 (B 50–1)** **C** unusually revises a Type Ia line to an extended Type IIIa scanning on |ð| / |θ|, possibly with counterpoint on |p|. *R–K* emend *palle* to *falle* (understood here as a scribal attempt to normalise the metre); but the likelihood of this verb's having been replaced in Cx (or in *x*[1], **p**) by the lexically harder *palle* (the assured reading of **B**) is remote. *thridde*: the right reading in both **B** and **C** (each shoring up the other), *B-M*'s source *m* evidently having erred by ⊗ from a γ ms. **55** *fayre* **x**: preferred to **p**, whose *wonder* may have been prompted by *ferly* 56. **60** *sonnere*: preferable on grounds of sense, with *somme* an easy visual error partly induced by its preceding occurrences in the a-half. The reading is clearly that of *x*[2] (> **pt**) and N[2] would seem to have been collated with a **p**-type source, as may D. It is not evident whether Y was too, or is a happy scribal correction, or an accurate independent reflex of y, as seems possible in the light of 75. The original of <XIP[2]D[2]> could have erred mechanically and U (< u) coincidentally. **63** *o*: 'one and the same [degree of]'; preferable on grounds of superior sense and presumably lost from several mss through haplography after *of*. **64** *sonnore*: though rejected as obscuring the wordplay on *sonne*, the *sannere* of XY is an authentic historical spelling-form derived from OE *sana* (see MED s.v. *sane* adv.), is instanced at Z 7.165, and could be original. **B 66** scans as Type IIIa on |s| and (*pace K–D Sch*[1]) no emendation is required. **70** *apples of o kynde*: 'fruit of one species'; the alternative without *o* preferred by *R–K* gives the sense 'natural fruit', which is acceptable, but does not repeat 62 so closely. **L**'s point is that whether the species is that of apples or of humankind, there is variation and difference, though one common species-nature. **75** *hete x*[2]: judged original on grounds of sense and metre. Of the five *x*[1] variants, only the Ø-reading preserved in N[2] (and coincidentally in the **p** copy W) could have generated the others and thus be the group-original. The unrelated *þei* and *sonne* point to a Ø-form in u, as *thre* does to Ø in y, since it seems suggested by the threefold category specified in 74. Y's variant indicates independent descent from y, the group <XIP[2]D[2]> here sharing a disjunctive reading. It would appear likely, therefore, that *x*[1] read **These haen þe [ ] of þe holi goest* and that two mss of this family (Y and D) have omitted *þe* (1) in smoothing after insertion of their respective conjecture (U's *sonne*, being a noun, does not require such smoothing). The reading at 75 is one of the most decisive indicators of two major sub-divisions in the Cx tradition (*x*[1] and *x*[2]), of a two-fold division in *x¹* (y and u), and of a possible sub-division within y into < XIP²D² > and Y. **83** The ampersand here is expanded as *and* following DPAVMG in order to treat the line as a double macaronic (like 16.202) and better integrate it with the structure of the whole sentence. **94** For the preferred order in the b-half, cf. 123b. **B 71 (C 97)** The Bx line (*pace K–D Sch¹*) scans as a T-type with wrenched stress on -*hóde* giving the first vocalic a-stave, *and* as a mute key-stave, and the b-staves on *r*. **101** The a-half is treated by *R–K* as a parenthetical interjection; but this seems forced and is unparalleled in **L**'s usage, while the thought in 101b–03a is not such as to be unattributable to Will. **102** The epithet *faire* **p** is to be rejected as a scribal insertion for added emphasis (cf. *wonder* **p** at 55) which sits uneasily with *inparfit* 103. **B 78** Duggan (1990:180) argues for transposing verbal and adverbial phrases in the b-verse on metrical grounds; but though inversion to prose order is common enough in the Bx tradition, emendation is not strictly necessary, since the suffix -*liche* is disyllabic here (see note on 1.177 above). Nor does occurrence of monosyllabic terminal -*ly* at 9.329 //AB (a core-line) count decisively against this, since **L** could have used variant forms of the suffix at his convenience. **120–21 (B 87–8)** The C line as here punctuated requires *hit aftur* 'threw' (MED s.v. *hitten* v. 2(b), illustrated only from **L**) to have an understood object *it* (= *shoriare* 119). But possibly *fley* 121 is a Ø-relative clause and *Filius* the object of this verb, like *Filius* in // B 88. **126 (B 92)** *iustice(s)*: in each case what seems to be the archetypal form is given, since either may be intended; if *iustice* 'justice' (MED s.v. *justice* n. 1), then the pun is on 'judge' (ibid., 5(a)), if *iustices*, then it is on 'justice'. A second pun on *sone / sonne* also seems clearly intended (see *Commentary* further). **128** *That* 'at which time, when', corresponding to *And þanne* **B**. *R–K* place a full stop after *rype* and treat *That* as a demonstrative adjective. **130 (B 96)** Understood in each case is an antecedent verb, hence 'to determine [who / which one]'; for a similar construction cf. 3.152 //. *fonge* **B** 'capture' (MED s.v. *fongen* v. 3): preferred on grounds of sense and closeness to revised **C**, though perhaps a felicitous correction. Either Bx read *fonde* 'try (for), attempt' (MED s.v. v. 8(a)) or else the reading of YCBLR is a ⇒ for Bx *fonge* 'undertake', 'endeavour' (MED s.v. 8), which overlaps semantically with *fonde*. The fittest meaning here however is 'get hold of' (= *fecche* **C**), since both Christ and Satan are to *try* for the fruit but only one will win it. **139 (B 103)** *hy*: the reading of *x²* and presumably also of *x¹* (if Y = y and U = u). It is preferred on grounds of sense, 'the fullness of time' (MED s.v. *heigh* 6(b)) translating the Latin of the a-half (and cf. *plener* in // B 103). Therefore *by* is to be taken as a visual error, which D coincidentally shares with the exclusive ancestor of <XIP²D²> (though I's reading is unknown, owing to the loss of a leaf).

B 110–50 110 (C 143) In spite of earlier doubts (*K–D, Sch¹*), 110 can now be accepted as scanning cognatively, with the **C** line offering a complete revision of the b-half. There are no real grounds for questioning 108–09, which employ a type of repetition-with-variation (*sike and synfulle*) well instanced elsewhere in **L**. **110a (C 142a)** Choice between α *male habentibus* (Vg and *VL*) and β *infirmis* (*apud* Ambrose, *Apologia*) is evenly divided. But *sanis* (Vg *valentibus*) is common to *VL* and Ambrose (AlfQ). **115 (C 146)** *as*: revised to *ar* in the direction of greater fidelity to the Vg source Jn 11: 35 (though the phrasing is that of Mt 26: 37). Though possibly the result of miscopying *r* as *s* (*K–DSch¹*), Bx *as* could as easily have been an authorial misrecollection of the Biblical sequence, so emendation is not justified. The a-half shows further revision in *miracle*, and the preceding and following lines are both changed. **121 (C 152)** scans either as Type IIIa on *ch* or cognatively as Type Ia on the related unvoiced and voiced sounds |tʃ| and |dʒ|; emendation in either case is otiose. On grounds of sense *iesus* must be correct and β a misreading of the exemplar's Latin abbreviation *ihc* or *i ch* [= *iesus christus*]. **125 (C 154)** The numerically indefinite *fisshes* of **B** is revised to the literally inaccurate *fyue fisches and loues.* Amongst the **B** sources, w has unnecessarily altered *fisshes* to *two fisshes*, M following doubtless by collation with its w-type source and F independently changing α. But **L** may have recalled that the feedings of the Five and the Four Thousand gave different quantities for the fishes (two in Mt 14: 17 // Mk / Lk/ Jn, 'a few' in Mt 15: 34). **136** *arne*: to be securely adopted on the basis of sense and the showing of **C** as the strong preterite of the SWM form *ernen*, on all grounds likely to be **L**'s authentic usage. The R variant is an ambiguous syllabicised reflex that was probably the reading of Bx (as it is of *C*-YI) and generated the β preterite of a supposed verb *to be*, with F coincidentally following the same substitution-process. **140** scans on cognative staves (|θ| |f| / |ð|), the last of them mute. Either *cene* or *maundee* could be original, the latter giving a T-type line. But on balance it would seem preferable to judge *maundee* a scribal ⇒ aimed at avoiding repetition of *cene* in *soper* 141; for one co-polyseme of *maunde* (MED s.v. n. 2 (d)) is the washing of hands and feet (Christ's *mandatum* 'command' of love), and that may have been understood by the scribe. **142** *som* 'a certain one' (MED s.v. *som* pron. 1 sg. (a)), for which α has the spelling-form that normally represents the pl. and β ⇒ of a non-alliterating but unambiguous synonym. Given that the pl. sense is contextually excluded, *som* sg. is to be judged as the harder and therefore the likelier original reading. **150** scans as a Type IIIa line with the four-syllable prelude-dip by no means unusual in lines of all types (cf. e.g. B 79). Although original **B** could have read **Iudas þe Iew*, echoing B 10.128 still more closely than does Bx, no emendation is required, since the full staves are evidently the two proper names. *K–D*'s conjecture *þus] so* is otiose and weakens the line by locating all three staves in non-lexical at the expense of semantically more important words (for *þus* functioning with full semantic weight, cf. 160, where it is a full stave in key-position).

169 (B 151) *þat ribaud; he* ? **p**: to be preferred to the pl. on grounds of sense, since it is Judas who is in question, and the reference of the identical form in **B** is not in doubt. The mss suggest, however, that the correction may have been made in *p¹*, with D² agreeing coincidentally and D possibly by correction from a **p** source. In the absence of K it remains uncertain whether *p²* had the pl. noun, N's *þys* being potentially pl. though the noun is *rybaude* sg. The error could be due to retrospective smoothing of the sg. noun and demonstrative after earlier misconstruction of **ȝede* as plural, while the noun in the exemplar could have had a number-ambiguous spelling **ribau(du)s*. But whether *p¹* here = **p** (< *x²*) or shows intelligent correction, it is intrinsically preferable as representing the probable original of (here unrevised) C. **175** *vsen* 'practise': contextually more appropriate than *vysen* 'devise' (so X); either could be a visual error for the other, or the latter a spelling-variant of the former, with *y* a graphemic indicator of length. **176 (B 158)** *and at*: reconstructed for Bx after C from the split variants *and* α, *at* β, with a liaisonal stave (possibly mute) in *at_youre*.

B 161 *his name*: because he is known as 'Jesus' during the early stages of the Passion, becoming 'Christ' only at the crucifixion. Since the importance of the *name* of Jesus is later brought out in Will's remonstrance to Conscience at B XIX (esp. 15–25) // C, it is decidedly not a 'pointless homœograph [for **ynome*]' (*K–D* p. 185). F's variant seems an obvious ⇒ (unconsciously induced by preceding *taken*) for an exemplar misreading *y nome* of α **ys nome*, whereas βR (= Bx) make an important point about *Iesus*, who receives the further name *Crist* at 164. But if a past participle form *ynome* were read, the half-line *would* ('pointlessly') repeat 160b. The notion plainly underlying *K–D*'s reconstruction of F's exemplar reading, that it is taken from a postulated superior lost **B** ms, finds scant support from argument of this order.

177 (B 159) *pays; pees*: apparently no more than spelling variants (MED s.v. *pes* n.), as the ↔ by WCr etc suggests (the less common *pays* form is found elsewhere only at Z 4.52). Although the different graphs need not denote distinct senses of the same lexeme, such senses may well be intimated, e.g. 4 (a) 'freedom from molestation' and 5 (b) 'cessation of hostilities' ('alone'; 'in peace' [*Sk*]). After this q has a line: *Sinite eos abire etcetera* (= Jn 18:8). **181 (B 169)** *Estwárd*: requiring wrenched stress to provide the first stave; decisive support for its correctness appears in the key-stave of B 228 // below (*afterwárd*).

202 (B 192) Both archetypal lines have the same defective metrical pattern *aa / xa*. Emendation must therefore be tentative (*K–D* emend Bx, *R–K* leave Cx unmetrical), but scribal inversion to prose order may be discerned in each case. The sense of Cx *se* will correspond closely to *knowe* Bx if the latter is taken as 'know by experience' (MED s.v. *knouen* v. 4(a)), signifying that God (*potencia*) acquires *experiential* 'knowledge' of his power (as light / life) by exercising / manifesting it through an intermediary (*sapiencia*). This reading is theoretically possible but theologically tortuous. A more lucid interpretation of *knowe* in **B** would be as 'make known, reveal, show' (MED s.v. 7(a)), which is more appropriate to God's self-disclosure through Christ. In that case the **C** revision, which alters only the verb, might be expected to read not *se* but *shewe*, which is here conjectured as the original (perhaps ambiguously spelled **sewen*) for which Cx is presumed to have read **suen* (see for the spelling forms MED s.v. *sen* v. (1) and *sheuen* v. (1)). The source of error in Cx's exemplar could have been auditory as much as visual, since **L** may have sounded *s* as |ʃ| before front vowels (for an earlier example see on 1.39 // ZBC). But an equally important contributory factor might have been the semantic overlap between the two verbs (see MED s.v. *scheuen* 1(a) 'see'). The sense of *shewe* here will be 7(a) 'make known' or 9 (a) 'disclose, reveal', both close to the meaning of *knowe* preferred for **B**. **203 (B 193)** *soffreth hem boþe*: the α reading confirmed by Cx as likely to be that of Bx, though the construction is idiosyncratic and the sense consequently difficult. Impersonal uses of *suffren* are not recorded in MED, which does not cite this example. Yet *hem boþe* must be necessarily the subject of the verb, despite its object case, since *what* as subject yields no ascertainable meaning. Presumably, therefore, *hem* registers the continuing force of the verb *shewe* in 202 = B 192 *knowe* and is thus accusative, while logically it functions as a nominative. The sense of 202–03 (B 192–93) might be rendered tentatively: 'power, and a means / intermediary to manifest his own power and that of / proceeding from his agent, and what they both undergo / experience'. Although the unexpected grammatical form troubled neither archetypal scribe, *B-β* has regularised by making the verb-subject nominative, though with no substantive change in the meaning postulated here. **208–10 (B 198–201)** The punctuation adopted for these lines of somewhat strained analogical thinking assumes that **L** has in mind the notion of Christ as the Church's divine bridegroom, not her divine father. The *children of charite* of 207 (B 197) are 'fathered' upon the Church (their mother) by Christ. In B 199 a full stop after *Chirche* (*SkK–D*) would grammatically require *Crist, Cristendom and alle Cristene* to have the complement *Holy Chirche* or else, if *Holy Chirche* forms an integral phrase with *alle Cristene*, the (anticipatory) complement *children*; but neither reading gives satisfactory sense. In the light of // **C** 210, which replaces B 200 with B 210, the three subjects of B 199 (with *alle Cristene Holy Chirche* the third of them) are therefore better read with 200–01 and a verb *ben* understood before *In menynge þat*, the sense of which phrase then corresponds exactly to **C**'s *Bitokeneth.* The meaning is that the triad 'Christ', 'Christianity' and 'the [whole community of] Christians constituting the Church' signify [by their unity as Christ's mystical body] that man must believe in God as One who is also Three. If this reading is correct, *alle C-***x***B-α* is to be preferred against Ø in *C-***p***B-β*. The analogy, which is now theologically coherent, would gain in clarity if B 201 were a Ø-relative clause qualifying God (200): 'believe in one God who...revealed himself as a trinity', so initial *And* 201 may be a Bx error visually induced by *And* 202 or intruded in response to the compressed grammar of 201. This line is also not free of lexical difficulty, since the impersonal *louede* as a doublet of *lykede* is an idiosyncratic use (not illustrated in MED but recurring at B 17.140 below) with the second verb depending on the force of the familiar *hym lykede*. However, *K–D*'s desperate insertion of *he* before *louede*, making the line scan vocalically on three pronouns (or two and a preposition), is metrically and stylistically too much at odds with the sense to contend as a possible original. The conjectured stave-word ******leodes*, used earlier at 181, has contextually just the required sense to have invited Bx ⇒ of a non-alliterating synonym in key-position (MED s.v. *led(e* n. (2) 'person'). However, even in the emended form of B 199–201 here given, the analogy suffers some loss of focus through being annexed to the earlier one in 198, where the Apostles are joined by two OT categories of 'children of charity' (patriarchs and prophets) who must be regarded as 'children of the *Church*' by retrospective adoption. This idea, theologically transparent in itself, was evidently judged important enough to be retained in **C**. The revision's clearer syntax, making the nouns of C 209 unambiguously the grammatical subject of *Bitokeneth* 210, was recognised by *Sk*, who nevertheless ignored its bearing on the punctuation of B 199 in his parallel-text. In consequence, where *K–D*'s line 201 scans poorly, *Sk*'s makes no sense. **215 (B 202)** The Bx line scans on |m| as an extended Type IIIa with counterpoint on |s| (*abb / ab*), so *K–D*'s emendation of the b-half is gratuitous. **B 213** *He*: the archetypal and probably original reading, wF severally correcting to a grammatically correct accusative after a transitive verb. But the phrase reads something like a free-standing title. **228–29** The sense is satisfactory, so that *R–K*'s re-division after *was* (following W) and emendation of *when* to *whom* seems unusually arbitrary. **229** *wye* ?*x²*: obviously right on grounds of sense, with *wey* a (possibly archetypal) spelling variant best avoided here since the potential

local ambiguity (with 'way') cannot be intended. For a closely similar case, cf. on B 9.113. **233–34** *Is and ay were*: the sg. *Is* relates solely to the Spirit in his procession from Father and Son (*of hem bothe is* translating B 223*a*); *were*, *worþ* (here pl.) refer elliptically to all three persons, with *þei* to be understood as subject. The t variant makes *was* and *worþ* appear to predicate eternity of the Spirit only. *and worþ withouten ende*: the final phrase echoing the doxology, and clearly necessary to provide the b-half of line 233, but apparently lost in *x¹* by assimilation of *worþ* to *were* in the a-half, and loss of *withouten ende* by homœoteleuton (*bote o mank*ynde). In theory, the *x¹* form of these lines would be metrically acceptable with division after *spirit*; but the notion of 'eternity' implied in *Is* and *were* feels incomplete without *worþ*. **236 (B 223)** The **C** line scans as Type Ia on |s|: *Só is Gòd Godes Sóne in thre persónes the Trinite.* The first word is the adverb (MED s.v. 1(a)), not the conjunction (ibid. 17), the subject of the verb being *Sone*, and the key-stave coming in the second syllable of *persónes,* which had shifting stress (cf. B 16.185n, Chaucer *CT* III 1161, Gower *CA* I 840, and contrast 234). *R–K*'s gratuitous emendation *God and godes sone is* yields strained sense, whereas Cx clearly gives two separate existential statements, one about the Son and the other about the Trinity. **242** scans cognatively as Type IIa (|g| |k| |g|) with a 'supplemental' |g| stave in position five (see *Intro.* IV § 44). *R–K*'s ↔ of *cam...thre* and *riʒt...gate* gives an unacceptable masculine ending or necessitates de-stressing the important word *thre.* **244 (B 228)** *her*: supported by **B** as also the probable original in **C**. The form *hes* (over an erasure in X, *he* in I) appears an attempt in y to harmonise the number of the possessive with sg. *hym* in 243, *he* in 245–46, whereas *they* 244b favours the pl. in this line at least, as in **B**, as referring to the 'angels' severally. **247 (B 230)** *when tyme cometh* **x**: preferred to **p**'s *what tyme*, since it alludes to an expected future meeting (to be achieved in the 'Harrowing' scene). It is not a mere memorial of the covenant as a past event, for Abraham is confident that he can point to his fidelity as grounds for his release from hell. The preterite verb-variant *mette* **p**uH² (adopted by *SkR–K*) clarifies the sense while compounding the error. **248 (B 231)** The **B** line scans as Type Ia with a liaisonal stave in *if Í louede.* **249–50 (B 232–33)** The six-syllable prelude-dip in 249 is presumably justified because of the particular contrastive stress required on 'hým' (1) with referent 'Isaac', and 'hým' (2), with 'God'. It is possible that this pattern is being repeated in 250 (with a four-syllable prelude dip), although in that line *I* could equally well be the first lift.

B 246–73 246 *leneden*: on grounds of sense the best resolution of a word palaeographically and contextually ambiguous. 'Believed' goes well enough with Abraham the 'father of faith', but 'leaned' better suits the *foot of feiþ* metaphor of 245. **264 (C 281)** appears genuine on intrinsic grounds and the showing of near-identical **C**. Loss from α here will have been by the 'omission of [an] intervening syntactical unit through grammatical attraction between *may...no buyrn...brynge us* 262, 263 and *Til* 265' (*K–D* p. 68). **287–90 (B 270–73)** The spurious lines in α (printed on p. 751) bear little relation in sense to those of β, the authenticity of which is guaranteed by their intrinsic quality and their presence in (virtually unrevised) **C**. *Allas* and *longe* in α 270 indicate that its exemplar was damaged at this point and patched by the α scribe with doggerel prompted by the verbs of motion (*come, wolde*) in 274–75.

Passus XIX (B XVII)

RUBRIC Agreement of *B*-β with the rubric of *C*-**x** against *C*-**p** may point to the form of the heading in Bx. R is one behind in numbering the Passus and has no section-heading; F, having been previously three passūs out, here gives up the ghost.

8 *R–K* follow G to read *croes* in the a-half and adopt *crist* **B** for Cx *croes* in the b-half. But this looks like a case of revision, with *hym* rather than *seel* becoming the antecedent of the relative's complement. Thus *cristendom* and *croes* are now the joint subject of *hange*, which acquires a semi-figurative sense for the first of these subjects. **10 (B 8)** The extra line that follows in α, whether in its truncated R form or as expanded to a Type Ia line in F (and so adopted by *K–D*), is to be rejected on the evidence of **C**, which shows no trace of it, and on grounds of intrinsic want of content, as patently scribal patching after loss of 7b through eyeskip from *so* to *soþe*. **13** *on*: in the light of **B** the correct preposition (against *in* and redundant *and*). **15 (B 13)** *gome*: the ON-derived form with palatal stop (MED s.v. *gome* n. (4)) is preferred to that with the palatal spirant as providing the *cauda* of a T-type line. **22 (B 19)** Both lines could be of Type IIIa or, with wrenched stress on *wommén* to facilitate homophonic wordplay on *men...meny* (cf. *somme* at 33), of Type Ia. **24** *quod Fayth*: unnecessary, and perhaps come in by anticipation of 26 (GN[2] omit); but such repetition is found. **26 (B 23)** is revised, somewhat unusually, from a Type Ia to a Type IIIa. Possibly Cx *quod* is for *saide* or *mo* a ⇒ for *biside*; but emendation here cannot be justified. **27** *ȝow*: the clear reading of **B** and **C**, giving good sense; so *R–K*'s alteration to *hem* is indefensible. **28 (B 25)** *lich*: conjectured as the difficult original for which Cx's synonym is a non-alliterating ⇒ (see MED s.v. *lich* n.). Although t's *lif* is identical with **B** and could represent *x²*, it is not difficult enough to have invited ⇒ of *body*, though this is recorded as one of its meanings (MED s.v. *lif* n.7). **L** is therefore presumed to have recognised the semantic overlap between the dominant sense of *lif* 'animate existence; animating principle, soul' (MED s.v. *lif*. n.1a (a)

and (b)) and that of *soule* (= *anima*) and made explicit the benefits of faith that extend to man's corporeal as well as his spiritual nature. In **B** *lif* and *soule* are linked by *and* (as in t), allowing equivalence rather than difference, in *C-x¹***p** by *or*, which requires a contrast. In the light of these considerations *lich* is recommended as the substantive reading in the b-half which, like the a-half, appears revised in detail. **34 (B 31)** The identical **C** line confirms β as the form of Bx and this as original and of Type IIIa. *K–D*'s gratuitous emendation *now*] *þanne* is sensibly avoided by *R–K*. **35 (B 32)** The sound of the key-stave is |s| and while the **x** form can be scanned as Type IIa by reading *súfficéde*, *x²*'s *so* is preferable on grounds of sense (cf. B 36). But possibly Cx read *so to* (the actual reading of MW), of which *so* and *to* could be split variants, *so* then being mute. **36 (B 33)** The Cx line, of Type IIIa, scans awkwardly with a four-syllable prelude and an abrupt caesura after *hath*, and *speketh* may have been lost by haplography after *Spes*, an omission all the easier if **C** had a Ø subject of the verb (thereby accounting for the variants *that* prn, *and* conj.). But the metrical weakness is not enough to warrant emendation.

B 37–47 These eleven β lines appear authentic on intrinsic grounds and the evidence of **C**'s (abbreviated) revision (cf. esp. C 43–7). Their omission from α is plausibly ascribed by *K–D* to resumption at the wrong point in the exemplar under inducement from repeated names and phrases in the sequence from 26–46 (*Abraham, thre... persones, lawe, Spes, beleeue and louye / louye and lene*), and eyeskip from *gome þat gooþ...heele* 37 to *Go...God helpe* 46 may have contributed. It is conceivable that the α version of **B** ran from 36 to 48 without break and that 37–47 are an addition in a second state of the text. But the transition would be very abrupt, and Will's objection to *Spes* in 31–6 insufficiently developed, as it lacks the two important points made in 40–1 and 43. **38** *teep*: tentatively conjectured as the lexically difficult stave-word for which the Bx ⇒ is a non-alliterating synonym caught up from 37. In principle, *Than he þat gooþ with* could form a dip before the heavily stressed *two*, but the Bx a-half is uncharacteristically flat in its repetition of 37a, and full stress on the grammatical word *to* in a Type III key-stave would be unparalleled. In the reading as emended, the key-stave *to* is now clearly mute, with *sighte* a blank stave carrying stress. If *sighte* were taken as key-stave, an alternative for the a-half might be *steppeþ*; but this would not seem difficult enough to invite ⇒, *gooþ* would not be an exact synonym, and the stress would be thrown off the semantically crucial *two*. On the conjectured verb, which is mainly SW, SWM or WM in distribution and well-illustrated from alliterative poetry, see MED s.v. *ten* v. (1), 1(a).

52 (B 52) *iaced* **C**: instanced only here (MED s.v. *jacen* v. 'hurry, rush') and of unknown etymology. If Skeat is right to link it with *jounce* 'bounce or jolt along', it may be a blend of the latter and the rare but attested *chacen* of **B**, 'a (partially) coined word, to make the alliteration more exact' (*Sk* IV:386). Given its presumed difficulty, *iaced* as the hypothetical **B** original could have invited ⇒ of the synonym *chaced* in Bx. But *iaced* did not cause wide difficulty to the C-Text scribes (U has *hased*, W *raked*), the line has detailed revision in both halves, *chacen* is apt in sense (see MED s.v. 5 (a) 'hurry') and cognative |tʃ| / |dʒ| alliteration in **B** may be safely accepted. *K–D*'s emendation of Bx to *iaced* is thus unwarranted (for similar revision of an originally cognative stave, cf. 20.48 B 18.48n). **54** *wilde wildernesse*: a collocation found earlier both at 10.62 (with // **B**) and at B 15.459. The Athlone editors gratuitously emend them all, reading *wide* here for *wilde*. **59 (B 58)** *of hym sihe*: the hardest variant, and clearly attested in the unrelated x^1 members YD^2 (< y) and D (< u). The sense is apparently 'perceived mentally' (MED s.v. *sen* v. 21 (a)), the implied notion being 'became aware of, grasped [the man's condition]'). It would presumably be a revision of **B**, a version of which is preserved with slight variations in t and (diversely) in **p**, both of which descend from x^2 (R–K read with **B**). The straightforward *hadde sihte of* attested at 63, 65 might in principle be divined as the reading of $<XIP^2>$ and U, with loss of *hadde* (so *Pe*). More plausibly, *of hym siht* could be a back-spelled form of the contracted-present variant **of hym sith*. This would both explain the expanded x^2 form and be hard enough to have generated *of hym sihe*. But given that all eighteen verbs in the sequence 48–64 are in the past tense, this seems improbable, and *of hym siht* is perhaps best seen as no more than a perplexed response from the scribes of $<XIP^2>$ and U to the rare construction preserved in YD^2 and D (< y + u, = $?x^1$). The **p** variants except $<RM>$ agree with t in *on* for *of*, so this is probably what x^2 read. But the adverb-verb order in x^2 is more likely to have been that of t than **p**. However, if *ferst had on him siʒt* represents x^2, it untypically has four syllables in the dip preceding the caesura and two following it. The adopted $<YD^2>$D form may therefore be read as a counterpointed Type Ie line (*aab / ab*) preserving y from x^1 (and < Cx). **63** *syke*: rejected for *segge* (with **B**) by R–K on the basis of D^2; but as this appears one of many revisions in the passage, there are no grounds for doubting Cx here. **70 (B 69)** The unquestionably authentic α line could have been lost from β by homoarchy (initial *And* the fourth successively in 66–9). **72 (B 71)** The **C** line's revised b-half shows the stave-sound to be |b| and provides some support for *K–D*'s conjecture *barm] lappe* in **B**. However, the Bx form will scan vocalically as a T-type with *Eńbawmed* as first stave, a blank second stave (*bond*) and the *cauda* in |l| after mute *his*. In its other two occurrences (13.106, 19.88) *enbaumed* bears stress on the root vowel; but with words of this type consisting of prefix and radical, the

stress was often shifting (contrast *inparfitly* B 10.465, *inpárfit* B 15.95 //; *Éxperimentis* A 11.160 and its revised parallel *Expériment3* B 10.214).

B 75–95 75 scans as a Type IIIa line with a three or four-syllable prelude dip containing a lexical verb, a pattern not uncommon in **L** (e.g. 33). In view of its appearance with stave-function in 76, *seide* here seems redundant, and without it the translineation from 74/5 would be smoother. But the repetition in 78 suggests a deliberate patterning and so the earlier conjecture *quod* for *seide* (Sch^1) is otiose. **78 (C 77)** will scan awkwardly if acceptably as Type IIIb on the vowels of non-lexical words; but if |s| is discerned as the stave-sound, an auxiliary **shal* may be conjectured as a mute key-stave lost before *make*, though there is no suggestion of this in **C**. Revision to consonantal scansion on lexical words is possible, but the simple reconstruction adopted merely presumes Bx verb-adverb ↔ to prose order. **81 (C 80)** *folweþ*: preferred on the showing of LR as the more likely Bx reading. Though this could be a mis-resolution of *folwet*, more probably γ and M have adapted the tense to fit the verb in the b-half. That tenses in co-ordinate clauses could be mixed is clear from *bystrideth* 78 (79) alongside *quod* preceding and *raped(e)* in following 80 (79). **C**, in eliminating one verb, keeps a simple preterite for the other. **82** *sprakliche*: adopted on the showing at 18.12 of α supported by **C** as the probable Bx form here of which *sparkliche* is a metathetised reflex. The sense could be 'quickly, at once' (MED s.v. *spakli* adv., quoting appositely *WPal* 3357 & *spakli gun ride*). But the identical form (s.v. *spakliche* adj.) appears as the β variant at 18.12 and *sprakliche* 'in a lively manner, quickly' (MED s.v. *sprakli* adv.) evidently existed, though cited only from here in the period. The more economic supposition is that **L** used one adverb with the form *spracliche* and the sense 'energetically, vigorously', which would fit equally well for Hope as later for the Samaritan. **86** *gome* α: to be identified (against Sch^1) as the Bx reading since it is contextually the harder, *groom* being a β ⇒ suggested in part aurally by the preceding and following stave-words in |gr|. There is overlap between a sub-sense of *grom* (MED s.v. 3(a) 'man of low station or birth' and (b) 'man') and the basic sense of *gome* (1(a) 'man'), and between a sub-sense of the latter (3(b) 'man servant') and sense 2(a) of the former 'male servant, retainer'. This may be illustrated from C 8.227 //, where Bx evidently read *gomes* for **ZAC** *grom(u)s* (with MED sense 3(a)) and only one **B** ms (M) has conjectured the correct word. **88** scans vocalically or, preferably, as a Type Ia line on |θ| |ð| / |θ| with *siþpe_Í* providing the key-stave by liaison. **90** scans *aax / xx* and lacks a key-stave. A possible conjecture would be *so* before *robbed*; but *segge* would seem safer, since the Bx tradition evidences ⇒ of *man* for *segge*, as at 11.265 in β. **92 (C 84)** *vnder molde*: confirmed for **B** by the secure reading of **C**, with the implied sense that no ordinary (herbal) remedy rooted in earth can save man, only *Loue...þe plonte of pees, most precious of vertues* (1.147). In the present figure, faith and hope are seen as 'earthly' virtues found in the old dispensation, whereas love belongs to the time of grace. *K–D*'s rejection of *molde* for *mone* (pp. 111–12) as 'contextually not meaningful' shows failure to understand the imagery and indifference to the textual evidence, and their claim that **C** 'here reproduces the corrupt reading of the **B** archetype' is self-refuting, since in 'reproducing' the reading **L** can hardly be inferred to have judged it 'corrupt'. *R–K* bow to fact and logic in abandoning the emendation. **95** *he*: syntactically necessary to provide articulation with the main clause in 97a and lost through visual assimilation to preceding *be* (cf. App. at C 91).

91 Cx scans in principle as a Type IIa line with cognative alliteration |b| |p| |p| and a 'compensatory' |p| stave in position five. However, this gives unnaturally heightened stress to *be* and it may therefore be safely supposed that verb-phrase and subject in the b-half have undergone ↔ to prose order. The order *priketh him* (adopted by *R–K*) is excluded as giving a masculine ending. **94** The phrase *And ȝut bote he leue* is to be construed as a second condition-setting clause dependent, if remotely, on *worth he neuere* 89. The first such clause (*And ȝut be plasterud* 91) requires *moot* to be understood, unless *be* is a p.p. = *ybe* (the former goes better with *leue* 94, the latter better with *haue eten* 90). But the syntax of 94 remains awkwardly elliptical, with an unexpressed apodosis ['he will never be saved] unless he believes faithfully...that the baby's body must be our ultimate remedy'. As here understood, *they* will be a mistaken Cx reflex of the exemplar's *a*, since a singular pronoun *he* fits better with the preceding *man* of 93.

B 112a–116 112a Loss in β is ascribed by *K–D* (p. 67) to rubricator's oversight. **113–24** Despite the suggestive circumstance of **C**'s resumption just where α takes up (C 96=B 125), the twelve lines attested by β are not open to question as authentic. Nor is there real reason for thinking them part of a post-Bx stage of transmission unique to one tradition. Their mechanical loss from α is convincingly ascribed by *K–D* (p. 68) to resumption at a wrong point induced by a succession of recurring similar words and phrases before and within the omitted passage (*Feith; feloun; felawe; folwen*). **114** *out comune*: rejected as meaningless by *K–D* (p. 183), who argue for *outcom(m)en* Cr²³ (MED s.v. *outcomen* v. 2(a) p.pl. 'foreign, alien'). Though attractive, this interpretation is hazardous in the absence of α and any **C** parallel. Both Cr²³ and B which (on the imperfect showing of its members) may have read *vnkonnande*, could be attempted corrections consequent upon failing to see *kennen out* as a phrasal verb (= 'lead out') and *Which...Ierusalem* as a noun-clause object of *knowen* 114 in apposition with its

direct noun-object *contree*. As here understood, the point is the importance of a particular theological virtue to the ordinary *wye in þis world* who needs direction *þoruȝ þat wildernesse* (99): *Faith*'s guidance consists in teaching about salvation through the passion and death of Christ, allegorically represented as *þe wey þat I wente, and wher forþ to Ierusalem*. **116** The β line scans *aax / xa*, and presumed loss of the key-stave through inversion to prose order is remedied by ↔ of subject + verb-phrase with the adverbial phrase.

100 (B 130–31) *o God x¹*: preferred to *God x²* both on intrinsic grounds and on the evidence of the **B** lines under revision and 109 below (both apparently overlooked by *R–K*). B 130 has a 'double-stave' structure, being a vocalic Type Ib with rhetorical stresses on grammatical words and having a secondary sequence of |g| alliteration on lexical words; but only the vocalic pattern, in which the reduced numeral is important, is retained in **C**. (In *C*-H² *o* is added *a.h.*, possibly from an *x¹* source). **106** *venge*: an absolute use not illustrated in MED (s.v. *avengen* v.). Reflexive *me* could have been coincidentally lost in *x¹* and *p²* by assimilation to following *ve-*; but *x¹* and *p²* might preserve from Cx a harder reading with the generalised sense 'take revenge / act vengefully', changed in *p¹* and t to a commoner form.

B 140–64 140 *hym louede* β: presumed the reading of Bx, since R has a visual error and F nonsense. *K–D*, adopting *hym likede*, **C**'s revision to a more familiar phrase, compound their earlier mistake of re-constructing the same phrase at 16.201. But these widely separated appearances of so idiosyncratic a usage could hardly be scribal replacements of the commonplace *hym lykede*, so their emendation amounts to 'scribal rewriting' in its indifference to the evidence (*R–K* wisely desist from these excesses). **142 (C 118)** may be scanned as a T-type in both texts. *purely*: a highly characteristic term that recurs at 174 (identical in **C**). *K–D*'s adoption of **C**'s *the pethe of* in its place has no justification. *forþ*: in *x²* but lost from *x¹* by virtual haplography after *-fereth*. **151 (C 128)** *Al*: perhaps providing a basis for preferring *Al* **p** to *And* **x** in **C**. But the lines, with those preceding and following, have been extensively revised, a connective is in place here, and the rest of the **p** form of 128 shows extensive corruption. **153** *in oon shéwýnge*: a 'monolexical' stave-phrase, of the rare type (*Intro.* IV § 38) instanced at 7.170 // (*K–D*'s ↔ of *in oon* and *shewynge* is therefore unwarranted). The requirement of a feminine ending indicates that the word be not the participle but the verbal noun (MED s.v. *scheuing(e* ger.1(a) 'manifestation'). **154** scans on |f| with *for* as a rhetorically-stressed first lift ('because', 'for the reason that'). The ?α *paume²* (for which F substitutes *it*) will give a Type IIb line scanning *aaa / bb* on |p| and |f|; but it has an awkward caesura after *forþ* and an impossibly heavy final dip [*fúst*] *bòþè*.

441

Though deserving consideration, R is therefore not to be preferred to β, which has the caesura after *fyngeres*. **164** The Bx line scans as Type IIIa with an awkward caesura after *in* (unless an even more awkward pattern with two lifts in *bilóngép* is accepted), and the semantically important *pre þynges* relegated to a prelude dip. The present emendation presumes subject and verb transposed to prose order, a very common occurrence in Bx. The line thus becomes an extended Type IIIa with semi-counterpoint (*abb / ax*), the important subject-phrase receives prominence as contrapuntal staves, and the caesura is located in its natural place before the preposition governing the indirect object. **133 (B 167)** *As*: the probable reading of Cx, *And as* a p^1 smoothing that happens to coincide with **B**. **134 (B 168)** *And* **x**: syntactically weak, and *So is* **p** (in the light of supporting **B**) likelier to represent x^2, with t having varied independently towards x^1. **136–38 (B 170–71)** The syntax of the **C** lines would flow more smoothly if *ne* were inserted before *worche*, since the two infinitives in 137 possess no subject or modal verb (as the text stands, they must be read as indirectly dependent on *worche*, which is joined prolatively to *sholde*. Possibly a wider reconstruction is required for 138a: *Ne worche sholde no wriht*, which would make *wriht sholde* govern all three infinitives. Although *no* u argues against *ne* y representing the reading of x^1 (contrast 143) the present reconstruction, though speculative, meets the need. **138** *hy*: reconstructed as the probable Cx form underlying the variants *they* (plural) and *he* (vocalic). *awey*: pronounced either with stress wrenched to the first syllable *áwèy* (as at B 5.108) or preferably as trisyllabic *aweye* (as at 12.148 //), with inserted final *–e*. **143 (B 176)** *pulte* C-y*B*-α: 'extend' (MED s.v. *pilten* v. 3(a)); clearly the harder reading and thus an unlikely ⇒ for original *putte* in either version. Here y is presumed to have preserved the x^1 reading, but since GN (= p^2) are also right, it seems less probable that x^2 had *putte* than that p^1, t and u severally varied to one more obvious. In the Bx tradition, only R retains the right reading (< α). Similar difficulties with *pulten* were experienced in earlier instances: in 10.95 **p** reads *putte*, but one p^1 copy (K) has *pulte* with **x**; in // **B** *pulte* is almost certainly the reading of Bx; in B 1.127 *pulte* is preserved by L (= β), here accompanied by Cr, and by R (= α) against *putte* γM, while in the // passage Ax reads *putte* against **Z** *pulte* (see the notes on these lines, and esp. the discussion of 1.128 // B 1.127). **144–46 (B 177–79)** The lines B 177b–179a, attested only in α, unquestionably genuine on intrinsic grounds and the showing of (partly revised) **C**, will have been lost from β by homoteleuton at the caesura (*fust* 177, 179; cf. B 184–85 below). **147** *Be he* **p**: preferable on grounds of sense, the reading of **x** being awkward even with Ø-punctuation after *liketh* and an understood object for *lat falle* supplied. Allowing

this possibility, the noun-clause of 146 could be made the object of *liketh* 145 if **x**'s variant were seen as a visual error for *Bote be he*, yielding the same substantive meaning as **p** (so *R–K*, who put a stop after *toucheth*. But it seems safer to accept **p** as = Cx than to reconstruct.

B 184–85 (C 152–53) The two half-lines 184b, 185a have been lost from γ by the same mechanical error noted at B 177–79, homoteleuton at the caesura (*hand...hand*). M's error will probably have been coincidental, consisting in omission of 184b (followed by erasure and restoration) and complete loss of 185 (followed by restoration in the margin by the same corrector, whether by reference back to the exemplar or to an L-type source). Cr, as a γ-ms, can only have corrected from such a source or from a **C** copy. The error here identifies γ as a major genetic group, while the omission of 186 further distinguishes g from w as a sub-division within that group.

158 (B 190) *R–K* diagnose omission from Cx of original lines corresponding to B 190b–192 through homoteleuton very like that noted at 152–53 (here *hand...hand* again) and restore these lines to **C**. It is an attractive emendation, but since the sense of Cx is satisfactory this could be a case of *authorial* abbreviation, aiming to avoid the repetition of B 186 (= C 154) found in B 191. *ypersed* **B**: in context having the substantive sense 'pierce', so that the hypothetical β reading **yper(is)ched* may be seen as a spelling-variant either influenced by *perisshen*, a verb of distinct etymology, or reflecting a pronunciation intermediate between |s| and |ʃ|. (For spellings with *sh* see MED s.v. *percen* v. (derived from OF *perc(i)er, perchier*) and compare the spelling with *-iss-* under *perishen* v. (derived from the extended stem of OF *perir*).

163a, 164 (B 198a, 199) *Spiritum Sanctum* C-**p**: the accusative required on grounds of sense, Bx appearing to have erred in both instances, C-**x** in the first, perhaps by initially missing the nasal suspension in 'spiritui 'and then by smoothing 'sanctui' to 'sancto'. The cause was presumably failure to grasp the sense of *in* 'against', though **L** so uses even English *in* (MED s.v. *in* prep. 20 (a)) at preceding 162 // 197 in free variation with *aȝeyn* 167 // (and see Apparatus to **B** for β's variant *in*). **171 (B 206)** *flaumynge fuyr* **x**: preferred on the showing of // **B** as the probable Cx form which **p** misread as a preterite, perhaps through missing a nasal suspension in an exemplar form spelled *flaumede (that Bx had the *-ende* form of the present participle is indicated by the spelling *flaumende* in *B*-LR). Loss of 171 (and also 172) in t will have been caused by homoarchy and homoteleuton (*And...togyderes* 170, 172) and is paralleled in the **p**-group copies QF and N. **174** *se*: the probable Cx reading, for while *wirche* may point to *swynke as the group-original of y, the Ø-reading of X suggests rather that the verb had been omitted and was independently supplied in YIP^2 (but in D^2 from another source of u, t or **p** type). The line, here taken to have been added in the revision to **C**, is held by *K–D* to have been lost by Bx 'through inducement to complete the correlative construction begun in 20[7]'. Though it was accepted for **B** in *Sch*[1], the reservation expressed there that the evidence is inconclusive is here held to tell against its inclusion (compare the cases of B 18.161, where revision still remains possible, and B 19.441, 20.261, where Cx preserves what appears a largely unrevised text of B[1]).

B 214–44 214 (C 180) Bx has the imperfect scansion *aa / xx* and *lowe* 'low' is conjectured as the required stave-word presumed lost through visual assimilation to *yblowe* at 213a or to a preceding identical exemplar form of the word for 'fire' (MED s.v. *loue* n. 2(a)). This last is found as a t variant to *leye* in C 180, in ms C at // **B** and as the text form at 20.140 (in MED s.v. 3 '(flash of) light'; cf. *lei(e* n. (2) (a)). **218–44 (C 184–210)** The authenticity of these *B*-β lines is guaranteed by their presence (lightly revised) in **C**. This longest omission from α may have been occasioned by resumption at a wrong point induced by several words and phrases occurring in and just before the passage (*K–D* p. 69). But loss for purely mechanical reasons (215 and 249 being identical) would have been more certain had the omission run from 216 to 248, which is approximately the content of a single page (the average *PP* ms has about 38 lines to the page [Green 1987:307]). **224 (C 190)** The line scans as a vocalic extended Type IIIc with full counterpoint (*abb / ab*), or as a normal Type IIIc characteristically reversing the stress-pattern of the phrase *Holy Góest* in C 189 // B 223 and making the emphatic comparative adverb *as* the key-stave. *K–D*'s emendation *glede unglade* for *glede* takes W's *glade*] *glede* as descended from the postulated group original. But this conjecture illustrating their obliviousness (in seeking a metrically unnecessary stave-word) to the force of **BC** agreement, is unpersuasive, given its 'more than usually complex presumption of split variation' (p. 207), and the logic of their footnote 163 suggests its implausibility. For the W variant is explicable as an error for an exemplar form spelled *gl(e)ade* (one C15th example of *glad* is cited by MED s.v. *gled(e* n. (2)). **196–97 (B 230–31)** The **p** form has defective metre in the first line (*aa / bb*) as a result of ↔ to prose order, perhaps arising from misreading *the grete myhte of þe Trinite*, the noun-phrase object of *melteth*, as appositional with *grace of þe Holi Gost* (on a possible fruitful ambiguity see *Commentary* further). The **p** form, however, gives the same sense as **x**, which is that of **B. 200 (B 234)** *noȝt*: restored in **B** as necessary for the sense and presumed lost by Bx for a mechanical reason. This, if the form was *nat* as in **C**, could have been *þat* (1) > < *þat* (2) attraction. Alternatively, a negative particle *ne* could have been lost through visual confusion with either syllable of following *mowe*. The defect in sense went unnoticed not only by all the scribes but also by *Sk*. **206 (B 240)** The **C** line retains

B's Type Ie or IIIc with counterpoint and mute key-stave (*aab / [a]b*) or (preferably) reads as a T-Type (*aa / [a]bb*). B-Y *faire* need not show ⊗ but accidental convergence with **C**'s revised epithet prompted by objection to the linking of *warm* with *flaumbe*. **212 (B 246)** *tasch* **CB**-α: a word instanced only here (MED s.v. *tach(e* n. (2) 'touchwood') and too hard not to be the Bx reading, for which β *tow* is ⇒ of a more familiar term ('kindling made from hemp or flax'). **220 (B 254)** *ingratus*: preferred not because *ingrat* is the easier reading (it is instanced only here in MED s.v.) but because it is likelier that an abbreviation for *-us* in the α and **p** exemplars was overlooked in copying than that a naturalised word was made Latin by the scribes of *x*[1], t and β. The metre is unaffected either way, the line scanning with rhetorical stresses on both privative particles or as a macaronic T-type with its *cauda* alliterating cognatively on |g|, |k|. **231** has been added in revision, and there is no warrant for inserting it (as do *K–D*) after B 264. In **B** line 265 serves to direct the audience towards the example of Dives, which is not elaborated; in **C**, it introduces seventeen new lines and *Minne ȝe nat.../ That* is inserted to effect the transition and connect Dives with the rich men of 229. **232** *dampned*: evidently the reading of y and probably that of **p**, various **x** and **p** mss intruding the understood verb *was* (cf. 241, where **p** and t diversely fill out the terse syntax of Cx). The presumed Cx form here is close to that of B 265; but there is no need to omit *and*, which introduces a characteristic ellipsis. **237** *his lycame werie*: a second subordinate clause, having a new subject, dependent (like *lyue*) on the main verb *sotiled*, with *myhte* understood. The inserted *on* in Dt, paralleled in N[2] (and adopted by *R–K* with omission of *on* in 236) smooths the abrupt but characteristic expression preserved in Cx. **240** *told*: preferred as harder and more precise in sense (MED s.v. *tellen* 18(b) 'consider'), *cald* y presumably resulting from *c / t* confusion. **242** *atymye*: a form of *atte(i)nen* in sense 1(a) 'attain' or (c) 'succeed in'. The spelling with *m* appears original, though it is unrecorded in MED, which does not cite the passage under *atteinen* v. Kane 2000:52–3 argues for derivation of the verb from OE *atemien* and the sense 'refrain from [fine living]'. But this is at variance with the entire context, since **L**'s point is that the rich should not be misers but should spend generously, so that others (including the poor) may benefit thereby. **251 (B 269)** *vnhynde*: 'ungenerous' (MED s.v. *hende* 2(c) + *vn-*), confused by several mss with its synonym (in this sense) under influence from the spelling-form and following *vnkyndenesse* 253. The word is probably, as **B** *vnkynde* must be, stressed on the privative prefix. **253 (B 271)** scans with two lifts in *vnkýndenésse* as Type IIIa, unusually revising a Type Ia, and possibly *þe contrarie* (as in **B**) has been lost through eyeskip from *kyn-* to *quen-* (so *PeR–K*). The insertion by t of a stave-word *kid* (so *Sk*) is palpably scribal, since the 'making known' or 'recognition' of this vice has small bearing on the matter. The loss of **B**'s 'elemental' idea weakens the **C** line, but grounds for emendation are not strong. **255–56 (B 273–74)** The line-division in the majority of **C** mss is unsatisfactory in giving 255 a masculine ending, and re-lineation as in **B** is desirable. The correct u form could derive from x^1 (< Cx) but is more probably a happy scribal re-arrangement. Misdivision might have occurred through associating *this corsede theues* 255 too closely with its parallel subject *Vnkynde Cristene men* in 256. **268 (B 286)** The line could have been lost from γ by resumption at the wrong point following confusion of *mercy* 287 with *mercy...mercy* in 286. Cr^1 or its manuscript exemplar presumably restored by collation with a **C** copy or a **B** copy of *l* or *m* type. **270 (B 288)** *Innócence*: so stressed to provide the first stave in this Type Ie line. **275–76 (B 293–94)** **C** omits B 294 and revises as two lines a single **B** line of Type IIa structure with an extra *l* stave in position five. The sense and metre both being satisfactory, *K–D*'s reconstruction, a blend of **C** and **B**, amounts to the creation of a conflated text. **B 294** *þat he pleyneþ þere*: ↔ of the adverb and relative clause to prose order to restore the key-stave *pléynéþ* in final position, producing the unmetrical pattern *aa / xa* and giving in its two lifts an unacceptable masculine ending. The adverb *þere* has its normal disyllabic form with final *-e* to provide the required feminine ending (cf. B 4.23, 36). **277 (B 295)** *nouthe* **C**: quite possibly also the form in **B** (and Bx), thus accounting for ?γ *nouht*. The emphatic form conveys the sense 'at this very moment', also one sense of *nou* (MED s.v. adv. 1(a)), and may stand in contrast with the rhetorically emphatic *now* of 278 / 296 (MED s.v. *nou* 7(f)). *K–D*'s adoption of *nouthe* in **B** is thus defensible, but the metre does not require it here (contrast 244 or B 13.184 above) and since the sense difference is small, *now* may be allowed to stand. **278 (B 296)** The second *Y* of **C** is also preferable in **B** to the Ø-reading of LR, which could be coincidental or a reflex of Bx (this occurs also at B 13.385 and at B 18.202, where LR are joined by Y). Such omission of a subject pronoun could in principle be an original feature. However, in another (second-person) instance at B 5.494 (*Feddest*), **C** confirms the reading (C 8.133), while in *fettest* 20.379 **C** omits and **B** has the pronoun, but the verbs in the added **C** line 20.380 both *lack* it. The first *Y*, which is *not* necessary, has presumably been intruded in *B*-WHmM for the sake of emphasis; but in **C** it may be a revision. **279 (B 297)** scans cognatively as a Type Ic on |k| and |g|. *K–D*'s emendation *Crist* is metrically unnecessary and theologically inexact (cf. the 'economic' precision of *bouhte* at 267) and the note in *Sch¹* largely otiose. *R–K* sensibly retain **C**. **290 (B 308)** will scan satisfactorily as an extended Type IIIa on vowels with semi-counterpoint on |l| or, preferably, as a T-type, with key-stave on |l| formed

by liaison of *til_hem* (*aa / [a]bb*). *PeR–K*'s emendation to the form of **B**'s b-half *lif* is unnecessary and should be rejected: the D variant *lif*, coming before *hem*, clearly aims at 'regularising' the metre. The *sense* of Cx is virtually equivalent to that of **B**, while alluding to a familiar proverbial expression.

B 309–39 (C 291–321) 309–10 Loss of these (obviously authentic) lines from β is hard to account for on mechanical grounds. *K–D* 's explanation ('distraction by the corrupt copy preceding', p. 67) would be implausible even if 308b were corrupt as they judge. But deliberate censorship of the lines as too pessimistic cannot be entirely excluded and invites comparison with the converse situation at B 316 (where α omits). **316 (C 298)** The exact form of the b-half is unascertainable in the absence of α, but *K–D*'s conjecture *swich* may be safely adopted on the showing of (slightly revised) **C** as the necessary key-stave for which β (?or Bx) *hym* is a non-alliterating ⇒ suggested by preceding *His*. *K–D* (p. 69) attribute the loss in α to 'resumption at a wrong point induced by *restitucion* 31[5], *satisfaccion* 3[16]'. But a mechanical explanation is not less convincing here than deliberate censorship, α rejecting a theological position judged too lenient, as β at 309–10 may have rejected one thought too severe (either tradition displaying a consistent moral posture in the two cases). **326 (C 308)** The Bx line could in principle scan as Type IIIa, though stress on *be* would lack semantic or rhetorical justification. Neither of the sub-archetypal variants is likely to be the source of the other, though both could be reflexes of the relatively more difficult noun adopted by *K–D* from // **C**. MED s.v. *burre* n. (1) 2(b) 'hoarseness' cites only this one example of the word and OED has no further examples before *c*.1600. **336 (C 318)** *ouhte*: a stronger reading and the likelier to be original in both versions. **339 (C 321)** *ben* *B*-wαC: presumably lost from gLM by visual attraction of *ben* > < *in*. The error could have been in β (> γLM) and independently corrected in w, since convergence of g, L and M seems improbable.

332 (B 350) *that his lyf amende*: tentatively discriminated as the Cx reading, *that* tightening **B**'s looser association of the will to charity with spiritual renewal. The larger divergence attested in **x** introduces a new notion, scribal in origin, of recovering from illness and then being converted, whereas the theme of 330–32 is patient endurance of illness as a spiritually meritorious act.

Passus XX (B XVIII)

RUBRICS *B*-β and *C*-**x** concur in regarding this passus, which is not through-numbered in **C**, as the third of *Dobet*, *C*-**p** as the fourth; *B*-α is out as before.
1 *Wollewaerd*: a rare word, only once instanced before L (MED s.v. *wolward* a.). The probable Cx spelling (with

-*ae*- for -*a*-), could account for **p**'s misunderstanding the sense of the second element as *weried* (as actually in QZ), with retrospective smoothing of the first element in some mss to an adverbial prefix (*wel, ful*); but the substantive reading is not in doubt. **2** revises to Type Ia a line of vocalic extended Type IIIc with counterpoint on |r| (*abb / ab*); for the pattern cf. B 19.452. Possibly Bx has inverted an original prose order (*réccheþ of nó wò*), which would give an acceptable b-half closer to **C** (so *K–DSch*[1]); but since revision appears with the omission of B 6, it cannot be ruled out here. **6–7 (B 6–8)** Re-positioning of the **B** lines is required by the failure of sense in Bx (unnoticed by *Sk*), which has no verb governing the indirect object in 9a (Bx 6). **C** solves the problem by omitting 9 and drops 6 for good measure (as perhaps lowering the tone). **7** *by organe*: preferred on the showing of **C** as the probable Bx reading, the β form *organye* being perhaps no more than a spelling variant. The special sense 'in *organum*' (vocal parts a fifth above or below the plainsong line, favoured by *Pe*), is instanced only from *c*.1400 (MED s.v. *organ(e* n.3); but the general sense in the period of *singen bi organe* is 'to sing to the accompaniment of instrumental music', whether the instruments are of strings or wind (MED s.v. ibid. 2., and see 1). Possibly, since the singers are processing, the instrument may be a portative organ (ibid. 2(a)). Trevisa's definition cited by MED s.v. *organum* shows the duality of contemporary reference ('general name of alle instrumentes of musik...specialliche...þe instrument...y-made of many pipes'), but omits the harmonic signification. **12 (B 14)** *and* **C**: a revision anticipated in *B*-g (and in Cr possibly by collation with a **C** source). The probable Bx reading *or* is unacceptable, since the shoes are not an *alternative* to the spurs, the significant item in the ceremony of knighting. F's *on*, an intelligent guess (unless it simply preserves α where R has erred visually with β), gives good enough sense to be adopted as the reading of **B**. **14 (B 16)** The superior spelling with final -*ous* is adopted to avoid possible confusion with the plural of the noun *auntur*. **24** *plates*: rejected for **B**'s *paltok* by *R–K*, who miss the pungent irony of one of **L**'s most forceful revisions. **30 (B 31)** The substantive sense is 'that he [Death] is lying', and αL *likth* may represent Bx in this sense (see MED s.v. *lien* v. (2), spelling-forms). The alternative sense 'what he [Life] pleases' is not so apt, and if β read thus, M could have altered from a γ-type source. But on the showing of *a lyeth* **C**, the αL reading is best interpreted as a spelling-variant, *likth* representing Bx **lyȝþ* or **lyg(h)þ* with the same sense ('lies') as in γ. **34–34a (B 35–35a)** *forbite*: a harder reading lexically, the word being almost exclusive to **L** (MED s.v. *forbiten* v.), whereas *forbeten*, also in *PP* at 22.198 //, is commoner. The verb, describing Life's fatal 'bite' at Death, recalls its earlier use to describe the action of sin upon charity at 18.39, where only X has the erroneous

reading *forbet*. Its originality is confirmed by the Latin of 34*a* (*morsus*), with its mordant pun on *Mors*, on the strength of which the completion of the quotation may be accepted into **B** in a form reconstructed from F's evidence to accord with **C**. Therefore *forbite* may be safely identified as the Bx reading preserved in α, from which βF have varied convergently under inducement from following *adoun*. It remains uncertain whether *and* Bx has been misplaced, since its present position requires *bale-deeþ* to be a compound object of the phrasal verb *adoun brynge*. Placed after *adoun* in **C**, perhaps in revision, *deth* becomes the direct object of *brynge*, while *bale* 'death' (MED s.v. 2b) becomes its indirect object. This gives clearer sense and smoother style, but grounds for emending Bx are insufficiently strong. More certain is it that *forbete* βF should be identified as a scribal ⇒ for the original **B** verb preserved in R. *R–K*'s adoption of *forbete* and re-ordering of the a-half to accord with **B** has nothing to recommend it. **36** *per x*[1] (here **p**lt): presumably an isolated spelling variant for the possessive, and not the adverb *þere*. It should be altered to *her* (*R–K*) as it is probably not archetypal. **37 (B 38)** *iustice*: pl. also in *B*-Cr[23]YOCBF, but presumably an error in Cx, as the only judge is the Roman Pilate and the text cannot refer to the Jewish authorities Herod and the High Priest. **38 (B 39)** *þe court* **C**B-γMF: either LR *her*] *þe* is a convergent scribal error, heightening the hostility of the 'court', or it represents Bx (< β + α), where γ, M (< γ) and F (? < **C**) substitute the more neutral expression. But it is unlikely to be original. **39 (B 40)** *pelour*: lexically difficult and found first here, with a precise and apt legal sense (see MED s.v. *pelour* n.). The word's rarity doubtless provoked its replacement in Bx by one which, though contextually inappropriate, was loosely used as a term of abuse for 'ruffian', 'scoundrel' (MED s.v. *pilour* n. (1) (c)). The substituted word occurs in *PP* in its normal senses, (a) 'pillager' and (b) 'one who deprives others of money or goods by undue force' (ibid., senses (a) and (b)) at 22.263 // and 21.418 // respectively, in the latter with the well-attested variant spelling *pelours* in X. **46** revises to a Type Ia (or Ic) a Type IIb line with *quod* as stave two. *K–D*'s rejection of Bx's b-half for **C**'s because 'more emphatic' (p. 91) strains belief. **48 C** revises to a standard Type Ia a **B** line scanning cognatively with the same pattern (|g| |k| / |g|) but rhetorical *repetitio* of the epithet from 47. *K–D* 's diagnosis of *kene* as a scribal ⇒ induced by preceding copy (mistakenly accepted in *Sch*[1]) fails to recognise **L**'s cognative staves. **49** *saide*: either in its normal sense (MED s.v *seien* 1(a)) with *quod* 50 pleonastic or, as preferable, absolute 'spoke' (ibid. 6(a)), as *K–D* take it (with a semi-colon better after *enuye*). **50** *þat ribaud* **C**B-β: *þe ribaudes* α, most simply accounted for as a mistaken pl. anticipating the implied pl. subject of *Nailed* 51 and the stated one of *þei putte* 52 (no pronoun in // **C**). In the light of C 50, however, it seems best to take the speaker of *Aue, raby* as the *other* of 47 who makes the crown of thorns. *vp*: reconstructed as the Cx form of the preposition in the relatively rare sense 'in physical opposition to' (MED s.v. *up* prep. 8 (b), 'in hostile encounter... attack on' (OED s.v. *Up* prep.[1] 3a). This was replaced in the **p** groups by *at* (as in // **B**) or *on*, while **x** treated *vp* as an adverb and added the preposition *to* (perhaps under suggestion from 52), thus overloading the dip. **51** *a*: one of two small revisions in this line; there is no reason to think B*x* *þe* unoriginal (as *K–D* hold). **53** revises *deep-yuel...ydone* doubtless in consequence of a changed understanding of the purpose of the *poysen* (Mk 15: 36, Jn 19: 297; see *Commentary*). *K–D* (p. 91) again reject B*x* for **C** because 'more emphatic'; but it could not fail to be (given what is being said), so as a reason for emending, this hardly signifies. **54 (B 54)** *saiden*: to be securely adopted in **B** on the showing of **C** as syntactically necessary after *And* before the quoted speech, and perhaps lost through distraction from preceding *beden* 53. **C** makes *saiden* a stave in revising to Type Ia a **B** line of Type IIIc that scanned on vowels and |s| (unless, as *K–D* judge, its b-half read *þiselue now þou helpe*, with the word-order of **C**). **55–6** In the light of near-identical **B**, Cx can be seen to have shortened two lines of unusual length. The product is three lines scanning *xa / ax*, as prose, *aa / ax*, only the last being of authentic form. Line 55 as now restored turns **B** *kynges sone* into a fully parenthetical phrase, sharpening up its theology to make Christ both Messiah and Divine Son. *R–K*'s replacement of *Crist, Godes sone* by *kynges sone* should be rejected; for being a king's son, as **L** seems to have realised, would not empower Jesus to come down from the cross, but being *God*'s son would. The wording of Mt 27:43 as well as 42 // is relevant. **61 C** revises a counterpointed Type Ie line, scanning *aab / ab* on |w| and |k|, to a form reconstructable from the evidence of the sub-archetypes. Thus *wal* moves from being stave one to being part of the prelude-dip, and the line's stave-sound is |t|, with staves three and five, *euene* and *peces*, blank not counterpointed as in **B**. It is presumed here on the evidence of y that x^1 contained a second adverb *al*, lost haplographically in x^2u before *a* 'in', the prepositional form still preserved in **p**. In P^2 both *al* and *a* were lost from y and *a* later added. The substantive key-stave, carrying full stress, is a numeral *two*, not the preposition; for *to* is the ambiguous orthographic variant (found also at 75) punning homophonically with *to* in the a-half, which bears rhetorical sentence-stress (contrast *to-* in 62). **63** *to-quasche*: the tense clearly past (*to-quaschete* in pUt) and the unique y spelling without preterite morpheme perhaps a 'false form', the verb being historically weak (it recurs at 257). **71 (B 69) C** revises **B**'s Type Ia to a Type IIIc scanning on vowels (*He*; *is*) and *s*. **73 (B 71) C** revises to Type Ia a Type IIIc in **B**. *K–D* 's metrically

unnecessary ↔ of *also* and *þat tyme* ignores **C**'s word-order, which confirms that of **B**. **75 (B 73)** In the light of **B**, the form of Cx may be discriminated as preserved in u ($< x^1$) and t ($< x^2$), **p** inverting the subject-verb order and padding out with an unnecessary adverb a line presumably judged too short. The intrusive phrase *of tho theues* (rejected as scribal after *Pe*) could have entered y from a marginal note in its exemplar designed to emphasize that only the thieves' legs, not Christ's, were broken (though its position misleadingly connects it with *cachepol*). This instance demonstrates N^2's primary descent from a y-type source. **78 (B 76)** *prowe* B-α: preferred for **B** as the harder reading, which **C** is judged to have revised to the more familiar *tyme*. B-β could have anticipated the change by ⇒ of a commoner synonym and need show no ⊗ from **C**. Conversely, α is unlikely to have substituted a lexically harder word for *tyme*; nor need Cx have replaced original *prowe*, as *R–K* judge, since the next line in **C** is also revised. **80 (B 78)** *blynde* **C**: an addition that anticipates 81b, for which reason *R–K* omit. However the threefold *repetitio* in 80, 84, 87 seems deliberate, and the word can be accepted as a blank stave in a Type Ie line. **84 (B 82)** *Iouste* x^1: more colloquial and arguably harder than x^2's form, though *To* could have been lost by haplography. The B*x* line has a defective metrical pattern *xx / aa* and could be emended to give a Type IIIb by reading *jauelot* as a neologism for which the synonym *spere* was substituted. However MED s.v. has no evidence of this word before 1440 and this conjecture, though possibly less drastic than the one adopted, is lexically more hazardous. *K–D* (p. 94) may be right that the line was rewritten to exclude the notion of Longinus as a Jew, since he was honoured as a Christian saint (see *Commentary*); so the **C** reading is accepted, tentatively, for **B**. 86 is revised in both halves and *R–K*'s wholesale adoption of **B** has no justification. **91 (B 89)** *A*: the unstressed colloquial form posited as underlying *And* **x** and *He* **p**. **94 (B 91)** *ruthe* **C**: adopted on the showing of **B** as the likely original for which *mercy* is a non-alliterating ⇒ of a synonym commoner in this type of context. Although Cx, scanning as Type IIIa with a six-syllable prelude dip, could be a revision offering a more strictly rational antithesis to *riȝt* than the affective *ruthe* (see *Commentary*), the reconstruction seems safe, with a gain in metrical smoothness and little loss of meaning (for the standard mercy / right contrast cf. 439–40). N^2's variant, while not the basis of the emendation, indicates the intelligent scribal dissatisfaction with imperfect metre shown at 400; but that it was corrected from a 'pre-archetypal copy' (*R–K* p. 102) is a logically unnecessary supposition. **95** *fouely* **C**: a revision emphasising the force of the abuse rather than the ferocity of the motivation. N^2's *felly*, preferred by *R–K*, may be identified as derived from **B**. **96–8 (B 93–5)** The incorrect line-division in **p** and TH^2 (but in this instance not Ch) may directly reflect the reading of x^2, and was probably occasioned by eyeskip from *for* to *For þis*. The x^1 lineation, as well as giving more satisfactory metre, is supported by **B**. The form of the last phrase in 97 is reconstructed by *R–K* from **x** and **p** in the light of **B** as **to ʒow falle*, retaining the preposition of **B** and **p**, the verb of **p** and the imprecatory form of **x**. But this is unnecessary, since 97–8 show changes in detail, notably the removal of *alle*, so as implicitly to re-direct the ban towards the Jews present and their offspring rather than the whole nation or race. The reading *falle* in *B*-WHmGC^2 is, moreover, unlikely to be that of Bx and may show ⊗ from **C** (or merely influence from the common collocation *vengeaunce falle*), just as *to ʒow alle* Ch could be echoing **B**. Given the signs of revision, it is better to let the archetypal readings stand, without seeking a common underlying form for both. **98 (B 95)** *the dede* x^1 (*hym þat was ded* **p**): 'the dead'. The singular t variant *þe dede þat ʒe dede* takes *dede* as 'deed' and *beten* as 'make amends for, atone for' (MED s.v. *beten* v. (2) 2(a)) or possibly *þat ʒe dede it* as an integral noun-phrase with *a boyes dede* as its complement (= 'that you did it was a rascally act'). M's flat extra line after 98 (adopted by *Sk*), while metrically and stylistically acceptable, is not necessitated by the syntax, and merely repeats 95, so is better interpreted as scribal over-insistence on the guilt of the Jews. **103** *ʒelde* x^1: a spelling variant of the contracted present found with its more usual unvoiced ending in x^2 and Bx. *recreaunt* x^2 **B**: *creaunt* x^1, a well-attested variant that cannot be original here since a first stave in |r| is required. *remynge* **C**: of a visual form such that the erroneous **C** variants support *K–D*'s view of Bx as a visual mistake for the same reading. But since *rennyng* 'fleeing' (MED s.v. *rennen* v. (1) 4 (a)) is in keeping with the metaphorical figure and revision is continuing here, grounds for emendation are insecure. **106 (B 103)** *into* x^1: less smooth metrically than the monosyllabic *to* and *in*, the reading of **B**; but these could be split variants of x^1 *into* (< Cx). **109 (B 106)** Both lines have 'dual' scansions, **C** as an extended Type IIIa on vowels with semi-counterpoint (*abb / ax*) or Type Ia with mute key-stave, and **B** as a Type IIb (with *But* as stave one) or as an extended Type IIIb on vowels with semi-counterpoint on |b|.

B 109–19 109 Because of **C**'s revision in both half-lines, the Bx form cannot be decisively discriminated. The absence of the final word in L could indicate a Ø-reading in β, with γ having supplied an appropriate verb on the basis of the Latin *cessabit*. This will have come into *m* from γ, and from a w-type ms M will have added *of*, a word necessary for the line's grammatical coherence after adoption of *cesse*. The α reading *lese* is not self-evidently superior to *cesse*, though it fits more idiomatically with *crowne* than does *cesse*, and accords well with B 7.159, where *The kyng lees his lordshipe* is close

to the present *hir kyngdom þe crowne sholde lese*. (On the sense of *crowne* 'sovereignty', see MED s.v. *coroune* n. 5a, which exactly corresponds with that of *lordshipe* n., ibid., 3(d)). **113 (C 116)** is of Type IIIa and revised in **C** to a Type Ia by replacing *coste* with a filler-phrase providing a second stave. *K–D*'s insertion of *Where* before *Oute* to normalise the line is too arbitrary to deserve consideration. **119 (C 122)** While **C** scans as a Type IIa, Bx has the defective pattern *aa / xx*. The third stave *and a clene* is presumed lost by Bx on account of the line's length and the phrase's placing after a noun already provided with an epithet qualified by an adverb, the combined weight of which promoted expectation of a caesura following the noun. The line was lacking in t and T has supplied the gap not from another **C** ms but from a post-Bx copy of **B**, which lacked the adjectival phrase, adding *and* and substituting a synonymous expression for *she hihte*. **131 (C 134)** *K–D* (p. 90) diagnose homœoarchic loss of *wommane* (here understood as a **C** addition for explicitness); but this must remain speculative, as the sense does not require it and the line will scan as standard with shifted stress on *Wiþouten*.

140 (B 137) *lowe* **x**: preferred (as a revision in **C**), despite agreement with **B** of p^1, N (by alteration) and P^2 (the last doubtless collated with a **p** source). A sense '(flash) of light' is illustrated by two MED quotations s.v. *loue* n. (2); but in one it is that of a lightning flash and there seems no doubt that the sense here is the basic one, 'fire' or 'flame' (ibid. 1(a)), **C** stressing the light's fiery (sun-like) quality as much as its brightness. **141** After this *R–K* insert B 139 and read *And* before *That* in 142. But no mechanical or other reason appears for the omission, and since the sense runs on satisfactorily and the antecedent of *herof* can be the noun-clause of 136–7, the case for adding it is weak. **151 (B 149)** *parfit* **C**: revising **B** to emphasise Job's moral stature rather than his dual character as OT prophet and 'patriarch'. So despite the converse appearance of *prophete* as a variant in *C*-mss W and N, *K–D*'s ⇒ of **C** on the grounds that Bx misread a contracted form is to be rejected. **153 (B 151)** *heo* **C**: a stave-word here, so the ambiguously-spelled *he* of x^1α and the non-alliterating *she* of β are rejected for the W and S pronoun-form probably original in **L**'s dialect. **157 (B 154)** Though Bx could scan (very awkwardly) on vowels as Type IIIa, this would be only if the important term *medicyne* is placed in the prelude-dip and the final lifts have the same structure as 155b. It seems safe therefore to suppose an original Type IIa structure as in **C** and Bx to be ⇒ of a non-alliterating semi-synonym. **158 (B 155)** Vocalic staves with semi-counterpoint seem intrinsically unlikely here, so the line may be scanned either cognatively on |t| |d| |d| as Type IIa (with a supplemental |t| stave in *destrúyeth*), or as Type Ia with 'monolexical' *déstrúyeth*, a pattern instanced at 320 (see *Intro*. IV § 38). *be*: omitted in ?**x** through *he* > < *ded* attraction but supplied (in different positions) by YCh and D²D. **162–64 (B 159–61)** The Bx form of these lines may be defended as not self-evidently defective in sense. But in the light of **C**, the contrast between the acts of guile and grace better prepares for the oxymoron of *good sleighte*; so a following line may be conjectured omitted by eyeskip from *good* 160 > *good* 161, with mechanical ⇒ of *sleighte* for *ende*. Its inclusion restores the lost antithesis between diabolic and divine *gile*, the stratagem (*sleighte*) being 'good' because its outcome (*ende*) proves so. In B 160 *al* is required for the syntax (since *bigan* is transitive) and for the sense (since the contrast with *ende* as restored otherwise fails). The **x** order is preferred for **C** as implicitly confirmed by 220 //; but because the position of *al* in **p** and *B*-C² (which may derive from a **p** copy) would equally explain its mechanical loss from Bx (by attraction to preceding *þat*), it may also be accepted in **B**. The ⇒ of *ende* in 160 could be a happy guess in YG, since there is no definitive sign of ⊗ as already in C². The form of B 159 is metrically defective (*xa / xa*) and it appears thin in content, with no qualifying term to distinguish Satan's kind of *gile* from God's. *K–D*'s emendation replaces 159 with C 162, ignoring such signs of revision as the repetition of *formost* from 161 and vaguely ascribing the corruption to 'imperfect recollection' (p. 94). But reconstruction here, though guided by **C**, does not reproduce it, since the original passive construction in **B** could have been later made active in C 162. A passive construction in the b-half here accordingly subsumes the content of C 162b, while in the a-half a possessive *gilours* is posited as lost through haplography occasioned by *gile (bi)giled* following. **168, 173 (B 165, 170)** *heo*: adopted for **B** and **C** as the clearest form, for which both archetypes have the (possibly original) gender-ambiguous *he*, though the spelling conceals the rounded vowel (see MED s.v. *he* pron. (2)). **172 (B 169)** is revised to scan on |l|, but Bx scans on |s| with a liaisonal key-stave *þis_light* (the emendation [*Loue*] in *Sch*² has been erroneously retained from *Sch*¹ and should read *he* as in *PT* Vol. I). **177 (B 174)** *And in*: the grammatically required form of the phrase (identical with **B**), of which *And* and *In* appear split variants; felicitously restored in D²Ch. **181–82 (B 178–79)** There is no good reason to question the authenticity of the archetypal b-halves *Mercy shal synge / haue* as do *K–D* (suggesting *merye shul synge* for **B**) and *Sch*¹ (adopting *synge* for **B**); Pe's note *ad loc* mistakenly suggests that *mery* is the reading of Bx, but it is that of only one ms, the **C** copy Ch. The phrase *I shal daunce þerto* in Bx presents no problem if the adverb means not 'also' but 'according with that [*sc.* the giving of Mercy]' (OED s.v. *Therto adv.* 2, MED s.v. 6c). *K–D*'s claim (p. 208) that *Mercy shal synge* makes 'poor sense because the speaker is replying to Righteousness, not Mercy' itself makes

poor sense, and *R–K*'s jocose restatement (p. 115) of their objection does not reassure. For that Peace should urge Righteousness to dance with her, declaring that (her close colleague) Mercy will provide the music of the *carole*, hardly baffles understanding. In the revision *þerto*, with *daunse* now adjoined to *synge*, means 'to it [*sc.* Mercy's song]' or 'also, likewise' (OED s.v. 1 and 3, MED s.v. 11). The pl. *shullen* **p** may reflect misunderstanding of *Moises* as subject and *Mercy* as addressee. **B 179** has presumably been lost from α by homœoarchy (*daunce* 179, *dawe* 180). **195 (B 190)** In the light of **B**, the caesura in **C** could be located after *God*, or before it, with *God* forming the key-stave (mute or full) in a Type IIIa line. There is insufficient reason for omitting *of the world* as scribal with *R–K*. **198 (B 193)** could scan either as Type Ia on |ð| and |f| or as an extended Type IIIb on vowels with semi-counterpoint on |t|, *of* as key-stave and a supplemental vocalic fifth stave (a pattern also possible in **B**). Given the unusual importance of this tree, stressing *a* 'a single' or 'a certain' and *þat* 'that particular' (MED s.v. *on* num. 3(a), 9 (a); *that* def. art. & adj. 2b (a)), would be preferable (on *a*, cf. at 397–98 //). *K–D*'s acceptance (p. 161) of *the trees* Hm for *þe* as the **B** original finds no support in **C**, and *R–K* defy the testimony of Cx in adopting their emendation into **C**. However, F's *of þe*] *þe* βR may be safely taken in the light of **C** as preserving α (from which R will have varied to converge with β). **203 (B 198)** Reasons for the line's loss from α are obscure. *K–D* (p. 69) suggest connotational attraction (*fend* 197, *peyne...perpetuel* 199) or pseudo-grammatical attraction (*wille* 197 > *That* 199), the latter of these seeming the more probable. The presence of the necessary pronoun *I* in ms L, here presumably preserving by pure descent from β or making a commonsense correction of an erroneous β reading preserved in γM, may be contrasted with its absence at 202. In the Cx tradition **pt** (= *x²*) has made a similar error but smoothed by adding *and* to give a sense compatible with Righteousness's being the speaker. **207 (B 202)** *Y*: clearly necessary, since the speaker is now not Righteousness but Peace. The omission in L (? < β) and R (? < α) might not seem noteworthy, given that the γ ms Y joins them, save for the fact that these two copies have already made the identical error twice, at 13.385 and 17.296. Thus, though Y's convergence here may be accidental, it is quite possible that these errors were in Bx and that γF independently made a commonsense insertion (similar to that of L noted at 198), with M doing so by correction from its usual w-type γ source. But whereas in those earlier instances an idiosyncratic usage may be in question, comparable to the omission of the 2 pers. sg. pronoun at C 20.379–80, *I* would here appear to be indispensable. Its loss, which shows no mechanical cause, may therefore be due to misunderstanding *recorde* as imperative, after a prior failure to register Righteousness as the speaker. *preye* **Cα**: preferable on grounds of sense in both versions. The modal *moet* here and in 208 should be taken to mean not 'must' (MED s.v. *moten* v. (2) 2a) but 'may' (*ibid.* 1a), a sense which overlaps with *mouen* (v. (3) 3). There is thus no substantive revision in 207–08, **B**'s *moot / mowe* variation (which is not a contrast) being perhaps eliminated for that reason. A tone of humble entreaty seems more appropriate to Peace than one of demonstration. *B*-β's misinterpretation of *moot* 202, together with the 'proof-like' appearance of the analogical argument in 204–16 and possible recollection of 152, may be what prompted ⇒ of *preue*. This is adopted by *K–D* and retained by *R–K* (partly on the witness of N²'s β–contaminated reading), but mistakenly. For whereas in 152 Mercy sets out to *preue by reson* a natural truth concerning poisons that involves *experience* (cf. *euydence* in // **C**), here the religious truth of man's coming salvation through Grace is a matter not of evidence but of faith and is therefore an object not of proof but of prayer. The suasive force of the analogies from experience in each case is a matter of their 'fitness' with God's nature as *Kynde*. **226 (B 217)** *gome*: the harder reading and necessary to provide the key-stave, assuming scansion on lexical words. The line as attested in x^I**p** could in principle scan on |f|, |v| with a liasonal stave on *of his*. *C*-t has either retained the correct reading from x^2 where **p** substituted the more familiar non-alliterating synonym convergently with x^I, or it has emended by felicitous conjecture. Influence from **B** here seems less likely, as it is not found elsewhere in t, whereas t's propensity for seeking metrical 'correctness' is widely evidenced. **231 (B 222)** scans on vowels, either as Type IIIa or, stressing *hath* and taking *soffred* as a blank third stave, as Type Ie (with *in* as muted key-stave). The line would undeniably read more smoothly with *see* for *wyte* (so *K–D*), and distraction from the preceding and following appearances of the latter verb in 229 (220) and 233 (224) might sufficiently explain its (unconscious) ⇒ here for a word not in itself difficult. But **C**'s ratification of Bx should quiet conjecture, especially given the pattern of rhetorical *repetitio* revealed in the mounting series [*To wite*] *what wele was...what he haþ suffred...what alle wo is*. To emend in such circumstances would be to interfere like a medieval scribe, as *R–K* seem to realise in not adopting *see*. **235** *loue*: a revision underlining the magnitude of concern shown in God's 'auntring' himself for man. *R–K*'s intrusion of **B**'s *langour* seems editorial *folye*, if not *synne*. **241 (B 232)** *Tho þat* **C**: apparently the only revision in a twelve-line sequence, unless Bx has inverted the words (as has *C*-F), seeing *þat* as a conjunction like the two following in 233–34; but no difference of sense arises. **242 (B 233)** *wyse* **Cβ**: contextually certain as the nominal adjective, not the noun *wyes* of which *B*-α *men* is a scribal reflex. **247 (B 238)** scans on |t| as a Type IIIa with a liasonal first stave in *That wéren* and a mute key-

stave in *token* 'compensated' by an internal full stave in *stella*, the word that contains the third lift, if the line is read with natural stressing. *K–D*'s conjecture *The oostes* for *Tho þat* is metrically unnecessary and textually unwarranted; the C-Text ratifies a reading in no way defective, as *R–K* apparently recognise by abandoning the emendation. **248 (B 239)** *tenden* **C**: preterite as in **B**, which has the uncontracted pl. form (MED s.v. *tenden* v. (3)). **250 (B 241)** *witnesseth*: preferred as giving a general statement about the elements' recognition of Christ's divinity (cf. 245 //). The preterite may be a misresolution of a tense-ambiguous BxCx form **witnesset*, induced by the tense of the preceding and following verbs. **252 (B 243)** After this *C*-F adds a line *Lord crist comaunde me to come to þe on watur* included by *Sk* which, though metrically acceptable, appears an evident translation of the following Latin with no claim to authenticity. **255 (B 246)** *heo*: the sun being feminine (*heresulue* 254) and as the clear vocalic form to be preferred here, though Cx probably read ambiguous *he*. *se* **Cβ**: preferred for **B** (although *mone* α gives a satisfactory T-type line) as both less obvious and more appropriate, the sun representing fire (along with the comet) as the third of the elements described in action so far. **260 (B 251)** *hit lihte*: conjectured as the Cx form of which *hit* x^2 and *lihte* x^I are diagnosed as split variants. It may be presumed that D has retained the x^I reading from u and U has converged with x^2, while N² has varied from its x^I primary source to the reading of its secondary **p** source. As reconstructed **C**, which scans as a Type Ic, is to be regarded as a revision, since Bx appears satisfactory in sense and metre and need not be judged imperfect like identical x^2 on comparison with x^I. **261–62 (B 252–53)** Loss of these lines from α may have been occasioned by the successive occurrences of *And* in 250–51, 254, 256–59 (*K–D* p. 69). Alternatively, it could be due to wrong resumption at 254 through identifying *Iesus* as the key-word but omitting the two preceding lines that respectively begin and end in a similar or the same word (an error all the easier had **B** read *Iesus* for *Gigas*, as *K–D* suppose). However, **C** is completely revised, and nothing in **B** (with its characteristic macaronic stave and wordplay) suggests scribal corruption even if, in the absence of α, Bx's exact form is not recoverable. **263** The reading of t N² *of helle alle þo* (*a. þo*] *hem* N²) for *alle of hem*, adopted by *PeR–K*, makes plausibly explicit the sense attested by x^I and **p**; but it has no real claim to represent Cx. *K–D* (p. 90) hold that this line (in the t form) has been lost by Bx through homoarchy and homœoteleuton (*And...liketh, And...lyue*); if so, it would probably have been in **B**¹, not a revision as here assumed. But since the sense does not require it, the case for its inclusion in **B** remains speculative. **272 (B 263)** *Principes* x^I: preferred as the harder reading in a line seen as revised to macaronic form. The singular in IP²U (and the English in **p**t) may result from the scribes' regarding Lucifer as the sole rather than the *immediate* addressee; but the Latin, being a direct quotation, should be given the pl. it has in the psalm-verse. *place* **x**: the likelier original, despite the possibility of irony in *palys* **p**, since **L** thinks of the devil not as ruler of a royal palace but as gaoler of a dungeon or overseer of a domain (it is *paradys* that properly bears the title of *palays* at 378). **288** *the carnel*: conjectured as the difficult but contextually appropriate original to which unsatisfactory *car(e)* '? chariot' (MED s.v. *carre n.* 3(a)) points as a reflex of a damaged or abbreviated original, while being itself the source of the smoothed and less apt variant *oure catel* of **p** (the word is found earlier in the description of Truth's court (7.234 //). The situation being one of war, it is the fortifications that they must first protect (*saue*), only thereafter the property within. Thus both *car* and *catel* should be rejected, while **Pe**'s conjecture *castel* seems too straightforward to have generated either. **293** *mangonel* **p**: the standard form of the word, perhaps spelled with omitted central vowel in x^2 (so tERQWF) and with *n* misread as *r* in x^1. **294** *And with*: the conjectured Cx form of which *And* and *With* appear split variants. Reconstructed thus, the syntax renders **x**'s third *and* redundant, but it may be a mistaken reflex of the proclitic *a-* **p**, here given in the fuller form (*en-*) attested in **M**. **299 (B 276)** *of his* **x**: preferred, despite **p**'s agreement with **B**, as offering characteristic wordplay on the grammatical particle (*of my, of his*). The motive for **p**'s ⇒ of the commoner *by* could have been to remove an apprehended ambiguity.

B 281–3 281 (C 304) *in deol*: conjectured on the showing of revised **C** as the required second stave in a Type IIa line, lost by *dwelle* > < *deueles* attraction in Bx, which scans *aa / xx*. **K–D**'s *driȝten* for *he*, providing the key-stave in a standard line, is unconvincing, since at 13.269, 14.101 (eliminated in **C**) the word has a tone of respectful loyalty inappropriate to the hostile speaker here. **282 (C 307)** *siþen*: conjectured not for the metre (since the line will scan as Type IIIa) but as giving the first of two reasons for Lucifer's confidence. It will have been lost by homœoarchy before *Sooþ-* or through anticipation of *siþen* (with different sense) in 283, and there may be an echo of it in C 308b, which revises the content of B 282. **283 (C 309)** *I sithen iseised*: the R form taken in the light of revised **C** as preserving that of α and thence Bx. F alters the subject + participle idiom to a full verb-phrase construction while β, omitting the first *I*, treats the second as a subject pronoun, not a participial proclitic, and makes the verb active. The two lines together give the sense 'And since he said...and I afterwards [was] given possession...' *seuenty hundred*: reconstructed in the light of revised **C** as closer to the traditional number (four or five thousand) and, being in the less usual form, easily liable to corruption. It is more likely that *seuene* was misread for *seuenty* than that *hundred* was substituted for

visually dissimilar *thousand*. (For a parallel formation cf. *ten hundred* at B 5.426//).

310 scans in Cx as Type IIIc on |n| or |w|. Possibly *þera-ȝeyne* has replaced *þerewiþ* in the same sense 'against it' (MED s.v. *therwith* adv. 1(a)) in a Type Ia line; but nothing is lost in the text accepted here. **R–K**'s emendation of *was* to *nas* is otiose. **320** scans with monolexical lifts in *bíhéstes,* a pattern that is rare but authentic (cf. on 158 above) but reduces the effect of the lexical word *fals.* One possible emendation would diagnose b-half inversion to prose order and read *bihéstes fálse* with the prefix as a mute key-stave but with full stress on the root and the important adjective. Alternatively, *thorw* could be seen as a Cx ⇒ for synonymous *bi*, a word that would facilitate a characteristic wordplay on grammatical morphemes (cf. on 299). However, it seems that **C** favours the causal preposition *thorw* (as at 395, where it replaces *by* in B 350 twice), so it is best taken as authentic here. **322 (B 291)** should perhaps in the light of **C** be spoken by Gobelyn in **B** (as **K–D** judge). But revision here is possible and B 291 as naturally ends Satan's speech as it begins Gobelyn's (cf. 325, where the replacement of *Certes* **B** by *Forthy* is the basis for identifying the 'Deuel' with 'Gobelyne'). **323 (B 292)** *And*: a revision of **B**, with which t's *For* has coincided, perhaps under inducement from a wish to tighten the link between the two clauses. **325 (B 294)** scans cognatively on |d| |d / |t|, though **K–D** see Bx *wol* as an error occasioned by attraction to *God wol* 292. But their conjecture *do* is unconvincing in diagnosing the mechanism of error, inaccurate in judging the metre inauthentic, imprudent in ignoring the confirmatory force of **C** and implausible in reducing Christ's active rôle by supposing that he will 'have them fetched' (no one accompanies *Treuthe* to hell since no one can). On all counts, it is firmly to be rejected, and **R–K** are wise to refrain from emending. **332 (B 298)** **C** revises a Type IIIa to a Type Ia line by adding as second stave *like a tidy man.* **K–D** diagnose its omission from **B** on account of the length of the line; yet usually such length produces not loss of interior phrases but misdivision followed by padding (as here in *C*-**p**), and errors of this type are not easy to parallel in Bx. This **C** line, like the next, shows **L** actively revising **B**, and apart from their metrical objection, which is ill-founded, there are no grounds for the Athlone editors' emendation. **333 (B 299)** The b-half in **B** contains a 'hanging participle' that could have misled the scribe of w (through failure to grasp the reference) to judge the word an error for a visually similar verb of motion. M has probably altered from a w source. **336 (B 303)** could be a revision of a Type Ib to a Type IIIc scanning on |s| and |ʃ| or to a vocalic Type Ib with stresses on contextually important grammatical words. **341 (B 306)** *seillynge hiderward* **B**: Bx's Type IIIc line scanning on vowel / *s* is acceptable, but in the light of **C** suggests scribal ↔ to the order more familiar in b-verses, with the adverb before the participle. *seillynge*: with sense 'gliding' attested by MED s.v. *seilen* v. 4 (citing this passage), overlapping with one sense of *sylinge* in **C**. The latter more effectively plays on this verb's two senses of 'sink, drop' and 'proceed, go' (MED s.v. *silen* v.(3) (a), (b) respectively) and therefore fits well with the local perspective of the speaker, to whom Christ's approach would be from above. Occurrences of *silen* appear confined virtually to alliterative verse and is lexically much harder than *seillynge*, which could be a Bx ⇒, if it is not simply a spelling variant (cf. *salid / syled* cited in MED s.v. ibid., from the two mss of *The Parliament of the Three Ages*, l. 657). On balance it seems better not to follow *K–D* in emending to **C**, since *seillynge* gives satisfactory sense and metre, and revision here cannot be ruled out. **343 (B 308)** *the fende* **C**: revising to Type Ia a **B** line of Type IIIc. *K–D* gratuitously judge *he* a Bx ⇒ under inducement from the rhyming monosyllables preceding. **344 (B 309)** *in his* **C**: a revision, taking the verb in the sense 'remain' (MED s.v. *abiden* v. 3(a)) rather than 'endure' or 'face' (ibid. 10(a), 12(a)). *B-F* could preserve Bx from α and R, like β, have lost *in* by haplography after preceding *abiden*; but the sense of βR is acceptable as it stands. **347–48 (B 312–13)** x^2B-α: on intrinsic grounds, the x^2 and α forms of these lines may be judged to represent respectively Cx and Bx, and x^1β to have lost the two half-lines as a result of homoarchy at the caesura (*lesynges* 347 [312], *lesing* 345 [313]). **349a (B 314a)** is possibly intended as a free-standing narratorial comment but is here taken as the clinching line of Satan's speech beginning at 341 and accordingly given in its expanded form as in the **C** copies RM and in **B**. **359–62 (B 315–20)** The revision is relatively free of uncertainty, the loss of 359b in x^1 being explained by eyeskip from *Lucifer* after the caesura to *Lucifer* 360 before the caesura; it drops the three pieces of appended Latin that seem to have occasioned the problems of order, lineation and metre in Bx and in both sub-archetypal traditions. The content is uniformly attested except for the omission of *soone* in R (corresponding to *aloude* in C 360) and sophistication by F of the phrase containing the adverb. *K–D* 's reconstruction yields a sequence logical in thought and correct in metre and is accordingly accepted as that of the probable original. Bx had defective metrical patterns in the lines here numbered 316–18, placing the first Latin phrase after present 317a and the second before 317b. The key to metrical correction is to recognise, in the light of // **C**, that none of the lines are macaronic but that the passage consists of English verse lines and Latin (prose) half-lines in alternation. Thus Lucifer's Latin question *Quis est iste* (316) answers Christ's command (315a), while Christ's Latin *Rex glorie* (318) answers Lucifer's English question (317a). Numbering these lines follows the practice

usual in this edition, only *Dominus virtutum* being treated as a 'citation-line' (319a), because it is syntactically free-standing. The sequence thus runs: 316 (*Quis*); 317 (*What lord*); 318 (*Rex*); 319 (*The lord*); 319a (*Dominus*). **365 (B 323)** *open*: either the adjective or the present-tense verb. Preterite *openede* is acceptable but easier and thus more likely to have been substituted under influence from the preterites *braek* 364 and *songen* 367. **372** *were*: a revision, referring to the original status of humanity. Posited Cx ⇒ for an original *be* (R–K) seems tenuous grounds for emendation. **379 (B 337)** *fettest*: containing no subject pronoun, the Ø-form of Cx presumably relying grammatically on the retained force of *thow* in 377. **381 (B 339)** While the revised line scans as Type Ia on |l|, **B** is a Type Ie with the key-stave generated by elision of *þ(e)_ólde*. **382 (B 340)** *be*: necessary for the sense and lost either by haplography in x^1 or through mistaking the verb as *giled*. **386** scans as Type Ic with the caesura after *lete* and with lyf^2 as key-stave. *anyentised*: spelled with *-issen* in Y, from the extended stem of OF *anientir* (MED s.v. *anientishen* v.); Cx may have read *aniente* as at 19.269 //. **B 343** The Bx line scans imperfectly *aa / xa* through fronting of the adverbial phrase, with consequent loss of the key-stave, and ↔ restores the metre. **393–94 (B 349–50)** The line-division in **C-p** gives an unmetrical 393 (*aa / xa*) with evident padding while that of **x**, though acceptable, awkwardly defers the adverb to the next line. In the light of B 349, which has an object pronoun after the verb, *here* is tentatively restored to the end of 393.

B 351–6 351 scans vocalically as Type IIIc on grammatical words (*in, álle*), the second bearing sentence-stress. The line would scan on |m| with *maugre* for *ayeins* (as in *K–D*) or *alle maner* for *alle*, the latter conjecture making the key-stave a lexical word. But given the lack of **C** support for either, Bx may stand. **356** *þyng* α: preferred as harder than *þo*, with the same terse stress-pattern as β (cf. B 10.127–28). But both may be split variants of Bx **þo þyng*.

397–98 (B 359–60) have *a* as a full stave, though 397 (359) is of Type Ia and 398 (360) of Type IIa (both vocalic). **400 (B 363)** *grettore* C-N^2B: required as the key-stave, Cx scanning *aa / bb*, and N^2's reading being a felicitous correction almost certainly from a **B** source. *wyddore* Cβ: preferable in **B** as providing a second dimension, *grettore* here (in the context of the metaphor of a growing plant or tree) denoting height. The α error exactly parallels that in Cx, ⇒ at the key-stave of a word familiar from a common repeating phrase, the consequence in both cases being to destroy the metre and conceal the locally discriminated sense of *grettore*. **405** *ne*: possibly unoriginal in its seeming to distinguish a metaphorical drink in the b-half from a literal one in the a-half, whereas the contrast intended is between *two* metaphorical 'drinks', one specific to the learned (*clergyse*), one shared by all (the *comune coppes* of 406). It could be that *ne* was shifted in Cx from a position before *wol* to one before *of*². **412** Y: required for the sense, as in **B**, and lost for no evident reason unless inducement from three preceding verbs in the 3rd person. **416 (B 375)** revises to Type Ia a **B** line of Type IIIa scanning on vowels (*át; -éuere*) or on |m| in the rhythmically parallel phrases 'mý bíddyng', 'mé líkeþ'. Conjecture of a Type Ia key-stave in |b| before *me* (*best K–D, be Sch¹*) is unnecessary. **419 (B 378)** *hole*: accepted on grounds of sense and the showing of **B** as referring to those who are 'entirely' Christ's brethren by sharing naturally in his humanity and sacramentally in his divinity. The ? t variant *holy* (shared by one **p**-ms, N) is a misreading of *hole* perhaps under influence from the sacramental aspect (baptism giving sanctifying grace); *halue* **p** a consequence of misunderstanding the sense (perhaps prompted by 436) or a smoothed reflex of a spelling variant *hale*; *owne* DF an attempt to simplify an idea found difficult. The line allows dual scansion as Type Ib on |b| or as a T-type on vowels and |b| (*aab / [a]bb*), varying 418 (which must scan on |b|), linking with it translinearly by making the latter's blank stave *alle* the first (full) stave of 419, and placing sentence-stress on *hole*. **420 (B 379)** revises to Type Ib a **B** line scanning either as Type Ia with a cognative liaisonal key-stave (|d| |d| / |t|) in *that_ís* or, if the key-stave is also muted, as a T-type: *that_is withóuten énde* (*aa / [a]bb*), the latter preferable for its more natural stress-pattern. *K–D*'s *dureþ* for *is* presumes metrical defect where none exists. **422 (B 381)** *hy*: the presumed pl. prn in **C** (with scansion on vowels like **B**), the advancing non-alliterating form being a Cx ⇒ and N a felicitous correction for the sake of the metre. N² has *he were a treitour* following *a felown* in 421, readings accepted by *R–K* (p. 102) as corrections from a superior lost **C** source but here judged ⊗ from **B**. **424 (B 383)** **C** offers no obvious difficulty of interpretation, the contrast of *deth oþer iewyse* presumably being between the execution and the judge's passing of sentence, at either of which events the king could arrive by chance (both 'execution' and 'sentence' were primary senses of *juwis(e* (MED s.v. n. 1(a)). The probable Bx reading *deep or ooþer wise* appears unsatisfactory because there is obviously no punishment other than death for which *life* could be granted in remission. Thus it seems likely that **B** read *iuwise*, though WHmGC² will have corrected independently or by reference to **C**, *els* Cr preserving w's reflex of *oþer wise* and M deriving the same reading from its w-type secondary source. To adopt *iuwise* for **B** but retain *or* will make *ooþer* here an adjective, implying for *iuwise* a punishment other than 'execution' (its usual meaning), e.g. mutilation. But as this conflicts with the logical sense of 384, it may be that **L** deleted *or* in **C** to leave *ooþer* as the conjunction 'or' with the clearer meaning spelled out above. Alternatively, the **B** reading was identical with

C (as judged by *K–D*) and *or* was intruded by Bx or its exemplar through failure to register the sense of *iuwise* as 'sentence to punishment (usually by death)'. This, and not 'execution of punishment (usually by death)', its other sense, is the one supported by *doem* 427 // (which clearly envisages the act of final *judgement*). The smoothing *wise* would then have followed after rejection of *ooþer iuwise* 'other [death] sentence' as illogical. The confusion may have arisen in **B** if **L**'s first thought was indeed the act of execution itself as being interrupted by the king's arrival (421–22). It would thus be acceptable to find no revision in **C** 423–29b and to reject *or* from B 383 as a Bx error. **434 (B 392)** scans vocalically either with an abrupt caesura after *wol* that heightens the stress on the contextually significant stave-word *here* or (less expressively) with the caesura after *wykkede*. The Bx line has the imperfect pattern *aa / xx* and *clene* is here conjectured as the required stave-word lost haplographically after *clensed, clerliche*. Although scansion of the emended line as Type IIa is possible, it reads better as Type Ia with muted key-stave and *clene* playing on its three main senses 'cleanly', 'properly' and 'completely' (MED s.v. *clene* adv. 1(a), 2(a), 3(a)). *K–D* justify their conjecture *keuered* as having been replaced by a 'more explicit' term (p. 198). But a mechanical explanation seems likelier, and the proposed phrase **clene wasshen* will recall an earlier reference to the purgation of sin by divine power at 10.228–29// (see *Commentary* further on the significance of this echo). **436** *halue-bretherne*: a reading adopted by *K–D* for **B** and defended by Donaldson (1982:72), though **B** contains implicitly what **C** will make explicit. **440 (B 398)** *and*: emended by *PeR–K* after **B**; but the latter is enforcing a deliberate contrast between *al helle* and *al mankynde*, both parts of which are eliminated in **C**. Accidental Cx ⇒ of *and* may be ruled out as improbable, so *and* may be taken as a revision of *al*, giving the non-trivial (and more certainly uncontroversial) meaning 'my mercy and my human nature [which I share with those I shall judge] will hold sway in heaven'. **444** *Tho ledis* t: possibly the *x²* reading from which *ledis* could have been lost by distraction from preceding *lede* (443) and following *leued* in both *x¹* and **p**, then smoothed in **p** to *Alle*; or else a felicitous conjecture in the t scribe's manner designed to correct the metre (see 226). The *x¹* reading scans as Type IIIa on *I* and in **p** (identical with *B-α*) as Type Ia with muted second and third staves; but both are unsatisfactory in throwing the stress off the important words that link Christ's *love* of the patriarchs with their *belief* in him. The *B-β* line (also Type IIIa) allows a more significant stress pattern (*me, my*), but likewise de-emphasises the verbs. On balance the t reading may therefore be tentatively adopted as the best on grounds of sense and as facilitating characteristic wordplay on *lede* 443 and *ledis*. It further guides conjectural reconstruction of

Bx, in which *ledes* must be presumed lost for the same mechanical reasons as in ?Cx. **448 (B 406)** *leste*: convincingly emended by *K–D* on the showing of **C** as the probable original in **B** for which *boldeste* is Bx's replacement of a non-alliterating term after failing (as did *Sch¹*) to appreciate that the 'fiendkins' (415) would have *less* to fear than the greater 'fiends'. Since **L**'s subtle logic here upsets the conventional expectation that 'daring' would be expected from the 'bold', this scribal (and editorial) error is unsurprising.

B 413 (C 457) For the next 532 lines the unique representative of *B-α* is **F**. But the readings of this wayward copy are cited in the Apparatus only where they appear intrinsically likely to represent α. Of the extensively sophisticated variants characteristic of F, a few are nonetheless considered when the text of **B** appears uncertain on the basis of sole β and // **C**.

460 (B 416) *That...ne*: adopted as the most unambiguous reading, though not impossibly *That* is elliptical for *But þat,* as seems to be the understanding of Hm, and this 'preclusive' use fits more naturally with the syntax of 461 (B 417). While the Bx reading cannot be finally established, it seems probable that Cx did not have *ne* (cf. on 6.312, 7.61 above). Like F, which may be an intelligent guess, N² also contains *ne* (probably from a *B-β* source). *louhynge*: read in XYI as *loulynge* by *R–K* and recorded as a substantive variant. But *louhynge* as an authentic (if little-instanced) spelling of the gerund seems quite possible as the underlying form of y, and may be accepted here. **464 (B 420)** The preterite *chydde* is unquestionably right on grounds of contextual sense; since Peace desires the sisters' smiles and embraces to cover all trace of their former discord, she cannot be intended to mean that they are still quarrelling. **466 (B 422)** must scan on |r| as a Type IIIa line with a five-syllable prelude, since scansion as Type IIa on |s| subordinates the speaker's name to the function-word *saide*, which will not naturally bear the stress required for position three in this type. **467 (B 423)** *here*: the spelling of the feminine sg. pronoun in Cx but modified in **B** to the normal spelling of the base ms (its potential ambiguity indicated by the substituted adverb in *B-G*). **470 (B 426)** *caroled C-xB-F*: discriminated as the harder and therefore more probably original reading in both **C** and in **B** (F < α = Bx), for which **p** and β *dauncede* is a neutral ⇒ unattended by ambiguous secular overtones (see MED s.v. *carolen* v., esp. the quotations from *Handlyng Synne* and *Cursor Mundi*). **473 (B 429)** *go*: accepted on the showing of **C** as the probable α reading (< Bx) lost in β by alliterative attraction of *Ariseþ* > *reuerenceþ.*

Passus XXI (B XIX)

In the last two passūs the texts represented, **Cx** (derived from *B²*, whether or not revised in details from *B¹*), and

Bx are here understood as independent witnesses to a single source from which both descend, *B-Ø*, the first scribal copy of the B-Text (see *Intro.* III B § 2). All the divergences between them are therefore noted, even if intrinsically unimportant, as each text contains potential evidence for the original reading of the other.

RUBRICS The Cx tradition is clear in regarding XXI–XXII as *Dobest* One and Two. *B-β* accords in part, implicitly treating XIX as the prologue of Dobest and denoting XX as Dobest One. But with no reliable evidence for α, the exact form of Bx remains uncertain.

12 *his(e)*: proposed in order to resolve the logical contradiction between the Cx reading *Cristes* (possibly *B-α*'s) and the adversative *ac* in 13b, which is supported by *B-β* (*om* F). *C-*p does this through ⇒ of the easier *and* (as have *B-CrC*, perhaps from a *C-*p copy). The *B-α* reading remains unknown, F having Ø in 13b; but there is no contradiction in β's *ac*, since the substantive β reading in 12 is *Piers*. It is uncertain, however, whether F *cristis* preserves α (and so represents Bx) or shows ⊗ from **C**. The reconstruction *his(e)* is difficult enough to have prompted two distinct and unrelated alternative readings. The 'logical' β variant depends on the figure's physical likeness to Piers and recalls Abraham's answers to Will's earlier question at 18.22–6. The 'theological' variant starts from the notion that Jesus after his 'conquest' on the cross bears the title 'Christ'. But since **L** understands his 'arms' (visible form) as belonging equally to the divine Son who assumed humanity and to the human nature he assumed, both of which are united in the person of 'Jesus Christ', the reading *Piers* would be satisfactory. Conversely, the contradiction in the *C-*x form would be avoided by reading with *C-*p, which could in theory preserve a revision in **C**. However, it seems improbable that **x** substituted *ac* for Cx *and* so as to render a lucid reading incoherent. On the assumption, therefore, that *ac* is the **BC** original, either *Piers* or the reconstructed form is likely to have been the common reading of B¹ and Bx. Although *Piers* would give good sense in **C** (and is so judged by *PeR–K*), *his(e)* better explains both *Piers* and *Cristes*, while allowing retention of the probable Cx reading *ac*. It is thus adopted as the postulated **BC** original for which Bx and B¹ substituted their respective resolutions. It should be noted that the **C** Apparatus entry omits to record that N² reads *Piers*. This N² reading, which *R–K* (p. 102) do not include with those they consider derived from a pre-Cx copy, is likely to be by ⊗ from a **B** source of β-type.

15 *callede* C: preferred on intrinsic grounds in **B** as almost certainly the reading of α, F's ⇒ being of a non-alliterating *preterite* synonym. *B-β calle(n)* may be a reflex of a tense-ambiguous form **callyt,* g an independent 'commonsense' correction. **18** The absence from **C** of the quotation later given as 80a indicates that its appearance here in F is more probably a scribal anticipation than a reflex of Bx. **21** *for to* **C** / *to* **B**: unlikely to be a revision; either could be the common original. **24** *more worthiore* CF: the harder reading, and if F = α here, likely to be that of Bx also (the *C*-mss ChQFG have *worþi*). **30** *Ac* C-**x**?*B*-β: preferred to *And* **p**B-g on contextual grounds as contrasting the title of conqueror, which is 'special' because not received from another, with the previous two (cf. on *ac* at 13 above). **38** *Baptist* CB-L: self-evidently the right reading, with *B*-L's source *l* presumably deriving directly from β and M varying to γ under influence from its usual w-type secondary source. F has smoothed by deleting the article and could have varied through failure to grasp the allusion (see *Commentary*). Although L could be an independent commonsense correction of *baptisme*, or corrected from a **C** source, it probably preserves the reading of Bx; but the α form remains uncertain in the absence of R. **39** *and* C: possibly a revision in **C**, which commonly smooths such 'harder' asyndetic constructions. But if F preserves α, it may be that β has simply lost the conjunction by *fra-* > < *fre* attraction (*C*-N² also omits *and*, perhaps following *B*-β). **40** *Iesu²*: distinguished from *Iesus* (at 25), though it is unclear whether **x**'s repetition retains the reading of **B** (the same) or ?β preserves a varied form revised in **C**. (For similar variation between **C** and **B** see at 48, where F is taken to stand for α). **47** *was*: the less common form in pl. use and therefore more probably original, perhaps preferred because *fendes* is a collective pl., or under influence from the number of the following noun. *B*-L preserves from β, F from α, and M has varied with γ, while *C*-**p** substitutes the customary form, with inversion to prose order.

56–9 may have been lost from β by homoarchy of *And* 56, *And* 60 (*K–D*). In the absence of any control from β or from R, F's text as representing α is assessed in the light of its marked tendency to vary word-order and sophisticate phrasing and expression. **56** **C**'s reading here does not appear a revision but the underlying form of **B**, which F may be judged to vary to prose order. **57** The **C** reading is more pregnant than that of F, even after correction of *his* (1) to *him*, the important idea being not that of Lucifer's *status* but of his actual *position*. F's reading may have been influenced by the preceding reference to *cherles* 55. **59** *lawe*: preferable since *lawe* here has the wider sense 'religion' (MED s.v. *laue* 4(a) or (b)) rather than the specific 'a (set of) rule(s) or ordinance(s)' (ibid. 1(a)).

60 scans as Type Ib with two staves in *lárgelíche*, or on vowels (*hé, álle*) as Type IIIc, so *R–K*'s object-adverb ↔ is unwarranted. *ʒeueth* **x**?α:preferred on grounds of sense to *ʒau(e)* **p**β as referring to Christ's continuing grant of heaven to the just. *Lege* C: the adjective as noun, marginally harder than the nominal form in **B**; either could be the common original or there may be a small revision here. **62** *be wel* **C** / *wel be* **B**: both acceptable, with no evidence of revision. **63** *his cros and his* **C** / *cros of his*

B-β: both acceptable, *þerwith* 64, 65 referring with equal propriety to the symbol alone or to the symbol and what it symbolises together (cf. B 14.190–91). If *his* (1) in F, which may reflect α, was also in Bx, it was presumably deleted in β to avoid the awkwardness of a reading **his cros of his passion*. The **C** reading could then be a revision to ease the latter (though **p** brings back some of the awkwardness by omitting *his* (1)). **74** *knelend*: preferable in **C** to the preterite, which may have come in by anticipation of 75 or failure to expand a nasal contraction in *kneléde*.

75–6 The context favours the presence of *(en)sense* in the common **BC** original, and its absence from Cx would indicate its omission from B¹. If F has here preserved it from α, the word will doubtless have been in Bx; but F could have provided at 76 a term judged necessary, as did *B*-Cot at the end of 75 (borrowing the β form at 86) and *C*-R at 76 (employing the native synonym conjectured at 90 below). The placing of the word in *K–DSch¹Pe* is at the end of 75. An explanation for its loss from that point might be failure to grasp the line's rare Type IIb structure; but an original positioning at the head of 76 as the prelude-dip in a long Type Ia line might more easily do so. (Lines with major lexical words in the initial dip are not uncommon, and one occurs below at 89). If **L** wrote the word in its apocopated form *sense*, it could have been lost in Bx / B¹ or their common ancestor B-Ø through being misconstrued as *sen(n)es* 'afterward' (MED s.v. *sitthenes* adv. (a), found at 78 below) and mistakenly deleted. The witness of B² here, as at 90, indicates that if **L** had indeed begun detailed revision of B¹, he did not make good all scribal omissions in his copy-text. **76** *withouten mercy askynge*: 'without asking for a "thank you" / 'any favour [in return]'. The text is entirely secure in both Bx and B² (< B¹) and the Cot reading *mercede* over an erasure may reflect both difficulty with this unusual use of *mercy* and acquaintance with an idiosyncratic term first introduced in C 3.290 and memorably elaborated there (*mede* registers similar awareness that the dominant senses of *mercy* would be inappropriate here). *K–D* (p. 160), however, support *mercede* on the grounds of likely direction of variation; they see it as capable of generating a gloss *mede* and a homœograph *mercy* and argue that lexical evidence for the sense 'thanks' is very poor and that the other uses in *PP* are non-analogous 'social gallicisms' (B 1.43 //; the other cases cited, at B 10.220 and 17.86, combine with 'graunt'). But analogous is exactly what this use is, as becomes clear if inverted commas are put around the word in the present instance. The Kings do not ask 'thanks' from their *conquerour noble* because they are subject rulers offering tribute to the *God þat al wrouhte* (20.246), who could say of their *ertheliche honeste þynges* what Christ says to Lucifer about the patriarchs: *Myne þei ben and of me — I may þe bet hem cleyme* (B

18.330). However, as well as 'thanks' (MED s.v. *merci* n. (1) 8(c)), there is present the sense 'favour' (ibid. *s.v.* 5(a)). The Kings seek *no* recognition from the *sovereyn /...of sand, sonne and see*, neither 'thanks' / 'favour' nor *eny kyne catel* (77) such as an earthly conqueror might be expected to offer tributaries in recognition of their homage. Thus while *mercede* could fit the context, there is insufficient reason to suppose it the original underlying *mercy*, and K–D 's emendation to **BC** should be rejected. **77** *knoweleched*: the preterite a better fit as the third main verb (coming as a climax after *knelede, offrede*) than as a second participle (after *askynge*). The correct form in F is presumably from α, that in G by felicitous conjecture. The β reading may result from misreading the pret. pl. termination *-eden* as *ende*, the older participial ending still attested in some copies as a relict form (e.g. at 3. 333 and at 74 above). **83** *Rihtfulness*: with the same primary sense 'justice' as *Rightwisnesse* (MED s.vv. 1(a)). Use of the latter (exactly synonymous, but more common) at 88 does not in itself argue against the former (uniquely instanced here in *PP*), as the virtues are assigned various synonyms between 83 and 93 (e.g. *Reuthe, Pite, Mercy* at 83, 92, 93). **84–7** are inserted in X in another hand; they may be presumed to have been lost by eyeskip from *offrede* 83 > *offrede* 87. **86** *sense*: the apocopated form preferred both as rhythmically smoother and as facilitating wordplay on the homophone *sense*, which overlaps semantically with *resoun* (MED s.v. *sense* n., *resoun* n. 10(a) 'meaning, signification'). **88–9** have an identical form in βC; F (? = α) will have lost 88b, 89a through eyeskip (from *gold* before the caesura in 88 to the relative *þat* at 89b after the caesura), partly induced by the presence of *Gold* as the initial word in 89. **90** *richeles*: conjectured as the harder native synonym for *(en)sense*, the word contextually required here (incense = 'reason', gold = 'justice'). The error was probably mechanical in origin, a superficially meaningless form *riche les* inviting ⇒ of a term (*gold*) often associated with the adjective *riche*. This confusion would have been facilitated by the further comparison of *Resoun* to *riht* and *treuthe*, the first of which forms the root of *Rihtwisnesse* ('Resones felawe'). B-F, after omitting 88b–89a, rewrites the a-half of 90 as *For it shal turne tresoun*. But the sequence of thought requires *it* to refer to *Rightwisnesse*, whereas the more natural referent would be *reed gold*, giving an unsuitable meaning here. *Resoun*, moreover, is left in F without any elaboration such as *Rightwisnesse* (B 88–9) and *Reuthe* (92–3) receive. K–D nonetheless argue for F's as the original reading supplanted through scribal censorship of a line 'mentioning treason in connection with kings'. Their objection to *riche gold* as unacceptable because at 86 incense signified 'reason' naturally holds; but the emendation offered above answers this, and is on all criteria one of the securest for any disputed reading

in the poem. By contrast, K–D's adoption of F appears exceptionally weak, in itself and for the reasons adduced in support; R–K's retention of it defies belief. **91** *cam þo* **C** (*trs* **B**): order of verb and adverb in the common original of Bx and B¹ could have been as here or transposed. *and kneled* CB-F: preferred as the Bx / B¹ reading, altered to a participle in β under inducement from *apperynge* 92, *knelynge* 95. **94** *Ertheliche* CB-F: preferred on grounds of sense as the common Bx / B¹ reading for which β will have substituted *Thre yliche* following mechanical ↔ of consonants in the first word (|r|, |θ|). **97** *comsed* **C**: possibly a revision of cognatively-alliterating *gan to*, but conjectured here as the original (cf. 106 below) replaced in Bx by a commoner synonym (Cx's ⇒ of *comsed* for *gan to* can be ruled out as improbable). **99** *For* / Ø: either could be original. **101** *durste*: presumably a revision of *hadde tyme to* Bx, which provides a cognative key-stave in a Type Ib line (with cognative b-staves). Conceivably Bx could be a ⇒ through objection to the tone of *durste*; but the motivation appears obscure. **108–9** *feste* / *Turned water into wyn* **C**: preferred as the probable reading of B-Ø and reconstructed as that of Bx. The latter appears with wrong line-division but correct word-order in ?α (though with insertion of *he* by F) and correct lineation but wrong word-order in β (here through inverting verb and noun to promote the idea judged most significant). R–K's emendation of Cx to read with β (as presumably harder) surprisingly ignores the witness of F. **111** *lyfholinesse* **C**: rhythmically better and conceptually superior, but not impossibly a revision (B-W's agreement with **C** is presumably coincidental). **113** *thus*: accepted here as a satisfactory original reading in both Bx and B¹, the variant *vs* (B-g, C-y) resulting from haplographic loss of initial *þ*. Conversely B-F's *þus vs* could preserve an original from which *vs* was lost by the same mechanism in B¹ and β; but the rhythm of the adopted form is clearly superior. **115** *þat* / *þe*: either could be original, B-WHm here converging coincidentally with **C**. **117** *only*: clearly right on grounds of sense. B-Cr's correction is possibly by collation with a C-Text, M's more probably independent. **134** *the* **C** / Ø β: either could be original, so F is not here adopted as representing α. C-WN² omit the article, the latter perhaps after comparison with a B-β copy. **135** is to be scanned as a 'licensed' macaronic with the anomalous pattern *aa* / *xx* found at 7.152 // above. The (possible) emendation of *et* to *sed et* would not be supported by the Biblical source in its well-established form. **140** *Herof* **C**: perhaps slightly preferable to *Wherof* β, but it is not a necessary stave-word and either could be original. Ø **C** / *of þe* **B**: either could be original, though the rhythm of the latter is smoother. **142** *on a* / *on*: either could be original or both reflexes of **a* 'on / one'. **148** *deuyned* **C**: 'foretold,' 'prophesied' (MED s.v. *divinen* v. 1(b)), found earlier in this sense at 17. 312 and B 15. 598; possibly a revision of *demede* **B** (MED s.v. *demen* v. 11b, c 'suppose, expect') with which senses 2(b), 3(b) of *divinen* partly overlap (*pace* the argument of *R–K,* p. 119). In both texts the referent of *men* is the *profetes* of 145, and *deuyned,* while an improvement in precision, is more in the nature of a repetition than *demede* (which could, however, be a visual error for the latter).

151–52 The *B*-β single-line form is plausible, but in the light of F unlikely to be that of Bx. F has, however, added an extra lift in the phrase *a mortuis* (independently accompanied here by the unrelated Cot) and substituted *he* in the b-half, perhaps through objection to applying a neuter *it* to Christ's risen body. Four unrelated **C** sources of the x^2 family insert *rex* in the a-half to make the line scan as a macaronic Type Ia, and this monosyllable could have been lost by haplography before *res-* (so *K–D*). But in the majority of **C** mss (= Cx) and in Bx the line will scan either as Type IIIa, with two lifts in *résúrgèns* or, preferably, as Type Ia with an internal |r| stave in *Christus.* The form of the Latin phrase, securely that of its Biblical source, is confirmed by its repetition at 160. **153** Ø CB-F /*he* β: either could be original (with F representing α), though more probably *he* was lost by *hem* > < *ȝede* attraction. **154** *preyede* (2) C: adopted for **B** as the likely original, with synonymous Bx *bisouȝte* (scanning in principle with a mute cognative stave *bi-*) a ⇒ following objection to the repeated verb (*K–D,* p. 95). The F line, except in preserving *þo,* appears not a reflexion of α but a scribal attempt to 'correct' the metre, *propre* having no ascertainable contextual appropriateness. There seems to be wordplay here on co-polysemes of *preien* (MED s.v.1a (a) and 1b (a)). But the repetition of a word with little real difference in sense has already been instanced at B 16.159 // (*pays; pees*), where F has characteristically sophisticated the b-half in a similar way. **159** *heo* **pB**: lost in **x**, perhaps through haplography if the exemplar form was *a.* **161a–62** C β: omitted by F for no immediate reason, unless eyeskip from *Christus* 160 to *Christum* 161 (though this does not explain loss of 162). **164** Ø / *for*: either could be original (cf. the converse situation at 21 above). **175** Ø / *Thow*: the 2nd pers. sg. preterite without pronoun, instanced earlier at 20.379–80 but not in // **B** and possibly a revision-feature in **C** or the reading of B-Ø, the <B¹Bx> source, smoothed to the more conventional form in Bx. **180** *be* CF: preferred to *alle be* β, here identifiable as a more emphatic scribal reading. **183** *thouhte*: to be preferred on grounds of sense as the original in **BC**, and not a **C** revision. Christ's intention is to perform an *act,* that of giving the sacramental power of forgiveness to the apostles; his *teaching* of them has been completed on Holy Thursday night. The Bx error could have been visual, though *t* for *th* is less frequent than *th* for *t* (cf. 239 below); the α reading is undiscernible through F's sophistication. **186** *To hym*: conjectured on the basis of

*Hym B-βC-***x**, the presumed reading of both Bx and B¹, as the reading underlying both, from which B-Ø will have lost the preposition through homoarchy (*To* at 185). The key point is that 'forgiveness' (MED s.v. *pardoun* n. 1(a)) may be granted to all, but ability to 'release from temporal penalty' (ibid. 1(b)) to Piers alone, this being the sacramental *power* specified in 180. Since that is the inescapable sense of the lines, *K–D*'s more drastic transference of *Hym*186 to final position in 184 and transposition of 185 with 186 is quite unnecessary. Indeed, if absolute *Hym* were an acceptable prepositionless dative, no emendation would be required; but since the usage sounds unidiomatic and reads confusingly, it is not retained. **187** The present subjunctive in Bx is as acceptable as the preterite (if *come* is taken as present), though formally less correct than WHm strive to be (see Vol. 1, Appendix One, *B-Text*). **C**'s preterite could be revision, or either might be original. **190** *to* / Ø: the probable archetypal readings are retained; again, either could be original. *elles*: preferred as both harder (MED s.v. *elles* adv. 5) and metrically smoother, β being presumably represented by L, α by F. For **L**'s use of this adverb in line-final position and in temporal sense, cf. Pr 89 //. The phrase *here or / ne elliswher,* found at 15.300 //, 19.163 // and *otherwhile elliswher,* found at 10.29 //, are placed only in the a-half. **194** *reddit*: the present tense, preferred to the future as the original since the second verb is also present, as is the English of 195 that translates it (*Payeth*). **197** scans as Type IIa, reading *dómesdáy,* with a supplementary stave in position five. **198** Ø / *þe*: the **C** reading arguably harder as implying the idea of *theosis*; but *þe* could have been lost through *gode* > < *God* attraction. **205–07** In Cβ; loss of these lines from F (though not necessarily from α) may have been by eyeskip from *Conscience* (205 end) to *Quod Conscience* (208 beginning). **206** *for* (1) C: with its characteristic wordplay arguably preferable for **B** as the harder reading (so *K–D*). In the absence of F, α is undeterminable, but *of* β makes good sense. The ?Bx line will scan satisfactorily as Type IIIc, as will Cx (which, however, has the alternative scansion *aab / ab* as Type Ie with counterpoint). **211–13** In Cβ, loss of the Latin in 211 after *wiþ* in F (perhaps through a rubricator's oversight), occasioned loss of 212–13, so that the scribe (whether of *f* or of α) picked up from *And thanne* 214 instead of *Thanne* 212. **212** *And...þo* C-**p** / *Thanne...song* B-β: the adverb seems confirmed as substantively archetypal on the showing of **p** and β; but *þo* could be an intruded **p** form (it substitutes at 214 for *And thenne* x**B**). Its position and the subject-verb order remain uncertain, though revision is unlikely here. *R–K* adopt the N² reading, that of *B*-β,(as again at 224 below). **213** scans as Type Ib on cognative staves (|k| |k| / |g| |g|). *K–D*'s emendation *Crist* for *God* is metrically superfluous and theologically imprecise, since it is the Holy Spirit who is being invoked in the Latin, not the Son, and *God of grace* appears an integral phrase. **214** *the*: a form that occurs in both versions at the end at 22.386 and is commoner than the Ø form. Cx gives, preferably, a Type IIb line and Bx can be scanned as Ia or T-type, so no alteration is warranted here. **217** *can* C**B**-LF: 'have mastery of' (MED s.v. *connen* v. 3(a)); required as the key-stave and self-evidently harder than *han*. F appears to attest α and L to preserve β, with M varying to the γ reading under presumed influence from its usual w-type source. *his(e)* C**B**-F: the harder reading, smoothed to the grammatically more logical pl. under the influence of *hir* 218 after *creatures*, which perhaps retains from the common source of <BxB¹> a pluralised form of a collective sg. *al kyn creature. **224** *And...and* C**B**-F: agreement with C here supports F's reading as that of α. *B*-β may have lost the first two words through promotion of the dominant notion (*Pride*) and the conjunction through alliterative attraction (*Pope* > < *prynce*). *R–K* adopt the reading of N², which is, as usual, that of *B*-β. **228** The variant *gom* is metrically otiose but illustrates t's readiness to retain or substitute alliterating synonyms for 'man' (cf. on 20.226, 444). Group t also omits the article *a* and the phrase *to gye with*. **229** *hem* C / *hym* **B**: the sg. fitting better with *vch man*, but the pl. according correctly with *gow* 226. It could be a revision or either could attest the common original. **230** *wyes*: conjectured as the required first stave-word which Cx has replaced with the common non-alliterating synonym and Bx omitted; as they stand, both scan *xa / ax*. The Ø-reading of Bx could have been the result of distraction from *wit* at the end of the a-half and again at the beginning of 231 (if its source read *wyes*), or from preceding *som(me)* if it read *men*. That Cx had *men* seems virtually certain, despite the fact that three unrelated C copies and one group read Ø. Though in principle t could here preserve the reading of *x²*, while both *x¹* and **p** severally could have substituted *men* for Ø, it is more probable that tP²EW have all lost *men* for the same reason as has Bx. **231** C could be revised, the sense being somewhat different. *K–D* reject Bx for C, but this is an unsafe emendation. For the former is not evidently scribal, and the small but significant change could easily have been made in **L**'s copy-text (B¹) without causing disarrangement of the lines. **B** could be rendered more economical by deleting *hir liflode* and reading *þat* for *as* (the latter the reading of C-t). This would make the postulated C revision a mere matter of omitting initial *Wit* (as one **B**-ms Cot has done) and then inserting *treuthe*; but reconstruction of **B** on these lines remains too speculative. **236** Both Cx and Bx have an unmetrical line (*xa / ax*), which *K–D* emend by reading *By* (the preposition already instanced in 233 and 234) for *Wiþ*. But while this facilitates characteristic wordplay on the key-stave *bilyue*, which may have its prefix stressed, it unnaturally emphasises the particle in its proposed initial position (contrast

the effect of stressed *by* at B Pr 80 // and B 3.10, the latter revised in **C**). The reading adopted here, with ↔ of the *lexical* words in the a-half, yields a Type IIIa line while retaining a natural stress-pattern. The inversion, whether occurring independently in BxB¹ or present in B-Ø, could have resulted from promoting the idea thought most prominent in 'winning one's livelihood' by trade, i.e. *selling*. As in an earlier instance (20.400 above), a single C-copy N² anticipates the present emendation; but its citation in the Apparatus here does not imply that it is any more than a felicitous scribal correction. **237–38** are in **C** and **B**-F, and loss of 237b and 238a is attributed to Bx by Chambers and Grattan (1931:6). But the error pertains to β, which will have lost it through homoteleuton at the caesura (*laboure...labour*), aided perhaps by unconscious suggestion from the collocation of *lelly to lyue* with *by labour* at 233 above. The resulting line's acceptable sense and metre would have effectively concealed the error from detection, as it did from *Sk*. **239–40** Differences between Bx and Cx appear here which could be due to revision. 239 scans with a mute key-stave *to* or in **B** possibly with a cognative full stave *dyche*. C 240 rewrites a line which both repeats in its a-half the sense of B 231a (itself re-written in **C**) and supplies a correct if unforceful b-half. However, B 240 scans acceptably as Type I with two lifts in *liflóde* (as earlier at B 14.48) and both this pattern and the position of *wiþ* reveal variation here as well as repetition of 231a. In 239 *K–D*'s complex argument (pp 174–5) for *coke* in place of *dyche* relies on too many suppositions to justify emendation. In the Cx tradition, *theche* as the first verb is not seriously in doubt, with *teche* being, as *Sk* recognised (Apparatus), merely a spelling variant of a kind paralleled in Bx at 183 above. *R–K*'s re-arrangement of the verbs (p. 125) presupposes non-revision without arguing for it. In 240, their replacement of **C** by B 240 is radical interposition on the slenderest grounds. **241** has the inauthentic scansion *aa / xx* in both Bx and Cx. *K–D*'s emendation (p. 207; so *R–K*) provides in *figures* (MED s.v. *figure* n. 6(a) 'numerical symbol') an apt and rare lexeme for which *noumbres* could well be a scribal ⇒ (perhaps a B-Ø marginal gloss incorporated into the text in Bx and B¹). An even apter and rarer term is *digit*, first instanced in Trevisa's *Bartholomew* (MED s.v.), which would give scansion on |d|. *Pe* omits *to kenne* after t, producing a line with cognative scansion (|t| |d| / |d|) but a stress-pattern with nothing to justify its deviance. The earlier emendation in *Sch¹* with *diuerse* as a key-stave judged lost through a combination of homoarchy and the length of the line is here abandoned for a less drastic conjecture *of* 'concerning' (MED s.v. *of* prep. 23a). This provides a stave by liaison (*of_noumbres*) so inconspicuous as easily to have suffered loss in Bx and again in Cx (if not omitted in B¹). **242** *some* **B**: easily omitted by homœoarchy before *com-*, its inclusion making the **C** line fit better with the pattern of the preceding categories introduced by *som(m)e*. But too little is lost by its absence for emendation of Cx here to be worthwhile. *craftily*: adopted from Bx as the second stave-word and judged lost through *com-* > < *col-* attraction in Cx (*C*-F has either conjectured independently or derived the adverb from comparison with a **B** source). The *first* stave *To keruen*, adopted by *PeR–K* (and by *K–D* for **B**), is attractive on grounds of sense and metre. But it appears more probably the t scribe's alteration of *to kenne*, which he omits from the end of 241, an easy mechanical error if his exemplar had the inconsequential reading **To kenne and to compace and coloures to make*. D²'s *keuer*, if intended for *keruen*, may be similarly accounted for, and H²'s *lernen* for *keruen* may point to *kenne* in t's source. It is possible that B¹ (and **B**) lacked an adverb, *cómpáce(n)* scanning with two lifts and *craftily* being a later Bx filler. But the insertion of adverbs is not a habitual feature of Bx, and as the sense of the whole phrase 'to practise architecture skilfully according to the rules of the profession' is convincingly non-trivial, it may be adopted as the intended reading in **C** (see MED s.vv. *compassen* v. 2(b) and *craftili* adv. (b)). **244** *wel* **B**: conjectured as the required key-stave presumed lost through *telle it* > < *it felle* attraction. The sense is either 'carefully' or 'successfully' (MED s.v. *wel* adv. 3a, 4a) or 'long' (ibid. 16). The b-half of **C** is adopted by *K–D* in place of Bx; but the former is scarcely hard enough to have invited 'substitution of a more explicit reading' (*K–D* p. 95). What this may be is a revision, perhaps to avoid the repetition in *er it fel* of *what sholde bifalle* 243, one that **L** could have easily made in his copy (B¹) by deletion of *telle...felle* and substitution of *and...bifore*. An alternative conjecture would be *wite*] *telle*, which is closer in sense to *be ywaer* **C** and could have been lost through partial haplography after *it* (and then smoothed). However, Bx's internal rhyme is demonstrably characteristic of **L**'s style (cf. B 1.33, 2.198 //, 3.265; C 10.303, 12.78) and the half-line may be judged substantively original, though having suffered mechanical loss of the adverb. **247** Either *men* **C** or *hem* *B*-β could be the common original, though *men* could have come in from 248 (*R–K* emend to *hem*). In the absence of F, lost doubtless through homoarchy (*And* 246, 248) assisted by the flow of thought from 246 (*recouere*) to 248 (*fecchen*), the α reading is irrecoverable, and it may be that Bx read as Cx. **252** shows what could well be revision, and despite Bx's imperfect metre, its substantive reading should not be rejected as 'more emphatic and explicit' (*K–D*, p. 95). The metrical defect in the b-half may be ascribed to Bx's ⇒ of the non-alliterating preterite under influence from the tense-sequence of the main verb (*forbad*). The construction may be understood as a mixture of indirect and semi-direct command, the present tense following without difficulty as in **C**, where it provides the key-stave conjectured here for **B**.

B 254–55 254 is followed by four lines of doggerel in F (printed *K–D*, p. 223) which the scribe has made no attempt to correct metrically and may represent an intrusion into its direct source *f*, or into α. But while in the absence of R their status remains undeterminable, they can be dismissed as of no textual interest. B 254 is judged spurious by *K–D* (p. 193) with no sufficient grounds and without discussion. But it scans satisfactorily as a Type IIIa with a six-syllable prelude dip, resembling in its rhythmic structure lines of unusual length like B 13.255 //. Moreover, its substantive content is not to be dismissed as due to 'scribal participation in the sense of a living text' (*K–D*); on the contrary, its quasi-egalitarian implications suffice to explain why, in a specific social context (see *Commentary*) **L** might have wished its removal. (It should emerge clearly from comparing B 254 with the pair after B 373, or with the other ten spurious lines in Bx [*Intro.* III *B* § 60 (iv)] why *K–D*'s judgement of it is rejected). C 254 now follows its omission of B 254 (as not 'scribal' but too radical) with a more conciliatory expression of the view that skill and knowledge are gifts of grace. **255** This line, to which C 254 actually corresponds, will scan acceptably on cognative staves (|g| |g| / |k|). But the a-half's sense is weak, *alle* referring unconvincingly to the addressees rather than to the *craft and connyng* that it qualifies in **C**. A simple reconstruction, bringing the line closer to the structure of **C** and incidentally generating characteristic homophonic wordplay, would be *þat al grace quod Grace* (the ease with which the Bx a-half could have been generated from such a reading is obvious). But the thought is banal and appears suspiciously like a dilution of the bolder idea that natural accomplishments and not just supernatural virtues are among the fruits of the Spirit's activity. The line as reconstructed is of Type Ia with a natural stress-pattern on cognative staves |k| |g| / |k|.

255 (B 256) Either *alle* Bx has come in from 255 or has been lost in Cx through visual assimilation to following *as* (especially if in the form *al*, the adverb). Revision seems unlikely here. **256 (B 257)** Either *he* **C** or *who* **B** could be original, although if both are reflexes of *ho, it is **B** that will be substantively right (as judged by *R–K*). **268 (B 269)** *sethe* **C** / *yit* ?*B*-α: either could be original and revision is unlikely. Given the closeness of F and **C**, β's altered Ø-reading (which offers no help in discriminating) is unlikely to represent Bx, and *K–DR–K*'s endorsement of it is ill-founded. **269 (B 270)** The infinitive *to harwen* *C*-p**B** following an implied verb of command is preferable to the preterite *to harwed* *C*-**x**, since the action does not occur till 273 (on the construction cf. 233 above). Thus **x** will have mistaken *to* for the numeral and *harwen* for present indicative and smoothed the verb to accord with the tense of *gaef* 268 (P²uW omitting the 'numeral' presumably as contradicting *foure* 268). **271 (B 272)** scans cognatively (|g| |g| |k|) as Type IIa with a supplemental voiced stop in position five. Transposing *Ieroem* and *þe gode* (K–DR–KSch¹) is accordingly superfluous. **272 (B 273)** Either *folewede* C or *folweþ* B could be a resolution of a tense-ambiguous original **folwyt.* The preterite goes better with 273, but mixing of tenses is frequent. **274 (B 275)** *aythes* C?α: preferred as the harder reading for which β will have substituted a commoner synonym that here alliterates acceptably. The word was very rare and is cited by MED s.v. *eithe* n. only from this line. F's spelling presumably reflects an α form **(h)ayptes,* with non-organic aspirate and subsequent *ȝ / þ* confusion. **276** *he*: lost in copies of B and C by haplography after preceding *set he.* **278 (B 279)** *þat* (2) xβ: preferred as the simpler reading, *frut* F being inappropriate in sense, *seed* p superfluous (though perhaps inserted to make the formula uniform with 283, 291, 300) but both scribal elaborations of a terse original. **281 (B 282)** *kele* C: a harder reading than *kepe* B, which could have been suggested by *saue* in the b-half. But the greater vividness may be due to revision, so rejection of Bx is unwarranted. The sense of **B** here is 'watch over, attend to' (MED s.v. *kepen* 14a). **285 (B 286)** scans cognatively on |ʃ| and |s| (found internally in the group |sk|), and failure to grasp this could have led β to insert an extra stave-word in |sk|. **286 (B 287)** *neuere* C / Ø B: added by Cx or lost from Bx by homoarchy (*ne, *nere*). **296 (B 297)** The substantive reading is not in doubt, though evidence is evenly divided in **C** as between the infinitive and the preterite (*plede[d]*), the verb co-ordinating either with *soffre* 295 or with *keuered* 297. The former is favoured as more likely to underlie the present tense in β, which has the wrong verb (presumably a corruption of a form spelled ambiguously **pleit*), though F's tense has cross-family support in the Cx tradition. While the contending verb-forms are distinct (though etymologically cognate) words, their primary senses overlap exactly (MED s.v. *pleden* v. (a), *pleten* v.1(a)). The metaphorical reference here is to the man with fortitude who will 'go to law' only by enduring injustice patiently. The sense of β *pleieþ* 'deal with, handle' (MED s.v. *pleien* v. 1, 8(b), citing only this case), is undeniably hard, and in the form **pleit* could as easily have invited ⇒ of more obvious *ple(t)e.* But the legal metaphor, which is lost by *pleieþ*, seems decisively indicated by the quotation at 298, which both concludes Fortitude and effects a transition to the next virtue, Justice (now specifically concerned with procedure in court). N²'s *plaieþ* is presumably taken by *R–K* as correction from a lost superior **C** source (though not listed on p. 102) but is here judged yet another case of this copy's ⊗ from a **B** ms of β–type. **300–01 (B 301–02)** The resolution *euene* C is preferred to *euere* as more apt in context, its implications of bal-

ance, exactness and consistency (MED s.v. *even* adv. 3, 7, 15) marginally better fitting with justice (*trewe / With God*) than that of constancy (*euere*) and echoed in the punning *eueneforth* at 310. Bx's error, doubtless visual, recurs in several **C** copies. **303 (B 304)** scans cognatively on |b| and the |p| staves internal to *aspyed* and *Spiritus*; emendation of *May* to *Shal* (K–DR–K) is therefore gratuitous. *thorw* C: preferred also in **B** as conveying precisely that justice is the agency through which good faith finds out guile. Although *for* overlaps with this sense (MED s.v. *for* prep. 4), the Bx reading is more probably an auditory error for *þoruȝ* than an original form revised in **C**, and if carrying a possible ambiguity (ibid. 1(a) 'on account of') that is better avoided. **304–05 (B 305–06)** Both Cx and Bx misdivide these two lines as three, presumably in consequence of their exceptional length, and only *C*-ms Y, probably by felicitous conjecture, gives the lineation adopted here. Of the Cx lines, the first scans as Type IIIb, the second is unmetrical and the third scans *aa / xa* (the final stave being cognative). In Bx the first and second lines are identical with Cx, the third (on the sole basis of β, since F is sophisticated) *ax / ax*, with cognative key-stave. Even after re-lineation, however, the b-verses of 305/306 remain discrepant, with a choice of **C** variants. The reconstruction here finds in the Bx and *C*-**p** expansions scribal reflexes of the postulated generalising expression *kynne(s)*, which now forms the key-stave. This involves taking *agulte* x, here uniquely (and doubtfully) attested as a noun (MED s.v. *agilt* n.), to be identical with *gilt* Bx (so C-DH²). The **p** variant *gulty* is then seen as a smoothing of this difficult word to the adjectival form, with *any þynge* **p** and *or in trespas* Bx being reflexes of the conjectured form *any [kynne]*. In the a-half, it may be that *kyng* (2) Cx was also in Bx; but this could have been a **C** revision of *he*, one easy to make by supralinear correction in B¹. The construction with repeated subject has a close parallel in 20.55 //, where **C** repeats *Crist* in revising, and thus there is no sufficient reason to emend the a-half of **B** as do *K–D* (p. 95). The scansions of the two lines, with their (identically) reconstructed b-halves, are now *aax / aa* for **B** (Type Ie with cognative supplemental stave in fifth position), and *aaa / aa* for **C** (Type Id with cognative fifth stave). **308 (B 309)** *dede þe lawe*: 'carried out the law', rigorous adherence to the detailed requirements of the law being here stressed (cf. 310). L may be presumed in the light of Cx to preserve β, and F to preserve α, against the looser γ reading with which the two **C** copies DG converge. The wider sense 'administered justice' is expressed in 310. **310 (B 311)** The two words forming the last lifts overlap in their sense 'ability to do' (MED s.v. *knouing(e* ger. 5, citing this line, and *pouer(e* n. 1(a)). **C** could be a revision, either could be original and the other a scribal ⇒, or both could be synonym-reflexes of a common original *conninge* (MED s.v.

ger. 1). Given the uncertainty, both should be allowed to stand, and *K–D*'s judgement of Bx as 'more emphatic' (p. 92) rejected. **316 (B 317)** *forthy* C: to be preferred on grounds of sense as the original for which Bx substituted a post-positional adjective, presumably through misinterpreting an exemplar form of the conjunction spelled *uorþi* (*u* representing the labial spirant with Southern voicing). The motivation for this could have been the apparently abrupt transition from exemplum to conclusion, an abruptness *C-p¹* eases by inserting *and*. The mislineation, giving an unmetrical line and an excessively long 318, will have resulted from mislocating the caesura after *vices*. **318 (B 319)** scans as Type Ia with a mute cognative key-stave in *cardinál(e)* rather than as Type IIa with wrenched stress on *aftúr*. *K–D*'s conjecture (p. 118) of *to* 'according to' (MED s.v. prep. 12a) for *after* (an easier reading) deserves consideration. **320 (B 321)** *Peres*: the obviously right reading on contextual grounds, *quod* in *B*-LMCr, *C-y*B-LM being a visual error induced by the immediate presence of *quod Peres* in the next line. *B*-WHmCr³ have corrected commonsensically, the last of these possibly by reference to a **C** source. **323 (B 324)** scans as Type Ic on cognative staves (|g| |g| |k| / |k|). *K–DR–K*'s conjectural emendation *garland*, having no metrical or other justification, is wholly gratuitous. **324 (B 325)** Despite the separate etymological origins of *peyned* C / *pyned* B 'suffered' (from OF and from OE respectively), one sense of *pyned* (MED s.v. *pinen* v. 3(b)) exactly coincides with that of *peinen* (s.v. 1(d)), and either could be original. *C*-D²ChG *pyned* endorse **B**'s (possibly intended) internal rhyme in the b-half (cf. 325b). **331 (B 332)** *deúýsed*: a rare but authentic 'monolexical' pattern found at 7.170, 20.158, 320 (and see *Intro.* IV § 38). **332 (B 333)** *hoem Peres* C: the securely conjectured original reading in **B** also, of which *?α hoom* and *Piers* β appear as classic split variants. **334 (B 335)** scans on vowels with wrenched stress on *-hóed* and *hym-* as mute key-stave. **336 (B 337)** *londe* C: preferred as also the original reading for **B** on grounds of contextual appropriateness. Under inducement from preceding *truþe* and following *lawe*, F, perhaps not representing α here, appears to have substituted an abstract term through failure to grasp the metaphor of the 'land of faith' (on other allegorical 'lands' cf. 11.169, 15.190 and *Commentary*). The line may have been lost from β as 'a delaying syntactical unit through attraction between *Piers* 33[6] and *Piers* 33[8]' (*K–D*, p. 67). **337 (B 338)** Omission of *and* **B** (so *K–DSch¹*) gives a terser line; but the change to Ø **C** could have been made by deletion in B¹ and it is therefore retained. **341 (B 342)** The figure of Presumption as a single sergeant-of-arms accompanied by a single spy (*Surquidous; sergeant* β) would seem to make superior sense, the word being well-attested (MED s.v. *surquidous* adj. (a), though with no other certain examples

of a personification), and C15th examples of the form *surquidour(s)* **C**?α are cited by MED s.v. *surquidrous* adj. If the *s*-ending of the latter is, like that of *paramours* at 16.105, not intended as a sign of plurality, *seriauntes* pl. may be a C*x* error based on wrongly inferring that it is. But if the pl. form attested in *B*-F's variant reflects α, the reading of Bx may well have been identical with that of C*x*. As the texts stand here, *Thise two* 344 in **B** refers to the Sergeant and the Spy-with-Two-Names, in **C** more naturally to the spy and another companion or, if Spill-Love and Speak-Evil are one, less naturally to *one* of the 'sergeants' despatched by Pride. Probably the most satisfactory solution would be to see *Surquidours* as the (idiosyncratic) original form of the name (constructed on the analogy of a word such as *paramours*) with *sergeaunt* sg. qualifying it, and *Surquidous* as a β normalisation of an unfamiliar form. On the evidence of F, unless ⊗ from **C** is posited, revision is probably to be ruled out and C*x seriauntes* could be fairly safely emended to the singular. **344–45 (B 345–46)** In the light of *C-p* the BxC-**x** lines appear unoriginal in their misdivision, which leads to loss of the first stave-word. Bx has also lost the second stave-word, perhaps through *Sire > Piers* attraction, with subsequential smoothing of the a-half in βF, and reconstruction after *C-p* restores *sedes* to its proper position. The correct verb in **B** can be reliably discerned as preterite, but given the corrupt condition of β and the sophistication of α in F, the precise form of Bx is undeterminable except for the misdivision and loss of *Sire*. The reason for the latter was perhaps objection to applying the customary title of a knight or priest to a ploughman (as he was earlier), though it is poetically appropriate to Piers in his new capacity as a symbolic pope-figure. **347 (B 348)** *and* (1): probably the reading of Cx*B-*β and acceptable as extending the threat to include the addressee, but without prefacing his name with the personal pronoun *3e*. *K–DR–K*'s omission is arguably preferable on stylistic grounds. *caples tweyne*: ↔ (following *K–D*) restoring the key-stave doubtless lost in B-Ø (< BxB¹) by inversion to prose order. The disyllabic form of the numeral, presumed altered in B-Ø to its usual pre-nominal form, is adopted to provide the necessary feminine ending. **348 (B 349)** The ↔ of the *partes penitentiae* in **p** to the more usual order is presumably a scribal 'correction'. But the Bx*C-***x** order *Confessioun; Contricioun C-***x**B has its own logical sequence: ritual act (personal and outward), spiritual disposition (personal and inward), religious condition (collective, outward and inward). **349 (B 350)** *oure*: clearly required by the sense; *3oure* may have come in mechanically by inducement from *3oure* in 347b, 348b. The Ø-readings may reflect deletions of *3oure* sensed (rightly) as inappropriate. **350–51 (B 351–52)** On the assumption that y has varied and that **p**ut preserve C*x* (confirmed by Bx), the two identical lines appear to scan somewhat awkwardly. 350 is either a

Type IIIb with the caesura after *nat* or (better) a Type Ia with 'monolexical' lifts in *Cóntrícioun*, 351 a Type IIIc, with caesura after *ho* or *is,* or (better) a Type IIIa with caesura after *Cónfessioún*, (metrically balancing 350b). *K–D* (p. 119) object to the metrical inadequacy of the second line (but not of the first, which presents much the same difficulty) and to 'the bad sense of the two' if they 'understand the allegory correctly' (this they may not). Pride's emissaries are asserting that because their guile will throw a veil of deception and confusion over the practice and administration of Penance, Conscience will be unable to tell from men's outward behaviour or from (what they erroneously consider) their inner disposition whether they really are Christian or not. *K–D* judge that *be Contricioun / Ne be Confession* was a 'misguided gloss' intruded in the common ancestor [of BxB¹ = B-Ø] with 'consequent redivision' (and *Pe* favours this view, though without emending). By removing the 'gloss' they generate a single line of superior metre (and sense): *That Conscience shal nat knowe ho is Cristene or hethene.* But despite this improvement of the metre without significant loss of meaning, *K–D* have not explained why the 'gloss' was intruded in the first place. A possible mechanism accounting for this would be the presumption that B-Ø read *knowe þerby*, the referent being necessarily understood as the two elements of Penance, which the 'gloss' then specified. The latter could thus be held to have been 'intruded' without being 'misguided', since it would merely spell out what the adverb implied. But with so little to be gained, *K–D*'s invitation to improve the text is better declined. **358 (B 359)** The Bx reading *to*] *we* **C** (shared by *C*-MN²) involves a change of construction in B 360, where *holde* becomes co-ordinate not subordinate, and the grammatically smoother form could be a revision. **360 (B 361)** Ø **C** / *And* **B**: the conjunction may have been added in Bx (as in *C*-t) to ease an abrupt transition. **365 (B 366)** Either *For* **B** or Ø **C** could be original, though Ø is usual in **L** after verbs of commanding, exhorting or entreating. *and diche*: harder than the nominal construction, induced by preceding *deluen*, which raises an expectation of an object. *al* *C*-**pB**-F / Ø *C*-**xβ**: a small word that makes an important point about the protection (an encircling moat), and possibly lost by visual assimilation to ab*oute* following, under inducement from the phrasal rhythm of *deluen and dyche* and misassignation of the caesura. But the line is of the rare Type IIb with a strong pause after the adverb *depe*, which expresses KYNDE WIT's first order, and a heavy stress on the second adverb *al,* with its complementary and still more important order (see *Commentary* further). **366 (B 367)** *in holinesse* **C**: obviously apt on grounds of sense, as made explicit in 383. The Bx reading could have been either Ø (leading to variant ⇒ in β and α) or *Vnitee*, the product of stylistic dissatisfaction with the supposedly pointless repetition of

holinesse, with F (or α) then replacing through objection to the perceived wrong sense. *were a pile* **C** / *trs* **B**: either possibly original and both giving good metre, *pil(e)* having mono- and disyllabic base forms. The substantive reading is clearly *pile* (MED s.v. n. 4 sense 2(a) 'castle, tower, stronghold') not 1(a) 'pillar', as taken by t. The *x¹* error *pole* will have resulted from mistaking the referent of *it.* **371 (B 372)** *riht* 'only' (MED s.v. *right(e* adv. Ib (d)): conjectured as the needed key-stave presumed lost in B-Ø by attraction of s*ynne* to s*aue* one. *K–DR–K* make the line scan on *s* by conjecturing *forsoke* as first stave. But this emendation, which presumes deliberate ⇒ not a mechanical cause, is unconvincing as it both relegates the crucial word *Repenteden* to the prelude-dip and replaces *refusede* with a word which, being familiar in the phrase *forsaken synne*, is easier, and so unlikely to have been supplanted by one less common. **372 (B 373)** Bx here has two lines, the first scanning *aa / xa*, the second unmetrical. The former can in principle be corrected by ↔ of the b-half nouns; but while the second line retains the b-half of // **C**, it has clearly replaced the a-half's neutral nouns with a negatively-toned term (*questemongere*) and a term of general opprobrium (*Lyeris*). The four abusive categories thus suggest a scribe enthusiastically specifying types presumed capable of perjury. Since support for the authenticity of the first line and the a-half of the second is so weak, it seems safe to recognise **C** as retaining the text of B-Ø intact. **373 (B 374)** *thei* **C** / Ø **B**: not strictly required, but easily enough omitted from Bx (as by N²), especially if the exemplar form was *hy*, before he*lden*. The two lines allow acceptable alternative stress-patterns, *with* being possibly a full stave in **B**, probably mute in **C**. **375 (B 376)** *ne was* **C**: the single negative arbitrating between the rival β and α variants, neither of which need represent Bx. **376 (B 377)** The Bx line does not appear scribal on grounds of sense or style and the meaning would be impoverished without it. Loss from Cx may be presumed for a syntactical and a mechanical reason, the parenthetical nature of the line breaking up the flow of thought from *Ther ne* 375 to *That he ne* (Cx 376) and eyeskip from *hadde* 375 to *halpe* 377. **378 (B 379)** *thorw* (1): preferred on *x¹*Bx agreement as the probable Cx form replaced in *x²* under inducement from following *be-, bi-,* and from *bi* in the b-half. *somme* (2): accepted on **pBx** agreement as indicating the Cx form presumed lost in *x¹*t by bi*ddynge* > < *bi* attraction. *bi* **C** / *þoruʒ* **B**: natural stressing guides scansion of **C** as having cognative key-staves (|b| |b| / |p|), the last word being a two lift 'monolexical' (*pilgrimáges*). In principle 378 could also scan on |s| as an extended Type IIIa with cognative *b / p* counterpoint. Both alternatives are likewise available for **B**, and either preposition could be the common original; so *K–D*'s emendation of *þoruʒ* to *bi* becomes otiose. Either pl. *pilgimages* **C** or sg. **Bt** could be original; but revision might have been made in order to produce a symmetrical balance with the two singular verbal nouns. **379 (B 380)** The corrupt state of F leaves it unclear whether *And B-β* = Bx or only β, but either this or *Or* **C** is acceptable. **384 (B 385)** *now* **C** / Ø **B**: perhaps lost from Bx by homœoarchy after *noȝt*; unlikely to have been added in revision or scribally for emphasis, like *now* in **p** at 386, but dropped by several *C*-mss, presumably because judged repetitious. **389 (B 390)** The title *the Plouhman* could have been added in revision or in Cx, or omitted in Bx as superfluous (so N²); but in either form the line scans as a T-type. **390 (B 391)** The bare noun *Myhte* in apposition with French-derived *power* (C-**x**B-?β) is more graphic and thus more likely to be original than the form with conjunction in **p**?α (the phrasing is reminiscent of 18.202). The pl. β is self-evidently inauthentic since only one power, that of consecration, is in question; *B-C* will have had the right reading by felicitous variation. *for to eten hit* **C** / *to ete it after* **B**: revision being unlikely here, choice between the variants is uncertain. Either *for* or *after* could have been added to a terse common original *to eten it* that exactly balanced *to maken it* in the a-half (Bx scans as a T-type). **394 (B 395)** scans either as a vocalic Type Ie with *vs* a rhetorically-stressed key-stave, or as a Type Ia on |k| with *quod* as first stave. The former alternative sits better with the tone of incredulity in 395[6], the latter makes a contrast with the vocalic alliteration of 395. **395 (B 396)** *or þat* **C**: perhaps a revision of *er* to achieve better balance as key-stave with *Ál þat* as first stave. **397 (B 398)** *Or* **C**B-F: 'beforehand, first' (MED s.v. *er* adv. 3), the first stage in a process of reconciliation with God, of which the next two are absolution and communion (398 [9]). The correct reading of Bx is retained by F from α, but β presumably mistook *or* for a conjunction implying (nonsensically) an *alternative* to the repayment of *debita* enjoined in B 396, and so rationalised the text by ⇒ of *That* to make the requirement of 398 parallel to that of 396, as it indeed is. *Or* is usually *er* in ms W, though at 10.417 it appears as *or*, perhaps punningly (see *Commentary*), and as *ar* in ms X; but both archetypes suggest that **L** spelled it *or* in stressed position. **400 (B 401)** The line scans as a standard macaronic of Type Ia with a characteristic 'monolexical' double lift in *Iústice*, as at 477 (for this pattern see on 331 and *Intro.* IV § 38). The line repeats the (duolexical) structure of 399 (*bé (y)rúled*), though the usual stress-pattern in *Iustíce* is that at 299, 303 and 408. *aftur* **C** / *wiþ* **B**: a small but significant change that could be a revision to produce symmetry with 401. N²'s *wiþ* (adopted R–K) will derive from a **B** copy. **401 (B 402)** *while Y can* t*B*-β: giving the best reading (so Pe), though t, joined by D² for *can*, may be an intelligent conjecture or (like N²) result from resort to a **B**-source to correct an exemplar reading found unsatisfactory. Agreement of **p** and *x¹* in *couthe* suggests that the preterite was the reading of *x²*

and so of Cx. The of *x¹* reading Ø] *while* is more likely to be archetypal than **p**'s *for*, which appears an attempt to link the clauses *Y wol nat* and *Y couthe*. In the Bx tradition, F has *but* for *while*, omitting *by Crist* and adding *wel* after *kan*. Here, if *but* could be filling out Ø in α, *wel* equally could be echoing *while*; but the sophistication in F precludes any certainty beyond the presence of *kan* in Bx. **402 (B 403)** Either *it* **B** was lost in Cx by assimilation to following *at* or inserted in β in anticipation of the direct object retained until 404. F's sophisticated reading *hole tappe* again conceals the form of α. The omission of *it* by O is presumably fortuitous. **403 (B 404)** The divergent conjunctions *and* **C** / *for* β arguably favour Ø F as attesting the common original. But F, which omits *ale* (2), could also have *lost* a conjunction (?*and*) by eyeskip from *þynne > þat*, so α must remain conjectural. N² again reads with β. **404 (B 405)** Either *to* **C** or Ø **B** is acceptable. **408 (B 409)** *Saue*: tentatively conjectured as the first stave in an extended Type IIIa line with semi-counterpoint (*abb / ax*). In principle, the line could be a 'licensed' macaronic (*aa / xx*), but in this passus it is noteworthy that **L** uniformly observes metrical norms where the names of the cardinal virtues appear. Alternatively, it could scan cognatively with a |p| stave found internally in *Spiritus* (|b| |b| / |p|), with which cf. 202 above. What seems virtually certain is that *Bote* was the reading of the common original B-Ø. However, this could have been caught up from *Bote* at 410 (411) or 407 (408), and the word conjectured here facilitates a characteristic pun on *ysaued* 409 (410). *Saue* as preposition occurs frequently (e.g. 371, 376); but it is not found as a conjunction in *PP*, though well instanced in the period (MED s.v. *sauf* prep., 4 [as conjunction] (a) 'except that, but; unless'). **410 (B 411)** *be thy comune fode*: reconstructed for **C** as the reading of **x** from the split variants *be* t (?=*x¹*) and *thy* (*x¹*) and felicitously preserved in D², a member of *C*-y. The substantive reading adopted for **C** is also that to be discriminated as preserved by F from α, and in B-C² in a form identical with t's, perhaps following collation with a t-type **C** copy. The variant *þe comune fede* of C-p*B*-β gives the same essential sense and (in **p** at least) may be an attempt to rationalise an exemplar reading like t's after omitting *be*. **411 (B 412)** *wel*: lost in **x** and by coincidence in **p**-G by haplography before *we*, but to be accepted on grounds of style, idiom, and the support of **B**. *we* **C** / *þei* β / *þou* FC-D²: the referent of *þei* being somewhat obscure, this may account for F's (or α's) ⇒ of *þou*. Presumably in Bx Conscience must be thinking of the *comune* who speak at 395, not just the Brewer he directly addresses here. It is therefore unlikely that *þou* is original, since it is both easier than *þei* and cannot underlie both the latter and *we* (a better reading ȝe, is not attested). C-D² may here show ⊗ from a **B** copy like F; but N²'s reading is clearly that of B-β. **412 (B 413)** *many* **C** / *many a* ?**B**: the form without the article is attested in the Bx tradition by L (which may = β) but lacking support from R (here absent), is not adopted; the article also appears in *C*-mss ChRMFN (so *R*–*K*), but is clearly not archetypal. *lede*: conjectured as the original for which BxB¹ (= B-Ø) have the more familiar *man* under inducement from preceding *many*. As they stand, CxBx scan *aab / bx* and a key-stave in ||l|| is required. *K*–*D*'s conjecture *lif* 'with punning implications' (p. 118) [*sc.* on 412] is attractive; but *lif* caused no difficulty to the Bx scribe (as at 3.294, 10.262, 11.91, 213, 13.17, 282, 332, 15.6 and 20.92) or to the Cx scribe at 18.105 or 19.276, and the lexical evidence is overwhelming that in the sense 'living creature, man' (MED s.v. n. 6(a)) *lif* presented no problem; so it is an unlikely original for which *man* was a ⇒. But *lede* was both restricted and recessive, evidently so at 20.444 (where *C*-t may well not represent Cx) and // B 18. 402, where it is restored as the omitted first stave in the light of *C*-t (cf. also the conjectural readings at B 15.393, 16.201, where *lede* offers itself as the best emendation of a defective key-stave). On these grounds, the reading of *C*-ms N² may be confidently adopted as representing, by felicitous conjecture, the probable original in **B** and **C**. Here, the second case (cf. 21.236) where N² has a better reading than both archetypes and could in principle show correction from a 'superior lost **C** copy', *R*–*K* again choose *not* to adopt it. **413 (B 414)** *kirke*: not certainly the reading of either Cx or Bx and not strictly necessary on metrical grounds (its adoption making the line of Type Ia rather than IIIa), but preferred here, as the less common variant (and one widely instanced in stave-position). **414 (B 415)** The spelling *Cardinales* with final -*s* (modelled on French plural adjectives) is the form in both archetypes on its first occurrence at 275 //. But thereafter the -*s* is mostly dropped (318 //, 345 //, 396 //, 410 //), and as no special reason appears for its use here (or at 455), either could be right. **415 (B 416)** *or an hennes* Cβ: unlikely to be 'a more emphatic reading' (*K*–*D* p. 156, *Sch*¹) substituted independently in *x*¹p and in β. Rather, omission in the unrelated D, t and WF, as in *B*-F, will have been due to the length of the line and its apparent rhythmical termination at *fether*. Since the phrase was in Cx and is not a fixed expression inseparable from the preceding one, it can be taken as almost certainly the reading of Bx (and hence of B-Ø), so there are no grounds for deleting it from the text. **418 (B 419)** *pelours* **C**: here only a spelling-variant of *pilours* (the form at 22.263), not the separate lexeme instanced at 20.39, *pilour* in Bx (and see MED s.vv. *pilour* n. (1) 1(a), *pelour* n.). The form with *e* may have been deliberately employed here in B-Ø so as to allow a pun on *pelure*, but if so was regularised in Bx. **420 (B 421)** *þat / þer(e)*: possibly split variants of *þere þat*; but **L**'s earlier use of *cometh ynne* has a simple relative pronoun (A 7.287 // Z). This reads more idiomatically here, and *þer* may have come in from 421, where it

occurs twice. **424 (B 425)** *helden* ?**CB**: the best resolution of a possible Cx form **heolden*, which must represent the preterite subjunctive. **425 (B 426)** scans awkwardly as a macaronic Type IIb with a wrenched stress in the third a-stave (*ámong*), and 425a might read better as the b-half of 424, with the Latin as a free-standing citation-line. **426 (B 427)** *wolde* **C**: more correct after the preterites *come*, *helden*; but since the obligation is perpetual, present *wole* **B** would be equally appropriate. **429 (B 430)** scans vocalically as a Type IIIb, the *B-F* reading (adopted by *K*–*DR*–*K*) being a characteristic attempt to 'correct' the alliteration. But the sense requires that the stressed words should be *newe* and *olde*, not *Peres* and *plouh*. This is only possible in a Type IIIb structure, which makes *newe* the second lift in the a-half (*his néwe ploùh*). *also* **C** / *ek with* **B**: either could be original, as revision is unlikely. **432 (B 433)** *soudeth* **C**: possibly a revision of **B** to increase force and precision. But the likelihood of visual error in Bx, partly induced by *sent* 436, is so great (it is also paralleled in three unrelated **C** sources) that the harder reading may be readily accepted as original in **B**. The implied point is not just that the Pope sends mercenaries against his opponents but that he misappropriates the *bona pauperum Christi* to pay them. **433 (B 434)** *Ac* **C**: reliably to be reconstructed for **B** on the evidence of F's sense and β's form (the latter doubtless induced visually by *And* 433). **434 (B 435)** A 'licensed' macaronic possibly scanning *xx / aa* (with *in*- stressed as keystave) or, with five-syllable prelude-dip on *ius-, iniús-,* as Type IIIa. The fixed nature of the Biblical phrase will have rendered complete metrical adaptation difficult. **435 (B 436)** *sonne*: the obviously mistaken *soule*, a reading criterial for the group *x*¹ and visibly corrected in three of its members, probably induced unconsciously by associations of *God...sent...sonne* and *saue* with the Son's mission to save man's soul. **438–40 (B 439–41)** The same mechanical error (homoteleuton at 438, 441) has caused the loss of 439–40 in F (or α) as of 441 in Bx. The line is not absolutely necessary on grounds of sense, but there seems a parallelism intended between the activity of God (436), who is praised at 444, and that of his deputy Piers (438), who is 'blessed' at 441. **438** In the absence of α, *and wenches* β is not certainly the Bx reading, though *or for a wenche* **C** may revise to give a closer balance with the first phrase of the line. **443 (B 444)** scans as a Type IIIc line on |b| and |w|. Inversion of *gode, wicke* to a less expected order would yield a Type Ia line, but there is no necessity for this. *K*–*DR*–*K* (rightly) leave the line unemended, though inconsistently with their own metrical criteria. **444 (B 445)** *som x*¹**B**: omitted by *x*² presumably through *til* > < *tyme* attraction, reinforced perhaps by the sense of one syllable too many in the b-half, though the word is necessary to provide the (mute) key-stave in this Type Ia line. **445 (B 446)** *the Pope amende*: simple

↔ of a subject and verb inverted to prose order in BxB[1] (< B-Ø) creates from a line scanning *xa / ax* a satisfactory line of Type IIIa. *K–D*'s fertile speculations (p. 208) on possible forms of the a-half terminate in the conjecture *Piers* for *God*. Certainly, Conscience has been speaking of both (440, 443); but it is *He þat wrouhte all, boþe gode and wicke* who is also the one that *may al amende* (B 10.439). Indeed, most references in **L** to transitive amending (esp. morally) have God as their subject: see, e.g., 13.199, 18. 288, 19.295. The prayer *God amende* here is echoed below by *Crist...saue* at 452. But *Piers* at this juncture is distinct in identity-function from Christ, so *K–D*'s conjecture, far from having 'strong indications' in its favour, seems not only 'arbitrary' but wide of the mark. **449 (B 450)** In this line, the text of Bx helps effectively to discriminate the **C** variants. It clearly supports *lawe* (2), which is in only two members of y, against the rest as surely the reading of **x** and thence, against p's sophisticated rewriting, of Cx. Conversely, in the b-half, **C** supports F (= α) as having here preserved the true reading of Bx. **451 (B 452)** scans as an extended Type IIIa on vowels with counterpoint on |r| (*abb / ab*), a pattern identical to that of B 18.2 or, if an oblique form with final -*e* is posited, as Type Ia, with two lifts in *rémenáunt(e)*. *He ?x?α / That he pβ*: the form without *that* after *semeth*, being terser and more colloquial, is likelier to be original. *Ø* **C** / *ne* **B**: metre and sense are unaffected by presence or absence of the double negative. **453 (B 454)** *for þe* **C** / *of* β; *to* F: the rhythm of **C** preferable, though possibly a revision. On the other hand, *for þe* could have come in by suggestion from *For the* 454, β is satisfactory in itself and could represent Bx. **455 (B 456)** *Cardinale(s)*: see on 414 above. **456 (B 457)** *sowne* **C**B-F; the reading *sowe* of *B*-L is an ambiguous reflex of an exemplar spelling with suspension, not a form of the past subjunctive of *sen* (MED s.v. *sen* v (1) 8a(a), *sen to* 'look at'), to which *Sk* mistakenly alters. But γ appears to have misread under inducement from following *sighte* and M to have adopted accordingly from a w-source or by the same mechanism. *K–D* rightly take F as preserving from α the **B** original. **460 (B 461)** Either *For x[1]?α* or *Ø x[2]β* is acceptable, and no reason appears for loss of the conjunction. But a connective eases the syntax, and the two Bx families offer split variants of the *C-x[1]* form, with ⇒ by F of a synonym for *ech*. **466–67 (B 467–68)** The lines scan as follows: 466 as a T-type on |t| and |r| with wrenched stress on -*tus* (1) and -*tus* (2), giving *aa / [a]bb*; 467 as a Type IIIa with two lifts in *Fórtitúdinis* and a five-syllable prelude dip. *wolle he, null he*: conjectured also as the reading of **B**, with β appearing a smoothing after presumed loss of *he nel he* at the end of a long line. It is the lord's minions who will do the 'fetching' from his tenants. **471 (B 472)** Either *þat* or *Ø*: is acceptable, but **B** gives smoother rhythm (so P[2]H[2]ChR–K). **473 (B 474)** Either *And* **C** or *For* **B** could be right, **C**'s conjunction

being repeated in the b-half, **B**'s repeating from 473b. **477 (B 478)** will scan as Type IIIa with two lifts in *Iústicie* as at 400. **481–82 (B 482–83)** The reading of Bx can be established in 481 on the agreement of βCx and scans acceptably as a normal Type Ia line, notwithstanding the objection of *K–D* (p. 175), mistakenly followed by *Sch[1]*. For 483, *K–D* identify the Bx reading in that of β; but in the light of Cx *That thow haue al thyn askyng* it must be transparent that F's *þat þou þyn lykyng haue* is a reflex of α but with characteristic ⇒ of a synonym for the noun and a minor ↔ of the same verb-phrase. It is α, not β, that may best be judged to have preserved Bx, and it remains to show that the reading of the two archetypes, effectively identical, makes adequate sense. The difficulty in the lines is entirely grammatical. Normally, the conditional present subjunctive of the protasis *In condicioun...þat þou conne defende.../ And rewle* would be expected to be followed by an indicative, and this is what β has indeed substituted (*Take þow may*). But surprisingly it is here followed by another subjunctive, of the 'jussive' type (*That thow haue* CF), possibly as a way of expressing the appropriate combination of deference and firmness towards the royal addressee. It is therefore unnecessary to read 482a as a purpose clause and, in seeking a main clause for it to follow, to emend *riht wel and in* (an adverbial phrase further modifying *rewle*) to *riht wol and*. The only emendation required is the slight one of reconstructing from F the α form of B 483, which is identical with C 482 but for the omission of *al*. The case for and against this important little word is finely balanced. **L**'s habitual reserve towards absolute power would question it; but the *Omnia* of 482a, unless it has been anticipated by the Cx scribe, would support it. Otherwise it may be a late revision reflecting a significant change of attitude (see *Commentary*).

Passus XXII (B XX)

Collation In the final passūs, the main Cx traditions *x[1]*, t and *p[1]* continue to be well supported, but for *p[2]* only N remains. By way of compensation, Bx is reliably represented with the return of the one sound α witness R.
7 *to lyue by* **C**B-F: presumed original in **B** on the strength of CF (= α) agreement. *R–K*'s preference of the easier β reading is dubious, their ⇒ of it for Cx remarkable. **8** If *As* LMCr is the reading of β and **p** it requires *That* 7 to be a conjunction (following an understood verb of 'saying') and strongly favours *þat* F in 9 (omitted β) as also a conjunction. By contrast, the **x** reading *Was*, indirectly supported by *B*-α as reconstructed from F & *þat was* (and preferred as slightly the harder) presupposes *That* as a relative pronoun subject (= *That which*) and allows *þat* 9 to be either another such or, with change of construction, a conjunction. The line scans as a standard macaronic with the key-stave found either in *Spiritús* or, preferably,

in *Témperáncie*. **11** The key-stave is apparently *for*, and polysemous wordplay with initial *For* (see MED s.v. *for* prep. 5b(b), 1(a)) is facilitated if the latter bears full stress in a Type Ie line (*aax / ax*). Alternatively, *thre* may be the first lift and the wordplay less significant. **12** Either *for* **C** or *and* **B** could be original, or *for* a revision to sharpen the sense. **13** The b-half seems fairly secure for both texts on the agreement of ?Cx and ?α. In the a-half, the substantive reading of the first stave-word is *wight*, clearly established in Bx and discernible as that of *C-x¹*. The **p** reading (shared by D) would seem to be a smoothing of **wit(eth)*, a mistaken reflex of *with*, the common reversed-spelling of *wyht* actually instanced in U. The error may have been prompted in part by the unexpected change of subject between *weldeth* 12 and *wol be* 13. Once *wyht* is adopted, Cx *þat* can be omitted as redundant, the clause following being Ø-relative. The readings *noon* β / *þat* ?α may be split variants of Bx **noon þat*, but the relative pronoun is not strictly needed for the sense. As here understood, β's a-half is taken to preserve correctly both Bx and the presumed B¹ source of Cx. **14** *cacche*: reconstructed as also the correct form of Bx, which β has levelled to a preterite, perhaps through misconstruing the tense of *come*. But the latter, like *come* in 16, is present subjunctive, as is shown decisively by the present indicatives in the apodosis of 17 and the second verb in the protasis of 16 (contrast 21. 424). **19** *dysch*: preferred in **C** as the unambiguous form of the word, of which *dych* is a recognised spelling (see MED s.v. *dish* n.) evidently archetypal in **B**. The notion (unhappily implied by *R–K*'s preference for *dych*) that the referent could be 'ditch' is obviously absurd. *deyde for furste* **C**: adopted also for **B** as the presumed common original, the alternative relying only on vocalic non-lexical stave-words *he, ech, er / he* (Bx has here, less usually, inverted an *original* prose order). The tense of the second verb is preferably past in **C** (as in **B**) after *wolde* 18, and in parallel with *dronke* in the a-half. **23** *be (v)er* C-x*B*-β: correct on grounds of sense, *for* being due to misreading *fer*. **25** Either *wel* ?**C** or *ful* **B** could be original, *wel* being perhaps even a y variant on *x¹ ful*; but no difference of sense or metre arises. **33a–36 (B 33a–35)** Both Cx and Bx evidently misdivided, although in neither case with the intrusion of spurious words or phrases as padding. The coincidence between *x²* and α may point to the respective forms of Cx and Bx; but the most satisfactory (and most probably correct) lineation is found by *K–D*, who treat 33a as a free-standing citation-line and not part of a macaronic. The first stave-word of 34 may be established for both versions as *God* on the showing of Cx, the Latin and the demands of sense and syntax (as antecedent of *hym* 35). It could have been lost from Bx by haplography before *gou-*, with subsequential smoothing. **35** Arguably *Ac* β yields a sharper contrast (when taken closely with *nexst*); but it may not stand for Bx here, given agree-

ment of ?α and **C** in *And*. **37** In Cα; omission of the line from β will have been by homoarchy (*nedeþ* 36, *nedy* 38). **48** *byde x¹*β: with the sense 'wait patiently' (MED s.v. *biden* v. 5(a)), the harder variant and to be preferred to *bydde x²*?αg. Although late spellings with single *d* of the verb meaning 'to beg' are recorded (MED s.v. *bidden* v.), the word here appears to echo *abyde* 46 (so spelled D²U) and the erroneous variant may have come in by contextual suggestion from *abasched...to be nedy*. Need is urging Will to endure because Christ did, not to beg because he endured (which is illogical), and he has advocated taking, not begging, if dire necessity compels (20). The wider context of thought also supports *byde*, and any interpretation that depends on reading *bydde* is questionable (cf. further Nede's words against begging at 238–9). **54** *tyd* **C**: plausibly conjectured as having been lost by Bx through *it > < ti(t)* attraction. **62–3** Correct lineation and substantives are not found together in any (sub)archetype, but both can be satisfactorily reconstructed. (*The*) *whiche fooles* is confirmed by *x²*Bx, presence or absence of the article having no effect on metre or sense (*C*-W also lacks it). The initial phrase would seem to have been lost from *x¹* by haplography after *onel*ich *foles* 61. The adverb *wel*, necessary as the key-stave, is confirmed by *x¹*β agreement; the mechanism of loss will have been repetition (after the caesura) of earlier *wel* (occurring *before* the caesura) in 61. The Cx misdivision may have been as in Bx; but *p¹*'s felicitous lineation must be correct, since it alone provides in *lyue* the needed first stave of 63, which scans *aa / xx* in Bx*C*-x*N*. **67** *her(e)* **C**: adopted also for **B** as the common original for which Bx *hem* may be a simple visual error. Although in principle *gile* could be a verb, the phrase *hem gile* 'them to be practising guile' sounds unidiomatic, as the ⇒ in β attests. **70** scans cognatively on |p| |b| / |b| in *B*-β*R*C-x and the variants *bar yt bare B*-F and *bar þat baner B*-Y*C*-p both appear attempts to lengthen the line and make it scan 'regularly' on |b| staves. *K–D* (p. 159) see the insertion of *baner* as an easier scribal reading (as indeed it appears), but judge the original to survive in F's *bare* with its 'superior meaning ..."uncased", "displayed as a sign of battle"' (MED s.v. *bar* adj. 13(a); accepted *Sch¹*). However, their observation that 'in the absence of R', F 'possibly represents its group (RF)', repeated on p. 165n86, is mistaken, since R (as *K–D*'s apparatus correctly reports) is not defective but reads as β and, as presumably representing α, indicates the reading of Bx. Thus, while it remains remotely possible that *bare* was thrice lost by haplography in β, R and **x**, and twice smoothed to *baner* in **p** and (coincidentally) in *B*-Y, it is far more probable that BxCx read Ø and that F (or its exemplar) inserted *bare* to supply a supposed metrical gap. The principle of cognative alliteration proves the 'absent' stave-word to be an unnecessary entity here. **72** The ⇒ of *And* for *That* seems to have no motive other than stylistic aversion to repetition. Alternatively, the common original had a Ø-relative (as at 86) and this was supplied in Bx and in y, U, <TH²>, q and p², while <eRM>, W and the two unrelated **x**-type mss D and Ch inserted *And* instead. **83** *scabbes* **C** / *scalles* **B**: effectively synonyms, *scalles* overlapping in sense with *scabbes* (MED s.v. *scale* n. (1), 2(a)), and neither more difficult, though **C** could be a revision. The reading *scabbes* in *B*-W is probably a visual error, since double *l* / *b* are easily confused and, as the same could have occurred either way in Bx and Cx, there is no case for reading *scalles* in **C** (with *R–K*). **87** Either *he* **C** or *hir* **B** is acceptable, and no reason for ⇒ of one for the other appears, though each could have been inserted to fill out a Ø-reading in the common original. **92** Hereafter *damaged readings of* ms **I** are not noted, and group **y** is represented by XYP²D². **97** *kyne* **C** / *kene* **B**: probably the same word (MED s.v. *kene* adj. 5(a) 'painful' and (d) 'noxious') with the *y* -spelling punningly alluding to Kynde, the author of the sores, and so possibly being the common original (on this grapheme of |e:| cf. *lyf* at 312 below). **103** The reading of the b-half in both versions is established on the agreement of Bx and *x¹*, with t representing the presumed text of *x²* (*neuere* for *euere*) and **p** a further stage of variation (↔ of verb and adverb). The substantive reading *euere* is not in doubt, the paronomasia on *euene* forming an essential element in the line's meaning. **104** *here lemmanes knyhtes* **C**: to be preferred on grounds of sense as the likely common original, the compound second subject of two apposed nouns ('lover-knights') being made to correspond with their ladies. In *B*-β, the b-half phrase effectively repeats that of the a-half and appears a mistaken alteration of the reading attested in R, that of α and probably preserving Bx. But Cx *hir*, giving sharper sense and smoother metre, does not look like revision and may be safely adopted for **B**. **106** *tho* **C**: yielding better sense, anticipating 109 and unlikely to be a revision, Bx *to* appearing a visual error for *tho* partly induced by *To* 107 (cf. *x¹* at 110). In other occurrences, the verb *bisechen* is always transitive (see 3.77, 115 and *IG* s.v.). **109** scans as a Type IIIa line, the *tho* of Kynde's response echoing that of Conscience's request (see note above). F's *sone* is a characteristic normalisation of the line to Type Ia unlikely to represent α: the sense 'immediately' (MED s.v. *sone* adv. 1a (a)) is inappropriate, 'shortly' (ibid. (b)) little less so; what matters is not the length of time but the fact that Kynde desisted *when* (or *after*) Conscience asked him and the people had begun to show signs of repenting. Adoption of *sone* by *R–K* (following *K–D*) is thus ill-advised, since both archetypes read *tho*. **110** *tho*: in the light of Bx, the Cx reading may be established as *to* (a poor spelling of *tho*), which *x¹* preserves correctly and P² etc. alter plausibly to the article (for the converse, *th* for *t*, cf. at 186). **113** *gadereth*: X's *gaderet* may here be a devoiced

form of the preterite (= *gadered* **B**) or a de-aspirated form of the present as elsewhere, e.g. at 17.247 (cf. the present / preterite alteration at 148-9 above).**117** *brode*: to be preferred as the common original of both versions (cf. 226), *blody* being induced by the martial context. Presumably *B*-WhmF corrected independently upon registering the inappropriateness of their exemplar's reading. **120** *Kirke* **B**: securely to be accepted on the showing of α as the form of Bx (and inferentially of B¹), from which β and Cx have convergently varied to the commoner form, with loss of the key-stave. Cr may well be an independent scribal correction. **126** *suede* **C**: to be accepted on grounds of sense as the **B** reading, perhaps found as *seude* in Bx, whence the form of R (< α). Thus spelled, it could have been misread as the preterite of *senden* (with voiced stop) and levelled to the commoner form *sente* found in βF. The context shows decisively that Symonye must be the one who 'preaches' and 'makes prelates', and who therefore first 'follows'. **127** On intrinsic grounds C's *presed on þe Pope* is a much stronger and bolder half-line than *preched to þe peple* and may preserve the common original replaced in Bx by a more innocuous phrase. The scribe's motive could have been censorship: acceptance of Death as abstract universal leveller (101) was one thing, a direct charge of simony against the reigning pontiff another. Against this, it should be noted that the Bx scribe does *not* censor the even more forthright criticism of the (actual) Pope at 19.446; so since the metre shows no defect, there could well be revision here. Alternatively, misreading of *presed* as *preced* and insertion of *to þe peple* by way of smoothing is proposed by Barney 2006:214. But K–D's adoption of the **C** reading lacks conclusiveness and is not recommended (see also at 130). **128** Either a group sg. *temperaltee* or the pl. could be original. **130** The Bx reading *kneled to* is less vivid than *knokked* Cx, but cannot easily be a visual error for it, nor does any precise motive for ⇒ appear (*K–D*'s explanation of 'misguided "improvement"' [p. 92] explains nothing). If 'submitted (hypocritically)' (*Sk*) is accepted as fitting well, there is no justification for rejecting *kneled to*, which may then be judged the second case within a few lines where a revising hand may be discerned (for another see on 380 below). **135** Either *vp* **B** or *on* **C** could be original, or both split variants of *vpon* (so P² with *on* added *a.h.*); but though *vp* is more typical of **L**'s style, each may be allowed to stand. **140** The position of the adverb *tho* is less certain in Cx than in Bx, but affects neither sense nor metre. Agreed *C*-**p**B-F give a simpler form (so *K–DR–K*) that is unlikely to be the common original. **149** Either *priketh* **C** or *priked* **B** could be the common original, or both be reflexes of a tense-ambiguous form **prikyt*. *B*-W's present, coinciding with the majority of **C** copies, may have been induced by following *preisep.* **155** *ȝowthe* **C** / *sorwe* **B**: a change to normative metre, Bx scanning as Type IIIc, but also with change of sense. Reminiscence of C 12.12, 11.196f is evident; but this begins with 154, as *Pe* notes, and need not be 'scribal' (*K–D* p. 209). A metonymic sense 'the sins of youth' is entirely apt in context and would be natural enough as a revision of *sorwe* 'contrition'. The tR variant *þouȝt* may be interpreted as the result of *þ* / *ȝ* confusion. While the common original could have read Ø through eyeskip from *forȝ*ete to *forȝ*eue, and both Cx and Bx have substituted independently a word judged appropriate, the change in thought and metre points rather to revision. *R–K*'s gratuitous rewriting of a Cx line sound in form and meaning as *And* [*s*]*o forȝete* [*sorwe*] *and* [*of synne ȝeue nouht*] invites comparison with the most intrusive scribal practice. **163** *sley* **C** / *war* **B**: an apparent revision of an extended Type IIIa line with semi-counterpoint on |w| to a Type Ie scanning on |s|. Both adjectives look authentic and there is no reason to see *war* as Bx ⇒ of a synonym by alliterative inducement (*K–D* p. 95), since *sley* is not a word of difficult meaning. However, *wex* g (so *K–D*) may indeed have been induced from *wax* 159 above and cannot be accepted as preserving β here against wLM. Its adoption by *R–K* (p. 127) for Cx is hazardous since, even if it is harder than *was*, a mechanical explanation of its appearance in g is at hand. **167** *shroef hym* **C** / *he shifte hym* **B**: here judged a revision in the direction of greater explicitness. The Bx verb (MED s.v. *shiften* v. 1(b), refl.) cannot well be a visual error for *shroef*, a verb of unmistakable sense that had no weak preterite *shrivede* at this period (see MED s.v. *shriven* v.). **171** The pl. *hertes* is judged the likely common original; for though less consistent than the sg., it conveys an intelligible distinction between the art of Physic personified and its practitioners severally, who become the subject of 172. **172** *gyuen*: to be accepted on the showing of Bx as also the probable form of B¹, the past tense having been induced from preceding *gaef* and a possible ambiguous Cx form (*g*)*euen*, as in T (cf. *wesched* 194 below). Mixture of present and preterite is characteristic of **L** and common in this section (e.g. 148–49). **183** As revision seems unlikely, the adverb *anoon* was either inserted in Bx or omitted by Cx. **198** *heo*: adopted on obvious grounds of sense as preferable to a possible B-Ø form *hee*. **202** Either Ø **B** could be original or *how* **C** a revision (in B-Text *delete misprinted* how). **212** Both *Y* **C** / *þere* **B**; Ø **C** / I **?B**: are acceptable and neither more obviously original, though the **C** order is less usual. If the common source B-Ø read *þere I*; then *þere* Bx, *Y* Cx may be split variants, Bx having read Ø in the b-half (so α > R) and β having commonsensically inserted a pronoun subject. **215** *soethly*: not a strong reading but metrically adequate, and plainly that of B-Ø. *K–D* (p. 117) see it as a ⇒ for a near-synonymous *sikerly* (MED s.v. *sikerli* adv. 1 (a)), but here with the sense 'firmly' (ibid. s.v. 2(a)). However, as neither this nor

soorly (*Sch*¹), likelier as a visual error, imposes itself, Bx and Cx should be left to stand. **219** *pissares*: emended by *K–D* (p. 184) to *purses and* on the basis of the GC² variant *and gypsers*, and argued for again by *R–K* 135–36, but founded on a nugatory objection to *Sk*'s explanation of the phrase as a cant term for armed retainers. The word, too vivid in itself to be scribal, could hardly have entered the common source B-Ø and persisted through both archetypal traditions if unintelligible to the copyists. Its allusion to such Biblical texts as III Kg 14:10, 16:11 or I Kg 25:22, 34 (where the Wycliffite Bible has *pissere* for Vg *mingentem*) displays **L**'s typical clerkly wit combined with the sort of humour shown in the established phrase *ballok knyf* at 15.124 (which compares a different part of the instrument and the male organ). Both examples reprove the aggressive sexuality of the clerk who comports himself like 'a very good blade, a very tall man' (*Romeo and Juliet* II iv. 31). **225** *hym* **C**: perhaps present in B-Ø and lost mechanically from Bx by attraction of *aye*in to wi*þ*; but not strictly required for the sense, and possibly added in Cx (as in YOCB of *B*-g). **227** *holynesse*: preferred on the showing of Bx, the commonsensical *holychurche* perhaps reflecting scribal unease with the idea of 'bringing down' a *moat* (cf. 21.383 above). **228** The rhythm of *or* **C** is better, but *ellis* could have been added in Bx or lost from Cx by *ell*is > < f*alle* attraction. **236** *cheytyftee pouertee*; on the showing of *C-x¹* and *B*-WLα the probable reading of each archetype, *chaitife x²B*-?γ M attempting to turn the first noun into an adjective governing the *second* noun. *Sk* adapts **B** to the adjectival form of **p**, which gives acceptable sense and metre, while *Pe* follows *K–D* (p.117) in judging *pouertee* an early scribal gloss incorporated in the <BxB¹> source (presupposing a phase before B-Ø). This gives a line with two lifts *chéytýftee*, an authentic 'monolexical' b-half pattern (see *Intro.* IV § 38). In its (older) variant AN-derived form *caytiftee* (9.255), the word caused no difficulty for the Cx scribe. Yet that fact argues not for but against viewing the present 'gloss' as scribal, since the spelling with central French *ch* is much the rarer (MED s.v. *caitifte* n.). It is therefore accepted here as an (authorial) 'internal gloss' skilfully integrated into the metrical pattern of the line. **238–39** will have been lost from α either by eyeskip from *And siþen* B 236 > *And siþen* B 240 (though without the expected loss of 237) or perhaps by the 'notional correspondence' (*K–D* p. 69) in *liflode...begge* / *liflode...beggeres* (238–39), *beggeres...foode* (241). **256** *newe* **B**: more probably omitted by **C** (or Cx) than added in Bx, though a mechanical loss would have been easier if *newe* came immediately before *nempned*, or else before *noumbrede* (as in α). However β is preferable to α, since it was the names not the numbering that would have been 'new'. The sense 'made or established for the first time, newly created' (MED s.v. *neue* adj.1 (a)) is appropriate, and

Donaldson's objection to it as pointless (1949:242, followed by *K–D*) is misguided. **261** cannot be an addition, since it is needed to complete the sense of the sentence beginning in 260 (as recognised by the scribe of *B*-C²), and so must have been present in B¹. It could have been lost from Bx by distraction from similar corresponding ideas as at 238–39 (*nombre /...wages* 259–60, *nombre... ywaged* 261). The line scans vocalically as Type Ia on non-lexical words or as an extended Type IIIa with semi-counterpoint on |n|. **270** will have been lost from XD²tW, as from *B*-Y, by homoteleuton (*nombre*). **271** Either Ø **C** or *þe* **B**: could be original, the noun in any case having shifting stress and the metre not being otherwise affected. **282** *They* C-t; Ø **B**: the correct reading is that of Bx, which requires *For* in 281 to be a conjunction, and that of t, which has presumably corrected by omitting *And*. The latter conjunction could have come into Cx as a consequence of reading *For* 281 as a preposition (MED s.v. *for* prep. 14 (a) 'as regards') or as a smoothing after addition of *þat* to a Ø-relative clause in the exemplar at 281b. **287** *leue* **C**: judged on the strength of L and α as the reading also of Bx, for which γ has ⇒ offers a more explicit expression. What the *folk* require is permission to postpone repayment of the loan, not a further loan (though the whole phrase will bear the equivalent sense 'extension of the period of re-payment of the loan'). The γ reading, which presumably arose as a visual error of a very common type (*lone* for *leue* by *e / o, n / u* confusion), and will have come into *B*-M from its usual w-type source, is shared by *C*-M (and adopted by *R–K*). **292–93** Both lines appear corrupt in the b-halves, having non-alliterating synonyms in place of the required key-staves on |p| and |r| respectively. The lineation is, however, correctly preserved in Bx and in *C*-x². Pe retains the x¹ reading but relineates after **p**, and *Sk* prints the **p** reading, emending P's *murþe* to *merye*. Both give lines scanning *aa / bb* and prose (unless *reménaunt* is pronounced with wrenched stress, making 293 a Type IIIa). *K–D* (p. 119) more drastically emend 292b to [*pleye*] *with þe remenaunt* and omit 293b. Hardly less drastic is [*purchace*] *hem mur*[*th*]*e* for 292 and *renkes* for *men* in 293, with omission from **B** of *þe residue and* in the light of // **C** (*Sch¹*). The present reconstruction of 292 accepts *K–D*'s original conjecture *pleyen* for the key-stave of 292 but retains *murye,* judging *maken* a *B*-Ø ⇒ under inducement from 289a as the expected word in this stock locution, where *murye* is an adjective not an adverb. Though there seems little likelihood of revision having occurred here, the a-halves of both archetypes are allowed to stand, since each gives a line acceptable in sense and metre. But there can be no certainty as to whether *þe residue and* was intruded in Bx or omitted in Cx. After adoption of the lexically restricted *renkes* as the key-stave in both lines (for which *men* is judged a *B*-Ø ⇒), the emended **B** line now scans as Type

Ia and that of **C** as Type IIIc. **301** scans as Type IIIa in Cx, as Type Ia in Bx, but the sense requires a pl. pronoun subject. The vocalic form *hy* original in **L**'s dialect, which probably underlies the mistaken sg. in Bx, may be safely presumed to have been the reading of B¹, and its adoption for **C** makes the line identical in both versions. **306** Either *To x²* or *Go x¹*?Bx could be the joint-original or both could be split variants of *To go*, the actual reading of *B*-W (cf. earlier 5.126//, and Apparatus for *to*] *go* ⇒); *R–K*'s readings of XYP²D²U as *Go* is here accepted. **308** scans as a Type IIIa line on |v| (*For; þei*), though not very satisfactorily. *K–D* (p. 119) alter to a Type Ia by conjecturing *mysfetes* for *mysdedes*, citing B 11.37[4], where this word (MED s.v. *misfait* n.) uniquely occurs (though for all its rarity, *mysfeet* there caused the Bx scribe no difficulty). It is also possible that, if *wrouht* is the key-stave (as its significance merits), the first lift was a stave-word in *w*, the unrecorded *wandedes conjectured at Z 5.152, a line unquestionably scanning on |w| (see note *ad loc*). A somewhat less speculative emendation would be a lexical word *wykkede* (so *C*-R) for the negative prefix *mys*-. More cautiously still, *hy* could be read for *þei*, giving a Type IIIb line with justifiable sentence-stress on *here*. This, however, involves accepting the vocalic allomorph of the subject-pronoun as the key-stave (but with full stress less clearly justified), so the line's scansion will still depend on non-lexical words. Given the want of a fully satisfactory emendation, the agreed reading (< B-Ø) should be retained. **309** *pardon* **C**: unlikely to have been added in revision of **B**, since it is contextually required for the sense, the line closely echoing B 19.393b–94, and for the metre, 309 being a true macaronic (of Type IIa) like B 19.394. Loss from Bx could have occurred by alliterative attraction (*Pi-* > < *pay-*). **312** *Lyf* **C**B-α: either a spelling variant of *leef* (so actually Z) or the substantive lexeme 'life', to be identified with the worldling Lyf of 143 ff, the name here meaning 'Life-to-be-lived-in-lechery', with a second (pun-ning) sense 'Love-to-live-in-lechery'. If it is the former, as seems quite probable, the α reading should be preferred in the B-Text, β eliminating the pun and with it the link with the earlier character who had turned to earthly Physic for help against Age (169 ff). (On the spelling of the close |e:| sound, cf. the note on *kyne* at 37 above). **314** Either *the* Cx or *þis* Bx could be original, though the Bx is the more explicit. **318** Ø **C** / *a* **B**: a sense-neutral variant of no metrical significance, the line being best taken to scan vocalically as an extended Type IIIa with semi-counterpoint on |m|. **326–27** scan as a Type Ia and Type IIIa respectively. *K–D*'s re-division after *haue* so as to standardise 327 and their omission of *a were* verge on editorial re-writing. **329** *coome* **B**: preferred also for **C**, where only N has (presumably by accident) the required form of the preterite subjunctive within an implied subordinate clause. The distinction between moods, generally preserved in Bx (*cam* 327, 330, 356, but *coom(e)* 329), is likely to have been original (but *coom* at 345 could be a non-significant local spelling variant). **338** *do þoþe* **B**: accepted here as also the form of Cx (< B¹), *done x²* and *bothe x¹* being diagnosable as split variants. **351** scans either as an extended Type IIIa on |s| with vocalic semi-counterpoint, or as a Type IIa on vowels. The former seems rhythmically preferable and its annominative chime between monosyllabic staves (*se, so*), is characteristic. **355** scans vocalically as Type IIIa, so *K–DR–K*'s noun-verb ↔ in the b-half to produce spirantal alliteration is otiose. **356** Ø **C** / *in* **B**: either inserted in Bx or lost in Cx through minim confusion (ca*m* / *in*). **360** *ben* **CB**-R: preferred as giving superior metre, although *B*-βF could read acceptably as not Type Ia with quadrisyllabic pre-final dip but as Type Ic with cognative key-stave and the caesura after the second subject. However, it is likely that *biten* has come in from 362 (a similar desire to heighten the tone of the b-half is shown by the *C*-t variant *pynen*). It seems preferable that *byte* 362 should make specific, not merely repeat the verb of 360. **361** Either *chaungen* **C** / *change hem* **B** may be an auditory error for the other, but the absolute fully inflected infinitive seems preferable. **366** *alle hem*: reconstructed as the reading of B-Ø, of which Bx *al* and Cx *hem* appear split variants. The form adopted, as appropriate in this case, is the plural; wordplay on *alle* / *al* is typical of **L** (cf. *alle* / *al* at 21. 394–95). **367** *and*: conjectured to provide a more natural-sounding pl. object for the pl. complement *freres* in 368 (*freres* is the BxCx reading (< B-Ø), obviously not impossible but nonetheless altered to the sg. by three **B** mss and one **C** ms). Presumably an ampersand could have been omitted by visual attraction of yo*w* > < *m*y, or loss of *and* could have been by assimilation to preceding *And*. The referent of *Lady* should be the penitent's wife or mistress, Friar Flatterer here displaying his address as a 'lady's man' in what appears a conscious echo of 3. 38ff. *Pe*'s interpretation of *my lady* in the sense 'a particular object of my prayers' is very forced (and not at all supported by *Purity* 1084, where *my lady* refers, quite naturally in context, to the Blessed Virgin Mary). *K–DR–K*'s adoption for both versions of *B*-F's scribal re-writing of an ostensibly difficult line evades the issue. Their notion that *my lady* could be a misreading of contracted *memoria,* and subsequent emendation to the latter, is unpersuasive (though it has contributed a phantom Latin word which figures as a 'quotation' in Alf*Q*, p.117). As to *R–K*'s objections to *and my lady* (p. 136, n. 65), these are nugatory. The fact that Contrition is being addressed does not logically preclude a second addressee, the situation pointedly recalling that evoked by Peace at 346 above, while the construction *maken...as freres* reads contextually with naturalness and in no way violates Middle English idiom. The key to the crux is *As freres* in

368, here accepted on the strength of Bx*C-x²* agreement as the probable reading of the common original. This necessitates that at least two persons are being promised tertiary membership of the order in return for their donation. While *al*[*le hem*] *that ye ben holden to* are being promised the friars' prayers, they are not all being promised fraternity, a privilege reserved for Contrition and his Lady, and echoing 3.53–4, 67. **371** Neither *bifore* **C** nor *to doone* **B** is difficult nor does any evident motive for ⇒ or revision appear. It may be that Cx and Bx are split variants of B-Ø **wont bifore to doone*, that Cx lost *doone* by visual anticipation of *For* 372, and Bx lost *bifore* by *wont* > < *doone* attraction. However, since both archetypes give acceptable sense and metre, with little to choose between them, they should be allowed to stand. **373** scans vocalically as an extended Type IIIa with *álle* as key-stave and double counterpoint on |s|. The superlative (*souerayneste* **B**) of an adjective already superlative in meaning (*souereyne* **C**) could be suspected as typical 'scribal over-emphasis'. But here the emphasis could equally be authorial (as at 1.146) and the -*st(e)* ending have been lost before following *s*- in Cx (TH² in fact have it). It is thus better to let each reading stand. The earlier emendation of *kynnes* to *skynnes* (*Sch¹*) retains plausibility but lacks necessity, so is abandoned. *K–DR–K*'s more drastic *synnes of kynde* for *kynnes synnes*, with its wider unwarranted theological implications, amounts to editorial re-writing. **376–77** *Clergie...helpe* **C**: on balance marginally superior to *and bad Clergie...for to* **B**, the form of the request in C 376 more authentic than the explicit one in // Bx. The latter may have anticipated *bad* from 377 and then smoothed by substituting *also,* subsequently omitting *come*, perhaps to shorten the line. *K–D*'s reconstruction follows Cx in the a-half, omitting only *to*, but Bx in the b-half, omitting Cx *helpe* in B 377. The latter looks suspicious as pointless repetition of *help* 376 //. But given the uncertainty, it seems better to let both readings stand, except for the insertion in **B** of *come* as second stave (since, of the word's two appearances in Cx, this is the likelier to have been in the common original). The lines are not wholly satisfactory in either archetype; but both are open to fewer objections than a wider reconstruction, and the sense of both is clear. **378** *adreint and dremeþ*: reconstructed by *K–D* as the original form underlying what they identify as the split variants *dremeþ* Bx / *adreint* Cx. Possibly the latter was a revision of the Bx form (inferentially also that of B¹) and both lines will scan acceptably as Type IIIa. But the sense of each seems defective and requires the other to complete the figure, 'drowned [in sleep] and dreaming'. If there has been revision, it was more probably to this reconstructed form, Cx (or B¹) subsequently having lost the part (*and dremeþ*) originally present in **B** and preserved in Bx. However, a mechanical explanation will best account for the readings: for if *and dremeþ* had been not conjunction + finite verb but a preposition + verbal noun (**adremeth* 'in a state of dreaming') the loss by each archetype of one word could have been the result of simple haplography through minim-confusion. **380** The difference in the a-halves *doth men drynke dwale þat men* **C** / *plastred hem so esily hij* **B** is so extreme that both may be original (**C** a revision), or one be a ⇒ for the other, or both a ⇒ for a lost form. The Cx version is striking enough to seem beyond suspicion; but that of Bx does not appear a variant of it, since its content is at once completely different and by no means patently scribal. The line's defective key-stave is easily remedied by adopting the vocalic allomorph of the plural pronoun and scanning the line on vowels (*hem, esily, hij*). *K–D*'s drastic adoption of **C**'s a-half is unacceptable, since the possibility of localised revision in **C** has never been stronger in these final passūs, and so the only proper course for the editor is to let each version speak for itself. **382** Either *wenden* **C** or *walken* **B** could be original, and revision seems improbable here: *wyde walken* appears as a set phrase at 7.175 //, 10.14 //, *wenden wide* at 10.200 and B Pr 4. *regneth* **C**: instanced only here in the sense 'extends' (MED s.v. *regnen* v. 4(f)), and so self-evidently difficult that there is no

justification for *K–DR–K*'s emendation of it to *renneþ*. There is clearly some play on this sense, even if it is not uppermost, at 13.185 *as wyde as thow regneste*, which alludes to the extent of Reason's immanence ('rule') in the natural world; so there would seem no grounds for questioning *regneth* here. But while *lasteþ* **B** could be an easier ⇒ for the latter, it could equally be the B[1] reading which **L** altered as a ?final act of revision. The sardonic pun on the prospects for Conscience in a situation where *þe world regneth* would strike experienced readers of *PP* as wholly characteristic. **386** The **B** form *þe Plowman* with the article, giving a T-type line, is preferred to Ø **C** as the sole one instanced in the last two passūs (21.6, 11, 188, 214, 259, 389, 433, 440, 22.77, 321). Its formal, quasi-titular quality is especially apt at this point. **Colophon** The archetypal forms of the final colophon are not securely recoverable. It may have been in two parts, the first as in *B-R* (? = α)*C*-**p** ([*Explicit*] *passus secundus de dobest*), the second containing a form like *Explicit dialogus vocatus pers / liber de petri plowman*. The ?*C*-**x** form *liber vocatus pers ploghman* is fairly close to the ascription in the **C** copy V (Dublin 212) concerning the authorship of the poem, *librum qui vocatur Perys ploughman*.

470

Typeset in 10.5/12.5 New Times Roman
Cover designed by Linda K. Judy
Composed by Tom Krol
Manufactured by Cushing-Malloy, Inc.

Medieval Institute Publications
College of Arts and Sciences
Western Michigan University
1903 W. Michigan Avenue
Kalamazoo, MI 49008-5432
http:/ /www.wmich.edu/medieval/mip